Ritchie

"The Laudon & Laudon Web site includes technology updates, interactive Web exercises and study guide, a virtual tour of Electronic Commerce sites, and new case studies."

www.prenhall.com/laudon

"This interactive student CD ROM includes bullet text to assist students in their understanding of the material in the text, audio and video tours, and links to the student's Web site exercises and study guide so users can continually check their progress in mastering the material."

Management Information Systems

Fifth Edition

New Approaches to Organization and Technology

Kenneth C. Laudon

New York University

Jane P. Laudon

Azimuth Corporation

PRENTICE HALL *Upper Saddle River, New Jersey 07458*

Library of Congress Cataloging-in-Publication Data
Laudon, Kenneth C.
    Management information systems: new approaches to organization and technology/
    Kenneth C. Laudon, Jane Price Laudon.—5th ed.
        p.   c m.
    Includes bibliographical references and index.
    ISBN 0–13–857723–4
    1. Management information systems.   I. Laudon, Jane Price.
    II. Title.
    T58.6.L376   1998
    658.4'038—dc21   97-32418
                                                                        CIP

Acquisitions Editor: David Alexander
Editor-in-Chief: P.J. Boardman
Assistant Editor: Audrey Regan
Editorial Assistant: Shane Gemza
Marketing Manager: Nancy Evans
Production: Carlisle Communications, Inc.
Production Coordinator: Cindy Spreder
Managing Editor: Katherine Evancie
Senior Manufacturing Supervisor: Paul Smolenski
Manufacturing Manager: Vincent Scelta
Design Director: Pat Smythe
Interior Design: Jill Yutkowitz
Cover Design: Cheryl Asherman
Cover Illustrator: Wendy Grossman
Composition: Carlisle Communications, Inc.

© 1998, 1996 by Prentice Hall, Inc.
A Simon & Schuster Company
Upper Saddle River, New Jersey 07458

Printed in the United States of America

10   9   8   7   6   5   4   3   2   1

ISBN 0-13-857723-4

Prentice-Hall International (UK) Limited, *London*
Prentice-Hall of Australia Pty. Limited, *Sydney*
Prentice-Hall Canada, Inc., *Toronto*
Prentice Hall Hispanoamericana, S. A., *Mexico*
Prentice-Hall of India Private Limited, *New Delhi*
Prentice-Hall of Japan, Inc., *Tokyo*
Simon & Schuster Asia Pte. Ltd., *Singapore*
Editora Prentice-Hall do Brasil, Ltda., *Rio de Janeiro*

Kenneth C. Laudon is a Professor of Information Systems at New York University's Stern School of Business. He holds a B.A. in Economics from Stanford and a Ph.D. from Columbia University. He has authored fourteen books dealing with information systems, organizations, and society. Professor Laudon has also written over seventy-five articles concerned with the social, organizational, and management impacts of information systems, privacy, ethics, and multimedia technology.

Professor Laudon's current research focuses on four areas: understanding the value of knowledge work; the social and organizational uses of information technology; privacy of personal information; and the development of multimedia, interactive digital higher education materials. He has received grants from the National Science Foundation to study the evolution of national information systems at the Social Security Administration, the IRS, and the FBI. A part of this research is concerned with computer-related organizational and occupational changes in large organizations, changes in management ideology, changes in public policy, and understanding productivity change in the knowledge sector.

Ken Laudon has testified as an expert before the United States Congress. He has been a researcher and consultant to the Office of Technology Assessment (United States Congress) and to the Office of the President, several executive branch agencies, and Congressional Committees. Professor Laudon also acts as a consultant on systems planning and strategy to several Fortune 500 firms.

Ken Laudon's hobby is sailing.

Jane P. Laudon is a management consultant in the information systems area and the author of seven books. Her special interests include systems analysis, data management, MIS auditing, software evaluation, and teaching business professionals how to design and use information systems.

Jane received her Ph.D. from Columbia University, her M.A. from Harvard University, and her B.A. from Barnard College. She has taught at Columbia University and the New York University Graduate School of Business. She maintains a lifelong interest in Oriental languages and civilizations.

The Laudons have two daughters, Erica and Elisabeth.

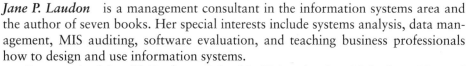

Management Information Systems: New Approaches to Organization and Technology reflects a deep understanding of MIS research and teaching as well as practical experience designing and building real world systems.

for Erica
and Elisabeth

BRIEF CONTENTS

CONTENTS

WINDOWS ON MIS

Management Information Systems: New Approaches to Organization and Technology (Fifth Edition) is based on the premise that it is difficult—if not impossible—to manage a modern organization without at least some knowledge of information systems—what information systems are, how they affect the organization and its employees, and how they can make businesses more competitive and efficient. Information systems have become essential for creating competitive firms, managing global corporations, and providing useful products and services to customers. This book provides an introduction to management information systems that undergraduate and MBA students will find vital to their professional success.

The Information Revolution in Business and Management: New Approaches to Organization and Technology

Globalization of trade, the emergence of information economies and the growth of the Internet and other global communications networks have recast the role of information systems in business and management. Companies can use information technology to design global business organizations linking factories, offices, and mobile sales forces around the clock. The Internet is becoming the foundation for new business models, new business processes, and new ways of distributing knowledge. Accordingly we have changed the title of this text to *Management Information Systems: New Approaches to Organization and Technology* because we believe these changes are creating new approaches to organization and management.

New to the Second Edition

This edition maintains the strengths of earlier editions while showing how the Internet and related technologies are transforming information systems and business organizations. The fifth edition was reworked from start to finish to integrate the issues surrounding the growing use of the Internet more fully into the MIS course. This new direction is reflected in the following changes:

The Internet and Electronic Commerce: The Internet and electronic commerce are introduced in Chapter 1 and integrated throughout the text and the entire learning package. A full chapter on the Internet and enterprise-wide networking (Chapter 10) describes the underlying technology, capabilities, and benefits of the Internet, with expanded

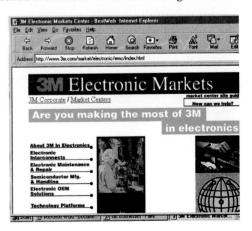

treatment of electronic commerce and Internet business models. The Part II case study is "Electronic Commerce Strategies: A Tale of Two Companies."

Internet Integrated into Every Chapter: Every chapter contains a Window On box, case study, or in-text discussion of how the Internet is changing a particular aspect of information systems. Intranets, extranets, "push" technology, Java software, intelligent agents, Internet-based group collaboration, and Internet security are among the topics given detailed coverage.

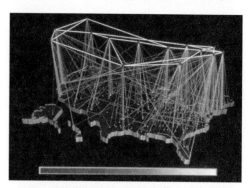

Laudon & Laudon Web site [http://www.prenhall.com/laudon] The Laudon & Laudon Web site has been enhanced to provide a wide array of capabilities for interactive learning and management problem-solving: They include:

- **The Internet Connection and Interactive Internet Projects. The Internet Connection** can be found in each chapter. The Internet Connection interactively shows students how to use the Internet for research and management problem-solving and helps professors integrate the Internet into the MIS course. The Internet Connection icon in the text directs students to various sites on the World Wide Web of the Internet where they can find interactive projects, additional case studies, or resources related to topics and organizations discussed in the chapter.

- **Interactive Electronic Commerce Projects.** The Web site features six interactive electronic commerce projects covering problems in international marketing, pricing, sales support, sales planning, customer support, logistics planning, and investment portfolio analysis. Students are presented with a problem requiring them to use interactive features of a Web site to develop a solution. They will be able to obtain the information required by the solution by inputting data on-line and using the software at that Web site to perform the required calculations or analysis.

- **A Virtual Tour of Electronic Commerce Sites:** Students are presented with a tour of electronic commerce sites where they can explore various Internet business models and electronic commerce capabilities. Students can use what they have learned on the tour to complete a more comprehensive electronic commerce project.

- **Additional case studies:** The Web site contains additional case studies with hyperlinks to the Web sites of the organizations they discuss.

- **Technology Updates:** The Web site provides technology updates to keep instructors and students abreast of leading-edge technology changes.

- **International Links:** Links to Web sites in Canada, Europe, Latin America, Asia, Australia, and Africa are provided for professors wishing more international coverage.

- **Interactive Study Guide:** The interactive study guide provides students with instant feedback as they take chapter by chapter quizzes of multiple choice, true/false, and matching exercises. The feedback includes hints and relevant page references to the text when students miss questions.

New leading-edge topics. The text includes up-to-date coverage of topics such as:

Intranets and extranets

Internet business models

Network computers

Java and the software revolution

"Push" technology

Internet security, firewalls, and electronic payment systems

Internet privacy issues

Supply chain management

Systems for knowledge management

Virtual organizations

On-line analytical processing (OLAP) and multidimensional data analysis

Intelligent agents

Data mining and knowledge discovery

Expanded treatment of business processes, business models, and their relationship to information technology. Business processes and business models receive new emphasis throughout the text. Chapter 11 presents an expanded discussion of business process redesign and reengineering. The text concludes with a Business Process Redesign Project. Throughout the text are examples of how the Internet has helped organizations redesign their business processes and create new business models.

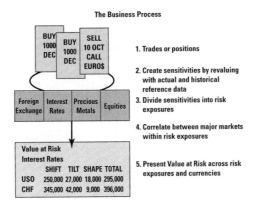

Management Wrap-Up sections at the end of each chapter summarize key issues using the authors' management, organization, and technology framework for analyzing and describing information systems.

Unique Features of This Text

Management Information Systems: New Approaches to Organization and Technology (Fifth Edition) has many unique features designed to create an active, dynamic learning environment.

- **Integrating Technology with Content:** The textbook is the only MIS textbook that provides a full array of interactive support tools for integrating technology into the MIS course. The text is accompanied by a CD-ROM and the Laudon Web site, providing an integrated learning system for the student. Highlights

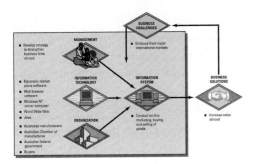

A special diagram accompanying each chapter-opening vignette graphically illustrates how management, organization, and technology elements work together to create an information system solution to the business challenges discussed in the vignette. The diagram can be used as a starting point to analyze any information system problem.

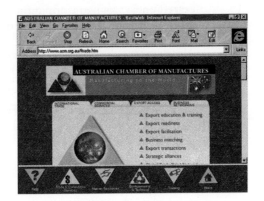

Each chapter opens with a vignette illustrating the themes of the chapter by showing how a real-world organization meets a business challenge using information systems.

include audio/video overviews explaining key concepts in the text, simulations, interactive Web exercises hyperlinked from the CD to the Web site, an interactive study guide for students supporting the chapter objectives, technology updates, additional cases, and more.

- **An integrated framework for describing and analyzing information systems.** An integrated framework portrays information systems as being composed of management, organization and technology elements. This framework is used throughout the text to describe and analyze information systems and information system problems.

- **Real-World Examples:** Real-world examples drawn from business and public organizations are used throughout to illustrate text concepts. More than 100 companies in the United States and over 100 organizations in Canada, Europe, Australia, Asia, and Africa are discussed.

Each chapter contains three Window On boxes (Window On Management, Window On Organizations, Window On Technology) that present real-world examples illustrating the management, organization, and technology issues in the chapter. Each Window On box concludes with a section called *To Think About* containing questions for students to apply chapter concepts to management problem solving. The themes for each box are:

 **WINDOW ON MANAGEMENT:** Management problems raised by systems and their solution; management strategies and plans; careers and experiences of managers using systems.

 **WINDOW ON TECHNOLOGY:** Hardware, software, telecommunications, data storage, standards, and systems-building methodologies.

 **WINDOW ON ORGANIZATIONS:** Activities of private and public organizations using information systems; experiences of people working with systems.

- **Attention to small businesses and entrepreneurs.** A SMALL BUSINESS icon identifies designated chapter-opening vignettes, Window On boxes, and ending case studies highlighting the experiences and challenges of small businesses and entrepreneurs using information systems

- **Pedagogy to encourage active learning and management problem-solving.**

Management Information Systems: New Approaches to Organization and Technology contains many features that encourage students to actively learn and to engage in management problem-solving.

Group projects: At the end of each chapter is a group project that encourages students to develop teamwork and oral and written presentation skills. For instance, students might be asked to work in small groups to analyze a business and to suggest appropriate strategic information systems for that particular business or to develop a corporate ethics code on privacy that considers E-mail privacy and monitoring employees using networks.

Management Challenges Section: Each chapter begins with several challenges relating to the chapter topic that managers are likely to encounter. These challenges are multifaceted and sometimes pose dilemmas. They make excellent springboards for class discussion. Some of these Management Challenges are finding the right Internet business model, the organizational obstacles to building a database environment, or agreeing on quality standards for information systems.

Case studies: Each chapter concludes with a case study based on a real-world organization. These cases help students synthesize chapter concepts and apply this new knowledge to real-world problems and scenarios. Major part-ending case studies, international case studies, and electronic case studies at the Laudon & Laudon Web site provide additional opportunities for management problem-solving.

- **A truly international perspective:** In addition to a full chapter on Managing International Information Systems, all chapters of the text are illustrated with real-world examples from over one hundred corporations in Canada, Europe, Asia, Latin America, Africa, Australia, and the Middle East. Each chapter contains at least one Window On box, case study or opening vignette drawn from a non-U.S. firm, and often more. The text concludes with five major international case studies contributed by leading MIS experts in Canada, Europe, Singapore, and Australia—Len Fertuck, University of Toronto (Canada); Helmut Krcmar, Stephen Wilczek and Gerhard Schwabe, University of Hohenheim (Germany); Donald Marchand, Thomas Vollmann, and Kimberly Bechler, International Institute for Management Development (Switzerland); Boon Siong Neo and Christina Soh, Nanyang Technological University (Singapore); and Peter Weill and J.B. Barolsky, University of Melbourne (Australia).

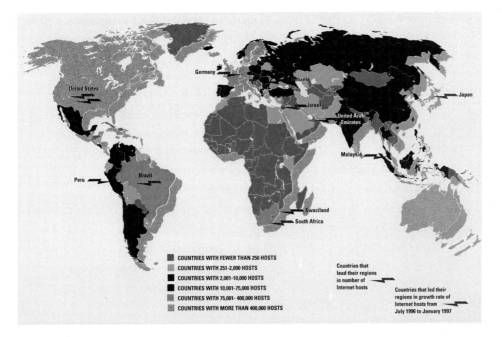

Book Overview

The five parts of the book are designed to be relatively independent of each other. Each instructor may choose to emphasize different parts.

Part One is concerned with the organizational foundations of systems and their emerging strategic role. It provides an extensive introduction to real-world systems, focusing on their relationship to organizations, management, and important ethical and social issues.

Part Two provides the technical foundation for understanding information systems, describing hardware, software, storage, and telecommunications technologies. Part Two concludes by describing how all of the information technologies work together in enterprise-wide networking and internetworking with other organizations through the Internet.

Part Three focuses on the process of redesigning organizations using information systems, including reengineering of critical business processes. We see systems analysis and design as an exercise in organizational design, one that requires great sensitivity to the right tools and techniques, quality assurance and change management.

Part Four describes the role of information systems in capturing and distributing organizational knowledge and in enhancing management decision-making. It shows how knowledge management, work group collaboration, and individual and group decision making can be supported by the use of knowledge work, artificial intelligence, decision support, and executive support systems.

Part Five concludes the text by examining the special management challenges and opportunities created by the pervasiveness and power of contemporary information systems: ensuring security and control and developing global systems. Throughout the text emphasis is placed on using information technology to redesign the organization's products, services, procedures, jobs and management structures, with numerous examples drawn from multinational systems and global business environments.

Chapter Outline

Each chapter contains the following:

- A detailed outline at the beginning to provide an overview.
- An opening vignette describing a real-world organization to establish the theme and importance of the chapter.
- A diagram analyzing the opening vignette in terms of the management, organization, and technology model used throughout the text.
- A list of learning objectives.
- Management challenges.
- Marginal glosses of key terms in the text.
- An Internet Connection icon directing students to related material on the Internet.
- A Management Wrap-Up tying together the key management, organization, and technology issues for the chapter, with questions for discussion.
- A chapter summary keyed to the learning objectives.
- A list of key terms that the student can use to review concepts.
- Review questions for students to test their comprehension of chapter material.
- A group project to develop teamwork and presentation skills.
- A chapter-ending case study that illustrates important themes.
- A list of references for further research on topics.

Instructional Support Materials

Software

A series of optional management software cases called *Solve it! Management Problem Solving with PC Software* has been developed to support the text. *Solve it!* consists of 10 spreadsheet cases, 10 database cases and 6 Internet projects drawn from real-world businesses, plus a data diskette with the files required by the cases. The cases are graduated in difficulty. The case book contains complete tutorial documentation showing how to use spreadsheet, database, and Web browser software to solve the problems. A new version of *Solve it!* with all new cases is published every year. *Solve it!* must be adopted for an entire class. It can be purchased directly from the supplier, Azimuth Corporation, 124 Penfield Ave., Croton-on-Hudson, New York 10520 (Telephone 914-271-6321).

Instructor's Manual

The Instructor's Manual, written by Dr. Glenn Bottoms of Gardner-Webb University, features an in-depth lecture outline and answers to key terms, review and discussion questions, case studies, and group projects, as well as additional Internet Resources.

Test Item File

New to this edition is a separate expanded Test Item File, written by Dr. Bindiganavale Vijayaraman of the College of Business Administration, University of Akron. This edition includes true/false, multiple choice, fill-ins and essay questions. Each question is section-referenced and rated according to difficulty level.

Video Cases

Video cases based on real-world corporations and organizations are available to adopters. The video cases illustrate the concepts in the text and can be used for class discussion or written projects.

Powerpoint Slides

Over 100 electronic color slides created by Dr. Edward Fisher of Central Michigan University are available to adopters. The slides, which illuminate and build upon key concepts in the text, can be customized to suit class needs.

Transparencies

One hundred full-color transparency acetates are also available to adopters. These transparencies, taken from figures in the text, provide additional visual support to class lectures.

Web Site

Please visit this book's Web site at http://www.prenhall.com/laudon. The site contains the instructor materials cited above, as well as an interactive study guide for students. Also available for students are additional cases not found in the text, links to Web resources for each chapter, interactive electronic commerce projects, and technology updates.

Acknowledgments

The production of any book involves many valued contributions from a number of persons. We would like to thank all of our editors for encouragement, insight, and strong support for many years. We are grateful to our editors, David Alexander and Jo-Ann DeLuca for their energy in guiding the development of this edition and to PJ Boardman and Richard Wohl for supporting the project. We thank Audrey Regan for directing the preparation of ancillary materials and commend Katherine Evancie for overseeing production of this text. We continue to be grateful to Nancy Evans for her outstanding marketing work. Special thanks to Patti Arneson for her focus group and market research work for this edition.

We remain deeply indebted to Marshall R. Kaplan for his invaluable assistance in the preparation of this edition. Special thanks to Dr. Glenn Bottoms of Gardner-Webb University and Dr. Bindiganavale Vijayaraman of the College of Business Administration, University of Akron for their work on supporting materials.

The Stern School of Business at New York University and the Information Systems Department provided a very special learning environment, one in which we and others could rethink the MIS field. Special thanks to Professors Edward Stohr, Jon Turner, Vasant Dhar, Ajit Kambil, and Stephen Slade for providing critical feedback and support where deserved. Professor William H. Starbuck of the Management Department at NYU provided valuable comments and insights.

Professors Al Croker and Michael Palley of Baruch College and NYU, Professor Kenneth Marr of Hofstra University, Professor Gordon Everest of the University of

Minnesota, Professor Sassan Rahmatian of California State University, Fresno, and Dr. Edward Roche provided additional suggestions for improvement.

The late Sara Tykol of Croton-on-Hudson, New York and the late Professor James Clifford of the Stern School made important contributions to the text. Sara helped us with the preparation of boxes, case materials and multimedia content. Jim offered valuable recommendations for improving our discussion of files and databases. Both Sara and Jim were wonderful colleagues and friends and we miss them deeply.

One of our goals was to write a book which was authoritative, synthesized diverse views in the MIS literature, and helped define a common academic field. A large number of leading scholars in the field were contacted and assisted us in this effort. Reviewers and consultants for *Management Information Systems: New Approaches to Organization and Technology* are listed in the back end papers of the book. We thank them for their contributions. Reviewers for the new edition are: Murray Jennex, University of Phoenix; Anthony Hendrickson, Iowa State; Carolyn Jacobson, Marymount University; John Tarjan, California State University at Bakersfield; Christopher Kimble, University of York, United Kingdom; Michel Benarcoh, Syracuse University; Charles Van Der Mast, Delft University of Technology, Netherlands; David Scanlan, California State University at Sacramento; Leah R. Pietron, University of Nebraska; Mats Daniels, Uppsala University. It is our hope that this group endeavor contributes to a shared vision and understanding of the MIS field.

K.C.L.
J.P.L.

Organizational Foundations of Information Systems

Part One places information systems in the context of organizations, highlighting their strategic role and their ethical and social implications.

CHAPTER 1

Information Systems: Challenges and Opportunities

Chapter 1 introduces the concept of an information system, detailing its management, organization, and technology dimensions. Information systems and the Internet are transforming contemporary organizations and the process of management, posing five key challenges.

CHAPTER 2

The Strategic Role of Information Systems

Chapter 2 highlights the critical role that information systems play in organizations with examples of key information system applications. The authors describe how information systems can be used to support different levels of strategy to provide a competitive advantage.

CHAPTER 3

Information Systems, Organizations, and Business Processes

Chapter 3 explores the relationship between information systems and organizations, with special attention to business processes. Information systems are shaped by organizational characteristics, but information technology can influence organizations as well.

CHAPTER 4

Information, Management, and Decision Making

Chapter 4 examines the three leading schools of management thought. Each offers a different vision of the management process and the role of information technology in the organization. The authors discuss the different levels, types, and stages of management decision making and the individual and organizational models of decision making that can be applied.

CHAPTER 5

Ethical and Social Impact of Information Systems

Chapter 5 describes how the widespread use of information systems has created new ethical and social problems. The issues of information rights (including privacy), intellectual property rights, accountability, liability, system quality, and quality of life must be carefully examined in light of the new power of information technology and surging use of the Internet.

PART ONE CASE STUDY

Chrysler and GM: Organization, Technology and Business Processes in the U.S. Auto Industry

This case illustrates how two giant American corporations have tried to use information technology to combat foreign and domestic competitors. The case explores the relationship between each firm's management strategy, organizational characteristics, business processes, and information systems.

Information Systems: Challenges and Opportunities

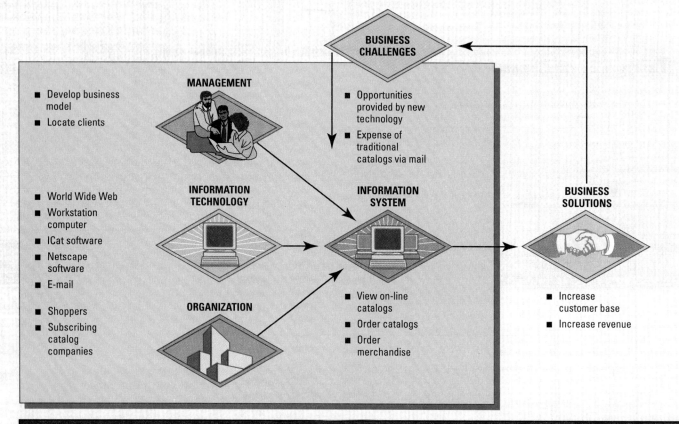

BUSINESS CHALLENGES

MANAGEMENT
- Develop business model
- Locate clients

- Opportunities provided by new technology
- Expense of traditional catalogs via mail

INFORMATION TECHNOLOGY
- World Wide Web
- Workstation computer
- ICat software
- Netscape software
- E-mail

- Shoppers
- Subscribing catalog companies

ORGANIZATION

INFORMATION SYSTEM
- View on-line catalogs
- Order catalogs
- Order merchandise

BUSINESS SOLUTIONS
- Increase customer base
- Increase revenue

Let the Internet Do the Walking

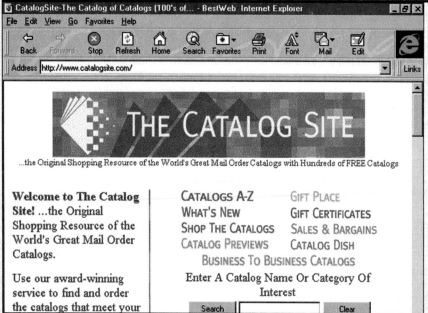

In 1872, Montgomery Ward & Co. launched the first mail-order catalogue in the United States, offering home goods to tens of thousands of people living in small towns and on farms. A century and a quarter later, Gary Baker is hoping that his electronic one-stop shop on the Internet will have a similar impact on the digital world. Baker created The Catalog Site on the World Wide Web as an electronic mall for companies selling their merchandise through catalogues.

Baker came up with this idea several years ago when he found himself grappling with an armful of catalogues crammed into his mailbox. He marveled at how well pro-

CHAPTER OUTLINE

LEARNING OBJECTIVES

After completing this chapter, you will be able to:

1. Define an information system.

2. Explain the difference between computer literacy and information systems literacy.

3. Explain why information systems are so important today and how they are transforming organizations and management.

4. Identify the major management challenges to building and using information systems in organizations.

---

duced they were and then proceeded to throw them all into his trash can. Baker concluded that mailing unsolicited telephone-book-size catalogues is no longer an efficient or cost-effective way to do business. Better to let people use networked information systems to do the walking.

The Catalog Site lists more than 200 companies that sell their wares through either on-line or traditional print catalogues. Visitors can scroll through this list of tenants or search for the goods they want by product type. When they click to select a company in which they are interested, they are taken to a templated storefront offering telephone and

fax numbers, store hours, types of payments accepted, and other essential information. They can then link to that company's own site on the World Wide Web to see its electronic catalogue of goods. If the company does not have a Web site, they can order a free paper catalogue by filling out an on-line order form. After inputting the name and address information required for the on-line catalogue, the visitor receives an order reference number for the catalogue order. Visitors can click on a View Orders button to see a summary of their orders.

Visitors can preview paper catalogues, find out what items are on sale, order gift certificates, or sign

up for a biweekly e-mail newsletter. The Catalog Site reviews many of the catalogues it lists, rating them on criteria such as design, originality, and ease of use. About half of The Catalog Site's clients have their own separate presence on the Web, and all but a handful produce paper catalogues.

The Catalog Site offers clients four basic levels of marketing service. The first provides an electronic order form for the company's paper catalogue and a single Web page. The second provides an additional Web page for the company to display its products. The third provides on-line ordering capabilities for the client's products themselves and an automatic link to the client's Web site. The basic service costs between $1200 and $1500 per year.

The Catalog Site runs on a Sun Microsystems Inc., Sparcstation 5 workstation computer and uses two pieces of software from ICat Corporation. One is Commerce Publisher, for catalogue creation. The other is Commerce Exchange, for secure credit card transactions. A third piece of software, Netscape Secure Server, sorts the thousands of orders for print catalogues and gift certificates.

When The Catalog Site opened in June 1995, its 30 clients received about 2500 catalogue requests per week. The number of requests has climbed to 17,000 per week. Each week 60,000 people "visit" the Web site to look around. The site is designed to help locate "qualified" customers who are seriously interested in buying something. All who access The Catalog Site must pass through several steps before requesting a catalogue, a process that weeds out casual visitors.

The company excels at finding customers for its more obscure clients, such as the John Rinehart Taxidermy Supply Co. and School of Exclusively Bar-B-Q Inc., a small, family-run mail-order business. Its owners believe it can do much more than traditional print catalogues because it offers interactivity and extra value. By harnessing the power of the Internet for electronic commerce, The Catalog Site believes it can find, for example, gardening customers that could not be reached by a single gardening catalogue in print. ∎

Source: Edward Engel, "Something for Everyone," *Webmaster*, February 1997.

The Catalog Site's innovative use of the Internet demonstrates how information systems can create new business opportunities for both small and large companies, helping them compete in today's global business environment. Information systems and global networks allow The Catalog Site and other companies to extend their reach to faraway locations, offer new products and services, reshape jobs and work flows, and perhaps profoundly change the way they conduct business. An understanding of information systems is essential for today's managers because most organizations need information systems to survive and prosper. This chapter starts our investigation of information systems and organizations by describing information systems from both technical and behavioral perspectives and by surveying the changes they are bringing to organizations and management.

1.1 WHY INFORMATION SYSTEMS?

Until recently, there was little need for this textbook or course. Information itself was not considered an important asset for the firm. The management process was considered a face-to-face, personal art and not a far-flung, global coordination process. But today few managers can afford to ignore how information is handled by their organization.

The Competitive Business Environment

Three powerful worldwide changes have altered the environment of business. The first change is the emergence and strengthening of the global economy. The second change is the transformation of industrial economies and societies into knowledge- and information-based service economies. The third is the transformation of the business enterprise. These changes in the business environment and climate, summarized in Table 1.1, pose a number of new challenges to business firms and their management.

Table 1.1 The Changing Contemporary Business Environment

Globalization

Management and control in a global marketplace

Competition in world markets

Global work groups

Global delivery systems

Transformation of Industrial Economies

Knowledge- and information-based economies

Productivity

New products and services

Knowledge: a central productive and strategic asset

Time-based competition

Shorter product life

Turbulent environment

Limited employee knowledge base

Transformation of the Enterprise

Flattening

Decentralization

Flexibility

Location independence

Low transaction and coordination costs

Empowerment

Collaborative work and teamwork

Emergence of the Global Economy

A growing percentage of the American economy—and other advanced industrial economies in Europe and Asia—depends on imports and exports. Foreign trade, both exports and imports, accounts for a little over 25 percent of the goods and services produced in the United States, and even more in countries such as Japan and Germany. This percentage will grow in the future. The success of firms today and in the future depends on their ability to operate globally.

Globalization of the world's industrial economies greatly enhances the value of information to the firm and offers new opportunities to businesses. Today, information systems provide the communication and analytic power that firms need for conducting trade and managing businesses on a global scale. Controlling the far-flung global corporation—communicating with distributors and suppliers, operating 24 hours a day in different national environments, servicing local and international reporting needs—is a major business challenge that requires powerful information system responses.

Globalization and information technology also bring new threats to domestic business firms: Because of global communication and management systems, customers now can shop in a worldwide marketplace, obtaining price and quality information reliably, 24 hours a day. This phenomenon heightens competition and forces firms to play in open, unprotected worldwide markets. To become effective and profitable participants in international markets, firms need powerful information and communication systems.

Transformation of Industrial Economies

The United States, Japan, Germany, and other major industrial powers are experiencing a third economic revolution. In the first revolution, the United States had by 1890 transformed itself from a colonial backwater to an agrarian powerhouse capable of feeding large segments of the world population. In the second revolution, the United States had by 1920 transformed itself from an agrarian nineteenth-century society to a first-class industrial power. In the third revolution, now in progress, the country is transforming itself into a knowledge- and information-based service economy while manufacturing has moved to low-wage countries. In a knowledge- and information-based economy, knowledge and information are key ingredients in creating wealth.

The knowledge and information revolution began at the turn of the twentieth century and has gradually accelerated. By 1976 the number of white-collar workers employed in offices surpassed the number of farm workers, service workers, and blue-collar workers employed in manufacturing (see Figure 1.1). Today, most people no longer work in farms or factories but instead are found in sales, education, health care, banks, insurance firms, and law firms; they also provide business services such as copying, computer software, or deliveries. These jobs primarily involve working with, distributing, or creating new knowledge and information. In fact, knowledge and information work now account for 60 percent of the American gross national product, and nearly 55 percent of the labor force.

Knowledge and information are becoming the foundation for many new services and products. **Knowledge- and information-intense products** such as computer games require a great deal of learning and knowledge to produce. Entire new information-based services have sprung up, such as Lexis, Dow Jones News Service, and America Online. These fields are employing millions of people.

Intensification of knowledge utilization in the production of traditional products has increased as well. This trend is readily seen throughout the automobile industry

knowledge- and information-intense products Products that require a great deal of learning and knowledge to produce.

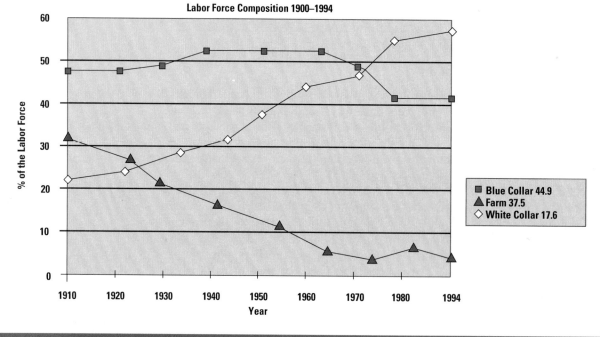

Labor Force Composition 1900–1994

Legend:
- Blue Collar 44.9
- Farm 37.5
- White Collar 17.6

Y-axis: % of the Labor Force

X-axis: Year — 1910, 1920, 1930, 1940, 1950, 1960, 1970, 1980, 1994

FIGURE 1.1

The growth of the information economy. Since the turn of the century, the United States has experienced a steady decline in the number of farm workers and blue-collar workers who are employed in factories. At the same time, the country is experiencing a rise in the number of white-collar workers who produce economic value using knowledge and information.

Sources: Adapted from U.S. Department of Commerce, Bureau of the Census, Statistical Abstract of the United States, 1994, *Table 644 and* Historical Statistics of the United States, Colonial Times to 1970, *Vol. 1, Series D 182–232.*

where both design and production now rely heavily upon knowledge-intensive information technology. Over the past decade, the automobile producers have sharply increased their hiring of computer specialists, engineers, and designers while reducing the number of blue-collar production workers.

New kinds of knowledge- and information-intense organizations have emerged that are devoted entirely to the production, processing, and distribution of information. For instance, environmental engineering firms, which specialize in preparing environmental impact statements for municipalities and private contractors, simply did not exist 30 years ago.

In a knowledge- and information-based economy, information technology and systems take on great importance. Knowledge-based products and services of great economic value such as credit cards, overnight package delivery, and worldwide reservation systems are based on new information technologies. Information technology constitutes more than 70 percent of the invested capital in service industries such as finance, insurance, and real estate.

Across all industries, information and the technology that delivers it have become critical, strategic assets for business firms and their managers (Leonard-Barton, 1995). Information systems are needed to optimize the flow of information and knowledge within the organization and to help management maximize the firm's knowledge resources. Because the productivity of employees will depend on the quality of the systems serving them, management decisions about information technology are critically important to the prosperity and survival of a firm.

Transformation of the Business Enterprise

The third major change in the business environment is the very nature of organization and management. There has been a transformation in the possibilities for organizing and managing. Some firms have begun to take advantage of these new possibilities.

The traditional business firm was—and still is—a hierarchical, centralized, structured arrangement of specialists that typically relies on a fixed set of standard operating procedures to deliver a mass-produced product (or service). The new style of business firm is a flattened (less hierarchical), decentralized, flexible arrangement of generalists who rely on nearly instant information to deliver mass-customized products and services uniquely suited to specific markets or customers. This new style of organization is not yet firmly entrenched—it is still evolving. Nevertheless, the direction is clear, and this new direction would be unthinkable without information technology.

The traditional management group relied—and still does—on formal plans, a rigid division of labor, formal rules, and appeals to loyalty to ensure the proper operation of a firm. The new manager relies on informal commitments and networks to establish goals (rather than formal planning), a flexible arrangement of teams and individuals working in task forces, a customer orientation to achieve coordination among employees, and appeals to professionalism and knowledge to ensure proper operation of the firm. Once again, information technology makes this style of management possible.

Information technology is bringing about changes in organization that make the firm even more dependent than in the past on the knowledge, learning, and decision making of individual employees. Throughout this book, we describe the role that information technology is now playing in the transformation of the business enterprise form.

What Is an Information System?

An **information system** can be defined technically as a set of interrelated components that collect (or retrieve), process, store, and distribute information to support decision

information system Interrelated components working together to collect, process, store, and disseminate information to support decision making, coordination, control, analysis, and visualization in an organization.

FIGURE 1.2

Functions of an information system. An information system contains information about an organization and its surrounding environment. Three basic activities—input, processing, and output—produce the information organizations need. Feedback is output returned to appropriate people or activities in the organization to evaluate and refine the input.

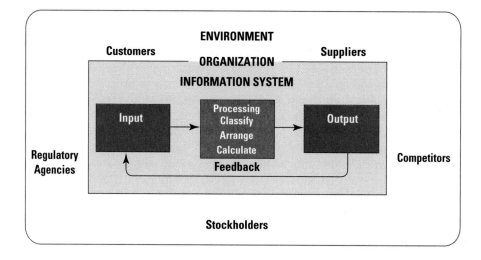

information Data that have been shaped into a form that is meaningful and useful to human beings.

data Streams of raw facts representing events occurring in organizations or the physical environment before they have been organized and arranged into a form that people can understand and use.

input The capture or collection of raw data from within the organization or from its external environment for processing in an information system.

processing The conversion, manipulation, and analysis of raw input into a form that is more meaningful to humans.

output The distribution of processed information to the people or activities where it will be used.

feedback Output that is returned to the appropriate members of the organization to help them evaluate or correct input.

computer-based information system (CBIS) An information system that relies on computer hardware and software for processing and disseminating information.

making and control in an organization. In addition to supporting decision making, coordination, and control, information systems may also help managers and workers analyze problems, visualize complex subjects, and create new products.

Information systems contain information about significant people, places, and things within the organization or in the environment surrounding it (see Figure 1.2). By **information** we mean data that have been shaped into a form that is meaningful and useful to human beings. **Data,** in contrast, are streams of raw facts representing events occurring in organizations or the physical environment before they have been organized and arranged into a form that people can understand and use.

Three activities in an information system produce the information that organizations need for making decisions, controlling operations, analyzing problems, and creating new products or services. These activities are input, processing, and output. **Input** captures or collects raw data from within the organization or from its external environment. **Processing** converts this raw input into a more meaningful form. **Output** transfers the processed information to the people or activities where it will be used. Information systems also require **feedback,** which is output that is returned to appropriate members of the organization to help them evaluate or correct the input stage.

In the information system used by The Catalog Site for ordering a print catalogue or gift certificate, the raw input consists of the name, address, and perhaps the telephone number, e-mail address, or credit card number of the person placing the order. The computer processes these data by sorting them into orders for catalogues and orders for gift certificates and assigning each order an order reference number to uniquely identify that order. Orders to the catalogue companies and the on-line reports of order summary information to the person placing the order become output. The system thus provides meaningful information such as lists of who ordered each catalogue or gift certificate, the total number of catalogues and gift certificates ordered from each catalogue company, the total number of people who accessed The Catalog Site, and the total number of people who ordered catalogues.

Our interest in this book is in a formal, organizational **computer-based information system (CBIS)** similar to those designed and used by The Catalog Site. A **formal system** rests on accepted and fixed definitions of data and procedures for collecting, storing, processing, disseminating, and using these data. The formal systems we describe in this text are structured; that is, they operate in conformity with predefined rules that are relatively fixed and not easily changed. For instance, The Catalog Site's catalogue ordering system requires that all orders for paper catalogues include the recipient's name and mailing address.

Informal information systems (such as office gossip networks) rely, by contrast, on implicit agreements and unstated rules of behavior. There is no agreement on what is information, or on how it will be stored and processed. Such systems are essential for the life of an organization, but an analysis of their qualities is beyond the scope of this text.

Formal information systems can be either computer based or manual. Manual systems use paper and pencil technology. These manual systems serve important needs, but they too are not the subject of this text. Computer-based information systems, in contrast, rely on computer hardware and software technology to process and disseminate information. From this point, when we use the term *information systems* we will be referring to computer-based information systems—formal organizational systems that rely on computer technology. The Window on Technology describes some of the typical technologies used in computer-based information systems today.

Although computer-based information systems use computer technology to process raw data into meaningful information, there is a sharp distinction between a computer and a computer program on the one hand, and an information system on the other. Electronic computers and related software programs are the technical foundation—the tools and materials—of modern information systems. Computers provide the equipment for storing and processing information. Computer programs, or software, are sets of operating instructions that direct and control computer processing. Knowing how computers and computer programs work is important in designing solutions to organizational problems, but computers are only part of an information system.

Housing provides an appropriate analogy. Houses are built with hammers, nails, and wood, but these do not make a house. The architecture, design, setting, landscaping, and all the decisions that lead to the creation of these features are part of the house and are crucial for finding a solution to the problem of putting a roof over one's head. Computers and programs are the hammer, nails, and lumber of a CBIS, but alone they cannot produce the information a particular organization needs. To understand information systems, one must understand the problems they are designed to solve, their architectural and design elements, and the organizational processes that lead to these solutions. Today's managers must combine computer literacy with information systems literacy.

A Business Perspective on Information Systems

From a business perspective, an information system is an organizational and management solution, based on information technology, to a challenge posed by the environment. Examine this definition closely because it emphasizes the organizational and management nature of information systems: To understand information systems—to be information systems literate as opposed to computer literate—a manager must understand the broader organization, management, and information technology dimensions of systems (see Figure 1.3) and their power to provide solutions to challenges and problems in the business environment.

Review the diagram at the beginning of the chapter, which reflects this expanded definition of an information system. The diagram shows how The Catalog Site's information systems provide a solution to the business challenges of trying to overcome high printing and mailing expenses to reach individual customers scattered over large geographic areas and of trying to take advantage of opportunities created by new technology—in this case, the Internet. The diagram also illustrates how management, technology, and organization elements work together to create these systems. We begin each chapter of the text with a diagram similar to this one to help you analyze the opening case. You can use this diagram as a starting point for analyzing any information system or information system problem you encounter.

formal system System resting on accepted and fixed definitions of data and procedures, operating with predefined rules.

UPS Competes Globally with Information Technology

United Parcel Service, the world's largest air and ground package distribution company, started in 1907 in a closet-sized basement office. Jim Casey and Claude Ryan—two teenagers from Seattle with two bicycles and one phone—promised the "best service and lowest rates." UPS has used this formula successfully for 90 years.

UPS still lives up to that promise today, delivering over 3 billion parcels and documents each year to any address in the United States and to more than 185 countries and territories. Critical to the firm's success has been its investment in advanced information technology. Technology has helped UPS boost customer service while keeping costs low and streamlining its overall operations.

Through its automated package tracking system, UPS can monitor packages throughout the delivery process. At various points along the route from sender to receiver, a bar-code device scans shipping information on the package label; the information is then fed into the central computer. Customer-service representatives can check the status of any package from desktop computers linked to the central computer and are able to respond immediately to inquiries from customers. UPS customers can also access this information directly from their own personal computers, using either the World Wide Web of the Internet or special package tracking software supplied by UPS.

Anyone with a package to ship can access the UPS Web site to check delivery routes, calculate shipping rates, and schedule a pickup. Eventually they will be able to use the Web to pay for their shipments on-line. The data collected at the UPS Web site are transmitted to the UPS central computer and then back to the customer after processing.

UPS's Inventory Express, launched in 1991, warehouses customers' products and ships them overnight to any destination the customer requests. Customers using this service can transmit electronic shipping orders to UPS by 1:00 A.M. and expect delivery by 10:30 that same morning. UPS is enhancing its information system capabilities so that it can guarantee that a particular package or group of packages will arrive at its destination at a specified time. If requested by the customer, UPS will be able to intercept a package prior to delivery and have it returned or rerouted.

Using a handheld computer called a Delivery Information Acquisition Device (DIAD), UPS drivers automatically capture customers' signatures along with pickup, delivery, and time card information. The drivers then place the DIAD into their truck's vehicle adapter, which is an information-transmitting device connected to the cellular telephone network. Package tracking information is then transmitted to UPS's computer network for storage and processing in UPS's main computer in Mahwah, New Jersey. From there, the information can be accessed worldwide to provide proof of delivery to the customer. The system can also generate a printed response to queries by the customer.

To Think About: What are the inputs, processing, and outputs of UPS's package tracking system? What technologies are used? How are these technologies related to UPS's business strategy? What would happen if these technologies were not available?

Sources: "UPS Launches New Delivery and Information Options," UPS Public Relations, January 2, 1997; Kim Nash, "Overnight Services Duke It Out On-Line," *Computerworld*, April 22, 1996; and Linda Wilson, "Stand and Deliver," *Information Week*, November 23, 1992.

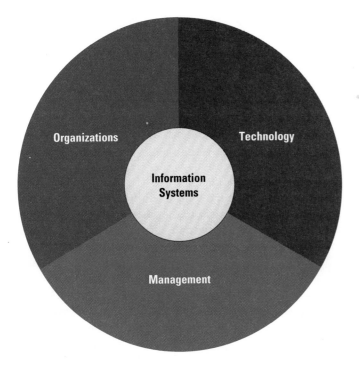

FIGURE 1.3

Information systems are more than computers. Using information systems effectively requires an understanding of the organization, management, and information technology shaping the systems. All information systems can be described as organizational and management solutions to challenges posed by the environment.

Organizations

Information systems are a part of organizations. Indeed, for some companies, such as credit reporting firms, without the system there would be no business. The key elements of an organization are its people, structure and operating procedures, politics, and culture. We introduce these components of organizations here and describe them in greater detail in Chapter 3. Formal organizations are composed of different levels and specialties. Their structures reveal a clear-cut division of labor. Experts are employed and trained for different functions, including sales and marketing, manufacturing, finance, accounting, and human resources. Table 1.2 describes these functions.

An organization coordinates work through a structured hierarchy and formal, standard operating procedures. The hierarchy arranges people in a pyramidal structure of rising authority and responsibility. The upper levels of the hierarchy consist of managerial, professional, and technical employees, whereas the lower levels consist of operational personnel.

Standard operating procedures (SOPs) are formal rules for accomplishing tasks that have been developed over a long time; these rules guide employees in a variety of procedures, from writing an invoice to responding to complaining customers.

standard operating procedures (SOPs) Formal rules for accomplishing tasks that have been developed to cope with expected situations.

Table 1.2	Major Organizational Functions
Function	**Purpose**
Sales and marketing	Selling the organization's products and services
Manufacturing	Producing products and services
Finance	Managing the organization's financial assets (cash, stocks, bonds, etc.)
Accounting	Maintaining the organization's financial records (receipts, disbursements, paychecks, etc.); accounting for the flow of funds
Human resources	Attracting, developing, and maintaining the organization's labor force; maintaining employee records

knowledge workers People such as engineers or architects who design products or services and create knowledge for the organization.

data workers People such as secretaries or bookkeepers who process an organization's paperwork.

production or **service workers** People who actually produce the products or services of the organization.

Most procedures are formalized and written down, but many others are informal work practices. Many of a firm's SOPs are incorporated into information systems—such as how to pay a supplier or how to correct an erroneous bill.

Organizations require many different kinds of skills and people. In addition to managers, **knowledge workers** (such as engineers, architects, or scientists) design products or services and create new knowledge, and **data workers** (such as secretaries, bookkeepers, or clerks) process the organization's paperwork. **Production** or **service workers** (such as machinists, assemblers, or packers) actually produce the products or services of the organization.

Each organization has a unique *culture,* or fundamental set of assumptions, values, and ways of doing things, that has been accepted by most of its members. Parts of an organization's culture can always be found embedded in its information systems. For instance, the concern with putting service to the customer first is an aspect of the organizational culture of United Parcel Service that can be found in the company's package tracking systems.

Different levels and specialties in an organization create different interests and points of view. These views often conflict. Conflict is the basis for organizational politics. Information systems come out of this cauldron of differing perspectives, conflicts, compromises, and agreements that is a natural part of all organizations. In Chapter 3 we will examine these features of organizations in greater detail.

Management

Managers perceive business challenges in the environment; they set the organizational strategy for responding and they allocate the human and financial resources to achieve the strategy and coordinate the work. Throughout, they must exercise responsible leadership. Management's job is to "make sense" out of the many situations faced by organizations and formulate action plans to solve organizational problems. The business information systems described in this book reflect the hopes, dreams, and realities of real-world managers.

But less understood is the fact that managers must do more than manage what already exists. They must also create new products and services and even re-create the organization from time to time. A substantial part of management is creative work driven by new knowledge and information. Information technology can play a powerful role in redirecting and redesigning the organization. Chapter 4 describes the activities of managers and management decision making in detail.

senior managers People occupying the topmost hierarchy in an organization who are responsible for making long-range decisions.

middle managers People in the middle of the organizational hierarchy who are responsible for carrying out the plans and goals of senior management.

operational managers People who monitor the day-to-day activities of the organization.

It is important to note that managerial roles and decisions vary at different levels of the organization. **Senior managers** make long-range strategic decisions about products and services to produce. **Middle managers** carry out the programs and plans of senior management. **Operational managers** are responsible for monitoring the firm's daily activities. All levels of management are expected to be creative: to develop novel solutions to a broad range of problems. Each level of management has different information needs and information system requirements.

Technology

computer hardware Physical equipment used for input, processing, and output activities in an information system.

computer software Detailed, preprogrammed instructions that control and coordinate the work of computer hardware components in an information system.

Information systems technology is one of many tools available to managers for coping with change. A CBIS uses computer hardware, software, storage, and telecommunications technologies. **Computer hardware** is the physical equipment used for input, processing, and output activities in an information system. It consists of the following: the computer processing unit; various input, output, and storage devices; and physical media to link these devices. Chapter 6 describes computer hardware in greater detail.

Computer software consists of the detailed preprogrammed instructions that control and coordinate the computer hardware components in an information system. Chapter 7 explains the importance of computer software in information systems.

Storage technology includes both the physical media for storing data, such as magnetic or optical disk or tape, and the software governing the organization of data on these physical media. More detail on physical storage media can be found in Chapter 6, whereas Chapter 8 treats data organization and access methods.

Communications technology, consisting of both physical devices and software, links the various pieces of hardware and transfers data from one physical location to another. Computers and communications equipment can be connected in networks for sharing voice, data, images, sound, or even video. A **network** links two or more computers to share data or resources such as a printer. Chapters 9 and 10 provide more details on communications and networking technology and issues.

Let us return to UPS's package tracking system in the Window on Technology and identify the organization, management, and technology elements. The organization element anchors the package tracking system in UPS's sales and production functions (the main product of UPS is a service—package delivery). It identifies the required procedures for identifying packages with both sender and recipient information, taking inventory, tracking the packages en route, and providing package status reports for UPS customers and customer-service representatives. The system must also provide information to satisfy the needs of managers and workers. UPS drivers need to be trained in both package pickup and delivery procedures and in how to use the package tracking system so that they can work more efficiently and effectively. UPS customers may need some training to use UPS in-house package tracking software or the UPS World Wide Web site. UPS's management is responsible for monitoring service levels and costs and for promoting the company's strategy of combining low cost and superior service. Management decided to use automation to increase the ease of sending a package via UPS and of checking its delivery status, thereby reducing delivery costs and increasing sales revenues. The technology supporting this system consists of handheld computers, bar-code scanners, wired and wireless communications networks, desktop computers, UPS's central computer, storage technology for the package delivery data, UPS in-house package tracking software, and software to access the World Wide Web. The result is an information system solution to a business challenge.

storage technology Physical media and software governing the storage and organization of data for use in an information system.

communications technology Physical devices and software that link various computer hardware components and transfer data from one physical location to another.

network Two or more computers linked to share data or resources such as a printer.

1.2 CONTEMPORARY APPROACHES TO INFORMATION SYSTEMS

Multiple perspectives on information systems show that the study of information systems is a multidisciplinary field; no single theory or perspective dominates. Figure 1.4 illustrates the major disciplines that contribute problems, issues, and solutions in the study of information systems. In general, the field can be divided into technical and behavioral approaches. Information systems are sociotechnical systems. Though they are composed of machines, devices, and "hard" physical technology, they require substantial social, organizational, and intellectual investments to make them work properly.

Technical Approach

The technical approach to information systems emphasizes mathematically based, normative models to study information systems, as well as the physical technology and formal capabilities of these systems. The disciplines that contribute to the technical approach are computer science, management science, and operations research. Computer science is concerned with establishing theories of computability, methods of computation, and methods of efficient data storage and access. Management science emphasizes the development of models for decision-making and management practices. Operations research focuses on mathematical techniques for optimizing selected parameters of organizations such as transportation, inventory control, and transaction costs.

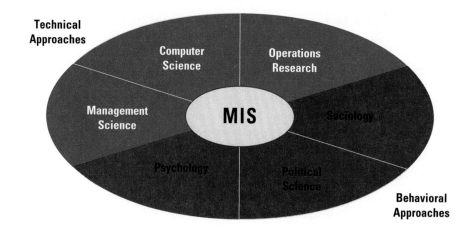

FIGURE 1.4

Contemporary approaches to information systems. The study of information systems deals with issues and insights contributed from technical and behavioral disciplines.

Behavioral Approach

A growing part of the information systems field is concerned with behavioral problems and issues. Many behavioral problems, such as system utilization, implementation, and creative design, cannot be expressed with the normative models used in the technical approach. Other behavioral disciplines also play a role. Sociologists focus on the impact of information systems on groups, organizations, and society. Political scientists investigate the political impacts and uses of information systems. Psychologists are concerned with individual responses to information systems and cognitive models of human reasoning.

The behavioral approach does not ignore technology. Indeed, information systems technology is often the stimulus for a behavioral problem or issue. But the focus of this approach is generally not on technical solutions; it concentrates rather on changes in attitudes, management and organizational policy, and behavior (Kling and Dutton, 1982).

Approach of This Text: Sociotechnical Systems

The study of management information systems (MIS) arose in the 1970s to focus on computer-based information systems aimed at managers (Davis and Olson, 1985). An MIS combines the theoretical work of computer science, management science, and operations research with a practical orientation toward building systems and applications. It also pays attention to behavioral issues raised by sociology, economics, and psychology.

Our experience as academics and practitioners leads us to believe that no single perspective effectively captures the reality of information systems. Problems with systems—and their solutions—are rarely all technical or all behavioral. Our best advice to students is to understand the perspectives of all disciplines. Indeed, the challenge and excitement of the information systems field is that it requires an appreciation and tolerance of many different approaches.

A sociotechnical systems perspective helps to avoid a purely technological approach to information systems. For instance, the fact that information technology is rapidly declining in cost and growing in power does not necessarily or easily translate into productivity enhancement or bottom-line profits.

In this book, we stress the need to optimize the performance of the system as a whole. Both the technical and behavioral components need attention. This means that technology must be changed and designed in such a way as to fit organizational and individual needs. At times, the technology may have to be "de-optimized" to accomplish this fit. Organizations and individuals must also be changed through training, learning, and planned organizational change to allow the technology to operate and prosper (see, for example, Liker et al., 1987). People and organizations change

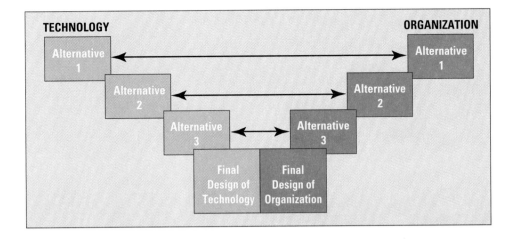

FIGURE 1.5

A sociotechnical perspective on information systems. In a sociotechnical perspective, the performance of a system is optimized when both the technology and the organization mutually adjust to one another until a satisfactory fit is obtained.
Source: Tornatsky et al., 1983.

to take advantage of new information technology. Figure 1.5 illustrates this process of mutual adjustment in a sociotechnical system.

1.3   THE NEW ROLE OF INFORMATION SYSTEMS IN ORGANIZATIONS

Information systems cannot be ignored by managers because they play such a critical role in contemporary organizations. Digital technology is transforming business organizations. The entire cash flow of most Fortune 500 companies is linked to information systems. Today's systems directly affect how managers decide, how senior managers plan, and in many cases what products and services are produced (and how). They play a strategic role in the life of the firm. Responsibility for information systems cannot be delegated to technical decision makers.

The Widening Scope of Information Systems

Figure 1.6 illustrates the new relationship between organizations and information systems. There is a growing interdependence between business strategy, rules, and procedures on the one hand, and information systems software, hardware, databases, and telecommunications on the other. A change in any of these components often requires changes in other components. This relationship becomes critical when management plans for the future. What a business would like to do in five years is often dependent on what its systems will be able to do. Increasing market share, becoming the high-quality or low-cost producer, developing new products, and increasing employee productivity depend more and more on the kinds and quality of information systems in the organization.

A second change in the relationship of information systems and organizations results from the growing complexity and scope of system projects and applications. Building systems today involves a much larger part of the organization than it did in the past (see Figure 1.7). Whereas early systems produced largely technical changes that affected few people, contemporary systems bring about managerial changes (who has what information about whom, when, and how often) and institutional "core" changes (what products and services are produced, under what conditions, and by whom).

In the 1950s, employees in the treasurer's office, a few part-time programmers, a single program, a single machine, and a few clerks might have used a computerized payroll system. The change from a manual to a computer system was largely technical—the computer system simply automated a clerical procedure such as check processing. In contrast, today's integrated human resources system (which includes payroll processing) may involve all major corporate divisions, the human resources department, dozens of

The interdependence between organizations and information systems. In contemporary systems there is a growing interdependence between organizational business strategy, rules, and procedures and the organization's information systems. Changes in strategy, rules, and procedures increasingly require changes in hardware, software, databases, and telecommunications. Existing systems can act as a constraint on organizations. Often, what the organization would like to do depends on what its systems will permit it to do.

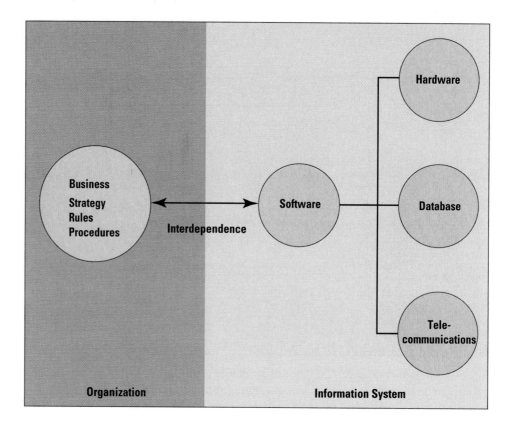

full-time programmers, a flock of external consultants, multiple machines (or remote computers linked by communications networks), and perhaps hundreds of end users in the organization who use payroll data to make calculations about benefits and pensions and to answer a host of other questions. The data, instead of being located in and controlled by the treasurer's office, are now available to hundreds of employees via desktop computers, each of which is as powerful as the large computers of the mid-1980s. This contemporary system embodies both managerial and institutional changes.

The Network Revolution and the Internet

One reason why systems play a larger role in organizations, and why they affect more people, is the soaring power and declining cost of the computer technology that is at the core of information systems. Computing power has been doubling every 18 months, so that the performance of microprocessors has improved 25,000 times since their invention 25 years ago. In today's organization, it is now possible to put

The widening scope of information systems. Over time, information systems have come to play a larger role in the life of organizations. Early systems brought about largely technical changes that were relatively easy to accomplish. Later systems affected managerial control and behavior; ultimately systems influenced "core" institutional activities concerning products, markets, suppliers, and customers.

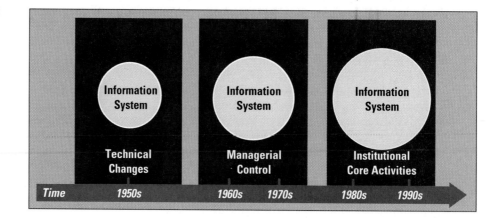

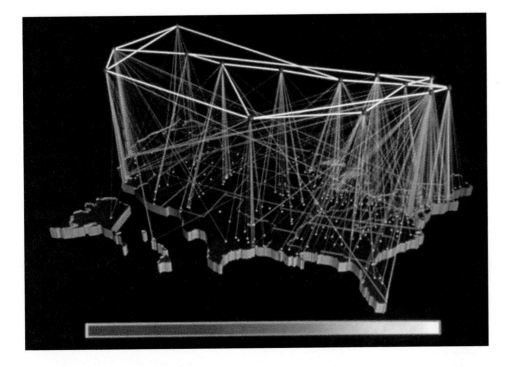

The Internet. This global network of networks provides a highly flexible platform for information-sharing. Digital information can be distributed at almost no cost to millions of people throughout the world.

the power of a large mainframe computer, which at one time took up nearly an entire floor of a company, on every desktop. With powerful, easy-to-use software, the computer can crunch numbers, analyze vast pools of data, or simulate complex physical and logical processes with animated drawings, sounds, and even tactile feedback.

The soaring power of computer technology has spawned powerful communication networks that organizations can use to access vast storehouses of information from around the world and to coordinate activities across space and time. As the source of the most important breakthroughs in information systems today, these networks are transforming the shape and form of business enterprises and even our society.

The world's largest and most widely used network is the **Internet.** The Internet is an international network of networks that are both commercial and publicly owned. The Internet connects hundreds of thousands of different networks from nearly 200 countries around the world. More than 60 million people working in science, education, government, and business organizations use the Internet to exchange information or perform business transactions with other organizations around the globe. The number of Internet users is supposed to surpass 250 million by the year 2000.

Internet International network of networks that is a collection of over 100,000 private or public networks.

The Internet is extremely elastic. If networks are added or removed or failures occur in parts of the system, the rest of the Internet continues to operate. Through special communication and technology standards, any computer can communicate with virtually any other computer linked to the Internet using ordinary telephone lines. Companies and private individuals can use the Internet to exchange business transactions, text messages, graphic images, and even video and sound, whether they are located next door or on the other side of the globe. Table 1.3 describes some of the Internet's capabilities.

The Internet is creating a new "universal" technology platform upon which to build all sorts of new products, services, strategies, and organizations. Its potential for reshaping the way information systems are used in business and daily life is vast and rich, and it is just beginning to be tapped. By eliminating many technical, geographic, and cost barriers obstructing the global flow of information, the Internet is accelerating the information revolution, inspiring new uses of information systems and new business models.

Table 1.3   What You Can Do on the Internet

	Function	Description
	Communicate and collaborate	Send electronic mail messages; transmit documents and data
	Access information	Search for documents, databases, and library card catalogues; read electronic brochures, manuals, books, and advertisements
	Participate in discussions	Join interactive discussion groups; conduct primitive voice transmission
	Obtain information	Transfer computer files of text, computer programs, graphics, animations, or videos
	Find entertainment	Play interactive video games; view short video clips; read illustrated and even animated magazines and books
	Exchange business transactions	Advertise, sell, and purchase goods and services

World Wide Web A system with universally accepted standards for storing, retrieving, formatting, and displaying information in a networked environment.

Of special interest to organizations and managers is the Internet capability known as the World Wide Web, because it offers so many new possibilities for doing business. The **World Wide Web** is a system with universally accepted standards for storing, retrieving, formatting, and displaying information in a networked environment. Information is stored and displayed as electronic "pages" that can contain text, graphics, animations, sound, and video. These Web pages can be linked electronically to other Web pages, regardless of where they are located, and viewed by any type of computer. By clicking on highlighted words or buttons on a Web page, one can link to related pages to find additional information, software programs, or still more links to other points on the Web. The Web can serve as the foundation for new kinds of information systems.

Web site The World Wide Web pages maintained by an organization or individual.

The Web pages created by an organization or individual are called a **Web site**. (The chapter-opening vignette describes The Catalog Site's Web site and illustrates one of its pages.) Businesses are creating Web sites with stylish typography, colorful graphics, push-button interactivity, and often sound and video to widely disseminate product information, to "broadcast" advertising and messages to customers, to collect electronic orders and customer data, and increasingly to coordinate far-flung sales forces and organizations on a global scale.

In Chapter 10 we describe the Web and other Internet capabilities in greater detail. We will also be discussing relevant features of the Internet throughout the text because the Internet affects so many aspects of information systems in organizations.

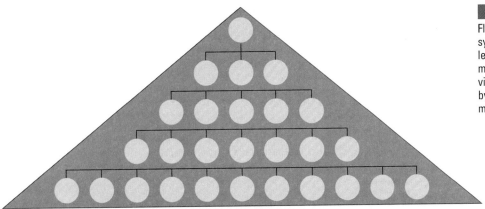

FIGURE 1.8

Flattening organizations. Information systems can reduce the number of levels in an organization by providing managers with information to supervise larger numbers of workers and by giving lower-level employees more decision-making authority.

A traditional hierarchical organization with many levels of management

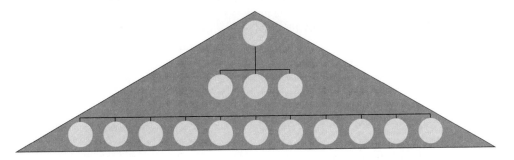

An organization that has been "flattened" by removing layers of management

New Options for Organizational Design

Information systems can become powerful instruments for making organizations more competitive and efficient. Information technology can be used to redesign and reshape organizations, transforming their structure, scope of operations, reporting and control mechanisms, work practices, work flows, products, and services. We now describe some of the major organizational design options that information technology has made available.

Flattening Organizations

Today, the large, bureaucratic organizations that developed before the explosive growth of information technology are often inefficient, slow to change, and uncompetitive. Some of these organizations have downsized, reducing the number of employees and the number of levels in their organizational hierarchies. For example, by 1994 heavy equipment manufacturer Caterpillar, Inc., was producing the same level of output as it did 15 years earlier, but with 40,000 fewer employees.

Flatter organizations have fewer levels of management, with lower-level employees being given greater decision-making authority (see Figure 1.8). Those employees are empowered to make more decisions than in the past, they no longer work standard 9-to-5 hours, and they no longer necessarily work in an office. Moreover, such employees may be scattered geographically, sometimes working half a world away from the manager.

Modern information systems have made such changes possible. They can make more information available to line workers so they can make decisions that previously had been made by managers. Networks of computers have made it possible for employees to work together as a team, another feature of flatter organizations. With the emergence of global networks such as the Internet, team members can collaborate closely even from distant locations. These changes mean that the management span of control has also been broadened, allowing high-level managers to manage and control more workers spread over greater distances. Many companies have eliminated thousands of middle managers as a result of these changes. AT&T, IBM, and General Motors are only a few of the organizations that have eliminated more than 30,000 middle managers in one fell swoop.

Separating Work from Location

It is now possible to organize globally while working locally: Information technologies such as e-mail, the Internet, and videoconferencing to the desktop permit tight coordination of geographically dispersed workers across time zones and cultures. Entire parts of organizations can disappear: Inventory (and the warehouses to store it) can be eliminated as suppliers tie into the firm's computer systems and deliver just what is needed and just in time.

Modern communications technology has eliminated distance as a factor for many types of work in many situations. Salespersons can spend more time in the field—with customers—and yet have more up-to-date information with them while carrying much less paper. Many employees can work remotely from their homes or cars, and companies can reserve space at a much smaller central office for meeting clients or other employees.

Collaborative teamwork across thousands of miles has become a reality as designers work on the design of a new product together even if they are located on different continents. Ford Motor adopted a cross-continent collaborative model when it undertook the design of the 1994 Ford Mustang. Supported by high-capacity communications networks and computer-aided design (CAD) software, Ford designers launched the Mustang design in Dunton, England. The design was worked on simultaneously by designers at Dearborn, Michigan, and Dunton, with some input from designers in Japan and Australia. Once the design was completed, Ford engineers in Turin, Italy, used it to produce a full-size physical model.

virtual organization
Organization using networks linking people, assets, and ideas to create and distribute products and services without being limited by traditional organizational boundaries or physical location.

Companies are not limited to physical locations or their own organizational boundaries for providing products and services. Networked information systems are allowing companies to coordinate their geographically distributed capabilities and even coordinate with other organizations as virtual corporations (or virtual organizations), sometimes called networked organizations. **Virtual organizations** use networks to link people, assets, and ideas, allying with suppliers and customers (and sometimes even competitors) to create and distribute new products and services without being limited by traditional organizational boundaries or physical location. One company can take advantage of the capabilities of another company without actually physically linking to that company. Each company contributes its core competencies, the capabilities that it does the best. These networked organizations last as long as the opportunity remains profitable. For example, one company might be responsible for product design, another for assembly and manufacturing, and another for administration and sales. Figure 1.9 illustrates the concept of a virtual organization.

Calyx and Corolla, which has its headquarters in San Francisco, created a networked virtual organization to sell fresh flowers directly to customers, bypassing the traditional flower shop. The company takes orders via a toll-free telephone number and enters them into a central computer, which transmits them directly to grower farms. Farmers pick the flowers and place them in waiting Federal Express refrigerated vans. Calyx and Corolla flowers are delivered within a day or two to their final destination. They are weeks fresher than flowers provided by traditional florists.

Increasing Flexibility of Organizations

Modern communications technology has enabled many organizations to organize in more flexible ways, increasing the ability of those organizations to respond to changes in the marketplace and to take advantage of new opportunities. Information systems can give both large and small organizations additional flexibility to overcome some of the limitations posed by their size. Table 1.4 describes some of the

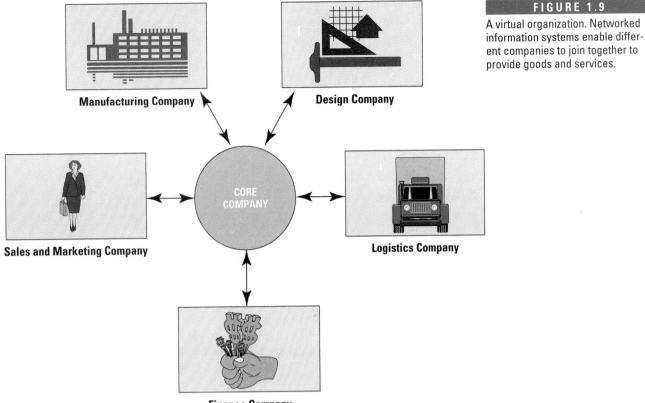

FIGURE 1.9

A virtual organization. Networked information systems enable different companies to join together to provide goods and services.

Manufacturing Company

Design Company

Sales and Marketing Company

CORE COMPANY

Logistics Company

Finance Company

ways in which information technology can help small companies act big and help big companies act "small." Small organizations can use information systems to acquire some of the muscle and reach of larger organizations. They can perform coordinating activities such as processing bids or keeping track of inventory and many manufacturing tasks with very few managers, clerks, or production workers. For example, Merig Design Equipment in Southcott Pines, Canada, is a one-man company that produces elaborate and intricate machine tool designs for the automotive industry

Table 1.4	How Information Technology Increases Organizational Flexibility

Small Companies

Desktop machines, inexpensive computer-aided design (CAD) software, and computer-controlled machine tools provide the precision, speed, and quality of giant manufacturers.

Information immediately accessed by telephone and communications links eliminates the need for research staff and business libraries.

Managers can more easily obtain the information they need to manage larger numbers of employees in widely scattered locations.

Large Companies

Custom manufacturing systems allow large factories to offer customized products in small quantities.

Massive databases of customer purchasing records can be analyzed so that large companies can know their customers' needs and preferences as easily as local merchants.

Information can be easily distributed down the ranks of the organization to empower lower-level employees and work groups to solve problems.

using a desktop Pentium PC and computer-aided design (CAD) software in the home of owner Roy Merkley. In the past, such work would have to be performed by teams of draftsmen and managers in conventional production offices (Warson, 1996). Large organizations can use information technology to achieve some of the agility and responsiveness of small organizations.

The Window on Management explores one aspect of this phenomenon—mass customization. In **mass customization,** software and computer networks are used to link the plant floor tightly with orders, design, and purchasing and to finely control production machines. The result is a dynamically responsive environment in which products can be turned out in greater variety and easily customized with no added cost for small production runs.

A related trend is micromarketing, in which information systems can help companies pinpoint tiny target markets for these finely customized products and services—as small as individualized "markets of one." We discuss micromarketing in more detail in Chapter 2.

Redefining Organizational Boundaries and Electronic Commerce

Networked information systems can enable transactions such as payments and purchase orders to be exchanged electronically among different companies, thereby reducing the cost of obtaining products and services from outside the firm. Organizations can also share business data, catalogues, or mail messages through such systems. These networked information systems can create new efficiencies and new relationships between an organization, its customers, and suppliers, thus redefining their organizational boundaries and the way they conduct business. For example, the Chrysler Corporation is networked to suppliers, such as the Budd Company of Rochester, Michigan. Through this electronic link, the Budd Company monitors Chrysler production and ships sheet metal parts exactly when needed, preceded by an electronic shipping notice. Chrysler and its suppliers have thus become linked business partners with mutually shared responsibilities.

The information system linking Chrysler and its suppliers is called an interorganizational information system. Systems linking a company to its customers, distributors, or suppliers are termed **interorganizational systems** because they automate the flow of information across organizational boundaries (Barrett, 1986–1987; Johnston and Vitale, 1988). Such systems allow information or processing capabilities of one organization to improve the performance of another or to improve relationships among organizations.

Interorganizational systems that provide services to multiple organizations by linking many buyers and sellers create an **electronic market.** Through computers and telecommunications, these systems function like electronic middlemen, with lowered costs for typical marketplace transactions such as selecting suppliers, establishing prices, ordering goods, and paying bills (Malone, Yates, and Benjamin, 1987). Buyers and sellers can complete purchase and sale transactions digitally regardless of their location.

The Internet is creating a global electronic marketplace where a vast array of goods and services are being advertised, bought, and exchanged worldwide. Companies are furiously creating eye-catching electronic brochures, advertisements, product manuals, and order forms on the World Wide Web. All kinds of products and services are available on the Web, including fresh flowers, books, real estate, musical recordings, electronics, steaks, and automobiles.

Many retailers maintain their own site on the Web, such as Virtual Vineyards (see Chapter 10) or Absolutely Fresh Flowers. Discovering such independent retailers can be difficult, however, so many prefer to offer their products through one of the electronic shopping malls, such as The Catalog Site. Another electronic shopping mall is the Internet Shopping Network, which is owned by the Home Shopping Network. Customers can locate products on this mall either by manufacturer, if they know what they want, or by product type and then order them directly.

mass customization Use of software and computer networks to finely control production so that products can be easily customized with no added cost for small production runs.

interorganizational systems Information systems that automate the flow of information across organizational boundaries and link a company to its customers, distributors, or suppliers.

electronic market A marketplace that is created by computer and communication technologies that link many buyers and sellers via interorganizational systems.

Mass Customization: The New Automation

For two decades after World War II, mass production reigned supreme. Mass-production techniques pushed companies into standardized one-size-fits-all products, long product life cycles, and rigid manufacturing emphasizing efficiency and low cost over flexibility. Special orders and made-to-order products cost more. But today's consumers are very choosy. They want quality, value, and products specially tailored to their needs—at the lowest possible price. Enter mass customization.

Mass customization uses state-of-the-art information technology to produce and deliver products and services designed to fit the specifications of individual customers. Companies can customize products in quantities as small as one with the same speed and low cost as mass-production methods. Mass-customization systems use information taken from the customer

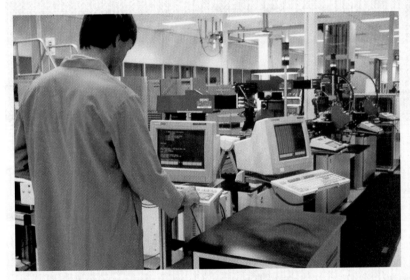

to control the flow of goods. For example, Motorola manufactures handheld pagers to individual customer specifications. Retailers use Macintosh PCs to help customers design the pager features they want. At Motorola's Boynton Beach, Florida, plant, orders stream in over toll-free telephone lines or e-mail for different colors and models. The data are digitized and flow immediately to the assembly line. Within 80 minutes, pick-and-place robots select the proper components for each order and humans assemble them into the final product. Often the customer can have the pager the same day or the day after. Instead of manufacturing, Motorola thinks of this process as rapidly translating data from customers into products.

The John Deere Harvester Works manufacturing plant in Moline, Illinois, produces a wide variety of crop planters, many of which sell for over $100,000. Customers can choose from scores of options, including liquid or dry fertilizer and row count, which amount to thousands of different configurations. Until 1992, the plant was a typical mass-production operation. It kept an inventory of about 300 planters, based on projected demand and production forecasts because it could not respond quickly to individual orders. Then Deere equipped the factory with new manufacturing scheduling software that would provide shorter lead times and greater flexibility. With this new system, the Deere plant can reschedule production each day in response to customer orders. The plant needs to keep only 20 finished machines in inventory.

Levi Strauss is equipping its stores with an option called Personal Pair, which allows customers to design jeans to their own specifications, rather than picking them off the rack. A "fit specialist" enters a customer's measurements into a personal computer, which then transmits the customer's specifications over a network to a factory in Tennessee. The company is able to produce the custom jeans on the same lines that manufacture its standard items.

Because of the marketing presumption that custom-made jeans are expensive, Levi Strauss can charge 20 percent more for Personal Pair jeans than for an off-the-rack pair. But by using mass-customization technology, Levi's actually eliminates 75 percent of the production cost because there are no warehousing, production overruns, and inventories. Customer satisfaction has risen from 28 percent to 99 percent as well. The service now accounts for 25 percent of women's jeans sales at Original Levi's stores.

To Think About: *How does mass customization change the way these companies do business? What are the management benefits of mass customization?*

Sources: John Landry, "Internet Strategies for Business Transformation," in *The Culpepper Letter*, December, 1996; Jeff Moad, "Let Customers Have It Their Way," in *Datamation*, April 1, 1995; and Gene Bylinsky, "The Digital Factory," in *Fortune*, November 14, 1994.

The Internet: The New Electronic Marketplace

Merrill Lynch and Co.'s worst nightmare could be a small investor such as Ed Harrison. He makes several stock trades a week, but he doesn't use a conventional brokerage firm. Instead, he buys and sells stocks directly from his desktop computer using the Internet.

Originally investors could only choose among full-service brokers. That changed in the 1980s when Charles Schwab Inc., began offering brokerage fee discounts of 50 percent and more. Discount brokers save by eliminating large research departments. People who actively trade stocks have flocked to the discount brokers because they make their own decisions and need a broker only to enter trades. Next, in the mid-1990s, some discount firms began offering deeper discounts to traders who enter their trades electronically via networked computers linked to proprietary networks. (Schwab charges $39 per electronic trade on its E-Schwab network.) Electronic trades bypass human contact, further reducing brokerage personnel costs. Now the newest step, use of a World Wide Web brokerage firm, has begun and may be the next revolution.

Internet trading offers further savings because Internet brokerage houses offer a bare-bones service. They maintain no research departments and have few offices, because customers linked to Internet can access their broker from their desktops. Because these companies link their account data to the Internet, their customers are able to monitor their portfolios via the Net at any time. They see the same up-to-the-minute information that their broker sees. Finally, these brokerage houses never "close." Customers enter their trades any time of the day or night, any day of the year. Internet brokerage sites also offer links to other sites where the investor can obtain stock quotes, charts, investment news, and all kinds of advice on-line. One Internet-accessible firm, Lombard Institutional Brokerage, offers free 30-minute delayed stock quotes and even stock graphs. Clients can use Lombard's Internet capabilities to make their home computers look like the same flashy terminals used by high-powered Wall Street traders. A window running across the top of the screen displays icon buttons that let investors click to obtain equity and option quotes, draw historical and intra-day trading graphs, or write and send e-mail. A vertical window along the left side of the screen contains icons for accessing portfolios, account activity, and research tools. These windows remain on the computer screen while users retrieve stock quotes and charts showing same-day trading activity.

Internet brokerage firms such as E*Trade Securities and Lombard charge commissions of $15 to $30 for most trades of any size. In comparison, full-service brokers such as Merrill Lynch, who provide stock selection advice, charge roughly $100 to $1100 for trades of 100 to 5000 stock shares. Live order takers at Fidelity's discount brokerage service charge $55 to $270 per trade. Recognizing the Web's convenience and popularity, Fidelity, Schwab, and other mutual fund companies are starting to provide trading services at their Web sites.

Will investor trading via the Internet replace conventional financial trading? Internet security is not yet adequate so that Net brokerage houses bill customers the old-fashioned way through the mail. Very few investors trade electronically, either on the Internet or through proprietary on-line services. Forrester Research estimates there are only about 1.5 million on-line or Internet brokerage accounts, compared with 60 million conventional brokerage accounts in the United States. Most Internet traders are young and computer literate. Big full-service retail brokerage firms do not offer electronic trading, but they have started to use the Internet to provide clients with account and money management data, watching warily as the electronic brokers expand. But over the years, as the population's comfort with computers expands, Internet securities trading will grow, and the traditional brokerage firms will have to adapt.

To Think About: How has the Internet changed the brokerage business? In what ways can using the Internet as an electronic marketplace affect other organizations?

Sources: Kathryn Haines, "Fund Firms See Savings on Web Trades," *The Wall Street Journal*, January 2, 1997; Leah Nathans Spiro and Linda Himelstein, "With the World Wide Web, Who Needs Wall Street?" *Business Week*, April 29, 1996; and Eric R. Chabrow, "Wall Street on the Desktop," *Information Week*, March 11, 1996.

Even electronic financial trading has arrived on the Web, offering electronic trading in stocks, bonds, mutual funds, and other financial instruments. The Window on Organizations examines the growing interest in Internet trading.

By creating electronic marketplaces and linking suppliers, buyers, and sellers, the Internet and other networking technologies are fueling the growth of electronic commerce. **Electronic commerce** is the process of buying and selling goods electronically by consumers and from company to company through computerized business transactions. By replacing manual and paper-based procedures with electronic alternatives, and by using information flows in new and dynamic ways, electronic commerce

electronic commerce The process of buying and selling goods electronically by consumers and from company to company through computerized business transactions.

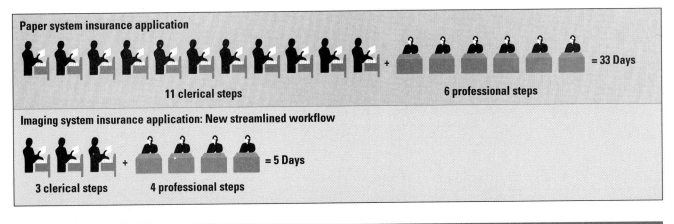

FIGURE 1.10

Redesigned work flow for insurance underwriting. An application requiring 33 days in a paper system would only take 5 days using computers, networks, and a streamlined work flow.

can accelerate ordering, delivery, and payment for goods and services while reducing companies' operating and inventory costs. We explore electronic commerce in greater detail in Chapter 10.

Reorganizing Work Flows

Since the first uses of information technology in business, information systems have been progressively replacing manual work procedures with automated work procedures, work flows, and work processes. Electronic work flows have reduced the cost of operations in many companies by displacing paper and the manual routines that accompany it. Improved workflow management has enabled many corporations to not only cut costs significantly but also to improve customer service at the same time. For instance, insurance companies can reduce processing of applications for new insurance from weeks to days (see Figure 1.10). Redesigned work flows can have a profound impact on organizational efficiency and can even lead to new organizational structures, products, and services. We will be discussing the impact of restructured work flows on organizational design in greater detail in Chapters 3 and 11.

The Changing Management Process

Information technology is recasting the process of management, providing powerful new capabilities to help managers strategize and plan, organize, lead, and control. For instance, it is now possible for managers to obtain information on organizational performance down to the level of specific transactions from just about anywhere in the organization at any time. Product managers at Frito-Lay Corporation, the world's largest manufacturer of salty snack foods, can know within hours precisely how many bags of Fritos were sold on any street in America at its customers' stores, how much they sold for, and what the competition's sales volumes and prices are. This new intensity of information makes possible far more precise planning, forecasting, and monitoring. Information technology has also opened new possibilities for leading. By distributing information through electronic networks, the new manager can effectively communicate frequently with thousands of employees and even manage far-flung task forces and teams—tasks which would be impossible in face-to-face traditional organizations.

New People Requirements

Managers must deal with new people issues because the changes brought about by information technology definitely require a new kind of employee. Employees need to be more highly trained than in the past as work shifts from production of goods to production of services and as more tasks become automated. High on this skill set is the ability to work in an electronic environment; the ability to digest new information and knowledge, and act upon that information; and the ability and willingness to learn new software and business procedures. Most important is the willingness to engage in a lifelong learning process. The new global worker, whether in factories or offices, is a multitalented college graduate who is exceptionally productive because of an ever-changing set of skills and competencies.

1.4   THE CHALLENGE OF INFORMATION SYSTEMS: KEY MANAGEMENT ISSUES

One message of this text is that despite, or perhaps because of, the rapid development of computer technology, there is nothing easy or mechanical about building workable information systems. Building, operating, and maintaining information systems are challenging activities for a number of reasons. We believe that managers should heed five key challenges:

1. The Strategic Business Challenge: How can businesses use information technology to design organizations that are competitive and effective? Investment in information technology amounts to more than half of the annual capital expenditures of most large service sector firms. Yet despite investing more in computers than any other country, the United States is grappling with a serious productivity challenge. Until recently, America's productivity growth rate of just under 2 percent per year has been far below those of other industrial countries. The productivity lag has been especially pronounced in the service sector. During the 1980s, white-collar productivity increased at an annual rate of only .28 percent (Roach, 1991).

Technical change moves much faster than humans and organizations are changing. The power of computer hardware and software has grown much more rapidly than the ability of organizations to apply and use this technology. To stay competitive, many organizations actually need to be redesigned. They will need to use information technology to simplify communication and coordination, eliminate unnecessary work, and eliminate the inefficiencies of outmoded organizational structures. If organizations merely automate what they are doing today, they are largely missing the potential of information technology. Organizations need to rethink and redesign the way they design, produce, deliver, and maintain goods and services.

2. The Globalization Challenge: How can firms understand the business and system requirements of a global economic environment? The rapid growth in international trade and the emergence of a global economy call for information systems that can support both producing and selling goods in many different countries. In the past, each regional office of a multinational corporation focused on solving its own unique information problems. Given language, cultural, and political differences among countries, this focus frequently resulted in chaos and the failure of central management controls. To develop integrated multinational information systems, businesses must develop global hardware, software, and communications standards and create cross-cultural accounting and reporting structures (Roche, 1992).

3. The Information Architecture Challenge: How can organizations develop an information architecture that supports their business goals? Creating a new system now means much more than installing a new machine in the basement. Today, this process typically places thousands of terminals or PCs on the desks of employees who have little experience with them, connecting the devices to powerful communications networks, rearranging social relations in the office and work locations, changing reporting patterns, and redefining business goals. Briefly, new systems today often require redesigning the organization and developing a new information architecture.

Information architecture is the particular form that information technology takes in an organization to achieve selected goals or functions. Information architecture in-

information architecture The particular form that information technology takes in a specific organization to achieve selected goals or functions.

cludes the extent to which data and processing power are centralized or distributed. Figure 1.11 illustrates the major elements of information architecture that managers will need to develop. Although the computer systems base is typically operated by technical personnel, general management must decide how to allocate the resources it has assigned to hardware, software, and telecommunications. Resting upon the computer systems base are the major business application systems, or the major islands of applications. Because managers and employees directly interact with these systems, it is critical for the success of the organization that these systems meet business functional requirements now and in the future.

Some MIS scholars prefer to use the term *IT infrastructure* rather than *architecture*, focusing on computer and communications technologies as the technical foundation of the organization's information systems capabilities (Weill and Broadbent, 1997). Human knowledge and skills convert these components into information technology services which then provide the foundation for the organization's information systems applications.

Here are typical questions regarding information architecture facing today's managers: Should the corporate sales data and function be distributed to each corporate remote site, or should they be centralized at headquarters? Should the organization purchase stand-alone PCs or build a more powerful centralized mainframe environment within an integrated telecommunications network? Should the organi-

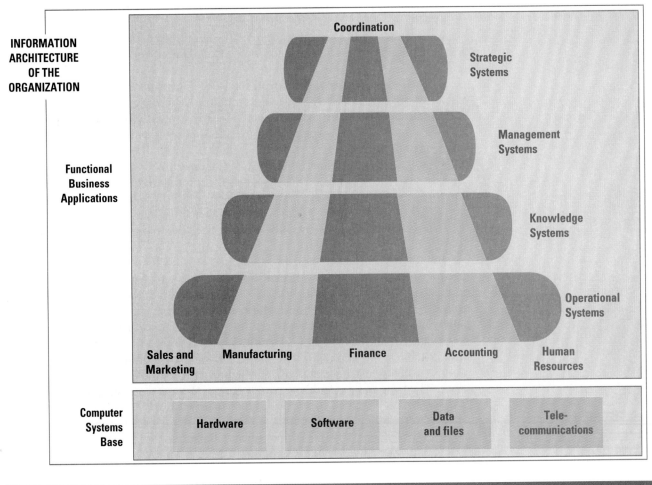

FIGURE 1.11

The information architecture of the firm. Today's managers must know how to arrange and coordinate the various computer technologies and business system applications to meet the information needs of each level of their organization, as well as the needs of the organization as a whole.

zation build its own data communications utility to link remote sites or rely on external providers such as the telephone company? There is no one right answer to these questions (see Allen and Boynton, 1991).

Even under the best of circumstances, combining knowledge of systems and the organization is itself a demanding task. For many organizations, the task is even more formidable because they are crippled by fragmented and incompatible computer hardware, software, telecommunications networks, and information systems. Integrating islands of information and technology into a coherent architecture is now a priority.

4. The Information Systems Investment Challenge: How can organizations determine the business value of information systems? A major problem raised by the development of powerful, inexpensive computers involves not technology but rather management and organizations. It's one thing to use information technology to design, produce, deliver, and maintain new products. It's another thing to make money doing it. How can organizations obtain a sizable payoff from their investment in information systems?

Engineering massive organizational and system changes in the hope of positioning a firm strategically is complicated and expensive. Is this an investment that pays off? How can you tell? Senior management can be expected to ask these questions: Are we receiving the kind of return on investment from our systems that we should be? Do our competitors get more? Although understanding the costs and benefits of building a single system is difficult enough, it is daunting to consider whether the entire systems effort is "worth it." Imagine, then, how a senior executive must think when presented with a major transformation in information architecture—a bold venture in organizational change costing tens of millions of dollars and taking many years.

5. The Responsibility and Control Challenge: How can organizations design systems that people can control and understand? How can organizations ensure that their information systems are used in an ethically and socially responsible manner? Information systems are so essential to business, government, and daily life that organizations must take special steps to ensure that they are accurate, reliable, and secure. Automated or semi-automated systems that malfunction or are poorly operated can have extremely harmful consequences. A firm invites disaster if it uses systems that do not work as intended, that do not deliver information in a form that people can interpret correctly and use, or that have control rooms where controls do not work or where instruments give false signals. The potential for massive fraud, error, abuse, and destruction is enormous.

Information systems must be designed so that they function as intended and so that humans can control the process. When building and using information systems, organizations should consider health, safety, job security, and social well-being as carefully as they do their business goals. Managers will need to ask: Can we apply high quality assurance standards to our information systems as well as to our products and services? Can we build information systems that respect people's rights of privacy while still pursuing our organization's goals? Should information systems monitor employees? What do we do when an information system designed to increase efficiency and productivity eliminates people's jobs?

This text is designed to provide future managers with the knowledge and understanding required to deal with these challenges. To further this objective, each succeeding chapter begins with a Management Challenges box that outlines the key issues of which managers should be aware.

Managers are problem solvers who are responsible for analyzing the many challenges confronting organizations and for developing strategies and action plans. Information systems are one of their tools, delivering the information required for solutions. Information systems both reflect management decisions and serve as instruments for changing the management process.

MANAGEMENT

Information systems are rooted in organizations, an outcome of organizational structure, culture, politics, work flows, and standard operating procedures. They are instruments of organizational change, making it possible to recast these organizational elements into new business models and redraw organizational boundaries. Advances in information systems are accelerating the trend toward globalized, knowledge-driven economies and flattened, flexible, decentralized organizations.

ORGANIZATION

A network revolution is underway. Information systems technology is no longer limited to computers but consists of an array of technologies that enable computers to be networked together to exchange information across great distances and organizational boundaries. The Internet provides global connectivity and a flexible platform for information sharing, creating new uses for information systems and revolutionizing the role of information systems in organizations.

TECHNOLOGY

For Discussion: Information systems are too important to be left to computer specialists. Do you agree? Why or why not?

SUMMARY

1. Define an information system. The purpose of a CBIS is to collect, store, and disseminate information from an organization's environment and internal operations for the purpose of supporting organizational functions and decision making, communication, coordination, control, analysis, and visualization. Information systems transform raw data into useful information through three basic activities: input, processing, and output.

2. Explain the difference between computer literacy and information systems literacy. Information systems literacy requires an understanding of the organizational and management dimensions of information systems as well as the technical dimensions addressed by computer literacy. Information systems literacy draws on both technical and behavioral approaches to studying information systems. Both perspectives can be combined into a sociotechnical approach to systems.

3. Explain why information systems are so important today and how they are transforming organizations and management. The kinds of systems built today are very important for the overall performance of the organization, especially in today's highly globalized and information-based economy. Information systems are driving both daily operations and organizational strategy. Powerful computers, software, and networks have helped organizations become more flexible, eliminate layers of management, separate work from location, and restructure work flows, giving new powers both to line workers and management. The Internet and other networks have redefined organizational boundaries, opening new opportunities for electronic markets and electronic commerce. To maximize the advantages of information technology, there is a much greater need to plan for the overall information architecture of the organization.

4. Identify the major management challenges to building and using information systems in organizations. There are five key management challenges to building and using information systems: (1) designing systems that are competitive and efficient; (2) understanding the system requirements of a global business environment; (3) creating an information architecture that supports the organization's goals; (4) determining the business value of information systems; and (5) designing systems that people can control, understand, and use in a socially and ethically responsible manner.

KEY TERMS

Knowledge- and information-intense products	Computer-based information system (CBIS)	Senior managers	World Wide Web
		Middle managers	Web site
		Operational managers	Virtual organization
Information system	Formal system	Computer hardware	Mass customization
Information	Standard operating procedures (SOPs)	Computer software	Interorganizational systems
Data		Storage technology	Electronic market
Input	Knowledge workers	Communications technology	Electronic commerce
Processing	Data workers		Information architecture
Output	Production or service workers	Network	
Feedback		Internet	

REVIEW QUESTIONS

1. Distinguish between a computer, a computer program, and an information system. What is the difference between data and information?

2. What activities convert raw data to usable information in information systems? What is their relationship to feedback?

3. What is information systems literacy?

4. What are the organization, management, and technology dimensions of information systems?

5. Distinguish between a behavioral and a technical approach to information systems in terms of the questions asked and the answers provided.

6. What major disciplines contribute to an understanding of information systems?

7. Why should managers study information systems?

8. What is the relationship between an organization and its information systems? How is this relationship changing over time?

9. What is the Internet? How has it changed the role played by information systems in organizations?

10. What is the relationship between the network revolution and electronic commerce?

11. Describe some major changes that information systems are bringing to organizations.

12. How are information systems changing the management process?

13. What do we mean by the information architecture of the organization?

14. What are the key management challenges involved in building, operating, and maintaining information systems today?

GROUP PROJECT

In a group with three or four classmates, find a description in a computer or business magazine of an information system used by an organization. Describe the system in terms of its inputs, processes, and outputs and in terms of its organization, management, and technology features. Present your analysis to the class.

David Battles Goliath for the Power of Information on the Internet

In an information-based economy, control of information is the key to power. Many believe that is the source of the 1995 conflict between the London Stock Exchange and a tiny startup, Electronic Share Information Ltd. The London Stock Exchange (LSE), the Goliath in the battle, was formally organized 250 years ago to replace a 150-year-old informal system of trading shares in London coffee houses. LSE has undergone some computerization, but some of its activities remain manual and paper based. Today, although LSE is one of the five premier stock exchanges in the world, it is coming under increasing competitive pressure. The European Association of Securities Dealers plans an automated screen-based trading system soon, while Tradepoint Financial Networks has already established a stock exchange that delivers its services electronically.

Electronic Share Information (ESI), the David in the battle, was established in June 1993 for the purpose of becoming the "world's first cyberspace stock market." Being a British company, it planned to start with British stocks, going head-to-head with the LSE. The new company's leadership was convinced that the Internet would change the way people do business, and it saw an opportunity to develop new tools to support the globalization of the financial markets.

The conflict originated with the plans of ESI to create the first on-line stock exchange. Its founders wanted to phase in the exchange, beginning with a conventional Internet-based information service that provided up-to-the-minute stock prices, company news, and analyst reports. During phase two they would develop an on-line stock exchange for small companies. Their planned service required

them to deliver instant real-time market data to the computers of paying customers. The only source for the data was the London Stock Exchange. In the spring of 1995 the LSE signed a contract to supply ESI with market data for a year. Originally ESI planned to develop the whole system itself; however, the World Wide Web of the Internet grew far faster than any of them (or anyone else) expected, and ultimately they decided to base their service on the Web.

Although ESI would not become a stock exchange during its first phase, it did need to offer a brokerage service to transact orders, something that it was not licensed to do. So it turned to David Jones, the founder and chief executive officer of ShareLink Ltd., an established retail brokerage firm that uses modern telecommunications to reduce the cost of brokerage services, thus enabling discount prices. Jones agreed to provide ESI with a Web-based full-brokerage service, including client portfolio tracking.

With everything in place the pilot began on May 20, 1995. The ESI pilot site offered free stock market information, including delayed stock prices, price histories, and company data. By the end of August, 3000 potential clients had registered, a positive enough response for ESI to decide to launch the service. The launch was scheduled for September 8.

On September 4 the LSE backed out, announcing its decision to discontinue the data feed to ESI and to end the contract to supply ESI with real-time market data. Without real-time data, ESI could not continue in business—real-time prices are a linchpin to any market trading service in the electronic information age. The feed was not cut immediately, and ESI decided to go ahead with the launch as planned but to challenge the LSE by

publicizing its action to explain its (ESI's) own lack of service. ESI also decided to fight the stock exchange because ESI's contract with LSE still had eight months to run.

On September 8, Jones gave a public TV interview in which he alleged that the LSE had improperly changed the terms of its contract with ESI. On September 11, the LSE cut its price feed in the middle of the afternoon, and on September 13 it held a press conference at which it rejected allegations that it had cut the feed to prevent a new competitor from being established. It announced a defamation suit against Jones, claiming that Jones's remarks on September 8 constituted "conduct detrimental to the interests of the Exchange."

The Office of Fair Trading, a British regulatory body, quickly undertook an investigation into whether the LSE's cancellation of the ESI contract was "intended to distort, restrict or prevent competition." With this great pressure on the LSE, secret negotiations commenced, and on September 27, both sides dropped their legal proceedings and the contract between them was renewed. The details of the settlement remain secret, but on September 28, the data feed to the ESI Web site resumed and soon thereafter Jones publicly apologized.

Jones later indicated his belief that the episode was a battle for control of information. He stated that the Internet undermines control of information, and therefore power, by giving individuals more direct access to information. The London Stock Exchange continues to claim that the whole affair was merely a contract dispute. Observers point out that the LSE is certainly unable to control the new Internet technology and has reason to be concerned about being undermined.

By early November 1995, ESI had 8500 users registered for the free service and 250 customers paying for access to the full on-line service, including real-time data and brokerage services. The company indicated that it expected to break even by the end of 1995, and early in 1996, ESI began another round of raising investment capital to begin the second phase, the development of a cyberspace stock market for small capitalized companies. By early 1996 the company already had 17 inquiries from groups in various countries interested in franchising its virtual stock exchange model. ∎

Sources: E. E. Baatz, "Hostile Exchanges," *WebMaster,* January/February 1996; Faegre & Benson Limited Liability Partnership, "London Stock Exchange—New Market to be Launched," http://www.faegre.com/areas/area_ib5.html.

Case Study Questions

1. How are the Internet and information technology changing the way stock exchanges are conducting business?

2. How important is the role of information systems in ESI's new venture? Discuss.

3. Describe the management, organization, and technical challenges to building this cyberspace stock exchange.

REFERENCES

Ackoff, R. L. "Management Misinformation System." *Management Science* 14, no. 4 (December 1967), B140–B116.

Alavi, Maryam, and Patricia Carlson. "A Review of MIS Research and Disciplinary Development." *Journal of Management Information Systems* 8, no. 4 (Spring 1992).

Allen, Brandt R., and Andrew C. Boynton. "Information Architecture: In Search of Efficient Flexibility." *MIS Quarterly* 15, no. 4 (December 1991).

Anthony, R. N. *Planning and Control Systems: A Framework for Analysis.* Cambridge, MA: Harvard University Press (1965).

Applegate, Lynda, and Janice Gogan. "Electronic Commerce: Trends and Opportunities." Harvard Business School 9-196-006 (October 6, 1995).

Armstrong, Arthur, and John Hagel III. "The Real Value of On-line Communities." *Harvard Business Review* (May–June 1996).

Bakos, J. Yannis. "A Strategic Analysis of Electronic Marketplaces." *MIS Quarterly* 15, no. 3 (September 1991).

Barrett, Stephanie S. "Strategic Alternatives and Interorganizational System Implementations: An Overview." *Journal of Management Information Systems* (Winter 1986–1987).

Benjamin, Robert, and Rolf Wigand. "Electronic Markets and Virtual Value Chains on the Information Superhighway." *Sloan Management Review* (Winter 1995).

Brown, Carol V., and Sharon L. Magill. "Alignment of the IS Functions with the Enterprise: Toward a Model of Antecedents." *MIS Quarterly* 18, no. 4 (December 1994).

Brynjolffson, E. T., T. W. Malone, V. Gurbaxani, and A. Kambil. "Does Information Technology Lead to Smaller Firms?" *Management Science* 40, no. 12 (1994).

Cash, James I., F. Warren McFarlan, James L. McKenney, and Lynda M. Applegate. *Corporate Information Systems Management,* 4th ed. Homewood, IL: Irwin (1996).

Clark, Thomas D., Jr. "Corporate Systems Management: An Overview and Research Perspective." *Communications of the ACM* 35, no. 2 (February 1992).

Davis, Gordon B., and Margrethe H. Olson. *Management Information Systems: Conceptual Foundations, Structure, and Development,* 2nd ed. New York: McGraw-Hill (1985).

Deans, Candace P., and Michael J. Kane. *International Dimensions of Information Systems and Technology.* Boston, MA: PWS-Kent (1992).

Fedorowicz, Jane, and Benn Konsynski. "Organization Support Systems: Bridging Business and Decision Processes." *Journal of Management Information Systems* 8, no. 4 (Spring 1992).

Feitzinger, Edward, and Hau L. Lee. "Mass Customization at Hewlett-Packard: The Power of Postponement." *Harvard Business Review* (January–February 1997).

Gilmore, James H., and B. Joseph Pine II. "The Four Faces of Mass Customization." *Harvard Business Review* (January–February 1997).

Gorry, G. A., and M. S. Scott Morton. "A Framework for Management Information Systems." *Sloan Management Review* 13, no. 1 (1971).

Johnston, Russell, and Michael J. Vitale. "Creating Competitive Advantage with Interorganizational Information Systems." *MIS Quarterly* 12, no. 2 (June 1988).

Keen, Peter G. W. *Shaping the Future: Business Design Through Information Technology.* Cambridge, MA: Harvard Business School Press (1991).

King, John. "Centralized vs. Decentralized Computing: Organizational Considerations and Management Options." *Computing Surveys* (October 1984).

Kling, Rob, and William H. Dutton. "The Computer Package: Dynamic Complexity," in *Computers and Politics,* edited by James Danziger, William H. Dutton, Rob Kling, and Kenneth Kraemer. New York: Columbia University Press (1982).

Laudon, Kenneth C. "A General Model for Understanding the Relationship Between Information Technology and Organizations." Working paper, Center for Research on Information Systems, New York University (1989).

Leonard-Barton, Dorothy. *Wellsprings of Knowledge.* Boston, MA: Harvard Business School Press (1995).

Liker, Jeffrey K., David B. Roitman, and Ethel Roskies. "Changing Everything All at Once: Work Life and Technological Change." *Sloan Management Review* (Summer 1987).

Lucas, Henry C., Jr., and Jack Baroudi. "The Role of Information Technology in Organization Design."

Journal of Management Information Systems 10, no. 4 (Spring 1994).

Malone, T. W., and J. F. Rockart. "Computers, Networks, and the Corporation." *Scientific American* 265, no. 3 (September 1991).

Malone, Thomas W., JoAnne Yates, and Robert I. Benjamin. "Electronic Markets and Electronic Hierarchies." *Communications of the ACM* (June 1987).

———. "The Logic of Electronic Markets." *Harvard Business Review* (May–June 1989).

McFarlan, F. Warren, James L. McKenney, and Philip Pyburn. "The Information Archipelago—Plotting a Course." *Harvard Business Review* (January–February 1983a).

———. "Governing the New World." *Harvard Business Review* (July–August 1983b).

McKenney, James L., and F. Warren McFarlan. "The Information Archipelago—Maps and Bridges." *Harvard Business Review* (September–October 1982).

Niederman, Fred, James C. Brancheau, and James C. Wetherbe. "Information Systems Management Issues for the 1990s." *MIS Quarterly* 15, no. 4 (December 1991).

Orlikowski, Wanda J., and Jack J. Baroudi. "Studying Information Technology in Organizations: Research Approaches and Assumptions." *Information Systems Research* 2, no. 1 (March 1991).

Rayport, J. F., and J. J. Sviokla. "Managing in the Marketspace." *Harvard Business Review* (November–December 1994).

Roach, Stephen S. "Technology and the Services Sector: The Hidden Competitive Challenge." *Technological Forecasting and Social Change* 34 (1988).

———. "Services Under Siege—The Restructuring Imperative." *Harvard Business Review* (September–October, 1991).

Roche, Edward M. "Planning for Competitive Use of Information Technology in Multinational Corporations." AIB UK Region, Brighton Polytechnic, Brighton, UK, Conference Paper, March 1992. Edward M. Roche, W. Paul Stillman School of Business, Seton Hall University.

Rockart, John F. "The Line Takes the Leadership—IS Management in a Wired Society." *Sloan Management Review* 29, no. 4 (Summer 1988).

Rockart, John F., and James E. Short. "IT in the 1990s: Managing Organizational Interdependence." *Sloan Management Review* 30, no. 2 (Winter 1989).

Scott Morton, Michael, ed. *The Corporation in the 1990s.* New York: Oxford University Press (1991).

Strassman, Paul. *The Information Payoff—The Transformation of Work in the Electronic Age.* New York: Free Press (1985).

Tornatsky, Louis G., J. D. Eveland, Myles G. Boylan, W. A. Hertzner, E. C. Johnson, D. Roitman, and J. Schneider. "The Process of Technological Innovation: Reviewing the Literature." Washington, DC: National Science Foundation (1983).

Upton, David M., and Andrew McAfee. "The Real Virtual Factory." *Harvard Business Review* (July–August 1996).

Warson, Albert. "Tool Time." *Forbes ASAP* (October 7, 1996).

Weill, Peter, and Marianne Broadbent. "Management by Maxim: How Business and IT Managers Can Create IT Infrastructures." *Sloan Management Review* (Spring 1997).

Winter, Susan J., and S. Lynne Taylor. "The Role of IT in the Transformation of Work: A Comparison of Post-Industrial, Industrial, and Proto-Industrial Organization." *Information Systems Research* 7, no. 1 (March 1996).

The Strategic Role of Information Systems

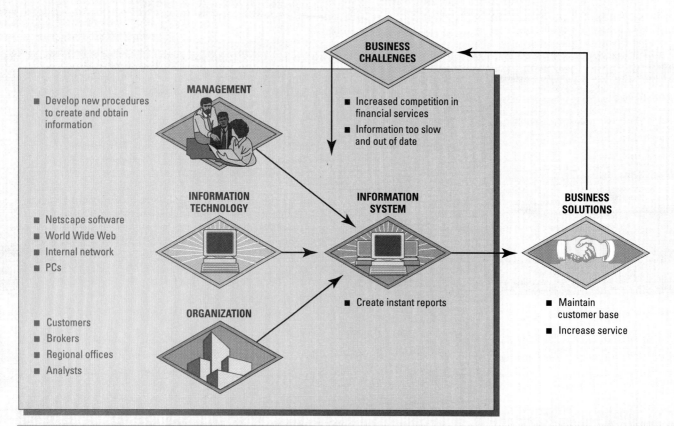

BUSINESS CHALLENGES

MANAGEMENT

- Develop new procedures to create and obtain information

- Increased competition in financial services
- Information too slow and out of date

INFORMATION TECHNOLOGY

- Netscape software
- World Wide Web
- Internal network
- PCs

INFORMATION SYSTEM

BUSINESS SOLUTIONS

- Create instant reports

- Maintain customer base
- Increase service

ORGANIZATION

- Customers
- Brokers
- Regional offices
- Analysts

Scotia Capital Markets: Internet Competitive Edge

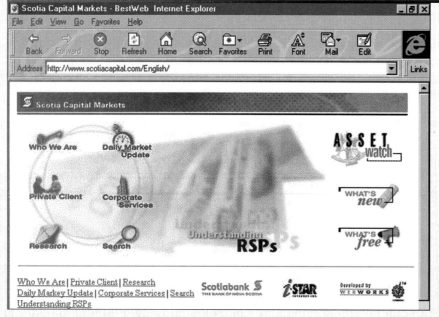

What good is information if it cannot be distributed and understood by those who need it? Nowhere is this problem more acute than in financial services, where seconds can mean the difference between a profitable stock purchase and a loss. The Toronto-based Scotia Capital Markets investment firm has decided to use Internet technology to slice an entire day off the length of time required to deliver stock analyst reports to its brokers, traders, and other analysts.

Scotia Capital Markets has 2500 employees spread out in 64 offices across Canada, and locations in New York, Boston, London, Singapore, Tokyo, Cologne, and

CHAPTER OUTLINE

LEARNING OBJECTIVES

After completing this chapter, you will be able to:

1. Describe the role played by the six major types of information systems in organizations.
2. Discuss the relationship between the various types of information systems.
3. Define a strategic information system and explain why information is now considered a strategic resource.
4. Describe how information systems can be used to support three levels of strategy used in business.
5. Explain why strategic information systems are difficult to build and sustain.

Geneva. In the past, Scotia serviced clients and staff with an outdated 10-year-old system which allowed for once-a-day updates of its analysts' reports. This meant reports were generally 24 hours out of date by the time they hit the brokers' desks, and even older by the time customers got the news. Although the old system met the regulatory requirements, customers were starting to turn elsewhere for timely investment information. And that meant customers were taking their trading business elsewhere.

Scotia turned to Internet technology to regain a competitive edge in its information-driven business. Scotia already had an internal home-grown network with thousands of PCs. It added to its network new Netscape software that could display and access information on the World Wide Web, creating a new information service. Using the Web and a private network based on Internet technology, brokers and customers can receive reports instantly, as soon as the analysts file their reports. This has sliced 24 hours off the information delivery cycle, and given Scotia an edge over its competitors who rely on much slower investment research systems. Another bonus of using Web technology is that the reports can include detailed graphics and color.

Scotia is finding new uses for this network. It plans to develop workflow applications such as expense reports, purchase orders, and travel reports and has created new investment services such as high-yield bonds. ■

Source: "Scotia Spreads Stock Information More Quickly via Intranet," *Computerworld*, October 14, 1996, and [http://www.scotiacapital.com].

MANAGEMENT CHALLENGES

Scotia Capital Markets is using Internet technology to rethink how it does business and to rearrange one of its business processes—the delivery of timely market information to brokers and customers. Scotia has temporarily gained a market advantage over its competitors by offering a service others cannot. But something more than a single technological leap is required to sustain this competitive edge. Managers need to discover ways of maintaining a competitive edge over many years. Specifically, managers need to address the following challenges:

1. **Sustainability of competitive advantage.** The competitive advantages conferred by information technology do not necessarily last long enough to ensure long-term profits. Competitors can retaliate and copy strategic systems. Moreover, these systems are often expensive; costs saved by some systems are expended immediately to maintain the system. Competitive advantage isn't always sustainable. Market conditions change. The business and economic environments change. Technology and customers' expectations change. The classic strategic information systems—American Airlines' SABRE computerized reservation system, Citibank's ATM system, and Federal Express' package tracking system—benefited by being the first in their respective industries. But then rival systems emerged. Information systems alone cannot provide an enduring business advantage (Kettinger et al., 1994; Mata et al., 1995; Hopper, 1990). Systems originally intended to be strategic frequently become tools for survival, something every firm has in order to stay in business. Rather than conferring long-term competitive advantage, they become critical for a company simply to keep abreast of the competition.

2. **Organizational barriers to strategic transitions.** Implementing strategic systems usually requires far-reaching sociotechnical changes. These sociotechnical changes are the real key for sustained advantage. But this goal is not easy to accomplish because organizational change is frequently resisted by middle and even senior managers. In fact, one of the greatest obstacles to strategic transitions may be resistance to change—both the changes that are imposed on an organization and those that employees experience as their jobs are reshaped. Even the identities of employees must change. One is no longer simply a salesperson or a member of the production department. These tasks become increasingly integrated through a single information network. To be successful, strategic transitions require changes in organizational culture (see Chapter 3). Interorganizational systems may also be resisted if one organization perceives that it will be worse off by closer coordination with another organization (Clemons and Row, 1993).

The experience of Scotia Capital Markets illustrates how critical information systems have become for supporting organizational goals and for enabling firms to stay ahead of the competition. In this chapter, we show the role played by the various types of information systems in organizations. We then look at the problems firms face from competition and the ways in which information systems can provide competitive advantage at three different levels of the business.

Scotia Capital Markets used information systems to provide a superior service that could not be matched by competitors. Information systems can also create competitive advantage by helping companies market products more accurately, reduce internal operating costs, and forge new relationships with customers and suppliers.

Because there are different interests, specialties, and levels in an organization, there are different kinds of systems. No single system can provide all the information an organization needs. Figure 2.1 illustrates one way to depict the kinds of systems found in an organization. In the illustration, the organization is divided into strategic, management, knowledge, and operational levels and then is further divided into functional areas such as sales and marketing, manufacturing, finance, accounting, and human resources. Systems are built to serve these different organizational interests (Anthony, 1965).

Different Kinds of Systems

Four main types of information systems serve different organizational levels: operational-level systems, knowledge-level systems, management-level systems, and strategic-level systems. **Operational-level systems** support operational managers by keeping track of the elementary activities and transactions of the organization, such

operational-level systems Information systems that monitor the elementary activities and transactions of the organization.

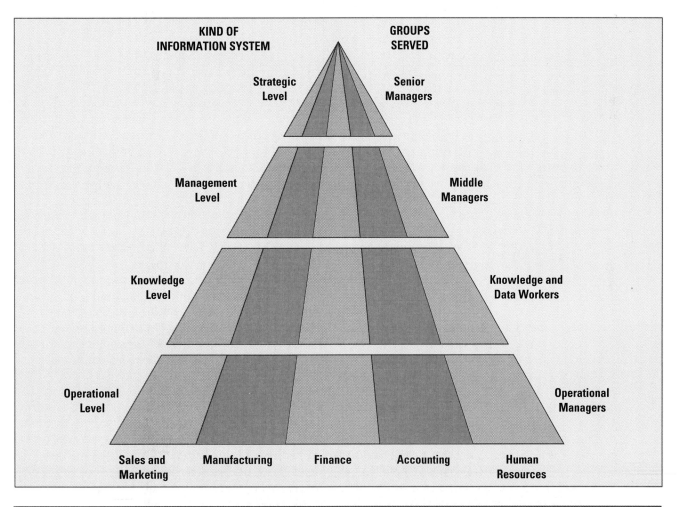

KIND OF INFORMATION SYSTEM

GROUPS SERVED

Strategic Level — Senior Managers

Management Level — Middle Managers

Knowledge Level — Knowledge and Data Workers

Operational Level — Operational Managers

Sales and Marketing   Manufacturing   Finance   Accounting   Human Resources

FIGURE 2.1

Types of information systems. Organizations and information systems can be divided into strategic, management, knowledge, and operational levels. They can be divided further into five functional areas: sales and marketing, manufacturing, finance, accounting, and human resources. Information systems serve each of these levels and functions. Strategic-level systems help senior managers with long-term planning. Management-level systems help middle managers monitor and control. Knowledge-level systems help knowledge and data workers design products, distribute information, and cope with paperwork. Operational-level systems help operational managers keep track of the firm's day-to-day activities.

as sales, receipts, cash deposits, payroll, credit decisions, and the flow of materials in a factory. The principal purpose of systems at this level is to answer routine questions and to track the flow of transactions through the organization. How many parts are in inventory? What happened to Mr. Williams's payment? To answer these kinds of questions, information generally must be easily available, current, and accurate. Examples of operational-level systems include a system to record bank deposits from automatic teller machines or one that tracks the number of hours worked each day by employees on a factory floor.

knowledge-level systems
Information systems that support knowledge and data workers in an organization.

Knowledge-level systems support knowledge and data workers in an organization. The purpose of knowledge-level systems is to help the business firm discover, organize, and integrate new knowledge into the business and to help the organization control the flow of paperwork (Dhar and Stein, 1997). Knowledge-level systems, especially in the form of workstations and office systems, are the fastest-growing applications in business today.

management-level systems
Information systems that support the monitoring, controlling, decision-making, and administrative activities of middle managers.

Management-level systems are designed to serve the monitoring, controlling, decision-making, and administrative activities of middle managers. The principal question addressed by such systems is: Are things working well? Management-level systems typically provide periodic reports rather than instant information on operations. An example is a relocation control system that reports on the total moving, house-hunting, and home financing costs for employees in all company divisions, noting wherever actual costs exceed budgets.

Some management-level systems support nonroutine decision making (Keen and Morton, 1978). They tend to focus on less structured decisions for which information requirements are not always clear. These systems often answer "what if" questions: What would be the impact on production schedules if we were to double sales in the month of December? What would happen to our return on investment if a factory schedule delayed for six months? Answers to these questions frequently require new data from outside the organization, as well as data from inside that cannot be drawn from existing operational-level systems.

strategic-level systems
Information systems that support the long-range planning activities of senior management.

Strategic-level systems help senior management tackle and address strategic issues and long-term trends, both in the firm and in the external environment. Their principal concern is matching changes in the external environment with existing organizational capability. What will employment levels be in five years? What are the long-term industry cost trends, and where does our firm fit in? What products should we be making in five years?

Information systems may also be differentiated by functional specialty. Major organizational functions, such as sales and marketing, manufacturing, finance, accounting, and human resources, are each served by their own information systems. In large organizations, subfunctions of each of these major functions also have their own information systems. For example, the manufacturing function might have systems for inventory management, process control, plant maintenance, computer-aided engineering, and material requirements planning.

A typical organization has operational-, management-, knowledge-, and strategic-level systems for each functional area. For example, the sales function generally has a sales system on the operational level to record daily sales figures and to process orders. A knowledge-level system designs promotional displays for the firm's products. A management-level system tracks monthly sales figures by sales territory and reports on territories where sales exceed or fall below anticipated levels. A system to forecast sales trends over a five-year period serves the strategic level.

Finally, different organizations have different information systems for the same functional areas. Because no two organizations have exactly the same objectives, structures, or interests, information systems must be custom-made to fit the unique characteristics of each. There is no such thing as a universal information system that can fit all organizations. Every organization does the job somewhat differently.

Information systems can thus be classified by functional specialty or by the organizational level they serve. Throughout this text are examples of systems supporting the various functional areas—sales systems, manufacturing systems, human resources systems, and finance and accounting systems. For professors and students requiring deeper analysis of information systems from a functional perspective, we have included additional material on the Laudon and Laudon Web site. This chapter analyzes the key applications of the organization primarily in terms of the organizational level and types of decisions they support.

Six Major Types of Systems

In this section we describe the specific categories of systems serving each organizational level and their value to the organization. Figure 2.2 shows the specific types of information systems that correspond to each organizational level. The organization has executive support systems (ESS) at the strategic level; management information systems (MIS) and decision-support systems (DSS) at the management level; knowledge work systems (KWS) and office automation systems (OAS) at the knowledge level; and transaction processing systems (TPS) at the operational level. Systems at each level in turn are specialized to serve each of the major functional areas. Thus,

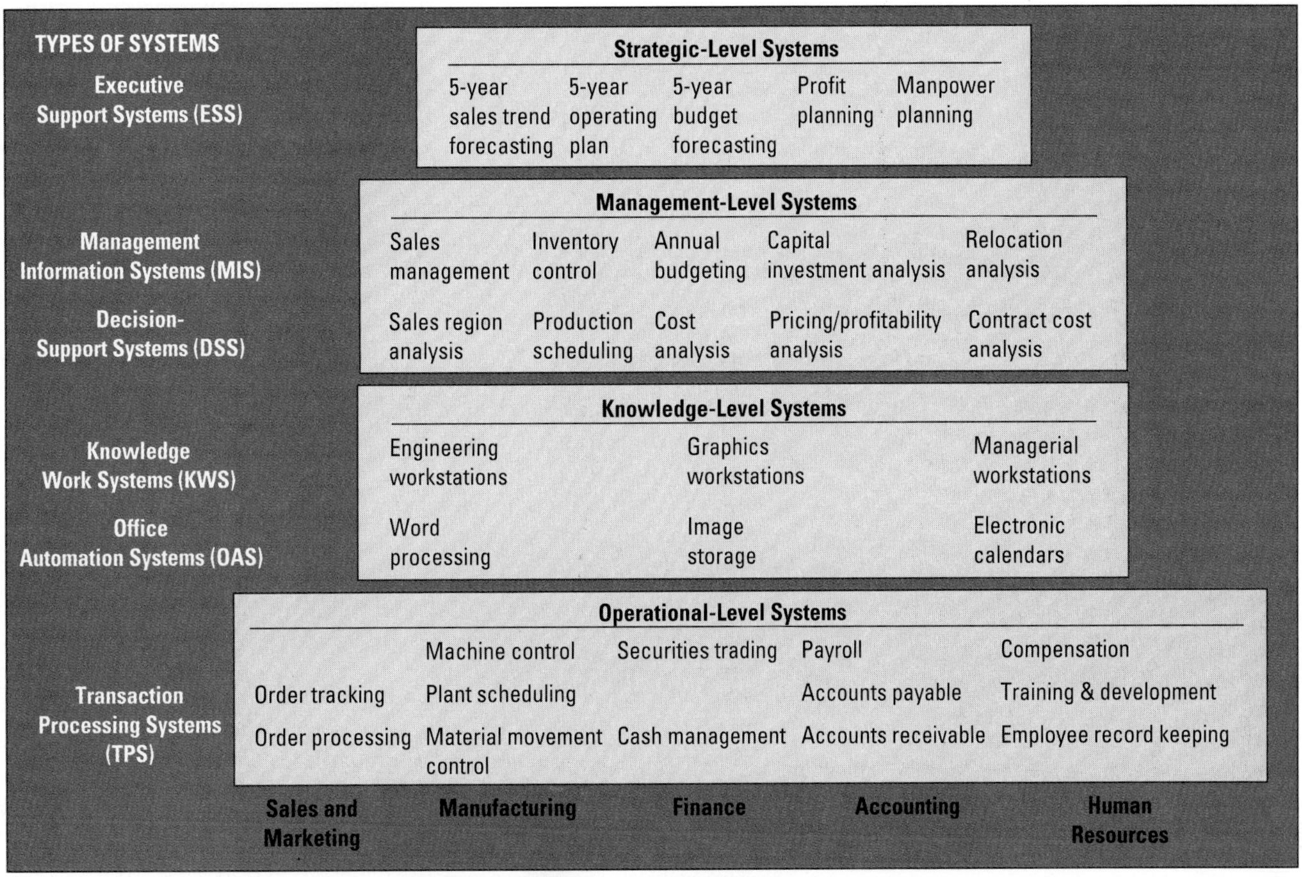

TYPES OF SYSTEMS	Strategic-Level Systems				
Executive Support Systems (ESS)	5-year sales trend forecasting	5-year operating plan	5-year budget forecasting	Profit planning	Manpower planning
	Management-Level Systems				
Management Information Systems (MIS)	Sales management	Inventory control	Annual budgeting	Capital investment analysis	Relocation analysis
Decision-Support Systems (DSS)	Sales region analysis	Production scheduling	Cost analysis	Pricing/profitability analysis	Contract cost analysis
	Knowledge-Level Systems				
Knowledge Work Systems (KWS)	Engineering workstations		Graphics workstations		Managerial workstations
Office Automation Systems (OAS)	Word processing		Image storage		Electronic calendars
	Operational-Level Systems				
Transaction Processing Systems (TPS)	Order tracking / Order processing	Machine control / Plant scheduling / Material movement control	Securities trading / Cash management	Payroll / Accounts payable / Accounts receivable	Compensation / Training & development / Employee record keeping
	Sales and Marketing	**Manufacturing**	**Finance**	**Accounting**	**Human Resources**

FIGURE 2.2

The six major types of information systems needed for the four levels of an organization. Information systems are built to serve each of the four levels of an organization. Transaction processing systems (TPS) serve the operational level of an organization. Knowledge work systems (KWS) and office automation systems (OAS) serve the knowledge level of an organization. Decision-support systems (DSS) and management information systems (MIS) serve the management level of the organization. Executive support systems (ESS) serves the strategic level of an organization.

Table 2.1	Characteristics of Information Processing Systems			
Type of System	Information Inputs	Processing	Information Outputs	Users
ESS	Aggregate data; external, internal	Graphics; simulations; interactive	Projections; responses to queries	Senior managers
DSS	Low-volume data or massive databases optimized for data analysis; analytic models	Interactive; simulations, analysis	Special reports; decision analyses; responses to queries	Professionals; staff managers
MIS	Summary transaction data; high-volume data; simple models	Routine reports; simple models; low-level analysis	Summary and exception reports	Middle managers
KWS	Design specifications; knowledge base	Modeling; simulations	Models; graphics	Professionals; technical staff
OAS	Documents; schedules	Document management; scheduling; communication	Documents; schedules; mail	Clerical workers
TPS	Transactions; events	Sorting; listing; merging; updating	Detailed reports; lists; summaries	Operations personnel; supervisors

the typical systems found in organizations are designed to assist workers or managers at each level and in the functions of sales and marketing, manufacturing, finance, accounting, and human resources.

Table 2.1 summarizes the features of the six types of information systems. It should be noted that each of the different kinds of systems may have components that are used by organizational levels and groups other than their main constituencies. A secretary may find information on an MIS, or a middle manager may need to extract data from a TPS.

Transaction Processing Systems

transaction processing system (TPS) Computerized system that performs and records the daily routine transactions necessary to conduct the business; these systems serve the operational level of the organization.

Transaction processing systems (TPS) are the basic business systems that serve the operational level of the organization. A transaction processing system is a computerized system that performs and records the daily, routine transactions necessary to conduct the business. Examples are sales order entry, hotel reservation systems, payroll, employee record-keeping, and shipping.

At the operational level, tasks, resources, and goals are predefined and highly structured. The decision to grant credit to a customer, for instance, is made by a lower-level supervisor according to predefined criteria. All that must be determined is whether the customer meets the criteria.

Figure 2.3 depicts a payroll TPS, which is a typical accounting transaction processing system found in most firms. A payroll system keeps track of the money paid to employees. The master file is composed of discrete pieces of information (such as a name, address, or employee number) called data elements. Data are keyed into the system, updating the data elements. The elements on the master file are combined in different ways to make up reports of interest to management and government agencies and paychecks sent to employees. These TPS can generate other report combinations of existing data elements.

Other typical TPS applications are identified in Figure 2.4. The figure shows the five functional categories of TPS: sales/marketing, manufacturing/production, finance/accounting, human resources, and other types of TPS that are unique to a particular industry. The UPS package tracking system described in Chapter 1 is an example of a manufacturing TPS. UPS sells package delivery services; the system keeps track of all its package shipment transactions.

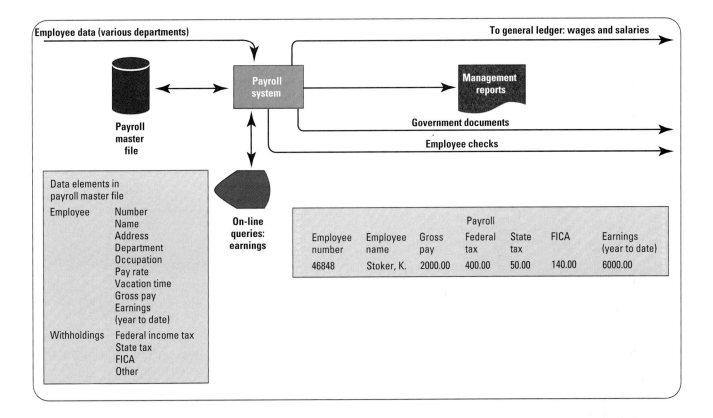

FIGURE 2.3

A symbolic representation for a payroll TPS.

	TYPE OF TPS SYSTEM				
	Sales/ marketing systems	Manufacturing/ production systems	Finance/ accounting systems	Human resources systems	Other types (e.g., university)
Major functions of system	Sales management	Scheduling	Budgeting	Personnel records	Admissions
	Market research	Purchasing	General ledger	Benefits	Grade records
	Promotion	Shipping/receiving	Billing	Compensation	Course records
	Pricing	Engineering	Cost accounting	Labor relations	Alumni
	New products	Operations		Training	
Major application systems	Sales order information system	Materials resource planning systems	General ledger	Payroll	Registration system
	Market research system	Purchase order control systems	Accounts receivable/payable	Employee records	Student transcript system
	Pricing system	Engineering systems	Budgeting	Benefit systems	Curriculum class control systems
		Quality control systems	Funds management systems	Career path systems	Alumni benefactor system
				Personnel planning systems	

FIGURE 2.4

Typical applications of TPS. There are five functional categories of TPS: sales/marketing, manufacturing/production, finance/accounting, human resources, and other types of systems specific to a particular industry. TPS support most business functions in most organizations. Within each of these major functions are subfunctions. For each of these subfunctions (e.g., sales management) there is a major application system.

All organizations have these five kinds of TPS (even if the systems are manual). Transaction processing systems are often so central to a business that a TPS failure for a few hours can spell the demise of a firm and perhaps other firms linked to it. Imagine what would happen to UPS if its package tracking system was not working! What would the airlines do without their computerized reservation systems?

Managers need TPS to monitor the status of internal operations and the firm's relations with the external environment. Transaction processing systems are also major producers of information for the other types of systems. (For example, the payroll system illustrated here along with other accounting TPS supply data to the company's general ledger system, which is responsible for maintaining records of the firm's income and expenses and for producing reports such as income statements and balance sheets.)

Knowledge Work and Office Automation Systems

Both **knowledge work systems (KWS)** and **office automation systems (OAS)** serve the information needs at the knowledge level of the organization. Knowledge work systems aid knowledge workers, whereas office automation systems primarily aid data workers (although they are also used extensively by knowledge workers).

In general, *knowledge workers* are people who hold formal university degrees and who are often members of a recognized profession, such as engineers, doctors, lawyers, and scientists. Their jobs consist primarily of creating new information and knowledge. A knowledge work system (KWS), such as a scientific or engineering design workstation, promotes the creation of new knowledge and ensures that new knowledge and technical expertise are properly integrated into the business. One example of a KWS is the computer-aided design system used by the Hong Kong Airport project described in the Window on Technology.

Data workers typically have less formal, advanced educational degrees and tend to process rather than create information. They consist primarily of secretaries, accountants, filing clerks, or managers whose jobs are principally to use, manipulate, or disseminate information. An office automation system (OAS) is an information technology application designed to increase the productivity of data workers in the office by supporting the coordinating and communicating activities of the typical office. Office automation systems coordinate diverse information workers, geographic units, and functional areas: The systems communicate with customers, suppliers, and other organizations outside the firm and serve as a clearinghouse for information and knowledge flows.

Typical office automation systems handle and manage documents (through word processing, desktop publishing, and digital filing), scheduling (through electronic calendars), and communication (through electronic mail, voice mail, or videoconferencing). **Word processing** refers to the software and hardware that creates, edits, formats, stores, and prints documents (see Chapter 7). Word processing systems represent the single most common application of information technology to office work, in part because producing documents is what offices are all about. **Desktop publishing** produces professional publishing–quality documents by combining output from word processing software with design elements, graphics, and special layout features.

Document imaging systems are another widely used knowledge application. **Document imaging systems** convert documents and images into digital form so that they can be stored and accessed by the computer. Figure 2.5 illustrates the imaging system used by the United Services Automobile Association, the largest direct writer of property and casualty insurance in the United States. USAA receives more than 100,000 letters and mails more than 250,000 items daily. USAA has developed the largest imaging system in the world, storing 1.5 billion pages. All incoming mail received each day by the policy department is scanned and stored on optical disk. The original documents are thrown away. Six of USAA's major regional offices across the

knowledge work system (KWS)
Information system that aids knowledge workers in the creation and integration of new knowledge in the organization.

office automation system (OAS)
Computer system, such as word processing, electronic mail system, and scheduling system, that is designed to increase the productivity of data workers in the office.

word processing Office automation technology that facilitates the creation of documents through computerized text editing, formatting, storing, and printing.

desktop publishing Technology that produces professional-quality documents combining output from word processors with design, graphics, and special layout features.

document imaging systems
Systems that convert documents and images into digital form so that they can be stored and accessed by the computer.

Hong Kong Airport Flies High with CAD

Hong Kong's Kai Tak Airport, the third busiest international airport in the world for passengers and second busiest for freight, reached its absolute capacity in 1994. To meet predicted traffic through the year 2040, Hong Kong's Provisional Airport Authority contracted to build the Chek Lap Kok Airport at a cost of $16 billion on land that will be reclaimed on a nearby island.

The new airport will be connected to Hong Kong by a 1500-yard bridge, the second largest suspension bridge in the world. It will include a highway, a rail link, and a complete town for 20,000 employees. It is one of the largest infrastructure projects in the world.

Designing the airport has been a massive undertaking involving a number of design firms and sophisticated ways to link the designers and their designs. The runway designers had to take into account local topology, the urban surroundings, prevalent wind patterns, and criteria from the International Civil Aviation Authority. The designers had to assume that the airport would be able to accommodate 900-passenger jets that are now only on the drawing boards. The Mott Consortium in charge of the project must keep track of a multidisciplinary team of more than 200 professionals handling architectural design, structural design, civil engineering, and production of specialized airport systems.

The client required all 10,000 design and construction drawings to be produced using CAD software. To integrate the work, the consortium purchased UNIX workstations and desktop PCs for each technician and linked them into a local area network. The consortium decided to use CAD software from Intergraph Corp. because it was especially well suited for large projects. When run on a UNIX workstation, Intergraph can process large amounts of data quickly. It also has file reference capabilities to coordinate the work of various design groups. The network allows any designer to easily call up his or her own work at any workstation or PC.

The team defined 15 aspects of design, such as vertical structure, horizontal structure, signage, and interior planning, to store in separate files. With the file reference capability, designers can overlay files to create composite drawings and they can see what changes have been made to the various aspects of design. All of the data can be related to the basic Hong Kong survey grid maps so that output can be used by the designs of more detailed plans of the airport.

Other facets of the project—including land reclamation, the bridge, the highway, the railway systems, and an analysis of the town and its infrastructure—are being designed by other companies using a wide array of specialized CAD programs. Each team is very dependent upon the output of work by other teams.

To integrate the work, the Mott Consortium uses an optical jukebox holding 54 read-only optical disks. Finished drawings are archived to the optical disks, where they are immediately available to all via a network. Each drawing has a version number so that it can be updated later if needed. When updates occur that might affect the work of other teams, earlier versions of the same document are marked with a warning.

So far, the airport project has been proceeding on target and under budget for a scheduled opening in April 1998.

> **To Think About:** Do you think this project could be attempted without CAD technology? Why or why not? What are the management benefits of using this technology?

Sources: "Franchises and Facilities Update," *Airport Authority—Hong Kong Newsletter,* July 1996; Anna Foley, "Design Firm Flies Through the Airport Project with CAD," *Computerworld,* September 5, 1994; and Ross Milburn, "Flying High," *Computer Graphics World,* February 1993.

country are hooked up to its imaging network. The network consists of image scanners, optical storage units, a mainframe computer, workstations, and a local area network (LAN) to link service representatives' workstations and the scanner workstations located in the firm's mailroom. Service representatives can retrieve a client's file on-line and view documents from desktop computers. About 2000 people use the network. Users believe that the imaging system reduces the amount of time their work would take with a paper-based system by one-third, saving paper and storage costs. Customer service has been improved because electronic documents can be accessed more rapidly (Lasher, Ives, and Jarvenpaa, 1991; "USAA Insuring Progress," 1992).

Management Information Systems

Management information systems (MIS) serve the management level of the organization, providing managers with reports and, in some cases, with on-line access to the organization's current performance and historical records. Typically, these systems

management information system (MIS) Information system at the management level of an organization that serves the functions of planning, controlling, and decision making by providing routine summary and exception reports.

FIGURE 2.5

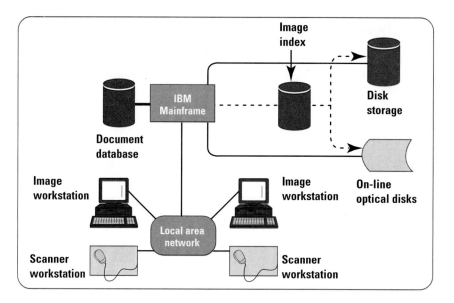

are oriented almost exclusively to internal, not environmental or external, events. MIS primarily serve the functions of planning, controlling, and decision making at the management level. Generally, these systems are dependent on underlying transaction processing systems for their data.

MIS summarize and report on the basic operations of the company. The basic transaction data from TPS are compressed and are usually presented in long reports that are produced on a regular schedule. Figure 2.6 shows how a typical MIS transforms transaction level data from inventory, production, and accounting into MIS files that are used to provide managers with reports. Figure 2.7 shows a sample report from this system.

MIS usually serve managers interested in weekly, monthly, and yearly results—not day-to-day activities—and generally address structured questions that are known well in advance. These systems are generally not flexible and have little analytical capability. Most of these systems use simple routines such as summaries and compar-

Computer-aided design (CAD) systems eliminate many manual steps in design and production by performing much of the de sign work on the computer.

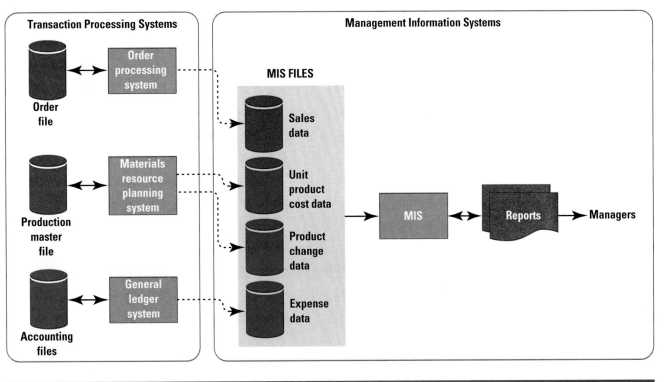

FIGURE 2.6

How management information systems obtain their data from the organization's TPS. In the system illustrated by this diagram, three TPS supply summarized transaction data at the end of the time period to the MIS reporting system. Managers gain access to the organizational data through the MIS, which provides them with the appropriate reports.

isons, as opposed to sophisticated mathematical models or statistical techniques. Table 2.2 describes the characteristics of typical management information systems.

Some researchers use the term *MIS* to include all the information systems that support the functional areas of the organization (Davis and Olson, 1985). However, in this book we prefer to use a computer-based information system (CBIS) as the umbrella term for all information systems and to consider management information systems as those specifically dedicated to management-level functions.

Consolidated Consumer Products Corporation
Sales by Product and Sales Region: 1997

PRODUCT CODE	PRODUCT DESCRIPTION	SALES REGION	ACTUAL SALES	PLANNED	ACTUAL VS. PLANNED
4469	Carpet Cleaner	Northeast	4,066,700	4,800,000	0.85
		South	3,778,112	3,750,000	1.01
		Midwest	4,867,001	4,600,000	1.06
		West	4,003,440	4,400,000	0.91
	TOTAL		16,715,253	17,550,000	0.95
5674	Room Freshener	Northeast	3,676,700	3,900,000	0.94
		South	5,608,112	4,700,000	1.19
		Midwest	4,711,001	4,200,000	1.12
		West	4,563,440	4,900,000	0.93
	TOTAL		18,559,253	17,700,000	1.05

FIGURE 2.7

A sample report that might be produced by the MIS in Figure 2.6.

Table 2.2	Characteristics of Management Information Systems

1. They support structured and semi-structured decisions at the operational and management control levels. However, they are also useful for planning purposes of senior management staff.

2. They are generally reporting and control oriented. They are designed to report on existing operations and therefore to help provide day-to-day control of operations.

3. They rely on existing corporate data and data flows.

4. They have little analytical capability.

5. They generally aid in decision making using past and present data.

6. They are relatively inflexible.

7. They have an internal rather than an external orientation.

8. The information requirements are known and stable.

9. They often require a lengthy analysis and design process.

Decision-Support Systems

decision-support system (DSS)
Information system at the management level of an organization that combines data and sophisticated analytical models to support semi-structured and unstructured decision making.

Decision-support systems (DSS) also serve the management level of the organization. DSS help managers make decisions that are semi-structured, unique, or rapidly changing, and not easily specified in advance. DSS have to be responsive enough to run several times a day in order to correspond to changing conditions. Although DSS use internal information from TPS and MIS, they often bring in information from external sources, such as current stock prices or product prices of competitors. Table 2.3 shows how contemporary DSS differ from MIS and TPS.

Clearly, by design, DSS have more analytical power than other systems; they are built explicitly with a variety of models to analyze data or they condense large amounts of data into a form where they can be analyzed by decision-makers. DSS are designed so that users can work with them directly; these systems explicitly include user-friendly software. DSS are interactive; the user can change assumptions, ask new questions, and include new data.

An interesting, small, but powerful DSS is the voyage-estimating system of a subsidiary of a large American metals company that exists primarily to carry bulk cargoes of coal, oil, ores, and finished products for its parent company. The firm owns some vessels, charters others, and bids for shipping contracts in the open market to carry general cargo. A voyage-estimating system calculates financial and technical voyage details. Financial calculations include ship/time costs (fuel, labor, capital), freight rates for various types of cargo, and port expenses. Technical details include a myriad of factors such as ship cargo capacity, speed, port distances, fuel and water consumption, and loading patterns (location of cargo for different ports). The system can answer questions such as the following: Given a customer delivery schedule

Table 2.3	Characteristics of Decision-Support Systems

1. They offer users flexibility, adaptability, and a quick response.

2. They allow users to initiate and control the input and output.

3. They operate with little or no assistance from professional programmers.

4. They provide support for decisions and problems whose solutions cannot be specified in advance.

5. They use sophisticated data analysis and modeling tools.

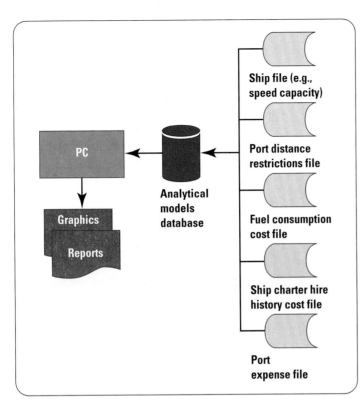

FIGURE 2.8

Voyage-estimating decision-support system. This DSS operates on a powerful PC. It is used daily by managers who must develop bids on shipping contracts.

Ship file (e.g., speed capacity)

Port distance restrictions file

Analytical models database

Fuel consumption cost file

PC

Graphics

Reports

Ship charter hire history cost file

Port expense file

and an offered freight rate, which vessel should be assigned at what rate to maximize profits? What is the optimum speed at which a particular vessel can optimize its profit and still meet its delivery schedule? What is the optimal loading pattern for a ship bound for the U.S. West Coast from Malaysia? Figure 2.8 illustrates the DSS built for this company. The system operates on a powerful desktop PC, providing a system of menus that makes it easy for users to enter data or obtain information. We will describe other types of DSS in Chapter 16.

Executive Support Systems

Senior managers use a category of information systems called **executive support systems (ESS)** to make decisions. ESS serve the strategic level of the organization. ESS address unstructured decisions and create a generalized computing and communications environment rather than providing any fixed application or specific capability. ESS are designed to incorporate data about external events such as new tax laws or competitors, but they also draw summarized information from internal MIS and DSS. These systems filter, compress, and track critical data, emphasizing the reduction of time and effort required to obtain information useful to executives. ESS employ the most advanced graphics software and can deliver graphs and data from many sources immediately to a senior executive's office or to a boardroom.

Unlike the other types of information systems, ESS are not designed primarily to solve specific problems. Instead, ESS provide a generalized computing and communications capacity that can be applied to a changing array of problems. Whereas, DSS are designed to be highly analytical, ESS tend to make less use of analytical models.

Questions that an ESS can assist in answering include the following: What business should we be in? What are the competitors doing? What new acquisitions would protect us from cyclical business swings? Which units should we sell to raise cash for acquisitions? (Rockart and Treacy, 1982). Figure 2.9 illustrates a model of an ESS. It consists of workstations with menus, interactive graphics, and communications capabilities that can access historical and competitive data from internal corporate

executive support system (ESS)
Information system at the strategic level of an organization designed to address unstructured decision making through advanced graphics and communications.

FIGURE 2.9

Model of a typical executive support system. This system pools data from diverse internal and external sources and makes them available to executives in an easy-to-use form.

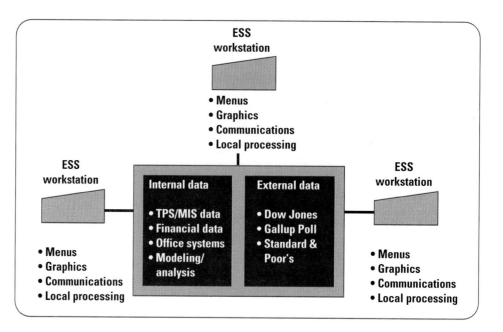

systems and external databases such as Dow Jones News/Retrieval or the Gallup Poll. Because ESS are designed to be used by senior managers who often have little, if any, direct contact or experience with computer-based information systems, they incorporate easy-to-use graphic interfaces. More details on leading-edge applications of both DSS and ESS can be found in Chapter 16.

Relationship of Systems to One Another: Integration

Figure 2.10 illustrates how the various types of systems in the organization are related to one another. A TPS is typically a major source of data for other systems, whereas the ESS is primarily a recipient of data from lower-level systems. The other types of systems may exchange data among one another as well.

FIGURE 2.10

Interrelationships among systems. The various types of systems in the organization do not work independently; rather, there are interdependencies between the systems. A TPS is a major producer of information that is required by the other systems which, in turn, produce information for other systems. These different types of systems are only loosely coupled in most organizations.

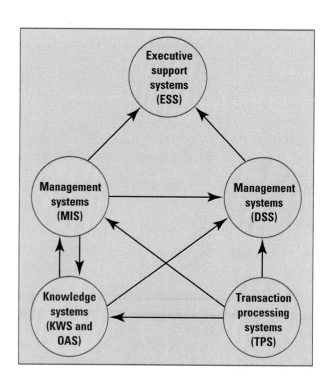

But how much can or should these systems be integrated? This is a difficult question to answer. It is definitely advantageous to have some measure of integration so that information can flow easily among different parts of the organization. But integration costs money, and integrating many different systems is extremely time consuming and complex. Each organization must weigh its needs for integrating systems against difficulties of mounting a large-scale systems integration effort. There is no one "right level" of integration or centralization (Allen and Boynton, 1991; King, 1984).

2.2 INFORMATION AS A STRATEGIC RESOURCE

Each of the major types of information systems described previously is valuable for helping organizations solve an important problem. In the last few decades, some of these systems and the knowledge that can be derived from them have become especially critical to the firm's long-term prosperity and survival. Such systems, which are powerful tools for staying ahead of the competition, are called strategic information systems.

What Is a Strategic Information System?

Strategic information systems change the goals, business processes, products, services, or environmental relationships of organizations to help them gain an edge over competitors. Systems that have these effects may even change the business of organizations. Merrill Lynch, for instance, used information systems to change from the stock brokerage business to the financial services business. State Street Bank and Trust Co. of Boston transformed its core business from traditional banking services, such as customer checking and savings accounts and loans, to electronic record keeping, providing data processing services for securities and mutual funds. Now it is moving beyond computerized record keeping into a broad array of financial information services, including a monitoring service that allows pension funds to keep better tabs on their money managers (Rebello, 1995).

Strategic information systems often change the organization as well as its products, services, and internal processes, driving the organization into new behavior patterns. As we will see, organizations may need to change their internal operations to take advantage of the new information systems technology. Such changes often require new managers, a new work force, and a much closer relationship with customers and suppliers.

strategic information systems
Computer systems at any level of an organization that change the goals, processes, products, services, or environmental relationships to help the organization gain a competitive advantage.

Changing Conceptions of Information and Information Systems

Behind the growing strategic uses of information systems is a changing conception of the role of information in organizations. Organizations now consider information a resource, much like capital and labor. This was not always the case.

Information as a Paper Dragon

In the past, information was often considered a necessary evil associated with the bureaucracy of designing, manufacturing, and distributing a product or service. Information was a "paper dragon" that could potentially strangle the firm and prevent it from doing its real work (see Table 2.4). Information systems of the 1950s focused on reducing the cost of routine paper processing, especially in accounting. The first information systems were semi-automatic check-processing, issuing, and canceling machines—so-called electronic accounting machines (EAM). The term *electronic data processing (EDP)* dates from this period.

Table 2.4 Changing Concepts of Information Systems

Time Period	Conception of Information	Information System	Purpose
1950–1960	Necessary evil Bureaucratic requirement A paper dragon	Electronic accounting machine (EAM)	Speed accounting and paper processing
1960s–1970s	General-purpose support	Management information system (MIS) Information factory	Speed general reporting requirements
1970s–1980s	Customized management control	Decision support system (DSS) Executive support system (ESS)	Improve and customize decision making
1985–2000	Strategic resource Competitive advantage Business foundation	Strategic system	Promote survival and prosperity of the organization

Information for General Support

By the 1960s, organizations started viewing information differently, recognizing that information could be used for general management support. Any information system of the 1960s and 1970s was frequently called a management information system (MIS) and was thought of as an information factory churning out reports on weekly production, monthly financial information, inventory, accounts receivable, accounts payable, and the like. To perform these tasks, organizations acquired general-purpose computing equipment that could support many functions rather than simply canceling checks.

Information for Management

In the 1970s and early 1980s information—and the systems that collected, stored, and processed it—were seen as providing fine-tuned, special-purpose, customized management control over the organization. The information systems that emerged during this period were decision-support systems (DSS) and executive support systems (ESS). Their purpose was to improve and speed up the decision-making process of specific managers and executives in a broad range of problems.

Information as a Strategic Resource

By the mid-1980s, the conception of information changed again. Information began to be viewed as a strategic asset or resource; it began to be seen as a source of strategic advantage, or a weapon to defeat and frustrate the competition. These changing conceptions of information reflected advances in strategic planning and theory (Porter, 1985).

Moving toward the year 2000, the arrival of ubiquitous computing and universal networking via the Internet have once again changed the business conception of information. Now information is viewed as the very foundation of business processes, products, and services. Firms are seen primarily as composed of knowledge assets which, if properly shared with vendors, customers, and employees, can become the foundation for sustained success and relative competitive advantage.

2.3 HOW INFORMATION SYSTEMS CAN BE USED FOR COMPETITIVE ADVANTAGE

Firms use information technology at three different levels of strategy: the business, the firm, and the industry level. See Table 2.5. There generally is no single all-encompassing strategic system, but instead a number of systems operating at differ-

Table 2.5	Strategy Levels and IT		
	Strategies	Models	IT Techniques
Industry	Cooperation vs Competition Licensing Standards	Competitive forces model Network economics	Electronic transactions Communication networks Interorganizational systems Information partnerships
Firm	Synergy Core competencies	Core competency	Knowledge systems Organization-wide systems
Business	Low cost Differentiation Scope	Value chain analysis	Datamining IT-based products/services Interorganizational systems Supply chain management Efficient customer response

ent levels. For each level of business strategy, there are strategic uses of systems. And for each level of business strategy, there is an appropriate model used for analysis.

Business-Level Strategy and the Value Chain Model

At the business level of strategy, the key question is "How can we compete effectively in this particular market?" The market might be lightbulbs, utility vehicles, or cable television. The most common generic strategies at this level are (1) become the low cost producer, (2) differentiate your product or service, and/or (3) change the scope of competition by either enlarging the market to include global markets or narrowing the market by focusing on small niches not well served by your competitors. Moving toward global markets, the firm can generate economies of scale. Moving toward niche markets, the firm can generate high margin products and services available nowhere else.

Leveraging Technology in the Value Chain

At the business level the most common analytic tool is value chain analysis. The **value chain model** highlights specific activities in the business where competitive strategies can be best applied (Porter, 1985) and where information systems are most likely to have a strategic impact. The value chain model identifies specific, critical leverage points where a firm can use information technology most effectively to enhance its competitive position. Exactly where can it obtain the greatest benefit from strategic information systems—what specific activities can be used to create new products and services, enhance market penetration, lock in customers and suppliers, and lower operational costs? This model views the firm as a series or "chain" of basic activities that add a margin of value to a firm's products or services. These activities can be categorized as either primary activities or support activities.

Primary activities are most directly related to the production and distribution of the firm's products and services that create value for the customer. Primary activities include inbound logistics, operations, outbound logistics, sales and marketing, and service. Inbound logistics include receiving and storing materials for distribution to production. Operations transforms inputs into finished products. Outbound logistics entail storing and distributing products. Marketing and sales includes promoting and selling the firm's products. The service activity includes maintenance and repair of the firm's goods and services. **Support activities** make the delivery of the primary activities possible and consist of organization infrastructure (administration and management), human resources (employee recruiting, hiring, and training), technology (improving products and the production process), and procurement (purchasing input).

value chain model   Model that highlights the primary or support activities that add a margin of value to a firm's products or services where information systems can best be applied to achieve a competitive advantage.

primary activities   Activities most directly related to the production and distribution of a firm's products or services.

support activities   Activities that make the delivery of the primary activities of a firm possible. Consist of the organization's infrastructure, human resources, technology, and procurement.

FIGURE 2.11

Activities of the value chain. Various examples of strategic information systems for the primary and support activities of a firm that would add a margin of value to a firm's products or services.

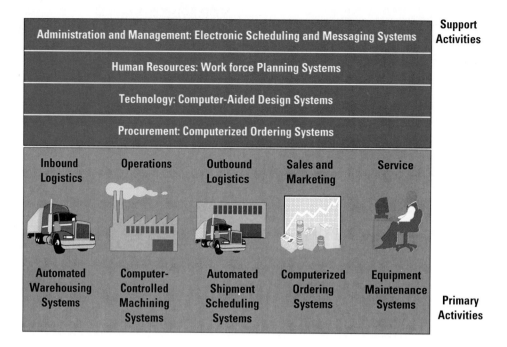

Organizations have competitive advantage when they provide more value to their customers or when they provide the same value to customers at a lower price. An information system could have strategic impact if it helped the firm provide products or services at a lower cost than competitors or if it provided products and services at the same cost as competitors but with greater value. Scotia Capital Market's systems described in the chapter-opening vignette create value by delivering high-quality information very rapidly and at very low cost. The value activities that add the most value to products and services depend on the features of each particular firm. Businesses should try to develop strategic information systems for the value activities that add the most value to their particular firm. Wal-Mart, for example, found it could achieve competitive advantage by focusing on logistics. Figure 2.11 illustrates the activities of the value chain, showing examples of strategic information systems that could be developed to make each of the value activities more cost effective.

For instance, a firm could save money in the inbound logistics activity by having suppliers make daily deliveries of goods to the factory, thereby lowering the costs of warehousing and inventory. A computer-aided design system might support the technology activity, helping a firm to reduce costs and perhaps to design more high-quality products than the competition produces. Such systems would be more likely to have strategic impact in a manufacturing firm, whereas an electronic scheduling and messaging system or office automation technology would more likely have strategic value in a law firm or consulting firm.

A strategic analysis might identify the sales and marketing activity as an area where information systems would provide the greatest productivity boost. The analysis might recommend a system similar to those used by American Express, Bank of America, or U.S. West for bringing together and analyzing data (described in this chapter's Window on Organizations) to reduce marketing costs by targeting marketing campaigns more efficiently. The system might also provide information that lets the firm develop products more finely attuned to its target market as well. Many different projects, or a series of linked systems, may be required to create a strategic advantage.

The role of information technology at the business level is to help the firm reduce costs, differentiate product, and serve new markets. Here are some leading examples of how firms use IT to lower costs, differentiate, and change the scope of competition.

Table 2.6	New Products and Services Based on Information Technology
New Product or Service*	**Underlying Technology**
On-line banking	Private communication networks; Internet
Cash management accounts	Corporate-wide customer account systems
Derivative investments (options, futures, complex variations)	Management and trader workstations; mainframe transaction systems
Global and national airline, hotel, and auto reservation systems	Worldwide telecommunication–based reservation systems
FedEx and other overnight package delivery	Nationwide package tracking systems
Mail-order retailing	Corporate customer databases
Voice mail systems (call services)	Company- and network-wide digital communication systems
Automatic teller machines	Customer account systems
Micro-customized clothing	Computer-aided design and manufacturing (CAD/CAM) systems

Many products and services that we take for granted are based on information technology and, of course, the creative insight of managers who dreamed up these products and services.

Information System Products and Services

Firms can use information systems to create unique new products and services that can be easily distinguished from those of competitors. Strategic information systems for **product differentiation** can prevent the competition from responding in kind so that firms with these differentiated products and services no longer have to compete on the basis of cost. Table 2.6 lists some of the new products and services that have been created with information technology.

Many of these information technology–based products and services have been created by financial institutions. Citibank developed automatic teller machines (ATMs) and bank debit cards in 1977. Seeking to tap the largest retail depository market in the United States, Citibank installed its ATMs throughout the New York metropolitan area, everywhere a depositor might find the time to use them to deposit or withdraw money. As a leader in this area, Citibank became at one time the largest bank in the United States. Citibank ATMs were so successful that Citibank's competitors were forced to counterstrike with their own ATM systems.

Citibank, Wells Fargo Bank, and others have continued to innovate by providing on-line electronic banking services so that customers can do most of their banking transactions with home computers linked to proprietary networks. Recently they have offered customers the option of reviewing their accounts using the World Wide Web. Madrid-based Banco Santander offers a similar service called Banca Supernet. Clients accessing the bank's Web site are presented with a list of their existing accounts and the current balance of each. They can trace the activities in each of these accounts over the past 12 months. Some companies such as Security First Network Bank in Atlanta, have used the Web to set up "virtual banks" offering a full array of banking services without any physical branches. (Customers mail in their deposits.)

In the retail world, manufacturers are starting to use information systems to create products and services that are custom-tailored to fit the precise specifications of individual customers. Andersen Windows created a "Window of Knowledge" system that allows customers in hardware stores and retail outlets to design their own windows. PCs transmit customers' window specifications to Andersen's manufacturing plant in Bayport, Minnesota. The system has given such a boost to Andersen's business that competitors are trying to copy it (Moad, 1995). Chapter 1 describes

product differentiation
Competitive strategy for creating brand loyalty by developing new and unique products and services that are not easily duplicated by competitors.

other instances when information technology is creating customized products and services while retaining the cost efficiencies of mass-production techniques.

Systems to Focus on Market Niche

focused differentiation Competitive strategy for developing new market niches for specialized products or services where a business can compete in the target area better than its competitors.

Businesses can create new market niches by identifying a specific target for a product or service that it can serve in a superior manner. Through **focused differentiation**, the firm can provide a specialized product or service for this narrow target market better than competitors.

An information system can give companies a competitive advantage by producing data for such finely tuned sales and marketing techniques. Such systems treat existing information as a resource that can be "mined" by the organization to increase profitability and market penetration. Information systems enable companies to finely analyze customer buying patterns, tastes, and preferences so that they efficiently pitch advertising and marketing campaigns to smaller and smaller target markets.

datamining Analysis of large pools of data to find patterns and rules that can be used to guide decision making and predict future behavior.

Sophisticated **datamining** software tools find patterns in large pools of data and infer rules from them. These patterns and rules can be used to guide decision making and forecast the effect of those decisions. For example, mining data about purchases at supermarkets might reveal that when potato chips are purchased, soda is also purchased 65 percent of the time. When there is a promotion, soda is purchased 85 percent of the time people purchase potato chips. Table 2.7 describes the various marketing techniques that can be supported by datamining. More detail on datamining can be found in Chapter 16.

Sears, Roebuck and Company continually mines its computerized data on its 60 million past and present credit card holders to target groups such as appliance buyers, tool buyers, gardening enthusiasts, and mothers-to-be. Datamining helps the firm practice what it calls "life-stage marketing." Sears knows that when a customer gets married or buys a home, that event is often reflected in what they purchase. When a customer buys a washer and dryer, Sears mails a postcard advertising an annual maintenance contract. Each year Sears will send out an annual maintenance contract renewal form or telephone customers to keep its maintenance business going. And Sears also knows when that washer and dryer need to be replaced.

| Table 2.7 | Datamining can be used for . . . |
Application	Description
Market segmentation	Identify the common characteristics of customers who buy the same products from your company.
Customer churn	Predict which customers are likely to leave your company and go to a competitor.
Fraud detection	Identify which transactions are most likely to be fraudulent.
Direct marketing	Identify which prospects should be included in a mailing list to obtain the highest response rate.
Interactive marketing	Predict what each individual accessing a Web site is most likely interested in seeing.
Market basket analysis	Understand what products or services are commonly purchased together, e.g., beer and diapers.
Trend analysis	Reveal the difference between a typical customer this month versus last.

Source: From "Strike it Rich" in *Datamation*, February 1997. Reprinted with permission from *Datamation*, copyright 1997 Cahners Publishing Company, a division of Reed Elsevier, Inc. *Datamation* is a trademark of Cahners Publishing Company, a division of Reed Elsevier, Inc. All rights reserved

This approach contrasts with earlier reliance on mass marketing, where the same message is directed at virtually everyone. The newest approach, commonly known as one-to-one marketing, consists of personal or individualized messages based upon likely individual preferences. Massive quantities of data are gathered on consumers and then analyzed to locate individual customers with specific interests or to determine the interests of a specific group of customers.

The data come from a range of sources—credit card transactions, demographic data, and purchase data from checkout counter scanners at supermarkets and retail stores. Some firms are starting to extract and analyze information provided when people access and interact with World Wide Web sites. For example, Stein Roe Investors, a mutual fund company, has a Web site describing its funds and services which includes software and hardware that capture and analyze data generated when people visit the site. They can use these data to create and manage profiles of Web site visitors and to target individuals and common interest groups with content, advertising, and incentives. Chapter 10 provides more detail on how the Web can be used for this purpose. Companies collect some of these data internally and purchase some from other organizations. By carefully analyzing people's past purchasing patterns, companies can develop a more precise picture of their purchasing interests, form relationships with those customers, and provide them with more personalized products and services (see the Window on Organizations). Some companies can target their marketing so finely that they can create a specialized targeted promotional offer for as few as 20 customers. The level of fine-grained customization provided by these datamining systems parallels that for custom manufacturing described in Chapter 1.

The cost of acquiring a new customer has been estimated to be five times that of retaining an existing customer. By carefully examining transactions of customer purchases and activities, firms can identify profitable customers and win more of their business. Likewise, companies can use these data to identify nonprofitable customers (Clemons and Weber, 1994).

Datamining is both a powerful and profitable tool, but it poses challenges to the protection of individual privacy. Datamining technology can combine information from many diverse sources to create a detailed "data image" about each of us—our income, a record of our purchases, our driving habits, our hobbies, our families, and our political interests. Many critics wonder whether companies should be allowed to

Ken Laudon
23 N. Division St.
Peekskill, NY 10566-2927

By mining its customer database, Sears, Roebuck and Company can identify customers for maintenance contracts or other promotional campaigns.

Dear Ken Laudon,

You've recently made an important investment in your new refrigerator and you want it to serve you well for many years. Surely you, and your refrigerator, deserve the Sears Maintenance Agreement to protect and maintain it.

You now qualify for a very special introductory offer -- Receive a 20% discount when you select the Sears Maintenance Agreement three-year coverage! You get Sears quality coverage and the best discount when you choose three years! Please reply by November 21, 1996.

We're delighted you bought your new refrigerator at our Sears Yorktown Hts store on September 7, 1996. We are confident that you will enjoy the convenience and value of this quality product. Of course, as you know, even the highest quality products may occasionally require repair.

Save 20% when you choose 3 years!

Enjoy Peace of Mind with the Sears Maintenance Agreement!

Striking It Rich with Datamining

Mass marketing is highly inefficient. Fewer than 2 percent of coupons are redeemed and the number of coupons issued is falling. A response rate of 3 percent to direct mail advertising is considered very good. Datamining and technologies for one-to-one marketing may be the answer.

American Express tries to treat each of its 30 million credit card holders as a "market of one" by using datamining to add personalized messages and offers in their invoices. If, for example, a customer purchases a dress at Saks Fifth Avenue department store, American Express might include in her next billing an offer of a discount on a pair of shoes purchased at the same store and charged on her American Express card. The two goals are to increase the customer's use of her American Express card and also to expand the presence of American Express at Saks. A cardholder residing in London, England, who recently took a British Airways flight to Paris might find an offer in a newsletter for a special discounted "getaway" weekend to New York. The company can draw on a gigantic pool of data culled from hundreds of billions in credit card purchases since 1991. Its one-to-one marketing system is capable of supporting hundreds of millions of promotions.

San Francisco–based Bank of America wanted to improve its relationships with existing checking account customers and to acquire new ones. Instead of cutting prices or offering free checking for life, it used datamining to figure out which of its customers were using what products. The bank also wanted to use its customer data to tell them if a different mix of products and services might better meet certain customers' needs. Bank of America merged various behavior patterns into a more exact profile of its customers, clustering them into smaller, more understandable groups with similar interests and needs. When it found customers who were using the wrong products, it contacted them by telephone or mail. Datamining also helped the bank expand its

Hispanic customer base. The bank learned that its Hispanic customers were growing in affluence and education and was able to develop a new set of products and promotions for this group.

U.S. West Communications, based in Denver, turned to datamining when competition overheated in the telecommunications industry. U.S. West wanted to determine customer trends based on household characteristics to draw additional business from existing subscribers and to sign up new ones. The company combined and reassembled data from its billing operations, line provision units, and data provided by R.R. Donnelly, an external vendor. It developed a system to derive customer trends and needs based on household characteristics such as family size, median ages of family members, types of spending patterns, location, and so forth. U.S. West's datamining project found that customers didn't simply want cheaper rates. That finding helped the company refocus its business strategy to put more emphasis on quality of service. The company was able to use non-cost-related items to save 45 percent of customer losses.

Although datamining has great potential benefits, some hurdles must be overcome. The technology is often costly, requiring supercomputers, vast amounts of data storage, and expensive software. Customers often feel their privacy has been invaded because companies know so much about them or sell their personal information to other businesses.

To Think About: *How could datamining change the way organizations conduct their business? What benefits does datamining provide? What problems might it create?*

Sources: "Strike It Rich!" *Datamation,* February 1997; and John Foley, "Ready, Aim, Sell!" *Information Week,* February 17, 1997.

---

collect such detailed information about individuals. We explore the privacy dimensions of datamining further in Chapter 5.

Supply Chain Management and Efficient Customer Response Systems

Inventory is just dead weight on a firm. When goods sit in warehouses, or when staff members are underutilized, the firm must pay financial costs without receiving any revenues. Therefore, many firms attempt to use IT to eliminate or greatly reduce inventory.

By keeping prices low and shelves well stocked, Wal-Mart has become the leading retail business in the United States. Wal-Mart uses a legendary inventory replenishment system triggered by point-of-sale purchases that is considered the best in the industry. The "continuous replenishment system" sends orders for new merchandise directly to suppliers as soon as consumers pay for their purchases at the cash register. Point-of-sale terminals record the bar code of each item passing the checkout

Wal-Mart's continuous inventory replenishment system uses sales data captured at the checkout counter to transmit orders to restock merchandise directly to its suppliers. The system enables Wal-Mart to keep costs low while fine-tuning its merchandise to meet customer demands.

counter and send a purchase transaction directly to a central computer at Wal-Mart headquarters. The computer collects the orders from all Wal-Mart stores and transmits them to suppliers. Because the system can replenish inventory with lightning speed, Wal-Mart does not need to spend much money on maintaining large inventories of goods in its own warehouses. The system also allows Wal-Mart to adjust purchases of store items to meet customer demands. Competitors such as Sears spend nearly 30 percent of each dollar in sales to pay for overhead (that is, expenses for salaries, advertising, warehousing, and building upkeep). Kmart spends 21 percent of sales on overhead. But by using systems to keep operating costs low, Wal-Mart pays only 15 percent of sales revenue for overhead.

Wal-Mart's continuous replenishment system is an example of efficient supply chain management. **Supply chain management** integrates the supplier, distributor, and customer logistics requirements into one cohesive process. The **supply chain** is a collection of physical entities such as manufacturing plants, distribution centers, conveyances, retail outlets, people, and information, which are linked through processes such as procurement or logistics, to supply goods or services from source through consumption. Goods or services start out as raw materials and move through the company's logistics and production system until they reach customers. To manage the supply chain, a company tries to eliminate delays and cut the amount of resources tied up along the way. This can be accomplished by streamlining the company's internal operations or by reducing inventory costs by asking suppliers to put off delivery of goods—and their payments—until the moment they are needed. Information systems make efficient supply chain management possible by integrating demand planning, forecasting, materials requisition, order processing, inventory allocation, order fulfillment, transportation services, receiving, invoicing, and payment. Supply chain management systems can create value not only by lowering inventory costs but also by delivering the product or service more rapidly to the customer.

Supply chain management can be used to create efficient customer response systems that respond to customer demands more efficiently. The convenience and ease of using these information systems raise **switching costs** (the cost of switching from one product to a competing product), discouraging customers from going to competitors.

supply chain management
Integration of supplier, distributor, and customer logistics requirements into one cohesive process.

supply chain A collection of physical entities, such as manufacturing plants, distribution centers, conveyances, retail outlets, people, and information, which are linked together into processes supplying goods or services from source through consumption.

switching costs The expense a customer or company incurs in lost time and expenditure of resources when changing from one supplier or system to a competing supplier or system.

Baxter Healthcare International's "stockless inventory" and ordering system uses supply chain management to create an efficient customer response system. Participating hospitals become unwilling to switch to another supplier because of the system's convenience and low cost. Baxter supplies nearly two-thirds of all products used by U.S. hospitals. It uses an information system originally developed by American Hospital Supply Corporation (which Baxter acquired in 1985) to become a full-line supplier for hospitals—a one-stop source for all hospital needs. This effort requires an inventory of more than 120,000 items. Maintaining a huge inventory is very costly. However, it is also costly *not* to have items in stock, because hospitals switch to competitors.

Terminals tied to Baxter's own computers are installed in hospitals. When hospitals want to place an order, they do not need to call a salesperson or send a purchase order—they simply use a Baxter computer terminal on-site to order from the full Baxter supply catalog. The system generates shipping, billing, invoicing, and inventory information, and the hospital terminals provide customers with an estimated delivery date. With more than 80 distribution centers in the United States, Baxter can make daily deliveries of its products, often within hours of receiving an order.

This system is similar to the just-in-time delivery systems developed in Japan and now being used in the American automobile industry. In these systems, automobile manufacturers such as GM or Chrysler enter the quantity and delivery schedules of specific automobile components into their own information systems. Then these requirements are automatically entered into a supplier's order entry information system. The supplier must respond with an agreement to deliver the materials at the time specified. Thus, automobile companies can reduce the cost of inventory, the space required for warehousing components or raw materials, and construction time.

Baxter has even gone one step further. Delivery personnel no longer drop off their cartons at a loading dock to be placed in a hospital storeroom. Instead, they deliver orders directly to the hospital corridors, dropping them at nursing stations, operating rooms, and stock supply closets. This has created in effect a "stockless inventory," with Baxter serving as the hospitals' warehouse. Stockless inventory substantially reduces the need for hospital storage space and personnel and lowers holding and handling costs (Caldwell, 1991). New Textron Automotive Interiors plants in Columbia, Missouri, and the Netherlands, which build instrument panels for Fords, use a similar stockless inventory system. Textron's suppliers deliver parts directly to its assembly lines.

Figure 2.12 compares stockless inventory with the just-in-time supply method and traditional inventory practices. While just-in-time inventory allows customers to reduce their inventories, stockless inventory allows them to eliminate their inventories entirely. All inventory responsibilities shift to the distributor, who manages the supply flow. The stockless inventory is a powerful instrument for "locking in" customers, thus giving the supplier a decided competitive advantage.

Strategic systems aimed at suppliers, such as Wal-Mart's continuous replenishment system, are designed to maximize the firm's purchasing power (and minimize costs) by having suppliers interact with its information system to satisfy the firm's precise business needs. If suppliers are unwilling to go along with this system, they may lose business to other suppliers who can meet these demands.

On the other hand, these information systems also provide benefits for suppliers. Suppliers can continually monitor product requirements, factory scheduling, and commitments of their customers against their own schedule to ensure that enough inventory will be available. The manufacturers and retailers are their customers. Once these systems are in place and working smoothly, their efficiency and convenience may help discourage the vendors' customers from switching to competitors.

Sometimes information systems provide value in multiple ways. For example, the package tracking systems developed by Federal Express, United Parcel Service, and other overnight delivery companies help these firms compete by offering new services

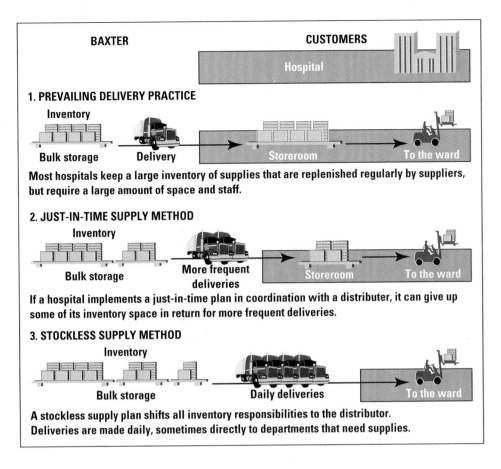

FIGURE 2.12

A comparison of traditional inventory and delivery practices to the *just-in-time supply method* and the *stockless inventory method.* Strategic systems for linking customers and suppliers have changed the way in which some companies handle the supply and inventory requirements of their businesses. The just-in-time supply method reduces inventory requirements of the customer whereas stockless inventory allows the customer to eliminate inventories entirely, resulting in a decided competitive advantage.

Adapted from "Removing the Warehouse from Cost-Conscious Hospitals," The New York Times, *March 3, 1991. Copyright © 1991; 1992 by The New York Times Company. Reprinted by permission.*

and also by remaining low-cost providers. The Window on Management shows how these companies are using the World Wide Web to enhance these capabilities.

Figure 2.13 illustrates the relationship among the various business-level strategies.

Firm-Level Strategy and Information Technology

A business firm is typically a collection of businesses. Often, the firm is organized financially as a collection of strategic business units, and the returns to the firm are directly tied to strategic business unit performance. The questions are, "How can the overall performance of these business units be achieved?" and "How can information technology contribute?"

There are two answers in the literature to these questions. One answer involves the concept of synergies: When outputs of some units can be used as inputs to other units, then unique nonmarket relationships can lower costs and generate profits. For instance, an investment bank such as Morgan Stanley in New York, which creates new financial products, requires a retail outlet to sell these financial products. This would suggest a merger with a strong securities retailing firm. Morgan Stanley merged in February 1997 with Dean Witter Reynolds, noted for its wide network of retail brokerages precisely for this purpose.

How can IT be used strategically here? One use of information technology in these synergy situations is to tie together the operations of disparate business units so that they can act as a whole. In the case of Morgan Stanley, the development of an internal information system, which will tightly couple the financial products group with the retailing service organization, is recommended. Such a system would lower retailing costs, increase customer access to new financial products, and speed up the process of marketing new instruments.

Package Tracking on the Web: The Race Is On

Carrier companies such as FedEx and United Parcel Service (UPS) have made great strides in recent years with the introduction of simple package tracking services. Now those same companies are racing to use the World Wide Web to gain market share by providing more sophisticated services to their customers. Their Web sites can handle package scheduling and pickup from start to finish.

Anyone in a major metropolitan area with a package to ship can use the UPS Web site to check delivery routes, calculate shipping charges, and schedule a pickup. Then they can track their packages en route by entering their package tracking numbers into a form provided by the Web site. UPS has found that this interactive Web site has helped it slash support costs with anticipated savings of $4 million to $6 million each year in tracking costs alone. UPS also uses Web applications for its time-in-transit calculator and dropoff locator, which lets users plug in a ZIP code to locate dropoff locations.

At FedEx's Web site customers can prepare their own shipping documents and request pickup. By filling in the pertinent information on an electronic form provided at the FedEx Web site, they can print out the documents with a freshly generated bar code. They can also send e-mail to a courier to schedule a pickup and track their packages by entering their package tracking numbers into a form on the Web site. FedEx users track over 26,000 packages daily this way. Each time a customer uses FedEx's Web site to track a package instead of inquiring by telephone, FedEx saves $8, amounting to millions of dollars of savings each year.

Use of the World Wide Web has enabled FedEx and UPS to create new business ventures which wouldn't have otherwise been feasible. Monorail, Inc. of Atlanta, a company that sells PCs for under $1000, depends on FedEx's on-line logistics services to manage its orders and deliveries. Monorail's PCs were designed to fit inside FedEx's 19-inch by 19-inch standard cardboard box. Currently orders are made over FedEx's proprietary networks, but an Internet version is expected to be introduced this year.

"We started with a business model rather than a product," said Dave Hocker, a cofounder of Monorail. "The notion of using FedEx was integral," he added. The arrangement with FedEx makes Monorail's business economically viable by eliminating the need for keeping inventory and cutting out the middlemen distributors. But, Hocker is eager to see FedEx move its order and delivery services to the Internet. "We dream of the day when a dealer doesn't have to call FedEx but can just send an e-mail."

RPS, Inc., a smaller delivery firm based in Pittsburgh, is introducing "pre alerts" on the Web for cash-on-delivery packages. The company uses Internet mail to notify customers of the time the delivery will arrive and informs them about how much it will cost when it does. Thirty percent of RPS's sales are from proprietary and Internet electronic data interchange services. Only three years ago those sales totaled less than 2 percent.

Both UPS and FedEx claim that their financial futures depend on having everything a customer does today done on-line with networks.

To Think About: *How much competitive advantage does the Internet provide UPS and Federal Express? What competitive strategies are supported by their use of the World Wide Web?*

Source: Thomas Hoffman and Kim S. Nash, "Couriers Deliver New 'Net Services," *Computerworld*, January 6, 1997; Kim Nash, "Overnight Services Duke It Out On-Line," *Computerworld*, April 22, 1996; and Amy Cortese, "Here Comes the Intranet," *Business Week*, February 26, 1996.

Enhancing Core Competencies

A second concept for firm-level strategy involves the notion of "core competency." The argument is that the performance of all business units can increase insofar as these business units develop, or create, a central core of competencies. A core competency is an activity at which a firm is a world-class leader. Core competencies may involve being the world's best fiber-optic manufacturer, the best miniature parts designer, the best package delivery service, or the best thin film manufacturer. In general, a core competency relies on knowledge which is gained over many years of experience (embedded knowledge), and a first-class research organization or just key people who follow the literature and stay abreast of new external knowledge (tacit knowledge).

How can IT be used to advance or create core competencies? Any system that encourages the sharing of knowledge across business units enhances competency. Such systems might encourage or enhance existing competencies and help employees become aware of new external knowledge; such systems might also help a business

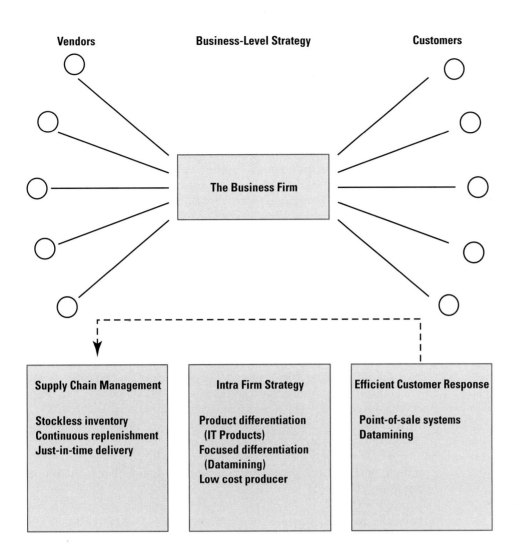

FIGURE 2.13

Business-level strategy. Efficient customer response and supply chain management systems are often interrelated, helping firms "lock in" customers and suppliers while lowering operational costs. Other types of systems can be used to support product differentiation, focused differentiation strategies, and low-cost producer strategies.

leverage existing competencies to related markets. Datamining can be seen as a knowledge generator—it helps a firm know its customers in a unique way. Datamining is therefore a competence enhancer at the firm level as well as at the business level.

Industry-Level Strategy and Information Systems: Competitive Forces and Network Economics

Firms together comprise industries, such as the automotive industry, telephone, television broadcasting, and forest products industry, to name a few. The key strategic question at this level of analysis is "How and when should we compete as opposed to cooperate with others in the industry?" Whereas most strategic analyses emphasize competition, a great deal of money can be made by cooperating with other firms in your industry or firms in related industries. For instance, firms can cooperate to develop industry standards in a number of areas; they can cooperate by working together to build customer awareness, and to work collectively with suppliers to lower costs.

Information Partnerships

Firms can form information partnerships, and even link their information systems to achieve unique synergies. In an **information partnership,** both companies can join forces without actually merging, by sharing information (Konsynski and McFarlan,

information partnership
Cooperative alliance formed between two corporations for the purpose of sharing information to gain strategic advantage.

1990). American Airlines has an arrangement with Citibank to award one mile in its frequent flier program for every dollar spent using Citibank credit cards. American benefits from increased customer loyalty, while Citibank gains new credit card subscribers and a highly creditworthy customer base for cross-marketing. Northwest Airlines has a similar arrangement with First Bank of Minneapolis. American and Northwest have also allied with MCI, awarding frequent flier miles for each dollar of long-distance billing.

Although falling sales caused Sears, Roebuck and Co. to close its "big book" general mail-order catalogue, it set up joint ventures with six partners to produce 14 smaller catalogues catering to specialized market niches such as workwear and auto accessories. Sears provides its partners access to its database of credit card customers and datamining analysis. Its partners then select the merchandise, mail the catalogue, and fill the orders using their own merchandise. Although the Sears name goes on the cover, the catalogues produced by the partners are similar to those mailed to their own customers, except that the partners tailor the merchandise selection to the buying patterns of Sears' customers. Sears shares the profits from each catalogue. Sears' partners, such as Hanover Direct Inc. in Weehawken, New Jersey, benefit from the powerful Sears merchandising name and access to Sears' customer base. This information partnership allows Sears to make money in the mail-order business even though it is no longer in catalogues (Chandler, 1994).

Such partnerships help firms gain access to new customers, creating new opportunities for cross-selling and targeting products. They can share investments in computer hardware and software. Sometimes traditional competitors (such as Sears and competing catalogue companies) can benefit from some of these partnerships. Baxter Healthcare International offers its customers medical supplies from competitors and office supplies through its electronic ordering channel. Even companies that were traditional competitors have found such alliances to be mutually advantageous.

At the industry level, two analytic models are used: the competitive forces model and network economics.

The Competitive Forces Model

competitive forces model
Model used to describe the interaction of external influences, specifically threats and opportunities, that affect an organization's strategy and ability to compete.

In the **competitive forces model,** which is illustrated in Figure 2.14, a firm faces a number of external threats and opportunities: the threat of new entrants into its market, the pressure from substitute products or services, the bargaining power of customers, the bargaining power of suppliers, and the positioning of traditional industry competitors.

Competitive advantage can be achieved by enhancing the firm's ability to deal with customers, suppliers, substitute products and services, and new entrants to its market, which in turn may change the balance of power between a firm and other competitors in the industry in the firm's favor.

How can information systems be used to achieve strategic advantage at the industry level? By working with other firms, industry participants can use information technology to develop industry-wide standards for exchanging information or business transactions electronically (see Chapters 9 and 10), which force all market participants to subscribe to similar standards. This increases industry efficiency—making substitute products less possible and perhaps raising entry costs—thus discouraging new entrants. Customers may be better served, and incur switching costs by using products of other industries. Also, industry members can build industry-wide IT-supported consortia, symposia, and communications networks to coordinate activities vis-à-vis government agencies, foreign competition, and competing industries.

For example, CommerceNet is an on-line consortium of over 140 companies in electronics, computer, financial services, and information service industries and other companies committed to electronic commerce. It provides on-line directories of companies, products, and services and is piloting electronic commerce ap-

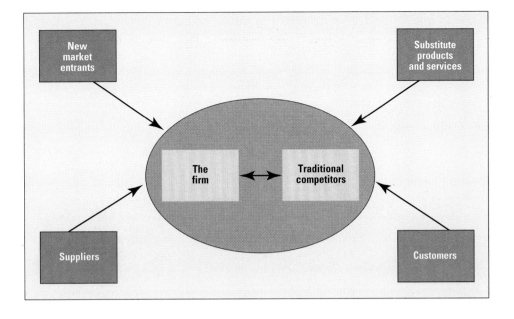

FIGURE 2.14

The competitive forces model. There are various forces that affect an organization's ability to compete and therefore greatly influence a firm's business strategy. There are threats from new market entrants and from substitute products and services. Customers and suppliers wield bargaining power. Traditional competitors constantly adapt their strategies to maintain their market positioning.

plications. The OASIS system on the Web for selling surplus electrical power described in the opening vignette for Chapter 3 is another example.

Network Economics

A second strategic concept useful at the industry level is **network economics.** In a network, the marginal costs of adding another participant are about zero, whereas the marginal gain is much larger. The larger the number of subscribers in a telephone system, or the Internet, the greater the value to all participants. Networks may not experience diminishing returns in the short run. It's no more expensive to operate a television station with 1000 subscribers than with 10 million subscribers. And the value of a community of people grows with size while the cost of adding new members is inconsequential.

From this network economics perspective, information technology can be strategically useful. Internet sites can be used by firms to build "communities of users"—like-minded customers who want to share their experiences. This can build customer loyalty and enjoyment, and build unique ties to customers. Microsoft Corporation—the world's dominant PC software manufacturer—uses information technology to build communities of software developers around the world. Using the Microsoft Developer's Network, these small software developer firms work closely with Microsoft to debug its operating system software, provide new applications ideas and extensions, supply customers with tips and new software applications, and in general participate in a powerful and useful network. Table 2.8 shows how the Internet can be used to support different levels of business strategy.

network economics Model based on the concept of a network where adding another participant entails zero marginal costs but can create much larger marginal gain. Used as a model for strategic systems at the industry level.

Managing Strategic Transitions

Adopting the kinds of strategic systems described in this chapter generally requires changes in business goals, relationships with customers and suppliers, internal operations, and information architecture. These sociotechnical changes, affecting both social and technical elements of the organization, can be considered **strategic transitions**—a movement between levels of sociotechnical systems.

How much sociotechnical change occurs depends on the specific circumstances. Clearly, however, there is a connection between the strategy of an organization and its internal structure. As companies move to make information systems part of the overall corporate strategy, their internal structure must also change to reflect these

strategic transitions A movement from one level of sociotechnical system to another. Often required when adopting strategic systems that demand changes in the social and technical elements of an organization.

Table 2.8	Strategic Uses of the Internet
Level of Strategy	Internet Application
Business	Security First Network Bank allows customers to view account statements, pay bills, check account balances, and obtain 24-hour customer service through the World Wide Web.
	Federal Express and UPS maintain World Wide Web sites where customers can track the status of their packages any time of the day by entering their package tracking numbers.
	Hyatt Hotels can track the activities of visitors to its TravelWeb site, which provides electronic information on participating hotels. It can analyze these usage patterns to tailor hospitality-related products more closely to customer preferences (see Chapter 10).
	J.B. Hunt Transport Services manages the transportation logistics for J.C. Penney. Penney employees can access Hunt's Web site to check the status of any shipment.
Firm	Allegany County (Maryland) Human Resources Development Commission provides client tracking and communications across various county agencies through file sharing and e-mail.
Industry	OASIS Web sites allow consortiums of electric utilities companies to sell their surplus power to wholesalers and locate the transmission facilities for moving it between the power source and the customer.

new developments. Managers struggling to boost competitiveness will need to redesign various organizational processes to make effective use of leading-edge information systems technology.

Such changes often entail blurring of organizational boundaries, both external and internal. This is especially true of telecommunications-based strategic systems (Cash and Konsynski, 1985; Keen, 1986). Suppliers and customers must become intimately linked and may share each other's responsibilities. For instance, in Baxter International's stockless inventory system, Baxter has assumed responsibility for managing its customers' inventories (Johnston and Vitale, 1988). With the help of information systems, the supplier actually makes the inventory replenishment decisions, based on orders, point-of-sale data, or warehouse data supplied by the customer. This approach to inventory management, called **vendor-managed inventory,** is based on the theory that suppliers are the product or "category" experts and thus can do the best job of making sure that supply meets demand. Managers will need to devise new mechanisms for coordinating their firms' activities with those of customers, suppliers, and other organizations (Kambil and Short, 1994).

Firms with successful strategic information systems have broken down organizational barriers that block the sharing of data across functions. Design, sales, and manufacturing departments must work together much more closely. Federal Express' package tracking system shares information among operations, customer service, and accounting functions. Firestone Tire & Rubber Company has made tire design information available to quality control, production, and testing groups as well as to customers' engineers. Over time, Baxter redesigned its work processes numerous times to continually improve its overall service level and business relationship to customers (Short and Venkatraman, 1992).

Other organizational changes may be required as well. Standard operating procedures may need to be redesigned. As companies examine their value chains for strategic opportunities, looking for the activities that add the most value, they are finding many wasted steps or procedures that could be eliminated. In redesigning a Celina, Ohio plant, Reynolds & Reynolds Co. of Dayton, Ohio, found that 90 separate steps were required to fill an order for its business forms. Using a new order-

vendor-managed inventory
Approach to inventory management that assigns the supplier the responsibility to make inventory replenishment decisions based on order, point-of-sale data, or warehouse data supplied by the customer.

ing information system that enters specifications for orders directly into the computer, Reynolds cut the steps to 20 and the elapsed time from quoting the order to shipment from three weeks to one (Bulkeley, 1994).

In some cases, reshaping an organization to remain competitive may necessitate an entirely new organizational structure. To produce the Saturn, a new low-cost car competitive with Japanese models, General Motors also created an entirely new automotive division with a new factory, a new sales force, and a new design team to utilize the new technologies. Not all strategic information systems require such massive change, but clearly, many do. The organizational change requirements surrounding new information systems are so important that they merit attention throughout this text. Chapters 3, 11, and 14 examine organizational change issues in great detail.

What Managers Can Do

Information systems are too important to be left entirely to a small technical group in the corporation. Managers must take the initiative to identify the types of systems that would provide a strategic advantage to the firm. Although some industries are far ahead of others in their use of information technology, some of those that are far behind may be so for a good reason: The technology may not be appropriate. Other industries have simply failed to keep up with the times and thus offer considerable opportunities for vast and rapid changes. Some of the important questions managers should ask themselves are as follows:

- What are some of the forces at work in the industry? What strategies are being used by industry leaders?
- How is the industry currently using information and communication technology? Which organizations are the industry leaders in the application of information systems technology?
- What are the direction and nature of change within the industry? From where are the momentum and change coming?
- Are significant strategic opportunities to be gained by introducing information systems technology into the industry? Can information systems alter the basis of competition, build in switching costs, generate new products, strengthen the firm's power in dealing with suppliers, or create barriers against new competitors?
- What kinds of systems are applicable to the industry? Does it require systems to create new products and services, supplier systems, and/or sales and marketing systems?

Once the nature of information systems technology in the industry is understood, managers should turn to their organization and ask other important questions:

- Is the organization behind or ahead of the industry in its application of information systems?
- What is the current business strategic plan, and how does that plan mesh with the current strategy for information services?
- Have the information technologies currently in use provided significant payoffs to the business? Do they largely support the business or drain its resources?
- Where would new information systems provide the greatest value to the firm?

Once these issues have been considered, managers can gain a keener insight into whether their firms are ready for strategic information systems.

Studies of successful strategic systems have found that they are rarely planned but instead evolve slowly over a long time, and they almost always originate with practical operational problems. For instance, SABRE, the American Airlines computerized reservation system that is often cited as a classic "strategic system," originated as a straightforward inventory control and order entry system (Copeland and McKenney, 1988; Hopper, 1990). Rather than sprouting from some magical methodology, strategic systems, like most new products, come from closely observing real-world business situations. This finding may provide a clue about how to look for powerful strategic impact systems.

MANAGEMENT WRAP-UP

MANAGEMENT

The key to strategic success with information technology is, of course, managers. Managers need to identify the right technology for the appropriate level of strategy (business, firm, and industry). Managers must identify the business process to be improved, the core competencies to be enhanced, and the relationships with others in the industry. Last, managers have to implement changes in business process and technology throughout the organization.

ORGANIZATION

There are many types of information systems in an organization which serve different purposes, from transaction processing to knowledge management and decision making. Each of these systems can contribute a strategic edge. Increasingly, organizations are recognizing that information is a strategic asset which can be leveraged into long-term market advantage, but meaningful strategic systems generally require sociotechnical change.

TECHNOLOGY

Information technology is used at the business, firm, and industry level of firm strategy to achieve competitive edge. Technology can be used to differentiate existing products, create new products and services, and nurture core competencies over the long haul. Perhaps the most important contribution of the technology per se is its potential for reducing management costs within the firm and transaction costs among firms.

For Discussion. Several information systems experts have claimed that there is no such thing as a sustainable strategic advantage. Do you agree? Why or why not?

SUMMARY

1. Describe the role played by the six major types of information systems in organizations. There are six major types of information systems in contemporary organizations that are designed for different purposes and different audiences. Operational-level systems are transaction processing systems (TPS), such as payroll or order processing, that track the flow of the daily routine transactions necessary to conduct business. Knowledge-level systems support clerical, managerial, and professional workers. They consist of office automation systems (OAS) for increasing the productivity of data workers and knowledge work systems (KWS) for enhancing the productivity of knowledge workers.

Management-level systems (MIS and DSS) provide the management control level with reports and access to the organization's current performance and historical records.

Most MIS reports condense information from a TPS and are not highly analytical. Decision-support systems (DSS) support management decisions when these decisions are unique, rapidly changing, and not specified easily in advance. These systems have more advanced analytical models and data analysis capabilities than MIS and often draw on information from external as well as internal sources. Executive support systems (ESS) support the strategic level by providing a generalized computing and communications environment to assist senior management's decision making. An ESS has limited analytical capabilities but can draw on sophisticated graphics software and many sources of internal and external information.

2. Discuss the relationship between the various types of information systems. The various types of systems in the organization exchange data with one another.

Transaction processing systems are a major source of data for other systems, especially MIS and DSS. Executive support systems are primarily recipients of data from lower-level systems. However, the different systems in an organization are only loosely integrated. The information needs of the various functional areas and organizational levels are too specialized to be served by a single system.

3. Define a strategic information system and explain why information is now considered a strategic resource. A strategic information system changes the goals, operations, products, services, or environmental relationships of organizations to help them gain an edge over competitors. Today information systems can so dramatically boost a firm's productivity and efficiency that businesses view information as a weapon against competition and a strategic resource. In the past, information used to be considered a bureaucratic nuisance.

4. Describe how information systems can be used to support three levels of strategy used in business. Information systems can be used to support strategy at the business, firm, and industry level. At the business level of strategy, information systems can be used to help firms become the low-cost producer, differentiate products, or serve new markets. Information systems can also be used to "lock in" customers and suppliers using efficient customer re-

sponse and supply chain management applications. Value chain analysis is useful at the business level to highlight specific activities in the business where information systems are most likely to have a strategic impact.

At the firm level, information systems can be used to achieve new efficiencies or to enhance services by tying together the operations of disparate business units so that they can function as a whole or promote the sharing of knowledge across business units. At the industry level, systems can promote competitive advantage by facilitating cooperation with other firms in the industry, creating consortia or communities for sharing information, exchanging transactions, or coordinating activities. The competitive forces model and network economics are useful concepts for identifying strategic opportunities for systems at the industry level.

5. Explain why strategic information systems are difficult to build and sustain. Not all strategic systems make a profit; they can be expensive and risky to build. Many strategic information systems are easily copied by other firms, so that strategic advantage is not always sustainable. Implementing strategic systems often requires extensive organizational change and a transition from one sociotechnical level to another. Such changes are called strategic transitions and are often difficult and painful to achieve.

KEY TERMS

Operational-level systems	Word processing	Strategic information system	Supply chain
Knowledge-level systems	Desktop publishing	Value chain model	Switching costs
Management-level systems	Document imaging systems	Primary activities	Information partnership
Strategic-level systems	Management information system (MIS)	Support activities	Competitive forces model
Transaction processing system (TPS)	Decision-support system (DSS)	Product differentiation	Network economics
Knowledge work system (KWS)	Executive support system (ESS)	Focused differentiation	Strategic transitions
Office automation system (OAS)		Datamining	Vendor-managed inventory
		Supply chain management	

REVIEW QUESTIONS

1. Identify and describe the four levels of the organizational hierarchy. What types of information systems serve each level?

2. List and briefly describe the major types of systems in organizations. How are they related to one another?

3. What are the five types of TPS in business organizations? What functions do they perform? Give examples of each.

4. Describe the functions performed by knowledge work and office automation systems and some typical applications of each.

5. What are the characteristics of MIS? How does a MIS differ from a TPS? From a DSS?

6. What are the characteristics of DSS? How do they differ from those of an ESS?

7. What is a strategic information system? What is the difference between a strategic information system and a strategic-level system?

8. Describe appropriate models for analyzing strategy at the business level and the types of strategies that can be used to compete at this level.

9. Describe the various ways that information systems can be used to support business-level strategies.

10. Describe the role of information systems in supporting strategy at the firm level.

11. How can the competitive forces model and network economics be used to identify strategies at the industry level?

12. How can industry-level strategies be supported by information systems?

13. Why are strategic information systems difficult to build?

14. How can managers find strategic applications in their firms?

GROUP PROJECT

With a group of two or three students identify a single business firm and the strategies it is pursuing with information technology at one or all of the three different levels (business, firm, and industry). Use resources such as *Fortune, Business Week,* and the *Wall Street Journal,* or government reports such as the 10-K form reported on the Edgar Web site. The Laudon and Laudon Web site has a link to this site. Present your findings to the class.

CASE STUDY

Procter & Gamble: Finding the Right Business Model

Like many consumer products companies, Procter & Gamble, Co. embraced micromarketing. The world's preeminent consumer products company began using information technology in the late 1980s to support a traditional make-sell business strategy. P&G developed capabilities to electronically exchange orders with its largest customers, and began to redevelop its order, billing, and shipping systems. But a major consolidation of grocery stores brought about by competition from large national chains such as Wal-Mart resulted in 40,000 retail outlets disappearing by the mid 1990s. P&G sales slowed.

P&G's answer was to (1) proliferate new products to give customers more choices, (2) develop marketing programs to push the product through the retail marketing channel to the customer, and (3) develop information systems that could track manufacturing, warehousing, shipping, and the hundreds of different price promotions used to push product down the channel to retailers. P&G used a series of information systems to collect and analyze retail sales data, using the information for finely tuned promo-

tional campaigns. For example, by analyzing scanner-based sales data in relationship to regional weather patterns, P&G measured the effects of the cough and flu season on sales of its Vicks Formula 44 and Nyquil cold products. It then developed consumer response programs, such as special sales or coupon giveaways in cold regions. P&G developed 35 different varieties of Bounce fabric softener in North America, his and her baby diapers, 31 different varieties of hair shampoo, and 50 versions of Crest toothpaste.

To move all this new product down the retail channel, P&G developed 27 different types of promotions from bonus packs (two products put together in a single pack) to cents-off campaigns, to goldfish giveaways (unfortunately, most of the goldfish froze to death before customers could retrieve them). P&G made 55 price changes per day, affecting 110 products, and offered 440 price promotions per year. It was the micromarketing product model gone completely wild.

In this period of the early 1990s, information systems were developed to make the existing business processes

and the business model more efficient. Marketing developed elaborate quota systems for salespeople, and carefully tracked sales force performance. To make new products successful, any sales force has to be given sales targets, and P&G salespeople were told to move product no matter what. The sales force was credited with a sale when the product was shipped out of the P&G warehouse, not when a consumer actually bought the product. And the recently modernized order, shipping, and billing system dutifully tracked how much product was shipped from the P&G warehouses. In fact, the sales force developed so many promotions and pricing formulas (17 different price lists for the same products) that it became difficult even with elaborate computer systems to keep the orders straight. Retailers would order cases at a promised $100 per case, but P&G would ship them at $125 a case; a special order–correction facility of 150 specialists was set up in Cincinnati to correct 27,000 orders per month, at a cost of $35 to $75 per order.

Retailers of course responded to aggressive price promotions. Econo-

---

mists call this a moral hazard: People are given incentives to do the wrong thing. Retailers built larger warehouses, and when P&G prices became very attractive, they would order trainloads of merchandise in what is called "forward buying." These huge orders presented P&G manufacturing with severe problems. Manufacturing began to build new plants, only to find that the new plants would sit idle as prices returned to normal. Meanwhile, retailers' warehouses were filled with aging coffee, shampoo, and diapers. Some items would be trapped for years in the warehouse system of retailers.

The combined result of the P&G business model, systems, and marketing strategy was to raise costs to everyone in the retail channel and to the consumer. Earnings of P&G fell and sales growth stopped. Consumers were confused. The average consumer, often a woman, takes only 21 minutes to do her supermarket shopping. In that time, she buys an average of 18 items from 30,000 to 40,000 choices, down 25 percent from five years ago. She doesn't bother to check prices, looking for the same product, in the same row, at the same price week after week.

Obviously a new business model with new business processes was needed, and in 1993 P&G began a major business strategy and process shift. The new business strategy had several components according to Durk Jager, president and chief operating officer.

P&G began by eliminating one-third of its products, some of which were sold to others. It reduced its labor force by 13,000 and eliminated dozens of factories. P&G then greatly reduced price promotions and met with retail channel executives to explain the new policies. A new policy was adopted for new products: If they failed to rise to the top two-thirds of product sales in a division they would be eliminated in one year. P&G moved from brand and product management toward customer management by assigning one P&G representative to a store to coordinate sales to individual supermarkets. Prior to this, up to seven P&G product managers would call on stores. To ensure the customer would always find the product they wanted on the shelf, P&G built systems that would trigger shipments only when customers actually bought product. Taking a cue from Wal-Mart, one of P&G's largest customers and well known for its continuous replenishment systems, P&G now uses point-of-sale data provided by retailers to generate orders. P&G trucks now deliver only what is needed based on customer sales. This has saved retailers over $250 million in inventory costs alone. Now, when dealing with highly automated retailers such as Wal-Mart, 40 percent of all orders are computer generated and based directly on actual sales recorded daily and weekly. The sales force was equipped with laptop computers, and they send daily reports to headquarters recording changes in customer buying habits—and the reasons for changes in those buying habits. At headquarters, sales and marketing specialists analyze the data and quickly adjust production schedules to both actual purchases and anticipated demand. Last, P&G began a program of sharing data with its retail customers to improve the profits of its "channel partners." In some instances this has meant some P&G products have been withdrawn from retail shelves because they did not sell well. Overall, P&G believes that sharing information with channel partners, optimizing their profits, is the way to build loyalty and stay in touch with what is actually selling in the marketplace. ∎

Sources: Raju Nariesetti, "P&G, Seeing Shoppers Were Being Confused, Overhauls Marketing," *The Wall Street Journal,* January 15, 1997; Zachary Schiller, Greg Burns, and Karen Lowry, "Make It Simple. That's P&G's New Mantra—and Its Spreading." *Business Week,* September 9, 1996; Ronald Henkoff, "P&G New and Improved," *Fortune,* October 14, 1996; Julia King, "Coral Lipstick? It Sells Big in Florida," *Computerworld,* May 11, 1992; and Harvard Business School Case Study, "Procter & Gamble: Improving Consumer Value Through Process Design," President and Fellows of Harvard College, 1995.

Case Study Questions

1. What was Procter & Gamble's business strategy during the 1980s and early 1990s? What level of business strategy did this represent?

2. How much strategic advantage was provided by P&G's information systems? Why?

3. What management, organization, and technology factors contributed to Procter & Gamble's problems?

4. How successful are the solutions Procter & Gamble developed? What kind of changes in strategy and systems did the solutions involve?

REFERENCES

Allen, Brandt R., and Andrew C. Boynton. "Information Architecture: In Search of Efficient Flexibility." *MIS Quarterly* 15, no. 4 (December 1991).

Anthony, R. N. *Planning and Control Systems: A Framework for Analysis.* Cambridge, MA: Harvard University Press (1965).

Bakos, J. Yannis, and Michael E. Treacy. "Information Technology and Corporate Strategy: A Research Perspective." *MIS Quarterly* (June 1986).

Barua, Anitesh, Charles H. Kriebel, and Tridas Mukhopadhyay. "An Economic Analysis of Strategic Information Technology Investments." *MIS Quarterly* 15, no. 5 (September 1991).

Beath, Cynthia Mathis, and Blake Ives. "Competitive Information Systems in Support of Pricing." *MIS Quarterly* (March 1986).

Bower, Joseph L., and Thomas M. Hout. "Fast-Cycle Capability for Competitive Power." *Harvard Business Review* (November–December 1988).

Bulkeley, William M. "The Latest Big Thing at Many Companies Is Speed, Speed, Speed." *The Wall Street Journal* (December 23, 1994).

Caldwell, Bruce. "A Cure for Hospital Woes." *Information Week* (September 9, 1991).

Cash, J. I., and Benn R. Konsynski. "IS Redraws Competitive Boundaries." *Harvard Business Review* (March–April 1985).

Cash, J. I., and P. L. McLeod. "Introducing IS Technology in Strategically Dependent Companies." *Journal of Management Information Systems* (Spring 1985).

Chandler, Susan. "Strategies for New Mail Order: Sears." *Business Week* (December 19, 1994).

Clemons, Eric K. "Evaluation of Strategic Investments in Information Technology." *Communications of the ACM* (January 1991).

Clemons, Eric K., and Michael Row. "McKesson Drug Co.: Case Study of a Strategic Information System." *Journal of Management Information Systems* (Summer 1988).

———. "Sustaining IT Advantage: The Role of Structural Differences." *MIS Quarterly* 15, no. 3 (September 1991).

———. "Limits to Interfirm Coordination through IT." *Journal of Management Information Systems* 10, no. 1 (Summer 1993).

Clemons, Eric K., and Bruce W. Weber. "Segmentation, Differentiation, and Flexible Pricing: Experience with Information Technology and Segment-Tailored Strategies." *Journal of Management Information Systems* 11, no. 2 (Fall 1994).

Copeland, Duncan G., and James L. McKenney. "Airline Reservations Systems: Lessons from History." *MIS Quarterly* 12, no. 3 (September 1988).

Culnan, Mary J. "Transaction Processing Applications as Organizational Message Systems: Implications for the Intelligent Organization." Working paper no. 88-10, Twenty-second Hawaii International Conference on Systems Sciences (January 1989).

Davis, Gordon B., and Margrethe H. Olson. *Management Information Systems: Conceptual Foundations, Structure, and Development,* 2nd ed. New York: McGraw-Hill (1985).

Dhar, Vasant, and Roger Stein. *Intelligent Decision Support Methods.* Upper Saddle River, NJ: Prentice-Hall (1997).

Eisenhardt, Kathleen M., and Claudia Bird Schoonhoven. "Resource-Based View of Strategic Alliance Formation: Strategic and Social Effects in Entrepreneurial Firms." *Organization Science* 7, no. 2 (March–April 1996).

Evans, Philip P. and Thomas S. Wurster. "Strategy and the New Economics of Information." *Harvard Business Review* (September–October 1997).

Feeny, David F., and Blake Ives. "In Search of Sustainability: Reaping Long-Term Advantage from Investments in Information Technology." *Journal of Management Information Systems* (Summer 1990).

Fisher, Marshall L. "What Is the Right Supply Chain for Your Product?" *Harvard Business Review* (March–April 1997).

Foley, John. "Ready, Aim, Sell!" *Information Week* (February 17, 1997).

Grant, Robert M. "Prospering in Dynamically Competitive Environments: Organizational Capability as Knowledge Integration." *Organization Science* 7, No. 4 (July–August 1996).

Henderson, John C., and John J. Sifonis. "The Value of Strategic IS Planning: Understanding Consistency, Validity, and IS Markets." *MIS Quarterly* 12, no. 2 (June 1988).

Hopper, Max. "Rattling SABRE—New Ways to Compete on Information." *Harvard Business Review* (May–June 1990).

Houdeshel, George, and Hugh J. Watson. "The Management Information and Decision Support (MIDS) System at Lockheed Georgia." *MIS Quarterly* 11, no. 1 (March 1987).

Huber, George P. "Organizational Information Systems: Determinants of Their Performance and Behavior." *Management Science* 28, no. 2 (1984).

Illinitch, Anne Y., Richard A. D'Aveni, and Arie Y. Lewin. "New Organizational Forms and Strategies for Managing in Hypercompetitive Environments." *Organization Science* 7, no. 2 (May–June 1996).

Ives, Blake, and Gerald P. Learmonth. "The Information System as a Competitive Weapon." *Communications of the ACM* (December 1984).

Ives, Blake, and Michael R. Vitale. "After the Sale: Leveraging Maintenance with Information Technology." *MIS Quarterly* (March 1986).

Johnston, H. Russell, and Shelley R. Carrico. "Developing Capabilities to Use Information Strategically." *MIS Quarterly* 12, no. 1 (March 1988).

Johnston, Russell, and Paul R. Lawrence. "Beyond Vertical Integration—The Rise of the Value-Adding Partnership." *Harvard Business Review* (July–August 1988).

Johnston, Russell, and Michael R. Vitale. "Creating Competitive Advantage with Interorganizational Information Systems." *MIS Quarterly* 12, no. 2 (June 1988).

Kambil, Ajit, and James E. Short. "Electronic Integration and Business Network Redesign: A Roles-Linkage Perspective." *Journal of Management Information Systems* 10, no. 4 (Spring 1994).

Keen, Peter G. W. *Competing in Time: Using Telecommunications for Competitive Advantage.* Cambridge, MA: Ballinger Publishing Company (1986).

———. *Shaping the Future: Business Design Through Information Technology.* Cambridge, MA: Harvard Business School Press (1991).

Keen, Peter G. W., and M. S. Morton. *Decision Support Systems: An Organizational Perspective.* Reading, MA: Addison-Wesley (1978).

Kettinger, William J., Varn Grover, Subashish Guhan, and Albert H. Segors. "Strategic Information Systems Revisited: A Study in Sustainability and Performance." *MIS Quarterly* 18, no. 1 (March 1994).

King, John. "Centralized vs. Decentralized Computing: Organizational Considerations and Management Options." *Computing Surveys* (October 1984).

Konsynski, Benn R., and F. Warren McFarlan. "Information Partnerships—Shared Data, Shared Scale." *Harvard Business Review* (September–October 1990).

Lasher, Donald R., Blake Ives, and Sirkka L. Jarvenpaa. "USAA-IBM Partnerships in Information Technology:

Managing the Image Project." *MIS Quarterly* 15, no. 4 (December 1991).

Lee, Hau L., V. Padmanabhan and Seugin Whang. "The Bullwhip Effect in Supply Chains." *Sloan Management Review* (Spring 1997).

Levy, David. "Lean Production in an International Supply Chain." *Sloan Management Review* (Winter 1997).

Liebeskind, Julia Porter, Amalya Lumerman Oliver, Lynne Zucker, and Marilynn Brewer. "Social Networks, Learning and Flexibility: Sourcing Scientific Knowledge in New Biotechnology Firms." *Organization Science* 7, No. 4 (July–August 1996).

Main, Thomas J., and James E. Short. "Managing the Merger: Building Partnership Through IT Planning at the New Baxter." *MIS Quarterly* 13, no. 4 (December 1989).

Mata, Franciso J., William L. Fuerst, and Jay B. Barney. "Information Technology and Sustained Competitive Advantage: A Resource-Based Analysis." *MIS Quarterly* 19, no. 4 (December 1995).

McCarthy, Vince. "Strike It Rich!" *Datamation* (February 1997).

McFarlan, F. Warren. "Information Technology Changes the Way You Compete." *Harvard Business Review* (May–June 1984).

Millar, Victor E. "Decision-Oriented Information." *Datamation* (January 1984).

Moad, Jeff. "Let Customers Have It Their Way." *Datamation* (April 1, 1995).

Nault, Barrie R., and Albert S. Dexter. "Added Value and Pricing with Information Technology." *MIS Quarterly* 19, No. 4 (December 1995).

Porter, Michael. *Competitive Strategy.* New York: Free Press (1980).

———. *Competitive Advantage.* New York: Free Press (1985).

———. "How Information Can Help You Compete." *Harvard Business Review* (August–September 1985a).

Rackoff, Nick, Charles Wiseman, and Walter A. Ullrich. "Information Systems for Competitive Advantage: Implementation of a Planning Process." *MIS Quarterly* (December 1985).

Rebello, Joseph. "State Street Boston's Allure for Investors Starts to Fade." *The Wall Street Journal* (January 4, 1995).

Rockart, John F., and Michael E. Treacy. "The CEO Goes On-Line." *Harvard Business Review* (January–February 1982).

Short, James E., and N. Venkatraman. "Beyond Business Process Redesign: Redefining Baxter's Business Network." *Sloan Management Review* (Fall 1992).

Sprague, Ralph H., Jr., and Eric D. Carlson. *Building Effective Decision Support Systems.* Englewood Cliffs, NJ: Prentice-Hall (1982).

Thomas, L. G., III. "The Two Faces of Competition: Dynamic Resourcefulness and Hypercompetitive Shift." *Organization Science* 7, no. 2 (May–June 1996).

"USAA Insuring Progress." *Information Week* (May 25, 1992).

Vitale, Michael R. "The Growing Risks of Information System Success." *MIS Quarterly* (December 1986).

Wiseman, Charles. *Strategic Information Systems.* Homewood, IL: Richard D. Irwin (1988).

Young, Greg, Ken G. Smith, and Curtis M. Grimm. "Austrian and Industrial Organization Perspectives on Firm-Level Competitive Activity and Performance." *Organization Science* 7, no. 2 (May–June 1996).

Information Systems, Organizations, and Business Processes

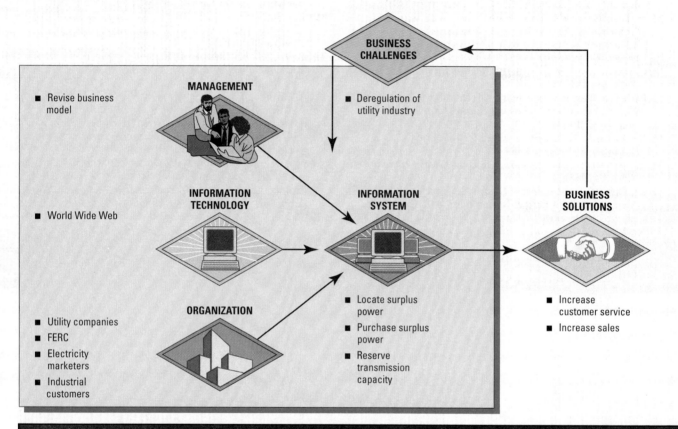

BUSINESS CHALLENGES

MANAGEMENT

- Revise business model

- Deregulation of utility industry

- World Wide Web

INFORMATION TECHNOLOGY

INFORMATION SYSTEM

BUSINESS SOLUTIONS

- Utility companies
- FERC
- Electricity marketers
- Industrial customers

ORGANIZATION

- Locate surplus power
- Purchase surplus power
- Reserve transmission capacity

- Increase customer service
- Increase sales

Wired on the Web

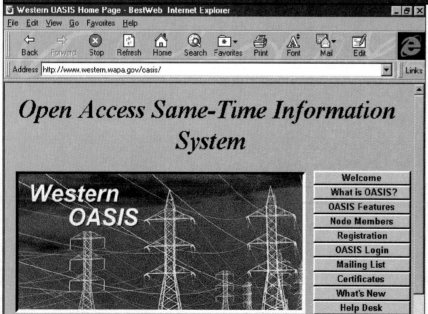

Western OASIS Home Page - BestWeb Internet Explorer

File Edit View Go Favorites Help

Back Forward Stop Refresh Home Search Favorites Print Font Mail Edit

Address http://www.western.wapa.gov/oasis/   Links

Open Access Same-Time Information System

Western OASIS

Welcome
What is OASIS?
OASIS Features
Node Members
Registration
OASIS Login
Mailing List
Certificates
What's New
Help Desk

Deregulation has ended nearly 90 years of monopoly status for gas and electric companies. Now they must face open markets and real competition. Any business or residential customer can purchase electricity from any provider anywhere. In the past, utility companies didn't need to care about what large customers thought about them. But now, customers are no longer limited to the utility company serving their area—they can pick and choose—so utilities must pay more attention to customer service.

To promote openness, the Federal Energy Regulatory Commission (FERC), the agency responsible for regulating utilities, has ordered

LEARNING OBJECTIVES

After completing this chapter, you will be able to :

1. Describe the salient characteristics of organizations.
2. Explain the changing role of information systems within the organization.
3. Compare models for describing the origins of systems in organizations.
4. Identify the major theories about organizations that help us understand their relationship with information systems.
5. Discuss the impact of information systems on organizational structure, culture, political processes, and management.
6. Describe the organizational implications for the design and implementation of systems.

electric companies to build sites on the World Wide Web, where wholesale electric customers can shop around and place orders freely. FERC officials chose the Web because it provides an easy-to-use and economical solution to the open-access problem, speeding the deregulation process. Before using the Web, wholesalers depended on personal contacts, faxes, and telephone calls to obtain the services they needed.

To comply, many electric utility companies in the United States banded together into regional power pool groups of 10 to 15 utilities. Each of these groups is to operate a Web site for its region, sharing develop-

ment and maintenance costs. The series of electric utility Web sites is called Oasis (open-access same-time information systems). Depending upon fluctuating demand, an electric utility might have surplus electricity that it could sell at a lower price to a "power marketer." The wholesaler would then resell the lower-priced power to its own industrial customers and find a way to move the electricity over competing power grids from its source to destination.

Oasis handles both the transactions for locating and purchasing the surplus power and the logistics of transmission. Electricity marketers accessing Oasis can check on the

price and availability of a utility's power grid and then schedule and reserve transmission capacity for the transfer of the wholesale electric power. A marketer working for a steel company, for example, could use Oasis to purchase electricity wherever it is cheapest and move it on the lines that lie between the power source and its customers. Oasis expects to handle between $25 and $50 billion in transactions in 1997, making the electric utilities the largest nationwide commercial-sector industry to implement business-to-business electronic commerce on the Web.

While many power companies are using Oasis to comply with FERC rulings, others have used the Web as an opportunity to change their business model. New England Electric System (NEES), the parent company of New England Power and other subsidiaries, announced in September 1996 that it would sell its power-generation plants as a result of deregulation. Instead of creating watts, the company will focus on transmitting, distributing, and marketing them using the Oasis system. Now the gas companies are taking a close look at Oasis and plan to implement a similar system. ■

Source: Lynda Radosevich, "Wired," *Webmaster*, February 1997.

MANAGEMENT CHALLENGES

The creation of Oasis illustrates the interdependence of business environments, organizational processes, management, and the development of information systems. Utility companies banded together to develop a new information system based on the World Wide Web in response to changes in competitive pressures and government regulations from their surrounding environment. The new information system has changed the way electric utilities run their business and make management decisions. The creation and use of this system and the topics discussed in this chapter raise the following management challenges:

1. **The difficulties of managing change.** Bringing about change through the development of information technology and information systems is slowed considerably by the natural inertia of organizations. Of course, organizations do change, and powerful leaders are often required to bring about these changes. Nevertheless, the process, as leaders eventually discover, is more complicated and much slower than is typically anticipated.

2. **Fitting technology to the organization (or vice versa).** On the one hand, it is important to align information technology to the organization's business plan, standard operating procedures, and business processes. Information technology is, after all, supposed to be the servant of the organization. On the other hand, these business plans, standard operating procedures, and business processes may all be very outdated or incompatible with the envisioned technology. In such instances, managers will need to change the organization to fit the technology or to adjust both the organization and the technology to achieve an optimal "fit."

3. **Understanding the limits of information technology.** We often look to technology to solve what are fundamentally human and organizational problems. We often fail to realize that information technology is no better than the skills of the knowledge and information workers who use it. Ultimately, the impact of computers is decided by the intelligence of the user. Information technology is a mirror for both organizations and individuals.

This chapter explores the complex relationship between organizations and information systems. Our goal is to introduce you to the salient features of organizations that you will need to know about as a manager when you envision, design, build, and operate information systems. First we will describe the features of organizations that are related to information systems—what we call the "salient" features. Then we will examine in greater detail precisely how information systems affect organizations, and just as important, how organizations affect information systems. The chapter concludes by describing some reasons why organizations are so difficult to change—with or without technology—and how you can use this knowledge to your advantage.

Can information systems "flatten" organizations by reducing their number of levels? Will information systems allow organizations to operate with fewer middle managers and clerical workers? Can they be used to "reengineer" organizations so they become lean, efficient, and hard hitting? Can organizations use information technology to decentralize power down to lower-level workers, thereby unleashing the creative talents of millions of employees? Can organizations use systems to rebuild their business processes? Can the Internet and World Wide Web substitute for organization?

These are among today's leading management questions. The issues raised by contemporary information systems—efficiency, creativity, bureaucracy, employment, quality of work life—are long-standing issues of industrial society, and they pre-date computers. No one can deny that information systems have contributed to organizational efficiency and effectiveness. Yet social and behavioral scientists who have studied organizations over a long time argue that no radical transformation of organizations has occurred except in isolated cases. And the long-term viability of new organizational forms is not known. Exactly what can information systems do for organizations?

The relationship between information technology and organizations is complex, and the interpretations of this relationship are controversial. Our goal is to present an overview of the relationship and a discussion of contemporary research so that you can understand the issues and join the debate.

The Two-Way Relationship

Let us start with a simple premise based on observation and a great deal of research: Information systems and organizations have a mutual influence on each other (see Figure 3.1). On the one hand, information systems must be aligned with the organization to provide information needed by important groups within the organization. At the same time, the organization must be aware of and must open itself to the influences of information systems to benefit from new technologies. Information systems affect organizations, and organizations necessarily affect the design of systems.

It is very convenient for journalists, scholars, and managers to think about "the impact of computers" on organizations as if it were like some ship colliding with an iceberg at sea. But the actual effect is much more complex. Figure 3.1 shows a great many mediating factors that influence the interaction between information technology and organizations. These include the organization's structure, standard operating procedures, politics, culture, surrounding environment, and management decisions (Orlikowski and Robey, 1991; Orlikowski, 1992). Managers, after all, decide what systems will be built, what the systems will do, how they will be implemented,

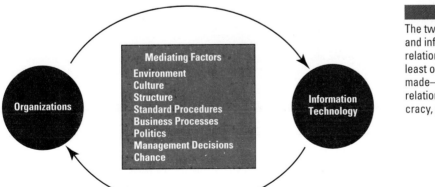

FIGURE 3.1

The two-way relationship between organizations and information technology. This complex two-way relationship is mediated by many factors, not the least of which are the decisions made—or not made—by managers. Other factors mediating the relationship are the organizational culture, bureaucracy, politics, business fashion, and pure chance.

and so forth. To a large extent, managers and organizations choose the "computer impacts" they want (or at least receive the impacts they deserve) (Laudon, 1986; Laudon and Marr, 1994; Laudon and Marr, 1995). Sometimes, however, the outcomes are the result of pure chance and of both good and bad luck.

Because there are many types of organizations, it stands to reason that the technology of information systems will have a different impact on different types of organizations. There is no singular effect of computers; one cannot, for example, conclude that "computers flatten hierarchies" in all organizations. Instead, different organizations in different circumstances experience different effects from the same technology. Before describing how each of these mediating factors affects information systems, we must first review the salient features of organizations.

What Is an Organization?

organization (technical definition)
A stable, formal social structure that takes resources from the environment and processes them to produce outputs.

An **organization** is a stable, formal social structure that takes resources from the environment and processes them to produce outputs. This technical definition focuses on three elements of an organization (see Figure 3.2). Capital and labor are primary production factors provided by the environment. The organization (the firm) transforms these inputs into products and services in a production function—a process that transforms capital and labor into a product.[1] The products and services are consumed by environments in return for supply inputs.

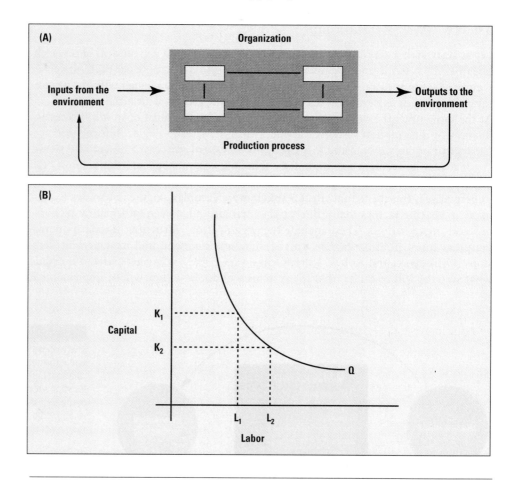

FIGURE 3.2

The technical microeconomic definition of the organization. In the microeconomic definition of organizations, capital and labor (the primary production factors provided by the environment) are transformed by the firm through the production process into products and services (outputs to the environment). The products and services are consumed by the environment, which supplies additional capital and labor as inputs in the feedback loop. (B) The microeconomic view is a technical model of the firm in which the firm combines capital and labor in a production function to produce a single product of the amount Q. The firm can freely substitute the capital for labor anywhere along the curve Q. In this view, the production process is unexamined, largely a black box.

---

1. A typical production function is given by $Q = A*(K,L)$, where Q is the quantity of output produced by a firm; K and L are factors of production, capital, and labor. A represents a parameter greater than 0 reflecting the productivity of available technology—factors such as education, knowledge, and changes in technique and technology—which can alter the output Q independent of capital and labor. See any microeconomics textbook for further background. An excellent reference is Robert S. Pindyck and Daniel L. Rubinfield, *Microeconomics* (New York: Macmillan, 1992). This text has several interesting chapters on information asymmetries, although like most microeconomics texts it is limited in its coverage of technology.

An organization is more stable than an informal group in terms of longevity and routineness. Organizations are formal because they are legal entities and must abide by laws. They have internal rules and procedures. Organizations are social structures because they are a collection of social elements, much as a machine has a structure— a particular arrangement of valves, cams, shafts, and other parts.

This definition of organizations is powerful and simple, but it is not very descriptive or even predictive of the real-world organizations to which most of us belong. A more realistic, behavioral definition of an **organization** is that it is a collection of rights, privileges, obligations, and responsibilities that are delicately balanced over time through conflict and conflict resolution (see Figure 3.3).

In this behavioral view of the firm, people who work in organizations develop customary ways of working; they gain attachments to existing relationships; and they make arrangements with subordinates and superiors about how work will be done, how much work will be done, and under what conditions. Most of these arrangements and feelings are not discussed in any formal rule book.

How do these definitions of organizations relate to information system technology? A technical microeconomic view of organizations encourages us to think that introducing new technology changes the way inputs are combined into outputs, like changing the spark plugs on an engine. The firm is seen as infinitely malleable, with capital and labor substituting for one another quite easily.

But the more realistic behavioral definition of an organization suggests that building new information systems or rebuilding old ones involves much more than a technical rearrangement of machines or workers. Instead, technological change requires changes in who owns and controls information, who has the right to access and update that information, and who makes decisions about whom, when, and how. For instance, the Oasis system opened access to information about electric utility companies' power supplies to new parties, recasting the relationship among utility companies and wholesalers and among the utility companies themselves. The more complex view forces us to look at the way work is designed and the procedures used to achieve outputs.

The technical and behavioral definitions of organizations are not contradictory. Indeed, they complement one another: The microeconomic definition tells us how thousands of firms in competitive markets combine capital and labor and information technology, whereas the behavioral model takes us inside the individual firm to see how, in fact, specific firms use capital and labor to produce outputs. Section 3.4 describes how theories based on each of these definitions of organizations can help explain the relationship between information systems and organizations.

Information systems can markedly alter life in the organization. Some information systems change the organizational balance of rights, privileges, obligations, responsibilities, and feelings that has been established over a long time. What this means is that managers cannot design new systems or understand existing systems without understanding organizations.

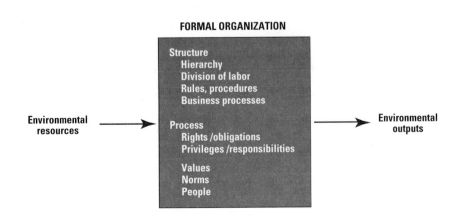

FIGURE 3.3

The behavioral view of organizations. The behavioral view of organizations emphasizes group relationships, values, and structures.

In this section, we introduce and discuss the major features of organizations of which managers should be aware when building information systems. These organizational features are mediating factors (review Figure 3.1) that influence the relationship between organizations and information technology.

Some features of organizations are common to all organizations; others distinguish one organization from another. Let us look first at the features common to all organizations.

Why Organizations Are So Much Alike: Common Features

You might not think that Apple Computer, United Airlines, or the Aspen Colorado Police Department have much in common, but they do. In some respects, all modern organizations are alike because they share the characteristics that are listed in Table 3.1. A German sociologist, Max Weber, was the first to describe these "ideal–typical" characteristics of organizations in 1911. He called organizations **bureaucracies** that have certain "structural" features (see Table 3.1).

According to Weber, all modern bureaucracies have a clear-cut division of labor and specialization. Organizations employ or train individuals who possess specific talents or skills. Organizations arrange specialists in a hierarchy of authority in which everyone is accountable to someone and authority is limited to specific actions. Authority and action are further limited by abstract rules or procedures (standard operating procedures or SOPs) that are interpreted and applied to specific cases. These rules create a system of impartial and universalistic decision making; everyone is treated equally. Organizations try to hire and promote employees on the basis of technical qualifications and professionalism (not personal connections). The organization itself is devoted to the principle of efficiency: maximizing output using limited inputs.

Bureaucracies are so prevalent, according to Weber, because they are the most efficient form of organization. They are much more stable and powerful than mercurial charismatic groups or formal aristocracies held together by the right of birth. Other scholars supplemented Weber, identifying additional features of organizations. All organizations develop standard operating procedures, politics, and a culture.

Standard Operating Procedures

All organizations, over time, stabilize to produce a given number of products and services. Over long periods of time, the organizations that survive become very efficient, producing a limited number of products and services by following standard routines. In this period of time, employees develop reasonably precise rules, procedures, and practices called **standard operating procedures (SOPs)** to cope with virtually all expected situations. Some of these rules and procedures are written down as formal procedures, but most are rules of thumb to be followed in selected situations.

bureaucracy Formal organization with a clear-cut division of labor, abstract rules and procedures, and impartial decision making that uses technical qualifications and professionalism as a basis for promoting employees.

standard operating procedures (SOPs) Precise, defined rules, procedures, and practices developed by organizations to cope with virtually all expected situations.

Table 3.1 Structural Characteristics of All Organizations
Clear division of labor
Hierarchy
Explicit rules and procedures
Impartial judgments
Technical qualifications for positions
Maximum organizational efficiency

A great deal of the efficiency that modern organizations attain has little to do with computers but a great deal to do with the development of standard operating procedures. For instance, in the assembly of a car, thousands of motions and procedures must be planned and executed in a precise fashion to permit the finished product to roll off the line. If workers had to decide how each vehicle was to be built, or if managers had to decide how each day's product was to be built, efficiency would drop dramatically. Instead, managers and workers develop a complex set of standard procedures to handle most situations. Any change in SOPs requires an enormous organizational effort. Indeed, the organization may need to halt the entire production process, or create a new and expensive parallel system, which must then be tested exhaustively before the old SOPs can be retired. For example, difficulty in changing standard operating procedures is one reason Detroit auto makers have been slow to adopt Japanese mass-production methods. Until recently, U.S. auto makers followed Henry Ford's mass-production principles. Ford believed that the cheapest way to build cars was to churn out the largest number of autos by having workers repeatedly perform a simple task. By contrast, Japanese auto makers have emphasized "lean production" methods where a smaller number of workers each performing several tasks can produce cars with less inventory, less investment, and fewer mistakes. Workers have multiple jobs and responsibilities and are encouraged to note every glitch and, if necessary, stop production to correct a problem.

Organizational Politics

Organizations are arranged so that people occupy different positions. Because these individuals have different concerns and specialties, they naturally have differences in viewpoint, perspective, and opinion about how resources, rewards, and punishments should be distributed. Because of these differences, political struggle, competition, and conflict occur in every organization. Sometimes political struggles occur when individuals or interest groups seek to exercise leadership and to gain advantages. Other times, entire groups compete, leading to clashes on a large scale. In either case, politics is a normal part of organizational life.

One difficulty of bringing about change in organizations—especially concerning the development of new information systems—is the political resistance that any important organizational change seems to bring forth. "Important" changes are those that directly affect who does what to whom, where, when, and how. Virtually all information systems that bring about significant changes in goals, procedures, productivity, and personnel are politically charged.

Organizational Culture

All organizations have bedrock, unassailable, unquestioned (by the members) assumptions that define the goals and products of the organization. **Organizational culture** is the set of fundamental assumptions about what the organization should produce, what business processes should be used and how they should be defined, how it should produce its products, where, and for whom. Generally, these cultural assumptions are taken totally for granted and rarely are publicly announced or discussed. They are simply assumptions that few people, if anyone (in their right mind), would question (Schein, 1985).

Everything else—technology, values, norms, public announcements, and so on— follows from these assumptions. You can see organizational culture at work by looking around your university or college. Some bedrock assumptions of university life are that professors know more than students, the reason students attend college is to learn, the primary purpose of the university is to create new knowledge and communicate knowledge to students, classes follow a regular schedule, and libraries are repositories of knowledge in the form of books and journals. Sometimes these cultural assumptions are true. Organizational culture is a powerful unifying force, which restrains political conflict and promotes common understanding, agreement

organizational culture The set of fundamental assumptions about what products the organization should produce, how and where it should produce them, and for whom they should be produced.

on procedures, and common practices. If we all share the same basic cultural assumptions, then agreement on other matters is more likely.

At the same time, organizational culture is a powerful restraint on change, especially technological change. Any technological change that threatens commonly held cultural assumptions will meet with a great deal of resistance. One reason why U.S. auto makers were slow to switch to "lean production" methods is because of long-standing assumptions that management should be authoritarian and does not need to listen to the opinions of workers. Not only did U.S. companies change the business processes and standard operating procedures on their assembly lines, but they also had to find ways to involve auto workers in improving factories. These deep-seated changes were difficult given the hierarchical and authoritarian culture of U.S. auto companies.

In general, organizational cultures are far more powerful than information technologies. Therefore, most organizations will do almost anything to avoid making changes in basic assumptions, and new technologies are almost always used at first in ways that support existing cultures.

On the other hand, there are times when the only sensible way to employ a new technology is directly opposed to an existing organizational culture. When this occurs, the technology is often stalled or delayed while the culture slowly adjusts. Organizational change requires far more time than technological change requires (Klotz, 1966).

Why Organizations Are So Different: Unique Features

Some features vary from one organization to another. Although all organizations have some common characteristics, no two organizations are identical. Organizations have different structures, goals, constituencies, leadership styles, tasks, and surrounding environments.

Different Organizational Types

One important way in which organizations differ is in their structure or shape. The differences among organizational structures are characterized in many ways. Mintzberg's classification is especially useful and simple, for it identifies the following five basic kinds of organizations:

Entrepreneurial structure: Organizations with simple structures tend to be young, small, entrepreneurial firms in fast-changing environments, dominated by a single entrepreneur and managed by a single chief executive officer. Information systems typically are poorly planned and significantly behind fast-breaking production developments.

Machine bureaucracy: The large, classic bureaucracy exists in slow-changing environments, producing standardized products. It is dominated by a strategic senior management that centralizes information flow and decision authority. It is likely to be organized into functional divisions, for example, manufacturing, finance, marketing, and human resources. Information systems tend to be mainframe-based. They are well planned, but are generally limited to accounting, finance, simple planning, and administrative applications.

Professional bureaucracy: This structure is typical of law firms, school systems, accounting firms, hospitals, and other knowledge-based organizations that depend on the knowledge and expertise of professionals. Professional bureaucracies are suitable for slow-changing environments and skill sets. They are dominated by department heads and have weak centralized authority. Professional members of the organization who have considerable information and authority create the product or service. Such organizations typically have primitive central information systems for time accounting and billing for professional services, and often have sophisticated knowledge work support systems for professionals. Knowledge work systems are described in greater detail in Chapter 15.

entrepreneurial structure
Young, small firm in a fast-changing environment dominated by a single entrepreneur and managed by a single chief executive officer.

machine bureaucracy Large bureaucracy organized into functional divisions that centralizes decision making, produces standard products, and exists in a slow-changing environment.

professional bureaucracy Knowledge-based organization such as a law firm or hospital that is dominated by department heads with weak centralized authority; operates in a slowly changing environment.

Divisionalized bureaucracy: This type of organization is the most common Fortune 500 form, a combination of many machine bureaucracies, each producing a different product or service, topped by a central headquarters. This type of organization is suited to slow-changing environments and standardized products, but because these kinds of organizations are divisionalized, they tend to operate in several different environments (one for each division or product line). Information systems typically are elaborate and complex so that they can support central headquarter's financial planning and reporting requirements on one hand, and the operational requirements of the divisions on the other hand.

Adhocracy: This "task force" organization is typically found in research organizations (such as the Rand Corporation), aerospace companies, medical, biomedical, electronic, and other high-tech firms that must respond to rapidly changing environments and markets or that derive revenue from government contracts. Such organizations are more innovative than machine bureaucracies, more flexible than professional bureaucracies, and have more sustained, effective power than the simple entrepreneurial firm. They are characterized by large groups of specialists organized into short-lived, multidisciplinary task forces focusing on new products and by weak central management that understands little of the technical work of its employees but is nevertheless expected to manage the flow of funds from the environment and deliver products in return. Information systems are poorly developed at the central level, but are often remarkably advanced within task forces where experts build their unique systems for narrow functions.

Organizations and Environments

Organizations reside in environments from which they draw resources and to which they supply goods and services. Organizations and environments have a two-way reciprocal relationship. On the one hand, organizations are open to, and dependent upon, the social and physical environment that surrounds them. Organizations need financial resources and political legitimacy (a set of laws by which to operate) provided by outside institutions and governments. Customers are significant members of the environment. And knowledge and technology are also a part of the environment: they are produced by other actors in the environment and purchased by the organization as educated labor or as pure knowledge assets (such as databases or other information flows).

Organizations can also influence their environments, at least in the short term. Organizations form alliances with others to influence the political process, often altering the tax environment to suit their needs, and they advertise to influence customer acceptance of their products. Organizations also choose to participate in certain environments: General Motors chooses every day to stay in the automobile business.

Information technology, specifically business systems, plays a significant role in helping organizations perceive changes in their environments, and also in helping organizations act on their environments (see Figure 3.4). Information systems are key tools for *environmental scanning*, helping managers identify external changes that might require an organizational response.

Environments generally change much faster than organizations. Organizational environments change for all the reasons described in Chapter 1: changing knowledge and technology, new values, new markets, and changes in the global distribution of wealth. Environmental change is a main cause of organizational failure. As environments change, they pose new problems for managers of organizations. New knowledge, for instance, can invalidate the existing knowledge of an entire industry. Consider the fate of the coal industry, the vacuum tube industry, and the horse carriage industry. The Lehigh Coal Company was one of America's Fortune top 10 business firms in 1919. It disappeared in the 1940s as the country shifted to gas and oil heat. Only about 10 percent of the 1919 Fortune 500 survive in 1997. What these organizations "knew how to do" was totally irrelevant to new techniques and newer

divisionalized bureaucracy
Combination of many machine bureaucracies, each producing a different product or service, under one central headquarters. Common form for Fortune 500 firms.

adhocracy Task force organization, such as a research organization, designed to respond to a rapidly changing environment and characterized by large groups of specialists organized into short-lived multidisciplinary task forces.

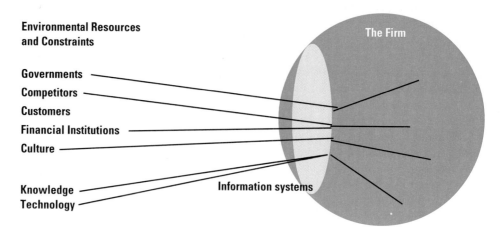

FIGURE 3.4

The Organization and Its Environment

Environments and organizations have a reciprocal relationship. Environments shape what organizations can do, but organizations can influence their environments and decide to change environments altogether. Information technology plays a critical role in helping organizations perceive environmental change, and in helping organizations act on their environment. Information systems act as a filter between organizations and their environments. They do not necessarily reflect reality, but instead refract environmental change through a number of built-in biases.

competencies. When environments become turbulent, complex, and resource constrained, the knowledge and skills that organizations once possessed can become useless, and even a hindrance to change.

Some organizations fail to perceive, or rather misperceive, changes in their environments. Even if correctly perceived, organizations react to environmental changes in a variety of ways. Some organizations "learn" how to survive in new and changing environments by adopting new information technologies, by changing their products and services and their production process, by reallocating assets of all kinds, and by altering their cultures—explanations of what they are doing. These organizations rapidly acquire new knowledge and technology, and employ these assets in production quickly.

Other organizations, perhaps most, are more resistant to change and they become dysfunctional and fail. These organizations learn by insulating themselves from their environments; they survive by relying on slack resources and savings and by developing rigid standard operating procedures. They become efficient at what they always did, such as learning how to run a traditional steel mill more efficiently. Eventually these coping and learning mechanisms are overwhelmed and the organizations fail.

Most people do not realize how fragile and short-lived formal organizations really are. Consider that less than 10 percent of Fortune 500 companies in 1918 survived more than 50 years; less than 4 percent of all federal government organizations ever created are still in existence; 50 percent of new private organizations are out of business within 5 years; and bigness per se is only marginally protective against extinction and may only slow the decline (Laudon, 1989).

The main reasons for organizational failure are an inability to adapt to a rapidly changing environment and the lack of resources—particularly among young firms—to sustain even short periods of troubled times (Freeman et al., 1983). New technologies, new products, and changing public tastes and values (many of which result in new government regulations) put strains on any organization's culture, politics, and people. In general, most organizations do not cope well with large environmental shifts.

From an organizational standpoint, technology is a major environmental factor that continually threatens existing arrangements. At times, technological changes occur so radically as to constitute a "technological discontinuity," a sharp break in industry practice that either enhances or destroys the competence of firms in an industry (Tushman and Anderson, 1986). Fast-changing technologies, such as information technology, pose a particular threat to organizations. For instance, Wang Laboratories, a leading manufacturer of minicomputers and word processors, was a dominant force in the computer industry during the 1970s and early 1980s. But when powerful desktop PCs reduced the need for minicomputers, Wang nearly went out of business because it failed to adapt its products to the new technology.

Other Differences Among Organizations

There are many reasons why organizations have different shapes or structures. Organizations differ in their ultimate goals and the types of power used to achieve them. Some organizations have coercive goals (e.g., prisons); other have utilitarian goals (e.g., businesses). Still others have normative goals (universities, religious groups). The kinds of power and incentives differ accordingly, as does the overall shape of the organization: A coercive organization will be very hierarchical whereas a normative organization will be less hierarchical.

Organizations serve different groups or have different constituencies. Some primarily benefit their members; others benefit clients, stockholders, or the public. The social roles or functions of organizations differ. Some organizations are primarily interested in politics (trying to change the distribution of benefits in society), whereas others play primarily economic roles (seeking to optimize the utilization of resources). Some organizations play integrative roles by trying to pull together diverse groups in a common enterprise; examples include hospitals devoted to the control of disease and courts devoted to the pursuit of justice. Still other organizations, such as universities, schools, and churches, work to preserve important social values (normative roles). In general, the wider the constituency that an organization serves, the less hierarchical the organization.

Clearly, the nature of leadership differs greatly from one organization to another, even in similar organizations devoted to the same goal. Some of the major leadership styles are democratic, authoritarian (even totalitarian), laissez-faire (leadership is absent), technocratic (according to technical criteria, formal models), or bureaucratic (strictly according to formal rules). These kinds of leadership can occur in any type of organization and seem to depend on chance and history.

Still another way organizations differ is by the tasks they perform and the technology they use. In some cases, organizations use routine tasks that could be programmed; that is, tasks may be reduced to formal rules that require little judgment (e.g., inventory reordering). Organizations that primarily perform routine tasks are typically like machine bureaucracies—they are hierarchical and run according to standard procedures. In other cases, organizations work with highly judgmental, nonroutine tasks (e.g., a consulting company that creates strategic plans for other companies).

Business Processes

Business processes refer to the manner in which work is organized, coordinated, and focused to produce a valuable product or service. On the one hand, business processes are concrete work flows of material, information, and knowledge—sets of activities. This definition falls into the technical–rational view of organizations, and the focus is on value-creating activities and their improvement.

But business processes also refer to the unique ways in which organizations coordinate work, information, and knowledge, and the ways in which management chooses to coordinate work. This definition focuses more on core competencies of the organization, management perceptions of work flow, and leadership of the organization. The behavioral model of the firm dominates in this definition of business process. In this view, business processes are primarily conceptual, and they result from management thinking about how the organization works.

Several contemporary management movements focus on business process: total quality management, business reengineering, time-based competition, team-based

business processes The unique ways in which organizations coordinate and organize work activities, information, and knowledge to produce a valuable product or service.

Lantech, Inc. redesigned its manufacturing process, replacing the traditional assembly line with microlines. Integrated teams of workers oversee the entire production process.

organization, networked organizations, and so-called learning organizations. We frequently discuss these movements throughout the book. The field of management originated with a focus on manufacturing processes in the late nineteenth century; the most widely known business process practitioner was Frederick Taylor who carefully examined the motions of production factory workers to improve their efficiency.

The contemporary interest with business processes comes from the recognition that strategic success ultimately depends on how well firms execute their primary mission of delivering the lowest cost, highest quality goods and services to customers. To a large extent, the new emphasis on business process is a reaction to the almost exclusive focus on corporate strategy which dominated the literature of the late 1980s.

Examples of processes are new product development, which turns an idea into a manufacturable prototype, or order fulfillment, which begins with the receipt of an order and ends when the customer has received and paid for the product. Figure 3.5 depicts the order management process at Procter & Gamble after it was improved through the development of an order, shipping, and billing system (OSB system). By breaking down the order management process into concrete steps or activities and their core processes, analysts were able to develop concrete performance measures and set improvement targets.

Processes, by nature, are generally cross functional, transcending the boundaries between sales, marketing, manufacturing, and research and development. Processes cut across the traditional organizational structure, grouping employees from different functional specialties to complete a piece of work.

The objectives for processes are more external and linked to meeting customer and market demands than are those for the traditional functional approach. Instead of evaluating how well each functional area is performing as a discrete business function, management would evaluate how well a group executes a process. For instance, instead of measuring manufacturing independently on how well it reduces the cost to produce each unit, and shipping independently on how quickly it ships out each unit, management might look at the entire logistics process from receipt of raw material to receipt by the customer.

Information systems can help organizations achieve great efficiencies by automating parts of these processes or by helping organizations rethink and streamline these processes through the development of workflow software. Chapter 11 will treat this subject in greater detail, as it is fundamental to systems analysis and design.

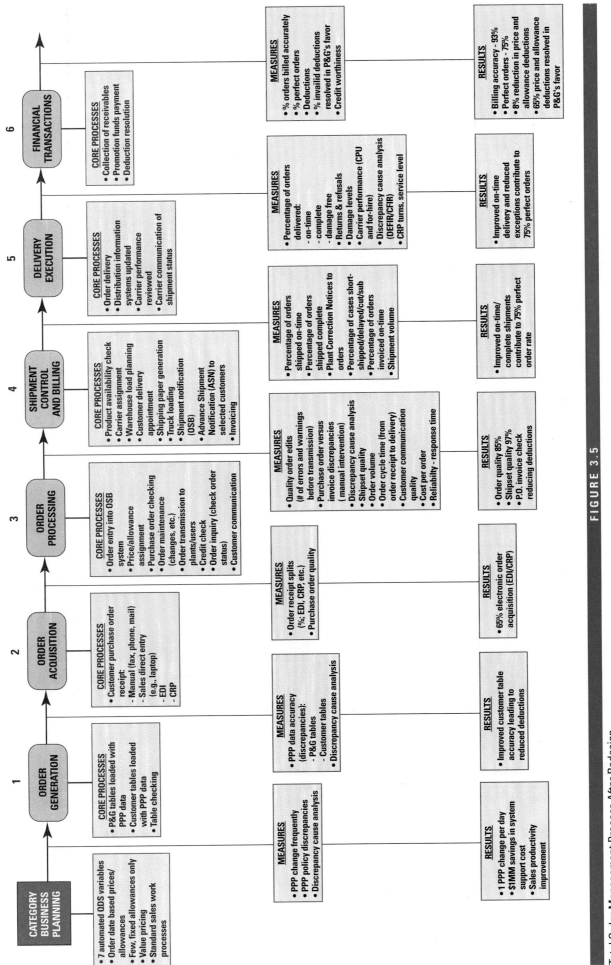

FIGURE 3.5

Total Order Management Process After Redesign

Source: "Procter & Gamble: Improving Consumer Value through Process Redesign," Exhibit 5, "Total Order Management Process After Redesign (1994), Harvard Business School, March 31, 1995. 9-195-126. Copyright © 1995 by the President and Fellows of Harvard College. Harvard Business School Publishing, Boston, MA 02163.

1 ORDER GENERATION

CORE PROCESSES
• 7 automated ODS variables
• Order date based prices/allowances
• Few, fixed allowances only
• Value pricing
• Standard sales work processes

MEASURES
• PPP change frequently
• PPP policy discrepancies
• Discrepancy cause analysis

RESULTS
• 1 PPP change per day
• $1MM savings in system support cost
• Sales productivity improvement

2 ORDER ACQUISITION

CORE PROCESSES
• Customer purchase order receipt:
  - Manual (fax, phone, mail)
  - Sales direct entry (e.g., laptop)
  - EDI
  - CRP

MEASURES
• Order receipt splits (%; EDI, CRP, etc.)
• Purchase order quality

RESULTS
• 65% electronic order acquisition (EDI/CRP)

3 ORDER PROCESSING

CORE PROCESSES
• Order entry into OSB system
• Price/allowance assignment
• Purchase order checking
• Order maintenance (changes, etc.)
• Order transmission to plants/users
• Credit check
• Order inquiry (check order status)
• Customer communication

MEASURES
• Quality order edits (# of errors and warnings before transmission)
• Purchase order versus invoice discrepancies (manual intervention)
• Discrepancy cause analysis
• Shipset quality
• Order volume
• Order cycle time (from order receipt to delivery)
• Customer communication quality
• Cost per order
• Reliability - response time

RESULTS
• Order quality 85%
• Shipset quality 97%
• P.O. invoice check reducing deductions

4 SHIPMENT CONTROL AND BILLING

CORE PROCESSES
• Product availability check
• Carrier assignment
• Warehouse load planning
• Customer delivery appointment
• Shipping paper generation
• Truck loading
• Shipment notification (OSB)
• Advance Shipment Notification (ASN) to selected customers
• Invoicing

MEASURES
• Percentage of orders shipped on-time
• Percentage of orders shipped complete
• Plant Correction Notices to orders
• Percentage of cases short-shipped/delayed/cut/sub
• Percentage of orders invoiced on-time
• Shipment volume

RESULTS
• Improved on-time/complete shipments contribute to 75% perfect order rate

5 DELIVERY EXECUTION

CORE PROCESSES
• Order delivery
• Distribution information systems updated
• Carrier performance reviewed
• Carrier communication of shipment status

MEASURES
• Percentage of orders delivered:
  - on-time
  - complete
  - damage free
• Returns & refusals
• Damage levels
• Carrier performance (CPU and for-hire)
• Discrepancy cause analysis (DEFIR/CFIR)
• CRP turns, service level

RESULTS
• Improved on-time delivery and reduced exceptions contribute to 75% perfect orders

6 FINANCIAL TRANSACTIONS

CORE PROCESSES
• Collection of receivables
• Promotion funds payment
• Deduction resolution

MEASURES
• % orders billed accurately
• % perfect orders
• Deductions
• % invalid deductions resolved in P&G's favor
• Credit worthiness

RESULTS
• Billing accuracy - 93%
• Perfect orders - 75%
• 8% reduction in price and allowance deductions
• 65% price and allowance deductions resolved in P&G's favor

CATEGORY BUSINESS PLANNING

MEASURES
• PPP data accuracy (discrepancies):
  - P&G tables
  - Customer tables
• Discrepancy cause analysis

RESULTS
• Improved customer table accuracy leading to reduced deductions

CORE PROCESSES
• P&G tables loaded with PPP data
• Customer tables loaded with PPP data
• Table checking

Backing Away from Technology

For 20 years, Lantech, Inc., a manufacturer of industrial packaging equipment, was heavily into automation, acquiring larger, more powerful computers as years rolled on. Today, Lantech's central computer room, once the nerve center of the factory, lies dark and shuttered, its computers unplugged or sold.

The Lantech plant now runs on technology that is 40 years old. Instead of using a shop filled with automated assembly machines and numerically controlled lathes, workers wield drill presses and hand tools. Managers use simple visual aids such as strips of tape to show the direction of production flow or cue cards to signal when to order new supplies. Since Lantech discarded its old high-tech system in 1992, productivity has risen almost 100 percent and production defects have been cut in half.

Lantech didn't just abandon automation—it replaced the dominant manufacturing model for U.S. industry, division of labor, with the Japanese style system of "lean production," based on generalization of labor. Instead of the traditional assembly line, where individuals toil repeatedly at a single task, Lantech workers are organized into collaborative "microlines," integrated teams that oversee the entire production process from start to finish.

Lantech led the industry in the manufacture of "unitizers," machines that bind items together so that they can be handled as a single package. The Lantech plant assembles machines that can stretch plastic wrap around items so that they are held together by the natural elasticity of the wrap. The basic components include roller conveyors, ramps, turntables, wrapping arms, frames, motors, belt drives, stretch-wrap threaders, safety shields, and control systems. However, assembly is complicated because a significant portion of the orders require custom designs. A "standard" machine can be ordered in thousands of different configurations.

For its first 20 years, Lantech used traditional mass-production methods. Its managers defined a set of core processes (sawing, machining, fabrication, painting, electrical assembly, and final assembly) and organized internal operating divisions around those processes. Productivity could be increased by raising the speed of the core processes, primarily by intensifying the division of labor and accelerating automation.

But in 1989 Lantech lost a key design patent and its lead in the wrapping-machine market. New competitors entered the field with aggressive pricing tactics. Business fell sharply. Pat Lancaster, Lantech's founder and chairman, decided to move toward the "lean production" model where higher productivity is achieved not by reducing costs per part but by lowering costs for the production cycle as a whole from design to manufacture to sales. Instead of trying to put peg A in hole B as quickly as possible, the job of each employee is to find a succession of better ways to get the entire cycle to meet the overarching objectives of the business—a philosophy of continuous improvement.

Lantech teams evaluated and redesigned every aspect of its production process. The company replaced its "hurry up and wait" pattern, in which inventory was moved in batches from one sector of the factory with a system composed of several microlines. Each microline is a production cell responsible for all the processes—sawing, welding, electrical wiring—that were once spread out throughout the factory. The new production process cut down on excess inventory and production delays because it made it possible for each component moving through production to correspond to a specific customer order. Under the old system, Lantech produced parts in lots and batches specified by projections.

Lantech's automated machines designed for mass-production methods were not compatible with the company's new production process. Redesigning its computer systems to fit lean production methods was too expensive, so Lantech reverted to manual methods. The company can complete orders in 12 hours instead of five weeks and is competitive once again.

To Think About: What business processes did Lantech change? Why? What management, organization, and technology issues had to be addressed when Lantech changed these processes?

Source: Fred Hapgood, "Keeping It Simple," *Inc. Technology,* March 19, 1996.

Automating business processes requires careful analysis and planning. When systems are used to strengthen the wrong business model or business processes, the business can become more efficient at doing what it should not do. And as a result, the strategic position of the firm suffers and it becomes vulnerable to competitors who may have discovered the right business model. Therefore, one important strategic decision that a firm can make is not deciding how to use computers to improve business processes, but instead to first understand what business processes need improvement (Keen, 1997). The choice of the business process to improve is critical. If you optimize the wrong process you waste money.

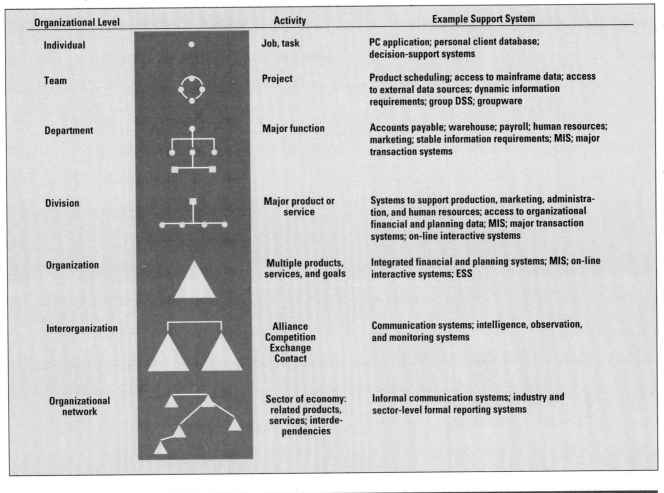

Organizational Level		Activity	Example Support System
Individual		Job, task	PC application; personal client database; decision-support systems
Team		Project	Product scheduling; access to mainframe data; access to external data sources; dynamic information requirements; group DSS; groupware
Department		Major function	Accounts payable; warehouse; payroll; human resources; marketing; stable information requirements; MIS; major transaction systems
Division		Major product or service	Systems to support production, marketing, administration, and human resources; access to organizational financial and planning data; MIS; major transaction systems; on-line interactive systems
Organization		Multiple products, services, and goals	Integrated financial and planning systems; MIS; on-line interactive systems; ESS
Interorganization		Alliance Competition Exchange Contact	Communication systems; intelligence, observation, and monitoring systems
Organizational network		Sector of economy: related products, services; interdependencies	Informal communication systems; industry and sector-level formal reporting systems

FIGURE 3.6

Organizational levels and support systems. Systems are designed to support various levels of the organization.

The Window on Organizations shows how one company achieved significant benefits by selecting the right set of business processes to improve, even though these improvements did not require automation.

Levels of Analysis

Within organizations, there are different levels, occupations, divisions, and groups. All organizations have levels, but each organization is quite different from others in terms of what the levels are, who occupies them, and what tasks are assigned to different levels. The impact of information systems will probably be different for different levels and groups within an organization.

Each organizational level has different concerns and a different framework of analysis. This can be seen in Figure 3.6, which describes the various organizational levels and the principal concerns at each level, providing examples of information systems that are appropriate for each level.

At the individual and small-group levels of organization, information systems apply to a particular job, task, or project. At the department and division levels, information systems deal with a particular business function, product, or service. At the organization, interorganizational, and organizational network levels, information systems support multiple products, services, and goals and facilitate alliances and coordination between two different organizations or groups of organizations.

Table 3.2 Work Groups, Problems, and Systems Support

Type of Work Group Support	Description	Problems	Systems
Hierarchical	Formal working relationship between manager and staff	Frequent meetings; dispersed work environments	Video conferencing; electronic mail (one to many)
Interdepartmental committees	Sequential activities; "expediters," "fixers"	Need occasional direct communication	Electronic messaging (one to one)
Project teams	Formally defined groups; close day-to-day interaction	Meeting schedules	Scheduling and communication software; meeting support tools; document interchange; Intranet
Committees	Formally defined groups; occasional interaction	High peak load; communications; intermittent	Electronic bulletin boards; video conferencing; electronic mail; computer conferencing
Task forces	Formally defined single-purpose groups	Rapid communication; access to internal and external data	Graphics display; information utility; document interchange; meeting support tools
Peer groups/social networks	Informal groups of similar-status individuals	Intense personal communication	Telephone; electronic mail
Problems of all work groups			
Making arrangements			
Attending meetings			
Long agendas			
Cost of meetings			
Between-meeting activities			

Perhaps one of the most important and least heralded contributions of information systems is its support of the large variety of work groups that spring up in organizations and that are not even part of the formal organization chart. Much of the work of an organization is done by informal task forces, interdepartmental committees, project teams, and committees. Table 3.2 presents the most important work groups and shows how systems can support them. These work groups generally have rapidly changing information needs, peak-load work schedules associated with project deadlines, and high communication requirements. Office automation systems, especially those with high-speed communication linkages, are one of the most recently developed system tools directed at work groups (see Chapter 15).

We have developed a rather long list of salient features you should know about when considering information systems in organizations (see Table 3.3). As you can see, the list of unique features of organizations is longer than the common features list. What this should suggest to you is that most organizations are quite unique. One consequence of this fact is that information systems are not completely portable from one organization to another. The impacts of systems will differ from one organization to another, and only by close analysis of a specific organization can a manager design and manage information systems.

Much of the organization's work is accomplished by task forces and project teams using their combined skills.

Table 3.3	A Summary of Salient Features of Organizations

Common Features	Unique Features
Formal structure	Organizational type
Standard operating procedures (SOPs)	Environments
Politics	Goals
Culture	Power
	Constituencies
	Function
	Leadership
	Tasks
	Technology
	Business processes
	Levels

3.3 HOW ORGANIZATIONS AFFECT INFORMATION SYSTEMS

We now can look more closely at the two-way relationship between information systems and organizations. We first need to explain how organizations affect technology and systems. Organizations have an impact on information systems through the decisions made by managers and employees. Managers make decisions about the design of systems; they also use information technology. Managers decide who will build and operate systems, and ultimately managers provide the rationale for building systems. There are four important questions to consider in studying this issue.

- How have organizations actually used information systems?
- How has the organizational role of information systems changed?
- Who operates information systems?
- Why do organizations adopt information systems in the first place?

Decisions About the Role of Information Systems

Organizations have a direct impact on information technology by making decisions about how the technology will be used and what role it will play in the organization. Chapters 1 and 2 described the ever-widening role of information systems in organizations. Supporting this changing role have been changes in the technical and organizational configuration of systems that have brought computing power and data much closer to the ultimate end users (see Figure 3.7).

Isolated "electronic accounting machines" with limited functions in the 1950s gave way to large, centralized mainframe computers that served corporate headquarters and a few remote sites in the 1960s. In the 1970s, mid-sized minicomputers located in individual departments or divisions of the organization were networked to large centralized computers. Desktop microcomputers first were used independently and then were linked to minicomputers and large computers in the 1980s.

In the 1990s, the architecture for a fully networked organization emerged. In this new architecture, the large central mainframe computer stores information (like a library) and coordinates information flowing among desktops and perhaps among hundreds of smaller local networks. These networks can be connected into a network that connects the entire enterprise or is linked to external networks, including the Internet. Chapter 10 provides a detailed discussion of this enterprise-wide information architecture and the way it has reshaped the delivery of information in the firm. Information systems have become integral, on-line interactive tools deeply involved in the minute-to-minute operations and decision making of large organizations. Organizations now are critically dependent on systems and could not survive even an occasional breakdown.

Decisions About the Computer Package: Who Delivers Information Technology Services?

A second way in which organizations affect information technology is through decisions about who will design, build, and operate the technology within the organization. Information systems require a package of services, organizations, and people—specialized organizational subunits, information specialists, and a host of other supportive groups (Kling and Dutton, 1982). Managers (and organizations in general) make the key decisions about the computer package: These decisions determine how technology services will be delivered, and by whom, how, and when.

information systems department
The formal organizational unit that is responsible for the information systems function in the organization.

The computer package is composed of three distinct entities (see Figure 3.8). The first is a formal organizational unit or function called an **information systems department.** The second consists of information systems specialists such as programmers, systems analysts, project leaders, and information systems managers. Also, external specialists such as hardware vendors and manufacturers, software firms, and consultants frequently participate in the day-to-day operations and long-term planning of information systems. A third element of the information systems package is the technology itself, both hardware and software.

Today the information systems group often acts as a powerful change agent in the organization, suggesting new business strategies and new information-based products and coordinating both the development of technology and the planned changes in the organization.

The size of the information systems department can vary greatly, depending on the role of information systems in the organization and on the organization's size. In most medium to large firms, the information systems group is composed of 100 to 400 people. The size of the information systems group and the total expenditures on computers and information systems are largest in service organizations (especially those that sell information products such as Dow Jones News), where information systems can consume more than 40 percent of gross revenues.

FIGURE 3.7

The development of information architecture of organizations. The last five decades have seen dramatic changes in the technical and organizational configurations of systems. During the 1950s organizations were dependent on computers for a few critical functions. The 1960s witnessed the development of large centralized machines. By the late 1970s and into the 1980s information architecture became complex and information systems included telecommunications links to distribute information. During the 1990s information architecture is an enterprise-wide information utility, which in turn is connected to vendors and customers through the World Wide Web.

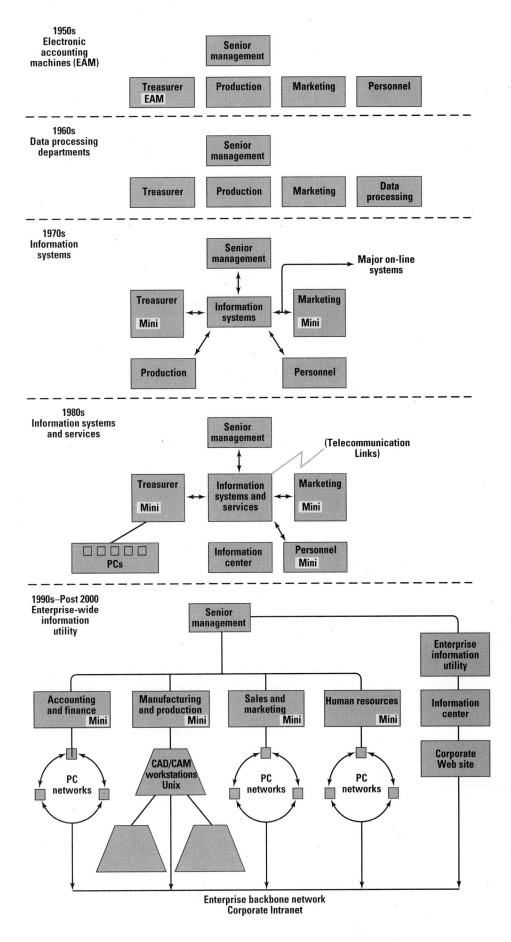

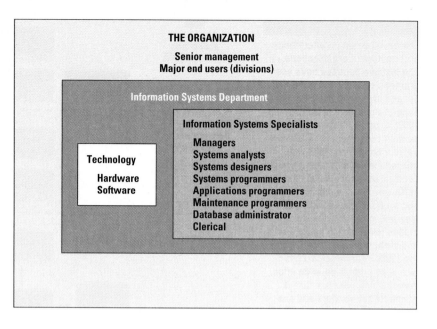

FIGURE 3.8

The computer package. Many groups, individuals, and organizations are involved in the design and management of information systems.

THE ORGANIZATION

Senior management
Major end users (divisions)

Information Systems Department

Information Systems Specialists

Managers
Systems analysts
Systems designers
Systems programmers
Applications programmers
Maintenance programmers
Database administrator
Clerical

Technology

Hardware
Software

programmers Highly trained technical specialists who write computer software instructions.

systems analysts Specialists who translate business problems and requirements into information requirements and systems, acting as liaison between the information systems department and the rest of the organization.

information systems managers Leaders of the various specialists in the information systems department.

end users Representatives of departments outside the information systems group for whom information systems applications are developed.

In the early years of the computer, when the role of information systems was limited, the information systems group was composed mostly of **programmers**, highly trained technical specialists who wrote the software instructions for the computer. Today, in most information systems groups, a growing proportion of staff members are systems analysts. **Systems analysts** constitute the principal liaison between the information systems group and the rest of the organization. It is the system analyst's job to translate business problems and requirements into information requirements and systems.

Information systems managers are leaders of teams of programmers and analysts; project managers; physical facility managers; telecommunications managers; heads of office automation groups; and, finally, managers of computer operations and data entry staff.

End users are representatives of departments outside the information systems group for whom applications are developed. These users are playing an increasingly large role in the design and development of information systems.

The last element of the computer package is the technology itself—the hardware and software instructions. Chapters 6 and 7 provide detailed discussions of these topics.

Decisions About Why Information Systems Are Built

Managers provide the public and private rationales for building information systems. Managers can choose to use systems primarily to achieve economies, or to provide better service, or to provide a better workplace. The impact of computers in any organization depends in part on how managers make decisions.

Systems today are, of course, built to increase efficiency and save money but they have become vitally important simply for staying in business. Information systems are as vital as are capital improvements such as modern buildings or corporate headquarters. Improvements in decision making (speed, accuracy, comprehensiveness), serving ever higher customer and client expectations, coordinating dispersed groups in an organization, complying with governmental reporting regulations, and exercising tighter control over personnel and expenditures, have become important reasons for building systems (Huff and Munro, 1985).

More recently, organizations have been seeking the competitive benefits of systems described in Chapter 2. What seems like an easy question to answer—Why do organizations adopt systems?—is actually quite complex. Some organizations are

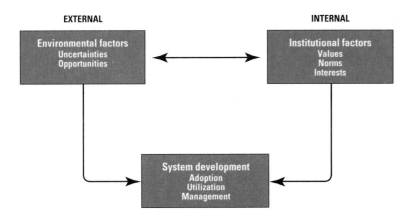

FIGURE 3.9

The systems development process. External environmental factors and internal institutional factors influence the types of information systems the organizations select, develop, and use.

simply more innovative than others. They have values that encourage any kind of innovation, regardless of its direct economic benefit to the company. In other cases, information systems are built because of the ambitions of various groups within an organization and the anticipated effect on existing organizational conflicts. And in some cases such as the electric utility companies, described in the chapter-opening vignette, changes in an organization's environment—including changes in government regulations, competitors' actions, and costs—demand a computer system response.

Figure 3.9 illustrates a model of the systems development process that includes many factors other than economic considerations. This model divides the explanations for why organizations adopt systems into two groups: external environmental factors and internal institutional factors (Laudon, 1985; King et al., 1994).

Environmental factors are factors that are external to the organization that influence the adoption and design of information systems. Some external environmental factors are rising costs of labor or other resources, the competitive actions of other organizations, and changes in government regulations. In general, these can be thought of as environmental constraints: At the same time, the environment also provides organizations with opportunities—new technologies, new sources of capital, the development of new production processes, the demise of a competitor, or a new government program that increases the demand for certain products.

Institutional factors are factors internal to the organization that influence the adoption and design of information systems. They include values, norms, and vital interests that govern matters of strategic importance to the organization. For instance, the top management of a corporation can decide that it needs to exercise much stronger control over the inventory process and therefore decides to develop an inventory information system. The resulting system is adopted, developed, and operated for purely internal, institutional reasons (for a similar model, see Kraemer et al., 1989).

environmental factors Factors external to the organization that influence the adoption and design of information systems.

institutional factors Factors internal to the organization that influence the adoption and design of information systems.

3.4 HOW INFORMATION SYSTEMS AFFECT ORGANIZATIONS

Now we shall look at the other side of the relationship between information technology and organizations, asking the following question: How do information systems affect organizations? To answer this question, we need to examine and quickly summarize a large body of research and theory. Some researchers base their work on economics, whereas others take a behavioral approach. In a single chart, Table 3.4 compares these theories and the hypothesized impacts of information technology on organizations. Table 3.4 is complex, and you should read the text first and then use the table for a convenient summary.

Table 3.4 The Impact of Information Systems on Organizations

Theories	(A) Economic Theories			(B) Behavioral Theories		
	Microeconomic	Transaction Cost	Agency	Decision/Control	Social Science*	Postindustrial
Unit of Analysis	The firm	Markets and the firm	The firm	The organization	The organization, subunits, players, environments	Macro and global society and economy
Core Concepts	Substitution of factors of production	Transactions costs Markets	Agents, principals, and contracts	Decision-making process and structure	SOPs, politics, culture, social history	Knowledge and information-intense work and products
Dynamics	Capital is substituted for labor as IT costs fall	IT reduces market transaction costs	IT reduces agency costs	IT replaces humans in the information and decision process	IT reflects bureaucratic, political, and cultural forces	IT encourages growth of information-intense occupations and goods
Impacts of IT Occupational Structure	Decline in middle managers and clericals	Decline in middle managers and clerical workers	Decline in middle managers and clerical workers	Decline in middle managers and clericals; growth in information and knowledge workers	IT has little impact per se on occupational structure; specialists try to use IT to their advantage	IT creates new occupations highly dependent on information
Organizational Structure Formal: Hierarchy Div. of Labor SOPs Authority	Reduced hierarchy Centralization	Reduced org. size Centralization of authority; decentralization of decisions; Reduction in hierarchy Less reliance on SOPs	Reduced org. size Centralization of authority, reduction in hierarchy	Authority more uniform Less specialization and less reliance on SOPs Reduction in hierarchy Formalization of information functions	Groups use IT to extend their influence, stabilize their position, and optimize performance of SOPs	IT results in more flexible, self-guided work, decentralization, flattening of hierarchies, and fluid division of labor
Informal: Info. flow Decision making Intelligence	Increased info. flow, more rapid decision making, more intelligence	Information access, timeliness, accuracy increase; decision-making units fewer and more efficient	Increased surveillance Information access, timeliness, accuracy increase; decision-making units fewer and more efficient	Information access, timeliness, accuracy increase; decision-making units fewer and more efficient	IT as a formal information system has little impact on informal channels of power and influence	Rigid hierarchic decision structures replaced by rich information-intense networks
Management Strategy	Employ technology to reduce labor costs	Employ IT to increase reliance on markets and reduce org. size, middle mgmt. and clericals	Senior managers employ IT to increase surveillance, reduce costs of management	Employ IT to improve decision making and restructure organization to optimize command and control technologies	Managers should understand and use IT to achieve their agendas	Managers should assist the emergence of less rigid organizations, encourage self-manager and networked organizations

*The social science reference disciplines are sociology, political science, anthropology, and social history.
Source: Azimuth Corporation, 1992

Economic Theories

Economics is the study of allocating scarce resources in markets populated by thousands of competing firms. It is also the study of national and global economies. Microeconomics focuses on individual firms and provides several models to describe the impact of information technology on organizations (see Gurbaxani and Whang, 1991).

Microeconomic Theory

The most widespread theory of how information technology affects thousands of firms is the **microeconomic model** portrayed in Figure 3.10. Information system technology is viewed as a factor of production that can be freely substituted for capital and labor. As the cost of information system technology falls, it is substituted for labor that historically has a rising cost. As information system technology transforms the production function—through the use of technology to automate previous manual activities or to streamline or to rethink how work is accomplished—the entire production function shifts inward. Over time, less capital and less labor are required for a given output. Moreover, the expansion trajectory of the firm is altered more toward increasing reliance on capital, and less toward reliance on labor—which historically has risen in cost (Pindyck and Rubinfield, 1992). Hence in microeconomic theory, information technology should result in a decline in the number of middle managers and clerical workers as information technology substitutes for their labor.

microeconomic model Model of the firm that views information technology as a factor of production that can be freely substituted for capital and labor.

Transaction Cost Theory

Transaction cost theory is based on the idea that a firm incurs costs when it buys on the marketplace what it does not make itself. These costs are referred to as transaction costs. Transaction costs are the equivalent of friction in physical systems. Firms and individuals seek to economize on transaction costs (much as they do on production costs). Using markets is expensive (Williamson, 1985) because of coordination costs such as locating and communicating with distant suppliers, monitoring contract compliance, buying insurance, obtaining information on products, and so forth. Traditionally, firms sought to reduce transaction costs by getting bigger: hiring more employees, vertically integrating (as General Motors did—see the section-ending case on Chrysler and GM), buying their own suppliers and distributors, growing hori-

transaction cost theory Economic theory that states that firms exist because they can conduct marketplace transactions internally more cheaply than they can with external firms in the marketplace.

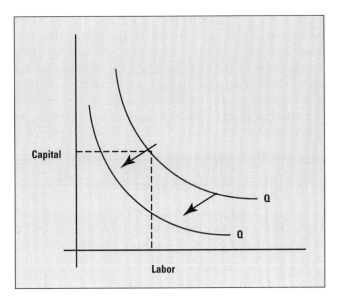

FIGURE 3.10

The microeconomic theory of the impact of information technology on the organization. Firms substitute IT for labor over time; when IT transforms the production function, the function shifts inward, lowering the amount of both capital and labor needed to produce level Q.

FIGURE 3.11

The transaction cost theory of the impact of information technology on the organization. Firms traditionally grew in size in order to reduce transaction costs. IT potentially reduces the costs for a given size, shifting the transaction cost curve inward, opening up the possibility of revenue growth without increasing size, or even revenue growth accompanied by shrinking size.

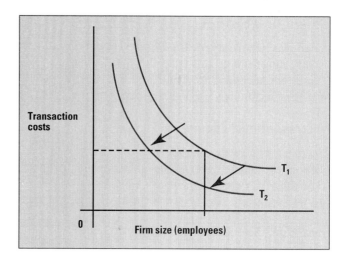

zontally by moving into new markets, taking over smaller companies, and even developing monopolies.

Information technology could help firms lower the cost of market participation (transaction costs), making it worthwhile for firms to contract with external suppliers instead of using internal sources of supply. The size of firms (measured by the number of employees) could stay constant or contract even though they increased their revenues. As transaction costs decrease, firm size (the number of employees) should shrink because it becomes easier and cheaper for the firm to contract the purchase of goods and services in the marketplace rather than to make the product or service inside. (For example, General Electric has reduced its workforce from about 400,000 people in the early 1980s to about 230,000 while increasing revenues 150 percent.) Why hire workers, grow bigger, and suffer rising management costs when the same volume of business and profit could be obtained if the firm contracted with outside suppliers and workers in an electronic marketplace? (See Figure 3.11.) These labor force reductions would probably affect middle managers and clerical workers in particular.

Agency Theory

agency theory Economic theory that views the firm as a nexus of contracts among self-interested individuals rather than a unified, profit-maximizing entity.

In **agency theory,** the firm is viewed as a "nexus of contracts" among self-interested individuals rather than as a unified, profit-maximizing entity (Jensen and Meckling, 1976). A principal (owner) employs "agents" (employees) to perform work on his or her behalf and delegates some decision-making authority to the agent. However, agents need constant supervision and management because they otherwise will tend to pursue their own interests rather than those of the owners. This factor introduces agency costs or coordination costs, the costs of supervising and managing employees. As firms grow in size and scope, management costs rise because owners must expend more and more effort monitoring agents, acquiring information, tracking inventory, and so on. Owners must delegate more decision-making authority to agents, who in turn may be untrustworthy.

Information technology, by reducing the costs of acquiring and analyzing information, permits organizations to reduce overall management costs, and allows them to grow in revenues while shrinking the numbers of middle management and clerical workers (see Figure 3.12). Each manager can oversee a larger number of employees. We have seen examples in earlier chapters where information technology expanded the power and scope of small organizations by allowing them to perform coordinating activities such as processing orders or keeping track of inventory with very few clerks and managers.

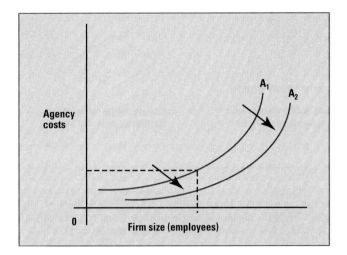

FIGURE 3.12

The agency cost theory of the impact of information technology on the organization. As firms grow in size and complexity, traditionally they experience rising agency costs. IT shifts the agency cost curve down and to the right, allowing firms to increase size while lowering agency costs.

Behavioral Theories

Although microeconomic theories try to explain how large numbers of firms act in the marketplace, most economists would agree they are quite poor at describing or predicting the actual behavior of any one particular real-world firm. In the real world, managers face unique problems such as minimizing inventory costs, meeting production schedules, devising diverse product mixes, managing a labor force, and obtaining financing. Behavioral theories from sociology, psychology, and political science generally are far more descriptive and predictive of the behavior of individual firms and managers than are economic theories.

Behavioral research has found little evidence that information systems automatically transform organizations, although the systems may be instrumental in accomplishing this goal once senior management decides to pursue this end. Instead, researchers have observed an intricately choreographed relationship in which organizations and information technology mutually influence each other. Because information systems are used to promote organizational values and interests, they are deeply affected by the organization.

What looks like an impact of information technology is often a reflection of what the organization and the system designers consciously intended (or unconsciously created). In behavioral models of the firm, the influence of information systems is not as simple and direct as the economic models suggest.

Decision and Control Theory

According to **decision and control theory,** the function of the organization is to make decisions under conditions of uncertainty and risk and under the constraint of bounded rationality. The theory holds that managers never have complete information and knowledge, and they can never examine all alternatives even though they would like to.[2] Organizations are decision-making structures, arranged so as to reduce uncertainty and to ensure survival. Because persons lower in the hierarchy do not have the information needed for making decisions, organizations must centralize decision making and create a hierarchy of decision makers. A large middle management group is necessary to gather information, analyze it, and pass it up to senior managers. In turn, senior managers require middle managers to implement policies because middle managers are in direct contact with lower-level operating units.

decision and control theory
Behavioral theory stating that the function of the organization is to make decisions under conditions of uncertainty and risk and that organizations centralize decision making and create a hierarchy of decision making to reduce uncertainty and to ensure survival.

2. See George P. Huber, "The Nature and Design of Post-Industrial Organizations." *Management Science* 30, no. 8 (August 1984). See also the classic statement of this view in James G. March and Herbert A. Simon, *Organizations* (New York: Wiley, 1958). See also Herbert A. Simon, "Applying Information Technology to Organization Design," *Public Administration Review* (May/June, 1973).

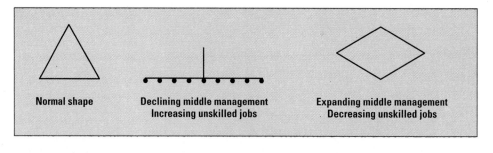

| Normal shape | Declining middle management
Increasing unskilled jobs | Expanding middle management
Decreasing unskilled jobs |

FIGURE 3.13

The impact of information systems on organizational structure. There are several hypotheses on how systems can change the structure of an organization. Three outcomes are represented here: Systems can have no effect; they may reduce the number of middle managers, creating an inverted *T* effect; or they may expand the capabilities and numbers of middle managers, producing the diamond effect.

Lower-level employees, in turn, rely on standard operating procedures designed by senior decision makers. If a situation does not fit the SOP, then senior managers must make a decision. The organization is a pyramidal structure in which authority and responsibility grow as one rises in the hierarchy.

Theoretically, information technology could change this rigid structure by lowering the costs of information acquisition and broadening the distribution of information (Malone, 1997). Information technology could bring information directly from operating units to senior managers through networked computers and communications. Alternatively, information technology could distribute information to lower-level workers who could then make their own decisions based on their own knowledge and information without management intervention (Applegate, Cash, and Mills, 1988).

Early speculation on the impact of information systems suggested that organizations would indeed become more centralized and that middle management would tend to disappear over time because computers would give central, high-level managers all the information they required to operate the organization without intervention from middle management (Leavitt and Whisler, 1958; Drucker, 1988).

Figure 3.13 illustrates this change in organizational structure. Before information technology, the organization had a triangular shape with decision making concentrated at the top. After the introduction of computer systems, the organization chart would start to look like an inverted *T*. Other research suggests that computerization gives more information to middle managers, empowering them to make more important decisions than in the past and reducing the need for large numbers of lower-level workers. Over time, this results in a diamondlike structure (Shore, 1983).

Sociological Theory: Oligarchies and Routines

sociological theory Behavioral theory stating that organizations develop hierarchical bureaucratic structures and standard operating procedures to cope in unstable environments and that organizations cannot change routines when environments change.

Sociological theory focuses on the growth of hierarchical, bureaucratic structures and standard operating procedures as primary coping tools for organizations trying to cope in unstable environments. Organizations hone and refine routines (SOPs) until they become extremely efficient. Unfortunately, organizations find it nearly impossible to change routines when their environment changes.

Information technology is embraced by managers in various subunits of the organization to help them implement existing rules and SOPs. They reject information technology if it threatens existing routines or subunits. Information technology adds little to the survivability of firms, and given reasonable time, most organizations fail. Change comes about because new organizations form around new technologies, and they incorporate the new technologies into their SOPs. Over time, these new organizations become old, bureaucratic, and brittle, and they too pass away.

The sociological view emphasizes the power of people and organizations to control the impacts of systems. Important groups in the organization determine, either consciously or unconsciously, the kinds of changes that will occur in organizational structure. Organizations adopt information technology because it suits the power interests of key subunits, divisions, and managers. Organizations can decide to centralize or decentralize power.

Postindustrial Theory: Knowledge-Intensive Structures and Shapes

According to theorists of postindustrial society—often sociologists and political scientists—advanced industrial countries entered a new kind of postindustrial economy and society sometime in the 1960s (Bell, 1973; Brzezinski, 1970; Masuda, 1980; Toffler, 1970; Martin, 1981). In a postindustrial society, the service sector dominates the economy,[3] favoring knowledge workers (scientists, engineers, and some managers) and data workers (secretaries, accountants, salespeople). In postindustrial global economies, industrial manufacturing is shifted to low-wage countries, and high-skilled, knowledge-based work grows rapidly in the developed, high-wage countries.

According to **postindustrial theory,** the transformation to a postindustrial society brings with it inherent changes in organizational structure: Authority should rely more on knowledge and competence, and not on mere formal position; the shape of organizations should flatten, because professional workers tend to be self-managing; and decision making should become more decentralized as knowledge and information become more widespread throughout (Drucker, 1988).

Information technology should lead then to "task force" networked organizations in which groups of professionals come together—face-to-face or electronically—for a short time to accomplish a specific task (e.g., designing a new automobile); once the task is accomplished, the individuals join other task forces. Clericals should be reduced because professionals maintain their own portable offices in the form of laptop and palmtop personal computers connected to powerful global networks. Firms could conceivably operate as virtual organizations, where work is no longer tied to geographic location because knowledge and information can be delivered anywhere and any time they are needed. Organizations should look more like Mintzberg's adhocracies described earlier.[4]

Who makes sure that self-managed teams do not head off in the wrong direction? Who decides which person works on what team and for how long? How can managers judge the performance of someone who is constantly rotating from team to team? How do people know where their careers are headed when there is no clear hierarchical ladder to ascend? The Window on Management explores some of these questions as it examines the impact of "virtual offices" and anytime, anywhere work environments.

No one knows the answer to these questions, and it is not clear that all modern organizations will undergo this transformation: General Motors may have many self-managed knowledge workers in certain divisions, but it still has a manufacturing division structured as a "machine bureaucracy," to use Mintzberg's category. Not all types of organizations can be "flattened." Behavioral research has found little evi-

postindustry theory Behavioral theory stating that the transformation of advanced industrial countries into postindustrial societies creates flatter organizations dominated by knowledge workers where decision making is more decentralized.

---

3. The names for this phenomenon—of societies based primarily on knowledge and information—differ, but the underlying rationale remains the same: the "technetronic society" (Brzezinski), "telematic society" (Martin), and Toffler's "future shock" and ad hoc organizations.

4. Postindustrial themes are echoed in Drucker's 1988 formulation of how IT affects organizations: "The typical large business 20 years hence will have fewer than half the levels of management of its counterpart today, and no more than a third the managers. . . . the typical business will be knowledge-based, an organization composed largely of specialists, who direct and discipline their own performance through organized feedback from colleagues, customers, and headquarters. For this reason, it will be what I call an information-based organization" (Drucker, 1988, p. 45).

In virtual offices, employees do not work from a permanent location. Here, work spaces are temporary with employees moving from desk to desk as vacancies open.

dence that information systems automatically transform organizational structures, although the systems may be instrumental in accomplishing this goal once senior management decides to pursue this end. No one knows if organizations designed along postindustrial process lines survive longer than traditional hierarchical organizations.

In general, the shape of organizations historically changes with the business cycle and with the latest management fashions. When times are good and profits are high, firms hire large numbers of supervisory and nonproduction personnel. When times are tough, they let go of many of these same people (Mintzberg, 1979). In the late 1980s, times were tough. Many U.S. firms, especially those in direct competition with foreign manufacturers, shrank their middle-level management and supervisory positions. This was also a period of extensive investment in computer technology. It is not known if the shrinkage of some firms' middle management resulted from hard times or from computerization. For firms not in direct foreign competition, and for firms that experienced good business environments, employment rose throughout the 1990s even as information technology exploded. In a period of intense computerization, employment has risen even while incomes have stagnated. What these observations suggest, then, is that the impact of information technology and systems on the entire population of organizations is not very well understood.

Cultural Theories: Information Technology and Fundamental Assumptions

cultural theory Behavioral theory stating that information technology must fit into an organization's culture or the technology will not be adopted.

Cultural theory (often discussed by anthropologists) argues that information technology must fit into the organization's culture or is unlikely to be adopted. The assumption at Ford, for instance, is that the company's primary activity is to make cars (rather than to operate a credit corporation), or at IBM it is the assumption that the primary purpose of the organization is to make large mainframe computers. These assumptions are rarely challenged by members, and if members do present challenges to these assumptions, the members are ostracized (Schein, 1985).

When the assumptions no longer fit reality, members of the culture may try to deny reality, ignore reality, or reinvent reality to fit the culture. Cultures change when the organizations that support them die off, or when radical fringe groups gain control and shift cultural assumptions. This feature is usually attended by massive senior management turnover, because it is the senior managers who support the old culture (indeed, they were recruited and promoted for precisely this reason).

Information technology can either threaten or support organizational culture. The emergence of personal computer technology, for instance, threatened both

Managing the Virtual Office

Cisco Systems, Ernst & Young, IBM, and other companies are eliminating offices and allowing employees to work from any location they choose. Some of their employees are supposed to work in "virtual offices," in any place such as a car, plane, train, or home where they can get work done. Virtual offices are possible because of cellular telephones, fax machines, portable computers, and other mobile computing and communications devices.

Cisco Systems, the red-hot maker of networking hardware, was expanding so rapidly that it outgrew its offices before it moved into them. Between the fall of 1996 and early 1997, its New York office staff quadrupled, from 50 to 200 employees. People were working on top of each other, yet they spent so much time calling on customers and working from home that they used their cubicles barely 30 percent per day. So Cisco introduced "nonterritorial offices" throughout its worldwide operations, eliminating permanent seating for everyone except secretaries and managers. (Secretaries would be allowed to work in fixed cubicles with their files and gear and managers would keep their private offices.)

Employees work at "hot desks," moving from cubicle to cubicle as vacancies open. Special telephone technology allows them to carry their phone extensions to any open desk. According to Marina VanOverbeek, Cisco's workplace strategist, "ideas mix faster when people aren't tethered to the same 48 square feet of space every day." Ms. VanOverbeek believes that hot-desking will save Cisco $7 million over its five-year lease for its New York office alone.

Ernst & Young, the accounting firm, began moving its Chicago-based accountants and consultants, including senior managers, from offices into a "hoteling" system in June 1992 in an effort to reduce office space and costs. Office spaces must be reserved at least one day in advance to bring in all the equipment and files required to do the work. Ernst & Young hopes to eliminate 1 million of the 7 million square feet of office space it rents nationwide, a savings of $40 million per year.

Eliminating private offices can cut down on real estate costs and increase the amount of time employees spend with customers. It may help firms comply with the U.S. government's Clean Air Act requiring companies with 200 or more employees in major metropolitan areas to reduce commuter automobile mileage 25 percent. Virtual office employees have more flexibility and control over their own time. But is the virtual office a better way of working? What is its impact on individual identity, worker satisfaction, and corporate community?

Some employees fear the virtual office will lead to downsizing, part-time work, and eventually the loss of their jobs. Others respond to the loss of daily social contact. A Bell Telephone study of employees working from home found that productivity and morale plunged precipitously unless they kept in close personal contact with the office. On the other hand, Ernst & Young reported 99 percent employee approval of its hoteling arrangement, with increased interaction among employees from different areas and between employees and their bosses.

To Think About: *What management, organization, and technology issues must be addressed when converting to a virtual office? Can all companies use virtual offices?*

Sources: Thomas Petzinger, Jr., "Cisco's Staff Conquers Separation Anxieties after Losing Desks," *The Wall Street Journal*, February 21, 1997; Montieth M. Illingworth, "Virtual Managers," *InformationWEEK*, June 13, 1994; and Phil Patton, "The Virtual Office Becomes Reality," *The New York Times*, October 28, 1993.

the manufacturers of large mainframe computers and their customers in large corporations—the managers of large information system departments in Fortune 1000 corporations. Resistance, denial, and efforts to redefine the reality followed in many of these organizations. On the other hand, information technology can be supportive of organizational cultures: The insurance industry welcomed computers to reduce costs in traditional claims processing.

Political Theories: Information Technology As a Political Resource

Organizations are divided into specialized subgroups (e.g., marketing, accounting, production). These groups have different values, and they compete for resources, producing competition and conflict. **Political theory** describes information systems as the outcome of political competition between organizational subgroups for influence over the policies, procedures, and resources of the organization (Laudon, 1974; Keen, 1981; Kling, 1980; Laudon, 1986).

political theory Behavioral theory that describes information systems as the outcome of political competition between organizational subgroups for influence over the policies, procedures, and resources of the organization.

Information systems inevitably become bound up in the politics of organizations because they influence access to a key resource—namely, information. Information systems can affect who does what to whom, when, where, and how in an organization. For instance, a major study of the efforts of the FBI to develop a national computerized criminal history system (a single national listing of the criminal histories, arrests, and convictions of over 36 million individuals in the United States) found that the state governments strongly resisted the FBI's efforts. The states felt that this information would give the federal government, and the FBI in particular, the ability to monitor how states use criminal histories and to control the interstate dissemination of criminal history information. This was a function that the states felt they could accomplish without federal interference. The states resisted the development of this national system quite successfully (Laudon, 1986).

How the Web Potentially Affects Organizations

With more than 50 million Web pages developed by over 50,000 organizations around the globe, the World Wide Web is beginning to have an important impact on the relationships between firms and external entities, and even on the organization of business processes inside the firm. We discuss the technical foundations and the impacts of the Web on business throughout the book and specifically in Chapter 10. Here we want only to discuss the organizational theoretic aspects of the Web–business link.

The World Wide Web alters the accessibility, storage, and distribution of information and knowledge for organizations. The Web has the following capabilities:

- It enlarges the potential to access information for all market and organizational participants; nearly any information can be available anywhere at anytime.

- It enlarges the scope, depth, and range of information and knowledge storage; with so many contributors to what constitutes a global encyclopedia, just about any extant knowledge or information is available.

- It lowers the cost and raises the quality of information and knowledge distribution; business interactive multimedia applications on the Web enhance the attention span of vendors, customers, and employees.

Because information and knowledge can be powerful determinants of organizational structure and activities, the Web potentially will have a large impact on business firms along the lines previously described in the chapter.

Figure 3.14 illustrates some of the capabilities of the Web in electronic commerce and within the firm. In essence, the Web is capable of reducing the transaction and agency costs facing most organizations. For instance, brokerage firms and banks in New York can now "deliver" their internal operations procedures manuals to their correspondent institutions by posting them on their corporate Web site, saving millions of dollars in distribution costs and update costs when compared with the old text-based method. A global sales force can receive nearly instant price or product information updates via the Web; employees at one firm can use a private corporate system based on Web technology to determine their benefits and incomes after retirement. Vendors of some large retailers can access the retailer internal Web sites directly for up-to-the-minute sales information, and initiate a replenishment order instantly.

While initially difficult to migrate key applications to the Web, many businesses are slowly rebuilding several key business processes based on the new Internet technology. If prior networking is any guide, one result will be simpler business processes, fewer employees, and much flatter organizations than was true in the past.

Organizational Resistance to Change

Because information systems potentially change an organization's structure, culture, politics, and work, there is often considerable resistance to them when they are in-

Vendors

The Firm

Customers

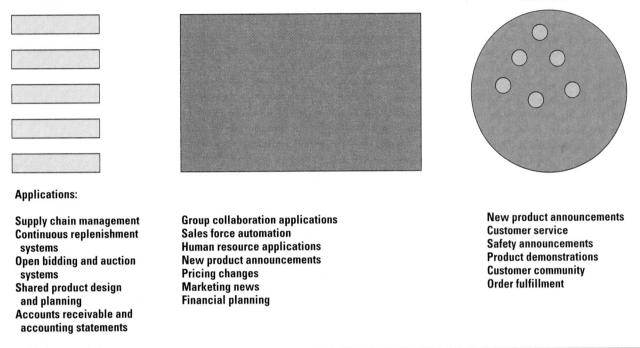

Applications:

Supply chain management
Continuous replenishment
  systems
Open bidding and auction
  systems
Shared product design
  and planning
Accounts receivable and
  accounting statements

Group collaboration applications
Sales force automation
Human resource applications
New product announcements
Pricing changes
Marketing news
Financial planning

New product announcements
Customer service
Safety announcements
Product demonstrations
Customer community
Order fulfillment

FIGURE 3.14

Applications of the World Wide Web to typical business processes potentially reduce the transaction and management (agency) costs faced by firms. In turn, these changes give managers new options for organizing work and developing corporate strategy.

troduced (see the Window on Technology). Microeconomic theories have no explanation for organizational resistance to change. In general, behavioral theories are superior for describing this phenomenon.

There are several ways to visualize organizational resistance. Leavitt (1965) used a diamond shape to illustrate the interrelated and mutually adjusting character of technology and organization (see Figure 3.15). Here, changes in technology are absorbed, deflected, and defeated by organizational task arrangements, structures, and people. In this model, the only way to bring about change is to change the technology, tasks, structure, and people simultaneously. Other authors have spoken about the need to "unfreeze" organizations before introducing an innovation, quickly implementing it, and "re-freezing" or institutionalizing the change (Kolb, 1970; Alter and Ginzberg, 1978).

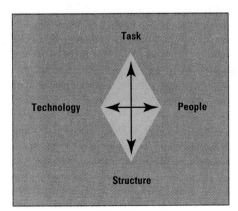

FIGURE 3.15

Organizational resistance and the mutually adjusting relationship between technology and the organization. Implementing information systems has consequences for task arrangements, structures, and people. According to this model, in order to implement change, all four components must be changed simultaneously. *Source:* Leavitt, 1965.

Paper Dies Hard on the Tokyo Stock Exchange

In 1987, the Tokyo Stock Exchange (TSE) eclipsed the New York Stock Exchange to become the world's largest stock market. With the collapse of Japan's "bubble economy" in the 1990s, the TSE has lost some of its luster, but it still acts as middleman and represents some of the largest, fast-paced, most powerful companies in the world. Yet the Tokyo Stock Exchange looks like a place where time has stopped. Market participants in Japan have no opportunity to use highly advanced automated trading systems that are commonplace in European and North American stock exchanges. Much of TSE's security trading is carried out the old-fashioned way, with traders shouting out buys and sells on the exchange floor, and order clerks manually inputting the information to complete the transaction.

TSE has tried several times to upgrade its computer systems. None of these efforts have succeeded. Opposition to automation comes from two traditional sources—the exchange's powerful labor unions and the order clerks, called Saitori. The Saitori perform functions similar to specialists at the New York Stock Exchange but lack the capacity to trade for their own account. Small and medium-size Japanese brokers are also wary of major upgrades.

In 1982 the Exchange installed a system called CORES (computer-assisted order routing and execution system), which used equipment provided by Hitachi Corp. to process large numbers of orders at high speeds. But this system is still not used to its full potential because of internal resistance. Nine years later TSE implemented another system using Fujitsu computers to simplify trading-floor paperwork. It connected brokers' order entry terminals to the TSE's main computer. This system is only utilized at the beginning of and during each trading session for trades of fewer than 3000 shares.

TSE justifies its reluctance to embrace technology by saying that it wants to maintain the spirit and drama of the traditional trading floor. But securities industry officials contend the real reason is pressure from labor unions and the Saitori against replacing jobs with computers. TSE also has no serious competitors. There is no other securities market operating in the same time zone that is capable of trading Japanese securities. Japan has eight regional stock exchanges, but they act like regional monopolies. There is no government effort to force them to compete.

It is unlikely that change will come quickly. The last time there was major discussion of reforming TSE was in the late 1970s, during the TSE's 100-year anniversary.

> **To Think About:** *What features of organizations explain the resistance to automation at the Tokyo Stock Exchange?*

Source: Gale Eisenstadt, "The Origami Effect: Paper Dies Hard on the Floor of the Tokyo Stock Exchange," *Forbes ASAP,* August 26, 1996.

Chapter 14 describes how organizational resistance causes many systems failures. Because of the difficulties of introducing new information systems, experienced systems observers approach social change through systems very cautiously. Briefly:

- Organizations do not innovate unless there is a substantial environmental change. Organizations adopt innovations only when necessary.

- Substantial forces resisting change are rooted in the organization's structures, values, and interest groups.

- Organizational innovation is difficult and complex to achieve. It involves more than simply purchasing technology. To reap the benefits of technology, innovations must be utilized and managed properly. This, in turn, requires changes in the values, norms, and interest-group alignments of the organization.

- The function of leaders is to take advantage of external circumstances to solidify their power. Leaders must use external opportunities to tilt the internal conflict in an organization in their favor and toward the successful development of their own agendas.

Implications for the Design and Understanding of Information Systems

The primary significance of this chapter is to show you that you should not take a narrow view of organizations and their relationship to information systems. Neither should you believe that technology will do the job for you—whatever that job is. For the information systems to work properly, you will have to manage the process actively, adjust the technology to the situation, and accept responsibility for success as well as failure.

You can develop a checklist of factors to consider in your plans when envisioning, designing, building, or managing information systems. In our experience, the following are the central organizational factors in rough rank order of importance:

- The *environment* in which the organization must function.
- The *structure* of the organization: hierarchy, specialization, standard operating procedures.
- The *culture* and *politics* of the organization.
- The *type* of organization.
- The extent of support and understanding of *top management*.
- The *level* of organization at which the system resides.
- The principal *interest groups* affected by the system.
- The *kinds of tasks, decisions,* and *business processes* that the information system is designed to assist.
- The *sentiments* and *attitudes* of workers in the organization who will be using the information system.
- The *history of the organization:* past investments in information technology, existing skills, important programs, and human resources.

MANAGEMENT WRAP-UP

ORGANIZATION

Information technology is providing new ways of organizing work. Unless organizations explore these new techniques, they will be quickly overwhelmed by new startup organizations that do understand the new technologies. Organizations should specifically examine how organizational structure can be simplified, made less hierarchical, and rely more on teamwork and task forces rather than on permanent organizational departments.

MANAGEMENT

A major contribution of information technology in the last decade has been the focus on organizational and business processes, on how things get done. There are few textbooks that tell managers how to manage organizations that are critically reliant on information technology. Managers will have to invent new techniques that utilize the Internet, and other network technologies to lead, coordinate, plan, and control the organization.

TECHNOLOGY

Information technology changes far more rapidly than organizations, and for this reason, IT is often a destroyer of organization competence. Yet information technology offers managers the opportunities for organizational survival and prosperity. Managers have to keep a keen eye on changes in IT to avoid losing organizational competencies and to exploit the opportunities provided by new technology.

For Discussion: It has been said that when we design an information system, we are redesigning the organization. As an example, discuss some of the challenges that might arise in developing a corporate Internet application which allowed customers to order products directly instead of working through the direct sales force or the retailers who traditionally carried the firm's products.

SUMMARY

1. Describe the salient characteristics of organizations. All modern organizations are hierarchical, specialized, and impartial. They use explicit standard operating procedures to maximize efficiency. All organizations have their own culture and politics arising from differences in interest groups. Organizations differ in goals, groups served, social roles, leadership styles, incentives, surrounding environments, types of tasks performed, and in their arrangement of business processes for accomplishing their work. These differences create varying types of organizational structures. Mintzberg classified organizations into five structures: the simple entrepreneurial structure, machine bureaucracy, divisionalized bureaucracy, professional bureaucracy, and adhocracy.

2. Explain the changing role of information systems within the organization. Computerized information systems are supported in organizations by a "computer package" consisting of a formal organizational unit or information systems department, information specialists, and computer technology. The roles of information systems and the computer package in the organization have become increasingly critical to both daily operations and strategic decision making.

3. Compare models for describing the origins of systems in organizations. Organizations adopt information systems for both external environmental reasons, such as to respond to competition or to promote changes in government regulations, and for internal institutional reasons, such as to promote the values or interests of top management.

4. Identify the major theories about organizations that help us understand their relationship with information systems. Theories that describe the relationship between information systems and organizations can be classified as based on either economic or behavioral models of the firm. Theories based on economic models of the firm include the microeconomic model, the transaction cost model, and agency theory. Theories based on behavioral models of the firm include decision and control theory, sociological theory, postindustrial theory, cultural theories, and political theories.

5. Discuss the impact of information systems on organizational structure, culture, political processes, and management. The impact of information systems on organizations is not unidirectional. Information systems and the organizations in which they are used interact with and influence each other. The introduction of a new information system will affect the organizational structure, goals, work design, values, competition between interest groups, decision making, and day-to-day behavior. At the same time, information systems must be designed to serve the needs of important organizational groups and will be shaped by the structure, tasks, goals, culture, politics, and management of the organization. The power of information systems to transform organizations radically by flattening organizational hierarchies has not yet been demonstrated for all types of organizations. The World Wide Web has a potentially large impact on organizational business processes and structure.

6. Describe the organizational implications for the design and implementation of systems. Salient features of organizations that must be addressed by information systems include organizational levels, organizational structures, types of tasks and decisions, the nature of management support, and the sentiments and attitudes of workers who will be using the system. The organization's history and external environment must be considered as well.

Implementation of a new information system is often more difficult than anticipated because of organizational change requirements. Because information systems potentially change important organizational dimensions, including the structure, culture, power relationships, and work activities, there is often considerable resistance to new systems.

KEY TERMS

Organization (technical definition)	Entrepreneurial structure	Programmers	Transaction cost theory
Organization (behavioral definition)	Machine bureaucracy	Systems analysts	Agency theory
	Professional bureaucracy	Information systems managers	Decision and control theory
Bureaucracy	Divisionalized bureaucracy		Sociological theory
Standard operating procedures (SOPs)	Adhocracy	End users	Postindustrial theory
	Business processes	Environmental factors	Cultural theory
Organizational culture	Information systems department	Institutional factors	Political theory
		Microeconomic model	

REVIEW QUESTIONS

1. What is an organization? How do organizations use information?

2. Compare the technical definition of organizations with the behavioral definition.

3. What features do all organizations have in common?

4. In what ways can organizations diverge?

5. What is meant by a business process? Give two views and two examples.

6. Describe the five basic kinds of organizational structures.

7. Name the levels of analysis for organizational behavior.

8. Name the changing applications of organizational information systems that existed from the 1950s to the 1990s. How has the role of information systems in the organization changed over this time period?

9. Name the three elements in the computer package. How has the role of each element in the organization changed over time?

10. Describe the two factors that explain why organizations adopt information systems.

11. Describe each of the economic theories that help explain how information systems affect organizations. What are their limitations?

12. Describe each of the behavioral theories that help explain how information systems affect organizations. What are their limitations?

13. Why should the Web change organizational structure or process?

14. What is the relationship between information systems and organizational culture?

15. What is the relationship between information systems and organizational politics?

16. Why is there considerable organizational resistance to the introduction of information systems? Describe two models that explain this resistance.

17. What aspects of organizations addressed by various theories of organizations must be considered when designing an information system?

GROUP PROJECT

With a group of two or three students, examine an organization such as a local drugstore or the bookstore, cafeteria, or registrar's office in your college or university. Describe some of the features of this organization, such as its standard operating procedures, business processes, culture, structure, and interest groups. Identify an information system or series of information systems that might improve the performance of this organization, and describe the changes that the organization would have to make to use information technology successfully.

CASE STUDY

Greyhound Seeks Salvation in a Strategic Reservation System

Greyhound Lines Inc., headquartered in Dallas, Texas, has long been the leading transcontinental bus company in the United States. However, the company share of interstate travel dropped from 30 percent in 1960 to 6 percent in the late 1980s, because of the rise in ownership of automobiles and discount airline service. The following chronology lists events that appear to be relevant to the problems Greyhound underwent.

JULY 1991

■ Frank Schmieder becomes Greyhound chief executive.

Schmieder gained a reputation as an intelligent though volatile boss. Union negotiators found him to be affable and were pleased that he occasionally rode the bus.

■ Michael Doyle, a former financial officer at Phillips Petroleum Co., becomes chief financial officer and works closely with Schmieder to run Greyhound.

AUGUST 1991

Schmieder begins to cut costs, upgrade buses and facilities, and settle labor disputes. Schmieder's and Doyle's policies include cutting the bus fleet from 3700 to 2400 and replacing current regional executives. They also replace most terminal workers with part-time workers who are paid about $6 an hour, whether they sweep floors or serve customers. These part-time workers are offered little opportunity to get a raise. Over the next three years, annual staff turnover of 30 percent becomes common, with some terminals reaching 100 percent annual turnover.

OCTOBER 1991

The Greyhound business plan includes a commitment to a computerized reservation system that financial market analysts focus on as the key to remaining competitive in the national market. The plan includes system support for more efficient use of buses and drivers.

Bus customers traditionally do not reserve seats in advance but rather arrive at the terminal, buy a ticket, and take the next bus. Few buses ever reserve seats. The primary use of bus-customer telephone lines has been to disseminate schedule information, not for reserving seats as is the case in the airline industry. Traditionally, clerks plotted journeys manually from thick bus schedule log books (Greyhound buses stop in several thousand towns in the United States). The process was very slow. Computerizing all the routes and stops would theoretically greatly reduce the time needed to plot journeys and issue tickets. The goals of an automated system were not only to speed the issuing of tickets, thereby reducing company service counter costs, but also simultaneously to improve customer service and customer relations.

The company had to manage several thousand buses and their drivers nationwide, making certain they were in the right locations at the right time. Greyhound assigned buses and bus drivers by hand, using data that were usually months old. The company kept buses and drivers in reserve to meet peak period demand, thereby enabling the company to remain the premier continent-wide bus company.

The new system, called Trips, was to handle both reservations and bus and driver allocations together because they were seen as tightly linked. The traditional bus strategy of no reservations, only walk-in riders, meant that many times buses departed nearly empty. Management hoped that adopting a reservation approach would allow them to reduce the number of near-empty buses. They also expected that the reservation portion of the system would provide Greyhound with reliable customer data so schedules could be more efficiently organized and so planners could determine where and when to reduce prices to fill seats. The plan for Trips was received very positively in the financial markets, giving Greyhound the ability to borrow funds and to offer new shares to raise capital.

EARLY SPRING 1992

The Trips project begins with a staff of 40 or so and a $6 million budget; Thomas Thompson, Greyhound senior vice president for network planning and operations, is placed in charge of Trips development.

A bus reservation system, by the nature of the operation of buses, is far more complex than airline reservation systems. A passenger might make one or two stops on an airline flight and cross the United States with one to two stops only, whereas bus passengers may make 10 or more stops on a trip, and a cross-country trip might involve scores of stops. Greyhound technicians estimated that a bus management system would need to manage 10 times the number of vehicle stops per day of an airline vehicle management system.

The average bus passenger is much less affluent than the average airline passenger. Several Greyhound executives later claimed to have raised the questions of how many bus passengers would have credit cards to enable them to purchase tickets in advance by telephone, and even how many have telephones available. American Airlines' SABRE reservation system had taken three years to develop and had cost several hundred million dollars, and the project had included a staff many times the size of the Trips staff.

NOVEMBER–DECEMBER 1992

- Greyhound stock price reaches $13.50.
- Greyhound management actively promotes Trips to investors, lenders, and security analysts as a key to the future success of Greyhound. Management publicly promises to launch the system in time for the 1993 summer busy season.

Trips had been developed by a consulting firm. Planned users of the system such as ticket clerks required 40 hours of training to learn to use it. Clerks had to deal with many screens to plot a trip between any two points. The system data bank was incomplete, with the result that clerks often had to pull out the log books and revert to plotting a ticket purchaser's planned trip manually. Clerk time to issue tickets doubled when they used the system. The system also crashed repeatedly.

Thompson decided to redesign the system and to introduce it in the Northeast corridor in the spring of 1993. After that initial introduction, no new sites would be added until the autumn of 1993, when the busiest travel season would be behind Greyhound. This approach would also give the team time to work out the bugs before the system was introduced nationally. However, he was overruled by Doyle, who had promised the new system to the financial community.

- Greyhound reports a profit of $11 million, its first profit since 1989.

MAY 1993

- Rollout of Trips begins, using the failed version because Thompson did not have enough time to develop the new version. When Trips reaches 50 locations, the computer terminals begin to freeze unpredictably.
- Greyhound stock hits a post–Chapter 11 high of $22.75. Securities analysts had been praising Greyhound management for reengineering the company and for cutting costs.

JUNE 1993

- The rollout of Trips continues.

- Doyle exercises an option to purchase 15,000 shares of Greyhound stock at $9.81.

- Greyhound stock holds above $20 as formal introduction of Trips nears.

- Doyle exercises options on 22,642 shares at $9.81 and immediately sells them at a profit of $179,000.

JULY 1993

- The new toll-free number telephone system begins serving the 220 terminals already hooked up to Trips to be used for making reservations.

The system could not handle all the calls, with many customers receiving busy signals. Customers often had to call as many as a dozen times to get through. The busy signals were caused by the switching mechanism and by the slow response time of Trips. The computer in Dallas sometimes took as long as 45 seconds to respond to just a single keystroke and could take up to five minutes to print a ticket. The system also crashed numerous times, causing many tickets to be written manually.

At some bus terminals, the passengers who arrived with manual tickets were told to wait in line so that they could be reissued a ticket by the computer. Long lines, delays, and confusion resulted. Many passengers missed their connections; others lost their luggage.

- On the same day as the initiation of the telephone system, Greyhound announces an increase in earnings per share and ridership and the introduction of a new discount-fare program; Greyhound stock rises 4.5 percent.

AUGUST 1993

Doyle sells 15,000 shares of stock at $21.75 on August 4. Two other Greyhound vice presidents sell a total of 21,300 shares of stock.

SEPTEMBER 1993

- Trips is closed down west of the Mississippi River because of its continuing problems and delays.

- On September 23, Greyhound announces ridership down by 12 percent in August and earnings also down; the press release does not mention Trips and blames the fall in ridership on the national economic environment.

- Greyhound stock, which was down 12 percent in August, falls to $11.75, or 24 percent in one day.

- Thompson is relieved of his duties on Trips; another vice president takes over responsibility.

MAY 1994

The company offers a $68 ticket for a trip anywhere in the United States with a three-day advance purchase. The crush of potential customers brings Trips to a halt. Buses and drivers are not available in some cities, resulting in large numbers of frustrated passengers stranded in terminals.

JULY 1994

- On-time bus performance falls to 59 percent, versus 81 percent at its peak.

- First-half operating revenues fall 12.6 percent, accompanied by a large dropoff in ridership; the nine largest regional carriers in the United States show an average rise in operating revenue of 2.6 percent.

AUGUST 1994

- Schmieder and Doyle both resign.

- Thomas G. Plaskett, a 50-year-old Greyhound director, is appointed interim CEO; Plaskett was the chairman and CEO of Pan Am Corporation and a former managing director of Fox Run Capital Associates investments.

NOVEMBER 1994

- Greyhound creditors file suit to attempt to force Greyhound back into protection under Chapter 11 of the Federal Bankruptcy Act.

- Greyhound stock falls to $1.875 per share.

- Greyhound announces its fourth consecutive quarterly loss.

- A financial restructuring agreement is reached that gives creditors 45 percent ownership of Greyhound. The agreement allows the company to avoid Chapter 11 bankruptcy.

- Craig Lentzcsh is appointed Greyhound's new permanent CEO.

JANUARY 1995

Greyhound announces that the Securities and Exchange Commission is investigating the company and former directors, officers, and employees for possible securities law violations. The investigation is examining possible insider trading, the adequacy of the firm's internal accounting procedures, and the adequacy of public disclosures related to the Trips system and the company's disappointing earnings in 1993. Greyhound says that it does not believe it has violated any securities laws and is cooperating fully. In addition to the SEC investigation, Greyhound is facing a raft of investors' lawsuits involving similar allegations and a Justice Department antitrust investigation into its terminal agreements with smaller carriers.

Lentzsch's first step in bringing the company back was to dismantle the "airline" model which relied on reservations. Greyhound today does not take reservations. If people want to travel by bus, they show up at the terminal and will get a seat on the bus at a reasonable price. If a bus fills up, Greyhound will roll out another until everyone has a seat.

Lentzsch then changed the company's pricing structure. Schmieder had raised the walk-up prices as high as possible while lowering prices of advanced purchased tickets to compete with the airlines. Lentzsch realized that Greyhound's core customers had incomes of less than $15,000 per year and wanted low-cost no-frills travel above all. Today Greyhound's maximum one-way walk-up fare averages half of airline discount prices.

Other steps toward profitability include adding more people to answer telephones, adding buses to popular routes, such as New York to Boston, and restoring long-haul routes to rural areas that Schmieder nearly abandoned. Lentzsch is also trying to rebuild the company's package express business, which at one time had generated 15 percent of Greyhound's total revenue. Greyhound can use its buses carrying passengers to deliver packages from urban to rural areas at a low cost.

Since Lentzsch took over, revenues and sales have grown and the company expects to be in the black again. But some Wall Street analysts question how much more the company can grow. Bus travel today only accounts for 1.5 percent of intercity travel, down from 5 percent in 1950. ∎

Sources: Wendy Zellner, "Leave the Driving to Lentzsch," *Business Week*, March 18, 1996; Bill Deener, "The Greyhound Turnaround," *Dallas Morning News*, January 14, 1996; Robert Tomsho, "Greyhound Says SEC Is Investigating Possible Violations of Securities Law," *The Wall Street Journal*, January 26, 1995; "How Greyhound Lines Re-Engineered Itself Right into a Deep Hole," *The Wall Street Journal*, October 20, 1994.

Case Study Questions

1. What was Greyhound's business strategy? How were its business processes related to that strategy?

2. How compatible was Trips with Greyhound's business processes and other organizational features?

3. What management, organization, and technology factors contributed to Greyhound's problems?

4. If you were a Greyhound manager, what solutions would you recommend? Would you suggest new business processes or information systems applications? If so, what would they do?

5. Does this case raise any ethical issues?

REFERENCES

Alter, Steven, and Michael Ginzberg. "Managing Uncertainty in MIS Implementation." *Sloan Management Review* 20, no. 1 (Fall 1978).

Anthony, R. N. *Planning and Control Systems: A Framework for Analysis.* Cambridge, MA: Harvard University Press (1965).

Applegate, Lynda M. "Managing in an Information Age: Organizational Challenges and Opportunities," Harvard Business School Note, 9-196-002 (September 1995). The President and Fellows of Harvard College, Cambridge, MA.

Applegate, Lynda M., James Cash Jr., and D. Quin Mills. "Information Technology and Tomorrows's Manager." *Harvard Business Review* (November–December 1988).

Argyris, Chris. *Interpersonal Competence and Organizational Effectiveness.* Homewood, IL: Dorsey Press (1962).

Attewell, Paul, and James Rule. "Computing and Organizations: What We Know and What We Don't Know." *Communications of the ACM* 27, no. 12 (December 1984).

Beer, Michael, Russell A. Eisenstat, and Bert Spector. "Why Change Programs Don't Produce Change." *Harvard Business Review* (November–December 1990).

Bell, Daniel. *The Coming of Post-Industrial Society.* New York: Basic Books (1973).

Bikson, T. K., and J. D. Eveland. "Integrating New Tools into Information Work." The Rand Corporation (1992) RAND/RP-106.

Blau, Peter, and W. Richard Scott. *Formal Organizations.* San Francisco: Chandler Press (1962).

Brzezinski, Z. *The Technetronic Society.* New York: Viking Press (1970).

Charan, Ram. "Now Networks Reshape Organizations—For Results." *Harvard Business Review* (September–October 1991).

DiMaggio, Paul J., and Walter W. Powell. "The Iron Cage Revisited: Institutional Isomorphism and Collective Rationality in Organizational Fields." *American Sociological Review* 48 (1983).

Drucker, Peter. "The Coming of the New Organization." *Harvard Business Review* (January–February 1988).

El Sawy, Omar A. "Implementation by Cultural Infusion: An Approach for Managing the Introduction of Information Technologies." *MIS Quarterly* (June 1985).

Etzioni, Amitai. *A Comparative Analysis of Complex Organizations.* New York: Free Press (1975).

Fayol, Henri. *Administration industrielle et generale.* Paris: Dunods (1950) (first published in 1916).

Fulk, Janet, and Geraldine DeSanctis. "Electronic Communication and Changing Organizational Forms." *Organization Science* 6, no. 4 (July–August 1995).

Freeman, John, Glenn R. Carroll, and Michael T. Hannan. "The Liability of Newness: Age Dependence in Organizational Death Rates." *American Sociological Review* 48 (1983).

Gorry, G. A., and M. S. Morton. "Framework for Management Information Systems." *Sloan Management Review* 13, no. 1 (Fall 1971).

Gouldner, Alvin. *Patterns of Industrial Bureaucracy.* New York: Free Press (1954).

Gurbaxani, V., and S. Whang, "The Impact of Information Systems on Organizations and Markets." *Communications of the ACM* 34, no. 1 (January 1991).

Herzberg, Frederick. *Work and the Nature of Man*. New York: Crowell (1966).

Hinds, Pamela, and Sara Kiesler. "Communication across Boundaries: Work, Structure, and Use of Communication Technologies in a Large Organization." *Organization Science* 6, no. 4 (July–August 1995).

Huber, George P. "The Nature and Design of Post-Industrial Organizations." *Management Science* 30, no. 8 (August 1984).

Huff, Sid L., and Malcolm C. Munro. "Information Technology Assessment and Adoption: A Field Study." *Management Information Systems Quarterly* (December 1985).

Jaques, Elliott. "In Praise of Hierarchy." *Harvard Business Review* (January–February 1990).

Jensen, M., and W. Meckling. "Theory of the Firm: Managerial Behavior, Agency Costs, and Ownership Structure." *Journal of Financial Economics* 3 (1976).

Keen, P. G. W. "Information Systems and Organizational Change." *Communications of the ACM* 24, no. 1 (January 1981).

Keen, P. G. W. *Every Managers Guide to Business Processes*. Cambridge, MA: Harvard Business School Press (1996).

Keen, Peter G. W. *The Process Edge*. Boston, MA: Harvard Business School Press (1997).

King, J. L., V. Gurbaxani, K. L. Kraemer, F. W. MacFarlan, K. S. Raman, and C. S. Yap. "Institutional Factors in Information Technology Innovation." *Information Systems Research* 5, no. 2 (June 1994).

Kling, Rob. "Social Analyses of Computing: Theoretical Perspectives in Recent Empirical Research." *Computing Survey* 12, no. 1 (March 1980).

Kling, Rob, and William H. Dutton. "The Computer Package: Dynamic Complexity." In *Computers and Politics*, edited by James Danziger, William Dutton, Rob Kling, and Kenneth Kraemer. New York: Columbia University Press (1982).

Klotz, B. *Industry Productivity Projections: A Methodological Study*. U.S. Department of Labor, Bureau of Labor Statistics (1966).

Kolb, D. A., and A. L. Frohman. "An Organization Development Approach to Consulting." *Sloan Management Review* 12, no. 1 (Fall 1970).

Kraemer, Kenneth, John King, Debora Dunkle, and Joe Lane. *Managing Information Systems*. Los Angeles: Jossey-Bass (1989).

Laudon, Kenneth C. *Computers and Bureaucratic Reform*. New York: Wiley (1974).

———. "Environmental and Institutional Models of Systems Development." *Communications of the ACM* 28, no. 7 (July 1985).

———. *The Dossier Society: Value Choices in the Design of National Information Systems*. New York: Columbia University Press (1986).

———. "A General Model of the Relationship Between Information Technology and Organizations." Center for Research on Information Systems, New York University. Working paper, National Science Foundation (1989).

Laudon, Kenneth C., and Kenneth L. Marr. "Productivity and the Enactment of a Macro Culture," International Conference on Information Systems, Vancouver, December 1994 and Working Paper, Center for Research on Information Systems, New York University (1994).

———. "Information Technology and Occupational Structure." Working paper, Center for Research on Information Systems, New York University (1995).

Lawrence, Paul, and Jay Lorsch. *Organization and Environment*. Cambridge, MA: Harvard University Press (1969).

Leavitt, Harold J. "Applying Organizational Change in Industry: Structural, Technological and Humanistic Approaches." In *Handbook of Organizations*, edited by James G. March. Chicago: Rand McNally (1965).

Leavitt, Harold J., and Thomas L. Whisler. "Management in the 1980s." *Harvard Business Review* (November–December 1958).

Leifer, Richard. "Matching Computer-Based Information Systems with Organizational Structures." *MIS Quarterly* 12, no. 1 (March 1988).

Malone, Thomas W. "Is Empowerment Just a Fad? Control, Decision-Making and IT." *Sloan Management Review* (Winter 1997).

March, James G., and Herbert A. Simon. *Organizations*. New York: Wiley (1958).

Martin, J. *The Telematic Society*. Englewood Cliffs, NJ: Prentice-Hall (1981).

Masuda, Y. *The Information Society*. Bethesda, MD: World Future Society (1980).

Mayo, Elton. *The Social Problems of an Industrial Civilization*. Cambridge, MA: Harvard University Press (1945).

Michels, Robert. *Political Parties*. New York: Free Press (1962) (original publication in 1915).

Millman, Zeeva, and Jon Hartwick. "The Impact of Automated Office Systems on Middle Managers and Their Work." *MIS Quarterly* 11, no. 4 (December 1987).

Mintzberg, Henry. *The Nature of Managerial Work*. New York: Harper & Row (1973).

———. *The Structuring of Organizations*. Englewood Cliffs, NJ: Prentice-Hall (1979).

Orlikowski, Wanda J. "The Duality of Technology: Rethinking the Concept of Technology in Organizations." *Organization Science* 3, no. 3 (August 1992).

———. "Improvising Organizational Transformation Over Time: A Situated Change Perspective." *Information Systems Research* 7, no. 1 (March 1996).

Orlikowski, Wanda J., and Daniel Robey. "Information Technology and the Structuring of Organizations." *Information Systems Research* 2, no. 2 (June 1991).

Parsons, Talcott. *Structure and Process in Modern Societies*. New York: Free Press (1960).

Perrow, Charles. *Organizational Analysis*. Belmont, CA: Wadsworth (1970).

Pindyck, Robert S., and Daniel L. Rubinfield. *Microeconomics*. Upper Saddle River, NJ: Prentice-Hall (1997).

Porat, Marc. *The Information Economy: Definition and Measurement*. Washington, D.C.: U.S. Department of Commerce, Office of Telecommunications (May 1977).

Robey, Daniel, and Sundeep Sahay. "Transforming Work through Information Technology: A Comparative Case Study of Geographic Information Systems in County Government." *Information Systems Research* 7, no. 1 (March 1996).

Roethlisberger, F. J., and W. J. Dickson. *Management and the Worker*. Cambridge, MA: Harvard University Press (1947).

Schein, Edgar H. *Organizational Culture and Leadership*. San Francisco: Jossey-Bass (1985).

Scott Morton, Michael S., ed. *The Corporation of the 1990s*. New York: Oxford University Press (1991).

Shore, Edwin B. "Reshaping the IS Organization." *MIS Quarterly* (December 1983).

Simon, Herbert A. "Applying Information Technology to Organization Design." *Public Administration Review* (May/June 1973).

Straub, Detmar, and James C. Wetherbe. "Information Technologies for the 1990s: An Organizational Impact Perspective." *Communications of the ACM* 32, no. 11 (November 1989).

Toffler, Alvin. *Future Shock*. New York: Random House (1970).

Turner, Jon A. "Computer Mediated Work: The Interplay Between Technology and Structured Jobs." *Communications of the ACM* 27, no. 12 (December 1984).

Turner, Jon A., and Robert A. Karasek, Jr. "Software Ergonomics: Effects of Computer Application Design Parameters on Operator Task Performance and Health." *Ergonomics* 27, no. 6 (1984).

Tushman, Michael L., and Philip Anderson. "Technological Discontinuities and Organizational Environments." *Administrative Science Quarterly* 31 (September 1986).

Tushman, Michael L., William H. Newman, and Elaine Romanelli. "Convergence and Upheaval: Managing the Unsteady Pace of Organizational Evolution." *California Management Review* 29, no. 1 (1986).

Weber, Max. *The Theory of Social and Economic Organization*. Translated by Talcott Parsons. New York: Free Press (1947).

Winter, Susan J., and S. Lynne Taylor. "The Role of IT in the Transformation of Work: A Comparison of Post-Industrial, Industrial, and Proto-Industrial Organization." *Information Systems Research* 7, no. 1 (March 1996).

Williamson, Oliver E. *The Economic Institutions of Capitalism*. New York: Free Press (1985).

Woodward, Joan. *Industrial Organization: Theory and Practice*. Oxford: Oxford University Press (1965).

Zack, Michael H., and James L. McKenney. "Social Context and Interaction in Ongoing Computer-Supported Management Groups." *Organization Science* 6, no. 4 (July–August 1995).

Information, Management, and Decision Making

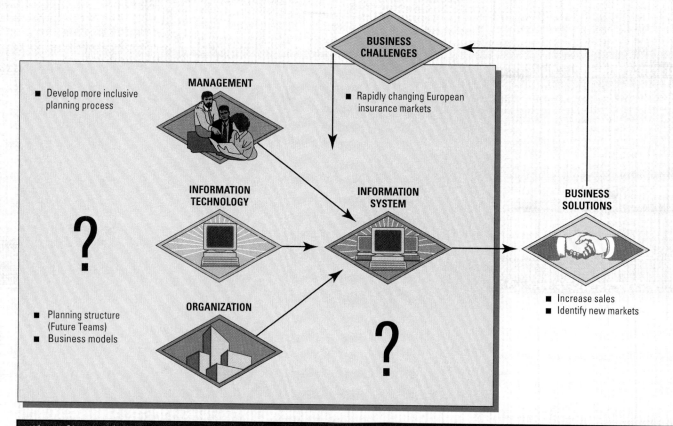

- Develop more inclusive planning process

MANAGEMENT

BUSINESS CHALLENGES

- Rapidly changing European insurance markets

INFORMATION TECHNOLOGY

INFORMATION SYSTEM

BUSINESS SOLUTIONS

?

ORGANIZATION

- Planning structure (Future Teams)
- Business models

- Increase sales
- Identify new markets

?

Skandia Rethinks Its Future

The 140-year-old Skandia Group dominates the Nordic countries with insurance and savings products, reporting over $7 billion in revenues in 1996. Now it is rethinking its future. Believing that the company's strategic planning was too slow, Leif Edvinsson, Skandia's "director of intellectual capital," created a future-focused think tank outside of Stockholm and populated it with a hand-picked group of 30 people from around the world. This elite group was asked to develop a vision of the future for the 150 senior executives comprising Skandia's corporate council.

The group split into Future Teams to explore five driving forces of the

LEARNING OBJECTIVES

After completing
this chapter, you will
be able to:

1. Understand the three main schools of management thinking.
2. Describe the levels, types, and stages of decision making.
3. Identify models for describing individual and organizational decision making.
4. Describe how information technology has changed the management process.
5. Explain how information systems can assist managers and improve managerial decision making.

business environment, including the European insurance market, demographics, technology, the global economy, and organization and leadership. Each Future Team had members from different functional roles, organizational experiences, and generations, ranging from employees in their twenties to their sixties.

Edvinsson was especially interested in the views of younger employees because they might offer fresh perspectives. For example, Lotta Karlsson, a 27-year-old "fast-tracker" managing some of Skandia's advanced high-tech in-

vestment products, used her three-minute presentation to challenge Skandia's existing business model of selling insurance and financial services through broker networks. She rattled off a series of direct-sales success stories as alternative approaches for the future. In the discussions that followed, even high-ranking executives whose careers were invested in the current business model were convinced to examine the issue. In another presentation, the demographic group made a case for the development of financial products geared toward

women, a significant yet largely ignored future market segment.

The meeting culminated in an on-line brainstorming session among 20 groups in different rooms, who responded to five core questions about Skandia's future. By using Future Teams and 150 brains working on the same problem simultaneously, Skandia emerged with a new strategic planning process. ■

Source: Polly LaBarre, "How Skandia Generates Its Future Faster," *Fast Company*, December–January 1997.

MANAGEMENT CHALLENGES

The challenges and decisions facing Leif Edvinsson and Skandia's managers are typical of those facing many senior executives. In companies both large and small, managers are asking such questions as "Where is our industry headed? Should we change our business model? How can we enlarge market share? What should our strategy be? How can we design a strategy?" There are no easy answers to these questions. In some instances, managers find solutions using information systems; in other situations, computers may be of little or no use. Applying information systems to the management process raises the following management challenges:

1. **Unstructured nature of important decisions.** Many important decisions, especially in the areas of strategic planning and knowledge, are not structured and require judgment and examination of many complex factors. Solutions cannot be provided by computerized information systems alone. System builders need to determine exactly what aspects, if any, of a solution can be computerized, and exactly how systems can support the process of arriving at a decision.

2. **Diversity of managerial roles.** Up to now, information systems have supported only a few of the roles managers play in organizations. System builders need to determine whether new technologies such as the Internet can create information systems to help managers in their interpersonal and decisional roles that previously were not backed up by formal systems. In addition to helping managers plan, organize, and coordinate, it is vital that systems help managers get things done through interpersonal communication, by implementing personal agendas, and by establishing networks throughout the organization. Such systems require a different vision of information systems that are less formal, offer more communications capabilities, are adjustable to managers' unique situations, and utilize diverse sources of information inside and outside the firm.

3. **Complexity of decision making.** Individual decision making is not a simple rational process, and is conditioned by decision makers' goals, psychological characteristics, and frames of reference. It is challenging to build systems that genuinely support decision making because they must provide multiple options for handling data and for evaluating information; they must support different personal styles, skills, and knowledge; and they should be easily modified as humans learn and clarify their values. Ideally, systems should not only be designed to support managers' predispositions but also to provide information supporting alternative points of view.

System builders must find new ways of building systems that support decision making in an organization as a group process, conditioned by bureaucratic struggles, political infighting, and the tendency to randomly attach solutions to problems.

The remainder of this text examines how information systems can be designed to support managers. In this chapter we scrutinize the role of a manager and try to identify areas where information systems can contribute to managerial effectiveness. We will also point out areas where information systems have limited value.

Decision making is a key task for managers at all levels in organizations large and small. Many existing systems improve or enhance management decision making, but challenges remain for systems designers seeking new forms of decision support.

To identify opportunities for information systems and to understand their proper role, we first look at what managers actually do. Then we examine the types of decisions managers make and the process of decision making by individuals and organizations.

4.1 WHAT MANAGERS DO

The responsibilities of managers range from making decisions about new products and services, to arranging birthday parties, to writing reports, to attending meetings and giving inspirational speeches to employees. To determine how information systems can benefit managers, we must first examine what managers do and what information they need for decision making. We must also understand how decisions are made and what kinds of decisions can be supported by formal information systems.

Putting Management and Information Systems in Context

Although the practice of management is ancient, the effort to systematically observe and theorize about management and organization did not begin until the last half of the nineteenth century. The formal study of management began in the 1880s as an offshoot of engineering. The very first articles on how to manage a modern business appeared in *Engineering Magazine* and publications of the American Society for Mechanical Engineers (ASME). "Management" as a discipline began to emerge as industrial organizations grew in size from 100 or so workers, to thousands of workers at a single site. In Europe similar forces produced the first literature on administration and bureaucracy, which in essence is the study of large organizations both public and private. Since then, three schools of management have emerged each with a distinct literature, a unique theme and viewpoint about how managers should behave to ensure the success of the organization.

After 100 years of writing about management, it comes down to the fact that organizational success has something to do with technical competence, organizational adaptability to environments, and finally with know-how and intimate knowledge of the product and production process. Theoretical schools and literatures have organized around these three observations. The literature that describes the role of technical competence we call the "technical–rational" school; the literature that emphasizes organizational adaptability to internal and external environments is usually called the "behavioral" school; and the literature that emphasizes the role of knowledge and managerial sense-making we will call the "cognitive" school. See Table 4.1.

Each of these theories are in use today as rationales for why information systems should be built and how managers should use information technology. These three schools are not contradictory but rather complement each other. You can think of

Table 4.1	The Three Main Schools In Management Theory.*
School Name	**Main Emphasis**
Technical–Rational	Emphasizes the precision with which a task can be done, the organization of tasks into jobs, and jobs into production systems.
Behavioral	Emphasizes how well the organization can adapt to its external and internal environment.
Cognitive	Emphasizes how well the organization learns and applies know-how and knowledge, and how well managers provide meaning to new situations.

Most of the literature on management and organizational theory can be divided into three schools of thought: technical–rational, behavioral, and cognitive.

each of these schools as representing an important dimension of both management and organizations.

Three Schools of Management

Figure 4.1 is a theory map which takes the three dimensions of management theory and places them on an historical time line. Figure 4.1 also places contemporary management movements, fads, and slogans into their respective theoretical camps (in italics).

The classical period begins in 1880, when the first widely circulated technical engineering journals appeared and began the systematic theorizing about what made factories, managers, and organizations efficient. During this time period, the technical–rational perspective was ascendant. The contemporary period begins in the late 1920s, spurred on by the growing disciplines of psychology and sociology and new ideas about human motivation and the nature of organizations. During the contemporary period, the behavioral perspective dominated. The postmodern period begins in the early 1960s, when a book entitled *The Production and Distribution of the Knowledge in the United States* began a period of intense speculation about the contribution of knowledge and know-how to organizational success, thus ushering in the cognitive perspective.

The influence of all those theories continues to reverberate throughout the literature and culture in different forms. Each theory describes an important element of being—or becoming—an efficient and effective organization. For instance, the concerns of the technical–rational school for understanding how workers perform tasks, the reduction in variance of output (the emphasis on standards and standard measurable

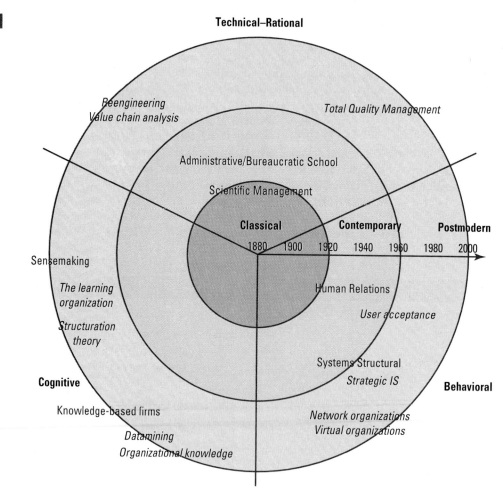

FIGURE 4.1

The Evolution of Management Theory. The history of management theory can be broken into three main historical periods. The classical period (1880–1927) is dominated by the technical–rational view, often held by engineers and "rationalistic" thinkers in scientific management; the contemporary period (1930–1962) is dominated by social psychologists, sociologists, and organizational behavior experts who emphasize individual and collective behavior; the postmodern period (1965–present) is dominated by economists, sociologists, management theorists, and others who emphasize the knowledge basis of organizations.

How to read this figure: Time line from the center outward (Classical, Contemporary, Postmodern); Major perspectives in bold (Technical–Rational; Behavioral; Cognitive); Variants and subschool in regular type; Contemporary applications in consulting and information technology in italic

outputs), and the way tasks are properly organized into jobs do not end in the 1920s but instead live on today as "reengineering" and "total quality management."

We can now take a brief but closer look at what each school discovered and what they believed.

The Technical–Rational Perspective

In the **technical–rational** or **classical perspective,** the organization is seen as a closed, mechanical system—much like a watch or an engine. Like an engine, the efficiency and effectiveness of the organization depend on the precision with which the parts are designed, and the cleverness of the designer in integrating the parts. The role of the manager is to design a more perfect mechanism by closely studying the parts (jobs, tasks, people, and machinery), redesigning the parts, and building an effective administration which can closely monitor the entire operation. There are two variations of the technical–rational perspective: the scientific management school and the administrative–bureaucratic school. The first focuses on factory settings and the second on white-collar administrative organizations.

Henri Fayol and other early writers first described the five functions of managers as planning, organizing, coordinating, deciding, and controlling (see Table 4.2). This description of formal management activities dominated management thought for a long time, and still is popular today.

The belief that the organization is a watchlike mechanism whose internal processes and operations can be continuously improved by management is reflected in the information systems field in such popular programs as reengineering, value chain analysis, business process design, and total quality management. Each of these programs argues that managers should use information technology to improve the mechanism of production.

But as a description of what managers actually do, these five terms are unsatisfactory. The terms do not address what managers do when they plan. How do they actually decide things? How do managers control the work of others? What is needed in a description is a more fine-grained understanding of how managers actually behave.

technical–rational "classical" perspective Descriptions of management and organizations that focus on the mechanistic aspects of organization and the formal management functions of planning, organizing, coordinating, deciding, and controlling.

The Behavioral Perspective

The **behavioral perspective** on management developed in reaction to the limitations of the technical school: its failure to consider the people who worked in organizations as human beings (rather than automaton-like machines), its failure to consider the role of small groups, group norms, and other sociological phenomena, and the failure of the technical school to consider the external environment in which the organization operated. The behavioral perspective in management theory began in the late 1920s and early 1930s, spurred on by the development of large scale, mass production of consumer goods for a national market, huge multilevel firms, social strife associated with the emergence of powerful labor unions, and the growing acceptance and influence of the social sciences such as sociology and psychology.

behavioral perspective Descriptions of management based on behavioral scientists' observations of how organizations actually behave and what managers actually do in their jobs.

Table 4.2   The Technical–Rational or Classical Model of Management Functions
Planning
Organizing
Coordinating
Deciding
Controlling

In the behavioral perspective the organization is seen as an open, biological organism much like a cell, or animal. Like a biological cell, the efficiency and effectiveness of the organization depend on its ability to adapt to its environment and its ability to arrange itself internally so that all its constituent parts are supported and sustained. The role of the manager is to assist the organization in its quest for survival by continually redesigning the organization so it can "fit" or adapt to its environment, and to ensure that the organization's employees are satisfied and functioning well. There are two major schools within the behavioral perspective: the human relations school which focuses on the psychological and social–psychological needs of employees; and the systems structural school which focuses on the structure of the organization and the needs of the organization to adapt to an ever-changing external environment.

The behavioral perspective on management has had a powerful impact on the information systems field: the literature on "user acceptance" of information systems which emphasizes the sociological and psychological aspects of system success; the "strategic IS" literature which emphasizes the ability of the organization to respond to and potentially dominate its environment; and the contemporary "network organization" and "virtual organization" literature which emphasize organizing labor forces without traditional hierarchies.

Contemporary behavioral scientists have discovered from observation that managers do not behave as the classical model of management led us to believe. Kotter (1982), for example, describes the morning activities of the president of an investment management firm.

> 7:35 A.M. Richardson arrives at work, unpacks his briefcase, gets some coffee, and begins making a list of activities for the day.
>
> 7:45 A.M. Bradshaw (a subordinate) and Richardson converse about a number of topics and exchange pictures recently taken on summer vacations.
>
> 8:00 A.M. They talk about a schedule of priorities for the day.
>
> 8:20 A.M. Wilson (a subordinate) and Richardson talk about some personnel problems, cracking jokes in the process.
>
> 8:45 A.M. Richardson's secretary arrives, and they discuss her new apartment and arrangements for a meeting later in the morning.
>
> 8:55 A.M. Richardson goes to a morning meeting run by one of his subordinates. Thirty people are there, and Richardson reads during the meeting.
>
> 11:05 A.M. Richardson and his subordinates return to the office and discuss a difficult problem. They try to define the problem and outline possible alternatives. He lets the discussion roam away from and back to the topic again and again. Finally, they agree on a next step.

In the behavioral perspective, the actual behavior of managers appears to be less systematic, more informal, less reflective, more reactive, less well organized, and much more frivolous than students of information systems and decision making generally expect. In our example, it is difficult to determine which activities constitute Richardson's planning, coordinating, and decision making.

A widely noted study of actual managerial behavior conducted by Mintzberg (1971) indicates that actual managerial behavior often contrasts with the classical description (see Table 4.3). First, modern researchers have found that the manager performs a great deal of work at an unrelenting pace and works at a high level of intensity. Some studies have found that managers engage in more than 600 different activities each day, with no break in their pace. Managers seem to have little free time. Even when they leave the office, general managers frequently take work home.

Second, managerial activities are fragmented and brief. Managers simply lack the time to get deeply involved in a wide range of issues. They shift their attention rapidly from one issue to another, with very little pattern. When a problem occurs, all other matters must be dropped until the issue is solved. Mintzberg found that

Table 4.3	The Behavioral Model of Management Activities
High-volume, high-speed work	
Variety, fragmentation, brevity	
Issue preference current, ad hoc, specific	
Complex web of interactions, contacts	
Strong preference for verbal media	
Control of the agenda	

most activities of general managers lasted for less than nine minutes, and only 10 percent of the activities exceeded one hour in duration.

Third, managers prefer speculation, hearsay, gossip—in brief, they enjoy current, up-to-date, although uncertain, information. They pay less attention to historical, routine information. Managers want to work on issues that are current, specific, and ad hoc.

Fourth, managers maintain a diverse and complex web of contacts that acts as an informal information system. Managers converse with clients, associates, peers, secretaries, outside government officials, and so forth.

Fifth, managers prefer verbal forms of communication to written forms because verbal media provide greater flexibility, require less effort, and bring a faster response. Communication is the work of the manager, and he or she uses whatever tools are available to be an effective communicator.

Despite the flood of work, the press of deadlines, and the random order of crises, Mintzberg found that successful managers appear to be able to control their own affairs. To some extent, higher-level managers are at the mercy of their subordinates, who bring to their attention crises and activities that must be attended to immediately. Nevertheless, successful managers can control the activities that they choose to get involved in on a day-to-day basis. By developing their own long-term commitments, their own information channels, and their own networks, senior managers can control their personal agendas. Less successful managers tend to be overwhelmed by problems brought to them by subordinates.

Managerial Roles: Mintzberg

Managerial roles are expectations of the activities that managers should perform in an organization. Mintzberg classified managerial activities into 10 roles that fall into three categories: interpersonal, informational, and decisional. Information systems, if built properly, can support these diverse managerial roles in a number of ways (see Table 4.4).

Interpersonal roles. Managers act as figureheads for the organization when they represent their companies to the outside world and perform symbolic duties such as giving out employee awards. Managers act as leaders, attempting to motivate, counsel, and support subordinates. Lastly, managers act as a liaison between various levels of the organization; within each of these levels, they serve as a liaison among the members of the management team. Managers provide time, information, and favors, which they expect to be returned.

Informational roles. Managers act as the nerve centers of their organization, receiving the most concrete, up-to-date information and redistributing it to those who need to be aware of it. Managers are therefore disseminators and spokespersons for their organization.

Decisional roles. Managers make decisions. They act as entrepreneurs by initiating new kinds of activities; they handle disturbances arising in the organization; they allocate resources to staff members who need them; and they negotiate conflicts and mediate between conflicting groups in the organization.

managerial roles Expectations of the activities that managers should perform in an organization.

interpersonal roles Mintzberg's classification for managerial roles where managers act as figureheads and leaders for the organization.

informational roles Mintzberg's classification for managerial roles where managers act as the nerve centers of their organizations, receiving and disseminating critical information.

decisional roles Mintzberg's classification for managerial roles where managers initiate activities, handle disturbances, allocate resources, and negotiate conflicts.

Table 4.4	Managerial Roles and Supporting Information Systems	
Role	Behavior	Support Systems
Interpersonal Roles		
Figurehead	--→	None exist
Leader	-----------------------Interpersonal-----------→	None exist
Liaison	---→	Electronic communication systems
Informational Roles		
Nerve center	--→	Management information systems
Disseminator	----------------Information------------→	Mail, office systems
Spokesman	--------------------processing------------→	Office and professional systems, workstations
Decisional Roles		
Entrepreneur	--→	None exist
Disturbance handler	---------Decision------------→	None exist
Resource allocator	-------------making--------------→	DSS systems
Negotiator	---→	None exist

Source: Kenneth C. Laudon and Jane P. Laudon; and Mintzberg 1971.

Table 4.4 enables us to see where systems can help managers and where they cannot. The table shows that information systems do not as of yet contribute a great deal to many areas of management life. These areas will undoubtedly provide great opportunities for future systems and system designers.

In the area of interpersonal roles, information systems are extremely limited and currently can make only indirect contributions. The systems act largely as a communications aid with some of the newer office automation and communication-oriented applications. These systems contribute more to the field of informational roles: A

Corporate chief executives learn how to use laptop computers during a "technology retreat." Many senior managers lack computer knowledge or experience and require systems that are extremely easy to use.

Table 4.5   Myths About Top Managers

Life is less complicated at the top of the organization.

The top managers also know everything, can command whatever resources are needed, and therefore can be decisive.

The top manager's job consists of making long-range plans.

The top manager's job is to meditate about the role of the company in society.

Source: Wrapp (1984).

manager's presentation of information is significantly improved with large-scale MIS systems, office systems, and professional workstations. In the area of decision making, only recently have DSS and PC-based systems begun to make important contributions (see Chapters 10 and 16).

How Managers Get Things Done: Kotter

Kotter (1982) uses the behavioral approach to modern management to describe how managers work. Building on the work of Mintzberg, Kotter argues that effective managers are involved in three critical activities. First, general managers spend significant time establishing personal agendas and goals, both short and long term. These personal agendas include both vague and specific topics and usually address a broad range of financial, product-oriented, and organizational issues.

Second—but perhaps most important—effective managers spend much time building an interpersonal network composed of people at virtually all levels of the organization, from warehouse staff to clerical support personnel to other managers and senior management. These networks, like their personal agendas, are generally consistent with the formal plans and networks of an organization, but they are different and apart. General managers build these networks using a variety of face-to-face, interactive tools, both formal and informal. Managers carefully nurture professional reputations and relationships with peers.

Third, Kotter found that managers use their networks to execute personal agendas. In his findings, general managers called on peers, corporate staff, subordinates three or four levels below them, and even competitors to help accomplish goals. There was no category of people that was never used.

What Managers Decide: Wrapp

In the technical–rational model of management, one might expect that managers make important decisions and that the more senior the manager, the more important and profound the decisions will be. Yet in a frequently cited article about general managers, H. Edward Wrapp (1984) found that good managers do not make sweeping policy decisions but instead give the organization a general sense of direction and become skilled in developing opportunities.

Wrapp found that good managers seldom make forthright statements of policy; often get personally involved in operating decisions; and rarely try to push through total solutions or programs for particular problems. Wrapp described a number of myths about modern managers and compared them with the reality that he came to know as a member of several corporate boards (see Table 4.5).

Wrapp was able to show that, contrary to popular belief, successful managers spend much time and energy getting involved in operational decisions and problems to stay well informed. These managers focus time and energy on a small subset of organizational problems that they can directly affect successfully; they are sensitive to the power structure of the organization because any major proposal requires the support of several organizational units and actors; and they appear imprecise in setting

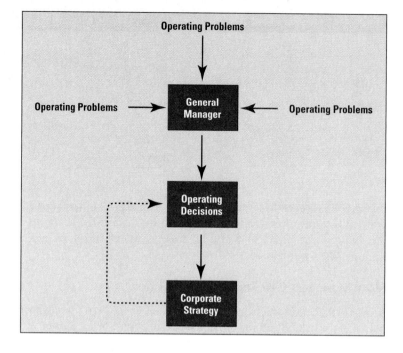

FIGURE 4.2

Wrapp's successful manager. According to Wrapp, successful general managers are highly involved in operational problems and decisions. Corporate strategy tends to not be systematic or comprehensive but instead is an outgrowth of day-to-day operating decisions.

overall organizational goals but nevertheless provide a sense of direction. In this way, managers maintain visibility but avoid being placed in a policy straitjacket.

In contrast to the classical description in which senior managers are thought of as making grand, sweeping decisions, Wrapp found that the contemporary manager tackles organizational decisions with a purpose, and does not seek to implement comprehensive, systematic, logical, well-programmed plans. Systematic, comprehensive plans are generally unable to exploit changes in the environment, and they are just as likely to create opposition in the organization as they are to gain support. For this reason, the manager seeks to implement plans one part at a time, without drawing attention to an explicit, comprehensive design.

Figure 4.2 illustrates Wrapp's conception of a good manager. Especially critical here is the notion of general managers becoming involved in operating problems and decisions. Corporate strategy derives from operating problems and decisions. This means that the corporate strategy is closely tied to operating problems and decisions as opposed to being an independent entity.

The Cognitive Perspective and Postmodern Era

cognitive perspective Descriptions of management and organization which emphasize the role of knowledge, core competency, and perceptual filters.

In the **cognitive perspective,** the organization is a knowing, sentient organism. Like a human being, organizations seek to make sense out of their environments, and can "learn" as well as "know" things. The efficiency and effectiveness of the organization depend on the correctness, the appropriateness of its sense-making judgments, as well as its ability to gather, create, store, disseminate, and use information and knowledge. The role of the manager in this perspective is to use his or her sense-making ability to properly define the situation of the organization so it can act (perceive problems and define solutions), and to build the information- and knowledge-processing infrastructure of the organization. Although the cognitive school has historical precedents, it is largely a child of the post-1960s computer age.

There are two schools within the cognitive perspective. The managerial sense-making school emphasizes the key role of the manager in correctly perceiving and interpreting environmental events, understanding and conceptualizing the problems faced by an organization, defining the solution set, and making the solution decision. Managers create mental models which can serve as the basis for the organization's action plans. The second cognitive school is the knowledge-based view of the firm which emphasizes the collection, storage, dissemination, and use of knowledge and information. Both theories address the same problem as earlier theories: What makes for an effective and efficient organization?

The cognitive perspective has had a large impact on contemporary thinking about information technology and the firm. For instance, the development of data-mining techniques and the use of "discovered knowledge" and intelligent software to assist management decision making argue that managers should use information technology primarily to increase the information and knowledge-processing infrastructure of the firm. There is a growing focus in the information systems field on the role of information technology in helping the organization learn about its environment, in responding to the environment more efficiently, and in storing and disseminating knowledge using the Internet, and interactive multimedia software which are far more effective in communicating knowledge. Finally, there is a small but important body of IS literature which illustrates how organizations use information technology to impose order on and make sense of their environments (Orlikowski, 1992).

Managerial Sense-making

The "managers as sense-makers" school is the collective work of sociologists, cognitive psychologists, information systems experts, computer scientists, and economists. The basic premise of the managerial sense-making school is that managers define the situation for both the employees and the firm. Managers increase firm value, effectiveness, and efficiency, insofar as they are correct in their sense-making. If they are incorrect, the organization loses effectiveness, efficiency, and ultimately fails. Some other premises include:

- Managers create knowledge structures—or mental maps—which transform the chaotic, ambiguous stream of events in the environment into tractable "problems," and become the foundation for organizational programs and policies for coping and survival. Managers do this by applying various filters to information from the environment (Starbuck and Milliken, 1988). The information filters and knowledge structures developed by managers are often wrong as much as they are right (Mintzberg, 1973).

- Managers are problem solvers and decision makers. Managers must make myriad number of high-speed, correct decisions, and in the process solve problems faced by the organization. Managers define problems for the organization. The success of any organization is largely the result of how well its managers solve problems and make decisions.

- Managers are information processors. The primary role of management is to process information from the external and internal environments of the firm. This information processing is increasingly aided by information technology tools and systems. The information process is both formal—the result of formally structured organizational systems—and informal, for example, gossip, hearsay, notes, and diagrams on the backs of envelopes and napkins (March and Sevon, 1984).

- Managers create information-processing structures, programs, and routines which scan external and internal environments in accordance with the managers' knowledge structures. Information does not simply land on the manager's desk in a random stream but instead is produced by the manager on the basis of his or her definition of the situation (Schwenk, 1984).

Figure 4.3 illustrates the managerial sense-making school.

The essence of this school is that it is the manager's role to impose an intellectual and mental order on a chaotic environment, to define the situation for employees and the organization as a whole. Once defined, products and services are designed, produced, and distributed to customers or users. The emphasis is on the creative role of the manager.

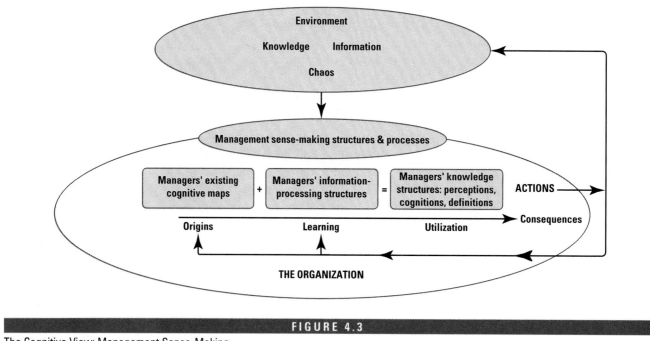

FIGURE 4.3

The Cognitive View: Management Sense-Making
Managers are problem-solvers who interpret environmental events, define the problems, and develop solutions for the organization.

The Knowledge-Based View of the Firm

The knowledge-based view of the firm focuses less on the manager than on the organization as a whole, reflecting the work of sociologists, information systems and computer scientists, and strategic planners. The basic premise of this school is that the success of the organization—survival and efficiency—depends on the organization's ability to gather, produce, maintain, and disseminate knowledge which is used to produce products and services. The key premises of this school include:

- Knowledge is the central productive and strategic asset of the firm (Arrow, 1972; Badaracco, 1991; Quinn, 1992).

- Knowledge can be explicit or tacit. Explicit knowledge is codified in books, manuals, pictures, and videos. Tacit knowledge is implicit know-how, or a social relationship needed to complete a task, built over years of experience. Tacit knowledge includes craftsmanship, teams that work together well, values, culture and attitudes which support learning, and decision-making patterns based on knowledge. Tacit knowledge is embedded in individuals and organizations, is not easily marketed, and tends to be sticky (Jensen and Meckling, 1992).

- Knowledge is a complex concept and includes information, social relations, personal know-how, and skills. Knowledge is an attribute of both individuals and organizations. Personal knowledge can be appropriated and encoded by the organization in the form of manuals, software, and operating procedures.

- Firms concentrate and manage explicit and tacit knowledge better than markets. Otherwise, organizations would not exist.

- Organizations and people can learn in the sense that they can change their behavior on the basis of new information or knowledge (Huber, 1991).

- All physical capital is an instance of knowledge. Knowledge can be embedded in machines (Machlup, 1962; Boulding, 1966).

- The creation of value by the organization requires the application of different types of specialized knowledge (Quinn, 1992).

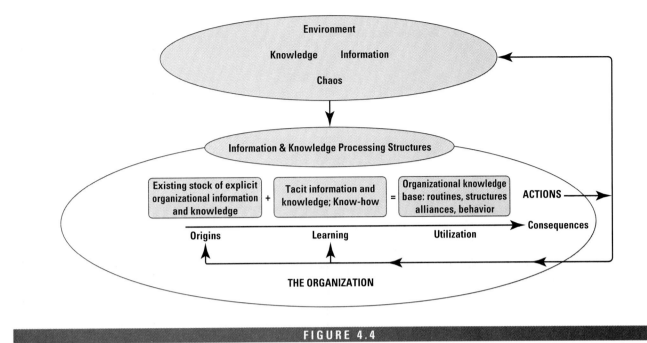

FIGURE 4.4

The Knowledge-Based View of the Firm. Knowledge is the core productive and strategic asset of the firm. The success of the organization hinges on its ability to manage its knowledge resources.

- The function of the firm is to create value—to survive and be efficient— through the integration of specialized knowledge.
- The strategy of the firm is to develop specialized expertise "core competencies" which other firms cannot copy easily and which cannot be marketed (Prahalad and Hamel, 1990).

Figure 4.4 illustrates the knowledge-based view of the firm.

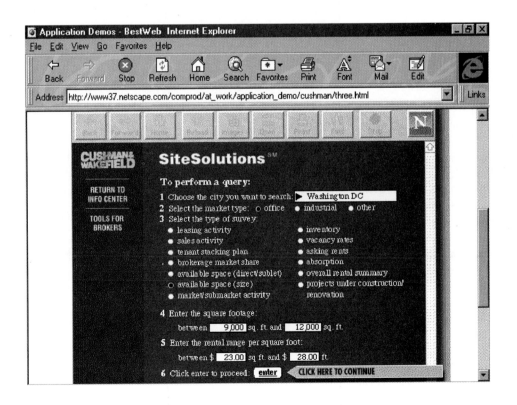

Cushman & Wakefield's property tracking system uses Web technology to provide managers with data on commercial properties. This is one of many ways that the Internet can help managers distribute and leverage knowledge.

Managers Turn to the Internet

Cushman & Wakefield (C&W), a large New York real estate firm, has 2000 employees and six major offices around the United States, plus many other smaller offices around the country and the world. The firm manages office buildings, factories, and other commercial properties in addition to being a commercial broker. Their management problem was the logistics nightmare of keeping personnel, benefits, and legal policies and procedures current at all their sites, particularly given the need to update them many times a year. C&W already had a proprietary network installed, and it also had many employees already using the Internet. The solution was obvious: Why not take advantage of the low-cost and interactive features of the Internet to create an internal network for employee communication?

To set up the new network, all C&W needed to do was develop the software. No new hardware or wires were needed; this new network would run over the company's existing network infrastructure. The firm's policies and procedures were already being stored electronically as Microsoft Word documents. C&W purchased commercial software to convert existing documents directly into documents that could be displayed on the World Wide Web of the Internet. C&W's employee resource system (ERS) was completed within three months. It cost less than $10,000 to develop. Once the policies were on-line, it became easy to keep every office up to date—simply type the new document using Microsoft Word, convert it through the conversion software, and it is done. No complex distribution is required. In addition, many employees found it easy to learn because they were already using the Internet.

C&W then added other Internet applications. One calculates employee commissions using an internal Internet-based network. Employee agents, and even contract brokers, can see the commission data they want. C&W plans to provide employees with Internet capabilities for on-line discussions and e-mail as well.

Site Solutions, C&W's property tracking system, is its biggest system made available through the internal network. This system maintains detailed data on thousands of commercial properties worldwide which the company manages, including available office space. It also contains data on all their commercial real estate ventures worldwide, whether planned, under construction, or completed. This system can be accessed by brokers throughout the company and by clients and employees. It will be easy for clients to access because the Internet is so widely used.

Managers at other companies are turning to the Internet as well. At Southern California Gas Co. (SoCal Gas), account executives use an internal Web-based application to access information about proposed new services or rate changes so that the change can be reviewed by regulators, customers, and advocacy groups. In the past, this information was more difficult to locate and keep up to date because it was kept in paper binders. Another Internet-based application called Pe Xchng allows SoCal Gas employees to send "competitive intelligence"—any information they glean while on the job of competitive interest—to managers at the firm's Los Angeles headquarters.

To Think About: *How can the Internet help managers manage? Suggest management uses for the Internet other than those described here.*

Sources: Alice LaPlante, "Start Small, Think Infinite," *Computerworld Premier 100*, February 24, 1997; and Clinton Wilder, "Location, Location, Location," *InformationWEEK*, March 25, 1996.

The knowledge-based view of the firm has important consequences for how organizations are managed and how they use information technology. If intellectual and knowledge-based activities are the very heart of an organization, then a manager's role should be focused more on how to manage knowledge workers; how to gather, acquire, store, and disseminate information and knowledge; and how to build new knowledge into the organization. Information technology applications should focus on knowledge workers and the management of knowledge. Teams and groups become more important in this view simply because problem solving often requires the input of many people who work in the problem area. And if intellectual and knowledge-based activities are central, then the long-term strategy of the firm should be to focus on strengthening its "core" knowledge competencies and building the knowledge base.

The Window on Technology describes some of the ways that the Internet can be used by managers to distribute and leverage knowledge. Each of the three main schools of management thinking—technical–rational, behavioral, and cognitive—

have important implications for managing and organizing information technology in today's contemporary organization. Each of the three schools shares a common focus on managerial decision making. Next we take a closer look at how information technology shapes the decision-making process.

4.2 INTRODUCTION TO DECISION MAKING

Decision making remains one of the more challenging roles of a manager. Information systems have helped managers communicate and distribute information; however, they have provided only limited assistance for management decision making. Because decision making is an area that system designers have sought most of all to affect (with mixed success), we now turn our attention to this issue. In this section we introduce the process; in the next two sections we examine models of individual and organizational decision making.

Levels of Decision Making

Differences in decision making can be classified by organizational level. Anthony (1965) grouped decision making in an organization into three categories: strategic, management control, and operational control. We include an additional category for knowledge-level decision making because Anthony did not envision the prominent role now played by knowledge work in organizations. These categories of decisions correspond to the strategic, management, knowledge, and operational levels of the organization introduced in Chapter 2.

strategic decision making
Determining the long-term objectives, resources, and policies of an organization.

Strategic decision making determines the objectives, resources, and policies of the organization. A major problem at this level of decision making is predicting the future of the organization and its environment and matching the characteristics of the organization to the environment. This process generally involves a small group of high-level managers who deal with complex, nonroutine problems.

management control
Monitoring how efficiently or effectively resources are utilized and how well operational units are performing.

Decision making for **management control** is principally concerned with how efficiently and effectively resources are utilized and how well operational units are performing. Management control requires close interaction with those who are carrying out the tasks of the organization; it takes place within the context of broad policies and objectives set out by strategic decision making; and, as the behaviorists have described, it requires an intimate knowledge of operational decision making and task completion.

knowledge-level decision making
Evaluating new ideas for products, services, ways to communicate new knowledge, and ways to distribute information throughout the organization.

Knowledge-level decision making deals with evaluating new ideas for products and services; ways to communicate new knowledge; and ways to distribute information throughout the organization.

Decision making for **operational control** determines how to carry out the specific tasks set forth by strategic and middle management decision makers. Determining which units in the organization will carry out the task, establishing criteria for completion and resource utilization, and evaluating outputs all require decisions about operational control.

operational control Deciding how to carry out specific tasks specified by upper and middle management and establishing criteria for completion and resource allocation.

Types of Decisions: Structured versus Unstructured

Within each of these levels of decision making, Simon (1960) classified decisions as being either programmed or nonprogrammed. Other researchers refer to these types of decisions as structured and unstructured, as we do in this book. **Unstructured decisions** are those in which the decision maker must provide judgment, evaluation, and insights into the problem definition. These decisions are novel, important, and nonroutine, and there is no well-understood or agreed-upon procedure for making them (Gorry and Scott-Morton, 1971). **Structured decisions,** by contrast, are repetitive, routine, and involve a definite procedure for handling so that they do not have

unstructured decisions Nonroutine decisions in which the decision maker must provide judgment, evaluation, and insights into the problem definition; there is no agreed-upon procedure for making such decisions.

structured decisions Decisions that are repetitive, routine, and have a definite procedure for handling them.

semistructured decisions
Decisions where only part of the problem has a clear-cut answer provided by an accepted procedure.

to be treated each time as if they were new. Some decisions are **semistructured decisions;** in such cases, only part of the problem has a clear-cut answer provided by an accepted procedure.

Types of Decisions and Types of Systems

Combining these two views of decision making produces the grid shown in Figure 4.5. In general, operational control personnel face fairly well-structured problems. In contrast, strategic planners tackle highly unstructured problems. Many problems encountered by knowledge workers are fairly unstructured as well. Nevertheless, each level of the organization contains both structured and unstructured problems.

In the past, most success in modern information systems came in dealing with structured, operational, and management control decisions. But now most of the exciting applications are occurring in the management, knowledge, and strategic planning areas, where problems are either semistructured or totally unstructured. Examples include general DSS, PC-based decision-making systems including spreadsheets and other packages, professional design workstations, and general planning and simulation systems (discussed in later chapters).

Stages of Decision Making

Making decisions is not a single activity that takes place all at once. The process consists of several different activities that take place at different times.

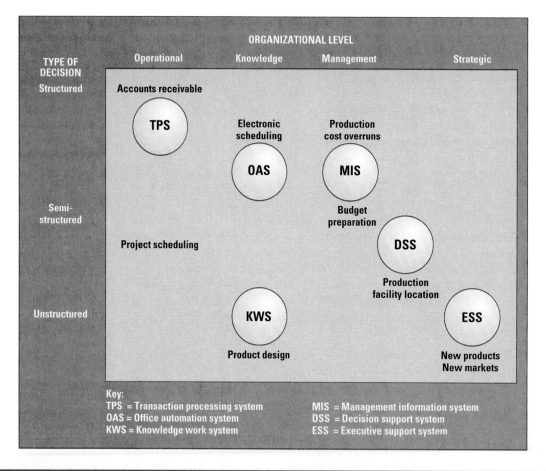

FIGURE 4.5

Different kinds of information systems at the various organizational levels support different types of decisions.
Source: Gorry and Scott-Morton, 1971.

Take any important decision that you as a student make—for example, whether to attend college—and ask yourself precisely when you decided to go to college. Chances are that you made the decision over time; you were influenced by friends, counselors, and parents; and you used different information sources to find out about each alternative. Let us try to divide decision making into its component stages.

The decision maker has to perceive and understand problems. Once perceived, solutions must be designed; once solutions are designed, choices have to be made about a particular solution; finally, the solution has to be implemented. Simon (1960) described four different stages in decision making (see Table 4.6): intelligence, design, choice, and implementation.

Intelligence consists of identifying the problems occurring in the organization. Intelligence indicates why, where, and with what effects a situation occurs. This broad set of information-gathering activities is required to inform managers how well the organization is performing and to let them know where problems exist. Traditional MIS systems that deliver a wide variety of detailed information can help identify problems, especially if the systems report exceptions (with added ability to call up text and additional detailed information).

During **design,** the second stage of decision making, the individual designs possible solutions to the problems. This activity may require more intelligence so that the manager can decide if a particular solution is appropriate. The design stage may also entail more carefully specified and directed information activities. Smaller DSS systems are ideal in this stage of decision making because they operate on simple models, can be developed quickly, and can be operated with limited data.

Choice, the third stage of decision making, consists of choosing among alternatives. Here a manager can use information tools that can calculate and keep track of the consequences, costs, and opportunities provided by each alternative designed in the second stage. The decision maker might need a larger DSS system to develop more extensive data on a variety of alternatives and to use complex analytic models needed to account for all the consequences.

The last stage in decision making is **implementation.** Here, managers can use a reporting system that delivers routine reports on the progress of a specific solution. The system will also report some of the difficulties that arise, will indicate resource constraints, and will suggest possible ameliorative actions. Support systems can range from full-blown MIS systems to much smaller systems as well as project-planning software operating on microcomputers.

Table 4.6 lists the stages in decision making, the general type of information required, and specific examples of information systems corresponding to each stage.

In general, the stages of decision making do not necessarily follow a linear path from intelligence to design, choice, and implementation. Think again about your decision to attend a *specific* college. At any point in the decision-making process, you may have to loop back to a previous stage (see Figure 4.6). For instance, one can often create several designs but may not be certain about whether a specific design meets the requirements for the particular problem. This situation requires additional

intelligence The first of Simon's four stages of decision making, when the individual collects information to identify problems occurring in the organization.

design Simon's second stage of decision making, when the individual conceives of possible alternative solutions to a problem.

choice Simon's third stage of decision making, when the individual selects among the various solution alternatives.

implementation Simon's final stage of decision making, when the individual puts the decision into effect and reports on the progress of the solution.

Table 4.6	Stages in Decision Making, Information Requirement, and Supporting Information Systems	
Stage of Decision Making	**Information Requirement**	**Example System**
Intelligence	Exception reporting	MIS
Design	Simulation prototype	DSS, KWS
Choice	"What-if" simulation	DSS; large models
Implementation	Graphics, charts	PC and mainframe decision aids

Source: Kenneth C. Laudon and Jane P. Laudon; and Scott-Morton, 1971.

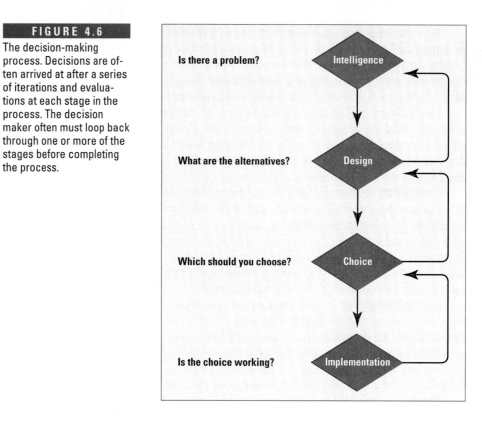

FIGURE 4.6

The decision-making process. Decisions are often arrived at after a series of iterations and evaluations at each stage in the process. The decision maker often must loop back through one or more of the stages before completing the process.

Is there a problem? — Intelligence

What are the alternatives? — Design

Which should you choose? — Choice

Is the choice working? — Implementation

intelligence work. Alternatively, one can be in the process of implementing a decision, only to discover that it is not working. In such a case, one is forced to repeat the design or choice stage.

4.3 INDIVIDUAL MODELS OF DECISION MAKING

A number of models attempt to describe how individuals make decisions (see Table 4.7). The basic assumption behind all these models is that human beings are in some sense rational.

The Rational Model

rational model   Model of human behavior based on the belief that people, organizations, and nations engage in basically consistent, value-maximizing calculations or adaptations within certain constraints.

The **rational model** of human behavior is built on the idea that people, organizations, and nations engage in basically consistent, value-maximizing calculations or adaptations within certain constraints. Since the time of Adam Smith, this assumption has been at the heart of consumer behavior theories and microeconomics, political philosophy (which hails the individual as a free-willed value maximizer), and social theory (which stresses the individual pursuit of prestige, money, and power).

The rational model works as follows: An individual has goals or objectives and has a payoff, utility, or preference function that permits that person to rank all possible alternative actions by the action's contribution to the desired goals. The actor is presented with and understands alternative courses of action. Each alternative has a set of consequences. The actor chooses the alternative and consequences that rank highest in terms of the payoff functions; that is, that contribute most to the ultimate goal. In a rigorous model of rational action, the actor has comprehensive rationality, can accurately rank all alternatives and consequences, and can perceive all alternatives and consequences.

There are three criticisms of the rational model. First, in a human time frame, the model is computationally impossible. In a "simple" chess game there are 10^{120}

Table 4.7   Models of Individual Decision Making

Name	Basic Concept	Inference Patterns
Rational model	Comprehensive rationality	Establish goals, examine all alternatives, and choose the best alternative.
Satisficing model	Bounded rationality	Establish goals, examine a few alternatives, and choose the first alternative that promotes the goals.
Muddling	Successive comparison	Examine alternatives to establish a mix of goals and consequences; choose policies that are marginally different from those of the past.
Psychological	Cognitive types	All decision makers choose goals, but they differ in terms of gathering and evaluating information. Systematic thinkers impose order on perceptions and evaluation; intuitive thinkers are more open to unexpected information and use multiple models and perspectives when evaluating information. Neither is more rational than the other.

moves, countermoves, and counter countermoves from start to finish, and it would take a machine 10^{95} years operating at a rate of 1 million instructions per second (MIPS) to decide the first move! Second, the model lacks realism in the sense that most individuals do not have singular goals and a consciously used payoff function, and they are not able to rank all alternatives and consequences. (To this it might be replied that realism is not required, only predictive accuracy.) Third, in real life the idea of a finite number of all alternatives and consequences makes no sense. In a maze constructed for a rat or in a game of tic-tac-toe, all alternatives and consequences can be meaningful and precise. In the real world of humans, specifying all of the alternatives and consequences is impossible.

Despite these criticisms, the rational model remains a powerful and attractive model of human decision making. It is rigorous, simple, and instructive.

Bounded Rationality and Satisficing

In answer to the critics, March and Simon (1958) and Simon (1960) proposed a number of adjustments to the rigorous rational model. Rather than optimizing, which presumes comprehensive rationality, Simon argues that people partake in **satisficing**— that is, choosing the first available alternative that moves them toward their ultimate goal. Instead of searching for all the alternatives and consequences (unlimited rationality), Simon proposes **bounded rationality,** that people limit the search process to sequentially ordered alternatives (alternatives not radically different from the current policy). When possible, people avoid new, uncertain alternatives and rely instead on tried-and-true rules, standard operating procedures, and programs. Individuals have many goals—not a single consistent set—and therefore they try to divide their goals into separate programs, avoiding interdependencies when possible. In this way, rationality is bounded.

satisficing   Choosing the first available alternative to move closer toward the ultimate goal instead of searching for all alternatives and consequences.

bounded rationality   Idea that people will avoid new, uncertain alternatives and stick with tried-and-true rules and procedures.

"Muddling Through"

In an article on the "science of **muddling through,**" Lindblom (1959) proposed the most radical departure from the rational model. He described this method of decision making as one of "successive limited comparisons." First, individuals and organizations have conflicting goals—they want both freedom and security, rapid economic growth and minimal pollution, faster transportation and minimal disruption due to highway construction, and so forth. People have to choose among policies that contain various mixes of conflicting goals. The values themselves cannot be discussed in the abstract; they become clear only when specific policies are considered. Everyone is against crime; there is little need to discuss this issue. But many object to permitting the police to search homes without a court order (as called for in the

muddling through   Method of decision making involving successive limited comparisons where the test of a good decision is whether people agree on it.

Fourth Amendment). Hence, values are chosen at the same time as policies, and there is no easy means-end analysis (if you believe in *X*, then choose policy *X*).

Because there is no easy means-end analysis, and because people cannot agree on values, the only test of a "good" choice is whether people agree on it. Policies cannot be judged by how much of *X* they provide, but rather by the agreement of the people making the policies. Labor and management can rarely agree on values, but they can agree on specific policies.

Because of the limits on human rationality, Lindblom proposes **incremental decision making,** or choosing policies most like the previous policy. Nonincremental policies are apolitical (not likely to bring agreement among important groups) and are dangerous because nobody knows to what they will lead.

Finally, choices are not "made." Instead, decision making is a continuous process in which final decisions are always being modified to accommodate changing objectives, environments, value preferences, and policy alternatives provided by decision makers.

Psychological Types and Frames of Reference

Modern psychology has provided a number of qualifications to the rational model. Psychologists have rarely challenged the basic premise that human beings are value maximizers and, in that sense, that they are rational. Instead, psychologists find that humans differ in *how they maximize their values* and in the *frames of reference* they use to interpret information and make choices (see the Window on Organizations).

Cognitive style describes underlying personality dispositions toward the treatment of information, the selection of alternatives, and the evaluation of consequences. McKenney and Keen (1974) described two cognitive styles that have direct relevance to information systems: systematic versus intuitive types. **Systematic decision makers** approach a problem by structuring it in terms of some formal method. They evaluate and gather information in terms of their structured method. **Intuitive decision makers** approach a problem with multiple methods, using trial and error to find a solution, and tend to not structure information gathering or evaluation. Neither type is superior to the other, but some types of thinking are more appropriate for certain tasks and roles in the organization.

The existence of different cognitive styles does not challenge the rational model of decision making. It simply says that there are different ways of being rational.

More recent psychological research poses strong challenges to the rational model by showing that humans have built-in biases that can distort decision making. Worse, people can be manipulated into choosing alternatives that they might otherwise reject simply by changing the *frame of reference.*

Tversky and Kahneman (1981), summarizing a decade of work on the psychology of decision making, found that humans have a deep-seated tendency to avoid risks when seeking gains but to accept risks to avoid losses. In other words, people are more sensitive to negative outcomes than to positive ones. College students refuse to bet $10, for instance, on a coin flip unless they stand to win at least $30. Other biases are listed in Table 4.8.

Because losses loom larger than gains, the credit card industry lobbied retailers aggressively to ensure that any price break given to cash customers would be presented publicly as a "cash discount" rather than a "credit card surcharge." Consumers would be less willing to accept a surcharge than to forgo a discount.

incremental decision making Choosing policies most like the previous policy.

cognitive style Underlying personality disposition toward the treatment of information, selection of alternatives, and evaluation of consequences.

systematic decision makers Cognitive style that describes people who approach a problem by structuring it in terms of some formal method.

intuitive decision makers Cognitive style that describes people who approach a problem with multiple methods in an unstructured manner, using trial and error to find a solution

4.4 ORGANIZATIONAL MODELS OF DECISION MAKING

For some purposes, it is useful to think of organizational decision making as similar to rational individual decision making. Organizations can be thought of as having singular goals, controlled by unitary rational decision makers who are completely in-

Table 4.8 Psychosocial Biases in Decision Making

1. People are more sensitive to negative consequences than to positive ones; for example, students generally refuse to flip a coin for $10 unless they have a chance to win $30.

2. People have no sensible model for dealing with improbable events and either ignore them or overestimate their likelihood; for example, one-in-a-million lotteries are popular, and people have an exaggerated fear of shark attacks.

3. People are more willing to accept a negative outcome if it is presented as a cost rather than a loss; for example, a man will continue playing tennis at an expensive club, despite a painful tennis elbow, by accepting the pain as a cost of the game rather than quit and accept the loss of an annual membership fee.

4. People given the same information will prefer alternatives with certain gains rather than alternatives with certain losses; people will gamble to avoid certain losses. For example, students and professional health workers were given the choice between alternative programs to fight a new disease that was expected to kill 600 people. When described in terms of lives saved, a large majority preferred a program that was certain to save 200 people over a program that had a possibility—but no certainty—of saving all 600. On the other hand, when presented in terms of lives lost, a large majority rejected a program that was guaranteed to lose 400 lives and preferred to gamble, against the odds, on a program that might save everyone but probably would lose everyone.

Source: A. Tversky and D. Kahneman, "The Framing of Decisions and The Psychology of Choice," in *Science*, 211, January, 1981.

formed, who choose among alternatives after weighing the consequences, and who act to maximize the goals of the organization. Thus, one can say, for instance, that General Motors "decided" to build a new type of automobile factory to make a profit on small cars.

But this simplified, shorthand way of talking about organizations should not conceal the fact that General Motors, and indeed any large organization, is composed of a number of specialized subgroups that are loosely coordinated, with each subgroup having a substantial life and capability of its own. What the organization ultimately does will be determined in large part by what the organizational subunits can do.

Organizations also are composed of a number of leaders who compete with each other for leadership. To a large extent, what the organization ultimately decides to do is the result of political competition among its leaders and staff.

Each of these perspectives reflects a different organizational model of decision making that is very different from the individual models previously described (see Table 4.9; also see Allison, 1971; Laudon, 1974; and Laudon, 1986, on which our analysis draws). An **organizational model** of decision making takes into account the structural and political characteristics of an organization. Bureaucratic, political, and even "garbage can" models have been proposed to describe how decision making takes place in organizations. We shall now consider each of these models.

organizational model Model of decision making that takes into account the structural and political characteristics of an organization.

Bureaucratic Models

The dominant idea of a **bureaucratic model** of decision making is that whatever organizations do is the result of standard operating procedures honed over years of active use. The particular actions chosen by an organization are an output of one or several organizational subunits (e.g., marketing, production, finance, human resources). The problems facing any organization are too massive and too complex to be attended by the organization as a whole. Problems are instead divided into their components and are parceled out to specialized groups. Competing with low-priced,

bureaucratic model Model of decision making where decisions are shaped by the organization's standard operating procedures (SOPs).

How do Juries Decide?

What is the difference between jury trials in England and in the United States? In England, the trial starts once jury selection ends; in the United States, the trial is already over. Recent research on the behavior of juries has supported this view. So goes an old lawyer's joke. But evidence is mounting that juries often hear evidence with a closed mind and reach verdicts using faulty reasoning.

Several studies have found that juries are susceptible to influence from the moment members are selected to the time of final deliberation. The research cites stories that juries tell themselves to make sense of the mounds of disconnected evidence they confront. Many jurors decide on a version of events based on a preliminary story that they find convincing, often at the time of opening arguments. These stories color jurors' interpretations so much that they seize on whatever fits their verdict and discount the rest. By the time such jurors enter the jury room for deliberation, they have already made up their minds.

A study conducted by Dr. Deanna Kuhn, a psychologist at the Columbia University Teachers College, attempted to simulate

jury decision making by having volunteers representing a typical jury view a videotaped reenactment of an actual murder trial and then explain how they reached their own verdicts. Close to one-third of the participants, those with the most flawed decision making, tended to be the most vehement about their certainty and argued for the most extreme verdicts as the jury deliberated. Instead of considering all alternatives, such jurors perceived their task as arguing for one version of events.

Because a trial boils down to two versions of a story—the prosecution's and the defense's, jury consultants explicitly identify the poor decision makers and then oppose or support them, depending on their point of view. Both sides then compete to devise the most dramatically compelling story to appeal to this group.

Another study conducted by Dr. Nancy Pennington, a University of Colorado psychologist, found that people do not listen to all the evidence and then evaluate it at the end. Instead, they process it as they go along, creating a continuing story throughout the trial so that they can make sense of what they are hearing. Jurors have little or nothing that will enable them to tie together all the facts presented at a trial unless an attorney suggests an interpretation in an opening statement that could provide a story line for them to follow.

Dr. Pennington, along with Dr. Reid Hastie, another University of Colorado psychologist, studied people called for jury duty who were not assigned to a trial and who were asked to participate as jurors for a simulated murder trial. When Dr. Pennington interviewed jurors to find out how they reached their verdicts, 45 percent of the references they made were to events that had not been included in the courtroom testimony, including inferences about the perpetrator and victim's motives and psychological states, and assumptions based on jurors' personal experiences. The stories the jurors told themselves pieced together the evidence in ways that could lead to opposite verdicts.

Jurors' backgrounds played a crucial role in the assumptions they brought to their stories. Middle-class jurors were more likely to find the defendant guilty than were working-class jurors, the difference hinging mainly on how these jurors interpreted the fact that the perpetrator had a knife with him during a struggle with the victim. Working-class jurors saw nothing incriminating about a man carrying a knife

for self-protection. Prosecutors seek out conservative and conformist jurors, while defense attorneys might look for people who are prone to conspiracy theories regarding crime labs and the police.

Other studies of jurors by psychologists have found that many tend to focus on the ability of victims to avoid being injured. Furthermore, Whites trust the honesty and fairness of the police far more than Blacks, and people who favor the death penalty tend to be pro-prosecution in criminal cases.

To Think About: *What do these studies of juries reveal about the decision-making process?*

Sources: Daniel Goleman, "Study Finds Jurors Often Hear Evidence with a Closed Mind," *The New York Times,* November 29, 1994; and "Jurors Hear Evidence and Turn It Into Stories," *The New York Times,* May 12, 1992.

Table 4.9 Models of Organizational Decision Making

Name	Basic Concept	Inference Pattern
Rational actor	Comprehensive rationality	Organizations select goals, examine all alternatives and consequences, and then choose a policy that maximizes the goal or preference function.
Bureaucratic	Organizational output Standard operating procedures	Goals are determined by resource constraints and existing human and capital resources; SOPs are combined into programs, programs into repertoires; these determine what policies will be chosen. The primary purpose of the organization is to survive; uncertainty reduction is the principal goal. Policies are chosen that are incrementally different from the past.
Political	Political outcome	Organizational decisions result from political competition; key players are involved in a game of influence, bargaining, and power. Organizational outcomes are determined by the beliefs and goals of players, their skills in playing the game, the resources they bring to bear, and the limits on their attention and power.
Garbage can	Nonadaptive organizational programs	Most organizations are nonadaptive, temporary, and disappear over time. Organizational decisions result from interactions among streams of problems, potential actions, participants, and chance.

high-quality Asian cars, for instance, is a complex problem. There are many aspects: production, labor relations, technology, marketing, finance, and even government regulation.

Each organizational subunit has a number of standard operating procedures (SOPs)—tried and proven techniques—that it invokes to solve a problem. Organizations rarely change these SOPs, because they may have to change personnel and incur risks. (Who knows if the new techniques work better than the old ones?)

SOPs are woven into the programs and repertoires of each subunit. Taken together, these repertoires constitute the range of effective actions that leaders of organizations can take. These repertoires are what the organization can do in the short term. As a U.S. president discovered in a moment of national crisis, his actions were largely constrained not by his imagination but by what his "pawns, bishops, and knights" were trained to do (see the Window on Management).

The organization generally perceives problems only through its specialized subunits. These specialized subunits, in turn, are concerned only with parts of the problem. They consciously ignore information not directly relevant to their part of the problem.

Blockade by the Book

In the evening of October 23, 1962, the Executive Committee of the President (EXCOM), a high-level working group of senior advisors to President John F. Kennedy, decided to impose a naval quarantine or blockade on Cuba to force the Soviet Union to remove its intermediate-range ballistic missiles from the island, located 90 miles south of Miami.

The naval blockade was chosen only after the Air Force reported that it could not conduct what the politicians in EXCOM called a "surgical air strike" to remove the missiles. Instead, the Air Force recommended a massive strategic air campaign against a number of ground, air, and naval Cuban targets. This was considered extreme by EXCOM, and the only other alternative seemed to be a blockade that would give Chairman Khrushchev plenty of time to think and develop several face-saving alternatives.

But EXCOM was worried that the Navy might blunder when implementing the blockade and cause an incident, which in turn could lead to World War III. Secretary of Defense Robert McNamara visited the Navy's chief of naval operations to make the point that the blockade was not intended to shoot Russians but rather to send a political message.

McNamara wanted to know the following: Which ship would make the first interception? Were Russian-speaking officers on board? In what way would submarines be handled? Would Russian ships be given the opportunity to turn back? What would the Navy do if Russian captains refused to answer questions about their cargo?

At that point, the chief of naval operations picked up the *Manual of Naval Regulations,* waved it at McNamara, and said "It's all in there." McNamara responded, "I don't give a damn what John Paul Jones would have done. I want to know what you are going to do tomorrow!"

The visit ended with the navy officer inviting the secretary of defense to go back to his office and let the Navy run the blockade.

To Think About: *What does this story tell you about decision making at a time of national crisis? Is such decision making rational?*

Source: Graham T. Allison, *Essence of Decision,* 1971.

Although senior management and leaders are hired to coordinate and lead the organization, they are effectively trapped by parochial subunits that feed information upward and that provide standard solutions. Senior management cannot decide to act in ways that the major subunits cannot support.

Some organizations do, of course, change; they learn new ways of behaving; and they can be led. But these changes require a long time. In general, organizations do not "choose" or "decide" in a rational sense; instead, they choose from among a very limited set of repertoires. The goals of organizations are multiple, not singular, and the most important goal is the preservation of the organization itself (e.g., the maintenance of budget, manpower, and territory). The reduction of uncertainty is another major goal. Policy tends to be incremental, only marginally different from the past, because radical policy departures involve too much uncertainty.

Political Models of Organizational Choice

Power in organizations is shared; even the lowest-level workers have some power. At the top, power is concentrated in the hands of a few. For many reasons, leaders differ in their opinions about what the organization should do. The differences matter, causing competition for leadership to ensue. Each individual in an organization, especially at the top, is a key player in the game of politics: Each is bargaining through a number of channels among players.

political model Model of decision making where decisions result from competition and bargaining among the organization's interest groups and key leaders.

In a **political model** of decision making, what an organization does is a result of political bargains struck among key leaders and interest groups. Actions are not necessarily rational, except in a political sense, and the outcome is not what any individual necessarily wanted. Instead, policy–organizational action is a compromise, a mixture of conflicting tendencies. Organizations do not invent "solutions" that are "chosen" to solve some "problem." They develop compromises that reflect the conflicts, the major stake holders, the diverse interests, the unequal power, and the confusion that constitutes politics.

Political models of organizations depict decision makers as having limited attention spans; participating in tens (sometimes hundreds) of games and issues; and being susceptible to misperception, extraneous influences, miscommunication, and pressures of impending deadlines. Players in the game focus almost entirely on the short-term problem: What decision must be made today? Long-term strategic thinking for the whole organization goes by the wayside as individual decision makers focus on their short-term interests and on the part of the problem in which they are interested.

"Garbage Can" Model

The preceding models of organizational choice take as their starting point the basic notion that organizations try to adapt, and for the most part do so successfully, to changing environmental conditions. Presumably, over the long run, organizations develop new programs and actions to meet their goals of profit, survival, and so on.

In Chapter 3 we pointed out that many organizations do not survive. There are surprisingly few theories that explicitly address the fact that organizations are quite short lived. One such theory of decision making, called the **"garbage can" model,** states that organizations are not rational. Decision making is largely accidental and is the product of a stream of solutions, problems, and situations that are randomly associated. That is, solutions become attached to problems for accidental reasons: Organizations are filled with solutions looking for problems and decision makers looking for work.

garbage can model Model of decision making that states that organizations are not rational and that decisions are solutions that become attached to problems for accidental reasons.

If this model is correct, it should not be surprising that the wrong solutions are applied to the wrong problems in an organization, or that, over time, a large number of organizations make critical mistakes that lead to their demise. The Exxon Corporation's delayed response to the 1989 Alaska oil spill is an example. Within an hour after the Exxon tanker *Valdez* ran aground in Alaska's Prince William Sound on March 29, 1989, workers were preparing emergency equipment; however, the aid was not dispatched. Instead of sending out emergency crews, the Alyeska Pipeline Service Company (which was responsible for initially responding to oil spill emergencies) sent the crews home. The first full emergency crew did not arrive at the spill site until at least 14 hours after the shipwreck. By the time the vessel was finally surrounded by floating oil containment booms, the oil had spread beyond effective control. Yet enough equipment and personnel had been available to respond effectively. Much of the 10 million gallons of oil fouling the Alaska shoreline in the worst tanker spill in American history could have been confined had Alyeska acted more decisively (Malcolm, 1989).

4.5   HOW INFORMATION TECHNOLOGY HAS CHANGED THE MANAGEMENT PROCESS

There is a vast difference between how traditional managers fulfilled the management functions we have just described, and how contemporary managers act. And there is a corresponding vast difference between how managers solved problems in the past and how they increasingly do it today. Researchers such as Rosabeth Moss Kanter and others have found contemporary organizations to be less hierarchical, more collaborative, more egalitarian, and more dependent on cross-functional teams. To manage organizations such as these, modern managers need to build networks among employees at all levels and to rely more on horizontal relationships than hierarchical ones (Kanter, 1989).

Information technology has played a role in the changing process of management by providing powerful tools for managers to carry out both their traditional and newer roles. Contemporary information systems permit managers rapidly to obtain, analyze, and comprehend vast quantities of data. Middle and senior managers can use management information systems (MIS) and executive support systems (ESS) to monitor day-to-day operations at any level of detail needed, from the most general down to the specific transaction, employee, or customer. Decision-support systems (DSS) and executive support systems (ESS) do not necessarily guarantee more accurate and predictive forecasting—that also depend upon many other factors such as the skill of the planner. But they do enable a more comprehensive examination of both the data and the issues (see Chapter 16). Additionally, they enable managers to respond more quickly to the rapidly changing business environment. Managers monitor, plan, and forecast with more precision and speed than ever before.

Managers can also use information systems to give employees more responsibility and decision-making power in the "new" organization. Employees are working more and more in electronic environments (as opposed to face-to-face environments). Electronic mail and other network-based forms of communication enable managers to broaden their span of control and manage workers and organizations wherever they are located. With new group communication and coordination technologies, including the Internet, managers can establish and manage flexible work groups and short-term task forces from around the world that bring together just the right mix of skills for the task at hand. Information can be rapidly distributed to workers so that they can act independently.

Traditional and Contemporary Management

Table 4.10 lists some of the differences between contemporary and traditional management and the role played by information technology. Although information technology supports new ways of managing and organizing, it is not the only reason why these changes are taking place. General cultural and economic changes in attitudes and the nature of work are important factors.

Many organizations today believe that the key assets of the organization are knowledge and core competencies from which all products and services derive. Without these, the financial and physical assets of the firm would be worthless. Contemporary views rely much more on the involvement, enabling, and empowering of lower-level managers and workers. The assumption here is that employees and managers know what to do, want to work hard and succeed, and believe in the goals of the firm. The job of management—especially senior management—is to make it possible for the employees to achieve their goals and the company's goals. A very important part of organizational success in the contemporary view is developing a proper understanding of the environment, opening the organization to outside influences, and in general adjusting the organization to contemporary social and ethical currents.

These contemporary views of management and organizations are often directly at odds with the old style of management and organizations. In these more traditional views, workers must be told what to do, do not want to work hard, and either do not know or do not care about the goals of the firm. In these circumstances, management must be micromanagement, involve extensive and costly control systems, and result in centralized organizations where senior management plays critical operational roles.

In older and larger organizations, traditional management styles are pervasive. In younger, entrepreneurial, and smaller organizations, more contemporary management styles are common although not universal. Many Fortune 500 firms are seeking to adopt contemporary management styles as their products, services, and employees change.

Implications for System Design

The research on management decision making has a number of implications for information systems design and understanding. First, managers use formal information systems to plan, organize, and coordinate. However, they also use them for a variety of other less obvious (but vital) tasks such as interpersonal communication, setting and carrying out personal agendas, and establishing a network throughout the organization. This should remind information system designers that there are multiple uses for their products and that the way systems are actually used may not, in fact, reflect the original intention of the designers.

Another implication of contemporary investigations of managers is that formal information systems may have limited impact on managers. Formal systems may have an important role to play at the operational level but are less critical at the middle and senior management levels. General managers may briefly glance at the output of formal information systems, but they rarely study them in great detail. Ad hoc (less formal) information systems that can be built quickly, use more current and up-to-date information, and can be adjusted to the unique situations of a specific group of managers are highly valued by the modern manager. Systems designers and builders should appreciate the importance of creating systems that can process information at the most general level; communicate with other sources of information, both inside and outside the organization; and provide an effective means of communication among managers and employees within the organization.

Research also shows that decision making is not a simple process, even in the rigorous rational model. There are limits to human computation, foresight, and analytical powers. Decision situations differ from one another in terms of the clarity of goals, the types of decision makers present, the amount of agreement among them, and the frames of reference brought to a decision-making situation. An important role of information systems is not to make the decision for humans but rather to support the decision-making process. How this is done will depend on the types of decisions, decision makers, and frames of reference.

The research on organizational decision making should alert students of information systems to the fact that decision making in a business is a group and organizational process. Systems must be built to support group and organizational decision making.

Systems must do more than merely promote decision making. They must also make individual managers better managers of existing routines, better players in the bureaucratic struggle for control of an organization's agenda, and better political players. Finally, for those who resist the "garbage can" tendencies in large organizations, systems should help bring a measure of power to those who can attach the right solution to the right problem.

As a general rule, research on management decision making indicates that information systems designers should design systems that have the following characteristics:

- They are flexible, with many options for handling data, evaluating information, and accommodating changes in individual and organizational learning and growth.

- They are capable of supporting a variety of styles, skills, and knowledge, and both individual and organizational processes of decision making.

- They are powerful in the sense of having multiple analytical and intuitive models for the evaluation of data and the ability to keep track of many alternatives and consequences.

- They reflect the bureaucratic and political requirements of systems, with features to accommodate diverse interests.

- They reflect an appreciation of the limits of organizational change in policy and in procedure and awareness of what information systems can and cannot do.

Table 4.10   Traditional and Contemporary Management

Management Schools	Traditional	Contemporary	Role of Information Technology
Technical–Rational School			
Analysis of work	Time/motion studies to increase efficiency of individual workers	Analyze groups of workers and entire business processes	Use IT to "reengineer" business processes, seeking quick but drastic increases in productivity
Administration	Develop intricate, hierarchical reporting structures	Analyze the flow of information	Use IT as "workflow" software making the movement of documents more efficient for information-intense service sector organizations
Behavioral School			
Planning	Top-down centralized planning by senior management	Decentralized involving all units and employees with management support	Use IT such as the Internet to involve more people in the planning process
Organizing	Management defines a stable division of labor	Enable employees to self-organize project teams	Use networks to facilitate self-organizing teams
Leading	Management inspires or threatens employees to perform	Enable employees to do their jobs as well as they can and know how; build and activate networks; all employees lead	Use networks to maintain contact with subordinates and to supervise their work
Controlling	Develop precise micromanagement control systems	Push controls down to project teams; use peer group controls; focus on overall results with computer-based systems	Use IT to develop real-time organizational controls
Innovating	Centralized, specialized product research and design units	Innovations come from customers, employees, and managers at all levels	Use electronic conferencing and other techniques to generate new ideas for business; groupware and group decision support tools helpful
Environments	Hostile and competitive, requires strong boundaries and defensive posture	Competitive but potential for alliances, resources, and coalitions; requires proactive adjustment, proper understanding to succeed	Use IT to continuously monitor key environmental changes; encourage use of nonroutine sources of information to overcome organizational biases
Cognitive School			
Sense-making	Individual managers impose "sense" on the situation of the firm	Formal and informal information systems affect group sense-making activities	Build information systems as reality checkers with much information that cannot be filtered out by biased individuals and groups
Organizational learning	Organizational knowledge is captured by the routines, procedures, and business processes of the firm	Organizational knowledge is captured by the information systems—formal and informal—which operate the organization	Use information technology explicitly to create, store, and disseminate organizational knowledge using datamining, multimedia, and the Internet
Knowledge base	Financial and physical assets are the foundation of the firm	Core competencies, knowledge, and knowledge workers are key assets	Use information technology to capture core competency in software where possible; use IT to coordinate and manage the work of knowledge workers to enhance their productivity

Information technology provides new tools for enhancing and transforming the management process. However, the central issue for management is whether the new information technologies such as the Web can overcome the built-in psychosocial biases that permeate middle and higher management ranks. The single most common cause of organizational failure is the management misperception of market environments. The second most common cause of organizational failure is the inability of management to bring about needed changes (assuming they have correctly perceived the problem).

MANAGEMENT

It's clear that there are new ways of organizing work which are enabled in part by new technology. The central organizational issue is whether traditional organizations can change their internal structures—their business processes—to permit new ways of organizing to emerge. Or, alternatively, will the competitive marketplace require the timely demise of traditional organizations and their replacement by entirely new organizations? The ability of organizations to adapt is still an issue.

ORGANIZATION

Each of the three schools of management can draw on information technology to enhance managerial effectiveness. Networks and communication and collaboration tools are especially useful for supporting managerial work in the "new" organization where more work is distributed among small groups and task forces and more responsibility given to employees.

TECHNOLOGY

For Discussion: How would each of the three schools of management use information systems to make managers and organizations more effective?

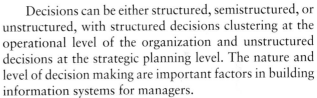

SUMMARY

1. Understand the three main schools of management thinking. The three main schools of management thinking are technical–rational, behavioral, and cognitive. Each of these schools provides a different perspective on the process of management. Early technical–rational (or classical) models of management stressed the design of job tasks and management functions of planning, organizing, coordinating, deciding, and controlling. Research from the behavioral school has examined the actual behavior of managers to show how managers get things done. Mintzberg found that managers' real activities are highly fragmented, variegated, and brief in duration, with managers moving rapidly and intensely from one issue to another. Other behavioral research has found that managers spend considerable time pursuing personal agendas and goals and that contemporary managers shy away from making grand, sweeping policy decisions. The behavioral school also emphasizes employee relations and organizational adaptation to its environment. The cognitive school emphasizes the role of knowledge in organizational effectiveness and managers as information processors and problem solvers.

2. Describe the levels, types, and stages of decision making. Decision making in an organization can be classified by organizational level: strategic, management control, knowledge, and operational control.

Decisions can be either structured, semistructured, or unstructured, with structured decisions clustering at the operational level of the organization and unstructured decisions at the strategic planning level. The nature and level of decision making are important factors in building information systems for managers.

Decision making itself is a complex activity at both the individual and the organizational level. Simon described four different stages in decision making: intelligence, design, choice, and implementation.

3. Identify models for describing individual and organizational decision making. Rational models of decision making assume that human beings can accurately choose alternatives and consequences based on the priority of their objectives and goals. The rigorous rational model of individual decision making has been modified by behavioral research that suggests that rationality is limited. People "satisfice," "muddle through" decisions incrementally, or select alternatives biased by their cognitive style and frame of reference.

Organizational models of decision making illustrate that real decision making in organizations takes place in arenas where many psychological, political, and bureaucratic forces are at work. Thus, organizational decision making may not necessarily be rational. The design of information systems must accommodate these realities, recognizing that decision making is never a simple process.

4. Describe how information technology has changed the management process. Information technology has changed all three dimensions of management. IT has made possible the realization of many dreams of the technical–rational school including rational design of business processes, fine-grained monitoring of organizational activities, and real-time management response to environmental changes. IT has changed the behavioral dimension of management by enabling decentralization, empowerment, self-organization, and the sharing of responsibility. At the same time, the cognitive dimension of management has received new importance by the emergence of technologies which can greatly expand the knowledge base of a firm.

5. Explain how information systems can assist managers and improve managerial decision making. If information systems are built properly, they can support individual and organizational decision making. Up to now, information systems have been most helpful to managers for performing informational and decisional roles; the same systems have been of very limited value for managers' interpersonal roles. Information systems that are less formal and highly flexible will be more useful than large, formal systems at higher levels of the organization.

The design of information systems must accommodate these realities. Designers must recognize that decision making is never a simple process. Information systems can best support managers and decision making if such systems are flexible, with multiple analytical and intuitive models for evaluating data and the capability of supporting a variety of styles, skills, and knowledge.

KEY TERMS

Technical–rational classical perspective	Management control	Choice	Systematic decision makers
Behavioral perspective	Knowledge-level decision making	Implementation	Intuitive decision makers
Managerial roles	Operational control	Rational model	Organizational model
Interpersonal roles	Unstructured decisions	Satisficing	Bureaucratic model
Informational roles	Structured decisions	Bounded rationality	Political model
Decisional roles	Semistructured decisions	Muddling through	Garbage can model
Cognitive perspective	Intelligence	Incremental decision making	
Strategic decision making	Design	Cognitive style	

REVIEW QUESTIONS

1. Describe the key ideas in the technical–rational (classical) school of management. What are the five functions of managers described in the classical model?

2. Describe the key ideas in the behavioral perspective on management. What characteristics of modern managers does the behavioral school emphasize?

3. What specific managerial roles can information systems support? Where are information systems particularly strong in supporting managers, and where are they weak?

4. What did Wrapp and Kotter discover about the way managers make decisions and get things done? How do these findings compare with those of the classical model?

5. Describe the key ideas of the cognitive perspective on management.

6. Define structured and unstructured decisions. Give three examples of each.

7. What are the four kinds of computer-based information systems that support decisions?

8. What are the four stages of decision making described by Simon?

9. Describe each of the four individual models of decision making. What is the name, basic concept, and dominant inference pattern of each? How would the design of information systems be affected by the model of decision making employed?

10. Describe each of the four organizational choice models. How would the design of systems be affected by the choice of model employed?

11. How has the management process changed? What is the role played by information technology?

GROUP PROJECT

Form a group with three to four of your classmates. Observe a manager for one hour. Classify the observed behavior in two ways, using the classical model and then the behavioral model. Compare the results and discuss the difficulties of coding the behavior. Present your findings to the class.

Fisher SpacePen's Management Time Warp

Paul Fisher, an economist with an interest in science, decided in 1948 to make his mark in business by designing a better ballpoint pen. The Fisher Pen Company thrived with its smooth-writing ink cartridges, but it was the 1960s space race that inspired Fisher's most exciting innovation. His SpacePen was a pressurized pen that could write under almost any condition, including zero gravity and vacuum. The pen became the standard issue for astronauts, and Fisher was able to parlay NASA's seal of approval and the nation's space craze into a booming business. By the early 1970s, Fisher's company was realizing annual sales of approximately $6 million. Fisher renamed his business the Fisher SpacePen Co.

But, the country's enthusiasm about the space program waned by the late 1970s and Fisher SpacePen Co. sales remained flat at around $7 million through the early 1980s. Fisher had no striking new products or sizzling marketing strategies to compensate.

Fisher's sons, Cary and Morgan, who by then had joined the business, realized the company's approach to marketing and finance was out of date, but their father refused to talk about new management tools. The senior Fisher, a scientist by nature, was so obsessed with perfecting ink formulas, which he believed was the only way to grow a successful company, that he couldn't make simple management decisions. He didn't even raise prices in one six-year period. Except for a few standalone PCs, a primitive accounting program, and a fax machine, nothing in the company was automated.

Sales operations were in shambles. The system for tracking sales leads was a notebook and some scraps of paper. With no way to organize sales

leads by region, a salesperson might travel to a state for only one sales call. The company didn't maintain historical sales data, making forecasting impossible. One year the company lost $400,000 because it miscalculated demand on certain products.

Fisher's management style was stifling any chance for growth. A technical infrastructure had to be built from the ground up to give sales the support it needed to function competitively, and to provide the information required to successfully market the company's products.

The Fisher sons knew that a technological overhaul was needed, but the elder Fisher could not be moved. It wasn't until 1992 that a chance meeting between Cary and a business consultant signaled the beginning of a new era for Fisher SpacePen. After meeting at an industry trade show, Cary hired Jim Jobin, a marketing director and longtime fan of the SpacePen. It was Jobin who ultimately convinced the elder Fisher of the benefits of the newer computer products. Jobin simply drew upon Fisher's fascination with gadgetry by playing up the technological marvels of computers. Fisher provided a $35,000 computer budget, and the company began its transformation.

Jobin and Cary bought PCs, linking them via a network and running wires through the company's offices on weekends. Once the network was up, Jobin bought ACT, a contact-management program from Symantec, and began creating a sales database. An 800 number connected the laptops of salespeople in the field to the D&B Market Place database on CD-ROM allowing salespeople to update leads while they were out on the road. The average number of sales calls needed before a sales close dropped from five

to two. Fifty-three new salespeople have been hired, many of them to work on international sales. The company has realized thousands of dollars on marketing materials since Jobin moved production in house.

The senior Fisher was persuaded to get on the Internet after Jobin showed him that other companies, including The Sharper Image, were making money selling SpacePens on the World Wide Web. The company set up its first Web site in February 1996.

In the past year sales at Fisher SpacePen Co. have skyrocketed from $3.5 million to $5.8 million. At the same time, administrative costs associated with sales have dropped by approximately 30 percent. The future is looking bright for Fisher SpacePen Co. ■

Source: Sarah Schafer, "A Space Odyssey Pen," *Inc. Technology,* June 18, 1996.

Case Study Questions

1. What problems did Fisher SpacePen Co. have? What management, organization, and technology factors were responsible for these problems?

2. How were the various management perspectives described in Section 4.1 reflected in the problems facing Fisher SpacePen Company?

3. What was the relationship between the company's management and its information systems?

4. Information-intensive management techniques have transformed business processes at the Fisher SpacePen Company. Do you agree? Why or why not?

REFERENCES

Adams, Carl. R., and Jae Hyon Song. "Integrating Decision Technologies: Implications for Management Curriculum." *MIS Quarterly* 13, no. 2 (June 1989).

Allison, Graham T. *Essence of Decision—Explaining the Cuban Missile Crisis*. Boston: Little, Brown (1971).

Anthony, R. N. "Planning and Control Systems: A Framework for Analysis." Harvard University Graduate School of Business Administration (1965).

Arrow, Kenneth J. *Information and Economic Behavior*. Stockholm: Federation of Swedish Industries (1972).

Badaracco, Joseph. *The Knowledge Link: How Firms Compete Through Strategic Alliances*. Boston: Harvard Business School Press (1991).

Boulding, Kenneth. "The Economics of Knowledge and the Knowledge of Economics." *American Economic Review* (May 1966).

Cohen, Michael, James March, and Johan Olsen. "A Garbage Can Model of Organizational Choice." *Administrative Science Quarterly* 17 (1972).

George, Joey. "Organizational Decision Support Systems." *Journal of Management Information Systems* 8, no. 3 (Winter 1991–1992).

Gorry, G. Anthony, and Michael S. Scott-Morton. "A Framework for Management Information Systems." *Sloan Management Review* 13, no. 1 (Fall 1971).

Grobowski, Ron, Chris McGoff, Doug Vogel, Ben Martz, and Jay Nunamaker. "Implementing Electronic Meeting Systems at IBM: Lessons Learned and Success Factors." *MIS Quarterly* 14, no. 4 (December 1990).

Huber, George P. "Cognitive Style as a Basis for MIS and DSS Designs: Much Ado About Nothing?" *Management Science* 29 (May 1983).

Huber, George. "Organizational Learning: The Contributing Processes and Literature." *Organization Science*, 2 (1991), pp. 88–115.

Isenberg, Daniel J. "How Senior Managers Think." *Harvard Business Review* (November–December 1984).

Ives, Blake, and Margrethe H. Olson. "Manager or Technician? The Nature of the Information Systems Manager's Job." *MIS Quarterly* (December 1981).

Jensen, M. C., and W. H. Meckling. "Specific and General Knowledge and Organizational Science." In *Contract Economics*, edited by L. Wetin and J. Wijkander. Oxford: Basil Blackwell (1992).

Jessup, Leonard M., Terry Connolly, and Jolene Galegher. "The Effects of Anonymity on GDSS Group Process with an Idea-Generating Task." *MIS Quarterly* 14, no. 3 (September 1990).

Kanter, Rosabeth Moss. "The New Managerial Work." *Harvard Business Review* (November–December 1989).

Kotter, John T. "What Effective General Managers Really Do." *Harvard Business Review* (November–December 1982).

Laudon, Kenneth C. *Computers and Bureaucratic Reform*. New York: Wiley, 1974.

———. *Dossier Society: Value Choices in the Design of National Information Systems*. New York: Columbia University Press, 1986.

Leonard-Barton, Dorothy. *Wellsprings of Knowledge: Building and Sustaining the Sources of Innovation*. Boston: Harvard Business School Press (1995).

Lindblom, C. E. "The Science of Muddling Through." *Public Administration Review* 19 (1959).

Machlup, Fritz. *The Production and Distribution of Knowledge in the United States*. Princeton, NJ: Princeton University Press (1962).

Malcolm, Andrew H. "How the Oil Spilled and Spread: Delay and Confusion Off Alaska." *The New York Times* (April 16, 1989).

March, James G., and G. Sevon. "Gossip, Information and Decision Making." In *Advances in Information Processing in Organizations*, edited by Lee S. Sproull and J. P. Crecine. vol. 1. Hillsdale, NJ: Erlbaum (1984).

March, James G., and Herbert A. Simon. *Organizations*. New York: Wiley (1958).

Markus, M. L. "Power, Politics, and MIS Implementation." *Communications of the ACM* 26, no. 6 (June 1983).

McKenney, James L., and Peter G. W. Keen. "How Managers' Minds Work." *Harvard Business Review* (May–June 1974).

Mintzberg, Henry. "Managerial Work: Analysis from Observation." *Management Science* 18 (October 1971).

———. *The Nature of Managerial Work*. New York: Harper & Row (1973).

Orlikowski, Wanda J. "The Duality of Technology: Rethinking the Concept of Technology in Organizations." *Organization Science* 3, no. 3 (August 1992).

Orlikowski, Wanda J., and Daniel Robey. "Information Technology and the Structuring of Organizations." *Information Systems Research* 2, no. 2 (June 1991).

Prahalad, C. K., and Gary Hamel. "The Core Competence of the Corporation," *Harvard Business Review* (May–June 1990).

Quinn, James B. *Intelligent Enterprise: A Knowledge and Service Based Paradigm for Industry*. New York: Free Press (1992).

Schwenk, C. R. "Cognitive Simplification Processes in Strategic Decision Making," *Strategic Management Journal*, 5 (1984).

Simon, H. A. *The New Science of Management Decision*. New York: Harper & Row (1960).

Starbuck, William H. "Organizations as Action Generators." *American Sociological Review* 48 (1983).

Starbuck, William H., and Frances J. Milliken. "Executives' Perceptual Filters: What They Notice and How They Make Sense." In *The Executive Effect: Concepts and Methods for Studying Top Managers*, edited by D. C. Hambrick. Greenwich, CT: JAI Press (1988).

Tversky, A., and D. Kahneman. "The Framing of Decisions and the Psychology of Choice." *Science* 211 (January 1981).

Wrapp, H. Edward. "Good Managers Don't Make Policy Decisions." *Harvard Business Review* (July–August 1984).

Ethical and Social Impact of Information Systems

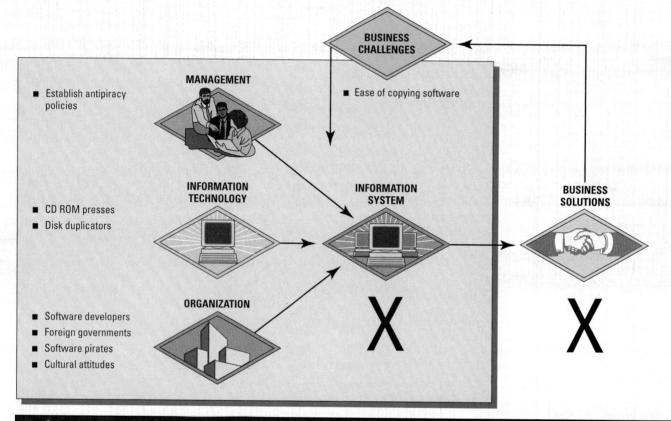

BUSINESS CHALLENGES

MANAGEMENT

- Establish antipiracy policies

■ Ease of copying software

INFORMATION TECHNOLOGY

- CD ROM presses
- Disk duplicators

INFORMATION SYSTEM

BUSINESS SOLUTIONS

ORGANIZATION

- Software developers
- Foreign governments
- Software pirates
- Cultural attitudes

X

X

Software Piracy Is Big Business

Almost everyone has been tempted to copy software. You might be low on funds. You might be too pressed for time to go out and buy a copy for yourself. Your manager might tell you to buy one copy of a product for your department and make copies to keep costs down. Many people copy the software and keep on working without a second thought, even though it's illegal.

What would happen if everyone around the world copied the software they used? For one thing, they would be cheating software developers out of billions of dollars. In 1995, software piracy around the world created losses of over $13.2 billion, an amount exceeding the

LEARNING OBJECTIVES

After completing this chapter, you will be able to:

1. Understand the relationship among ethical, social, and political issues raised by information systems.
2. Identify the main moral dimensions of an information society and apply them to specific situations.
3. Apply an ethical analysis to difficult situations.
4. Understand specific ethical principles for conduct.
5. Develop corporate policies for ethical conduct.

---

combined revenues of the ten largest PC software companies. And in some countries, software piracy is big business. In China, Russia, the Philippines, and El Salvador, more than 90 percent of the software in use was copied illegally. These are some key findings of a study released by the Software Publishers Association (SPA) and the Business Software Alliance. The SPA is the principal trade association of the desktop software industry and is active in protecting intellectual property rights around the world.

On another occasion, the SPA noted in its annual "Special 301" review of unfair international trade practices for the U.S. Trade Repre-sentative (USTR) that Indonesia and Vietnam have piracy rates of 98 percent. The SPA called them "one-copy" countries, where the entire country's demand could be satisfied by copying a single, legitimate piece of software.

SPA credited the Chinese government with raiding pirate CD-ROM factories and with trying to establish a software title verification program to deter them. Nevertheless, the software piracy rate in China remains 95 percent, virtually unchanged. The SPA applauded the raids reported by the Chinese government but noted that there were no reports indicating fines or prison sentences for the offenders, nor were there any indica-tions that the pirated software was taken off the market.

Enforcement of anti-piracy laws in Russia is impeded by the weakness of the country's police and court system. Despite a new criminal code, criminal penalties remain low. A huge "installed base" of pirated software cannot be eradicated because software created by U.S. authors before 1993 is unprotected by copyright.

The software piracy rate is lower in the United States. The culture respects intellectual property and there are effective enforcement mechanisms. According to Ken Wasch, president of SPA, the only companies using illegally copied software who are safe in the United States "are those who have no disgruntled employees." About 95 percent of the calls SPA receives each day reporting software piracy come from current or former employees of the companies being reported.

Users are hurt by software piracy as well as the software developers because they pay higher prices to offset the losses. If piracy could be curbed, many software firms would have the resources to invest more in research and development to improve their products. Large software companies can survive piracy, but many small firms cannot afford to lose 30 to 50 percent of their revenue. According to Greg Wrenn, corporate counsel at Adobe Systems Inc. in Mountain View, California, "The loss to consumers is the innovation they bring." ∎

Sources: Software Publishers Association, "Argentina, China and Russia Among Top Priorities in SPA 'Special 301' Report," February 18, 1997; and Gary H. Anthes, "Software Pirates Booty Topped $13B, Study Finds," *Computerworld*, January 6, 1997.

MANAGEMENT CHALLENGES

Technology can be a double-edged sword. It can be the source of many benefits. One great achievement of contemporary computer systems is the ease with which digital information can be so easily transmitted and shared among many people. But at the same time, this powerful capability creates new opportunities for breaking the law or taking benefits away from others. Copying software and other digital media is one of the compelling ethical issues raised by contemporary information systems. As you read this chapter, you should be aware of the following management challenges:

1. **Understanding the moral risks of new technology.** Rapid technological change means that the choices facing individuals also rapidly change, and the balance of risk and reward and the probabilities of apprehension for wrongful acts change as well. Software copying has emerged as a new ethical issue precisely for this reason, in addition to other issues described in this chapter. In this environment it will be important for management to conduct an ethical and social impact analysis of new technologies. One might take each of the moral dimensions described in this chapter and briefly speculate on how a new technology will impact each dimension. There will be no right answers for how to behave but there should be considered management judgment on the moral risks of new technology.

2. **Establishing corporate ethics policies that include information systems issues.** As managers you will be responsible for developing corporate ethics policies and for enforcing them and explaining them to employees. Historically the information systems area is the last to be consulted and much more attention has been paid to financial integrity and personnel policies. But from what you will know after reading this chapter, it is clear your corporation should have an ethics policy in the information systems area covering such issues as privacy, property, accountability, system quality, and quality of life. The challenge will be in educating non-IS managers to the need for these policies, as well as educating your work force.

S oftware piracy challenges traditional protections of intellectual property rights and is one of the new ethical issues raised by the widespread use of information systems. Others include establishing information rights, including the right to privacy; establishing accountability for the consequences of information systems; setting standards to safeguard system quality that protect the safety of the individual and society; and preserving values and institutions considered essential to the quality of life in an information society. This chapter describes these issues and suggests guidelines for dealing with these questions.

5.1 UNDERSTANDING ETHICAL AND SOCIAL ISSUES RELATED TO SYSTEMS

Ethics refers to the principles of right and wrong that can be used by individuals acting as free moral agents to make choices to guide their behavior. Information technology and information systems raise new ethical questions for both individuals and societies because they create opportunities for intense social change, and thus threaten existing distributions of power, money, rights, and obligations. Like other technologies, such as steam engines, electricity, telephone, and radio, information technology can be used to achieve social progress, but it can also be used to commit crimes and threaten cherished social values. The development of information technology will produce benefits for many, and costs for others. In this situation, what is the ethical and socially responsible course of action?

ethics Principles of right and wrong that can be used by individuals acting as free moral agents to make choices to guide their behavior.

A Model for Thinking about Ethical, Social, and Political Issues

Ethical, social, and political issues are of course tightly coupled together. The ethical dilemma you may face as a manager of information systems typically is reflected in social and political debate. One way to think about these relationships is given in Figure 5.1. Imagine society as a more or less calm pond on a summer day, a delicate ecosystem in partial equilibrium with individuals and with social and political institutions. Individuals know how to act in this pond because social institutions (family, education, organizations) have developed well-honed rules of behavior, and these are backed by laws developed in the political sector that prescribe behavior and promise sanctions for violations. Now toss a rock into the center of the pond. But imagine instead of a rock that the disturbing force is a powerful shock of new information technology and systems hitting a society more or less at rest. What happens? Ripples, of course.

Suddenly individual actors are confronted with new situations often not covered by the old rules. Social institutions cannot respond overnight to these ripples—it may take years to develop etiquette, expectations, social responsibility, "politically correct" attitudes, or approved rules. Political institutions also require time before developing new laws and often require the demonstration of real harm before they act. In the meantime, you may have to act. You may be forced to act in a legal "gray area."

We can use this model as a first approximation to the dynamics which connect ethical, social, and political issues. This model is also useful for identifying the main moral dimensions of the "information society" which cut across various levels of action—individual, social, and political.

Five Moral Dimensions of the Information Age

A review of the literature on ethical, social, and political issues surrounding systems identifies five moral dimensions of the information age that we introduce here and explore in greater detail in Section 5.3. The five moral dimensions are as follows:

- *Information rights and obligations:* What **information rights** do individuals and organizations possess with respect to information about themselves? What can they protect? What obligations do individuals and organizations have concerning this information?

- *Property rights:* How will traditional intellectual property rights be protected in a digital society in which tracing and accounting for ownership is difficult, and ignoring such property rights is so easy?

information rights The rights that individuals and organizations have with respect to information which pertains to themselves.

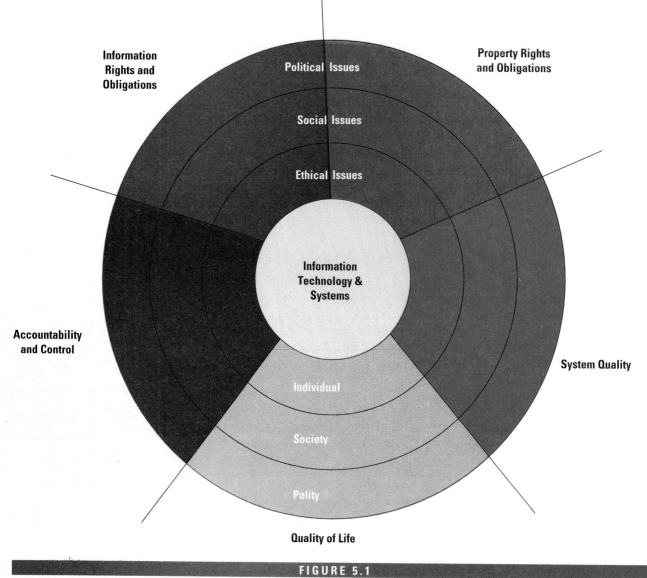

FIGURE 5.1

The relationship between ethical, social, and political issues in an information society. The introduction of new information technology has a ripple effect, raising new ethical, social, and political issues that must be dealt with on the individual, social, and political levels. These issues have five moral dimensions: information rights and obligations, property rights and obligations, system quality, quality of life, and accountability and control.

- *Accountability and control:* Who can and will be held accountable and liable for the harm done to individual and collective information and property rights?
- *System quality:* What standards of data and system quality should we demand to protect individual rights and the safety of society?
- *Quality of life:* What values should be preserved in an information- and knowledge-based society? What institutions should we protect from violation? What cultural values and practices are supported by the new information technology?

Before we analyze these dimensions let us briefly review the major technology and system trends which have heightened concern about these issues.

Key Technology Trends That Raise Ethical Issues

These ethical issues long preceded information technology—they are the abiding concerns of free societies everywhere. Nevertheless, information technology has heightened ethical concerns, put stress on existing social arrangements, and made existing laws obsolete or severely crippled. There are four key technological trends responsible for these ethical stresses.

The doubling of computing power every 18 months has made it possible for most organizations to utilize information systems for their core production processes. As a result, our dependence on systems and our vulnerability to system errors and poor data quality have increased. Occasional system failures heighten public concern over our growing dependence on some critical systems. Social rules and laws have not yet adjusted to this dependence. Standards for ensuring the accuracy and reliability of information systems (see Chapter 17) are not universally accepted or enforced.

Advances in data storage techniques and rapidly declining storage costs have been responsible for the multiplying databases on individuals—employees, customers, and potential customers—maintained by private and public organizations. These advances in data storage have made the routine violation of individual privacy both cheap and effective. For example, EMASS Storage Systems of Denver has a DataTower mass storage facility that can hold between 1 to 6 trillion characters of data in approximately 25 square feet of space, with a record access time of a few seconds. Consider that the Social Security Master Beneficiary File with over 50 million names could be put on this EMASS system and take up only a fraction of the space! Already massive data storage systems are cheap enough for regional and even local retailing firms to use in identifying customers.

Advances in datamining techniques for large databases are a third technological trend that heightens ethical concerns, because they enable companies to find out much detailed, personal information about individuals. The Window on Organizations in Chapter 2 describes how American Express, Bank of America, and others can use datamining on very large pools of data from multiple sources to rapidly identify buying patterns of customers and suggest individualized responses.

Making a purchase with a credit card can make personal information available to market researchers, telephone marketers, and direct mail companies. Advances in information technology facilitate the invasion of privacy.

Last, *advances in telecommunications infrastructure* such as Integrated Services Digital Network (ISDN—see Chapter 10) and the Internet promise to reduce greatly the cost of moving large quantities of data, and open the possibility of mining large data sets remotely using smaller desktop machines.

Information technology advances are starting to permit the invasion of privacy on a scale and precision heretofore unimaginable. Even the Census Bureau would lose its shelter: With commonly available census data on blocks, along with other data, we could easily pick out information about individuals with great regularity. The Window on Organizations in Chapter 8, describing how companies can combine data from visitors to Web sites with other internal data and census data, shows how this is starting to happen.

The development of global digital superhighway communication networks widely available to individuals and businesses poses many ethical and social concerns. Who will account for the flow of information over these networks? Will you be able to trace information collected about you? What will these networks do to the traditional relationships between family, work, and leisure? How will traditional job designs be altered when millions of "employees" become subcontractors using mobile offices that they themselves must pay for?

In the next section we will consider some ethical principles and analytical techniques for dealing with these kinds of ethical and social concerns.

5.2 ETHICS IN AN INFORMATION SOCIETY

Ethics is a concern of humans who have freedom of choice. Ethics is about individual choice: When faced with alternative courses of action, what is the correct moral choice? What are the main features of "ethical choice"?

Basic Concepts: Responsibility, Accountability, and Liability

Ethical choices are decisions made by individuals who are responsible for the consequences of their actions. Responsibility is a feature of individuals and is a key element of ethical action. **Responsibility** means that you accept the potential costs, duties, and obligations for the decisions you make. **Accountability** is a feature of systems and social institutions: it means that mechanisms are in place to determine who took responsible action, who is responsible. Systems and institutions in which it is impossible to find out who took what action are inherently incapable of ethical analysis or ethical action. Liability extends the concept of responsibility further to the area of laws. **Liability** is a feature of political systems in which a body of law is in place which permits individuals to recover the damages done to them by other actors, systems, or organizations. **Due process** is a related feature of law-governed societies, and is a process in which laws are known and understood and there is an ability to appeal to higher authorities to ensure that the laws were applied correctly.

responsibility Accepting the potential costs, duties, and obligations for the decisions one makes.

accountability The mechanisms for assessing responsibility for decisions made and actions taken.

liability The existence of laws that permit individuals to recover the damages done to them by other actors, systems, or organizations.

due process A process in which laws are well known and understood and there is an ability to appeal to higher authorities to ensure that laws are applied correctly.

These basic concepts form the underpinning of an ethical analysis of information systems and those who manage them. First, as discussed in Chapter 3, information technologies are filtered through social institutions, organizations, and individuals. Systems do not have "impacts" by themselves. Whatever information system impacts exist are a product of institutional, organizational, and individual actions and behaviors. Second, responsibility for the consequences of technology fall clearly on the institutions, organizations, and individual managers who choose to use the technology. Using information technology in a "socially responsible" manner means that you can and will be held accountable for the consequences of your actions. Third, in an ethical political society, individuals and others can recover damages done them through a set of laws characterized by due process.

Ethical Analysis

When confronted with a situation that seems to present ethical issues, how should you analyze and reason about the situation? Following is a five-step process that should help:

- *Identify and describe clearly the facts.* Find out who did what to whom, and where, when, and how. You will be surprised in many instances at the errors in the initially reported facts, and often you will find that simply getting the facts straight helps define the solution. It also helps to get the opposing parties involved in an ethical dilemma to agree on the facts.

- *Define the conflict or dilemma and identify the higher-order values involved.* Ethical, social, and political issues always reference higher values. The parties to a dispute all claim to be pursuing higher values (e.g., freedom, privacy, protection of property, and the free enterprise system).

    Typically, an ethical issue involves a dilemma: two diametrically opposed courses of action that support worthwhile values. For example, the Window on Technology in this chapter illustrates two competing values: the need of companies to use marketing to become more efficient and the need to protect individual privacy.

- *Identify the stakeholders.* Every ethical, social, and political issue has stakeholders: players in the game who have an interest in the outcome, who have invested in the situation, and usually who have vocal opinions. Find out the identity of these groups and what they want. This will be useful later when designing a solution.

- *Identify the options that you can reasonably take.* You may find that none of the options satisfy all the interests involved, but that some options do a better job than others. Sometimes arriving at a "good" or ethical solution may not always be a "balancing" of consequences to stakeholders.

- *Identify the potential consequences of your options.* Some options may be ethically correct, but disastrous from other points of view. Other options may work in this one instance, but not be generalizable to other similar instances. Always ask yourself, "What if I choose this option consistently over time?"

    Once your analysis is complete, what ethical principles or rules should you use to make a decision? What higher-order values should inform your judgment?

Candidate Ethical Principles

Although you are the only one who can decide which among many ethical principles you will follow, and how you will prioritize them, it is helpful to consider some ethical principles with deep roots in many cultures that have survived throughout recorded history.

1. Do unto others as you would have them do unto you (the Golden Rule). Putting yourself into the situation of others, and thinking of yourself as the object of the decision, can help you think about "fairness" in decision making.

2. If an action is not right for everyone to take, then it is not right for anyone (**Immanuel Kant's Categorical Imperative**). Ask yourself, "If everyone did this, could the organization, or society, survive?"

3. If an action cannot be taken repeatedly, then it is not right to be taken at any time (**Descartes' rule of change**). This is the slippery-slope rule: An action may bring about a small change now that is acceptable, but if repeated would bring unacceptable changes in the long run. In the vernacular, it might be stated as "once started down a slippery path you may not be able to stop."

Immanuel Kant's Categorical Imperative A principle that states that if an action is not right for everyone to take it is not right for anyone.

Descartes' rule of change A principle that states that if an action cannot be taken repeatedly, then it is not right to be taken at any time.

Utilitarian Principle Principle that assumes one can put values in rank order and understand the consequences of various courses of action.

Risk Aversion Principle Principle that one should take the action that produces the least harm or incurs the least cost.

ethical "no free lunch" rule Assumption that all tangible and intangible objects are owned by someone else unless there is a specific declaration otherwise and that the creator wants compensation for this work.

4. Take the action that achieves the higher or greater value (the **Utilitarian Principle**). This rule assumes you can prioritize values in a rank order, and understand the consequences of various courses of action.

5. Take the action that produces the least harm, or the least potential cost (**Risk Aversion Principle**). Some actions have extremely high failure costs of very low probability (e.g., building a nuclear generating facility in an urban area), or extremely high failure costs of moderate probability (speeding and automobile accidents). Avoid these high failure cost actions, with greater attention obviously to high failure cost potential of moderate to high probability.

6. Assume that virtually all tangible and intangible objects are owned by someone else unless there is a specific declaration otherwise. (This is the **ethical "no free lunch" rule**.) If something created by someone else is useful to you, it has value and you should assume the creator wants compensation for this work.

Unfortunately, these ethical rules have too many logical and substantive exceptions to be absolute guides to action. Nevertheless, actions that do not easily pass these rules deserve some very close attention and a great deal of caution if only because the appearance of unethical behavior may do as much harm to you and your company as actual unethical behavior.

Professional Codes of Conduct

When groups of people claim to be professionals, they take on special rights and obligations. As professionals, they enter into special, even more constraining, relationships with employers, customers, and society given their special claims to knowledge, wisdom, and respect. Professional codes of conduct are promulgated by associations of professionals such as the American Medical Association (AMA), the American Bar Association (ABA), and the American Society of Mechanical Engineers (ASME). These professional groups take responsibility for the partial regulation of their professions by determining entrance qualifications and competence. Codes of ethics are promises by the profession to regulate themselves in the general interest of society. In return, professionals seek to raise both the pay and the respect given their profession.

Certain professional computer societies in the United States, such as the Data Processing Management Association (DPMA), the Institute for Certification of Computer Professionals (ICP), the Information Technology Association of America (ITAA), and the Association of Computing Machinery (ACM), have drafted codes of ethics (Oz, 1992). Table 5.1 describes the code of professional conduct with moral imperatives of the ACM, the oldest of these societies.

Extensions to these moral imperatives state that ACM professions should consider the health, privacy, and general welfare of the public in the performance of their work and that professionals should express their professional opinion to their employer regarding any adverse consequences to the public (see Oz, 1994).

Some Real-World Ethical Dilemmas

The recent ethical problems described in this section illustrate a wide range of issues. Some of these issues are obvious ethical dilemmas, in which one set of interests is pitted against another. Others represent some type of breach of ethics. In either instance, there are rarely any easy solutions.

Continental Can: Based in Norwalk, Connecticut, Continental Can Company developed a human resources database with files on all of its employees. Besides the typical employee data, the system included the capability to "red flag" employees nearing retirement or approaching the age at which a pension would be vested in the individual. Throughout the 1980s, when the red flag went up, management would fire the person even after decades of loyal service. In 1991 a federal district court in

Table 5.1 Association of Computing Machinery Code of Professional Conduct

Recognition of professional status by the public depends not only on skill and dedication but also on adherence to a recognized code of professional conduct.

General Moral Imperatives

Contribute to society and human well-being.

Avoid harm to others.

Be honest and trustworthy.

Honor property rights including copyrights and patents.

Give proper credit for intellectual property.

Access computing resources only when authorized.

Respect the privacy of others.

Source: Excerpted from *ACM's Code of Ethics and Professional Conduct. Communications of the ACM*, 36, #12. © 1993 Association of Computing Machinery. Reprinted by permission.

Newark, New Jersey, awarded ex-employees $445 million for wrongful dismissal (McPartlin, 1992).

Downsizing with Technology at the Telephone Company: Many of the large telephone companies in the United States are using information technology to reduce the size of their work force. For example, AT&T is using voice recognition software to reduce the need for human operators by allowing computers to recognize a customer's responses to a series of computerized questions. New algorithms called "word spotting" allow the computer to recognize speech that is halting, stuttering, paused, or ungrammatical. AT&T expects that the new technology will eliminate 3000 to 6000 operator jobs nationwide, 200 to 400 management positions, and 31 offices in 21 states.

GTE Corporation reengineered its customer-service function to reduce the number of repair technicians. Customer-service workers who in the past had passed customer complaints on to repair technicians have been authorized to resolve the problems themselves by performing remote tests on customers' lines. The company also merged 12 operations centers into a single center to monitor the company's entire nationwide network. These and other changes have relied on technology to eliminate 17,000 jobs (Andrews, 1994; Levinson, 1994).

E-mail privacy at EPSON: In March 1990, e-mail administrator Alana Shoars filed a suit in Los Angeles Superior Court alleging wrongful termination, defamation, and invasion of privacy by her former employer, Epson America Inc. of Torrance, California. She sought $1 million in damages. In July 1990, Shoars filed a class suit seeking $75 million for 700 Epson employees and approximately 1800 outsiders whose e-mail may have been monitored. Shoars contends that she was fired because she questioned the company's policy of monitoring and printing employee's e-mail messages. Epson claims that Shoars was fired because she opened an MCI:Mail account without permission. Many firms claim that they have every right to monitor the electronic mail of their employees because they own the facilities, intend their use to be for business purposes only, and create the facility for a business purpose (Bjerklie, 1994; Rifkin, 1991).

In each instance, you can find competing values at work, with groups lined on either side of a debate. A company may argue, for example, that it has a right to use information systems to increase productivity and reduce the size of its work force to keep down costs and stay in business. Employees displaced by information systems may argue that employers have some responsibility for their welfare. A close analysis of the facts can sometimes produce compromised solutions that give each side "half a loaf." Try to apply some of the described principles of ethical analysis to each of these cases. What is the right thing to do?

In this section, we take a closer look at the five moral dimensions of information systems first described in Figure 5.1. In each dimension we identify the ethical, social, and political levels of analysis and illustrate with real-world examples the values involved, the stakeholders, and the options chosen.

Information Rights: Privacy and Freedom in an Information Society

privacy The claim of individuals to be left alone, free from surveillance or interference from other individuals, organizations, or the state.

Privacy is the claim of individuals to be left alone, free from surveillance or interference from other individuals or organizations including the state. Claims to privacy are also involved at the workplace: Millions of employees are subject to electronic and other forms of high-tech surveillance. Information technology and systems threaten individual claims to privacy by making the invasion of privacy cheap, profitable, and effective.

The claim to privacy is protected in the U.S., Canadian, and German constitutions in a variety of different ways, and in other countries through various statutes. In the United States, the claim to privacy is protected primarily by the First Amendment guarantees of freedom of speech and association and the Fourth Amendment protections against unreasonable search and seizure of one's personal documents or home, and the guarantee of due process.

Due process has become a key concept in defining privacy. Due process requires that a set of rules or laws exist which clearly define how information about individuals will be treated, and what appeal mechanisms are available. Perhaps the best statement of the due process in record keeping is given by the Fair Information Practices Doctrine developed in the early 1970s.

fair information practices (FIP) A set of principles originally set forth in 1973 that governs the collection and use of information about individuals and forms the basis of most U.S. and European privacy laws.

Most American and European privacy law is based on a regime called fair information practices (FIP) first set forth in a report written in 1973 by a federal government advisory committee (U.S. Department of Health, Education, and Welfare, 1973). **Fair information practices (FIP)** is a set of principles governing the collection and use of information about individuals. The five fair information practices principles are shown in Table 5.2.

FIP principles are based on the notion of a "mutuality of interest" among the record holder and the individual. The individual has an interest in engaging in a transaction, and the record keeper—usually a business or government agency—requires information about the individual to support the transaction. Once gathered, the individual maintains an interest in the record, and the record may not be used to support other activities without the individual's consent.

Fair Information Practices form the basis of 13 federal statutes listed in Table 5.3 that set forth the conditions for handling information about individuals in such areas as credit reporting, education, financial records, newspaper records, cable communications, electronic communications, and even video rentals. The Privacy Act of

Table 5.2 Fair Information Practices Principles
1. There should be no personal record systems whose existence is secret.
2. Individuals have rights of access, inspection, review, and amendment to systems that contain information about them.
3. There must be no use of personal information for purposes other than those for which it was gathered without prior consent.
4. Managers of systems are responsible and can be held accountable and liable for the damage done by systems for their reliability and security.
5. Governments have the right to intervene in the information relationships among private parties.

1974 is the most important of these laws, regulating the federal government's collection, use, and disclosure of information. Most federal privacy laws apply only to the federal government. Only credit, banking, cable, and video rental industries have been regulated by federal privacy law.

In the United States, privacy law is enforced by individuals who must sue agencies or companies in court to recover damages. European countries and Canada define *privacy* in a similar manner to that in the United States, but they have chosen to enforce their privacy laws by creating privacy commissions or data protection agencies to pursue complaints brought by citizens.

Internet Challenges to Privacy

The Internet introduces technology which poses new challenges to the protection of individual privacy. Information sent over this vast network of networks may pass through many different computer systems before it reaches its final destination. Each of these systems is capable of monitoring, capturing, and storing communications that pass through it.

It is possible to record many on-line activities, including which on-line newsgroups or files a person has accessed and which Web sites he or she has visited. This information can be collected by both a subscriber's own Internet service provider and the system operators of remote sites which a subscriber visits. The Window on Technology describes some of the challenges to individual privacy posed by this technology.

Ethical Issues

The ethical privacy issue in this information age is as follows: Under what conditions should I (you) invade the privacy of others? What legitimates intruding into others' lives through unobtrusive surveillance, through market research, or by whatever means? Do we have to inform people that we are eavesdropping? Do we have to inform people that we are using credit history information for employment screening purposes?

Table 5.3   Federal Privacy Laws in the United States
(1) General Federal Privacy Laws
Freedom of Information Act, 1968 as Amended (5 USC 552)
Privacy Act of 1974 as Amended (5 USC 552a)
Electronic Communications Privacy Act of 1986
Computer Matching and Privacy Protection Act of 1988
Computer Security Act of 1987
Federal Managers Financial Integrity Act of 1982
(2) Privacy Laws Affecting Private Institutions
Fair Credit Reporting Act of 1970
Family Educational Rights and Privacy Act of 1978
Right to Financial Privacy Act of 1978
Privacy Protection Act of 1980
Cable Communications Policy Act of 1984
Electronic Communications Privacy Act of 1986
Video Privacy Protection Act of 1988

Are the Cookies Eating Your Privacy?

When you surf the Net, you are being observed. The only questions are by whom and for what purposes? Tools to monitor your visits to the World Wide Web have been developed for commercial reasons—to help organizations determine how to better target their offerings, and to determine who is visiting their Web sites. For example, many commercial sites log the number of visitors and which site pages they visit to collect marketing information about user interests and behaviors. One key issue arises from this data collection—do they know who you are? If so, then what do they do with such data, and are these uses appropriate, legal, and ethical? In other words, is your privacy being improperly invaded?

Do they know who you are? The answer is—maybe! Of course you are known if you register at a site to purchase a product or service. This situation is the same as using a credit card to purchase any product or service. In addition some sites offer you a free service, such as information, in exchange for your agreeing to register, and when you register they have you identified. This is probably no different from your signing up for a supermarket's frequent shopper or discount card—you voluntarily give up some of your privacy in exchange for something you want. In both cases, the company collects the information to use in its own marketing research and to target specific offers to you. They also might sell it to other companies or organizations, raising the privacy issues discussed elsewhere in this chapter.

But what if you do not volunteer personal information at a site? Can they gather it anyway, without your consent and without your knowledge? The answer seems to be yes, with the help of Internet technology. Observers generally agree that the logging products previously described here can obtain your domain name (the portion of your Internet address to the right of the @ symbol) which does not identify you but gives them a piece of the building block. Most also claim these tools cannot obtain your personal identifier (to the left of your address @ symbol), although as technology is developed, that may be changing. Another new tool, the cookie, is now in widespread use that may have that capability.

Cookies are tiny data files that are deposited on your computer by interested Web sites when you visit those sites. Cookies track your visits to the Web site. When you return to a site that has stored a cookie, it will search your computer, find the

cookie, and "know" what you have done in the past. It may also update the cookie, depending on your activity this visit. In this way, the site can customize its contents for your interests (assuming your past activities indicate your current interest). If you are a regular Web user, search your hard drive for files named "cookie.txt" and you are likely to find some. Many claim these cookies cannot gather your name or e-mail address from your computer, but technology is changing and will be able to collect your identity in time. The site may use the data from its cookies for itself, or it too may sell that data to others. If you want more information on cookies, visit the Laudon and Laudon Web site.

Web search engines are another source of privacy invasion. They monitor and store data on who searches and for what, and that data too is becoming public. For example, you can visit McKinley's Magellan site to see a sample of what topics people have searched using Magellan (http://voyeur.mckinley.com/voyeur.cgi). While Magellan does not display the identity of the searchers, they have that technical capacity. And they could sell it to interested parties. You are also monitored as you use Usenet newsgroups. Deja News publicly catalogues 15,000 Usenet groups and monitors their visitors. Visit its site (http://dejanews.com) and you can view a profile of your own (or other person's) use of Usenet groups—how many times you posted messages and in which newsgroups. You may not want this information released. For example, you may be part of a political newsgroup that you want kept confidential. That information is available for others to see and may even be sold to interested parties.

To Think About: *How would you balance the rights of individuals to privacy against the desire of companies to use this technology to improve their marketing and to better target their products to the interests of individuals?*

Sources: Matthew Hahn, "Easy Now to Keep Tabs on Users' Internet Postings," *The New York Times,* January 6, 1997; James Taschek, "Analyzing Your Website," *ZD Internet Magazine,* April 1997; Thomas E. Weber, "Browsers Beware: The Web Is Watching," *The Wall Street Journal,* June 27, 1996; and Stephen H. Wildstrom, "Privacy and the 'Cookie' Monster," *Business Week,* December 16, 1996.

Social Issues

The social issue of privacy concerns the development of "expectations of privacy" or privacy norms, as well as public attitudes. In what areas of life should we as a society encourage people to think they are in "private territory" as opposed to public view? For instance, should we as a society encourage people to develop expectations of privacy when using electronic mail, cellular telephones, bulletin boards, the postal system, the workplace, the street? Should expectations of privacy be extended to criminal conspirators?

Political Issues

The political issue of privacy concerns the development of statutes which govern the relations between record keepers and individuals. Should we permit the FBI to prevent the commercial development of encrypted telephone transmissions so they can eavesdrop at will (Denning et al., 1993)? Should a law be passed to require direct marketing firms to obtain the consent of individuals before using their names in mass marketing (a consensus database)? Should e-mail privacy—regardless of who owns the equipment—be protected in law? In general, large organizations of all kinds—public and private—are reluctant to remit the advantages which come from the unfettered flow of information on individuals. Civil liberties and other private groups have been the strongest voices supporting restraints on large organization, information-gathering activities.

Property Rights: Intellectual Property

Contemporary information systems have severely challenged existing law and social practice which protect private intellectual property. **Intellectual property** is considered to be intangible property created by individuals or corporations. Information technology has made it difficult to protect intellectual property because computerized information can be so easily copied or distributed on networks. Intellectual property is subject to a variety of protections under three different legal traditions: trade secret, copyright, and patent law (Graham, 1984).

intellectual property Intangible property created by individuals or corporations which is subject to protections under trade secret, copyright, and patent law.

Trade Secrets

Any intellectual work product—a formula, device, pattern, or compilation of data—used for a business purpose can be classified as a **trade secret,** provided it is not based on information in the public domain. Trade secrets have their basis in state law, not federal law, and protections vary from state to state. In general, trade secret laws grant a monopoly on the ideas behind a work product, but it can be a very tenuous monopoly.

Software that contains novel or unique elements, procedures, or compilations can be included as a trade secret. Trade secret law protects the actual ideas in a work product, not only their manifestation. To make this claim, the creator or owner must take care to bind employees and customers with nondisclosure agreements and to prevent the secret from falling into the public domain.

The limitation of trade secret protection is that although virtually all software programs of any complexity contain unique elements of some sort, it is difficult to prevent the ideas in the work from falling into the public domain when the software is widely distributed.

trade secret Any intellectual work or product used for a business purpose that can be classified as belonging to that business provided it is not based on information in the public domain.

Copyright

Copyright is a statutory grant that protects creators of intellectual property against copying by others for any purpose for a period of 28 years. Since the first Federal Copyright Act of 1790, and the creation of the copyright office to register copyrights and enforce copyright law, Congress has extended copyright protection to books, periodicals, lectures, dramas, musical compositions, maps, drawings, artwork of any kind, and motion pictures. Since the earliest days, the congressional intent behind copyright laws has been to encourage creativity and authorship by ensuring that creative people receive the financial and other benefits of their work. Copyright provides a limited monopoly on the commercial use of a work, but does not protect the ideas behind a work. Most industrial nations have their own copyright laws, and

copyright A statutory grant which protects creators of intellectual property against copying by others for any purpose for a period of 28 years.

there are several international conventions and bilateral agreements through which nations coordinate and enforce their laws.

In the mid-1960s the Copyright Office began registering software programs, and in 1980 Congress passed the Computer Software Copyright Act which clearly provides protection for source and object code and for copies of the original sold in commerce, and sets forth the rights of the purchaser to use the software while the creator retains legal title.

Copyright protection is explicit and clear-cut: It protects against copying of entire programs or their parts. Damages and relief are readily obtained for infringement. The drawback to copyright protection is that the underlying ideas are not protected, only their manifestation in a work. A competitor can use your software, understand how it works, and build new software that follows the same concepts without infringing on a copyright.

"Look and feel" copyright infringement lawsuits are precisely about the distinction between an idea and its expression. For instance, in the early 1990s Apple Computer sued Microsoft Corporation and Hewlett-Packard Inc. for infringement of the expression of Apple's Macintosh interface. Among other claims, Apple claimed that the defendants copied the expression of overlapping windows. The defendants counterclaimed that the idea of overlapping windows can only be expressed in a single way, and therefore was not protectable under the "merger" doctrine of copyright law. When ideas and their expression merge, the expression cannot be copyrighted. In general, courts appear to be following the reasoning of a 1989 case—*Brown Bag Software vs. Symantec Corp.*—in which the court dissected the elements of software alleged to be infringing. The court found that neither similar concept, function, general functional features (e.g., drop-down menus), nor colors are protectable by copyright law (*Brown Bag vs. Symantec Corp.*, 1992).

Patents

patent A legal document that grants the owner an exclusive monopoly on the ideas behind an invention for 17 years; designed to ensure that inventors of new machines or methods are rewarded for their labor while making widespread use of their inventions.

A **patent** grants the owner an exclusive monopoly on the ideas behind an invention for 17 years. The congressional intent behind patent law was to ensure that inventors of new machines, devices, or methods receive the full financial and other rewards of their labor and yet still make widespread use of the invention possible by providing detailed diagrams for those wishing to use the idea under license from the owner of the patent. The granting of a patent is determined by the Patent Office and relies on court rulings.

The key concepts in patent law are originality, novelty, and invention. The Patent Office did not accept applications for software patents routinely until a 1981 Supreme Court decision which held that computer programs could be a part of a patentable process. Since that time hundreds of patents have been granted and thousands await consideration.

The strength of patent protection is that it grants a monopoly on the underlying concepts and ideas of software. The difficulty is passing stringent criteria of nonobviousness (e.g., the work must reflect some special understanding and contribution), originality, and novelty, as well as years of waiting to receive protection.

Challenges to Intellectual Property Rights

Contemporary information technologies, especially software, pose a severe challenge to existing intellectual property regimes, and therefore create significant ethical, social, and political issues. Digital media differ from books, periodicals, and other media in terms of ease of replication; ease of transmission; ease of alteration; difficulty classifying a software work as a program, book, or even music; compactness—making theft easy; and difficulties in establishing uniqueness (see Samuelson, October 1991).

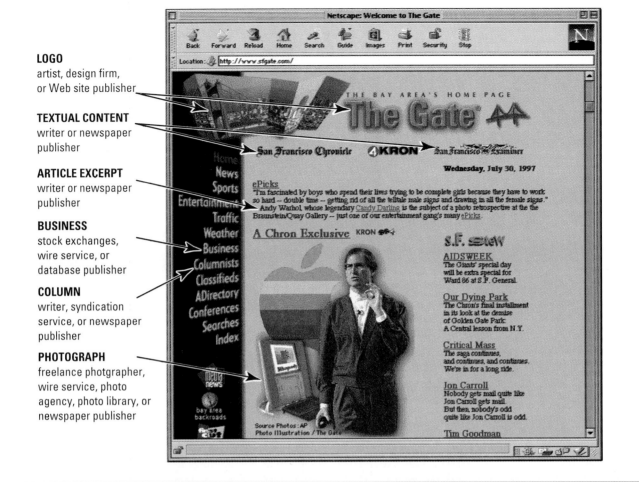

LOGO
artist, design firm,
or Web site publisher

TEXTUAL CONTENT
writer or newspaper
publisher

ARTICLE EXCERPT
writer or newspaper
publisher

BUSINESS
stock exchanges,
wire service, or
database publisher

COLUMN
writer, syndication
service, or newspaper
publisher

PHOTOGRAPH
freelance photgrapher,
wire service, photo
agency, photo library, or
newspaper publisher

FIGURE 5.2

Who Owns the Pieces? Anatomy of a Web page. Web pages are often constructed with elements from many different sources, clouding issues of ownership and intellectual property protection. © *The San Francisco Chronicle.* Reprinted with permission.

The proliferation of electronic networks, including the Internet, has made it even more difficult to protect intellectual property. Before widespread use of networks, copies of software, books, magazine articles, or films had to be stored on physical media, such as paper, computer disks, or videotape, creating some hurdles to distribution. Using networks, information can be more widely reproduced and distributed (Johnson, 1997). With the World Wide Web in particular, one can easily copy and distribute virtually anything to thousands and even millions of people around the world, even if they are using different types of computer systems. The Internet was designed to transmit information freely around the world, including copyrighted information. Intellectual property that can be easily copied is likely to be copied (Chabrow, 1996).

The manner in which information is obtained and presented on the Web further challenges intellectual property protections (Okerson, 1996). Web pages can be constructed from bits of text, graphics, sound, or video that may come from many different sources. Each item may belong to a different entity, creating complicated issues of ownership and compensation (see Figure 5.2). Web sites can also use a capability called "framing" to let one site construct an on-screen border around content obtained by linking to another Web site. The first site's border and logo stay on screen, making the content of the new Web site appear to be "offered" by the previous Web site. For example, TotalNews Inc., based in Phoenix, maintains a Web site linked to the Web sites of more than 1100 news organizations and frames virtually all of them.

The film adaptation of George Orwell's novel *1984* portrayed a frightening vision of the future. "Big Brother" kept a constant surveillance over every aspect of the daily lives of all citizens.

In December 1996 negotiators from 160 countries sponsored by the World Intellectual Property Organization, a United Nations body, signed two international treaties to broaden copyright protection of digital material. International law would specify that copyright protection includes the right to control the distribution of copyrighted materials over networks. Current international copyright laws protecting recorded music would be extended to include computer-generated copies of recordings. Negotiators agreed to delete language that would have treated even temporary copies of material downloaded from the Internet as possible violations of international copyright law. Mechanisms are being developed to sell and distribute books, articles, and other intellectual property on the Internet, but publishers continue to worry about copyright violations because intellectual property can now be copied so easily.

Ethical Issues

The central ethical issue posed to individuals concerns copying software: Should I (you) copy for my own use a piece of software protected by trade secret, copyright, and/or patent law? In the information age, it is so easy to obtain perfect, functional copies of software, that the software companies themselves have abandoned software protection schemes to increase market penetration, and enforcement of the law is so rare. However, if everyone copied software, very little new software would be produced because creators could not benefit from the results of their work.

Social Issues

There are several property-related social issues raised by new information technology. Most experts agree that the current intellectual property laws are breaking down in the information age. The vast majority of Americans report in surveys that they routinely violate some minor laws—everything from speeding to taking paper clips from work to copying software. The ease with which software can be copied contributes to making us a society of lawbreakers. These routine thefts threaten significantly to reduce the speed with which new information technologies can and will be introduced, and thereby threaten further advances in productivity and social well-being (see the chapter-opening vignette).

A Corporate Software Code of Ethics

This code of ethics is to state our organization's policy concerning software duplication. All employees shall use software only in accordance with the license agreement. Unless otherwise provided in the license, any duplication of licensed software except for backup and archival purposes is a violation of the law. Any unauthorized duplication of copyrighted computer software violates the law and is contrary to the organization's standards of conduct. The following points are to be followed in order to comply with software license agreements.

1. We will use all software in accordance with our license agreements.

2. Legitimate software will promptly be provided to all employees who need it. No employee of the company will make any unauthorized copies of any software under any circumstances. Anyone found copying software other than for backup purposes is subject to termination.

3. We will not tolerate the use of any unauthorized copies of software in our company. Any person illegally reproducing software can be subject to civil and criminal penalties including fines and imprisonment. We do not condone illegal copying of software under any circumstances and anyone who makes, uses, or otherwise acquires unauthorized software shall be appropriately disciplined.

4. No employee shall give software to any outsiders (including clients, customers, and others).

5. Any employee who determines that there may be a misuse of software within the company shall notify their Department Manager or legal counsel.

6. All software used by the organization on company computers will be properly purchased through appropriate procedures.

I have read the company's software code of ethics. I am fully aware of our software policies and agree to abide by those policies.

To Think About: Try to find out your university's policy regarding software. Is there a software code of ethics on campus? If an employee finds routine copying of software in a firm, should the person (a) call the firm's legal counsel, or (b) call SPA on the anti-piracy hotline? Are there any circumstances in which software copying should be allowed?

Source: *Software Management Guide: A Guide for Software Asset Management, version 1.0.* Courtesy of Software Publishers Association, 1992.

Political Issues

The main property-related political issue concerns the creation of new property protection measures to protect investments made by creators of new software. Apple, Microsoft, and 900 other hardware and software firms formed the Software Publishers Association (SPA) to lobby for new protection laws and enforce existing laws. SPA has distributed more than 30,000 copies of SPA audit—a software inventory management tool used by corporations to establish control over software used on individual PCs; established a toll-free anti-piracy hotline for employees to report on their corporations; completed over 75 surprise audits or raids; sent hundreds of cease and desist letters, and filed more than 100 lawsuits since its inception (80 percent against corporations, 20 percent against bulletin board operators, training facilities, schools, and universities). The SPA has developed a model Software Code of Ethics described in the Window on Organizations.

Allied against SPA are a host of groups and millions of individuals who resist efforts to strengthen anti-piracy laws, and instead encourage situations in which software can be copied. These groups believe that software should be free, that anti-piracy laws cannot in any event be enforced in the digital age, or that software should be paid for on a voluntary basis (shareware software). According to these groups, the greater social benefit results from the free distribution of software and the "benefits" of software should accrue to the creators in the form of greater prestige, perhaps, but not in the form of profits.

Accountability, Liability, and Control

Along with privacy and property laws, new information technologies are challenging existing liability law and social practices for holding individuals and institutions accountable. If a person is injured by a machine controlled, in part, by software, who should be held accountable and therefore held liable? Should a public bulletin board or an electronic service such as Prodigy or CompuServe permit the transmission of pornographic or offensive material (as broadcasters), or should they be held harmless against any liability for what users transmit (as is true of common carriers such as the telephone system)? What about the Internet? If you outsource your information processing, can you hold the external vendor liable for injuries done to your customers? Try some real-world examples.

Some Recent Liability Problems

In February 1992, hackers penetrated the computer network of Equifax, Inc. in Atlanta, Georgia, one of the world's largest credit-reporting bureaus that sells 450 million reports annually. Consumer files, credit card numbers, and other confidential information were accessed. The company is working with police and reviewing all files to catch the criminals. When finished, it will notify all affected customers. Who is liable for any damages done to individuals (King, 1992)?

On March 13, 1993, a blizzard hit the East Coast of the United States, knocking out an Electronic Data Systems Inc. (EDS) computer center in Clifton, New Jersey. The center operated 5200 ATM machines in 12 different networks across the country involving more than 1 million card holders. In the two weeks required to recover operations, EDS informed its customers to use alternative ATM networks operated by other banks or computer centers, and offered to cover more than $50 million in cash withdrawals. Because the alternative networks did not have access to the actual customer account balances, EDS was at substantial risk of fraud. Cash withdrawals were limited to $100 per day per customer to reduce the exposure. Most service was restored by March 26. Although EDS had a disaster recovery plan, it did not have a dedicated backup facility. Who is liable for any economic harm caused individuals or businesses who could not access their full account balances in this period (Joes, 1993)?

In April 1990, a computer system at Shell Pipeline Corporation failed to detect a human operator error. As a result, 93,000 barrels of crude oil were shipped to the wrong trader. The error cost $2 million because the trader sold oil that should not have been delivered to him. A court ruled later that Shell Pipeline was liable for the loss of the oil because the error was due to a human operator who entered erroneous information into the system. Shell was held liable for not developing a system that would prevent the possibility of misdeliveries (King, 1992). When would you have held liable—Shell pipeline? The trader for not being more careful about deliveries? The human operator who made the error?

These cases point out the difficulties faced by information systems executives who ultimately are responsible for the harm done by systems developed by their staffs. In general, insofar as computer software is part of a machine, and the machine injures someone physically or economically, the producer of the software and the operator can be held liable for damages. Insofar as the software acts more like a book, storing and displaying information, courts have been reluctant to hold authors, publishers, and booksellers liable for contents (the exception being instances of fraud or defamation), and hence courts have been wary of holding software authors liable for "booklike" software.

In general, it is very difficult (if not impossible) to hold software producers liable for their software products when those products are considered like books, regardless of the physical or economic harm which results. Historically, print publishers, books, and periodicals have not been held liable because of fears that liability claims would interfere with First Amendment rights guaranteeing freedom of expression.

What about "software as service"? ATM machines are a service provided to bank customers. Should this service fail, customers will be inconvenienced and perhaps harmed economically if they cannot access their funds in a timely manner. Should liability protections be extended to software publishers and operators of defective financial, accounting, simulation, financial, or marketing systems?

Software is very different from books. Software users may develop expectations of infallibility about software; software is less easily inspected than a book, and more difficult to compare with other software products for quality; and software claims actually to perform a task rather than describe a task like a book; people come to depend on services essentially based on software. Given the centrality of software to everyday life, the chances are excellent that liability law will extend its reach to include software even when it merely provides an information service.

There are virtually no liabilities imposed on book publishers, bookstores, or newspapers (outside of outright defamation and certain local restrictions on pornographic materials) because of their historic role in the evolution of First Amendment rights. Telephone systems have not been held liable for the messages transmitted because they are regulated "common carriers." In return for their monopoly on telephone service, they must provide access to all, at reasonable rates, and achieve acceptable reliability. But broadcasters and cable television systems are subject to a wide variety of federal and local constraints on content and facilities.

Liability and accountability are also at the heart of debates over the responsibility and freedoms of computer bulletin boards and networks. The second Window on Organizations describes recent lawsuits seeking to establish liability of Web site owners and bulletin board providers.

Ethical Issues

The central liability-related ethical issue raised by new information technologies is whether individuals and organizations who create, produce, and sell systems (both hardware and software) are morally responsible for the consequences of their use (see Johnson and Mulvey, 1995). If so, under what conditions? What liabilities (and responsibilities) should the user assume, and what should the provider assume?

Social Issues

The central liability-related social issue concerns the expectations that society should allow to develop around service-providing information systems. Should individuals (and organizations) be encouraged to develop their own backup devices to cover likely or easily anticipated system failures, or should organizations be held strictly liable for system services they provide? If organizations are held strictly liable, what impact will this have on the development of new system services? Can society permit networks and bulletin boards to post libelous, inaccurate, and misleading information that will harm many persons? Or should information service companies become self-regulating, self-censoring?

Political Issues

The leading liability-related political issue is the debate between information providers of all kinds (from software developers to network service providers) who want to be relieved of liability insofar as possible (thereby maximizing their profits), and service users—individuals, organizations, communities—who want organizations to be held responsible for providing high-quality system services (thereby maximizing the quality of service). Service providers argue they will withdraw from the marketplace if they are held liable, whereas service users argue that only by holding providers liable can we guarantee a high level of service and compensate injured parties. Should legislation impose liability or restrict liability on service providers? This fundamental cleavage is at the heart of numerous political and judicial conflicts.

Liability on the Internet

How exposed is an organization with an Internet site to liability suits? How can it protect itself from such suits? We cannot answer this question with any certainty because telecommunications liability is a newly developing field. However, companies linked to the Internet may have exposure for such areas as libel, copyright infringement, pornography, and fraud.

When will your organization be held liable for content on its site? Clearly the Web site owner can be held liable for objectionable content if that content was posted by its own organization, regardless if management authorized it. For example, if an employee posts libelous material without authorization, the company may still be responsible. However, responsibility may not end there. On-line services such as Prodigy and CompuServe and many Web sites may be liable for postings by their customers or visitors. A court recently awarded Stratton Oakmont, a New York investment bank, $200 million from Prodigy after determining that a Prodigy subscriber posted libelous statements. The court compared Prodigy with a publisher which has editorial control over content because Prodigy screens all postings for unacceptable words. This ruling would probably have held CompuServe blameless for subscribers' statements because it does not screen messages before posting and so would be considered like a bookstore which has no editorial control.

Many companies fear being held responsible for content on someone else's site. Some Web sites contain *hot buttons*—electronic links to other sites. Some believe that the site with the hot button can be held liable for content on the screen the consumer reaches using that hot button. For this reason, AMR Corporation (parent to American Airlines) prohibits any hot link on its site.

Another major question is jurisdiction—can a viewer of content in one jurisdiction sue the owner for content located in a different jurisdiction? For example, can a viewer in New York sue a Web site located in California if that site contains pornographic materials? Amateur Action, a computer bulletin board in Milpitis, California, was convicted under Tennessee state pornography laws, which have tougher standards than those of California.

The global reach of the Internet adds new challenges. A scathing on-line message that may be protected under the First Amendment in the United States could be considered libelous in Great Britain, Canada, or Australia, which have more restrictions on free speech.

Companies can take some protective steps, such as seeking legal advice prior to establishing a Web site; adopting clear and well-publicized guidelines that limit what employees can post; enforcing guidelines by punishing offenders; and posting disclaimer notices on the site. For example, *Penthouse's* Web site warns visitors of potentially offensive adult materials; it also warns visitors to not proceed if they are "accessing . . . from any country or locality where adult material is specifically prohibited by law," and the site lists 25 such countries.

To Think About: What management, organization, and technology issues should be addressed by companies trying to prevent libelous or offensive material from being distributed through the Internet?

Sources: Kate Maddox and Clinton Wilder, "Net Liability," *Information Week,* January 8, 1996; and Mitch Betts, Ellis Booker, and Gary H. Anthes, "On-Line Boundaries Unclear," *Computerworld,* June 5, 1995.

System Quality: Data Quality and System Errors

The debate over liability and accountability for unintentional consequences of system use raises a related but independent moral dimension: What is an acceptable, technologically feasible level of system quality (see Chapter 13)? At what point should system managers say, "Stop testing, we've done all we can to perfect this software. Ship it!" Individuals and organizations may be held responsible for avoidable and foreseeable consequences, which they have a duty to perceive and correct. And the gray area is that some system errors are foreseeable and correctable only at very great expense, an expense so great that pursuing this level of perfection is not feasible economically—no one could afford the product. For example, although software companies try to debug their products before releasing them to the marketplace, they knowingly ship buggy products because the time and cost of fixing all minor errors would prevent these products from ever being released (Rigdon, 1995). What if the product was not offered on the marketplace, would social welfare as a whole not advance and perhaps even decline? Carrying this further, just what is the responsibility

Table 5.4   Illustrative Reported Data Quality Problems

- An airline inadvertently corrupted its database of passenger reservations while installing new software and for months planes took off with half loads.

- A manufacturer attempted to reorganize its customer files by customer number only to discover the sales staff had been entering a new customer number for each sale because of special incentives for opening new accounts. One customer was entered 7000 times. The company scrapped the software project after spending $1 million.

- A manufacturing company nearly scrapped a $12 million data warehouse project because of inconsistently defined product data.

- J. P. Morgan, a New York bank, discovered that 40 percent of the data in its credit-risk management database was incomplete, necessitating double-checking by users.

- Several studies have established that 5 to 12 percent of bar-code sales at retail grocery and merchandise chains are erroneous and that the ratio of overcharges to undercharges runs as high as 5:1, with 4:1 as a norm. The problem tends to be human error in keeping shelf prices accurate and corporate policy which fails to allocate sufficient resources to price checking, auditing, and development of error-free policies.

Sources: Catherine Yang and Willy Stern, "Maybe They Should Call Them Scammers," *Business Week,* January 16, 1995; William Bulkeley, "Databases Plagued by a Reign of Error," *Wall Street Journal,* May 26, 1992; and Doug Bartholomew, "The Price is Wrong," *InformationWeek,* September 14, 1992.

of a producer of computer services—should they withdraw the product that can never be perfect, warn the user, or forget about the risk (let the buyer beware)?

Three principal sources of poor system performance are software bugs and errors, hardware or facility failures due to natural or other causes, and poor input data quality. Chapter 13 shows why zero defects in software code of any complexity cannot be achieved and the seriousness of remaining bugs cannot be estimated. Hence, there is a technological barrier to perfect software and users must be aware of the potential for catastrophic failure. The software industry has not yet arrived at testing standards for producing software of acceptable but not perfect performance (Collins et al., 1994).

Although software bugs and facility catastrophe are likely to be widely reported in the press, by far the most common source of business system failure is data quality. A total of 70 percent of IS executives in a recent survey reported data corruption as a source of business delay, 69 percent said their corporate data accuracy was unacceptable, and 44 percent said no systems were in place to check database information quality (Wilson, 1992). Table 5.4 describes some of these data quality problems.

Ethical Issues

The central quality-related ethical issue raised by information systems is at what point should I (or you) release software or services for consumption by others? At what point can you conclude that your software or service achieves an economically and technologically adequate level of quality? What are you obliged to know about the quality of your software, its procedures for testing, and its operational characteristics?

Social Issues

The leading quality-related social issue once again deals with expectations: Do we want as a society to encourage people to believe that systems are infallible, that data errors are impossible? Do we instead want a society where people are openly skeptical and questioning of the output of machines, where people are at least informed of the risk? By heightening awareness of system failure, do we inhibit the development of all systems which in the end contribute to social well-being?

Political Issues

The leading quality-related political issue concerns the laws of responsibility and accountability. Should Congress establish or direct the National Institute of Science and Technology (NIST) to develop quality standards (software, hardware, data quality) and impose those standards on industry? Or should industry associations be encouraged to develop industry-wide standards of quality? Or should Congress wait for the marketplace to punish poor system quality, recognizing that in some instances this will not work (e.g., if all retail grocers maintain poor quality systems, then customers have no alternatives)?

Quality of Life: Equity, Access, Boundaries

The negative social costs of introducing information technologies and systems are beginning to mount along with the power of the technology. Many of these negative social consequences are not violations of individual rights, nor are they property crimes. Nevertheless, these negative consequences can be extremely harmful to individuals, societies, and political institutions. Computers and information technologies potentially can destroy valuable elements of our culture and society even while they bring us benefits. If there is a balance of good and bad consequences to the use of information systems, who do we hold responsible for the bad consequences? Next, we briefly examine *some* of the negative social consequences of systems, considering individual, social responses, and political responses.

Balancing Power Center versus Periphery

An early fear of the computer age was that huge, centralized mainframe computers would centralize power at corporate headquarters and in the nation's capital, resulting in a Big Brother society suggested in George Orwell's novel, *1984*. The shift toward highly decentralized computing, coupled with an ideology "empowerment" of thousands of workers, and the decentralization of decision making to lower organizational levels, have reduced fears of power centralization in institutions. Yet much of the "empowerment" described in popular business magazines is trivial. Lower-level employees may be empowered to make minor decisions, but the key policy decisions may be as centralized as in the past.

Rapidity of Change: Reduced Response Time to Competition

Information systems have helped to create much more efficient national and international markets. The now more-efficient global marketplace has reduced the normal social buffers which permitted businesses many years to adjust to competition. "Time-based competition" has an ugly side: The business you work for may not have enough time to respond to global competitors and may be wiped out in a year, along with your job. We stand the risk of developing a "just-in-time society" with "just-in-time jobs" and "just-in-time" workplaces, families, and vacations.

Maintaining Boundaries: Family, Work, Leisure

Parts of this book were produced on trains, planes, as well as on family "vacations" and what otherwise might have been "family" time. The danger to ubiquitous computing, telecommuting, nomad computing, and the "do anything anywhere" computing environment is that it might actually come true. If so, the traditional boundaries that separate work from family and just plain leisure will be weakened. While authors have traditionally worked just about anywhere (typewriters have been portable for nearly a century), the advent of information systems, coupled with the growth of knowledge work occupations, means that more and more people will be working when traditionally they would have been playing or communicating with family and friends. The "work umbrella" now extends far beyond the eight-hour day.

While people may enjoy the convenience of working at home, the "do anything anywhere" computing environment can blur the traditional boundaries between work and family time.

Weakening these institutions poses clear-cut risks. Family and friends historically have provided powerful support mechanisms for individuals, and they act as balance points in a society by preserving "private life," providing a place for one to collect one's thoughts, think in ways contrary to one's employer, and dream.

Dependence and Vulnerability

Our businesses, governments, schools, and private associations such as churches are incredibly dependent now on information systems and are therefore highly vulnerable. Table 5.5 lists the biggest system disasters culled from a list of more than 300 begun in 1987. With systems now as ubiquitous as the telephone system, it is startling to remember that there are no regulatory or standard-setting forces in place similar to telephone, electrical, radio, television, or other public utility technologies. The

Table 5.5	The Largest Information System Catastrophes		
Date	Event	Location	Number of Data Centers Affected
8/14/87	Flood	Chicago	64
5/8/88	Network outage	Hinsdale, Ill.	175
5/11/88	Pakistani virus	Nationwide	90+
5/16/88	Internet virus	Nationwide	500+
10/17/89	Earthquake	San Francisco	90
8/13/90	Power outage	New York	320
4/13/92	Flood	Chicago	400
5/1/92	Riot	Los Angeles	50
8/24/92	Hurricane Andrew	Southeast	150
3/15/93	Blizzard	East coast	50

Sources: "Days of Infamy: The 10 Worst IT Disasters," *InformationWeek*, January 10, 1994; and "The Largest System Catastrophes," *InformationWeek*, March 8, 1993.

absence of standards and the criticality of some system applications will probably call forth demands for national standards and perhaps regulatory oversight.

Computer Crime and Abuse

computer crime The commission of illegal acts through the use of a computer or against a computer system.

Many new technologies in the industrial era have created new opportunities for committing crime. Technologies including computers create new valuable items to steal, new ways to steal them, and new ways to harm others. **Computer crime** can be defined as the commission of illegal acts through the use of a computer or against a computer system. Computers or computer systems can be the object of the crime (destroying a company's computer center or a company's computer files) as well as the instrument of a crime (stealing computer lists by illegally gaining access to a computer system using a home microcomputer). Simply accessing a computer system without authorization, or intent to do harm, even by accident, is now a federal crime. **Computer abuse** is the commission of acts involving a computer which may not be illegal but are considered unethical.

computer abuse The commission of acts involving a computer that may not be illegal but are considered unethical.

No one knows the magnitude of the computer crime problem—how many systems are invaded, how many people engage in the practice, or what is the total economic damage. Many companies are reluctant to report computer crimes because they may involve employees. The most economically damaging kinds of computer crime are introducing viruses, theft of services, disruption of computer systems, and theft of telecommunications services. Computer crime has been estimated to cost over $1 billion in the United States, and an additional $1 billion if corporate and cellular phone theft is included. "Hackers" is the pejorative term for persons who use computers in illegal ways. Hacker attacks are on the rise, posing new threats to organizations linked to the Internet (see Chapter 17).

Computer viruses (see Chapter 17) have grown exponentially during the past decade. More than 1000 viruses have been documented. The average corporate loss for a bad virus outbreak is $250,000 and the probability of a large corporation experiencing a significant computer virus infection in a single year is 50 percent according to some experts. Although many firms now use anti-virus software, the proliferation of computer networks will surely increase the probability of infections.

Following are some illustrative computer crimes:

- On May 29, 1996, the Federal Trade Commission announced it had obtained a temporary restraining order to freeze the assets of Fortuna Alliance of Bellingham, Washington. Fortuna had allegedly taken in over $6 million from thousands of people in an illegal investors' pyramid scheme advertised on the Internet. Fortuna placed ads at several Web sites inviting thousands of customers on the Web to invest $250 to $1750 with the promise of earning at least $5000 per month if they could persuade others to invest. The FTC called Fortuna its largest fraud case to date on the Internet (Wilder, 1996).

- In July 1992, a federal grand jury indicted a national network of 1000 hackers calling themselves MOD—Masters of Deception. Their's was one of the largest thefts of computer information and services in history. The hackers were charged with computer tampering, computer fraud, wire fraud, illegal wiretapping, and conspiracy. The group broke into over 25 of the largest corporate computer systems in the United States, including Equifax, Inc. (a credit reporting firm with 170 million records), Southwestern Bell Corporation, New York Telephone, and Pacific Bell. The group stole and resold credit reports, credit card numbers, and other personal information. Federal investigators used court-ordered wiretaps to monitor the calls of members. The firms blamed their own lax security and a philosophy of "openness" for not detecting the hackers themselves—all of whom were under 22 years of age. The hackers all pleaded guilty. Their convicted leader, Mark Abene, spent 10 months in prison (Gabriel, 1995; Tabor, 1992).

- At AT&T's British headquarters in London, three technicians set up their company in 1992, assigned it a 900 number, and then programmed AT&T computers to dial the number often. The loss amounted to just under $500,000 before the fraud was accidentally detected.

In general, it is employees—insiders—who have inflicted the most injurious computer crimes because they have the knowledge, access, and frequently a job-related motive to commit such crimes.

Congress responded to the threat of computer crime in 1986 with the Computer Fraud and Abuse Act. This act makes it illegal to access a computer system without authorization. Most states have similar laws, and nations in Europe have similar legislation. Other existing legislation covering wiretapping, fraud, and conspiracy by any means, regardless of technology employed, are adequate to cover computer crimes committed thus far.

Employment: Trickle-Down Technology and Reengineering Job Loss

Reengineering work (see Chapter 11) is typically hailed in the information systems community as a major benefit of new information technology. It is much less frequently noted that redesigning business processes could potentially cause millions of middle-level managers and clerical workers to lose their jobs. Worse, if reengineering actually worked as claimed, these workers could not find similar employment in the society because of an actual decline in demand for their skills. One economist has raised the possibility that we will create a society run by a small "high tech elite of corporate professionals . . . in a nation of the permanently unemployed" (Rifkin, 1993). Some have estimated that if reengineering were seriously undertaken by the Fortune 1000 companies, about 25 percent of the U.S. labor force could be displaced. Reengineering has been seriously used at only 15 percent of American service and manufacturing companies.

Economists are much more sanguine about the potential job losses. They believe relieving bright, educated workers from reengineered jobs will result in these workers moving to better jobs in fast-growth industries. Left out of this equation are blue-collar workers, and older, less well-educated middle managers. It is not clear that these groups can be retrained easily for high-quality (high-paying) jobs. Careful planning and sensitivity to employee needs can help companies redesign work to minimize job losses, as illustrated in the Window on Management.

Equity and Access: Increasing Racial and Social Class Cleavages

Does everyone have an equal opportunity to participate in the digital age? Will the social, economic, and cultural gaps which exist in American and other societies be reduced by information systems technology? Or will the cleavages be increased, permitting the "better off" to become still better off? When and if computing becomes ubiquitous, does this include the poor as well as the rich?

The answers to these questions are clearly not known; the differential impact of systems technology on various groups in society is not well studied. What is known is that information and knowledge, and access to these resources through educational institutions and public libraries, are inequitably distributed. Access to computers is distributed inequitably along racial and social class lines as are many other information resources. Left uncorrected, we could end up creating a society of information haves, computer literate and skilled, versus a large group of information have-nots, computer illiterate and unskilled.

The Clinton administration and public interest groups want to narrow this "digital divide" by making digital information services—including the Internet—available to "virtually everyone" just as basic telephone service is now. An amendment to the Telecommunications Act of 1996, which widened telecommunications deregulation, stipulates subsidies for schools and libraries so that people of all backgrounds

The Internet for All?

The Internet is making dramatic changes within corporations. But what happens if some employees cannot reap Internet benefits simply because they have no access to a computer? Or because they lack the computer skills? Management in many companies is facing this problem today. If some employees cannot use the company's information systems based on Internet technology, the company could fail to gain from all their talents and creativity. The employees too might lose by not being able to develop their own skills and advance their own careers. Some management is sensitive to this issue and is responding by searching for ways to include all their employees, to the benefit of all.

The Tribune Company, a Chicago-based publishing and broadcasting firm, began in 1996 to focus on potential benefits of information systems based on Internet technology. Like many companies, the Tribune first reacted with an external search for people with the required information systems skills. Yet quality information systems development requires both creativity and technical knowledge. Given the nature of their business, the company already employed many creative people, such as graphic designers and artists. Management realized this and concluded creative, artistic people could be taught the technical skills needed to use information systems based on the Internet. They quit looking outside and instead gave their employees the opportunity to advance into a new field. The company quickly gained a very creative Internet development staff which developed over 100 pages on the Tribune Company's Web site within the first two months. In addition, because the development staff was integrated into other company units, many Tribune employees quickly began using the Web-based system. According to Jeff Scherb, the company's senior vice president and chief technology officer, the Tribune's goal is to "get to the point where people don't think twice about Web publishing."

One problem many companies face is how to make Internet-based applications available to the whole staff. After all, not all employees have access to computers. The *Los Angeles Times* wanted to use Internet technology to establish an information system to expand human resources and workflow applications. Although most of its over 4000 employees have computer access, many do not. Some whole departments, such as printing, have no computers. The company is considering installing strategically placed kiosks as a solution to this problem. Kraft Foods, Inc., the Northfield, Illinois, food giant with 43,000 employees, is also considering kiosks. It has a number of uses for Internet-based applications, including putting human resources manuals on-line. Such manuals would benefit the organization through reduced printing costs, while the employees would gain easy access to up-to-date company policy information. But Kraft also has many employees without computer access. A total solution based on kiosks in strategic locations at all sites was rejected as too expensive. Karen Isaacson, associate director of human resources, estimates that each kiosk would cost about $100,000, and, she adds, "You put them in 100 plants and you still don't get the [mobile] salespeople." So rather than rely on a single technical solution for all sites, Kraft management decided to develop site-by-site solutions, rolling the system out one site at a time until all employees have access. The company will begin by deploying the system at headquarters, using whatever technology is necessary.

To Think About: What are the arguments for and against companies spending the time and funds to bring Internet technology to every employee? Think about social and ethical issues as well as those relating to profit.

Sources: Julie King, "Tribune Co. Trains 'Net Pros In-house," *Computerworld*, January 20, 1997; and Kim S. Nash, "Missing the Intranet Boat," *Computerworld*, October 21, 1996.

---

have access to the tools of information technology (Lohr, 1996). This is only a partial solution to the problem.

Health Risks: RSI, CVS, and Technostress

repetitive stress injury (RSI)
Occupational disease that occurs when muscle groups are forced through repetitive actions with high-impact loads or thousands of repetitions with low-impact loads.

The most important occupational disease today is **repetitive stress injury (RSI)**. RSI occurs when muscle groups are forced through repetitive actions often with high-impact loads (such as tennis) or tens of thousands of repetitions under low-impact loads (such as working at a computer keyboard).

The single largest source of RSI is computer keyboards. Forty-six million Americans use computers at work, and 185,000 cases of RSI are reported each year according to the National Center for Health Statistics. The most common kind of computer-related RSI is **carpal tunnel syndrome (CTS)** in which pressure on the median nerve through the wrist's bony structure called a "carpal tunnel" produces pain. The

carpal tunnel syndrome (CTS)
Type of RSI in which pressure on the median nerve through the wrist's bony carpal tunnel structure produces pain.

Repetitive stress injury (RSI) is the leading occupational disease today. The single largest cause of RSI is computer keyboard work.

pressure is caused by constant repetition of keystrokes: In a single shift, a word processor may perform 23,000 keystrokes. Symptoms of carpal tunnel syndrome include numbness, shooting pain, inability to grasp objects, and tingling. So far, 1.89 million workers have been diagnosed with carpal tunnel syndrome.

RSI is avoidable. Designing workstations for a neutral wrist position (using a wrist rest to support the wrist), proper monitor stands, and footrests all contribute to proper posture and reduced RSI. New ergonomically correct keyboards are also an option, although their efficacy has yet to be clearly established. These measures should be backed by frequent rest breaks, rotation of employees to different jobs, and moving toward voice or scanner data entry.

RSI is not the only occupational illness caused by computers: back and neck pain, leg stress, and foot pain also result from poor ergonomic designs of workstations (see Tables 5.6 and 5.7).

Computer vision syndrome (CVS) refers to any eye strain condition related to computer display screen use. Its symptoms are headaches, blurred vision, and dry and irritated eyes. The symptoms are usually temporary (Furger, 1993).

The newest computer-related malady is **technostress,** defined as stress induced by computer use and whose symptoms are aggravation, hostility toward humans, impatience, and enervation. The problem according to experts is that humans working continuously with computers come to expect other humans and human institutions to behave like computers, providing instant response, attentiveness, and with an absence of emotion. Computer-intense workers are aggravated when put on hold dur-

computer vision syndrome (CVS) Eye strain condition related to computer display screen use, with symptoms including headaches, blurred vision, and dry, irritated eyes.

technostress Stress induced by computer use whose symptoms include aggravation, hostility toward humans, impatience, and enervation.

Table 5.6   OSHA Ergonomic Risk Factors
Intermittent keying
Intensive keying
Neck twisting/bending
Wrist bending
Prolonged mouse use
Prolonged sitting
Sitting without solid foot support
Lighting (poor illumination or glare)

Source: Mary E. Thyfault, "OSHA Clamps Down," *Information Week,* November 21, 1995.

Table 5.7	Computer-Related Diseases
Disease/Risk	Incidence
RSI	185,000 new cases a year
Other joint diseases	Unknown
Computer Vision Syndrome	10 million cases a year
Miscarriage	Unknown. Related to manufacturing chemicals
Technostress	5 to 10 million cases
VDT Radiation	Unknown impacts

ing a phone call, become incensed or alarmed when their PCs take a few seconds longer to perform a task, lack empathy for humans, and seek out friends who mirror the characteristics of their machines. Technostress is thought to be related to high levels of job turnover in the computer industry, high levels of early retirement from computer-intense occupations, and elevated levels of drug and alcohol abuse.

The incidence of technostress is not known but is thought to be in the millions in the United States and growing rapidly. Although frequently denied as a problem by management, computer-related jobs now top the list of stressful occupations based on health statistics in several industrialized countries. The costs worldwide of stress are put at $200 billion.

To date the role of radiation from computer display screens in occupational disease has not been proved. Video display terminals (VDTs) emit nonionizing electric and magnetic fields at low frequencies. These rays enter the body and have unknown effects on enzymes, molecules, chromosomes, and cell membranes. Early studies suggesting a link between low-level electromagnetic fields (EMFs) and miscarriages have been contradicted by one later, superior study published in 1991 (Schnorr, 1991; Stevens, 1991). Longer-term studies are investigating low-level EMFs and birth defects, stress, low birth weight, and other diseases. All manufacturers have reduced display screen emissions since the early years of 1980, and European countries such as Sweden have adopted stiff radiation emission standards.

The computer has become a part of our lives—personally as well as socially, culturally, and politically. It is unlikely the issues and our choices will become easier as information technology continues to transform our world. The growth of the Internet and the information economy suggests that all the ethical and social issues we have described will be heightened further as we move into the first digital century.

Management Actions: A Corporate Code of Ethics

Some corporations have developed far-reaching corporate IS codes of ethics—Federal Express, IBM, American Express, and Merck and Co. Most firms, however, have not developed these codes of ethics, which leaves them at the mercy of fate, and leaves their employees in the dark about expected correct behavior. There is some dispute concerning a general code of ethics versus a specific information systems code of ethics. As managers, you should strive to develop an IS-specific set of ethical standards for each of the five moral dimensions:

- *Information rights and obligations.* A code should cover topics such as employee e-mail privacy, workplace monitoring, treatment of corporate information, and policies on customer information.

- *Property rights and obligations.* A code should cover topics such as software licenses, ownership of firm data and facilities, ownership of software created by employees on company hardware, and software copyrights. Specific guidelines for contractual relationships with third parties should be covered as well.

- *Accountability and control.* The code should specify a single individual responsible for all information systems, and underneath this individual others who are responsible for individual rights, the protection of property rights, system quality, and quality of life (e.g., job design, ergonomics, employee satisfaction). Responsibilities for control of systems, audits, and management should be clearly defined. The potential liabilities of systems officers and the corporation should be detailed in a separate document.

- *System quality.* The code should describe the general levels of data quality and system error that can be tolerated with detailed specifications left to specific projects. The code should require that all systems attempt to estimate data quality and system error probabilities.

- *Quality of life.* The code should state that the purpose of systems is to improve the quality of life for customers and for employees by achieving high levels of product quality, customer service, and employee satisfaction and human dignity through proper ergonomics, job and workflow design, and human resource development.

MANAGEMENT WRAP-UP

MANAGEMENT

Managers are ethical rule makers for their organizations (Green, 1994). They are charged with creating the policies and procedures to establish ethical conduct, including the ethical use of information systems. Managers are also responsible for identifying, analyzing, and resolving the ethical dilemmas that invariably crop up as they balance conflicting needs and interests.

ORGANIZATION

Rapid changes fueled by information technology are creating new situations where existing laws or rules of conduct may not be relevant. New "gray areas" are emerging in which ethical standards have not yet been codified into law. A new system of ethics for the information age is required to guide individual and organizational choices and actions.

TECHNOLOGY

Information technology is introducing changes that create new ethical issues for societies to debate and resolve. Increasing computing power, storage, and networking capabilities—including the Internet—can expand the reach of individual and organizational actions and magnify their impact. The ease and anonymity with which information can be communicated, copied, and manipulated in on-line environments are challenging traditional rules of right and wrong behavior.

For Discussion: Should producers of software-based services such as ATMs be held liable for economic injuries suffered when their systems fail?

SUMMARY

1. Understand the relationship among ethical, social, and political issues raised by information systems. Ethical, social, and political issues are closely related in an information society. Ethical issues confront individuals who must choose a course of action, often in a situation in which two or more ethical principles are in conflict (a

dilemma). Social issues spring from ethical issues. Societies must develop expectations in individuals about the correct course of action, and social issues then are debates about the kinds of situations and expectations that societies should develop so that individuals behave correctly. Political issues spring from social conflict and have to do largely with laws that prescribe behavior and seek to use the law to create situations in which individuals behave correctly.

2. Identify the main moral dimensions of an information society and apply them to specific situations. There are five main moral dimensions that tie together ethical, social, and political issues in an information society. These moral dimensions are information rights and obligations, property rights, accountability and control, system quality, and quality of life.

3. Apply an ethical analysis to difficult situations. An ethical analysis is a five-step methodology for analyzing a situation. The method involves identifying the facts, values, stakeholders, options, and consequences of actions. Once completed, you can begin to consider what ethical principle you should apply to a situation to arrive at a judgment.

4. Understand specific ethical principles for conduct. Six ethical principles are available to judge your own conduct (and that of others). These principles are derived independently from several cultural, religious, and intellectual traditions. They are not hard and fast rules and may not apply in all situations. The principles are the Golden Rule, Immanuel Kant's Categorical Imperative, Descartes' rule of change, the Utilitarian Principle, the Risk Aversion Principle, and the ethical "no free lunch" rule.

5. Develop corporate policies for ethical conduct. For each of the five moral dimensions, corporations should develop an ethics policy statement to assist individuals and to encourage the correct decisions. The policy areas are as follows. Individual information rights: spell out corporate privacy and due process policies. Property rights: clarify how the corporation will treat property rights of software owners. Accountability and control: clarify who is responsible and accountable for information. System quality: identify methodologies and quality standards to achieve. Quality of life: identify corporate policies on family, computer crime, decision making, vulnerability, job loss, and health risks.

KEY TERMS

Ethics	Descartes' rule of change	Trade secret	Carpal tunnel
Information rights	Utilitarian Principle	Copyright	syndrome (CTS)
Responsibility	Risk Aversion Principle	Patent	Computer vision
Accountability	Ethical "no free lunch" rule	Computer crime	syndrome (CVS)
Liability	Privacy	Computer abuse	Technostress
Due process	Fair Information	Repetitive stress	
Immanuel Kant's	Practices (FIP)	injury (RSI)	
Categorical Imperative	Intellectual property		

REVIEW QUESTIONS

1. In what ways are ethical, social, and political issues connected? Give some examples.

2. What are the key technological trends that heighten ethical concerns?

3. What are the differences between responsibility, accountability, and liability?

4. What are the five steps in an ethical analysis?

5. Identify six ethical principles.

6. What is a professional code of conduct?

7. What are meant by "privacy" and "fair information practices"? How is the Internet challenging the protection of individual privacy?

8. What are the three different regimes that protect intellectual property rights? What challenges to intellectual property rights are posed by the Internet?

9. Why is it so difficult to hold software services liable for failure or injury?

10. What is the most common cause of system quality problems?

11. Name four "quality of life" impacts of computers and information systems.

12. What is technostress, and how would you measure it?

13. Name three management actions that could reduce RSI injuries.

GROUP PROJECT

1. With three or four of your classmates, develop a corporate ethics code on privacy. Be sure to consider e-mail privacy and employer monitoring of worksites as well as hallways, entrances, and restrooms. You should also consider corporate use of information about employees concerning their off-job behavior (e.g., lifestyle, marital arrangements, and so forth). Present your ethics code to the class.

2. With three or four of your classmates, interview managers of your university information systems department concerning university ethics policies in the systems area. Does your university have an ethics policy for students and employees? What is it? You could also interview a local firm rather than university officials. Present your findings to the class.

Fished Out with Computers

In the early 1970s small commercial fishing operations in the United States embraced technology as an indispensable lifeline in a fiercely competitive industry. Now, more than 20 years later, those same fishing operations are finding that the very technology which afforded them a major edge threatens to devastate the limited resource on which their livelihoods depend.

Fishing boats outfitted with sophisticated electronic fish-finding equipment, global-positioning systems, and satellite communications gear have radically changed the commercial fishing industry. "Man-with-technology versus fish is a whole other thing than man versus fish," observed Vito J. Calomo, executive director of the Fisheries Commission in Gloucester, Massachusetts.

In the late 1960s the U.S. fishing fleet was overwhelmed by foreign fleets of huge technologically sophisticated boats fishing in U.S. waters. Many of these "floating factories" were from the Soviet Union. These 300-feet-long steel boats, equipped with sonar and massive refrigeration units, could catch and process hundreds of thousands more fish than their U.S. counterparts. During this period the total catch from the U.S. fleet plummeted.

In 1976, the U.S. Congress adopted the Magnuson Fishery Management and Conservation Act in an effort to protect U.S. fishermen from the competitive crush of foreign fleets

of huge, technologically sophisticated boats fishing in U.S. waters. The act declared a 200-mile zone off the U.S. coastline off-limits to non-U.S. fishermen. In addition, the government helped make low-interest loans available to fishermen who wanted to upgrade their boats. Both novice and experienced fishermen took advantage of a market that was flooded with inexpensive ex-military technology. For example LORAN—developed to give the Defense Department a long-range, highly accurate radio navigation system—afforded even unskilled fishermen with the ability to search out fish with precision. Inexpensive versions of Echo sounders—a technology used to pinpoint the location of enemy submarines—gave fishermen the ability to seek out schools of fish, ascertain depth, and even map the ocean floors.

The combined effect of eliminating competition from foreign boats, low-interest loans, and inexpensive technology resulted in a major increase in the fish catch for U.S. fishermen. In 1980, New England fishermen landed more than 117 million pounds of cod, the largest haul since 1945. But the resurgence of the golden days proved to be fleeting. No longer limited by experience and skill, more and more would-be fishermen joined the fray. What they lacked in sea-smarts they made up for with cutting-edge technology, intensifying the competition for all fishermen. By the early 1980s the catches again began to decline. Commercial fishermen re-

sponded by acquiring even more sophisticated technology. "Essentially what we did was replace the foreign fleet with a more powerful American fleet," noted Anthony D. DiLernia, a professor of marine education at Kingsboro Community College. "Unfortunately, you cannot have the same number of boats, fishing with ever-increasing technology, and still maintain the ecosystem."

In 1995, 27 million pounds of fish were sold, a decline of 4 million pounds from 1993. The traditional New England catch of groundfish stocks fell 30 percent from 1990 to 1992. In 1994 alone, groundfish landings in the Gulf of Maine dropped 25 percent from the previous year. Halibut and haddock, two New England staples, are for commercial purposes extinct in George's Bank, long famed as richly fertile fishing ground. In turn, the government has placed both geographic and time limits on fishing in an effort to provide some protection for diminished fish populations. Strict limits on commercial fishing in New England forced some fishermen to South America where the government has yet to place similar limits on threatened fish populations. The Clinton administration spent $2 million and plans to spend an additional $25 million this year to buy out struggling groundfish enterprises. In many cases the government-subsidized "superboats" built in the 1980s are sunk to serve as artificial reefs to support budding fish populations.

The experience of the New England fishing industry is significant because it directly links the introduction of information and communications technologies with the depletion of a resource. The saga of the New England fishing industry may well serve as a bellwether for other industries whose business interests also rely on a finite, shared pool of resources.

For example, the fierce competition in the oil industry and technological advancements in the ability to extract oil have led to a similar irony. Because oil cannot be owned until it is extracted from the ground, oil companies rush to lease and drill on oil-rich lands. The rapid extraction of oil destroys natural pressures in the ground leaving much of the oil trapped. The result? Extraction costs increase, hiking the costs of oil and forcing greater dependency on foreign sources.

Internet bandwidth, the information carrying capacity of the network, isn't given much thought today as millions rush to set up technologically sophisticated Web sites. However, there is a limit to the capacity of the Internet bandwidth. In the future, the bandwidth may become so clogged with information that traffic on the Internet will slow to a virtual standstill.

As growing businesses in all industries become more adept at taking advantage of state-of-the-art technology thereby becoming increasingly efficient, it is likely that more industries will simply run out of key resources. ■

Source: Sarah Schafer, "Fished Out," *Inc. Technology,* 1996.

Case Study Questions

1. What managerial, organizational, and technological factors were responsible for the problems facing the U.S. fishing industry?

2. Perform an ethical analysis of the plight of the fishing industry. Is there an ethical dilemma or conflict? Who are the stakeholders? What options can be taken to solve the problem? What are the consequences of these options?

3. Which of the six ethical principles apply here?

REFERENCES

Anderson, Ronald E., Deborah G. Johnson, Donald Gotterbarn, and Judith Perrolle. "Using the New ACM Code of Ethics in Decision Making." *Communications of the ACM 36*, no. 2 (February 1993).

Andrews, Edmund L. "AT&T Will Cut 15,000 Jobs to Reduce Costs." *The New York Times* (February 11, 1994).

Baase, Sara. *A Gift of Fire: Social, Legal, and Ethical Issues in Computing.* Upper Saddle River, NJ: Prentice-Hall, 1997.

Barlow, John Perry. "Electronic Frontier: Private Life in Cyberspace," *Communications of the ACM 34*, no. 8 (August 1991).

Bjerklie, David. "Does E-Mail Mean Everyone's Mail?" *Information Week* (January 3, 1994).

Brod, Craig. *Techno Stress—The Human Cost of the Computer Revolution.* Reading, MA: Addison-Wesley (1982).

Brown Bag Software vs. Symantec Corp. 960 F2D 1465 (Ninth Circuit, 1992).

Bulkeley, William M. "Databases Plagued by a Reign of Error." *The Wall Street Journal* (May 26, 1992).

Cafasso, Rosemary. "Rethinking Reengineering." *Computerworld* (March 15, 1993).

Caldwell, Bruce, with John Soat. "The Hidden Persuader." *Information Week* (November 19, 1990).

Carley, William M. "Rigging Computers For Fraud or Malice Is Often an Inside Job." *The Wall Street Journal* (August 27, 1992).

Carvajal, Dorren. "Book Publishers Worry about Threat of Internet." *The New York Times* (March 18, 1996).

Chabrow, Eric R. "The Internet: Copyrights." *Information Week* (March 25, 1996).

Collins, W. Robert, Keith W. Miller, Bethany J. Spielman, and Phillip Wherry. "How Good is Good Enough? An Ethical Analysis of Software Construction and Use." *Communications of the ACM 37*, no. 1 (January 1994).

Computer Systems Policy Project, "Perspectives on the National Information Infrastructure." January 12, 1993.

Couger, J. Daniel. "Preparing IS Students to Deal with Ethical Issues." *MIS Quarterly 13*, no. 2 (June 1989).

Dejoie, Roy, George Fowler, and David Paradice, eds. *Ethical Issues in Information Systems.* Boston: Boyd & Fraser (1991).

Denning, Dorothy E. et al., "To Tap or Not to Tap." *Communications of the ACM 36*, no. 3 (March 1993).

Diamond, Edwin, and Stephen Bates. "Law and Order Comes to Cyberspace." *Technology Review* (October 1995).

Equifax Report on Consumers in the Information Age, A National Survey. Equifax Inc., 1992.

Feder, Barnaby J. "As Hand Injuries Mount, So Do the Lawsuits." *The New York Times* (June 8, 1992).

Furger, Roberta. "In Search of Relief for Tired, Aching Eyes." *PC World* (February 1993).

Gabriel, Trip. "Reprogramming a Convicted Hacker." *The New York Times* (January 14, 1995).

George, Joey F. "Computer-Based Monitoring: Common Perceptions and Empirical Results." *MIS Quarterly 20*, no. 4 (December 1996).

Graham, Robert L. "The Legal Protection of Computer Software." *Communications of the ACM* (May 1984).

Green, R. H. *The Ethical Manager.* New York: Macmillan (1994).

Hagel, John III, and Jeffrey F. Rayport. "The Coming Battle for Customer Information." *Harvard Business Review* (January–February 1997).

Harrington, Susan J. "The Effect of Codes of Ethics and Personal Denial of Responsibility on Computer Abuse Judgments and Intentions." *MIS Quarterly 20*, no. 2 (September 1996).

Huff, Chuck, and C. Dianne Martin. "Computing Consequences: A Framework for Teaching Ethical Computing." *Communications of the ACM 38*, no. 12 (December 1995).

Joes, Kathryn. "EDS Set to Restore Cash-Machine Network." *New York Times* (March 26, 1993).

Johnson, Deborah G. "Ethics Online." *Communications of the ACM* 40, no. 1 (January 1997).

Johnson, Deborah G., and John M. Mulvey. "Accountability and Computer Decision Systems." *Communications of the ACM* 38, no. 12 (December 1995).

King, Julia. "It's CYA Time." *Computerworld* (March 30, 1992).

Kling, Rob. "When Organizations Are Perpetrators: The Conditions of Computer Abuse and Computer Crime." In *Computerization & Controversy: Value Conflicts & Social Choices*, edited by Charles Dunlop and Rob Kling. New York: Academic Press (1991).

Laudon, Kenneth C. "Ethical Concepts and Information Technology." *Communications of the ACM* 38, no. 12 (December 1995).

Levinson, Marc. "Thanks. You're Fired." *Newsweek* (May 23, 1994).

Lohr, Steve. "A Nation Ponders Its Growing Digital Divide." *New York Times* (October 21, 1996).

Markoff, John. "Computer Viruses: Just Uncommon Colds After All?" *New York Times* (November 1, 1992).

———. "Though Illegal, Copied Software is Now Common." *New York Times* (July 27, 1992).

Mason, Richard O. "Applying Ethics to Information Technology Issues." *Communications of the ACM* 38, no. 12 (December 1995).

———. "Four Ethical Issues in the Information Age. *MIS Quarterly* 10, no. 1 (March 1986).

McPartlin, John P. "A Question of Complicity." *InformationWeek* (June 22, 1992).

———. "Environmental Agency 'Held Hostage' by Outsourcer." *InformationWeek* (March 9, 1992).

———. "Ten Years of Hard Labor." *InformationWeek* (March 29, 1993).

———. "The Terrors of Technostress." *InformationWeek* (July 30, 1990).

Milberg, Sandra J., Sandra J. Burke, H. Jeff Smith, and Ernest A. Kallman. "Values, Personal Information Privacy, and Regulatory Approaches." *Communications of the ACM* 38, no. 12 (December 1995).

Mykytyn, Kathleen, Peter P. Mykytyn, Jr., and Craig W. Slinkman, "Expert Systems: A Question of Liability," *MIS Quarterly* 14, no. 1 (March 1990).

Neumann, Peter G. "Inside RISKS: Computers, Ethics and Values." *Communications of the ACM* 34, no. 7 (July 1991).

———. "Inside RISKS: Fraud by Computer." *Communications of the ACM* 35, no. 8 (August 1992).

Nissenbaum, Helen. "Computing and Accountability." *Communications of the ACM* 37, no. 1 (January 1994).

Okerson, Ann. "Who Owns Digital Works?" *Scientific American* (July 1996).

Oz, Effy, "Ethical Standards for Information Systems Professionals," *MIS Quarterly* 16, no. 4 (December 1992).

———. *Ethics for the Information Age.* Dubuque, Iowa: W.C. Brown (1994).

Pollack, Andrew. "San Francisco Law on VDTs is Struck Down." *The New York Times* (February 14, 1992).

Ramirez, Anthony. "AT&T to Eliminate Many Operator Jobs." *The New York Times* (March 4, 1992).

Rifkin, Glenn. "The Ethics Gap." *Computerworld* (October 14, 1991).

Rifkin, Jeremy. "Watch Out for Trickle-Down Technology." *The New York Times* (March 16, 1993).

Rigdon, Joan E. "Frequent Glitches in New Software Bug Users." *The Wall Street Journal* (January 18, 1995).

Rotenberg, Marc. "Communications Privacy: Implications for Network Design." *Communications of the ACM* 36, no. 8 (August 1993).

———. "Inside RISKS: Protecting Privacy." *Communications of the ACM* 35, no. 4 (April 1992).

Samuelson, Pamela. "Computer Programs and Copyright's Fair Use Doctrine." *Communications of the ACM* 36, no. 9 (September 1993).

———. "Copyright's Fair Use Doctrine and Digital Data." *Communications of the ACM* 37, no. 1 (January 1994).

———. "Digital Media and the Law." *Communications of the ACM* 34, no. 10 (October 1991).

———. "First Amendment Rights for Information Providers?" *Communications of the ACM* 34, no. 6 (June 1991).

———. "Liability for Defective Electronic Information." *Communications of the ACM* 36, no. 1 (January 1993).

———. "Self Plagiarism or Fair Use?" *Communications of the ACM* 37, no. 8 (August 1994).

———. "The Ups and Downs of Look and Feel." *Communications of the ACM* 36, no. 4, (April 1993).

———. "Updating the Copyright Look and Feel Lawsuits." *Communications of the ACM* 35, no. 9, (September 1992).

Schnorr, Teresa M. "Miscarriage and VDT Exposure." *New England Journal of Medicine* (March 1991).

Sipior, Janice C., and Burke T. Ward. "The Ethical and Legal Quandary of E-mail Privacy." *Communications of the ACM* 38, no. 12 (December 1995).

Smith, H. Jeff. "Privacy Policies and Practices: Inside the Organizational Maze." *Communications of the ACM* 36, no. 12 (December 1993).

Smith, H. Jeff, Sandra J. Milberg, and Sandra J. Burke. "Information Privacy: Measuring Individuals' Concerns about Organizational Practices." *MIS Quarterly* 20, no. 2 (June 1996).

Sterling, Bruce. *The Hacker Crackdown: Law and Disorder on the Computer Frontier.* New York: Bantam Books 1992.

Stevens, William K. "Major U.S. Study Finds No Miscarriage Risk From Video Terminals." *New York Times* (March 14, 1991).

Straub, Detmar W. Jr., and Rosann Webb Collins. "Key Information Liability Issues Facing Managers: Software Piracy, Proprietary Databases, and Individual Rights to Privacy." *MIS Quarterly* 14, no. 2 (June 1990).

Straub, Detmar W. Jr., and William D. Nance. "Discovering and Disciplining Computer Abuse in Organizations: A Field Study." *MIS Quarterly* 14, no. 1 (March 1990).

Tabor, Mary W., with Anthony Ramirez. "Computer Savy, With an Attitude." *The New York Times* (July 23, 1992).

The Telecommunications Policy Roundtable. "Renewing the Commitment to a Public Interest Telecommunications Policy." *Communications of the ACM* 37, no. 1 (January 1994).

United States Department of Health, Education and Welfare. *Records, Computers, and the Rights of Citizens.* Cambridge: MIT Press (1973).

Wilder, Clinton. "Feds Allege Internet Scam." *InformationWeek* (June 10, 1996).

Wilson, Linda. "Devil in Your Data." *InformationWeek* (August 31, 1992).

Weisband, Suzanne P., and Bruce A. Reinig. "Managing User Perceptions of E-mail Privacy." *Communications of the ACM* 38, no. 12 (December 1995).

Wolinsky, Carol, and James Sylvester. "Privacy in the Telecommunications Age." *Communications of the ACM* 35, no. 2 (February 1992).

CHRYSLER AND GM: ORGANIZATION, TECHNOLOGY, AND BUSINESS PROCESSES IN THE U.S. AUTO INDUSTRY

This case illustrates how two giant American corporations, Chrysler and General Motors, have tried to use information technology to combat foreign and domestic competitors. The case explores the relationship between each firm's management strategy, organizational characteristics, business processes, and information systems. It poses the following question: How has information technology addressed the problems confronting the U.S. automobile industry?

On October 26, 1992, Robert C. Stempel resigned as chairman and CEO of the General Motors Corporation. Stempel was pressured to resign because he had not moved quickly enough to make the changes required to ensure the automotive giant's survival. To counter massive financial losses and plummeting market share, Stempel had announced 10 months earlier that GM would have to close 21 of its North American plants and cut 74,000 of its 370,000 employees over three years. Stempel was replaced by a more youthful and determined management team headed by Jack Smith.

GM's plight reflected the depths of the decline of the once vigorous American automobile industry in the late 1980s. Year after year, as Americans came to view American-made cars as low in quality or not stylish, car buyers purchased fewer and fewer American cars, replacing them mostly with Japanese models.

Ironically, at about the same time, the Chrysler Corporation announced strong 1992 third-quarter earnings of $202 million. During the 1980s, Chrysler had struggled with rising costs and declining sales of mass-market cars. However, demand was strong for its minivans and the hot Jeep Grand Cherokee. A stringent cost-cutting crusade eliminated $4 billion in operating costs in only three years. The rest of the U.S. auto industry was still in a slump from prolonged recession and losses of market share to the Japanese.

Ten years before, Chrysler had been battling bankruptcy and GM was flush with cash. Had Chrysler finally turned itself around? Was this the beginning of the end for the world's largest automobile maker? What is the role of information systems in this tale of two auto makers and in the future of the U.S. automobile industry?

General Motors

General Motors, the world's largest auto maker, has more than 700,000 employees in 35 countries, and is bigger than AT&T, Federal Express, IBM, and Microsoft combined. In the early 1990s, GM's U.S. auto business accounted for about 1.5 percent of the U.S. economy, down from 5 percent in the 1950s. Its sheer size has proved to be one of GM's greatest burdens. For 70 years, GM operated along the lines laid down by CEO Alfred Sloan, who rescued the firm from bankruptcy in the 1920s. Sloan separated the firm into five separate operating groups and divisions (Chevrolet, Pontiac, Oldsmobile, Buick, and Cadillac). Each division functioned as a semiautonomous company with its own mar-

keting operations. GM's management was a welter of bureaucracies.

GM covered the market with low-end Chevys and high-end Caddies. At the outset, this amalgam of top-down control and decentralized execution enabled GM to build cars at lower cost than its rivals; but it could also charge more for the quality and popularity of its models. By the 1960s, GM started having trouble building smaller cars to compete with imports and started eliminating differences among divisions. By the mid-1980s, GM had reduced differences among the divisions to the point that customers could not tell a Cadillac from a Chevrolet; the engines in low-end Chevys were also found in high-end Oldsmobiles. Its own brands started to compete with each other.

Under Roger Smith, CEO from 1981 to 1990, GM moved boldly, but often in the wrong direction. GM remained a far-flung vertically integrated corporation that at one time manufactured up to 70 percent of its own parts. Its costs were much higher than either its U.S. or Japanese competitors. Like many large manufacturing firms, its organizational culture resisted change. GM has made steady improvements in car quality, but its selection and styling have lagged behind its U.S. and Japanese rivals. GM's market share plunged from a peak of 52 percent in the early 1960s to just 33 percent today. In 1979, GM's market share was 46 percent.

GM created an entirely new Saturn automobile with a totally new division, labor force, and production system based on the Japanese "lean production" model. Saturn workers and managers share information, authority, and decision making. The Saturn car was a market triumph. But Saturn took seven years to roll out the first model and drained $5 billion from other car projects. GM had been selling Saturn at a loss to build up market share.

In 1992, GM's labor costs were $2358 per car, compared with $1872 for Chrysler and $1563 for Ford. That made GM 40 percent less productive than Ford. These figures do not begin to approach those of the Japanese, whose automotive productivity surpasses all U.S. corporations.

Chrysler

In auto industry downturns, Chrysler was always the weakest of Detroit's Big Three auto makers (GM, Ford, and Chrysler). Founded in the 1930s by Walter P. Chrysler through a series of mergers with smaller companies such as Dodge and DeSoto, Chrysler prided itself on superior engineering, especially in engines and suspensions. In the 1940s and 1950s, Chrysler grew into a small, highly centralized firm with very little vertical integration. Unlike Ford and GM, Chrysler relied on external suppliers for 70 percent of its major components and subassemblies, becoming more an auto assembler than a huge vertically integrated manufacturer such as GM. Unlike its larger competitors, Chrysler did not develop a global market for its cars to cushion domestic downturns. Chrysler's centralized and smaller firm could potentially move faster and be more innovative than its larger competitors.

During the late 1980s, Chrysler lost several hundred thousand units of sales annually because it did not make improvements in engine development and in its mass-market cars—the small subcompacts and large rear-wheel drive vehicles. There was no new family of mid-priced, mid-sized cars to rival Ford's Taurus or Honda's Accord. Customers could not distinguish Chrysler's key car models and brands from each other, and thus migrated to other brands. Chrysler's re-

sponse, the Spirit and Acclaim, brought out in 1988, were ultraconservative in styling. Yet Chrysler lavished funds on specialty niches such as coupes and convertibles. By the early 1990s, fierce price cutting had upped Chrysler's breakeven point (the number of cars the firm had to sell to start making a profit) to 1.9 million units, up from 1.4 million.

GM's Information Systems Strategy

Despite heavy investment in information technology, GM's information systems were virtually archaic. It had more than 100 mainframes and 34 computer centers but had no centralized system to link computer operations or to coordinate operations from one department to another. Each division and group had its own hardware and software so that the design group could not interact with production engineers via computer.

GM adopted a "shotgun" approach, pursuing several high-technology paths simultaneously in the hope that one or all of them would pay off. GM also believed it could overwhelm competitors by outspending them. GM does spend more than its competitors on information systems. It spends 2.5 percent of sales on information systems, whereas Ford spends 1.6 percent and Chrysler 0.9 percent of sales on information systems budgets. GM also tried to use information technology to totally overhaul the way it does business.

Recognizing the continuing power of the divisions and the vast differences among them, Roger Smith, CEO of GM from 1981 to 1990, sought to integrate the manufacturing and administrative information systems by purchasing Electronic Data Systems (EDS) of Dallas for $2.5 billion. EDS has supplied GM's data processing and communications services. EDS and its talented system designers were charged with conquering the administrative chaos in the divisions: more than 16 different electronic mail systems, 28 different

word processing systems, and a jumble of factory floor systems that could not communicate with management. Even worse, most of these systems were running on completely incompatible equipment.

EDS consolidated its 5 computing centers and GM's 34 computing centers into 21 uniform information-processing centers for GM and EDS work. EDS replaced the hundred different networks that served GM with the world's largest private digital telecommunications network. In 1993, EDS launched the Consistent Office Environment project to replace its hodgepodge of desktop models, network operating systems, and application development tools with standard hardware and software for its office technology.

GM's Integrated Scheduling project is designed to replace 30 different materials and scheduling systems with one integrated system to handle inventory, manufacturing, and financial data. Factory managers can receive orders from the car divisions for the number and type of vehicles to build and then can create an estimated 20-week manufacturing schedule for GM and its suppliers. The system also sends suppliers schedules each morning on what materials need to be delivered to what docks at what hour during that manufacturing day.

Smith earmarked $40 billion for new plants and automation, but not all investments were fruitful. He spent heavily on robots to paint cars and install windshields, hoping to reduce GM's unionized work force. At first, however, the robots accidentally painted themselves and dropped windshields onto the front seats. Although a number of these problems were corrected, some robots stand unused today. The highly automated equipment never did what was promised because GM did not train workers properly to use it and did not design its car models for easy robot assembly. Instead of reducing its work force, GM had workers stay on the line because of frequent robotic breakdowns.

Chrysler's Information Systems Strategy

In 1980, with $2.8 billion in debt, Chrysler seemed headed for bankruptcy. Its financial crisis galvanized its management to find new ways to cut costs, increase inventory turnover, and improve quality. Its new management team led by Lee Iacocca instituted an aggressive policy to bring its computer-based systems under management control. Chrysler didn't have the money to invest in several high-technology paths at once. It adopted a "rifle" approach to systems: Build what was absolutely essential, and build what would produce the biggest returns. Chrysler focused on building common systems—systems that would work in 6000 dealer showrooms, 25 zone offices, 22 parts depots, and all of its manufacturing plants.

Chrysler built integrated systems. When an order is captured electronically at the dealer, the same order is tied to production, schedules, invoices, parts forecasts, projections, parts and inventory management, and so forth.

Chrysler's low degree of vertical integration put the company in a better position to concentrate on only a few technologies. Because it was more of an auto assembler and distributor than a manufacturer, it had less need for leading-edge manufacturing technologies such as vision systems, programmable controllers, and robotics, all of which are far more important to GM and Ford.

Chrysler directed most of its information systems budget to corporate-wide communications systems and just-in-time inventory management. Just-in-time (JIT) inventory management is obviously critical to a company that has 70 percent of its parts made by outside suppliers. (JIT supplies needed parts to the production line on a last-minute basis. This keeps factory inventory levels as low as possible and holds down production costs.) During the 1980s, Chrysler achieved a 9 percent reduction in inventory and an increase in average quarterly inventory turnover from 6.38 times to 13.9 times.

A single corporation-wide network connects Chrysler's large and mid-sized computers from various vendors and gives engineering workstations access to the large computers. This makes it easier to move data from one system, stage of production, or plant to another and facilitates just-in-time inventory management.

Even before the 1980s, Chrysler had decided it needed a centralized pool of computerized CAD specifications that was accessible to all stages of production. In 1981, it installed a system to provide managers in all work areas and in all nine Chrysler plants with the same current design specifications. Tooling and design can access this data concurrently, so that a last-minute change in design can be immediately conveyed to tooling and manufacturing engineers. Chrysler created centralized business files for inventory, shipping, marketing, and a host of other related activities.

All this centralized management information makes scheduling and inventory control much easier to coordinate. Chrysler's cars and trucks share many of the same parts. Chrysler launched a satellite communication network in 1982 that provides one-way video and two-way data transmission to nearly 5000 of its dealerships and offices around the country. It is being expanded to sites outside the United States.

Chrysler set up electronic links between its computers and those of its suppliers, such as the Budd Company of Rochester, Michigan, which supplies U.S. auto companies with sheet metal parts, wheel products, and frames. Budd can extract manufacturing releases electronically through terminals installed in all work areas and can deliver the parts exactly when Chrysler needs them. A new enhancement verifies the accuracy of advanced shipping notices electronically transmitted by suppliers and helps Chrysler track inventory levels and payment schedules more closely.

Learning from the Japanese

In the mid-1980s, MIT researchers found that the Toyota Motor Corporation's production system represented a sharp departure from Henry Ford's mass-production techniques. In "lean manufacturing," Japanese auto makers focused on minimizing waste and inventory and utilizing workers' ideas. The emphasis is on maximizing reliability and quality, and minimizing waste. The ideal "lean" factory has parts built just as they are needed and has a level of quality so high that inspection is virtually redundant.

After studying Honda Motor Company, Chrysler started to cut $1 billion a year in operating costs and began to rethink virtually everything it did, from designing engines to reporting financial results. Chrysler overhauled its top-down autocratic management structure. It replaced its traditional rigid departments, such as the engine division, with nimble Honda-like "cross-functional platform teams." The teams combined experts from diverse areas such as design, manufacturing, marketing, and purchasing together in one location and were given the power to make basic decisions ranging from styling to choice of suppliers.

The platform teams work with suppliers early in the design process and give them more responsibilities. More than 300 resident engineers from supplier firms work side by side with Chrysler employees. A single supplier is held accountable for the design prototypes and production of a specific system or part, including responsibility for cost, quality, and on-time delivery. In the past, Chrysler chose suppliers on the basis of competitive bids. Development time was stretched because suppliers were not chosen until after designs were finalized. Chrysler spent 12 to 18 months sending out bids for quotations, analyzing bids, and negotiating contracts with suppliers before suppliers were selected. Additional time would be wasted correcting problems with the suppliers' parts or systems that were discovered during manufacturing. Under this new collaborative relationship, Chrysler has reduced the number of suppliers by over 50 percent and shortened the production cycle.

Chrysler has asked suppliers to suggest operational changes that it could make to reduce its own costs as well as those of suppliers. Suppliers can use an on-line system to submit suggestions for making improvements. Chrysler and its suppliers can communicate using a common e-mail system. Nearly all suppliers have purchased Catia, Chrysler's preferred CAD/CAM software to further coordinate their work.

Chrysler now has five separate platform teams to design its large cars, small cars, jeeps, minivans, and trucks. Hourly workers provide input to help Chrysler eliminate wasted steps in the assembly process. Toyota cut waste by diagramming every step of its assembly process. It moved tools closer to the workers and eliminated unnecessary motions. Chrysler is now redesigning its assembly lines to be more like those of Toyota. Ten years ago, it took 6000 workers to build 1000 cars a day. Now Chrysler can achieve the same output with half that many workers.

Involving suppliers early in the design process, along with the platform team approach, has cut product development time by 20 to 40 percent while increasing quality. For example, Chrysler was able to develop its Durango utility vehicle in only 24 months. The Dodge Viper sports car was designed in only 36 months, a process that traditionally had taken Chrysler 4.5 years. Consequently, Chrysler's profit per vehicle has leaped from an average of $250 in the 1980s to $2110 in 1994.

To support its new approach to product development, Chrysler built a new 3.5-million-square-foot Chrysler Technology Center (CTC) 30 miles north of Detroit in Auburn Hills, Michigan. Chrysler leaders expect the CTC to further enhance productivity by providing the technology that will enable Chrysler to engineer things only once and not repeat them. For instance, a failed crash test in the past might have left engineers scratching their heads. Now they can compare crash data from a test with theoretical predictions, moving closer to a solution with each successive prediction cycle. Only when they need to test a solution would they actually have to crash another car. Because hand-built prototypes cost $250,000 to $400,000, avoiding a few crash tests has a large payoff. Using this approach, engineers designed the LH car so that it passed its crash test the first time out.

Every room in the CTC has eight-inch raised floors covering a total of 10,000 fiber-optic cables that can transmit massive volumes of data at high speed. These cables link CTC's buildings to its main data center. The CTC itself is scheduled to house 10 mainframe computers, 2 supercomputers, and control systems for all the center's data and computer networks. A total of 7000 people work there.

With a three-story atrium, the grandiose building goes far beyond functionality. It cost the cash-strapped Chrysler over $1 billion. Chrysler management claims the CTC technology makes reengineering of the automobile design process possible, but industry experts point out that you could put platform teams in much less elaborate quarters. Hundreds of millions of the dollars spent on the CTC could have been used to bring Chrysler cars to market even sooner. Is the CTC symbolic of Chrysler's overall predicament? Although Chrysler plans to spend $3 billion annually on product development through 1997, it could not find $100 million for a full-sized wind tunnel to test car designs—less money than what the

monumental features of CTC added to the building's cost.

GM similarly revamped its approach to production and product development. The company is moving away from traditional assembly lines into smaller working units called *cells,* in which workers have more opportunity to design their own processes and improve output. To combat GM's old culture of fiefdoms and interdivisional fighting that stifled innovation, Jack Smith replaced the old committee system with a single strategy board on which GM's top executives from manufacturing, engineering, sales and marketing, finance, human resources, logistics, purchasing, and communications work together on common goals. Every new GM car or truck must be explicitly targeted to 1 of 26 precisely defined market segments, such as small sporty cars or full-size pickup trucks. No two vehicles are allowed to overlap. A new launch center at GM's engineering headquarters north of Detroit acts as a filter for all design ideas. Teams of engineers, designers, and marketers evaluate car and truck proposals for cost, marketability, and compatibility with other GM products. But unlike Chrysler and Japanese auto makers, GM's teams are not empowered to make the important product development decisions. The power of the functional departments such as engineering and purchasing is still maintained.

Jack Smith has put even more emphasis than his predecessors on standardizing GM's business processes and parts, along with its information systems. He called for reducing the number of basic car platforms from 12 to 5. In the past, GM cars were built in plants dedicated to a single model; they seldom ran at full capacity. By reducing the potential variations of each model, GM can now build several models in the same plant; with fewer parts per car, the cars are much easier to assemble. With fewer platforms, GM can operate with fewer engineers, simpler more flexible factories, smaller inventories, more common parts, and greater economies of scale.

GM named J. Ignacio Lopez de Arriortua in April 1992 as its worldwide purchasing director to make GM's high parts costs more competitive. Before leaving the company, Arriortua consolidated 27 worldwide purchasing operations into one at Detroit. He made GM's company-owned suppliers bid against outside suppliers and pressured outside suppliers for immediate 20 percent price reductions and reductions of up to 50 percent in the next few years. At that time about 40 percent of GM parts were coming from outside suppliers versus 70 percent of the parts in Chrysler and 50 percent at Ford.

GM is also in the process of rolling out a satellite network for its 8500 dealerships, racing to catch up with Chrysler and Nissan Motor Corporation, who already have such networks in place. All these efforts have translated into more efficient and quality-driven production and lower costs. From 1991 until the beginning of 1994, GM removed $2800 in costs, before taxes, for every vehicle it manufactured. Assembly time for the Chevrolet Cavalier and the Pontiac Sunfire takes 40 percent less than the models they replaced. The number of parts for these vehicles has been cut by 29 percent.

Under Jack Smith, GM went from a $10.7 billion loss in 1991 to a $362 million profit in 1993, an $11 billion swing. Earnings have continued to improve. The company has benefited from strong and diverse overseas operations and gradual reductions in labor and manufacturing costs in North America. More significantly, GM earned an average of $1000 for each car and light truck sold in North America, up from $500 per vehicle a year earlier. It sold relatively more high-profit vehicles.

Yet GM is still less efficient than its competitors. It still takes GM longer to make a Cavalier than it does Ford to make cars at its most efficient plants.

The production cycle of a new model, from initial design to start-up production, still takes about 46 months, compared with 27 months for Toyota and 29 months for Chrysler. Production costs remain high because GM still buys a smaller proportion of its parts from outside suppliers than its competitors. (Ford earns $400 more per vehicle and Chrysler $600 more per vehicle than GM for this reason.) Even after strengthening its brand images, its 82 models are still too many. GM is finally introducing competitive vehicles such as the Chevrolet Cavalier and the Pontiac Sunfire in certain market segments, and demand for its sports-utility vehicles is very strong. However, engineering problems and parts shortages have crimped production. Implementing new programs and flexible manufacturing, combined with stringent cost cutting, has proved extremely difficult. GM has yet to show that it can once again become an auto-making star.

From near collapse, Chrysler has emerged as a highly profitable cash machine. It continues to dominate the minivan market, and has launched successful new models such as the Jeep Grand Cherokee, the Chrysler Neon, the Chrysler Concorde, and Eagle Vision. One in six vehicles sold in the United States comes from Chrysler, up from one in seven in 1995. The question for Chrysler, too, is whether it can sustain its successes over the long haul.

Chrysler still needs to work on quality and productivity. Although its cars and trucks are more reliable than they were a decade ago, they still do not match the competition. While Detroit appears to have stopped losing ground to Japanese autos, Japanese car makers are continuing to improve plant efficiency and reduce their product development time. Nissan and Mazda introduced assembly lines that can make half a dozen different vehicles, whereas most Big Three plants only make one or two different cars.

The principal challenge for Detroit's auto makers is to keep their comeback in perspective. Some of their spectacular growth in sales and earnings was due to the increasing value of the yen in 1993 and 1994, which made some Japanese cars more expensive than comparable Big Three models. Even with enormous price gaps, Japanese cars still captured 23 percent of U.S. car and truck sales, compared with 20 percent 10 years before. Can the U.S. auto industry sustain its turnaround momentum? ∎

Sources: Jerry Flint, "Company of the Year: Chrysler," *Forbes*, January 13, 1997; Jeffrey H. Dyer, "How Chrysler Created an American Keiretsu," *Harvard Business Review*, July–August 1996; Keith Bradsher, "What's New at GM? Cars, for a Change," *The New York Times*, September 8, 1996; David Woodruff et al., "Target Chrysler," *Business Week*, April 24, 1995; Alex Taylor III, "GM's $11,000,000,000 Turnaround," *Fortune*, October 12, 1994, and "Can GM Remodel Itself?" *Fortune*, January 13, 1992; Steve Lohr with James Bennet, "Lessons in Rebounds from GM and IBM," *The New York Times*, October 24, 1994; Kathleen Kerwin, "GM's Aurora," *Business Week*, March 21, 1994; John Greenwald, "What Went Wrong?" *Time Magazine*, November 9, 1992; Maryann Keller, *Rude Awakening: The Rise, Fall, and Struggle for Recovery of General Motors*, New York: Harper Collins Publishers, 1990; David Woodruff with Elizabeth Lesly, "Surge at Chrysler," *Business Week*, November 9, 1992; and Edward Cone, "Chrysler," *Information Week*, September 7, 1992.

Case Study Questions

1. Compare the roles played by information systems at Chrysler and GM. How did they affect the structure of the automobile industry itself?

2. How much did information systems contribute to GM's and Chrysler's success or failure?

3. What management, organization, and technology issues explain the differences in the way Chrysler and GM used information systems?

4. What management, organization, and technology factors were responsible for Chrysler's and GM's problems?

5. How did GM and Chrysler redesign their business processes to compete more effectively?

6. How important are information systems in solving the problems of the American automobile industry? What are some of the problems that technology cannot address?

Technical Foundations
of Information Systems

Part Two lays out the technical foundations of information systems: hardware, software, storage, and communications technologies.

CHAPTER 6

Computers and Information Processing

Chapter 6 surveys the features of computer hardware which help determine the capabilities of an information system. These features include the central processing unit, primary and secondary storage, and input and output devices. Emerging technologies include massively parallel processing, multimedia, and network computers.

CHAPTER 7

Information Systems Software

Chapter 7 describes the role of computer software in processing information, showing its interdependence with the capabilities of computer hardware. Systems software and application software are being enhanced with Internet capabilities. Java and object-oriented programming could potentially revolutionize software development and use.

CHAPTER 8

Managing Data Resources

Chapter 8 describes how information can be organized in files and databases. The chapter describes the components of a database management system and the three principal database models. Managing data as a resource requires organizational discipline as well as the appropriate data management technology.

CHAPTER 9

Telecommunications

Chapter 9 describes the components of a communications system, the major types of communications networks, and the costs and benefits of alternative communications technologies. Telecommunications applications such as electronic data interchange (EDI), electronic mail, digital information services, groupware, and videoconferencing can provide competitive advantage.

CHAPTER 10

The Internet and Enterprise Networking

Chapter 10 describes the underlying technology, benefits, and management challenges created by the Internet and enterprise networking as organizations create companywide networks and link to networks from many different organizations. Both enterprise networking and the Internet are fueling electronic commerce and providing opportunities for new business models.

6

Computers and Information Processing

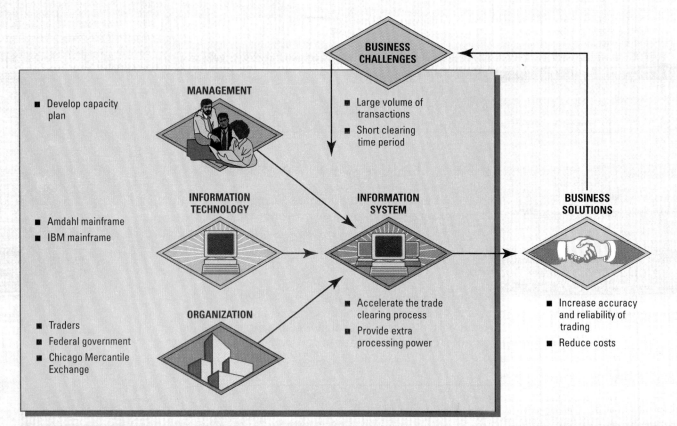

BUSINESS CHALLENGES

MANAGEMENT

- Develop capacity plan

INFORMATION TECHNOLOGY

- Amdahl mainframe
- IBM mainframe

ORGANIZATION

- Traders
- Federal government
- Chicago Mercantile Exchange

INFORMATION SYSTEM

- Large volume of transactions
- Short clearing time period

- Accelerate the trade clearing process
- Provide extra processing power

BUSINESS SOLUTIONS

- Increase accuracy and reliability of trading
- Reduce costs

The Chicago Mercantile Exchange Swaps Computers

The Chicago Mercantile Exchange is where yellow-jacketed traders furiously buy and sell pork belly futures, wheat crop options, and foreign currency instruments. A critical trade clearing system makes sure that the money behind these transactions—amounting to between $200 million and $300 million each business day, correctly changes hands.

This world-renowned commodities market had been running the clearing system on an IBM mainframe computer, but started looking around for additional computer processing power. When trading activity is very high, the system needs more processing power to clear all

LEARNING OBJECTIVES

After completing this chapter, you will be able to:

1. Identify the hardware components in a typical computer system.
2. Describe how information is represented and processed in a computer system.
3. Distinguish between generations of computer hardware.
4. Contrast the capabilities of mainframes, minicomputers, PCs, workstations, and supercomputers.
5. Describe the various media for storing data and programs in a computer system.
6. Compare the major input and output devices and approaches to input and processing.
7. Describe multimedia, network computers, and future information technology trends.

---

the trades. For instance, when the federal government raised interest rates in 1994, the exchange had to clear 2.5 million trades in one day. According to Mike Kelly, the exchange's chief information officer, "Our trades are not predictable, and we have to lay in a lot of excess capacity in a flexible way." The exchange does computer capacity planning from trading peak to trading peak rather than from year to year.

The IBM mainframe was very reliable, but the Mercantile Exchange decided to replace it with a Millennium CMOS mainframe from the Amdahl Corporation. Evaluating computers from both companies, the exchange found that the Millennium, a four-processor mainframe rated at 60 MIPS, cost $1000 less for each MIPS (millions of instructions per second) of processing power than the IBM mainframe. The Amdahl computer reduced processing costs, accelerated the trade clearing process, and gave the exchange additional flexibility to add processing power quickly if business required. Amdahl also agreed to provide an additional processor for emergencies at no extra cost. An IBM mainframe acts as a backup system for the Millennium.

By processing transactions more quickly, the Amdahl computer made the trade clearing system faster. Trade clearing is now completed on the same day, whereas in the past it had to take place overnight as a batch process. The new computer gave the exchange 30 to 40 minutes of additional time in the same day, so that it could pick later prices and have a more accurate view of the day's results. ∎

Source: Tim Ouellette, "Amdahl
Rates a Buy," *Computerworld*,
February 24, 1997.

By shifting from its IBM mainframe computer to a mainframe from another manufacturer, the Chicago Mercantile Exchange was able to provide more computing power for its business operations at a lower price. To make this decision, the Mercantile Exchange's management needed to understand how much computer processing capacity was required by its business processes and how to evaluate the price and performance of various types of computers. It had to know why mainframe computers were required for its processing needs and it had to plan for future processing requirements. Management also had to understand how the computer itself worked with related storage, input/output, and communications technology. Selecting appropriate computer hardware raises the following management challenges:

1. **Keeping abreast of technological change.** Because the technology is growing in power so rapidly and is changing basic patterns of information processing, managers must keep abreast of changes in the field. This requires time and resources. In medium to large firms, a person or small group must be assigned the task of tracking new technological developments and encouraging prototypes within the firm.

2. **Making wise purchasing decisions.** Soon after having made an investment in information technology, managers find the completed system is obsolete and too expensive, given the power and lower cost of new technology. In this environment it is very difficult to keep one's own systems up to date. A rather considerable amount of time must be spent anticipating and planning for technological change.

3. **Training the information systems staff and all employees.** In the transition from mainframe computing to desktops, enormous changes in perspective, skills, and attitudes are required on the part of an organization's information systems staff. Typically, staff members must be completely retrained every five years. All employees likewise will require extensive retraining simply to keep abreast of new ways of doing business with new information technologies.

In this chapter we describe the typical hardware configuration of a computer system, explaining how a computer works and how computer processing power and storage capacity are measured. We then compare the capabilities of various types of computers and related input, output, and storage devices.

6.1 WHAT IS A COMPUTER SYSTEM?

To understand how computers process data into information, you need to understand the components of a computer system and how computers work. No matter what their size, computers represent and process data using the same basic principles.

System Configuration

A contemporary computer system consists of a central processing unit, primary storage, secondary storage, input devices, output devices, and communications devices (see Figure 6.1). The central processing unit manipulates raw data into a more use-

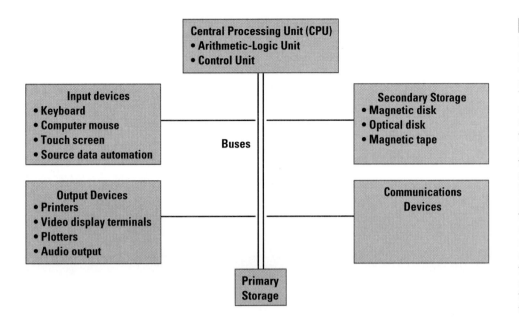

FIGURE 6.1

Central Processing Unit (CPU)
• Arithmetic-Logic Unit
• Control Unit

Input devices
• Keyboard
• Computer mouse
• Touch screen
• Source data automation

Output Devices
• Printers
• Video display terminals
• Plotters
• Audio output

Buses

Secondary Storage
• Magnetic disk
• Optical disk
• Magnetic tape

Communications Devices

Primary Storage

Hardware components of a computer system. A contemporary computer system can be categorized into six major components. The central processing unit manipulates data and controls the other parts of the computer system; primary storage temporarily stores data and program instructions during processing; secondary storage feeds data and instructions into the central processor and stores data for future use; input devices convert data and instructions for processing in the computer; output devices present data in a form that people can understand; and communications devices control the passing of information to and from communications networks.

ful form and controls the other parts of the computer system. Primary storage temporarily stores data and program instructions during processing, while secondary storage devices (magnetic and optical disks, magnetic tape) store data and programs when they are not being used in processing. Input devices, such as a keyboard or mouse, convert data and instructions into electronic form for input into the computer. Output devices, such as printers and video display terminals, convert electronic data produced by the computer system and display it in a form that people can understand. Communications devices provide connections between the computer and communications networks. Buses are paths for transmitting data and signals between the various parts of the computer system.

Bits and Bytes: How Computers Represent Data

For information to flow through a computer system and be in a form suitable for processing, all symbols, pictures, or words must be reduced to a string of binary digits. A binary digit is called a **bit** and represents either a 0 or a 1. In the computer, the presence of an electronic or magnetic signal means "one" and its absence signifies "zero." Digital computers operate directly with binary digits, either singly or strung together to form bytes. A string of 8 bits that the computer stores as a unit is called a **byte.** Each byte can be used to store a decimal number, a symbol, a character, or part of a picture (see Figure 6.2).

Figure 6.3 shows how decimal numbers are represented using true binary digits. Each position in a decimal number has a certain value. Any number in the decimal system (base 10) can be reduced to a binary number. The binary number system (base 2) can express any number as a power of the number 2. The table at the bottom of the figure shows how the translation from binary to decimal works. By using a binary number system a computer can express all numbers as groups of zeroes and ones. True binary cannot be used by a computer because, in addition to representing numbers, a computer must represent alphabetic characters and many other symbols used in natural language, such as $ and &. This requirement led manufacturers of computer hardware to develop standard binary codes.

There are two common codes: EBCDIC and ASCII, which are illustrated in Table 6.1. The first is the **Extended Binary Coded Decimal Interchange Code (EBCDIC—** pronounced ib-si-dick). This binary code, developed by IBM in the 1950s, represents every number, alphabetic character, or special character with 8 bits.

bit A binary digit representing the smallest unit of data in a computer system. It can only have one of two states, representing 0 or 1.

byte A string of bits, usually eight, used to store one number or character in a computer system.

Extended Binary Coded Decimal Interchange Code (EBCDIC) Binary code representing every number, alphabetic character, or special character with 8 bits, used primarily in IBM and other mainframe computers.

FIGURE 6.2

Bits and bytes. Bits are represented by either a 0 or 1. A string of 8 bits constitutes a byte, which represents a character. The computer's representation for the word "ALICE" is a series of five bytes, where each byte represents one character (or letter) in the name.

0 or **1** One bit

Characters are represented by one byte for each letter.

1 0 1 0 0 0 0 1 One byte for character A

The computer representation in ASCII for the name Alice is

A 1 0 1 0 0 0 0 1

L 1 0 1 0 1 1 0 0

I 1 0 1 0 1 0 0 1

C 1 0 1 0 0 0 1 1

E 1 0 1 0 0 1 0 1

FIGURE 6.3

True binary digits. Each decimal number has a certain value that can be expressed as a binary number. The binary number system can express any number as a power of the number 2.

10100, which is equal to:
$$0 \times 2^0 = 0$$
$$0 \times 2^1 = 0$$
$$1 \times 2^2 = 4$$
$$0 \times 2^3 = 0$$
$$1 \times 2^4 = \underline{16}$$
$$20$$

Place	5	4	3	2	1
Power of 2	2^4	2^3	2^2	2^1	2^0
Decimal value	16	8	4	2	1

American Standard Code for Information Interchange (ASCII) A 7- or 8-bit binary code used in data transmission, PCs, and some large computers.

pixel The smallest unit of data for defining an image in the computer. The computer reduces a picture to a grid of pixels. The term *pixel* comes from picture element.

millisecond One-thousand of a second.

microsecond One-millionth of a second.

The second code is the **American Standard Code for Information Interchange (ASCII)**, which was developed by the American National Standards Institute (ANSI) to provide a standard code that could be used by many different manufacturers to make machinery compatible. ASCII was originally designed as a 7-bit code, but most computers use 8-bit versions. EBCDIC is used in IBM and other mainframe computers, whereas ASCII is used in data transmission, PCs, and some larger computers.

How can a computer represent a picture? The computer stores a picture by creating a grid overlay of the picture. In this grid or matrix, the computer measures the light or color in each box or cell, called a **pixel** (picture element). The computer then stores this information on each pixel. A high-resolution computer terminal has a 1024×768 VGA standard grid, creating more than 700,000 pixels. Whether pictures or text are stored, it is through this process of reduction that a modern computer is able to operate in a complex environment.

Time and Size in the Computer World

Table 6.2 presents some key levels of time and size that are useful in describing the speed and capacity of modern computer systems. Very slow hardware or secondary storage devices measure machine cycle times in **milliseconds** (thousandths of a second). More powerful machines use measures of **microseconds** (millionths of a second)

Table 6.1 EBCDIC and ASCII Codes

Character	EBCDIC Binary	Character	ASCII-8-Binary
A	1100 0001	A	1010 0001
B	1100 0010	B	1010 0010
C	1100 0011	C	1010 0011
D	1100 0100	D	1010 0100
E	1100 0101	E	1010 0101
F	1100 0110	F	1010 0110
G	1100 0111	G	1010 0111
H	1100 1000	H	1010 1000
I	1100 1001	I	1010 1001
J	1101 0001	J	1010 1010
K	1101 0010	K	1010 1011
L	1101 0011	L	1010 1100
M	1101 0100	M	1010 1101
N	1101 0101	N	1010 1110
O	1101 0110	O	1010 1111
P	1101 0111	P	1011 0000
Q	1101 1000	Q	1011 0001
R	1101 1001	R	1011 0010
S	1110 0010	S	1011 0011
T	1110 0011	T	1011 0100
U	1110 0100	U	1011 0101
V	1110 0101	V	1011 0110
W	1110 0110	W	1011 0111
X	1110 0111	X	1011 1000
Y	1110 1000	Y	1011 1001
Z	1110 1001	Z	1011 1010
0	1111 0000	0	0101 0000
1	1111 0001	1	0101 0001
2	1111 0010	2	0101 0010
3	1111 0011	3	0101 0011
4	1111 0100	4	0101 0100
5	1111 0101	5	0101 0101
6	1111 0110	6	0101 0110
7	11111 0111	7	0101 0111
8	11111 1000	8	0101 1000
9	11111 1001	9	0101 1001

nanosecond One-billionth of a second.

kilobyte One thousand bytes (actually 1024 storage positions). Used as a measure of PC storage capacity.

megabyte Approximately one million bytes. Unit of computer storage capacity.

gigabyte Approximately one billion bytes. Unit of computer storage capacity.

or **nanoseconds** (billionths of a second). Very powerful computers measure machine cycles in *picoseconds* (trillionths of a second). A large computer has a machine cycle time of less than 10 nanoseconds. Thus such computers can execute over 200 million instructions per second. MIPS, or millions of instructions per second, is a common benchmark for measuring the speed of larger computers.

Size, like speed, is an important consideration in a system. Information is stored in a computer in the form of 0s and 1s (binary digits, or bits), which are strung together to form bytes. One byte can be used to store one character, such as the letter *A*. A thousand bytes (actually 1024 storage positions) is called a **kilobyte**. Small PCs used to have internal primary memories of 640 kilobytes. A large PC today can store 40 megabytes of information in primary memory. Each **megabyte** is approximately 1 million bytes. This means, theoretically, that the machine can store up to 40 million alphabetic letters or numbers. Modern secondary storage devices, such as hard disk drives in a PC or disk packs in a large mainframe, store millions and billions of bytes of information. A PC may have a 810-megabyte disk, whereas a large mainframe may have many disk drives, each capable of holding 8 gigabytes. A **gigabyte** is approximately 1 billion bytes. Some large organizations such as the Social Security Administration or the Internal Revenue Service have a total storage capacity adding up all their disk drive capacities measured in trillions of bytes. And if all their records were put together, including those stored on paper records and tapes, the total would be at the terabyte (thousands of billions of bytes) level of information storage.

The vast differences in the size and speed of the major elements of computer systems introduce problems of coordination. For instance, while central processing units operate at the level of nanoseconds, ordinary printers operate at the level of only a few hundred to a few thousand characters per second. This means that the central processing unit can process information far faster than a printer can print it out. For this reason, additional memory and storage devices must be placed between

---

Table 6.2 Size and Time in the Computer World

Time

Second	1	Time required to find a single record on a tape
Millisecond	1/1000 second	Time needed to find a single name on a disk, 1 millisecond
Microsecond	1/1,000,000 second	IBM PC instruction speed, 0.1 microseconds per instruction
Nanosecond	1/1,000,000,000 second	Mainframe instruction speed, one instruction each 10 nanoseconds
Picosecond	1/1,000,000,000,000 second	Speed of experimental devices

Size

Byte	String of 8 bits	Amount of computer storage for 1 character or number
Kilobyte	1000 bytes*	Early PC primary memory, 640 kilobytes
Megabyte	1,000,000 bytes	PC primary memory16 megabytes
Gigabyte	1,000,000,000 bytes	External storage disk and tape
Terabyte	1,000,000,000,000 bytes	Social security programs and records

Actually 1024 storage positions

---

the central processing unit and the printer so that the central processing unit is not needlessly held back from processing more information as it waits for the printer to print it out.

6.2 THE CENTRAL PROCESSING UNIT AND PRIMARY STORAGE

The **central processing unit (CPU)** is the part of the computer system where the manipulation of symbols, numbers, and letters occurs, and it controls the other parts of the computer system. The CPU consists of a control unit and an arithmetic-logic unit (see Figure 6.4). Located near the CPU is **primary storage** (sometimes called primary memory or main memory), where data and program instructions are stored temporarily during processing. Three kinds of buses link the CPU, primary storage, and other devices in the computer system. The data bus moves data to and from primary storage. The address bus transmits signals for locating a given address in primary storage. The control bus transmits signals specifying whether to read or write data to or from a given primary storage address, input device, or output device. The characteristics of the CPU and primary storage are very important in determining the speed and capabilities of a computer.

central processing unit (CPU)
Area of the computer system that manipulates symbols, numbers, and letters, and controls the other parts of the computer system.

primary storage Part of the computer that temporarily stores program instructions and data being used by the instructions.

Primary Storage

Primary storage has three functions. It stores all or part of the program that is being executed. Primary storage also stores the operating system programs that manage the operation of the computer. (These programs are discussed in Chapter 7.) Finally, the primary storage area holds data that are being used by the program. Data and programs are placed in primary storage before processing, between processing steps, and after processing has ended, prior to being returned to secondary storage or released as output.

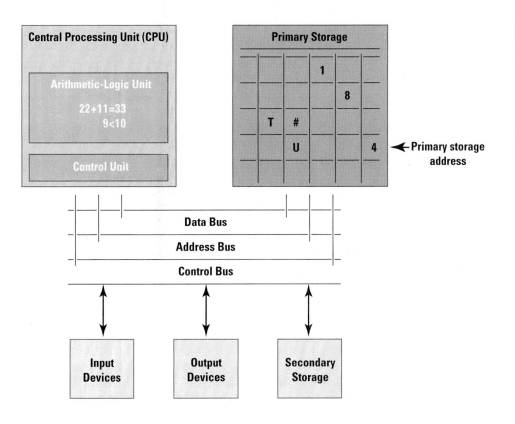

FIGURE 6.4

The CPU and primary storage. The CPU contains an arithmetic-logic unit and a control unit. Data and instructions are stored in unique addresses in primary storage that the CPU can access during processing. The data bus, address bus, and control bus transmit signals between the central processing unit, primary storage, and other devices in the computer system

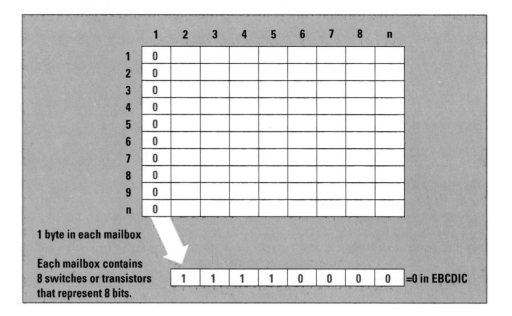

FIGURE 6.5

Primary storage in the computer. Primary storage can be visualized as a matrix. Each byte represents a mailbox with a unique address. In this example, mailbox [n,1] contains eight bits representing the number 0 (as coded in EBCDIC).

1 byte in each mailbox

Each mailbox contains 8 switches or transistors that represent 8 bits.

| 1 | 1 | 1 | 1 | 0 | 0 | 0 | 0 | =0 in EBCDIC |

random access memory (RAM)
Primary storage of data or program instructions that can directly access any randomly chosen location in the same amount of time.

semiconductor An integrated circuit made by printing thousands and even millions of tiny transistors on a small silicon chip.

read-only memory (ROM)
Semiconductor memory chips that contain program instructions. These chips can only be read from; they cannot be written to.

programmable read-only memory (PROM) Subclass of ROM chip used in control devices because it can be programmed once.

erasable programmable read-only memory (EPROM) Subclass of ROM chip that can be erased and reprogrammed many times.

How is it possible for an electronic device such as primary storage to actually store information? How is it possible to retrieve this information from a known location in memory? Figure 6.5 illustrates primary storage in an electronic digital computer. Internal primary storage is often called **random access memory** or **RAM**. It is called RAM because it can directly access any randomly chosen location in the same amount of time. The advantage of electronic information storage is the ability to store information in a precise known location in memory and to retrieve it from that same location.

Figure 6.5 shows that primary memory is divided into storage locations called bytes. Each location contains a set of eight binary switches or devices, each of which can store one bit of information. The set of 8 bits found in each storage location is sufficient to store one letter, one digit, or one special symbol (such as $) using either EBCDIC or ASCII. Each byte has a unique address—similar to a mailbox, indicating where it is located in RAM. The computer can remember where the data in all the bytes are located simply by keeping track of these addresses.

Most of the information used by a computer application is stored on secondary storage devices such as disks and tapes, located outside the primary storage area. For the computer to do work on information, information must be transferred into primary memory for processing. Therefore, data are continually being read into and written out of the primary storage area during the execution of a program.

Types of Semiconductor Memory

Primary storage is actually composed of semiconductors. A **semiconductor** is an integrated circuit made by printing thousands and even millions of tiny transistors on a small silicon chip. There are several different kinds of semiconductor memory used in primary storage. Random access memory or RAM is used for short-term storage of data or program instructions. RAM is volatile: Its contents will be lost when the computer's electric supply is disrupted by a power outage or when the computer is turned off. **Read-only memory** or **ROM** can only be read from; it cannot be written to. ROM chips come from the manufacturer with programs already burned in, or stored. ROM is used in general-purpose computers to store important or frequently used programs (such as computing routines for calculating the square roots of numbers).

There are two other subclasses of ROM chips: **programmable read-only memory** or **PROM**, and **erasable programmable read-only memory** or **EPROM**. PROM chips are used by manufacturers as control devices in their products. They can be programmed

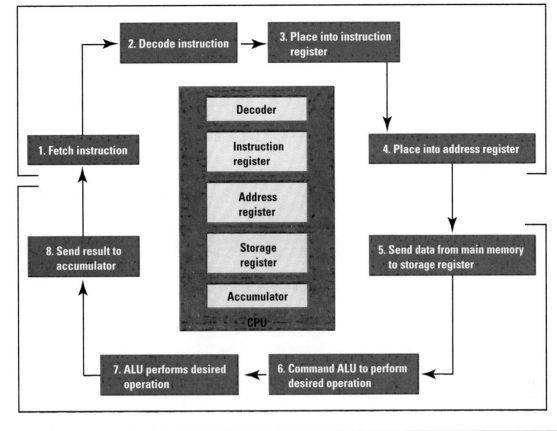

FIGURE 6.6

The various steps in the machine cycle. The machine cycle has two main stages of operation: the instruction cycle (I-cycle) and the execution cycle (E-cycle). There are several steps within each cycle required to process a single machine instruction in the CPU.

once. In this way, manufacturers avoid the expense of having a specialized chip manufactured for the control of small motors, for instance; instead, they can program into a PROM chip the specific program for their product. PROM chips, therefore, can be made universally for many manufacturers in large production runs. EPROM chips are used for device control, such as in robots, where the program may have to be changed on a routine basis. With EPROM chips, the program can be erased and reprogrammed.

The Arithmetic-Logic Unit and Control Unit

The **arithmetic-logic unit (ALU)** performs the primary logical and arithmetic operations of the computer. It adds, subtracts, multiplies, and divides, determining whether a number is positive, negative, or zero. In addition to performing arithmetic functions, an ALU must be able to determine when one quantity is greater than or less than another and when two quantities are equal. The ALU can perform logical operations on the binary codes for letters as well as numbers.

The **control unit** coordinates and controls the other parts of the computer system. It reads a stored program, one instruction at a time, and directs other components of the computer system to perform the tasks required by the program. The series of operations required to process a single machine instruction is called the **machine cycle.** As illustrated in Figure 6.6, the machine cycle has two parts: an instruction cycle and an execution cycle.

During the instruction cycle, the control unit retrieves one program instruction from primary storage and decodes it. It places the part of the instruction telling the ALU what to do next in a special instruction register and places the part specifying

arithmetic-logic unit (ALU) Component of the CPU that performs the principal logical and arithmetic operations of the computer.

control unit Component of the CPU that controls and coordinates the other parts of the computer system.

machine cycle Series of operations required to process a single machine instruction.

the address of the data to be used in the operation into an address register. (A register is a special temporary storage location in the ALU or control unit that acts like a high-speed staging area for program instructions or data being transferred from primary storage to the CPU for processing.)

During the execution cycle, the control unit locates the required data in primary storage, places it in a storage register, instructs the ALU to perform the desired operation, temporarily stores the result of the operation in an accumulator, and finally places the result in primary memory. As the execution of each instruction is completed, the control unit advances to and reads the next instruction of the program.

6.3 THE EVOLUTION OF COMPUTER HARDWARE

There have been four major stages, or computer generations, in the evolution of computer hardware, each distinguished by a different technology for the components that do the computer's processing work. Each generation has dramatically expanded computer processing power and storage capabilities while simultaneously lowering costs. For instance, the cost of performing 100,000 calculations plunged from several dollars in the 1950s to less than $0.025 in the 1980s and approximately $.00004 in 1995. These generational changes in computer hardware have been accompanied by generational changes in computer software (see Chapter 7) that have made computers increasingly more powerful, inexpensive, and easy to use.

Generations of Computer Hardware

The first and second generations of computer hardware were based on vacuum tube and transistor technology, whereas the third and fourth generations were based on semiconductor technology.

First Generation: Vacuum Tube Technology, 1946–1956

The first generation of computers relied on vacuum tubes to store and process information. These tubes consumed a great deal of power, were short-lived, and generated a great deal of heat. Colossal in size, first-generation computers had extremely limited memory and processing capability and were used for very limited scientific and engineering work. The maximum main memory size was approximately 2000 bytes (2 kilobytes), with a speed of 10 kiloinstructions per second. Rotating magnetic drums were used for internal storage and punched cards for external storage. Jobs such as running programs or printing output had to be coordinated manually.

Second Generation: Transistors, 1957–1963

In the second computer generation, transistors replaced vacuum tubes as the devices for storing and processing information. Transistors were much more stable and reliable than vacuum tubes, they generated less heat, and they consumed less power. However, each transistor had to be individually made and wired into a printed circuit board—a slow, tedious process. Magnetic core memory was the primary storage technology of this period. It was composed of small magnetic doughnuts (about 1 mm in diameter), which could be polarized in one of two directions to represent a bit of data. Wires were strung along and through these cores to both write and read data. This system had to be assembled by hand and, therefore, was very expensive. Second-generation computers had up to 32 kilobytes of RAM memory and speeds reaching 200,000 to 300,000 instructions per second. The enhanced processing power and memory of second-generation computers enabled them to be used more widely for scientific work and for such business tasks as automating payroll and billing.

Third Generation: Integrated Circuits, 1964–1979

Third-generation computers relied on integrated circuits, which were made by printing hundreds and later thousands of tiny transistors on small silicon chips. These devices were called semiconductors. Computer memories expanded to 2 megabytes of RAM memory, and speeds accelerated to 5 MIPS. Third-generation computer technology introduced software that could be used by people without extensive technical training, making it possible for computers to enlarge their role in business.

Fourth Generation: Very Large-Scale Integrated Circuits, 1980–Present

The fourth generation extends from 1980 to the present. Computers in this period use very large-scale integrated circuits (VLSIC), which are packed with hundreds of thousands and even millions of circuits per chip. Costs have fallen to the point where desktop computers are inexpensive and widely available for use in business and everyday life. The power of a computer that once filled a large room can now reside on a small desktop. Computer memory sizes have mushroomed to over 2 gigabytes in large commercial machines; processing speeds have exceeded 200 MIPS. In Section 6.7, we discuss the next generation of hardware trends.

VLSIC technology has fueled a growing movement toward microminiaturization—the proliferation of computers that are so small, fast, and cheap that they have become ubiquitous. For instance, many of the intelligent features that have made automobiles, stereos, toys, watches, cameras, and other equipment easier to use are based on microprocessors.

What Is a Microprocessor? What Is a Chip?

Very large-scale integrated circuit technology, with hundreds of thousands (or even millions) of transistors on a single chip, integrates the computer's memory, logic, and control on a single chip; hence the name **microprocessor,** or computer on a chip. Some

microprocessor Very large-scale integrated circuit technology that integrates the computer's memory, logic, and control on a single chip.

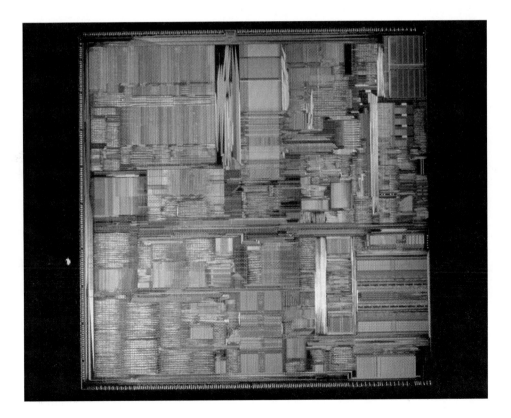

The Pentium Pro microprocessor contains more than 5 million transistors and provides mainframe and supercomputer-like processing capabilities.

Table 6.3	Examples of Microprocessors				
Name	Microprocessor Manufacturer	Word Length	Data Bus Width	Clock Speed (MHz)	Used In
80486	Intel	32	32	20–100	IBM and other PCs
68040	Motorola	32	32	25–40	Mac Quadras
Pentium	Intel	32	64	60–150+	IBM and other PCs
Pentium Pro	Intel	32	64	150–200	High-end PCs and workstations
Pentium II	Intel	32	64	233+	High-end PCs and workstations
PowerPC	Motorola, IBM, Apple	32	64	100–250+	High-end PCs and workstations
Alpha	DEC	64	64	300+	DEC workstations

word length The number of bits that can be processed at one time by a computer. The larger the word length, the greater the speed of the computer.

megahertz A measure of cycle speed, or the pacing of events in a computer; one megahertz (MHz) equals one million cycles per second.

data bus width The number of bits that can be moved at one time between the CPU, primary storage, and the other devices of a computer.

reduced instruction set computing (RISC) Technology used to enhance the speed of microprocessors by embedding only the most frequently used instructions on a chip.

popular chips are shown in Table 6.3. Chips are measured in several ways. You will often see chips labeled as 8-bit, 16-bit, or 32-bit devices. These labels refer to the **word length,** or the number of bits that can be processed at one time by the machine. An 8-bit chip can process 8 bits, or 1 byte, of information in a single machine cycle. A 32-bit chip can process 32 bits or 4 bytes in a single cycle. The larger the word length, the greater the speed of the computer.

A second factor affecting chip speed is cycle speed. Every event in a computer must be sequenced so that one step logically follows another. The control unit sets a beat to the chip. This beat is established by an internal clock and is measured in **megahertz** (abbreviated MHz, which stands for millions of cycles per second). The Intel 8088 chip, for instance, originally had a clock speed of 4.47 megahertz, whereas the Intel Pentium Pro chip has a clock speed that ranges from 150 to 200 megahertz.

A third factor affecting speed is the **data bus width.** The data bus acts as a highway between the CPU, primary storage, and other devices, determining how much data can be moved at one time. The 8088 chip used in the original IBM personal computer, for example, had a 16-bit word length but only an 8-bit data bus width. This meant that data were processed within the CPU chip itself in 16-bit chunks but could only be moved 8 bits at a time between the CPU, primary storage, and external devices. On the other hand, the Alpha chip has both a 64-bit word length and a 64-bit data bus width. Obviously, to get a computer to execute more instructions per second and work through programs or handle users expeditiously, it is necessary to increase the word length of the processor, the data bus width, or the cycle speed—or all three.

Microprocessors can be made faster by using **reduced instruction set computing (RISC)** in their design. Some instructions that a computer uses to process data are actually embedded in the chip circuitry. Conventional chips, based on complex instruction set computing, have several hundred or more instructions hard-wired into their circuitry, and usually take several clock cycles to execute a single instruction. In many instances, only 20 percent of these instructions are needed for 80 percent of the computer's tasks. If the little-used instructions are eliminated, the remaining instructions can execute much faster.

Reduced instruction set (RISC) computers have only the most frequently used instructions embedded in them. A RISC CPU can execute most instructions in a single machine cycle and sometimes multiple instructions at the same time. RISC is most appropriate for scientific and workstation computing, in which repetitive arithmetic and logical operations on data or applications calling for three-dimensional image rendering occur.

Champions of RISC claim that a PC or workstation with RISC technology can offer the performance of much larger computers costing ten times as much. But critics believe that gains in RISC processing speed may be offset by difficulties created by dropping complex instruction-set computing. Programs written for conventional processors cannot automatically be transferred to RISC machines; new software is required. Many RISC suppliers are adding more instructions to appeal to a greater number of customers, and designers of conventional microprocessors are streamlining their chips to execute instructions more rapidly.

6.4 CATEGORIES OF COMPUTERS

Computers represent and process data the same way, but there are different classifications. We can use size and processing speed to categorize contemporary computers as mainframes, minicomputers, PCs, workstations, and supercomputers.

Mainframes, Minis, and PCs

A **mainframe** is the largest computer, a powerhouse with massive memory and extremely rapid processing power. It is used for very large business, scientific, or military applications in which a computer must handle massive amounts of data or many complicated processes. A **minicomputer** is a mid-range computer, about the size of an office desk, often used in universities, factories, or research laboratories. A **personal computer (PC)**, which is sometimes referred to as a microcomputer, is one that can be placed on a desktop or carried from room to room. PCs are used for personal and business applications. A **workstation** also fits on a desktop but has more powerful mathematical and graphics processing capability than a PC and can perform more complicated tasks at the same time than can a PC. Workstations are used for scientific, engineering, and design work that requires powerful graphics or computational capabilities. A **supercomputer** is a highly sophisticated and powerful machine used for tasks requiring extremely rapid and complex calculations with hundreds of thousands of variable factors. Supercomputers have traditionally been used in scientific and military work, but they are also starting to be used in business.

The problem with this classification scheme is that the capacity of the machines changes so rapidly. A PC today has the computing power of a mainframe from the 1980s or the minicomputer of a few years ago. Powerful PCs have sophisticated graphics and processing capabilities similar to workstations. PCs still cannot perform as many tasks at once as mainframes, minicomputers, or workstations (see the discussion of operating systems in Chapter 7); nor can they be used by as many people simultaneously as these larger machines. Even these distinctions will become less pronounced in the future. In another decade, some PCs might have the power and processing speed of today's supercomputers.

Any of these categories of computers can be designed to support a computer network, enabling users to share files, software, peripheral devices such as printers, or other network resources. **Server computers** are specifically optimized for network use, with large memory and disk storage capacity, high-speed communications capabilities, and powerful CPUs.

Mainframes, minicomputers, and PCs can be linked to form companywide information networks that share hardware, software, and data resources. The use of multiple computers linked by a communication network for processing is called **distributed processing**. In contrast with **centralized processing**, in which all processing is accomplished by one large central computer, distributed processing distributes the processing work among various PCs, minicomputers, and mainframes linked together.

Downsizing and Cooperative Processing

In some firms PCs have actually replaced mainframes and minicomputers. The process of transferring applications from large computers to smaller ones is called **downsizing**. Downsizing has many advantages. The cost per MIPS on a mainframe is almost

mainframe Largest category of computer, used for major business processing.

minicomputer Middle-range computer.

personal computer (PC) Small desktop or portable computer.

workstation Desktop computer with powerful graphics and mathematical capabilities and the ability to perform several tasks at once.

supercomputer Highly sophisticated and powerful computer that can perform very complex computations extremely fast.

server computer Computer specifically optimized to provide software and other resources to other computers over a network.

distributed processing The distribution of computer processing work among multiple computers linked by a communication network.

centralized processing Processing that is accomplished by one large central computer.

downsizing The process of transferring applications from large computers to smaller ones.

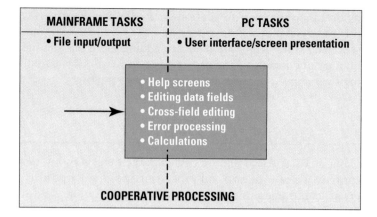

FIGURE 6.7

Cooperative processing. In cooperative processing, an application is divided into tasks that run on more than one type of computer. This example shows the tasks that a PC is best at performing; the tasks that a mainframe computer is best at performing, and those tasks that each type is able to perform.

100 times greater than on a PC; a megabyte of mainframe memory costs about 10 times more than the same amount of memory on a PC. For some applications PCs may also be easier for nontechnical specialists to use and maintain. The decision to downsize involves many factors besides the cost of computer hardware, including the need for new software, training, and perhaps new organizational procedures.

Another computing pattern divides processing work for transaction-based applications among mainframes and PCs. Each type of computer is assigned the functions it performs best, and each shares processing (and perhaps data) over a communications link. For example, the PC might be used for data entry and validation, whereas the mainframe would be responsible for file input and output. This division of labor is called **cooperative processing**. PCs are utilized because they can provide the same processing power much more economically than a mainframe or because they are superior at some tasks, such as at providing screen presentations for the user interface. Figure 6.7 illustrates cooperative processing.

cooperative processing Type of processing that divides the processing work for transaction-based applications among mainframes and PCs.

PCs and Workstations

What distinguishes a PC from a workstation? Workstations have more powerful graphics and mathematical processing capabilities than PCs, and can easily perform several tasks at the same time. They are typically used by scientists, engineers, and other knowledge workers but are spreading to the financial industry because they have the computing power to simultaneously analyze portfolios, process securities trades, and provide financial data and news services (see Chapter 15). Workstations are especially useful for computer-aided design (CAD) and for complex simulations and modeling. They can represent fully rendered multiple views of a physical object such as an airplane wing, rotate the object three-dimensionally, and present design history and cost factors.

Powerful high-end PCs have many of the same capabilities as low-end workstations. As PCs become increasingly graphics-oriented, the distinctions between the two types of computers are likely to blur further. Moreover, workstations themselves have increased in power, so that the most sophisticated workstations have some of the capabilities of earlier mainframes and supercomputers (Thomborson, 1993).

Supercomputers and Parallel Processing

A supercomputer is an especially sophisticated and powerful type of computer that is used primarily for extremely rapid and complex computations with hundreds or thousands of variable factors. Supercomputers have traditionally been used for classified weapons research, weather forecasting, and petroleum and engineering applications, all of which use complex mathematical models and simulations. Although extremely expensive, supercomputers are beginning to be employed in business, as the Window on Technology demonstrates.

Parallel Processing Goes Commercial

Parallel processing computers—often known as supercomputers—have long been viewed as tools exclusively for scientists and engineers. Now, their great power is fast resulting in their finding new roles as commercial computers.

Parallel processors have not been widely used for commercial applications until recently, primarily for two related reasons. First, they have been difficult to cost-justify for commonplace commercial uses. In addition, few corporate or IS managers have envisioned any uses for so much intense computing power—what would they do with them? Technology has progressed, resulting in the lowering of prices, while management has responded to the growing power of computers with new ideas on how the power might be used.

Wal-Mart Stores, Inc., the Bentonville, Arkansas, discounting giant and largest retailer in the United States, processes 20 million point-of-sale updates daily in its 2100 stores, storing trillions of bytes of data used to keep their inventory current and to spot sales trends. Wal-Mart needs supercomputers to process approximately 2300 queries per day against this massive collection of data. Trimark Investment Management, a Toronto, Canada, mutual funds company, has seen its account base shoot from 250,000 customers in 1992 to 800,000 two years later. To post its accounts at the end of 1992, its more traditional IBM System 38 required 18 to 24 hours of processing. Today the company would not even be able to post the data for more than triple the number of customers the 1992 way—the computer simply could not handle all that data. However, in 1994, using a Pyramid Technology Niles 150 with six processors, Trimark posted all the customers in eight hours.

The SABRE Group, the reservation and ticketing organization that is owned by American Airlines but also services 52 other carriers plus a large number of travel agencies, uses an IBM Parallel Enterprise Server (PES) to price its tickets. SABRE processes a massive amount of data, normally handling about 3000 messages per second. SABRE's parallel processors have successfully processed a peak load of 4100 messages per second. Financial firms are starting to use supercomputers for derivatives pricing and portfolio optimization, which require numerous elements of computational analysis. For example, Atlantic

Portfolio Analytics and Management in Orlando, Florida, uses a Cray EL98 supercomputer to keep track of and evaluate a portfolio of more than 600,000 securities. Companies are turning to parallel processing computers to improve customer service. Because parallel processing computers can search large databases so rapidly, companies are finding they can answer customer queries much more rapidly than with single-processor technology.

Perhaps the applications that generate the most intense interest have come to be known as datamining (see Chapter 2). Organizations mine data—search through and analyze massive pools of data—to find hidden but useful information. For example, retail companies of all types, including Wal-Mart, are now analyzing huge databases to identify changing buying patterns and customer tastes, information that can then be used to support marketing or to drive the new product development process. Others are mining data to determine the consequences of a particular action. Max D. Hopper, chairman of the SABRE Group AA, Inc., offers an example of just such an application: "If Dallas–Fort Worth has a severe weather problem that affects 50 arriving or departing flights with 5000 passengers, the [parallel processing] technology has the power to let us see the impact on every flight, including aircraft, crew, maintenance, and passengers." It might take a large mainframe several days or a week to come up with the answer, yet a parallel processing computer might deliver results within a few hours.

> **To Think About:** How is selection of parallel processor technology related to the business strategies of the firms described here? What management, organization, and technology criteria would you use in deciding whether to purchase a parallel processor?

Sources: Dean Tomasula, "Entering a Parallel Universe," *Wall Street and Technology* 14, no. 4, April 1996; Michael Alexander, "Mine for Gold with Parallel Systems," *Datamation*, November 15, 1994; Willie Schatz, "Out of the Lab, Into the Office," *Information Week*, May 16, 1994; and Craig Stedman, "Sabre Parallel Systems Reduce Transaction Costs," *Computerworld*, November 17, 1994.

Supercomputers can perform complex and massive computations almost instantaneously because they can perform billions and even hundreds of billions of calculations per second—many times faster than the largest mainframes. Supercomputers do not process one instruction at a time but instead rely on **parallel processing.** As illustrated in Figure 6.8, multiple processing units (CPUs) break down a problem into smaller parts and work on it simultaneously. Some experimental supercomputers use up to 64,000 processors. Getting a group of processors to attack the same problem at once is easier said than done. It requires rethinking the problems and special software that can divide problems among different processors in the most efficient

parallel processing Type of processing in which more than one instruction can be processed at a time by breaking down problems into smaller parts and processing them simultaneously with multiple processors.

FIGURE 6.8

Sequential and parallel processing. During sequential processing, each task is assigned to one CPU that processes one instruction at a time. In parallel processing, multiple tasks are assigned to multiple processing units to expedite the result.

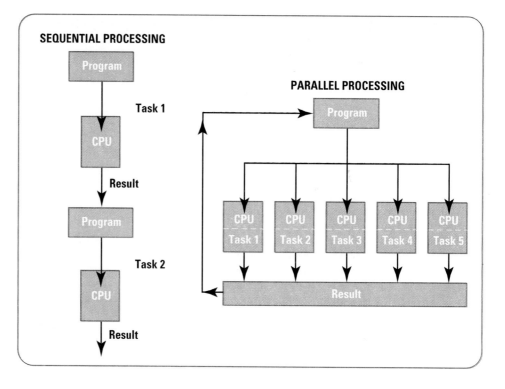

possible way, providing the needed data, and reassembling the many subtasks to reach an appropriate solution.

6.5 SECONDARY STORAGE

secondary storage Relatively long-term, nonvolatile storage of data outside the CPU and primary storage.

register Temporary storage location in the ALU or control unit where small amounts of data and instructions reside for thousandths of a second just before use.

cache Memory area for high-speed storage of frequently used instructions and data.

magnetic disk A secondary storage medium in which data are stored by means of magnetized spots on a hard or floppy disk.

hard disk Magnetic disk resembling a thin steel platter with an iron oxide coating; used in large computer systems and in many PCs.

In addition to primary storage, where information and programs are stored for immediate processing, modern computer systems use other types of storage to accomplish their tasks. Information systems need to store information outside the computer in a nonvolatile state (not requiring electrical power) and to store volumes of data too large to fit into a computer of any size today (such as a large payroll or the U.S. census). The relatively long-term storage of data outside the CPU and primary storage is called **secondary storage.**

Primary storage is where the fastest, most expensive technology is used. As shown in Table 6.4, there are actually three different kinds of primary memory: register, cache, and RAM. **Register** is the fastest and most expensive memory, in which small amounts of data and instructions reside for thousandths of a second just prior to use, followed by **cache** memory (for high-speed storage of frequently used instructions and data) and RAM memory for large amounts of data. Access to information stored in primary memory is electronic and occurs almost at the speed of light. Secondary storage is nonvolatile and retains data even when the computer is turned off. There are many kinds of secondary storage; the most common are magnetic disk, optical disk, and magnetic tape. These media can transfer large bodies of data rapidly to the CPU. But because secondary storage requires mechanical movement to gain access to the data, in contrast to primary storage, it is relatively slow.

Magnetic Disk

The most widely used secondary storage medium today is **magnetic disk.** There are two kinds of magnetic disks: floppy disks (used in PCs) and **hard disks** (used on commercial disk drives and PCs). Hard disks are thin steel platters with an iron oxide coating. In larger systems, multiple hard disks are mounted together on a vertical

Table 6.4 Data Storage Devices in a PC

Type of Memory	Total Storage Capacity	Access Time
Primary Storage		
Register	1 kilobyte	.01 microseconds
Cache	1 kilobyte	.1 microseconds
RAM	8–64 megabytes	.5 microseconds
Secondary Storage		
Hard disk	2.1 gigabytes	15 milliseconds
High-density diskette (3.5″)	2.8 megabytes	200 milliseconds
Optical disk	660 megabytes	200–500 milliseconds
Magnetic tape backup	2 gigabytes	1–2 seconds

shaft. Figure 6.9 illustrates a commercial hard disk pack for a large system. It has 11 disks, each with two surfaces, top and bottom. However, although there are 11 disks, no information is recorded on the top or bottom surfaces; thus, there are only 20 recording surfaces on the disk pack. On each surface, data are stored on tracks. The disk pack is generally sealed from the environment and rotates at speeds of about 3500 to 7000 rpm, creating an air-stream speed of about 50 mph at the disk surface.

Information is recorded on or read from the disk by read/write heads, which literally fly over the spinning disks. Unlike a home stereo, the heads never actually touch the disk (which would destroy the data and cause the system to crash) but hover a few thousandths of an inch above it. A smoke particle or a human hair is sufficient to crash the head into the disk.

The read/write heads move horizontally (from left to right) to any of 200 positions called cylinders. At any one of these cylinders, the read/write heads can read or write information to any of 20 different concentric circles on the disk surface areas (called **tracks**). The **cylinder** represents the circular tracks on the same vertical line within the disk pack. Read/write heads are directed to a specific record using

track Concentric circle on the surface area of a disk on which data are stored as magnetized spots; each track can store thousands of bytes.

cylinder Represents circular tracks on the same vertical line within a disk pack.

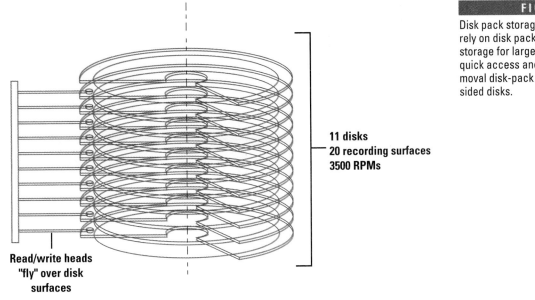

Read/write heads "fly" over disk surfaces

11 disks
20 recording surfaces
3500 RPMs

FIGURE 6.9

Disk pack storage. Large systems often rely on disk packs, which provide reliable storage for large amounts of data with quick access and retrieval. A typical removal disk-pack system contains 11 two-sided disks.

an address consisting of the cylinder number, the recording surface number, and the data record number.

The speed of access to data on a disk is a function of the rotational speed of the disk and the speed of the access arms. The read/write heads must position themselves, and the disk pack must rotate until the proper information is located. Each track contains several records. The entire disk pack is housed in a disk drive or disk unit. Large mainframe or minicomputer systems have multiple disk drives because they require immense disk storage capacity.

Disk drive performance can be further enhanced by using a disk technology called **redundant array of inexpensive disks (RAID)**. RAID devices package more than a hundred 6.25-inch disk drives, a controller chip, and specialized software into a single large unit. While traditional disk drives deliver data from the disk drive along a single path, RAID delivers data over multiple paths simultaneously, accelerating disk access time. Smaller RAID systems provide 10 to 20 gigabytes of storage capacity, while larger systems provide over 700 gigabytes. RAID is potentially more reliable than standard disk drives because other drives are available to deliver data if one drive fails.

PCs usually contain hard disks, which can store over 2 gigabytes. PCs also use **floppy disks,** which are flat, 3.5-inch disks of polyester film with a magnetic coating (5.25-inch floppy disks are becoming obsolete). These disks have a storage capacity of up to 2.8 megabytes and a much slower access rate than hard disks. Floppy disks and cartridges and packs of multiple disks use a **sector** method of storing data. As illustrated in Figure 6.10, the disk surface is divided into pie-shaped pieces. Each sector is assigned a unique number. Data can be located using an address consisting of the sector number and an individual data record number.

Magnetic disks on both large and small computers have several important advantages. First, they permit direct access to individual records. Each record can be given a precise physical address in terms of cylinders and tracks, and the read/write head can be directed to go to that address and access the information in about several milliseconds, depending on the storage system being used. This means that the computer system does not have to search the entire file, as in a sequential tape file, to find the person's record. Disk storage is often referred to as a **direct access storage device (DASD)**.

For on-line systems requiring direct access, disk technology provides the only practical means of storage today. Records can be easily and rapidly retrieved. DASD is, however, more expensive than magnetic tape. Updating information stored on a disk destroys the old information because the old data on the disk are written over if changes are made. The disk drives themselves are susceptible to environmental dis-

---

redundant array of inexpensive disks (RAID) Disk storage technology to boost disk performance by packaging more than 100 smaller disk drives with a controller chip and specialized software in a single large unit to deliver data over multiple paths simultaneously.

floppy disk Removable magnetic disk storage primarily used with PCs.

sector Method of storing data on a floppy disk in which the disk is divided into pie-shaped pieces or sectors. Each sector is assigned a unique number so that data can be located using the sector number.

direct access storage device (DASD) Refers to magnetic disk technology that permits the CPU to locate a record directly, in contrast to sequential tape storage that must search the entire file.

FIGURE 6.10

The sector method of storing data. Each track of a disk can be divided into sectors. Disk storage location can be identified by sector and data record number.

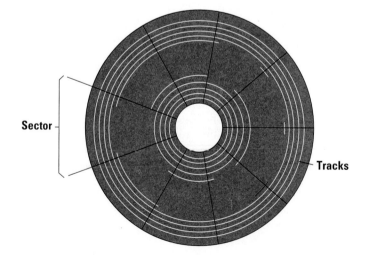

turbances; even smoke particles can disrupt the movement of read/write heads over the disk surface. Therefore, the environment must be relatively pure and stable. That is why disk drives are sealed in a clean room.

Optical Disks

Optical disks, also called compact disks or laser optical disks, store data at densities many times greater than those of magnetic disks and are available for both PCs and large computers. Data are recorded on optical disks when a laser device burns microscopic pits in the reflective layer of a spiral track. Binary information is encoded by the length of these pits and the space between them. Optical disks can thus store massive quantities of data, including not only text but also pictures, sound, and full-motion video, in a highly compact form. The optical disk is read by having a low-power laser beam from an optical head scan the disk.

The most common optical disk system used with PCs is called **compact disk read-only memory (CD-ROM).** A 4.75-inch compact disk can store up to 660 megabytes, nearly 300 times more than a high-density floppy disk. Optical disks are most appropriate for applications where enormous quantities of unchanging data must be stored compactly for easy retrieval, or for storing graphic images and sound. CD-ROM is also less vulnerable than floppy disks to magnetism, dirt, or rough handling.

CD-ROM is read-only storage. No new data can be written to it; it can only be read. CD-ROM has been most widely used for reference materials with massive amounts of data, such as encyclopedias, directories, or on-line databases and for storing multimedia applications that combine text, sound, and images (see Section 6.7). For example, financial databases from Dow Jones or Dun and Bradstreet are available on CD-ROM. The U.S. Department of Defense has initiated a system of networks and optical imaging to reduce the mountains of paper generated by technical design information and administrative data for weapons systems.

compact disk read-only memory (CD-ROM) Read-only optical disk storage used for imaging, reference, and database applications with massive amounts of data and for multimedia.

Because a single CD-ROM can store vast quantities of data, the technology is often used for storing images, sound, and video, as well as text.

write once/read many (WORM)
Optical disk system that allows users to record data only once; data cannot be erased but can be read indefinitely.

Write once/read many (WORM) optical disk systems allow users to record data only once on an optical disk. Once written, the data cannot be erased, but can be read indefinitely. WORM has been used as an alternative to microfilm for archiving digitized document images. The disadvantages of CD-ROM and WORM optical disks are that their contents cannot easily be erased and written over, as with magnetic disks, and that the access speed is slower than that of magnetic disks.

Rewritable magneto-optical disks are starting to become cost effective for data storage. The disk surface is coated with a magnetic material that can change magnetic polarity only when heated. To record data, a high-powered laser beam heats tiny spots in the magnetic medium that allow it to accept magnetic patterns. Data can be read by shining a lower-powered laser beam at the magnetic layer and reading the reflected light. The magneto-optical disk is erasable and can be written on nearly a million times. The access speed of optical disks, although slower than that of a magnetic disk, is continuing to improve, making the optical disk an attractive storage technology in the coming years.

digital video disk (DVD) High-capacity optical storage medium that can store full-length videos and large amounts of data.

CD-ROM storage is likely to become more popular and more powerful in years to come. **Digital video disks (DVDs)** (also called digital versatile disks) are optical disks the same size as CD-ROM but of even higher capacity. They can hold up to 5 gigabytes of data, enough to store a full-length motion picture. DVDs will initially be used to store movies and multimedia applications using large amounts of video and graphics, but may replace CD-ROMs because they can store digitized text, graphics, audio, and video data.

Magnetic Tape

magnetic tape Inexpensive and relatively stable secondary storage medium in which large volumes of information are stored sequentially by means of magnetized and nonmagnetized spots on tape.

Magnetic tape is an older storage technology that is still employed for secondary storage of large volumes of information. It is used primarily in mainframe batch applications and for archiving data. Magnetic tape for large systems comes in 14-inch reels that are up to 2400 feet long and 0.5 inches wide. It is very similar to home cassette recording tape, but of higher quality. Information can be stored on magnetic tape at different densities. Low density is 1600 bytes per inch (bpi), and densities of up to 6250 bpi are common. Tape cartridges with much higher density (6000 to over 60,000 bpi) and storage capacity are replacing reel-to-reel tapes in mainframe and minicomputer systems. PCs and some minicomputers use small tape cartridges resembling home audiocassettes to store information.

The principal advantages of magnetic tape are that it is inexpensive, that it is relatively stable, and that it can store large volumes of information. Moreover, magnetic tape can be used repeatedly, although it does age with time and computer users must handle it carefully.

The principal disadvantages of magnetic tape are that it stores data sequentially and is relatively slow compared with the speed of other secondary storage media. To find an individual record stored on magnetic tape, such as your employment record, the tape must be read from the beginning to the location of the desired record. Hence, magnetic tape is not a good medium when it is necessary to find information rapidly (such as for an airline reservation system). Tape can also be damaged and is labor intensive to mount and dismount. Tape represents a fading technology, but it continues to exist in changing forms.

6.6 INPUT AND OUTPUT DEVICES

Human beings interact with computer systems largely through input and output devices. Advances in information systems rely not only on the speed and capacity of the CPU but also on the speed, capacity, and design of the input and output devices. Input/output devices are often called *peripheral devices*.

Input Devices

The traditional method of data entry has been by keyboarding. Today, most data are entered directly into the computer using a data entry terminal and they are processed on-line. For instance, on-line airline reservation and customer information systems have reservation clerks or salespeople enter transactions directly while dealing with the customer, and their systems are updated immediately.

Some applications developed during an earlier era in computing might still use keypunching to obtain input. Data entry clerks use a keypunch machine to code characters on an 80-column card, designating each character with a unique punch in a specific location on the card. An electromechanical card reader senses the holes and solid parts of the cards. A single card could store up to 80 bytes of information (80 columns). Key-to-tape or key-to-disk machines allowed data to be keyed directly onto magnetic tape or disk for later computer processing.

The Computer Mouse

The point-and-click actions of the **computer mouse** have made it an increasingly popular alternative to keyboard and text-based commands. A mouse is a handheld device that is usually connected to the computer by a cable. The computer user moves the mouse around on a desktop to control the position of the cursor on a video display screen. Once the cursor is in the desired position, the user can push a button on the mouse to select a command. The mouse can also be used to "draw" images on the screen.

computer mouse Handheld input device whose movement on the desktop controls the position of the cursor on the computer display screen.

Touch Screens

Touch screens are easy to use and are appealing to people who can't use traditional keyboards. Users can enter limited amounts of data by touching the surface of a sensitized video display monitor with a finger or a pointer. With colorful graphics, sound, and simple menus, touch screens allow the user to make selections by touching specified parts of the screen. Touch screens are proliferating in retail stores, restaurants, shopping malls, and even in some schools. The Window on Organizations shows how touch screens in kiosks became an important element of one bank's business strategy.

touch screen Input device technology that permits the entering or selecting of commands and data by touching the surface of a sensitized video display monitor with a finger or a pointer.

Touch screens allow users to enter small amounts of data by touching words, numbers, or specific points on the screen.

La Caixa Bank Pioneers Touch-Screen Kiosks

A tradition for embracing cutting-edge technology has helped to make Caja de Ahorros y Pensiones de Barcelona (Barcelona Savings and Pensions Bank) or "la Caixa" the largest bank in Spain and the second largest bank in Europe. Because of the bank's pioneering computer automation, by 1964 la Caixa's customers could already conduct their banking business from any branch.

Technology has also played a significant role in keeping la Caixa a lean operation. Through development and massive use of self-service systems, la Caixa averages only four employees at each of its 2425 branches. La Caixa was the first bank in Europe to install enhanced automatic teller machines (ATMs) able to operate with passbooks. This innovation has made it possible for the bank's customers to record running balances conveniently 24 hours a day, at any of the banks 3200 ATM locations.

Now, with the help of IBM, la Caixa has transformed the ATM into a sophisticated touch-screen kiosk capable of delivering a far-richer array of services to its customers. The kiosks have provided the bank with new ways to attract customers and have created new sources of revenue while keeping costs down. Integrated bar-code and credit card readers, passbook scanner/printers, ticket printers, and the touch-screen interface help to make la Caixa's kiosks capable of handing just about any transaction imaginable. No longer limited to banking services, the IBM kiosks—which will be placed in more than 640 convenient locations—can dispense tickets for public transportation, sporting events, movies, and concerts. Customers can also use the multipurpose kiosks to pay gas and electric bills and even their taxes.

Moreover, these new multimedia, easy-to-use kiosks provide a great new revenue generator for la Caixa. For example, the bank offers on-line information on real estate sales and is thereby able to direct business to its mortgage and insurance divisions by catching renters as soon as they show an interest in buying.

Because the kiosks are capable of doing the business of more than one institution, the bank can sell "kiosk time" to other vendors as well, providing an almost limitless potential. Major vendors use la Caixa's kiosks to offer exclusive product promotions. Customers are offered and will often impulse buy all sorts of specialty and new products which are then delivered to their homes or to others as gifts. Vendors are charged, usually on a transaction basis, for the privilege of using kiosks so the bank actually gains commission revenues for services delivered by other companies.

In addition, a wide variety of services can be offered to win customer loyalty. For example, using the kiosks, customers can look for jobs and schedule employment interviews on-line. The bank expects that the wide variety of services offered by the kiosks will make their use a part of the customer's routine. "We want people to be able to enter the branch and use the kiosk to perform almost any transaction, all at the same place," says Victoria Matia Agell, director of electronic banking services at la Caixa. "People will quickly get comfortable with this technology and find that it can accomplish many of their needs. As a result, these kiosks will become sought after as a marketing venue for many companies."

To Think About: *How is the use of kiosks and touch screens related to la Caixa's business strategy? What business processes does this technology support?*

Sources: Geoff Amthor, " 'La Caixa' Touch-Screen Teller," *Multimedia Today,* October–November–December 1995.

Source Data Automation

source data automation Input technology that captures data in computer-readable form at the time and place the data are created.

Source data automation captures data in computer-readable form at the time and place they are created. Point-of-sale systems, optical bar-code scanners used in supermarkets, and other optical character recognition devices are examples of source data automation. One advantage of source data automation is that the many errors that occur when people use keyboards to enter data are almost eliminated. Bar-code scanners make fewer than one error in 10,000 transactions, whereas skilled keypunchers make about one error for every 1000 keystrokes.

The principal source data automation technologies are magnetic ink character recognition, optical character recognition, pen-based input, digital scanners, voice input, and sensors.

magnetic ink character recognition (MICR) Input technology that translates characters written in magnetic ink into digital codes for processing.

Magnetic ink character recognition (MICR) technology is used primarily in check processing for the banking industry. The bottom portion of a typical check contains characters that are preprinted using a special ink. Characters identify the bank, checking account, and check number. An MICR reader translates the characters on checks that have been cashed and sent to the bank for processing into digital form for the computer. The amount of the check, which is written in ordinary ink, must be keyed in by hand.

Optical character recognition (OCR) devices translate specially designed marks, characters, and codes into digital form. The most widely used optical code is the **bar code**, which is used in point-of-sale systems in supermarkets and retail stores. Bar codes are also used in hospitals, libraries, military operations, and transportation facilities. The codes can include time, date, and location data in addition to identification data; the information makes them useful for analyzing the movement of items and determining what has happened to them during production or other processes. (The discussion of the United Parcel Service in Chapter 1 and the case concluding this chapter show how valuable bar codes can be for this purpose.)

Handwriting-recognition devices such as pen-based tablets, notebooks, and notepads are promising new input technologies, especially for people working in the sales or service areas or for those who have traditionally shunned computer keyboards. These **pen-based input** devices usually consist of a flat-screen display table and a penlike stylus.

With pen-based input, users print directly onto the tablet-sized screen. The screen is fitted with a transparent grid of fine wires that detects the presence of the special stylus, which emits a faint signal from its tip. The screen can also interpret tapping and flicking gestures made with the stylus. Pen-based input devices transform the letters and numbers written by users on the tablet into digital form, where they can be stored or processed and analyzed. For instance, the United Parcel Service replaced its drivers' familiar clipboard with a battery-powered delivery information acquisition device (DIAD) to capture signatures (see the Chapter 1 Window on Technology) along with other information required for pickup and delivery. This technology requires special pattern-recognition software to accept pen-based input instead of keyboard input. At present, most pen-based systems cannot recognize freehand writing very well.

Digital scanners translate images such as pictures or documents into digital form and are an essential component of image processing systems. **Voice input devices** convert spoken words into digital form. Voice-recognition software compares the electrical patterns produced by the speaker's voice with a set of prerecorded patterns. If the patterns match, the input is accepted. Sophisticatd voice systems have vocabularies of 30,000 words, but most voice systems accept only very simple commands. For instance, some branches of the U.S. Postal Service are using voice-recognition systems to make sorting packages and envelopes more efficient. In one application, users can speak out ZIP codes instead of keying them in, so that both hands can manipulate a package.

Sensors are devices that collect data directly from the environment for input into a computer system. For instance, sensors are being used in General Motors cars with onboard computers and screens that display the map of the surrounding area and the driver's route. Sensors in each wheel and a magnetic compass supply information to the computer for determining the car's location.

Batch and On-Line Input and Processing

The manner in which data are input into the computer affects how the data can be processed. Information systems collect and process information in one of two ways: through batch or through on-line processing. In **batch processing**, transactions such as orders or payroll time cards are accumulated and stored in a group or batch until the time when, because of some reporting cycle, it is efficient or necessary to process them. This was the only method of processing until the early 1960s, and it is still used today in older systems or some systems with massive volumes of transactions. In **on-line processing**, which is now common, the user enters transactions into a device

optical character recognition (OCR) Form of source data automation in which optical scanning devices read specially designed data off source documents and translate the data into digital form for the computer.

bar code Form of OCR technology widely used in supermarkets and retail stores in which identification data are coded into a series of bars.

pen-based input Input devices such as tablets, notebooks, and notepads consisting of a flat-screen display tablet and a penlike stylus that digitizes handwriting.

digital scanners Input devices that translate images such as pictures or documents into digital form for processing.

voice input device Technology that converts the spoken word into digital form for processing.

sensors Devices that collect data directly from the environment for input into a computer system.

batch processing A method of collecting and processing data in which transactions are accumulated and stored until a specified time when it is convenient or necessary to process them as a group.

on-line processing A method of collecting and processing data in which transactions are entered directly into the computer system and processed immediately.

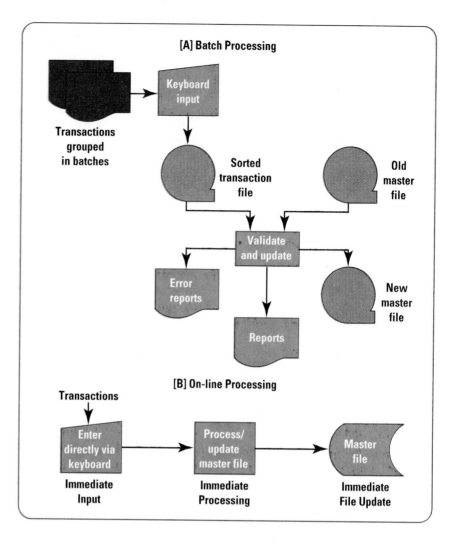

that is directly connected to the computer system. The transactions are usually processed immediately.

The demands of the business determine the type of processing. If the user needs periodic or occasional reports or output, as in payroll or end-of-the-year reports, batch processing is most efficient. If the user needs immediate information and processing, as in an airline or hotel reservation system, then the system should use on-line processing.

Figure 6.11 compares batch and on-line processing. Batch systems often use tape as a storage medium, whereas on-line processing systems use disk storage, which permits immediate access to specific items of information. In batch systems, transactions are accumulated in a **transaction file,** which contains all the transactions for a particular time period. Periodically this file is used to update a **master file,** which contains permanent information on entities. (An example is a payroll master file with employee earnings and deductions data. It is updated with weekly time card transactions.) Adding the transaction data to the existing master file creates a new master file. In on-line processing, transactions are entered into the system immediately and the system usually responds immediately. The master file is updated continually. In on-line processing, there is a direct connection to the computer for input and output.

Output Devices

The major data output devices are cathode ray tube (CRT) terminals (sometimes called video display terminals or VDTs) and printers. The **cathode ray tube (CRT)** is

---

transaction file In batch systems, a file in which all transactions are accumulated to await processing.

master file A file that contains all permanent information and is updated during processing by transaction data.

cathode ray tube (CRT) terminal A screen, also referred to as a video display terminal (VDT). Provides a visual image of both user input and computer output. Displays text or graphics as either color or monochrome images.

---

probably the most popular form of information output in modern computer systems. It works much like a television picture tube, with an electronic gun shooting a beam of electrons to illuminate the pixels on the screen. The more pixels per screen, the higher the resolution. CRT monitors can be classified as monochrome or color and by their display capabilities. Some display only text, whereas others display both text and graphics. Display devices for graphics often utilize bit mapping. **Bit mapping** allows each pixel on the screen to be addressed and manipulated by the computer (as opposed to blocks of pixels in character addressable displays). This requires more computer memory but permits finer detail and the ability to produce any kind of image on the display screen. Special-purpose graphics terminals used in CAD/CAM and commercial art have very high-resolution capabilities (1280 × 1024 pixels).

bit mapping The technology that allows each pixel on the screen to be addressed and manipulated by the computer.

Printers and Plotters

Printers produce a printed hard copy of information output. They include impact printers (a standard typewriter or a dot matrix) and nonimpact printers (laser, inkjet, and thermal transfer printers). Most printers print one character at a time, but some commercial printers print an entire line or page at a time. In general, impact printers are slower than nonimpact printers.

printer A computer output device that provides paper hard copy output in the form of text or graphics.

High-quality graphics documents can be created using **plotters** with multicolored pens to draw (rather than print) computer output. Plotters are much slower than printers, but are useful for outputting large-size charts, maps, or drawings.

plotter Output device using multicolored pens to draw high-quality graphic documents.

Other Output Devices

Microfilm and microfiche have been used to compactly store output as microscopic filmed images, and they are used mainly by insurance companies or other firms that need to output and store large numbers of documents. These media are cumbersome to search through and will be replaced by optical disk technology.

A **voice output device** converts digital output data back into intelligible speech. Sounds are prerecorded, coded, and stored on disk, to be translated back as spoken words. For instance, when you call for information on the telephone, you may hear a computerized voice respond with the telephone number you requested.

voice output device A converter of digital output data into spoken words.

6.7 INFORMATION TECHNOLOGY TRENDS

Over the last 30 years, computing costs have dropped by a factor of 10 each decade and capacity has increased by a factor of at least 100 each decade. Today's microprocessors can put a mainframe on a desktop, and eventually into a briefcase or shirt pocket. Chapter 10 shows how the traditional mainframe is being supplanted by networks of powerful desktop machines, although the mainframe will never be eliminated. The future will see even more intelligence built into everyday devices, with mainframe and perhaps even supercomputer-like computing power packed in a pocket- or notebook-sized computer. Pen, notebook, and palmtop computers will be as pervasive as handheld calculators. Computers on a chip will increasingly guide automobiles, military weapons, robots, and everyday household devices. Computers and related information technologies will blend data, images, and sound, sending them coursing through vast networks that can process all of them with equal ease. More information and knowledge will be represented visually, through graphics (Lieberman, 1996). Potentially, computer technology could be so powerful and integrated into daily experiences it would appear essentially invisible to the user (Weiser, 1993). People will increasingly interact with the computer in more intuitive and effortless ways—through writing, speech, touch, eye movement, and other gestures (Selker, 1996). We can see how this might be possible through the use of multimedia, network computers, and fifth-generation computers.

One of the principal applications of multimedia today is for interactive corporate training.

Multimedia

Multimedia is defined as the technologies that facilitate the integration of two or more types of media, such as text, graphics, sound, voice, full-motion video, still video, or animation into a computer-based application. Multimedia is becoming the foundation of new consumer products and services, such as electronic books and newspapers, electronic classroom presentation technologies, full-motion video conferencing, imaging, graphics design tools, and video and voice mail. Many World Wide Web sites are multimedia.

By pressing a button, a person using a computer can call up a screenful of text; another button might bring up related video images. Still another might bring up related talk or music. For instance, Bell Canada, which provides residential and business telephone services across Canada, uses a multimedia application to help diagnose and repair problems on the network. The application contains hundreds of repair manuals that have been scanned, digitized, and made available on-line to technicians and network analysts as they work on repairing off-site network components. Each multimedia workstation can display maps of the network, sound alarms when problems occur on specific equipment, and fax maps on-line to repair personnel who have trouble locating their appointments. A voice-message annotation feature lets users click on an icon to hear new information or additional comments on specific diagnostic or repair cases (De Pompa, 1993).

A simple multimedia system consists of a personal computer with a 32-bit microprocessor, a high-resolution color monitor, a high-capacity hard disk drive, and a CD-ROM disk drive. (A 5-inch optical disk holding more than 600 megabytes of information can store an hour of music, several thousand full-color pictures, several minutes of video or animation, and millions of words.) Stereo speakers are useful for amplifying audio output.

The most difficult element to incorporate into multimedia information systems has been full-motion video, because so much data must be brought under the digital

Table 6.5	Examples of Multimedia Web Sites
Web Site	Description
Internet TV	Playlist includes live concerts, music videos, and hourly newscasts.
FedNet	Tracks congressional activities with live and archived floor debates and proceedings.
Newsworld Online	Provides news from Canada, including live video, 24 hours a day.
Movielink	Provides sneak previews of movies in several formats and the ability to order tickets on-line.

control of the computer. The massive amounts of data in each video image must be digitally encoded, stored, and manipulated electronically, using techniques that compress the digital data. Special adapter cards are used to digitize sound and video.

Microprocessors optimized for multimedia have been developed to improve processing of visually intensive applications. Intel's *MMX (MultimMedia eXtension)* microprocessor is a Pentium chip that has been modified to increase performance in many applications featuring graphics and sound. Multimedia applications such as games and video will be able to run more smoothly, with more colors, and be able to perform more tasks simultaneously. For example, multiple channels of audio, high-quality video or animation, along with Internet communication could all be running in the same application.

The possibilities of this technology are endless, but multimedia seems especially well suited for training and presentations. For training, multimedia is appealing because it is interactive and permits two-way communication. People can use multimedia training sessions any time of the day, at their own pace (Hardaway and Will, 1997). Instructors can easily integrate words, sounds, pictures, and both live and animated video to produce lessons that capture students' imaginations. For example, Duracell, the $2.3 billion battery manufacturer, taught new employees at its Chinese manufacturing facility how to use battery-making machinery with an interactive multimedia program. Workers can use computer simulations to "stop," "start," and control equipment (Kay, 1997).

People are now using multimedia on the Internet, creating interactive Web pages replete with graphics, sound, animations, and full-motion video. For example, the TerraQuest Web site features "virtual explorations" on the Web to exotic destinations such as Antarctica or the Galápagos Islands. At Virtual Galápagos, an interactive tour of the Galápagos Islands, one can read letters from voyagers, content by experts in natural history and expedition travel, view film clips, photos, or maps or participate in on-line chat sessions with other visitors to the site. Table 6.5 lists examples of other multimedia Web sites.

Network Computers

Companies are starting to use network computers as an alternative to expensive desktop computers with powerful processing and storage technology. **Network computers** are smaller, simpler, and cheaper versions of the traditional personal computer that do not store software programs or data permanently. Instead, users download whatever software or data they need from a central computer over the Internet or an organization's own internal network. The central computer also saves information for the user and makes it available for later retrieval, effectively eliminating the need for hard disks, floppy disks, CD-ROMs, and their drives. A network computer may consist of little more than a stripped-down PC, a monitor, a keyboard, and a network connection.

network computer Simplified desktop computer that does not store software programs or data permanently. Users download whatever software or data they need from a central computer over the Internet or an organization's own internal network.

Proponents of network computer systems claim that NCs could reduce the costs of owning and operating a desktop computer by as much as 80 percent. Network computers are less expensive to purchase than full-function PCs, costing between $500 and $1000 per unit. Most estimates place a firm's annual cost of owning a PC between $5000 and $12,000. This includes maintenance, software upgrades, training, and troubleshooting help. Network computers have fewer parts than conventional PCs, and thus are less likely to malfunction. Software programs and applications would not have to be purchased, installed, and upgraded for each user because software would be delivered and maintained from one central point.

Network computers would increase management control over the organization's computing function. All users' work could be saved on one backup system. It would be more difficult for users to leak sensitive information or secretly copy software because they would have no way of copying from their machines to a secondary storage tool such as a disk drive. The chance of infection from computer viruses would be lessened, because users could not input potentially tainted software or data from an external source. With management controlling the software available to employees, productivity might increase because employees wouldn't have access to software for computer games or other distractions. And if the network computers use a programming language such as Java, the firm would not have to pay for writing different versions of software to run on different brands of computers or specific operating systems (see Chapter 7).

Not everyone agrees that network computers will bring benefits. Some researchers believe that centralizing control over computing would stifle worker initiative and creativity. Several studies of the cost of owning PCs question whether the savings promised by network computers will actually be realized. Companies might need to invest in more powerful computers that could deliver required software and data to the network computers. Very little software has yet to be designed for the network computing model. Because the technology is so new, cost savings from network computing have not been fully ascertained. If a network failure occurs, hundreds or thousands of employees would not be able to use their computers, whereas people could keep on working if they had full-function PCs. A poorly supervised network computer system could prove to be just as inefficient as PCs sometimes are. Companies should closely examine how network computers would fit into their information technology infrastructure. These issues are explored in the Window on Management.

Simplified network computers are being promoted by Sun Microsystems Inc., the creator of the Java programming language (see Chapter 7). Sun launched its Javastation network computer in the fall of 1996. IBM and Oracle have also aligned themselves on the side of the simplified network unit. Microsoft and Intel initially dismissed the network computing concept as a step backward in information technology. They subsequently developed the Net PC, their own version of a network computer, acknowledging the need for a more economical desktop machine. Unlike Sun's Javastation, which operates only with a network, the NetPC has some independent processing and storage capability. Computer manufacturers such as Compaq, Hewlett-Packard, Digital, and NEC indicated they would support the NetPC.

Superchips and Fifth-Generation Computers

In addition to improving their design, microprocessors have been made to perform faster by shrinking the distance between transistors. This process gives the electrical current less distance to travel. The narrower the lines forming transistors, the larger the number of transistors that can be squeezed onto a single chip, and the faster these circuits will operate. The Pentium Pro microprocessor, for example, squeezes 5.5 million transistors on a postage-stamp–size silicon pad. Figure 6.12 shows that line widths have shrunk from the diameter of a hair to less than one micron and should reach one-fifth of a micron by the year 2000. The lower part of the figure shows the

Network Computers: A New Management Option

Are network computers (NCs) the next phase in corporate computing? Some companies think so. Pizza Hut Inc. and Charles Schwab & Co. are evaluating whether to replace some of their desktop PCs with network computers, and other companies have already made the switch. They point to low purchase and maintenance costs as their rationale for switching to NCs.

Management at UniHealth, a health services provider in Burbank, California, believes network computers will reduce the company's capital and ongoing maintenance costs. UniHealth plans to use NCs to improve coordination of patient services across its four divisions—hospitals, physician groups, home health care units, and a health maintenance organization. NCs will initially be installed to link these divisions internally. Eventually UniHealth hopes to equip its customers with network computers so that they can access personal health information.

Retired Persons Services Inc. in Alexandria, Virginia, the pharmaceutical arm of the American Association of Retired Persons (AARP), installed 1000 units of @Workstation, a $700 network computing device from HDS Network Systems at three locations, with 200 more to be installed later. According to Don Resh, the company's senior vice president and chief information officer (CIO), "There's nothing a user can do to screw them up." The NC system requires much less technical support than 1000 PCs. Resh calculates that five years of support and maintenance for 1000 PCs would cost $35 million, compared with $2.5 million for the network computer system.

Some managers have decided against NCs because of the unreliability of both internal networks and the Internet. Dayna Aronson, information systems manager at Norpac Food Sales, the Lake Oswego, Oregon, division of Norpac Foods, Inc., is not planning to adopt the NC model for many years to come. He worries about hundreds of users twiddling their thumbs if the network goes down. Having local processing power and data "provides a level of autonomy and redundancy worth far more than saving $1000."

John Holmwood, a technical analyst at Nova Gas Transmission in Calgary, British Columbia, believes that network computers save management and support costs. The majority of a company's total costs for networked desktop computers are at the desktop, particularly managing the various pieces of hardware and software maintained on each user's desktop throughout the company. Although Nova's main focus is to decrease support costs as much as possible, the company is not committed to network computers. It is debating whether to use NCs or "dataless" workstations. These "dataless" workstations are standard PCs linked to a network, but most of the data and applications they use are stored on centralized computers. Nova will move to network computers only if it can prove that support and management costs will be significantly lower than such costs with standard PCs.

Zona Research released a study predicting that shipments of network computers will top 4.2 million units by the end of the decade. However, International Data Corporation, a Framingham, Massachusetts, consulting firm, isn't as optimistic. According to IDC analyst Ted Julian, the idea that you can sit at your desk and download what you need from the network is appealing, "but there's a lot of infrastructure for distributing, managing, and using that model that isn't there yet."

To Think About: If you were a manager, what people, organization, and technology factors would you consider in deciding whether to use network computers in your organization?

Sources: Edward Cone, "NCs Impress," *Information Week*, March 31, 1997; Mary Hayes, "The NC Arrives," *InformationWeek*, November 18, 1996; and David Simpson, "Who Needs a Network Computer?" *Datamation*, October 1996.

---

number of transistors on some prominent microprocessors and memory chips. Because the number of transistors that can fit economically onto a single silicon chip is doubling every 18 months, between 50 and 100 million transistors could soon conceivably be squeezed onto a single microprocessor. Researchers have recently found a way to double the power of memory chips, further accelerating chip performance (Markott, 1997).

Conventional computers are based on the Von Neumann architecture, which processes information serially, one instruction at a time. In the future, more computers will use parallel processing and massively parallel processing to blend voice, images, and massive pools of data from diverse sources, using artificial intelligence and intricate mathematical models.

Massively parallel computers, illustrated in Figure 6.13, have huge networks of processor chips interwoven in complex and flexible ways. As opposed to parallel processing, in which small numbers of powerful but expensive specialized chips are

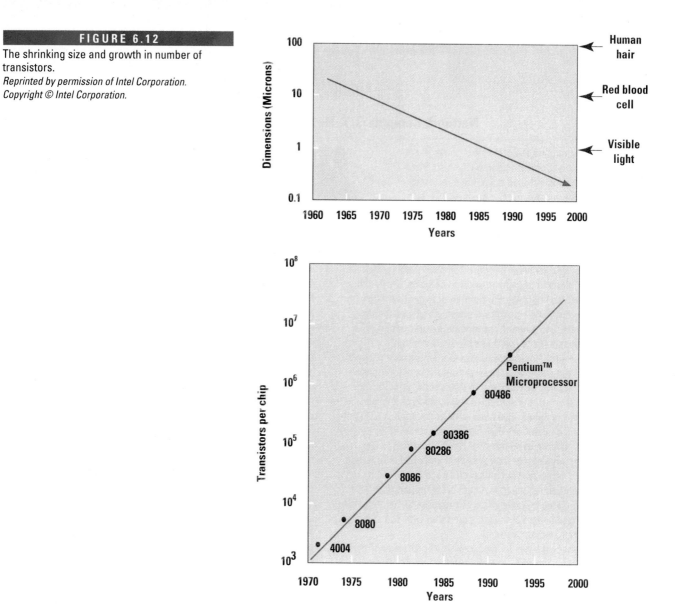

FIGURE 6.12
The shrinking size and growth in number of
transistors.
Reprinted by permission of Intel Corporation.
Copyright © Intel Corporation.

massively parallel computers
Computers that use hundreds or
thousands of processing chips
to attack large computing problems simultaneously.

linked together, **massively parallel computers** chain hundreds or even thousands of inexpensive, commonly used chips to attack large computing problems, attaining supercomputer speeds. For instance, Wal-Mart uses its massively parallel machine to
sift through an inventory and sales trend database with 24 trillion bytes of data.

Massively parallel systems have cost advantages over conventional computers
because they can take advantage of off-the-shelf chips. They may be able to accomplish processing work for one-tenth to one-twentieth the cost of traditional mainframes or supercomputers.

Today's supercomputers can perform hundreds of billions of calculations per second. Some supercomputers can now perform more than a trillion mathematical calculations each second—a teraflop. The term *teraflop* comes from the Greek "teras,"
which for mathematicians means one trillion, and "flop," which is an acronym for
floating point operations per second. (A floating point operation is a basic computer
arithmetic operation, such as addition, on numbers that include a decimal point.)
Teraflop machines can support projects such as mapping the surface of planets, designing new computers, or testing the aerodynamics of supersonic airplanes, where
trillions of calculations are required.

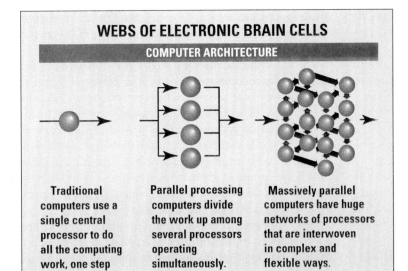

WEBS OF ELECTRONIC BRAIN CELLS

COMPUTER ARCHITECTURE

Traditional computers use a single central processor to do all the computing work, one step at a time.

Parallel processing computers divide the work up among several processors operating simultaneously.

Massively parallel computers have huge networks of processors that are interwoven in complex and flexible ways.

FIGURE 6.13

Computer architecture. A comparison of traditional serial processing, parallel processing, and massively parallel processing.

From John Markoff, "Foray Into Mainstream for Parallel Computing." The New York Times, *June 15, 1992. Copyright © 1991; 1992 by the New York Times Co. Reprinted by permission.*

MANAGEMENT WRAP-UP

Selection of computer hardware technology for the organization is a key business decision, and should not be left to just technical specialists. General managers should understand the capabilities of various computer processing, input, output, and storage options as well as price-performance relationships. They should be involved in hardware capacity planning and decisions to distribute computing, downsize, or use network computers.

MANAGEMENT

Computer hardware technology can either enhance or impede organizational performance. Selection of appropriate computer hardware technology should consider how well the technology meshes with the culture and structure of the organization as well as its information-processing requirements.

ORGANIZATION

Information technology today is not limited to only computers but must be viewed as an array of digital devices networked together. Organizations have many computer processing options, including mainframes, workstations, PCs, and network computers and many different ways of configuring hardware components to create systems.

TECHNOLOGY

For Discussion: A firm would like to introduce computers into its order entry process but feels that it should wait for a new generation of machines to be developed. After all, any machine bought now will be quickly out of date and less expensive a few years from now. Do you agree? Why or why not?

SUMMARY

1. Identify the hardware components in a typical computer system. The modern computer system has six major components: a central processing unit (CPU), primary storage, input devices, output devices, secondary storage, and communications devices.

2. Describe how information is represented and processed in a computer system. Digital computers store and process information in the form of binary digits called bits. A string of 8 bits is called a byte. There are several coding schemes for arranging binary digits into characters. The most common are EBCDIC and ASCII. The CPU is the center of the computer, where the manipulation of symbols, numbers, and letters occurs. The CPU has two components: an arithmetic-logic unit and a control unit. The arithmetic-logic unit performs arithmetic and logical operations on data, while the control unit controls and coordinates the other components of the computer.

The CPU is closely tied to primary memory, or primary storage, which stores data and program instructions temporarily before and after processing. Several different kinds of semiconductor memory chips are used with primary storage: RAM (random access memory) is used for short-term storage of data and program instructions, while ROM (read-only memory) permanently stores important program instructions. Other memory devices include PROM (programmable read-only memory) and EPROM (erasable programmable read-only memory).

3. **Distinguish between generations of computer hardware.** Computer technology has gone through four generations, from vacuum tubes to transistors, integrated circuits, and very large-scale integrated circuits, each dramatically increasing computer-processing power while shrinking the size of computing hardware.

4. **Contrast the capabilities of mainframes, minicomputers, PCs, workstations, and supercomputers.** Depending on their size and processing power, computers are categorized as mainframes, minicomputers, PCs, workstations, or supercomputers. Mainframes are the largest computers; minicomputers are mid-range machines; PCs are desktop or laptop machines; workstations are desktop machines with powerful mathematical and graphic capabilities; and supercomputers are sophisticated, powerful computers that can perform massive and complex computations because they use parallel processing. Server computers are optimized to support networks. The capabilities of microprocessors used in these computers can be gauged by their word length, data bus width, and cycle speed. Because of continuing advances in microprocessor technology, the distinctions between these various types

of computers are constantly changing. PCs are now powerful enough to perform much of the work that was formerly limited to mainframes and minicomputers.

5. **Describe the various media for storing data and programs in a computer system.** The principal forms of secondary storage are magnetic tape, magnetic disk, and optical disk. Tape stores records in sequence and can only be used in batch processing. Disk permits direct access to specific records and is much faster than tape. Disk technology is used in on-line processing. Optical disks can store vast amounts of data compactly. CD-ROM disk systems can only be read from, but rewritable optical disk systems are becoming available.

6. **Compare the major input and output devices and approaches to input and processing.** The principal input devices are keyboards, computer mice, touch screens, magnetic ink and optical character recognition, pen-based instruments, digital scanners, sensors, and voice input. The principal output devices are video display terminals, printers, plotters, voice output devices, and microfilm and microfiche. In batch processing, transactions are accumulated and stored in a group until the time when it is efficient or necessary to process them. In on-line processing, the user enters transactions into a device that is directly connected to the computer system. The transactions are usually processed immediately.

7. **Describe multimedia, network computers, and future information technology trends.** Multimedia integrates two or more types of media, such as text, graphics, sound, voice, full-motion video, still video, and/or animation into a computer-based application. Network computers are pared-down desktop machines that download their data and software from a network rather than storing them independently. The future will see steady and impressive progress toward faster chips at lower cost and microprocessors with the power of today's mainframes or supercomputers. Hardware using massively parallel processing will be utilized more widely, and computers and related information technologies will be able to blend data, images, and sound.

KEY TERMS

Bit	Kilobyte	Erasable programmable read-only memory (EPROM)	Mainframe
Byte	Megabyte		Minicomputer
Extended Binary Coded Decimal Interchange Code (EBCDIC)	Gigabyte	Arithmetic-logic unit (ALU)	Personal computer (PC)
	Central processing unit (CPU)	Control unit	Workstation
American Standard Code for Information Interchange (ASCII)	Primary storage	Machine cycle	Supercomputer
	Random access memory (RAM)	Microprocessor	Server computer
Pixel	Semiconductor	Word length	Distributed processing
Millisecond	Read-only memory (ROM)	Megahertz	Centralized processing
Microsecond	Programmable read-only memory (PROM)	Data bus width	Downsizing
Nanosecond		Reduced instruction set computing (RISC)	Cooperative processing
			Parallel processing
			Secondary storage

Register	Compact disk read-only	Optical character	Cathode ray tube (CRT)
Cache	memory (CD-ROM)	recognition (OCR)	terminal
Magnetic disk	Write once/read many	Bar code	Bit mapping
Hard disk	(WORM)	Pen-based input	Printer
Track	Digital video disk (DVD)	Digital scanners	Plotter
Cylinder	Magnetic tape	Voice input device	Voice output device
Redundant array of	Computer mouse	Sensors	Multimedia
inexpensive disks (RAID)	Touch screen	Batch processing	Network computer
Floppy disk	Source data automation	On-line processing	Massively parallel
Sector	Magnetic ink character	Transaction file	computers
Direct access storage	recognition (MICR)	Master file	
device (DASD)			

REVIEW QUESTIONS

1. What are the components of a contemporary computer system?

2. Distinguish between a bit and a byte.

3. What are ASCII and EBCDIC, and why are they used? Why can't true binary be used in a computer as a machine language?

4. Name and define the principal measures of computer time and storage capacity.

5. What problems of coordination exist in a computing environment and why?

6. Name the major components of the CPU and the function of each.

7. Describe how information is stored in primary memory.

8. What are the four different types of semiconductor memory, and when are they used?

9. Describe the major generations of computers and the characteristics of each.

10. Name and describe the factors affecting the speed and performance of a microprocessor.

11. What are downsizing and cooperative processing?

12. List the most important secondary storage media. What are the strengths and limitations of each?

13. List and describe the major input devices.

14. What is the difference between batch and on-line processing? Diagram the difference.

15. List and describe the major output devices.

16. What is multimedia? What technologies are involved?

17. What is a network computer? How does it differ from a conventional PC?

18. Distinguish between serial, parallel, and massively parallel processing.

GROUP PROJECT

It has been predicted that notebook computers will be available that have 10 times the power of a current personal computer, with a touch-sensitive color screen on which one can write or draw with a stylus or type when a program displays a keyboard. Each will have a small, compact, rewritable, removable CD-ROM disk that can store the equivalent of a set of encyclopedias. In addition, the computers will have elementary voice-recognition capabilities, including the ability to record sound and give voice responses to questions. The computer will be able to carry on a dialogue by voice, graphics, typed words, and displayed video graphics. Thus, computers will be about the size of a thick pad of letter paper and just as portable and convenient, but with the intelligence of a computer and the multimedia capabilities of a television set. Such a computer is expected to cost about $2000. Form a group with three or four of your classmates and develop an analysis of the impacts such developments would have on university education. Explain why you think the impact will or will not occur.

Storage and Strategy

No company wants to fix a system that isn't broken. But sometimes systems that have operated smoothly for many years come to a crossroads. Distributed computing, along with widespread use of the Internet and multimedia are putting new strains on firms' data storage capabilities. New technology arrangements are required because so much data is being generated.

A key part of the business of Schlumberger Geco Prakla, headquartered in Gatwick, England, is selling seismic data to oil and gas companies to guide their exploration. Schlumberger's reservoir of approximately 3 terabytes of on-line data will climb rapidly after an automated data collection system and 3-D seismic mapping techniques and engineering applications enabled by a more powerful internal communications network become operational in 1997.

For the past 15 years, the company stored its data using backup tape technology. When a customer requested seismic data, an employee had to search among 1.5 million warehoused reels of tape and then copy the information to whatever storage format the customer needed. This inefficient, time-consuming process could take up to two weeks. Schlumberger experienced throughput problems because its storage capacity wasn't keeping up with the soaring power of its computers and networks.

The company installed Storage Computer's OmniRAID, a continuously available storage system. OmniRAID can move data at a rate of 12 megabytes per second. (Schlumberger's previous small computer interface technology could move data at only 3 to 5 megabytes per second.) Also in use are Storage Technology's PowderHorn

Automated Cartridge System silos, which house 5000 50-gigabyte D3 tape cartridges. The silos and the OmniRAID system can deliver data very rapidly when requested by customers and transfer it to their choice of media for overnight delivery. Instead of taking weeks, Schlumberger's new storage system can deliver seismic data to customers overnight. Customers belonging to the ARIES network (a nationwide network linking the National Aeronautic and Space Administration (NASA), supercomputing centers, and various private firms) can have their data delivered over the network almost instantaneously.

San Francisco–based Fritz Companies, an import-export broker that handles customs clearance and other logistics for Wal-Mart, Federal Express, Sears, and other companies, was forced to change its hardware technology. Fritz used a Unisys A16 mainframe for its major business transaction processing related to customs clearance and also for its accounting system. Computer activity for its main business is very intense for only a few hours each day. The accounting department was able to run its programs on the mainframe during other less busy times.

The accounting system used commercial software supplied by an external vendor. The vendor announced that it would stop supporting its software running on mainframes in favor of software running on mid-range systems. Fritz's management wanted to keep using the vendor's accounting package, so it moved the accounting system to a Hewlett-Packard HP 9000 minicomputer. The rest of Fritz's business remained on the mainframe.

Performance of the HP 9000 system fell off drastically. Reports and

batch operations that used to take three or four hours on the mainframe were taking 20 or more hours on the mid-range system. The time required to output reports necessary to manage field offices rose from one to three days. Both managers and rank-and-file employees were screaming.

The bottleneck proved not to be in the computer's processing speed but in its input/output activities, even though the system used high-performance disk controllers and HP Fast/Wide SCSI 2-gigabyte disk drives. Fritz then acquired a Zitel CASD-II/Enterprise storage system, which offers high-capacity solid-state memory caching. Cache memory resides between the CPU and the array of disk drives. Data can be read into and out of the system at close to the speed of the CPU. Because the system no longer had to wait for an input/output event, processor utilization doubled. There was a 300 to 400 percent improvement in accounting operations. Performance returned to the level it was when the system ran on the mainframe. The time required to run the company's month-end fixed asset closing shrank from 3 hours to 45 minutes. A batch update program that used to take 13 hours can now run in 3 to 4 hours. ∎

Source: Nick Wreden, "Putting Data in Its Place," *Beyond Computing*, April 1997.

Case Study Questions

1. What problems did Schlumberger Geco Prakla and Fritz Companies experience? What management, organization, and technology factors were responsible for these problems?

2. How are the capabilities of an information system affected by its input, output, and storage devices?

3. How were Fritz's and Schlumberger's business processes affected by their choice of data storage systems?

4. What management, organization, and technology issues should be considered when selecting a data storage system?

REFERENCES

Bell, Gordon. "The Future of High Performance Computers in Science and Engineering." *Communications of the ACM* 32, no. 9 (September 1989).

———. "Ultracomputers: A Teraflop Before Its Time." *Communications of the ACM* 35, no. 8 (August 1992).

Burgess, Brad, Nasr Ullah, Peter Van Overen, and Deene Ogden. "The PowerPC 603 Microprocessor." *Communications of the ACM* 37, no. 6 (June 1994).

Camp, W. J., S. J. Plimpton, B. A. Hendrickson, and R. W. Leland. "Massively Parallel Methods for Engineering and Science Problems." *Communications of the ACM* 37, no. 4 (April 1994).

De Pompa, Barbara. "Multimedia Isn't the Message." *Information Week* (July 19, 1993).

Demasco, Patrick W., and Kathleen F. McCoy. "Generating Text from Compressed Input: An Intelligent Interface for People with Severe Motor Impairments." *Communications of the ACM* 35, no. 5 (May 1992).

Emmett, Arielle. "Simulations on Trial." *Technology Review* (May–June 1994).

Fitzmaurice, George W. "Situated Information Spaces and Spatially Aware Palmtop Computers." *Communications of the ACM* 36, no. 7 (July 1993).

Halfhill, Tom R. "Cheaper Computing." *Byte* (April 1997).

Hardaway, Don, and Richard P. Will. "Digital Multimedia Offers Key to Educational Reform." *Communications of the ACM* 40, no. 4 (April 1997).

Kay, Emily. "Hello Mr. Chips! Multimedia in the Classroom." *Technology Training* (June 1997).

Lambert, Craig. "The Electronic Tutor." *Harvard Magazine* (November–December 1990).

Lieberman, Henry. "Intelligent Graphics." *Communications of the ACM* 39, no. 8 (August 1996).

Lohr, Steve. "The Network Computer as the PC's Evil Twin," *The New York Times* (November 4, 1996).

Markott, John. "Innovation to Double Chip Power May Cut Life Span of Computers." *The New York Times* (September 17, 1997).

Nelson, Neal. "The Reality of RISC." *Computerworld* (March 22, 1993).

Peleg, Alex, Sam Wilkie and Uri Weiser. "Intel MMX for Multimedia PCs." *Communications of the ACM* 40, no. 1 (January 1997).

Press, Larry. "Compuvision or Teleputer?" *Communications of the ACM* 33, no. 3 (September 1990).

———. "Personal Computing: Dynabook Revisited—Portable Computers Past, Present, and Future." *Communications of the ACM* 35, no. 3 (March 1992).

Selker, Ted. "New Paradigms for Using Computers." *Communications of the ACM* 39, no. 8 (August 1996).

Smarr, Larry, and Charles E. Catlett, "Metacomputing." *Communications of the ACM* 35, no. 6 (June 1992).

Thomborson, Clark D. "Does Your Workstation Computation Belong to a Vector Supercomputer?" *Communications of the ACM* 36, no. 11 (November 1993).

Thompson, Tom. "The Macintosh at 10." *Byte* (February 1994).

Vaughan-Nichols, Steven J. "To NC or Not to NC?" *NetWorker* 1, no. 1 (March/April 1997).

Weiser, Mark. "Some Computer Science Issues in Ubiquitous Computing." *Communications of the ACM* 36, no. 7 (July 1993).

Williamson, Miday. "High-Tech Training." *Byte* (December 1994).

Wood, Elizabeth. "Multimedia Comes Down to Earth." *Computerworld* (August 1, 1994).

CHAPTER 7

Information Systems Software

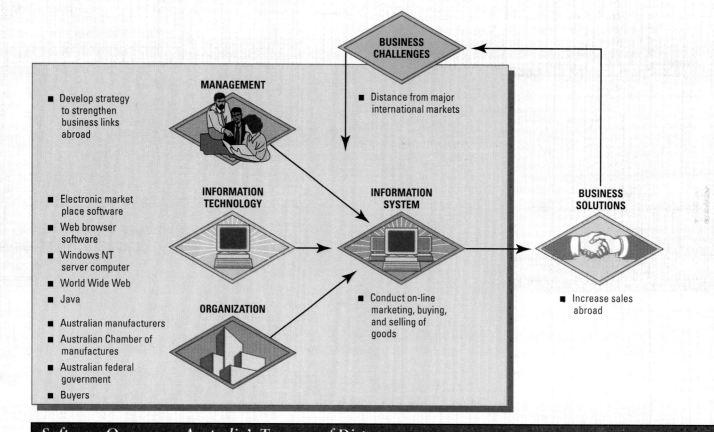

Software Overcomes Australia's Tyranny of Distance

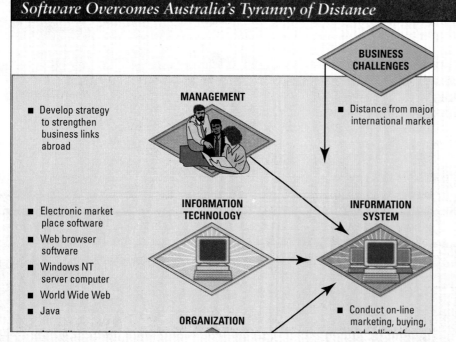

Australian manufacturers are used to talking about the "tyranny of distance," their country's geographical isolation from the world's largest trade centers. Companies from "down under" typically require two years to break into international markets, a long time for small or medium-sized businesses without income. That time is usually spent conducting preliminary market research, establishing supply chains, and developing and growing their market.

Now, Australia's government and business leaders are hoping to use software and the Internet to shrink those distances from the rest of the world. The Australian federal

LEARNING OBJECTIVES

After completing
this chapter, you will
be able to:

1. Describe the major types of software.
2. Describe the functions of system software and compare leading PC operating systems.
3. Explain how software has evolved and how it will continue to develop.
4. Compare strengths and limitations of the major application programming languages and software tools.
5. Describe new approaches to software development.

government has launched an "Innovate Australia" initiative to strengthen Australian businesses' links to other countries. It funded a project to band together manufacturers to conduct trade over the Internet. The project created a "live" trading floor on which on-line marketing, bidding, buying, and selling of goods and services can take place on the Internet using Java-capable Web browser software. Trade'ex, a Tampa, Florida, vendor of electronic marketplace software, developed the system in cooperation with the Australian Chamber of Manufactures (ACM), the nation's largest multi-industry employer organization for manufacturers.

Here's how the system works: Trade'ex Marketplace Server software runs on a Windows NT server computer at ACM headquarters, storing information about the manufacturers' products such as product descriptions, pricing, and inventory figures. This computer also runs software that allows buyers to shop and place orders and for sellers to fulfill those orders. Registered purchasers can purchase products directly on-line using a secure purchasing "swipe" debit card to which they have been assigned. Manufacturers can even use the Market Administrator system to customize their product information over the Internet. They can set up special pro-

motions or multitiered pricing arrangements by company or region.

About 1500 Australian manufacturers from various industries, including information technology, telecommunications, printing, office equipment, and stationery, have participated. The government has invested about $462,000 in the project, while the time and resources invested by the ACM and its partners have been about double that amount. The ACM plans to collect a small percentage of each sales transaction. It predicts that by 2001, half of all purchasing transactions in the manufacturing sector will be made on-line and it expects to capture a significant amount of this business.

The system was initially launched in a pilot version which was limited to domestic trading activities, but is being widened for international trade. Pilot participants have been enthusiastic, noting that other systems could not provide information to distribution channels fast enough. The system also required much less effort and expense than having each manufacturer set up its own Web site. The ACM is now rebuilding the system with Sun Microsystems Java technology to enable larger manufacturers to link the system with their existing systems to facilitate invoicing, payment, and account collection. ∎

Source: Louisa Bryan, "Reaching Out from Down Under," *Computerworld Global Innovators*, March 10, 1997.

MANAGEMENT CHALLENGES

To use the Internet and the World Wide Web for electronic commerce, Australian manufacturers had to develop special software. They had to know the capabilities of various types of software, including Web browsers and Java, and they had to select software that could provide a foundation for buying and selling on the Internet. Selecting and developing the right software can improve organizational performance, but it raises the following management challenges:

1. **Increasing complexity and software errors.** Although some software for desktop systems and for some Internet applications can be rapidly generated, a great deal of what software will be asked to do remains far-reaching and sophisticated, requiring programs that are large and complex. Citibank's automatic teller machine application required 780,000 lines of program code, written by hundreds of people, each working on small portions of the program. Large and complex systems tend to be error-prone, with software errors or "bugs" that may not be revealed for years until exhaustive testing and actual use. AT&T, for instance, found 300 errors for every 1000 lines of code in its large programs. Researchers do not know if the number of bugs grows exponentially or proportionately to the number of lines of code, nor can they tell for certain whether all segments of a complex piece of software will always work in total harmony. The process of designing and testing software that is reliable and "bug-free" is a serious quality control and management problem (see Chapter 13).

2. **The application backlog.** Advances in computer software have not kept pace with the breathtaking productivity gains in computer hardware. Developing software has become a major preoccupation for organizations. A great deal of software must be intricately crafted. Moreover, the software itself is only one component of a complete information system that must be carefully designed and coordinated with other people, as well as with organizational and hardware components. Managerial, procedural, and policy issues must be carefully researched and evaluated apart from the actual coding. The "software crisis" is actually part of a larger systems analysis, design, and implementation issue, which will be treated in detail in Part III. Despite the gains from fourth-generation languages, personal desktop software tools, object-oriented programming, and software tools for the World Wide Web, many businesses continue to face a backlog of two to three years in developing the information systems they need, or they will not be able to develop them at all.

The usefulness of computer hardware depends a great deal on available software and the ability of management to evaluate, monitor, and control the utilization of software in the organization. This chapter shows how software turns computer hardware into useful information systems, describes the major types of software, provides criteria for selecting software, and presents new approaches to software development.

7.1 WHAT IS SOFTWARE?

Software is the detailed instructions that control the operation of a computer system. Without software, computer hardware could not perform the tasks we associate with computers. The functions of software are to (1) manage the computer resources of the organization; (2) provide tools for human beings to take advantage of these resources; and (3) act as an intermediary between organizations and stored information. Selecting appropriate software for the organization is a key management decision.

software The detailed instructions that control the operation of a computer system.

Software Programs

A software **program** is a series of statements or instructions to the computer. The process of writing or coding programs is termed *programming,* and individuals who specialize in this task are called programmers.

The **stored program concept** means that a program must be stored in the computer's primary storage along with the required data in order to execute, or have its instructions performed by the computer. Once a program has finished executing, the computer hardware can be used for another task when a new program is loaded into memory.

program A series of statements or instructions to the computer.

stored program concept The idea that a program cannot be executed unless it is stored in a computer's primary storage along with required data.

Major Types of Software

There are two major types of software: system software and application software. Each kind performs a different function. **System software** is a set of generalized programs that manage the resources of the computer, such as the central processor, communications links, and peripheral devices. Programmers who write system software are called *system programmers.*

Application software describes the programs that are written for or by users to apply the computer to a specific task. Software for processing an order or generating a mailing list is application software. Programmers who write application software are called *application programmers.*

The types of software are interrelated and can be thought of as a set of nested boxes, each of which must interact closely with the other boxes surrounding it. Figure 7.1 illustrates this relationship. The system software surrounds and controls access to the hardware. Application software must work through the system software in order to operate. End users work primarily with application software. Each type of software must be specially designed to a specific machine to ensure its compatibility.

system software Generalized programs that manage the resources of the computer, such as the central processor, communications links, and peripheral devices.

application software Programs written for a specific application to perform functions specified by end users.

7.2 SYSTEM SOFTWARE

System software coordinates the various parts of the computer system and mediates between application software and computer hardware. The system software that manages and controls the activities of the computer is called the **operating system.** Other system software consists of computer language translation programs that convert programming languages into machine language and utility programs that perform common processing tasks.

operating system The system software that manages and controls the activities of the computer.

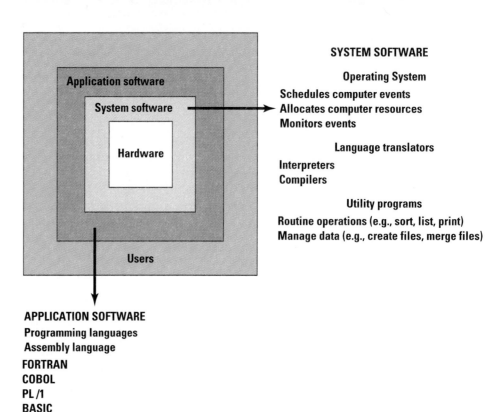

FIGURE 7.1

The major types of software. The relationship between the system software, application software, and users can be illustrated by a series of nested boxes. System software—consisting of operating systems, language translators, and utility programs—controls access to the hardware. Application software, such as the programming languages and "fourth-generation" languages, must work through the system software to operate. The user interacts primarily with the application software.

Application software

System software

Hardware

Users

SYSTEM SOFTWARE

Operating System
Schedules computer events
Allocates computer resources
Monitors events

Language translators
Interpreters
Compilers

Utility programs
Routine operations (e.g., sort, list, print)
Manage data (e.g., create files, merge files)

APPLICATION SOFTWARE
Programming languages
Assembly language
FORTRAN
COBOL
PL /1
BASIC
PASCAL
C
"Fourth-generation" languages

Functions of the Operating System

One way to look at the operating system is as the system's chief manager. Operating system software decides which computer resources will be used, which programs will be run, and the order in which activities will take place.

An operating system performs three functions. It allocates and assigns system resources; it schedules the use of computer resources and computer jobs; and it monitors computer system activities.

Allocation and Assignment

The operating system allocates resources to the application jobs in the execution queue. It provides locations in primary memory for data and programs and controls the input and output devices such as printers, terminals, and telecommunication links.

Scheduling

Thousands of pieces of work can be going on in a computer simultaneously. The operating system decides when to schedule the jobs that have been submitted and when to coordinate the scheduling in various areas of the computer so that different parts of different jobs can be worked on at the same time. For instance, while a program is executing, the operating system is scheduling the use of input and output devices. Not all jobs are performed in the order they are submitted; the operating system must schedule these jobs according to organizational priorities. On-line order processing may have priority over a job to generate mailing lists and labels.

Monitoring

The operating system monitors the activities of the computer system. It keeps track of each computer job and may also keep track of who is using the system, of what

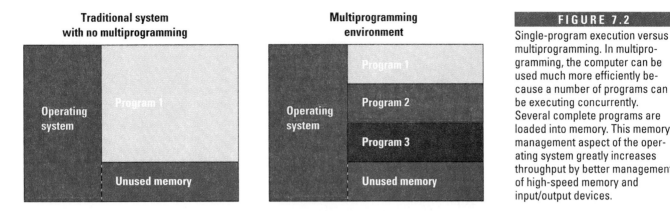

Traditional system with no multiprogramming

Operating system

Program 1

Unused memory

Multiprogramming environment

Operating system

Program 1

Program 2

Program 3

Unused memory

FIGURE 7.2

Single-program execution versus multiprogramming. In multiprogramming, the computer can be used much more efficiently because a number of programs can be executing concurrently. Several complete programs are loaded into memory. This memory management aspect of the operating system greatly increases throughput by better management of high-speed memory and input/output devices.

programs have been run, and of any unauthorized attempts to access the system. Information system security is discussed in detail in Chapter 17. Obviously, the operating system of a major mainframe computer is itself a very large program. For this reason, only parts of the operating system are actually stored in the primary storage area. Most of the operating system is stored in a copy on a disk, to which primary storage has very rapid access. When parts of the operating system are required by a given application, they are transferred from the disk and loaded into primary storage. The device on which a complete operating system is stored is called the **system residence device.**

system residence device The secondary storage device on which a complete operating system is stored.

Multiprogramming, Virtual Storage, Time Sharing, and Multiprocessing

How is it possible for 1000 or more users sitting at remote terminals to use a computer information system simultaneously if, as we stated in the previous chapter, most computers can execute only one instruction from one program at a time? How can computers run thousands of programs? The answer is that the computer has a series of specialized operating system capabilities.

Multiprogramming

The most important operating system capability for sharing computer resources is **multiprogramming.** Multiprogramming permits multiple programs to share a computer system's resources at any one time through concurrent use of a CPU. By concurrent use, we mean that only one program is actually using the CPU at any given moment but that the input/output needs of other programs can be serviced at the same time. Two or more programs are active at the same time, but they do not use the same computer resources simultaneously. With multiprogramming, a group of programs takes turns using the processor.

multiprogramming A method of executing two or more programs concurrently using the same computer. The CPU executes only one program but can service the input/output needs of others at the same time.

Figure 7.2 shows how three programs in a multiprogramming environment can be stored in primary storage. The first program executes until an input/output event is read in the program. The operating system then directs a channel (a small processor limited to input and output functions) to read the input and move the output to an output device. The CPU moves to the second program until an input/output statement occurs. At this point, the CPU switches to the execution of the third program, and so forth, until eventually all three programs have been executed. Notice that the interruptions in processing are caused by events that take place in the programs themselves. In this manner, many different programs can be executing at the same time, although different resources within the CPU are actually being utilized.

The first operating systems executed only one program at a time. Before multiprogramming, when a program read data off a tape or disk or wrote data to a printer, the entire CPU came to a stop. This was a very inefficient way to use the computer. With multiprogramming, the CPU utilization rate is much higher.

Multitasking

multitasking The multiprogramming capability of primarily single-user operating systems, such as those for PCs.

Multitasking refers to multiprogramming on single-user operating systems such as those in personal computers. One person can run two or more programs concurrently on a single computer. For example, a sales representative could write a letter to prospective clients with a word processing program while simultaneously using a database program to search for all sales contacts in a particular city or geographic area. Instead of terminating the session with the word processing program, returning to the operating system, and then initiating a session with the database program, multitasking allows the sales representative to display both programs on the computer screen and work with them at the same time.

Virtual Storage

virtual storage A way of handling programs more efficiently by the computer by dividing the programs into small fixed- or variable-length portions with only a small portion stored in primary memory at one time.

Virtual storage handles programs more efficiently because the computer divides the programs into small fixed- or variable-length portions, storing only a small portion of the program in primary memory at one time. If only two or three large programs can be read into memory, a certain part of main memory generally remains under-utilized because the programs add up to less than the total amount of primary storage space available. Given the limited size of primary memory, only a small number of programs can reside in primary storage at any given time.

page A small fixed-length section of a program, which can be easily stored in primary storage and quickly accessed from secondary storage.

Only a few statements of a program actually execute at any given moment. Virtual storage breaks a program into a number of fixed-length portions called **pages** or into variable-length portions called *segments*. Each of these portions is relatively small (a page is approximately 2 to 4 kilobytes). This permits a very large number of programs to reside in primary memory, inasmuch as only one page of each program is actually located there (see Figure 7.3).

All other program pages are stored on a peripheral disk unit until they are ready for execution. Virtual storage provides a number of advantages. First, the central processor is utilized more fully. Many more programs can be in primary storage because only one page of each program actually resides there. Second, programmers no longer have to worry about the size of the primary storage area. With virtual storage, programs can be of infinite length and small machines can execute a program of any size (admittedly, small machines will take longer than big machines to execute a large program).

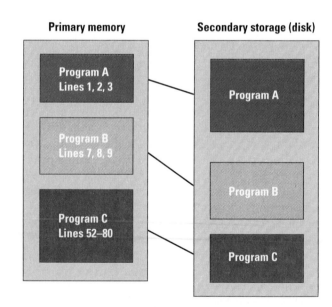

FIGURE 7.3

Virtual storage. Virtual storage is based on the fact that, in general, only a few statements in a program can actually be utilized at any given moment. In virtual storage, programs are broken down into small sections called pages. Individual program pages are read into memory only when needed. The rest of the program is stored on disk until it is required. In this way, very large programs can be executed by small machines, or a large number of programs can be executed concurrently by a single machine.

Primary memory

Program A
Lines 1, 2, 3

Program B
Lines 7, 8, 9

Program C
Lines 52–80

Secondary storage (disk)

Program A

Program B

Program C

Time Sharing

Time sharing is an operating system capability that allows many users to share computer processing resources simultaneously. It differs from multiprogramming in that the CPU spends a fixed amount of time on one program before moving on to another. In a time-sharing environment, thousands of users are each allocated a tiny slice of computer time (2 milliseconds). In this time slot, each user is free to perform any required operations; at the end of this period, another user is given a 2-millisecond time slice of the CPU. This arrangement permits many users to be connected to a CPU simultaneously, with each receiving only a tiny amount of CPU time. But because the CPU is operating at the nanosecond level, a CPU can accomplish a great deal of work in 2 milliseconds.

Multiprocessing

Multiprocessing is an operating system capability that links together two or more CPUs to work in parallel in a single computer system. The operating system can assign multiple CPUs to execute different instructions from the same program or from different programs simultaneously, dividing the work between the CPUs. While multiprogramming uses concurrent processing with one CPU, multiprocessing uses simultaneous processing with multiple CPUs.

Language Translation and Utility Software

When computers execute programs written in languages such as COBOL, FORTRAN, or C, the computer must convert these human-readable instructions into a form it can understand. System software includes special language translator programs that translate higher-level language programs written in programming languages such as BASIC, COBOL, and FORTRAN into machine language that the computer can execute. This type of system software is called a *compiler* or *interpreter*. The program in the high-level language before translation into machine language is called **source code**. A **compiler** translates source code into machine code called **object code**. Just before execution by the computer, the object code modules are joined with other object code modules in a process called *linkage editing*. The resulting load module is what is actually executed by the computer. Figure 7.4 illustrates the language translation process.

Some programming languages such as BASIC do not use a compiler but an **interpreter,** which translates each source code statement one at a time into machine code and executes it. Interpreter languages such as BASIC provide immediate feedback to the programmer if a mistake is made, but they are very slow to execute because they are translated one statement at a time.

An assembler is similar to a compiler, but it is used to translate only assembly language (see Section 7.3) into machine code.

System software includes **utility programs** for routine, repetitive tasks, such as copying, clearing primary storage, computing a square root, or sorting. If you have worked on a computer and have performed such functions as setting up new files, deleting old files, or formatting diskettes, you have worked with utility programs. Utility programs are prewritten programs that are stored so that they can be shared by all users of a computer system and can be rapidly used in many different information system applications when requested.

Graphical User Interfaces

When users interact with a computer, even a PC, the interaction is controlled by an operating system. The user interface is the part of an information system that users interact with. Users communicate with an operating system through the user interface of that operating system. Early PC operating systems were command-driven, but

time sharing The sharing of computer resources by many users simultaneously by having the CPU spend a fixed amount of time on each user's program before proceeding to the next.

multiprocessing An operating system feature for executing two or more instructions simultaneously in a single computer system by using multiple central processing units.

source code Program instructions written in a high-level language that must be translated into machine language to be executed by the computer.

compiler Special system software that translates a higher-level language into machine language for execution by the computer.

object code Program instructions that have been translated into machine language so that they can be executed by the computer.

interpreter A special translator of source code into machine code that translates each source code statement into machine code and executes them, one at a time.

utility program System software consisting of programs for routine, repetitive tasks, which can be shared by many users.

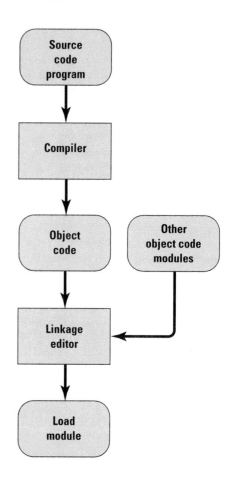

FIGURE 7.4

The language translation process. The source code, the program in a high-level language, is translated by the compiler into object code so that the instructions can be "understood" by the machine. These are grouped into modules. Prior to execution, the object code modules are joined together by the linkage editor to create the load module. It is the load module that is actually executed by the computer.

graphical user interface (GUI)
The part of an operating system that users interact with that uses graphic icons and the computer mouse to issue commands and make selections.

the **graphical user interface**, often called a **GUI**, makes extensive use of icons, buttons, bars, and boxes to perform the same task. It has become the dominant model for the user interface of PC operating systems.

Older PC operating systems such as DOS, described on the following page, are command-driven, requiring the user to type in text-based commands using a keyboard. For example, to perform a task such as deleting a file named DATAFILE, the user must type in a command such as *DELETE C:\DATAFILE*. Users need to remember these commands and their syntax to work with the computer effectively. An operating system with a graphical user interface uses graphical symbols called *icons* to depict programs, files, and activities. Commands can be activated by rolling a mouse to move a cursor about the screen and clicking a button on the mouse to make selections. Icons are symbolic pictures and they are also used in GUIs to represent programs and files. For example, a file could be deleted by moving the cursor to a Trash icon. Many graphical user interfaces use a system of pull-down menus to help users select commands and pop-up boxes to help users select among various command options. Windowing features allow users to create, stack, size, and move around various boxes of information.

Proponents of graphical user interfaces claim that they save learning time because computing novices do not have to learn different arcane commands for each application. Common functions such as getting help, saving files, or printing output are performed the same way. A complex series of commands can be issued simply by linking icons. Graphical user interfaces can promote superior screen and print output communicated through graphics. On the other hand, GUIs may not always simplify complex tasks if the user has to spend too much time first pointing to icons and then selecting operations to perform on those icons (Morse and Reynolds, 1993). Graphical symbols themselves are not always easy to understand unless the GUI is well designed. Existing GUIs are modeled after an office desktop, with files, docu-

Table 7.1   Leading PC Operating Systems

Operating System	Features
DOS	Operating system for IBM (PC-DOS) and IBM-compatible (MS-DOS) PCs. Limits program use of memory to 640 K.
Windows 95 and Windows 98	32-bit operating system with a streamlined graphical user interface. Has multitasking and powerful networking capabilities and can be integrated with the information resources of the Web.
Windows NT	32-bit operating system for PCs, workstations, and network servers not limited to Intel microprocessors. Supports multitasking, multiprocessing, intensive networking.
OS/2 (Operating System/2)	Operating system for the IBM PCs. Can take advantage of the 32-bit microprocessor. Supports multitasking and networking.
UNIX	Used for powerful PCs, workstations, and minicomputers. Supports multitasking, multi-user processing, and networking. Is portable to different models of computer hardware.
Mac OS	Operating system for the Macintosh computer. Supports networking and multitasking and has powerful multimedia capabilities. Supports connecting to and publishing on the Internet.

ments, and actions based on typical office behavior, making them less useful for nonoffice applications in control rooms or processing plants (Mandelkern, 1993).

PC Operating Systems

Like any other software, personal computer software is based on specific operating systems and computer hardware. A software package written for one PC operating system generally cannot run on another. The PC operating systems themselves have distinctive features—such as whether they support multitasking or graphics work—that determine the types of applications for which they are suited.

Multitasking is one of the principal strengths of operating systems such as Microsoft's Windows 95 (and Windows 98), IBM's OS/2 (Operating System/2), or UNIX. PC-DOS and MS-DOS, the older operating system for IBM personal computers and IBM-PC clones, do not allow multitasking, although the Microsoft Corporation markets Windows software to create a multitasking environment for DOS programs.

Table 7.1 compares the leading PC operating systems—Windows 95 (and Windows 98), Windows NT, OS/2, UNIX, the Macintosh operating system, and DOS. **DOS** was the most popular operating system for 16-bit PCs. It is still used today with older PCs based on the IBM PC standard because so much available application software has been written for systems using DOS. (PC-DOS is used exclusively with IBM PCs. MS-DOS, developed by Microsoft, is used with other 16-bit PCs that function like the IBM PC.) DOS itself does not support multitasking and limits the size of a program in memory to 640 K.

DOS is command-driven, but it can present a graphical user interface by using Microsoft **Windows,** a highly popular graphical user interface shell that runs in conjunction with the DOS operating system. Windows supports multitasking and some forms of networking but shares the memory limitations of DOS. It is not considered to run very efficiently in a multitasking environment. Early versions of Windows had some problems with application crashing when multiple programs competed for the same memory space.

DOS Operating system for 16-bit PCs based on the IBM personal computer standard.

Windows A graphical user interface shell that runs in conjunction with the DOS PC operating system. Supports multitasking and some forms of networking.

Windows 95 A 32-bit operating system, with a streamlined graphical user interface, that features multitasking, multi-threading, and powerful networking capabilities.

Microsoft's **Windows 95** is a 32-bit operating system designed to remedy many of the deficiencies of Windows sitting atop DOS. A 32-bit operating system can run faster than DOS (which could only address data in 16-bit chunks) because it can address data in 32-bit chunks. Windows 95 provides a streamlined graphical user interface that arranges icons to provide instant access to common tasks. It can support software written for DOS and Windows but it can also run programs that take up more than 640 K of memory. Windows 95 features multitasking, multithreading (the ability to manage multiple independent tasks simultaneously), and powerful networking capabilities, including the capability to integrate fax, e-mail, and scheduling programs.

Windows 98 New version of the Windows operating system that is more closely integrated with the Internet.

The **Windows 98** version of the Windows operating system will be integrated with the multimedia technology of the World Wide Web. Microsoft's Internet Explorer Web browser software (see Section 7.3) will become an integral part of the operating system, making the information resources of World Wide Web more accessible to computer users. Users will be able to work with the traditional Windows interface or a new browserlike interface that displays information in the form of a multimedia Web page. Each piece of material created on a personal computer will be more easily embellished with images, audio, and video and more easily distributed on the Web.

Windows NT Powerful operating system developed by Microsoft for use with 32-bit PCs and workstations based on Intel and other microprocessors. Supports networking, multitasking, and multiprocessing.

Windows NT is another operating system developed by Microsoft with features that make it appropriate for critical applications in large networked organizations. It is used as an operating system for high-performance workstations and network servers. Windows NT uses the same graphical user interface as Windows, but it has powerful networking, multitasking, and memory management capabilities. Windows NT can support existing software written for DOS and Windows, and it can provide mainframe-like computing power for new applications with massive memory and file requirements. It can address data in 32-bit chunks if required and can even support multiprocessing with multiple CPUs. Unlike OS/2, Windows NT is not tied to computer hardware based on Intel microprocessors. A company might choose Windows NT if it values flexibility and wants to use an operating system that can run different types of applications on a variety of computer hardware platforms using a common interface that is familiar to users.

Microsoft's Windows 95 is a powerful operating system with networking capabilities and a streamlined graphical user interface.

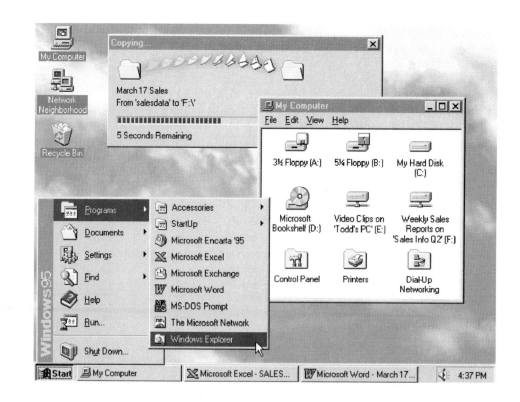

OS/2 is a robust operating system that is used with 32-bit IBM PCs or IBM-compatible PCs with Intel microprocessors. OS/2 is being used for more complex memory-intensive applications or those that require networking, multitasking, or large programs. OS/2 supports multitasking, accommodates larger applications, allows applications to be run simultaneously, supports networked multimedia and pen computing applications, and is a much more protected operating system. One application that crashes is less likely to bring the whole operating system and other applications down with it. OS/2 provides powerful desktop computers with mainframe operating system capabilities, such as multitasking and supporting multiple users in networks. Credit Industriel et Commercial de Paris, a major French bank, adopted OS/2 for its networked branch office systems because its stability and support for multitasking made it suitable for serious financial applications (Greenbaum, 1994).

OS/2 has its own graphical user interface, which provides users with a consistent graphical user interface across applications. OS/2 supports DOS applications and can run Windows and DOS applications at the same time in its own resizable windows. The latest version of OS/2 is called OS/2 Warp. OS/2 Warp now provides support for the Internet, Java (see Section 7.4), and network computing.

UNIX was developed at Bell Laboratories in 1969 to help scientific researchers share data and programs while keeping other information private. It is an interactive, multi-user, multitasking operating system. Many people can use UNIX simultaneously to perform the same kind of task, or one user can run many tasks on UNIX concurrently. UNIX was developed to connect various machines together and is highly supportive of communications and networking.

UNIX was initially designed for minicomputers but now has versions for PCs, workstations, and mainframes. UNIX can run on many different kinds of computers and can be easily customized. It can also store and manage a large number of files. At present, UNIX is primarily used for workstations, minicomputers, and inexpensive multi-user environments in small businesses, but its use in large businesses is growing because of its machine independence. Application programs that run under UNIX can be ported from one computer to run on a different computer with little modification.

UNIX is accused of being unfriendly to users. It is powerful but very complex. It has a legion of commands, some of which are very cryptic and terse. A typing error on a command line can easily destroy important files. UNIX cannot respond well to problems caused by the overuse of system resources such as jobs or disk space. UNIX also poses some security problems, because multiple jobs and users can access the same file simultaneously. Finally, UNIX requires huge amounts of random access memory and disk capacity, limiting its usefulness for less powerful microcomputers.

Mac OS 8, the latest version of Macintosh system software, features multitasking as well as powerful multimedia and networking capabilities and a mouse-driven graphical user interface (illustrated in Figure 7.5). Users can integrate video clips, stereo sound, and animated sequences with conventional text and graphics software. (Recall the discussion of multimedia in Chapter 6.) New features of this operating system allow users to connect to, explore, and publish on the Internet and World Wide Web.

Selecting a PC Operating System

How should a firm go about choosing the operating system for its PC-based applications? Should the decision be made only on the basis of technical merits? Should companies look at other issues such as ease of use, training, and cost of hardware and software that use the operating system? This brief survey suggests that there are many factors to consider.

If a firm wants an operating system for its mainstream business applications, it needs an operating system that is compatible with the software required by these applications. The operating system should be easy to use and install. The user interface

OS/2 Powerful operating system used with 32-bit IBM/PCs or workstations that supports multitasking, networking, and more memory-intensive applications than DOS.

UNIX Operating system for PCs, minicomputers, and mainframes, which is machine independent and supports multi-user processing, multitasking, and networking.

Mac OS 8 Operating system for the Macintosh computer that supports multitasking, has access to the Internet, and has powerful graphics and multimedia capabilities.

FIGURE 7.5

Mac OS 8, the newest version of the Macintosh operating system, provides powerful support for networking, multitasking, multimedia, and access to the Internet.

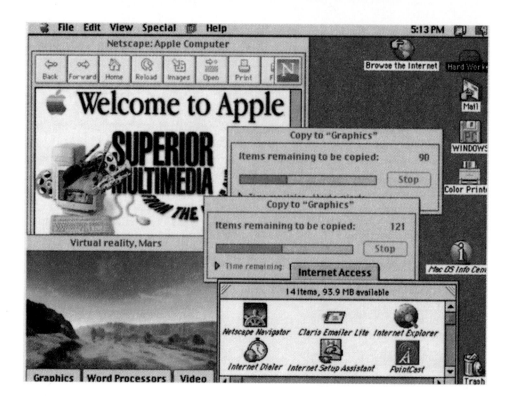

features of the operating system should be easy to learn. Mission-critical applications have special operating system requirements, because businesses depend on them for their continuing operation and survival. For such applications an operating system that provides reliable support for multitasking and memory management is essential. The operating system should be able to run multiple applications quickly without having the system crash because applications are contending for the same memory space. Mission-critical applications typically have large volumes of transactions to process and require operating systems that can handle large complex software programs and massive files.

7.3   APPLICATION SOFTWARE

Application software is primarily concerned with accomplishing the tasks of end users. Many different languages can be used to develop application software. Each has different strengths and drawbacks.

Generations of Programming Languages

machine language   A programming language consisting of the 1s and 0s of binary code.

To communicate with the first generation of computers, programmers had to write programs in **machine language**—the 0s and 1s of binary code. End users who wanted applications had to work with specialized programmers who could understand, think, and work directly in the machine language of a particular computer. Programming in 0s and 1s (reducing all statements such as add, subtract, and divide into a series of 0s and 1s) made early programming a slow, labor-intensive process.

As computer hardware improved and processing speed and memory size increased, computer languages changed from machine language to languages that were easier for humans to understand. Generations of programming languages developed to correspond with the generations of computer hardware. Figure 7.6 shows the development of programming languages over the last 50 years as the capabilities of hardware have increased. The major trend is to increase the ease with which users can interact with the hardware and software.

A. Generations

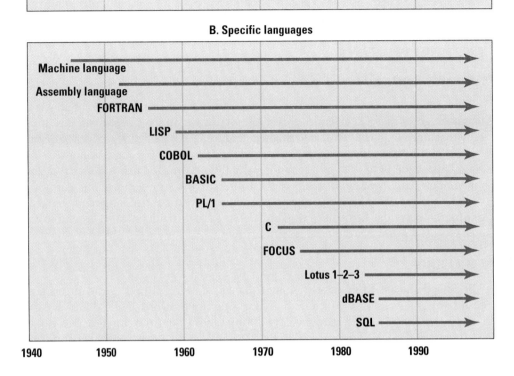

FIGURE 7.6

Generations of programming languages. As the capabilities of hardware increased, programming languages developed from the first generation of machine and second generation of assembly languages of the 1950s to 1960, through the third-generation high-level languages such as FORTRAN and COBOL developed in the 1960s and 1970s, to today's fourth-generation languages and tools.

Machine language was the first-generation programming language. The second generation of programming languages occurred in the early 1950s with the development of assembly language. Instead of using 0s and 1s, programmers could now substitute languagelike acronyms and words such as *add*, *sub* (subtract), and *load* in programming statements. A language translator called a *compiler* converted the Englishlike statements into machine language.

When the third hardware generation was underway, programming languages entered their third generation as well. From the mid-1950s to the 1970s, the first higher-level languages emerged. These languages permitted mathematicians for the first time to work with computers through the use of languages such as FORTRAN (FORmula TRANslator program). Mathematicians were now able to define variables with statements such as $Z = A + B$. The software translated these definitions and mathematical statements into a series of 0s and 1s. COBOL (COmmon Business Oriented Language) permitted the use of English statements such as *print* and *sort* to be used by programmers, who did not have to think in terms of 0s and 1s.

These **high-level languages** are so called because each statement in FORTRAN or COBOL generates multiple statements at the machine-language level. The use of these higher-level languages requires much faster, more efficient compilers to translate higher-level languages into machine codes.

Fourth-generation computer languages emerged in the late 1970s, and their development is still in progress. These languages dramatically reduce programming time and make software tasks so easy that nontechnical computer users can develop applications without the help of professional programmers. Fourth-generation tools also include prewritten application software packages that can be used directly by

high-level language Programming languages in which each source code statement generates multiple statements at the machine-language level.

end users. Using the software package Lotus 1-2-3, for instance, users can create their own financial spreadsheets and manipulate data without programmer intervention. Such sophistication by nonspecialists using FORTRAN would have been impossible in the 1960s and 1970s.

Popular Programming Languages

Most managers need not be expert programmers, but they should understand how to evaluate software applications and to select programming languages that are appropriate for their organization's objectives. We will now briefly describe the more popular high-level languages.

Assembly Language

assembly language A programming language developed in the 1950s that resembles machine language but substitutes mnemonics for numeric codes.

Many programmers still prefer to write programs in assembly language because this language gives them close control over the hardware and very efficient execution. Like machine language, **assembly language** (Figure 7.7) is designed for a specific machine and specific microprocessors. Each operation in assembly corresponds to a machine operation. On the other hand, assembly language makes use of certain mnemonics (e.g., *load, sum*) and assigns addresses and storage locations automatically. While assembly language gives programmers great control, it is costly in terms of programmer time, difficult to read and debug, and difficult to learn. Assembly language is used primarily today in system software.

FORTRAN

FORTRAN (FORmula TRANslator)
A programming language developed in 1956 for scientific and mathematical applications.

FORTRAN (FORmula TRANslator) (Figure 7.8) was developed in 1956 to provide an easier way of writing scientific and engineering applications. FORTRAN is especially useful in processing numeric data. Many kinds of business applications can be written in FORTRAN, it is relatively easy to learn, and contemporary versions provide sophisticated structures for controlling program logic. FORTRAN is not very good at providing input/output efficiency or in printing and working with lists. The syntax is very strict and keying errors are common, making the programs difficult to debug.

COBOL

COBOL (COmmon Business Oriented Language) The predominant programming language for business applications because it can process large data files with alphanumeric characters.

COBOL (COmmon Business Oriented Language) (Figure 7.9) came into use in the early 1960s. It was originally developed by a committee representing both government and industry because the Defense Department wished to create a common administrative language for internal and external software. Rear Admiral Grace M. Hopper was a key committee member who played a major role in COBOL development. COBOL was designed with business administration in mind, for processing large data files with alphanumeric characters (mixed alphabetic and numeric data), and for performing repetitive tasks such as payroll. Its primary data structures are records, files, tables, and lists. The weakness of COBOL is a result of its virtue. It is poor at complex mathematical calculations. Also, there are many versions of COBOL, and not all are compatible with each other.

BASIC

BASIC (Beginners All-purpose Symbolic Instruction Code) A general-purpose programming language used with PCs and for teaching programming.

BASIC (Beginners All-purpose Symbolic Instruction Code) was developed in 1964 by John Kemeny and Thomas Kurtz to teach students at Dartmouth College how to use computers. Today it is a popular programming language on college campuses and for PCs. BASIC can do almost all computer processing tasks from inventory to mathematical calculations. It is easy to use, demonstrates computer capabilities well, and requires only a small interpreter. The weakness of BASIC is that it does few tasks well even though it does them all. It has no sophisticated program logic control or data

```
AR 5, 3
```

FIGURE 7.7

Assembly language. This sample assembly language command adds the contents of register 3 to register 5 and stores the result in register 5.

```
READ (5,100) ID, QUANT, PRICE
TOTAL = QUANT * PRICE
```

FIGURE 7.8

FORTRAN. This sample FORTRAN program code is part of a program to compute sales figures for a particular item.

```
MULTIPLY QUANT-SOLD BY UNIT-PRICE GIVING SALES-TOTAL.
```

FIGURE 7.9

COBOL. This sample COBOL program code is part of a routine to compute total sales figures for a particular item.

structures, which makes it difficult to use in teaching good programming practices. Different versions of BASIC programs often cannot be moved from one machine to another.

PL/1

PL/1 (Programming Language 1) was developed by IBM in 1964. It is the most powerful general-purpose programming language because it can handle mathematical and business applications with ease, is highly efficient in input/output activities, and can handle large volumes of data.

Unfortunately, the huge volume of COBOL and FORTRAN programs written in the private sector at great cost cannot simply be jettisoned when a newer, more powerful language comes along. PL/1 has not succeeded largely because programmers trained in COBOL could not be convinced to learn an entirely new language, and business organizations could not be convinced to spend millions of dollars rewriting their software. PL/1 is, moreover, somewhat difficult to learn in its entirety.

PL/1 (Programming Language 1) A programming language developed by IBM in 1964 for business and scientific applications.

Pascal

Named after Blaise Pascal, the seventeenth-century mathematician and philosopher, **Pascal** was developed by the Swiss computer science professor Niklaus Wirth of Zurich in the late 1960s. Pascal programs can be compiled using minimal computer memory, so they can be used on PCs. With sophisticated structures to control program logic and a simple, powerful set of commands, Pascal is used primarily in computer science courses to teach sound programming practices. The language is weak at file handling and input/output and is not easy for beginners to use.

Pascal A programming language used on PCs and to teach sound programming practices in computer science courses.

Ada

Ada was developed in 1980 to provide the United States Defense Department with a structured programming language to serve as the standard for all its applications. Ada was named after Ada, Countess of Lovelace, a nineteenth-century mathematician whose father was the English poet Lord Byron. The Countess is sometimes called the first programmer because she developed the mathematical tables for an

Ada A programming language that is portable across different brands of hardware; is used for both military and nonmilitary applications.

early calculating machine. This language was initially conceived for weapons systems, where software is developed on a processor and then imbedded into the weapon. It was explicitly designed so that it could be uniformly executed in diverse hardware environments. The language also promotes structured software design. U.S. government experts hope Ada will produce more cost-effective software because it facilitates more clearly structured code than COBOL.

Ada is used in nonmilitary government applications as well. The language can also be used for general business applications because it can operate on microcomputers and is portable across different brands of computer hardware.

C

C A powerful programming language with tight control and efficiency of execution; is portable across different microprocessors and is used primarily with PCs.

C was developed at AT&T's Bell Labs in the early 1970s and is the language in which much of the UNIX operating system is written. C combines some of the tight control and efficiency of execution features of assembly language with machine portability. In other words, it can work on a variety of computers rather than on just one. Much commercial PC software has been written in C, but C is gaining support for some minicomputer and mainframe applications. C is unlikely to dislodge COBOL for mainframe business applications, but it will be used increasingly for commercial PC software and for scientific and technical applications.

LISP and Prolog

LISP (designating LISt Processor) and Prolog are widely used in artificial intelligence. LISP was created in the late 1950s by M.I.T. mathematician John McCarthy and is oriented toward putting symbols such as operations, variables, and data values into meaningful lists. LISP is better at manipulating symbols than at ordinary number crunching.

Prolog, introduced around 1970, is also well suited to symbol manipulation and can run on general-purpose computers, whereas LISP usually runs best on machines configured especially to run LISP programs.

Fourth-Generation Languages

fourth-generation language A programming language that can be employed directly by end users or less skilled programmers to develop computer applications more rapidly than conventional programming languages.

Fourth-generation languages consist of a variety of software tools that enable end users to develop software applications with minimal or no technical assistance or that enhance the productivity of professional programmers. Fourth-generation languages tend to be nonprocedural or less procedural than conventional programming languages. Procedural languages require specification of the sequence of steps, or procedures, that tell the computer what to do and how to do it. Nonprocedural languages need only specify what has to be accomplished rather than provide details about how to carry out the task. Thus, a nonprocedural language can accomplish the same task with fewer steps and lines of program code than a procedural language.

There are seven categories of fourth-generation languages: query languages, report generators, graphics languages, application generators, very high-level programming languages, application software packages, and PC tools. Figure 7.10 illustrates the spectrum of these tools and some commercially available products in each category.

Query Languages

query language A high-level computer language used to retrieve specific information from databases or files.

Query languages are high-level languages for retrieving data stored in databases or files. They are usually interactive, on-line, and capable of supporting requests for information that are not predefined. They are often tied to database management systems (see Chapter 8) and PC tools (see the following discussion). Query languages can search a database or file, using simple or complex selection criteria to display information relating to multiple records. Available query language tools have different

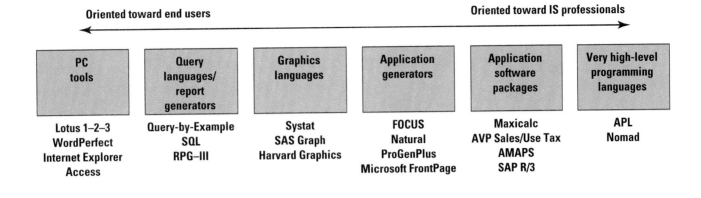

Oriented toward end users ← → **Oriented toward IS professionals**

PC tools	Query languages/ report generators	Graphics languages	Application generators	Application software packages	Very high-level programming languages
Lotus 1–2–3 WordPerfect Internet Explorer Access	Query-by-Example SQL RPG–III	Systat SAS Graph Harvard Graphics	FOCUS Natural ProGenPlus Microsoft FrontPage	Maxicalc AVP Sales/Use Tax AMAPS SAP R/3	APL Nomad

FIGURE 7.10

Fourth-generation languages. The spectrum of major categories of fourth-generation languages and commercially available products in each category is illustrated. Tools range from those that are simple and designated primarily for end users to complex tools designed for information systems professionals.

kinds of syntax and structure, some being closer to natural language than others (Vassiliou, 1984–1985). Some support updating of data as well as retrieval. An example of a typical ad hoc query is, "List all employees in the payroll department." Figure 7.11 illustrates how two different query languages, Query-by-Example and FOCUS, express this request.

Report Generators

Report generators are facilities for creating customized reports. They extract data from files or databases and create reports in many formats. Report generators generally provide more control over the way data are formatted, organized, and displayed than query languages. The more powerful report generators can manipulate data with complex calculations and logic before they are output. Some report generators are extensions of database or query languages. The more complex and powerful report generators may not be suitable for end users without some assistance from professional information systems specialists.

report generator Software that creates customized reports in a wide range of formats that are not routinely produced by an information system.

Graphics Languages

Graphics languages retrieve data from files or databases and display them in graphic format. Users can ask for data and specify how they are to be charted. Some graph-

graphics language A computer language that displays data from files or databases in graphic format.

Query: "List all employees in the Payroll department."

Using Query-by-Example:

EMPLOYEE	EMPLOYEE #	NAME	DEPARTMENT
		P.	PAYROLL

Using FOCUS:

```
>> TABLE FILE EMPDEPT
>PRINT EMP_NAME IF DEPT EQ 'PAYROLL'
>END
```

FIGURE 7.11

Query languages. This figure illustrates how the simple query, "List all employees in the Payroll department," would be handled by the two different query languages: Query-by-Example and FOCUS.

ics software can perform arithmetic or logical operations on data as well. SAS, Harvard Graphics, and Lotus Freelance Graphics are popular graphics tools.

Application Generators

application generator   Software that can generate entire information system applications; the user needs only to specify what needs to be done, and the application generator creates the appropriate program code.

Application generators contain preprogrammed modules that can generate entire applications, greatly speeding development. A user can specify what needs to be done, and the application generator will create the appropriate code for input, validation, update, processing, and reporting. Most full-function application generators consist of a comprehensive, integrated set of development tools: a database management system, data dictionary, query language, screen painter, graphics generator, report generator, decision support/modeling tools, security facilities, and a high-level programming language. Application generators now include tools for developing full-function Web sites. For unique requirements that cannot be met with generalized modules, most application generators contain *user exits* where custom-programmed routines can be inserted. Some application generators are interactive, enabling users sitting at a terminal to define inputs, files, processing, and reports by responding to questions on-line.

Very High-Level Programming Languages

very high-level programming language   A programming language that uses fewer instructions than conventional languages. Used primarily as a professional programmer productivity tool.

Very high-level programming languages are designed to generate program code with fewer instructions than conventional languages such as COBOL or FORTRAN. Programs and applications based on these languages can be developed in much shorter periods of time. Simple features of these languages can be employed by end users. However, these languages are designed primarily as productivity tools for professional programmers. APL and Nomad2 are examples of these languages.

Application Software Packages

software package   A prewritten, precoded, commercially available set of programs that eliminates the need to write software programs for certain functions.

A **software package** is a prewritten, precoded, commercially available set of programs that eliminates the need for individuals or organizations to write their own software programs for certain functions. There are software packages for system software, but the vast majority of package software is application software.

Sophisticated graphics software tools can present data in the form of three-dimensional charts.

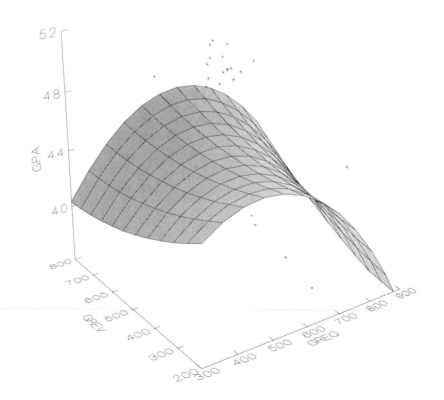

Mapping Solutions with Geographic Information Systems

If you were a manager at a television station, would you want demographic information about your viewers presented as columns of numbers or in a graphic format? To Rod Brown of Big Horn Computer Services in Buffalo, Wyoming, the answer is clear. A graphical presentation of a complex set of numbers is unquestionably preferred. Brown is working on an application for a national television network. The network has collected a massive amount of demographic data on its viewers and wants management of its local affiliate stations to have access to that data. The application Brown is developing uses software technology known as *geographic information systems (GIS)*. The software maps any data that has a spatial quality. For the television station, the data will display maps that have areas shaded according to income, viewing habits, or whatever data the viewer wants to see. This particular application is prized by the network's management for another reason—the affiliated stations will be able to view the data through the Internet. As a result, the network need only install and keep up-to-date one copy of the software and data. The local stations will use their Web browser to view the data relevant to their own market.

Mapping tools are proving valuable as management tools in many ways. For example, to wireless telecommunications giant Bell South, the technology means lower customer support costs, while to its more than 50,000 wireless customers it means improved customer service. Bell South customers constantly want to know how far their service reaches. Traditionally, customer-service representatives took several minutes to rifle through paper files to find the answer—an expensive routine. Now, using a GIS system, the same representatives can visually see the answer displayed on a map in only seconds.

Managers in retail firms are finding many uses for mapping software. Johanna Dairies of Union, New Jersey, is using GIS software to display its customers on a map and then to design the most efficient delivery routes, creating savings of $100,000 per year for each route that can be eliminated. Quaker Oats uses GIS software to display and analyze sales and customer data by store locations. This information aids Quaker Oats customers to tailor the products they carry in their stores and to design advertising campaigns targeted specifically to each store's customers.

Retail stores also use GIS software to track their competition and, with the use of census data, to analyze their customer pool. Management at Sonny's Bar-B-Q, the Gainesville, Florida-based restaurant chain, uses mapping software to determine where to open new outlets. Sonny's well-thought-out growth plan specifies that the company will expand only into regions where barbecued food is very common but where the number of barbecue restaurants is small. The company also requires that location sites are no closer than seven miles from any other Sonny's. The company looks at a range of factors when determining the suitability of a given territory, including traffic count, median age, household income, total population, and population distribution. The data come from local and federal census bureaus and is purchasable in computer format. Reading and understanding mountains of statistics in numeric form is an almost impossible task. To Michael Turner, director of franchise services at Sonny's, the only answer was GIS software. That software has been central to Sonny's ability to open 15 to 20 restaurants a year (from a base of 83 in 1994).

To Think About: What are the management benefits of geographic information system software. What management, organization, and technology issues should be addressed when deciding whether to use GIS?

Sources: April Jacobs, "Mapping Software Puts an End to Paper Chase," *Computerworld*, March 3, 1997; John Swenson, "Maps on the Web," *Information Week*, July 8, 1996; and Tony Seideman, "You Gotta Know the Territory," *Profit*, November–December 1994.

Application software packages consist of prewritten application software that is marketed commercially. These packages are available for major business applications on mainframes, minicomputers, and PCs. They contain customization features so that they can be tailored somewhat to an organization's unique requirements. Although application packages for large complex systems must be installed by technical specialists, many application packages, especially those for PCs, are marketed directly to end users. Systems development based on application packages is discussed in Chapter 12.

The Window on Management provides examples of geographic information systems software, a type of leading-edge application package software that is proving very useful for businesses.

Geographic information system (GIS) software presents and analyzes data geographically, tying business data to points, lines, and areas on a map. GIS tools are now available for use on the World Wide Web.

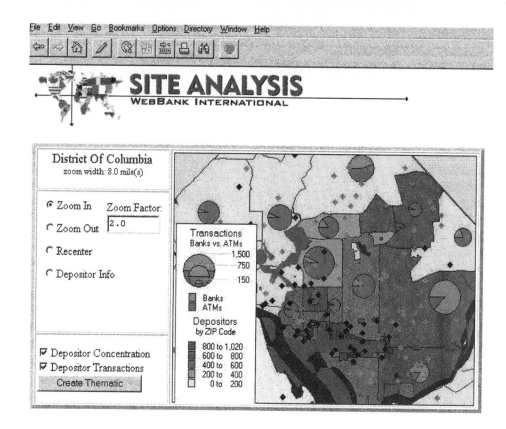

PC Tools

Some of the most popular and productivity-promoting fourth-generation tools are the general-purpose application packages that have been developed for PCs, especially word processing, spreadsheet, data management, graphics, integrated software packages, and Web browsers.

word processing software
Software that handles electronic storage, editing, formatting, and printing of documents.

WORD PROCESSING SOFTWARE. **Word processing software** stores text data electronically as a computer file rather than on paper. The word processing software allows the user to make changes in the document electronically in memory. This eliminates the need to retype an entire page to incorporate corrections. The software has formatting options to make changes in line spacing, margins, character size, and column width. Microsoft Word and WordPerfect are popular word processing packages. Figure 7.12 illustrates a Microsoft Word screen displaying text, graphics, and major menu options.

Most word processing software has advanced features that automate other writing tasks: spelling checkers, style checkers (to analyze grammar and punctuation), thesaurus programs, and mail merge programs (which link letters or other text documents with names and addresses in a mailing list). The newest versions of this software can create and access Web pages.

spreadsheet Software displaying data in a grid of columns and rows, with the capability of easily recalculating numerical data.

SPREADSHEETS. Electronic **spreadsheet** software provides computerized versions of traditional financial modeling tools such as the accountant's columnar pad, pencil, and calculator. An electronic spreadsheet is organized into a grid of columns and rows. The power of the electronic spreadsheet is evident when one changes a value or values, because all other related values on the spreadsheet will be automatically recomputed.

Spreadsheets are valuable for applications in which numerous calculations with pieces of data must be related to each other. Spreadsheets are also useful for applications that require modeling and what-if analysis. After the user has constructed a set of mathematical relationships, the spreadsheet can be recalculated instanta-

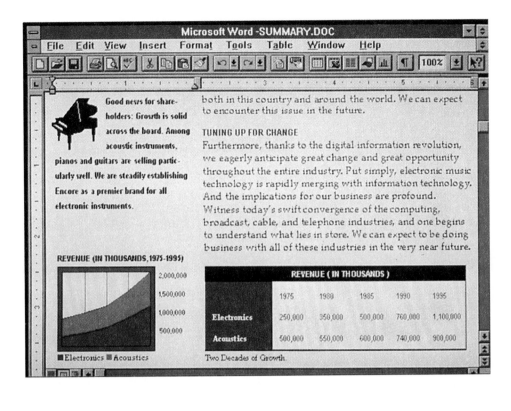

FIGURE 7.12

Text and some of the options available in Microsoft Word for Windows. Word processors provide many easy-to-use options to create and output a text document to meet a user's specifications.
Courtesy of Microsoft.

neously using a different set of assumptions. A number of alternatives can easily be evaluated by changing one or two pieces of data without having to rekey in the rest of the worksheet. Many spreadsheet packages include graphics functions that can present data in the form of line graphs, bar graphs, or pie charts. The most popular spreadsheet packages are Microsoft Excel and Lotus 1-2-3. The newest versions of this software can read and write Web files.

Figure 7.13 illustrates the output from a spreadsheet for a breakeven analysis and its accompanying graph.

DATA MANAGEMENT SOFTWARE.   Although spreadsheet programs are powerful tools for manipulating quantitative data, **data management software** is more suitable for creating and manipulating lists and for combining information from different files. PC database management packages have programming features and easy-to-learn menus that enable nonspecialists to build small information systems.

Data management software typically has facilities for creating files and databases and for storing, modifying, and manipulating data for reports and queries. A detailed treatment of data management software and database management systems can be found in Chapter 8. Popular database management software for the personal computer includes Microsoft Access, which has been enhanced to publish data on the Web. Figure 7.14 shows a screen from Microsoft Access illustrating some of its capabilities.

INTEGRATED SOFTWARE PACKAGES AND SOFTWARE SUITES.   **Integrated software packages** combine the functions of the most important PC software packages, such as word processing, spreadsheets, graphics, and data management. This integration provides a more general-purpose software tool and eliminates redundant data entry and data maintenance. For example, the breakeven analysis spreadsheet illustrated in Figure 7.13 could be reformatted into a polished report with word processing software without separately keying the data into both programs. Integrated packages are a compromise. Although they can do many things well, they generally do not have the same power and depth as single-purpose packages.

data management software
Software used for creating and manipulating lists, creating files and databases to store data, and combining information for reports.

integrated software package   A software package that provides two or more applications, such as word processing and spreadsheets, providing for easy transfer of data between them.

FIGURE 7.13

Spreadsheet software. Spreadsheet software organizes data into columns and rows for analysis and manipulation. Contemporary spreadsheet software provides graphing abilities for clear visual representation of the data in the spreadsheets. This sample breakeven analysis is represented as numbers in a spreadsheet as well as a line graph for easy interpretation.

Total fixed cost	19,000.00
Variable cost per unit	3.00
Average sales price	17.00
Contribution margin	14.00
Breakeven point	1,357

Custom Neckties Pro Forma Income Statement

Units sold	0.00	679	1,357	2,036	2,714
Revenue	0	11,536	23,071	34,607	46,143
Fixed cost	19,000	19,000	19,000	19,000	19,000
Variable cost	0	2,036	4,071	6,107	8,143
Total cost	19,000	21,036	23,071	25,107	27,143
Profit/Loss	(19,000)	(9,500)	0	9,500	19,000

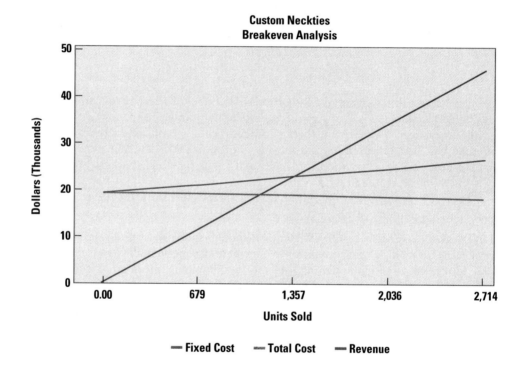

Custom Neckties Breakeven Analysis

Integrated software packages should be distinguished from software suites, which are collections of applications software sold as a unit. Microsoft Office 97 is an example. This software suite contains Word word processing software, Excel spreadsheet software, Access database software, PowerPoint presentation graphics software, and Outlook, a set of tools for e-mail, scheduling, and contact management. Software suites have some features of integrated packages, such as the ability to share data among different applications, but they consist of full-featured versions of each type of software.

WEB BROWSERS. **Web browsers** are easy-to-use software tools for accessing the World Wide Web and the Internet. Web browser software features a point-and-click graphical user interface that can be employed throughout the Internet so that it can

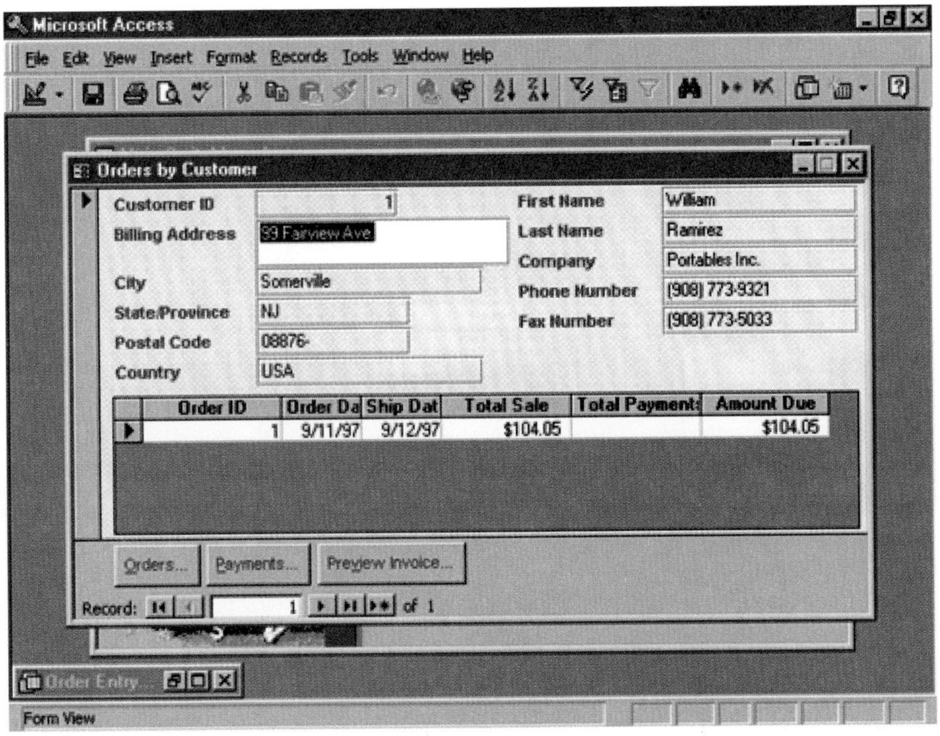

FIGURE 7.14

Data management software. This screen from Microsoft Access illustrates some of its powerful capabilities for managing and organizing information.

access and display information stored on computers at other Internet sites. Browsers can display or present graphics, audio, and video information as well as traditional text and they allow you to click on-screen buttons or highlighted words to link to related Web sites. Netscape Navigator (along with Netscape Communicator) and Microsoft's Internet Explorer are the leading commercial Web browsers, with additional features for using e-mail, on-line bulletin boards and discussion groups, and other Internet services.

As Chapter 12 will discuss, fourth-generation tools are applicable only to specific areas of application development. Nevertheless, fourth-generation tools have provided many productivity and cost-cutting benefits for businesses.

web browser An easy-to-use software tool for accessing the World Wide Web and the Internet.

7.4 NEW SOFTWARE TOOLS AND APPROACHES

A growing backlog of software projects and the need for businesses to fashion systems that are flexible and quick to build have spawned new approaches to software development with object-oriented programming tools and a programming language called Java.

Object-Oriented Programming

Traditional software development methods have treated data and procedures as independent components. A separate programming procedure must be written every time someone wants to take an action on a particular piece of data. The procedures act on data that the program passes to them.

What Makes Object-Oriented Programming Different?

Object-oriented programming combines data and the specific procedures that operate on those data into one *object*. The object combines data and program code. Instead of passing data to procedures, programs send a message for an object to perform a procedure that is already embedded into it. (Procedures are termed *methods* in

object-oriented programming An approach to software development that combines data and procedures into a single object.

With visual programming tools such as SQL Windows, working software programs can be created by drawing, pointing, and clicking instead of writing program code.
Source: Courtesy of the Gupta Corporation.

object-oriented languages.) The same message may be sent to many different objects, but each will implement that message differently.

For example, an object-oriented financial application might have Customer objects sending debit and credit messages to Account objects. The Account objects in turn might maintain Cash-on-Hand, Accounts-Payable, and Accounts-Receivable objects.

An object's data are hidden from other parts of the program and can only be manipulated from inside the object. The method for manipulating the object's data can be changed internally without affecting other parts of the program. Programmers can focus on what they want an object to do, and the object decides how to do it.

Because an object's data are encapsulated from other parts of the system, each object is an independent software building block that can be used in many different systems without changing the program code. Thus, object-oriented programming is expected to reduce the time and cost of writing software by producing reusable program code or software *chips* that can be reused in other related systems. Future software work can draw upon a library of reusable objects, and productivity gains from object-oriented technology could be magnified if objects were stored in reusable software libraries and explicitly designed for reuse (Fayad and Cline, 1996).

Object-oriented programming has spawned a new programming technology known as **visual programming.** With visual programming, programmers do not write code. Rather, they use a mouse to select and move around programming objects, copying an object from a library into a specific location in a program, or drawing a line to connect two or more objects. The Window on Technology more fully describes *drag-and-drop,* one visual programming method.

visual programming The construction of software programs by selecting and arranging programming objects rather than by writing program code.

Object-Oriented Programming Concepts

Object-oriented programming is based on the concepts of class and inheritance. Program code is not written separately for every object but for classes, or general categories of similar objects. Objects belonging to a certain class have the features of that class. Classes of objects in turn can inherit all the structure and behaviors of a more general class and then add variables and behaviors unique to each object. New

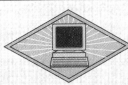

Power Short-Circuits in Object-Oriented Development

Ontario Hydro, the Toronto-based and government-owned utility, faces an enormous task in maintaining its 69 hydroelectric power stations, eight fossil-fuel generators, and five nuclear power plants. It is the Northern hemisphere's biggest electric utility, servicing one of the most electricity-intensive economies of any high-population state or province. When an unscheduled shutdown of a plant does occur, it can cost the company as much as $1 million a day. It also can affect the 8 million customers served by this $8.3 billion (Canadian) power utility. Mike Benjamin, an Ontario Hydro project manager, had an idea for an information system that would reduce unscheduled shutdowns by assisting on-site maintenance staff in their performance of plant component predictive maintenance. Much of the information the staff required to enable it to predict problems was already available, but in scattered existing systems. Benjamin launched a project that combined data from a hodgepodge of existing systems—from simulation packages to commercial databases and artificial intelligence—running on various computers so that all operators could monitor operations and even predict equipment failure. To build the system rapidly, Benjamin first developed a pilot system using object-oriented technology. Ontario Hydro plans to roll it out to all its plants. This system won't prevent shutdowns, but it should decrease the frequency of shutdowns and the amount of downtime.

The key software tool Ontario Hydro used to program the objects was Xshell from Expersoft Corp. of San Diego, California, which relies on a programming technique known as *drag-and-drop*. Drag-and-drop is a visually oriented and easy-to-use object-oriented programming method that is gaining popularity. It relies on object request brokers (or ORBs) that are hidden to the programmer but are the elements that allow objects to communicate with each other. PC users who work under Microsoft's Windows (or Apple Macintosh computer users) are familiar with two functions of ORBs. If you copy data from one Windows application to another, such as from Microsoft's Excel spreadsheet into WordPerfect's word processor, the tool that makes this transfer of data possible is an ORB called OLE (Microsoft's Object Linking and Embedding). All the user needs to do is highlight the data to be copied from the first application, click the Copy command with the mouse, move the cursor to the appropriate place in the other application, click the Paste command, and the data

are there. Similarly, many Windows users easily customize their button bars in many of their applications. They do so by pointing the mouse at the button they want to add to the bar and dragging it to the bar. In fact, a Windows application button is nothing more than an object.

Benjamin's pilot system, which was developed on a Sun Microsystems workstation, is a database of plant component data that Ontario Hydro operators need if they are to do predictive and preventive maintenance. To program it, he first had to convert the relevant sections of the various Ontario Hydro applications into objects. Then, all Benjamin had to do to create the pilot application (or any future application) was to click and drag each of the needed objects to the appropriate place in the new program and then drop them there by releasing the mouse button.

Although object-oriented programming is proving effective and thus expanding in use, that expansion is slowed by two technical problems. One is the use of ORBs. Although programmers should not have to concern themselves with ORBs, the problem is that no ORB standard yet exists. Software developers do not have one ORB they can use to communicate with all their software applications.

A second technical problem is the difficulties programmers encounter in their use of object libraries for the reuse of objects. Reuse of code is one major benefit of object-oriented programming, but reuse turns out to be difficult to learn.

The time and cost to start using the technology is another major hurdle companies must overcome. Object-oriented startup requires a long-range commitment by management and a significant investment in hardware, software, and retraining.

To Think About: How was object-oriented development related to Ontario Hydro's business needs? What management, technology, and organization factors would you consider before making a recommendation to use object-oriented development?

Sources: "Don't Water Down Ontario Hydro Privatization," *The Wall Street Journal*, March 15, 1996; Emily Kay, "Code That's Ready to Go," *Information Week*, August 22, 1994; Lamont Wood, "The Future of Object Systems," *Information Week*, November 21, 1994.

---

classes of objects are created by choosing an existing class and specifying how the new class differs from the existing class, instead of starting from scratch each time.

Classes are organized hierarchically into superclasses and subclasses. For example, a *car* class might have a *vehicle* class for a superclass, so that it would inherit all the methods and data previously defined for *vehicle*. The design of the *car* class would only need to describe how cars differ from vehicles. A banking application could define a Savings-Account object that is very much like a Bank-Account object

class The feature of object-oriented programming so that all objects belonging to a certain class have all of the features of that class.

inheritance The feature of object-oriented programming in which a specific class of objects receives the features of a more general class.

with a few minor differences. Savings-Account inherits all the Bank-Account's state and methods and then adds a few extras.

We can see how class and **inheritance** work in Figure 7.15, which illustrates a tree of classes concerning employees and how they are paid. Employee is the common ancestor of the other four classes. Contractor and Paid weekly are subclasses of Employee, whereas Hourly and Salaried are subclasses of Paid weekly. The variables for the class are in the top half of the box, and the methods are in the bottom half. Shaded items in each box are inherited from some ancestor class. (For example, by following the tree upward, we can see that Name and Title in the Contractor, Paid weekly, Hourly, and Salaried subclasses are inherited from the Employee superclass [ancestor class].) Unshaded methods, or class variables, are unique to a specific class and they override, or redefine, existing methods. When a subclass overrides an inherited method, its object still responds to the same message, but it executes its definition of the method rather than its ancestor's. Whereas Print is a method inherited from some superclass, the method Make_weekly_paycheck is specific to the Paid weekly class, and Make_weekly_paycheck-OVERRIDE is specific to the Hourly class. The Salaried class uses its own Print-OVERRIDE method.

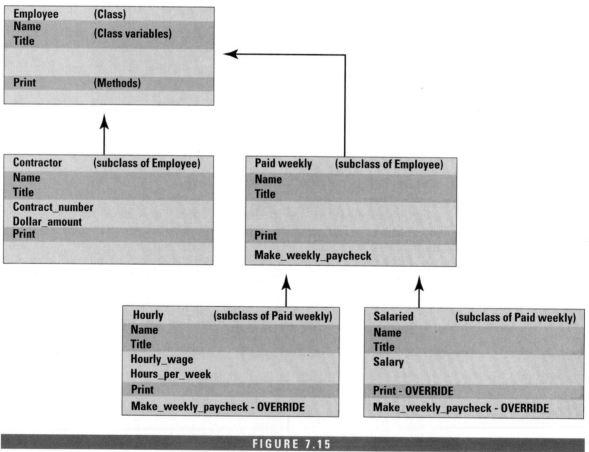

FIGURE 7.15

Class, subclasses, inheritance, and overriding. This figure illustrates how a message's method can come from the class itself or an ancestor class. Class variables and methods are shaded when they are inherited from above.
Hypercard 2.2 © 1987–1991, 1993 Apple Computer, Inc. Apple ®, the Apple logo and Hypercard ® are registered trademarks of Apple Computer, Inc. Used with permission. All rights reserved.

Java and the Software Revolution

Java is a programming language named after the many cups of coffee its Sun Microsystems developers drank along the way. It has the potential to revolutionize both computer software and hardware.

Traditional application software packages address a single, general function and include all of its subfunctions in one package. For example, a popular word processor includes not only the functions we all would use—such as setting margins, indenting, line spacing, and bolding—but also the ability to use automatic bullets and numbering, to use footnotes or endnotes, to insert graphics, to merge documents with mailing lists, to check grammar or spelling, and many more special features. Few people use any more than a small subset of the many functions contained in each of these packages, and no one uses more than a few functions at a time. Such software requires a computer with a large amount of storage, memory, and processing power to execute. The software must be run on the specific platform for which it was designed, such as a Microsoft Windows operating system running on an Intel-type microprocessor.

The Technology of Java

Technically, Java is an object-oriented language, combining the data with the specific functions for processing that data. Java is designed so that its users can build small *applets*—tiny Java programs that execute one small function that until now was obtained only as part of larger applications. For example, if you wished to access and modify data on an employee's dependents, rather than run a whole personnel system to modify that data, you would be able to run a tiny Java applet for that specific function only. Now, if you assume that the personnel system is programmed in Java applets and resides on a network rather than on the user's computer, all you (the user) would need to do on the network would be to ask for dependent data on a specific individual. The data would arrive with whatever processing functionality you need. When you are finished, you would save the data through the network, and the data and software would disappear from your personal computer. Note that with this system you never have to purchase a copy of the software, never have to install it on your computer, never have to upgrade the software to the latest version, and never have to worry about the compatibility of the software with your hardware platform or data. Java enables all processing software to be stored on the network, downloaded as needed, and then erased from the local computer when the processing is completed.

Java was developed specifically for use on the Internet, although it is also being used as a general-purpose programming language in other areas. Any computer that adheres to Internet technology standards is able to access the network and communicate with any other connected computer, regardless of the specific hardware and software used on each computer. An Apple Macintosh, an IBM personal computer running Windows, and a DEC computer running UNIX can all exchange data with each other. Hence, Java is platform-independent, which means that a Java program could be transferred from any computer to any other computer regardless of which PC or operating system both use. Both of the computers will have to have either an operating system containing a Java virtual machine (JVM) or a very small virtual computer control unit (CPU). (The Java Virtual Machine is a compact program that enables the computer to run Java applications. A Java Virtual Machine is incorporated into Netscape Web browser software.) Java is also a very robust language that is able to handle text, data, graphics, sound, and video, all within one program if needed.

Because Java was designed for use on networks, security was given high priority by the Sun developers. Sun claims that no Java program can penetrate the rest of your computer, making it safe from viruses and other types of damage that might occur when downloading more conventional programs off a network. The language has other network-specific facilities built in.

Java An object-oriented programming language that can deliver only the software functionality needed for a particular task as a small applet downloaded from a network; can run on any computer and operating system.

Table 7.2	The Promise of Java	
	Today	Five Years from Now
Hardware/software independence	Application software must run on the specific hardware and operating system for which it was written.	Platform-independent applications will run on any computer and operating system.
Program size	Giant applications with more functionality than needed and which require large, powerful computers to run	Small applets, which deliver only the functionality needed and which run on small computers and handheld devices.
Software distribution	Vast, costly distribution chain including packaging, wholesalers, retailers, advertising, and catalogue companies with users needing to upgrade every two years	Distribution chain eliminated; software comes to desktop from network as needed with latest upgrades

How Java Is Changing the Way Software Is Developed and Used

It will take years before we see a large number of full-blown applications available through networks in the manner promised by Java. When Java software development does catch on, software developers will no longer need to create separate versions for the UNIX, Microsoft Windows, Macintosh, IBM mainframe, and other environments—one version will run on all of them.

Java will change the way software is distributed. If the model proves effective, more work than ever will be done through networks. Functionality will be stored with data on the network and both will be downloaded only as needed. Many users will no longer purchase software packages to run on their personal computers, eliminating many software wholesale and retail organizations. As software improvements are completed, they will immediately be installed on the network and so become available to everyone instantly. Table 7.2 summarizes the impact that Java could have on software development and use.

Management and Organizational Benefits of Java

Java and Java-like systems promise many potential benefits for organizations. These benefits include the following:

- Companies will no longer need to purchase hundreds or thousands of copies of commercial software to run on individual computers. Instead they will purchase one network copy made of Java applets; the way such software is paid for may also change dramatically—companies could be charged for each usage much like companies are charged today for telephone or photocopying service.

- Companies will no longer need to purchase such powerful personal computers for most employees. If most computers will only download applets when needed and do not need to store the software on their computers, this cost can be reduced to $500 for a network computer, including a monitor, that has far less memory and storage (see Chapter 6).

- Organizations will have less need to set IT standards (software, hardware, telecommunications), because all development can now be done without concern for the platform on which it will be run. All types of computing devices, including cellular phones or television sets, could run Java applets.

Europe Is Banking on Java

Why has Java become the language of choice in a number of different European banks? Robert Gualini, head of information systems at Banca Popolare di Bergamo–Credito Varesino, says that "The main advantage of Java is its portability." Banca Popolare di Bergamo, which is headquartered near Milan, wants to improve its position among Italy's small to medium-sized businesses as well as among retail customers. Their answer is a range of financial products that will make banking easier for customers. One product, for example, will provide customers with an overview of relationships they have with the bank. Other products to be introduced will be banking both by phone and by Internet.

In the past, Banca Popolare was more concerned with the internal efficiency of its information systems. Now it is more interested in developing stronger relationships with customers using sophisticated marketing and cross-selling techniques.

Most of the bank's existing applications are already distributed to its more than 300 branches. Only aggregate data are transmitted to Banca Popolare di Bergamo's headquarters. Therefore, to fit in with their distributed architecture, any new software must be able to run on the wide range of hardware and operating systems already in place in the branches. In the bank's eyes, Java is the answer, not only because it is very portable and so will run on all branch computers, but also because it is much easier to program than other highly portable languages such as C++.

London-based National Westminster Bank (NatWest) is also turning to Java. Their primary motivation was cost savings. NatWest is moving into the home banking market but does not want to develop large, locally based applications because they would generate large support costs with a large number of external users. Java programs can be relatively simple, partly because they can use Java applets to perform individual banking tasks. Applets are tiny programs that are downloaded to the desktop when needed and then are erased when users finish their work. Because they are not stored on the user's machine, they do not require local support. The bank is using applets, for example, for such interactive features as loan repayment calculations and budget planning. Customers can use their PCs to view their ac-

counts or pay bills 24 hours a day. The Java applets check to make sure that account transfers are allowed. By using Java, most of the code maintenance that might be needed will take place on the bank's own computers, not on those of the users.

NatWest is doing other things to keep their costs low. For example, it is building its home banking application around a customized version of Netscape's Navigator Web browser. Again, because this is a third-party application, it is a software product that the bank will not have to maintain on the clients' computers. In addition, the bank "deliberately did not use graphics because people want only their own information and they want it quickly," according to Charlie Herbert, the manager of new delivery channels at NatWest Retail Banking Services. This approach not only gives the customers what they want (speed), but it also reduces development costs because graphics programming can be expensive. Java offers other benefits as well. The bank sees Java as providing "a high level of functionality at the front end," according to Herbert. "Just as important," he adds, "it has allowed a high level of security."

The home banking application dials into the bank at local telephone call rates and connects the user's PC to the bank's mainframe using a secure connection. Customers can carry out the usual branch activities from their PCs, such as viewing transactions and paying bills. Java applets check that account transfers are allowed. NatWest piloted the system with 2000 users as a test of its online banking strategy, making sure that it could be used with individual customers and very small businesses. This trial was very important to show that the bank could improve service to customers without adding more cost to its delivery channels.

To Think About: *How was the use of Java related to the business goals of these banks? What organizational implications are there in the choice of a programming language?*

Sources: "Armchair Accounting" and "Ready to Serve," *Open Finance,* Spring 1997.

■ Companies will have better control over both data and software—both major corporate investments—because both will be controlled at the center on network computers. Upgrades will occur on one machine instead of on thousands.

The Window on Organizations illustrates how Java is helping some companies pursue their business goals.

MANAGEMENT

Management should be aware of the strengths and weaknesses of various software tools, the tasks for which they are best suited, and whether these tools fit into the firm's long-term strategy and information architecture. Tradeoffs between efficiency, ease of use, and flexibility should be carefully analyzed. These organizational considerations have long-term cost implications.

ORGANIZATION

Software can either enhance or impede organizational performance, depending on the software tools selected and how they are used. Organizational needs should drive software selection. The software tool selected should be easy for the firm's IS staff to learn and maintain and flexible enough so that it can grow with the organization. Software for non-IS specialists should have easy-to-use interfaces and be compatible with the firm's other software tools.

TECHNOLOGY

A range of system and application software technologies are available to organizations. Key technology decisions include the appropriateness of the software tool for the problem to be addressed, compatibility with the firm's hardware, the efficiency of the software for performing specific tasks, vendor support of software packages, and other support capabilities for debugging, documentation, and reuse.

For Discussion: Why is selecting both system and application software for the organization an important management decision?

SUMMARY

1. Describe the major types of software. The major types of software are system software and application software. Each serves a different purpose. System software manages the computer resources and mediates between application software and computer hardware. Application software is used by application programmers and some end users to develop systems and specific business applications. Application software works through system software, which controls access to computer hardware.

2. Describe the functions of system software and compare leading PC operating systems. System software coordinates the various parts of the computer system and mediates between application software and computer hardware. The system software that manages and controls the activities of the computer is called the operating system. Other system software includes computer language translation programs that convert programming languages into machine language and utility programs that perform common processing tasks.

The operating system acts as the chief manager of the information system, allocating, assigning, and scheduling system resources and monitoring the use of the computer. Multiprogramming, multitasking, virtual storage, time sharing, and multiprocessing enable system resources to be used more efficiently so that the computer can attack many problems at the same time.

Multiprogramming (multitasking in PC environments) allows multiple programs to use the computer's resources concurrently. Virtual storage splits up programs into pages so that main memory can be utilized more efficiently. Time sharing enables many users to share computer resources simultaneously by allocating each user a tiny slice of computing time. Multiprocessing is the use of two or more CPUs linked together working in tandem to perform a task.

In order to be executed by the computer, a software program must be translated into machine language via special language translation software—a compiler, an assembler, or an interpreter.

PC operating systems have developed sophisticated capabilities such as multitasking and support for multiple users on networks. Leading PC operating systems include Windows 95 (and Windows 98), Windows NT, OS/2, UNIX, Mac OS 8, and DOS. PC operating systems with graphical user interfaces have gained popularity over command-driven operating systems. Windows is a popular graphical user interface shell for the DOS operating system.

3. Explain how software has evolved and how it will continue to develop. Software has evolved along with hardware. The general trend is toward user-friendly high-level languages that both increase professional programmer productivity and make it possible for complete amateurs to use information systems. There have been four generations of software development: (1) machine language; (2) symbolic languages such as assembly language; (3) high-level languages such as FORTRAN and COBOL; and (4) fourth-generation languages, which are less procedural and closer to natural language than earlier generations of software. Software is starting to incorporate both sound and graphics and to support multimedia and applications.

4. Compare strengths and limitations of the major application programming languages and software tools. The most popular conventional programming languages are assembly language, FORTRAN, COBOL, BASIC, PL/1, Pascal, C, and Ada. Conventional programming languages make more efficient use of computer resources than fourth-generation languages and each is designed to solve specific types of problems.

Fourth-generation languages include query languages, report generators, graphics languages, application generators, very high-level programming languages, application software packages, and PC tools. They are less procedural than conventional programming languages and enable end users to perform many software tasks that previously required technical specialists.

5. Describe new approaches to software development. Object-oriented programming combines data and procedures into one *object*, which can act as an independent software building block. Each object can be used in many different systems without changing program code.

Java is an object-oriented programming language designed to operate from the Internet. It can deliver only the software functionality needed for a particular task as a small *applet* that is downloaded from a network. Java can run on any computer and operating system and could potentially eliminate the need for many powerful desktop computers.

KEY TERMS

Software	Interpreter	COBOL (COmmon Business	Very high-level
Program	Utility program	Oriented Language)	programming language
Stored program concept	Graphical user interface (GUI)	BASIC (Beginners All-	Software package
System software	DOS	purpose Symbolic	Word processing software
Application software	Windows	Instruction Code)	Spreadsheet
Operating system	Windows 95	PL/1 (Programming	Data management software
System residence device	Windows 98	Language 1)	Integrated software
Multiprogramming	Windows NT	Pascal	package
Multitasking	OS/2	Ada	Web browser
Virtual storage	UNIX	C	Object-oriented
Page	Mac OS 8	Fourth-generation language	programming
Time sharing	Machine language	Query language	Visual programming
Multiprocessing	High-level language	Report generator	Class
Source code	Assembly language	Graphics language	Inheritance
Compiler	FORTRAN (FORmula	Application generator	Java
Object code	TRANslator)		

REVIEW QUESTIONS

1. What are the major types of software? How do they differ in terms of users and uses?

2. What is the operating system of a computer? What does it do?

3. Describe multiprogramming, virtual storage, time sharing, and multiprocessing. Why are they important for the operation of an information system?

4. Define multitasking.

5. What is the difference between an assembler, a compiler, and an interpreter?

6. Define graphical user interfaces.

7. Compare the major PC operating systems.

8. What are the major generations of software and approximately when were they developed?

9. What is a high-level language? Name three high-level languages. Describe their strengths and weaknesses.

10. Define fourth-generation languages and list the seven categories of fourth-generation tools.

11. What is the difference between fourth-generation languages and conventional programming languages?

12. What is the difference between an application generator and an application software package?

13. Name and describe the most important PC software tools.

14. What is object-oriented programming? How does it differ from conventional software development?

15. What is Java? How could it change the way software is created and used?

Is Windows NT better than Windows 95? Your instructor will divide the class into two groups to discuss this question from both a technical and a business standpoint.

Use articles from computer magazines to help prepare your group's analysis.

CASE STUDY

The Year 2000 Problem

The year 1999 is followed immediately by what year? That's easy for us—we all know that it is the year 2000, and we even know it is also a new century and a new millennium. But "ask" any computer and a great many of them will give a strange answer—1999 is followed by the year 1900. And this is an enormous problem. Let us see why.

Imagine that you were born in 1940 and are a citizen of the United States. You expect that when you turn 65 in the year 2005, you will collect Social Security benefits. But, if the computer calculates the year to be 1905, you will receive no payments, because you will not be eligible. In fact, you won't have even been born yet. Now assume that in 1980 you took out a 30-year mortgage on your house, scheduled to be paid off in 2010, a year that will never arrive if 1999 is followed by the year 1900. However, depending on how the computer handles its dates, it could calculate that your mortgage already ended in the year 1910—so you would need to make no payments after 1999. You certainly would love that, but your mortgage company would likely go bankrupt. Finally, assume that you are in charge of maintenance for one of your company's large plants. Your computer runs a maintenance system that schedules plant equipment maintenance, and for that maintenance schedules the purchase of supplies and allocates the staff time. You have scheduled maintenance in 1995, 1998, and 2001. If your computer jumps to

1900 and so never reaches the year 2000, your plant and your whole operation will be in chaos.

Why do many computer programs fail to handle the turn-of-the-century properly? Check your computer programs. You will probably find that for many date fields, the dates are stored as six digits, two digits each for the day, month, and year (MM-DD-YY). Programs have been written this way for decades because it saved data entry time and storage space if the century number "19" does not have to be entered. Imagine, for example, the data entry time needed just to enter 19 for every one of the millions of checks that each major bank processes each day. This presents no problem if the date is used only for display purposes. Human beings reading it will have no problem interpreting it. But if the date is used for calculations, it could mean confusion if not disaster.

To solve the problem before 2000 arrives, organizations need to comb through their programs to locate all coding in which dates are used. They then must determine whether each of those places is a problem. Many companies have computer programs amounting to many millions of lines of code, making this a daunting task. Where problems are found, they must be corrected. Two types of corrections are possible. One approach is to fix each date field by increasing the year field to four digits and inserting the century number. The other ap-

proach is to change the program code to compensate for the problem. The year 2000 affects all organizations—business, nonprofit, and government alike. We will look at two federal government agencies, the Department of Defense and the Central Intelligence Agency, to help us better understand the problem and the steps needed to address it.

The Department of Defense (DOD) has over 7000 computer systems with perhaps 360 million lines of code. These systems do everything from managing inventories to controlling weaponry. Failure to address the year 2000 problem could easily result in complete chaos. Transportation and other logistics systems, maintenance systems, accounting, and many other systems are very date dependent. Many weapons systems are also date dependent. The failure of these systems in a time of military crisis could easily be "catastrophic," according to Pentagon Chief Information Officer Emmett Paige, Jr. One reason for the urgency felt by many in the DOD is that one never knows when or from whom a military threat will come, and so the military must always be ready. As explained by Bryce Ragland, the head of a year 2000 task force team at the Air Force Software Support Center, "There's a real risk that some wacko in another country might decide to launch an attack against the U.S. a few seconds after midnight just to see if our defenses can handle it."

One common approach to addressing the problem is first to review each system, placing each program into one of three groups. Group 1 applications are already year 2000 compliant (probably because they were developed within the last few years when people were already aware of the problem). Group 2 applications are those that are mission-critical, technically sound, and not going to be replaced, but not yet year 2000 compliant. These must be addressed. Group 3 applications are those not being kept (the DOD, like many organizations, sees the year 2000 problem also as an opportunity to eliminate a lot of dead wood). Next, the necessary changes for group 2 systems must be made. Finally, all changes must be thoroughly tested, a massive job which will take up at least half the total year 2000 effort. All programs must be tested not only for how they handle the change from 1999 to 2000, but also for the years before and after 2000. In addition, all links to other programs must be tested so that programmers are certain that wrong data are neither sent to nor received from other programs and systems.

Changing programs or stored data presents a massive problem to the DOD because, like most of industry, it has had poor development practices over the years. The DOD used obscure, specialty programming languages, such as Jovial, for which few analytical and debugging tools are available to aid in solving the year 2000 problems. Quality documentation does not exist for most systems, documentation that would have enabled the staff to review the programs quickly or that would have enabled programmers to quickly make changes. Moreover, like most organizations, the DOD has had few programming standards, so that date calculations were written differently by different programmers, adding confusion to the problem.

The costs of scanning over 7000 computer systems and identifying and fixing the trouble spots are enormous. The problem is so massive that, according to an April 1996 survey conducted by the House of Representatives, the DOD hadn't yet finished inventorying its roughly 358 million lines of program code. The DOD has an annual IT budget of $3 billion, but this is surely too little for such an enormous task. Congress, which is well aware of the year 2000 problem, has budgeted $2.3 billion to address the problem for the whole federal government. But a study of 24 federal agencies by Federal Sources Inc. estimates that it will cost about $5.6 billion for the federal government to rewrite all of its code to be year 2000 compliant. That's about 2.5 times higher than an estimate submitted to Congress in February by the Office of Management and Budget. Without Congress allocating a major increase in funds, the DOD will have to focus on identifying the problems and making the changes, ignoring testing, or testing superficially at best. That means many systems will have to be put back in production with many hidden problems in them. Nor can the deadline for the changes be extended—the year 2000 will arrive on schedule, no matter what. By early 1997 the DOD had only 302 systems that were fully compliant with the year 2000. That actually puts them in better shape than not only most government agencies but also most businesses. Nonetheless, with nearly 7000 systems remaining, the task the department faces is gargantuan to say the least.

The Central Intelligence Agency (CIA) first realized it had a problem when it found a rather mundane failure—the system that projects dividends for the agency's employee thrift savings plan malfunctioned for any period beyond the year 1999. The CIA faces the same basic problems as the DOD and most companies—budget, poor program documentation, a lack of standards. It runs 3000 mostly homegrown applications among hundreds of fragmented, departmentalized "mini" agencies. In addition, like most organizations, the CIA has its own special situations.

For the agency, the overriding need is for security and secrecy, which adds another level of complications. Almost all data and programs are tightly protected, with access granted only on a need-to-know basis. Therefore, the agency does not know what programs and systems even exist, much less whether they have problems. In addition, the CIA systems share massive amounts of data with such outside organizations as the FBI, state and local police departments, and other law enforcement and security agencies, making them highly dependent on those other organizations. (What happens if the CIA fixes its year 2000 problem but New York and California law enforcement agencies do not?) Moreover, the agency is under a congressional mandate that it must not make changes to any fields within its historical computer records, making it impossible for them to make changes to date fields. They must find another way to solve their problems. The CIA is actually in good shape, however, because its management expects to have the code changes completed in 1997, leaving ample time to test them. ∎

Sources: Robert L. Scheier, Gary H. Anthes, and Allan E. Alter, "Year 2000 May Ambush U.S. Military," *Computerworld*, February 24, 1997; "The CIA's Biggest Issue is Sharing App Information," *Software Magazine*, March 1997; Bruce Caldwell and Bob Violino, "Year 2000 Costs Climb," *InformationWeek*, April 7, 1997; Robert L. Scheier, "Congress Examines Date-Change Progress," *Computerworld*, February 24, 1997; Richard Adhikari, "Approaching 2000," *InformationWeek*, October 7, 1996; and Bob Violino, "Getting Down To The Wire," *InformationWeek*, February 10, 1997.

Case Study Questions:

1. Why is the year 2000 problem a serious management issue?

2. What management, organization, and technology factors were responsible for causing the year 2000 problem at the Defense Department and CIA?

3. How well are the Department of Defense and the CIA handling the year 2000 problem?

4. What management, organizational, and technical issues must be considered when planning to address the year 2000 problem?

5. It has been said that if information systems were all thoroughly object oriented, the year 2000 problem would probably be a minor annoyance. Do you agree or disagree?

REFERENCES

Abdel-Hamid, Tarek K. "The Economics of Software Quality Assurance: A Simulation-Based Case Study." *MIS Quarterly* 12, no. 3 (September 1988).

Apte, Uday, Chetan S. Sankar, Meru Thakur, and Joel E. Turner. "Reusability-Based Strategy for Development of Information Systems: Implementation Experience of a Bank." *MIS Quarterly* 14, no. 4 (December 1990).

Barrett, Jim, Kevin Knight, Inderject Man, and Elaine Rich. "Knowledge and Natural Language Processing." *Communications of the ACM* 33, no. 8 (August 1990).

Bochenski, Barbara. "GUI Builders Pay Price for User Productivity." *Software Magazine* (April 1992).

Borning, Alan, "Computer System Reliability and Nuclear War." *Communications of the ACM* 30, no. 2 (February 1987).

Cortese, Amy with John Verity, Kathy Rebello, and Rob Hof. "The Software Revolution." *Business Week* (December 4, 1995).

Fayad, Mohamed, and Marshall P. Cline. "Aspects of Software Adaptability." *Communications of the ACM* 39, no. 10 (October 1996).

Flynn, Jim, and Bill Clarke. "How Java Makes Network-Centric Computing Real." *Datamation* (March 1, 1996).

Freedman, David H. "Programming Without Tears." *High Technology* (April 1986).

Frye, Colleen. "Catch the Millennium Bug Before It's Too Late." *Software Magazine* (January 1997).

Greenbaum, Joshua. "The Evolution Revolution." *Information Week* (March 14, 1994).

Haavind, Robert. "Software's New Object Lesson," *Technology Review* (February/March 1992).

Jalics, Paul J. "Cobol on a PC: A New Perspective on a Language and Its Performance." *Communications of the ACM* 30, no. 2 (February 1987).

Joyce, Edward J. "Reusable Software: Passage to Productivity?" *Datamation* (September 15, 1988).

Kim, Chai, and Stu Westin. "Software Maintainability: Perceptions of EDP Professionals." *MIS Quarterly* 12, no. 2 (June 1988).

Korson, Timothy D., and Vijay K. Vaishnavi. "Managing Emerging Software Technologies: A Technology Transfer Framework." *Communications of the ACM* 35, no. 9 (September 1992).

Korson, Tim, and John D. McGregor. "Understanding Object-Oriented: A Unifying Paradigm." *Communications of the ACM* 33, no. 9 (September 1990).

Layer, D. Kevin, and Chris Richardson. "LISP Systems in the 1990s." *Communications of the ACM* 34, no. 9 (September 1991).

Littlewood, Bev, and Lorenzo Strigini. "The Risks of Software." *Scientific American* 267, no. 5 (November 1992).

Mandelkern, David. "Graphical User Interfaces: The Next Generation." *Communications of the ACM* 36, no. 4 (April 1993).

Monarchi, David E., and Gretchen I. Puhr. "A Research Typology for Object-Oriented Analysis and Design." *Communications of the ACM* 35, no. 9 (September 1992).

Morse, Alan, and George Reynolds. "Overcoming Current Growth Limits in UI Development." *Communications of the ACM* 36, no. 4 (April 1993).

Mukhopadhyay, Tridas, Stephen S. Vicinanza, and Michael J. Prietula. "Examining the Feasibility of a Case-Based Reasoning Model for Software Effort Estimation," *MIS Quarterly* 16, no. 2 (June 1992).

Nance, Barry. "Windows NT and OS/2 Compared." *Byte* (June 1992).

Nerson, Jean-Marc. "Applying Object-Oriented Analysis and Design." *Communications of the ACM* 35, no. 9 (September 1992).

Nielsen, Jakob. "Noncommand User Interfaces." *Communications of the ACM* 36, no. 4 (April 1993).

Pancake, Cherri M. "The Promise and the Cost of Object Technology: A Five-Year Forecast." *Communications of the ACM* 38, no. 10 (October 1995).

Schonberg, Edmond, Mark Gerhardt, and Charlene Hayden. "A Technical Tour of Ada," *Communications of the ACM* 35, no. 11 (November 1992).

Semich, Bill, and David Fisco. "Java: Internet Toy or Enterprise Tool?" *Datamation* (March 1, 1996).

Swanson, Kent, Dave McComb, Jill Smith, and Don McCubbrey. "The Application Software Factory: Applying Total Quality Techniques to Systems Development." *MIS Quarterly* 15, no. 4 (December 1991).

Vassiliou, Yannis, "On the Interactive Use of Databases: Query Languages." *Journal of Management Information Systems* 1 (Winter 1984–1985).

White, George M. "Natural Language Understanding and Speech." *Communications of the ACM* 33, no. 8 (August 1990).

Wiederhold, Gio, Peter Wegner, and Stefano Ceri. "Toward Megaprogramming." *Communications of the ACM* 35, no. 11 (November 1992).

Wilkes, Maurice V. "The Long-Term Future of Operating Systems." *Communications of the ACM* 35, no. 11 (November 1992).

Managing Data Resources

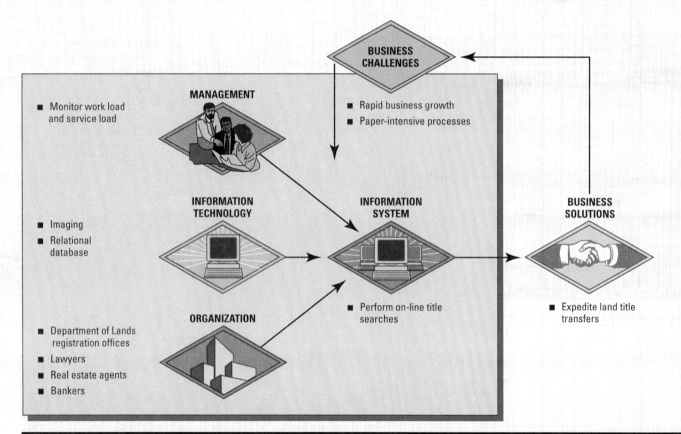

MANAGEMENT

- Monitor work load and service load

INFORMATION TECHNOLOGY

- Imaging
- Relational database

ORGANIZATION

- Department of Lands registration offices
- Lawyers
- Real estate agents
- Bankers

BUSINESS CHALLENGES

- Rapid business growth
- Paper-intensive processes

INFORMATION SYSTEM

- Perform on-line title searches

BUSINESS SOLUTIONS

- Expedite land title transfers

A Land Title System That Makes a Difference

Queensland, Australia's "Sunshine State," has been undergoing strong business growth for a number of years. As a result the Queensland Department of Lands has been very busy, with no letup in sight. The department tracks and administers all Queensland land transactions. With an annual operating budget of A$100 million (U.S. $75 million), it employs 1500 people in its 34 offices. In the past all land title transfer registration had to go through three of those offices (Brisbane, Rockhampton, and Townsville), which also stored all certificates of title in leather-bound volumes. As business boomed the department had to continually increase its staff to manually handle

LEARNING OBJECTIVES

After completing this chapter, you will be able to:

1. Describe traditional file organization and management techniques.
2. Explain the problems of the traditional file environment.
3. Describe how a database management system organizes information.
4. Describe the three principal database models and some principles of database design.
5. Discuss new database trends.
6. Explain the managerial and organizational requirements for creating a database environment.

---

the daily workload of registering, filing, and searching through titles. Moreover, the whole system was slow—land title transfer registration took several weeks to complete, and title searches required that photocopies and faxes be sent between the three registration offices and the office where a lawyer or other interested party wanted to search a specific title (users now conduct about 55,000 searches a month).

In the early 1990s management saw no end in sight to the staff growth to handle the increase or to the concomitant rise in costs. It decided to automate the manual title registration and search processes to bring the growing costs to an end.

Any new information system would have to store the title certificates on-line and make them available for title searches at all the offices. The system would have to store older documents as well as new titles.

The new system, Automated Titles System (ATS), was completed in 1995 at a cost of A\$13 million (U.S. \$9.75 million). Title certificate data are now available on-line, with older certificates stored through document imaging technology. The registration process had to be redesigned so that a title registration, which used to be handled by a number of people, is now essentially completed by one person. The redesign still restricted the final step in the new process to

only five centers, however, because that step requires specially trained, highly skilled staff, an expense too costly to implement at all the offices. The users of the ATS did have to undergo training. Today, land title transfers take only a few days while lawyers, real estate agents, bankers, and Department clerks can undertake on-line title searches at all the 34 offices or, for a fee, from their own computers in their own company offices. The new system is able to handle up to 300 concurrent users.

To accomplish the department's goals, ATS uses a relational database that is able to store all needed data from a vast number of registration certificates—at present it holds

25 gigabytes of data. Moreover, its relational database management system is flexible enough to accommodate rapid growth of data without any problems. In the relational database, the user-friendly database interface software makes it easy for all to search the database and quickly retrieve the data they need. ■

Source: Keith Power, "Australian Agency Breaks New Ground," *International Software Magazine*, February 1996.

MANAGEMENT CHALLENGES

The Automated Titles System illustrates how much the effective use of information depends on how data are stored, organized, and accessed. Proper delivery of information not only depends on the capabilities of computer hardware and software but also on the organization's ability to manage data as an important resource. It has been very difficult for organizations to manage their data effectively. Three challenges stand out.

1. **Organizational obstacles to a database environment.** Implementing a database requires widespread organizational change in the role of information (and information managers), the allocation of power at senior levels, the ownership and sharing of information, and patterns of organizational agreement. A database management system (DBMS) challenges the existing arrangements in an organization and for that reason often generates political resistance. In a traditional file environment, each department constructed files and programs to fulfill its specific needs. Now, with a database, files and programs must be built that take into account the full organization's interest in data. Although the organization has spent the money on hardware and software for a database environment, it may not reap the benefits it should because it is unwilling to make the requisite organizational changes.

2. **Cost/benefit considerations.** The costs of moving to a database environment are tangible, up front, and large in the short term (three years). Most firms buy a commercial DBMS package and related hardware. The software alone can cost $0.5 million for a full-function package with all options. New hardware may cost an additional $1 to 2 million annually. It soon becomes apparent to senior management that a database system is a huge investment.

   Unfortunately, the benefits of the DBMS are often intangible, back loaded, and long term (five years). Several million dollars have been spent over the years designing and maintaining existing systems. People in the organization understand the existing system after long periods of training and socialization. For these reasons, and despite the clear advantages of the DBMS, the short-term costs of developing a DBMS often appear to be nearly as great as the benefits. When the short-term political costs are added to the equation, it is convenient for senior management to defer the database investment. The obvious long-term benefits of the DBMS tend to be severely discounted by managers, especially those unfamiliar with (and perhaps unfriendly to) systems. Moreover, it may not be cost effective to build organization-wide databases that integrate all the organization's data (Goodhue et al., September 1992).

3. **Organizational placement of the data management function.** Many organizations, seeking to avoid large commitments and organizational change, begin (and end) by buying a DBMS package and placing it in the hands of a low-level database group in the information systems department. Generally this leads to a piecemeal approach to database use; that is, small database systems will be developed for various divisions, functional areas, departments, and offices. Eventually this results in incompatible databases throughout the company, and fails to address the key organizational issue: What is the role of information and who will manage it for the organization as a whole? Senior management must be persuaded to implement a data administration function and data planning methodology at the highest corporate level.

This chapter examines the managerial and organizational requirements as well as the technologies for managing data as a resource. First we describe the traditional file management technologies that have been used for arranging and accessing data on physical storage media and the problems they have created for organizations. Then we describe the technology of database management systems, which can overcome many of the drawbacks of traditional file management. We end the chapter with a discussion of the managerial and organizational requirements for successful implementation of database management systems.

8.1 ORGANIZING DATA IN A TRADITIONAL FILE ENVIRONMENT

An effective information system provides users with timely, accurate, and relevant information. This information is stored in computer files. When the files are properly arranged and maintained, users can easily access and retrieve the information they need.

You can appreciate the importance of file management if you have ever written a term paper using 3×5 index cards. No matter how efficient your storage device (a metal box or a rubber band), if you organize the cards randomly your term paper will have little or no organization. Given enough time, you could put the cards in order, but your system would be more efficient if you set up your organizational scheme early on. If your scheme is flexible enough and well documented, you can extend it to account for any changes in your viewpoint as you write your paper.

The same need for file organization applies to firms. Well-managed, carefully arranged files make it easy to obtain data for business decisions, whereas poorly managed files lead to chaos in information processing, high costs, poor performance, and little, if any, flexibility. Despite the use of excellent hardware and software, many organizations have inefficient information systems because of poor file management. In this section we describe the traditional methods that organizations have used to arrange data in computer files. We also discuss the problems with these methods.

File Organization Terms and Concepts

A computer system organizes data in a hierarchy that starts with bits and bytes and progresses to fields, records, files, and databases (see Figure 8.1). A *bit* represents the smallest unit of data a computer can handle. A group of bits, called a *byte*, represents a single character, which can be a letter, a number, or another symbol. A grouping of characters into a word, a group of words, or a complete number (such as a person's name or age), is called a **field**. A group of related fields, such as the student's name, the course taken, the date, and the grade comprise a **record;** a group of records of the same type is called a **file**. For instance, the student records in Figure 8.1 could constitute a course file. A group of related files make up a database. The student course file illustrated in Figure 8.1 could be grouped with files on students' personal histories and financial backgrounds to create a student database.

A record describes an entity. An **entity** is a person, place, thing, or event on which we maintain information. An order is a typical entity in a sales order file, which maintains information on a firm's sales orders. Each characteristic or quality describing a particular entity is called an **attribute**. For example, order number, order date, order amount, item number, and item quantity would each be an attribute of the entity order. The specific values that these attributes can have can be found in the fields of the record describing the entity *order* (see Figure 8.2).

Every record in a file should contain at least one field that uniquely identifies that record so that the record can be retrieved, updated, or sorted. This identifier field is called a **key field**. An example of a key field is the order number for the order record illustrated in Figure 8.2 or an employee number or social security number for

field A grouping of characters into a word, a group of words, or a complete number, such as a person's name or age.

record A group of related fields.

file A group of records of the same type.

entity A person, place, thing, or event about which information must be kept.

attribute A piece of information describing a particular entity.

key field A field in a record that uniquely identifies instances of that record so that it can be retrieved, updated, or sorted.

FIGURE 8.1

The data hierarchy. A computer system organizes data in a hierarchy that starts with the bit, which represents either a 0 or a 1. Bits can be grouped to form a byte to represent one character, number, or symbol. Bytes can be grouped to form a field, and related fields can be grouped to form a record. Related records can be collected to form a file, and related files can be organized into a database.

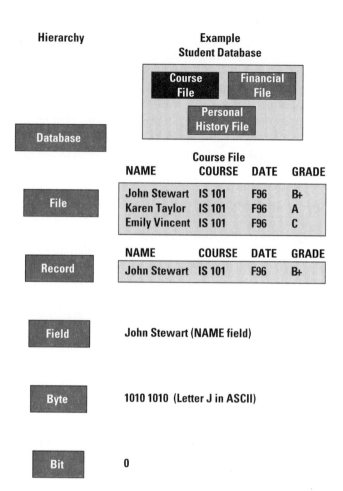

sequential file organization A method of storing data records in which the records must be retrieved in the same physical sequence in which they are stored.

direct or **random file organization** A method of storing data records in a file so that they can be accessed in any sequence without regard to their actual physical order on the storage media.

a personnel record (containing employee data such as the employee's name, age, address, job title, and so forth).

Accessing Records from Computer Files

Computer systems store files on secondary storage devices. Records can be arranged in several ways on storage media, and the arrangement determines the manner in which individual records can be accessed or retrieved. One way to organize records is sequentially. In **sequential file organization**, data records must be retrieved in the same physical sequence in which they are stored. In contrast, **direct** or **random file organization** allows users to access records in any sequence they desire, without regard to actual physical order on the storage media.

FIGURE 8.2

Entities and attributes. This record describes the entity called ORDER and its attributes. The specific values for order number, order date, item number, quantity, and amount for this particular order are the fields for this record. Order number is the key field because each order is assigned a unique identification number.

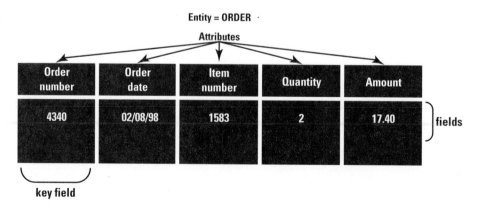

Sequential file organization is the only file organization method that can be used on magnetic tape. This file organization method is no longer popular, but some organizations still use it for batch processing applications in which they access and process each record sequentially. A typical application using sequential files is payroll, in which all employees in a firm must be paid one by one and issued a check. Direct or random file organization is utilized with magnetic disk technology (although records can be stored sequentially on disk if desired). Most computer applications today utilize some method of direct file organization.

The Indexed Sequential Access Method

Although records may be stored sequentially on direct access storage devices, individual records can be accessed directly using the **indexed sequential access method (ISAM)**. This access method relies on an index of key fields to locate individual records. An **index** to a file is similar to the index of a book, as it lists the key field of each record and where that record is physically located in storage to expedite location of that record. Figure 8.3 shows how a series of indexes identifies the location of a specific record. Records are stored on disk in their key sequence. A cylinder index shows the highest value of the key field that can be found on a specific cylinder. A track index shows the highest value of the key field that can be found on a specific track. To locate a specific record, the cylinder index and then the track index are searched to locate the cylinder and track containing the record. The track itself is then sequentially read to find the record. If a file is very large, the cylinder index might be broken down into parts and a master index created to help locate each part of the cylinder index. ISAM is used in applications that require sequential processing of large numbers of records but that occasionally require direct access of individual records.

indexed sequential access method (ISAM) A file access method to directly access records organized sequentially using an index of key fields.

index A table or list that relates record keys to physical locations on direct access files.

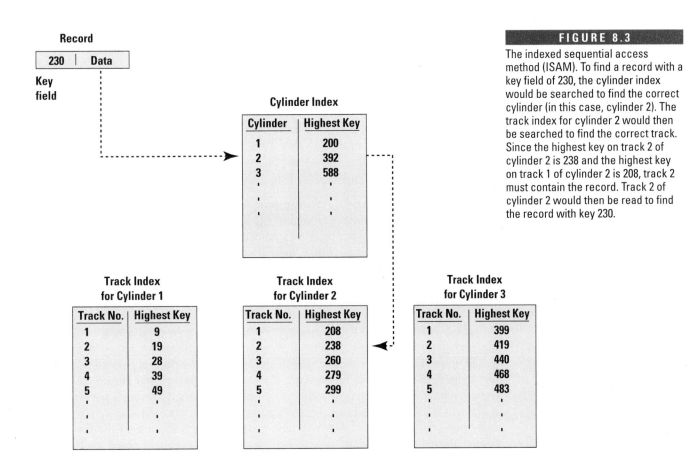

FIGURE 8.3

The indexed sequential access method (ISAM). To find a record with a key field of 230, the cylinder index would be searched to find the correct cylinder (in this case, cylinder 2). The track index for cylinder 2 would then be searched to find the correct track. Since the highest key on track 2 of cylinder 2 is 238 and the highest key on track 1 of cylinder 2 is 208, track 2 must contain the record. Track 2 of cylinder 2 would then be read to find the record with key 230.

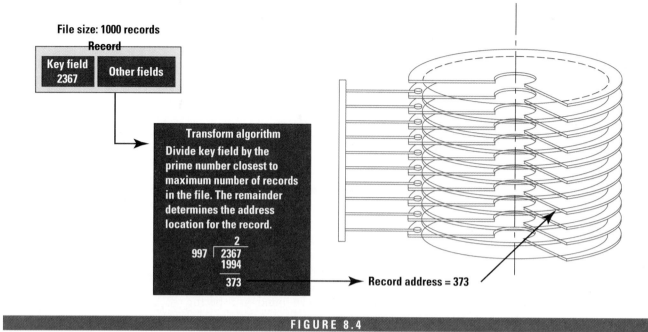

File size: 1000 records

Record

| Key field 2367 | Other fields |

Transform algorithm
Divide key field by the prime number closest to maximum number of records in the file. The remainder determines the address location for the record.

$$997 \overline{\smash{\big)}\, 2367} \atop \underline{1994} \atop 373 \quad \genfrac{}{}{0pt}{}{2}{}$$

Record address = 373

FIGURE 8.4

The direct file access method. Records are not stored sequentially on the disk but are arranged according to the results of some mathematical computation. Here, the transform algorithm divides the value in the key field by the prime number closest to the maximum number of records in the file (in this case, the prime number is 997). The remainder designates the storage location for that particular record.

Direct File Access Method

direct file access method A method of accessing records by mathematically transforming the key fields into the specific addresses for the records.

transform algorithm A mathematical formula used to translate a record's key field directly into the record's physical storage location.

The **direct file access method** is used with direct file organization. This method uses a key field to locate the physical address of a record. However, the process is accomplished using a mathematical formula called a **transform algorithm** to translate the key field directly into the record's physical storage location on disk. The algorithm performs some mathematical computation on the record key, and the result of that calculation is the record's physical address. This process is illustrated in Figure 8.4.

This access method is most appropriate for applications in which individual records must be located directly and rapidly for immediate processing only. A few records in the file need to be retrieved at one time, and the required records are found in no particular sequence. An example might be an on-line hotel reservation system.

Problems with the Traditional File Environment

Most organizations began information processing on a small scale, automating one application at a time. Systems tended to grow independently, and not according to some grand plan. Each functional area tended to develop systems in isolation from other functional areas. Accounting, finance, manufacturing, human resources, and marketing all developed their own systems and data files. Figure 8.5 illustrates the traditional approach to information processing.

Each application, of course, required its own files and its own computer program to operate. For example, the human resources functional area might have a personnel master file, a payroll file, a medical insurance file, a pension file, a mailing list file, and so forth until tens, perhaps hundreds, of files and programs existed.

In the company as a whole, this process led to multiple master files created, maintained, and operated by separate divisions or departments. Figure 8.6 shows three separate master files: customer, personnel, and sales. Creating a simple report such as that listed in this example, sales personnel by annual sales and by principal customers, required a complex matching program that read each of the three files, copied pertinent records, and recombined the records into an intermediate file. This

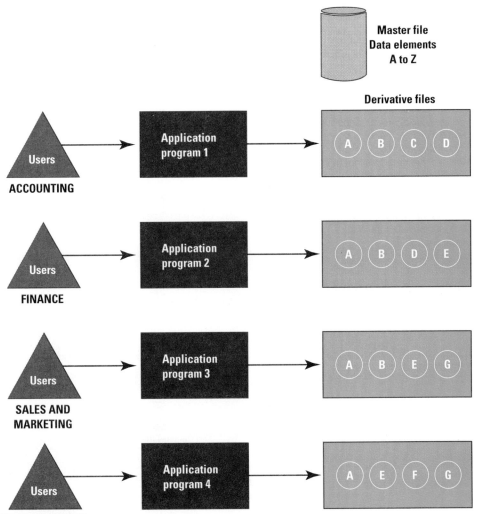

FIGURE 8.5

Traditional file processing. The use of a traditional approach to file processing encourages each functional area in a corporation to develop specialized applications. Each application requires a unique data file that is likely to be a subset of the master file. These subsets of the master file lead to data redundancy, processing inflexibility, and wasted storage resources.

intermediate file had to be sorted in the desired sequence (sales personnel ranked by highest sales) before a final report could be printed.

There are names for this situation: the **traditional file environment;** the *flat file organization* (because most of the data are organized in flat files); and the *data file approach* (because the data and business logic are tied to specific files and related programs). By any name, the situation results in growing inefficiency and complexity.

As this process goes on for five or ten years, the firm becomes tied up in knots of its own creation. The organization is saddled with hundreds of programs and applications, with no one who knows what they do, what data they use, and who is using the data. There is no central listing of data files, data elements, or definitions of data. The organization is collecting the same information in far too many files. The resulting problems are data redundancy, program-data dependence, inflexibility, poor data security, and inability to share data among applications.

traditional file environment A way of collecting and maintaining data in an organization that leads to each functional area or division creating and maintaining its own data files and programs.

Data Redundancy and Confusion

Data redundancy is the presence of duplicate data in multiple data files. Data redundancy occurs when different divisions, functional areas, and groups in an organization independently collect the same piece of information. For instance, within the commercial loans division of a bank, the marketing and credit information functions might collect the same customer information. Because it is collected and maintained in so many different places, the same data item may have different meanings in dif-

data redundancy The presence of duplicate data in multiple data files.

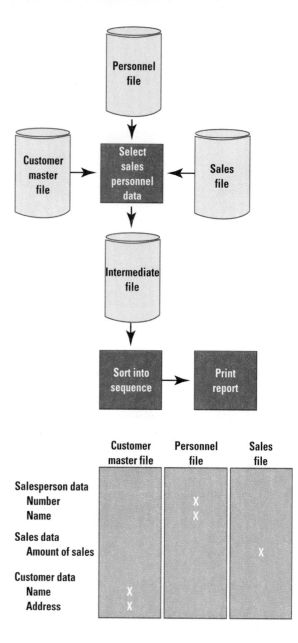

FIGURE 8.6

Creating a report using traditional file processing. In this example, three separate files—customer, personnel, and sales—have been created and are maintained by each respective division or department. To create a simple report consisting of a list of sales personnel by annual sales and principal customers, the three files had to be read, and an intermediate file had to be created. This required writing several programs. The table in the figure shows the information selected from each file.

	Customer master file	Personnel file	Sales file
Salesperson data			
Number		X	
Name		X	
Sales data			
Amount of sales			X
Customer data			
Name	X		
Address	X		

ferent parts of the organization. Simple data items such as the fiscal year, employee identification, and product code can take on different meanings as programmers and analysts work in isolation on different applications.

Program-Data Dependence

program-data dependence The close relationship between data stored in files and the software programs that update and maintain those files. Any change in data organization or format requires a change in all the programs associated with those files.

Program-data dependence is the tight relationship between data stored in files and the specific programs required to update and maintain those files. Every computer program has to describe the location and nature of the data with which it works. In a traditional file environment, any change in data requires a change in all programs that access the data. Changes, for instance, in tax rates or ZIP-code length require changes in programs. Such programming changes may cost millions of dollars to implement in each program that requires the revised data.

Lack of Flexibility

A traditional file system can deliver routine scheduled reports after extensive programming efforts, but it cannot deliver ad hoc reports or respond to unanticipated information requirements in a timely fashion. The information required by ad hoc requests is somewhere in the system but too expensive to retrieve. Several programmers would have to work for weeks to put together the required data items in a new file.

Poor Security

Because there is little control or management of data, access to and dissemination of information are virtually out of control. What limits on access exist tend to be the result of habit and tradition, as well as of the sheer difficulty of finding information.

Lack of Data Sharing and Availability

The lack of control over access to data in this confused environment does not make it easy for people to obtain information. Because pieces of information in different files and different parts of the organization cannot be related to one another, it is virtually impossible for information to be shared or accessed in a timely manner.

8.2   A MODERN DATABASE ENVIRONMENT

Database technology can cut through many of the problems created by traditional file organization. A more rigorous definition of a **database** is a collection of data organized to serve many applications efficiently by centralizing the data and minimizing redundant data. Rather than storing data in separate files for each application, data are stored physically to appear to users as being stored in only one location. A single database services multiple applications. For example, instead of a corporation storing employee data in separate information systems and separate files for personnel, payroll, and benefits, the corporation could create a single common human resources database. Figure 8.7 illustrates the database concept.

database A collection of data organized to service many applications at the same time by storing and managing data so that they appear to be in one location.

Database Management Systems

A **database management system (DBMS)** is simply the software that permits an organization to centralize data, manage them efficiently, and provide access to the stored data by application programs. As illustrated in Figure 8.8, the DBMS acts as an interface between application programs and the physical data files. When the application program calls for a data item such as gross pay, the DBMS finds this item in the database and presents it to the application program. Using traditional data files the programmer would have to define the data and then tell the computer where they are. A DBMS eliminates most of the data definition statements found in traditional programs.

A database management system has three components:

- A data definition language
- A data manipulation language
- A data dictionary

The **data definition language** is the formal language used by programmers to specify the content and structure of the database. The data definition language defines each data element as it appears in the database before that data element is translated into the forms required by application programs.

Most DBMS have a specialized language called a **data manipulation language** that is used in conjunction with some conventional third- or fourth-generation programming languages to manipulate the data in the database. This language contains commands that permit end users and programming specialists to extract data from the database to satisfy information requests and develop applications. The most prominent data manipulation language today is **Structured Query Language,** or **SQL.**

database management system (DBMS) Special software to create and maintain a database and enable individual business applications to extract the data they need without having to create separate files or data definitions in their computer programs.

data definition language The component of a database management system that defines each data element as it appears in the database.

data manipulation language A language associated with a database management system that is employed by end users and programmers to manipulate data in the database.

Structured Query Language (SQL) The emerging standard data manipulation language for relational database management systems.

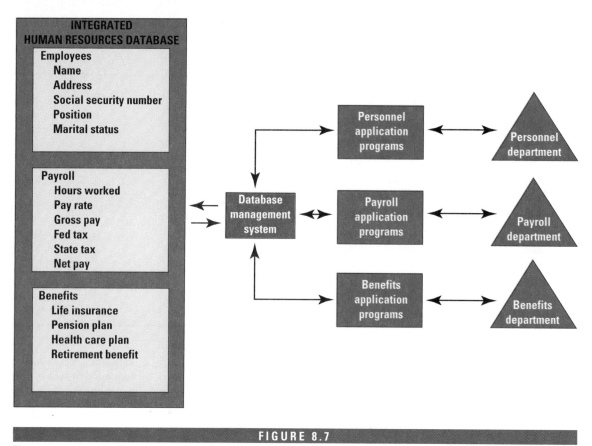

FIGURE 8.7

The contemporary database environment. A single human resources database serves multiple applications and also allows a corporation to easily draw together all the information on various applications. The database management system acts as the interface between the application programs and the data.

Complex programming tasks cannot be performed efficiently with typical data manipulation languages. However, most mainframe DBMSs are compatible with COBOL, FORTRAN, and other third-generation programming languages, permitting greater processing efficiency and flexibility.

The third element of a DBMS is a **data dictionary.** This is an automated or manual file that stores definitions of data elements and data characteristics such as usage, physical representation, ownership (who in the organization is responsible for maintaining the data), authorization, and security. Many data dictionaries can produce lists and reports of data utilization, groupings, program locations, and so on. Figure 8.9

data dictionary An automated or manual tool for storing and organizing information about the data maintained in a database.

FIGURE 8.8

Elements of a database management system. In an ideal database environment, application programs work through a database management system to obtain data from the database. This diagram illustrates a database management system with an active data dictionary that not only records definitions of the contents of the database but also allows changes in data size and format to be automatically utilized by the application programs.

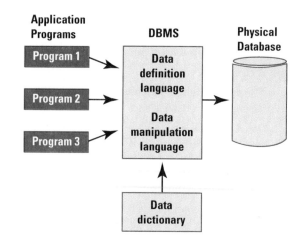

FIGURE 8.9

NAME: AMT-PAY-BASE
FOCUS NAME: BASEPAY
PC NAME:　　SALARY

DESCRIPTION: EMPLOYEE'S ANNUAL SALARY

SIZE: 9 BYTES
TYPE: N　　(NUMERIC)
DATE CHANGED: 01/01/85
OWNERSHIP: COMPENSATION
UPDATE SECURITY: SITE PERSONNEL
ACCESS SECURITY: MANAGER, COMPENSATION PLANNING AND RESEARCH
　　　　　　　　　MANAGER, JOB EVALUATION SYSTEMS
　　　　　　　　　MANAGER, HUMAN RESOURCES PLANNING
　　　　　　　　　MANAGER, SITE EQUAL OPPORTUNITY AFFAIRS
　　　　　　　　　MANAGER, SITE BENEFITS
　　　　　　　　　MANAGER, CLAIMS PAYING SYSTEMS
　　　　　　　　　MANAGER, QUALIFIED PLANS
　　　　　　　　　MANAGER, SITE EMPLOYMENT/EEO
BUSINESS FUNCTIONS USED BY: COMPENSATION
　　　　　　　　　　　　　　　HR PLANNING
　　　　　　　　　　　　　　　EMPLOYMENT
　　　　　　　　　　　　　　　INSURANCE
　　　　　　　　　　　　　　　PENSION
　　　　　　　　　　　　　　　ISP

PROGRAMS USING: PI01000
　　　　　　　　　PI02000
　　　　　　　　　PI03000
　　　　　　　　　PI04000
　　　　　　　　　PI05000

REPORTS USING:　　REPORT 124 (SALARY INCREASE TRACKING REPORT)
　　　　　　　　　REPORT 448 (GROUP INSURANCE AUDIT REPORT)
　　　　　　　　　REPORT 452 (SALARY REVIEW LISTING)
　　　　　　　　　PENSION REFERENCE LISTING

Sample data dictionary report. The sample data dictionary report for a human resources database provides helpful information such as the size of the data element, which programs and reports use it, and which group in the organization is the owner responsible for maintaining it. The report also shows some of the other names that the organization uses for this piece of data.

illustrates a sample data dictionary report that shows the size, format, meaning, and uses of a data element in a human resources database. A **data element** represents a field. Besides listing the standard name (AMT-PAY-BASE), the dictionary lists the names that reference this element in specific systems and identifies the individuals, business functions, programs, and reports that use this data element.

data element　A field.

By creating an inventory of the pieces of data contained in the database, the data dictionary serves as an important data management tool. For instance, business users could consult the dictionary to find out exactly what pieces of data are maintained for the sales or marketing function or even to determine all the information maintained by the entire enterprise. The dictionary could supply business users with the name, format, and specifications required to access data for reports. Technical staff could use the dictionary to determine what data elements and files must be changed if a program is changed.

Most data dictionaries are entirely passive; they simply report. More advanced types are active; changes in the dictionary can be automatically utilized by related programs. For instance, to change ZIP codes from five to nine digits, one could simply enter the change in the dictionary without having to modify and recompile all application programs using ZIP codes.

With a database program that permits users to share and integrate employee health statistics, the Epidemiology group of Texaco Inc. can track unusual patterns of employee disease.

In an ideal database environment, the data in the database are defined once and consistently, and used for all applications whose data reside in the database. Application programs (which are written using a combination of the data manipulation language of the DBMS and a conventional language such as COBOL) request data elements from the database. Data elements called for by the application programs are found and delivered by the DBMS. The programmer does not have to specify in detail how or where the data are to be found.

Logical and Physical Views of Data

Perhaps the greatest difference between a DBMS and traditional file organization is that the DBMS separates the logical and physical views of the data, relieving the programmer or end user from the task of understanding where and how the data are actually stored.

The database concept distinguishes between logical and physical views of data. The **logical view** presents data as they would be perceived by end users or business specialists, whereas the **physical view** shows how data are actually organized and structured on physical storage media.

Suppose, for example, that a professor of information systems wanted to know at the beginning of the semester how students performed in the prerequisite computer literacy course (Computer Literacy 101) and the students' current majors. Using a database supported by the registrar, the professor would need something similar to the report shown in Figure 8.10.

Ideally, for such a simple report, the professor could sit at an office terminal connected to the registrar's database and write a small application program using the data manipulation language to create this report. The professor first would develop the desired logical view of the data (Figure 8.10) for the application program. The DBMS would then assemble the requested data elements, which may reside in several different files and disk locations. For instance, the student major information may be located in a file called *Student*, whereas the grade data may be located in a file called *Course*. Wherever they are located, the DBMS would pull these pieces of information together and present them to the professor according to the logical view requested.

logical view A representation of data as they would appear to an application programmer or end user.

physical view The representation of data as they would be actually organized on physical storage media.

Student Name	ID No.	Major	Grade in Computer Literacy 101
Lind	468	Finance	A-
Pinckus	332	Marketing	B+
Williams	097	Economics	C+
Laughlin	765	Finance	A
Orlando	324	Statistics	B

FIGURE 8.10

The report required by the professor. The report requires data elements that may come from different files but can easily be pulled together with a database management system if the data are organized into a database.

```
SELECT Stud_name, Stud.stud_id, Major, Grade
FROM Student, Course
WHERE Stud.stud_id = Course.stud_id
AND Course_id = "CL101"
```

FIGURE 8.11

The query used by the professor. This example shows how Structured Query Language (SQL) commands could be used to deliver the data required by the professor. These commands join two files, the student file (Student) and the course file (Course), and extract the specified pieces of information on each student from the combined file.

The query using the data manipulation language constructed by the professor may resemble that shown in Figure 8.11. Several DBMSs working on both mainframes and PCs permit this kind of interactive report creation.

Advantages of Database Management Systems

The preceding discussion illustrates the advantages of a DBMS:

- Complexity of the organization's information system environment can be reduced by central management of data, access, utilization, and security.
- Data redundancy and inconsistency can be reduced by eliminating all isolated files in which the same data elements are repeated.
- Data confusion can be eliminated by providing central control of data creation and definitions.
- Program-data dependence can be reduced by separating the logical view of data from its physical arrangement.
- Program development and maintenance costs can be radically reduced.
- Flexibility of information systems can be greatly enhanced by permitting rapid and inexpensive ad hoc queries of very large pools of information.
- Access and availability of information can be increased.

Given these benefits of DBMS, one might expect all organizations to change immediately to a database form of information management. But it is not that easy, as we will see later.

8.3   DESIGNING DATABASES

There are alternative ways of organizing data and representing relationships among data in a database. Conventional DBMSs use one of three principal logical database models for keeping track of entities, attributes, and relationships. The three principal logical database models are hierarchical, network, and relational. Each logical model has certain processing advantages and certain business advantages.

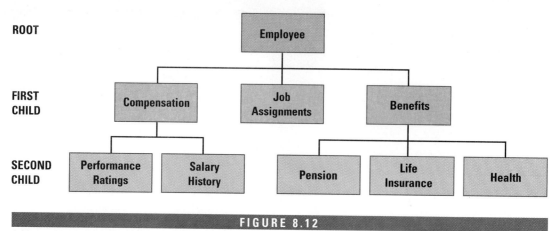

ROOT

FIRST CHILD

SECOND CHILD

FIGURE 8.12

A hierarchical database for a human resources system. The hierarchical database model looks like an organizational chart or a family tree. It has a single root segment (Employee) connected to lower-level segments (Compensation, Job Assignments, and Benefits). Each subordinate segment, in turn, may connect to other subordinate segments. Here, Compensation connects to Performance Ratings and Salary History. Benefits connects to Pension, Life Insurance, and Health Care. Each subordinate segment is the child of the segment directly above it.

Hierarchical Data Model

hierarchical data model One type of logical database model that organizes data in a treelike structure. A record is subdivided into segments that are connected to each other in one-to-many parent-child relationships.

The earliest DBMSs were hierarchical. The **hierarchical data model** presents data to users in a treelike structure. The most common hierarchical DBMS is IBM's IMS (Information Management System). Within each record, data elements are organized into pieces of records called *segments*. To the user, each record looks like an organization chart with one top-level segment called the *root*. An upper segment is connected logically to a lower segment in a parent-child relationship. A parent segment can have more than one child, but a child can have only one parent.

Figure 8.12 shows a hierarchical structure that might be used for a human resources database. The root segment is Employee, which contains basic employee information such as name, address, and identification number. Immediately below it are three child segments: Compensation (containing salary and promotion data), Job Assignments (containing data about job positions and departments), and Benefits (containing data about beneficiaries and various benefit options). The Compensation segment has two children below it: Performance Ratings (containing data about employees' job performance evaluations) and Salary History (containing historical data about employees' past salaries). Below the Benefits segment are child segments for Pension, Life Insurance, and Health, containing data about these various benefit plans.

pointer A special type of data element attached to a record that shows the absolute or relative address of another record.

Behind the logical view of data are a number of physical links and devices to tie the information together into a logical whole. In a hierarchical DBMS the data are physically linked to one another by a series of **pointers** that form chains of related data segments. Pointers are data elements attached to the ends of record segments on the disk directing the system to related records. In our example, the end of the Employee segment would contain a series of pointers to all Compensation, Job Assignments, and Benefits segments. In turn, at the end of the Compensation and Benefits segments are pointers to their respective child segments.

Network Data Model

network data model A logical database model that is useful for depicting many-to-many relationships.

The **network data model** is a variation of the hierarchical data model. Indeed, databases can be translated from hierarchical to network and vice versa to optimize processing speed and convenience. Whereas hierarchical structures depict one-to-many relationships, network structures depict data logically as many-to-many relationships. In other words, parents can have multiple children, and a child can have more than one parent.

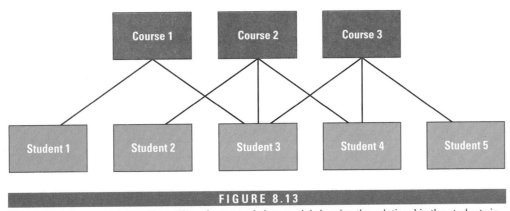

The network data model. This illustration of a network data model showing the relationship the students in a university have to the courses they take represents an example of logical many-to-many relationships. The network model reduces the redundancy of data representation through the increased use of pointers.

A typical many-to-many relationship in which a network DBMS excels in performance is the student-course relationship (see Figure 8.13). There are many courses in a university and many students. A student takes many courses and a course has many students. The data in Figure 8.13 could be structured hierarchically. But this could result in considerable redundancy and a slowed response to certain types of information queries; the same student would be listed on the disk for each class he or she was taking instead of only once. Network structures reduce redundancy and, in certain situations (when many-to-many relationships are involved), respond more quickly. However, there is a price for this reduction in redundancy and increased speed: The number of pointers in network structures rapidly increases, making maintenance and operation potentially more complicated.

Relational Data Model

The **relational data model,** the most recent of these three database models, overcomes some of the limitations of the other two models. The relational model represents all data in the database as simple two-dimensional tables called *relations*. The tables appear similar to flat files, but the information in more than one file can be easily extracted and combined. Sometimes the tables are referred to as files.

Figure 8.14 shows a supplier table, a part table, and an order table. In each table the rows are unique records and the columns are fields. Another term for a row or record in a relation is a **tuple.** Often a user needs information from a number of relations to produce a report. Here is the strength of the relational model: It can relate data in any one file or table to data in another file or table *as long as both tables share a common data element.*

To demonstrate, suppose we wanted to find in the relational database in Figure 8.14 the names and addresses of suppliers who could provide us with part number 137 or part number 152. We would need information from two tables: the supplier table and the part table. Note that these two files have a shared data element: SUPPLIER-NUMBER.

In a relational database, three basic operations are used to develop useful sets of data: select, project, and join. The *select* operation creates a subset consisting of all records in the file that meet stated criteria. *Select* creates, in other words, a subset of rows that meet certain criteria. In our example, we want to select records (rows) from the part table where the part number equals 137 or 152. The *join* operation combines relational tables to provide the user with more information than is available in individual tables. In our example we want to join the now shortened part table (only parts numbered 137 or 152 will be presented) and the supplier table into a single new result table.

relational data model A type of logical database model that treats data as if they were stored in two-dimensional tables. It can relate data stored in one table to data in another as long as the two tables share a common data element.

tuple A row or record in a relational database.

Table (Relation)

Columns (Fields)

ORDER

ORDER-NUMBER	ORDER-DATE	DELIVERY-DATE	PART-NUMBER	PART-AMOUNT	ORDER-TOTAL
1634	02/02/98	02/22/98	152	2	144.50
1635	02/12/98	02/29/98	137	3	79.70
1636	02/13/98	03/01/98	145	1	24.30

Rows (Records, Tuples)

PART

PART-NUMBER	PART-DESCRIPTION	UNIT-PRICE	SUPPLIER-NUMBER
137	Door latch	26.25	4058
145	Door handle	22.50	2038
152	Compressor	70.00	1125

SUPPLIER

SUPPLIER-NUMBER	SUPPLIER-NAME	SUPPLIER-ADDRESS
1125	CBM Inc.	44 Winslow, Gary IN 44950
2038	Ace Inc.	Rte. 101, Essex NJ 07763
4058	Bryant Corp.	51 Elm, Rochester NY 11349

FIGURE 8.14

The relational data model. Each table is a *relation* and each row or record is a *tuple.* Each column corresponds to a field. These relations can easily be combined and extracted to access data and produce reports, provided that any two share a common data element. In this example, the ORDER file shares the data element "PART-NUMBER" with the PART file. The PART and SUPPLIER files share the data element "SUPPLIER-NUMBER."

The *project* operation creates a subset consisting of columns in a table, permitting the user to create new tables that contain only the information required. In our example, we want to extract from the new result table only the following columns: PART-NUMBER, SUPPLIER-NUMBER, SUPPLIER-NAME, and SUPPLIER-ADDRESS.

Leading mainframe relational database management systems include IBM's DB2 and Oracle from the Oracle Corporation. Microsoft Access is a PC relational database management system.

Advantages and Disadvantages of the Three Database Models

The principal advantage of the hierarchical and network database models is processing efficiency. For instance, a hierarchical model is appropriate for airline reservation transaction processing systems, which must handle millions of structured routine requests each day for reservation information.

Hierarchical and network structures have several disadvantages. All the access paths, directories, and indices must be specified in advance. Once specified, they are not easily changed without a major programming effort. Therefore, these designs have low flexibility. For instance, if you queried the human resources database illustrated in Figure 8.12 to find out the names of the employees with the job title of administrative assistant, you would discover that there is no way that the system can find the answer in a reasonable amount of time. This path through the data was not specified in advance.

Table 8.1	Comparison of Database Alternatives			
Type of Database	Processing Efficiency	Flexibility	End-User Friendliness	Programming Complexity
Hierarchical	High	Low	Low	High
Network	Medium–high	Low–medium	Low–moderate	High
Relational	Lower but improving	High	High	Low

Both hierarchical and network systems are programming intensive, time consuming, difficult to install, and difficult to remedy if design errors occur. They do not support ad hoc, English language–like inquiries for information.

The strengths of relational DBMS are great flexibility in regard to ad hoc queries, power to combine information from different sources, simplicity of design and maintenance, and the ability to add new data and records without disturbing existing programs and applications. However, these systems are somewhat slower because they typically require many accesses to the data stored on disk to carry out the select, join, and project commands. Selecting one part number from among millions, one record at a time, can take a long time. Of course the database can be indexed and tuned to speed up prespecified queries. Relational systems do not have the large number of pointers carried by hierarchical systems.

Large relational databases may be designed to have some data redundancy to make retrieval of data more efficient. The same data element may be stored in multiple tables. Updating redundant data elements is not automatic in many relational DBMSs. For example, changing the employee status field in one table will not automatically change it in all tables. Special arrangements are required to ensure that all copies of the same data element are updated together.

Hierarchical databases remain the workhorse for intensive high-volume transaction processing. Banks, insurance companies, and other high-volume users continue to use reliable hierarchical databases such as IBM's IMS, developed in 1969. Many organizations have converted to DB2, IBM's relational DBMS for new applications, while retaining IMS for traditional transaction processing. For example, Dallas-based Texas Instruments depends on IMS for its heavy processing requirements. Texas Instruments bases its complete operations, including inventory, accounting, and manufacturing, on IMS. The firm has built up a huge library of IMS applications over 20 years, and a complete conversion to DB2 would take 10 more years. As relational products acquire more muscle, firms will shift away completely from hierarchical DBMS, but this will happen over a long period of time. Table 8.1 compares the characteristics of the different database models.

Creating a Database

To create a database, one must go through two design exercises: a conceptual design and a physical design. The conceptual design of a database is an abstract model of the database from a business perspective, whereas the physical design shows how the database is actually arranged on direct access storage devices. Physical database design is performed by database specialists, whereas logical design requires a detailed description of the business information needs of actual end users of the database. Ideally, database design will be part of an overall organizational data planning effort (see Chapter 11).

The conceptual database design describes how the data elements in the database are to be grouped. The design process identifies relationships among data elements and the most efficient way of grouping data elements together to meet information

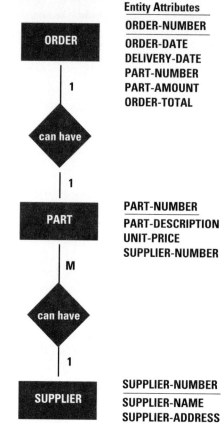

FIGURE 8.15

An entity-relationship diagram. This diagram shows the relationships between the entities OR-DER, PART, and SUPPLIER that were used to develop the relational database illustrated in Figure 8.14.

Entity Attributes

ORDER-NUMBER

ORDER-DATE
DELIVERY-DATE
PART-NUMBER
PART-AMOUNT
ORDER-TOTAL

PART-NUMBER
PART-DESCRIPTION
UNIT-PRICE
SUPPLIER-NUMBER

SUPPLIER-NUMBER
SUPPLIER-NAME
SUPPLIER-ADDRESS

entity-relationship diagram A methodology for documenting databases illustrating the relationship between various entities in the database.

normalization The process of creating small stable data structures from complex groups of data when designing a relational database.

requirements. The process also identifies redundant data elements and the groupings of data elements required for specific application programs. Groups of data are organized, refined, and streamlined until an overall logical view of the relationships among all the data elements in the database emerges.

Database designers document the conceptual data model with an **entity-relationship diagram**, illustrated in Figure 8.15. The boxes represent entities and the diamonds represent relationships. The *1* or *M* on either side of the diamond represents the relationship among entities as either one-to-one, one-to-many, or many-to-many. Figure 8.15 shows that the entity ORDER can have only one PART and a PART can only have one SUPPLIER. Many parts can be provided by the same supplier. The attributes for each entity are listed next to the entity and the key field is underlined.

To use a relational database model effectively, complex groupings of data must be streamlined to eliminate redundant data elements and awkward many-to-many relationships. Figures 8.16 and 8.17 illustrate this process. In the particular business modeled here, an order can have more than one part but each part is provided by only one supplier. If we had built a relation called ORDER with all the fields included here, we would have to repeat the name, description, and price of each part on the order and name and address of each part vendor. This relation contains what are called *repeating groups* because there can be many parts and suppliers for each order and it actually describes multiple entities—parts and suppliers as well as orders. A more efficient way to arrange the data is to break down ORDER into smaller relations, each of which describes a single entity. The process of creating small, stable data structures from complex groups of data is called **normalization.** If we go step by step and normalize the relation ORDER, we emerge with the relations illustrated in Figure 8.17.

If a database has been carefully considered, with a clear understanding of business information needs and usage, the database model will most likely be in some

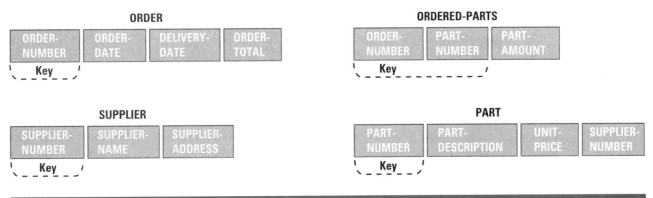

ORDER

ORDER-NUMBER	PART-AMOUNT	PART-NUMBER	PART-DESCRIPTION	UNIT-PRICE	SUPPLIER-NUMBER	SUPPLIER-NAME	SUPPLIER-ADDRESS	ORDER-DATE	DELIVERY-DATE	ORDER-TOTAL

FIGURE 8.16

An unnormalized relation for ORDER. In an unnormalized relation there are repeating groups. For example, there can be many parts and suppliers for each order. There is only a one-to-one correspondence between ORDER-NUMBER and ORDER-DATE, ORDER-TOTAL, and DELIVERY-DATE.

ORDER

ORDER-NUMBER	ORDER-DATE	DELIVERY-DATE	ORDER-TOTAL

Key

ORDERED-PARTS

ORDER-NUMBER	PART-NUMBER	PART-AMOUNT

Key

SUPPLIER

SUPPLIER-NUMBER	SUPPLIER-NAME	SUPPLIER-ADDRESS

Key

PART

PART-NUMBER	PART-DESCRIPTION	UNIT-PRICE	SUPPLIER-NUMBER

Key

FIGURE 8.17

A normalized relation for ORDER. After normalization, the original relation ORDER has been broken down into four smaller relations. The relation ORDER is left with only three attributes and the relation ORDERED-PARTS has a combined, or concatenated, key consisting of ORDER-NUMBER and PART-NUMBER.

normalized form. Many real-world databases are not fully normalized because this may not be the most sensible way to meet business information requirements. Note that the relational database illustrated in Figure 8.14 is not fully normalized because there could be more than one part for each order. The designers chose to not use the four relations described in Figure 8.17 because this particular business has a business rule specifying that a separate order must be placed for each part. The designers might have felt that there was no business need for maintaining four different tables.

8.4 DATABASE TRENDS

Recent database trends include the growth of distributed databases and the emergence of object-oriented and hypermedia databases.

Distributed Processing and Distributed Databases

Information processing became more distributed with the growth of powerful telecommunications networks and the decline in computer hardware costs. Instead of relying on a single centralized mainframe computer to provide service to remote terminals, organizations began to install minicomputers and PCs at remote sites. These distributed processors directly serve local and regional branch offices and factories and are generally linked together in networks. The dispersion and use of computers among multiple geographically or functionally separate locations so that local computers handle local processing needs is called **distributed processing.** Chapters 9 and 10 will describe the various network arrangements for distributed processing.

It is only a short step from distributed processing to distributed databases. Although early distributed systems worked with a single centralized database, over time the smaller local systems also began to store local databases. It soon became obvious that the central database could be entirely distributed to local processors as

distributed processing The distribution of computer processing among multiple geographically or functionally separate locations linked by a communications network.

long as some mechanism existed to provide proper updating, integrity of data, sharing of data, and central administrative controls.

A **distributed database** is one that is stored in more than one physical location. Parts of the database are stored physically in one location and other parts are stored and maintained in other locations. There are two main ways of distributing a database (see Figure 8.18). The central database (see Figure 8.18a) can be partitioned so that each remote processor has the necessary data on customers to serve its local area. Changes in local files can be justified with the central database on a batch basis, often at night. Another strategy is to replicate the central database (Figure 8.18b) at all remote locations. For example, Lufthansa Airlines replaced its centralized mainframe database with a replicated database to make information more immediately available to flight dispatchers. Any change made to Lufthansa's Frankfort DBMS is automatically replicated in New York and Hong Kong. This strategy also requires updating of the central database on off hours.

Still another possibility—one used by very large databases such as the FBI's National Crime Information Center—is to maintain only a central name index and to store complete records locally (Figure 8.18c). A query to the central name index identifies a location where the full record can be found. Here there is no central database and no updating costs. National Westminster Bank in London uses a similar approach to maintain its customer account information in two massive fragmented DB2 databases. Specially developed software allows each of its 22,000 users to access the data on either database with a global catalogue of where the data are stored. Another variation is an ask-the-network scheme (Figure 8.18d). There is no central index of names in this design. Instead, all remote processors are polled to find a complete record. The complete record is then transferred to whatever processor requests it (Laudon, 1986).

Both distributed processing and distributed databases have benefits and drawbacks. Distributed systems reduce the vulnerability of a single, massive central site. They permit increases in systems' power by purchasing smaller, less expensive minicomputers. Finally, they increase service and responsiveness to local users. Distributed systems, however, are dependent on high-quality telecommunications lines, which themselves are vulnerable. Moreover, local databases can sometimes depart from central data standards and definitions, and pose security problems by widely distributing access to sensitive data. The economies of distribution can be lost when remote sites buy more computing power than they need.

Despite these drawbacks, distributed processing is growing rapidly. With the advent of PCs and powerful telecommunications systems, more and more information services will be distributed. For large national organizations working in several regions, the question is no longer whether to distribute but how to distribute in such a way as to minimize costs and improve responsiveness without sacrificing data and system integrity.

Object-Oriented and Hypermedia Databases

Conventional database management systems were designed for homogeneous data that can be easily structured into predefined data fields and records. But many applications today and in the future will require databases that can store and retrieve not only structured numbers and characters but also drawings, images, photographs, voice, and full-motion video (see Figure 8.19). Conventional DBMS are not well suited to handling graphics-based or multimedia applications. For instance, design data in a CAD database consist of complex relationships among many types of data. Manipulating these kinds of data in a relational system requires extensive programming to translate these complex data structures into tables and rows. An **object-oriented database,** on the other hand, stores the data and procedures as objects that can be automatically retrieved and shared. The Window on Technology describes how firms can benefit from these new capabilities.

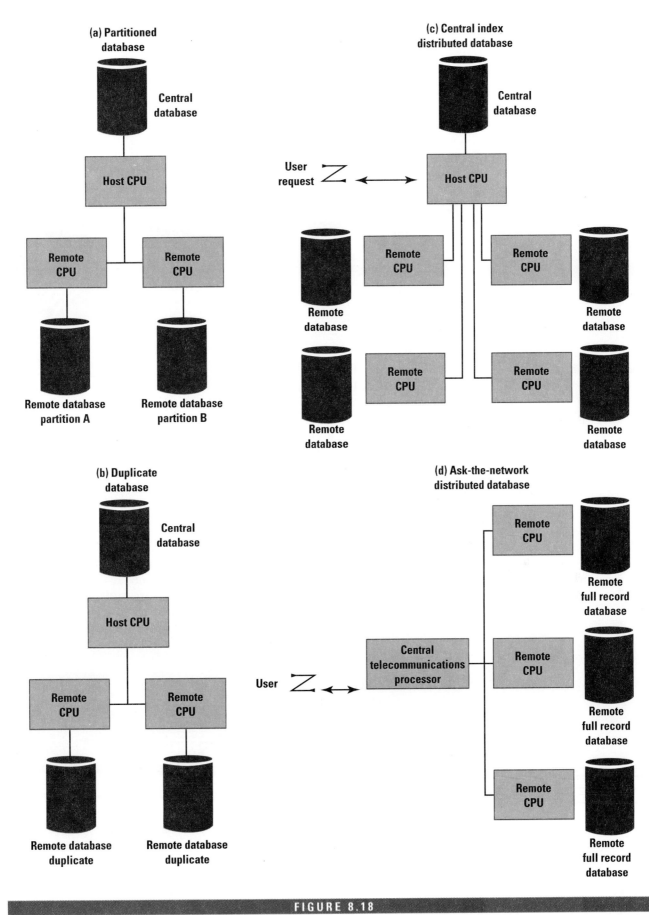

(a) Partitioned database

Central database

Host CPU

Remote CPU — Remote CPU

Remote database partition A

Remote database partition B

(b) Duplicate database

Central database

Host CPU

Remote CPU — Remote CPU

Remote database duplicate

Remote database duplicate

(c) Central index distributed database

Central database

User request — Host CPU

Remote CPU

Remote database

Remote CPU

Remote database

Remote CPU

Remote database

Remote CPU

Remote database

(d) Ask-the-network distributed database

User — Central telecommunications processor

Remote CPU

Remote full record database

Remote CPU

Remote full record database

Remote CPU

Remote full record database

FIGURE 8.18

Distributed databases. There are alternative ways of distributing a database. The central database can be partitioned (a) so that each remote processor has the necessary data to serve its own local needs. The central database can also be duplicated (b) at all remote locations. In the central index distributed database (c) complete records are stored locally and can be located using a central name index. In an ask-the-network distributed database (d), the network polls its remote processors to locate a record and transfers the complete record to whatever processor requests it.

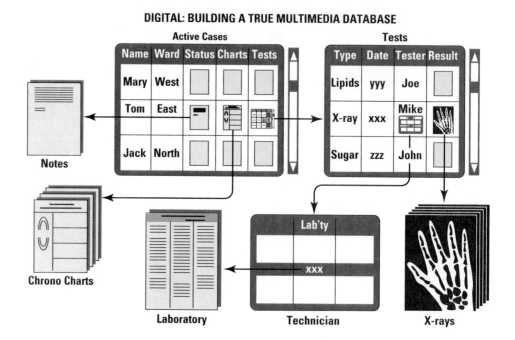

FIGURE 8.19

An object-oriented multimedia database. Medical data on patients in a hospital might likely be stored in a multimedia database such as this. Doctors could access patient files including vital medical images to generate the reports and derive the information they need to deliver quality health care quickly.

Reprinted by permission of Digital Equipment Corporation, Maynard, MA.

hypermedia database An approach to data management that organizes data as a network of nodes linked in any pattern established by the user; the nodes can contain text, graphics, sound, full-motion video, or executable programs.

The **hypermedia database** approach to information management transcends some of the limitations of traditional database methods by storing chunks of information in the form of nodes connected by links established by the user (see Figure 8.20). The nodes can contain text, graphics, sound, full-motion video, or executable computer programs. Searching for information does not have to follow a predetermined organization scheme. Instead, one can branch instantly to related information in any kind of relationship established by the author. The relationship between records is less structured than in a traditional DBMS. In most systems each node can be displayed on a screen. The screen also displays the links between the node depicted and other nodes in the database.

While object-oriented and hypermedia databases can store more complex types of information than relational DBMS, they are relatively slow compared with relational DBMS for processing large numbers of transactions. *Hybrid* object-relational systems are now available to provide capabilities of both object-oriented and relational DBMS. A hybrid approach can be accomplished in three different ways: by using tools that offer object-oriented access to relational DBMS, by using object-oriented extensions to existing relational DBMS, or by using a hybrid object-relational database management system.

FIGURE 8.20

Hypermedia. In a hypermedia database, the user can choose his or her own path to move from node to node. Each node can contain text, graphics, sound, full-motion video, or executable programs.

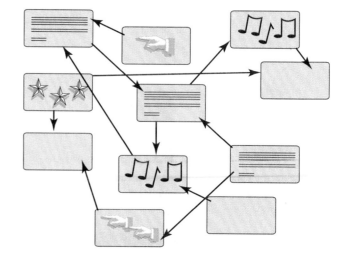

Air France Flies with Object Technology

Can an object database help Air France increase its revenue by 1 percent? Management at the Paris-based airline thinks so, and so does AMR Corporation (parent of American Airlines). With a current revenue of about $7 billion, a 1 percent increase in Air France's revenue would mean an extra $70 million per year.

The problem the airline faces is that too many of its seats are filled by lower-paying customers, while higher-paying customers are often unable to find seats. The current mainframe-based reservation system enables the reservation personnel to track individual flight segments only, such as the nonstop Paris–to–New York segment. A customer whose trip originates elsewhere might be paying more money to fly and might need to connect to that same flight. The current system cannot check that segment in conjunction with flights originating elsewhere, and so that higher-paying customer will not be able to fill a seat on that flight. The seat instead may be filled by lower-paying customers whose flight originates in Paris. If the airline could fill the same seat instead with a customer who is paying more for the ticket, it will increase Air France's revenue without any increase in the number of passengers. To address this problem, Air France is purchasing a new system using object database technology.

Like other airlines, Air France has depended on a mainframe to handle all reservations and to process all tickets. Air France will continue to keep its heavy transaction processing for reservations and tickets on its Unisys mainframe, but it will use a new system for revenue and yield management applications. According to Air France's Pierre Gandois, the manager of this project, the new system will be tracking "a combination of flights rather than looking at each flight as a single unit." In that way it will become easier for reservation clerks to sell seats to customers who purchase higher-priced tickets but are connecting from another flight.

This new system runs on a Unix server and an object-oriented database. It will perform yield management to determine the best mix of full-fare and discount seat prices for a given flight that produces the highest revenue. The database sets parameters for ticket availability and discounts, automatically opening or closing discount offers as business conditions change. This will help the airline sell seats on a continuation flight for higher prices. The server will receive nightly updates on ticket sales from the mainframe. The system on the server will approve or deny bookings as flights are filling up. Once a request for a booking is approved by the new system, the mainframe will process the ticket as in the past. Thus the new system would increase revenue, not by increasing the passenger load but by filling some of the seats it is already filling with passengers who are paying higher prices for their tickets.

The reservation application was written and is being marketed by Sabre Decision Technologies, the software development company of AMR Corporation. Versant Object Technology Corporation supplied the object-oriented database. Air France's system represents one of the first companies outside the financial and telecommunications industries to use an object-oriented database for a core transaction processing application.

The new system will control about 20 percent of the airline's 500 daily flights. Sabre is also trying to market the system to other airlines, but they are having trouble. According to Vic Nilson, Sabre's Air France project director, managements at other airlines "are scared to go into an object database" because they believe the technology is too new. Many feel it is still unproved for heavy transaction processing applications such as flight reservations.

To Think About: *Analyze Air France using the competitive forces and value chain models. Will the use of the object database reservation system enhance its competitive position? Why or why not? What management, organization, and technology issues did the new object-oriented system address?*

Source: Craig Stedman, "Object Project Flies," *Computerworld,* February 10, 1997.

Multidimensional Data Analysis

Sometimes managers need to analyze data in ways that cannot be represented by traditional database models. For example, a company selling four different products—apples, bananas, oranges, and pears—in three regions, East, West, and Central—might want to know actual sales by product for each region and might also want to compare them with projected sales. This analysis requires a multidimensional view of data.

To provide this type of information, organizations can use either a specialized multidimensional database or a tool that creates multidimensional views of data in relational databases. Multidimensional analysis enables users to view the same data

FIGURE 8.21

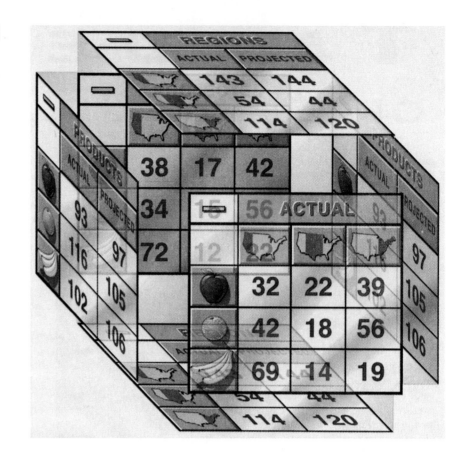

Only one view can be seen at a time on a two-dimensional computer monitor, in this case the original view, or product versus region. But if you rotate the cube 90 degrees horizontally, the face showing will be product versus actual and projected sales. If you rotate the cube 90 degrees vertically, you're looking at region versus actual and projected sales. Rotate 180 degrees from the original view, and you have projected sales, product versus region. And views can be nested within views to build complex, yet useful data matrices.

Source: Mike Ricciuti, "Winning the Competitive Game," Datamation, February 15, 1994. Reprinted with permission from Datamation copyright 1997 Cahners Publishing Company, a division of Reed Elsevier, Inc. All rights reserved.

on-line analytical processing (OLAP) Capability for manipulating and analyzing large volumes of data from multiple perspectives.

in different ways using multiple dimensions. Each aspect of information—product, pricing, cost, region, or time period—represents a different dimension. So a product manager could use a multidimensional data analysis tool to learn how many pears were sold in the East in June, how that compares with the previous month and the previous June, and how it compares with the sales forecast. Another term for multidimensional data analysis is **on-line analytical processing (OLAP)**.

Figure 8.21 shows a multidimensional model that could be created to represent products, regions, actual sales, and projected sales. A matrix of actual sales can be stacked on top of a matrix of projected sales to form a cube with six faces. If you rotate the cube 90 degrees horizontally, the face showing will be product versus actual and projected sales. If you rotate the cube 90 degrees vertically, you can see region versus actual and projected sales. If you rotate 180 degrees from the original view, you can see projected sales and product versus region. Cubes can be nested within cubes to build complex views of data.

Data Warehousing

Decision makers need concise, reliable information about current operations, trends, and changes. What has been immediately available at most firms is current data only (historical data was available through special IS reports that took a long time to produce). Data are often fragmented in separate operational systems such as sales or payroll so that different managers make decisions from incomplete knowledge bases. Data warehousing addresses this problem by integrating key operational data from around the company in a form that is consistent, reliable, and easily available for reporting.

What Is a Data Warehouse?

data warehouse A database, with reporting and query tools, that stores current and historical data extracted from various operational systems and consolidated for management reporting and analysis.

A **data warehouse** is a database, with tools, that stores current and historical data of potential interest to managers throughout the company. The data originate in many

Table 8.2   Comparison of Data Warehouse and Operational Data

Operational Data	Data Warehouse Data
Isolated data stored in and used by isolated legacy systems	Enterprise-wide integrated data collected from legacy systems
Contains current operational data	Contains recent data as well as historical data
Data are stored on multiple platforms	Data are stored on a single platform
Individual fields (such as customer number) may be inconsistent across the enterprise	A single, agreed-upon definition exists for every field stored in the system
Data are organized from an operational or functional view—such as sales, production, purchasing, payroll, order processing	Data are organized around major business informational subjects—such as customer or product
Data are volatile to support operations within a company	Data are stabilized for decision making

core operational systems and are copied into the data warehouse database as often as needed—hourly, daily, weekly, monthly. The data are standardized and consolidated so that they can be used across the enterprise for management analysis and decision making. The data are available for anyone to access as needed but cannot be altered. A data warehouse system includes a range of ad hoc and standardized query tools, analytical tools, and graphical reporting facilities. These systems can perform high-level analysis of patterns or trends, but they can also drill into more detail where needed. Table 8.2 shows how data warehouse data differ from operational data.

Building a Data Warehouse

Building a data warehouse can be a very difficult process because of the organizational obstacles to enterprise-wide information management that we have already described. Most successful data warehousing projects include the following steps:

1. Defining the mission and business objectives for the data warehouse at a high level of the organization, and mapping those objectives to the mission and objectives of the whole organization

2. Identifying data from all operational databases required for the data warehouse

3. Defining the data items by standardizing data names and meanings across the company. It is usually too big a job to make these data items consistent in existing operational systems. Instead, the project manager needs to identify any problems and eliminate inconsistencies as data are copied from the legacy systems into the data warehouse.

4. Designing the database

5. Developing a policy for archiving older data so storage space does not become too large and so queries do not become too slow

6. Extracting the production data, cleaning them up, and loading them into the warehouse databases

Benefits of a Data Warehouse

Data warehouses not only offer improved information, but they make it easy for decision makers to obtain it. They even include the ability to model and remodel the data. These systems also enable decision makers to access data as often as they need without affecting the processing performance of the operational systems.

The Environmental Protection Agency (EPA) created a Web site where employees and the general public can access its Envirofacts data warehouse. More and more organizations are using the World Wide Web to provide an interface to internal databases.

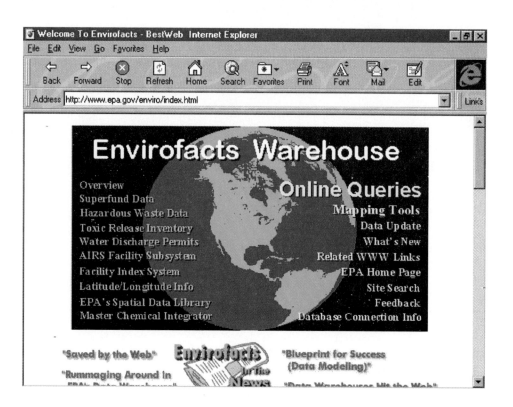

For example, financial controllers at Philips Electronics, Sunnyvale, California, were wasting enormous amounts of time tracking product information from around the world. The firm's data warehouse helped it integrate sales, returns, and marketing expense data.

Victoria's Secret Stores had been spending too much time trying to locate information and not enough time analyzing it. Through data warehousing, the lingerie chain learned that its system of allocating merchandise to its 678 shops, based on a mathematical store average, was wrong. For example, an average store sells equal pieces of black and ivory lingerie, but Miami-area consumers buy ivory designs by a margin of 10 to 1. Geographic demand patterns also showed that some stores did not need to discount merchandise. Data warehousing gave this firm a more precise understanding of customer behavior (Goldberg and Vijayan, 1996).

The Window on Management explores another promising database trend, the linking of internal databases to the Internet. The interactive features of the Internet's World Wide Web can provide an easy-to-use user interface to these databases for inside and outside the organization.

8.5 MANAGEMENT REQUIREMENTS FOR DATABASE SYSTEMS

Much more is required for the development of database systems than simply selecting a logical database model. Indeed, this selection may be among the last decisions. The database is an organizational discipline, a method, rather than a tool or technology. It requires organizational and conceptual change.

Without management support and understanding, database efforts fail. The critical elements in a database environment are (1) data administration, (2) data planning and modeling methodology, (3) database technology and management, and (4) users. This environment is depicted in Figure 8.22 and will now be described.

The EPA Cleans Up Its Own Mess Through the Internet

The Environmental Protection Agency (EPA) is charged with monitoring and cleaning up the environment. Nevertheless, it has had a longstanding mess of its own that needed cleaning up. The EPA's management recently decided to do just that. Part of its problem arose from the fact that over the years the EPA had built a series of databases in response to laws passed by Congress. Separate databases were established to support, among other things: the Clean Air Act; permits for waste water discharge; the Superfund Authorization Bill for cleaning up hazardous waste sites; the classification of more than 300 chemicals as toxic that have been or could be released into the environment; the issuing of more than 450,000 site permits for hazardous cleanup activities; record keeping on the more than 675,000 facilities regulated or monitored by the EPA; and an index of the chemical data in the various databases. These databases were so isolated from each other that they used five different database management systems, including Oracle and IBM's DB2.

The other EPA problem is the popularity of the data combined with their slow, expensive method of making the data available. Many thousands of people, such as EPA employees, chemical industry employees, environmental organizations, and residents of specific local areas, want some part of the information that is stored in those databases. However, because the data are not integrated, they have been extremely difficult to access. Those who wanted access, including most EPA employees, had to call an EPA information systems specialist who then had to retrieve the data for them, a very slow, time-consuming, and expensive operation.

Management has found a better way, relying on more advanced information technology, including the Internet. The first issue, the need to integrate the data, was addressed through a data warehouse known as Envirofacts. While the independent databases remain, an integrated data warehouse database was completed in 1995. It combines data from five of the EPA databases, with more databases to be added soon. The data stored in Envirofacts are automatically updated monthly from the five isolated databases. EPA employees gain access through a proprietary EPA interface called Gateway. Using the Gateway and Envirofacts, EPA employees are able to quickly access most of the data they need. The Gateway interface was installed on many of the EPA's 24,000 desktop PCs. They access Envirofacts through an EPA network.

Nonemployees were also able to access the data directly through a dial-up line. The new system not only made it quicker for many people to procure the data they needed, but it also greatly reduced the workload for the EPA's information systems staff, freeing them for more productive work than simply retrieving data.

Nonetheless, problems remained. Support of the Gateway, installed on thousands of machines, required a great deal of information systems staff time. Moreover, for those who were not EPA employees, access through a dial-up line was slow, difficult, and costly. So management has now turned to the Internet to allow access to anyone. The Internet offers several advantages. First, no special interface, such as the Gateway, is needed. Instead, all anyone needs is the popular Netscape Navigator Web browser software that many people use for all their Internet access. Moreover, the public no longer needs to gain access through an EPA dial-up line. Instead, they use their own Internet access providers. EPA employees have also been given access in this manner. Eventually, the EPA is going to phase out the use of the Gateway. However, that will be done slowly so that employees who prefer to access that way can continue to do so. Ultimately the Gateway will be retired totally and all access will be achieved through the Internet.

In addition to adding more databases to Envirofacts, the EPA has also launched another project to enhance access to the data people need. The agency will be adding to its Web site hot links to other government agencies and universities that also make environmental data available to the public. In that way, both the EPA and other organizations of all kinds will have quick and easy access to the data they need to help clean up and protect our environment.

> **To Think About:** *What are the management benefits of Envirofacts? of making Envirofacts available through the Internet? What do you think might be management drawbacks?*

Source: Richard Adhikari, "Saved by the Web," *Information Week*, March 17, 1997.

Data Administration

Database systems require that the organization recognize the strategic role of information and begin actively to manage and plan for information as a corporate resource. This means that the organization must develop a **data administration** function with the power to define information requirements for the entire company and with direct access to senior management. The chief information officer (CIO) or vice president of information becomes the primary advocate in the organization for database systems.

data administration A special organizational function for managing the organization's data resources, concerned with information policy, data planning, maintenance of data dictionaries, and data quality standards.

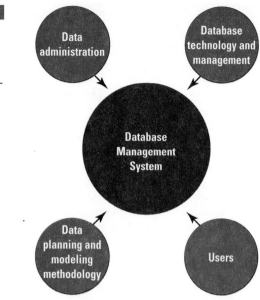

FIGURE 8.22

Key organizational elements in the database environment. For a database management system to flourish in any organization, data administration functions and data planning and modeling methodologies must be coordinated with database technology and management. Resources must be devoted to train end users to use databases properly.

Data administration is responsible for the specific policies and procedures through which data can be managed as an organizational resource. These responsibilities include developing information policy, planning for data, overseeing logical database design and data dictionary development, and monitoring the usage of data by information system specialists and end-user groups.

The fundamental principle of data administration is that all data are the property of the organization as a whole. Data cannot belong exclusively to any one business area or organizational unit. All data are to be made available to any group that requires them to fulfill its mission. An organization needs to formulate an **information policy** that specifies its rules for sharing, disseminating, acquiring, standardizing, classifying, and inventorying information throughout the organization. Information policy lays out specific procedures and accountabilities, specifying which organizational units share information; where information can be distributed; and who has responsibility for updating and maintaining the information. Although data administration is a very important organizational function, it has proved very challenging to implement.

information policy Formal rules governing the maintenance, distribution, and use of information in an organization.

Data Planning and Modeling Methodology

Because the organizational interests served by the DBMS are much broader than those in the traditional file environment, the organization requires enterprise-wide planning for data. Enterprise analysis, which addresses the information requirements of the entire organization (as opposed to the requirements of individual applications), is needed to develop databases. The purpose of enterprise analysis is to identify the key entities, attributes, and relationships that constitute the organization's data. These techniques are described in greater detail in Chapter 11.

Database Technology and Management

Databases require new software and a new staff specially trained in DBMS techniques as well as new management structures. Most corporations develop a database design and management group within the corporate information system division that is responsible for the more technical and operational aspects of managing data. The functions it performs are called **database administration**. This group does the following:

database administration Refers to the more technical and operational aspects of managing data, including physical database design and maintenance.

- Defines and organizes database structure and content
- Develops security procedures to safeguard the database

Linking Databases to the Web: A New Threat to Privacy?

Modern database technology allows organizations to combine many pieces of information about you, which are stored on computers. These organizations probably know more about you than you would like. You generate computer information about yourself in many ways: charge card purchases, video rentals, telephone calls, magazine subscriptions, mail-order purchases, court and police records, travel tickets, and so on. Put together and mined properly, this information could create a detailed "data image," revealing your driving habits, your hobbies, your political interests, and your tastes.

Companies that mine their data often sell it to marketing companies so that it can be used by other firms to target their marketing more efficiently. For example, if you buy "upscale" merchandise from one catalogue, the catalogue company might sell your name to another catalogue mail-order company.

The World Wide Web has opened new avenues for sharing and selling personal data. Organizations can link their internal databases or data warehouses to the World Wide Web, where they can be accessed by their business partners. Outsiders can query and analyze the data stored in the databases. A considerable amount of personal information can be obtained this way, especially when data about individuals from one company are combined with data from another.

MicroStrategy, Inc. in Vienna, Virginia, which sells on-line analytical processing (OLAP) software to work with relational DBMS, is promoting the idea of "consumerizing" data warehouses by making them accessible via the Web. Outsiders would be allowed to query and analyze warehoused data. Michael Saylor, MicroStrategy's CEO, believes that corporations will want to enrich their Web-accessible warehouses with demographic data on U.S. households including names, addresses, phone numbers, approximate incomes, and "psychographic" data such as hobbies and interests. MicroStrategy is working on an agreement with Acxiom Corporation in Conway, Arkansas, which accumulates data on 95 percent of U.S. households, to "content-enable" its decision-support software so that clients can combine their internal data with Acxiom's demographic data. According to Saylor, thousands of organizations would be interested in such information. Corporations could charge up to $100 per person per month to let others analyze warehouse data.

Source Informatics in Phoenix plans to use MicroStrategy's DSS Web to broaden its customer base by distributing data via the Web to thousands of pharmaceutical sales representatives. It has a database of pharmaceutical information gathered from pharmacies around the United States.

Some companies have found that marketing personal data has backfired. Word that the information service provider Lexis-Nexis was making critical information such as Social Security numbers and maiden names available for sale spread quickly by e-mail. The company's Dayton, Ohio, headquarters received a deluge of communications from individuals who requested that their names be deleted from Lexis-Nexis' P-Trak service. When the furor died down, it was revealed that the service only provided Social Security numbers for a very short time. The remainder of the data provided through P-Trak (name, address, two prior addresses, maiden name, birth date, and telephone numbers) are header information from credit reports, and are not protected by the Fair Credit Reporting Act. (The Fair Credit Reporting Act restricts the use of consumer credit data. See Chapter 5.) Furthermore, Lexis-Nexis screens its clients before allowing them to use P-Trak.

In response to the Lexis-Nexis incident, the Federal Trade Commission is proposing tighter rules on how personal data are used. The FTC has recommended extending the confidentiality guidelines of the Fair Credit Reporting Act to cover items such as Social Security numbers, birth dates, former addresses, and mothers' maiden names. The Senate even designated a subcommittee to explore the dangers of circulating personal data publicly. The subcommittee recognizes that a great deal of data has already reached the public arena, but it wants to investigate whether the data's presence on the Internet makes the problem much more severe because its information is easy to find and easy to access.

To Think About: *Should the Web be used to allow outsiders to view internal corporate data on people? Why or why not? What management, organization, and technology factors need to be addressed in using the Web for accessing internal corporate databases?*

Source: John Foley and Bruce Caldwell, "Dangerous Data," *Information Week*, September 30, 1996.

- Develops database documentation
- Maintains the database management software

In close cooperation with users, the design group establishes the physical database, the logical relations among elements, and the access rules and procedures.

Users

A database serves a wider community of users than traditional systems. Relational systems with fourth-generation query languages permit employees who are not computer specialists to access large databases. In addition, users include trained computer specialists. To optimize access for nonspecialists, more resources must be devoted to training end users. Professional systems workers must be retrained in the DBMS language, DBMS application development procedures, and new software practices.

Database technology has provided many organizational benefits, but it allows firms to maintain large databases with detailed personal information that pose a threat to individual privacy. Chapter 2 described how businesses can benefit strategically from well-designed customer databases. Linking these internal databases to the World Wide Web could make privacy problems grow larger. The Window on Organizations describes what might happen when organizations allow internal databases and data warehouses containing personal information to be accessed by outsiders using the Web.

MANAGEMENT WRAP-UP

MANAGEMENT

Selecting an appropriate data model and data management technology for the organization is a key management decision. Managers will need to evaluate the costs and benefits of implementing a database environment and the capabilities of various DBMS or file management technologies. Management should ascertain that organizational databases are designed to meet management information objectives and the organization's business needs.

ORGANIZATION

The organization's data model should reflect its key business processes and decision-making requirements. Data planning may need to be performed to make sure that the organization's data model delivers information efficiently for its business processes and enhances organizational performance. Designing a database is an organizational endeavor.

TECHNOLOGY

Many database and file management options are available for organizing and storing information. Key technology decisions should consider the efficiency of accessing information, flexibility in organizing information, the type of information to be stored and arranged, compatibility with the organization's data model, and compatibility with the organization's hardware and operating systems.

For Discussion: It has been said that you do not need database management software to create a database environment. Discuss.

SUMMARY

1. Describe traditional file organization and management techniques. In a traditional file environment, data records are organized using either a sequential file organization or a direct or random file organization. Records in a sequential file can be accessed sequentially or they can be accessed directly if the sequential file is on disk and uses an indexed sequential access method. Records on a file with direct file organization can be accessed directly without an index.

2. Explain the problems of the traditional file environment. By allowing different functional areas and groups in the organization to maintain their own files independently, the traditional file environment creates problems such as data redundancy and inconsistency, program-data dependence, inflexibility, poor security, and lack of data sharing and availability.

3. Describe how a database management system organizes information. A database management system

(DBMS) is the software that permits centralization of data and data management. A DBMS includes a data definition language, a data manipulation language, and a data dictionary capability. The most important feature of the DBMS is its ability to separate the logical and physical views of data. The user works with a logical view of data. The DBMS software translates user queries into queries that can be applied to the physical view of the data. The DBMS retrieves information so that the user does not have to be concerned with its physical location. This feature separates programs from data and from the management of data.

4. Describe the three principal database models and some principles of database design. There are three principal logical database models: hierarchical, network, and relational. Each has unique advantages and disadvantages. Hierarchical systems, which support one-to-many relationships, are low in flexibility but high in processing speed and efficiency. Network systems support many-to-many relationships. Relational systems are relatively slow but are very flexible for supporting ad hoc requests for information and for combining information from different sources. The choice depends on the business requirements. Designing a database requires both a logical design and a physical design. The process of creating small, stable data structures from complex groups of data when designing a relational database is termed normalization.

5. Discuss new database trends. It is no longer necessary for data to be centralized in a single, massive database. A complete database or portions of the database can be distributed to more than one location to increase responsiveness and reduce vulnerability and costs. There are two major types of distributed databases: *replicated databases* and *partitioned databases*. Object-oriented, hypermedia, and multidimensional databases may be alternatives to traditional database structures for certain types of applications. Object-oriented and hypermedia databases can store graphics and other types of data in addition to conventional text data to support multimedia applications. Hypermedia databases allow data to be stored in nodes linked together in any pattern established by the user. A multidimensional view of data represents relationships among data as a multidimensional structure, which can be visualized as cubes of data and cubes within cubes of data, allowing for more sophisticated data analysis. Data can be more conveniently analyzed across the enterprise by using a data warehouse, in which current and historical data are extracted from many different operational systems and consolidated for management decision making.

6. Explain the managerial and organizational requirements for creating a database environment. Development of a database environment requires much more than selection of technology. It requires a change in the corporation's attitude toward information. The organization must develop a data administration function and a data planning methodology. The database environment has developed more slowly than was originally anticipated. There is political resistance in organizations to many key database concepts, especially to sharing of information that has been controlled exclusively by one organizational group. There are difficult cost/benefit questions in database management. Often, to avoid raising difficult questions, database use begins and ends as a small effort isolated in the information systems department.

KEY TERMS

Field	Direct file access method	Data dictionary	Distributed database
Record	Transform algorithm	Data element	Object-oriented database
File	Traditional file environment	Logical view	Hypermedia database
Entity	Data redundancy	Physical view	On-line analytical
Attribute	Program-data dependence	Hierarchical data model	processing (OLAP)
Key field	Database	Pointer	Data warehouse
Sequential file organization	Database management	Network data model	Data administration
Direct or random file	system (DBMS)	Relational data model	Information policy
organization	Data definition language	Tuple	Database administration
Indexed sequential access	Data manipulation language	Entity-relationship diagram	
method (ISAM)	Structured Query	Normalization	
Index	Language (SQL)	Distributed processing	

REVIEW QUESTIONS

1. Why is file management important for overall system performance?

2. Describe how indexes and key fields enable a program to access specific records in a file.

3. Define and describe the indexed sequential access method and the direct file access method.

4. List and describe some of the problems of the traditional file environment.

5. Define a database and a database management system.

6. Name and briefly describe the three components of a DBMS.

7. What is the difference between a logical and a physical view of data?

8. List some benefits of a DBMS.

9. Describe the three principal database models and the advantages and disadvantages of each.

10. What is normalization? How is it related to the features of a well-designed relational database?

11. What is a distributed database, and how does it differ from distributed data processing?

12. What are object-oriented and hypermedia databases? How do they differ from a traditional database?

13. Describe the capabilities of on-line analytical processing (OLAP) and multidimensional data analysis.

14. What is a data warehouse? How can it benefit organizations?

15. What are the four key elements of a database environment? Describe each briefly.

16. Describe and briefly comment on the major management challenges in building a database environment.

GROUP PROJECT

Form a group with half of your classmates. Consider two strategies for building a database environment. One strategy recommends that a small group be created in the information systems department to begin exploring database applications throughout the firm. The other strategy recommends the creation of a vice president of information and subsequent development of important database applications. Debate the costs and benefits of each strategy with the other group.

CASE STUDY

Glaxo's Data Warehouse Prescription

How can a pharmaceuticals manufacturer monitor its own sales in an era dominated by HMOs? GlaxoWellcome plc faced this question, and its response was the development and installation of a new data warehouse application. GlaxoWellcome is the world's largest pharmaceutical provider, the result of a merger between both Britain's Glaxo and Wellcome companies. Headquartered in London and in Research Triangle, North Carolina, the firm has 54,000 employees in 70 countries and $8.5 billion in sales in 1995. Its major drugs include Zantac, used in the treatment of ulcers, Serevant and Flovent, used to treat asthma, and Epivir and Retrovir, used to treat AIDS.

Prior to the rise of HMOs (health maintenance organizations), the sale of pharmaceuticals was dominated by doctors who prescribed the drugs to be taken by their patients. Therefore, the marketing was directed entirely at them. Keeping track was fairly simple. Pharmaceutical firms only needed to keep track of what the doctors ordered.

Today, the market is dominated by HMOs, hospitals, insurance companies, and other third-party organizations that heavily influence what drugs are prescribed and in what quantity. The drug producers need to know which drugs (both their own and their competitors') are on the approved lists of these third-party groups, both for marketing purposes and for production planning. The drive toward managed care has also increased pressure to keep prices and inventories low.

To keep up with this information GlaxoWellcome, like other pharmaceutical houses, relies on reports from two audited data services, IMS America in Philadelphia and Source Informatics in Phoenix. These two organizations report on such drug market statistics as the sales volume, wholesale and retail price of each drug. They report on the shipment of drugs from wholesalers to retailers. They even publish the average dose and the number of tablets per prescription. Each month, GlaxoWellcome buys detailed reports summarizing this information.

In the past GlaxoWellcome analyzed these data manually, combining them with its own internal sales, shipment, and inventory information. The purchased market data came in a book-length paper-based report. To access the data, company executives, marketers, and market analysts had to search through the report until they found the information they needed. The data would then have to be combined with GlaxoWellcome's internal data, frequently in a Microsoft Excel spreadsheet. "We couldn't get at the data easily, and it wasn't integrated," recalls Jay Short, the director of information marketing. Oftentimes this task was farmed out to an analyst. Preparation of such a report was a slow process, often taking analysts two or three days to complete. Such a process was also quite expensive. Each month the company created a 50-page product performance report that would be distributed to about 110 people at an average cost of $100 per copy. Hundreds of other similar reports were also created monthly, making the overall company reporting cost extremely high. Worse, the reports would be outdated the moment they were printed, according to Jay Short, director of GlaxoWellcome's information marketing department. Management at GlaxoWellcome used this slow, expensive information system as best as they could to plan marketing; analyze sales, inventory and prescription data; support its distribution process; and plan its production.

To attempt to give better information to management of these various functions in the day of HMOs, the company built an information system called GWis (GlaxoWellcome Information System). The system is a data warehouse application based on MicroStrategy Inc.'s relational on-line analytical processing (ROLAP) technology. It works with a relational DBMS to integrate internal data with data from external sources. Users at their own desktop computers can easily access and combine internal sales, inventory, and prescription data with external market data. Users launch the process by entering various search criteria to create a report tailored to their own needs. They can, for example, quickly determine how a specific drug is selling. Using those criteria, the computer searches the data warehouse. It stores data collected from both internal and external systems. Users get back tabular reports within a matter of seconds or a few minutes for the most complex queries. They do not need the involvement of an analyst.

The company paid special attention to the interface. It had to be easy for everyone to use—a difficult requirement given the varying skill level of users. To meet the needs of their users, they designed a scalable interface which enables each user to select from three levels of complexity. As Julia Pastor, a project consultant from MicroStrategy, explained, "they needed something that was simple enough for novices, but wouldn't bore the power users."

The cost of the whole project was less than $500,000 while its benefits appear to be large. Because the reports are on-line and based on an up-to-date data warehouse, the reports are no longer out-of-date. GlaxoWellcome can use this information to closely monitor its distribution process and reduce operational costs. Moreover, reports can be produced without the need to rely on special analysts for preparing them. Gone are the $100-per-copy cost for many hundreds of reports. Even the information technology department has reaped major benefits because it was taken out of the daily reporting loop, according to Bill Almand, director of IT marketing. He claims that "all the reporting functions that fell on us as an organization are now pushed out to the business side." Although access to the new system was limited at first, the plan is to make it available to anyone who needs it, including its 2500 salespeople in the field in the United States. The company is now constructing an internal network based on Internet technology and the application will be made available through it when construction is complete.

How has the system worked? It faced its first major test during the summer of 1996 when GlaxoWellcome released studies showing that when Epivir and Retrovir are used in combination, they are effective in treating AIDS. Doctors began writing massive numbers of prescriptions for both drugs immediately. In the past the company would not have had a way to manage inventories when faced with such a deluge and would likely have ended up with shortages. But GWis made a difference. Using the new system, market analysts were able to monitor the sources of the demand and its size. Reports were often generated within minutes. Using these reports to manage production, inventories, and distribution, the company reports that its wholesalers around the world never ran out of either drug. ∎

Source: Bronwyn Fryer, "Fast Data Relief," *Information Week*, December 2, 1996.

Case Study Questions

1. Analyze GlaxoWellcome from the viewpoint of the competitive forces and value chain models.

2. What management, organization, and technology problems did GlaxoWellcome have? What business processes were affected?

3. Did GWis enhance the company's competitive position, and if so, how?

4. Discuss the significance of the choices made in the interface.

5. What management, organization, and technology factors should have been considered when the company was deciding to develop and install the GWis system?

6. To what extent is selection of data warehouse application a decision to be made by technicians and to what extent is it an important business decision?

REFERENCES

Belkin, Nicholas J., and W. Bruce Croft. "Information Filtering and Information Retrieval: Two Sides of the Same Coin?" *Communications of the ACM* 35, no. 12 (November 1992).

Butterworth, Paul, Allen Otis, and Jacob Stein, "The GemStone Object Database Management System." *Communications of the ACM* 34, no. 10 (October 1991).

Carmel, Erran, William K. McHenry, and Yeshayahu Cohen. "Building Large, Dynamic Hypertexts: How Do We Link Intelligently?" *Journal of Management Information Systems* 6, no. 2 (Fall 1989).

Clifford, James, Albert Croker, and Alex Tuzhilin. "On Data Representation and Use in a Temporal Relational DBMS." *Information Systems Research* 7, no. 3 (September 1996).

Date, C. J. *An Introduction to Database Systems.* 5th ed. Reading, MA: Addison-Wesley (1990).

Everest, G. C. *Database Management: Objectives, System Functions, and Administration.* New York: McGraw-Hill Book Company (1986).

Fiori, Rich. "The Information Warehouse." *Relational Database Journal* (January–February 1995).

Fryer, Bronwyn. "Zeneca Takes its Medicine." *Information Week* (March 18, 1996).

Goldberg, Michael, and Jaikumar Vijayan. "Data 'Wearhouse' Gains." *Computerworld* (April 8, 1996).

Goldstein, R. C., and J. B. McCririck. "What Do Data Administrators Really Do?" *Datamation* 26 (August 1980).

Goodhue, Dale L., Judith A. Quillard, and John F. Rockart. "Managing the Data Resource: A Contingency Perspective." *MIS Quarterly* (September 1988).

Goodhue, Dale L., Laurie J. Kirsch, Judith A. Quillard, and Michael D. Wybo. "Strategic Data Planning: Lessons from the Field." *MIS Quarterly* 16, no. 1 (March 1992).

Goodhue, Dale L., Michael D. Wybo, and Laurie J. Kirsch. "The Impact of Data Integration on the Costs and Benefits of Information Systems." *MIS Quarterly* 16, no. 3 (September 1992).

Grover, Varun, and James Teng. "How Effective Is Data Resource Management?" *Journal of Information Systems Management* (Summer 1991).

Gupta, Amarnath and Ranesh Jain. "Visual Information Retrieval." *Communications of the ACM* 40, no. 5 (May 1997).

Hackathorn, Richard. "Data Warehousing Energizes Your Enterprise." *Datamation* (February 1, 1995).

Inman, W. H. "The Data Warehouse and Data Mining." *Communications of the ACM* 39, no. 11 (November 1996).

Kahn, Beverly K. "Some Realities of Data Administration." *Communications of the ACM* 26 (October 1983).

Kahn, Beverly, and Linda Garceau. "The Database Administration Function." *Journal of Management Information Systems* 1 (Spring 1985).

Kent, William. "A Simple Guide to Five Normal Forms in Relational Database Theory." *Communications of the ACM* 26, no. 2 (February 1983).

King, John L., and Kenneth Kraemer. "Information Resource Management Cannot Work." *Information and Management* (1988).

Kroenke, David. *Database Processing: Fundamentals, Design, and Implementation.* 6th ed. Upper Saddle River, NJ: Prentice-Hall (1997).

Laudon, Kenneth C. *Dossier Society: Value Choices in the Design of National Information Systems.* New York: Columbia University Press (1986).

Madnick, Stuart E., and Richard Y. Wang. "Evolution Toward Strategic Application of Databases through Composite Information Systems." *Journal of Management Information Systems* 5, no. 3 (Winter 1988–1989).

March, Salvatore T., and Young-Gul Kim. "Information Resource Management: A Metadata Perspective." *Journal of Management Information Systems* 5, no. 3 (Winter 1988–1989).

Martin, James. *Managing the Data-Base Environment.* Englewood Cliffs, NJ: Prentice-Hall (1983).

Ricciuti, Mike. "Winning the Competitive Game," *Datamation* (February 15, 1994).

Silberschatz, Avi, Michael Stonebraker, and Jeff Ullman, eds. "Database Systems: Achievements and Opportunities." *Communications of the ACM* 34, no. 10 (October 1991).

Smith, John B., and Stephen F. Weiss. "Hypertext." *Communications of the ACM* 31, no. 7 (July 1988).

Telecommunications

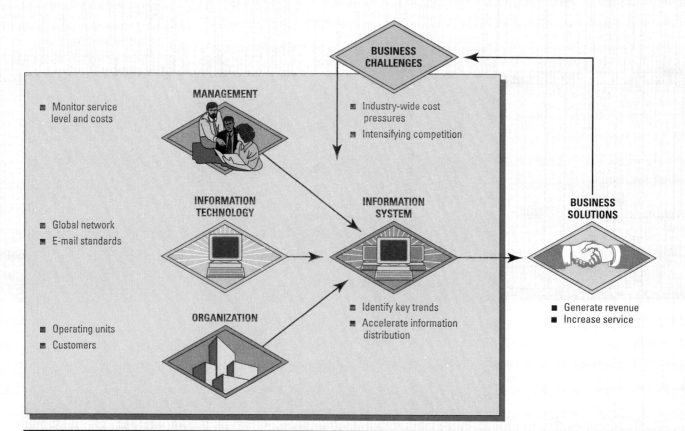

BUSINESS CHALLENGES

MANAGEMENT

- Monitor service level and costs

- Industry-wide cost pressures
- Intensifying competition

INFORMATION TECHNOLOGY

- Global network
- E-mail standards

INFORMATION SYSTEM

BUSINESS SOLUTIONS

ORGANIZATION

- Identify key trends
- Accelerate information distribution

- Operating units
- Customers

- Generate revenue
- Increase service

Smith-Kline Beecham's Global Knowledge Network

The pharmaceutical industry today is more competitive than ever, with health care reform and managed care posing additional pressure to cut costs. Any improvement in communication with physicians, suppliers, distributors, or testing laboratories can translate into savings and even strategic advantage. Smith-Kline Beecham, P.L.C., the United Kingdom–based drug manufacturer, developed a global network for this purpose.

As a global organization, Smith-Kline is interested in anything that can shrink the distance between operating units in different locations and between itself and outside companies. The firm uses a global mes-

CHAPTER OUTLINE

saging network to collect vast quantities of information about shipments and customer feedback. The company then compiles these data, analyzes them, and identifies key trends and statistics, such as growing demand for a particular drug or an unusually high incidence of a particular side effect. It then uses the global network to distribute this information back to its customers, either as a value-added service or increasingly as a product for which customers pay.

Smith-Kline built its global network with a unified messaging infrastructure that can support a broad range of communications media and services. The effort took several years. The network uses the Simple Mail Transfer Protocol (SMTP) and the X.400 standard for e-mail, providing a seamless, reliable flow of information to support the end-to-end process of marketing, manufacturing, and delivering pharmaceuticals. ■

Source: Elisabeth Horwitt and Ron Condon, "Right Here, Right Now," *Computerworld/Network World*, September 9, 1996.

Smith-Kline Beecham, P.L.C., like many companies from all over the world, is finding it can benefit from telecommunications to coordinate its internal activities and to communicate more efficiently with customers, suppliers, and other external organizations. Uses of telecommunications are multiplying for research, customer support, and organizational coordination and control, but they raise several management challenges.

1. **Selecting a telecommunications platform.** There is such a bewildering array of hardware, software, and network standards that managers may have trouble choosing the right telecommunications platform for the firm's information architecture. Telecommunications systems based on one standard may not be able to be linked to telecommunications based on another without additional equipment, expense, and management overhead. Networks that meet today's requirements may lack the connectivity for domestic or global expansion in the future. Not all standards problems can be solved by using the Internet.

2. **Managing Local Area Networks.** Although local area networks (LANs) appear to be flexible and inexpensive ways of delivering computing power to new areas of the organization, they must be carefully administered and monitored. LANs are especially vulnerable to network disruption, loss of essential data, access by unauthorized users, and infection from computer viruses (see Chapters 5 and 17). Dealing with these problems or even installing popular applications such as spreadsheets or data management software on a network, requires special technical expertise that is not normally available in end-user departments and remains in short supply.

Many of the features of contemporary information systems, such as on-line processing and direct access to data, are based on telecommunications technology. Telecommunications has become so essential to the conduct of business life that managers will be making telecommunications-related decisions throughout their careers. This chapter describes the components of telecommunications systems, showing how they can be arranged to create various types of networks and network-based applications that can increase the efficiency and competitiveness of an organization. It provides a method for determining the organization's telecommunications requirements.

9.1 THE TELECOMMUNICATIONS REVOLUTION

telecommunications The communication of information by electronic means, usually over some distance.

Telecommunications can be defined as the communication of information by electronic means, usually over some distance. We are currently in the middle of a telecommunications revolution that has two components: rapid changes in the technology of communications and equally important changes in the ownership, control, and marketing of telecommunications services. Today's managers need to understand the capabilities, costs, and benefits of alternative communications technologies and how to maximize their benefits for their organizations.

The Marriage of Computers and Communications

For most of the last 120 years since Alexander Bell invented the first singing telegraph in 1876, telecommunications was a monopoly of either the state or a regulated private firm. In the United States, American Telephone and Telegraph (AT&T) was the largest regulated monopoly, providing virtually all telecommunications services. In Europe and in the rest of the world, there is a state post, telephone, and telegraph authority (PTT). In the United States the monopoly ended in 1984, when the Justice Department forced AT&T to give up its monopoly and allow competing firms to sell telecommunications services and equipment.

The end of AT&T's monopoly widened the market for new telecommunications technologies and devices, from cheaper long-distance service to telephone answering equipment, cellular telephones, and private satellite services. AT&T itself started marketing computing services and equipment.

Changes in the telecommunications industry were accompanied by changes in telecommunications technology. Previously, telecommunications meant voice transmission over telephone lines. Today, much telecommunications transmission is digital data transmission, using computers to transmit data from one location to another. On-line information systems and remote access to information would be impossible without telecommunications. Table 9.1 shows some of the common tasks performed by computer systems that would be impossible without advanced telecommunications.

The Information Superhighway

Deregulation and the marriage of computers and communications has also made it possible for the telephone companies to expand from traditional voice

Table 9.1	Common Tasks Performed by Computer Systems Requiring Telecommunications	
Application	**Example**	**Requirements**
Business		
On-line data entry	Inventory control	Transactions occurring several times/second, direct response required
On-line text retrieval	Hospital information systems; library systems	Response required in real-time; high character volumes
Inquiry/response	Point-of-sale system; airline reservation system; credit checking	Transactions several times/second; instant response within seconds
Administrative message switching	Electronic mail	Short response and delivery times (minutes to hours)
Process control	Computer-aided manufacturing (CAM); numeric control of machine tools	Continuous input transactions and on-line responses required
Intercomputer data exchange	International transfer of bank funds	Infrequent but high-volume bursts of information; transfer of large data blocks; on-line immediate response
Home		
Inquiry response	Home banking; shopping; ordering	On-line transactions collected with high frequency
Text retrieval	Home education	High-volume, rapid transmission
Special entertainment	Sports; polling and political participation	High-capacity video and data capabilities

communications into new information services, such as providing transmission of news reports, stock reports, television programs, and movies. The telecommunications revolution has allowed the telephone companies created by the breakup of AT&T to move into the information service business.

Their efforts are laying the foundation for the **information superhighway**, a vast web of high-speed digital telecommunications networks delivering information, education, and entertainment services to offices and homes. The networks comprising the highway are national or worldwide in scope and accessible by the general public rather than restricted to use by members of a specific organization or set of organizations such as a corporation. Some analysts believe the information superhighway will have as profound an impact on economic and social life in the twenty-first century as railroads and interstate highways did in the past.

The press has stressed the home entertainment implications of this technology, extolling movies on demand with VCR-like forward and reverse controls. This technology has also been touted for its ability to offer an almost unlimited number of cable television channels—the standard number quoted is 500. Users will be able to read newspapers and magazines via these networks, and many predict the decline of paper-based news media as a result. The technology will make possible interactive communications between the televised programs and the viewers at home. While all of this is indeed an important aspect of the information superhighway, the concept is much broader and richer than indicated in these popular press reports. It involves new ways to obtain and disseminate information that virtually eliminate the barriers of time and place. The business implications of this new superhighway are only now beginning to emerge. The most well-known and easily the largest implementation of the information superhighway is the Internet.

Another aspect of the information superhighway is a national computing network proposed by the U.S. federal government. The Clinton administration envisions this network linking universities, research centers, libraries, hospitals, and other institutions that need to exchange vast amounts of information while being accessible in homes and schools.

9.2   COMPONENTS AND FUNCTIONS OF A TELECOMMUNICATIONS SYSTEM

information superhighway
High-speed digital telecommunications networks that are national or worldwide in scope and accessible by the general public rather than restricted to use by members of a specific organization or set of organizations such as a corporation.

telecommunications system   A collection of compatible hardware and software arranged to communicate information from one location to another.

A **telecommunications system** is a collection of compatible hardware and software arranged to communicate information from one location to another. Figure 9.1 illustrates the components of a typical telecommunications system. Telecommunications systems can transmit text, graphic images, voice, or video information. This section describes the major components of telecommunications systems. Subsequent sections describe how the components can be arranged into various types of networks.

Telecommunications System Components

The following are essential components of a telecommunications system:
1. Computers to process information
2. Terminals or any input/output devices that send or receive data
3. Communications channels, the links by which data or voice are transmitted between sending and receiving devices in a network. Communications channels use various communications media, such as telephone lines, fiber-optic cables, coaxial cables, and wireless transmission.
4. Communications processors, such as modems, multiplexers, controllers, and front-end processors, which provide support functions for data transmission and reception
5. Communications software that controls input and output activities and manages other functions of the communications network

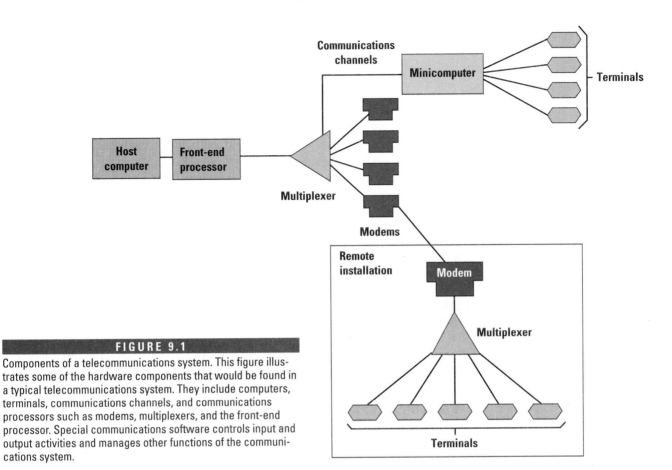

Components of a telecommunications system. This figure illustrates some of the hardware components that would be found in a typical telecommunications system. They include computers, terminals, communications channels, and communications processors such as modems, multiplexers, and the front-end processor. Special communications software controls input and output activities and manages other functions of the communications system.

Functions of Telecommunications Systems

To send and receive information from one place to another, a telecommunications system must perform a number of separate functions, which are largely invisible to the people using the system. A telecommunications system transmits information, establishes the interface between the sender and the receiver, routes messages along the most efficient paths, performs elementary processing of the information to ensure that the right message gets to the right receiver, performs editorial tasks on the data (such as checking for errors and rearranging the format), and converts messages from one speed (say, the speed of a computer) into the speed of a communications line or from one format to another. Lastly, the telecommunications system controls the flow of information. Many of these tasks are accomplished by computer.

Protocols

A telecommunications network typically contains diverse hardware and software components that need to work together to transmit information. Different components in a network can communicate by adhering to a common set of rules that enable them to talk to each other. This set of rules and procedures governing transmission between two points in a network is called a **protocol**. Each device in a network must be able to interpret the other device's protocol.

The principal functions of protocols in a telecommunications network are to identify each device in the communication path, to secure the attention of the other device, to verify correct receipt of the transmitted message, to determine that a message requires retransmission if it is incomplete or has errors, and to perform recovery when errors occur.

Although business, government, and the computer industry recognize the need for common communications standards, the industry has yet to put a universal

protocol A set of rules and procedures that govern transmission between the components in a network.

standard into effect. Chapter 10 discusses the question of telecommunications standards in greater detail.

Types of Signals: Analog and Digital

Information travels through a telecommunications system in the form of electromagnetic signals. Signals are represented in two ways: analog and digital signals. An **analog signal** is represented by a continuous waveform that passes through a communications medium. Analog signals are used to handle voice communications and to reflect variations in pitch.

A **digital signal** is a discrete, rather than a continuous, waveform. It transmits data coded into two discrete states: 1-bits and 0-bits, which are represented as on–off electrical pulses. Most computers communicate with digital signals, as do many local telephone companies and some larger networks. But if a telecommunications system, such as a traditional telephone network, is set up to process analog signals—the receivers, transmitters, amplifiers, and so forth—a digital signal cannot be processed without some alterations. All digital signals must be translated into analog signals before they can be transmitted in an analog system. The device that performs this translation is called a **modem**. (*Modem* is an abbreviation for MOdulation/DEModulation.) A modem translates the digital signals of a computer into analog form for transmission over ordinary telephone lines, or it translates analog signals back into digital form for reception by a computer (see Figure 9.2).

Types of Communications Channels

Communications **channels** are the means by which data are transmitted from one device in a network to another. A channel can utilize different kinds of telecommunications transmission media: twisted wire, coaxial cable, fiber optics, terrestrial microwave, satellite, and wireless transmission. Each has certain advantages and limitations. High-speed transmission media are more expensive in general, but they can handle higher volumes (which reduces the cost per bit). For instance, the cost per bit of data can be lower via satellite link than via leased telephone line if a firm uses the satellite link 100 percent of the time. There is also a wide range of speeds possible for any given medium depending on the software and hardware configuration.

Twisted Wire

Twisted wire consists of strands of copper wire twisted in pairs and is the oldest transmission medium. Most of the telephone systems in a building rely on twisted wires installed for analog communication. Most buildings have additional cables installed for future expansion, and so there are usually a number of twisted-pair cables unused in every office of every building. These unused cables can be used for digital communications. Although it is low in cost and is already in place, **twisted wire** is relatively slow for transmitting data, and high-speed transmission through this medium causes interference called *crosstalk*. On the other hand, new software and hardware

analog signal A continuous waveform that passes through a communications medium. Used for voice communications.

digital signal A discrete waveform that transmits data coded into two discrete states as 1-bits and 0-bits, which are represented as on–off electrical pulses; used for data communications.

modem A device for translating digital signals into analog signals and vice versa.

channels The links by which data or voice are transmitted between sending and receiving devices in a network.

twisted wire A transmission medium consisting of pairs of twisted copper wires. Used to transmit analog phone conversations but can be used for data transmission.

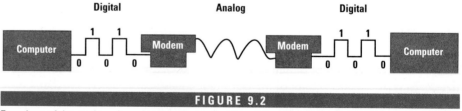

FIGURE 9.2

Functions of the modem. A modem is a device that translates digital signals from a computer into analog form so that they can be transmitted over analog telephone lines. The modem is also used to translate analog signals back into digital form for the receiving computer.

have raised the capacity of existing twisted-wire cables up to 10 megabits per second, which is often adequate for connecting PCs and other office devices.

Coaxial Cable

Coaxial cable, such as that used for cable television, consists of thickly insulated copper wire, which can transmit a larger volume of data than twisted wire. It is often used in place of twisted wire for important links in a telecommunications network because it is a faster, more interference-free transmission medium, with speeds of up to 200 megabits per second. However, coaxial cable is thick, is hard to wire in many buildings, and cannot support analog phone conversations. It must be moved when computers and other devices are moved.

coaxial cable A transmission medium consisting of thickly insulated copper wire. Can transmit large volumes of data quickly.

Fiber Optics

Fiber-optic cable consists of thousands of strands of clear glass fiber, each the thickness of a human hair, which are bound into cables. Data are transformed into pulses of light, which are sent through the fiber-optic cable by a laser device at a rate of 500 kilobits to several billion bits per second. On the one hand, fiber-optic cable is considerably faster, lighter, and more durable than wire media and is well suited to systems requiring transfers of large volumes of data. On the other hand, fiber-optic cable is more difficult to work with, more expensive, and harder to install. It is best used as the backbone of a network and not for connecting isolated devices to a backbone. In most networks fiber-optic cable is used as the high-speed trunk line, while twisted wire and coaxial cable are used to connect the trunk line to individual devices.

fiber-optic cable A fast, light, and durable transmission medium consisting of thin strands of clear glass fiber bound into cables. Data are transmitted as light pulses.

Wireless Transmission

Wireless transmission that sends signals through air or space without any physical tether has emerged as an important alternative to tethered transmission channels such as twisted wire, coaxial cable, and fiber optics. Today, common uses of wireless data transmission include pagers, cellular telephones, microwave transmissions, communication satellites, mobile data networks, personal communications services, personal digital assistants, and even television remote controls.

The wireless transmission medium is the *electromagnetic spectrum*, illustrated in Figure 9.3. Some types of wireless transmission, such as microwave or infrared, by nature occupy specific spectrum frequency ranges (measured in megahertz). Other types of wireless transmissions are actually functional uses, such as cellular telephones and paging devices, that have been assigned a specific range of frequencies by national regulatory agencies and international agreements. Each frequency range has its own strengths and limitations, and these have helped determine the specific function or data communications niche assigned to it.

Microwave systems, both terrestrial and celestial, transmit high-frequency radio signals through the atmosphere and are widely used for high-volume, long-distance, point-to-point communication. Because microwave signals follow a straight line and do not bend with the curvature of the earth, long-distance terrestrial transmission systems require that transmission stations be positioned 25 to 30 miles apart, adding to the expense of microwave.

microwave A high-volume, long-distance, point-to-point transmission in which high-frequency radio signals are transmitted through the atmosphere from one terrestrial transmission station to another.

This problem can be solved by bouncing microwave signals off **satellites,** enabling them to serve as relay stations for microwave signals transmitted from terrestrial stations. Communication satellites are cost effective for transmitting large quantities of data over long distances. Satellites are typically used for communications in large, geographically dispersed organizations that would be difficult to tie together through cabling media or terrestrial microwave. For instance, the Rite Aid pharmacy chain uses a satellite network to provide instant two-way communications between its stores and its corporate mainframe in Camp Hill, Pennsylvania. Each store has a server (a powerful PC dedicated to storing data and programs—see Section 9.3)

satellite The transmission of data using orbiting satellites to serve as relay stations for transmitting microwave signals over very long distances.

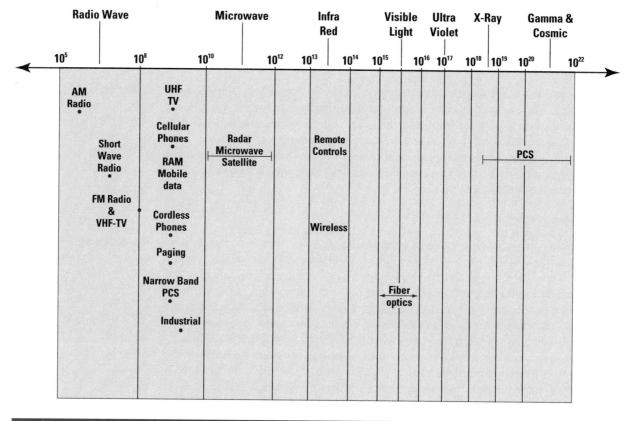

FIGURE 9.3

Frequency ranges for communications media and devices. Each telecommunications transmission medium or device occupies a different frequency range, measured in megahertz, on the electromagnetic spectrum.

which supports cash registers, pharmacy terminals, and the manager's terminal and tracks inventory. The server can communicate with the central mainframe via satellite to post sales and to fill prescriptions stored in the mainframe database (see Figure 9.4).

Conventional communication satellites move in stationary orbits approximately 22,000 miles above the earth. A newer satellite medium, the **low-orbit satellite,** is beginning to be deployed. These satellites travel much closer to the earth and so are able to pick up signals from weak transmitters. They also consume less power and cost less to launch than conventional satellites. With such wireless networks, business persons will be able to travel virtually anywhere in the world and have access to full communication capabilities, regardless of the adequacy of the telecommunications infrastructure of the country they are in.

Other wireless transmission technologies have recently been developed and are being used in situations requiring mobile computing power. **Paging systems** have been in common use for several decades, originally just beeping when the user receives a message and requiring the user to telephone an office to learn what the message is. Today, paging devices can receive short alphanumeric messages that the user reads on the pager's screen. Paging is useful for communicating with mobile workers such as repair crews; one-way paging can also provide an inexpensive way of communicating with workers in offices. For example, Ethos Corporation in Boulder, Colorado, markets mortgage-processing software that uses a paging system that can deliver daily changes in mortgage rates to thousands of real estate brokers. The data transmitted through the paging network can be downloaded and manipulated, saving brokers approximately one and a half hours of work each week.

Cellular telephones (sometimes called mobile telephones) work by using radio waves to communicate with radio antennas (towers) placed within adjacent geo-

low-orbit satellite Satellites that travel much closer to the earth than traditional satellites and so are able to pick up signals from weak transmitters while consuming less power.

paging system A wireless transmission technology in which the pager beeps when the user receives a message; used to transmit short alphanumeric messages.

cellular telephone A device that transmits voice or data, using radio waves to communicate with radio antennas placed within adjacent geographic areas called *cells.*

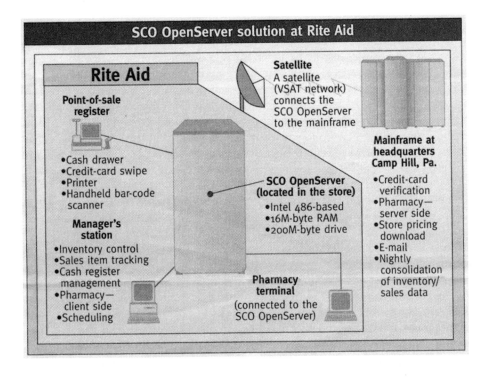

SCO OpenServer solution at Rite Aid

Rite Aid

Point-of-sale register
- Cash drawer
- Credit-card swipe
- Printer
- Handheld bar-code scanner

Manager's station
- Inventory control
- Sales item tracking
- Cash register management
- Pharmacy—client side
- Scheduling

SCO OpenServer (located in the store)
- Intel 486-based
- 16M-byte RAM
- 200M-byte drive

Pharmacy terminal
(connected to the SCO OpenServer)

Satellite
A satellite (VSAT network) connects the SCO OpenServer to the mainframe

Mainframe at headquarters Camp Hill, Pa.
- Credit-card verification
- Pharmacy—server side
- Store pricing download
- E-mail
- Nightly consolidation of inventory/sales data

FIGURE 9.4

Satellite transmission at Rite Aid. Satellites help the Rite Aid pharmacy chain transmit data between its 2960 stores and its corporate mainframe in Camp Hill, Pennsylvania.
Copyright August 1, 1994, by Computerworld, Inc., Framingham, MA 01701. Reprinted from Computerworld. *Reprinted by permission.*

graphic areas called *cells*. A telephone message is transmitted to the local cell by the cellular telephone and then is handed off from antenna to antenna—cell to cell—until it reaches the cell of its destination, where it is transmitted to the receiving telephone. As a cellular signal travels from one cell into another, a computer that monitors signals from the cells switches the conversation to a radio channel assigned to the next cell. The radio antenna cells normally cover eight-mile hexagonal cells, although their radius is smaller in densely populated localities. Although the cellular telephone infrastructure has primarily been used for voice transmission, recent developments have made it capable of two-way digital data transmission. The breakthrough came in the form of a transmission standard called Cellular Digital Packet Data (CDPD), with the support of such telecommunications giants as AT&T, Bell

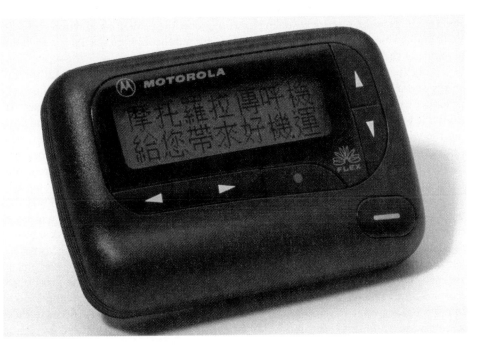

Pagers are increasingly used for wireless transmission of brief messages in China and throughout the globe.

Atlantic, Sprint, and McCaw Cellular. CDPD uses the pauses in voice communication, when the transmission channel is idle, filling them with packets of data.

Wireless networks explicitly designed for two-way transmission of data files are called **mobile data networks.** These radio-based networks transmit data to and from handheld computers. Another type of mobile data network is based on a series of radio towers constructed specifically to transmit text and data. RAM Mobile Data (jointly owned by Ram Broadcasting and Bell South) and Ardis (jointly owned by IBM and Motorola) are two publicly available networks that use such media for national two-way data transmission. Mastercard uses the RAM Mobile Data network for wireless credit card verification terminals at county fairs or merchants' sidewalk kiosks. Otis Elevators uses the Ardis network to dispatch repair technicians around the country from a single office in Connecticut and to receive their reports. Value-added companies are now beginning to offer services built on those mobile data networks. For instance, RadioMail has introduced a wireless fax service at only 99 cents per domestic page. The cellular telephone network is also starting to be used for this purpose.

Wireless support is becoming more common in both computer hardware and software. Portable computers, using either internal or external wireless modems, can now be linked to wireless networks.

One new wireless cellular technology that should soon be available for both voice and data is called **personal communication services (PCS).** PCS uses lower-power, higher-frequency radio waves than does cellular technology. Because of the lower power, PCS cells are much smaller and so must be more numerous and closer together. The higher-frequency signals enable PCS devices to be used in many places where cellular telephones are not effective, such as in tunnels and inside office buildings. Moreover, because PCS telephones need less power, they can be much smaller (shirt-pocket size) and less expensive than cellular telephones. According to some estimates PCS networks will offer better service and quality than existing cellular telephones while being 20 times more efficient. Also, because they operate at higher, less-crowded frequencies than cellular telephones (see Figure 9.3), they will have the bandwidth to offer video and multimedia communication.

Personal digital assistants (PDAs) are small, pen-based, handheld computers capable of entirely digital communications transmission. They have built-in wireless telecommunications capabilities as well as work organization software. A well-known example is the one-pound Apple Newton MessagePad. It can function as a pager and can transmit e-mail, faxes, documents for printing, and data to other computers. The Newton also includes an electronic scheduler, calendar, and notepad software and is able to accept handwriting input entered through its special stylus. Some versions of the Newton provide Internet access.

JC Penney Co., the fourth largest retailer in the United States with 1200 retail stores and a large catalogue business, provides an example of a mundane but very practical use of wireless technology. The company operates three warehouses nationwide with a combined storage area of 3.3 million square feet. Receiving and storing the goods and later locating, pulling, and shipping them consumes a great deal of time and effort and is very costly. JC Penney has made both processes more efficient, faster, and less expensive through the use of computers and wireless telecommunications, as illustrated in Figure 9.5. As shipments arrive the goods are immediately bar coded. Wireless handheld scanners then transmit the data on each box to a warehouse computer, which immediately assigns a storage location and wirelessly transmits this data to the forklift operator. The company selected wireless scanners to be used in receiving to free the warehouse workers from the inconvenience and potential dangers of strapped-on wired scanners. Later, when goods are to be picked and placed on a conveyor belt that brings them to the shipping dock, the forklift operator is sent a picking list with location data by wireless transmission. Scanners used to read and transmit data on goods on the conveyor belt are wired. (Because these scanners are stationary—the goods pass under them—the designers found no gain in

mobile data networks Wireless networks that enable two-way transmission of data files cheaply and efficiently.

personal communication services (PCS) A new wireless cellular technology that uses lower-power, higher-frequency radio waves than does cellular technology and so can be used with smaller-sized telephones inside buildings and tunnels.

personal digital assistant (PDA) Small, pen-based, handheld computers with built-in wireless telecommunications capable of entirely digital communications transmission.

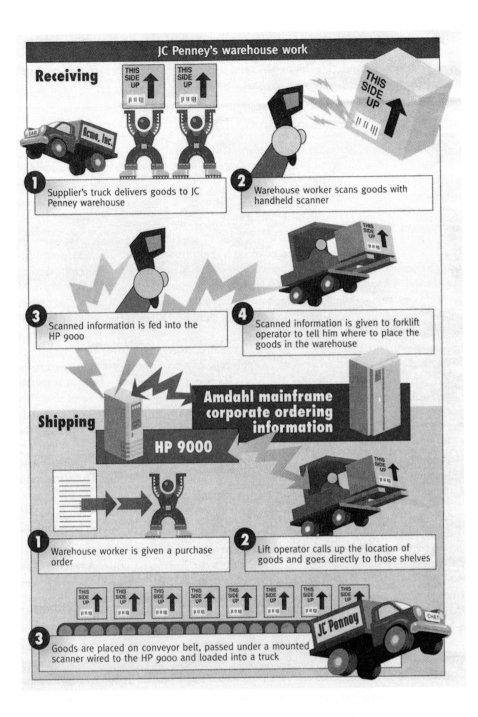

FIGURE 9.5

Wireless transmission at JC Penney's. JC Penney uses wireless handheld scanners to locate goods for shipping and receiving at its three massive warehouses throughout the United States. *Copyright September 12, 1994, by Computerworld, Inc., Framingham, MA 01701. Reprinted from Computerworld. Reprinted by permission.*

JC Penney's warehouse work

Receiving

1. Supplier's truck delivers goods to JC Penney warehouse

2. Warehouse worker scans goods with handheld scanner

3. Scanned information is fed into the HP 9000

4. Scanned information is given to forklift operator to tell him where to place the goods in the warehouse

Amdahl mainframe corporate ordering information

HP 9000

Shipping

1. Warehouse worker is given a purchase order

2. Lift operator calls up the location of goods and goes directly to those shelves

3. Goods are placed on conveyor belt, passed under a mounted scanner wired to the HP 9000 and loaded into a truck

using wireless technology for this task.) JC Penney claims a 23 percent improvement in accuracy as a result of the system, as well as enhanced productivity. The company also expects the system to eliminate the expensive twice-yearly inventory warehouse shutdowns.

Although wireless telecommunications holds great potential for the expansion of communication worldwide, the technology does have limitations. Wireless transmission is highly error prone because it is susceptible to many kinds of environmental disturbance, from magnetic interference from the sun to automobile ignition emissions. Bandwidth and energy supply in wireless devices require careful management from both hardware and software standpoints (Imielinski and Badrinath, 1994). Security and privacy will be more difficult to maintain because wireless transmission can be easily intercepted (see Chapter 17). Wireless networks require complex error-correcting capabilities that result in repeated transmission of message segments, slowing actual transmission throughput speeds. Software and hardware technology advances and agreement on standards are all needed before transmission between various wireless networks becomes seamless.

Characteristics of Communications Channels

The characteristics of the communications channel help determine the efficiency and capabilities of a telecommunications system. These characteristics include the speed of transmission, the direction in which signals may travel, and the mode of transmission.

Transmission Speed

The total amount of information that can be transmitted through any telecommunications channel is measured in bits per second (BPS). Sometimes this is referred to as the *baud rate*. A **baud** is a binary event representing a signal change from positive to negative or vice versa. The baud rate is not always the same as the bit rate. At higher speeds a single signal change can transmit more than one bit at a time, so the bit rate will generally surpass the baud rate.

Because one signal change, or cycle, is required to transmit one or several bits per second, the transmission capacity of each type of telecommunications medium is a function of its frequency, the number of cycles per second that can be sent through that medium, measured in *hertz* (see Chapter 6). The range of frequencies that can be accommodated on a particular telecommunications channel is called its **bandwidth**. The bandwidth is the difference between the highest and lowest frequencies that can be accommodated on a single channel. The greater the range of frequencies, the greater the bandwidth and the greater the channel's telecommunications transmission capacity. Table 9.2 compares the transmission speed and relative costs of the major types of transmissions media.

Transmission Modes

There are several conventions for transmitting signals; these methods are necessary for devices to communicate when a character begins or ends. **Asynchronous transmission** (often referred to as *start–stop transmission*) transmits one character at a time over a line, each character framed by control bits—a start bit, one or two stop bits, and a parity bit for error checking. Asynchronous transmission is used for low-speed transmission.

baud A change in signal from positive to negative or vice versa that is used as a measure of transmission speed.

bandwith The capacity of a communications channel as measured by the difference between the highest and lowest frequencies that can be transmitted by that channel.

asynchronous transmission The low-speed transmission of one character at a time.

Table 9.2 Typical Speeds and Costs of Telecommunications Transmission Media		
Medium	Speed	Cost
Twisted wire	300 BPS–10 MBPS	Low
Microwave	256 KBPS–100 MBPS	
Satellite	256 KBPS–100 MBPS	
Coaxial cable	56 KBPS–200 MBPS	
Fiber-optic cable	500 KBPS–10 GBPS	High

BPS = bits per second
KBPS = kilobits per second
MBPS = megabits per second
GBPS = gigabits per second

Synchronous transmission transmits groups of characters simultaneously, with the beginning and ending of a block of characters determined by the timing circuitry of the sending and receiving devices. Synchronous transmission is used for transmitting large volumes of data at high speeds.

Transmission Direction

Transmission must also consider the direction of data flow over a telecommunications network. In **simplex transmission** data can travel only in one direction at all times. In **half-duplex transmission** data can flow two ways but can travel in only one direction at a time. In **full-duplex transmission** data can be sent in both directions simultaneously.

Communications Processors

Communications processors, such as front-end processors, concentrators, controllers, multiplexers, and modems, support data transmission and reception in a telecommunications network.

The **front-end processor** is a small computer (often a programmable minicomputer) dedicated to communications management and is attached to the main, or host, computer in a large computer system. The front-end processor performs special processing related to communications such as error control, formatting, editing, controlling, routing, and speed and signal conversion. It takes some of the load off the host computer. The front-end processor is largely responsible for collecting and processing input and output data to and from terminals and grouping characters into complete messages for submission to the CPU of the host computer.

A **concentrator** is a programmable telecommunications computer that collects and temporarily stores messages from terminals until enough messages are ready to be sent economically. The concentrator bursts signals to the host compA **controller,** which is often a specialized minicomputer, supervises communications traffic between the CPU and peripheral devices such as terminals and printers. The controller manages messages from these devices and communicates them to the CPU. It also routes output from the CPU to the appropriate peripheral device.

A **multiplexer** is a device that enables a single communications channel to carry data transmissions from multiple sources simultaneously. The multiplexer divides the communications channel so that it can be shared by multiple transmission devices. The multiplexer may divide a high-speed channel into multiple channels of slower speed or may assign each transmission source a very small slice of time for using the high-speed channel.

Telecommunications Software

Special **telecommunications software** is required to control and support the activities of a telecommunications network. This software resides in the host computer, front-end processor, and other processors in the network. The principal functions of telecommunications software are network control, access control, transmission control, error detection/correction, and security.

Network control software routes messages, polls network terminals, determines transmission priorities, maintains a log of network activity, and checks for errors. Access control software establishes connections between terminals and computers in the network, establishing transmission speed, mode, and direction. Transmission control software enables computers and terminals to send and receive data, programs, commands, and messages. Error-control software detects and corrects errors, then retransmits the corrected data. Security-control software monitors utilization, log ons, passwords, and various authorization procedures to prevent unauthorized access to a network. More detail on security software can be found in Chapter 17.

---

synchronous transmission The high-speed simultaneous transmission of large blocks of data.

simplex transmission A transmission in which data can travel in only one direction at all times.

half-duplex transmission A transmission in which data can flow two ways but in only one direction at a time.

full-duplex transmission A transmission in which data can travel in both directions simultaneously.

communications processors Hardware that supports data transmission and reception in a telecommunications network.

front-end processor A small computer managing communications for the host computer in a network.

concentrator Telecommunications computer that collects and temporarily stores messages from terminals for batch transmission to the host computer.

controller A specialized computer that supervises communications traffic between the CPU and the peripheral devices in a telecommunications system.

multiplexer A device that enables a single communications channel to carry data transmissions from multiple sources simultaneously.

telecommunications software Special software for controlling and supporting the activities of a telecommunications network.

A number of different ways exist to organize telecommunications components to form a network and hence provide multiple ways of classifying networks. Networks can be classified by their shape, or **topology**. Networks can also be classified by their geographic scope and the type of services provided. Wide area networks, for example, encompass a relatively wide geographic area, from several miles to thousands of miles, whereas local networks link local resources such as computers and terminals in the same department or building of a firm. This section will describe the various ways of looking at networks.

topology The shape or configuration of a network.

Network Topologies

One way of describing networks is by their shape, or topology. As illustrated in Figures 9.6 to 9.8, the three most common topologies are the star, bus, and ring.

The Star Network

The **star network** (see Figure 9.6) consists of a central host computer connected to a number of smaller computers or terminals and is used primarily in mainframe systems. This topology is useful for applications in which some processing must be centralized and some can be performed locally. One problem with the star network is its vulnerability. All communication between points in the network must pass through the central computer. Because the central computer is the traffic controller for the other computers and terminals in the network, communication in the network will come to a standstill if the host computer stops functioning.

star network A network topology in which all computers and other devices are connected to a central host computer. All communications between network devices must pass through the host computer.

The Bus Network

The **bus network** (see Figure 9.7) links a number of computers by a single circuit made of twisted wire, coaxial cable, or fiber-optic cable. All the signals are broadcast in both directions to the entire network, with special software to identify which components receive each message (there is no central host computer to control the net-

bus network Network topology linking a number of computers by a single circuit with all messages broadcast to the entire network.

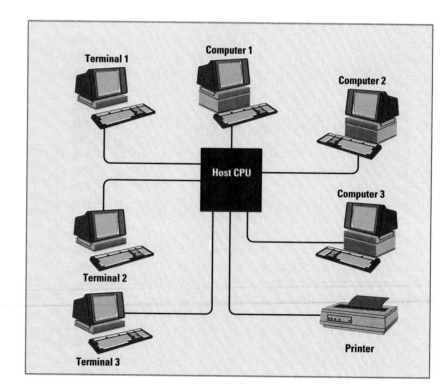

FIGURE 9.6

A star network topology. In a star network configuration a central host computer acts as a traffic controller for all other components of the network. All communication between the smaller computers, terminals, and printers must first pass through the central computer.

work). If one computer in the network fails, none of the other components in the network is affected. This topology is commonly used for local area networks (LANs), discussed in the following section.

The Ring Network

Like the bus network, the **ring network** (see Figure 9.8) does not rely on a central host computer and will not necessarily break down if one of the component computers malfunctions. Each computer in the network can communicate directly with any other computer, and each processes its own applications independently. However, in ring topology, the connecting wire, cable, or optical fiber forms a closed loop. Data are passed along the ring from one computer to another and always flow in one direction.

The token ring network is a variant of the ring network. In the token ring network all the devices on the network communicate using a signal, or token. The token is a predefined packet of data, which includes data indicating the sender, receiver, and whether the packet is in use. The tokens may contain a message or be empty.

ring network A network topology in which all computers are linked by a closed loop in a manner that passes data in one direction from one computer to another.

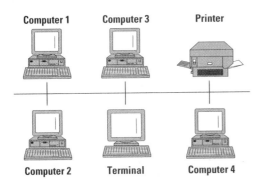

FIGURE 9.7

A bus network topology. This topology allows for all messages to be broadcast to the entire network through a single circuit. There is no central host, and messages can travel in both directions along the cable.

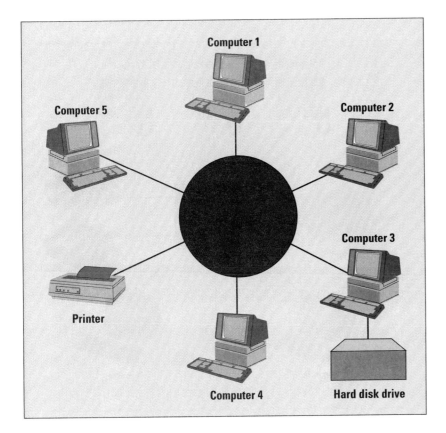

FIGURE 9.8

A ring network topology. In a ring network configuration, messages are transmitted from computer to computer, flowing in a single direction through a closed loop. Each computer operates independently so that if one fails, communication through the network is not interrupted.

A token moves from device to device in the network, and each device examines the token as it passes. If the token contains data and is meant for that device, the device accepts the data and marks the packet as empty. If a computer wants to send a message, it finds an available token; supplies sender, receiver, and message data; loads the message onto the token; and marks it as used. If no message is pending, the token passes unchanged. The token ring configuration is most useful for transmitting large volumes of data between PCs or for transmission between PCs and a larger computer.

Private Branch Exchanges and Local Area Networks

Networks may be classified by geographic scope into local networks and wide area networks. Local networks consist of private branch exchanges and local area networks.

Private Branch Exchanges

private branch exchange (PBX)
A central switching system that handles a firm's voice and digital communications.

A **private branch exchange (PBX)** is a special-purpose computer designed for handling and switching office telephone calls at a company site. Today's PBXs can carry both voice and data to create local networks.

While the first PBXs performed limited switching functions, they can now store, transfer, hold, and redial telephone calls. PBXs can also be used to switch digital information among computers and office devices. For instance, you can write a letter on a PC in your office, send it to the printer, then dial up the local copying machine and have multiple copies of your letter created. All this activity is possible with a digital PBX connecting smart machines in the advanced office. Figure 9.9 illustrates a PBX system.

The advantage of digital PBXs over other local networking options is that they utilize existing telephone lines and do not require special wiring. A phone jack can be found almost anywhere in the office building. Equipment can therefore be moved when necessary with little worry about having to rewire the building. A hard-wired computer terminal or microcomputer connected to a mainframe with coaxial cable

FIGURE 9.9

A PBX system. A PBX can switch digital information among telephones and among computers, copiers, printers, fax machines, and other devices to create a local network based on ordinary telephone wiring.

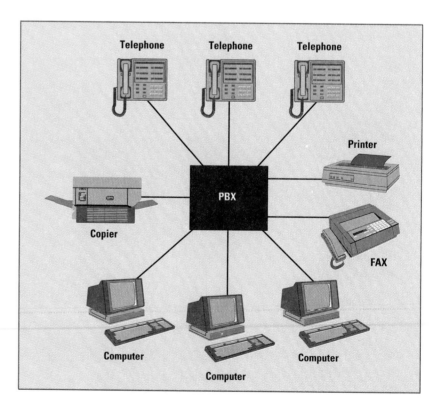

must be rewired at considerable cost each time it is moved. A PC connected to a network by telephone can simply be plugged or unplugged anywhere in the building, utilizing the existing telephone lines. PBXs are also supported by commercial vendors such as the local telephone company, so that the organization does not need special expertise to manage them.

The geographic scope of PBXs is limited, usually to several hundred feet, although the PBX can be connected to other PBX networks or to packet-switched networks (see the discussion of value-added networks in this section) to encompass a larger geographic area. The primary disadvantages of PBXs is that they are limited to telephone lines and they cannot easily handle very large volumes of data.

Local Area Networks

A **local area network (LAN)** encompasses a limited distance, usually one building or several buildings in close proximity. Most LANs connect devices located within a 2000-foot radius and have been widely used to link PCs. LANs require their own communications channels.

LANs generally have higher transmission capacities than PBXs. A very fast PBX can have a maximum transmission capacity of over 2 megabits per second. LANs typically transmit at a rate of 256 kilobits per second to over 100 megabits per second. They are recommended for applications requiring high volumes of data and high transmission speeds. For instance, because a picture consumes so many bits of information, an organization may require a LAN for video transmissions and graphics.

LANs are totally controlled, maintained, and operated by end users. This produces the advantage of allowing user control, but it also means that the user must know a great deal about telecommunications applications and networking.

LANs allow organizations to share expensive hardware and software. For instance, several PCs can share a single printer by being tied together in a LAN. LANs can promote productivity because users are no longer dependent on a centralized computer system (which can fail) or on the availability of a single peripheral device such as a printer. Finally, there are many new applications—such as electronic mail, graphics, video teleconferencing, and on-line applications—requiring high-capacity networks.

The most common use of LANs is for linking personal computers within a building or office to share information and expensive peripheral devices such as laser printers. Another popular application of LANs is in factories, in which they link computers and computer-controlled machines.

Figure 9.10 illustrates a LAN. The **server** acts as a librarian, storing various programs and data files for network users. The server determines who gets access to what and in what sequence. Servers may be powerful PCs with large hard disk capacity, workstations, minicomputers, or mainframes, although specialized computers are now available for this purpose. The server typically contains the LAN's **network operating system,** which manages the server and routes and manages communications on the network.

The network **gateway** connects the LAN to public networks, such as the telephone network, or to other corporate networks so that the LAN can exchange information with networks external to it. A gateway is generally a communications processor that can connect dissimilar networks by translating from one set of protocols to another. (A bridge connects two networks of the same type. A router is used to route messages through several connected LANs or to a wide area network.)

LAN technology consists of cabling (twisted wire, coaxial, or fiber-optic cable) or wireless technology that links individual computer devices, network interface cards (which are special adapters serving as interfaces to the cable), and software to control LAN activities. The LAN interface card specifies the data transmission rate, the size of message units, the addressing information attached to each message, and network topology (Ethernet utilizes a bus topology, for example).

local area network (LAN) A telecommunications network that requires its own dedicated channels and that encompasses a limited distance, usually one building or several buildings in close proximity.

server The computer in a network that stores various programs and data files for users of the network. Determines access and availability in the network.

network operating system Special software that manages the server in a LAN and routes and manages communications on the network.

gateway A communications processor that connects dissimilar networks by providing the translation from one set of protocols to another.

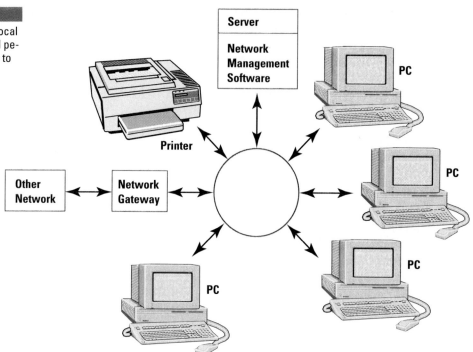

FIGURE 9.10

A local area network (LAN). A typical local area network connects computers and peripheral devices that are located close to each other, often in the same building.

baseband LAN channel technology that provides a single path for transmitting only text, graphics, voice, or video data at one time.

broadband LAN channel technology that provides several paths for transmitting text, graphics, voice, or video data so that different types of data can be transmitted simultaneously.

wide area network (WAN) Telecommunications network that spans a large geographical distance. May consist of a variety of cable, satellite, and microwave technologies.

switched lines Telephone lines that a person can access from a terminal to transmit data to another computer, the call being routed or switched through paths to the designated destination.

dedicated lines Telephone lines that are continuously available for transmission by a lessee. Typically conditioned to transmit data at high speeds for high-volume applications.

LAN technologies for physically connecting devices employ either a baseband or a broadband channel technology. **Baseband** products provide a single path for transmitting text, graphics, voice, or video data, and only one type of data at a time can be transmitted. **Broadband** products provide several paths so that different types of data can be transmitted simultaneously.

LAN capabilities are also defined by the network operating system. The network operating system can reside on every computer in the network, or it can reside on a single designated server for all applications on the network.

The primary disadvantages of LANs are that they are more expensive to install than PBXs and are more inflexible, requiring new wiring each time the LAN is moved. LANs require specially trained staff to manage and run them.

Wide Area Networks

Wide area networks (WANs) span broad geographical distances, ranging from several miles to across entire continents. Common carriers (companies licensed by the government to provide communications services to the public, such as AT&T or MCI) typically determine transmission rates or interconnections between lines, but the customer is responsible for telecommunications contents and management. It is up to the individual firm to establish the most efficient routing of messages, and to handle error checking, editing, protocols, and telecommunications management.

WANs may consist of a combination of switched and dedicated lines, microwave, and satellite communications. **Switched lines** are telephone lines that a person can access from a terminal to transmit data to another computer, the call being routed or switched through paths to the designated destination. **Dedicated lines,** or nonswitched lines, are continuously available for transmission, and the lessee typically pays a flat rate for total access to the line. The lines can be leased or purchased from common carriers or private communications media vendors. Dedicated lines are often conditioned to transmit data at higher speeds than switched lines and are more appropriate for higher-volume transmissions. Switched lines, on the other hand, are less expensive and more appropriate for low-volume applications requiring only occasional transmission.

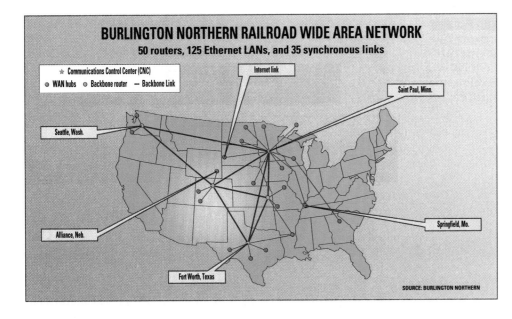

BURLINGTON NORTHERN RAILROAD WIDE AREA NETWORK

50 routers, 125 Ethernet LANs, and 35 synchronous links

★ Communications Control Center (CNC)
● WAN hubs   ● Backbone router   — Backbone Link

Internet link

Saint Paul, Minn.

Seattle, Wash.

Springfield, Mo.

Alliance, Neb.

Fort Worth, Texas

SOURCE: BURLINGTON NORTHERN

FIGURE 9.11

Burlington Northern's WAN plays a critical role in keeping its trains moving.
Source: Adapted from Peggy Wallace, "Burlington Northern Puts Down WAN Tracks," illustrator G. Boren, Infoworld, *December 20, 1993. Reprinted by permission of Infoworld.*

Individual business firms may maintain their own wide area networks. Figure 9.11 illustrates a wide area network used by the Burlington Northern Railroad to help keep its trains moving. The WAN carries traffic controls from dispatch offices to various rail locations, relaying information to make trains stop and start. But private wide area networks are expensive to maintain, or firms may not have the resources to manage their own wide area networks. In such instances, companies may choose to use commercial network services to communicate over vast distances.

Value-Added Networks

Value-added networks are an alternative to firms designing and managing their own networks. **Value-added networks (VANs)** are private, multipath, data-only, third-party-managed networks that can provide economies in the cost of service and in network management because they are used by multiple organizations. The value-added network is set up by a firm that is in charge of managing the network. That firm sells subscriptions to other firms wishing to use the network. Subscribers pay only for the amount of data they transmit plus a subscription fee. The network may utilize twisted-pair lines, satellite links, and other communications channels leased by the value-added carrier.

The term *value added* refers to the extra value added to communications by the telecommunications and computing services these networks provide to clients. Customers do not have to invest in network equipment and software or perform their own error checking, editing, routing, and protocol conversion. Subscribers may achieve savings in line charges and transmission costs because the costs of using the network are shared among many users. The resulting costs may be lower than if the clients had leased their own lines or satellite services. VANs are attractive for firms such as Continental Grain because they provide special services such as electronic mail and access to foreign telecommunications systems.

Continental Grain switched from a private network to GE Information Services' (GEIS) value-added network to link its 175 domestic locations with its 45 branch locations in South America, the Far East, and Europe. Continental found that switching to the value-added network reduced costs and reduced operational problems associated with networks. International VANs such as GEIS have representatives with language skills and knowledge of various countries' telecommunications administrations. The VANs have already leased lines from foreign telecommunications authorities or can arrange access to local networks and equipment abroad.

value-added network (VAN)
Private, multipath, data-only third-party-managed networks that are used by multiple organizations on a subscription basis.

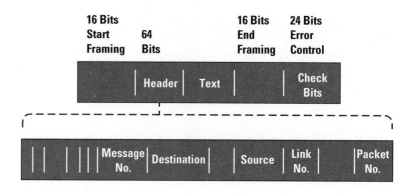

FIGURE 9.12

Packet switched networks and packet communications. Data are grouped into small packets, framed by identifying information, which are transmitted independently via various communication channels to maximize the potential of the paths in a network.

The leading international value-added networks provide casual or intermittent users international services on a dial-up basis and can provide a private network using dedicated circuits for customers requiring a full-time network. (Maintaining a private network may be most cost effective for organizations with a high communications volume.)

Another way value-added networks provide economies is through **packet switching.** Packet switching breaks up a lengthy block of text into small, fixed bundles of data (often 128 bytes each) called *packets* (see Figure 9.12). The VAN gathers information from many users, divides it into small packets, and continuously uses various communications channels to send the packets. Each packet travels independently through the network (this contrasts to one firm using a leased line, for example, for one hour and then not using it for three or four hours). Packets of data originating at one source can be routed through different paths in the network, and then may be reassembled into the original message when they reach their destination. Packet switching enables communications facilities to be utilized more fully by more users.

Frame relay is a faster and less expensive variant of packet switching. Frame relay is a shared network service that packages data into frames that are similar to packets. Frame relay, however, does not perform error correction. This is because so many of today's digital lines are cleaner than in the past and networks are more adept at correcting transmission problems. Frame relay can communicate at transmission speeds up to 1.544 megabits per second. Frame relay is essentially used for transmitting data. It is not recommended for any transmissions that are sensitive to varying delay, such as voice or digital video traffic, and it cannot easily control network congestion. Frame relay works successfully only over reliable lines that do not require frequent retransmission because of error.

Most corporations today use separate networks for voice, private-line services, and data, each of which is supported by a different technology. An emerging networking technology called **asynchronous transfer mode (ATM)** may overcome some of these problems because it can seamlessly and dynamically switch voice, data, images, and video between users. ATM also promises to tie LANs and wide area networks together more easily (LANs are generally based on lower-speed protocols, whereas WANs operate at higher speeds). ATM technology parcels information into uniform cells, each with 53 groups of 8 bytes, eliminating the need for protocol conversion. It can pass data between computers from different vendors and permits data to be transmitted at any speed the network handles (Vetter, 1995). ATM currently requires fiber-optic cable, but it can transmit up to 2.5 GBPS.

packet switching Technology that breaks blocks of text into small, fixed bundles of data and routes them in the most economical way through any available communications channel.

frame relay A shared network service technology that packages data into bundles for transmission but does not use error-correction routines. Cheaper and faster than packet switching.

asynchronous transfer mode (ATM) A networking technology that parcels information into 8-byte cells, allowing data to be transmitted between computers from different vendors at any speed.

9.4 HOW ORGANIZATIONS USE TELECOMMUNICATIONS FOR COMPETITIVE ADVANTAGE

Baxter International, described in Chapter 2, realized the strategic significance of telecommunications. The company placed its own computer terminals in hospital supply rooms and provided a direct telecommunications link with its central headquar-

Capespan's Global Network Delivers Fresh Produce

The emergence of the supermarket in Europe, combined with the growing economic unity of Europe, has forced Capespan International PLC to examine its organization and turn to a new telecommunications network to meet its customers' needs. Although Capespan is headquartered in Farnham Royal, England, it is a South African exporter of produce to Europe. (Capespan is jointly owned by Outspan International in Pretoria and Unifruco Ltd. in Capetown, two South African fruit exporting firms.) Their major exports include oranges, plums, apples, mangos, and avocados. In 1995, the company recorded $825 million in sales, and they expect that number to increase to $1.5 billion by the year 2000.

Traditionally the company loaded its tens of millions of cartons of produce on its ships in South African ports with the products being tracked only by the number of cartons of each product. When the shipment arrived in a European port, the sales staff sold the cartons to customers and then they were distributed. Most information was gathered manually. There was no time for last-minute decisions such as customer-specific labeling requests or changes in delivery times.

According to Gwynne Foster, Capespan's manager of information services, this "previous view of the world—that we bring in the product en mass to local sales offices—doesn't fit the trading environment moving into the future." In other words, the company had to change its whole method of sales and distribution. The immediate driving force was the emergence of supermarkets in Europe in the 1980s. Because the supermarket environment places an emphasis on quality, the products must arrive on time and in good condition. Name branding became important. "When you walk into a supermarket in the UK, every apple has a label on it," points out Foster. No longer can the supplier simply distribute and ship massive numbers of cartons of products. The products now need specific brands, and specific cartons must go to designated customers—Unifroco's Granny Smith apples and Outspan's navel oranges must get to specific stores branded in a precise way.

Capespan developed a new information system to help it thrive in the new market. The new Capespan system maintains details on each carton, including such details as the grower, the packaging, the chemical treatment of the product, and inspection information. The data are fed into the system at the South African shipping dock, where each carton is scanned using a handheld scanner. The product is then tracked as it travels to Europe and eventually to customers. Also, a manifest is created listing what is on each vessel. The manifest data are transmitted to Europe as soon as they are available, using Capespan's new network. The network operates through IBM Global Network and ties the organization together, linking more than half of its 200 trading partners.

Each sales office and receiving port receives the manifest, enabling the sales office to know what is available for sale and the port to plan for the off-loading of the goods. The sales office then sells the specific products to customers, and both the seller and the customer can plan in advance for customer-specific labeling. Delivery to the customer can also be planned, and the customer knows what to expect. As Foster explained, "The whole thrust of the system is to get information about the product in the chain before the product comes through the chain." She adds, "Had we not taken dramatic steps, we would not have supported our customers."

Foster believes the new system has also given the company the flexibility to respond to changes in the market as Europe continues to unify. No one knows just what market changes will occur, although a new system of buying based on pan-European fruit buyers has already emerged. Prior to the installation of this system, Capespan had little flexibility and little capacity to respond rapidly to pan-European buyers or to any other coming changes. Now the company believes that although its technology will certainly have to change as the market evolves, the technology has the foundation to enable Capespan to make those changes.

To Think About: *How did market changes force Capespan to make changes in its business processes? What management, organization, and technology issues did Capespan have to face to make the required changes?*

Source: Jeanette Borzo, "African-European Network Means Peachy Prospects for Capespan," *Computerworld Global Innovators,* March 10, 1997.

ters via a VAN. Customers could dial up a local VAN node and send their orders directly to the company. Since then, many other corporations have realized the strategic potential of networked computer systems (see the Window on Organizations).

Telecommunications has helped eliminate barriers of geography and time, enabling organizations to accelerate the pace of production, to speed decision making, to forge new products, to move into new markets, and to create new relationships with customers and suppliers. Many of the strategic applications described in

Chapter 2 would not be possible without telecommunications. Firms that fail to consider telecommunications in their strategic plans will fall behind (Keen, 1986).

Facilitating Applications

Some of the leading telecommunications applications for communication, coordination, and speeding the flow of transactions, messages, and information throughout business firms are electronic mail, voice mail, facsimile (fax) machines, digital information services, teleconferencing, dataconferencing, videoconferencing, electronic data interchange, and groupware.

Electronic Mail

electronic mail (e-mail) The computer-to-computer exchange of messages.

Electronic mail, or **e-mail,** is the computer-to-computer exchange of messages. A person can use a PC attached to a modem or a terminal to send notes and even lengthier documents just by typing in the name of the message's recipient. Many organizations operate their own internal electronic mail systems, but communications companies such as MCI and AT&T offer these services, as do commercial on-line information services such as America Online, CompuServe, and Prodigy and public networks on the Internet (see Chapter 10). E-mail eliminates telephone tag and costly long-distance telephone charges, expediting communication between different parts of the organization. Nestlé SA, the Swiss-based multinational food corporation, installed an electronic mail system to connect its 60,000 employees in 80 countries. Nestlé's European units can use the electronic mail system to share information about production schedules and inventory levels to ship excess products from one country to another.

E-mail systems present security problems because without adequate protection, electronic eavesdroppers can read the mail as it moves through a network. We discuss such security problems in Chapter 17. The Window on Management looks at the privacy of e-mail messages from a different perspective, examining whether monitoring employees using e-mail, the Internet, and other network facilities is ethical.

Voice Mail

voice mail A system for digitizing a spoken message and transmitting it over a network.

A **voice mail** system digitizes the spoken message of the sender, transmits it over a network, and stores the message on disk for later retrieval. When the recipient is ready to listen, the messages are reconverted to audio form. Various store-and-forward capabilities notify recipients that messages are waiting. Recipients have the option of saving these messages for future use, deleting them, or routing them to other parties.

Facsimile Machines

facsimile (fax) machine A machine that digitizes and transmits documents with both text and graphics over telephone lines.

Facsimile (fax) machines can transmit documents containing both text and graphics over ordinary telephone lines. A sending fax machine scans and digitizes the document image. The digitized document is then transmitted over a network and reproduced in hard copy form by a receiving fax machine. The process results in a duplicate, or facsimile, of the original.

Digital Information Services

Powerful and far-reaching digital electronic services now enable networked PC and workstation users to obtain information from outside the firm instantaneously without leaving their desks. Stock prices, historical references to periodicals, industrial supplies catalogs, legal research, news articles, reference works, weather forecasts, and travel information are just some of the electronic databases that can be accessed on-line. Many of these services have capabilities for electronic mail, electronic bulletin boards, and for on-line discussion groups, shopping, and travel reservations. Table 9.3 describes the leading commercial digital information services. An extension

Monitoring Employees on Networks: Unethical or Good Business?

Should managers monitor employees using networks? Is it unethical or is it just good business? Although many view monitoring employee e-mail as unethical and even an illegal invasion of privacy, many companies consider it to be legitimate. They claim they need to know that the business facilities they own are being used to further their business goals. Some also argue that they need to be able to search electronic mail messages for evidence of illegal activities, racial discrimination, or sexual harassment. Others argue that the company needs access to business information stored in e-mail files just the same as if it were stored in paper file cabinets.

E-mail privacy within a company is not covered by U.S. federal law. The Electronic Communications Privacy Act of 1986 only prohibits interception or disclosure of e-mail messages by parties outside the company where the messages were sent without a proper warrant. Lawsuits have so far failed to limit the right of companies to monitor e-mail. For example, when Alana Shoars, a former e-mail administrator at Epson America Inc. discovered that her supervisor was copying and reading employees' e-mail, she sued in the Los Angeles, California, courts, alleging invasion of privacy. Later she filed a class action suit in the name of 700 Epson employees and 1800 outsiders also charging privacy invasion. Both cases were dismissed on the grounds that e-mail does not fall within the state's wiretapping laws.

Despite the lack of legal restrictions, many observers see electronic mail privacy as serious. Michael Godwin, legal adviser for the Electronic Frontier Foundation, recommends that employers who intend to monitor e-mail establish a stated policy to that effect. Various companies have such policies, including Nordstrom, Eastman Kodak, and Federal Express, all of which claim the right to intercept and read employee e-mail. General Motors and Hallmark Cards have policies that grant employees greater privacy.

The Internet presents different issues—the use of company facilities for nonbusiness purposes, and even for illegal uses such as retrieving pornography. Management can use new Web monitoring tools to monitor what employees are doing on the Internet. These tools can track what Web sites users visit, the files they download, and even the categories of information they search for using Web information-searching tools. Some employers want to make sure that employees aren't wasting company time by surfing the Web to check sports scores or plan for vacations. Systems administrators can also use these tools to make sure that valuable network resources aren't being wasted on non-business-related activities.

Some employers take a tough stance. Sixty-four employees at Sandia Labs in Albuquerque, New Mexico, were disciplined for reading pornography at work on company time—or on their own time. Many were suspended without pay. Other firms, including Eli Lilly, publish a clear policy and then leave it to individual managers to enforce it if they so choose. Many, however, take a middle-of-the-road position. At Chicago's WMS Industries, the IS department logs the amount of time each employee spends on the Net and sends such reports to managers to use as they wish.

To Think About: Do you believe management should have the right to monitor employee e-mail and Internet usage? Why or why not? Describe the problems such monitoring might present to management.

Sources: Sharon Machlis, "Gotcha! Monitoring Tools Check Web Surfing at Work," *Computerworld,* April 7, 1997; Alice LaPlante, "Firms Spell Out Appropriate Use of Internet for Employees," *Computerworld,* February 5, 1996; and "Does E-Mail Mean Everyone's Mail?" *Information Week,* January 3, 1994.

of the Windows 95 operating system will let users use Microsoft Network, Microsoft's on-line information service featuring interactive publishing tools. In the following chapter we describe the capabilities of the Internet, a publicly available system of networks offering access to many thousands of databases throughout the world.

Teleconferencing, Dataconferencing, and Videoconferencing

People can meet electronically—even though they are hundreds or thousands of miles apart—by using teleconferencing, dataconferencing, or videoconferencing. **Teleconferencing** allows a group of people to confer simultaneously via telephone or via electronic mail group communication software. Teleconferencing that includes the ability of two or more people at distant locations to work on the same document or data simultaneously is called **dataconferencing.** With dataconferencing, two or more users at distant locations are able to edit and directly modify data (text, such as word processing documents; numeric, such as spreadsheets; and graphic) files simultaneously.

teleconferencing The ability to confer with a group of people simultaneously using the telephone or electronic mail group communication software.

dataconferencing Teleconferencing in which two or more users are able to edit and directly modify data files simultaneously.

Table 9.3	Commercial Digital Information Services
Provider	Type of Service
America Online	General interest/business information
CompuServe	General interest/business information
Prodigy	General interest/business information
Microsoft Network	General interest/business information
Dow Jones News Retrieval	Business/financial information
Quotron	Financial information
Dialog	Business/scientific/technical information
Lexis	Legal research
Nexis	News/business information

videoconferencing Teleconferencing with the capability of participants to see each other over video screens.

Teleconferencing that also has the capability to let participants see each other face-to-face over video screens is termed *video teleconferencing,* or **videoconferencing.**

These various forms of electronic conferencing are growing in popularity because they save travel time and cost. Legal firms might use videoconferencing to take depositions and to convene meetings between lawyers in different branch offices. For example, the firm of Howrey & Simon with 300 lawyers in Los Angeles has several expensive teleconferencing rooms that are busy almost constantly, linking them with their staff counterparts in Washington, D.C. Designers and engineers use videoconferencing for remote collaboration. The cosmetics manufacturer Estée Lauder is using desktop videoconferencing to enable staff in Manhattan and Melville, Long Island, to view products under design along with the talking heads of meeting par-

Department stores such as Marshall Fields, a unit of Dayton Hudson, use electronic commerce services to track inventory from the warehouses to the truck and into its stores. By helping companies coordinate their supply chains, telecommunications applications can provide a competitive advantage.

Videoconferencing on the Internet

The Internet has opened many new ways for people to communicate, and videoconferencing is one of the most exciting. For the cost of a local telephone call, you can have a conference or work collaboratively on a whiteboard with anyone in the world. One leading Internet videoconferencing tool is CU-SeeMe. CU-SeeMe is an Internet-based videoconferencing program developed at Cornell University that can run on Windows or Macintosh computers connected to the Internet. By using a "reflector" program, which mirrors transmissions to every videoconferencing participant, multiple parties at different locations can use their desktop computers to participate in a CU-SeeMe conference.

CU-SeeMe supports up to eight "windows" to other parties on a computer screen. The biggest advantage to Internet-based systems is the price. A pared-down version of CU-SeeMe is available as free shareware, but many businesses prefer Enhanced CU-SeeMe, a mature production version of the software, marketed by White Pine Software for $499. CU-SeeMe requires little extra equipment, and virtually none for parties that only need to sit in on a conference or use a whiteboard. This tool is very well suited for "talking head" applications, in which people are mainly sitting at their desks and not giving elaborate presentations.

Those with a Windows PC system that need to be an active part of a meeting would need a videocamera, a video capture board (if not bundled with their camera), a sound card, and a microphone (if one is not built into their computer system). New multimedia systems by Compaq, IBM, and Packard Bell include a mix of preloaded conferencing software and cameras. No extra hardware is required to speed up data transmission, because the software does all the data compression and decompression. CU-SeeMe is easy to install.

The World Bank, the Washington, D.C.–based development institution, has offices or partner organizations in 180 countries and thus an urgent need for global communications. It operates with tight budgets and limited travel resources. The World Bank uses the White Pines software commercial version of CU-SeeMe to conduct small meetings and "virtual seminars" among employees in the United States, Egypt, Russia, and other countries. Although the video image that CU-SeeMe produces does not measure more than four inches square, and the feed does not always appear very smooth, its low cost allows the World Bank to let more employees work collaboratively from far-away locations. Users can brainstorm on a common electronic whiteboard, and they will soon be able to use CU-SeeMe to share applications as well. For large group meetings and training sessions, the World Bank uses PictureTel's videoconferencing system, a high-end desktop product.

To Think About: What business processes can be streamlined through videoconferencing? What management, organization, and technology factors would you consider to decide whether to use Internet-based videoconferencing?

Sources: Jose Alvear and Ronen Yaari, "You've Got a Video Call on Your Desktop," *NetGuide,* February 1997; and Lynda Radosevich, "Sizzle and Steak," *WebMaster,* November 1996.

---

ticipants. Hospitals, universities, and even corporate researchers are using videoconferencing to fill in personnel expertise gaps (Brandel, 1995; Frye, 1995). Electronic conferencing is even useful in supporting telecommuting, enabling home workers to meet with or collaborate with their counterparts working in the office or elsewhere.

Videoconferencing has usually required special video conference rooms and videocameras, microphones, television monitors, and a computer equipped with a codec device that converts video images and analog sound waves into digital signals and compresses them for transfer over communications channels. Another codec on the receiving end reconverts the digital signals back into analog for display on the receiving monitor. PC-based desktop videoconferencing systems where users can see each other and simultaneously work on the same document are reducing videoconferencing costs so that more organizations can benefit from this technology.

Desktop videoconferencing systems typically provide a local window, in which you can see yourself, and a remote window to display the individual with whom you are conversing. Most desktop systems provide audio capabilities for two-way real-time conversations and a whiteboard. The whiteboard is a built-in shared drawing program that lets multiple users collaborate on projects by modifying images and text on-line. Desktop videoconferencing software is now available for use on the Internet, as the Window on Technology describes.

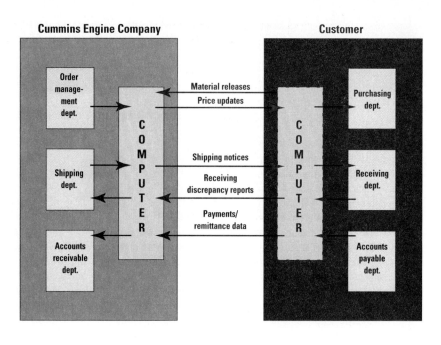

Electronic Data Interchange

electronic data interchange (EDI)
The direct computer-to-computer exchange between two organizations of standard business transaction documents.

Electronic data interchange (EDI) is the direct computer-to-computer exchange between two organizations of standard business transaction documents such as invoices, bills of lading, or purchase orders. EDI saves money and time because transactions can be transmitted from one information system to another through a telecommunications network, eliminating the printing and handling of paper at one end and the inputting of data at the other. EDI may also provide strategic benefits by helping a firm lock in customers, making it easier for customers or distributors to order from them rather than from competitors.

EDI differs from electronic mail in that it transmits an actual structured transaction (with distinct fields such as the transaction date, transaction amount, sender's name, and recipient's name) as opposed to an unstructured text message such as a letter.

Figure 9.13 illustrates how EDI operates at the Cummins Engine Company. Cummins implemented EDI to automate purchasing, shipping, and payment transactions with its customers. Cummins transmits price updates and shipping notices directly to its customers' computer system. Customers in turn transmit material releases, reports on receiving discrepancies, and payment and remittance data directly to Cummins's computer system. EDI has replaced paper for these transactions.

EDI lowers routine transaction processing costs and turnaround time because there is less need to transfer data from hard copy forms into computer-ready transactions. EDI reduces transcription errors and associated costs that occur when data are entered and printed out many times. Chapter 2 has shown how EDI can also curb inventory costs by minimizing the amount of time components are in inventory. Organizations can most fully benefit from EDI when they integrate the data supplied by EDI with applications such as accounts payable, inventory control, shipping, and production planning (Premkumar, Ramamurthy, and Nilakanta, 1994). However, to use EDI successfully, companies must standardize the form of the transactions they use with other firms and comply with legal requirements for verifying that the transactions are authentic.

As intelligent agent technology and commercial networks open new electronic marketplaces, they will lead to more flexible forms of EDI in which exchange of

Table 9.4	Groupware Capabilities
Group writing and commenting	
Electronic mail distribution	
Scheduling meetings and appointments	
Shared files and databases	
Shared time lines and plans	
Electronic meetings	

purchase and sale transactions are not limited to the computer systems of two organizations.

Groupware

Groupware provides functions and services to support the collaborative activities of work groups. Groupware includes software for information sharing, electronic meetings, scheduling, and e-mail, and a network to connect the members of the group as they work on their own desktop computers, often in widely scattered locations. The groupware definition of groups is fluid, allowing users to define the work groups, with multiple group definitions allowed. For example, a manager may define a group of only those people who work for him. A group may be established for all employees dealing with a specific customer. A companywide group may be established. Of course, an individual may belong to as many of those groups as is appropriate. Table 9.4 describes the capabilities of groupware.

Groupware enhances collaboration by allowing the exchange of ideas (in the form of electronic messages) on a given topic. All the messages on that topic will be saved in a group, stamped with the date, time, and author. Any group member can

groupware Software that recognizes the significance of groups in offices by providing functions and services that support the collaborative activities of work groups.

Lotus Notes groupware facilitates collaboration by enabling members of a group to share documents, schedule meetings, and discuss activities, events, and issues.

review the ideas of others at any time and add ideas of his or her own. Similarly, individuals can post a document for other members of the group to comment on or edit. Members of a group can post requests for help from the group, and any member of the group can respond and can view the responses of other members of the group. Finally, if a group so chooses, the members of that group can store their work notes on the groupware so that all others in the group can see what progress is being made, what problems occur, and what activities are planned.

The leading commercial groupware product has been Lotus Notes from the Lotus Development Corporation. The Internet can be used for many groupware functions (see Chapters 10 and 15). Microsoft Internet Explorer 4.0 and Netscape Communicator include groupware functions.

The Emergency Operations Center of Pacific Gas and Electric (PG&E) uses Lotus Notes groupware to receive damage reports and repair requests from 150 offices throughout the 93,000 square miles in Northern California. While management in San Francisco may use the database to view a chronological list of outages, the local offices will use it to produce a listing of outages that still need repairing. ABB Area Brown, Ltd., the world's largest electrical engineering firm, uses Notes to standardize its office applications worldwide. Chapter 15 provides more detail on how organizations are using groupware to coordinate and distribute knowledge.

9.5   MANAGEMENT ISSUES AND DECISIONS

The starting point for rational planning of telecommunications is to forget about the features of systems and instead try to understand the requirements of one's organization. A telecommunications plan is more likely to succeed if it advances the key business goals of the company. Cutting costs and installing advanced systems for their own sake is rarely a sufficient reason to justify large telecommunications projects.

The Telecommunications Plan

Telecommunications has enormous potential for enhancing a firm's strategic position, but managers need to determine exactly how the firm's competitive position could be enhanced by telecommunications technology. Managers need to ask how telecommunications can reduce costs by increasing the *scale* and *scope* of operations without additional management costs; they need to determine if telecommunications technology can help them *differentiate* products and services; or if telecommunications technology can improve the firm's *cost structure* by eliminating intermediaries such as distributors or by accelerating business processes.

There are steps to implementing a strategic telecommunications plan. First, start with an audit of the communications functions in your firm. What are your voice, data, video, equipment, staffing, and management capabilities? Then identify priorities for improvement.

Second, you must know the long-range business plans of your firm. Your plan should include an analysis of precisely how telecommunications will contribute to the specific five-year goals of the firm and to its longer-range strategies (e.g., cost reduction, distribution enhancement).

Third, identify critical areas where telecommunications currently does or can have the potential to make a large difference in performance. In insurance, these may be systems that give field representatives quick access to policy and rate information; in retailing, inventory control and market penetration; and in industrial products, rapid, efficient distribution and transportation.

Implementing the Plan

Once an organization has developed a business telecommunications plan, it must determine the initial scope of the telecommunications project. Managers should take eight factors into account when choosing a telecommunications network.

The first and most important factor is *distance*. If communication will be largely local and entirely internal to the organization's buildings and social networks, there is little or no need for VANs, leased lines, or long-distance communications.

Along with distance, one must consider the *range of services* the network must support, such as electronic mail, EDI, internally generated transactions, voice mail, videoconferencing, or imaging, and whether these services must be integrated in the same network.

A third factor to consider is *security*. The most secure means of long-distance communications is through lines that are owned by the organization. The next most secure form of telecommunications is through dedicated leased lines. VANs that slice up corporate information into small packets are among the least secure modes. Finally, ordinary telephone lines, which can be tapped at several locations, are even less secure than VANs.

A fourth factor to consider is whether *multiple access* is required throughout the organization or whether it can be limited to one or two nodes within the organization. A multiple-access system requirement suggests that there will be perhaps several thousand users throughout the corporation; therefore, a commonly available technology such as installed telephone wire and the related technology of a PBX is recommended. However, if access is restricted to fewer than 100 high-intensity users, a more advanced, higher-speed technology such as a fiber-optic or broadband LAN system may be recommended.

A fifth and most difficult factor to judge is *utilization*. There are two aspects of utilization that must be considered when developing a telecommunications network: the frequency and the volume of communications. Together, these two factors determine the total load on the telecommunications system. On the one hand, high-frequency, high-volume communications suggest the need for high-speed LANs for local communication and leased lines for long-distance communication. On the other hand, low-frequency, low-volume communications suggest dial-up, voice-grade telephone circuits operating through a traditional modem.

A sixth factor is *cost*. How much does each telecommunications option cost? Total costs should include costs for development, operations, maintenance, expansion, and overhead. Which cost components are fixed? Which are variable? Are there any hidden costs to anticipate? It is wise to recall the *thruway effect*. The easier it is to use a communications path, the more people will want to use it. Most telecommunications planners estimate future needs on the high side and still often underestimate the actual need. Underestimating the cost of telecommunications projects or uncontrollable telecommunications costs are principal causes of network failure.

Seventh, you must consider the difficulties of *installing* the telecommunications system. Are the organization's buildings properly constructed to install fiber optics? In some instances, buildings have inadequate wiring channels underneath the floors, which makes installation of fiber-optic cable extremely difficult.

Eighth, you must consider how much *connectivity* would be required to make all of the components in a network communicate with each other or to tie together multiple networks. There are so many different standards for hardware, software, and communication systems that it may be very difficult to distribute information from one network to another. The Internet cannot always solve these connecting problems. Chapter 10 treats connectivity issues in greater detail. Table 9.5 summarizes these implementation factors.

Table 9.5	Implementation Factors in Telecommunications Systems
Distance	
Range of services	
Security	
Multiple access	
Utilization	
Cost	
Installation	
Connectivity	

MANAGEMENT

Managers need to be deeply involved in telecommunications decisions because telecommunications is so deeply ingrained in today's information systems and business processes. Management should identify the business opportunities linked to telecommunications, establish the business criteria to be used in selecting the firm's telecommunications platform, and make the economic case for telecommunications investments (Keen and Cummins, 1994).

ORGANIZATION

By using telecommunications to reduce transaction and coordination costs, organizations can extend their reach and even offer new products and services. An organization's telecommunications infrastructure should support its business processes and its business strategy.

TECHNOLOGY

Telecommunications technology is intertwined with all the other information technologies and deeply embedded in most contemporary applications. Networks are becoming more pervasive and powerful, with growing capabilities to transmit voice, data, and video over long distances. Selection of transmission media and network design are key technology decisions.

For Discussion: Network design is a key business decision as well as a technology decision. Discuss.

SUMMARY

1. Describe the basic components of a telecommunications system. A telecommunications system is a set of compatible devices that are used to develop a network for communication from one location to another by electronic means. The essential components of a telecommunications system are computers, terminals, or other input/output devices, communications channels, communications processors (such as modems, multiplexers, controllers, and front-end processors), and telecommunications software. Different components of a telecommunications network can communicate with each other with a common set of rules termed *protocols*.

Data are transmitted throughout a telecommunications network using either analog signals or digital signals. A modem is a device that translates from analog to digital and vice versa.

2. Measure the capacity of telecommunications channels and evaluate transmission media. The capacity of a telecommunications channel is determined by the range of frequencies it can accommodate. The higher the range of frequencies, called *bandwidth*, the higher the capacity (measured in bits per second). The principal transmission media are twisted copper telephone wire, coaxial copper cable, fiber-optic cable, and wireless transmission utilizing microwave, satellite, low frequency radio, or infrared waves.

Transmission media use either synchronous or asynchronous transmission modes for determining where a character begins or ends and when data are transmitted from one computer to another. Three different transmission modes governing the direction of data flow over a transmission medium are simplex, half-duplex, and full-duplex transmission.

3. Describe the three basic network topologies. The three common network topologies are the *star* network, the *bus* network, and the *ring* network. In a star network, all communications must pass through a central computer. The bus network links a number of devices to a single channel and broadcasts all the signals to the entire network, with special software to identify which components receive each message. In a ring network, each computer in the network can communicate directly with any other computer but the channel is a closed loop. Data are passed along the ring from one computer to another.

4. Classify the various types of telecommunications networks. Networks can be classified by their shape or configuration or by their geographic scope and type of services provided. *Local area networks (LANs)* and *private branch exchanges (PBXs)* are used to link offices and buildings in close proximity. *Wide area networks (WANs)* span a broad geographical distance, ranging from several miles to entire continents and are private networks that are independently managed. *Value-added networks (VANs)* also encompass a wide geographic area but are managed by a third party, which sells the services of the network to other companies.

5. Identify telecommunications applications that can provide competitive advantage to organizations. Using information systems for strategic advantage increasingly depends on telecommunications technology and applications such as electronic mail, voice mail, fax, digital information services, teleconferencing, dataconferencing, videoconferencing, electronic data interchange (EDI), and groupware. Electronic data interchange (EDI) is the direct computer-to-computer exchange between two organizations of standard business transaction documents such as invoices, bills of lading, and purchase orders. Groupware allows people working in groups to collaborate and share information.

6. Explain the criteria used in planning for telecommunications systems. Firms should develop strategic telecommunications plans to ensure that their telecommunications systems serve business objectives and operations. Important factors to consider are distance, range of services, security, access, utilization, cost, installation, and connectivity.

KEY TERMS

Telecommunications	Mobile data networks	Multiplexer	Dedicated lines
Information superhighway	Personal communication	Telecommunications	Value-added network (VAN)
Telecommunications	services (PCS)	software	Packet switching
system	Personal digital	Topology	Frame relay
Protocol	assistant (PDA)	Star network	Asynchronous transfer
Analog signal	Baud	Bus network	mode (ATM)
Digital signal	Bandwidth	Ring network	Electronic mail (e-mail)
Modem	Asynchronous transmission	Private branch	Voice mail
Channels	Synchronous transmission	exchange (PBX)	Facsimile (fax) machine
Twisted wire	Simplex transmission	Local area network (LAN)	Teleconferencing
Coaxial cable	Half-duplex transmission	Server	Dataconferencing
Fiber-optic cable	Full-duplex transmission	Network operating system	Videoconferencing
Microwave	Communications	Gateway	Electronic data
Satellite	processors	Baseband	interchange (EDI)
Low-orbit satellites	Front-end processor	Broadband	Groupware
Paging system	Concentrator	Wide area network (WAN)	
Cellular telephone	Controller	Switched lines	

REVIEW QUESTIONS

1. What is the significance of telecommunications deregulation for managers and organizations?

2. What is a telecommunications system? What are the principal functions of all telecommunications systems?

3. Name and briefly describe each of the components of a telecommunications system.

4. Distinguish between an analog and a digital signal.

5. Name the different types of telecommunications transmission media and compare them in terms of speed and cost.

6. What is the relationship between bandwidth and the transmission capacity of a channel?

7. What is the difference between synchronous and asynchronous transmission? Between half-duplex, duplex, and simplex transmission?

8. Name and briefly describe the different kinds of communications processors.

9. Name and briefly describe the three principal network topologies.

10. Distinguish between a PBX and a LAN.

11. Define a wide area network (WAN).

12. Define the following:
   - Modem
   - Baud
   - Gateway
   - Value-added network (VAN)
   - Packet switching
   - Asynchronous transfer mode (ATM)

13. Name and describe the telecommunications applications that can provide strategic benefits to businesses.

14. What are the principal factors to consider when developing a telecommunications plan?

GROUP PROJECT

With a group of two or three of your fellow students, describe in detail the various ways that telecommunications technology can provide a firm with competitive advantage. Use the companies described in Chapter 2 or other chapters you have read about so far to illustrate the points you make, or select examples of other companies using telecommunications from business or computer magazines. Present your findings to the class.

CASE STUDY

Rosenbluth International Travels a Telecommunications Route to Success

The travel service industry is in trouble. Airlines have capped the commissions they will pay to travel agents, and these commissions have been the main source of their income. Travel agents can no longer afford to pay major corporate clients for the right to handle their travel business. In addition, global competition has forced many corporations to cut back on all expenses, including travel. Finally, the World Wide Web now makes it easy for individuals (whether as private persons or employees) to investigate and book their own travel arrangements. Management at Rosenbluth International Travel had to face this formidable reality and find a way to thrive in the face of these developments.

Rosenbluth Travel, a privately held, family-owned company, is the third (some say second) largest travel services firm in the world, with American Express being number one. Rosenbluth has $2.5 billion in annual sales and nearly 3500 employees in over 1000 locations in 41 countries. Headquartered in Philadelphia, Pennsylvania, the company was founded in 1892 and was a relatively small company when Hal Rosenbluth joined the firm in 1974. When, in 1984, he obtained a contract to provide all of DuPont Corporation's travel services, the company's explosive growth began. Rosenbluth was a success with DuPont because he managed to save the company $150 million in travel and entertainment (T&E) expenses.

The company now is perhaps best known because of Hal Rosenbluth's management style—a focus on making employees happy. He believes that by creating a humane working environment, and by genuinely putting employees (called "associates" at Rosenbluth) first, they will give more to the company, resulting in the company offering better service to its customers. "Our only sustainable competitive advantage," Rosenbluth maintains, "are the associates and the environment in which we work." Although his approach remains central to the company, by itself it would not continue to make the company successful in the radically new environment. The strategy that has worked begins with understanding the value that Rosenbluth International can add to its clients by helping them manage their travel and entertainment costs.

How can Rosenbluth add value and help companies manage their T&E costs? The company relies heavily on cutting-edge information technology. First, at the level of the individual trip, it has lowered airline costs by developing a way to search for the lowest fares that will meet the requirements of the traveler. DACODA is Rosenbluth's yield management system. The software focuses on the client company's optimal air program worldwide. One of its functions is to sort through the complex airline databases, analyzing their pricing and discounting schemes. Travelers are then given a list of choices from which to select within the time, date, and location parameters they have given. Through its software, Rosenbluth also tracks and manages a series of qualitative preferences that can offer its clients a better trip for the same cost. For example, the system combines personal preference information with flight data to enable many travelers to spend less time on the ground between connections. The software also maintains such data as seating preferences for each client, including traveler concerns about placement related to the wings.

As client employees travel, much of their travel data, both booked and billed, is automatically stored into Rosenbluth's databases, making it very easy for travelers and their employers to record and monitor expenses. VISION is the proprietary Rosenbluth real-time software package that instantly collects client travel data. The traveler is presented with a simple, easy-to-use interface to enter, submit, and track expenses during the trip. This software package even enforces the client company's travel policies for each trip. It integrates the data regardless of where the reservation is made or which airline reservation system is used. This software is the source of management reports that are customized to meet client-specific needs. Thus, management can easily monitor and control all its corporate travel and entertainment expenses.

Rosenbluth's global distribution network (GDN) is a worldwide telecommunication network through which the airline reservation systems are accessible. All Rosenbluth agents are connected to GDN, as are most of the company's travel software applications. Clients planning trips can either use the network to research and book their travel arrangements, or they can work through a Rosenbluth agent. Moreover, clients can choose to use a local Rosenbluth agent, or they can turn to specific agents of their choice located anywhere in the world.

Wal-Mart is a good example of a satisfied customer. Every traveler within the giant retailing company has access to a Rosenbluth reservation through a desktop or laptop computer connected to Wal-Mart's local area network. The company's 7000 frequent travelers book their own hotel, air, and auto rental reservations by calling up Rosenbluth's reservation system. They enter their name, travel dates, times, and cities of origin, destination, and stopover. Rosenbluth's software then creates a grid of flight options that adhere to Wal-Mart travel policies. The employee clicks a few buttons and the reservations are completed. Some other companies accomplish the same thing by having their employees access Rosenbluth software through Rosenbluth's new World Wide Web site. This approach is particularly cost effective for Rosenbluth clients, because the clients only need to give their employees Web browser software and a connection to the Internet.

The BOC group is another satisfied customer, one of many companies that have turned to Rosenbluth because of what they offer in this new travel environment. BOC is a British-based company with specialties in gases, vacuum technology, and health care. It is a giant, with sales of over $6 billion and 40,000 employees in over 1200 sites within 60 countries. By 1998 Rosenbluth will be handling all BOC travel worldwide.

In addition to aiding their clients, Rosenbluth has been forced to cut its own costs to the bone to survive in the new environment. To accomplish this, they also have relied heavily on technology. For example, the agents use the same software the clients use so that they too can easily and quickly locate the lowest fares, book flights for their clients, and otherwise enable them to serve the clients quickly. The company has also examined the working methods of its agents to find ways for the agents to work more efficiently. Rosenbluth himself noticed that his agents typed the same words repeatedly. So he ordered their computer interface be modified where possible to present prompts that required only "yes" and "no" responses. The developers also changed the programs to display the client company's travel guidelines on the screen so that the agent would not waste time creating options for a client that are outside the company guidelines. As a result of these changes, agents experienced a 75 percent reduction in keystrokes, a significant increase in productivity.

The global network also makes an enormous contribution to reducing Rosenbluth costs. Because of the network, it does not matter where the travel agent is physically located. As a result, Rosenbluth has been able to establish a series of centralized reservation centers, known as "intellicenters." These centers are located in North Dakota, Delaware, and Allentown, Pennsylvania, all locations where labor costs are low but the work ethic is high. Costs are low enough in these centers that Rosenbluth is able to offer its clients a significant reduction in costs for booking through one of the intellicenters. The network also is managed so that if one reservation center becomes overloaded, excess calls are immediately and automatically routed to another center where current volume is lower. For example, during the great East Coast blizzard of January 1996, about 21,000 calls were rerouted in this way without any problem. Customers didn't even know they were being rerouted. ∎

Source: Rob Walker, "Back to the Farm," *Fast Company*, February/March 1997; and http://www.boc.com;http://www.captura.com;http://www.rosenbluth.com.

REFERENCES

Berst, Jesse. "Deciphering Lotus' Notes." *Computerworld* (May 18, 1992).

Brandel, Mary. "Videoconferencing Slowly Goes Desktop." *Computerworld* (February 20, 1995).

Dertouzos, Michael. "Building the Information Marketplace." *Technology Review* (January 1991).

Donovan, John J. "Beyond Chief Information Officer to Network Manager." *Harvard Business Review* (September–October 1988).

Etzioni, Oren, and Daniel Weld. "A Softbot-Based Interface to the Internet." *Communications of the ACM 37*, no. 7 (July 1994).

Frye, Colleen. "Talking Heads: Coming to a Desktop Near You." *Software Magazine* (May 1995).

Gilder, George. "Into the Telecosm." *Harvard Business Review* (March–April 1991).

Grief, Irene. "Desktop Agents in Group-Enabled Projects." *Communications of the ACM 37*, no. 7 (July 1994).

Grover, Varun, and Martin D. Goslar. "Initiation, Adoption, and Implementation of Telecommunications Technologies in U.S. Organizations." *Journal of Management Information Systems 10*, no. 1 (Summer 1993).

Hall, Wayne A., and Robert E. McCauley. "Planning and Managing a Corporate Network Utility." *MIS Quarterly* (December 1987).

Hammer, Michael, and Glenn Mangurian. "The Changing Value of Communications Technology." *Sloan Management Review* (Winter 1987).

Hansen, James V., and Ned C. Hill. "Control and Audit of Electronic Data Interchange." *MIS Quarterly 13*, no. 4 (December 1989).

Imielinski, Tomasz, and B. R. Badrinath. "Mobile Wireless Computing: Challenges in Data Management." *Communications of the ACM 37*, no. 10 (October 1994).

Johansen, Robert. "Groupware: Future Directions and Wild Cards." *Journal of Organizational Computing 1*, no. 2 (April–June 1991).

Keen, Peter G. W. *Competing in Time.* Cambridge, MA: Ballinger Publishing Company (1986).

Keen, Peter G. W. *Shaping the Future: Business Design Through Information Technology.* Cambridge, MA: Harvard Business School Press (1991).

Keen, Peter G. W., and J. Michael Cummins. *Networks in Action: Business Choices and Telecommunications Decisions.* Belmont, California: Wadsworth Publishing Company (1994).

Kim, B. G., and P. Wang. "ATM Network: Goals and Challenges." *Communications of the ACM 38*, no. 2 (February 1995).

Massetti, Brenda, and Robert W. Zmud. "Measuring the Extent of EDI Usage in Complex Organizations: Strategies and Illustrative Examples." *MIS Quarterly 20*, no. 3 (September 1996).

Mueller, Milton. "Universal Service and the Telecommunications Act: Myth Made Law." *Communications of the ACM 40*, no. 3 (March 1997).

Orlikowski, Wanda J. "Learning from Notes: Organizational Issues in Groupware Implementation." Sloan Working Paper no. 3428, Cambridge, MA: Sloan School of Management, Massachusetts Institute of Technology.

Press, Lawrence. "Lotus Notes (Groupware) in Context." *Journal of Organizational Computing 2*, no. 3 and 4 (1992b).

Premkumar, G., K. Ramamurthy, and Sree Nilakanta. "Implementation of Electronic Data Interchange: An Innovation Diffusion Perspective." *Journal of Management Information Systems 11*, no. 2 (Fall 1994).

Railing, Larry, and Tom Housel. "A Network Infrastructure to Contain Costs and Enable Fast Response." *MIS Quarterly 14*, no. 4 (December 1990).

Roche, Edward M. *Telecommunications and Business Strategy.* Chicago: The Dryden Press (1991).

Rochester, Jack B. "Networking Management: The Key to Better Customer Service." *I/S Analyzer 27*, no. 12 (December 1989).

Rowe, Stanford H. II. *Business Telecommunications.* New York: Macmillan (1991).

Schultz, Brad. "The Evolution of ARPANET." *Datamation* (August 1, 1988).

Selker, Ted. "Coach: A Teaching Agent that Learns." *Communications of the ACM 37*, no. 7 (July 1994).

Stahl, Stephanie, and John Swenson. "Groupware Grows Up." *Information Week* (March 4, 1996).

Torkzadeh, Gholamreza, and Weidong Xia. "Managing Telecommunications Strategy by Steering Committee." *MIS Quarterly 16*, no. 2 (June 1992).

Vetter, Ronald J. "ATM Concepts, Architectures, and Protocols." *Communications of the ACM 38*, no. 2 (February 1995).

The Internet and Enterprise Networking

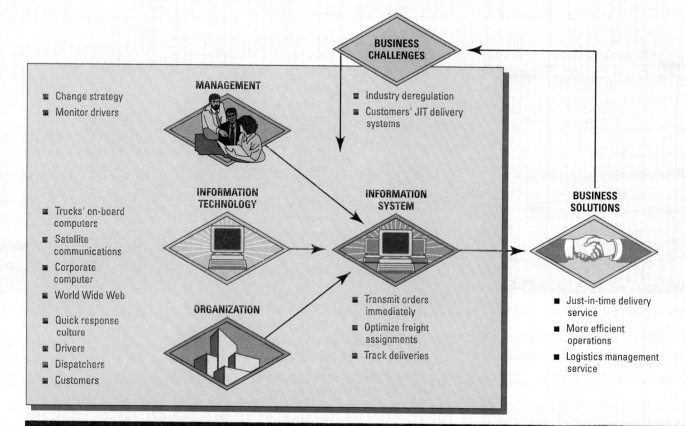

BUSINESS CHALLENGES

MANAGEMENT
- Change strategy
- Monitor drivers

- Industry deregulation
- Customers' JIT delivery systems

INFORMATION TECHNOLOGY

- Trucks' on-board computers
- Satellite communications
- Corporate computer
- World Wide Web

- Quick response culture
- Drivers
- Dispatchers
- Customers

ORGANIZATION

INFORMATION SYSTEM

- Transmit orders immediately
- Optimize freight assignments
- Track deliveries

BUSINESS SOLUTIONS

- Just-in-time delivery service
- More efficient operations
- Logistics management service

Schneider National Keeps On Trucking with the Internet

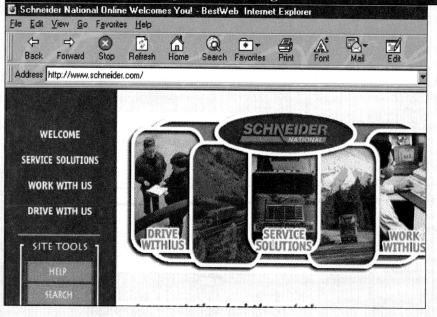

Deregulation changed the whole business of the trucking industry overnight. Competition among trucking firms for customers heated up. Customers could easily change carriers because they were no longer hampered by regulations about what kind of freight to carry and where to take it. Large retailers and manufacturers were also trying to slash inventory and warehouse costs by installing just-in-time delivery systems. They wanted to use trucking firms to transport their shipments right away. The large trucking firms had to worry much more about their prices and service.

Schneider National, based in Green Bay, Wisconsin, one of North

LEARNING OBJECTIVES

After completing
this chapter, you will
be able to:

1. Describe the characteristics and technologies of enterprise networking and explain how it is changing organizations.
2. Identify the capabilities of the Internet and describe the benefits it offers organizations.
3. Describe how the Internet can be used for electronic commerce.
4. Describe important standards used for linking hardware, software, and networks to achieve connectivity, including the use of intranets and Java.
5. Identify problems posed by enterprise networking and the Internet and recommend solutions.

America's largest trucking, transportation, and logistics companies, responded to this challenge with a multipronged strategy. First, it tried to make sweeping changes in its corporate culture to emphasize efficiency and customer responsiveness. CEO Don Schneider democratized the organization by calling all employees "associates" and removing status symbols such as reserved parking places. He encouraged everyone, from drivers on up, to speak out on ways to improve operations. He also instituted an extra bonus paycheck based solely on performance.

Second, Schneider deployed new information systems to support these changes. The firm equipped each truck with a computer and a rotating antenna. A satellite tracks every rig, making sure it adheres to schedule. When an order comes into headquarters, dispatchers know exactly which truck to assign to the job. The dispatchers send an order directly by satellite to the driver's on-board terminal, complete with directions to the destination and instructions on what gate to use and papers to collect with the merchandise. Within 15 to 30 minutes of sending an order to Schneider's

computer, customers know which trucks to expect and when.

Schneider has started using its information systems to provide the entire logistics management function for other companies, setting up a separate division, Schneider Logistics Inc., for this purpose. Among its clients is General Motors Corporation. Schneider manages every shipment of GM service parts, amounting to 435,000 outbound "order lines" daily to more than 9000 GM dealers, warehouse distributors, and mass merchandisers. While other providers use only their own trucks, planes, and trains, Schneider uses its information systems to provide solutions that use the best medium for moving freight, even if it is not Schneider-owned trucks.

To make shipment information more accessible to clients, Schneider Logistics created a Web site with electronic commerce capabilities. Designated customers can use the Web site to "paperlessly" send new load requests directly to Schneider Logistics. Preassigned passwords are provided to each customer, ensuring the security of confidential shipment information. The Web site is being enhanced so that clients can use it to track the status of their shipments. ■

Sources: "Website Features Interactive Electronic Commerce Capabilities," *Schneider National Logistics,* February 18, 1997; Mark Levinson, "Riding the Data Highway," *Newsweek,* March 21, 1994; and Stephen Barr, "Delivering the Goods," *CFO,* August 1994.

MANAGEMENT CHALLENGES

Schneider National is one of many organizations that has become more competitive and efficient by using the Internet and a networked computing architecture. It has rearranged its hardware, software, and communications capabilities into an enterprise-wide network and has developed communications links to other organizations. It has started using the Internet for electronic commerce. Enterprise networking and the Internet can help companies achieve new levels of competitiveness and productivity, but they raise the following management challenges.

1. **Enterprise networking and Internet computing require a complete change of mindset.** To implement networked and Internet-based computing successfully, companies may need to make organizational changes. They must examine and perhaps redesign an entire business process rather than throw new technology at existing business practices. Companies must consider a different organizational structure, changes in organizational culture, a different support structure for information systems, and different procedures for managing employees and networked processing functions.

2. **Finding a successful Internet business model.** Companies are racing to put up Web sites in the hope of generating revenue from electronic commerce. However, many electronic commerce sites have yet to turn a profit or to make a tangible difference in firms' sales and marketing efforts (Halper, 1997). Cost savings or access to new markets promised by the Web may not materialize. Companies need to think carefully about whether they can create a genuinely workable business model on the Internet and how the Internet relates to their overall business strategy.

3. **Reviving the centralization versus decentralization debate.** A long-standing issue among IS managers and CEOs has been the question of centralization. Should processing power and data be distributed to departments and divisions, or should they be concentrated at a central location? Enterprise networking facilitates decentralization, but the use of network computers and Java favors a centralized model. Which is the best for the organization? Each organization will have a different answer. Managers need to make sure that the computing model they select genuinely supports organizational goals.

M any organizations today are linking mainframes, minicomputers, PCs, and smaller networks into companywide networks or using the Internet to link their networks to those of other organizations. This chapter examines the ways in which enterprise networking and the Internet are transforming organizations and fueling electronic commerce. Despite the benefits of linking networks, the

Internet and enterprise networking have created new management problems. We describe these problems and their solutions so that organizations can maximize the benefits of this new information architecture.

10.1 ENTERPRISE NETWORKING

In Chapter 1 we defined *information architecture* as the particular form that information technology takes in an organization to achieve selected goals. An organization's information architecture consists of its computer hardware and software, telecommunications links, and data files. In **enterprise networking** the components of the information architecture are arranged to place more of the organization's computing power on the desktop and to create networks that link entire enterprises.

Figure 10.1 illustrates the implementation of enterprise networking at the National Basketball Association (NBA). As the diagram shows, NBA employees may work at its main offices in Manhattan and Secaucus, New Jersey, or in regional and international offices. The computers in the main offices are linked in local area networks (LANs). An enterprise-wide network links all these sites, NBA teams, and sports arenas together into one large network. Operating on these networks are a range of hardware, including IBM server computers, desktop Pentium Pro PCs

enterprise networking An arrangement of the organization's hardware, software, telecommunications, and data resources to put more computing power on the desktop and create a companywide network linking many smaller networks.

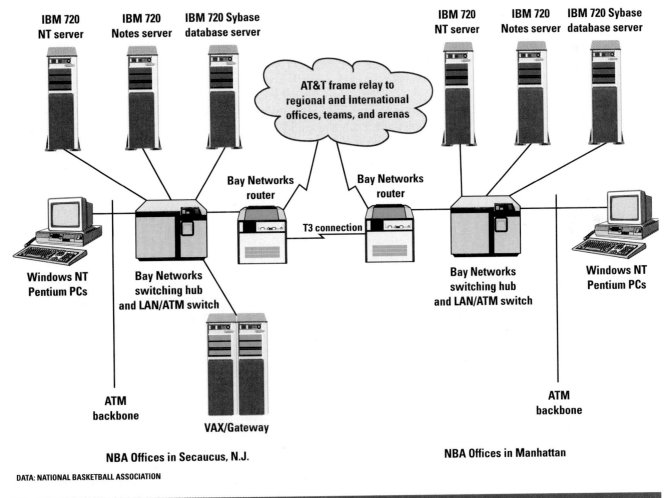

FIGURE 10.1

Enterprise networking at the National Basketball Association (NBA). The NBA's enterprise-wide network links desktop workstations and servers at its main, regional, and international offices, providing information to NBA employees, teams, and arenas.

Source: Copyright © 1996 by CMP Media, Inc., 600 Community Drive, Manhasset, NY 11030. Reprinted from Information Week *with permission.*

running Windows NT, a Digital Equipment Corporation (DEC) VAX computer used as a gateway, and various routers and switching hubs. These networked systems run applications developed with Visual Basic, PowerBuilder, Lotus Notes groupware, and Sybase databases such as a player-contract management system and an information kiosk for fans with full-motion video based on Lotus Notes.

In earlier information systems, mainframes and minicomputers from the same computer manufacturer, using proprietary operating systems, were responsible for most of the firm's information processing. PCs and workstations were used independently by individual users or were linked into small localized networks. By adopting an enterprise-wide information architecture, the NBA uses a mixture of computer hardware supplied by different hardware vendors. Much of the firms' computer processing takes place on the desktop. Large, complex databases that need central storage are found on mainframes, minis, or specialized servers, whereas smaller databases and parts of large databases are loaded on PCs and workstations.

The system is a network. In fact, for all but the smallest organizations the system is composed of multiple networks. A high-capacity backbone network connects many local area networks and devices. The backbone may be connected to many external networks such as the Internet. The linking of separate networks, each of which retains its own identity, into an interconnected network is called **internetworking**.

The Client/Server Model of Computing

In enterprise networking, the primary way of delivering computing power to the desktop is known as the client/server model. In the **client/server model** of computing, data and processing power are distributed into the enterprise rather than being centrally controlled. A client/server system is a user-centric system that emphasizes the user's interaction with the data. Client/server computing splits processing between "clients" and "servers." Both are on the network, but each machine is assigned functions it is best suited to perform. Ideally, the user will experience the network as a single system with all functions, both client and server, integrated and accessible. The **client** is the user point-of-entry for the required function and is normally a desktop computer, workstation, or laptop computer. The user generally interacts directly with only the client portion of the application, typically through a graphical user interface. The user typically utilizes it to input data and query a database to retrieve data. Once the data have been retrieved, the user can analyze and report on them, using fourth-generation packages such as spreadsheets, word processors, and graphics applications available on the client machine on the user's own desktop. The **server** satisfies some or all the user's request for data and/or functionality and might be anything from a supercomputer or mainframe to another desktop computer. Servers store and process shared data and also perform back-end functions not visible to users, such as managing peripheral devices and controlling access to shared databases (see Figure 10.2).

Figure 10.3 illustrates five different ways that the components of an application could be partitioned between the client and the server. The *presentation* component is essentially the application interface—how the application appears visually to the user. The *application logic* component consists of the processing logic, which is shaped by the organization's business rules. (An example might be that a salaried employee is only to be paid monthly.) The *data management* component consists of the storage and management of the data used by the application.

The client/server model requires that application programs be written as two or more separate software components that run on different machines but that appear to operate as a single application. The exact division of tasks depends on the requirements of each application including its processing needs, the number of users, and the available resources. For example, client tasks for a large corporate payroll might include inputting data (such as enrolling new employees and recording hours worked), submitting data queries to the server, analyzing the retrieved data, and displaying results on the screen or on a printer. The server portion will fetch the entered

internetworking The linking of separate networks, each of which retains its own identity, into an interconnected network.

client/server model A model for computing that splits the processing between "clients" and "servers" on a network assigning functions to the machine most able to perform the function.

client The user point-of-entry for the required function in a client/server computing application. Normally a desktop computer, workstation, or laptop computer.

server A computer in a client/server network that satisfies some or all the user's request for data and/or functionality, such as storing and processing shared data.

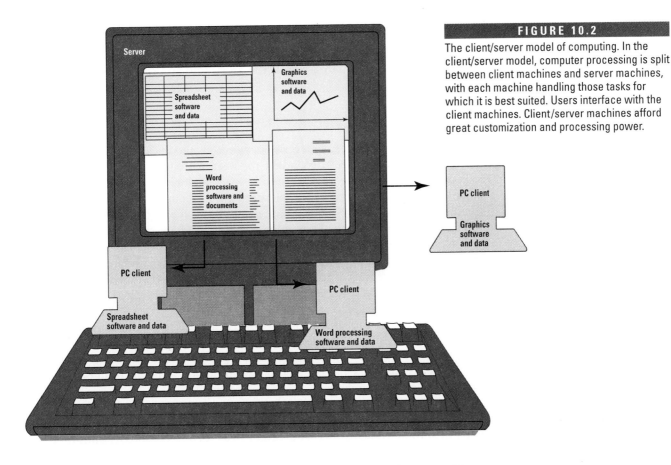

FIGURE 10.2

The client/server model of computing. In the client/server model, computer processing is split between client machines and server machines, with each machine handling those tasks for which it is best suited. Users interface with the client machines. Client/server machines afford great customization and processing power.

data and process the payroll. It will also control access so that only users with appropriate security can view or update the data. In the NBA network, the clients are fully functional PCs and the servers are used for storing the server portions of Notes groupware and Windows NT, as well as the company's Sybase database.

The client/server model does have limitations. It is difficult to write software that divides processing among clients and servers, although more and more client/server software is commercially available. A specific server can get bogged down quickly

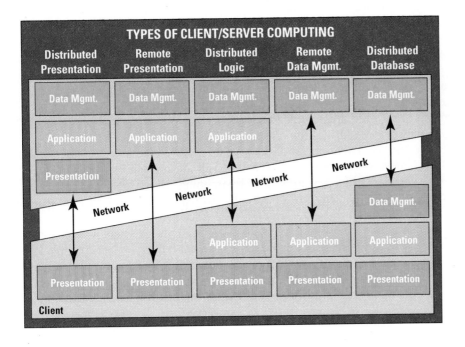

TYPES OF CLIENT/SERVER COMPUTING

FIGURE 10.3

Types of client/server computing. There are a variety of ways in which the presentation, application logic, and data management components of an application can be divided among the clients and servers in a network.
Source: "Discover the Fountain of Youth: How to Revitalize Host Systems for Client/Server Computing," "Attachmate" advertising section, DATAMATION Magazine, April 1, 1995. Reprinted by permission of the Gartner Group.

when too many users simultaneously want service. PCs with independent processing power are more difficult to coordinate and administer on a network. We explore management issues raised by client/server computing and enterprise networking in Section 10.4.

Business Drivers of Enterprise Networking

Organizations have adopted enterprise networking and client/server computing for compelling business reasons, including the need to reduce costs, maintain global competitiveness, and take advantage of new technologies. Chapters 6 and 9 have shown that the enhanced power of microprocessors, coupled with falling prices and reliable and accessible communications technology, make it both technically and economically feasible to transfer computing power to workers' desktops and to arrange resources into client/server–based networks. Today's desktop machines provide capabilities lacking in traditional mainframes—graphical user interfaces, productivity-promoting software such as spreadsheets and word processors, and access to on-line information services and interactive audiovisual computing involving multiple media such as sound, moving pictures, and text.

The growing number of knowledge workers in the information economy require easy access to all kinds of information. Client/server systems enhance their productivity and effectiveness by placing that access at their fingertips through their powerful desktop computers and the wealth of information available from digital information services and networks.

Enterprise networking and client/server computing support a business environment of flattening organizations and decentralized management better than traditional mainframe systems. A client/server infrastructure is more decentralized and able to deliver more information at all organizational levels. Individuals using a networked desktop computer have more control over their own work. Networked computers also allow teams to work closely together, even when members of those teams are hundreds or thousands of miles apart.

In addition, a networked platform is flexible enough to support a nimble organization because it can be transformed rapidly in response to changing competitive needs of the current marketplace. In many instances, adding a few hundred or a few thousand staff members to a network can be done in several weeks or months without degradation of service. Adding that many to a mainframe computer may require a major upgrade project that would consume a year or more.

Independent Telecommunications Network Inc. (ITN), an $18 million Overland Park, Kansas, provider of telephone company billing and credit service, installed client/server–based accounting systems because the company is growing fast and needs systems that can grow with it. The systems run on a central server on which the data are also stored. The client/server system allows employees to access the data wherever they are and use whichever desktop computer they are already using (including Apples and IBM compatible PCs, and UNIX workstations). The number of users can easily be expanded as the company grows.

The new business environment requires that employees be more productive—a goal which client/server systems can also help to fulfill. Conversion to a client/server system can support and even stimulate streamlining of business processes (see Chapter 11). Sun Microsystems of Palo Alto, California, a leading producer of workstations, turned to the client/server model when it decided to renovate its financial systems. In designing the new system, Sun realized it had to overhaul its accounting department. Now, rather than a centralized department relying on a centralized system with frozen printed reports, 200 users worldwide are able to customize and analyze the data in graphic format. The process of moving to client/server computing also revealed many process bottlenecks. Ultimately Sun cut headcount substantially while reducing its time to close its books from twenty-three days to eight.

An increasingly important way that both public and private organizations are networking internally and with other organizations is through the Internet. The Internet is perhaps the most well-known—and the largest—implementation of internetworking, linking hundreds of thousands of individual networks all over the world. The Internet has a range of capabilities that organizations are using to exchange information internally or to communicate externally with other organizations. This giant network of networks has become a major catalyst for electronic commerce.

The Internet began as a United States Department of Defense network to link scientists and university professors around the world. Even today individuals cannot directly connect to the Net, although anyone with a computer and a modem and the willingness to pay a small monthly usage fee can access it through an Internet service provider. An **Internet service provider (ISP)** is a commercial organization with a permanent connection to the Internet which sells temporary connections to subscribers. Individuals can also access the Internet through such popular on-line services as CompuServe, Prodigy, and America Online and through networks established by such giants as Microsoft and AT&T.

One puzzling aspect of the Internet is that no one owns it and it has no formal management organization. As a creation of the Defense Department for sharing research data, this lack of centralization was purposeful, to make it less vulnerable to wartime or terrorist attacks. To join the Internet, an existing network need only to pay a small registration fee and agree to certain standards based on the TCP/IP reference model (Transmission Control Protocol/Internet Protocol, described in Section 10.3). Costs are low because the Internet owns nothing and so has no real costs to offset. Each organization, of course, pays for its own networks and its own telephone bills, but those costs usually exist independent of the Internet. Regional Internet companies have been established to which member networks forward all transmissions. These Internet companies route and forward all traffic, and the cost is still only that of a local telephone call. The result is that the cost of e-mail and other Internet connections tends to be far lower than equivalent voice, postal, or overnight delivery costs, making the Net a very inexpensive communications medium. It is also a very fast method of communication, with messages arriving anywhere in the world in a matter of seconds or a minute or two at most.

The value of the Internet lies precisely in its ability to easily and inexpensively connect so many diverse people from so many places all over the globe. Anyone who has an Internet address can log onto a computer and reach virtually every other computer on the network, regardless of location, computer type, or operating system. We will now briefly describe the most important Internet capabilities.

Internet service provider (ISP)   A commercial organization with a permanent connection to the Internet which sells temporary connections to subscribers.

Internet Capabilities

The Internet is based on client/server technology. Users of the Net control what they do through client applications, using graphical user interfaces or character-based products that control all functions. All the data, including e-mail messages, databases, and Web sites, are stored on servers. Servers dedicated to the Internet or even to specific Internet functions are the heart of the information on the Net (see Figure 10.4).

Major Internet capabilities include e-mail, Usenet newsgroups, LISTSERVs, chatting, Telnet, FTP, gophers, Archie, Veronica, WAIS, and the World Wide Web. These are all standards and tools to retrieve and offer information. Table 10.1 lists these capabilities and describes the functions they support.

People-to-People Communications

ELECTRONIC MAIL (E-MAIL).   The Net has become the most important e-mail system in the world because it connects so many people from all over the world,

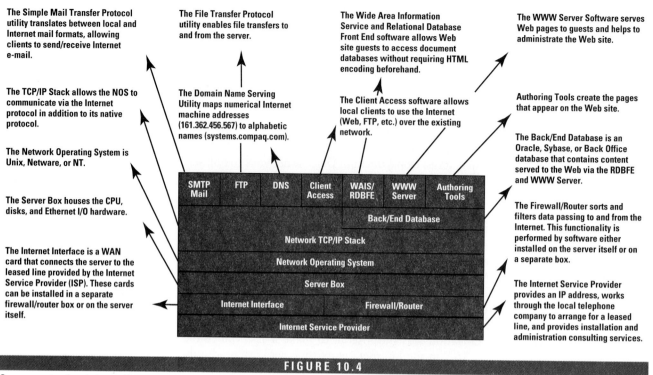

The Simple Mail Transfer Protocol utility translates between local and Internet mail formats, allowing clients to send/receive Internet e-mail.

The TCP/IP Stack allows the NOS to communicate via the Internet protocol in addition to its native protocol.

The Network Operating System is Unix, Netware, or NT.

The Server Box houses the CPU, disks, and Ethernet I/O hardware.

The Internet Interface is a WAN card that connects the server to the leased line provided by the Internet Service Provider (ISP). These cards can be installed in a separate firewall/router box or on the server itself.

The File Transfer Protocol utility enables file transfers to and from the server.

The Domain Name Serving Utility maps numerical Internet machine addresses (161.362.456.567) to alphabetic names (systems.compaq.com).

The Wide Area Information Service and Relational Database Front End software allows Web site guests to access document databases without requiring HTML encoding beforehand.

The Client Access software allows local clients to use the Internet (Web, FTP, etc.) over the existing network.

The WWW Server Software serves Web pages to guests and helps to administrate the Web site.

Authoring Tools create the pages that appear on the Web site.

The Back/End Database is an Oracle, Sybase, or Back Office database that contains content served to the Web via the RDBFE and WWW Server.

The Firewall/Router sorts and filters data passing to and from the Internet. This functionality is performed by software either installed on the server itself or on a separate box.

The Internet Service Provider provides an IP address, works through the local telephone company to arrange for a leased line, and provides installation and administration consulting services.

FIGURE 10.4

Components of an Internet Server

Source: © Copyright 1994, 1995, 1996, 1997 Compaq Computer Corporation.

creating a productivity gain that observers have compared with Gutenberg's development of movable type in the fifteenth century. Private individuals typically use Internet e-mail facilities to keep in touch with friends. Organizations use it to facilitate communication between employees and between offices, to communicate with customers and suppliers, and to keep in touch with the outside world.

Researchers use this facility to share ideas, information, even documents. E-mail over the Net has also made possible many collaborative research and writing projects even though the participants are thousands of miles apart. With proper software, the

Table 10.1	Major Internet Capabilities
Capability	**Functions Supported**
E-mail	Person-to-person messaging; document sharing
Usenet Newsgroups	Discussion groups on electronic bulletin boards
LISTSERVs	Discussion groups using e-mail mailing list servers
Chatting	Interactive conversations
Telnet	Log on to one computer system and do work on another
FTP	Transfer files from computer to computer
Gophers	Locate information using a hierarchy of menus
Archie	Search database of documents, software, and data files available for downloading
Veronica	Speed searching of gopher sites by using keywords
WAIS	Locate files in databases using keywords
World Wide Web	Retrieve, format, and display information (including text, audio, graphics, and video) using hyptertext links

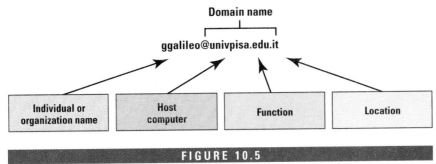

FIGURE 10.5

Analysis of an Internet address. In English, the e-mail address of physicist and astronomer Galileo Galilei would be translated as 'G. Galileo @ University of Pisa, educational institution, Italy'. The domain name to the right of the @ symbol contains a country indicator, a function indicator, and the location of the host computer.

user will find it easy to attach documents and files when sending a message to someone or to broadcast a message to a predefined group. Figure 10.5 illustrates the components of an Internet e-mail address.

The portion of the address to the left of the @ symbol in Net e-mail addresses is the name or identifier of the specific individual or organization. To the right of the @ symbol is the domain name. The **domain name** is the unique name of a collection of computers connected to the Internet. The domain contains subdomains separated by a period. The domain that is farthest to the right is the top level domain, and each domain to the left helps further define the domain by network, department, and even specific computer. The top level domain name may be either a country indicator (such as 'it' for Italy), a function indicator such as 'com' for a commercial organization, 'edu' for an educational institution, or 'gov' for a government institution. All e-mail addresses end with a country indicator except those in the United States, which do not use one. In this example, *it,* the top level domain, is a country indicator, indicating that the address is in Italy; *edu* indicates that the address is an educational institution; *univpisa* (in this case, University of Pisa), indicates the specific location of the host computer.

domain name The unique name of a collection of computers connected to the Internet.

USENET NEWSGROUPS (FORUMS). **Usenet** newsgroups are worldwide discussion groups in which people share information and ideas on a defined topic such as colorimetry or rock bands. Discussion takes place in large electronic bulletin boards where anyone can post messages on the topic for others to read. Over 15,000 such groups exist on almost any conceivable topic. Each Usenet site is financed and administered independently.

Usenet On-line forums in which people share information and ideas on a defined topic through large electronic bulletin boards where anyone can post messages on the topic for others to see.

LISTSERVS. A second type of public forum, **LISTSERV**s, are also discussion groups, but they use e-mail mailing list servers instead of bulletin boards for communications. If you find a LISTSERV topic in which you are interested, you may subscribe to a mailing list. From then on, through your e-mail, you will receive all messages sent by others concerning that topic. You can, in turn, send a message to your LISTSERV mailing list server and it will automatically be broadcast to the other subscribers. Tens of thousands of LISTSERV groups exist discussing every conceivable topic.

LISTSERV On-line discussion groups using e-mail mailing list servers instead of bulletin boards for communications.

CHATTING. **Chatting** allows people who are simultaneously connected to the Internet to hold live, interactive written conversations. Only people who happen to be signed on at the same time are able to "talk" because messages are not stored for later viewing as they are on Usenet newsgroups. On the other hand, this function can be an effective business tool if people who can benefit from interactive conversations set an appointment to "meet" and "talk" on a particular topic. The limitation of this is that the topic is open to all without security so that intruders can participate.

chatting Live, interactive conversations over a public network.

TELNET. We have included **Telnet** in this section even though it actually serves a different purpose—allowing someone to be on one computer system while doing work on another. Telnet is the protocol that establishes an error-free, rapid link between

Telnet Network tool that allows someone to log on to one computer system while doing work on another.

the two computers, allowing you, for example, to log in to your business computer from a remote computer when you are on the road or working from your home. You can also log in and use third-party computers that have been made accessible to the public, such as using the catalogue of the United States Library of Congress. Telnet will use the computer address you supply to locate the computer you want to reach and connect you to it.

Information Retrieval on the Internet

Information retrieval is a second basic Internet function. Many hundreds of library catalogues are on-line through the Internet, including those of such giants as the Library of Congress, the University of California, and Harvard University. In addition, users are able to search many thousands of databases that have been opened to the public by corporations, governments, and nonprofit organizations. Individuals can gather information on almost any conceivable topic stored in these databases and libraries. For example, teachers interested in finding information on hyperactive children can quickly search computer databases and locate many articles, papers, books, and even conference reports from universities and other organizations worldwide. They can then download the information for their reading and use at their leisure. Many use the Internet to locate and download some of the free, quality computer software that has been made available by developers on computers all over the world.

Because the Internet is a voluntary, decentralized effort with no central listing of participants or sites, much less a listing of the data located at all those sites, a major problem is finding what you need from among the vast storehouses of data found in databases and libraries all over the world. Here we will introduce five major methods of accessing computers and locating the files you need. We will describe additional information retrieval methods in our discussion of the World Wide Web.

File Transfer Protocol (FTP) Tool for retrieving and transferring files from a remote computer.

FILE TRANSFER PROTOCOL. **File Transfer Protocol (FTP)** is used to access a remote computer and retrieve files from it. FTP is a quick and easy method if you know the remote computer site in which the file is stored. Once you have logged on to the remote computer, you can move around directories that have been made accessible for FTP to search for the file(s) you want to retrieve. Once located, FTP makes transfer of the file to your own computer very easy.

Archie A tool for locating FTP files on the Internet that performs keyword searches on an actual database of documents, software, and data files available for downloading from servers around the world.

ARCHIE. **Archie** is a tool that can be used to search the files at FTP sites. It monitors hundreds of FTP sites regularly and updates a database of software, documents, and data files available for downloading called an Archie server. Although no individual Archie database can list more than a very tiny percentage of the files in the world, clicking on a relevant listing from one Archie server will bring you to another computer system where other relevant files are stored. There, the Archie server may have yet other relevant references, allowing you to continue your search for pertinent files, moving from database to database, library to library, until you locate what you need. Archie database searches use subject key words you enter, such as "Beijing," "telecommuting," "polymers," or "inflation," resulting in a list of sites that contain files on that topic.

gopher A tool that enables the user to locate information stored on Internet gopher servers through a series of easy-to-use, hierarchical menus.

GOPHERS. Most files and digital information that are accessible through FTP are also available through gophers. A **gopher** is a computer client tool that enables the user to locate information stored on Internet gopher servers through a series of easy-to-use, hierarchical menus. The Internet has thousands of gopher server sites throughout the world. Each gopher site contains its own system of menus listing subject-matter topics, local files, and other relevant gopher sites. One gopher site might have as many as several thousand listings within various levels of its menus. When you use gopher software to search a specific topic and select a related item from a menu, the server will automatically transfer you to the appropriate file on that server or to the selected server wherever in the world it is located. Once on the distant server, the process continues—you are presented with more menus of files and other gopher server sites that might interest you. You thus can move from site to site, narrowing your search as you go, locating information that you want anywhere in the world. When you do find information or files you want, you are free to browse, read them on-line, or download them onto your own computer for more leisurely reading or printing. With descriptive menu listings linked to other gopher sites, you do not need to know in advance where relevant files are stored or the exact FTP address of a specific computer.

VERONICA. **Veronica** (which stands for Very Easy Rodent-Oriented Netwide Index to Computer Archives) is an additional capability for searching gopher sites. When the user enters a key word, Veronica will search through thousands of gopher sites to find titles that contain that keyword. It then places these files onto a temporary menu on your own local server so that you can browse through them, making file retrieval by topic much easier.

Veronica Capability for searching for text that appears in gopher menus by using key words.

WAIS. **WAIS** (Wide Area Information Servers) is yet a fourth way to handle the problem of locating files around the world. WAIS is the most thorough way to locate a specific file, but it requires that you know the names of the databases you want searched. Once you specify database names and key identifying words, WAIS searches for the key words in all the files in those databases. When the search has been completed, you will be given a menu that lists all the files that contain your key words.

WAIS A tool for locating data on the Internet that requires the name of the databases to be searched based on a key word.

The World Wide Web

The **World Wide Web** (the Web) is at the heart of the explosion in the business use of the Net. The Web is a system with a universally accepted set of standards for storing, retrieving, formatting, and displaying information using a client/server architecture. It was originally developed to allow collaborators in remote sites to share their ideas on all aspects of a common project. If the Web was used for two independent projects and later relationships were found between the projects, information could flow smoothly between the projects without making major changes (Berners-Lee et al., 1994).

World Wide Web A system for storing, retrieving, formatting, and displaying information using a client/server architecture, graphical user interfaces, and a hypertext language that enables dynamic links to other documents.

Whereas the other methods of accessing information on the Net are primarily character based, the Web combines text, hypermedia, graphics, and sound. Together they can handle all types of digital communication while making it easy to link resources that are on the other side of the globe. The Web uses graphical user interfaces for easy viewing. It is based on a hypertext language called **Hypertext Markup Language (HTML)** that formats documents and incorporates dynamic links to other documents and pictures stored in the same or remote computers. Using these links, the user need only point at a highlighted key word or graphic, click on it, and immediately be transported to another document, probably on another computer somewhere else in the world. Users are free to jump from place to place following their own logic and interest.

Hypertext Markup Language (HTML) A programming tool that uses hypertext to establish dynamic links to other documents stored in the same or remote computers.

Those who offer information through the Web must first establish a **home page**— a text and graphical screen display that usually welcomes the user and explains the organization that has established the page. For most organizations, the home page will lead the user to other pages, with all the pages of an organization or individual being known as a *Web site*. For a corporation to establish a presence on the Web, therefore, it must set up a Web site of one or more pages. Most Web pages offer a way to contact the organization or individual.

home page A World Wide Web text and graphical screen display that welcomes the user and explains the organization that has established the page.

To access a Web site, the user must use a special software tool known as a *Web browser* which is programmed according to HTML standards (see Chapter 7). Because the standard is universally accepted, anyone using a browser can access any of the millions of Web sites anywhere in the world. Browsers use hypertext's point-and-click ability to enable the user to easily navigate (or *surf*—move from site to site on the Web) to another desired site. They also include an arrow or Back button to enable the user to retrace steps, navigating back, site by site. Microsoft's Internet

Explorer and Netscape Navigator from Netscape Communications Inc. are currently the most popular Web browsers.

Searching for Information on the Web

Locating information on the Web is a critical function given the tens of millions of Web sites in existence, and the Web is growing by an estimated 300,000 pages per week. No comprehensive catalogue of Web sites exists. The principal methods of locating information on the Web are Web site directories, search engines, and broadcast or "push" technology.

Several companies have created directories of Web sites and their addresses, providing search tools for locating information on specified topics. Yahoo! is an example. People or organizations submit sites of interest, which are then classified. To search the directory, you enter one or more keywords and will quickly see displayed a list of categories and sites with those key words in the title (see Figure 10.6).

Other search tools do not require Web sites to be preclassified and will search Web pages on their own automatically. Such tools, called **search engines,** can find Web sites that people might not know about. They contain software that looks for Web pages containing one or more of the search terms entered by the user, then displays matches ranked by a method that usually involves the location and frequency of the search terms. These search engines do not display information about every site on the Web, but create indexes of the Web pages they visit. The search-engine software then locates Web pages of interest by searching through these indexes. AltaVista, Lycos, and Infoseek are examples of these search engines. Some are more comprehensive or current than others, depending on how their components are tuned. Some also classify Web sites by various subject categories.

Broadcast and "Push" Technology

Instead of spending hours scouring the Web you can have the information in which you are interested delivered automatically to your desktop through **"push" technology.** A computer broadcasts information of interest directly to you, rather than having you "pull" content from Web sites.

search engine A tool for locating specific sites or information on the Internet. Primarily used to search the World Wide Web.

"push" technology Method of obtaining relevant information on the Internet by having a computer broadcast information directly to the user based on prespecified interests.

"Push" comes from *server push,* a term used to describe the streaming of Web page contents from a Web server to a Web browser. When you register for a push delivery service, you download client software on your computer. You can customize its interface to deliver only certain channels or categories of information offered by content providers such as news, sports, financial data, and so forth. You also specify how often you want this information updated. A profile is submitted to the push delivery service and stored on a database. Special software programs monitor Web sites and other information sources. The push client software runs in the background of your computer while you use it for other tasks. Upon finding information of interest to you, the push programs serve the information to the push client, notifying you by e-mail, playing a sound, displaying an icon on the desktop, sending full articles or Web pages, or displaying headlines on a screen saver. When you click for more details, you might be launched into the Web sites of interest.

Some of the leading push delivery platforms include PointCast, BackWeb, Marimba Castanet, and Intermind Communicator. BackWeb (see Figure 10.7) and Marimba Castanet feature richer multimedia capabilities, with Castanet capable of delivering Java software and applications.

The audience for push technology is not limited to individual users. Companies are using push technology to set up their own channels to broadcast important internal information. For example, Fruit of the Loom is using PointCast to alert managers to updated inventory information stored on its IBM AS/400 intranet Web server. The company is considering push technology to deliver internal information to distributors as part of its effort to streamline inventory management and ordering (Maddox, 1997).

Internet Benefits to Organizations

Organizations are deriving many benefits from the Internet, reducing communication costs, enhancing communication and coordination, accelerating the distribution of knowledge, and facilitating electronic commerce.

FIGURE 10.7
Delivering information through "push" technology. Subscribers to the BackWeb "push" delivery service can select channels to deliver information on topics of interest from the Internet or corporate intranets.

Reducing Communication Costs

Prior to the Net, to realize the communications benefits to be described, organizations had to build their own wide area networks or subscribe to a value-added network service. Employing the Internet, although far from cost-free, is certainly more cost effective for many organizations than building one's own network or paying VAN subscription fees. Moreover, companies are finding that by using the Net to fulfill a range of their communication needs, they are lowering other communication costs, including their network management expenses and their telephone and fax costs. For instance, one estimate is that a direct mailing or faxing to 1200 customers within the United States will cost $1200 to $1600, whereas the same coverage through the Net will cost only about $10. Adding 600 more recipients who are spread through six other countries would increase the cost only another $10.

Each time Federal Express clients use FedEx's Web site to track the status of their packages instead of inquiring by telephone, FedEx saves $8, amounting to $2 million in operating costs each year (Cortese, 1996). Although all companies can benefit from lower costs, small businesses find reduced communication costs particularly beneficial because it sometimes enables them to compete with larger companies in markets that would otherwise be closed to them.

Enhancing Communication and Coordination

As organizations expand and globalization continues, the need to coordinate activities in far-flung locations is becoming more critical. The Internet has become an important instrument for that coordination. Cygnus Support, a software developer with only 125 employees with offices in both Mountain View, California, and Somerville, Massachusetts, originally turned to the Internet to link their offices inexpensively via e-mail. Later, Cygnus established an internal Web site to keep employees informed about company developments. Through the Web, employees are able to see a company calendar, the employee policy manual, company financial data, even the number of customer problems and the speed of their resolution. The site is an important tool to help manage the large number of telecommuters that work for the company.

The Internet has made it easier and less expensive for companies to coordinate small staffs when opening new markets or working in isolated places because they do not have to build their own networks. For example, Schlumberger Ltd., the New York and Paris oil drilling equipment and electronics producer, operates in 85 countries, and in most of them their employees are in remote locations. To install their own network for so few people at each remote location would have been prohibitively expensive. Using the Net, Schlumberger engineers in Dubai (on the Persian Gulf) can check e-mail and effectively stay in close contact with management at a very low cost. In addition, the field staff is able to follow research projects as easily as can personnel within the United States. Schlumberger has found that since it converted to the Net from its own network, its overall communications costs are down 2 percent despite a major increase in network and IT infrastructure spending. The main reason for these savings is the dramatic drop in voice traffic and in overnight delivery service charges (they attach complete documents to their e-mail messages).

Accelerating the Distribution of Knowledge

In today's information economy, rapid access to knowledge is critical to the success of many companies. Yet new knowledge is expanding so swiftly that keeping up is an immense task that requires management's attention. The Internet system helps with this problem. Organizations are using e-mail and access to databases to gain easy access to information resources in such key areas as business, science, law, and government. With blinding speed, the Internet can link a lone researcher sitting at a computer screen to mountains of data (including graphics) all over the world, otherwise too expensive and too difficult to tap. For example, scientists can obtain photographs taken by NASA space probes within an hour. Hubble telescope data is made available over the Internet. Research teams in different locations can analyze data from these sources (O'Leary, Kuokka, and Plant, 1997). It has become easy and inexpensive for corporations to obtain the latest U.S. Department of Commerce statistics, current weather data, or laws of legal entities from all over the globe.

General Motors claims that Internet library access is vital to its product development research. Entek Manufacturing, of Lebanon, Oregon, manufactures equipment to produce plastic sheeting for automobile batteries. The sheeting sometimes develops microscopic holes as a result of the high temperatures of today's automobile motors. Engineer Ron Cordell needed to find a material for patching these holes and so presented his problem on a polymer forum on the Net. Several hours later an Australian responded via e-mail with the name of an adhesive that did the job. Cordell participates in other forums as well, gathering information that is vital to the running of his business. For example, he is part of a forum on machine vision because Entek uses videocameras to perform detailed microscopic analysis of their manufacturing processes.

The Internet and Electronic Commerce

Enterprise networking and the Internet are enabling organizations to build new business models in which they are directly linked to customers and suppliers as well as to other parts of their organizations. In other chapters, we described an array of information technologies that are transforming the way products are produced, marketed, shipped, and sold. Companies are using WANs, VANs, the Internet, electronic data interchange (EDI), e-mail, shared databases, digital image processing, bar coding, and interactive software to replace telephone calls and traditional paper-based procedures for product design, marketing, ordering, delivery, payment, and customer support. Trading partners can directly communicate with each other, bypassing middlemen and inefficient multilayered procedures.

A computer scientist updates pages on the World Wide Web at CERN, a European particle physics laboratory. By enabling scientists and other professionals to exchange ideas and research instantaneously, the Internet has accelerated the pace of scientific collaboration and the spread of knowledge.

The Mars Pathfinder mission broadcast images from Mars to 25 Web sites, where they could be reviewed by waiting scientists and the general public. This photo, which was taken on July 4, 1997, shows the roving vehicle Sojourner in the foreground in its position on a solar panel of the lander. The horizon is the rock strewn Martian surface.

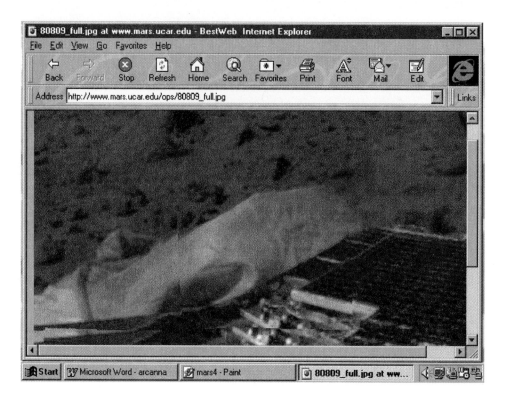

Electronic Commerce on the Internet

The Internet is rapidly becoming the technology of choice for electronic commerce because it offers businesses an even easier way to link with other companies or individuals at very low cost. The Internet's global connectivity and ease of use can provide companies with access to businesses or individuals that would normally be outside their reach. Web sites are available to consumers 24 hours a day. Marketers can use the interactive features of the Web to hold consumers' attention and can tailor communications precisely to individual customers. The Web shifts more marketing and selling activities to the customer, as customers fill out their own on-line order forms (Hoffman, Novak, and Chatterjee, 1995). New marketing and sales channels can be created. Businesses can find new outlets for their products and services abroad because the Internet facilitates cross-border transactions and information flows (Quelch and Klein, 1996). Handling transactions electronically can reduce transaction costs and delivery time for some goods, especially those that are purely digital (such as software, text products, images, or videos).

Companies large and small are using the Internet to make product information, ordering, and customer support immediately available and to help buyers and sellers make contact. TravelWeb is a Web site that offers to prospective vacationers pictures and electronic information on more than 16,000 hotels in 138 countries. Travelers can book reservations with a credit card number if they are using a secure Internet browser. Participating hotel chains believe the Net is well suited for the travel and hospitality industries because it is easy to keep the Web information up-to-date as compared with printed brochures. The interactive nature of the system helps potential customers believe the information is more relevant to them. The system runs 24 hours per day, whether or not a specific hotel's reservation desk is open. Hyatt Hotels is also using the system for market research. It tracks the origin of each user and the screens and hypertext links that user accesses. By analyzing these data Hyatt learns a great deal about customer preferences. For instance, the hotel chain has found that Japanese users are most interested in the golf facilities of a resort, valuable information in shaping market strategies and for developing hospitality-related products.

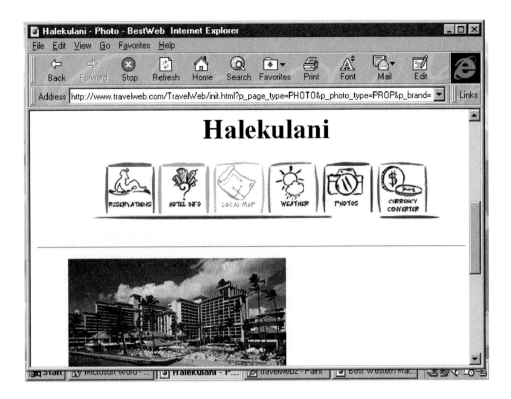

Prospective travelers can use TravelWeb any time of the day or night to make hotel reservations or to find out information on hotel rooms, rates, and nearby sight-seeing attractions in the United States or the Caribbean. By analyzing usage data from this Web site, participating hotels can learn more about customer preferences.

Digital Equipment Corporation (DEC) uses the Internet to allow its customers and software developers from all over the world to log on to its DEC Alpha AXP computer and run their own software as a test of the DEC computer. DEC also gives customers access to more than 3000 documents including sales brochures and technical manuals.

Using the Internet and the Web offers businesses new flexibility because they can update their Web page offerings as often as needed. AMP, Inc., a $5 billion electronic components manufacturer, publishes 400 catalogues a year at an annual cost of $8 to $10 million. By placing its catalogues on the Web, the company hopes to reduce and eventually eliminate these costs while offering catalogues that are always up-to-date. AMP Connect, AMP's Web-based product catalogue, has 30,000 registered users and 33,000 hits per day. AMP is capitalizing on its success by creating AMP eMerce Internet Solutions, a division that will help manufacturers and other companies develop Internet-based product catalogues and selling mechanisms.

Companies find that through e-mail they can answer customer questions rapidly and usually at lower cost than by staffing a telephone system. Dell Computer has established a Dell newsgroup on the Net and other on-line services to receive and handle customer complaints and questions. They answer about 90 percent of the questions within 24 hours. Dell also does free market research through these newsgroups rather than paying a professional for the same information. Recently, for example, the company gathered customer reaction to a potential change in the color of desktop cases. Internet presence is important enough to Dell that it assigns a staff of seven people, who are active 24 hours a day, keeping up with any mention of Dell and the other computer producers in the newsgroups and answering questions on-line.

The Internet is also performing electronic marketplace functions, directly connecting buyers and sellers. By bypassing intermediaries such as distributors or retail outlets, purchase transaction costs can be reduced. The Window on Organizations describes how the Internet is supplanting traditional middlemen in some industries

and creating new opportunities for others. For Internet-based commerce, distributors with warehouses of goods may be replaced by intermediaries specializing in helping Internet users efficiently obtain product and price information.

The Internet is automating purchase and sales transactions from business to business as well as transactions between businesses and individuals. AMP's clients are primarily other businesses. Cisco Systems, a leading manufacturer of networking equipment, sells more than $1 billion per year through its Web site. Order taking, credit checking, production scheduling, technical support, and routine customer support activities are handled on-line. Companies can use their own Web site or conduct sales through Web sites set up as on-line marketplaces for business-to-business commerce. Industrial malls such as IBM's and Nets Inc.'s Industry.net allow companies to exchange blueprints, electronic spreadsheets, and even digitized training videos as well as bids and prices (Lohr, 1997). Figure 10.8 illustrates how an Internet electronic commerce marketplace works.

Internet Business Models

Some of these Internet electronic commerce initiatives represent automation of traditional paper-based business processes, whereas others represent new business models. For example, A.G. Russell Knives, one of the companies on The Catalog Site described in the opening vignette for Chapter 1, uses the Web to offer an electronic version of its traditional print catalogue. Orders must still be placed by fax or telephone. But The Catalog Site itself is an example of a new type of business—an on-line mall—made possible by the Web, as is the Security First Network Bank, the virtual bank described in Chapter 2. AMP's experience building its own Web-based catalogue inspired it to create a new line of business, providing electronic commerce software and services for others.

New business models have been created utilizing the rich communication capabilities of the Internet. Onsale is an on-line auction forum, using e-mail and other interactive features of the Web. People can make on-line bids for items such as computer equipment, sports collectibles, wines, rock concert tickets, and electronics. The winning bidders' initials appear on the screen with their home cities. The system ac-

The Internet Becomes the Middleman

The World Wide Web performs one function exceedingly well—putting people in direct touch with each other, cutting out the middleperson. Professions such as brokers, dealers, and agents—the middlepersons in many marketplace transactions—may be threatened.

A series of Web sites now provide services that used to be provided by insurance agents. Insure Market lets users buy life insurance policies on-line. Visitors to the site can research product offerings, fill out policy applications, receive immediate rate quotes, and pay policy premiums on-line. Conversely, InsWeb, representing auto, life, and health insurance providers, doesn't sell policies itself. Visitors to the site can compare quotes from several insurance companies, and when they are ready to buy, InsWeb sends the information to brokers or insurance companies.

Many believe that travel agents will be threatened as people make their own airline and hotel reservations through the Web. A site called Travelocity offers live chat forums with travel experts, searchable restaurant and entertainment listings, and even luggage for sale—features that can't be found at the average travel agency. Will travel agents disappear? Observers say no. Travel agents offering reliable, personal service will survive and thrive.

Real estate will be affected. Real estate agents charge the seller a commission, often 6 percent of the sale price ($12,000 on a $200,000 home), a powerful incentive for sellers to seek other avenues to advertise their properties. Real estate listings on the Web can include pictures and floor plans as well as descriptive information. These Web sites typically only charge the seller a small fee, as little as $15 per month, for the listing. Buyers view listings for free. Some sites, such as Properties OnLine, include listings from anywhere and rely on powerful search engines to help visitors locate what they want. Others, such as BayNet World, Inc., focus on a specific area, in this case the San Francisco Bay area. The more traditional real estate firms, such as Coldwell Banker, are also establishing a presence on the Web, trying to capture part of the cyberspace business. However, they still charge commissions.

In businesses impacted by the Internet, middlemen will have to adjust their services to fit the new business model or create new services based on the model. So many real estate sites have appeared on the Internet that a new type of middleman has emerged to sort them out.

Entrepreneur Jerry Caviston set up a Web-based service called Matchpoint which operates a customized search engine for locating homes for sale on-line. The service is free to prospective buyers, making its profit by charging realtors a small fee for each listing.

Not all middlemen will disappear, because there are services that the Web simply cannot replicate. Web-based dealers such as Auto-By-Tel and DealerNet enable people to search for particular models and makes of cars offered by participating dealers, but people cannot simply purchase a car on the Web and drive it away. They need to test drive and have the car serviced, functions that can best be performed by the auto dealers. The Web may be useful for comparing insurance rates, but life insurance policies have to be underwritten by agents and require a medical examination and blood testing. Moreover, many life insurance products are too complicated for most consumers to understand. Consumers may need to meet face-to-face with agents to find out what they need.

To Think About: How is the Internet changing the business model of these organizations? Suggest and discuss how other organizations might be affected by the Web.

Sources: Thomas Hoffman, "Net Not Ideal for Selling Insurance, Survey Finds," *Computerworld,* February 17, 1997; David Bank, "Middlemen Find Ways to Survive Cyberspace Shopping," *The Wall Street Journal,* December 12, 1996; Elizabeth Baatz, "Will the Web Cut Your Job?" *Webmaster,* May/June 1996; and Mary Brandel, "The Exchange," *Computerworld,* April 29, 1996.

cepts bids for items entered on the Internet, evaluates the bids, and identifies the highest bidder. Onsale's e-mail system automatically notifies high bidders when they have been outbidded and warns them about how much time they have left to raise the ante. To pay for the merchandise, successful bidders can submit their credit card numbers over the Internet or telephone them using an 800 number. Even with a limited range of offerings, Onsale's revenues are rising 50 percent a month, 20 percent of which comes from international buyers.

The Internet has created on-line communities, where people can exchange ideas and opinions with people who have similar interests in many different locations. Some of these virtual communities are providing the foundation for new businesses. Electric Minds, a cyberspace community for people interested in technology and culture, generates revenue from advertisers who place banners on its Web site. In exchange, the sponsors have access to pockets of potential customers. Tripod attracts

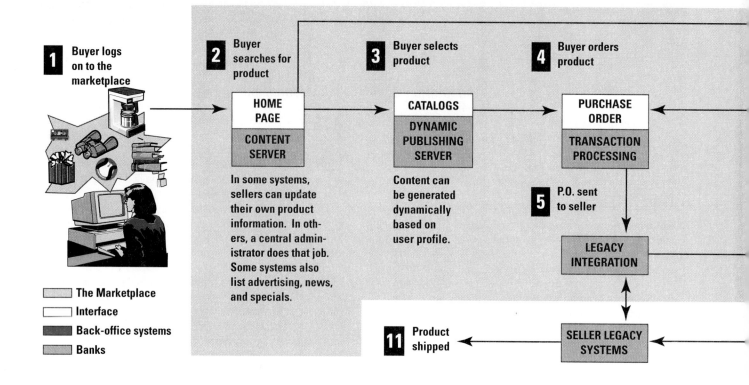

1 Buyer logs on to the marketplace

2 Buyer searches for product

3 Buyer selects product

4 Buyer orders product

HOME PAGE
CONTENT SERVER

In some systems, sellers can update their own product information. In others, a central administrator does that job. Some systems also list advertising, news, and specials.

CATALOGS
DYNAMIC PUBLISHING SERVER

Content can be generated dynamically based on user profile.

PURCHASE ORDER
TRANSACTION PROCESSING

5 P.O. sent to seller

LEGACY INTEGRATION

11 Product shipped

SELLER LEGACY SYSTEMS

The Marketplace
Interface
Back-office systems
Banks

college students and young college graduates by providing "tools for life"—practical information about careers, health, personal finance, and travel—a resume distribution service and a facility to maintain a personal Web page. Members can participate in on-line discussion groups on women's issues, work and money, or the arts. Tripod's revenue comes from providing ways for corporate clients to target customers in the 18- to 30-year-old age group. In addition to selling electronic advertising space, Tripod allows corporate customers to sell products on its Web site and receives a percentage of each transaction (Eckerson, 1996).

Table 10.2 compares some of these Internet-based business models. Some replace internal organizational processes, some replace existing businesses, and some represent completely new kinds of businesses. All in one way or another add value—they provide the customer with a new product or service, they provide additional information or service with a traditional product or service, or they provide a product or service at much lower cost than traditional means (Mougayar, 1996).

Internet Commerce Challenges

The Internet presents challenges to the business user, largely stemming from the fact that most of the technology and functions are relatively immature. Electronic commerce requires careful management of the firm's various divisions, production sites, and sales offices as well as close partnering relationships with customers, suppliers, banks, and other trading partners. Another issue that must be addressed is that of the security of electronic transactions. One major stumbling block to the growth of electronic commerce is that many people consider the Internet too risky for payment transactions and are awaiting proof that electronic payment systems are truly secure. Electronic payment systems for Internet-based commerce are relatively new. We discuss the security of the Internet and electronic payment systems in detail in Chapter 17.

To make extensive use of the Internet, some companies need more expensive telecommunications connections, workstations, or higher-speed computers that can handle transmission of bandwidth-hungry graphics. To establish a presence on the

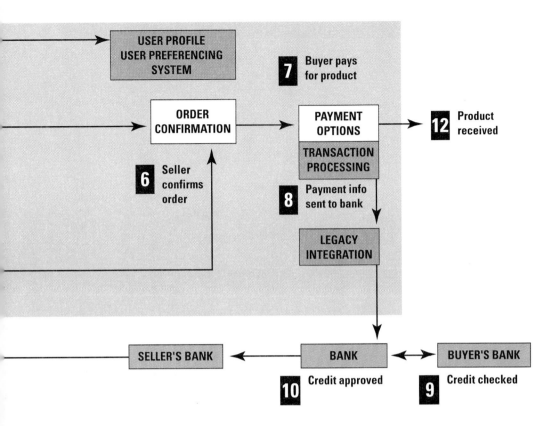

FIGURE 10.8

Portrait of an electronic commerce marketplace. Buyers can locate, order, and pay for products through an electronic mall, such as the one illustrated here for Industry.net or through an individual vendor's Web site.
Source: Copyright April 28, 1997, by Computerworld, Inc., Farmingham, MA 01701. Reprinted from Computerworld.

World Wide Web, they may require an information systems specialist with skills related specifically to the Internet. Individuals and organizations in less developed countries with poor telephone lines, limited hardware and software capacity, or government controls on communications will not be able to take full advantage of Internet resources (Goodman, Press, Ruth, and Rutkowski, 1994).

Laws governing electronic commerce are mostly nonexistent or are just being written. Legislatures, courts, and international agreements will have to settle such still open questions as the legality and force of e-mail contracts, including the role of electronic signatures, and the application of copyright laws to electronically copied documents. For instance, if a product is offered for sale in Australia via a server in Japan and the purchaser lives in Hungary, whose law applies? Internet electronic commerce will benefit when these issues are clarified.

10.3 CONNECTIVITY, STANDARDS, AND INTRANETS

Telecommunications and networks are most likely to increase productivity and competitive advantage when digitized information can move through a seamless web of electronic networks, connecting different kinds of machines, people, sensors, databases, functional divisions, departments, and work groups. They require **connectivity**—the ability of computers and computer-based devices to communicate with one another and "share" information in a meaningful way without human intervention. Internet technology and Java software provide some of this connectivity, but the Internet cannot be used as a foundation for all the organization's information systems. Most organizations will still require their own proprietary networks, especially for heavy-duty transaction processing applications. They will need to develop their own connectivity solutions to make different kinds of hardware, software, and communications systems work together. In this section we describe typical connectivity problems and show where Internet technology and other connectivity standards can provide solutions.

connectivity A measure of how well computers and computer-based devices communicate and share information with one another without human intervention.

Table 10.2   Examples of Internet Business Models

Category	Description	Examples
Virtual Storefront	Sells physical goods or services on-line instead of through a physical storefront or retail outlet. Delivery of nondigital goods and services takes place through traditional means.	Amazon.com Virtual Vineyards Security First Network Bank
Marketplace Concentrator	Concentrates information about products and services from multiple providers at one central point. Purchasers can search, comparison-shop, and sometimes complete the sales transaction.	Internet Shopping Network DealerNet Industry.net InsureMarket
Information Brokers	Provide product, pricing, and availability information. Some facilitate transactions, but their main value is in the information they provide.	PartNet Travelocity Auto-by-Tel
Transaction Brokers	Buyers can view rates and terms, but the primary business activity is to complete the transaction.	Etrade Lombard Institutional Brokerage
Electronic Clearinghouses	Provide auctionlike settings for products where price and availability are constantly changing, sometimes in response to customer actions.	Internet Liquidators Onsale
Digital Product Delivery	Sells and delivers software, multimedia, and other digital products over the Internet.	CyberSource Megasoft Build-a-Card PhotoDisc SonicNet
Content Provider	Creates revenue by providing content. The customer may pay to access the content or revenue may be generated by selling advertising space or by having advertisers pay for placement in an organized listing in a searchable database.	Wall Street Journal Interactive QuoteCom Pathfinder Catalog Mart Home Page Tripod
Online Service Provider	Provide service and support for hardware and software users.	Cyber Media Tune Up.com

Connectivity Problems

The following are some common examples of the absence of connectivity:

- Desktop PCs often cannot use data from the corporate mainframe, often cannot share information among different brands of PCs, and many times cannot share information meaningfully even among different pieces of software operating on the same personal computer.

- Some corporations have multiple e-mail systems within their own firms that cannot communicate with one another.

- IBM and other hardware vendors sell machines and software that cannot communicate with others even of the same brand because of different hardware designs and operating systems.

- Companies operating overseas have tremendous difficulty building global networks that can seamlessly tie their operations together. Different countries have different telecommunications infrastructures, many owned by national PTTs (post, telegraph, and telephone monopolies) that use disparate networking standards.

These connectivity problems arose because there were no standards for either hardware or software manufacturers prior to the 1980s, and hardware and software vendors themselves encouraged product differentiation. Moreover, the process of setting standards is largely political and involves many powerful interest groups, such as private-sector industry associations of equipment, the U.S. federal government, and professional groups such as the Institute of Electrical and Electronic Engineers (IEEE), the American National Standards Institute (ANSI), the International Organization for Standardization (ISO), and the International Telegraph and Telephone Consultative Committee (CCITT).

The inability to link different systems encompasses more than just networking. Issues of information portability and interoperability are involved. **Information portability** is the sharing of computer files among different types of computer hardware and different software applications. **Interoperability** is the ability of a single piece of software to operate on two different kinds of computer hardware, showing users an identical interface and performing the same tasks. In conventional systems one typically cannot run a piece of application software developed for one brand of hardware or operating system on another, nor can data be shared among applications with different hardware and software platforms.

Interoperability and information portability require open systems. Open systems promote connectivity because they enable disparate equipment and services to work together. **Open systems** are built on public, nonproprietary operating systems, user interfaces, application standards, and networking protocols. In open systems, software can operate on different hardware platforms and in that sense be "portable." Internet technology and Java software, described in Chapter 7, can be used to create an open system environment. The UNIX operating system supports open systems because it can operate on many different kinds of computer hardware. However, there are different versions of UNIX, and no one version has been accepted as an open systems standard. Moreover, the effort to make UNIX the operating systems standard has encountered considerable opposition. Hardware vendors have split into two warring camps over the issue of what version of UNIX to support, led by IBM and DEC on one side and AT&T and Sun Corporation on the other.

We first describe standards for achieving connectivity in conventional systems and then describe the connectivity that can be provided through Internet technology.

Standards for Achieving Connectivity

Achieving connectivity requires standards for networking, operating systems, and user interfaces. This section describes the most important standards that are being used today.

Models of Connectivity for Networks

Because of the many interests involved in connectivity and standard setting, there are different models for achieving connectivity in telecommunications networks. A **reference model** is a generic framework for thinking about a problem. It is a logical breakdown of some activity (such as communications) into a number of distinct steps or parts. Specific protocols are required to implement a reference model. A **protocol** is a statement that explains how a specific task, such as transferring data, will be performed. Reference models and protocols become **standards** when they are approved by important standard-setting groups or when industry builds or buys products that support the models and protocols.

Network connectivity can also be achieved without reference models or protocols by using gateways. Firms develop gateways between two disparate networks when it is impossible or too costly to integrate them by complying with reference models or standards. However, gateways are expensive to build and maintain, and they can be slow and inefficient. We now describe the most important models of network connectivity.

information portability The sharing of computer files among different hardware platforms and software applications.

interoperability The ability of a single piece of software to operate on two different machine platforms showing users an identical interface and performing the same tasks.

open systems Software systems that can operate on different hardware platforms because they are built on public nonproprietary operating systems, user interfaces, application standards, and networking protocols.

reference model A generic framework for thinking about a problem.

protocol A statement that explains how a specific task will be performed.

standard Approved reference models and protocols as determined by standard-setting groups for building or developing products or services.

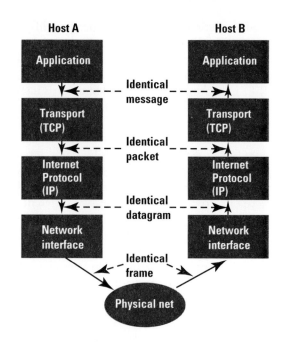

FIGURE 10.9

The Transmission Control Protocol/
Internet Protocol (TCP/IP) reference
model. This figure illustrates the five
layers of the TCP/IP reference model
for communications.

**Transmission Control
Protocol/Internet Protocol
(TCP/IP)** U.S. Department of
Defense reference model for
linking different types of computers and networks. Used in
the Internet.

The **Transmission Control Protocol/Internet Protocol (TCP/IP)** model was developed by the U.S. Department of Defense in 1972 and is used in the Internet. Its purpose was to help scientists link disparate computers. Because it is one of the oldest communications reference models (and is the model on which the Internet is based), TCP/IP is widely used. Figure 10.9 shows that TCP/IP has a five-layer reference model.

1. *Application:* Provides end-user functionality by translating the messages into the user/host software for screen presentation.

2. *Transmission Control Protocol (TCP):* Performs transport, breaking application data from the end user down into TCP packets called *datagrams.* Each packet consists of a header with the address of the sending host computer, information for reassembling the data, and information for ensuring that the packets do not become corrupted.

3. *Internet Protocol (IP):* The Internet Protocol receives datagrams from TCP and breaks the packets down further. An IP packet contains a header with address information and carries TCP information and data. IP routes the individual datagrams from the sender to the recipient. IP packets are not very reliable, but the TCP level can keep resending them until the correct IP packets get through.

4. *Network interface:* Handles addressing issues, usually in the operating system, as well as the interface between the initiating computer and the network.

5. *Physical net:* Defines basic electrical transmission characteristic for sending the actual signal along communications networks.

Two different computers using TCP/IP would be able to communicate, even if they were based on different hardware and software platforms. Data sent from one computer to the other would pass downward through all five layers, starting with the application layer of the sending computer and passing through the physical net. Once the data reach the recipient host computer, they travel up the layers. The TCP level would assemble the data into a format the receiving host computer can use. If the receiving computer found a damaged packet, it would ask the sending computer to retransmit it. This process would be reversed when the other computer responds.

Open Systems Interconnect (OSI)
International reference model
for linking different types of
computers and networks.

The **Open Systems Interconnect (OSI)** model is an international reference model developed by the International Standards Organization for linking different types of computers and networks. It was designed to support global networks with large volumes of transaction processing. OSI enables a computer connected to a network to

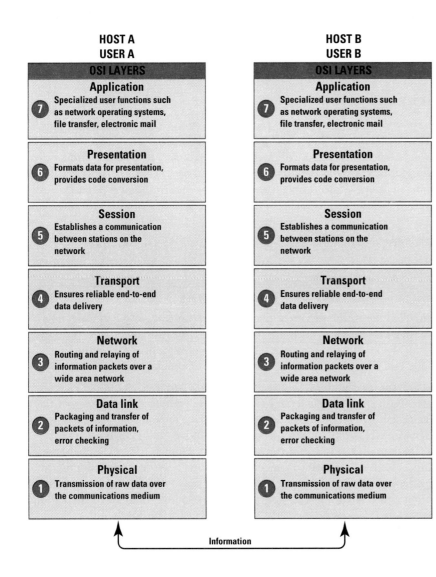

HOST A
USER A

OSI LAYERS

Application
7 Specialized user functions such as network operating systems, file transfer, electronic mail

Presentation
6 Formats data for presentation, provides code conversion

Session
5 Establishes a communication between stations on the network

Transport
4 Ensures reliable end-to-end data delivery

Network
3 Routing and relaying of information packets over a wide area network

Data link
2 Packaging and transfer of packets of information, error checking

Physical
1 Transmission of raw data over the communications medium

HOST B
USER B

OSI LAYERS

Application
7 Specialized user functions such as network operating systems, file transfer, electronic mail

Presentation
6 Formats data for presentation, provides code conversion

Session
5 Establishes a communication between stations on the network

Transport
4 Ensures reliable end-to-end data delivery

Network
3 Routing and relaying of information packets over a wide area network

Data link
2 Packaging and transfer of packets of information, error checking

Physical
1 Transmission of raw data over the communications medium

Information

FIGURE 10.10

The Open Systems Interconnect (OSI) reference model. The figure illustrates the seven layers defining the communication functions for the flow of information over an OSI network.

communicate with any other computer on the same network or a different network, regardless of the manufacturer, by establishing communication rules that permit the exchange of information between dissimilar systems.

The OSI model divides the telecommunications process into seven layers (see Figure 10.10). Each layer in the OSI model deals with a specific aspect of the communications process. Two different computers using OSI standards would each have software and hardware that correspond to each layer of the OSI model.

For example, if an officer at a local bank wanted information about a particular client's checking account that was stored in the bank's central host computer, the officer would enter the instructions to retrieve the client's account records into his or her terminal under control of layer 7, the application layer. The presentation layer (layer 6) would change this input data into a format for transmission. Layer 5 (the session layer) initiates the session. Layer 4 (the transport layer) checks the quality of the information traveling from user to host node. Layers 3 and 2 (the network and data link layers) transmit the data through layer 1 (the physical layer). When the message reaches the host computer, control moves up the layers back to the user, reversing the sequence.

The most widely used proprietary networking standard is **Systems Network Architecture (SNA),** developed by IBM in 1974. SNA is similar to OSI in that it takes a layered approach to the problem of communications among users and performs similar communications functions. However, the layers do not correspond completely,

Systems Network Architecture (SNA) Proprietary telecommunications reference model developed by IBM.

and SNA is not entirely compatible with OSI. SNA is a limited connectivity solution. Applications for one IBM host computer often cannot be operated on other IBM host computers, minicomputers, or PCs.

Other Networking Standards

Integrated Services Digital Network (ISDN) International standard for transmitting voice, image video, and data to support a wide range of service over public telephone lines.

Standards have also been developed for transmitting digital data over public switched networks. **Integrated Services Digital Network (ISDN)** is an international digital public switched network standard for transmitting voice, data, image, and video over phone lines. ISDN was developed in the late 1970s by the CCITT (International Telegraph and Telephone Consultative Committee), an international standards body representing over 150 countries. ISDN combines in one single service the following features:

- Complete voice, data, and video connection to anywhere in the world
- Complete digital connection to any other digital device in the world, from one next door to one halfway around the world
- Simultaneous use of voice, video, and digital devices
- User-controlled definition of video, digital, and data lines. You can use a line for digital personal service this hour, reconfigure the same phone line as an incoming 800 WATS line the next hour, and in the next hour redefine the line as a video line carrying pictures of a group videoconferencing session.

Modems are not used with ISDN except when they are needed to link up with a non-ISDN user. With some simple technology changes, ordinary twisted copper telephone wire can be more fully utilized without expensive recabling.

There are two levels of ISDN service: Basic Rate ISDN and Primary Rate ISDN. Basic Rate ISDN serves a single desktop with three channels. Two channels are B (bearer) channels with a capacity to transmit 64 kilobits per second of digital data (voice, data, video). A third delta channel (D channel) is a 16-kilobit-per-second channel for signaling and control information (such as the phone number of the calling party). Primary Rate ISDN offers 1.5 MBPS of bandwidth. The bandwidth is divided into 23 B channels and one D channel. This service is intended to meet the telecommunications needs of large users. Plans are underway to increase ISDN transmission capacity and to stitch together isolated ISDN "islands" into a national network.

Table 10.3 summarizes the standards we have described and lists other important standards for graphical user interfaces, electronic mail, packet switching, and electronic data interchange. Any manager wishing to achieve some measure of connectivity in an organization should try to use these standards when designing networks, purchasing hardware and software, or developing information system applications.

Intranets and Java

Some connectivity problems can be solved by using Java and by creating internal networks based on Internet technology. Companies can use Java to develop software applications that can run on any computer (see Chapter 7). Java applets can run on a smart cellular phone, a personal digital assistant (PDA), a laptop running Windows 95, a UNIX workstation or server, or an IBM minicomputer or mainframe.

To run Java applets, a computer needs a Java Virtual Machine (JVM). The Java Virtual Machine is a compact program, embedded in a computer operating system such as Windows 95 or UNIX, that enables the computer to run Java applications. (A Java Virtual Machine is incorporated into Netscape Web browser software.) The JVM lets the computer simulate an ideal standardized Java computer, complete with disk drives, memory, display, everything that would be needed on a computer to run the program. The Virtual Machine executes Java programs by interpreting their commands one by one and commanding the underlying computer to perform all the tasks specified by the command.

Table 10.3   Standards for Achieving Connectivity

Area	Standard or Reference Model	Description
Networking	TCP/IP, OSI, SNA	Computer-to-computer communications
Digital public switched network transmission	ISDN	Transmission of voice, video, and data over public telephone lines
Fiber-optic transmission	FDDI	100 MBPS data transmission over dual fiber-optical ring
Electronic mail	X.400	Permits e-mail systems operating on different hardware to communicate
Packet switching	X.25	Permits different international and national networks to communicate
EDI	X.12 Edifact (Europe)	Standardized transaction format
Graphical user interface	X Windows	High-level graphics description for standardized window management
Operating system	UNIX	Software portable to different hardware platforms

Organizations can achieve enterprise-wide connectivity by creating internal networks called *intranets* based on Internet networking standards and Web technology. An **intranet** is an internal organizational network based on Internet technology that can provide access to data across the enterprise. It uses the existing company network infrastructure along with Internet connectivity standards and software developed for the World Wide Web. Intranets can create networked applications that can run on many different kinds of computers throughout the organization.

An intranet was able to solve some of the connectivity problems of Santa Clara County, California. The county was spending an estimated $1 billion per year to support nearly 50 client/server platforms used by 40 departments and agencies. The county's client/server environment had been built without a central technology organization and without standards. Different agencies and departments, such as Santa Clara Valley's Medical Center (using DEC VAX minicomputers and Novell Netware LANs) and the Social Services division (using Sun SparcServers and other Unix-based systems), could not communicate with each other. Six different e-mail systems handled communications within but not among agencies. The county was able to tie together these client/server islands by building a $4.3 million intranet called Claranet in 1996. Now thousands of county workers can use Claranet to share electronic files (Fryer, 1996).

intranet An internal network based on Internet and World Wide Web technology.

Intranet Technology

The principal difference between the Web and an intranet is that while the Web is open to anyone, the intranet is private and is protected from public visits by **firewalls**—security systems with specialized software to prevent outsiders from invading private networks. The firewall consists of hardware and software placed between an organization's internal network and an external network, including the Internet. The firewall is programmed to intercept each message packet passing between the two networks, examine its characteristics, and reject unauthorized messages or access attempts.

Intranets require no special hardware and thus can run over an existing network infrastructure. Intranet software technology is the same as that of the World Wide Web. Intranets use HTML hypertext markup language to program Web pages and to establish dynamic, point-and-click hypertext links to other sites. The Web browser and Web server software used for intranets are the same as those being used on the Web. A simple intranet can be created by linking a client computer with a Web browser to a computer with Web server software via a TCP/IP network. A firewall keeps unwanted visitors out.

firewall Hardware and software placed between an organization's internal network and an external network to prevent outsiders from invading private networks.

Whereas most companies, particularly the larger ones, must support a multiplicity of computer platforms that cannot communicate with each other, Internet technology overcomes these platform differences, uniting all computers into a single, virtually seamless network system. Web software presents users with a uniform interface, reducing the user training requirements. Companies can connect their intranet to company databases just as is done with the Web, enabling employees to take actions central to a company's operations. For instance, through the US West intranet, the company's customer representatives are able to turn on customer services such as call waiting through the intranet while the customer is still on the telephone. In the past, customers had to wait hours or even days (see Figure 10.11).

For companies with an installed network infrastructure, intranets are very inexpensive to build and to run. All an organization needs to do is to install Web software on its internal TCP/IP networks, develop some home pages, connect any databases, and do some user training. Software costs are exceedingly low. Programming Web pages is quick and easy; some employees are programming their own Web pages. In addition, intranet networks cost very little to maintain, other than the cost

A DAY IN THE LIFE OF THE CORPORATE WEB AT US WEST

▪ At this Baby Bell, 15,000 employees rely on the company's intranet, Global Village, all day long. Typically, they log on to the home page shown below and select one of five icons. Then they point and click to information stored on computers around the company. The web relays the data back to their desktop PC.

LAB
11 A.M.: A project manager clicks on to the lab page to check out software being designed for a new service she wants to offer. She can test-drive the program from her desktop computer.

GATE
4 P.M.: An engineer researching the design of a new network component gets on to the global Internet via this "gateway" built into the home page. He visits World Wide Web sites belonging to possible suppliers, then clicks back to the internal web and updates his colleagues via E-mail.

VIRTUAL ROOM
9 P.M.: After tucking in the kids, a busy exec logs on to the corporate web via his home PC. He catches up on E-mail and checks out his team's project page for tomorrow's schedule. Finally, he looks over the volunteer page. After deciding to help paint a neighborhood center on Sunday, he signs off.

MODELS
1 P.M.: Squirrels are wreaking havoc on phone lines in Golden, Colorado. Repair technicians in Golden and supervisors at Denver HQ use the web to share a map of the damage and the results of trials of new materials for insulating wires. Together, they explore different strategies for repelling the critters.

LIBRARY
7:30 A.M.: A sales consultant in the Denver office begins his day by checking what's going on around the company. He pulls up News of the Day, an internal newsletter. Today's items include an update on winter storms that have knocked out company telephone lines in the Midwest. He also checks US West's stock price.

FIGURE 10.11

The U.S. West intranet. Companies are finding many uses for internal networks based on World Wide Web technology. From Alison L. Sprout, "The Internet Inside Your Company" in *Fortune*, November 27, 1995. Fortune Magazine, New York, NY. ©1995 Time, Inc. All rights reserved. Reprinted by permission. Graphic reprinted by permission of U.S. West Communications. U.S. West is a registered trademark of U.S. West, Inc.

of maintaining the infrastructure itself. The intranet provides a universal e-mail system, a remote access method, a set of group collaboration tools, an electronic library, an application sharing system, and a company communications network.

Benefits of Intranets

Companies are using their intranets in many ways. They are making customer profiles, product inventories, policy manuals, and company telephone directories available to their employees. Made available in this way, these documents are always up-to-date, eliminating paper, printing, and distributing costs. Some companies are using their intranets for virtual conferencing. Intranets are simple, cost-effective communication tools.

Earlier, we described how Cygnus Support uses its intranet for organizational communication and coordination. Silicon Graphics installed an intranet to connect its 7200 employees, enabling them to create reports from corporate databases using easy point-and-click technology. In addition to documents, the intranet delivers video and audio material to employees. Compaq Computers employees use their intranet to reallocate funds in their 401K savings plans. Mitre Corporation of Bedford, Massachusetts, uses its intranet for virtual conferencing, discussion groups, and even for news feeds. The animation division of DreamWorks SKG, the entertainment production company founded by Steven Spielberg, Jeffrey Katzenberg, and David Geffen, has set up its own divisional intranet to track the daily status of projects, including animation objects, and to coordinate movie scenes. The intranet also supports the production of live-action films, music, television shows, and digital media products.

The Window on Management illustrates some of the management benefits provided by intranets used for group collaboration and coordination.

WINDOW ON MANAGEMENT

Researchers Cross-Pollinate on Roche Bioscience's Intranet

Roche Bioscience, the Palo Alto division of the Swiss Roche Holding Ltd., specializes in research on nervous system and inflammatory problems such as arthritis and urinary tract disorders. Aleve, a popular over-the-counter medication to relieve pain and inflammation, is one of its inventions. Roche Bioscience created an intranet to connect several divisions worldwide, and it has promoted information sharing among groups separated by technical specialty or by geography. The intranet uses Netscape Communications Corporation's Web servers and Web browsers running on PCs, Macintoshes, and Unix machines.

Roche Bioscience's first intranet application was a simple telephone directory, followed by a company newsletter. Roche scientists now use the intranet to share research results, discuss findings, and to connect on-line to public information resources. They can coordinate with colleagues in Japan and England working on similar programs. In the past, much of the cross-pollination of ideas among chemists and physiologists or other groups took place around the watercooler or in other casual encounters.

According to Phyllis Whiteley, head of Roche's inflammation and immunomodulation department, meetings are more productive and decisions are made more quickly because participants come to meetings prepared. The scientists have already discussed and exchanged information on-line beforehand, so meeting time does not have to be spent presenting data. "Meetings are where decisions are made about which direction to take or which experiments to perform," Whiteley says. Whiteley's departmental Web site contains meeting minutes, new research findings, discussion forums, and links to outside libraries.

Before the intranet was built, inflammation and immunomodulation department members exchanged data using shared drives on networked file servers. This technology did not work well for graphics nor was it easy to use with scientists working on different types of computers. The scientists using Macintoshes had to be reminded to name files so that those using PCs could find them.

To Think About: *What were the management benefits of using an intranet at Roche Bioscience?*

Source: Kim S. Nash, "Bionet: Intranet Helps Researchers Cross-Pollinate," *Computerworld,* July 29, 1996.

Marshall Industries' Web site provides additional value and service along with its on-line catalogue of electronic parts. Engineers can test designs of TI chips at Marshall's Electronic Design Center, register for training, or access industry news and other information resources.

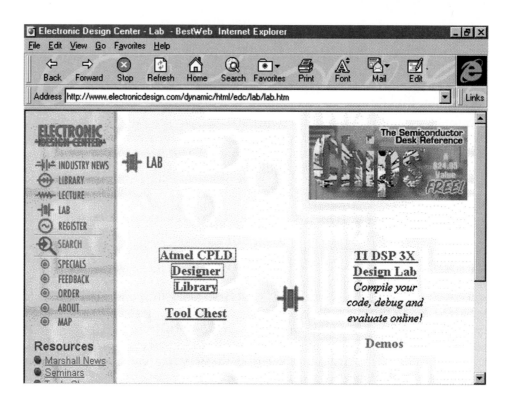

Extranets

Some firms are allowing people and organizations from the outside to have limited access to their internal intranets. For example, authorized buyers could dial into a portion of a company's intranet from the public Internet to obtain information about the cost and features of its products. Private intranets that are accessible to select outsiders are sometimes called **extranets.** The company can use firewalls to ensure that access to its internal data is limited and remains secure.

extranet A private intranet that is accessible to select outsiders.

Extranets are especially useful for linking organizations with customers or business partners, with many used for providing product availability, pricing, and shipment data. For example, Mobil Corp., based in Fairfax, Virginia, created an extranet application that allows its 300 lubricant distributors worldwide to submit purchase

Table 10.4	Examples of Intranet and Extranet Applications
Function	Description
Management	A manager can view daily progress reports from staff or projects, post the minutes of meetings, or post assignments from work groups.
Communication	A group can collaborate on projects on-line. Each member can post notes and changes.
Reference	Employees can access manuals, directories, and databases on-line.
Sales and Marketing	Sales staff can dial in for updates on pricing, promotions, rebates, or customers or obtain information about competitors. They can access presentations and sales documents and customize them for specific customers.
Purchasing	Authorized buyers check on new products, prices, and availability, research features, or obtain catalogues. Some can place orders on-line.
Customer Support	Customer-service representatives have a single point of access for customer order forms, invoices, procedure guides, and other support materials.
Human Resources	New employees can receive training information from multimedia pages, access policy and procedure manuals, or take on-line competency tests. Employees can enroll in health and pension benefits on-line.

Marshall Industries' Virtual Distribution System

If you're serious about selling on the Web, take a look at Marshall Industries. Its Web site averages more than 1 million hits per week from over 60 countries. Visitors can view more than 100,000 pages of data sheets, up-to-date pricing and inventory information from 150 major suppliers, and information on 170,000 parts numbers. Information can be customized on demand. Users can quickly locate products in Marshall's on-line catalogue using a sophisticated search engine. The site links up to United Parcel Service (UPS) Web site where customers can track the status of their shipments. Sales representatives have secure intranet access so that they can check sales and activity status in their territory only.

According to Kerry Young, Marshall's director of distributed computing, Marshall can "tell the world about new products faster than anybody else in the industry." Marshall has converted almost all the processes it performed physically to a digital service on the Net.

The added value and service provided by Marshall's Web site can be a source of competitive advantage, both to Marshall and its customers. Kevin McGarity, senior vice president of worldwide marketing for Texas Instruments (TI), calls Marshall's Web site "a major weapon" for its most important product, digital signal processors (DSPs). DSP chips improve the performance of high-tech products such as computer hard disks, headphones, and power steering in cars. TI expects to ship more than $1 billion of DSPs in 1997.

Marshall's Web site is critical to TI because it provides direct access to thousands of engineers worldwide who might use its DSPs in their products. For instance, an engineer designing a new piece of multimedia hardware might want to know how TI's DSP could enhance its performance. Until a few years ago, the engineer had to call Marshall, request technical literature, and wait for technical literature and a developer's kit to be mailed out. The process might take weeks. Today, the engineer can visit Marshall's Electronic Design Center on the Web. There the engineer can find technical specifications and even simulate designs using TI chips. The engineer would download sample code, modify the code to suit the product being built, test it on a "virtual chip" attached to the Web, and analyze its performance. If the engineer liked the results, Marshall could download the code, burn it into physical chips, and send back samples for designing prototypes. The entire process takes minutes.

For volume testing, the engineer can order shipments via MarshallNet, the company's secure extranet linked to suppliers and customers. Each customer sees a Web site modified to its specific needs. If someone is building multimedia entertainment products, that customer would see prices and quantities for parts that are relevant to that business. After ordering the chips, MarshallNet connects the engineer to its internal proprietary database. Customers can view the same shipment data that are available to Marshall's sales staff. An average of 1250 customers use MarshallNet each day.

And that's not all. Marshall's Web site provides after-sale training so that engineers don't have to attend special training classes or meetings in faraway locations. Marshall links to NetSeminar, a Web site where Marshall's customers can register for and receive educational programs developed for them by their suppliers using video, audio, and real-time chat capabilities.

To Think About: *How did Marshall Industries' use of the Web transform its business process? What kinds of competitive advantage does it provide?*

Source: "Web Sites that Sell," *Fast Company*, June–July 1997.

orders (Maloff, 1997). Marshall Industries, a $1 billion electronic parts distribution business headquartered in Los Angeles, at one time published a comprehensive paper catalogue of all its suppliers' products. In July 1994 it launched a Web site that includes an intranet system providing customers with access to its internal databases. The Window on Technology describes its capabilities.

Table 10.4 summarizes some of the uses of intranets and extranets.

Intranets (and extranets) have important limitations. They usually cannot replace such complex business programs as payrolls, accounting, manufacturing, and marketing systems because Web systems are too slow for high-speed transaction processing. Although companies use intranets to support group work (see Chapter 15), they currently lack the functionality of specialized groupware systems such as Lotus Notes. Because Web technology is designed for open communications, appropriate security measures are required (see Chapter 17). Effective intranets require careful management planning (*IS/Analyzer*, May 1996).

Implementing enterprise networking and Internet computing has created problems as well as opportunities for organizations. Managers need to address these problems as they design and build networks and Internet-based applications for their organizations.

Problems Posed by Enterprise Networking and the Internet

The rapid, often unplanned, development of networks, PCs, and workstations has created some problems. In addition to connectivity problems created by incompatible network components and standards, four additional problems stand out: loss of management control over information systems; the need for organizational change; the hidden costs of client/server and Internet computing; and the difficulty of ensuring network reliability and security (see Table 10.5).

Loss of Management Control Over Information Systems

Managing both information systems technology and corporate data is proving much more difficult in a distributed environment because of the lack of a single central point where needed management can occur. Desktop computing and networks have empowered end users to become independent sources of computing power capable of collecting, storing, and disseminating data and software. Users can create their own Web pages and distribute them on corporate intranets. Data and software are no longer confined to the mainframe and the management of the traditional information systems department.

Under enterprise networking, it becomes increasingly difficult to determine where data are located and to ensure that the same piece of information, such as a product number, is used consistently throughout the organization. User-developed applications may combine incompatible pieces of hardware and software. Uncontrolled proliferation of Web pages may saddle the organization's employees with information overload. Yet observers worry that excess centralization and management of information resources will stifle the independence and creativity of end users and reduce their ability to define their own information needs. The dilemma posed by enterprise networking is one of central management control versus end-user creativity and productivity.

Organizational Change Requirements

Decentralization also results in changes in corporate culture and organizational structure. Although enterprise-wide computing and intranets create opportunities to reengineer the organization into a more effective unit, they will only create problems or chaos if the underlying organizational issues are not fully addressed.

Hidden Costs of Client/Server and Internet Computing

Many companies have found that the savings they expected from client/server computing did not materialize because of unexpected costs. Hardware acquisition sav-

Table 10.5   Problems Posed by Enterprise Networking and the Internet
Connectivity problems
Loss of management control over systems
Organizational change requirements
Hidden costs of client/server and Internet computing
Network reliability and security

ings resulting from significantly lower costs of MIPS on PCs are often offset by high annual operating costs for additional labor and time required for network and system management. The Gartner consulting group of Stamford, Connecticut, estimated that the cost of owning a client/server system can be three to six times greater than for a comparable mainframe system, with software tools for managing and administering client/server costing two and one-half times more than mainframe tools (Caldwell, 1996).

The most difficult to evaluate and control are the hidden costs that accompany a decentralized client/server system. Considerable time must be spent on such tasks as network maintenance, data backup, technical problem solving, and hardware, software, and software-update installations. As illustrated in Figure 10.12, the largest cost component for both large and small client/server sites is operations staff.

Internet technology on the whole tends to be less expensive to implement and use than traditional information systems technology. However, Internet computing has some hidden costs of which managers should be aware, the largest being the cost of setting up TCP/IP networks. Another is productivity loss when users place information on intranets or Web sites not properly organized or integrated with the organization's legacy systems.

Network Reliability and Security

Network technology is still immature and highly complex. The networks themselves have dense layers of interacting technology, and the applications too are often intricately layered. Enterprise networking is highly sensitive to different versions of operating systems and network management software, with some applications requiring specific versions of each. It is difficult to make all the components of large heterogeneous networks work together as smoothly as management envisions (see Figure 10.13). **Downtime**—periods of time in which the system is not operational—remains much more frequent in client/server and Internet based systems than in established mainframe systems and should be considered carefully before one takes essential applications off the mainframe.

downtime Periods of time in which an information system is not operational.

Tools for managing distributed networks are still immature. Adequate, easy-to-use tools are lacking for such vital system functions as system configuration, tuning, systemwide backup and recovery, security, upgrading both system and application software, capacity planning, and the pinpointing of bottlenecks. Performance monitoring tools for client/server networks (for instance, monitoring CPU usage) are also

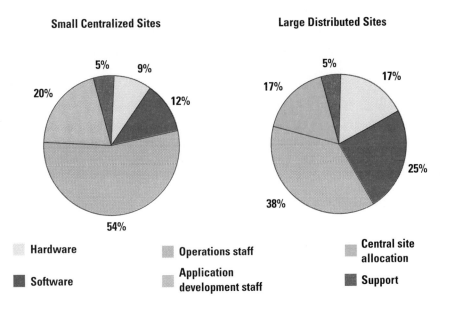

Small Centralized Sites

5% 9% 20% 12% 54%

Large Distributed Sites

5% 17% 17% 25% 38%

- Hardware
- Software
- Operations staff
- Application development staff
- Central site allocation
- Support

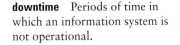

FIGURE 10.12

Cost breakdowns for client/server computing. The cost of operations staff, the largest cost component in client/server computing, is frequently underestimated when organizations downsize.
Source: Copyright April 30, 1996 by Computerworld, Inc., Framingham, MA 01701. Reprinted from Computerworld.

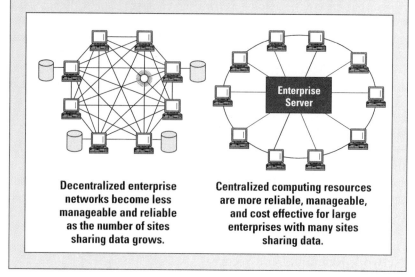

CENTRALIZED COMPUTING NETWORKS REDUCE ENTERPRISE NETWORK COST AND COMPLEXITY

Enterprise Server

Decentralized enterprise networks become less manageable and reliable as the number of sites sharing data grows.

Centralized computing resources are more reliable, manageable, and cost effective for large enterprises with many sites sharing data.

not as well developed or sophisticated as are the tools available for mainframes or minicomputers.

Security is of paramount importance in organizations in which information systems make extensive use of networks. Networks present end users, hackers, and thieves with many points of access and opportunities to steal or modify data in networks. How can an organization rely on data if one cannot prove where the data came from and who modified them along the way? Moreover, because users may simultaneously access several different computers (their client plus one or more servers) with different security systems, access can become overly complex and seriously interfere with the user's productivity.

Internet-based systems are even more vulnerable because the Internet was designed to be virtually open to everyone. Many people have the skill and technology to intercept and spy on streams of electronic information as it flows through the Internet and all other open networks. Any information, including e-mail as it flows through the Net, passes through many computer systems before it reaches its destination. It can be monitored, captured, and stored at any of these points along the route. Valuable data that might be intercepted include credit card numbers and names, private personnel data, marketing plans, sales contracts, product development and pricing data, negotiations between companies, and other information that might be of value to competition.

Some Solutions

Organizations can counteract problems created by enterprise networking and Internet computing by planning for and managing the business and organizational changes, increasing end-user training, asserting data administration disciplines, and considering connectivity and cost controls when planning their information architecture.

Managing the Change

To gain the full benefit of any new technology, including the Internet, organizations must carefully plan for and manage the change. Business processes may need to be reengineered to ensure that the organization fully benefits from the new technology (see Chapter 11). The company's information architecture must be redrawn to shape the new client/server environment or to incorporate Internet computing. Management must address the organizational issues that arise from shifts in staffing, function, power, and organizational culture. Data models must be developed, training given, network support assigned, and network management tools acquired.

Education and Training

A well-developed training program can help end users overcome problems resulting from the lack of management support and understanding of desktop computing (Westin et al., 1985; Bikson et al., 1985). Technical specialists will need training in client/server and intranet development and in network support methods. End users will need training on how to use client/server systems and Internet tools efficiently.

Data Administration Disciplines

The role of data administration (see Chapter 8) becomes even more important when networks and intranets link many different applications and business areas. Organizations must systematically identify where their data are located, which groups are responsible for maintaining each piece of data, and which individuals and groups are allowed to access and use that data. They need to develop specific policies and procedures to ensure that their data are accurate, available only to authorized users, and properly backed up.

Planning for Connectivity

Senior management must take a long-term view of the firm's information architecture and must ensure that its systems have the right degree of connectivity for its current and future information needs. Clearly, complete connectivity is usually not needed in most corporations. It is usually too expensive to achieve systemic connectivity for older applications. It is far more sensible to identify classes of connectivity problems and general solutions.

A longer-term strategy accepts the reality of today's incompatible systems but maintains a vision of the future, where connectivity is an important goal. Procurement strategy should then focus on new systems and follow the simple rule that, from today, systems will be developed only if (1) they support connectivity standards developed by the firm, and (2) they build on existing networks and user applications in a seamless fashion. Management can establish policies to keep networks as homogeneous as possible, limiting the number of hardware, software, and network operating systems from different vendors or encouraging development of intranets wherever appropriate.

MANAGEMENT

To obtain meaningful benefits from enterprise networking and the Internet, managers need to determine how these technologies support their business goals. Planning should carefully consider network costs, the costs and benefits of client/server computing, and connectivity issues. Managers should also anticipate making organizational changes to take advantage of these technologies and the need to maintain some measure of management control as more independent computing power becomes decentralized on the desktop.

ORGANIZATION

Organizational processes can be enhanced by using enterprise networks and the Internet to make communication and coordination more efficient. Organizations can also benefit by using the Internet and other networks for electronic commerce, exchanging purchase and sale transactions with customers and suppliers. The Internet can dramatically reduce transaction and agency costs and is fueling new business models. To take advantage of these opportunities, organizational processes will have to be redesigned.

TECHNOLOGY

Enterprise networks and the Internet are both based on the client/server computing model and the use of connectivity standards that enable disparate computing devices to communicate with each other. The Internet is creating a universal computing platform by using the TCP/IP network reference model and other standards for storing, retrieving, formatting, and displaying information. Organizations can create intranets, internal networks based on Internet and Web technology, to reduce network costs and overcome connectivity problems. Key technology decisions should consider network reliability, security, bandwidth, and connectivity as well as the capabilities of Internet and other networking technologies.

For Discussion: The Internet is creating a business revolution and transforming the role of information systems in organizations. Do you agree? Why or why not?

SUMMARY

1. Describe the characteristics and technologies of enterprise networking and explain how it is changing organizations. Enterprise networking has produced a mixed environment composed mostly of networked desktop workstations and PCs. Although it often contains minicomputers and mainframes, computing power tends to take place on the desktop. The organization's hardware, software, and data are much more controlled from the desktop by the professional who uses the desktop machine. The system is a network or multiple networks connecting many local area networks and devices. Enterprise networking provides flexibility for organizations trying to coordinate their activities without excess centralization because it can help eliminate layers of bureaucracy and invest lower-level line workers with more responsibility and authority. It also allows organizations to link directly with customers and suppliers, facilitating electronic commerce.

Enterprise networking uses the client/server computing model, which splits computer processing between "clients" and "servers," connected via a network. Each

function of an application is assigned to the machine best suited to perform that function. The exact division of tasks between client and server depends on the nature of the application.

2. Identify the capabilities of the Internet and describe the benefits it offers organizations. The Internet is used for communications, including e-mail, public forums on thousands of topics, and live, interactive conversations. It is also used for information retrieval from hundreds of libraries and thousands of library, corporate, government, and nonprofit databases from around the world. It has developed into an effective way for individuals and organizations to offer information and products through a web of graphical user interfaces and easy-to-use links worldwide. Major Internet capabilities include e-mail, Usenet, LISTSERV, chatting, Telnet, FTP, gophers, Archie, Veronica, WAIS, and the World Wide Web.

Organizations benefit from the Internet in a number of ways. Many use the Net to reduce their communications costs when they coordinate organizational activities and communicate with employees. Researchers and knowledge workers are finding the Internet a quick, low cost way to both gather and disperse knowledge.

3. Describe how the Internet can be used for electronic commerce. The Internet facilitates electronic commerce, creating new channels for marketing, sales, and customer support and eliminating middlemen in buy-and-sell transactions. Businesses can link with individuals or other businesses at very low cost, connecting easily to different types of computers. There are many different business models for electronic commerce on the Internet including virtual storefronts, marketplace concentrators, information brokers, content providers, digital content delivery, and electronic clearinghouses. Internet electronic commerce is still in its infancy. Successful Internet electronic commerce initiatives require secure payment systems and the development of business models that genuinely generate revenue or reduce costs.

4. Describe important standards used for linking hardware, software, and networks to achieve connectivity, including the use of intranets and Java. Connectivity is a measure of how well computers and computer-based devices can communicate with one another and "share" information in a meaningful way without human intervention. It is essential in enterprise-wide computing where different hardware, software, and network components must work together to transfer information seamlessly from one part of the organization to another. Open systems, information portability, and interoperability are all aspects of connectivity.

There are several different models for achieving connectivity in networks. Public standards such as OSI and TCP/IP are recognized as important reference models for network connectivity. Each divides the communications process into layers. TCP/IP is becoming more widely utilized because it is the standard for the Internet. ISDN is an emerging standard for digital transmission over twisted-pair telephone lines. UNIX is an operating system standard that can be used to create open systems.

Another way of achieving connectivity is to use Internet technology. Java software can run on all types of computers. Intranets are internal networks that use Web servers, Web browsers, and TCP/IP networking standards, creating applications that can run on many different kinds of computers throughout the organization.

5. Identify problems posed by enterprise networking and the Internet and recommend solutions. Problems posed by enterprise networking and the Internet include: connectivity issues; loss of management control over systems; the need to carefully manage organizational change; the difficulty of ensuring network reliability and security; and controlling the hidden costs of client/server and Internet computing.

Solutions include planning for and managing the business and organizational changes associated with enterprise networking and Internet computing, increasing end-user training, asserting data administration disciplines, and considering connectivity and cost controls when planning information architecture.

KEY TERMS

Enterprise networking	Telnet	"Push" technology	Open Systems
Internetworking	File Transfer Protocol (FTP)	Connectivity	Interconnect (OSI)
Client/server model	Archie	Information portability	Systems Network
Client	Gopher	Interoperability	Architecture (SNA)
Server	Veronica	Open systems	Integrated Services Digital
Internet service	WAIS	Reference model	Network (ISDN)
provider (ISP)	World Wide Web	Protocol	Intranet
Domain name	Hypertext Markup	Standard	Firewall
Usenet	Language (HTML)	Transmission Control	Extranet
LISTSERV	Home page	Protocol/Internet	Downtime
Chatting	Search engine	Protocol (TCP/IP)	

REVIEW QUESTIONS

1. Define enterprise networking. List three of its characteristics. How is it related to internetworking?

2. What is client/server computing? What is the difference between the client and the server? What are the different roles each fulfills?

3. Why are organizations adopting enterprise networking and client/server computing?

4. What is the Internet? List and describe its principal capabilities.

5. Why is the World Wide Web so useful for individuals and businesses? Describe the various ways of locating information on the Web.

6. Describe the benefits of the Internet to organizations.

7. How can the Internet facilitate electronic commerce?

8. Describe four business models for electronic commerce on the Internet.

9. Describe some obstacles to electronic commerce on the Internet.

10. What is connectivity? Why is it a goal for enterprise networking? Give three examples of connectivity problems.

11. Compare TCP/IP, OSI, and SNA as solutions to network connectivity problems.

12. Describe ISDN and explain why it is important.

13. How can intranets and Java promote connectivity?

14. Give four examples of problems posed by enterprise networking and the Internet.

15. What are some solutions to the problems raised in the previous question?

GROUP PROJECT

Form a group with three or four of your classmates. Locate a business using a popular business magazine or find a local business that could benefit from using the Internet. Develop an Internet strategy for that business, explaining what Internet capabilities should be used, technical requirements, and how the Internet could change the company's business model. Present your findings to the class.

CASE STUDY

Virtual Vineyards' Virtual Storefront

Peter Granoff had spent the better part of two decades serving various functions in the wine industry, serving as a teacher, taster, consultant, and sommelier in San Francisco's restaurants and clubs. He is the thirteenth American to be admitted to the British Court of Master Sommeliers. He watched sadly as the wine industry followed the lead of other retail-oriented businesses by creating superstores appealing to the consumers' call for lower prices. Such stores kept an abundance of wines in stock, but purchased fewer varieties, using their clout to squeeze lower prices from wine producers. And by simplifying their stock, they could substitute regular salesclerks for wine experts who received higher wages. These savings were passed on to the customers, most of whom were willing to sacrifice knowledgeable service for convenient shopping and savings. The retail outlets relied on the large producers with advertising budgets to educate consumers.

Consequently, smaller wineries had no one to sell their product to because they could not provide the output or the discounts that superstores demanded. Small wine producers were responsible for many of the industry's best wines, but they couldn't survive under the new order. Hundreds of small wineries producing less than 5000 cases of wine per year were abandoned by their distributors.

Granoff knew that a market still existed for specialty labels and quality wines. The question was how to tap it, because it was geographically diffuse and too fragmented to be addressed by superstores. He found his answer by teaming up with his brother-in-law, Robert Olson, who had headed a Silicon Graphics marketing team selling software for interactive television. Olson wanted to apply what he knew to on-line retailing, and the World Wide Web seemed like the perfect medium.

Olson and Granoff believed that there were three advantages to using the Web for on-line retailing: (1) Computers are perfectly suited for the task of searching for key words and comparing numbers. (2) On-line retail reduces marketing costs because it is available to potential customers 24 hours a day, 365 days a year (at very low cost compared with, for example, the price of placing four half-page ads per year in the New York Times). (3) A Web site can sell directly to customers, eliminating middlemen and distribution costs.

Olson and Granoff pooled their expertise to found Virtual Vineyards, an on-line market that would serve as an agent for both the vineyard and the consumer. Its proprietor would taste and evaluate everything in stock. Earnings would be based on commissions on sales. In essence, Olson and Granoff would be selling wines traditionally using the most leading-edge technology.

Virtual Vineyards opened its virtual storefront in late January 1995. Since then, business has been increasing by approximately 20 percent per month, and sales have topped $1 million. It is not the only Web site selling wine. What it offers, in addition to convenience and low prices, is information—the expertise supplied by Peter Granoff, an authority in his field.

Other Web sites retailing goods typically feature links to reviews by other experts, mailing lists, on-line discussion groups, newsletters, journals, and so forth. Virtual Vineyards has none of these—only a clean line running to Granoff. Virtual Vineyards does not even have links to the wine producers' sites where customers can wander to read product presentations from different vendors. The information comes only from one source.

Granoff provides the winery descriptions, which demonstrate his knowledge of the industry and the operations of specific producers. For example, "The tiny Ahlgren Vineyard in the Santa Cruz Mountains . . . has earned a reputation for producing wines that balance concentrated varietal character with finesse and complexity. Total production is approximately 2000 cases, and vineyards in the Livermore Valley, the Santa Clara Valley, and the Santa Cruz Mountains are sources for the small lots of handmade wines . . . Dexter Ahlgren's philosophy is to interfere as little as possible during the entire winemaking process. The results speak volumes about the wisdom of a minimalist approach." In the Virtual Vineyards advice column, Granoff answers questions on topic ranging from investment, wineglass selection, and wine storage methods. Virtual Vineyards wants to educate its visitors as well as sell them products. Visitors learn as they shop. For example, the Portfolio option describing wines on sale describes each label with a few sentences but also provides information about the class of wine. The Portfolio Option includes Peter's Tasting Chart for each label, with seven parallel horizontal lines, each representing a dimension of wine taste (intensity, sweetness or dryness, body, acidity, tannin, oak, and complexity). Each line represents a range. A red diamond, placed anywhere from far left to far right, indicates where the label under discussion falls within that range for that particular dimension. The chart conveys a great deal of information at a glance.

Virtual Vineyard's Web pages are clean and load quickly. The menus are uncluttered with links, the graphics compact. The site assembles its pages on the fly by modifying data from forms. This process makes it easy to standardize the amount of information that appears about each entry. The look and feel of the site and the performance of its software reinforce its message of a strong voice tied to a specific person. Virtual Vineyards stocks about 300 labels from about 100 wineries.

Virtual Vineyards' information-based approach to sales and marketing presents some difficulties. Past a certain level of detail, the expert's command of his product starts to weaken, and the software becomes too elaborate to use easily. The information-based model raises prices. The expert has to be paid adding to the retailer's markup. Customers theoretically could use the site to find out information and then purchase what they like somewhere else—at a lower price.

Virtual Vineyards hopes to surmount these difficulties by personalizing its service. For instance, Olson can learn about customer preferences from their order histories and then use that information to suggest new labels to try. Virtual Vineyards recently added food and gift items to its wares. It is considering opening a gourmet farmer's market to sell produce during peak seasons, but must first overcome transportation problems. ■

Source: Fred Hapgood, "What Makes Virtual Vineyards Rule?" *Inc. Technology*, no. 2, 1996; and Mark Glaser, "Selling Online: Electronic Storefronts that Work," *New Media*, October 28, 1996.

Case Study Questions

1. Analyze Virtual Vineyards using the value chain and competitive forces models.

2. Why is Virtual Vineyards successful? What role does the Web play in its business model? How does Virtual Vineyards provide value?

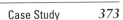

Summary: Sleek, aromatic and elegant: not for the rugby set. ☻) 94% Cabernet Sauvignon, 6% Cabernet Franc, unfined and unfiltered. 774 cases produced. This wine is currently on special. $18.00

Peter's Tasting Chart

Perception of...

INTENSITY	delicate	powerful
DRY OR SWEET	bone dry	dessert
BODY	light body	very full body
ACIDITY	soft, gentle	very crisp
TANNIN	none	heavy tannins
OAK	none	heavy oak
COMPLEXITY	direct	very complex

REFERENCES

Applegate, Lynda, and Janice Gogan. "Paving the Information Superhighway: Introduction to the Internet," Harvard Business School 9-195-202 (August 1995).

Berners-Lee, Tim, Robert Cailliau, Ari Luotonen, Henrik Frystyk Nielsen, and Arthur Secret. "The World-Wide Web." *Communications of the ACM* 37, no. 8 (August 1994).

Bikson, Tora K., Cathleen Stasz, and Donald A. Mankin. "Computer-Mediated Work: Individual and Organizational Impact on One Corporate Headquarters." *Rand Corporation* (1985).

Bikson, Tora K., J. D. Eveland, and Barbara A. Gutek. "Flexible Interactive Technologies for Multi-Person Tasks: Current Problems and Future Prospects." *Rand Corporation* (December 1988).

Bowman, C. Mic, Peter B. Danzig, Udi Manger, and Michael F. Schwartz. "Scalable Internet Resource Discovery: Research Problems and Approaches." *Communications of the ACM* 37, no. 8 (August 1994).

Caldwell, Bruce. "Can It Be Saved?" *Information Week* (April 8, 1996).

Chabrow, Eric R. "On-line Employment," *Information Week* (January 23, 1995).

Cortese, Amy. "Here Comes the Intranet." *Business Week* (February 26, 1996).

Crede, Andreas. "Electronic Commerce and the Banking Industry: The Requirement and Opportunities for New Payment Systems Using the Internet." *JCMC* 1, no. 3 (December 1995).

Darling, Michael. "The Internet: Hot or Just Cool?" *Stern Business* (Spring 1996).

Dearth, Jeffrey, and Arnold King, "Negotiating the Internet." *InformationWeek* (January 9, 1995).

De Pompa, Barbara. "More Power at Your Fingertips." *InformationWeek* (December 30, 1991).

Eckerson, Wayne. "Doing Business on the Web." Patricia Seybold Group's Notes on Information Technology (April 1996).

Fisher, Sharon. "TCP/IP." *Computerworld* (October 7, 1991).

Flynn, Laurie. "Browsers Make Navigating the World Wide Net a Snap." *The New York Times* (January 29, 1995).

Fryer, Bronwyn. "Silicon Valley Gets Wired." *Information Week* (June 17, 1996).

Goldman, Kevin. "Ad Agencies Slowly Set Up Shop At New Address on the Internet." *Wall Street Journal* (December 29, 1994).

Goodman, S. E., L. I. Press, S. R. Ruth, and A. M. Rutkowski. "The Global Diffusion of the Internet: Patterns and Problems." *Communications of the ACM* 37 no. 8 (August 1994.)

Guimaraes, Tom. "Personal Computing Trends and Problems: An Empirical Study." *MIS Quarterly* (June 1986).

Halper, Mark. "Meet the New Middlemen." *Computerworld Emmerce* (May 5, 1997).

Hoffman, Donna L., Thomas P. Novak, and Patrali Chatterjee. "Commercial Scenarios for the Web: Opportunities and Challenges." *JCMC* 1, no. 3 (December 1995).

Hoffman, Donna L., William D. Kalsbeek, and Thomas P. Novak. "Internet and Web Use in the U.S." *Communications of the ACM* 39, no. 12 (December 1996).

Horwitt, Elisabeth. "Intranet Intricacies." *Computerworld Client/Server Journal* (February 1996).

"How to Use Intranets to Support Business Applications." *I/S Analyzer Case Studies* 35, no. 5 (May 1996).

Huff, Sid, Malcolm C. Munro, and Barbara H. Martin. "Growth Stages of End-User Computing." *Communications of the ACM* (May 1988).

Johnson, Jim. "A Survival Guide for Administrators." *Software Magazine* (December 1992).

Kantor, Andrew. "The Best of the Lot." *Internet World* (January 1995).

Kautz, Henry, Bart Selman, and Mehul Shah. "ReferralWeb: Combining Social Networks and Collaborative Filtering." *Communications of the ACM* 40, no. 3 (March 1997).

King, Julia, and Rosemary Cafasso, "Client/Server Trimmings." *Computerworld* (December 19, 1994).

Laudon, Kenneth C. "From PCs to Managerial Workstations." In *Managers, Micros, and Mainframes,* edited by Matthias Jarke. New York: John Wiley (1986).

Lee, Denis M. "Usage Pattern and Sources of Assistance for Personal Computer Users." *MIS Quarterly* (December 1986).

Lee, Sunro, and Richard P. Leifer. "A Framework for Linking the Structure of Information Systems with Organizational Requirements for Information Sharing." *Journal of Management Information Systems* 8, no. 4 (Spring 1992).

Leiner, Barry M. "Internet Technology." *Communications of the ACM* 37 no. 8 (August 1994).

Lewis, Peter H. "Getting Down to Business on the Net." *The New York Times* (June 19, 1994).

Lohr, Steve. "Business to Business in the Internet." *The New York Times* (April 28, 1997).

Maddox, Kate. "Online Data Push." *Information Week* (February 24, 1997).

Maglitta, Joseph, and Ellis Booker, "Seller Beware." *Computerworld* (October 24, 1994).

Maloff, Joel. "Extranets: Stretching the Net to Boost Efficiency." *Net Guide Magazine* (August 1997).

Markoff, John. "Commerce Comes to the Internet." *The New York Times* (April 13, 1994).

Meeker, Mary, and Chris DePuy. *The Internet Report.* New York: Morgan Stanley & Co. (1996).

Mossberg, Walter S. "Before You Cruise the Internet, Get the Right Road Map." *The Wall Street Journal* (January 19, 1995).

Mougayar, Walid. *Opening Digital Markets: Advanced Strategies for Internet-Driven Commerce.* CYBER Management (1996).

Nouwens, John, and Harry Bouwman. "Living Apart Together in Electronic Commerce: The Use of Information and Communication Technology to Create Network Organizations." *JCMC* 1, no. 3 (December 1995).

O'Leary, Daniel E., Daniel Koukka, and Robert Plant. "Artificial Intelligence and Virtual Organizations." *Communications of the ACM* 40, no. 1 (January 1997).

"Plans and Policies for Client/Server Technology." *I/S Analyzer* no. 4 (April 1992).

Pyburn, Philip J. "Managing Personal Computer Use: The Role of Corporate Management Information Systems." *Journal of Management Information Systems* (Winter 1986–87).

Quelch, John A., and Lisa R. Klein. "The Internet and International Marketing." *Sloan Management Review* (Spring 1996).

Richard, Eric. "Anatomy of the World Wide Web." *Internet World* (April 1995).

Richardson, Gary L., Brad M. Jackson, and Gary W. Dickson. "A Principles-Based Enterprise Architecture: Lessons from Texaco and Star Enterprise." *MIS Quarterly* 14, no. 4 (December 1990).

Sarkar, Mitra Barun, Brian Butler, and Charles Steinfield. "Intermediaries and Cybermediaries: A Continuing Role for Mediating Players in the Electronic Marketplace." *JCMC* 1, no. 3 (December 1995).

Semich, J. William. "The World Wide Web: Internet Boomtown?" *Datamation* (January 15, 1995).

Sinha, Alok. "Client-Server Computing." *Communications of the ACM* 35, no. 7 (July 1992).

Smarr, Larry, and Charles E. Catlett. "Metacomputing." *Communications of the ACM* 35, no. 6 (June 1992).

Sprout, Alison L. "The Internet Inside Your Company." *Fortune* (November 27, 1995).

Steinfield, Charles. "The Impact of Electronic Commerce on Buyer-Seller Relationships." *JCMC* 1, no. 3 (December 1995).

Tash, Jeffrey B., and Paul Korzeniowski. "Theory Meets Reality for New Breed of APPs." *Software Magazine* (May 1992).

Tetzeli, Rick. "The INTERNET and Your Business." *Fortune* (March 7, 1994).

Ubois, Jeffrey. "CFOs in Cyberspace." *CFO* (February, 1995).

United States General Accounting Office. "FTS 2000: An Overview of the Federal Government's New Telecommunications System." *GAO/IMTEC-90-17FS* (February 1990).

Vacca, John R. "Mosaic: Beyond Net Surfing." *Byte* (January 1995).

Verity, John W. with Robert D. Hof. "The Internet: How It Will Change the Way You Do Business." *Business Week* (November 14, 1994).

Westin, Alan F., Heather A. Schwader, Michael A. Baker, and Sheila Lehman. *The Changing Workplace.* New York: Knowledge Industries (1985).

Wigand, Rolf T., and Robert Benjamin. "Electronic Commerce: Effects on Electronic Markets." *JCMC* 1, no. 3 (December 1995).

Wilder, Clinton. "The Internet Pioneers." *Information Week* (January 9, 1995).

Withers, Suzanne. "The Trader and the Internet." *Technical Analysis of Stocks & Commodities* (March 1995).

Xeniakis, John J. "Moving to Mission Critical." *CFO* (September 1994).

ELECTRONIC COMMERCE STRATEGIES: A TALE OF TWO COMPANIES

Electronic commerce (EC) is burgeoning all around us, but it is based on technologies that are not simple to use. General Electric and 3M are two of the giant corporations that have integrated EC into their business strategies. Both have been using EC for a number of years, and yet their strategies are different. Together they illustrate the complexities involved in gaining value from electronic commerce as well as some of the many uses of EC technology.

GENERAL ELECTRIC

General Electric (GE) is a huge company. In 1996 it was the most profitable company in the United States. Its 12 business units generated sales of $79.2 billion and earnings of $7.28 billion. The company is highly diversified, although primarily a manufacturer. Electronic commerce is not new at GE: The company has been a long-time leader in the use of electronic data interchange (EDI). Today that leadership continues as GE now does more business over the Internet than any other noncomputer manufacturer.

Over time GE has changed its view on the value of information technology. According to GE's 1996 annual report, information technology "is making the huge transition from the 'function' it was in the 1980s—with its own language, rituals and priesthood—to the indispensable competi-

tive tool, the central nervous system of virtually every operation in the Company." GE's perspective on electronic commerce has evolved in just the same way. Traditionally EC was viewed as a set of niche products, offering such functions as EDI to ease the burden of the exchange of business transaction documents. More recently GE's EC portfolio has expanded to include the use of credit card purchases over the Internet. "But [now] we have a much broader definition of electronic commerce," explains John McKinley, chief technology and information officer at GE Capital (Stamford, Connecticut). "It's a ubiquitous network business model for prospecting customers, order management, and order fulfillment." The annual report stresses that "information technology has drawn us closer to customers via inventory management systems," which are electronic commerce systems in action. GE also sees EC as a major element of its Six Sigma quality program. Six Sigma, which was established in 1995, is headed by General Electric's CEO, Jack Welch. Its goals include improving overall quality, improving customer service, and cutting costs. According to General Electric's CIO, Gary Reiner, "We are relying on Six Sigma to continue to grow our earnings in double digits, and we are heavily relying on electronic commerce to get there."

The prize of GE's electronic commerce strategy is its Web-based automated procurement systems, particularly the GE Trading Process Network (TPN). The center of TPN is its secure Web site, which was originally established in mid-1996 for GE Lighting in Cleveland, Ohio. GE touts the site as a

"revolutionary new way of doing business on the Internet." One goal for TPN is to replace GE's EDI network which requires the use of proprietary EDI software with an open, Internet browser-based system. The Web site gives access to two main functions—customized bidding and automated purchasing. GE uses TPN to send bidding packages via the Net to regular suppliers. These packages contain drawings, requisition forms, and any other needed information. The TPN site is linked directly to GE Lighting's manufacturing resource planning (MRP) software. This enables GE purchasing agents quickly and easily to post directly from the factory floor its latest needs in the form of up-to-date product blueprints.

The system appears to be a success. Suppliers like it because they do not need expensive proprietary EDI software to submit bids. They also find the system to be much more flexible than is GE's EDI system. Moreover, under the old EDI system, the bidder had to be on-line Friday at 5 P.M. to obtain a contract. "If you couldn't be at a terminal at 5 P.M. on a Friday when they accepted the electronic bids, that took you right out of it," explains Rich Wilson, Matrix Tool & Machine, Inc. operations manager. That is no longer the case. Wilson believes, "Now it's a lot more fair, and it has definitely made it easier to do business with them."

From GE Lighting's perspective, TPN is also viewed as a success. It has cut average purchasing cycle time from between 14 and 21 days to 7 days. Costs have been lowered—after one year the procurement group has eliminated paper and mailing costs. GE also finds that it is paying 10 to 15

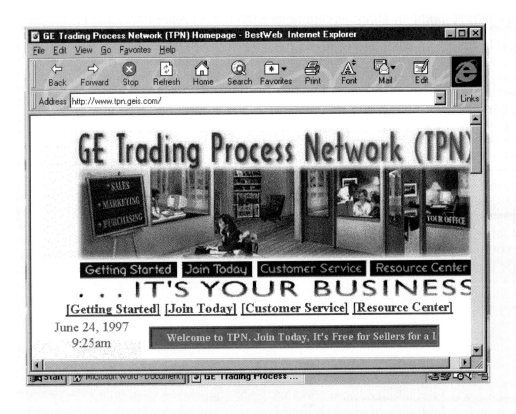

GE's Trading Process Network can be used for customized bidding and automated purchasing. Use of this Web site has reduced procurement time and costs.

percent lower prices as a result of the system. According to Orville Bailey, the global director of purchasing and supplier productivity at GE Information Services GEIS (which developed and administers TPN), "Suppliers aren't sure who else is out there bidding. The immediacy," he explains, "is causing more competitive pricing earlier in the process." All of GE has noticed TPN's success. During the first half of 1997, seven more GE units transferred part of their purchasing processes onto the site, including aircraft engines, medical systems, transportation, and power systems. GE estimates that in 1997 the company will purchase over $1 billion through TPN.

Another GE unit, GE Supply, has also developed a new EC system. GE Supply is a $1.6 billion electrical products distribution unit. GE SupplyNet, the new system, automates some processes linking GE with its customers. It is a Web-based ordering and order-tracking service and is the on-line front end to GE Supply's order entry, inventory, and distribution systems.

In addition to cutting costs and improving relations with partners, General Electric also sees electronic commerce as a way to generate revenue. GE has genuine advantages in this field. First, it has a base of thousands of trading partners (GE claims their trading community to be more than 40,000 companies), giving it both experience and the ability to test any new EC system. In addition, the company has plenty of funds to finance any venture it wishes to undertake.

To accomplish its revenue goal, GE now finds itself in new businesses. GE Capital Services provides EC consulting services within its own organization. It soon will be offering these same consulting services to outside customers. GE is also using its expertise in EC to develop and sell software to others. Actra Business Systems, which was formed in 1996, is a partnership between GEIS and Netscape Communications. Its first product is Business Document Gateway. This system converts a company's conventional EDI software

into Internet formats, enabling EDI users to do the same business on the Internet. GEIS has produced GE TradeWeb, a product that handles the counterpart to the issue addressed by Business Document Gateway. GE TradeWeb enables companies without EDI to use the Net to link to companies that rely on EDI.

TPN is also becoming a revenue generator. In early 1997 GE began offering it to other manufacturers for their own use. GE promotes TPN as a "productivity tool for business." Companies can sign up for it on the Web and use it through GE's Web site. Within the first several months, half a dozen companies already had begun using it. GE makes money by charging the buyer for the service and by collecting a fee from the seller if a transaction is completed. GE is also considering other specialized revenue-generating projects. For example, the company is considering developing a system for procurement of nonmedical supplies for hospitals.

3M

For 3M, commerce is an enormous challenge because it produces and sells about 60,000 products. The company is viewed as highly innovative, primarily rising from the fact that it has a perpetual goal that 30 percent of its revenues must come from products introduced within the past four years. This atmosphere of innovation spills over to its information technology staff. Electronic commerce has been a force at 3M since the early 1980s in the form of EDI. Its early goals were eliminating paperwork, reducing labor by automating reports, and speeding up purchase-order processing.

Today the vision has become much broader and more central. EC has come to include electronic catalogues, direct sales, and Web-based customer service. "The objective isn't to introduce electronic commerce; it's to improve the business," says Pete Jacobs, 3M manager of electronic commerce. He adds, "We're expanding from a focus mainly on the transactional side . . . to the electronic marketplace in its broader sense." 3M management sees two key EC approaches that can help to drive 3M growth: encouraging supply chain excellence by streamlining the supply chain, and building customer loyalty by simplifying the buying process.

The technology 3M uses for EC is extremely broad. The company supports any method of electronic commerce its customers prefer, including VAN, Web, direct connection, and fax. If the customer isn't really ready for a new technology, GM does not pressure them to change. If customers want to move into a new technology, 3M will help, relying on its own vast experience and knowledge. But they do not push. Interestingly, the dominant form of technology preferred by its customers is neither the Wcb nor EDI. Instead, it remains the fax. 3M automatically faxes to 3000 customer locations, whereas on-line updates are used by customers at only about 1500 locations. Web-based automatic EDI

accounts, of course, are new. Their use did not begin until 1996.

Thus it is not surprising that at 3M, in contrast to GE, EDI is still very much alive. In 1996 in the United States, 3M was still using EDI with about 1100 suppliers, 800 customers (including distributors), and 200 financial institutions and transportation carriers. In fact, the number of EDI partners is growing, while EDI transactions are increasing at an annual rate of 20 percent. More than 30 percent of customer purchase orders are received via EDI, and 3M sends 65 percent of its purchase orders through EDI. 3M also uses it for sending advance shipping notices. 3M's tracking application, InfoMyWay, enables customers to log in at any time to know where their shipment is and when it will arrive on their (the customer's) dock. EDI is also used for electronic fund transfers and to support vendor-managed inventory.

At 3M, customer response to EDI has been very positive, while the company's flexibility in accommodating other companies' technology preferences has strengthened customer loyalty. For example, the traditional EDI-based InfoMyWay enables them to streamline their own receiving processes by automating the check-in of newly arrived inventory. Another example is in the tightly managed retail market industry. "There are only so many spaces on a grocery shelf, and there's tremendous competition for those spaces," explains Denny Sullivan, the channel logistics manager for grocery and commercial products in 3M's consumer and office markets group. By enabling customers to maintain tight control over shipping, EDI has helped them reduce the amount of inventory they need to maintain. In addition, it contributes to paperwork reduction in their purchasing processes. Thus, customers like working with 3M, and they allocate more shelf space to its products. Suppliers also respond positively to the continued use of EDI because EDI helps in becoming a preferred supplier.

3M has made a major foray into electronic catalogues. Customers find

electronic catalogues quite useful. They aid customers in finding the correct product because the customer can search the catalogue electronically by specifications. Moreover, customers find they obtain correct responses more quickly and more easily than if they were using a paper catalogue. Electronic catalogues also enable one-stop shopping for customers. Many customers buy from more than one 3M business unit, dealing with each independently. Now, using 3M's electronic catalogue, customers are able to purchase all products from one source, making it more convenient and, in turn, more likely that customers will purchase more 3M products. For instance, a hospital must purchase both surgical and cleaning products. Traditionally, these products have been purchased from two very different channels, one (or both) of which might not be 3M. Now it is easy for a hospital to meet both types of needs through only one channel. 3M likes these catalogues for these reasons. In addition they find that electronic catalogues free up some customer-support personnel for other functions.

The company maintains two types of electronic catalogues—its own comprehensive catalogue that customers can access, and customized catalogues provided to individual customers. In the past, the comprehensive catalogue has been available primarily to distributors. However, now the Web is emerging as the key catalogue platform because it is easily available not only to distributors but also to all customers, including consumers. Customized catalogues are used by many customers, including the General Services Administration (GSA) of the United States government. The GSA maintains its own central catalogue of products for the use of employees in all its own departments. The 3M products are part of that catalogue, and 3M maintains its own product and price information in that catalogue electronically (using its EDI technology) so that it is always up to date.

3M is beginning to experiment with individualized customer marketing using personalized catalogues.

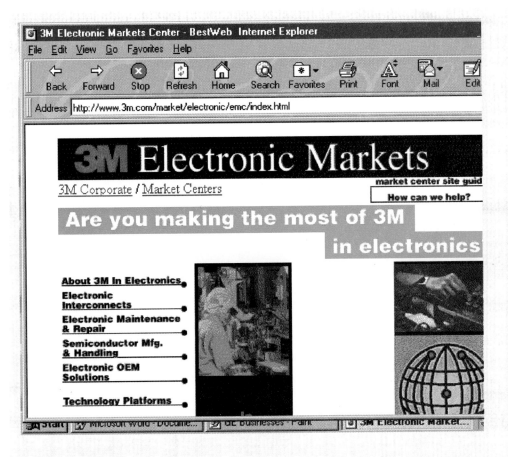

3M uses the Web for its electronic catalogues. The catalogues provide one-step stopping for customers who purchase from more than one 3M business unit.

This style of one-to-one marketing is based on customer data gathered online. For example, 3M might discover that a doctor who buys medical supplies has a sailboat and is interested in buying products for that. Once he logs on to the 3M Web site, instead of making him wade through 15,000 Web pages, 3M would greet him with a page of only those products in which he's interested. This will save customers time while appealing specifically to their individual interests, making it more likely they will purchase from 3M.

The technology for these catalogues is complex. According to Jim Radford, manager of interactive customer communications at 3M, and its Webmaster, the catalogues "are not rich enough, not deep enough, not fat enough." These catalogues will be significantly increasing in size. Building and maintaining the catalogues is also not easy. With 60,000 products to be listed, this work cannot be done by one group. The problem is further complicated by the existence of so many customized catalogues that need to be kept current at a multitude of customer locations. 3M's solution is based on companywide navigation and corporate identity standards. Each market center is responsible for its own product data, stored and kept up to date in databases based on these standards. IT has developed product data repositories that draw from these databases. 3M's EC group in turn uses the repositories to keep all catalogues current.

Electronic catalogues present nontechnical problems as well. Direct selling through electronic catalogues circumvents 3M's very large and profitable distributor network. 3M must find ways to protect that network while continuing to customize catalogues for customers and consumers. Another issue is that direct sales to customers results in smaller purchase orders. As a result, 3M will find itself shipping smaller-sized orders, resulting in higher shipping costs per product. This, in turn, could consume much of the profit. ∎

Sources: Leigh Buchanan, "Procurative Powers," *Webmaster*, May 1997;

"General Electric 1996 Annual Report," http://www.ge.com/annual96/; Derek Slater, "Sticking With Strategy," *CIO*; Mark Halper, "Meet the New Middlemen," *ComputerWorld Emmerce* (http://computerworld.com/ecommerce), May 5, 1997; and Clinton Wilder and Marianne Kolbasuk McGee, "GE: The Net Pays Off," *InformationWeek*, January 27, 1997.

Case Study Questions

1. Compare the business strategies of GE and 3M. What is the role of electronic commerce in their strategies? What accounts for their different approaches?

2. How does each company use information technology to support electronic commerce?

3. What management, organization, and technology problems did GE and 3M face when trying to move into electronic commerce? When moving into EC systems that are based on newer technology?

Building Information Systems: Contemporary Approaches

Anew information system represents an opportunity for organizational problem solving and planned organizational change. Alternative approaches for building systems have been devised to minimize the risks in this process. Ensuring information systems quality and managing the implementation process are essential.

CHAPTER 11

Redesigning the Organization with Information Systems

Chapter 11 is an overview of systems development, showing how building a new information system can redesign and reshape an organization. Plans for new information systems should carefully assess their business value and ensure that they support organizational goals.

CHAPTER 12

Alternative Systems-Building Methods

Chapter 12 describes the major alternative approaches for building information systems: the traditional systems life cycle, prototyping, software packages, end-user development, and outsourcing. Each approach has its own strengths and limitations.

CHAPTER 13

Ensuring Quality with Information Systems

Chapter 13 shows how information systems can contribute to total quality management in the firm. It also describes the principal problems with ensuring information systems quality: software reliability and maintainability. Software quality assurance methods include analysis and design methodologies, metrics, and computer-aided software engineering (CASE).

CHAPTER 14

System Success and Failure: Implementation

Chapter 14 looks at the factors responsible for the success and failure of information systems (including those based on the Internet), which are largely organizational in nature. To better understand these factors, one must examine the entire process of implementation and organizational change.

PART THREE CASE STUDY:

System Modernization at the Social Security Administration: 1982–1997

The story of the Social Security Administration's systems modernization efforts illustrates themes from this section and from the entire text: planning for systems, using systems to redesign organizations, assessing the benefits of information system investments, management of large-scale information systems projects, and organizational obstacles to strategic transitions.

Redesigning the Organization with Information Systems

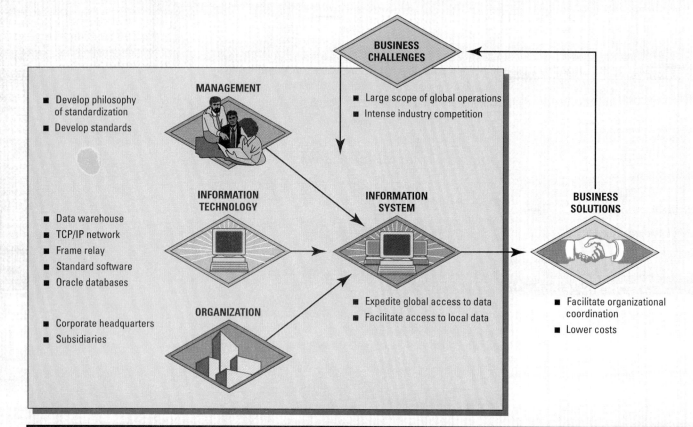

BUSINESS CHALLENGES

MANAGEMENT

- Develop philosophy of standardization
- Develop standards

- Large scope of global operations
- Intense industry competition

INFORMATION TECHNOLOGY

- Data warehouse
- TCP/IP network
- Frame relay
- Standard software
- Oracle databases

INFORMATION SYSTEM

BUSINESS SOLUTIONS

- Expedite global access to data
- Facilitate access to local data

- Facilitate organizational coordination
- Lower costs

ORGANIZATION

- Corporate headquarters
- Subsidiaries

Building the Toshiba Global Infrastructure

With 630 subsidiaries worldwide and over 186,000 employees in nearly 40 countries, Toshiba Corporation has an interest in keeping things simple. Pick up a Toshiba laptop computer anywhere in the world, and you will find nearly all components identical. Toshiba's success in the PC business has been based on its ability to keep costs low by spreading them over a large volume of machines based on standard parts. But keeping things simple is a complex job. To keep track of its sales, products, inventories, and personnel, Toshiba had to build a worldwide global information systems infrastructure.

Following its philosophy of standardization, Toshiba decided to build

LEARNING OBJECTIVES

After completing this chapter, you will be able to:

1. Understand why building new systems is a process of organizational change.
2. Explain how the organization can develop information systems that fit its business plan.
3. Identify the core activities in the systems development process.
4. Describe various models for determining the business value of information systems.

a single global infrastructure rather than adapt information systems to local requirements. The three key objectives of the new architecture were agility, globalization, and productivity. "We believe a global business needs a global IS system. Group companies need a common foundation to share business processes and information with other partners," argues Kyosuke Tsuruta, Toshiba's senior manager of the IS Architecture Group.

Toshiba's information systems department designed a system that will provide a standard architecture to 100 companies, representing Toshiba's key overseas subsidiaries. One main element that will tie to-gether the diverse operating elements of Toshiba is a data warehouse. The warehouse will provide details of the company's entire product line, parts, and prices, as well as sales and planning information to employees worldwide. In addition to this global focus, Toshiba learned from its employees after a lengthy systems analysis effort that they wanted the same system to provide local applications and local data. So the warehouse will act as a central repository for local and regional data, such as local market demand and pricing, for products solely produced and sold by local units.

The infrastructure Toshiba built consists of a global TCP/IP-based network using frame relay. Each worker is equipped with Lotus Notes groupware, Microsoft Office, and a choice of Netscape's Navigator or Microsoft Internet Explorer for a Web browser. Specialized local database needs will be handled by Oracle Corporation's database applications. With this new architecture, Toshiba is creating a single global warehouse that can tell managers precisely the daily demand for memory chips, the opening of a new business venture in Shanghai, or the announcement of a deal in Cairo to help build a new metro line system.

Although these capabilities and objectives appear simple on paper, massive information gathering efforts and analysis of the existing systems were required to understand the requirements of employees and subsidiaries worldwide. The solution was not simply technological, but instead involved an organized information gathering campaign and careful design to ensure the new architecture could meet local needs. Implementation also posed unique problems. For instance, with a single global system how would the instructions for installing and using software be written so that people with different languages and cultures could understand the software? As the world becomes a more integrated global economy, systems analysis and design become global efforts. ■

Source: Rob Guth, "Toshiba Corp.: From Toasters to DRAMs, This Global System Fits All," *Computerworld* Global Innovators Series, March 10, 1997.

MANAGEMENT CHALLENGES

Toshiba's new global infrastructure illustrates the many factors at work in the development of a new information system for global enterprises. Building the new system entailed analyzing Toshiba's problems with existing information systems, assessing its employees' information needs, selecting appropriate technology, and redesigning procedures and jobs on a global scale. Management had to monitor the system-building effort and evaluate its benefits and costs. The new information system represented a process of planned organizational change that took over three years to implement.

But building information systems that operate 24 hours a day without fault and quickly become the central nervous system of the entire business presents many challenges. Here are some challenges to consider:

1. **Understanding major risks and uncertainties in systems development.** Information systems development has major risks and uncertainties that make it difficult for the systems to achieve their goals. Sometimes the cost of achieving them is too high. One problem is the difficulty of establishing information requirements, both for individual end users and for the organization as a whole. The requirements may be too complex or subject to change. In such global systems as Toshiba's, these problems are magnified. Another problem is that the time and cost factors to develop an information system are very difficult to analyze, especially in large projects. Chapters 12 and 14 describe some ways of dealing with these risks and uncertainties, but the issues remain major management challenges.

2. **Determining benefits of a system when they are largely intangible.** As the sophistication of systems grows, they produce fewer tangible and more intangible benefits. By definition, there is no solid method for pricing intangible benefits. Organizations could lose important opportunities if they only use strict financial criteria for determining information systems benefits. On the one hand, organizations could make very poor investment decisions if they overestimate intangible benefits. On the other hand, intangible benefits must someday translate into bottom-line tangible revenues. How long should managers wait for a return?

3. **Managing change.** Although building a new information system is a process of planned organizational change, this does not mean that change can always be planned or controlled. Individuals and groups in organizations have varying interests, and may resist changes in procedures, job relationships, and technologies. Sustaining the commitment of organizational players to systems development is a major problem. Chapter 14, on implementation, describes the problems of change management in greater detail.

T his chapter describes how new information systems are conceived, built, and installed, with special attention to organizational design issues and business reengineering. It describes systems analysis and design and other core activities that must be performed to build any information system. The chapter explains how to establish the business value of information systems and how to ensure that new systems are linked to the organization's business plan and information requirements. The Web poses some interesting problems of cost and benefit calculation that we also address in this chapter.

11.1 SYSTEMS AS PLANNED ORGANIZATIONAL CHANGE

This text has emphasized that an information system is a sociotechnical entity, an arrangement of both technical and social elements. The introduction of a new information system involves much more than new hardware and software. It also includes changes in jobs, skills, management, and organization. In the sociotechnical philosophy, one cannot install new technology without considering the people who must work with it (Bostrom and Heinen, 1977). When we design a new information system, we are redesigning the organization.

One important thing to know about building a new information system is that this process is one kind of planned organizational change. Frequently, new systems mean new ways of doing business and working together. The nature of tasks, the speed with which they must be completed, the nature of supervision (its frequency and intensity), and who has what information about whom will all be decided in the process of building an information system. This is especially true in contemporary systems, which deeply affect many parts of the organization. System builders must understand how a system will affect the organization as a whole, focusing particularly on organizational conflict and changes in the locus of decision making. Builders must also consider how the nature of work groups will change under the impact of the new system. Builders determine how much change is needed.

Systems can be technical successes but organizational failures because of a failure in the social and political process of building the system. Analysts and designers are responsible for ensuring that key members of the organization participate in the design process and are permitted to influence the ultimate shape of the system. Information system builders (see Chapter 14) must carefully orchestrate this activity. As it turns out, managing the systems development process is exceedingly complex and requires very close monitoring by managers to ensure success (or avoid disaster) (Kirsch, 1996).

Linking Information Systems to the Business Plan

Deciding what new systems to build should be an essential component of the organizational planning process. Organizations need to develop an information systems plan that supports their overall business plan (Reich and Benbasat, 1996). Once specific projects have been selected within the overall context of a strategic plan for the business and the systems area, an **information systems plan** can be developed. The plan serves as a road map indicating the direction of systems development, the rationale, the current situation, the management strategy, the implementation plan, and the budget (see Table 11.1).

The plan contains a statement of corporate goals and specifies how information technology supports the attainment of those goals. The report shows how general goals will be achieved by specific systems projects. It lays out specific target dates and milestones that can be used later to judge the progress of the plan in terms of how many objectives were actually attained in the time frame specified in the plan. An important part of the plan is the management strategy for moving from the current situation to the future. Generally, this will indicate the key decisions made by managers

information systems plan A road map indicating the direction of systems development, the rationale, the current situation, the management strategy, the implementation plan, and the budget.

Table 11.1   Information Systems Plan

1. Purpose of the Plan
   - Overview of plan contents
   - Changes in firm's current situation
   - Firm's strategic plan
   - Current business organization
   - Management strategy

2. Strategic Business Plan
   - Current situation
   - Current business organization
   - Changing environments
   - Major goals of the business plan

3. Current Systems
   - Major systems supporting business functions
   - Major current capabilities
     - Hardware
     - Software
     - Database
     - Telecommunications
   - Difficulties meeting business requirements
   - Anticipated future demands

4. New Developments
   - New system projects
     - Project descriptions
     - Business rationale

   New capabilities required
   - Hardware
   - Software
   - Database
   - Telecommunications

5. Management Strategy
   - Acquisition plans
   - Milestones and timing
   - Organizational realignment
   - Internal reorganization
   - Management controls
   - Major training initiatives
   - Personnel strategy

6. Implementation Plan
   - Detailed implementation plan
   - Anticipated difficulties in implementation
   - Progress reports

7. Budget Requirements
   - Requirements
   - Potential savings
   - Financing
   - Acquisition cycle

concerning hardware acquisition; telecommunications; centralization/decentralization of authority, data, and hardware; and required organizational change. Although planning for global information systems is essentially the same as domestic systems, special legal, cultural, and organizational requirements—such as 24-hour availability—must be considered (Tractinsky and Jarvenpaa, 1995).

The implementation plan generally outlines stages in the development of the plan, defining milestones and specifying dates. In this section, organizational changes are usually described, including management and employee training requirements; recruiting efforts; and changes in authority, structure, or management practice.

Establishing Organizational Information Requirements

To develop an effective information systems plan, the organization must have a clear understanding of both its long- and short-term information requirements. Two principal methodologies for establishing the essential information requirements of the organization as a whole are enterprise analysis and critical success factors.

Enterprise Analysis (Business Systems Planning)

enterprise analysis An analysis of organization-wide information requirements by looking at the entire organization in terms of organizational units, functions, processes, and data elements; helps identify the key entities and attributes in the organization's data.

Enterprise analysis (also called *business systems planning*) argues that the information requirements of a firm can only be understood by looking at the entire organization in terms of organizational units, functions, processes, and data elements. Enterprise analysis can help identify the key entities and attributes of the organization's data. This method starts with the notion that the information requirements of a firm or a division can be specified only with a thorough understanding of the entire organization. This method was developed by IBM in the 1960s explicitly for establishing the relationship among large system development projects (Zachman, 1982).

PROCESS/ ORGANIZATION MATRIX

Group	PROCESSES \ ORGANIZATIONS	Commissioner	DC programs and policy	–AC disability insurance	–AC retirement and survivors ins.	–AC supp. security income	–AC governmental affairs	–AC policy	–0 actuary	–0 hearings and appeals	DC management and assessment	–AC assessment	– –0 field assessment	–0 human resources	–0 material resources	–0 financial resources	–0 training	DC systems	–AC system integration	–AC system requirements	–AC system operations	DC operations	–AC field operations	– –Region	– – –District/branch	– – –Teleservice center	–AC Central operations	– –0 Program service center	– – –Process center	– – – –Module	– –D International opers.	– – –Module	– –0 Disability opers.	– – –Module	– –Central records	– – –Module (cert. and coverage)	– – –Data operations centers	Disability determination service
PLANNING	Develop agency plans	M	M	M	M	M		M	M	M	M	S	S	S	S	S	S	M	M	M	M	M	M	S			M	S					S		S			
PLANNING	Administer agency budget	M	M	M	S	S	S	S	M	M	M	M	S	M	M	M	M	M	S	S	S	M	M	S	S		M	M	M		M		M		M		S	M
PLANNING	Formulate program policies	M	M	M	M	M		M		M	M	S	S			S	S	M	S	M	S	M	M	M			M	M	S				M		S			
PLANNING	Formulate admin. policies	M	M								M			M	M	M	M	M				M																
PLANNING	Design work processes		M	M	M	M	S	S		M	M	M	S	S	S		S	M	M	M	M	M	M	M	M	S	M	M	M	M	S	M	M	M	M	M	M	M
GENERAL MANAGEMENT	Manage public affairs	M	M	M	S	M	M	S		S	S	S	S		S		S	S	M	M	M	S	S	M	M	M	S	M	S		M	S	M	S		M	S	M
GENERAL MANAGEMENT	Manage intergovernmental affairs	M	M	M	M	M	M	M		M	M	M	S	M	M	S	S	S	M	M	M	S		M	S	S	S	S	S		M	S	M	S		S		M
GENERAL MANAGEMENT	Exchange data		M	M	M	M	M	M	M	S	M	M	S	M	S	S	S	M	M	M	M	S	M	M	M	S	M	S		M	M	M		M		M		
GENERAL MANAGEMENT	Maintain administrative accounts			M	S	S	S	S	S	S	M				M	M			S		S			M					S		S						S	S
GENERAL MANAGEMENT	Maintain programmatic accounts		M			M					M					M					S						M		M		M		M			S		
GENERAL MANAGEMENT	Conduct audits										M	S	S			S							M	S			M	S	S		S		S		S			
GENERAL MANAGEMENT	Establish organizations		M	M	M	M	M	M	M	M	M	M	M	M	M	M	M	M	M	M	M	M	M	M	M	M	M	M	M	M	M	M	M	M	M	M	M	M
GENERAL MANAGEMENT	Manage human resources		M	M	M	M	M	M	M	M	M	S	M	M	M	M	M	M	M	M	M	M	M	M	M	M	M	M	M	M	M	M	M	M	M	M	M	M
GENERAL MANAGEMENT	Provide security									S	M				M			M	M	M	M	M	S	S	S	S	S	S	S	S	S	S	S	S	S	S	S	S
GENERAL MANAGEMENT	Manage equipment		S				M			M	M	S	S		M		M	M	M		M	S	M	M	M	M	M	M	S	S	S	S	M	S	M	S	M	
GENERAL MANAGEMENT	Manage facilities			S						S	M	S	S		M		M	M	S		M	S	M	M	M	M	M	M	M		S		M		M		M	
GENERAL MANAGEMENT	Manage supplies		S	S	S	S	S	S	S	M	M	S	S		M		M	M	S		M	S	M	S	M	M	M	M	S	S	S	M	M	S	M	S	M	
GENERAL MANAGEMENT	Manage data		M	M	M	M		M										M	M	M	M	S	S	S	S	S	S	S	S	S	S	S	S	S	S	S	S	S
GENERAL MANAGEMENT	Manage workloads	M	M	M	M	M	M	M	M	M	M	M	M	M	M	M	M	M	M	M	M	M	M	M	M	M	M	M	M	M	M	M	M	M	M	M	M	M
PROGRAM ADMIN.	Issue social security numbers											S			S						S				M	M						M					S	
PROGRAM ADMIN.	Maintain earnings		S								S				S						S				M	M				S		S		S	M	M	M	
PROGRAM ADMIN.	Collect claims information																				S				M	M				M		M		M	M	S		
PROGRAM ADMIN.	Determine eligibility/entitlement		M	M	M	M		S		M		M	M								S				M	S			M	M		M	M	M	M	M	S	M
PROGRAM ADMIN.	Compute payments																				S				M	S	M			M		M		M	M			
PROGRAM ADMIN.	Administer debt management		S					S			M					M					S	M		M	M	S	M	M	M	M	M	M	M	M				
SUPPORT	Generate notices																				S				M	M				M		M		M		M		
SUPPORT	Respond to programmatic inquiries		M	M	M	M	M	M	M	M	M	M	S								S	M	S	M	M	M	S	M	S	M	M	M	M	M	M	M	S	M
SUPPORT	Provide quality assessment	M									M	M	M																									

KEY

M = major involvement
S = some involvement

DC = deputy commissioner
AC = associate commissioner
0 = office

FIGURE 11.1A

Process/organization matrix. This chart indicates who in the organization participates in specific processes and the nature of their involvement.

The central method used in the enterprise analysis approach is to take a large sample of managers and ask them how they use information, where they get the information, what their environment is like, what their objectives are, how they make decisions, and what their data needs are.

The results of this large survey of managers are aggregated into subunits, functions, processes, and data matrices (see Figure 11.1). Figure 11.1 shows parts of two matrices developed at the Social Security Administration as part of a very-large-scale systems redevelopment effort called the Systems Modernization Plan, which began in 1982.

Figure 11.1A shows a process/organization matrix identifying those persons in the organization who participate in specific processes, such as planning. Figure 11.1B

	LOGICAL APPLICATION GROUPS / PROCESSES \ DATA CLASSES	Actuarial estimates	Agency plans	Budget	Program regs./policy	Admin. regs./policy	Labor agreements	Data standards	Procedures	Automated systems documentation	Educational media	Public agreements	Intergovernmental agreements	Grants	External	Exchange control	Administrative accounts	Program expenditures	Audit reports	Organization/position	Employee identification	Recruitment/placement	Complaints/grievances	Training resources	Security	Equipment utilization	Space utilization	Supplies utilization	Workload schedules	Work measurement	Enumeration I.D.	Enumeration control	Earnings	Employer I.D.	Earnings control	Claims characteristics	Claims control	Decisions	Payment	Collection/waiver	Notice	Inquiries control	Quality appraisal
PLANNING	Develop agency plans	C	C	C	U	U									U																												
PLANNING	Administer agency budget	C	C	C	U	U						U	U	U		U	U	U		U	U					U	U	U		U		U			U		U			U		U	U
PLANNING	Formulate program policies	U	U		C				U						U				U				U															U					U
PLANNING	Formulate admin. policies		U		U	C	C		U						U				U	U			U																				
PLANNING	Formulate data policies		U	U		U		C	U	U															U	U	U	U															
PLANNING	Design work processes		U		U	U			C	C		U	U						U																			U					U
GENERAL MANAGEMENT	Manage public affairs		U		U	U			U		C	C	C																														
GENERAL MANAGEMENT	Manage intrgovt. affairs	U	U		U	U			U		U		C	C	C															U	U		U	U		U			U				
GENERAL MANAGEMENT	Exchange data				U				U			U	U	U	U	C	U	U												U													
GENERAL MANAGEMENT	Maintain admin. accounts			U		U			U			U	U				C				U					U	U	U								U			U				
GENERAL MANAGEMENT	Maintain prog. accounts			U	U				U			U	U					C														U			U		U	U	U	U		U	
GENERAL MANAGEMENT	Conduct audits				U	U			U	U							U	U	C		U								U														
GENERAL MANAGEMENT	Establish organizations			U		U			U											C	U								U	U													U
GENERAL MANAGEMENT	Manage human resources			U		U	U		U											C	C	C	C	C																			
GENERAL MANAGEMENT	Provide security				U	U		U	U	U															C	C	C	C		U													
GENERAL MANAGEMENT	Manage equipment			U		U		U	U	U															C	C	C	C															
GENERAL MANAGEMENT	Manage facilities			U		U			U																U	U	C																
GENERAL MANAGEMENT	Manage supplies			U		U			U																C	U	U	C															
GENERAL MANAGEMENT	Manage workloads	U		U	U	U			U							U										U	U	U	C	C		U			U		U					U	U
PROGRAM ADMIN.	Issue social security nos.								U				U		U																C	C											
PROGRAM ADMIN.	Maintain earnings								U				U	U	U																U		C	C	C	U							
PROGRAM ADMIN.	Collect claims information				U	U			U						U																U	U				C	C	U	U	U			
PROGRAM ADMIN.	Determine elig/entlmt.								U																						U	U	U			U		C	U	U			
PROGRAM ADMIN.	Compute payments				U				U									U													U		U			U		U	C	C			
PROGRAM ADMIN.	Administer debt mgmt.				U				U									U																					U	C			
SUPPORT	Generate notices								U						U																U		U			U		U	U	U	C		
SUPPORT	Respond to prog. inquiries				U				U		U																				U		U	U		U		U	U	U	U	C	
SUPPORT	Provide quality assessment				U	U			U	U																					U		U			U		U			U		C

KEY
C = creators of data U = users of data

FIGURE 11.1B

Process/data class matrix. This chart depicts what data classes are required to support particular organizational processes and which processes are the creators and users of data.

shows a process/data class matrix depicting what information is required to support a particular process, which process creates the data, and which uses it. (*C* in an intersection stands for "creators of data"; *U* stands for "users of data.")

The shaded boxes in Figure 11.1B indicate a *logical application group*—a group of data elements that supports a related set of organizational processes. In this case, actuarial estimates, agency plans, and budget data are created in the planning process. The planning process, in turn, is performed by the commissioner's office, along with deputy commissioners and associate commissioners. This suggests then that an information system focused on actuarial, agency plan, and budget data elements should be built for the commissioners to support planning.

One strength of enterprise analysis is that it gives a comprehensive view of the organization and of systems/data uses and gaps. Enterprise analysis is especially suitable for start-up or massive change situations. For instance, it is one method used by

Table 11.2 Critical Success Factors and Organizational Goals

Example	Goals	CSF

Profit concern	Earnings/share
	Return on investment
	Market share
	New product
		Automotive industry
		  Styling
		  Quality dealer system
		  Cost control
		  Energy standards

Nonprofit	Excellent health care Meeting government regulations Future health needs	Regional integration with other hospitals Efficient use of resources Improved monitoring of regulations

Source: Rockart (1979).

the Social Security Administration to bring about a long-term strategic change in its information processing activities. This organization had never before performed a comprehensive analysis of its information requirements. Instead, it had relied on a bottom-up method of responding to whatever users requested, as well as on by-product approaches in which most emphasis was placed on simply performing elementary transaction processing. Enterprise analysis was used to develop a comprehensive view of how the Social Security Administration has used information.

The weakness of enterprise analysis is that it produces an enormous amount of data that are expensive to collect and difficult to analyze. It is a very expensive technique with a bias toward top management and data processing. Most of the interviews are conducted with senior or middle managers, with little effort to collect information from clerical workers and supervisory managers. Moreover, the questions frequently focus not on the critical objectives of management and where information is needed, but rather on what existing information is used. The result is a tendency to automate whatever exists. In this manner, manual systems are automated. But in many instances, entirely new approaches to how business is conducted are needed, and these needs are not addressed.

Strategic Analysis: Critical Success Factors

The strategic analysis or critical success factor approach argues that the information requirements of an organization are determined by a small number of **critical success factors (CSFs)** of managers. CSFs are operational goals. If these goals can be attained, the success of the firm or organization is ensured (Rockart, 1979; Rockart and Treacy, 1982).

The industry, the firm, the manager, and the broader environment shape CSFs. This broader focus, in comparison with that of previous methods, accounts for the description of this technique as strategic. An important premise of the strategic analysis approach is that there are a small number of objectives that managers can easily identify and on which information systems can focus.

The principal method used in CSF analysis is personal interviews—three or four—with a number of top managers to identify their goals and the resulting CSFs. These personal CSFs are aggregated to develop a picture of the firm's CSFs. Then systems are built to deliver information on these CSFs. (See Table 11.2 for examples of CSFs. For the method of developing CSFs in an organization, see Figure 11.2.)

The strength of the CSF method is that it produces a smaller data set to analyze than enterprise analysis. Only top managers are interviewed, and the questions focus on a small number of CSFs rather than a broad inquiry into what information is used or needed. This method can be tailored to the structure of each industry, with different competitive strategies producing different information systems. The

critical success factors (CSFs)
A small number of easily identifiable operational goals shaped by the industry, the firm, the manager, and the broader environment that are believed to ensure the success of an organization. Used to determine the information requirements of an organization.

CSF method also depends on the industry position and even the geographical location. Therefore, this method produces systems that are more custom tailored to an organization.

A unique strength of the CSF method is that it takes into account the changing environment with which organizations and managers must deal. This method explicitly asks managers to look at the environment and consider how their analysis of it shapes their information needs. It is especially suitable for top management and for the development of DSS and ESS. Last, the method produces a consensus among top managers about what is important to measure in order to gauge the organization's success. Like enterprise analysis, the CSF method focuses organizational attention on how information should be handled.

The weakness of this method is that the aggregation process and the analysis of the data are art forms. There is no particularly rigorous way in which individual CSFs can be aggregated into a clear company pattern. Second, there is often confusion among interviewees (and interviewers) between individual and organizational CSFs. They are not necessarily the same. What can be critical to a manager may not be important for the organization. Moreover, this method is clearly biased toward top managers because they are the ones (generally the only ones) interviewed. Indeed, the method seems to apply only to management reporting systems, DSS, and ESS. It assumes that successful TPSs already exist. Last, it should be noted that this method does not necessarily overcome the impact of a changing environment or changes in managers. Environments and managers change rapidly, and information systems must adjust accordingly. The use of CSFs to develop a system does not mitigate these factors.

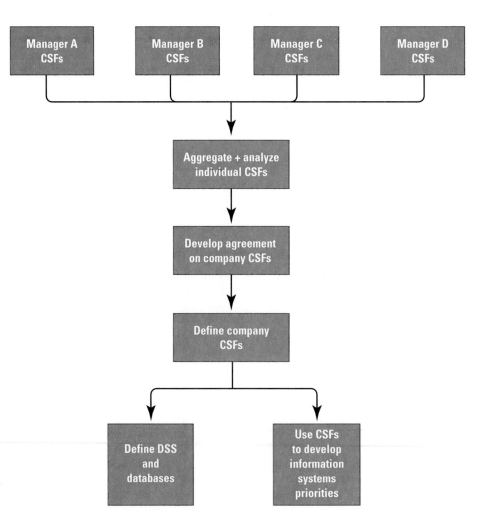

New information systems can be powerful instruments for organizational change, enabling organizations to redesign their structure, scope, power relationships, work flows, products, and services. Table 11.3 describes some of the ways that information technology is being used to transform organizations.

The Spectrum of Organizational Change

Information technology can promote various degrees of organizational change. Figure 11.3 shows the four kinds of structural organizational change which are enabled by information technology: automation, rationalization, reengineering, and paradigm shifts. Each carries different rewards and risks.

The most common form of IT-enabled organizational change is **automation.** The first applications of information technology involved assisting employees perform their tasks more efficiently and effectively. Calculating paychecks and payroll registers, giving bank tellers instant access to customer deposit records, and developing a nationwide network of airline reservation terminals for airline reservation agents are all examples of early automation. Automation is akin to putting a larger motor in an existing automobile.

A deeper form of organizational change—one that follows quickly from early automation—is **rationalization of procedures.** Automation frequently reveals new bottlenecks in production, and makes the existing arrangement of procedures and structures painfully cumbersome. Rationalization of procedures is the streamlining of standard operating procedures, eliminating obvious bottlenecks so that automation can make operating procedures more efficient. For example, Toshiba's new global infrastructure is effective not only because it utilizes state-of-the-art computer

automation Using the computer to speed up the performance of existing tasks.

rationalization of procedures The streamlining of standard operating procedures, eliminating obvious bottlenecks so that automation makes operating procedures more efficient.

Table 11.3 How Information Technology Can Transform Organizations	
Information Technology	**Organizational Change**
Global networks	International division of labor: the operations of a firm are no longer determined by location; the global reach of firms is extended; costs of global coordination decline. Transaction costs decline.
Enterprise networks	Collaborative work and teamwork: the organization of work can now be coordinated across divisional boundaries; a customer and product orientation emerges; widely dispersed task forces become the dominant work group. The costs of management (agency costs) decline. Business processes are changed.
Distributed computing	Empowerment: individuals and work groups now have the information and knowledge to act. Business processes are redesigned, streamlined. Management costs decline. Hierarchy and centralization decline.
Portable computing	Virtual organizations: work is no longer tied to geographic location. Knowledge and information can be delivered anywhere they are needed, anytime. Work becomes portable. Organizational costs decline as real estate is less essential for business.
Graphical user interfaces	Accessibility: everyone in the organization—even senior executives—can access information and knowledge; work flows can be automated, contributed to by all from remote locations. Organizational costs decline as work flows move from paper to digital image, documents, and voice.

FIGURE 11.3

Organizational change carries risks and rewards. The most common forms of organizational change are automation and rationalization. These relatively slow-moving and slow-changing strategies present modest returns but little risk. Faster and more comprehensive change—such as reengineering and paradigm shifts—carry high rewards but offer a substantial chance of failure.

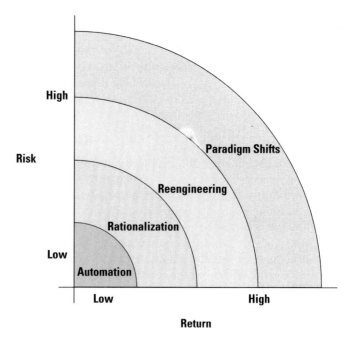

technology but also because its design allows Toshiba operating units, no matter where they are located, to operate more efficiently. To achieve this result, Toshiba had to first rationalize its business procedures down to the level of installation manuals and software instruction before it could reap the benefits of the technology. The company had to create standard names and formats for the data items in its global data warehouse. The procedures of Toshiba or of any organization must be rationally structured to achieve this result. Without a large amount of business process rationalization at Toshiba, its computer technology would have been useless.

A more powerful type of organizational change is **business reengineering,** in which business processes are analyzed, simplified, and redesigned. Reengineering involves radically rethinking the flow of work and the business processes used to produce products and services with a mind to radically reduce the costs of business. Table 11.4 describes various ways that information technology can impact business processes. Using information technology, organizations can rethink and streamline their business processes to improve speed, service, and quality. Business reengineering reorganizes work flows, combining steps to cut waste and eliminating repetitive, paper-intensive tasks (sometimes the new design eliminates jobs as well). It is much more ambitious than rationalization of procedures, requiring a new vision of how the process is to be organized.

A widely cited example of business reengineering is Ford Motor Company's invoiceless processing. Ford, with over five hundred people in its North American accounts payable organization alone, discovered that the Mazda Motor Corporation's accounts payable organization employed only five people. When Ford management analyzed the company's existing system, it discovered that the accounts payable clerks spent most of their time matching purchase orders against receiving documents and invoices and then issuing payments. Mismatches where the purchase order, receiving document, or invoice disagreed were common, forcing the accounts payable clerks to investigate the discrepancies and delay payments. Ford found that reengineering its entire accounts payable process could prevent mismatches in the first place. The company instituted invoiceless processing in which the purchasing department enters a purchase order into an on-line database that can be checked by the receiving department when the ordered items arrive. If the received goods match the purchase order, the system automatically generates a check for accounts payable to send to the vendor. There is no need for vendors to send invoices. After reengineer-

business reengineering The radical redesign of business processes, combining steps to cut waste and eliminating repetitive, paper-intensive tasks to improve cost, quality, and service and to maximize the benefits of information technology.

Table 11.4	IT Capabilities and Their Organizational Impacts
Capability	Organizational Impact/Benefit
Transactional	IT can transform unstructured processes into routinized transactions
Geographical	IT can transfer information with rapidity and ease across large distances, making processes independent of geography
Automational	IT can replace or reduce human labor in a process
Analytical	IT can bring complex analytical methods to bear on a process
Informational	IT can bring vast amounts of detailed information into a process
Sequential	IT can enable changes in the sequence of tasks in a process, often allowing multiple tasks to be worked on simultaneously
Knowledge Management	IT allows the capture and dissemination of knowledge and expertise to improve the process
Tracking	IT allows the detailed tracking of task status, inputs, and outputs
Disintermediation	IT can be used to connect two parties within a process that would otherwise communicate through an intermediary (internal or external)

Source: Reprinted from "The New Industrial Engineering: Information Technology and Business Process Redesign," Thomas H. Davenport and James E. Short by *Sloan Management Review* 11, Vol. 31, No. 4, Summer 1990. Copyright © 1990 by Sloan Management Review Association. All rights reserved.

ing the accounts payable process, Ford was able to reduce headcount by 75 percent and produce more accurate financial information (Hammer and Champy, 1993).

Rationalizing procedures and redesigning business processes are limited to specific parts of a business. New information systems can ultimately affect the design of the entire organization by actually transforming how the organization carries out its business or even the nature of the business itself. For instance, Schneider National, described in Chapter 10, used new information systems to create a competitive on-demand shipping service and to develop a new sideline business managing the logistics of other companies. Baxter International's stockless inventory system, described in Chapter 2, transformed Baxter into a working partner with hospitals and into a manager of its customers' supplies. The new system redrew organizational boundaries, allowing Baxter to take over its customers' warehousing functions.

This still more radical form of business change is called a **paradigm shift**. A paradigm shift involves rethinking the nature of the business and the nature of the organization itself. Banks, for instance, may decide not to automate, rationalize, or reengineer the jobs of tellers. Instead they may decide to eliminate branch banking altogether and seek less expensive sources of funds, such as international borrowing. Retail customers may be forced to use the Internet to conduct all their business, or a proprietary network. A paradigm shift is akin to rethinking not only the automobile, but transportation itself.

How much change is good? Should change be incremental or global? There is some reason to believe that reengineering produces the largest value when it is part of a global change program affecting organizational structure, decision authority, business process, and incentive systems (Barua, Lee, and Whinston, 1996). Nothing is free and simply creating radical change in some parts of the business is not the key to overall business success. Reengineering projects may not choose the right business process to improve, simply the most obvious targets. Deciding which business process to get right is half the challenge (Keen, 1997). Paradigm shifts and reengineering often fail because extensive organizational change is so difficult to orchestrate and manage (see Chapter 14). Some experts believe that 70 percent of the time programmatic reengineering efforts fail. Why then do so many corporations

paradigm shift Radical reconceptualization of the nature of the business and the nature of the organization.

Redesigning with the Internet

Many businesses are using the Internet to redesign their work flows, products, and services. Here are a few examples:

New York–based J.P. Morgan & Company, one of the most prestigious banks in the world, turned to the Internet because its IT vendors took too long providing technical help. David Spector, vice president of corporate technology, decided the quickest way to report problems to vendors and get back software modifications was through the Net. Spector claims that problems that once took days to fix are now remedied in hours or minutes. Word of the Net quickly spread, and now Morgan employees worldwide use it to gather information such as corporate financial or government census data. Later Morgan decided to become a Web information provider. It established a service, known as RiskMetrics, that provides daily risk measurement data on more than 300 financial instruments, including complex financial derivatives, government bonds, and mortgage refinance and mortgage purchase indices. Morgan claims that thousands of investors access its site each day. "The goal is to establish ourselves as a leader in providing information," says Spector. "Being positioned as experts is good for our business."

Trane Company, the LaCrosse, Wisconsin, heating and air-conditioning manufacturer, reengineered its business to reduce the time to manufacture a custom-designed commercial air-conditioning system from thirty-six days to six days. The company wanted "dramatic improvements in customer service and double revenues." Nonetheless, its paperwork still took 46 days using its mainframe-based network. To shrink its office cycles, the com-pany installed desktop computers at its 120 locations—sales offices, warehouses, corporate offices—connecting them via the Net. In addition, sales staff was issued laptops. Trane staff, vendors, collaborators, and customers now exchange sales bids and all other documents instantly. Using the Net, rather than installing their own wide area network, cut setup costs by at least 25 percent.

RoweCom facilitates library and research institute purchases of journal subscriptions. Richard Rowe was paying $2 million annually for leased lines. Now he uses the Net, saving his clients 7 to 9 percent on purchases. Through software developed by RoweCom, customers enter journal orders directly on the Internet. (Traditional subscription agencies act as intermediaries for these transactions.) The orders are then transmitted via the Internet to BancOne. The bank in turn collects the funds, forwards the subscription to the publisher, and pays the customer. Setup costs were also much lower because they used the Net. Development and complete testing by RoweCom and BancOne took only a few months, rather than several years as is common for such an operation.

To Think About: *How are these companies using the Internet for organizational design? What types of organizational change are taking place?*

Sources: L. Buchonon, "A Subscription for Change," *Webmaster*, January/February, 1996; and Clinton Wilder, "The Internet Pioneers," *InformationWeek*, January 9, 1995.

entertain such radical change? Because the rewards are equally high (see Figure 11.3). In many instances firms seeking paradigm shifts and pursuing reengineering strategies achieve stunning, order-of-magnitude increases in their returns on investment (or productivity). Some of these success stories and some failure stories are included throughout this book and in the Window on Organizations.

Redesigning Business Processes

Many companies today are focusing on building new information systems in which they can redesign business processes. To a large extent, business process redesign today has become the generic label for all sorts of change programs from simple automation to rationalization, reengineering, and paradigm shift. The idea is to choose an "important" business process—one that consumes a considerable amount of organizational time and costs—and then greatly improve the process through judicious application of information technology.

The home mortgage industry is a leading example in the United States of how major corporations have applied business process redesign. The cost of obtaining a mortgage is one of the leading factors that has led to a decline in home ownership in the United States from 66 percent to 64 percent of households in 1997. The application process for a mortgage is about six to eight weeks currently, and costs about $3000. The goal of many mortgage banks is to lower that cost to $1000 and the time to obtain a mortgage to about one week. Led by fast-growing mortgage banks such as BancOne Corporation, BancBoston, and Countrywide Funding Corporation, other banks are radically simplifying the mortgage application process.

Figure 11.4 illustrates how the mortgage application process is being redesigned by leading banks. The mortgage application process is divided into three stages: origination, servicing, and secondary marketing. Business process redesign is being used at each of these stages.

In the past, a mortgage applicant filled out a paper loan application. The bank entered the application transaction into its computer system. Specialists such as credit analysts and underwriters from eight different departments accessed and evaluated the application individually. If the loan application was approved, the closing was scheduled. After the closing, bank specialists dealing with insurance or funds in escrow serviced the loan. This desk-to-desk assembly-line approach might take up to 17 days.

Leading banks have replaced the sequential desk-to-desk approach with a speedier work-cell or team approach. Now, loan originators in the field enter the mortgage application directly into laptop computers. Software checks the application transaction to make sure the information is correct and complete. The loan originators transmit the loan applications using a dial-up network to regional production centers. Instead of working on the application individually, the credit analysts, loan underwriters, and other specialists convene electronically, working as a team to approve the mortgage. Some banks provide customers with a nearly instant credit lock-in of a guaranteed mortgage so they can find a house that meets their budget immediately. Such preapproval of a credit line is truly a radical reengineering of the traditional business process.

Reengineered mortgage processing at Banc One. Mortgage loan applications entered via laptop computers can now be evaluated by many people simultaneously, expediting the mortgage application process.

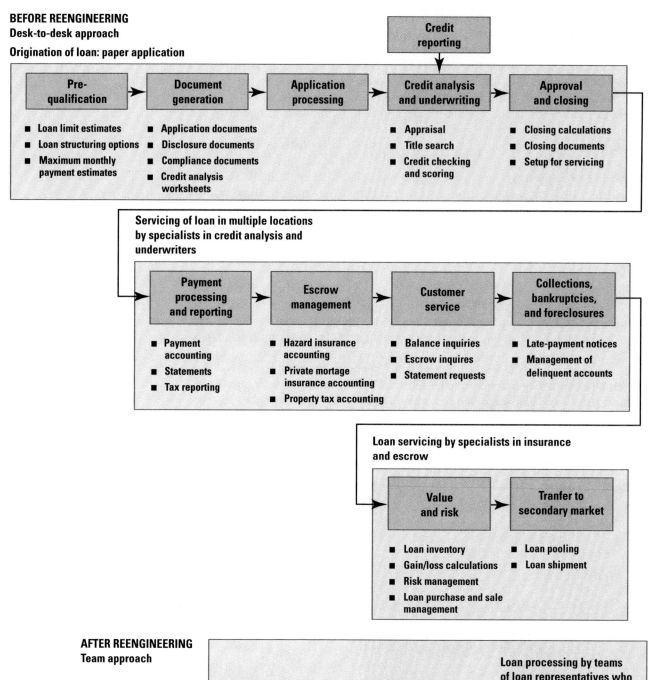

BEFORE REENGINEERING
Desk-to-desk approach

Origination of loan: paper application

Credit reporting

Pre-qualification	Document generation	Application processing	Credit analysis and underwriting	Approval and closing

- Loan limit estimates
- Loan structuring options
- Maximum monthly payment estimates

- Application documents
- Disclosure documents
- Compliance documents
- Credit analysis worksheets

- Appraisal
- Title search
- Credit checking and scoring

- Closing calculations
- Closing documents
- Setup for servicing

Servicing of loan in multiple locations by specialists in credit analysis and underwriters

Payment processing and reporting	Escrow management	Customer service	Collections, bankruptcies, and foreclosures

- Payment accounting
- Statements
- Tax reporting

- Hazard insurance accounting
- Private mortage insurance accounting
- Property tax accounting

- Balance inquiries
- Escrow inquires
- Statement requests

- Late-payment notices
- Management of delinquent accounts

Loan servicing by specialists in insurance and escrow

Value and risk	Tranfer to secondary market

- Loan inventory
- Gain/loss calculations
- Risk management
- Loan purchase and sale management

- Loan pooling
- Loan shipment

AFTER REENGINEERING
Team approach

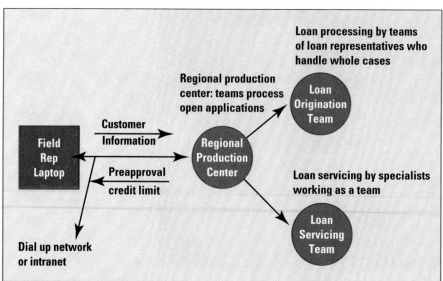

Loan processing by teams of loan representatives who handle whole cases

Regional production center: teams process open applications

Field Rep Laptop

Customer Information →

Preapproval credit limit

Regional Production Center

Loan Origination Team

Loan servicing by specialists working as a team

Loan Servicing Team

Dial up network or intranet

FIGURE 11.4

Redesigning mortgage processing in the United States. By redesigning their mortgage processing system and the mortgage application process, mortgage banks will be able to reduce the costs of processing the average mortgage from $3000 to $1000, and reduce the time of approval from six weeks to one week or less. Some banks are even pre-approving mortgages and locking interest rates on the same day as the customer applies.
Source: The Tower Group, Wellesley, MA.

Workflow Software: Conquering the Paper Mountain

Who was the last person to sign a document? Who authored the document? Where is it now? Why was this document sent to the wrong sales group? The idea of work group software is to strengthen management control over the flow of information in an electronic environment. In an organization with 10,000 to 80,000 employees, similar to many international banks or many governments, these are important questions which have to be answered every day by laboriously checking on the status of paper. The advent of corporate-wide, global, groupwork systems such as Lotus Notes has opened up the frightening possibility that millions of documents can spin through networks in completely unauthorized ways.

Workflow software automates and keeps track of documents, information, and tasks which are passed from one person to another in a way that is governed by rules or procedures. This software also establishes the officially approved routing of information in an organization, establishes rules for who can see what information, and the order information passes through corporate control points. CSE Systems of Austria is one of the world's premier providers of workflow software. Recently, they were awarded the job of automating the work flow in paper documents, tasks, and other objects such as plans and photos for Deutsche Telekom, the German telecommunications utility. CSE will provide total document control for over 90,000 employees at Deutsche Telekom.

Many companies are beginning to realize that they cannot simply eliminate paper documents entirely because of legal, cultural, or other reasons. For instance, utility companies still must send out physical invoices to customers or obtain signed documents from contractors. One alternative to eliminating paper is to automate its processing and tracking.

For instance, Con Edison, the $5 billion utility company, was looking for a way to cut costs, boost efficiency, and improve service to its 3 million gas and electricity customers in New York City and lower Westchester County. Its 1300 customer-service representatives were handling 1 million pieces of paper in 20 different offices. When a document was lodged on someone's desktop, no one knew what was happening. The company decided to reconfigure its work processes using workflow software.

Workflow software is often used in conjunction with imaging and document management software, which converts reports, blueprints, file folders, and other paper-based documents into electronic form for storage and access on the computer (see Chapter 15). Both are key tools for streamlining and reengineer-

ing paper-based business processes because they speed the flow of tasks, facilitate document sharing, and reduce paper documents and paperwork decisions.

Con Edison installed Omni-Desk workflow software from Sigma Imaging Systems Inc. of New York. The software runs in a client/server environment. Con Edison's customer service area is using this software on 1350 PCs running the OS/2 operating system and 85 Compaq superservers connected to each other in a local area network and linked to a database manager over high-capacity telephone lines. In addition to providing better customer service, Con Edison expects the workflow software to reduce expenses by consolidating jobs. The company expects to save between $2 and 3 million by eliminating up to 150 clerical positions.

The San Francisco office of Young & Rubicam Inc. turned to workflow software to provide better service to Chevron Corporation, its largest advertising client. The office had used a nine-step, paper-based, order-tracking and routing system when dealing with Chevron. Managers, when examining what the office actually did, uncovered redundancies, missing steps, and holes in the process. For example, they found that some account coordinators were omitting vital information on forms.

Y & R implemented an application based on Workflow Management System from Action Technologies, Inc. in Alameda, California. Twelve Y&R account coordinators use PCs linked via a LAN to an OS/2-compatible file server. With this system, electronic forms cannot be passed onto the next stage until all the fields have been filled out. When the system was first introduced as a pilot project, overtime was slashed in half, rework of incorrect papers was down 64 percent, and the office improved its on-time record for delivering information to Chevron by 63 percent.

To Think About: How did workflow management software change the business processes of Con Edison and Young & Rubicam? What management, organization and technology issues should be addressed when using workflow and document management software?

Sources: CSE Systems, "Workflow Fulfills its Promise," December 1996; and Paula Klein, "Go with the Flow," and Anne Fischer Lent, "Documenting Change," *InformationWeek,* March 28, 1994.

After closing, another team of specialists sets up the loan for servicing. The entire loan application process can take as little as two days. Loan information is also easier to access than before, when the loan application could be in eight or nine different departments. Loan originators can also dial into the bank's network to obtain information on mortgage loan costs or to check the status of a loan for the customer.

The secondary marketing of mortgages to other institutions such as Fannie Mae and Freddie Mac (two corporations originated by the federal government to securitize mortgages and develop a secondary market) is also being radically changed. Both Fannie Mae and Freddie Mac have developed expert systems to automate the credit authorization process, and reduce processing time from twenty to thirty days down to two days to obtain approval.

By redesigning their entire approach to mortgage processing, mortgage banks have achieved remarkable efficiencies. They have not focused on redesigning simply a single business process but instead they have reexamined the entire set of logically connected processes required to obtain a mortgage. Instead of automating the previous method of mortgage processing, they have completely rethought the entire mortgage application process. To streamline the paperwork in the mortgage application process, many banks have turned to workflow and document management software, described in the Window on Technology.

Steps in Business Reengineering

Business reengineering entails developing a business process model of how activities function, analyzing relationships among business units, and implementing changes that would eliminate redundant processes and make business units more effective. Reengineering experts have outlined five major steps for reengineering business processes (Davenport and Short, 1990):

1. *Develop the business vision and process objectives.* Senior management needs to develop a broad strategic vision, which calls for redesigned business processes. For example, Proctor & Gamble's management looked for breakthroughs to lower costs and accelerate service that would enable the firm to regain its competitive stature in the consumer products industry (see Chapters 2 and 3).

2. *Identify the processes to be redesigned.* Companies should identify a few core business processes to be redesigned, focusing on those with the greatest potential payback. Symptoms of inefficient processes include excessive data redundancy and reentering information, too much time spent handling exceptions and special cases, or too much time spent on corrections and rework. The analysis should identify what organizational group owns the process, what organizational functions or departments are involved in the process, and what changes are required. The methods for identifying organizational information requirements described earlier in this chapter may be useful here.

3. *Understand and measure the performance of existing processes.* If, for example, the objective of process redesign is to reduce time and cost in developing a new product or filling an order, the organization needs to measure the time and cost consumed by the unchanged process. Table 11.5 provides examples of metrics that have been used for the reengineering analysis.

4. *Identify the opportunities for applying information technology.* The conventional method of designing systems establishes the information requirements of a business function or process and then determines how they can be supported by information technology. However, information technology can create new design options for various processes because it can be used to challenge longstanding assumptions about work arrangements that used to inhibit organizations. Table 11.6 provides examples of innovations that have overturned these assumptions using companies discussed in the text. Information technology should be allowed to influence process design from the start.

5. *Build a prototype of the new process.* The organization should design the new process on an experimental basis (see Chapter 12), anticipating a series of revisions and improvements until the redesigned process wins approval. For instance, Mutual Benefit Life implemented a pilot project to redesign its individual life

Table 11.5   Achieving Operating Excellence: Selected Examples

Example	Activity	Base	Reengineered	Reference Definitions
Productivity indices				
Staffing efficiency: PLAINS COTTON COOPERATIVE ASSN. (TELCOT)	Transaction processing	9	450	Base = industry average, thousands of units processed per worker per year, 1991
Staffing levels: PHILLIPS PETROLEUM COMPANY	Corporate staff	36	12	Corporate staff per 100 employees, 1986–1989
Transaction costs: C. R. ENGLAND & SONS, INC.	Invoicing	$5.10	$.15	Cost of sending invoice, 1989–1991
Asset turnover: TOYOTA MOTOR CORP.	Work in process	16	215	Asset turnover, industry average annual turnover, 1990
Velocity PROGRESSIVE INSURANCE	Claims settlement	31 days	4 hours	Base = industry vs. Progressive's Immediate Response service, 1991
Quality FLORIDA POWER & LIGHT CO.	Power delivery	7 hours	32 min.	Base = competitor, power outage per customer per year, 1992
Business precision FARM JOURNAL, INC.	Product variety	1	1200 +	Number of unique editions per issue, 1985–1990
Customer service L. L. BEAN, INC.	Order fulfillment	61%	93%	Base = industry average, percent of orders filled in 24 hours

Source: Reprinted with permission from *IBM Systems Journal*, Vol. 32, No. 1. Copyright 1993 International Business Machines Corporation.

Table 11.6   New Process Design Options with Information Technology

Assumption	Technology	Option	Examples
Field personnel need offices to receive, store, and transmit information	Wireless communications	Personnel can send and receive information wherever they are	Cisco Systems Ernst & Young
Information can appear in only one place at one time	Shared databases	People can collaborate on the same project from scattered locations; information can be used simultaneously wherever it is needed	Hong Kong Airport BancOne Roche Bioscience
People are needed to ascertain where things are located	Automatic identification and tracking technology	Things can tell people where they are	United Parcel Service Schneider National
Businesses need reserve inventory to prevent stockouts	Telecommunications networks and EDI	Just-in-time delivery and stockless supply	Wal-Mart Baxter International

insurance underwriting process. The process involved 40 steps with over 100 people in 12 functional areas. Hoping to raise productivity by 40 percent, MBL centralized all underwriting tasks under a case manager using a workstation application that could draw together data from all over the company. After a brief start-up period, the firm realized that it needed to add specialists such as lawyers or physicians on some underwriting cases ("The Role of IT," 1993).

Following these steps does not automatically guarantee that reengineering will always be successful. The term *reengineering* itself is somewhat misleading, suggesting that there are some recognized principles that if followed will always produce predicted outcomes. In fact, the majority of reengineering projects do not achieve breakthrough gains in business performance. Michael Hammer, a leading proponent of reengineering, states that 70 percent of reengineering efforts he has observed have failed (Hammer and Stanton, 1995). Other estimates of unsuccessful engineering projects are equally high (King, 1994; Moad, 1993). Problems with reengineering are part of the larger problem of orchestrating organizational change, a problem that attends the introduction of all innovations, including information systems. Managing change is neither simple nor intuitive. A reengineered business process or a new information system inevitably affects jobs, skill requirements, work flows, and reporting relationships. Fear of these changes breeds resistance, confusion, and even conscious efforts to undermine the change effort. In addition, what happens after reengineering? How will the "change" program be sustained over time to remain competitive (Harkness, Kettinger, and Segars, 1996)? The organizational change requirements for new information systems are so important that we devote an entire chapter (Chapter 14) to this topic.

11.3 OVERVIEW OF SYSTEMS DEVELOPMENT

Whatever their scope and objectives, new information systems are an outgrowth of a process of organizational problem solving. A new information system is built as a solution to some type of problem or set of problems the organization perceives it is facing. The problem may be one in which managers and employees realize that the organization is not performing as well as expected, or it may come from the realization that the organization should take advantage of new opportunities to perform more successfully.

Review the diagrams at the beginning of each chapter of this text. They show an information system that is a solution to a particular set of business challenges or problems. The resulting information system is an outgrowth of a series of events called systems development. **Systems development** refers to all the activities that go into producing an information systems solution to an organizational problem or opportunity. Systems development is a structured kind of problem solving with distinct activities. These activities consist of systems analysis, systems design, programming, testing, conversion, and production and maintenance.

Figure 11.5 illustrates the systems development process. The systems development activities depicted here usually take place in sequential order. But some of the activities may need to be repeated or some may be taking place simultaneously, depending on the approach to system building that is being employed (see Chapter 12). Note also that each activity involves interaction with the organization. Members of the organization participate in these activities and the systems development process creates organizational changes. Chapter 14 describes the challenge of managing these organizational changes surrounding system building.

systems development The activities that go into producing an information systems solution to an organizational problem or opportunity.

Systems Analysis

systems analysis The analysis of a problem that the organization will try to solve with an information system.

Systems analysis is the analysis of the problem that the organization will try to solve with an information system. It consists of defining the problem, identifying its causes,

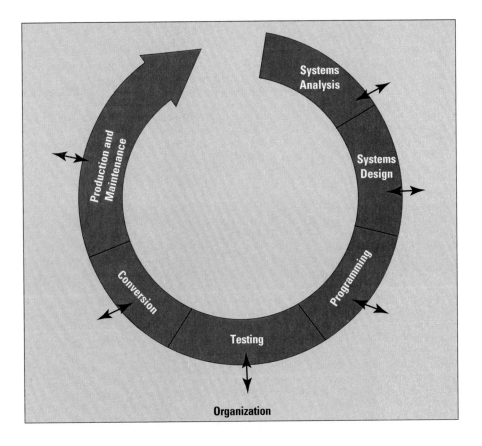

FIGURE 11.5

The systems development process. Each of the core systems development activities entails interaction with the organization.

specifying the solution, and identifying the information requirements that must be met by a system solution.

The key to building any large information system is a thorough understanding of the existing organization and system. Thus, the systems analyst creates a road map of the existing organization and systems, identifying the primary owners and users of data in the organization. These stakeholders have a direct interest in the information affected by the new system. In addition to these organizational aspects, the analyst also briefly describes the existing hardware and software that serve the organization.

From this organizational analysis, the systems analyst details the problems of existing systems. By examining documents, work papers, and procedures; observing system operations; and interviewing key users of the systems, the analyst can identify the problem areas and objectives to be achieved by a solution. Often the solution requires building a new information system or improving an existing one.

Feasibility

In addition to suggesting a solution, systems analysis involves a **feasibility study** to determine whether that solution is feasible, or achievable, given the organization's resources and constraints. Three major areas of feasibility must be addressed:

1. **Technical feasibility:** whether the proposed solution can be implemented with the available hardware, software, and technical resources.

2. **Economic feasibility:** whether the benefits of the proposed solution outweigh the costs. We explore this topic in greater detail in Section 11.4, Understanding the Business Value of Information Systems.

3. **Operational feasibility:** whether the proposed solution is desirable within the existing managerial and organizational framework.

feasibility study As part of the systems analysis process, the way to determine whether the solution is achievable, given the organization's resources and constraints.

technical feasibility Determines whether a proposed solution can be implemented with the available hardware, software, and technical resources.

economic feasibility Determines whether the benefits of a proposed solution outweigh the costs.

operational feasibility Determines whether a proposed solution is desirable within the existing managerial and organizational framework.

Building successful information systems requires close cooperation among end users and information systems specialists throughout the systems development process.

Normally the systems analysis process will identify several alternative solutions that can be pursued by the organization. The process will then assess the feasibility of each. Three basic solution alternatives exist for every systems problem:

1. To do nothing, leaving the existing situation unchanged

2. To modify or enhance existing systems

3. To develop a new system

There may be several solution design options within the second and third solution alternatives. A written systems proposal report will describe the costs and benefits, advantages, and disadvantages of each alternative. It is then up to management to determine which mix of costs, benefits, technical features, and organizational impacts represents the most desirable alternative.

Establishing Information Requirements

Perhaps the most difficult task of the systems analyst is to define the specific information requirements that must be met by the system solution selected. This is the area where many large system efforts go wrong and the one that poses the greatest difficulty for the analyst. At the most basic level, the **information requirements** of a

information requirements A detailed statement of the information needs that a new system must satisfy; identifies who needs what information, and when, where, and how the information is needed.

new system involve identifying who needs what information, where, when, and how. Requirements analysis carefully defines the objectives of the new or modified system and develops a detailed description of the functions that the new system must perform. Requirements must consider economic, technical, and time constraints, as well as the goals, procedures, and decision processes of the organization. Faulty requirements analysis is a leading cause of systems failure and high systems development costs (see Chapter 14). A system designed around the wrong set of requirements either will have to be discarded because of poor performance or will need to be heavily revised. Therefore, the importance of requirements analysis must not be underestimated.

Developing requirements specifications may involve considerable research and revision. A business function may be very complex or poorly defined. A manual system or routine set of inputs and outputs may not exist. Procedures may vary from individual to individual. Such situations will be more difficult to analyze, especially if the users are unsure of what they want or need (this problem is extremely common). To derive information systems requirements, analysts may be forced to work and rework requirements statements in cooperation with users. Although this process is laborious, it is far superior to and less costly than redoing and undoing an entire system. There are also alternative approaches to eliciting requirements that help minimize these problems (see Chapter 12).

In many instances, business procedures are unclear or users disagree about how things are done and should be done. Systems analysis often makes an unintended contribution to the organization by clarifying procedures and building organizational consensus about how things should be done. In many instances, building a new system creates an opportunity to redefine how the organization conducts its daily business.

Some problems do not require an information system solution, but instead need an adjustment in management, additional training, or refinement of existing organizational procedures. If the problem is information related, systems analysis may still be required to diagnose the problem and arrive at the proper solution.

Systems Design

While systems analysis describes what a system should do to meet information requirements, **systems design** shows how the system will fulfill this objective. The design of an information system is the overall plan or model for that system. Like the blueprint of a building or house, it consists of all specifications that give the system its form and structure. Information systems design is an exacting and creative task demanding imagination, sensitivity to detail, and expert skills.

systems design Details how a system will meet the information requirements as determined by the systems analysis.

Systems design has three objectives. First, the systems designer is responsible for considering alternative technology configurations for carrying out and developing the system as described by the analyst. This may involve analyses of the performance of different pieces of hardware and software, security capabilities of systems, network alternatives, and the portability or changeability of systems hardware.

Second, designers are responsible for the management and control of the technical realization of systems. Detailed programming specifications, coding of data, documentation, testing, and training are all the responsibility of the design staff. In addition, designers are responsible for the actual procurement of the hardware, consultants, and software needed by the system.

Third, the systems designer details the system specifications that will deliver the functions identified during systems analysis. These specifications should address all the managerial, organizational, and technological components of the system solution. Table 11.7 lists the types of specifications that would be produced during systems design.

Table 11.7   Design Specifications

Output	**Controls**
Medium	Input controls (characters, limit,
Content	reasonableness)
Timing	Processing controls (consistency, record
	counts)
Input	Output controls (totals, samples of
Origins	output)
Flow	Procedural controls (passwords, special
Data entry	forms)
User interface	**Security**
Simplicity	Access controls
Efficiency	Catastrophe plans
Logic	Audit trails
Feedback	
Errors	**Documentation**
	Operations documentation
Database design	Systems documents
Logical data relations	User documentation
Volume and speed requirements	
File organization and design	**Conversion**
Record specifications	Transfer files
	Initiate new procedures
Processing	Select testing method
Computations	Cut over to new system
Program modules	
Required reports	**Training**
Timing of outputs	Select training techniques
	Develop training modules
Manual procedures	Identify training facilities
What activities	
Who performs them	**Organizational changes**
When	Task redesign
How	Job design
Where	Process design
	Office and organization structure design
	Reporting relationships

Logical and Physical Design

The design for an information system can be broken down into logical and physical design specifications. **Logical design** lays out the components of the system and their relationship to each other as they would appear to users. It shows what the system solution will do as opposed to how it is actually implemented physically. It describes inputs and outputs, processing functions to be performed, business procedures, data models, and controls. (Controls specify standards for acceptable performance and methods for measuring actual performance in relation to these standards. They are described in detail in Chapter 17.)

Physical design is the process of translating the abstract logical model into the specific technical design for the new system. It produces the actual specifications for hardware, software, physical databases, input/output media, manual procedures, and specific controls. Physical design provides the remaining specifications that transform the abstract logical design plan into a functioning system of people and machines.

Like houses or buildings, information systems may have many possible designs. They may be centralized or distributed, on-line or batch, partially manual or heavily automated. Each design represents a unique blend of all the technical and organizational factors that shape an information system. What makes one design superior to

logical design Lays out the components of the information system and their relationship to each other as they would appear to users.

physical design The process of translating the abstract logical model into the specific technical design for the new system.

others is the ease and efficiency with which it fulfills user requirements within a specific set of technical, organizational, financial, and time constraints.

Before the design of an information system is finalized, analysts will evaluate various design alternatives. Based on the requirements definition and systems analysis, analysts construct high-level logical design models. They then examine the costs, benefits, strengths, and weaknesses of each alternative.

The Role of End Users

Technical specialists cannot direct information systems design alone. It demands a very high level of participation and control by end users. User information requirements drive the entire systems-building effort. Users must have sufficient control over the design process to ensure that the system reflects their business priorities and information needs, not the biases of the technical staff.

Working on design increases users' understanding and acceptance of the system, reducing problems caused by power transfers, intergroup conflict, and unfamiliarity with new system functions and procedures. As Chapter 14 points out, insufficient user involvement in the design effort is a major cause of system failure.

Some MIS researchers have suggested that design should be user led. However, other researchers point out that systems development is not an entirely rational process. Users leading design activities have used their position to further private interests and gain power rather than to enhance organizational objectives. Users controlling design can sabotage or seriously impede the systems-building effort (Franz and Robey, 1984).

The nature and level of user participation in design vary from system to system. There is less need for user involvement in systems with simple or straightforward requirements than in those with requirements that are elaborate, complex, or vaguely defined. Transaction processing or operational control systems have traditionally required less user involvement than strategic planning, information reporting, and decision-support systems. Less structured systems need more user participation to define requirements and may necessitate many versions of design before specifications can be finalized.

Different levels of user involvement in design are reflected in different systems development methods. Chapter 12 describes how user involvement varies with each development approach.

Completing the Systems Development Process

The remaining steps in the systems development process translate the solution specifications established during systems analysis and design into a fully operational information system. These concluding steps consist of programming, testing, conversion, and production and maintenance.

Programming

The process of translating design specifications into software for the computer constitutes a smaller portion of the systems development cycle than design and perhaps the testing activities. But it is here, in providing the actual instructions for the machine, that the heart of the system takes shape. During the **programming** stage, system specifications that were prepared during the design stage are translated into program code. On the basis of detailed design documents for files, transaction and report layouts, and other design details, specifications for each program in the system are prepared.

Some systems development projects assign programming tasks to specialists whose work consists exclusively of coding programs. Other projects prefer programmer/analysts who both design and program functions. Because large systems entail many programs with thousands—even hundreds of thousands—of lines of code,

programming The process of translating the system specifications prepared during the design stage into program code.

programming teams are frequently used. Moreover, even if a single individual can program an entire system, the quality of the software will be higher if it is subject to group review (see Chapter 13).

Testing

testing The exhaustive and thorough process that determines whether the system produces the desired results under known conditions.

Exhaustive and thorough **testing** must be conducted to ascertain whether the system produces the right results. Testing answers the question, "Will the system produce the desired results under known conditions?"

The amount of time needed to answer this question has been traditionally underrated in systems project planning (see Chapter 13). As much as 50 percent of the entire software development budget can be expended in testing. Testing is also time consuming: Test data must be carefully prepared, results reviewed, and corrections made in the system. In some instances, parts of the system may have to be redesigned. Yet the risks of glossing over this step are enormous.

Testing an information system can be divided into three types of activities:

unit testing The process of testing each program separately in the system. Sometimes called *program testing.*

Unit testing, or program testing, consists of testing each program separately in the system. Although it is widely believed that the purpose of such testing is to guarantee that programs are error free, this goal is realistically impossible. Testing should be viewed instead as a means of locating errors in programs, focusing on finding all the ways to make a program fail. Once pinpointed, problems can be corrected.

system testing Tests the functioning of the information system as a whole to determine if discrete modules will function together as planned.

System testing tests the functioning of the information system as a whole. It tries to determine if discrete modules will function together as planned and whether discrepancies exist between the way the system actually works and the way it was conceived. Among the areas examined are performance time, capacity for file storage and handling peak loads, recovery and restart capabilities, and manual procedures.

acceptance testing Provides the final certification that the system is ready to be used in a production setting.

Acceptance testing provides the final certification that the system is ready to be used in a production setting. Systems tests are evaluated by users and reviewed by management. When all parties are satisfied that the new system meets their standards, the system is formally accepted for installation.

It is essential that all aspects of testing be carefully considered and that they be as comprehensive as possible. To ensure this, the development team works with users to devise a systematic test plan. The **test plan** includes the preparations for the series of tests previously described.

test plan Prepared by the development team in conjunction with the users; it includes the preparations for the series of tests to be performed on the system.

Figure 11.6 shows an example of a test plan. The general condition being tested here is a record change. The documentation consists of a series of test-plan screens maintained on a database (perhaps a PC database) that is ideally suited to this kind of application.

Users play a critical role in the testing process. They understand the full range of data and processing conditions that may occur within their system. Moreover, programmers tend to be aware only of the conditions treated in their programs; the test data they devise are usually too limited. Therefore, input from other team members and users will help ensure that the range of conditions included in the test data is complete. Users can identify frequent and less common transactions, unusual conditions to anticipate, and most of the common types of errors that may occur when the system is in use. User input is also decisive in verifying the manual procedures for the system.

Conversion

conversion The process of changing from the old system to the new system.

Conversion is the process of changing from the old system to the new system. It answers the question, "Will the new system work under real conditions?" Four main conversion strategies can be employed: the parallel strategy, the direct cutover strategy, the pilot study strategy, and the phased approach strategy.

parallel strategy A safe and conservative conversion approach in which both the old system and its potential replacement are run together for a time until everyone is assured that the new system functions correctly.

In a **parallel strategy,** both the old system and its potential replacement are run together for a time until everyone is assured that the new one functions correctly.

FIGURE 11.6

Procedure	Address and Maintenance "Record Change Series"		Test Series 2		
Prepared By:		Date:	Version:		
Test Ref.	Condition Tested	Special Requirements	Expected Results	Output On	Next Screen
2	Change records				
2.1	Change existing record	Key field	Not allowed		
2.2	Change nonexistent record	Other fields	"Invalid key" message		
2.3	Change deleted record	Deleted record must be available	"Deleted" message		
2.4	Make second record	Change 2.1 above	OK if valid	Transaction file	V45
2.5	Insert record		OK if valid	Transaction file	V45
2.6	Abort during change	Abort 2.5	No change	Transaction file	V45

A sample test plan to test a record change. When developing a test plan, it is imperative to include the various conditions to be tested, the requirements for each condition tested, and the expected results. Test plans require input from both end users and information system specialists.

This is the safest conversion approach, because in the event of errors or processing disruptions, the old system can still be used as a backup. However, this approach is very expensive, and additional staff or resources may be required to run the extra system.

The **direct cutover strategy** replaces the old system entirely with the new system on an appointed day. At first glance, this strategy seems less costly than parallel conversion strategy. However, it is a very risky approach that can potentially be more costly than parallel activities if serious problems with the new system are found. There is no other system to fall back on. Dislocations, disruptions, and the cost of corrections may be enormous.

The **pilot study strategy** introduces the new system only to a limited area of the organization, such as a single department or operating unit. When this pilot version is complete and working smoothly, it is installed throughout the rest of the organization, either simultaneously or in stages.

The **phased approach strategy** introduces the new system in stages, either by functions or by organizational units. If, for example, the system is introduced by functions, a new payroll system might begin with hourly workers who are paid weekly, followed six months later by adding salaried employees who are paid monthly to the system. If organizational units introduce the system, corporate headquarters might be converted first, followed by outlying operating units four months later.

A formal **conversion plan** provides a schedule of all the activities required to install the new system. The most time-consuming activity is usually the conversion of data. Data from the old system must be transferred to the new system, either manually or through special conversion software programs. The converted data then must be carefully verified for accuracy and completeness.

Moving from an old system to a new one requires that end users be trained to use the new system. Detailed **documentation** showing how the system works from both a technical and end-user standpoint is finalized during conversion time for use in training and everyday operations. Lack of proper training and documentation contributes to system failure (see Chapter 14), so this portion of the systems development process is very important.

direct cutover strategy A risky conversion approach in which the new system completely replaces the old one on an appointed day.

pilot study strategy A strategy to introduce the new system to a limited area of the organization until it is proven to be fully functional; only then can the conversion to the new system across the entire organization take place.

phased approach strategy Introduces the new system in stages either by functions or by organizational units.

conversion plan Provides a schedule of all activities required to install a new system.

documentation Descriptions of how an information system works from either a technical or end-user standpoint.

Table 11.8	Systems Development
Core Activity	**Description**
Systems analysis	Identify problem(s) Specify solution Establish information requirements
Systems design	Create logical design specifications Create physical design specifications Manage technical realization of system
Programming	Translate design specifications into program code
Testing	Unit test Systems test Acceptance test
Conversion	Plan conversion Prepare documentation Train users and technical staff
Production and Maintenance	Operate the system Evaluate the system Modify the system

Production and Maintenance

production The stage after the new system is installed and the conversion is complete; during this time the system is reviewed by users and technical specialists to determine how well it has met its original goals.

maintenance Changes in hardware, software, documentation, or procedures to a production system to correct errors, meet new requirements, or improve processing efficiency.

After the new system is installed and conversion is complete, the system is said to be in **production**. During this stage, the system will be reviewed by both users and technical specialists to determine how well it has met its original objectives and to decide whether any revisions or modifications are in order. Changes in hardware, software, documentation, or procedures to a production system to correct errors, meet new requirements, or improve processing efficiency are termed **maintenance.**

Studies of maintenance have examined the amount of time required for various maintenance tasks (Lientz and Swanson, 1980). Approximately 20 percent of the time is devoted to debugging or correcting emergency production problems; another 20 percent is concerned with changes in data, files, reports, hardware, or system software. But 60 percent of all maintenance work consists of making user enhancements, improving documentation, and recoding system components for greater processing efficiency. The amount of work in the third category of maintenance problems could be reduced significantly through better system analysis and design practices. Table 11.8 summarizes the systems development activities.

Chapter 3 has described the many ways in which organizations can differ. Systems likewise differ in terms of their size, technological complexity, and the organizational problems they are meant to solve. Because there are different kinds of systems and situations in which each is conceived or built, a number of methods have been developed to build systems. We describe these various methods in the next chapter.

11.4 UNDERSTANDING THE BUSINESS VALUE OF INFORMATION SYSTEMS

Information systems can have several different values for business firms. As we have pointed out in earlier chapters, information systems can provide a temporary competitive advantage to firms. A consistently strong information technology infrastructure can, over the longer term, play an important strategic role in the life of the firm. Looked at less grandly, information systems can permit firms simply to survive. In many cases, survival even at a mediocre level will dictate investment in systems. In addition, government regulations may require these survival investments.

It is important also to realize that systems can have value but that the firm may not capture all or even some of the value. Although system projects can result in firm benefits such as profitability and productivity, some or all of the benefit can go directly to the consumer in the form of lower prices or more reliable services and products (Hitt and Brynjolfsson, 1996). Society can reward firms which enhance consumer surplus by allowing them to survive or by rewarding them with increases in business revenues. Competitors who fail to enrich consumers will not survive. But from a management point of view, the challenge is to retain as much of the benefit of systems investments as is feasible in current market conditions.

Strategy cannot be pursued when a firm is financially unsound. The worth of systems from a financial perspective essentially revolves around the question of return on invested capital. The value of systems from a financial view comes down to one question: Does a particular IS investment produce sufficient returns to justify its costs? There are many problems with this approach, not the least of which is how to estimate benefits and count the costs.

Capital Budgeting Models

Capital budgeting models are one of several techniques used to measure the value of investing in long-term capital investment projects. The process of analyzing and selecting various proposals for capital expenditures is called **capital budgeting.** Firms invest in capital projects to expand production to meet anticipated demand, or to modernize production equipment to reduce costs. Firms also invest in capital projects for many noneconomic reasons, such as to install pollution control equipment, or to convert to a human resources database to meet some government regulations, or to satisfy nonmarket public demands. Information systems are considered long-term capital investment projects.

capital budgeting The process of analyzing and selecting various proposals for capital expenditures.

Six capital budgeting models are used to evaluate capital projects:

The payback method

The accounting rate of return on investment (ROI)

The cost-benefit ratio

The net present value

The profitability index

The internal rate of return (IRR)

Cash Flows

All capital budgeting methods rely on measures of cash flows into and out of the firm. Capital projects generate cash flows into and out of the firm. The investment cost is an immediate cash outflow caused by the purchase of the capital equipment. In subsequent years, the investment may cause additional cash outflows that will be balanced by cash inflows resulting from the investment. Cash inflows take the form of increased sales of more products (for reasons including new products, higher quality, or increasing market share), or reduction in costs of production and operation. The difference between cash outflows and cash inflows is used for calculating the financial worth of an investment. Once the cash flows have been established, several alternative methods are available for comparison among different projects and decision making about the investment.

Limitations of Financial Models

Financial models are used in many situations: to justify new systems, explain old systems post hoc, and to develop quantitative support for a political position. Political decisions made for organizational reasons have nothing to do with the cost and benefits of a system.

Financial models assume that all relevant alternatives have been examined, that all costs and benefits are known, and that these costs and benefits can be expressed in a common metric, specifically, money. When one has to choose among many complex alternatives, these assumptions are rarely met in the real world, although they may be approximated. Table 11.9 lists some of the more common costs and benefits of systems. **Tangible benefits** can be quantified and assigned a monetary value. **Intangible benefits,** such as more efficient customer service or enhanced decision making, cannot be immediately quantified but may lead to quantifiable gains in the long run. Indeed, if intangible benefits do not at some reasonable point lead to tangible benefits, then they may not be "worth" much.

Information Systems as a Capital Project

Many well-known problems emerge when financial analysis is applied to information systems (Dos Santos, 1991). Financial models do not express the risks and uncertainty of their own cost and benefits estimates. Costs and benefits do not occur in the same time frame—costs tend to be upfront and tangible, whereas benefits tend to be back loaded and intangible. Inflation may affect costs and benefits differently. Technology—especially information technology—can change during the course of the project, causing estimates to vary greatly. Intangible benefits are difficult to quantify. These factors play havoc with financial models.

The difficulties of measuring intangible benefits give financial models an application bias: Transaction and clerical systems that displace labor and save space always produce more measurable, tangible benefits than management information systems, decision-support systems, or computer-supported collaborative work systems (see Chapter 15).

tangible benefits Benefits that can be quantified and assigned monetary value; they include lower operational costs and increased cash flows.

intangible benefits Benefits that are not easily quantified; they include more efficient customer service or enhanced decision making.

Table 11.9	Costs and Benefits of Information Systems
Costs	**Benefits**
Hardware	**Tangible**
	Cost savings
Telecommunications	Increased productivity
	Low operational costs
Software	Reduced work force
	Lower computer expenses
Services	Lower outside vendor costs
	Lower clerical and professional costs
Personnel	Reduced rate of growth in expenses
	Reduced facility costs
	Intangible
	Improved asset utilization
	Improved resource control
	Improved organizational planning
	Increased organizational flexibility
	More timely information
	More information
	Increased organizational learning
	Legal requirements attained
	Enhanced employee goodwill
	Increased job satisfaction
	Improved decision making
	Improved operations
	Higher client satisfaction
	Better corporate image

There is some reason to believe that investment in information technology requires special consideration in financial modeling. Capital budgeting historically concerned itself with manufacturing equipment and other long-term investments such as electrical generating facilities and telephone networks. These investments had expected lives of more than one year and up to twenty-five years. Computer-based information systems are similar to other capital investments in that they produce an immediate investment cost, and are expected to produce cash benefits over a term greater than one year.

Information systems differ from manufacturing systems in that their expected life is shorter. The very high rate of technological change in computer-based information systems means that most systems are seriously out of date in five to eight years. Although parts of old systems survive as code segments in large programs—some programs have code that is fifteen to twenty years old—most large-scale systems after five years require significant investment to redesign or rebuild them.

The high rate of technological obsolescence in budgeting for systems means simply that the payback period must be shorter, and the rates of return higher than typical capital projects with much longer useful lives.

The bottom line with financial models is to use them cautiously and to put the results into a broader context of business analysis. Let us look at an example to see how these problems arise and can be handled. The following case study is based on a real-world scenario, but the names have been changed.

Case Example: Primrose, Mendelson, and Hansen

Primrose, Mendelson, and Hansen is a 250-person law partnership on Manhattan's West Side. Founded in 1923, Primrose has excelled in corporate, taxation, environmental, and health law. Its litigation department is also well known.

The Problem

Spread out over three floors of a new building, each of the hundred partners has a secretary. Many partners still have 486 PCs on their desktops but rarely use them except to read the e-mail. Virtually all business is conducted face-to-face in the office, or when partners meet directly with clients on the clients' premises. Most of the law business involves marking up (editing), creating, filing, storing, and sending documents. In addition, the tax, pension, and real estate groups do a considerable amount of spreadsheet work.

With overall business off 10 percent since 1995, the chairman, Edward W. Hansen III, is hoping to use information systems to cut costs, enhance service to clients, and bring partner profits back up.

First, the firm's income depends on billable hours, and every lawyer is supposed to keep a diary of his or her work for specific clients in 30-minute intervals. Generally, senior lawyers at this firm charge about $500 an hour for their time. Unfortunately, lawyers are not good record keepers; they often forget what they have been working on, and must go back to reconstruct their time diaries. The firm hopes that there will be some automated way of tracking billable hours.

Second, much time is spent communicating with clients around the world, with other law firms both in the United States and overseas, and especially with Primrose's branches in Los Angeles, Tokyo, London, and Paris. The fax machine has become the communication medium of choice, generating huge bills and developing lengthy queues. The firm looks forward to using some sort of secure e-mail, perhaps Lotus Notes or even the Internet. Law firms are wary of breaches in the security of confidential client information.

Third, Primrose has no client database! A law firm is a collection of fiefdoms—each lawyer has his or her own clients and keeps the information about them private. This, however, makes it impossible for management to find out who is a client of the

Information systems can provide attorneys and legal researchers with legal data to expedite their research and recording processes.

firm, who is working on a deal with whom, and so forth. The firm maintains a billing system, but the information is too difficult to search. What Primrose needs is an integrated client management system that would take care of billing, hourly charges, and making client information available to others in the firm. Even overseas offices want to have information on who is taking care of a particular client in the United States.

Fourth, there is no system to track costs. The head of the firm and the department heads who compose the executive committee cannot identify what the costs are, where the money is being spent, who is spending it, and how the firm's resources are being allocated. Perhaps, for instance, health law is declining and the firm should trim associates (nonpartnered lawyers). A decent accounting system that could identify the cash flows and the costs a bit more clearly than the existing journal would be a big help.

The Solution

There are many problems at Primrose; information systems could obviously have some survival value and perhaps could grant a strategic advantage to Primrose if a system were correctly built and implemented. We will not go through a detailed systems analysis and design here. Instead, we will sketch the solution that in fact was adopted, showing the detailed costs and estimated benefits. These will prove useful for estimating the overall business value of the new system—both financial and nonfinancial.

The technical solution adopted was to create a local area network composed of 100 fully configured Pentium multimedia desktop PCs, three Windows NT file servers, and an Ethernet 10 MBS (megabit per second) local area network on a coaxial cable. Multimedia computers are required because lawyers access a fair amount of information stored on CD-ROM. The network connects all the lawyers and their secretaries into a single integrated system, yet permits each lawyer to configure his or her desktop with specialized software and hardware. The older 486 machines were given away to charity.

All desktop machines were configured with Windows 95 and Office 97 application software, while the file servers ran Windows NT. A networked relational database was installed to handle client accounting and mailing functions. Lotus Notes was chosen as the internal mail system because it provided an easy-to-use interface and good links to external networks (including the Internet) and mail systems. Frequently the partners send documents to Paris and San Francisco where the firm maintains satellite offices. The Internet was specifically rejected as an e-mail technology because of its uncertain security. Lotus Notes is still much more versatile than the Web at groupware functions and accounting functions such as simple client management and billing applications. Notes can also incorporate spreadsheets. The Primrose local area network is linked to external networks so that the firm can obtain information on-line from Lexis (a legal database) and several financial database services.

The new system required Primrose to hire a chief information officer and director of systems—a new position for most law firms. Four systems personnel were required to operate the system and train lawyers. Outside trainers were also hired for a short period.

Figure 11.7 shows the estimated costs and benefits of the system. The system had an actual investment cost of $1,210,500 in the first year (Year 0) and total cost over six years of $3,683,000. The estimated benefits total $6,075,000 after six years. Was the investment worthwhile? If so, in what sense? There are financial and nonfinancial answers to this question. Let us look at the financial models first. They are depicted in Figure 11.8.

The Payback Method

The **payback method** is quite simple: It is a measure of time required to pay back the initial investment of a project. The payback period is computed as

$$\frac{\text{Original investment}}{\text{Annual net cash inflow}} = \text{Number of years to pay back}$$

payback method A measure of the time required to pay back the initial investment of a project.

In the case of Primrose, it will take about 2.3 years to pay back the initial investment. (Since cash flows are uneven, annual cash inflows are summed until they equal the original investment in order to arrive at this number.) The payback method is a popular method because of its simplicity and power as an initial screening method. It is especially good for high-risk projects in which the useful life is difficult to know. If a project pays for itself in two years, then it matters less how long after two years the system lasts.

The weakness of this measure is its virtues: The method ignores the time value of money, the amount of cash flow after the payback period, the disposal value (usually zero with computer systems), and the profitability of the investment.

Accounting Rate of Return on Investment (ROI)

Firms make capital investments to earn a satisfactory rate of return. Determining a satisfactory rate of return depends on the cost of borrowing money, but other factors can enter into the equation. Such factors include the historic rates of return expected by the firm. In the long run, the desired rate of return must equal or exceed the cost of capital in the marketplace. Otherwise, no one will lend the firm money.

The **accounting rate of return on investment (ROI)** calculates the rate of return from an investment by adjusting the cash inflows produced by the investment for depreciation. It gives an approximation of the accounting income earned by the project.

To find the ROI, first calculate the average net benefit. The formula for the average net benefit is as follows:

$$\frac{(\text{Total benefits–Total cost–Depreciation})}{\text{Useful life}} = \text{Net benefit}$$

accounting rate of return on investment (ROI) Calculation of the rate of return from an investment by adjusting cash inflows produced by the investment for depreciation. Approximates the accounting income earned by the investment.

This net benefit is divided by the total initial investment to arrive at ROI (Rate of Return on Investment). The formula is

$$\frac{\text{Net benefit}}{\text{Total initial investment}} = \text{ROI}$$

Primrose, Mendelson, and Hansen
Intellex Legal Information System (ILIS)
Estimated Costs and Benefits 1998–2003

		0 1998	1 1999	2 2000	3 2001	4 2002	5 2003	
Costs								
Hardware								
File Servers	3@20000	$ 60,000.00	$ 10,000.00	$ 10,000.00	$ 10,000.00	$ 10,000.00	$ 10,000.00	
PCs	100@3000	$ 300,000.00	$ 10,000.00	$ 10,000.00	$ 10,000.00	$ 10,000.00	$ 10,000.00	
Network cards	100@100	$ 10,000.00	$ -	$ -	$ -	$ -	$ -	
Scanners	6@500	$ 3,000.00	$ 500.00	$ 500.00	$ 500.00	$ 500.00	$ 500.00	
Telecommunications								
Gateways	3@5000	$ 15,000.00	$ 1,000.00	$ 1,000.00	$ 1,000.00	$ 1,000.00	$ 1,000.00	
Cabling	150000	$ 150,000.00	$ -	$ -	$ -	$ -	$ -	
Telephone connect costs	50000	$ 50,000.00	$ 50,000.00	$ 50,000.00	$ 50,000.00	$ 50,000.00	$ 50,000.00	
Software								
Database	50000	$ 15,000.00	$ 15,000.00	$ 15,000.00	$ 15,000.00	$ 15,000.00	$ 15,000.00	
Network	10000	$ 10,000.00	$ 2,000.00	$ 2,000.00	$ 2,000.00	$ 2,000.00	$ 2,000.00	
Groupware	100@500	$ 50,000.00	$ 3,000.00	$ 3,000.00	$ 3,000.00	$ 3,000.00	$ 3,000.00	
Windows OS 97	100@150	$ 15,000.00	$ -	$ -	$ 15,000.00	$ -	$ -	
Services								
Nexis	50000	$ 50,000.00	$ 50,000.00	$ 50,000.00	$ 50,000.00	$ 50,000.00	$ 50,000.00	
Training	300hrs@75/hr	$ 22,500.00	$ 10,000.00	$ 10,000.00	$ 10,000.00	$ 10,000.00	$ 10,000.00	
0								
CIO	100000	$ 100,000.00	$ 100,000.00	$ 100,000.00	$ 100,000.00	$ 100,000.00	$ 100,000.00	
Systems Personnel	4@60000	$ 240,000.00	$ 240,000.00	$ 240,000.00	$ 240,000.00	$ 240,000.00	$ 240,000.00	
Trainers	2@60000	$ 120,000.00	$ -	$ -	$ -	$ -	$ -	
Total Costs		$1,210,500.00	$491,500.00	$491,500.00	$506,500.00	$491,500.00	$491,500.00	$3,683,000.00
Benefits								
1. Billing enhancements		$ 350,000.00	$400,000.00	$ 500,000.00	$ 500,000.00	$ 500,000.00	$ 500,000.00	
2. Reduced paralegals		$ 50,000.00	$100,000.00	$ 150,000.00	$ 150,000.00	$ 150,000.00	$ 150,000.00	
3. Reduced clerical		$ 50,000.00	$100,000.00	$ 100,000.00	$ 100,000.00	$ 100,000.00	$ 100,000.00	
4. Reduced messenger		$ 15,000.00	$ 30,000.00	$ 30,000.00	$ 30,000.00	$ 30,000.00	$ 30,000.00	
5. Reduced telecommunications		$ 10,000.00	$ 10,000.00	$ 10,000.00	$ 10,000.00	$ 10,000.00	$ 10,000.00	
6. Lawyer efficiencies		$ 120,000.00	$240,000.00	$ 360,000.00	$ 360,000.00	$ 360,000.00	$ 360,000.00	
Total Benefits		$ 595,000.00	$880,000.00	$1,150,000.00	$1,150,000.00	$1,150,000.00	$1,150,000.00	$6,075,000.00

FIGURE 11.7

Costs and benefits of the Intellex Legal Information System (ILIS). This spreadsheet analyzes the basic costs and benefits of implementing an information system for the law firm. The costs for hardware, telecommunications, software, services, and personnel are analyzed over a six-year period.

Year:	0	1	2	3	4	5
Net Cash Flow	$ (615,500.00)	$ 388,500.00	$ 658,500.00	$ 643,500.00	$ 658,500.00	$ 658,500.00

(1) Payback Period = 3 years

Initial investment $ 1,210,500.00

Cumulative Cash Flow

Year 1	$ 388,500.00	$ 388,500.00
Year 2	$ 658,500.00	$ 1,047,000.00
Year 3	$ 643,500.00	$ 1,690,500.00
Year 4	$ 658,500.00	$ 2,349,000.00
Year 5	$ 658,500.00	$ 3,007,500.00

(2) Accounting rate of return

$$\frac{\text{(Total benefits–Total Costs–Depreciation)/Useful life}}{\text{Total initial investment}}$$

Total Benefits	$ 6,075,000.00
Total Costs	$ 3,683,000.00
Depreciation	$ 1,210,500.00
	$ 1,181,500.00
Life	6 years
Initial investment	$ 1,210,500.00

$$\text{ROI} = \frac{1,181,500/6}{1,210,500} = 16.27\%$$

(3) Cost-Benefit Ratio

$$\frac{\text{Total Benefits}}{\text{Total Costs}} = \frac{\$6,075,000.00}{\$3,683,000.00} = 1.65$$

(4) Net Present Value

@NPV(0.05,D46:I46) $ 1,871,771.40

Net present value 1,871,771–1,210,500 $ 661,271.40

(5) Profitability Index

NPV/Investment $1,871,771/$1,210,500   1.55

(6) Internal Rate of Return (IRR)

@IRR(B17D46:146)+B49   82%

FIGURE 11.8

Financial models. To determine the financial basis for a project, a series of financial models helps determine the return on invested capital. These calculations include the payback period, the accounting rate of return (ROI), the cost-benefit ratio, the net present value, the profitability index, and the internal rate of return (IRR).

In the case of Primrose, the average rate of return on the investment is 16.27 percent. The cost of capital (the prime rate) has been hovering around 8 to 10 percent, and returns on invested capital in corporate bonds are at about 10 percent. On the surface, this investment returns more than other financial investments. On the other hand, 16.27 percent would be too low to pass the hurdle rate at many firms, who seek over 25 percent returns for internal projects.

The weakness of ROI is that it can ignore the time value of money. Future savings are simply not worth as much in today's dollars as are current savings. On the other hand, ROI can be modified (and usually is) so that future benefits and costs are calculated in today's dollars. (The present value function on most spreadsheets will perform this conversion.)

Net Present Value

Evaluating a capital project requires that the cost of an investment (a cash outflow usually in year 0) be compared with the net cash inflows that occur many years later. But these two kinds of inflows are not directly comparable because of the time value of money. Money you have been promised to receive three, four, and five years from now is not worth as much as money received today. Money received in the future has to be discounted by some appropriate percentage rate—usually the prevailing

present value The value, in current dollars, of a payment or stream of payments to be received in the future.

interest rate, or sometimes the cost of capital. **Present value** is the value in current dollars of a payment or stream of payments to be received in the future. It can be calculated by using the following formula:

$$\text{Payment} \times \frac{1 - (1 + \text{interest})^{-n}}{\text{Interest}} = \text{Present Value}$$

Thus, to compare the investment (made in today's dollars) with future savings or earnings, you need to discount the earnings to their present value and then calculate the net present value of the investment. The **net present value** is the amount of money an investment is worth, taking into account its cost, earnings, and the time value of money. The formula for net present value is

Present value of expected cash flows − Initial investment cost = Net present value

net present value The amount of money an investment is worth, taking into account its cost, earnings, and the time value of money.

In the case of Primrose, the present value of the stream of benefits is $1,871,771 and the cost (in today's dollars) is $1,210,500, giving a net present value of $661,271. In other words, the net present value of the investment is $661,271 over a six-year period. For a $1.2 million investment today, the firm will receive over $600,000. This is a good rate of return on investment.

Cost-Benefit Ratio

A simple method for calculating the returns from a capital expenditure is to calculate the **cost-benefit ratio,** which is the ratio of benefits to costs. The formula is

cost-benefit ratio A method for calculating the returns from a capital expenditure by dividing the total benefits by total costs.

$$\frac{\text{Total benefits}}{\text{Total costs}} = \text{Cost-benefit ratio}$$

In the case of Primrose, the cost-benefit ratio is 1.65, meaning that the benefits are 1.65 times greater than the costs. The cost-benefit ratio can be used to rank several projects for comparison. Some firms establish a minimum cost-benefit ratio that must be attained by capital projects. The cost-benefit ratio can of course be calculated using present values to account for the time value of money.

Profitability Index

One limitation of net present value is that it provides no measure of profitability. Neither does it provide a way to rank order different possible investments. One simple solution is provided by the profitability index. The **profitability index** is calculated by dividing the present value of the total cash inflow from an investment by the initial cost of the investment. The result can be used to compare the profitability of alternative investments.

profitability index Used to compare the profitability of alternative investments; it is calculated by dividing the present value of the total cash inflow from an investment by the initial cost of the investment.

$$\frac{\text{Present value of cash inflows}}{\text{Investment}} = \text{Profitability index}$$

In the case of Primrose, the profitability index is 1.55. The project returns substantially more than its cost. Projects can be rank ordered on this index, permitting firms to focus on only the most profitable projects.

Internal Rate of Return (IRR)

Internal rate of return (IRR) is a variation of the net present value method. It takes into account the time value of money. **Internal rate of return (IRR)** is defined as the rate of return or profit that an investment is expected to earn. IRR is the discount (interest) rate that will equate the present value of the project's future cash flows to the initial cost of the project (defined here as a negative cash flow in year 0 of $615,500). In other words, the value of R (discount rate) is such that Present value − Initial cost = 0. In the case of Primrose, the IRR is 82 percent. This seems to be a healthy rate of return.

internal rate of return (IRR) The rate of return or profit that an investment is expected to earn.

Results of the Capital Budgeting Analysis

Using methods that take into account the time value of money, the Primrose project is cash-flow positive over the time period and returns more benefits than it costs. Against this analysis, one might ask what other investments would be better from an efficiency and effectiveness standpoint? Also, one must ask if all the benefits have been calculated. It may be that this investment is necessary for the survival of the firm, or necessary to provide a level of service demanded by its clients. What are other competitors doing? In other words, there may be other intangible and strategic business factors to take into account.

For example, JC Penney Co. has established a capital appropriations committee for all technology investments that exceed $150,000. The committee includes JC Penney CEO W. R. Howell and six other top managers. Proposals to this committee must include a traditional ROI based on costs and benefits. In addition, the proposers are required to include a section devoted to examining competitive considerations. The proposals describe both quantifiable and nonquantifiable benefits. Some projects come in with no quantifiable benefits yet are considered competitive necessities. After a project is completed, the company evaluates whether the anticipated costs and benefits were realized. At Conoco, Inc., the Houston, Texas, energy company, developers use an interview form to hold numerous in-depth interviews on potential benefits prior to applying for project funding. In all affected departments, the department head and frequent users are interviewed for 30 to 60 minutes each. Summaries of the interviews are included in the management report on costs and benefits. Many firms—such as Amdahl Corporation, the mainframe manufacturer—have established firm-wide Web councils composed of business subunit Web directors. The Web council identifies both tangible and intangible benefits of corporate intranet proposals (Campbell, 1997).

Nonfinancial and Strategic Considerations

Other methods of selecting and evaluating information system investments involve nonfinancial and strategic considerations. When the firm has several alternative investments from which to select, it can employ portfolio analysis and scoring models. Several of these methods can be used in combination.

Portfolio Analysis

Rather than using capital budgeting, a second way of selecting among alternative projects is to consider the firm as having a portfolio of potential applications. Each application carries risks and benefits. The portfolio can be described as having a certain profile of risk and benefit to the firm (see Figure 11.9). Although there is no ideal profile for all firms, information-intensive industries (e.g., finance) should have a few high-risk, high-benefit projects to ensure that they stay current with technology. Firms in noninformation-intensive industries should focus on high-benefit, low-risk projects.

The general risks are as follows:

- Benefits may not be obtained.
- Costs of implementation may exceed budgets.
- Implementation time frames are exceeded.
- Technical performance is less than expected.
- The system is incompatible with existing software or hardware.

Risks are not necessarily bad. They are tolerable as long as the benefits are commensurate. In general, there are three factors that increase the risks of a project: project size, organizational experience, and project task complexity (Ein-Dor and Segev, 1978; McFarlan, 1981; Laudon, 1989). These are described in Chapter 14.

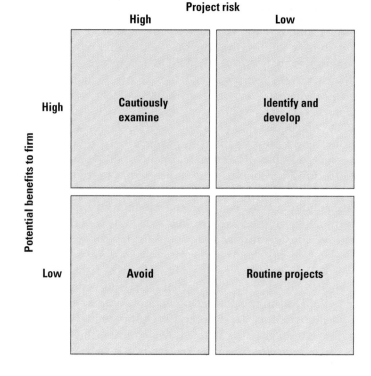

FIGURE 11.9

A system portfolio. Companies should examine their portfolio of projects in terms of potential benefits and likely risks. Certain kinds of projects should be avoided altogether and others developed rapidly. There is no ideal mix. Companies in different industries have different profiles.

portfolio analysis An analysis of the portfolio of potential applications within a firm to determine the risks and benefits and select among alternatives for information systems.

Once strategic analyses have determined the overall direction of systems development, a **portfolio analysis** can be used to select alternatives. Obviously, one can begin by focusing on systems of high benefit and low risk. These promise early returns and low risks. Second, high-benefit, high-risk systems should be examined; low-benefit, high-risk systems should be totally avoided; and low-benefit, low-risk systems should be reexamined for the possibility of rebuilding and replacing them with more desirable systems having higher benefits.

Scoring Models

scoring model A quick method for deciding among alternative systems based on a system of ratings for selected objectives.

A quick and sometimes compelling method for arriving at a decision on alternative systems is a **scoring model**. Scoring models give alternative systems a single score based on the extent to which they meet selected objectives (the method is similar to the objective attained model) (Matlin, 1989; Buss, 1983).

In Table 11.10 the firm must decide among three alternative office automation systems: (1) an IBM AS 400 client/server system with proprietary software, (2) a UNIX-based client/server system using an Oracle database, and (3) a Windows NT client/server system using Windows and Lotus Notes. Column 1 lists the criteria that decision makers may apply to the systems. These criteria are usually the result of lengthy discussions among the decision-making group. Often the most important outcome of a scoring model is not the score but simply agreement on the criteria used to judge a system (Ginzberg, 1979; Nolan, 1982). Column 2 lists the weights that decision makers attach to the decision criterion. The scoring model helps to bring about agreement among participants concerning the rank of the criteria. Columns 3 to 5 use a 1-to-5 scale (lowest to highest) to express the judgments of participants on the relative merits of each system. For example, concerning the percentage of user needs that each system meets, a score of 1 for a system argues that this system when compared with others being considered will be low in meeting user needs.

As with all objective techniques, there are many qualitative judgments involved in using the scoring model. This model requires experts who understand the issues and the technology. It is appropriate to cycle through the scoring model several times, changing the criteria and weights, to see how sensitive the outcome is to reasonable

Table 11.10   Scoring Model Used to Choose Among Alternative Office Automation Systems*

Criterion	Weight	AS400		UNIX		Windows NT	
Percentage of user needs met	0.40	2	0.8	3	1.2	4	1.6
Cost of the initial purchase	0.20	1	0.2	3	0.6	4	0.8
Financing	0.10	1	0.1	3	0.3	4	0.4
Ease of maintenance	0.10	2	0.2	3	0.3	4	0.4
Chances of success	0.20	3	0.6	4	0.8	4	0.8
Final score			1.9		3.2		4.0

Scale: 1 = low, 5 = high

One of the major uses of scoring models is in identifying the criteria of selection and their relative weights. In this instance, an office automation system based on Windows NT appears preferable.

WINDOW ON MANAGEMENT

Intranet Sites with 1000% ROIs?

It may be difficult to make money on the Web, but making money on corporate intranets appears to be a hard proposition to lose. Recent research claims that corporations such as Amdahl Corporation, Booz, Allen and Hamilton, Southern California Gas, Silicon Graphics, and Lockheed—to name a few—are getting returns on investment of 1000 percent! Here's why: corporations—for better or worse—print more paper than all the publishers in all markets in the United States put together. In other words, most corporations are publishing machines. Corporate intranets turn out to be an ideal electronic distributor of information. But buyer beware! The costs are often hidden, and what you improve may not be worth improving all that much in the long run. But you decide.

Costs. The major cost categories of intranet sites are the hardware, software, telecommunications, management, design, content, and the staff required to keep the site up to date. Many firms fail to include one or more of these costs, and especially they fail to account for the costs of developing the content in the first place (or second place if it must be rekeyed and reformatted to fit Web software). Information is definitely not free.

Benefits. There are two business benefits: new revenue and cost reduction. And then there are the intangibles. New revenues will include direct sales, accepting advertising fees for banners, and fees for Web-based services. Generally, intranet sites are cost reducers: reduced printing costs, reduction in force employee workforce, scaled back use of proprietary networks, lower management costs, reduced transaction costs, cheaper electronic data sharing with vendors, and so forth. Intangibles may include better customer service, marketing value, and better employee access to corporation information.

An example of the tremendous returns possible from an intranet site is Amdahl Corporation, a California-based mainframe computer manufacturer. Prior to the corporate intranet, Amdahl relied on paper and e-mail over proprietary networks. In 1995 Amdahl began a corporate expansion out of the mainframe niche into data center management software, services, and consulting. In two years it doubled in size. Amdahl's strategy involved creating a Web Council of representatives from all the major business units and divisions. The Web Council decided to build a unified corporate electronic library, which would permit all the divisions to share needed information. In 1995 senior management supported building a Web infrastructure—servers, software, and networks. Each division and unit is responsible for maintaining its Web pages in over 100 separate intranet directories. Today over 6500 pages are maintained on the intranet.

Some benefits of the corporate library are to make information from research firms available throughout the corporation, to reduce calls to the help desk by putting reference material on hand, to increase accuracy and currency of information, and to widely distribute a competitive analysis book (which before the intranet was a monthly three-inch-thick publication!). Time savings for employees is one of the biggest benefits. To calculate this, IDC sent a questionnaire to a sample of users and asked them to compare how much time the intranet saved them. IDC realized that only about 70 percent of this estimated time saving resulted in new additional work being done (because many employees could just waste time saved). Nevertheless, time saving was the largest benefit of the system.

The spreadsheet illustrated in Figure 11.10 shows how Amdahl calculated its ROI of 2063 percent.

To Think About: *Do you think Amdahl has correctly estimated all the important costs of their site? The time savings of employees is a big element in the benefits column, but how much of the time saved by an employee is actually translated into useful work?*

Source: http://www.netscape.com. Look in Netscape Columns and search the back-listed columns for "ROI." Find a preliminary report called "The Main Thing: Many Happy Returns" by International Data Corporation.

Financial Worksheet For:
Amdahl

Annual Savings	Base	Year 1	Year 2	Year 3
Personnel Savings	$0	$6,000,000	$6,000,000	$6,000,000
ISO 9000	$0	$28,246	$28,246	$28,246
Document Distribution	$0	$334,000	$334,000	$334,000
Total Savings Per Period	$0	$6,362,246	$6,362,246	$6,362,246

Depreciation Schedule*	Initial	Year 1	Year 2	Year 3**
Software	$110,000	$22,000	$22,000	$22,000
Total Per Period	$110,000	$22,000	$22,000	$22,000

Expensed Costs	Initial	Year 1	Year 2	Year 3
Maintenance	$0	$23,750	$23,750	$23,750
Network Upgrades	$45,000	$15,000	$15,000	$15,000
Hardware	$30,000	$0	$0	$0
Personnel	$384,358	$1,110,000	$1,110,000	$1,080,000
Training	$0	$133,923	$76,923	$76,923
Total Per Period	$459,358	$1,282,673	$1,225,673	$1,195,673

Basic Financial Assumptions	
All Federal and State Taxes	50%
Discount Rate	15%
Depreciation * Straight Line (Years)	5

Net Cash Flows	Initial	Year 1	Year 2	Year 3
Total Benefits		$6,362,246	$6,362,246	$6,362,246
Less: Total Costs	$569,358	$1,282,673	$1,225,673	$1,195,673
Less: Depreciation		$22,000	$22,000	$22,000
Net Profit Before Tax	$569,358	$5,057,573	$5,114,573	$5,144,573
Net Profit After Tax	$284,679	$2,528,787	$2,557,287	$2,572,287
Add: Depreciation		$22,000	$22,000	$22,000
Net Cash Flow After Taxes	$284,679)	$2,550,787	$2,579,287	$2,594,287

Financial Analysis	Results	Year 1	Year 2	Year 3
Annual ROI		779%	146%	206%
3-Year ROI	2063%			
Payback (Years)	0.13			
3-Year IRR	896%			
3-Year NPV	$5,589,493			

*Hardware and software costs totalling more than $100,000 are depreciated over five years on a straight-line basis. All other costs are treated as expenses in the initial year.

**Any software upgrade is treated as a depreciable asset if greater than $100,000; otherwise it is included as an expensed cost for the year.

FIGURE 11.10

Amdahl achieved a three-year ROI of 2063% from its corporate intranet investment. This spreadsheet shows how the company arrived at this figure.

changes in criteria. Scoring models are used most commonly to confirm, to rationalize, and to support decisions, rather than being the final arbiters of system selection.

If Primrose had other alternative systems projects to select from, it could have used the portfolio and scoring models as well as financial models to establish the business value of its systems solution.

Primrose did not have a portfolio of applications which could be used to compare the proposed system. Senior lawyers felt the project was low in risk using well-understood technology. They felt the rewards were even higher than the financial models stated. In particular they believed the financial models focused too much on cost savings, and not enough on new business creation. For instance, the ability to communicate with other law firms, with clients, and with the international staff of lawyers in remote locations was not even considered in the financial analysis.

The Window on Management explores the issue of returns on investment from corporate intranets.

MANAGEMENT WRAP-UP

The key management issues with building systems are to stay in control of the process (avoid runaway systems) and to lead the effort toward planned and sustained organizational change. Managers must link any systems development to the strategy of the firm, and identify precisely which systems should be changed to achieve large-scale improvements in results for the corporation as a whole. In other words, understanding what process to improve from the firm perspective is more important than blindly reengineering whatever business process happens to need fixing or happens to yield a huge ROI. There are many projects that have huge ROIs but in the scheme of things don't amount to much for the business as a whole.

MANAGEMENT

In large corporations a properly organized corporate-wide systems-building organization is required lest operating units and divisions go off on their own and develop unique solutions. This can result in chaos. The leading organizational issue here is how to balance local interests with corporate interests, and how to ensure that the overall strategy of the business dominates the system-building direction of local units. Many organizations have developed multitiered business processes to control the systems-building process as well as to permit local interests, a significant voice in the development of centralized infrastructure. Unfortunately, these firm-wide control structures can become unwieldy, bureaucratic, and political and stifle local initiatives.

ORGANIZATION

The key technological issues in system building involve how to use new technologies to enhance the system-building process and selection of the right technology for the system solution. Some new technologies help the actual organizational process of design, whereas other new technologies have only limited impacts on technical design. Technologies such as the Web and other network technologies are very useful in solving some of the management and organizational issues by soliciting the views of local units, and aggregating opinions through chat groups and e-mail discussion groups as well as providing technology solution options. Selecting a technology that fits the constraints of the problem to be solved and the organization's overall information technology infrastructure is a key decision.

TECHNOLOGY

SUMMARY

1. Understand why building new systems is a process of organizational change. Building a new information system is a form of planned organizational change that involves many different people in the organization. Because information systems are sociotechnical entities, a change in information systems involves changes in work, management, and the organization. The four levels of change that can result from the introduction of information technology are automation, rationalization of procedures, business process redesign (business reengineering), and paradigm shift. Business reengineering has the potential to dramatically improve productivity by streamlining work flows and redundant processes.

2. Explain how the organization can develop information systems that fit its business plan. Organizations should develop an information systems plan that describes how information technology supports the attainment of their goals. The plan indicates the direction of systems development, the rationale, implementation strategy, and budget. Enterprise analysis and critical success factors (CSFs) can be used to elicit organization-wide information requirements that must be addressed by the plan.

3. Identify the core activities in the systems development process. The core activities in systems development are systems analysis, systems design, programming, testing, conversion, and production and maintenance. Systems analysis is the study and analysis of problems of existing systems and the identification of requirements for their solution. Systems design provides the specifications for an information system solution, showing how its technical and organizational components fit together.

4. Describe various models for determining the business value of information systems. Capital budgeting models such as the payback method, accounting rate of return on investment (ROI), cost-benefit ratio, net present value, profitability index, and internal rate of return (IRR) are the primary financial models for determining the business value of information systems. Portfolio analysis and scoring models include nonfinancial considerations and can be used to evaluate alternative information systems projects.

KEY TERMS

Information systems plan	Technical feasibility	Test plan	Intangible benefits
Enterprise analysis	Economic feasibility	Conversion	Payback method
Critical success factors (CSFs)	Operational feasibility	Parallel strategy	Accounting rate of return on investment (ROI)
Automation	Information requirements	Direct cutover strategy	
Rationalization of procedures	Systems design	Pilot study strategy	Present value
	Logical design	Phased approach strategy	Net present value
Business reengineering	Physical design	Conversion plan	Cost-benefit ratio
Paradigm shift	Programming	Documentation	Profitability index
Systems development	Testing	Production	Internal rate of return (IRR)
Systems analysis	Unit testing	Maintenance	Portfolio analysis
Feasibility study	System testing	Capital budgeting	Scoring model
	Acceptance testing	Tangible benefits	

REVIEW QUESTIONS

1. Why can a new information system be considered planned organizational change? Describe four kinds of oganizational change that are evaluated by information technology.

2. What are the major categories of an information systems plan?

3. How can enterprise analysis and critical success factors be used to establish organization-wide information system requirements?

4. What is business process redesign (business reengineering)? How does it differ from traditional rationalization of procedures?

5. List and describe the five steps suggested for business reengineering.

6. What is the difference between systems analysis and systems design?

7. What is feasibility? Name and describe each of the three major areas of feasibility for information systems.

8. What are information requirements? Why are they difficult to determine correctly?

9. What is the difference between the logical design and the physical design of an information system?

10. Why is the testing stage of systems development so important? Name and describe the three stages of testing for an information system.

11. What is conversion? Why is it important to have a detailed conversion plan?

12. What roles do programming, production, and maintenance play in systems development?

13. Name and describe the capital budgeting methods used to evaluate information systems projects.

14. What are the limitations of financial models for establishing the value of information systems?

15. Describe how portfolio analysis and scoring models can be used to establish the worth of systems.

16. Why should corporate intranet projects—or certain other projects—be excluded from traditional and rigorous financial analysis?

GROUP PROJECT

With three or four of your classmates, read the following case or a description of another system in this text. Prepare a report describing (on the basis of the information provided) some of the design specifications that might be appropriate for the system you select. Present your findings to the class.

Alternatively, examine carefully the Amdahl spreadsheet in the Window on Management box. Calculate two different financial ratios and discuss in a report to your class.

Digital Bites at the Chicago Board of Trade

The Chicago Board of Trade (CBOT) is the world's largest trading exchange for futures and options. The 149-year-old institution moved recently to its new $182 million trading building which can accommodate up to 8000 traders, brokers, and support staff. The new floor can also accommodate the simultaneous use of 20,000 electronic devices, including 12,000 computers, 6000 wired or wireless phones, and 2000 video devices. Underneath the floor, 27,000 miles of cable provide members flexibility to organize their voice and data traffic.

But much of this leading-edge trading floor will not be utilized to conduct trading electronically. In fact, the traders—who own the CBOT—have resisted electronic trading vociferously and successfully so far over the last decade. Brokers for the most part, however, are avoiding the use of the new electronic trading devices, and instead continue to rely on the open-outcry auction style of trading which demands that traders stand together in open pits to bark out buy and sell or-

ders. CBOT traders claim that only by being physically present can they "get a sense of the marketplace," see what's happening in other pits and markets, and, of course, make money for their own accounts.

Worldwide electronic trading in futures and options rose to 18 percent of all trading in 1997 (up from 8 percent in 1989). The growth in electronic trading has occurred because of several advantages: transaction costs are cheaper, execution times are faster, 24-hour trading is possible around the world's time zones, there is better access to external sources of information (such as news broadcasts), and of course there is no need for paper in an electronic trading environment. In the electronic model, office-bound brokers and traders use mathematical models and multiple digital information feeds (including prices, news, announcements, and other market developments) to make deals with other similar traders around the world. Although the London International Financial Futures and Options Exchange has

nearly ended open-outcry trading and moved entirely to electronic trading, the CBOT has devised ways to preserve the jobs of its members and maintain the open-outcry method in the electronic age. Here's how the CBOT reengineered the old outcry system.

As Figure 11.11 illustrates, all brokers have shifted over to a semiautomated form of open-outcry trading. The traders still rub shoulders with one another, but orders are at least entered into a computer before execution, an electronic clerk tracks the trade, and back-office computers can confirm the order to the broker who placed the order from a remote site. Coupled with huge overhead electronic bulletin boards, which flash news, the semiautomatic system has moved the CBOT into paperless trading. Overall, it takes about six seconds to execute a trade with the new system, which is about as fast as the London exchange.

The CBOT, however, still faces problems. It created a Project A experiment to do complete electronic

Buying Bushels in the Digital Age

Tomorrow, the Chicago Board of Trade wades slowly into the digital age. Instead of using hand signals and paper tickets to execute trades, members will have access to computers that do most of the job. But the old-fashioned way of making a transaction takes only about six seconds, so members with a clear line of sight to their clerks may be slow to change. Here is a comparison of the old system and the new one.

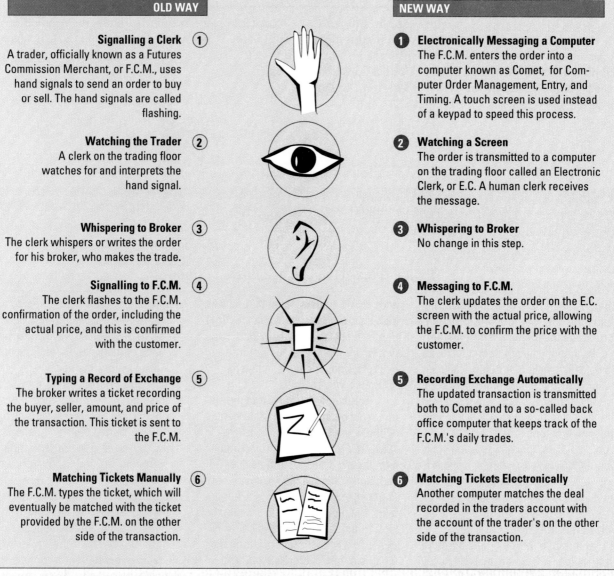

OLD WAY		NEW WAY

Signalling a Clerk (1)
A trader, officially known as a Futures Commission Merchant, or F.C.M., uses hand signals to send an order to buy or sell. The hand signals are called flashing.

Electronically Messaging a Computer (1)
The F.C.M. enters the order into a computer known as Comet, for Computer Order Management, Entry, and Timing. A touch screen is used instead of a keypad to speed this process.

Watching the Trader (2)
A clerk on the trading floor watches for and interprets the hand signal.

Watching a Screen (2)
The order is transmitted to a computer on the trading floor called an Electronic Clerk, or E.C. A human clerk receives the message.

Whispering to Broker (3)
The clerk whispers or writes the order for his broker, who makes the trade.

Whispering to Broker (3)
No change in this step.

Signalling to F.C.M. (4)
The clerk flashes to the F.C.M. confirmation of the order, including the actual price, and this is confirmed with the customer.

Messaging to F.C.M. (4)
The clerk updates the order on the E.C. screen with the actual price, allowing the F.C.M. to confirm the price with the customer.

Typing a Record of Exchange (5)
The broker writes a ticket recording the buyer, seller, amount, and price of the transaction. This ticket is sent to the F.C.M.

Recording Exchange Automatically (5)
The updated transaction is transmitted both to Comet and to a so-called back office computer that keeps track of the F.C.M.'s daily trades.

Matching Tickets Manually (6)
The F.C.M. types the ticket, which will eventually be matched with the ticket provided by the F.C.M. on the other side of the transaction.

Matching Tickets Electronically (6)
Another computer matches the deal recorded in the traders account with the account of the trader's on the other side of the transaction.

Source: From Barnaby J. Feder, "Face Lift at Board of Trade: High Tech, Say Hello to Primal Instinct," in The New York Times, *February 17, 1997. Copyright © 1997 The New York Times Co. Reprinted by permission.*

trading in afternoon and evening sessions. Younger brokers flocked to this experiment and trading tripled in the last year, thus creating a new electronic digital constituency at the CBOT in the process. A traditional open-outcry evening session, added to compete with 24-hour electronic trading around the world, is losing money as most skilled brokers are too wary to trade at night. But tradition dies slowly, and CBOT members refuse to stop open-outcry trading at night. As one trader noted, "Bringing computers to a venerable institution like CBOT is a political nightmare. Even replacing the open-outcry evening session with an all-electronic session is an emotional issue that flies in the face of some attitudes at the CBOT."

To implement truly paperless trading at CBOT, orders and records would have to be kept electronically from start to finish. The people in the pits would have to use handheld electronics tied into computer networks. Without such technology to cut costs, speed up recordkeeping, and provide clearer audit trails, the exchange might survive for decades but would continue to lose market share to computer-equipped office traders. ■

Sources: Aaron Lucchetti, "Some Traders Cry, but CBOT After Dark is High-Tech," *The Wall Street Journal*, February 27, 1997 and Barnaby J. Feder, "Face Lift at Board of Trade: High Tech, Say Hello to Primal Instinct," by *The New York Times Co.*, February 17, 1997.

Case Study Questions

1. Compare the process of executing a trade before and after the new CBOT system was installed. How efficient did the reengineered process become?

2. What management, organization, and technology issues had to be addressed in reengineering CBOT's trading process? How successfully were these issues addressed in the new system?

3. Do you think an all-electronic environment for trading will dominate world trading? What management strategies can you recommend to speed the transition to an all electronic environment?

REFERENCES

Ahituv, Niv, and Seev Neumann. "A Flexible Approach to Information System Development." *MIS Quarterly* (June 1984).

Alter, Steven, and Michael Ginzberg. "Managing Uncertainty in MIS Implementation." *Sloan Management Review* 20 (Fall 1978).

Bacon, C. James. "The Uses of Decision Criteria in Selecting Information Systems/Technology Investments." *MIS Quarterly* 16, no. 3 (September 1992).

Banker, Rajiv D., Robert J. Kauffman, and M. Adam Mahmood. *Strategic Information Technology Management: Perspectives on Organizational Growth and Competitive Advantage.* Harrisburg, PA: Idea Group Publishing (1993).

Barki, Henri, and Jon Hartwick. "User Participation, Conflict and Conflict Resolution: The Mediating Roles of Influence." *Information Systems Research* 5, no. 4 (December 1994).

Barua, Anitest, Sophie C.H. Lee, and Andrew B. Whinston, "The Calculus of Reengineering." *Information Systems Research* 7, no. 4 (December 1996).

Beath, Cynthia Mathis, and Wanda J. Orlikowski. "The Contradictory Structure of Systems Development Methodologies: Deconstructing the IS-User Relationship in Information Engineering." *Information Systems Research* 5, no. 4 (December 1994).

Bostrum, R. P., and J. S. Heinen. "MIS Problems and Failures: A Socio-Technical Perspective"; Part I: The Causes. *MIS Quarterly* 1 (September 1977); Part II: The Application of Socio-Technical Theory. *MIS Quarterly* 1 (December 1977).

Bullen, Christine, and John F. Rockart. *A Primer on Critical Success Factors.* Cambridge, MA: Center for Information Systems Research, Sloan School of Management (1981).

Buss, Martin D. J. "How to Rank Computer Projects." *Harvard Business Review* (January 1983).

Campbell, Ian. "The Intranet: Slashing the Cost of Business." *International Data Corporation*, 1997.

Cerveny, Robert P., Edward J. Garrity, and G. Lawrence Sanders. "A Problem-Solving Perspective on Systems Development." *Journal of Management Information Systems* 6, no. 4 (Spring 1990).

Davenport, Thomas H. *Process Innovation: Reengineering Work through Information Technology.* Boston, MA: Harvard Business School Press (1993).

Davenport, Thomas H., and James E. Short. "The New Industrial Engineering: Information Technology and Business Process Redesign." *Sloan Management Review* 31, no. 4 (Summer 1990).

Davidson, W. H. "Beyond Engineering: The Three Phases of Business Transformation." *IBM Systems Journal* 32, no. 1 (1993).

Davis, Gordon B. "Determining Management Information Needs: A Comparison of Methods." *MIS Quarterly* 1 (June 1977).

Davis, Gordon B. "Information Analysis for Information System Development." In *Systems Analysis and Design: A Foundation for the 1980s*, edited by W. W. Cotterman, J. D. Cougar, N. L. Enger, and F. Harold. New York: John Wiley (1981).

Davis, Gordon B. "Strategies for Information Requirements Determination." *IBM Systems Journal* 1 (1982).

Dennis, Alan R., Robert M. Daniels, Jr., Glenda Hayes, and Jay F. Nunamaker, Jr. "Methodology-Driven Use of Automated Support in Business Process Re-Engineering." *Journal of Management Information Systems* 10, no. 3 (Winter 1993–1994).

Doll, William J. "Avenues for Top Management Involvement in Successful MIS Development." *MIS Quarterly* (March 1985).

Dos Santos, Brian. "Justifying Investments in New Information Technologies." *Journal of Management Information Systems* 7, no. 4 (Spring 1991).

Ein-Dor, Philip, and Eli Segev. "Strategic Planning for Management Information Systems." *Management Science* 24, no. 15 (1978).

El Sawy, Omar, and Burt Nanus. "Toward the Design of Robust Information Systems." *Journal of Management Information Systems* 5, no. 4 (Spring 1989).

Emery, James C. *Cost/Benefit Analysis of Information Systems.* Chicago: Society for Management Information Systems Workshop Report No. 1 (1971).

Flatten, Per O., Donald J. McCubbrey, P. Declan O'Riordan, and Keith Burgess. *Foundations of Business Systems*, 2nd ed. Fort Worth, TX: Dryden Press (1992).

Franz, Charles, and Daniel Robey. "An Investigation of User-Led System Design: Rational and Political Perspectives." *Communications of the ACM* 27 (December 1984).

Gerlach, James H., and Feng-Yang Kuo. "Understanding Human-Computer Interaction for Information Systems Design." *MIS Quarterly* 15, no. 4 (December 1991).

Ginzberg, Michael J. "Improving MIS Project Selection." *Omega, Internal Journal of Management Science* 6, no. 1 (1979).

Ginzberg, Michael J. "The Impact of Organizational Characteristics on MIS Design and Implementation." Working paper CRIS 10, GBA 80-110. New York University Center for Research on Information Systems, Computer Applications and Information Systems Area (1980).

Goodhue, Dale L., Laurie J. Kirsch, Judith A. Quillard, and Michael D. Wybo. "Strategic Data Planning: Lessons from the Field." *MIS Quarterly* 16, no. 1 (March 1992).

Gould, John D., and Clayton Lewis. "Designing for Usability: Key Principles and What Designers Think." *Communications of the ACM* 28 (March 1985).

Grudnitski, Gary. "Eliciting Decision Makers' Information Requirements." *Journal of Management Information Systems* (Summer 1984).

Hammer, Michael. "Reengineering Work: Don't Automate, Obliterate." *Harvard Business Review* (July–August 1990).

Hammer, Michael, and James Champy. *Reengineering the Corporation*. New York: HarperCollins (1993).

Hammer, Michael, and Steven A. Stanton. *The Reengineering Revolution*. New York: HarperCollins (1995).

Harkness, Warren L., William J. Kettinger, and Albert H. Segars, "Sustaining Process Improvement in the Information Services Function: Lessons at the Bose Corporation." *MIS Quarterly* (September 1996).

Hitt, Lorin M., and Erik Brynjolfsson, "Productivity, Business Profitability, and Consumer Surplus: Three Different Measures of Information Technology Value." *MIS Quarterly* 20, no. 2 (June 1966).

Keen, Peter G. W. *The Process Edge*. Boston, MA: Harvard Business School Press (1997).

Keil, Mark. "Pulling the Plug: Software Project Management and the Problem of Project Escalation." *MIS Quarterly* (December 1995).

Keil, Mark, and Erran Carmel. "Customer-Developer Links in Software Development." *Communications of the ACM* 38, no. 5 (May 1995).

Keil, Mark, Richard Mixon, Timo Saarinen, and Virpi Tuunainen. "Understanding Runaway Information Technology Projects: Results from an International Research Program Based on Escalation Theory." *Journal of Management Information Systems* 11, no. 3 (Winter 1994–1995).

Kendall, Kenneth E., and Julie E. Kendall. *Systems Analysis and Design*, 4th ed. Englewood Cliffs, NJ: Prentice Hall (1998).

Kim, Chai, and Stu Westin. "Software Maintainability: Perceptions of EDP Professionals." *MIS Quarterly* (June 1988).

King, Julia. "Re-engineering Slammed." *Computerworld* (June 13, 1994).

King, William R. "Alternative Designs in Information System Development." *MIS Quarterly* (December 1982).

Kirsch, Laurie J. "The Management of Complex Tasks in Organizations: Controlling the Systems Development Process." *Organization Science* 7, no. 1 (January–February 1996).

Konsynski, Benn R. "Advances in Information System Design." *Journal of Management Information Systems* 1 (Winter 1984–1985).

Laudon, Kenneth C. "CIOs Beware: Very-Large-Scale Systems." New York: Center for Research on Information Systems, New York University Stern School of Business, working paper (1989).

Lientz, Bennett P., and E. Burton Swanson. *Software Maintenance Management*. Reading, MA: Addison-Wesley (1980).

Mahmood, Mo Adam, and Gary J. Mann. "Measuring the Organizational Impact of Information Technology Investment." *Journal of Management Information Systems* 10, no. 1 (Summer 1993).

Matlin, Gerald. "What Is the Value of Investment in Information Systems?" *MIS Quarterly* 13, no. 3 (September 1989).

McFarlan, F. Warren. "Portfolio Approach to Information Systems." *Harvard Business Review* (September–October 1981).

Moad, Jeff. "Does Reengineering Really Work?" *Datamation* (August 1, 1993).

Newman, Michael, and Rajiv Sabherwal, "Determinants of Commitment to Information Systems Development: A Longitudinal Investigation." *MIS Quarterly*, no. 1 (March 1996).

Nolan, Richard L. "Managing Information Systems by Committee." *Harvard Business Review* (July–August 1982).

Parker, M. M. "Enterprise Information Analysis: Cost-Benefit Analysis and the Data-Managed System." *IBM Systems Journal* 21 (1982).

Premkumar, G., and William R. King. "Organizational Characteristics and Information Systems Planning: An Empirical Study." *Information Systems Research* 5, no. 2 (June 1994).

Raghunathan, Bhanu, and T. S. Raghunathan. "Adaptation of a Planning System Success Model to Information Systems Planning." *Information Systems Research* 5, no. 3 (September 1994).

Reich, Blaize Horner, and Itzak Benbasat. "Measuring the Linkage Between Business and Information Technology Objectives." *MIS Quarterly* (March 1996).

Rockart, John F. "Chief Executives Define Their Own Data Needs." *Harvard Business Review* (March–April 1979).

Rockart, John F., and Michael E. Treacy. "The CEO Goes on Line." *Harvard Business Review* (January–February 1982).

"The Role of IT in Business Reengineering." *I/S Analyzer* 31, no. 8 (August 1993).

Shank, Michael E., Andrew C. Boynton, and Robert W. Zmud. "Critical Success Factor Analysis as a Methodology for MIS Planning." *MIS Quarterly* (June 1985).

Short, James E., and N. Venkatranan. "Beyond Business Process Redesign: Redefining Baxter's Business Network." *Sloan Management Review* (Fall 1992).

Tractinsky, Noam, and Sirka L. Jarvenpaa. "Information Systems Design Decisions in a Global Versus Domestic Context." *MIS Quarterly* (December 1995).

Venkatranan N. "Beyond Outsourcing: Managing IT Resources as a Value Center." *Sloan Management Review* (Spring 1997).

Vessey, Iris, and Sue Conger. "Learning to Specify Information Requirements: The Relationship between Application and Methodology." *Journal of Management Information Systems* 10, no. 2 (Fall 1993).

Vitalari, Nicholas P. "Knowledge as a Basis for Expertise in Systems Analysis: Empirical Study." *MIS Quarterly* (September 1985).

Wagner, Ina. "A Web of Fuzzy Problems: Confronting the Ethical Issues." *Communications of the ACM* 36, no. 4 (June 1993).

Wetherbe, James. "Executive Information Requirements: Getting It Right." *MIS Quarterly* 15, no. 1 (March 1991).

Zachman, J. A. "Business Systems Planning and Business Information Control Study: A Comparison." *IBM Systems Journal* 21 (1982).

Zmud, Robert W., William P. Anthony, and Ralph M. Stair, Jr. "The Use of Mental Imagery to Facilitate Information Identification in Requirements Analysis." *Journal of Management Information Systems* 9, no. 4 (Spring 1993).

CHAPTER 12

Alternative Systems-Building Methods

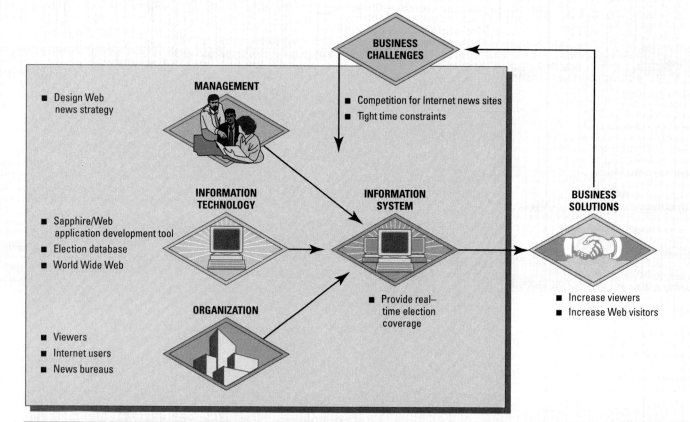

- Design Web news strategy

MANAGEMENT

BUSINESS CHALLENGES

- Competition for Internet news sites
- Tight time constraints

INFORMATION TECHNOLOGY

- Sapphire/Web application development tool
- Election database
- World Wide Web

INFORMATION SYSTEM

BUSINESS SOLUTIONS

- Increase viewers
- Increase Web visitors

ORGANIZATION

- Provide real–time election coverage

- Viewers
- Internet users
- News bureaus

CBS News Meets Its Web Site Deadline

CBS News found itself up against an unusually tight deadline when it decided to broadcast the 1996 election results on a Web site. There was no time for a drawn-out analysis and design cycle. Management wanted to provide Internet users with worldwide access to dynamically generated charts and graphs of election and exit poll results for local and national races. This real-time election data had to be linked to CBS News' legacy database so that Web pages would be updated with election information every one to three minutes. Time was running out.

With only one week to go before elections, CBS was still having trouble linking its database with election

LEARNING OBJECTIVES

After completing
this chapter, you will
be able to :

1. Distinguish between the various systems-building alternatives: the traditional systems life cycle, prototyping, application software packages, end-user development, and outsourcing.
2. Understand the strengths and limitations of each approach.
3. Describe the types of problems for which each approach is best suited.
4. Describe the solutions to the management problems created by these approaches.

data. Bluestone, Inc., the Mt. Laurel, New Jersey, Web development company that had worked on the CBS News Web site, was called in to troubleshoot. Bluestone decided to use its Sapphire/Web application-development tool to solve this problem. Sapphire/Web lets developers build Web applications and access databases with a minimum amount of programming using drag-and-drop methods. It also encourages reuse of existing application capabilities, allowing developers to focus on the unique aspects of each application. A team led by Ray Bentz, Bluestone's consulting manager, delivered a working prototype within 30 hours. Sapphire/Web created HTML pages dynamically from the election database while making use of existing subsystems at CBS.

At 5:00 P.M. on election day the CBS News site cut over to the new capabilities. Web users flooded the site, making several million hits within a few hours. The election system worked as planned. Web users were able to access only the election results they wanted as the vote counts came in. ■

Source: David Baum, "Web Goal: See It Now," *Information Week*, March 31, 1997.

Like CBS News, many organizations are examining alternative methods of building new information systems. Although they are designing and building some applications entirely on their own, they are also turning to rapid application development tools, software packages, external consultants, and other strategies to reduce time, cost, and inefficiency. The availability of alternative systems-building approaches raises the following management challenges.

1. **Determining the right systems development strategy to use.** Sometimes organizations encounter problems that cannot be addressed by any of the systems development strategies described in this chapter. For instance, a large complex system may have some unstructured features. The ultimate configuration of the system cannot be decided beforehand because information requirements or the appropriate technology is uncertain. Alternatively, a proposed system calls for major organizational and technical changes. In such instances, a firm may need to pursue a strategy of phased commitment in which systems projects are broken down into smaller portions and developed piece-by-piece in phases, or a firm may need to postpone the project altogether.

2. **Controlling information systems development outside the information systems department.** There may not be a way to establish standards and controls for end-user development that are appropriate. Standards and controls that are too restrictive may not only generate user resistance but may also stifle end-user innovation. If controls are too weak, the firm may encounter serious problems with data integrity and connectivity. It is not always possible to find the right balance.

3. **Selecting a systems development strategy that fits into the firm's information architecture and strategic plan.** End-user development, application software packages, or outsourcing may be appropriate short-term solutions, but they may not be in the best long-term interests of the firm. These solutions may result in disparate applications that cannot be easily integrated into the firm's overall information architecture. Organizations need to evaluate carefully the long-term impact of their applications-development strategies.

This chapter examines the use of prototyping, application software packages, end-user development, and outsourcing as systems-building alternatives to the traditional systems life cycle method of building an entire information system from scratch. There is no one approach that can be used for all situations and types of systems. Each of these approaches has advantages and disadvantages, and each provides managers with a range of choices. We describe and compare the various approaches so that managers know how to choose among them.

12.1   THE TRADITIONAL SYSTEMS LIFE CYCLE

The **systems life cycle** is the oldest method for building information systems and is still used today for complex medium or large systems projects. This methodology assumes that an information system has a life cycle similar to that of any living organism, with a beginning, a middle, and an end. The life cycle for an information system has six stages: project definition, systems study, design, programming, installation,

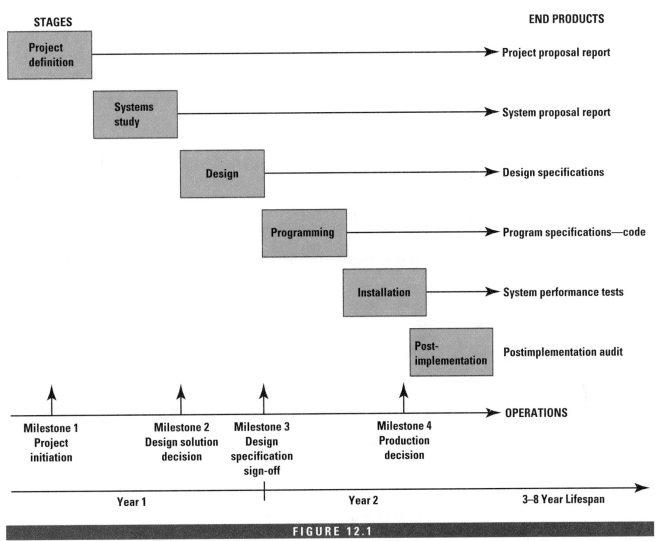

STAGES

Project definition
Systems study
Design
Programming
Installation
Post-implementation

END PRODUCTS

Project proposal report
System proposal report
Design specifications
Program specifications—code
System performance tests
Postimplementation audit

OPERATIONS

Milestone 1
Project initiation

Milestone 2
Design solution decision

Milestone 3
Design specification sign-off

Milestone 4
Production decision

Year 1   Year 2   3–8 Year Lifespan

FIGURE 12.1

The life cycle methodology for system development. The life cycle methodology divides systems development into six formal stages with specifics for milestones and end products at each stage. A typical medium-sized development project requires two years to deliver and has an expected life span of three to eight years.

and postimplementation. Figure 12.1 illustrates these stages. Each stage consists of basic activities that must be performed before the next stage can begin.

The life cycle methodology is a very formal approach to building systems. It partitions the systems development process into distinct stages and develops an information system sequentially, stage by stage. The life cycle methodology also has a very formal division of labor between end users and information systems specialists. Technical specialists such as systems analysts and programmers are responsible for much of the systems analysis, design, and implementation work; end users are limited to providing information requirements and reviewing the work of the technical staff. Formal sign-offs or agreements between end users and technical specialists are required as each stage is completed.

Figure 12.1 also shows the product or output of each stage of the life cycle that is the basis for such sign-offs. The project definition stage results in a proposal for the development of a new system. The systems study stage provides a detailed systems proposal report, outlining alternative solutions and establishing the feasibility of proposed solutions. The design stage results in a report on the design specifications for the system solution that is selected. The programming stage results in actual software code for the system. The installation stage outputs the results of tests

systems life cycle Traditional methodology for developing an information system that partitions the systems development process into six formal stages that must be completed sequentially with a very formal division of labor between end users and information systems specialists.

to assess the performance of the system. The postimplementation stage concludes with a postimplementation audit to measure the extent to which the new system has met its original objectives. We now describe the stages of the life cycle in detail.

Stages of the Systems Life Cycle

The **project definition** stage tries to answer the questions, "Why do we need a new system project?" and "What do we want to accomplish?" This stage determines whether the organization has a problem and whether that problem can be solved by building a new information system or by modifying an existing one. If a system project is mandated, this stage identifies its general objectives, specifies the scope of the project, and develops a project plan that can be shown to management.

The **systems study** stage analyzes the problems of existing systems (manual or automated) in detail, identifies objectives to be attained by a solution to these problems, and describes alternative solutions. The systems study stage examines the feasibility of each solution alternative for review by management. This stage tries to answer the questions, "What do the existing systems do?" "What are their strengths, weaknesses, trouble spots, and problems?" "What should a new or modified system do to solve these problems?" "What user information requirements must be met by the solution?" "What alternative solution options are feasible?" "What are their costs and benefits?"

Answering these questions requires extensive information gathering and research; sifting through documents, reports, and work papers produced by existing systems; observing how these systems work; polling users with questionnaires; and conducting interviews. All the information gathered during the systems study phase will be used to determine information system requirements. Finally, the systems study stage describes in detail the remaining life cycle activities and the tasks for each phase.

The **design** stage produces the logical and physical design specifications for the solution. Because the life cycle emphasizes formal specifications and paperwork, many of the design and documentation tools described in Chapter 13, such as data flow diagrams, structure charts, or system flowcharts, are likely to be utilized.

The **programming** stage translates the design specifications produced during the design stage into software program code. Systems analysts work with programmers to prepare specifications for each program in the system. These program specifications describe what each program will do, the type of programming language to be used, inputs and outputs, processing logic, processing schedules, and control statements such as those for sequencing input data. Programmers write customized program code typically using a conventional third-generation programming language such as COBOL or FORTRAN or a high-productivity fourth-generation language. Because large systems have many programs with hundreds of thousands of lines of program code, entire teams of programmers may be required.

The **installation** stage consists of the final steps to put the new or modified system into operation: testing, training, and conversion. The software is tested to make sure it performs properly from both a technical and a functional business standpoint. (More detail on testing can be found in Chapter 13.) Business and technical specialists are trained to use the new system. A formal conversion plan provides a detailed schedule of all the activities required to install the new system, and the old system is converted to the new one.

The **postimplementation** stage consists of using and evaluating the system after it is installed and is in production. It also includes updating the system to make improvements. Users and technical specialists will go through a formal postimplementation audit that determines how well the new system has met its original objectives and whether any revisions or modifications are required. After the system has been fine-tuned it will need to be maintained while it is in production to correct errors, meet requirements, or improve processing efficiency. Over time, the system may require so much maintenance to remain efficient and meet user objectives that it will

project definition Stage in the systems life cycle that determines whether the organization has a problem and whether the problem can be solved by launching a system project.

systems study Stage in the systems life cycle that analyzes the problems of existing systems, defines the objectives to be attained by a solution, and evaluates various solution alternatives.

design Stage in the systems life cycle that produces the logical and physical design specifications for the systems solution.

programming Stage in the systems life cycle that translates the design specifications produced during the design stage into software program code.

installation Systems life cycle stage consisting of testing, training, and conversion; the final steps required to put a system into operation.

postimplementation The final stage of the systems life cycle in which the system is used and evaluated while in production and is modified to make improvements or meet new requirements.

come to the end of its useful life span. Once the system's life cycle comes to an end, a completely new system is called for and the cycle may begin again.

Limitations of the Life Cycle Approach

The systems life cycle is still used for building large transaction processing systems (TPS) and management information systems (MIS) where requirements are highly structured and well defined. It will also remain appropriate for complex technical systems such as space launches, air traffic control, and refinery operations. Such applications need a rigorous and formal requirements analysis, predefined specifications, and tight controls over the systems-building process. However, the systems life cycle methodology has serious limitations and is not well suited for small desktop systems.

THE LIFE CYCLE APPROACH IS VERY RESOURCE INTENSIVE. A tremendous amount of time must be spent gathering information and preparing voluminous specification and sign-off documents. It may take years before a system is finally installed. If development time is too prolonged, the information requirements may change before the system is operational. The system that takes many years and dollars to build may be obsolete while it is still on the drawing board.

THE LIFE CYCLE APPROACH IS INFLEXIBLE AND INHIBITS CHANGE. The life cycle approach does allow for revisions to the system to ensure that requirements are met. Whenever requirements are incorrect or an error is encountered, the sequence of life cycle activities can be repeated. But volumes of additional documents must be generated, substantially increasing development time and costs. Because of the time and cost to repeat the sequence of life cycle activities, the methodology encourages freezing of specifications early in the development process. This means that changes cannot be made. Once users approve specification documents, the specifications are frozen. However, users traditionally have had trouble visualizing a final system from specification documents. In reality, they may need to see or use a system to make sure they know what it is they need or want. Because this is not possible with the life cycle approach, it is common for users to sign off on specification documents without fully comprehending their contents, only to learn during programming and testing that the specifications are incomplete or not what they had in mind. Proper specifications cannot always be captured the first time around, early enough in the life cycle when they are easy to change.

THE LIFE CYCLE METHOD IS ILL SUITED TO DECISION-ORIENTED APPLICATIONS. Decision making can be rather unstructured and fluid. Requirements constantly change or decisions may have no well-defined models or procedures. Decision makers often cannot specify their information needs in advance. They may need to experiment with concrete systems to clarify the kinds of decisions they wish to make. Formal specification of requirements may inhibit systems builders from exploring and discovering the problem structure (Fraser et al., 1994). This high level of uncertainty cannot be easily accommodated by the life cycle approach.

Some of these problems can be solved by the alternative strategies for building systems that are described in the remainder of this chapter.

12.2 PROTOTYPING

Prototyping consists of building an experimental system rapidly and inexpensively for end users to evaluate. By interacting with the prototype, users can get a better idea of their information requirements. The prototype endorsed by the users can be used as a template to create the final system.

The **prototype** is a working version of an information system or part of the system, but it is meant to be only a preliminary model. Once operational, the prototype

prototyping Process of building an experimental system quickly and inexpensively for demonstration and evaluation so that end users can better determine information requirements.

prototype Preliminary working version of an information system for demonstration and evaluation purposes.

iterative Process of repeating the steps to build a system over and over again.

will be further refined until it conforms precisely to users' requirements. For many applications, a prototype will be extended and enhanced many times before a final design is accepted. Once the design has been finalized, the prototype can be converted to a polished production system.

The process of building a preliminary design, trying it out, refining it, and trying again has been called an **iterative** process of systems development because the steps required to build a system can be repeated. We noted earlier that the traditional life cycle approach involved some measure of reworking and refinement. However, prototyping is more explicitly iterative than the conventional life cycle, and it actively promotes system design changes. It has been said that prototyping replaces unplanned rework with planned iteration, with each version more accurately reflecting users' requirements.

The prototype version will not have all the final touches of the complete system. Reports, sections of files, and input transactions may not be complete; processing may not be very efficient, but a working version of the system or part of the system will be available for users to evaluate. They can start interacting with the system, deciding what they like and dislike, what they want or do not want. Because most users cannot describe their requirements fully on paper, prototyping allows them to work with a system to determine exactly what they need. The methodology anticipates that they will change their minds; these changes can be incorporated easily and inexpensively during an early stage of development.

Prototyping is less formal than the life cycle method. Instead of generating detailed specifications and sign-off documents, prototyping quickly generates a working model of a system. Requirements are determined dynamically as the prototype is constructed. Systems analysis, design, and implementation all take place at the same time.

Steps in Prototyping

Figure 12.2 shows a four-step model of the prototyping process. The steps consist of the following:

1. *Identify the user's basic requirements.* The system designer (usually an information systems specialist) works with the user only long enough to capture the user's basic information needs.

2. *Develop a working prototype.* The system designer creates a working prototype quickly, most likely using the fourth-generation software tools described in Chapter 7 that speed application development. Some features of computer-aided software engineering (CASE) tools described in Chapter 13 can be used for prototyping, as can multimedia software tools that present users with interactive storyboards that sketch out the tasks of the proposed system for evaluation and modification (Madsen and Aiken, 1993). The prototype may only perform the most important functions of the proposed system, or it may consist of the entire system with a restricted file.

3. *Use the prototype.* The user is encouraged to work with the system to determine how well the prototype meets his or her needs and to make suggestions for improving the prototype.

4. *Revise and enhance the prototype.* The system builder notes all changes requested by the user and refines the prototype accordingly. After the prototype has been revised, the cycle returns to step 3. Steps 3 and 4 are repeated until the user is satisfied.

When no more iterations are required, the approved prototype then becomes an operational prototype that furnishes the final specifications for the application. Sometimes the prototype itself is adopted as the production version of the system. Prototyping is more rapid, iterative, and informal than the systems life cycle method has proven to be.

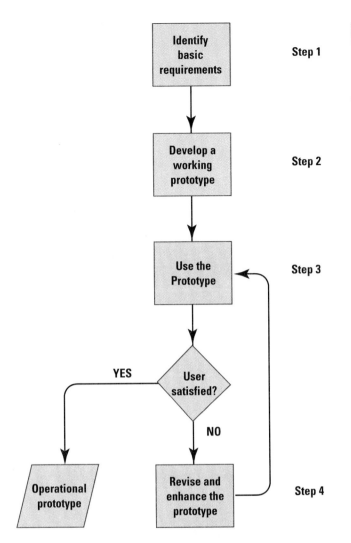

FIGURE 12.2

The prototyping process. The process of developing a prototype can be broken into four steps. Because a prototype can be developed quickly and inexpensively, the developers can go through several iterations, repeating steps 3 and 4, to refine and enhance the prototype before arriving at the final operational one.

Advantages and Disadvantages of Prototyping

Prototyping is most useful when there is some uncertainty about requirements or design solutions. Requirements may be difficult to specify in advance or they may change substantially as implementation progresses. This is particularly true of decision-oriented applications, where requirements tend to be very vague. Management realizes that better information is needed but is unsure of what this entails. For example, a major securities firm requests consolidated information to analyze the performance of its account executives. But what should the measures of performance be? Can the information be extracted from the personnel system alone, or must data from client billings also be incorporated? What items should be compared on reports? Will intermediate processing based on some form of statistical analysis be involved? For many decision-support applications such as this one, it is unlikely that requirements can be fully captured on the initial written specifications. The final system cannot be clearly visualized because managers cannot foresee how the system will work.

Prototyping is especially valuable for the design of the **end-user interface** of an information system (the part of the system with which end users interact, such as online display and data entry screens or reports). User needs and behavior are not entirely predictable (Gould and Lewis, 1985) and are strongly dependent on the context of the situation. The prototype enables users to react immediately to the parts of the system with which they will be dealing. Figure 12.3 illustrates the prototyping process for an on-line calendar for retail securities brokers. The first version of the

end-user interface The part of an information system through which the end user interacts with the system, such as on-line screens and commands.

FIGURE 12.3

Prototyping a portfolio management application. This figure illustrates the process of prototyping one screen for the Financial Manager, a client and portfolio management application for securities brokers. Figure 12.3A shows an early version of the on-line appointment screen. Based on the special needs of a client, Figure 12.3B has two enhancements: a "done" indicator to show whether the task has been completed and a "link" to reference information maintained by the system on the client with whom the broker has an appointment.

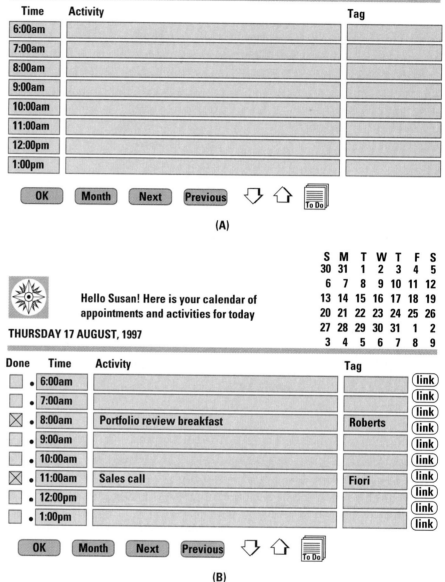

(A)

(B)

screen was built according to user-supplied specifications for a calendar to track appointments and activities. But when users actually worked with the calendar screen, they suggested adding labels for month and year to the screen and a box to indicate whether the appointment had been met or an activity completed. The brokers also found that they wanted to access information that was maintained in the system about clients with whom they had appointments. The system designer added a link enabling brokers to move directly from the calendar screen to the clients' records.

Prototyping encourages intense end-user involvement throughout the systems development life cycle. Users interact with a working system much earlier in the design process. As they react to and refine each version of the prototype, users become more intimately involved in the design effort (Cerveny et al., 1986). Prototyping is more likely to produce systems that fulfill user requirements, especially when it is used for decision-support applications. User satisfaction and morale are usually heightened because users can be presented with an actual working system, preliminary though it may be, in a very short time.

However, prototyping may not be appropriate for all applications. It should neither substitute for careful requirements analysis, structured design methodology, or thorough documentation, nor totally replace traditional development methods and tools. Both the method and the development tools currently used for prototyping have very real limitations.

Applications that are oriented to simple data manipulation and decision support are considered good candidates for prototyping. However, systems that are based on batch processing or that rely on heavy calculations and complex procedural logic are generally unsuitable for the prototyping process. Prototyping is better suited for smaller applications. Large systems must be subdivided so that prototypes can be built one part at a time (Alavi, 1984). Subdividing a large system may not be possible without a thorough requirements analysis using the conventional approach, because it may be hard to see at the outset how the different parts will affect each other.

Rapid prototyping can gloss over essential steps in systems development. Basic systems analysis and requirements analysis cannot be short-circuited. The appeal of an easily and rapidly developed prototype may encourage the development team to move too quickly toward a working model without capturing even a basic set of requirements. This may be especially problematic when a large system is under development. It may not be clear how prototypes can be created for a big system or parts of the system unless prototyping is preceded by a comprehensive and thorough requirements analysis.

The final steps to convert the prototype into a polished production system may not be carried out. Once finished, the prototype often becomes part of the final production system. If the prototype works reasonably well, management may not see the need for reprogramming and redesign. Some of these hastily constructed systems may be difficult to maintain and support in a regular production environment. Because prototypes are not carefully constructed, their technical performance may be very inefficient. They may not easily accommodate large quantities of data or a large number of users in a production environment.

Prototyped systems still need to be fully documented and tested, but often these steps are shortchanged. Because prototypes are constructed so effortlessly, managers may assume that testing can be handled by users on their own; any oversights in testing can be corrected later. Because the system is so easily changed, documentation may not be kept up to date. Prototyping as a development approach needs careful management and mechanisms for defining expectations, assigning resources, signaling problems, and measuring progress (Baskerville and Stage, 1996).

12.3 DEVELOPING SYSTEMS WITH APPLICATION SOFTWARE PACKAGES

Another alternative strategy is to develop an information system by purchasing an application software package. As introduced in Chapter 7, an **application software package** is a set of prewritten, precoded application software programs that are commercially available for sale or lease. Application software packages may range from a simple task (e.g., printing address labels from a database on a microcomputer) to over 400 program modules with 500,000 lines of code for a complex mainframe system. When an appropriate software package is available, it eliminates the need for writing software programs when an information system is developed and reduces the amount of design, testing, installation, and maintenance work as well. Table 12.1 provides examples of applications for which packages are commercially available.

Packages have flourished because organizations have many common information requirements for functions such as payroll, accounts receivable, general ledger,

application software package
Set of prewritten, precoded application software programs that are commercially available for sale or lease.

Table 12.1　Examples of Applications for Which Application Packages Are Available

Accounts payable	Human resources
Accounts receivable	Internet telephone
Architectural design	Inventory control
Banking systems	Job accounting
Bond and stock management	Job costing
Check processing	Library systems
Computer-aided design	Life insurance
Construction costing	Mailing labels
Data management systems	Mathematical/statistical modeling
Document imaging	Order entry
Electrical engineering	Payroll
Education	Performance measurement
E-mail	Process control
Financial control	Real estate management
Forecasting and modeling	Route scheduling
Forms design	Sales and distribution
General ledger	Savings systems
Government purchasing	Stock management
Graphics	Tax accounting
Health care	Web browser
Health insurance	Word processing
Hotel management	Work scheduling

or inventory control. For such universal functions with standard accounting practices, a generalized system will fulfill the requirements of many organizations. Therefore, it is not necessary for a company to write its own programs; the prewritten, predesigned, pretested software package can fulfill the requirements and can be substituted instead. Because the package vendor has already done most of the design, programming, and testing, the time frame and costs for developing a new system should be considerably reduced.

Packages are likely to be chosen as a development strategy under the following circumstances:

1. *Where functions are common to many companies.* For example, every company has a payroll system. Payroll systems typically perform the same functions: They calculate gross pay, net pay, deductions, and taxes. They also print paychecks and reports. Consequently, application software packages have been widely used for developing payroll systems.

2. *Where information systems resources for in-house development are in short supply.* With trained and experienced systems professionals in limited supply, many companies do not have staff that is either available or qualified to undertake extensive in-house development projects. Under such circumstances, packages may be the only way to enable a new system to be developed. Most companies also lack the budget to develop all their systems in house. Consequently, the most cost-effective development strategy is likely to involve an application software package.

3. *When desktop microcomputer applications are being developed for end users.* Numerous easy-to-use application packages have been developed for microcomputers and are the primary source of applications for desktop systems.

Advantages and Disadvantages of Software Packages

Application software packages can facilitate system design, testing, installation, maintenance support, and organizational acceptance of a new system. Packages also have serious limitations.

Advantages of Packages

Design activities may easily consume up to 50 percent or more of the development effort. Because design specifications, file structure, processing relationships, transactions, and reports have already been worked out by the package vendor, most of the design work has been accomplished in advance. Software package programs are usually pretested before they are marketed to eliminate major technical problems. Testing the installed package can be accomplished in a relatively shorter period. Many vendors supply sample test data and assist with the testing effort. Vendors also supply tools and assistance in installing major mainframe or minicomputer systems and provide much of the ongoing maintenance and support for the system. For systems such as human resources or payroll, the vendor is responsible for making changes to keep the system in compliance with changing government regulations. The vendor supplies periodic enhancements or updates; these are relatively easy for the client's in-house staff to apply.

Fewer internal information systems resources are necessary to support a package-based system. Because 50 to 80 percent of information systems budgets can be consumed by maintenance costs, the package solution is one way to cut these costs and free internal staff for other applications. The package vendor maintains a permanent support staff with expert knowledge of the specific application package. If a client's information systems personnel terminate or change jobs, the vendor remains a permanent source of expertise and help. System and user documentation are prewritten and kept current by the vendor.

An added benefit of packages is the way they can reduce some of the organizational bottlenecks in the systems development process. The need to work and rework design specifications is reduced because the package specifications are already fixed; users must accept them as is. External design work is often perceived as being superior to an in-house effort. The package offers a fresh start by a third party who is in a stronger position to take advantage of other companies' experiences and state-of-the-art technology. Management can be more easily convinced to support a new information system based on packaged software because major software costs appear to be fixed. Problems with the system can be attributed to the limitations of the package rather than to internal sources. Thus, the major contribution of packages may be their capacity to end major sources of organizational resistance to the systems development effort.

Disadvantages of Packages

Rarely noted are the disadvantages of packages, which can be considerable and even overwhelming for a complex system. Commercial software has not yet achieved the level of sophistication and technical quality needed to produce multipurpose packages that can do everything well that users want in a specific application. It is much easier to design and code software that performs one function very well than to create a system with numerous complex processing functions. For example, many human resources package vendors had to develop specialized packages for processing employee retirement benefits or applicant tracking because these functions were not handled well by the more comprehensive, multipurpose human resources packages.

customization The modification of a software package to
meet an organization's unique
requirements without destroying the integrity of the package
software.

Packages may not meet all of an organization's requirements. To maximize market appeal, packages are geared to the most common requirements of all organizations. But what happens if an organization has unique requirements that the package does not address? To varying degrees, package software developers anticipate
this problem by providing features for customization that do not alter the basic software. **Customization** features allow a software package to be modified to meet an organization's unique requirements without destroying the integrity of the package
software. For instance, the package may allocate parts of its files or databases to
maintain an organization's unique pieces of data. Some packages have a modular design that allows clients to select only the software functions with the processing they
need from an array of options. Packages can also be customized with user exits,
places in the package program code in which clients can exit from the processing performed by package programs to call software modules they write themselves for their
unique processing functions.

It is standard policy among vendors to refuse to support their products if changes
have been made that altered the package's source code. Some packages have been so
heavily modified with user source code changes that they are virtually unrecogniz-
able and unmaintainable.

So much modification and additional programming may be required to customize a package that implementation is seriously prolonged. Customization that is
allowed within the package framework may be so expensive and time consuming
that it eliminates many advantages of the package. Figure 12.4 shows how package
costs in relation to total implementation costs rise with the degree of customization.

The initial purchase price of the package can be deceptive because of these hidden implementation costs. An internal study by one company of the cost and time re-

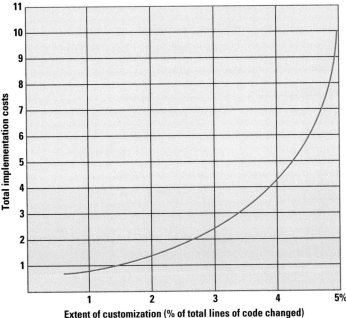

FIGURE 12.4

The effects of customizing a software package on total implementation costs. As the modifications to a software package rise, so does the cost of implementing the package. Sometimes the savings promised by the package are whittled away by excessive changes. As the number of lines of program code changed approaches 5 percent of the total lines in the package, the costs of implementation rise fivefold.

quired to install six major application packages (including manufacturing resources planning, the general ledger, accounts receivable, and fixed assets) showed that total implementation costs ranged from 1.5 times to 11 times the purchase price of the package. The ratio was highest for packages with many interfaces to other systems. The same study showed that management and support costs for the first year following installation averaged twice the original package purchase price.

Selecting Software Packages

Applications software packages must be thoroughly evaluated before they can be used as the foundation of a new information system. The most important evaluation criteria are the functions provided by the package, flexibility, user friendliness, hardware, software resources, database requirements, installation and maintenance effort, documentation, vendor quality, and cost.

The package evaluation process is often based on a **Request for Proposal (RFP)**, which is a detailed list of questions submitted to vendors of packaged software. The RFP is likely to include questions such as the following.

Package Evaluation Criteria

Functions Included   The functions included vary by application. But for the specific application, the following considerations are important:

- How many of the functional requirements will the package meet?
- Which functions can be supported only by modifying the package code?
- How extensive are the modifications required?
- Which functions cannot be supported at all by the package?
- How well will the package support future and current needs?

Flexibility

- How easy is the package to modify?
- What customization features are included?
- Is the vendor willing to modify the software for the client?

Request for Proposal (RFP)
Detailed list of questions submitted to vendors of packaged software or other computer services to determine if the vendor's product can meet the organization's specific requirements.

User Friendliness

- How easy is the package to use from a nontechnical standpoint?
- How much training is required to understand the package system?
- How much user control does the package allow?

Hardware and Software Resources

- On what model computer can the package run?
- What operating system is required?
- How much CPU and storage resources does the package utilize?
- How much computer time is needed to run the package?

Database/File Characteristics

- What kind of database/file structure does the package use?
- Do the standard fields in the package file correspond to the data elements specified by the application requirements?
- Does the database or file design support the client's processing and retrieval requirements?
- Are there provisions to add customized user fields for data elements that are not standard with the package?

Installation Effort

- How much change in procedures would the package necessitate?
- How difficult would it be to convert from the current system to the package system?

Maintenance

- Does the vendor supply updates or enhancements to the system?
- How easy are these changes to apply?
- What is the minimum internal staff necessary for ongoing maintenance and support (applications programmers, analysts, database specialists)?
- Is the source code clear, structured, and easy to maintain?

Documentation

- What kind of documentation (system and user) is provided with the package?
- Is it easy to understand and use?
- Is the documentation complete, or must the client write additional instructions to use the package?

Vendor Quality

- Is the vendor experienced in this application area?
- Does the vendor have a strong sales and financial record?
- Will the vendor continue to remain in business and support the package?
- What kinds of support facilities does the vendor provide for installation and maintenance (support staff, hotlines, training facilities, research and development staff)?
- Is the vendor responsive to clients' suggestions for improvements?
- Does the vendor have an active user group that meets regularly to exchange information on experiences with the package?

Cost

- What is the purchase or lease price of the basic software?
- What does the purchase price include (add-on modules; on-line, retrieval, or screen generator facilities; consulting time; training; installation support)?

- Is there a yearly maintenance fee and contract?
- What are the annual operating costs for the estimated volume of processing expected from the package?
- How much would it cost to tailor the package to the user's requirements and install it?

Packaged Software and the Systems Development Process

Table 12.2 illustrates how the use of an application software package affects the systems development process. Systems analysis will include a package evaluation effort that is usually accomplished by sending out requests for proposals (RFPs) to various package vendors. The responses to the RFP will be compared with the system requirements generated during this phase, and the software package that best meets these requirements will be selected. Design activities will focus on matching requirements to package features. Instead of tailoring the systems design specifications directly to user requirements, the design effort will consist of trying to mold user requirements to conform to the features of the package.

Table 12.2   Application Package Development Cycle
Systems Analysis
Identify problem
Identify user requirements
Identify solution alternatives
Identify package vendors
Evaluate package versus in-house development
Evaluate packages
Select package
Systems Design
Tailor user requirements to package features
Train technical staff on package
Prepare physical design
Customize package design
Redesign organizational procedures
Programming, Testing, and Conversion
Install package
Implement package modifications
Design program interfaces
Produce documentation
Convert to package system
Test the system
Train users on package
Production and Maintenance
Correct problems
Install updates or enhancements to package

One principal theme of this book has been the need to design systems that fit well with the organizations they serve. But when a package solution is selected, such a fit may be much harder to attain. The organization no longer has total control over the systems design process. Even with the most flexible and easily customized package, there are limits to the amount of tailoring allowed. Firms experienced in using packaged software for major business applications have noted that even the best packages cannot be expected to meet more than 70 percent of most organizations' requirements. But what about the remaining 30 percent? They will have to go unmet by the package or be satisfied by other means. If the package cannot adapt to the organization, the organization would have to adapt to the package and change its procedures. One far-reaching impact of software packages is their potential effect on organizational procedures. The kind of information a company can store for an application such as accounts receivable, for example, and the way in which the company organizes, classifies, inputs, and retrieves this information could be largely determined by the package it is using.

12.4   END-USER DEVELOPMENT

end-user development The development of information systems by end users with little or no formal assistance from technical specialists.

In many organizations, end users are developing a growing percentage of information systems with little or no formal assistance from technical specialists. This phenomenon is called **end-user development**. End-user development has been made possible by the special fourth-generation software tools introduced in Chapter 7. Even though these tools are less computer efficient than conventional programming languages, decreasing hardware costs have made them technically and economically feasible. With fourth-generation languages, graphics languages, and PC tools, end users can access data, create reports, create Web pages, and develop entire information systems on their own, without professional systems analysts or programmers. Alternatively, end users may rely on information systems specialists for technical support but may perform many systems development activities themselves that had previously been undertaken by the information systems department. Many of these end-user developed systems can be created much more rapidly than those using the traditional systems life cycle. Figure 12.5 illustrates the concept of end-user development.

End-User Computing Tools: Strengths and Limitations

End-user computing tools have increased the speed and ease with which certain kinds of applications can be created. Many fourth-generation tools have application design knowledge built in. For instance, when fourth-generation languages are linked to a database, the database has already been organized and defined. Many fourth-generation tools can easily access data, produce reports or graphics, or even generate simple data entry transactions.

Many organizations have reported appreciable gains in application-development productivity by using fourth-generation tools. Productivity enhancements based on conventional programming languages, such as structured programming (see Chapter 13), have resulted in a maximum productivity improvement of only 25 percent (Jones, 1979). In contrast, some studies of organizations developing applications with fourth-generation tools have reported productivity gains of 300 to 500 percent (Green, 1984–1985; Harel and McLean, 1985). Although these gains are not on the order of the magnitude of ten times initially claimed for fourth-generation methods, they are still very impressive. Finally, fourth-generation tools have new capabilities, such as graphics, spreadsheets, modeling, Web page design, and ad hoc information retrieval, that meet important business needs.

Unfortunately, fourth-generation tools still cannot replace conventional tools for some business applications because their capabilities remain limited. Most of these

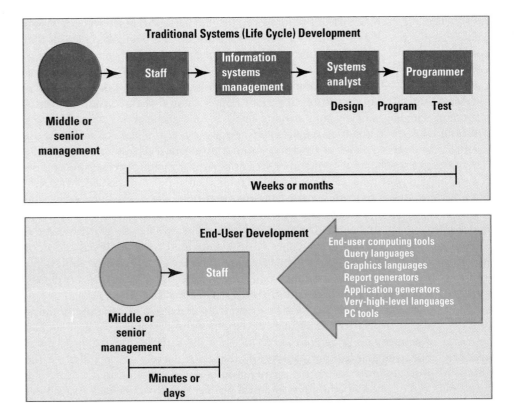

FIGURE 12.5

End user versus system life cycle development. End users can access computerized information directly or develop information systems with little or no formal technical assistance. On the whole, end-user developed systems can be completed more rapidly than those developed through the conventional systems life cycle.
Source: Adapted from James Martin, Applications Development without Programmers, © *1982, p. 119. Adapted by permission of Prentice Hall, Englewood Cliffs, NJ.*

tools were designed for simple systems manipulating small files. Fourth-generation processing is relatively inefficient, and the languages consume large amounts of computer resources. Most fourth-generation languages process individual transactions too slowly and at too high a cost to make these systems suitable for large transaction processing systems. Slow response time and computer performance degradation often

Features such as the easy-to-use graphical interface and natural language capabilities of Esperant's query software allow end users to develop some applications on their own.

result when large files are used. For instance, the New Jersey State Division of Motor Vehicles had a backlog of 1.4 million vehicle registration and ownership records that could not be processed quickly because the department had built its new vehicle registration system using Ideal, a fourth-generation tool. Part of the system had to be reprogrammed in COBOL to accommodate the high transaction volume.

Most fourth-generation tools are more nonprocedural than conventional programming languages. They thus cannot easily handle applications with extensive procedural logic and updating requirements. For example, applications such as those used for the design of nuclear reactors, optimal production scheduling, or tracking daily trades of stocks, bonds, and other securities require complex processing and often the matching of multiple files. Procedural logic must be used to specify processing functions, utility functions, error-handling conditions, specialized interfaces, and highly customized reporting. The logic for such functions is more easily expressed and controlled by conventional procedural code. The specification of procedural logic with fourth-generation languages is slow compared with the specification of nonprocedural functions, such as the generation of screens, reports, or graphics. For applications based on a large amount of specialized procedural logic, the overall productivity advantage of fourth-generation tools may be lost (Martin, 1982).

Fourth-generation tools make their greatest contribution to the programming and detail design aspects of the systems development process but have little impact on other systems-building activities. Productivity in systems analysis, procedural changes, conversion, and other aspects of design are largely independent of the choice of programming tool. Fourth-generation languages alone cannot overcome traditional organizational and infrastructural problems such as the lack of well-defined and well-integrated databases, standardized data management techniques, and integrated communications networks that typically hamper information system implementations (Grant, 1985).

Fourth-generation and rapid development tools are most likely to create systems rapidly and effectively when system builders lay the appropriate groundwork. The Window on Organizations illustrates a rapid development effort that was successful because the systems development team had carefully elicited information requirements, modeled business processes, and prepared the organization.

Management Benefits and Problems

Because end users can create many applications entirely on their own or with minimal assistance from information systems specialists, end-user–developed information systems can be created much more rapidly and informally than traditional systems. This situation has created both benefits and problems for organizations because these systems are outside the constraints of the formal information systems environment. Without question, end-user development provides many benefits to organizations. These include the following:

- *Improved requirements determination.* With users developing their own systems, there is less need to rely on information systems specialists for requirements analysis and less chance that user requirements will be misinterpreted by technical specialists.

- *User involvement and satisfaction.* Users are more likely to use and approve of systems they design and develop themselves.

- *Control of the systems development process by users.* Fourth-generation tools enable end users to take a more active role in the systems development process. Users can create entire applications themselves or with minimal assistance from information systems professionals. The tools often support prototyping, allowing end users to create experimental systems that can be revised quickly and inexpensively to meet changing requirements. With end users playing a much larger role in application creation, fourth-generation tools have helped

Credit Suisse Tackles Rapid Application Development

Like many financial institutions, Credit Suisse, an international investment bank with trading desks in major global locations, wanted to be able to measure the risk exposure of its various financial products. The problem was management wanted a global risk management system right away.

Credit Suisse already had a Value at Risk system implemented in its home office in Zurich, but its major branches had varying degrees of success implementing local risk management systems. What was missing was the ability to evaluate risk at a local and global level using identical analytics and procedures, so that management could easily compare "apples to apples."

The short-term goal was to provide a daily view of Value at Risk and to implement trading limits based on these risk figures. The long-term goal was to provide the ability to break down Value at Risk into its actual component trades and to educate traders on how different trading practices create different risk profiles. Could such a system be built quickly with minimal changes to Credit Suisse's front- and back-office trading systems and local accounting practices? And could it be built in six weeks to satisfy management?

The answer turned out to be yes. Credit Suisse's home office began by using Microsoft Excel spreadsheet software, Visual Basic, and internally developed libraries for advanced options analysis to develop an application called CS Risk Calculator. CS Risk Calculator accepted risk data from various back-office systems and then made correlations between major markets, various holding periods, and confidence levels. Major trading locations could not use this application, however, until it acquired sensitivities as input. Sensitivities demonstrate how a particular trade or position will react to a specific change in underlying market conditions. Although the Zurich systems provided this data, most international systems could not incorporate this requirement and apply it across products.

The company decided that a "least common denominator" approach should be taken. The final system should accept the most basic position data from front- and back-office systems and process these data in a manner identical to those in Zurich before feeding the CS Risk Calculator for further processing and presentation.

Before the first lines of program code were written, Credit Suisse provided the major international branches with an interface specification that included a record format for the various types of money market, foreign exchange, and precious metals positions and enough detail to ascertain risk. Each location was asked to produce the position data in the required format within a few weeks.

For its development team, Credit Suisse paired "financial engineers" who were specialists in risk analysis with an information systems specialist. The system was developed using the Windows NT operating system because most company branches had experience with NT and a number of rapid development aids were available, such as Visual Basic, Open Database Connectivity (ODBC), and Object Linking and Embedding (OLE). The information systems specialists on the team were highly experienced Windows NT developers. The development team visited seven locations around the world within two weeks.

All this preimplementation planning paid off. By supplying the branches with interface specifications and testing their results, development became largely a matter of travel planning. The international branches supplied risk figures. The team was able to quickly model the business process for risk management (see Figure 12.6). The project produced over 12,000 lines of code that were developed in Switzerland in just four weeks.

> **To Think About:** What management, organization, and technology factors enabled Credit Suisse to develop its risk management system so quickly?

Source: Daniel Globerson, "VaR On Demand," *Wall Street and Technology*, November 1996.

---

break down the barrier between users and programmers that has hampered conventional systems development.

- *Reduced application backlog.* User-developed systems can help relieve the application backlog by transferring the responsibility for development from the information systems staff to end users. The productivity of professional information systems specialists can also be boosted by the use of fourth-generation languages.

At the same time, end-user computing poses organizational risks because it occurs outside of traditional mechanisms for information systems management and control. Most organizations have not yet developed strategies to ensure that end-user–developed applications meet organizational objectives or meet quality assurance standards appropriate to their function. The most critical challenges posed by end-user computing are the following:

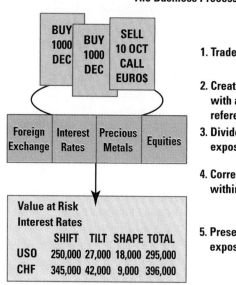

FIGURE 12.6

Credit Suisse's risk management process. This stripped-down view of risk management helped Credit Suisse speed development of its global risk management system.

Source: From Daniel Globerson, "VaR on Demand" in Wall Street and Technology, *Vol. 14, No. 11, November, 1996, page 86. Copyright © 1996 Miller Freeman, Inc.*

The Business Process

1. Trades or positions

2. Create sensitivities by revaluing with actual and historical reference data

3. Divide sensitivities into risk exposures

4. Correlate between major markets within risk exposures

5. Present Value at Risk across risk exposures and currencies

- *Insufficient review and analysis when user and analyst functions are no longer separate.* Without formal information systems analysts, user-developed applications have no independent outside review. There are no independent sources of problem analysis or alternative solutions. It may also be difficult for users to specify complete and comprehensive requirements.

- *Lack of proper quality assurance standards and controls.* User-developed systems are often created rapidly, without a formal development methodology. Although there are productivity and design advantages to be gained by avoiding conventional development methodologies, user-developed systems often lack appropriate standards, controls, and quality assurance procedures. There may not be adequate disciplines for testing and documentation. User-developed systems may lack controls for the completeness and validity of input and updating, audit trails, operating controls, project controls, and standards for stable interfaces among subsystems (Chapter 17 provides more detail on these controls).

- *Uncontrolled data.* With end-user computing tools, end-user groups outside the traditional information systems department can easily create their own applications and files. Many of these end-user–created files will contain the identical pieces of information, but each user application may update and define these data in a different way. Without formal data administration disciplines, it will become increasingly difficult to determine where data are located and to ensure that the same piece of information (such as product number or annual earnings) is used consistently throughout the organization (more details on the problem of uncontrolled data can be found in Chapter 8).

- *Proliferation of "private" information systems.* Users can use fourth-generation tools to create their own "private" information systems that are hidden from the rest of the organization. Such systems can conceal information from other groups. An undocumented private system cannot be easily turned over to another individual when the creator of that system leaves the job (Davis and Olson, 1985).

Managing End-User Development

How can organizations maximize the benefits of end-user applications development while keeping it under management control? A number of strategies have been suggested. Some have already been described in Chapter 10. Additional measures include using information centers and other training and support facilities for end-user development, establishing application development priorities, and establishing well-defined controls for end-user–developed applications.

Information Centers

One way both to facilitate and to manage end-user application development is to set up an information center. The **information center** is a special facility that provides training and support for end-user computing. Information centers feature hardware, software, and technical specialists that supply end users with tools, training, and expert advice so that they can create information system applications on their own. With information-center tools, users can create their own computer reports, spreadsheets, Web pages, or graphics, or extract data for decision making and analysis with minimal technical assistance. Information-center consultants are available to instruct users and to assist in the development of more complex applications.

Information-center staff members combine expert knowledge of the hardware, software, and databases for end-user applications with strong interpersonal communications skills. They function primarily as teachers and consultants to users, but they may also take part in the analysis, design, and programming of more complex applications.

Information centers provide many management benefits:

- They can help end users find tools and applications that will make them more productive.
- They prevent the creation of redundant applications.
- They promote data sharing and minimize integrity problems (see Chapter 8).
- They ensure that the applications developed by end users meet audit, data quality, and security standards.

Another important benefit of information centers is that they can help establish and enforce standards for hardware and software so that end users do not introduce many disparate and incompatible technologies into the firm (Fuller and Swanson, 1992). The information center generally works with the firm's information systems department to establish standards and guidelines for hardware and software acquisition. The information center will assist users only with hardware and software that have been approved by management.

information center A special facility within an organization that provides training and support for end-user computing.

Retail staff receive instruction in this New Jersey computer management class. An important function of information centers is to make end users feel proficient with computers.

Policies and Procedures to Manage End-User Computing

In addition to using information centers, managers can pursue other strategies to ensure that end-user computing serves larger organizational goals (see Alavi, Nelson, and Weiss, 1987–1988; Rockart and Flannery, 1983).

Managers can supplement central information centers with smaller distributed centers that provide training and computing tools tailored to the needs of different operating units and business functional areas. Managers can also make sure that the support provided is attuned to the needs of different types of end-user application developers. For instance, end users who use only high-level commands or simple query languages to access data will require different training and tools than end users who can actually write software programs and applications using fourth-generation tools (Rockart and Flannery, 1983). Training and support should also consider individual users' attitudes toward computers, educational levels, cognitive styles, and receptiveness to change (Harrison and Rainer, 1992).

Management should not allow end-user applications to be developed randomly. The organization should incorporate end-user systems into its strategic systems plans. The methodologies for establishing organization-wide information requirements that were described in Chapter 11 can help identify end-user applications with organization-wide benefits.

Management should also develop controls on end-user computing. These could include the following:

- Cost justification of end-user information system projects
- Hardware and software standards for user-developed applications
- Companywide standards for microcomputers, word processing software, database management systems, graphics software, and query and reporting tools
- Quality assurance reviews, specifying whether only individual end users or whether specialists from the information systems or internal audit departments should review end-user–developed information systems
- Controls for end-user–developed applications covering testing, documentation, accuracy, and completeness of input and update, backup, recovery, and supervision

These controls are described in detail in Chapter 17. The control process should flag critical applications that supply data to other important systems. Such systems warrant more rigorous standards. For instance, Northwest Airlines, Inc. established policies and guidelines for end-user development that ask users to classify the applications they develop according to critical nature so that the firm can take special steps to ensure data integrity and security (McMullen, 1992).

User-developed Web pages and Web sites have created a new area requiring management oversight and supervision. The Window on Management describes what some companies have done to control the proliferation of uncontrolled information on company Web sites.

12.5 OUTSOURCING INFORMATION SYSTEMS

outsourcing The practice of contracting computer center operations, telecommunications networks, or applications development to external vendors.

If a firm does not want to use its own internal resources to build and operate information systems, it can hire an external organization that specializes in providing these services to do the work. The process of turning over an organization's computer center operations, telecommunications networks, or applications development to external vendors of these services is called **outsourcing.**

Because information systems play such a large role in contemporary organizations, information technology now accounts for about half of most large firms' capital expenditures. In firms where the cost of information systems function has risen

Managing Web Site Content

It has become so easy to create Web pages with desktop software tools that many end users are publishing millions of Web pages. Nearly all new versions of the major PC word processing and spreadsheet software packages include some capability to output files in the Web's HTML (hypertext markup language) page formatting language. Users can save documents in HTML format, download HTML pages, or embed hypertext links in documents. The result? Corporate Web sites are becoming overcrowded and difficult to navigate.

Companies are appointing special Web coordinators or Web editors who are responsible for managing the internal content of intranets or the external content of Web sites. Their responsibilities are part editorial, part project management. They typically work in their companies' business units, such as the marketing department and they understand both business information needs and the demands of the Web. Whereas independent departments best understand their own content, the company's Web site needs some level of consistency in its message and navigational means. These gatekeepers are responsible for weaving together the news, information, and promotional messages of numerous contributors while ensuring that their material is accurate, timely, and within legal guidelines.

Millipore Corporation, a manufacturer of purification products for the microelectronics, biopharmaceutical, and analytical laboratory markets, dealt with this issue by apportioning pieces of its corporate Web site among its four product divisions and 31 offices. Millipore has an internal intranet, but uses an external Web site as a public place where company units can communicate directly with customers and with one another.

Most of the foreign office pages are primarily devoted to contact information posted by Millipore's corporate Webmaster. Bertil Thulin, managing director for Millipore's Swedish subsidiary, wanted his pages to speak directly to Swedish customers. He was not pleased with the results when Swedish content was filtered through the corporate Web team. Thulin now publishes directly to his portion of Millipore's corporate site. He added a few touches to give his pages a local feel, such as pictures and biographies of staff members, a Swedish user's club, and a map showing how to get to Millipore's office in Sandbyberg, Sweden.

As local interest groups such as Thulin's emerge, coordinating local and central needs becomes more of a challenge. Millipore has addressed this issue by assigning its corporate marketing and communications group responsibility for common standards for content and design and for gatekeeping. "Content" includes not only traditional text but graphics and even HTML links to other Web pages. A group of five "Web Uploaders" headed by the corporate Webmaster is responsible for ensuring that Web content is posted to the right areas.

> **To Think About:** *Should end users be allowed to create their own Web pages? Why or why not? What management issues need to be addressed when users publish on the Web?*

Source: Nina Berkson, "Authors, Authors Everywhere." *Webmaster,* January 1997.

---

rapidly, managers are seeking ways to control those costs and are treating information technology as a capital investment instead of an operating cost of the firm. One option for controlling these costs is to outsource.

Advantages and Disadvantages of Outsourcing

Outsourcing is becoming popular because some organizations perceive it as being more cost effective than it would be to maintain their own computer center and information systems staff. The provider of outsourcing services can benefit from economies of scale (the same knowledge, skills, and capacity can be shared with many different customers) and is likely to charge competitive prices for information systems services. Outsourcing allows a company with fluctuating needs for computer processing to pay for only what it uses rather than to build its own computer center to stand underutilized when there is no peak load. Some firms outsource because their internal information systems staff cannot keep pace with technological change. But not all organizations benefit from outsourcing, and the disadvantages of outsourcing can create serious problems for organizations if they are not well understood and managed.

Canadian Users Revolt

When Canadian government agencies needed to procure anything, including jet aircraft or pencils, they had to use a mainframe system built in the 1980s. Staff members hated it. Use of the system took weeks of training and supervision for users to master its 270 screens on dumb terminals. The word processor was incapable of handling certain procurement processes. The system could only support 85 percent of the workload for processing $8 billion (Canadian) in purchases for agencies nationwide.

The system also had a data quality problem. Users had to rekey information into the database. Because the data weren't captured automatically, reports often weren't filed until three months after a procurement. Errors sprung up. A new system was desperately needed.

The information systems department of the Canadian Public Works and Government Services ministry wanted to develop a new $200 million mainframe-based procurement application internally. But end users countered with a proposal for a client/server application that would be almost as powerful at 10 percent of the cost—approximately $25 million (Canadian). Development would be outsourced, with end users rather than the central IS department in charge of the project.

The Public Works department wanted the contractors to maximize the investment in software, meet all end-user requirements, and ensure that its own IS department could maintain and enhance the system after it was completed and in production. Because of ever-changing regulations and procedures, it was essential that the system be developed quickly. The system was completed in a little over a year and rolled out nationwide in December 1995.

The new client/server system, called Automated Buyers Environment (ABE), links 31 offices of the ministry's procurement arm and handles 100,000 requisitions per year (see Figure 12.7). It uses American Management Systems Inc. Procurement Desktop, a customizable software package with a proprietary workflow engine that supports all steps in the procurement process. Flexible workflow components route requests through the approval and rejection processes, automatically carrying forward information from the purchase request, vendor database, and quote sheet to the contract and to the database archives. This prevents data quality problems such as those encountered in the old mainframe system.

American Management Systems (AMS) was given the contract to do the work. It used Sybase's PowerBuilder to modify Procurement Desktop for bilingual (French and English) use. It also customized the software to work with the Canadian government's procurement forms to coordinate reporting and data sharing among offices around the country. ABE provides on-line support for the procurement process and access to the ministry's data warehouse of contract and vendor information. Templates for solicitations and contracts reduce word processing requirements, and tracking systems manage the procurement process from beginning to end. Supplier records can be searched using a number of different criteria. The system works with Microsoft Mail and Adobe Acrobat to enable Public Works procurement specialists and suppliers to share documents and exchange messages.

One of the largest problems appeared to be user training. It still takes four days for end users to learn the system. Many had no experience with Microsoft Windows. Some resented having to learn anything new at all and wanted to keep their old stand-alone systems.

> **To Think About:** What were the advantages and disadvantages of outsourcing the Automated Buyers Environment System? What management, organization, and technology issues had to be considered when making the outsourcing decision for this project?

Source: Bruce Caldwell, "User Revolt Pays Off in Canada," *InformationWeek,* November 18, 1996.

Advantages of Outsourcing

The most popular explanations for outsourcing are the following:

ECONOMY. Outsourcing vendors are specialists in the information systems services and technologies they provide. Through specialization and economies of scale, they can deliver the same service and value for less money than the cost of an internal organization (see the Window on Technology). For instance, American Standard reported saving $2 million annually from outsourcing its financial and payroll operations. Although some outsourcing vendors have promised annual reductions of 50 percent in information technology costs, savings of 15 to 30 percent are more common (Loh and Venkatraman, 1992).

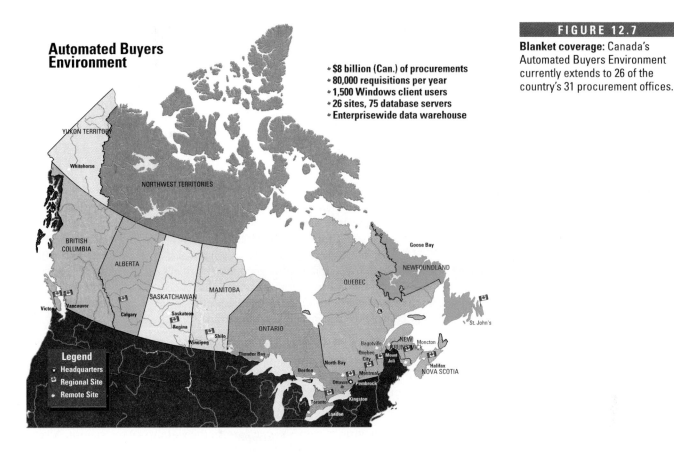

Automated Buyers Environment

- $8 billion (Can.) of procurements
- 80,000 requisitions per year
- 1,500 Windows client users
- 26 sites, 75 database servers
- Enterprisewide data warehouse

Legend
- ★ Headquarters
- ● Regional Site
- ♦ Remote Site

FIGURE 12.7

Blanket coverage: Canada's Automated Buyers Environment currently extends to 26 of the country's 31 procurement offices.

SERVICE QUALITY.   Because outsourcing vendors will lose their clients if the service is unsatisfactory, companies often have more leverage over external vendors than over their own employees. The firm that outsources may be able to obtain a higher level of service from vendors for the same or lower costs.

PREDICTABILITY.   An outsourcing contract with a fixed price for a specified level of service reduces uncertainty of costs.

FLEXIBILITY.   Business growth can be accommodated without making major changes in the organization's information systems infrastructure. As information technology permeates the entire value chain of a business, outsourcing may provide superior control of the business because its costs and capabilities can be adjusted to meet changing needs (Loh and Venkatraman, Summer 1992).

MAKING FIXED COSTS VARIABLE.   Some outsourcing agreements, such as running payroll, are based on the price per unit of work done (such as the cost to process each check). Many outsourcers will take into account variations in transaction processing volumes likely to occur during the year or over the course of the outsourcing agreement. Clients only need to pay for the amount of services they consume, as opposed to paying a fixed cost to maintain internal systems that are not fully utilized.

FREEING UP HUMAN RESOURCES FOR OTHER PROJECTS.   Scarce and costly talented individuals within an organization can refocus on activities with higher value and payback than they would find in running a technology factory.

FREEING UP FINANCIAL CAPITAL.   Some agreements with outsourcers include the sale for cash of the outsourced firm's technology capital assets to the vendor. For instance, when Blue Cross and Blue Shield of Massachusetts outsourced its computer operations and systems development to Electronic Data Systems (EDS), EDS paid

Blue Cross with cash and a promissory note for its computer center and other computer equipment (Caldwell, 1992).

Disadvantages of Outsourcing

Not all organizations obtain these benefits from outsourcing, and the disadvantages of outsourcing can create serious problems for organizations if they are not well-understood and managed (Earl, 1996). There are dangers in placing the information systems functions outside the organization. Outsourcing can create serious problems such as loss of control, vulnerability of strategic information, and dependence on the fortunes of an external firm.

LOSS OF CONTROL. When a firm farms out the responsibility for developing and operating its information systems to another organization, it can lose control over its information systems function. Outsourcing places the vendor in an advantageous position in which the client has to accept whatever the vendor does and whatever fees the vendor charges. If a vendor becomes the firm's only alternative for running and developing its information systems, the client must accept whatever technologies the vendor provides. This dependency could eventually result in higher costs or loss of control over technological direction.

VULNERABILITY OF STRATEGIC INFORMATION. Trade secrets or proprietary information may leak out to competitors because a firm's information systems are being run or developed by outsiders. This could be especially harmful if a firm allows an outsourcer to develop or to operate applications that give it some type of competitive advantage.

DEPENDENCY. The firm becomes dependent on the viability of the vendor. A vendor with financial problems or deteriorating services may create severe problems for its clients.

When to Use Outsourcing

Because outsourcing has both benefits and liabilities and is not meant for all organizations or all situations, managers should assess the role of information systems in their organization before making an outsourcing decision. There are a number of circumstances under which outsourcing makes a great deal of sense:

■ *When there is only a limited opportunity for the firm to distinguish itself competitively through a particular information systems application or series of applications.* For instance, both the development and operation of payroll systems are frequently outsourced to free the information systems staff to concentrate on activities with a higher potential payoff, such as customer-service or manufacturing systems. Figure 12.8 illustrates a matrix that could help firms determine appropriate applications for outsourcing. Applications such as payroll or cafeteria accounting, for which the firm obtains little competitive advantage from excellence, are strong candidates for outsourcing. If carefully developed, applications such as airline reservations or plant scheduling could provide a firm with a distinct advantage over competitors. The firm could lose profits, customers, or market share if such systems have problems.
Applications in which the rewards for excellence are high and the penalties for failure are high should probably be developed and operated internally.

Companies may also continue to develop applications internally while outsourcing their computer center operations when they do not need to distinguish themselves competitively by performing their computer processing on-site. For instance, the Eastman Kodak Co., a pioneer in outsourcing, initially farmed out its information systems operations—including mainframe processing, telecommunica-

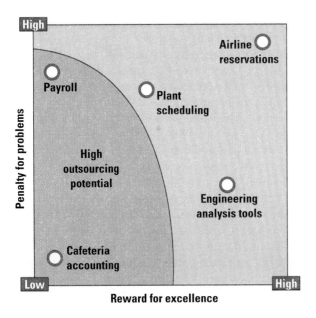

FIGURE 12.8

Rewards and penalties of outsourcing. This reward/penalty matrix shows that those applications with low reward for excellence and low penalty for problems are good candidates for outsourcing.

Source: Copyright September 2, 1991 by Computerworld, Inc., Framingham, MA 01701. Reprinted from Computerworld.

tions, and personal computer support—to IBM and DEC. It kept application development and support in house because it felt that these activities had competitive value (Clermont 1991).

■ *When the predictability of uninterrupted information systems service is not important.* For instance, airline reservations or catalogue shopping systems are too "critical" to be trusted outside. If these systems failed to operate for a few days or even a few hours, they could close down the business (see Chapter 2). On the other hand, a system to process employee insurance claims could be more easily outsourced because uninterrupted processing of claims is not critical to the survival of most firms.

■ *When outsourcing does not strip the company of the technical know-how required for future information systems innovation.* If a firm outsources some of its systems but maintains its own internal information systems staff, it should ensure that its staff remains technically up to date and has the expertise to develop future applications.

■ *When the firm's existing information systems capabilities are limited, ineffective, or technically inferior.* Some organizations use outsourcers as an easy way to revamp their information systems technology. For instance, they might use an outsourcer to help them make the transition from traditional mainframe-based computing to a client/server—distributed computing environment. On the other hand, outsourcing new technology projects can be risky because the organization may lack the expertise to negotiate a sound contract and may remain too dependent on the vendor after implementation (Lacity, Willcocks, and Feeny, 1996).

Despite the conventional wisdom on when to outsource, companies sometimes do outsource strategic functions. In any case, if systems development and the information systems function are well managed and productive, there may not be much immediate benefit that can be provided by an external vendor.

Managing Outsourcing

To obtain value from outsourcing, organizations need to make sure the process is properly managed. With sound business analysis and an understanding of outsourcing's strengths and limitations, managers can identify the most appropriate applications to outsource and develop a workable outsourcing plan.

Segmenting the firm's range of information systems activities into pieces that potentially can be outsourced makes the problem more manageable and also helps companies match an outsourcer with the appropriate job. Noncritical applications are usually the most appropriate candidates for outsourcing. Firms should identify mission-critical applications and mission-critical human resources required to develop and manage these applications. This would allow the firm to retain its most highly skilled people and focus all of its efforts on the most mission-critical applications development (Roche, 1992). Setting technology strategy is one area that companies should not abdicate to outsourcers. This strategic task is best kept in house.

Ideally, the firm should have a working relationship of trust with an outsourcing vendor. The vendor should understand the client's business and work with the client as a partner, adapting agreements to meet the client's changing needs. For instance, defense contractor General Dynamics Corporation in Falls Church, Virginia, chose Computer Sciences Corp. (CSC) of El Segundo, California, to take over its data center management, network operations, applications development, and other information services. General Dynamics signed a 10-year contract worth $3 billion with CSC because CSC knew the defense business; it understood the regulations and the critical success factors for the industry. General Dynamics would have had to teach other contractors the rules of the defense environment before they could do the work (Livingston, 1992).

Firms should clearly understand the advantages provided by the vendor and what they will have to give up to obtain these advantages. For lower operating costs, can the client live with a five-second response time during peak hours or next-day repair of PCs in remote offices?

Organizations must not abdicate management responsibility by outsourcing. They need to manage the outsourcer as they would manage their own internal information systems department by setting priorities, ensuring that the right people are brought in, and guaranteeing that information systems are running smoothly. They should establish criteria for evaluating the outsourcing vendor that include performance expectations and measurement methods for response time, transaction volumes, security, disaster recovery, backup in the event of a catastrophe (see Chapter 17), processing requirements of new applications, and distributed processing on PCs, workstations, and LANs.

Firms should design outsourcing contracts carefully so that the outsourcing services can be adjusted if the nature of the business changes. For instance, Zale Corp. signed a seven-year outsourcing agreement with SHL Systemhouse Inc., an Ottawa-based unit of MCI, to acquire more control over the outsourcing relationship. The contract acknowledges that part of SHL's earnings will depend on Zales' store performance (Caldwell, 1996). Organizations should constantly reevaluate their vendors and decisions to outsource in light of changing business conditions and the growing pool of available outsourcing services (Lacity, Willcocks, and Feeny, 1995).

Table 12.3 compares the advantages and disadvantages of each of the systems-building alternatives described in this chapter.

Table 12.3   Comparison of Systems Development Approaches

Approach	Features	Advantages	Disadvantages
Systems life cycle	Sequential step-by-step formal process Written specifications and approvals Limited role of users	Necessary for large complex systems and projects	Slow and expensive Discourages changes Massive paperwork to manage
Prototyping	Requirements specified dynamically with experimental system Rapid, informal, and iterative process Users continually interact with the prototype	Rapid and inexpensive Useful when requirements uncertain or when end-user interface is important Promotes user participation	Inappropriate for large, complex systems Can gloss over steps in analysis, documentation, and testing
Application software package	Commercial software eliminates need for internally developed software programs	Design, programming, installation, and maintenance work reduced Can save time and cost when developing common business applications Reduces need for internal information systems resources	May not meet organization's unique requirements May not perform many business functions well Customization raises development costs
End-user development	Systems created by end users using fourth-generation software tools Rapid and informal Minimal role of information systems specialists	Users control systems building Saves development time and cost Reduces application backlog	Can lead to proliferation of uncontrolled information systems Systems do not always meet quality assurance standards
Outsourcing	Systems built and sometimes operated by external vendor	Can reduce or control costs Can produce systems when internal resources not available or technically deficient	Loss of control over the information systems function Dependence on the technical direction and prosperity of external vendors

MANAGEMENT WRAP-UP

Selection of a systems-building approach can have a large impact on the time, cost, and end product of systems-building efforts. Managers should be aware of the strengths and weaknesses of each systems-building approach and the types of problems for which each is best suited.

MANAGEMENT

Organizational needs should drive the selection of a systems-building approach. The impact of application software packages and outsourcing should be carefully evaluated before they are selected because these approaches give organizations less control over the systems-building process.

ORGANIZATION

Various technologies and methodologies are available to support the systems-building process. Key technology decisions should be based on the organization's familiarity with the methodology or technology and its compatibility with the organization's information requirements and information architecture.

TECHNOLOGY

For Discussion: Why is selecting a systems development approach an important business decision? Who should participate in the selection process?

SUMMARY

1. Distinguish between the various systems-building alternatives: the traditional systems life cycle, prototyping, application software packages, end-user development, and outsourcing. The traditional systems life cycle—the oldest method for building systems—breaks the development of an information system into six formal stages: project definition, systems study, design, programming, installation, and postimplementation. The stages must proceed sequentially, have defined outputs, and require formal approval before the next stage can commence.

Prototyping consists of building an experimental system rapidly and inexpensively for end users to interact with and evaluate. The prototype is refined and enhanced until users are satisfied that it captures all their requirements and can be used as a template to create the final system.

Developing an information system using an application software package eliminates the need for writing software programs when developing an information system. Using a software package reduces the amount of design, testing, installation, and maintenance work required to build a system.

End-user development is the development of information systems by end users, either alone or with minimal assistance from information systems specialists. End-user developed systems can be created rapidly and informally using fourth-generation software tools.

Outsourcing consists of using an external vendor to build (or operate) a firm's information systems. The system may be custom built or may use a software package. In either case, the work is done by the vendor rather than by the organization's internal information systems staff.

2. Understand the strengths and limitations of each approach. The traditional systems life cycle is still useful for large projects that need formal specifications and tight management control over each stage of systems building. However, the traditional method is very rigid and costly for developing a system, and is not well suited for unstructured, decision-oriented applications in which requirements cannot be immediately visualized.

Prototyping encourages end-user involvement in systems development and iteration of design until specifications are captured accurately. The rapid creation of prototypes can result in systems that have not been completely tested or documented or that are technically inadequate for a production environment.

Application software packages are helpful if a firm does not have the internal information systems staff or financial resources to custom-develop a system. To meet an organization's unique requirements, packages may require extensive modifications that can substantially raise development costs. A package may not be a feasible solution if implementation necessitates extensive customization and changes in the organization's procedures.

The primary benefits of end-user development are improved requirements determination, reduced application backlog, and increased end-user participation in and control of the systems development process. However, end-user development, in conjunction with distributed computing, has introduced new organizational risks by propagating information systems and data resources that do not necessarily meet quality assurance standards and that are not easily controlled by traditional means.

Outsourcing can save application development costs or allow firms to develop applications without an internal information systems staff, but it can also make firms lose control over their information systems and make them too dependent on external vendors.

3. Describe the types of problems for which each approach is best suited. The traditional systems life cycle is appropriate for large transaction processing systems (TPS) and management information systems (MIS) with complex processing and requirements that need rigorous and formal requirements analyses, predefined specifications, and tight controls over the systems-building process.

Prototyping is useful for simple applications in which requirements are vague or unstructured or for designing the end-user interface portions of large complex systems. Prototyping is not suitable for designing all aspects of large systems that require batch processing or complex processing logic.

Software packages are best suited for applications with requirements common to many organizations and a limited number of functions that can be supported by commercial software.

The best candidates for end-user development are applications with relatively simple processing logic and small files that can be developed easily with fourth-generation tools.

Outsourcing is appropriate for applications that are not sources of competitive advantage or that require technical expertise not provided by the firm.

4. Describe the solutions to the management problems created by these approaches. Organizations can overcome some of the limitations of using software packages by performing a thorough requirements analysis and using rigorous package selection procedures to determine the extent to which a package will satisfy its requirements. The organization can customize the package or modify its procedures to ensure a better fit with the package.

Information centers help promote and control end-user development. They provide end users with appropriate hardware, software, and technical expertise to create their own applications and encourage adherence to application-development standards. Organizations can also develop new policies and procedures concerning systems-development standards, training, data administration, and controls to manage end-user computing effectively.

Organizations can benefit from outsourcing by outsourcing only part of their information systems, by thoroughly understanding what information systems functions are appropriate to outsource, by designing and managing outsourcing contracts carefully, and by trying to build a working partnership with the outsourcing vendor.

KEY TERMS

Systems life cycle	Installation	End-user interface	End-user development
Project definition	Postimplementation	Application software	Information center
Systems study	Prototyping	package	Outsourcing
Design	Prototype	Customization	
Programming	Iterative	Request for Proposal (RFP)	

REVIEW QUESTIONS

1. What is the traditional systems life cycle? What are its characteristics?

2. Describe each step in the systems life cycle.

3. What are the advantages and disadvantages of building an information system using the traditional systems life cycle?

4. What do we mean by information system prototyping?

5. Under what conditions is prototyping a useful systems development approach? What kinds of problems can it help solve?

6. Describe five ways in which prototyping differs from the traditional systems life cycle.

7. List and describe the steps in the prototyping process.

8. List and describe four limitations of prototyping.

9. What is an application software package? Under what circumstances should packages be used to build information systems?

10. What are the principal advantages of using application software packages to develop an information system? Why do packages have a strong appeal to management?

11. List and describe several disadvantages of software packages.

12. What is package customization? Under what circumstances can it become a problem when implementing an application software package?

13. List the main criteria for evaluating an application software package.

14. How is the systems development process altered when an application software package is being considered and selected?

15. What do we mean by end-user development?

16. What are the advantages and disadvantages of end-user development? For what kinds of problems is it suited?

17. What is an information center? How can information centers solve some of the management problems created by end-user development?

18. Name some policies and procedures for managing end-user development.

19. What is outsourcing? Under what circumstances should it be used for building information systems?

20. What are the advantages and disadvantages of outsourcing?

21. Describe some solutions to the management problems created by outsourcing.

GROUP PROJECT

With a group of your classmates, obtain product information or attend a demonstration for a PC application software package such as DacEasy Accounting/Payroll, Quicken, Peachtree Business Internet Suite, or Microsoft Money. Write an analysis of the strengths and limitations of the package you select. Present your findings to the class.

Can a German Software Giant Provide Client/Server Solutions?

SAP A.G., based in Walldorf, Germany, is Europe's largest vendor of software running on IBM mainframe computers and is an emerging leader in software packages for client/server environments. It currently controls $5.2 billion of the world's client/server enterprise applications business and has mushroomed into the world's fourth largest software company. Among its clients are the Dow Chemical Company, E.I. du Pont de Nemours & Company, Chevron Corporation, Microsoft Corporation, Apple Computer, IBM, Intel, and the Exxon Corporation.

SAP's R/3 software package for client/server environments automates a wide range of business processes in human resources, plant management, and manufacturing. The software modules are integrated, so that they can automatically share data between them and they have their own common database management system. The programs come in 12 foreign languages. Specific versions are tailored to accommodate different currencies, tax laws, and accounting practices. Managers can generate reports in their own local languages and currencies yet have the same reports generated in the language and currency that are used as the corporate standard by top management.

Businesses appreciate the multinational flavor of the software, especially its ability to overcome language and currency barriers fluently and to connect divisions and operating units spread around the world. Marion Merrel Dow Inc. is using SAP software for its financial, sales, and service departments because it believes that no other available packages can handle its global business needs. Nearly 7000 companies use R/3.

Despite being a standard software package, SAP software can be customized by approximately 10 percent. The software can be customized to multinational currencies and accounting practices. SAP makes this flexibility one of its key selling points. As another selling point, SAP promotes the package as a platform for business reengineering.

R/3 is an integrated, client/server, distributed system with a graphical user interface. It can operate on a wide range of computers, including UNIX-based machines, PowerPC-enabled IBM AS/400 minicomputers, and other servers. The back-end server and front-end client portions of R/3 can run on a number of different operating systems, including five variations of UNIX, Digital Equipment Corporation's VAX/VMS operating system, and Hewlett-Packard's MPE operating system. Versions for OS/2, Windows NT, and other operating systems are also being developed.

The R/3 package includes integrated financial accounting, production planning, sales and distribution, cost-center accounting, order-costing, materials management, human resources, quality assurance, fixed assets management, plant maintenance, and project planning applications. Users do not have to shut down one application to move to another; they can simply click on a menu choice. R/3 also provides word processing, filing systems, e-mail, and other office support functions.

R/3 can be configured to run on a single hardware platform, or it can be partitioned to run on separate machines (such as in whatever combination users choose to minimize network traffic and place data where users need it the most). For instance, a firm could put the data used most frequently by its accounting department on a file server located close to the accounting department to minimize network traffic. A central data dictionary keeps track of data and its location to maintain the integrity of distributed data. SAP will sell clients a blueprint of R/3's information, data, and function models and software tools to facilitate custom development and integration of existing applications into R/3.

The management of SAP America, Inc. (the Lester, Pennsylvania, subsidiary of SAP A.G.), thinks that the most important feature of R/3 may be the way it helps organizations automate and even redesign their business processes. By adopting the system design offered by the package, companies can evaluate and streamline their business processes. The promise of reengineering was what initially attracted the Eastman Kodak Company to SAP software. Kodak launched a pilot project in 1991 that installed SAP programs to redefine the job of order taking. The SAP package lets order takers make immediate decisions about granting customers credit and lets them access production data online so that they can tell customers exactly when their orders will be available for shipment. The project resulted in a 70 percent reduction in the amount of time it took to deliver products; response time to customers was also cut in half. These results prompted Kodak to use SAP software as the global architecture for all its core systems.

The intricate and sophisticated features of SAP software deeply affect the infrastructure of a corporation. Installing SAP's fully integrated suite of software modules with all the business alterations required is a complex process with many interdependent options which can overwhelm smaller firms lacking the resources of top-tier large corporations.

Because R/3 is so complicated, it is usually less expensive to change organizational procedures than to change the way the system works. Many companies installing R/3 experience intense organizational upheaval.

Owens-Corning Fiberglass Corporation adopted R/3 as part of its effort to double sales of its building products worldwide. Until recently, customers had to call an Owens-Corning shingle plant for a load of shingles, and place more calls to order insulation or siding. Each plant had its own product lines, pricing schedules, and trucking carriers. Factories limped along with decades-old PCs. The company operated like a collection of autonomous fiefdoms. Glen Hiner, the company's CEO, adopted R/3 as an engine for broad company overhaul.

R/3 demanded that the entire corporation adopt a single product list and a single price list. Staff members initially resisted. The company grossly underestimated the cost of training employees to use the new computers and software. Planners expected to devote 6 percent of the total project budget to training, whereas actual training costs are expected to be closer to 13 percent.

On the other hand, Owens-Corning expects R/3 to save the company $15 million in 1997 and $50 million in 1998 by streamlining business processes and eliminating jobs. Factory-floor employees will be able to use R/3 to confirm shipments of insulation or roofing shingles as the products leave the plant. The shipping information will automatically update the general ledger. But if someone makes a mistake and doesn't catch it right away, R/3's internal logic will force the company's finance staff to hunt for that transaction to balance the books.

So far, Owens-Corning has spent $100 million on its R/3 project. Other implementations of R/3 may not be as extensive, but the product is considered notoriously difficult to install. It took Mitsubishi Corporation's Sunnyvale, California, electronic device group twice as long, with far more cost to implement R/3 financial and distribution modules than had been originally estimated. Forrester Research in Cambridge, Massachusetts, estimates that for every dollar spent on SAP R/3 software, five more must be spent on training and systems integration.

SAP has a large internal staff to support its software packages, but it also uses legions of consultants from consulting firms such as Price Waterhouse, Andersen Consulting, EDS Corporation, and Coopers & Lybrand. These external consultants work with SAP clients to install the SAP packages. Because SAP is growing so fast, there is a worldwide shortage of SAP experts with experience implementing R/3.

Louis Dingerdissen, vice president of MIS for Kodak's health group, observed that experts in SAP software are in short supply, and that it can take 16 weeks of training to get end users up to speed on SAP software—far too long. With SAP quickly signing up new clients, the support situation could worsen before it gets better, or SAP may have to slow down its growth a bit.

One reason for the shortage of SAP consultants is that it can take years for even experienced technologists to understand all the complexities and methodologies of SAP software. SAP vice chairman and cofounder Hasso Plattner admitted that it takes about three years, or two or three installations of the package, before a consultant becomes an expert in the software. (R/3 was built with SAP's own internally developed programming language called Abap. Users need to work with Abap to modify or extend the SAP software package.) SAP pairs one or more if its seasoned 8- to 10-year German veterans with less experienced U.S. consultants at each installation. But according to Greg Staszko, a partner at the Cincinnati branch of Deloitte & Touche (a leading accounting and consulting firm), the SAP experts tend to be troubleshooters or product experts, rather than business consultants, so clients do not necessarily get the best advice on how to integrate the software into their business operations most efficiently and painlessly. The perception remains among some U.S. companies that even an on-site SAP expert who knows the financial accounting module cannot correct a bug in the sales and distribution module.

To augment the ranks of qualified consultants, SAP built a world training headquarters in Walldorf, costing an estimated $50 to 60 million. It recruited more consultants by signing agreements with new consulting firms such as Cap Gemini America and Coopers & Lybrand, and deemphasized its relationship with firms such as Computer Sciences Corporation and KPMG Peat Marwick, which it felt have not worked out well.

SAP recently introduced AcceleratedSAP (ASAP), a program that promises to cut implementation time by as much as half. ASAP provides tools, templates, and questionnaires for companies to create a step-by-step road map that lets users clearly define each task. The templates incorporate "best practices" that show how things are done and will help users figure out where to begin. ASAP might have helped Mitsubishi. Jerry Karr, vice president of business process reengineering for Mitsubishi's electronics device group, believes that one major reason for the company's problems with R/3 is that it didn't devise a clear reengineering strategy before it implemented the software package. ∎

Sources: "This German Software is Complex, Expensive—and Wildly Popular," *The Wall Street Journal*, March 14, 1997; Tom Stein, "Fast Deployment," *Information Week*, February 3, 1997; Emily Kay, "Desperately Seeking SAP Support," *Datamation*, February 6, 1996; Doug Bartholomew, "SAP Goes One Further," *Information Week*, October 31, 1994; and "SAP America: R/2 + R/3 = ?," *Information Week*, January 10, 1994.

Case Study Questions	2. Analyze the specific strengths and weaknesses of SAP software packages.	ness application software, would you choose SAP? Why or why not? What management, organization, and technology factors would you consider?
1. What advantages and disadvantages of application software packages are illustrated by SAP?	3. If you were the manager of a corporation looking for new busi-	

REFERENCES

Alavi, Maryam. "An Assessment of the Prototyping Approach to Information System Development." *Communications of the ACM* 27 (June 1984).

Alavi, Maryam, R. Ryan Nelson, and Ira R. Weiss. "Strategies for End-User Computing: An Integrative Framework." *Journal of Management Information Systems* 4, no. 3 (Winter 1987–1988).

Anderson, Evan A. "Choice Models for the Evaluation and Selection of Software Packages." *Journal of Management Information Systems* 6, no. 4 (Spring 1990).

Arthur, Lowell Jay. "Quick and Dirty." *Computerworld* (December 14, 1992).

Baskerville, Richard L., and Jan Stage. "Controlling Prototype Development through Risk Analysis." *MIS Quarterly* 20, no. 4 (December 1996).

Bersoff, Edward H., and Alan M. Davis. "Impacts of Life Cycle Models on Software Configuration Management." *Communications of the ACM* 34, no. 8 (August 1991).

Caldwell, Bruce. "Blue Cross, in Intensive Care, Beeps EDS." *InformationWeek* (January 27, 1992).

Caldwell, Bruce. "The New Outsourcing Partnership." *InformationWeek* (June 24, 1996).

Carr, Houston H. "Information Centers: The IBM Model vs. Practice." *MIS Quarterly* (September 1987).

Cerveny, Robert P., Edward J. Garrity, and G. Lawrence Sanders. "The Application of Prototyping to Systems Development: A Rationale and Model." *Journal of Management Information Systems* 3 (Fall 1986).

Clermont, Paul. "Outsourcing Without Guilt." *Computerworld* (September 9, 1991).

Cotterman, William W., and Kuldeep Kumar. "User Cube: A Taxonomy of End Users." *Communications of the ACM* 32, no. 11 (November 1989).

Cross, John. "IT Outsourcing: British Petroleum's Competitive Approach." *Harvard Business Review* (May–June 1995).

Davis, Gordon B., and Margrethe H. Olson. *Management Information Systems,* 2nd ed. New York: McGraw-Hill (1985).

Davis, Sid A., and Robert P. Bostrum. "Training End Users: An Experimental Investigation of the Role of the Computer Interface and Training Methods." *MIS Quarterly* 17, no. 1 (March 1993).

Earl, Michael J. "The Risks of Outsourcing IT." *Sloan Management Review* (Spring 1996).

Fraser, Martin D., Kuldeep Kumar, and Vijay K. Vaishnavi. "Strategies for Incorporating Formal Specifications in Software Development." *Communications of the ACM* 37 no. 10 (October 1994).

Fuller, Mary K., and E. Burton Swanson. "Information Centers as Organizational Innovation." *Journal of Management Information Systems* 9, no. 1 (Summer 1992).

Gould, John D., and Clayton Lewis. "Designing for Usability: Key Principles and What Designers Think." *Communications of the ACM* 28 (March 1985).

Grant, F. J. "The Downside of 4GLs." *Datamation* (July 1985).

Green, Jesse. "Productivity in the Fourth Generation." *Journal of Management Information Systems* 1 (Winter 1984–1985).

Gutert, Fred. "How to Manage Your Outsourcer." *Datamation* (March 1, 1996).

Harel, Elie C., and Ephraim R. McLean. "The Effects of Using a Nonprocedural Computer Language on Programmer Productivity." *MIS Quarterly* (June 1985).

Harrison, Allison W., and R. Kelly Rainer, Jr. "The Influence of Individual Differences on Skill in End-User Computing." *Journal of Management Information Systems* 9, no. 1 (Summer 1992).

Holtzblatt, Laren, and Hugh Beyer. "Making Customer-Centered Design Work for Teams." *Communications of the ACM* 36, no. 10 (October 1993).

Huff, Sid L., Malcolm C. Munro, and Barbara H. Martin. "Growth Stages of End User Computing." *Communications of the ACM* 31, no. 5 (May 1988).

Janson, Marius, and L. Douglas Smith. "Prototyping for Systems Development: A Critical Appraisal." *MIS Quarterly* 9 (December 1985).

Jenkins, A. Milton. "Prototyping: A Methodology for the Design and Development of Application Systems." *Spectrum* 2 (April 1985).

Johnson, Richard T. "The Infocenter Experience." *Datamation* (January 1984).

Jones, T. C. "The Limits of Programming Productivity." Guide and Share Application Development Symposium, Proceedings. New York: Share (1979).

Kozar, Kenneth A., and John M. Mahlum. "A User-Generated Information System: An Innovative Development Approach." *MIS Quarterly* (June 1987).

Kraushaar, James M., and Larry E. Shirland. "A Prototyping Method for Applications Development by End Users and Information Systems Specialists." *MIS Quarterly* (September 1985).

Lacity, Mary C., Leslie P. Willcocks, and David F. Feeny. "IT Outsourcing: Maximize Flexibility and Control." *Harvard Business Review* (May–June 1995).

Livingston, Dennis. "Outsourcing: Look Beyond the Price Tag." *Datamation* (November 15, 1992).

Loh, Lawrence, and N. Venkatraman. "Determinants of Information Technology Outsourcing." *Journal of Management Information Systems* 9, no. 1 (Summer 1992).

Loh, Lawrence, and N. Venkatraman. "Diffusion of Information Technology Outsourcing: Influence Sources and the Kodak Effect." *Information Systems Research* 3, no. 4 (December 1992).

Lucas, Henry C., Eric J. Walton, and Michael J. Ginzberg. "Implementing Packaged Software." *MIS Quarterly* (December 1988).

McMullen, John. "Developing a Role for End Users." *InformationWeek* (June 15, 1992).

Madsen, Kim Halskov, and Peter H. Aiken. "Experience Using Cooperative Interactive Storyboard Prototyping." *Communications of the ACM* 36, no. 4 (June 1993).

Martin, James. *Application Development without Programmers.* Englewood Cliffs, NJ: Prentice Hall (1982).

Martin, J., and C. McClure. "Buying Software Off the Rack." *Harvard Business Review* (November–December 1983).

Mason, R. E. A., and T. T. Carey. "Prototyping Interactive Information Systems." *Communications of the ACM* 26 (May 1983).

Matos, Victor M, and Paul J. Jalics. "An Experimental Analysis of the Performance of Fourth-Generation Tools on PCs." *Communications of the ACM* 32, no. 11 (November 1989).

McLean, Ephraim, Leon A. Kappelman, and John P. Thompson. "Converging End-User and Corporate Computing." *Communications of the ACM* 36, no. 12 (December 1993).

Panko, Raymond. *End-User Computing.* New York: Wiley and Sons (1988).

Rivard, Suzanne, and Sid L. Huff. "Factors of Success for End-User Computing." *Communications of the ACM* 31, no. 5 (May 1988).

Roche, Edward M. *Managing Information Technology in Multinational Corporations.* New York: Macmillan (1992).

Rockart, John F., and Lauren S. Flannery. "The Management of End-User Computing." *Communications of the ACM* 26, no. 10 (October 1983).

Schatz, Willie. "Bailoutsourcing." *Computerworld* (January 25, 1993).

Timmreck, Eric M. "Performance Measurement: Vendor Specifications and Benchmarks." In *The Information Systems Handbook,* edited by F. Warren McFarlan and Richard C. Nolan. Homewood, IL: Dow-Jones-Richard D. Irwin (1975).

Trauth, Eileen M., and Elliot Cole. "The Organizational Interface: A Method for Supporting End Users of Packaged Software." *MIS Quarterly* 16, no. 1 (March 1992).

White, Clinton E., and David P. Christy. "The Information Center Concept: A Normative Model and a Study of Six Installations." *MIS Quarterly* (December 1987).

Willis, T. Hillman, and Debbie B. Tesch. "An Assessment of Systems Development Methodologies." *Journal of Information Technology Management* 2, no. 2 (1991).

Zahniser, Richard A. "Design by Walking Around." *Communications of the ACM* 36, no. 10 (October 1993).

Ensuring Quality with Information Systems

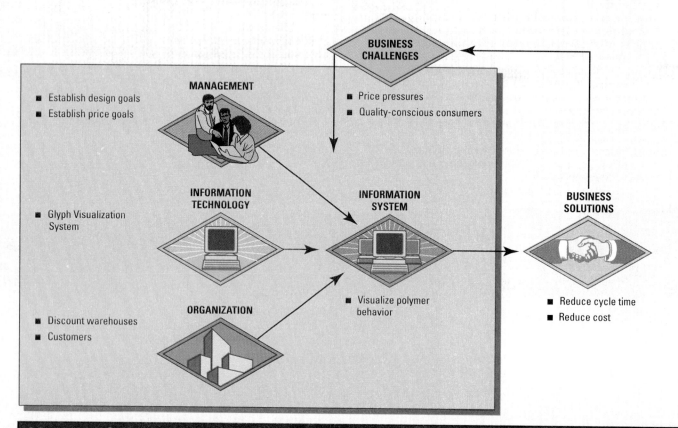

- Establish design goals
- Establish price goals

MANAGEMENT

BUSINESS CHALLENGES

- Price pressures
- Quality-conscious consumers

- Glyph Visualization System

INFORMATION TECHNOLOGY

INFORMATION SYSTEM

BUSINESS SOLUTIONS

- Discount warehouses
- Customers

ORGANIZATION

- Visualize polymer behavior

- Reduce cycle time
- Reduce cost

Maytag and Eastman Chemicals Build a Better Refrigerator

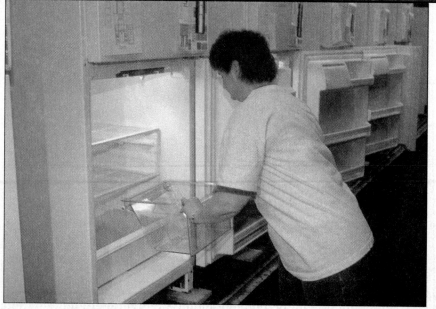

Informed, demanding customers and the emergence of discount superstores have made home appliances one of the most competitive durable goods today. About 80 percent of all refrigerators are now sold through low-price superstore "warehouses." The prices of refrigerators have not gone up as manufacturing costs have risen.

To remain competitive in this environment, Maytag Galesburg Refrigeration Products is constantly looking for ways to improve the appearance and performance of its products while keeping down costs. In its pursuit of quality, Maytag

LEARNING OBJECTIVES

After completing this chapter, you will be able to:

1. Describe how information systems can contribute to total quality management in an organization.
2. Explain why information systems must pay special attention to software quality assurance.
3. Identify the principal solutions to information systems quality problems.
4. Describe the traditional tools and methodologies for promoting information systems quality. ·
5. Describe new approaches for promoting information systems quality.

---

teamed with Eastman Chemical Company to develop a cost-effective material for several larger interior features of Maytag refrigerators.

Today's consumers are attracted to a high-style high-tech look, light colors, clear design, and features such as crystal-clear vegetable crisper pans that show contents at a glance. Eastman developed a copolymer that could meet Maytag's aesthetic goals as well as the physical and mechanical properties required of large crisper pans and meat keepers. These refrigerator containers must stand up to food chemicals and remain crystal-clear through cleanings with normal household products. A one-piece design keeps spills inside the containers.

The structural details are molded into these refrigerator components. Molten polymer is injected under controlled pressure and rate into a steel mold of the finished part. When the part cools and solidifies, it is ejected from the mold and the cycle is repeated. This one-step injection molding is very cost efficient. When the molding cycle for a crisper pan is completed at Maytag's Galesburg, Illinois, plant, the pan is ready for installation. No extra labor-intensive assembly is required.

The Maytag/Eastman design team used computer-based systems to predict how the polymer would behave in the mold. The molten polymer must flow into all sections of the mold to produce a complete part and this must be done within a specified time that keeps the rest of Maytag's production line running. Reducing cycle time by a few seconds can make a big difference. The team used Eastman's Glyph Visualization System to address such processing variables as temperature and injection pressure simultaneously.

The system produced information essential for modifying a design or changing materials. Maytag made some modifications to the tooling to accommodate the use of a replacement material. These changes speeded the production process, and by further reducing cycle time by a few seconds Maytag created large savings. ■

Source: "Maytag Teams with Eastman Chemical to Build a Better Refrigerator," *American Business Review,* November 1996.

MANAGEMENT CHALLENGES

The experience of Maytag and Eastman Chemicals illustrates some of the ways in which information systems and the information systems function can be used to improve quality throughout the firm. Yet few organizations have used information systems in this manner, and information systems have special quality problems of their own. The pursuit of quality in information systems raises the following management challenges.

1. **Applying quality assurance standards in large system projects.** The goal of zero defects in large, complex pieces of software is impossible to achieve. If the seriousness of remaining bugs cannot be ascertained, what constitutes an acceptable if not perfect performance? And even if meticulous design and exhaustive testing could eliminate all defects, software projects have time and budget constraints that often prevent management from devoting as much time to thorough testing as it should. Under these circumstances it will be difficult for managers either to define a standard for software quality or to enforce it.

2. **Enforcing a standard methodology.** Although structured methodologies have been available for 25 years, very few organizations have been able to enforce them. One survey found that only 15 to 20 percent of all organizations it studied used structured analysis and design in a consistent manner. It is impossible to use CASE or newer object-oriented methods effectively unless all participants in system building adopt a common development methodology and common development tools. Methodologies are organizational disciplines.

3. **Agreeing on what constitutes quality in information systems.** Many information systems professionals tend to view system problems as primarily technical issues. Yet many quality problems related to information systems, including software quality assurance, are not merely technical issues. Information systems specialists need to work in partnership with other areas of the organization to develop a shared sense of quality linked to larger business goals.

We have explored various facets of quality in information systems throughout this text, but quality is the special focus of this chapter. Here we will examine the ways in which information systems can contribute to improving quality throughout the organization. We will then outline the quality problems peculiar to information systems, focusing on the need for quality assurance in the development of software. Finally we will describe traditional and new methodologies and tools for improving software quality and overall system effectiveness.

The emergence of a global economy has stimulated worldwide interest in achieving quality. Companies can no longer be satisfied with producing goods and services that compete only with goods produced within their own country—consumers can now select from a broad range of products and services produced anywhere in the world. Before examining how information systems can contribute to quality throughout the organization, we must first define the term **quality.**

Traditional definitions for quality have focused on the conformance to specifications (or the absence of variation from those specifications). With this definition, a producer can easily measure the quality of its products. A wristwatch manufacturer, for example, might include a specification for reliability that requires that 99.995 percent of the watches will neither gain nor lose more than one second per month. Another requirement might be that 99.995 percent of the watches are sturdy enough to withstand being dropped 25 times onto a carpet or a linoleum floor from a height of seven feet. Simple tests will enable the manufacturer to measure precisely against these specifications.

However, achieving quality is not quite that simple and direct. A customer's perspective is much broader. Customers normally apply three criteria. First, customers are concerned with the quality of the physical product. They want to know if the product is durable, how safe it is, its reliability, its ease of use and installation, its stylishness, and how well the producer supports the product. Second, customers are concerned with the quality of service, by which they mean the accuracy and truthfulness of the advertising, the timeliness and accuracy of the billing process, responsiveness to warranties (implied as well as specified), and ongoing product support. Finally, customer concepts of quality include the psychological aspects: how well do the sales and support staff know their products, the courtesy and sensitivity of the staff, and even their neatness, and the reputation of the product. For companies to compete globally, they need to include a customer perspective in any definition of quality.

Management has been questioning the idea that quality costs more. Today many senior executives have come to the conclusion that the lack of quality is actually a significant expense. Although we all understand that product returns and repairs result in added costs for repair (labor, parts replacement, and additional shipping), only recently has management focused on the many previously hidden costs that arise from producing products that are not high quality. Assume, for example, that nine of every one hundred watches the wristwatch manufacturer produces are defective. Some of the previously unnoticed costs in producing those nine watches include:

- Materials used to manufacture nine defective watches
- Labor needed to manufacture nine defective watches
- A 9 percent increase in the wear and tear on production machinery, resulting in a 9 percent increase in maintenance, parts replacement, and eventual equipment replacement
- A 9 percent increase in inventory cost for raw material, work-in-process, and finished products
- A 9 percent increase in the cost of storage space to store the raw materials, work-in-process, and finished products
- A 9 percent increase in the inspection staff needed to inspect the nine defective watches
- An increase in liability insurance and legal defense costs to protect and defend the manufacturer from lawsuits.

quality   Conformance to producer specifications and satisfaction of customer criteria such as quality of physical product, quality of service, and psychological aspects.

Today more businesses are turning to an idea known as total quality management. **Total quality management (TQM)** is a concept that makes quality the responsibility of all people within an organization. TQM holds that the achievement of quality control is an end in itself. Everyone is expected to contribute to the overall improvement of quality—the engineer who avoids design errors, the production worker who spots defects, the sales representative who presents the product properly to potential customers, and even the secretary who avoids typing mistakes. Total quality management encompasses all functions within an organization.

TQM is based on quality management concepts developed by American quality experts such as W. Edwards Deming and Joseph Juran, but was popularized by the Japanese. Japanese management adopted the goal of zero defects, focusing on improving their products or services prior to shipment rather than correcting them after they have been delivered. Japanese companies often give the responsibility for quality consistency to the workers who actually make the product or service, as opposed to a quality control department. Studies have repeatedly shown that the earlier in the business cycle a problem is eliminated, the less it costs for the company to eliminate it. Thus the Japanese quality approach not only brought a shift in focus to the workers and an increased respect for product and service quality but also lowered costs.

As the quality movement has spread to Europe and the United States, both quality within information systems departments and the role of information systems in corporatewide quality programs have come under intense scrutiny. How can information systems contribute to overall quality in the organization? How can quality be promoted in information systems themselves?

How Information Systems Contribute to Total Quality Management

Information systems can fill a special role in corporate quality programs for a number of reasons. First, IS is deeply involved with the daily work of other departments throughout the organization. IS analysts usually have taken a leading role in designing, developing, and supporting such varied departmental systems as corporate payrolls, patent research systems, chemical process control systems, logistics systems, and sales support systems. IS professionals also maintain their knowledge of these departments through their participation in departmental information planning. In addition, IS personnel are usually key to the sharing of data between departments because they have unique knowledge of the relationships between various departments. Often, only IS personnel know where certain data originate, how other departments use and store them, and which other functions would benefit from having access to them. With this broad understanding of the functional integration of the corporation, IS personnel can be valuable members of any quality project team.

The IS staff in effective information systems departments have three skills that are critical to the success of a quality program. First, they are specialists in analyzing and redesigning business processes. Second, many IS technicians are experienced in quantifying and measuring procedures and critical activities in any process. Typically, IS departments have long been involved with measurements of their own service. Third, IS project managers are skilled in managing tasks and projects. Project manager training has long been a staple of better IS departments; such training includes the use of project management software. These skills can contribute a great deal to any serious quality program, which will normally be organized as a project and will usually be heavily task oriented.

The information systems staff is the source of ideas on the application of technology to quality issues; often they are also the people who can make that technology available to the quality project. For example, with the help of IS departments, statistical analysis software is becoming more widely used in the drive for quality. Goodmark Foods, Inc., the leading U.S. producer of snack meats, received support from its information systems group to apply such software to their manufacturing.

The software helps workers see when and by how much each piece of snack meat deviates from the specified weight (Mandell, 1992).

Let us discuss some of the more significant approaches companies follow in their quality programs and illustrate contributions IS can make.

SIMPLIFYING THE PRODUCT, THE PRODUCTION PROCESS, OR BOTH. Quality programs usually have a "fewer-is-better" philosophy—the fewer steps in a process, the less time and opportunity for an error to occur. A few years ago Carrier Corporation, the Syracuse, New York, manufacturing giant, was faced with an eroding market share. It believed it was not communicating effectively with customers. One reason: a 70 percent error rate in using their manual order entry system to match customers and products when ordering Carrier's commercial air-conditioning units. The system required so many steps to process an order that mistakes were all but inevitable. Errors sometimes went undetected until the end of the manufacturing line, where workers might discover a wrong coil or some other similar problem. Big mistakes occasionally affected customers. In 1988, the company finally instituted a TQM program in which information technology played a large role. Carrier now coordinates everything from sales to manufacturing by using an expert system (LaPlante, 1992). When IS professionals were able to reduce the number of steps, the number of errors dropped dramatically, manufacturing costs dropped, and Carrier found itself with happier customers.

BENCHMARK. Many companies have been effective in achieving quality by setting strict standards for products, services, and other activities, and then measuring performance against those standards. Companies may use external industry standards, standards set by other companies, internally developed high standards, or some combination of the three.

PHH FleetAmerica, the $1 billion fleet leasing unit of Hunt Valley, Maryland's PHH Corporation, recently turned to benchmarking to add value to its customer services. The firm analyzed every process and defined the 16 key ones that run its business. Then, for each of these 16 processes, the company developed a set of benchmark standards that is based on two external sets, the standards its competitors meet and its customer expectations. Having established these new standards, the company reengineered many of the processes. Now it is benchmarking all of them.

L. L. Bean Inc., the Freeport, Maine, mail-order clothing company, uses benchmarking to achieve an order shipping accuracy of 99.9 percent. In fact, during one period in the spring of 1994, the company shipped 500,000 packages consecutively without a single error. L. L. Bean has been so successful that copier giant Xerox Corporation of Rochester, New York, turned to it to learn how to use benchmarking for its copier parts shipping function.

IS contributes to these efforts in many ways. IS staff participates in reengineering projects and helps to design and build the systems that make the quality processes possible. Any study of quality programs shows that information is a top concern to those involved, and IS is often central to the collection of that information. To improve production or sales, for example, management needs data to determine both what is being done right and what is being done wrong. IS is usually the key to making that information available in a timely fashion and in a format useful to those who need it for quality purposes. For instance, manufacturing data have traditionally been supplied to management in summary form at the end of the manufacturing process. In effect it is historical data that at best can be used to reduce future problems. Real-time data are needed to correct problems as they occur, as the quality team at Continental General Tire, in Charlotte, North Carolina, realized. It installed a local area network that gives plant floor operators real-time data on raw materials as those materials arrive at the plant. In this way, flawed raw material batches are discovered very quickly, before the plant uses them to produce substandard tires.

To provide better information for benchmarking, information systems specialists can work with business specialists either to design new systems or to analyze

The quality assurance technician at Continental General Tire in Charlotte, North Carolina, is gathering real-time data for the manufacturing production process.

quality-related data found in existing systems. For instance, credit memo transactions stored in accounting systems contain a wealth of detail on customer returns. Mail-order firms such as L. L. Bean typically ask customers returning merchandise to select "reason codes" explaining why each item was returned (see Figures 13.1A and 13.1B). They and other mail-order companies have designed their information systems to analyze these return transactions. A report from these systems showing return transaction frequency and dollar value summarized by week or month and broken down by the reason for the returns will help management target areas in which mistakes are being made.

Inventory systems may contain data showing that customers are not being shipped their products in a timely manner or that other problems are occurring. Relevant metrics include

- Vendor promises versus actual delivery dates
- Frequency of rejected shipments at the receiving department
- Credit approval turnaround time for new customers
- Inventory value over time
- Work orders for scrap and rework

USE CUSTOMER DEMANDS AS A GUIDE TO IMPROVING PRODUCTS AND SERVICES. Improving customer service, making customer service the number one priority, will improve the quality of the product itself, as is clear from the Carrier example. The Window on Organizations shows how one small business, 800-FLOWERS, addressed the question of customer satisfaction in a quality program. It also shows the contribution of information systems in building a system and making needed information available when required. Systems that provide information on service levels from external customers, competitors' customers, and the firm's own employees can help companies improve their service quality (Berry and Parasuraman, 1997).

Figure 13.2 shows how Pizza Hut designed its information systems to reflect its new emphasis on quality in its business strategy. Facing falling profits, Pizza Hut's management decided to focus less on minimizing costs and more on keeping its customers happy. It launched a customer satisfaction measurement system in January 1995 that monitors customer satisfaction on a weekly basis. The system uses the

Building an Organization to Sell Flowers

Jim McCann bought 800-FLOWERS because it was the best marketing idea he had seen. But the company was $7 million in debt and spending way too much money attracting new customers. It relied on a large and costly telemarketing center and expensive national advertising. McCann recognized that selling flowers is a "nickel-and-dime" business that cannot afford expensive advertising. To be successful, he would have to rely on repeat customers. The underlying problem was that few customers came back because of poor service and inconsistent quality. So McCann rebuilt his organization to give customers

quality service—service that would bring them back repeatedly. 800-FLOWERS is now posting profits and expanding.

800-FLOWERS had a network of 8000 florists around the country to design and deliver all orders. McCann decided that he needed fewer florists, but these florists must be held to high standards for design, flower freshness, and delivery. He replaced the existing network with 2500 florists who agreed to his standards,

including a guarantee of same-day delivery for all orders received by 1:00 P.M. McCann then hired a staff of 15 quality-control experts who spot-checked the florists to make certain they sold only fresh flowers. Next, he moved the 800-FLOWERS telemarketing center from its 55,000-square-foot facility in Dallas, Texas, to much smaller facilities in Bayside, New York. He added 30 more telereps to his staff and trained them in customer service, instructing them to personalize each conversation. 800-FLOWERS offered the customer guarantees that wilted floral arrangements could be returned within seven days and arrangements that the customer didn't like could be returned when they arrived.

Making a sale required a number of steps: writing the order, obtaining credit card approval, determining which 800-FLOWERS florist is closest to the delivery location, describing and deciding on a floral arrangement, and forwarding the order to the florist. Each step in the manual process increased the chance of human error, and thus the possibility of a wrong delivery. McCann purchased a $4 million NCR midrange computer to centrally process orders more efficiently. The system reduces processing time from ten minutes to less than five. The computer system includes computer images of floral arrangements that the telereps can use to aid them as they talk with customers. Connection to the network brought the organization of 2500 florists into the whole process. A computer, a modem (to connect them to the network), and a printer was installed in each florist shop. McCann found that the data from the computer system also had other uses. For example, by tracking the orders, he has been able to anticipate the volume on any given day, allowing both 800-FLOWERS and the 2500 florists to have available added staff and product on days of predicted high volume.

To Think About: *How did technology promote quality at 800-FLOWERS? What business processes were affected? Could technology alone have solved 800-FLOWERS' quality problems? What was the relationship between quality, technology, and 800-FLOWERS' business strategy?*

Sources: Richard D. Smith, "From One Little Shop, an 800-Flowers Garden Grows," *New York Times*, January 8, 1995; and Leah Ingram, "One Blooming Business," *Profit*, May/June 1994.

company's customer database which tracks the buying patterns of more than 25 million delivery customers. These customer sales data are captured by a point-of-sale system when a customer buys a pizza. Each week, the customer satisfaction measurement system downloads 50,000 customer names and telephone numbers to the Gallup Organization. Gallup calls those customers and polls them about speed of service, quality of food, and willingness to repurchase food at Pizza Hut. The results are

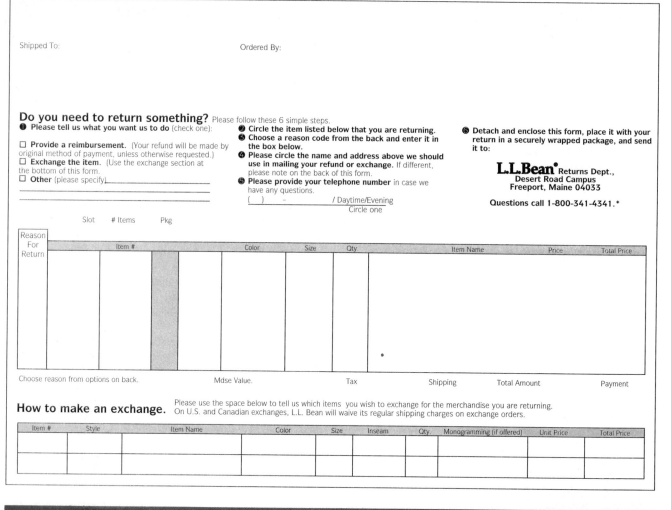

Shipped To:

Ordered By:

Do you need to return something? Please follow these 6 simple steps.

❶ **Please tell us what you want us to do** (check one):

☐ **Provide a reimbursement.** (Your refund will be made by original method of payment, unless otherwise requested.)
☐ **Exchange the item.** (Use the exchange section at the bottom of this form.
☐ **Other** (please specify)_____

❷ **Circle the item listed below that you are returning.**
❸ **Choose a reason code from the back and enter it in the box below.**
❹ **Please circle the name and address above we should use in mailing your refund or exchange.** If different, please note on the back of this form.
❺ **Please provide your telephone number** in case we have any questions.
( )   -   / Daytime/Evening
            Circle one

❻ **Detach and enclose this form, place it with your return in a securely wrapped package, and send it to:**

L.L.Bean® Returns Dept.,
Desert Road Campus
Freeport, Maine 04033

Questions call 1-800-341-4341.*

Slot	# Items	Pkg

Reason For Return	Item #		Color	Size	Qty	Item Name	Price	Total Price

Choose reason from options on back.   Mdse Value.   Tax   Shipping   Total Amount   Payment

How to make an exchange. Please use the space below to tell us which items you wish to exchange for the merchandise you are returning. On U.S. and Canadian exchanges, L.L. Bean will waive its regular shipping charges on exchange orders.

Item #	Style	Item Name	Color	Size	Inseam	Qty.	Monogramming (if offered)	Unit Price	Total Price

---

FIGURE 13.1A

Quality indicators in information systems. A company's information systems can be mined for data that might indicate quality problems. Companies such as L. L. Bean carefully analyze the codes indicating the reasons why customers return their purchases to identify items with quality problems.
Reprinted with permission of L. L. Bean Inc., Freeport, Maine.

analyzed by management to help identify and correct problems. The data are also used to construct a "loyalty index" for calculating management bonuses. Although this system costs approximately $5 million annually to operate, Pizza Hut research shows that a customer is worth $7200 over his or her lifetime, making the system worth more than any marketing program the company has devised to date (McWilliams, 1995).

The Window on Technology describes some of the issues that need to be addressed when a company wants to ensure a high level of customer service in many different parts of the world.

REDUCE CYCLE TIME. Experience indicates that the single best way to address quality problems is to reduce the amount of time from the beginning of a process to its end (cycle time). Reducing cycle time usually results in fewer steps, an improvement right there. But reducing cycle time has other advantages. With less time between beginning and end, workers will be better aware of what came just before, and so are less likely to make mistakes. Shorter cycles mean that errors are often caught earlier in production (or logistics or design or whatever the function), often before the product is complete, eliminating many of the hidden costs listed above. Fred

Reasons for return.

Letting us know why you are returning an item will help us speed your refund or exchange, and provide even better products in the future. Find the reason that best matches why you are making the return. Then write the code number in the left hand column of the return area on the other side of this form.

FIT & SIZING

TOO SMALL	TOO LARGE
21 Chest/bust	31 Chest/bust
22 Waist	32 Waist
23 Hip	33 Hip
24 Rise	34 Rise
25 Too narrow	35 Too wide
26 Too short	36 Too long
28 Overall	38 Overall

DURABILITY/PERFORMANCE
41 Excessive shrinkage
42 Color faded or bled
46 Does not work
47 Didn't last or hold up
48 Did not perform as intended
49 Not waterproof

SERVICE
51 Arrived too late
52 Wrong item shipped
53 Damaged in transit
55 Coordinate not received

SATISFACTION
61 Returning a gift
62 Changed my mind
66 Didn't like styling
67 Didn't like material
68 Didn't like color
69 Priced too high for item received

QUALITY
71 Faulty zipper
72 Material defect
73 Seam defective
74 Marked or soiled
75 Not well made
76 Components differ in shade
77 Finish unacceptable
78 Difficult to assemble
79 Part missing*

CATALOG
81 Item not as described
82 Item not as pictured
83 Color not as shown
84 Fit not as shown

*Have any questions? Part missing? Please call one of our Customer Service Representatives at 1-800-341-4341, (If outside U.S. or Canada call 207-865-3161), and let them know so that we can straighten it all out. We carry most replacement parts in stock, and we'll try to ship the part out right away.

New or different address?

If you are making a return, and want your refund or exchange sent to a new or different address, please write the new shipping information here and mark the appropriate box below:

Name

Address   Apt. no.

City   State   Zip Code

□ Gift? □ Address for this shipment only □ Permanent change of address

We'd enjoy hearing from you.

We welcome your comments and suggestions. Use the space below, and mail it to:

L.L.Bean®
Freeport, Maine 04033

FIGURE 13.1B

Bean provides a detailed list of codes describing reasons why customers might return merchandise.
Reprinted with permission of L. L. Bean, Inc.

Wenninger, CEO of disk drive producer Iomega Corporation in Roy, Utah, explains that "When your cycle is 28 days and you spot a defect at the end of the line, you can imagine how hard it is to isolate the problem." Iomega was spending $20 million a year to fix defective drives at the end of its 28-day production cycle. Reengineering the production process allowed them to reduce cycle time to a day and a half, eliminating this problem and winning the prestigious Shingo Prize for Excellence in American Manufacturing. The Continental General Tire example cited earlier also demonstrates the value of reducing cycle time.

IMPROVE THE QUALITY AND PRECISION OF THE DESIGN. Quality and precision in design will eliminate many production problems. Computer-aided design (CAD) software has made dramatic quality improvements possible in a wide range of businesses from aircraft manufacturing to production of razor blades. Alan R. Burns, a mining engineer from Perth, Australia, was able to use CAD to invent and design a new product that promises to have a major impact on the tire industry. His concept was a modular tire composed of a series of replaceable modules or segments so that when one segment is damaged, only that segment would need replacing rather than replacing the whole tire. The modules are not pneumatic and so cannot deflate.

FIGURE 13.2

Pizza Hut's customer satisfaction measurement system. Pizza Hut designed an information system that uses point-of-sale data to identify customers to survey each week about their impressions of Pizza Hut's food and service.

Source: Copyright February 13, 1995 by Computerworld, Inc., Framingham, MA 01701. Reprinted from Computerworld.

THE MEASURE OF LOYALTY

Last month, Pizza Hut launched a new program to monitor customer satisfaction on a weekly basis. The program uses the company's impressive customer database system, which Pizza Hut has used to track the buying patterns of more than 25 million delivery customers.

1. Customer buys pizza (delivery or dine-in)

2. POS information (name, address, phone, order details) is added to 25 million customer database in Wichita, Kan., headquarters

3. 50,000 customer records are downloaded to Gallup each week for a three-minute phone survey with each customer

4. Survey data is uploaded and tabulated by system; repurchase willingness ("loyalty index") calculated for each customer

5. Survey results available for on-line management decision support; company can make operational adjustments quickly to correct problems

6. Annual bonuses for management tied to improvement in loyalty index (target: 10% improvement annually)

Moreover they can be changed quickly and easily by one person. Burns researched the tire field and discovered that his new tire would likely find a ready market in the heavy equipment vehicle market (such as the backhoes and earthmovers used in construction). He established a company, Airboss, and proceeded to design his product. He first established quality performance measurements for such key tire characteristics as load, temperature, speed, wear life, and traction. He then entered this data into a CAD software package to design the modules. Using the software, he was able iteratively to design and test until he was satisfied with the results. He did not need to develop an actual working model until the iterative design process was almost complete. The product he produced was of much higher quality than would have been possible through manual design and testing because of the speed and accuracy of the CAD software.

INCREASE THE PRECISION OF PRODUCTION. For many products, one key way to achieve quality is to tighten production tolerances. CAD software has also made this possible. Most CAD software packages include a facility to translate design specifications into specifications both for production tooling and for the production process itself. In this way, products with more precise designs can also be produced more efficiently. Once his tire segment design was completed, Burns used the CAD software to design his manufacturing process, testing via computer just as he had done with product design. In his testing he discovered, for example, that the segment would cool unevenly. He was able to correct the problem even before developing the pro-

Delivering Quality Service Anywhere in the World

For Xerox Corporation, service within the United States is relatively easy because the infrastructure is in place to support quality maintenance. But Xerox is a $17.4 billion corporation with over 86,000 employees in more than 130 countries—and customers everywhere. In some of those countries, the infrastructure does not support the kind of maintenance Xerox believes is vital to its success. Yet the company's service arm, Team Xerox, has been very successful. It has been able to present such consistent and unified service around the world that Team Xerox has garnered both the Malcolm Baldridge Award and the Deming Prize for quality. How do they do it?

First, let's look at the problems they faced in many parts of the world. In the United States, someone with a copier problem will pick up the telephone and call for service or go on-line to troubleshoot the problem. One goal of Team Xerox is to serve the whole world alike. In some areas of the world, including South America, telecommunications is so costly that many clients cannot afford to have and use telephones, much less access worldwide networks. In the past, Xerox relied on a mainframe-based customer support system named GlobalView. The product worked fine in that "we could communicate very well among ourselves," says Pat Wallington, chief information officer at Xerox. "But," she adds, "not with the outside world. And they could not communicate with us." In addition, to better serve remote places, Team Xerox wanted to rely on mobile computers. However, building interfaces between GlobalView and these computers proved to be difficult.

In 1995 Xerox turned to Electronic Data Systems Inc. (EDS) and outsourced many of its IS departments to them. EDS was given the responsibility for developing a maintenance system that would focus on the needs of all employees and customers worldwide. By the end of 1996 the new system was 96 percent complete and was running at 700 sites worldwide. The system is client/server based and relies on standard Windows-based software for its interface. The system enables a Team Xerox maintenance person to travel with a laptop computer, hook that laptop up with the copier that needs maintenance, and run diagnostics right there with no state-of-the-art infrastructure or networking.

Now all customers everywhere are given the same high-quality service. "Our service is not consistent," claims Chuck Ray, vice president of customer-service delivery at Xerox. Instead, "It is the level of service to the customer that is consistent." His meaning? The company can now meet the needs of its customers regardless of the state of their economy, their culture, their business climate. Service can now be tailored to a local area.

To Think About: What do you think is the role of quality maintenance in Xerox's business strategy? In what ways is technology central to this strategy?

Source: Staiti, Chris, "Xerox Corp., A Worldwide System Delivers Service That's Anything But Carbon-Copy," *Computerworld Global Inovators,* March 10, 1997.

duction equipment. He was also able to design a shorter production cycle, improving quality while increasing his ability to meet customer demand more quickly.

Komag of Milpitas, California, the world's largest supplier of 5 1/4-inch and smaller sputtered thin-film disks for disk drives in all types of computers, must control hundreds of variables in its manufacturing process. Through carefully controlled application of materials, machines, robotics, instrumentation, and skilled production professionals, the process transforms uncoated aluminum disks into highly technical precision products. Komag also needed more precision in its production process. It implemented MESA, from Camstar Systems Inc., a Manufacturing Execution System (MES). MESA is designed to meet information requirements of manufacturing shop-floor management in complex batch/log process manufacturing environments. This system allows Komag to monitor hundreds of process manufacturing execution steps to analyze yield, productivity, and machine utilization. System capabilities include real-time lot movement and inventory tracking, generation of process control charts, lot history and process data, application of process parameters per operation step, and immediate response to out-of-control process variances and yield problems. Managers can obtain data on key production variables by product, process, machine, and shift. Within six months after implementing the new system, Komag doubled output (Komag, 1994).

Cerveceria y Malteria Quilmes, S.A., which makes Argentina's most popular beer, used an extranet to increase the precision of its supply chain management. Some of its distributors are located over 400 miles away from Quilmes' breweries. If Quilmes' production system causes an order to be off by several dozen cases, the distributor needs to know before its trucks arrive at Quilmes' loading dock.

Previously, the distributors had spent $2600 per month using Argentina's overpriced telephone system to obtain Quilmes' inventory data. Quilmes added a Web interface to its production planning systems and made daily sales reports and truck loading information available to 100 of its more than 600 distributors via an expanded intranet. Distributors can now instantly check the status of their orders, noting discrepancies if they occur and organize their trucks more efficiently. The intranet provides a higher level of service to Quilmes' distributors as well as more precise information to guide its supply chain (Fabris, 1997).

INCLUDE LINE WORKERS IN ANY QUALITY PROCESS. Experience has shown that involvement of the people who perform the function is critical to achieving quality in that function. One reason L. L. Bean was able to attain nearly error-free picking was the involvement of warehouse workers in the design of the picking process. These workers suggested, for example, that high-volume items be stored close to packing stations. They also plotted their own picking movements on flowcharts to identify other inefficient movements.

Although the information systems area could potentially make many more contributions like these, its involvement in corporate quality programs has provoked a great deal of controversy. IS has been criticized for a reluctance to become involved in organization-wide quality programs. Often IS focuses exclusively on technological capabilities while not reaching out to aid the rest of the company in the ways described earlier. For example, many IS departments are criticized for failure to use customer demands as a guide to improving their products and services. On the other hand, non-IS departments often fail to consider contributions the IS staff might make to their quality project and so do not reach out to involve them. It is not uncommon for IS to be viewed only as technical support with little to contribute to the planning or content of the quality program.

The Need for Software Quality Assurance

Another reason that information systems fall short of helping the organization meet its quality goals is that the systems themselves do not perform as required. The underlying quality issue for information systems departments is software quality assurance.

Producing software of high quality is critical to most large organizations because of software's central function in so many departments—payroll, accounts receivable, manufacturing, sales, research, management. An undiscovered error in a company's credit software or process control software can result in millions of dollars of losses. For more and more companies, software has even become an integral part of the products sold. Computer software is now part of automobile fuel consumption systems, dishwasher and VCR controls, and fax machines. Several years ago, a hidden software problem in AT&T's long-distance system brought down that system, bringing the New York–based financial exchanges to a halt and interfering with billions of dollars of business around the country for a number of hours. Modern passenger and commercial vehicles are increasingly dependent on computer programs for critical functions. A hidden software defect in a braking system could result in the loss of lives.

Like other types of production, software production is unique and presents its own set of problems. One special characteristic of software development is that its usual goal is to build only one copy of the final product (except for companies developing software for public sale). For most manufactured products—aircraft, automobiles, paperclips, socks—once development begins, hundreds, thousands, or even millions of copies of the product are manufactured. With software, quality problems must be solved the first time; the design must be of high quality on the first try.

Meeting user needs can be difficult in a process where the end user commits to the product before that product has been built. In effect, the final system is "purchased" in advance, bought "sight unseen." Defining user needs and judging the quality of the completed system have proved to be major challenges. Most systems development projects begin by defining user information requirements and specifications in the form of systems analysis and design documents.

The problem is that meeting specifications does not necessarily guarantee quality. The completed system may in fact meet the specifications but not satisfy the user's needs. This occurs because of inaccurate, incomplete, or improperly detailed specifications, omitting functions in the specifications, or changing user needs during the development period. Specifications often fail to consider the system from the perspective of the users. Although designers will concentrate on functionality, they frequently overlook ease of learning and use, unquestioned accuracy and reliability, or speed of response. All these factors are important to the success of a system.

Often quality is not quantified in the specifications so that judgments about system quality become subjective, making it difficult to determine if the system actually meets the users' needs. We treat the issue of user satisfaction again in Chapter 14.

The Maintenance Nightmare

Computer software has traditionally been a nightmare to maintain. Maintenance, the process of modifying a system in production use, is the most expensive phase of the systems development process. Table 13.1 indicates the size of the maintenance problem. In one-fifth of information systems departments, 85 percent of personnel hours are allocated to maintenance, leaving little time for new systems development. In most organizations, nearly half of information systems staff time is spent in the maintenance of existing systems. One estimate attributes 60 percent of all business expenditures on computing to maintenance of COBOL software (Freedman, 1986).

Why are maintenance costs so high? One major reason is organizational change. The firm may experience large internal changes in structure or leadership, or change may come from its surrounding environment. These organizational changes affect information requirements. Another reason appears to be software complexity, as measured by the number and size of interrelated software programs and sub-programs and the complexity of the flow of program logic between them (Banker, Datar,

Table 13.1 The Maintenance Problem	
Annual personnel hours	
Maintain and enhance current systems	48.0%
Develop new systems	46.1%
Other	5.9%
20% of the survey allocated 85% of its efforts to maintenance and enhancements	
Frequency of activity	
Errors—emergency	17.4%
Change—data, inputs, files, hardware	18.2%
Improve—user enhancements, efficiency, documentation, etc.	60.3%
Other	4.1%

Sources: Bennett P. Lientz and E. Burton Swanson, *Software Maintenance Management*, Reading, MA: Addison-Wesley 1980; and L. H. Putnam and A. Fitzsimmons, "Estimating Software Costs," *Datamation,* September 1979, October 1979, and November 1979.

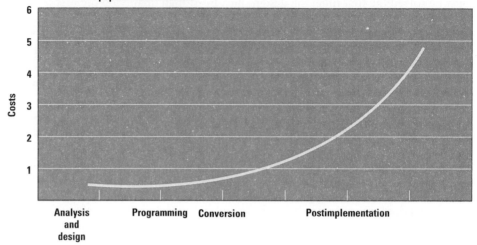

(A) Estimate of the relative cost of repairing errors based on consultant reports and the popular trade literature

(B) Origin, frequency, and severity of errors in large national defense and space programs

Error Type	% of Total Errors	Relative Severity	% of Total Cost of Errors
Design	66%	2.5	83+%
Logic	17%	1.0	8+%
Syntax	17%	1.0	8+%

FIGURE 13.3

The cost of errors over the systems development cycle. The most common, most severe, and most expensive system errors develop in the early design stages. They involve faulty requirements analysis. Errors in program logic or syntax are much less common, less severe, and less costly to repair than design errors.
Source: Alberts, 1976.

Kemerer, and Zweig, 1993). A third common cause of long-term maintenance problems is faulty systems analysis and design, especially information requirements analysis. Some studies of large TPS systems by TRW, Inc. have found that a majority of system errors—64 percent—result from early analysis errors (Mazzucchelli, 1985).

Figure 13.3 illustrates the cost of correcting errors during different stages of development. Part A is based on the experience of consultants reported in the literature. Part B shows the results of a quality assurance study of large national defense software projects.

If errors are detected early, during analysis and design, the cost to the systems development effort is small. But if they are not discovered until after programming, testing, or conversion has been completed, the costs can soar astronomically. A minor logic error, for example, that could take one hour to correct during the analysis and design stage could take 10, 40, or 90 times as long to correct during programming, conversion, or postimplementation.

To be able to handle maintenance quickly and inexpensively, a software system must be flexible. A flexible system can more quickly and easily be modified when problems occur or business requirements change over the years—which they most certainly will. For example a sales system must be able to accommodate new products, new sales staff, and even new offices with little or no problems. Otherwise, a system that may be successful in the short run becomes a long-run failure. Many designers do not consider the aspect of change as they design new systems. However, even if they do design a flexible system, flexibility can seem to be expensive and time consuming. Its benefits are not always understood or appreciated by the users. Target dates and cost limitations often pressure management to make developers sacrifice flexibility to complete a project as promised or as wanted. Unfortunately, the corporation may pay a much heavier price at a later time.

Bugs and Defects

A major problem with software is the presence of hidden **bugs** or program code defects. Studies have shown that it is virtually impossible to eliminate all bugs from large programs. The main source of bugs is the complexity of decision-making code. Even a relatively small program of several hundred lines will contain tens of decisions leading to hundreds or even thousands of different paths. Important programs within most corporations are usually much larger, containing tens of thousands or even millions of lines of code, each with many times the choices and paths of the smaller programs. Such complexity is difficult to document and design—designers document some reactions wrongly or fail to consider some possibilities.

bugs Program code defects or errors.

Zero defects, a goal of the total quality management movement, cannot be achieved in larger programs. Complete testing is simply not possible. Fully testing programs that contain thousands of choices and millions of paths would require thousands of years. Eliminating software bugs is an exercise in diminishing returns, because it would take proportionately longer testing to detect and eliminate obscure residual bugs (Littlewood and Strigini, 1993). Even with rigorous testing, one could not know for sure that a piece of software was dependable until the product proved itself after much operational use. The message? We cannot eliminate all bugs, and we cannot know with certainty the seriousness of the bugs that do remain.

Even when bugs are found, they are difficult to remove. Experience has shown that bug fixes often do not work. In many cases, the effort to fix a bug will introduce an entirely new bug or series of bugs. Studies by the Predictably Dependable Computing Systems research project have shown that once a bug has been "repaired," there is only a 50–50 chance that the program will function without failure as long as it did before the attempt to fix the bug (Littlewood and Strigini, 1992).

To achieve quality in software development, an organization must first reach agreement as to what quality is. Some developers view quality as the absence of programming defects. Clearly the presence of too many bugs will lower the quality of a system, but we have just learned that although zero defects may be an appropriate goal, such a situation can never be achieved in software development. Even if a system had no bugs, if it were slow, difficult to use, missing critical functions or inflexible, it certainly would not be a quality system. Any definition of quality must be viewed from the user perspective. It must be broad in scope and specific enough to encompass the satisfaction of user needs. A quality system must do the following:

- Achieve the business goals articulated by the user department
- Operate at an acceptable cost, commensurate with the value produced for the firm
- Meet carefully defined performance standards (such as response time and system availability)
- Produce accurate, reliable output with assurance that its dependability is "good enough" for the purpose intended
- Be easy to learn and use
- Be flexible

Some Solutions to Information System Quality Problems

Information systems are complex, and solutions to quality problems are equally complex. They include the use of an appropriate systems development methodology, proper resource allocation during systems development, the use of metrics, attention to testing, and the use of quality tools.

The Role of Methodologies

To limit problems and increase quality when building systems, developers must begin with a disciplined methodology that sets standards for all phases of the project. Good systems development methodologies will normally include the following:

- Proven methods for determining and documenting both system specifications and system design

- Programming standards that result in understandable, maintainable code that is not overly complex

- Guidelines for developing quality measurements to be agreed on by all interested parties prior to development

- Standards and methods for testing the system

- Software tools to be used at every phase to standardize the work in the project and to improve the quality of the output

- Project control methods, including numerous project milestones at which user approval will be required (see Chapter 14)

development methodology A collection of methods, one or more for every activity within every phase of a development project.

A **development methodology** is actually a collection of methods, one or more for every activity within every phase of a development project. The user of a methodology seldom uses every method within it because most projects do not require every possible activity. Numerous useful development methodologies exist, some suited to specific technologies, others reflecting differing development philosophies. Information systems departments, in conjunction with management of other departments, select the methodology they believe best fits the needs of their company. Larger corporations, employing multiple technologies, may select multiple methodologies to be used with differing technologies. However, the key to quality development is to select an appropriate methodology and then enforce its use. We will discuss several specific methodologies in Sections 13.2 and 13.3.

Because a quality system must achieve the business goals established by the user, it stands to reason that system quality begins with complete, detailed, accurate specifications documented in a form that users can understand. Some methodologies document specifications using flowcharts and diagrams, others use verbal descriptions. One popular method, prototyping, is discussed in Chapter 12. Specifications must also include agreed-upon measures of system quality so that the system can be evaluated objectively while it is being developed and once it is completed. We cannot overemphasize that quality specifications—clear, precise representations of user needs—are critical to the development of a quality system.

Resource Allocation During Systems Development

resource allocation Determination of how costs, time, and personnel are assigned to different activities of a systems development project.

Views on **resource allocation** during systems development have changed significantly over the years. Resource allocation determines the way the costs, time, and personnel are assigned to different phases of the project. In earlier times, developers focused on programming, with only about 1 percent of the time and costs of a project being devoted to systems analysis (determining specifications). As the information systems professionals have moved closer to a business or user perspective on quality, they have come to understand the central role of specifications. Moreover, technology that is now being used for systems development forces expenditures in analysis and design work to expand. Consequently, significant project resources are being shifted to earlier stages in the project cycle. More time is being spent in specifications and systems analysis, decreasing the proportion of programming time, and reducing the need for so much maintenance time. Figure 13.4 demonstrates the shift, although the ideal allocation of time represented in the figure is now considered to be outdated. Current

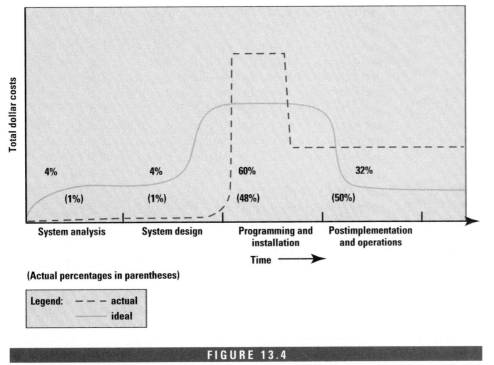

Ideal and actual software development costs. Ideally, relatively balanced amounts of time are allowed for analysis, design, programming, and installation. About 8 percent of costs are allocated ideally to analysis and design, 60 percent to programming and installation, and 32 percent to long-term maintenance. Actually, however, the early stages of analysis and design receive far fewer resources than is desirable. Programming and installation (including all important testing) also receive less time and fewer resources than is desirable, reflecting pressure to deliver a workable system as soon as possible. As a result, systems maintenance is far more expensive than is desirable—about 50 percent of the total software costs over the expected life span of the system.
Source: Alberts, 1976.

literature suggests that about one-quarter of a project's time and cost should be expended in specifications and analysis, with perhaps 50 percent of its resources being allocated to design and programming. Installation and postimplementation ideally should require only one-quarter of the project's resources.

Software Metrics

Software metrics can play a vital role in increasing the quality of a project. **Software metrics** are objective assessments of the system in the form of quantified measurements. Ongoing use of metrics allows the IS department and the user jointly to measure the performance of the system and identify problems as they occur. Software metrics include input metrics, output metrics, capacity metrics, performance/quality metrics, and value metrics.

The educational and experience level of system developers is an example of an input metric. The number of transactions that can be processed in a specified unit of time is an example of a capacity metric. Response time is a performance metric in an on-line system. The number of checks printed per hour is a system output metric for a payroll system. One metric for programming quality is the number of bugs per hundred lines of code. The business value of a transaction is an example of a value metric.

A widely used output metric is function points, which can help measure the productivity of software developers and the efficiency of the software itself regardless of the programming language employed. **Function point analysis** measures the number of inputs, outputs, inquiries, files, and external interfaces to other software used in an application. The results can be used to calculate the cost per function point of

software metrics Objective assessments of the software used in a system in the form of quantified measurements.

function point analysis Software output metric that measures the number of inputs, outputs, inquiries, files, and external interfaces used in an application. Used to assess developer productivity and software efficiency.

writing a piece of software and the number of function points written per programmer in a specified unit of time.

Unfortunately, most manifestations of quality are not so easy to define in metric terms. In those cases the developers must find indirect measurements. For example, an objective measurement of the ease of use of a newly developed system might be the average amount of time operators take to learn it. Ease of use might be measured by the number of calls for help the IS staff receives per month from system operators. For metrics to be successful, they must be carefully designed, formal, and objective. They must measure significant aspects of the system. One warning, however: Software metrics will be effective in judging the quality of the system only if users and IS staff agree to the measurements in advance. Finally, metrics are of no value unless they are used consistently. Few IS departments make wide use of formal, objective metrics today even though studies show they can significantly improve quality.

Testing

Early, regular, and thorough testing will contribute significantly to system quality. In general, software testing is often misunderstood. Many view testing as a way to prove the correctness of work they have done. In fact, we know that all sizable software is riddled with errors. The reason we test must be to uncover these errors.

Testing begins at the design phase. Because no coding yet exists, the test normally used is a **walkthrough**—a review of a specification or design document by a small group of people carefully selected based on the skills needed for the particular objectives being tested. Once coding begins, coding walkthroughs also can be used to review program code. However, completed code must be tested by computer runs. When errors are discovered, the source is found and eliminated through a process called **debugging**.

Chapter 11 describes the various stages of testing required to put an information system in operation—program testing, system testing, and acceptance testing. Testing will be successful only if planned properly. Early in the project, before any testing begins, a test plan must be prepared. The plan must include test cases so that the developers can be certain that they have tested an appropriate range of valid and invalid input. Invalid input must be tested to be certain the system handles errors appropriately.

Although testing is vital, it is time consuming and costly. The Window on Management explores the question of how to demonstrate the value of testing to management.

Quality Tools

Finally, system quality can be significantly enhanced by the use of quality tools. Today, many tools have been developed to address every aspect of the systems development process. Information systems professionals are using project management software to manage their projects. Products exist to document specifications and system design in text and graphic forms. Programming tools include data dictionaries, libraries to manage program modules, and tools that actually produce program code (see Chapters 7, 8, and 12). The most recent set of tools automates much of the preparation for comprehensive testing. We will discuss various types of tools in Sections 13.2 and 13.3.

Although many automated debugging tools exist, their usefulness appears to be more limited. The debugging process remains largely one of trial and error (Lieberman, 1997). Environments that enable programmers to graphically visualize how software programs work or to collaborate on debugging with other programmers may be promising future directions (Baecker, DiGiano, and Marcus, 1996; Domingue and Mulholland, 1997).

---

walkthrough A review of a specification or design document by a small group of people carefully selected based on the skills needed for the particular objectives being tested.

debugging The process of discovering and eliminating the errors and defects—the bugs—in program code.

When Testing Is Vital

Proper testing is too often sacrificed when new systems are being developed. As a result, expensive and sometimes catastrophic problems emerge later. Why is testing so often neglected? One reason is that testing can be very expensive and time consuming. Another is the difficulty of proving the value of testing to management.

Baylor Health Care Systems, Dallas, Texas, is a 1000-bed hospital with eight attached community medical centers and a transplant center. The software that keeps track of Baylor's blood supplies is crucial to the operation of its blood bank. When a patient has need for blood, the operator enters the blood type, and the system comes back with a list of the matching blood supplies. The system must respond with 100 percent accuracy. Anything less can be catastrophic. Errors are exceedingly dangerous because there are some combinations of blood that are basically lethal.

Management's response has been to retest the software on a regular basis. But this testing presented a problem. It would take about 1800 man-hours to do this manually each and every time the software is tested. Manually testing the system is in fact so time consuming and expensive it probably would not be done, despite the risk. However, testing software (in this case Teststream from Cyrano of Newburyport, Massachusetts) can accomplish the same task in about an hour. Thus, Teststream has literally become a life saver. In addition, the cost of the software is small compared with the cost of a multimillion-dollar lawsuit.

At Charles Schwab & Co. the issue is not one of life or death but of many billions of dollars of clients' money. The San Francisco–based discount brokerage firm is the largest such firm in the country. Its many brokers rely on Schwab computers and software applications to service their customers, and a failure in any of them could cost the customers—and perhaps even Schwab itself—millions of dollars. Moreover, in the investment brokerage business, time is of the essence—when a customer wants to place a trade, the company must be able to execute it instantly. The result of slow or down systems would be the loss of customers. Schwab's brokers applications are mostly purchased from third parties, and they tend to work well independently. But, because Schwab uses between 30 and 40 such applications together, its problem is constantly testing them to make sure they work well cooperatively. Schwab uses SQA Robot to create and run automated tests on its Windows client/server applications. The firm also uses SQA LoadTest to test the ability of the brokerage networks to handle all the traffic coming from the many brokers.

In both of these cases, the organization has not really been able to put a dollar value on the testing. Management simply knows testing is vital. However, in many companies management will not support extensive testing with expensive testing tools unless they know a dollar value. To satisfy these managers, Brendan Conway, research director with the Gartner Group, has developed a metric to calculate the return on investment (ROI) for automated testing tools. His metric examines productivity savings from the perspective of early defect removal—it is generally agreed that the later an error is discovered, the more expensive it is to correct, with cost increasing by a magnitude of 10 for each development phase it is not found and corrected. The metric also looks at the staff time saved by automating the process as compared with the cost of hiring additional staff to do the tasks manually. Finally the metric looks at the speed of development as a result of automating the testing. For management not wanting to invest in testing, this metric should certainly help.

To Think About: What criteria should managers use for determining the amount of information systems testing to perform?

Source: Paul Connolly, "Blood Test: the ROI of Testing Tools," *Datamation,* May 1997.

13.2 TRADITIONAL TOOLS AND METHODOLOGIES FOR QUALITY ASSURANCE

Structured methodologies have been used to document, analyze, and design information systems since the 1970s. **Structured** refers to the fact that the techniques are instructions that are carefully drawn up, often step-by-step, with each step building on the previous step, progressing from the highest, most abstract level to the lowest level of detail—from the general to the specific. For example, the highest level of a top-down depiction of a human resources system would show the main human resources functions, such as personnel, benefits, employment, and Equal Economic Opportunity (EEO). Each of these would then be exploded or decomposed down to the next layer. Benefits, for example, might include pension, employee savings, health

structured Refers to the fact that techniques are instructions that are carefully drawn up, often step-by-step, with each step building on a previous one.

Systems that keep track of blood supplies require the highest degree of accuracy and must be carefully tested

care, and insurance. Each path is broken down, layer by layer, until the material at the lowest level is easily graphed and documented.

The traditional structured methodologies are process oriented rather than data oriented. The process-oriented methodologies focus on how the data are transformed rather than on the data themselves. These methodologies are largely linear—each phase must be completed before the next one can begin. Despite growing interest in other methodologies, top-down structured methodologies remain an important approach today.

The methodologies discussed in this section include structured analysis, structured design, structured programming, and flowcharts. Using these methodologies can promote quality by improving communication, reducing errors caused by faulty program logic or unclear specifications, and creating software that is easier to understand and maintain.

Structured Analysis

Structured analysis is a widely used top-down method for defining system inputs, processes, and outputs. It offers a logical graphic model of information flow, partitioning a system into tiers of modules that show manageable levels of detail. It rigorously specifies the processes or transformations that occur within each module and the interfaces that exist between them. Its primary tool is the **data flow diagram (DFD)**, a graphic representation of a system's component processes and the flow of data between them.

Data Flow Diagrams

Data flow diagrams show how data flow to, from, and within an information system and the processes that transform the data. DFDs are constructed using four basic symbols, illustrated in Figure 13.5. These symbols consist of the following:

1. The data flow symbol, an arrow showing the flow of data.

2. The process symbol, rounded boxes or bubbles depicting processes that transform the data.

structured analysis Top-down method for defining system inputs, processes, and outputs and for partitioning systems into subsystems or modules that show a logical graphic model of information flow.

data flow diagram (DFD) Primary tool in structured analysis that graphically illustrates a system's component processes and the flow of data between them.

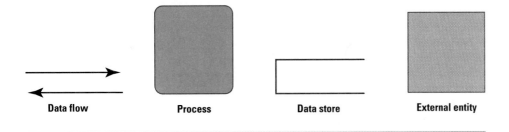

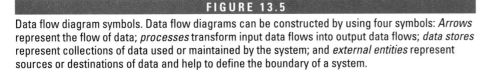

| Data flow | Process | Data store | External entity |

FIGURE 13.5

Data flow diagram symbols. Data flow diagrams can be constructed by using four symbols: *Arrows* represent the flow of data; *processes* transform input data flows into output data flows; *data stores* represent collections of data used or maintained by the system; and *external entities* represent sources or destinations of data and help to define the boundary of a system.

3. The data store symbol, an open rectangle indicating where data are stored.

4. The external entity symbol, either a rectangle or a square indicating the sources or destinations of data.

Data flows show the movement of data between processes, external entities, and data stores. They always contain packets of data, with the name or content of each data flow listed beside the arrow. The flows are of known composition and represent data that are manual or automated. Data flows are labeled with the name of the data flow, which could be reports, documents, or data from a computer file.

Processes portray the transformation of input data flows to output data flows. An example is a process that transforms a sales order into an invoice or that calculates an employee's gross pay from a time card. The convention for naming a process consists of combining a strong verb with an object. For example, we could call the process that calculates gross pay *Calculate gross pay*. Each process has a unique reference number (such as 1.0, 2.3, etc.) so that it can be easily distinguished from other processes in the data flow diagram.

Data stores are either manual or automated inventories of data. They consist of computer files or databases, file cabinets, card files, microfiche, or a binder of paper reports. The name of the data store is written inside the data store symbol.

External entities are originators or receivers of information. They consist of customers, suppliers, or government agencies external to the organization, or employees or departments within the organization but outside the current system. External entities are sometimes called *outside interfaces* because they are outside the boundary or scope of the system treated by the data flow diagram.

Figure 13.6 shows a simple data flow diagram for a mail-in university course registration system. Students submit registration forms with their name, identification number, and the numbers of the courses they wish to take. In process 1.0, the system verifies that each course selected is still open by referencing the university's course file. The file distinguishes courses that are still open from those that have been canceled or filled. Process 1.0 then determines which of the student's selections can be accepted or rejected. Process 2.0 enrolls the student in the courses for which he or she has been accepted. It updates the university's course file with the student's name and identification number and recalculates the class size. If maximum enrollment has been reached, the course number is flagged as closed. Process 2.0 also updates the university's student master file with information about new students or changes in address. Process 3.0 then sends each student applicant a confirmation of registration letter listing the courses for which he or she is registered and noting the course selections that could not be fulfilled.

The diagrams can be used to depict higher-level processes as well as lower-level details. Through leveled data flow diagrams, a complex process can be broken into

data flows The movement of data between processes, external entities, and data stores in a data flow diagram.

processes Portray the transformation of input data flows to output data flows in a data flow diagram. Each has a unique reference number and is named with a verb–object phrase.

data stores Manual or automated inventories of data.

external entities Originators or receivers of information outside the scope of the system portrayed in the data flow diagram. Sometimes called *outside interfaces*.

FIGURE 13.6

Data flow diagram for mail-in
university registration system.
The system has three processes.
Verify availability (1.0), Enroll
student (2.0), and Confirm registration (3.0). The name and content of each of the data flows
appear adjacent to each arrow.
There is one external entity in
this system, the student. There
are two data stores: the student
master file and the course file.

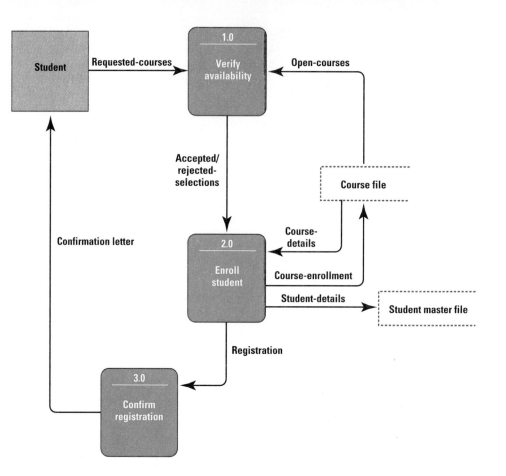

context diagram Overview data
flow diagram depicting an
entire system as a single process
with its major inputs and
outputs.

successive levels of detail. An entire system can be divided into subsystems with a
high-level data flow diagram. Each subsystem, in turn, can be divided into additional
subsystems with second-level data flow diagrams, and the lower-level subsystems can
be broken again until the lowest level of detail has been reached.

Figures 13.7A, 13.7B, and 13.7C show leveled data flow diagrams for a pension
recordkeeping and accounting system. Figure 13.7A is the most general picture of the
system. It is called a context diagram. The **context diagram** always depicts an entire
system as a single process with its major inputs and outputs. Subsequent diagrams
can then break the system into greater levels of detail.

The next level of detail, Figure 13.7B, shows that the system is composed of five
major processes: tracking participation in the pension plan (1.0); tracking service
that can be credited to pension benefits (2.0); capturing employee earnings data (3.0);
maintaining actuarial tables (4.0); and calculating pension benefits (5.0).
Figure 13.7C explodes process 5.0, Calculate benefit, into greater detail. It shows
that this process can be further decomposed into processes to calculate final average
earnings (5.1); the normal retirement benefit (5.2); the early retirement benefit (5.3);
the survivor's benefit (5.4); and a process to generate benefits statements (5.5).

Other Structured Analysis Tools

Other tools for structured analysis include a data dictionary, which we first described
in Chapter 8. In structured analysis, the data dictionary contains information about
individual pieces of data and data groupings within a system. The data dictionary defines the contents of data flows and data stores so that system builders understand
exactly what pieces of data they contain. The dictionary also provides information

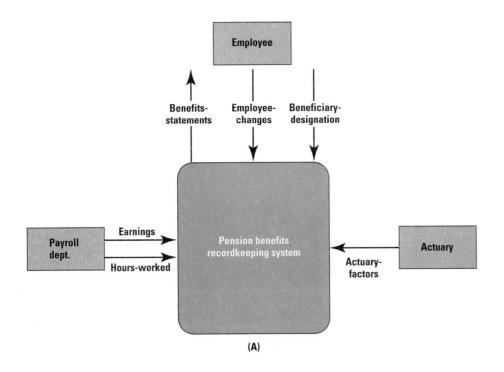

FIGURE 13.7A

Context diagram for a pension benefits recordkeeping and accounting system. This diagram provides an overview of the entire pension benefits recordkeeping and accounting system, showing its major inputs and outputs. The context diagram depicts the entire system as a single process that can be exploded into more detailed data flow diagrams at lower levels. Data flow to and from this pension benefits recordkeeping and accounting system. The external entities are the payroll department, the actuary, and the employee.

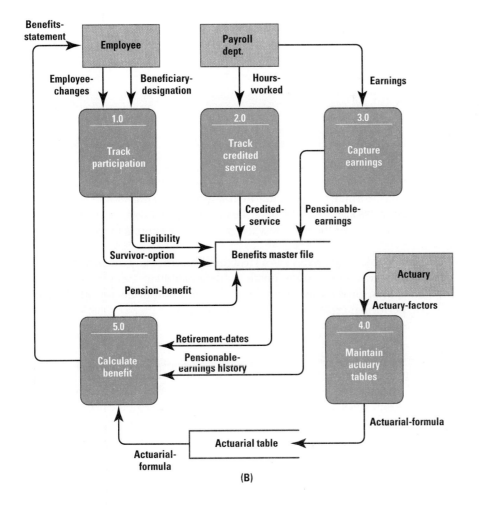

FIGURE 13.7B

Zero-level data flow diagram for a pension benefits recordkeeping and accounting system. This data flow diagram explodes the context diagram into a more detailed picture of the pension benefits recordkeeping and accounting system. It shows that the system consists of five major processes that can, in turn, be broken into more detailed data flow diagrams.

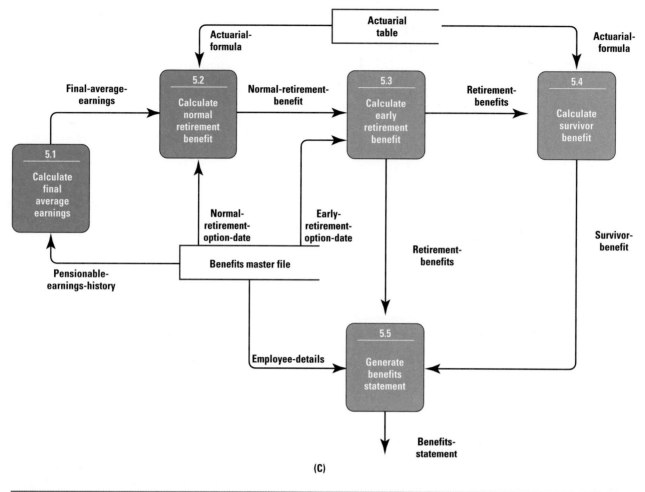

(C)

FIGURE 13.7C

First-level data flow diagram for a pension benefits recordkeeping and accounting system. This data flow diagram breaks down the process *Calculate benefit* (5.0) into further detail. It illustrates that calculating pension benefits entails processes to calculate final average earnings (5.1), normal retirement benefit (5.2), early retirement benefit (5.3), survivor benefit (5.4), and a process to generate a benefits statement (5.5).

process specifications Describe the logic of the transformations occurring within the lowest-level processes of the data flow diagrams.

on the meaning and format of each data item and the data flows and data stores where it is used. **Process specifications** describe the transformations occurring within the lowest-level processes of the data flow diagrams. They express the logic for each process.

The output of structured analysis is a structured specification document that includes data flow diagrams for system functions, data dictionary descriptions of data flows and data stores, process specifications, input and output documents, and security, control, performance, and conversion requirements.

Structured Design

structured design Software design discipline, encompassing a set of design rules and techniques for designing a system from the top down in a hierarchical fashion.

Structured design is primarily a software design discipline, but it is often associated with structured analysis and other structured approaches. **Structured design** encompasses a set of design rules and techniques that promotes program clarity and simplicity, thereby reducing the time and effort required for coding, debugging, and maintenance. Sometimes structured design is also referred to as *top-down design* or *composite design*. The main principle of structured design is that a system should be designed from the top down in hierarchical fashion and refined to greater levels of detail. The design should first consider the main function of a program or system,

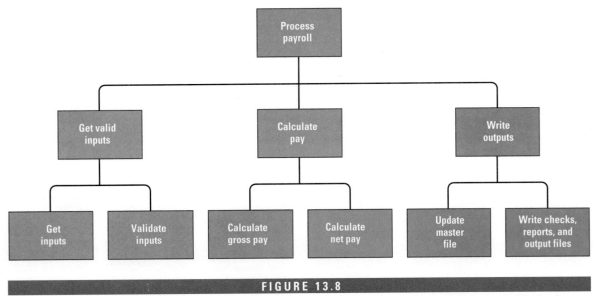

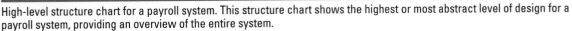

FIGURE 13.8

High-level structure chart for a payroll system. This structure chart shows the highest or most abstract level of design for a payroll system, providing an overview of the entire system.

then break this function into subfunctions and decompose each subfunction until the lowest level of detail has been reached. In this manner, all high-level logic and the design model are developed before detailed program code is written. If structured analysis has been performed, the structured specification document can serve as input to the design process.

As the design is formulated, it is documented in a structure chart. The **structure chart** is a top-down chart, showing each level of design, its relationship to other levels, and its place in the overall design structure. Figure 13.8 shows a structure chart that can be used for a payroll system. If a design has too many levels to fit onto one structure chart, it can be broken down further on more detailed structure charts. A structure chart may document one program, one system (a set of programs), or part of one program.

structure chart System documentation showing each level of design, the relationship among the levels, and the overall place in the design structure; can document one program, one system, or part of one program.

Structured Programming

Structured programming extends the principles governing structured design to the writing of programs. It also is based on the principle of modularization, which follows from top-down development.

Structured programming is a method of organizing and coding programs that simplifies control paths so that the programs can be easily understood and modified. Structured programming reduces the complexity created when program instructions jump forward and backward to other parts of the program, obscuring the logic and flow of the program.

Each of the boxes in the structure chart represents a component **module.** Programs can be partitioned into modules, each of which constitutes a logical unit that performs one or a small number of functions. Ideally, modules should be independent of each other. They should be interconnected so that they have only one entry to and exit from their parent modules. They should share data with as few other modules as possible. Minimizing connections among modules minimizes paths by which errors can be spread to other parts of the system.

Each module should also be kept to a manageable size. An individual should be able to read the program code for the module and easily keep track of its functions. Within each module, program instructions should not wander and should be executed in top-down fashion.

structured programming Discipline for organizing and coding programs that simplifies the control paths so that the programs can be easily understood and modified. Uses the basic control structures and modules that have only one entry point and one exit point.

module A logical unit of a program that performs one or a small number of functions.

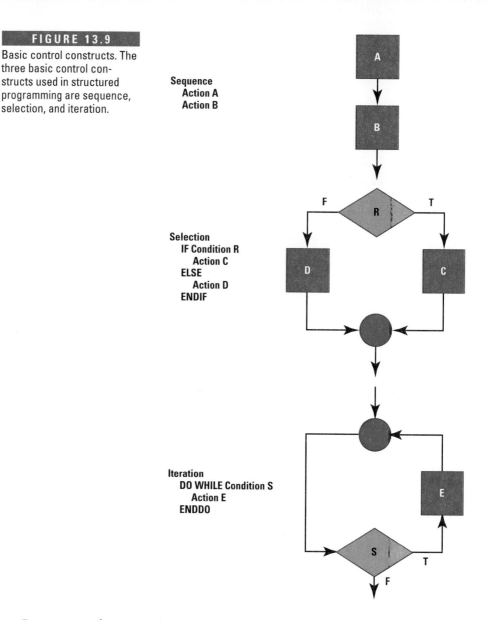

FIGURE 13.9

Basic control constructs. The three basic control constructs used in structured programming are sequence, selection, and iteration.

Sequence
Action A
Action B

Selection
IF Condition R
Action C
ELSE
Action D
ENDIF

Iteration
DO WHILE Condition S
Action E
ENDDO

sequence construct The sequential single steps or actions in the logic of a program that do not depend on the existence of any condition.

selection construct The logic pattern in programming in which a stated condition determines which of two or more actions can be taken depending on which satisfies the stated condition.

iteration construct The logic pattern in programming in which certain actions are repeated while a specified condition occurs or until a certain condition is met.

Proponents of structured programming have shown that any program can be written using three basic control constructs, or instruction patterns: (1) simple sequence, (2) selection, and (3) iteration. These control constructs are illustrated in Figure 13.9.

The **sequence construct** executes statements in the order in which they appear, with control passing unconditionally from one statement to the next. The program will execute statement A and then statement B.

The **selection construct** tests a condition and executes one of two or more alternative instructions based on the results of the test. Condition R is tested. If R is true, statement C is executed. If R is false, statement D is executed. Control then passes to the next statement.

The **iteration construct** repeats an instruction as long as the results of a conditional test remain true. Condition S is tested. If S is true, statement E is executed and control returns to the test of S. If S is false, E is skipped and control passes to the next statement.

Any one or any combination of these control structures can accommodate any kind of processing logic required by a program. There is a single entry and exit point for each structure so that the path of the program logic remains clear.

Flowcharts

Flowcharting is an old design tool that is still in use. **System flowcharts** detail the flow of data throughout an entire information system. Program flowcharts describe the processes taking place within an individual program in the system and the sequence in which they must be executed. Flowcharting is no longer recommended for program design because it does not provide top-down modular structure as effectively as other techniques. However, system flowcharts may still be used to document physical design specifications because they can show all inputs, major files, processing, and outputs for a system and they can document manual procedures.

Using specialized symbols and flow lines, the system flowchart traces the flow of information and work in a system, the sequence of processing steps, and the physical media on which data are input, output, and stored. Figure 13.10 contains the basic symbols for system flowcharting. The plain rectangle is a general symbol for a major computer processing function. Flow lines show the sequence of steps and the direction of information flow. Arrows are employed to show direction if it is not apparent in the diagram.

Figure 13.11 illustrates a high-level system flowchart of a payroll system.

Limitations of Traditional Methods

The traditional structured approach is valuable, but it has shortcomings. Most critics consider structured methodologies to be slow and unresponsive to today's fast-changing business world. The process is very linear. Completion of structured analysis is required before structured design can begin, and structured programming must await the completed deliverables from structured design. The slowness translates into increased cost. A change in specifications requires that the analysis documents and then the design documents must be modified before the programs can be changed to reflect the new requirement.

Structured methodologies are function oriented. They focus on the processes that transform the data. The storage of the data is described as an appendage to those processes. Yet, business management has come to understand that the most valuable portion of information systems is the data. Data generated by one department may be used by many other departments, each of which will process them differently. For example, production quality data might be used by the production department, research labs, marketing and sales staffs, corporate management, and even customers. Systems that focus on data can be smaller and more flexible, making them easier to modify and more responsive to changing business needs.

Despite the fact that specific groups of data are usually processed the same way in different programs, a separate programming procedure must be written every time someone wants to take an action on a particular piece of data. Why take the time and pay the cost to rewrite the code each time a tax calculation needs to be done or a specific chemical needs to be analyzed? Hopes that program modularization would solve this problem of reusability have not been fulfilled. Critics believe we must look beyond structured approaches to find solutions to this critical productivity issue.

Techniques have been developed to address many of these problems. For example, **joint application design (JAD)** is a design method that brings users and IS professionals into a room together for an interactive design of the system. Properly prepared and facilitated, JAD sessions can significantly speed the design phase while involving users in the design at a level previously not possible. (Traditional methods of system specification may still be used with JAD.) Prototyping (discussed in Chapter 12) also speeds design while involving users and increasing the flexibility of the whole process. Nonetheless, the IS profession has been trying to develop other methodologies in an attempt to replace structured methodologies.

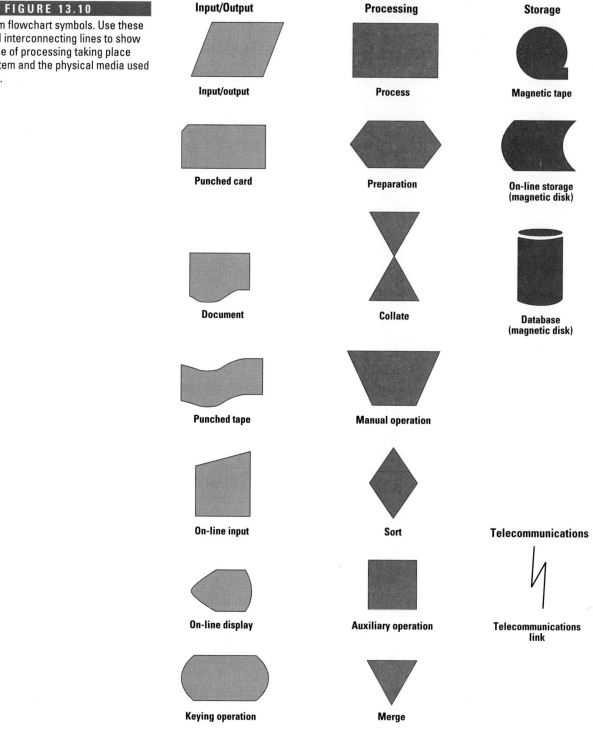

FIGURE 13.10

Basic system flowchart symbols. Use these symbols and interconnecting lines to show the sequence of processing taking place within a system and the physical media used in each step.

Input/Output

Input/output

Punched card

Document

Punched tape

On-line input

On-line display

Keying operation

Processing

Process

Preparation

Collate

Manual operation

Sort

Auxiliary operation

Merge

Storage

Magnetic tape

On-line storage (magnetic disk)

Database (magnetic disk)

Telecommunications

Telecommunications link

13.3 NEW APPROACHES TO QUALITY

In addition to the traditional methodologies and tools, system builders are turning to object-oriented development, computer-aided software engineering (CASE), and software reengineering to help cope with information systems quality problems.

Object-Oriented Software Development

We have already introduced object-oriented programming in Chapter 7. Object-oriented programming is part of a larger approach to systems development called

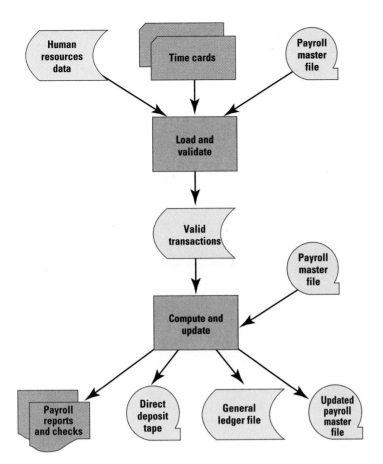

FIGURE 13.11

System flowchart for a payroll system. This is a high-level system flowchart for a batch payroll system. Only the most important processes and files are illustrated. Data are input from two sources: time cards and payroll-related data (such as salary increases) passed from the human resources system. The data are first edited and validated against the existing payroll master file before the payroll master is updated. The update process produces an updated payroll master file, various payroll reports (such as the payroll register and hours register), checks, a direct deposit tape, and a file of payment data that must be passed to the organization's general ledger system. The direct deposit tape is sent to the automated clearinghouse that serves the banks offering direct deposit services to employees.

object-oriented development. **Object-oriented software development** differs from traditional methodologies in the way it handles the issue of process versus data. Traditional structured analysis and design put procedures first. They first view a system in terms of what it is intended to *do* and then develop models of procedures and data. Object-oriented software development deemphasizes procedures. The focus shifts from modeling business processes and data to combining data and procedures into objects. The system is viewed as a collection of classes and objects and the relationships among them. The objects are defined, programmed, documented, and saved for use with future applications.

Proponents of object-oriented development claim that objects can be more easily understood by users than traditional representations of a system. For example, accounts receivable personnel tend to think of entities such as customers, credit limits, and invoices—the same level at which objects are built. Object-oriented analysis (OOA) and object-oriented design (OOD) are based on these objects and are believed to more closely model the real world than previous methods, which describe a system in terms of inputs, outputs, and data flows. However, some research shows that object-oriented software development methods may be more difficult to use for specifying information requirements than traditional structured methods (Vessey and Conger, 1994). Only more experience will tell if object-oriented software development is an improvement.

Benefits of an Object-Oriented Approach

Because objects are reusable, object-oriented software development directly addresses the issue of reusability and is expected to reduce the time and cost of writing software as well as the incidence of defects (Basili, Briand, and Melo, 1996). Of course, no organization will see savings from reusability until it builds up a library of classes and objects to draw upon. Maintenance costs are also lowered by reducing multiple

object-oriented software development Approach to software development that deemphasizes procedures and shifts the focus from modeling business processes and data to combining data and procedures to create objects.

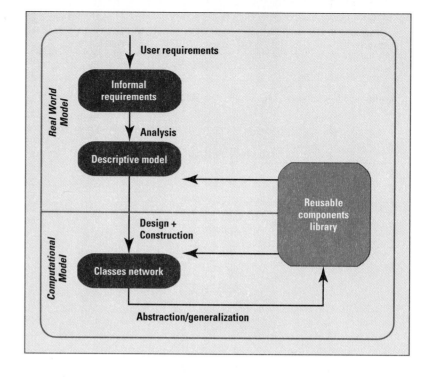

FIGURE 13.12

The object-oriented software life cycle.
Source: From Jean-Marc Nerson, "Applying Object-Oriented Analysis and Design" in Communications of the ACM, *Vol. 35, No. 9, September, 1992. Copyright © 1992 Association For Computing Machinery.*

maintenance changes. For example, when the U.S. postal system changed the ZIP code from five to nine digits, each program within a company had to be changed. If a company's programs were object-oriented, the programmer would only have had to modify the code within the object, and the change would be reflected in all the programs using that object.

Object-oriented software development is leading to other changes in methods. Once a library of objects exists, design and programming often can begin without waiting for analysis documents (see Figure 13.12). Rather, in theory, design and programming can be carried out together, beginning as soon as requirements are completed. Developers—users and IS professionals—use iterations of rapid prototyping to design the system. The prototype, when completed, will encompass a great deal of the programming needed for the completion of the system.

Obstacles to Using Object-Oriented Techniques

Although the demand for training in object-oriented techniques and programming tools is exploding, object-oriented software development is still in its infancy and is too unproven for most companies to adopt it. No agreed-upon object-oriented methodology yet exists, although several have been proposed. Moreover, many companies are hesitant to try it because it requires extensive staff training and a major methodological reorientation. Management is also aware that a complete switch to object-oriented development will take a long time. Most companies have a major investment in existing structured systems that would have to be maintained until the time came that they needed replacement. Until then, the IS departments would have to retain expertise in both structured and object-oriented methods.

New technology needs to be developed for the use of object-oriented methods. Data dictionaries for storing structured data definitions and program code are not appropriate for object-oriented programming. New object-oriented dictionaries need to be developed. CASE tools (discussed below) have been developed to support structured methodologies and are just starting to be redesigned for use with object-oriented development. Even new metrics need to be developed, as many of the metrics now used to evaluate system quality cannot be applied to object-oriented coding. Object-oriented development techniques by themselves cannot guarantee that software will be more flexible. Developers must know how to explicitly design the software for adaptability in the places where it can provide the greatest benefit (Fayad and Cline, 1996).

Computer-Aided Software Engineering (CASE)

Computer-aided software engineering (CASE)—sometimes called computer-aided systems engineering—is the automation of step-by-step methodologies for software and systems development to reduce the amount of repetitive work the developer needs to do. By automating many routine software development tasks and enforcing adherence to design rules, CASE can free the developer for more creative problem-solving tasks. CASE tools can facilitate creation of clear documentation and coordination of team development efforts (Forte and Norman, 1992). Team members can share their work more easily by accessing each other's files to review or modify what has been done. Systems developed with CASE and the newer methodologies have been found to be more reliable and require less maintenance (Dekleva, 1992). Many CASE tools are PC based, with powerful graphical capabilities.

computer-aided software engineering (CASE) The automation of step-by-step methodologies for software and systems development to reduce the amount of repetitive work the developer needs to do.

CASE tools provide automated graphics facilities for producing charts and diagrams, screen and report generators, data dictionaries, extensive reporting facilities, analysis and checking tools, code generators, and documentation generators. Most CASE tools are based on one or more of the popular structured methodologies. Some are starting to support object-oriented development and support for building client/server applications. In general, CASE tools try to increase productivity and quality by doing the following:

- Supporting a standard development methodology and design discipline. The design and overall development effort will have more integrity.
- Improving communication between users and technical specialists. Large teams and software projects can be coordinated more effectively.
- Organizing and correlating design components and providing rapid access to them via a design repository.
- Automating tedious and error-prone portions of analysis, design, and code generation.
- Automating testing and controlling rollout.

Key elements of CASE are described in Table 13.2.

Table 13.2 Elements of CASE
Diagramming tools: Graphics tools for drawing symbols for data flow diagrams, structure charts, entity-relationship diagrams, or other types of diagrams associated with a particular methodology.
Syntax verifier: Verifies the accuracy and completeness of information entered into a system in conformance with the rules of a particular structured methodology.
Prototyping tools: Screen, report, and menu generators that allow the analyst to paint desired screen and report layouts or menu paths through a system without complex formatting specifications or programming.
Information repository: A central information database which serves as a mechanism for storing all types of software assets—screen and report layouts, diagrams, data definitions, program code, project schedules, and other documentation. The repository coordinates, integrates, and standardizes the different pieces of information so they can be easily accessed, shared by analysts, and reused in future software work.
Code generators: These can generate modules of executable code from higher-level specifications. Some CASE tools use icons to indicate various program functions and translate these symbols into programs.
Development methodology: Some CASE products contain checklists or narratives detailing an entire development methodology that help monitor and control the entire systems development project.
Project management tools: Some CASE tools integrate their components with popular stand-alone tools for project scheduling and resource estimation, whereas others incorporate project management software into the CASE tool kit.

Table 13.3	What CASE Tools Can and Cannot Do

CASE Tools Can:

1. Automate many manual tasks of systems development.

2. Promote standardization based on a single methodology.

3. Promote greater consistency and coordination during a development project.

4. Generate a large portion of the documentation for a system, such as data flow diagrams, data models, structure charts, or other specifications.

CASE Tools Cannot:

1. Automatically provide a functional, relevant system. It is just as easy to produce a bad system as to produce a good system using CASE tools.

2. Interface easily with databases and fourth-generation languages.

3. Automatically force analysts to use a prescribed methodology or create a methodology when one does not exist.

4. Radically transform the systems analysis and design process.

Examples of CASE Tools

CASE tools have been classified in terms of whether they support activities at the front end or the back end of the systems development process. Front-end CASE tools focus on capturing analysis and design information in the early stages of systems development. They automate the process of creating data flow diagrams, structure charts, entity-relationship diagrams, and other specifications so that they can be easily revised to improve design before coding begins. Table 13.3 describes the strengths and limitations of CASE tools.

Back-end CASE tools address coding, testing, and maintenance activities and include text editors, formatters, syntax checkers, compilers, cross-reference generators, linkers, symbolic debuggers, execution profilers, code generators, and application generators. Back-end tools help convert specifications automatically into program code.

More fully integrated tools are starting to support the entire systems development process, including project management and automatic generation of program code for routine parts of an application.

Analysts use CASE tools to help capture requirements and specifications by storing the information in a CASE database, where it can be easily retrieved and revised. The CASE tools facilitate up-front design and analysis work, so that there are fewer errors to correct later. CASE text and graphics editors help the analyst create technically correct diagrams, process descriptions, and data dictionary entries. The analyst can draw diagrams by choosing from a set of standard symbols and positioning the symbols on the screen. Text information can be added to the diagram to describe processes and data flows using the CASE tool's text editor.

Many CASE tools automatically tie data elements to the processes wherein they are used. If a data flow diagram is changed from one process to another, the elements in the data dictionary would be altered automatically to reflect the change in the diagram. CASE tools also contain features for validating design; included in these features are automatic balancing of data flow diagrams and checking diagrams and specifications for completeness and consistency. Some tool kits contain prototyping features such as screen and report painters, which allow analysts to draw screen or report formats for users to review. CASE tools thus support iterative design by automating revisions and changes and providing prototyping facilities.

A central element in the CASE tool kit is the information repository, which stores all the information defined by the analysts during the project. The repository includes data flow diagrams, structure charts, entity-relationship diagrams, data definitions,

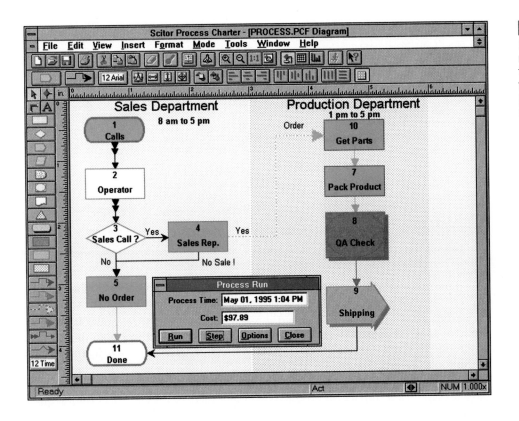

FIGURE 13.13

Process Charter provides tools to map out business processes and to simulate the processes in real-time with flashing colors. The process models include time and cost information.

process specifications, screen and report formats, notes and comments, test results and evaluations, source code, status and audit information, and time and cost estimates. The CASE database can be shared by members of a project team and contains features to restrict changes to only specified analysts.

CASE tools now have features to support client/server applications, object-oriented programming, and business process redesign. For example, Sterling Software's integrated suite of Key CASE tools contains modules for visual object-oriented development and modules to help designers model and generate code for client/server applications. A tool suite for a complete client/server–development environment is also available. Sterling's KEY:Model includes a workflow diagrammer and related tools to generate models of an organization's work flows and processes that can be used for business process redesign work.

Specialized tool sets for business process redesign are also available. Scitor's Process Charter for Windows is a flowcharting and process analysis software package that lets developers diagram and document business processes with information such as resource requirements, costs, efficiencies, and delays. Developers can use this tool to visualize how processes are affected by internal and external factors (see Figure 13.13), to perform "what-if" analyses to test important ideas before they are implemented, and to see how a process might be affected by different constraints (see Figures 13.14 and 13.15)

The Challenge of Using CASE

To be used effectively, CASE tools require more organizational discipline than the manual approach. Every member of a development project must adhere to a common set of naming conventions, standards, and development methodologies. Without this discipline, analysts and designers will cling to their old ways of developing systems and will attempt to incorporate the CASE tool in the process. This can actually be counterproductive because of the incompatibility between the old approach and new tools. The best CASE tools enforce common methods and standards,

FIGURE 13.14

Process Charter allows developers to define and store critical variables such as average wait time or total cost in a Key Value Spreadsheet on which they can test different assumptions and scenarios.

Scitor Process Charter - [PROCESS.PCF Spreadsheet]

File   Edit   View   Insert   Format   Mode   Tools   Window   Help

Activities | Resources | Assignments | **Key Values** | Flow Objects

Description	Current	Baseline 1	Baseline 2	Baseline 3	Baseline 4
Name	PROCESS.PCF	PROCESS.PCF	PROCESS.PCF	PROCESS.PCF	PROCESS.PCF
Time Last Run	13 Dec 16:37:05	13 Dec 16:36:31	13 Dec 16:35:11	13 Dec 16:33:44	13 Dec 16:32:56
Process Total Effort	36h 57.5m	36h 57.5m	37h 33.5m	37h 33.5m	44h 17.5m
Process Total Cost	$802.23	$775.30	$823.68	$795.95	$1,015.35
QA Check Max Copies	3	3	2	2	1
Prod. Engineer Rate	$16/hr	$12/hr	$16/hr	$12/hr	$12/hr
Prod. Engineer Quantity	3	3	2	2	1
Prod. Engineer Total Effort	6h 44m	6h 44m	6h 56m	6h 56m	9h
Prod. Engineer Total Cost	$107.73	$80.80	$110.93	$83.20	$108.00

Ready   Act 1: Calls   CAP NUM

which may discourage their use in situations when organizational discipline is lacking. Effective use of CASE requires strong support from management (Iivari, 1996).

Actual productivity gains from CASE remain difficult to define. A few firms have reported tangible cost savings from using CASE, whereas others note more rapid generation of systems or higher-quality software once developers have learned to use CASE tools (Banker, Kaufmann and Kumar, 1991–1992). Some studies have found that CASE tools improve productivity whereas others have found that CASE tools have no significant impact on productivity and a relatively weak effect on the quality of specifications (Vessey, Jarvenpaa, and Tractinsky, 1992). The issue remains clouded because productivity gains in software development have traditionally been difficult to measure and to quantify.

Although it facilitates some aspects of systems development, CASE is not a magic cure-all. It can accelerate analysis and design and promote iterative design, but it does not enable systems to be designed automatically or ensure that business re-

FIGURE 13.15

Process Charter automatically creates graphs that show how processes are affected by different constraints.

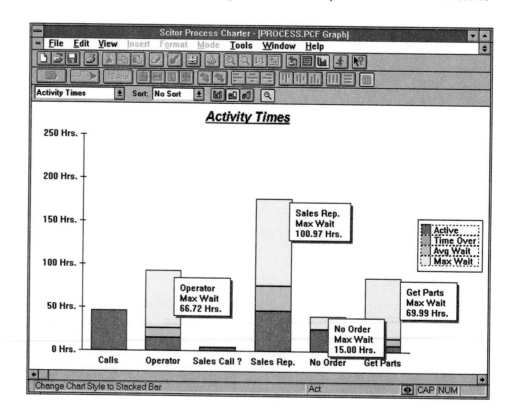

quirements are met. Systems designers still have to understand what a firm's business needs are and how the business works. Systems analysis and design are still dependent on the analytical skills of the analyst/designer. Some of the productivity gains attributed to CASE may actually be the result of systems developers improving communication, coordination, and software integrity by agreeing on a standard methodology rather than from the use of automated CASE tools themselves.

CASE provides a set of labor-saving tools that automate software development work. But the actual software development process to be automated is defined by a methodology. If a firm lacks a methodology, CASE tools may be used to automate disparate, and often incompatible, practices rather than integrating or standardizing a firm's systems development approach.

Software Reengineering

Software reengineering is a methodology that addresses the problem of aging software. A great deal of the software that organizations use was written without the benefit of structured analysis, design, and programming. Such software is difficult to maintain or update. However, the software may serve the organization well enough to continue to be used, if only it could be more easily maintained. The purpose of reengineering is to salvage such software by upgrading it so that the users can avoid a long and expensive replacement project. In essence, developers use reengineering to extract intelligence from existing systems, thereby creating new systems without starting from scratch. Reengineering involves three steps: reverse engineering, revision of design and program specifications, and forward engineering.

Reverse engineering entails extracting the underlying business specifications from existing systems. Older, nonstructured systems do not have structured documentation to clarify the business functions the system is intended to support. Nor do they have adequate documentation of either the system design or the programs. Reverse engineering tools, such as those supplied by Bachman Information Systems of Cambridge, Massachusetts, read and analyze the program's existing code, file, and database descriptions and produce structured documentation of the system. The output will show design-level components, such as entities, attributes, and processes. With structured documentation, the project team can revise the design and specifications to meet current business requirements. In the final step, **forward engineering,** the revised specifications are used to generate new, structured code for a structured and maintainable system. In Figure 13.16, you can follow the reengineering process.

Reengineering can have significant benefits. It allows a company to develop a modern system at a much lower cost than would be the case if it had to develop an entirely new system. The newly reengineered system will reflect current business requirements, and it will be capable of being modified as those requirements change. During the revision phase of the project, the technology of the system can also be upgraded, so that, for example, the new system can be networked or the code can be generated using relational database technology. Finally, unstructured programs contain a large amount of redundant code. Reengineering allows the developers to eliminate redundancy, thus reducing the size and complexity of the programs, resulting in fewer opportunities for current and future bugs.

It should be pointed out that software reengineering is a very complex undertaking, requiring much more than simply running old code through a CASE tool to produce a new system. Additional research and analysis are usually required to determine all business rules and data requirements for the new system (Aiken, Muntz, and Richards, 1994).

software reengineering Methodology that addresses the problem of aging software by salvaging and upgrading it so that the users can avoid a long and expensive replacement project.

reverse engineering The process of taking existing programs' code, file, and database descriptions and converting them into corresponding design-level components that can then be used to create new applications.

forward engineering The final step in reengineering when the revised specifications are used to generate new, structured program code for a structured and maintainable system.

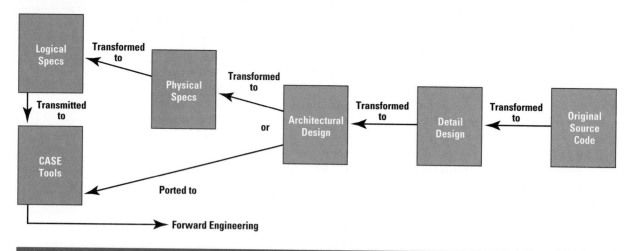

FIGURE 13.16

Steps in the reverse engineering process. The primary function of reverse engineering is to capture the functional capabilities—the process logic—of the existing system in a simplified form that can be revised and updated for the basis of the new structured replacement system.

Source: Thomas J. McCabe and Eldonna S. Williamson, "Tips on Reengineering Redundant Software," Datamation, *April 15, 1992. Reproduced with permission from DATAMATION©.*

MANAGEMENT WRAP-UP

MANAGEMENT

Establishing quality standards for the organization's products, services, business processes, and software systems are key management decisions. It is management's responsibility to ensure that proper financial and people resources have been allocated to meet these standards.

ORGANIZATION

The characteristics of the organization play a large role in determining its approach to quality and quality programs. Some organizations are more quality conscious than others. Their cultures and business processes support high standards of quality and quality programs and a high level of quality embedded in their information systems. Creating a quality-minded organization can be a process of lengthy organizational change.

TECHNOLOGY

A number of technologies and methodologies are available for improving software quality. They include software metrics, systems development methodologies, and tools to automate analysis, code generation, and testing. Organizational discipline is required to use these technologies effectively.

For Discussion: How much software testing is "enough"? What management, organization, and technology issues would you consider in answering this question?

SUMMARY

1. Describe how information systems can contribute to total quality management in an organization. Information systems can contribute to total quality management by helping other business functions perform their work more effectively, by helping to analyze and redesign business processes, by suggesting new ways to apply technology to enhance quality, and by sharing their experience in quantifying and measuring procedures with other areas of the organization. Information systems can help organizations simplify their products and production processes, meet benchmarking standards, improve customer service, reduce production cycle time, and improve the quality and precision of design and production.

2. Explain why information systems must pay special attention to software quality assurance. Software plays a central role in most organizations and is an integral part of daily operations, products, and services. However, it presents quality problems because of the difficulty in developing software that captures user specifications accurately, because of the high costs of maintaining software and correcting errors, and because software bugs may be impossible to eliminate.

3. Identify the principal solutions to information systems quality problems. Information systems quality problems can be minimized by using structured systems development methodologies, software metrics, thorough testing procedures, quality tools, and by reallocating resources to put more emphasis on the early stages of the systems development cycle.

4. Describe the traditional tools and methodologies for promoting information systems quality. Structured analysis highlights the flow of data and the processes through which data are transformed. Its principal tool is the data flow diagram. Structured design and programming are software design disciplines that produce reliable, well-documented software with a simple, clear structure that is easy for others to understand and maintain. System flowcharts are useful for documenting the physical aspects of system design.

5. Describe new approaches for promoting information systems quality. Object-oriented software development is expected to reduce the time and cost of writing software and of making maintenance changes because it models a system as a series of reusable objects that combine both data and procedures. Computer-aided software engineering (CASE) automates step-by-step methodologies for systems development. It promotes standards and improves coordination and consistency during systems development. CASE tools help system builders build a better model of a system and facilitate revision of design specifications to correct errors. Software reengineering helps system builders reconfigure aging software to conform to structured design principles, making it easier to maintain.

KEY TERMS

Quality	Debugging	Process specifications	Joint application
Total quality	Structured	Structured design	design (JAD)
management (TQM)	Structured analysis	Structure chart	Object-oriented software
Bugs	Data flow diagram (DFD)	Structured programming	development
Development methodology	Data flows	Module	Computer-aided software
Resource allocation	Processes	Sequence construct	engineering (CASE)
Software metrics	Data stores	Selection construct	Software reengineering
Function point analysis	External entities	Iteration construct	Reverse engineering
Walkthrough	Context diagram	System flowchart	Forward engineering

REVIEW QUESTIONS

1. What is total quality management? How can information systems contribute to it?

2. Describe some approaches that companies follow in their quality programs and the way that they can be supported by information systems.

3. Why can software become such an important quality problem for information systems? Describe two software quality problems.

4. Name and describe four solutions to software quality problems.

5. What is structured analysis? What is the role of the following in structured analysis: data flow diagrams, data dictionaries, process specifications?

6. What are the principles of structured design? How can structured design promote software quality?

7. What is the relationship of structured programming to structured design?

8. Describe the use of system flowcharts.

9. What is the difference between object-oriented software development and traditional structured methodologies?

10. What is CASE? How can it promote quality in information systems?

11. What are some key elements of CASE tools?

12. What are software reengineering and reverse engineering? How can they promote quality in information systems?

Form a group with two or three other students. Use one of the Web search tools to locate a site describing a CASE tool or business process reengineering tool or refer to Chapter 13 of the Laudon & Laudon Web site for some suggestions. Select one of these toolsets to analyze. On the basis of the information provided by the Web site, describe its capabilities and where such a tool might be most useful. Present your findings to the class.

CASE STUDY

Quality for Customer Self-Service

How do you define quality when you are using new technology for customer service? Many companies are asking that question because there are so many ways that information systems are being used to help customers or to create situations in which customers can help themselves.

To Online Vacation Mall (OVM), a Web-based business that lets people make their own vacation reservations, the answer seemed clear—offer all functions the customers will need directly on the home page. And make the site attractive with lots of jazzy artwork. OVM, established by MarkNet World of Mequon, Wisconsin, is in the travel reservation business. The stakes are enormous. John Ricks, vice president of marketing at MarkNet, cites a Forrester Research study that estimates sales via the Internet will reach $6.5 billion in the year 2000. Although computer products will account for the largest share of those dollars, according to this study, travel expenditures will come in second.

Web users can already go to many different sites to make airline,

automobile rental, and hotel reservations. However, the central OVM vision is that it should be easier for the potential traveler—they should be able to do it all in one place. Customers should be able to make all reservations at one Web site, and that site is OVM. They are able to book their reservations themselves with only one transaction rather than having to book flights, cars, and hotels in separate transactions. OVM management believes their's is the only such site on the Web.

Online Vacation Mall made its debut on the Web in March 1996. Web users were greeted with a jazzy home page interface designed partially with attractive cartoonlike pictures. The image at the top of the site gave users immediate choices to hot-link to travel destinations at the start. Links to nearly all OVM site pages (several score of them) were listed along the left side of the page in a vertical bar. The site contained an enormous amount of information (nearly 45 MB of data). To present the information to the customer, the programmers used the most sophisticated browser technology, frames, which essentially act as pages within a page, giving the programmer a great deal of functionality with which to work. The site even featured partnerships with such familiar travel providers as United Vacations and Southwest Airlines, adding an air of solidity to the site.

Everything on the site appeared to be of very high quality when it was launched—OVM was determined to be successful. The problems only became clear once the system went live, and they were many and serious. In fact, the interface was not user friendly. On December 13, 1996, after all but starting from scratch again, OVM installed a newly developed interface, abandoning the failing original one. The underlying problem seemed to be that the designers had focused on the wrong issues. The designers had not understood clearly what a quality interface would look like from either the perspective of the customer or even the eyes of OVM designers. Let us examine the problems.

The most obvious difficulty was the list of links along the left side. The designers saw them as helpful to the customer because by using them customers could immediately jump to the precise screen they wanted. Their belief was that this would save the users time and energy as they would not need to navigate through a number of levels to get to a specific function. However, to the users the list of links and the whole home page appeared to be very busy and too disorganized. The hot-link list was long, with three columns and illustrated graphics. It was so enormous that it overwhelmed many potential customers—they could not deal with so many choices in one window. Doug Frede, a MarkNet application developer, described MarkNet's conclusion: "The old home page was too confusing. It was like trying to show everything at once instead of leading them through the site." A new approach had to be found.

The graphics also presented major problems. The cartoonlike graphics were meant to entice potential travelers. In addition to these pictures, OVM's site also displayed many maps because they are such an essential part of travel planning. The designers had taken great care in making the maps as detailed and beautiful as possible. However, the clarity and beauty of the graphics carried a heavy price. Graphics-laden pages are very slow to download, and of course this proved to be the case for OVM customers, even for customers using a relatively fast 28.8 baud modem. But the problem was even worse because the designers had forgotten that many Web users still had modems as slow as 14.4 and even 9.6 bauds. The frustratingly sluggish download undermined OVM's basic strategy of making reservations easier for travelers. For these users, simply downloading the 60 KB Online Vacation Mall home page was virtually interminable. The screens simply had to work faster.

Problems appeared not only from the perspective of the customer, however. The main image at the top of the home page presented a problem to Online Vacation Mall because the image proved to be inflexible. Modification was so difficult that when the company decided to add links to new ski and golfing package offerings, they were not able. They realized they needed to reprogram the home page using more flexible technology, technology that allowed them to respond to the rapid pace of change in the travel business.

In addition, the support staff found that their use of frames did not work well and often made the site more difficult for customers. The frames were incompatible with some browsers (although they worked with the two major browsers—Netscape's

and Microsoft's). Moreover, the pages often had too many frames to fit onto the screen with smaller monitors. Finally, the technical staff discovered too late that the search engine they were using had problems searching the whole page when multiple frames were on that page. As a result, often the user would be directed to the wrong frame. Ultimately the staff decided that frames presented too many problems and they should abandon them.

The OVM team had one other problem. They felt that the cartoonlike graphics did not present the level of professionalism they wanted. They were too "cartoony." They decided that most of the picture graphics needed to be replaced with photographs that would present a more appropriate image.

The result is that the whole interface had to be redesigned. The new design was based on a new navigational system that reduced all locations into five content paths. Each of the five major areas is represented by its own color. Customers are presented with the five areas on the home page. They navigate within one of the five areas to the specific sites needed. By using five area colors, navigational arrows, and navigation bar listings, users easily now know just where they are and where they need to go next. And buttons to the other four major areas are available on each page so they can jump elsewhere when desired.

The vacation maps were redesigned to make them easier to understand. The new maps, for example, contained more redundancy. At the same time the maps were made smaller. The new ones totaled only about 10 KB each versus 25 KB with the old maps. Photographs replaced most of the "cartoony" graphics. Finally, frames were completely eliminated. As a result of these changes, the new site is now much easier to navigate. The evidence of this is that the overall site hit count has gone down while the number of users has risen by 15 percent. Dan Early, director

of business development for MarkNet, explains that we "can actually handle more users when [our] site is put together well."

Poor quality resulting from a failure to focus on the right issues when adopting a new technology is not limited to the Web. It seems to arise from the failure to understand the underlying issues of new technology. For example, Digital Equipment Corporation had a similar experience when designing a system to handle responses to its marketing campaigns. Stimulated by major marketing campaigns, the company was receiving 3000 telephone calls per day asking for more information on advertised products. Labor accounts for 70 percent of call center costs, and telephone automation could greatly reduce this expense. When the caller is only seeking information, it can often be supplied without human intervention. Digital decided to turn to integrated voice response (IVR), the relatively new but rapidly growing automation technology, to help them handle all those calls while reducing costs. Most of us have experienced this technology when we make a call and are forced to select from a menu of choices by pressing a digit on the telephone. Digital's approach made a great deal of sense when viewed both from the perspective of Digital's costs and from that of the customers seeking information.

The biggest problem was that the IVR system ran seven layers deep, keeping the caller busy pushing buttons. It did not come as a surprise to some at Digital that the system resulted in a very high hang-up rate. "We didn't need surveys to tell us we weren't doing well," commented Eric Hjerpe, director of IT for Digital's Systems Business Unit Americas. The customers did not like it. Moreover, Digital marketing didn't like it either. The system was a missed opportunity from their perspective because it did not tell Digital anything about either the callers or the effectiveness of Digital's marketing campaigns. The system did not even record to which ad the caller was responding. Nor could the company tell if the ads were generating new revenue.

Digital's response was to modify the IVR system, combining it with a new multimillion-dollar call center oriented toward the customer. "We've replaced our voice response units with people," explains Hjerpe. Digital now guarantees that all calls will be answered by a customer-service representative within four rings. Both Digital and their potential customers appear to be much happier. ∎

Sources: Lori Piquet, "The Virtual World," *ZD Internet,* March 1997; Deborah Ashrand, "Is Your Automated Customer Service Killing You?" *Datamation,* May 1997; and Tom Field, "Help Yourself," *Webmaster,* March 1997.

Case Study Questions

1. How were Online Vacation Mall and Digital's IVR system supposed to provide quality? What business processes were supposed to be improved by these systems?

2. How well did OVM and Digital's IVR enhance the quality of customer service? Why?

3. What management, organization, and technology factors were responsible for the problems that Online Vacation Mall and Digital Equipment experienced with these systems?

4. If you were helping to design OVM's Web site or Digital's IVM, what could you have done to avoid the problems they countered? What management, organization, and technology issues would you have considered?

REFERENCES

Abdel-Hamid, Tarek K. "The Economics of Software Quality Assurance: A Simulation-Based Case Study." *MIS Quarterly* (September 1988).

Aiken, Peter, Alice Muntz, and Russ Richards. "DOD Legacy Systems: Reverse Engineering Data Requirements." *Communications of the ACM 37,* no. 5 (May 1994).

Alberts, David S. "The Economics of Software Quality Assurance." Washington D.C.: National Computer Conference, 1976 proceedings.

Baecker, Ron, Chris DiGiano, and Aaron Marcus. "Software Visualization for Debugging." *Communications of the ACM 40,* no. 4 (April 1997).

Banker, Rajiv D., Srikant M. Datar, Chris F. Kemerer, and Dani Zweig. "Software Complexity and Maintenance Costs." *Communications of the ACM 36,* no. 11 (November 1993).

Banker, Rajiv D., Robert J. Kaufmann, and Rachna Kumar. "An Empirical Test of Object-Based Output Measurement Metrics in a Computer-Aided Software Engineering (CASE) Environment." *Journal of Management Information Systems 8,* no. 3 (Winter 1991–1992).

Banker, Rajiv D., and Chris F. Kemerer. "Performance Evaluation Metrics in Information Systems Development: A Principal-Agent Model." *Information Systems Research 3,* no. 4 (December 1992).

Basili, Victor R., Lionel C. Briand, and Walcelio L. Melo. "How Reuse Influences Productivity in OO Systems." *Communications of the ACM 39,* no. 10 (October 1996).

Berry, Leonard L. and A. Parasuraman. "Listening to the Customer—The Concept of a Service—Quality Information System." *Sloan Management Review* (Spring 1997).

Blum, Bruce I. "A Taxonomy of Software Development Methods." *Communications of the ACM 37,* no. 11 (November 1994).

Boehm, Barry W. "Understanding and Controlling Software Costs." *IEEE Transactions on Software Engineering 14,* no. 10 (October 1988).

Booch, Grady. *Object Oriented Design with Applications.* Redwood City, California: Benjamin Cummings (1991).

Bouldin, Barbara M. "What Are You Measuring? Why Are You Measuring It?" *Software Magazine* (August 1989).

Coad, Peter, with Edward Yourdon. *Object-Oriented Analysis.* Englewood Cliffs, NJ: Prentice-Hall (1989).

Dekleva, Sasa M. "The Influence of Information Systems Development Approach on Maintenance." *MIS Quarterly 16,* no. 3 (September 1992).

DeMarco, Tom. *Structured Analysis and System Specification.* New York: Yourdon Press (1978).

Dijkstra, E. "Structured Programming," in *Classics in Software Engineering,* edited by Edward Nash Yourdon. New York: Yourdon Press (1979).

Domingue, John, and Paul Mulholland. "Fostering Debugging Communities on the Web." *Communications of the ACM 40,* no. 4 (April 1997).

Fabris, Peter. "Going South." *Webmaster* (April 1997).

Fayad, Mohammed, and Marshall P. Cline. "Aspects of Software Adaptability." *Communications of the ACM 39,* no. 10 (October 1996).

Flatten, Per O., Donald J. McCubbrey, P. Declan O'Riordan, and Keith Burgess. *Foundations of Business Systems,* 2nd ed. Fort Worth, TX: The Dryden Press (1992).

Forte, Gene, and Ronald J. Norman. "Self-Assessment by the Software Engineering Community." *Communications of the ACM 35,* no. 4 (April 1992).

Freedman, David H. "Programming Without Tears." *High Technology 6* no. 4 (April 1986).

Gane, Chris, and Trish Sarson. *Structured Systems Analysis: Tools and Techniques.* Englewood Cliffs, NJ: Prentice-Hall (1979).

Henderson-Sellers, Brian, and Julian M. Edwards. "The Object-Oriented Systems Life Cycle." *Communications of the ACM 33,* no. 9 (September 1990).

Iivari, Juhani. "Why are CASE Tools Not Used?" *Communications of the ACM 39,* no. 10 (October 1996).

International Data Corporation. "Object Technology: A Key Software Technology for the '90s." *Computerworld* (May 11, 1992).

Keyes, Jessica. "New Metrics Needed for New Generation." *Software Magazine* (May 1992).

King, Julia. "Quality Conscious." *Computerworld* (July 19, 1993).

"Komag Chooses MES for Production Control." *Datamation* (September 15, 1994).

Korson, Tim, and John D. McGregor. "Understanding Object Oriented: A Unifying Paradigm." *Communications of the ACM* 33, no. 9 (September 1990).

Krajewski, Lee J., and Larry P. Ritzman. *Operations Management: Strategy and Analysis*, 4th ed. Reading, MA: Addison-Wesley (1996).

LaPlante, Alice. "For IS, Quality is Job None." *Computerworld* (January 6, 1992).

Lieberman, Henry. "Introduction: The Debugging Scandal and What to Do About It." *Communications of the ACM* 40, no. 4 (April 1997).

Lientz, Bennett P., and E. Burton Swanson. *Software Maintenance Management*. Reading, MA: Addison-Wesley (1980).

Littlewood, Bev, and Lorenzo Strigini. "The Risks of Software." *Scientific American* (November 1992).

Littlewood, Bev, and Lorenzo Strigini. "Validation of Ultrahigh Dependability for Software-Based Systems." *Communications of the ACM* 36, no. 11 (November 1993).

Maletz, Mark C. "KBS Circles: A Technology Transfer Initiative that Leverages Xerox's Leadership through Quality Program." *MIS Quarterly* 14, no. 3 (September 1990).

Mandell, Mel. "Statistical Software Rings in Quality." *Computerworld* (January 6, 1992).

Martin, James, and Carma McClure. *Structured Techniques: The Basis of CASE*. Englewood Cliffs, NJ: Prentice-Hall (1988).

Mazzucchelli, Louis. "Structured Analysis Can Streamline Software Design." *Computerworld* (December 9, 1985).

McIntyre, Scott C., and Higgins, Lexis F. "Object-Oriented Analysis and Design: Methodology and Application." *Journal of Management Information Systems* 5, no. 1 (Summer 1988).

McWilliams, Brian. "Coming Back for More." *Computerworld* (February 13, 1995).

Moran, Robert. "The Case against CASE." *InformationWeek* (February 17, 1992).

Nerson, Jean-Marc. "Applying Object-Oriented Analysis and Design." *Communications of the ACM* 35, no. 9 (September 1992).

Norman, Ronald J., and Jay F. Nunamaker, Jr. "CASE Productivity Perceptions of Software Engineering Professionals." *Communications of the ACM* 32, no. 9 (September 1989).

Palley, Michael A., and Sue Conger. "Health Care Information Systems and Formula-Based Reimbursement: An Empirical Study of Diagnosis-Related Groups, Patient Account Systems, and Hospital Compliance Costs." *Health Care Management Review* 20, no. 2 (1995).

Putnam, L. H., and A. Fitzsimmons. "Estimating Software Costs." *Datamation* (September 1979, October 1979, and November 1979).

Radding, Alan. "Quality is Job No. 1." *Datamation* (October 1, 1992).

Rettig, Marc. "Software Teams." *Communications of the ACM* 33, no. 10 (October 1990).

Rigdon, Joan E. "Frequent Glitches in New Software Bug Users." *Wall Street Journal* (January 18, 1995).

Swanson, Kent, Dave McComb, Jill Smith, and Don McCubbrey. "The Application Software Factory: Applying Total Quality Techniques to Systems Development." *MIS Quarterly* 15, no. 4 (December 1991).

Vessey, Iris, and Sue A. Conger. "Requirements Specification: Learning Object, Process, and Data Methodologies." *Communications of the ACM* 37, no. 5 (May 1994).

Vessey, Iris, Sirkka I. Jarvenpaa, and Noam Tractinsky. "Evaluation of Vendor Products: CASE Tools as Methodology Companions." *Communications of the ACM* 35, no. 4 (April 1992).

Yourdon, Edward, and L. L. Constantine, *Structured Design*. New York: Yourdon Press (1978).

Zultner, Richard E. "TQM for Technical Teams." *Communications of the ACM* 36, no. 10 (October 1993).

System Success and Failure: Implementation

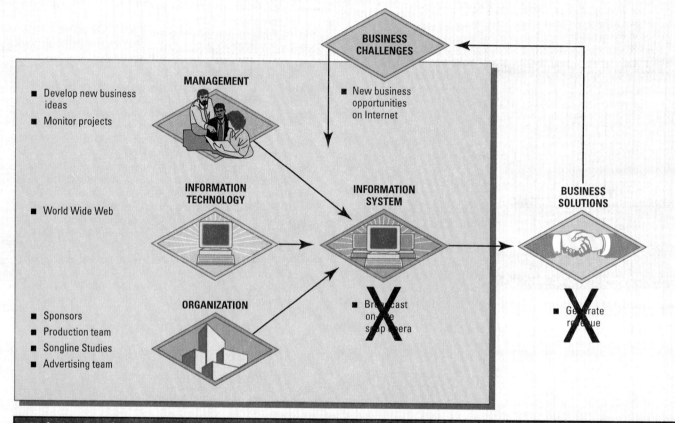

MANAGEMENT

- Develop new business ideas
- Monitor projects

INFORMATION TECHNOLOGY

- World Wide Web

ORGANIZATION

- Sponsors
- Production team
- Songline Studies
- Advertising team

BUSINESS CHALLENGES

- New business opportunities on Internet

INFORMATION SYSTEM

- Broadcast on-the soap opera

BUSINESS SOLUTIONS

- Generate revenue

Web Site Failures

Although the World Wide Web offers exciting new ways of doing business, it also has created new opportunities for failure. Ferndale, an on-line multimedia soap opera, proved that launching a Web site carries significant risks no matter how much effort is vested in it. The site received notice of its cancellation after a run of four months, not a very long life span for a project that seemed to have all the resources required for success. Dale Dougherty, president and CEO of Songline Studios Inc., commissioned Tom Arriola to create Ferndale. Songline was not a run-of-the-mill operation, counting America Online Inc. among its owners. Arriola himself repre-

LEARNING OBJECTIVES	
After completing this chapter, you will be able to:	1. Identify major problem areas in information systems.
	2. Determine whether a system is successful.
	3. Describe the principal causes of information system failure.
	4. Describe the relationship between the implementation process and system outcome.
	5. Describe appropriate strategies to manage the implementation process.

sented a known quantity in the field of Web site development, having been responsible for the provocative Crime Scene site which allows guests to participate in a chillingly lifelike murder probe. The marriage of Songline's capital and Arriola's talent appeared promising.

Ferndale, which acquired its name when Dougherty changed it from Arriola's Avondale, presented the lives of patients and workers at an exclusive, upscale mental hospital. The plan called for daily episodes which would reveal their story lines in the form of patient files and e-mail messages. Dougherty approved the idea, and set his creator free to begin production. Arriola

employed a professional screenwriter, and after a lengthy search, settled on a designer. The latter would result in Ferndale's first setback, as an early missed deadline resulted in the dismissal of the design company that had been hired. By the time production began, Arriola had added 25 individuals to the staff which boasted a costume designer, a makeup artist, and others that would normally contribute to a television or film production. A month and a half into the project, the budget had soared into the six-figure region.

Songline did not erupt into an immediate panic. The company had established a scheme for funding

the Ferndale venture. Receipts would arrive in the form of advertising and payments from host AOL, which pays its contributors a fee for each user that logs on to one of their features. Then the project began to fail. Earnings from AOL did not reach their anticipated level, netting only about $5000 a month. Songline's advertising team set their campaign in high gear, attempting to land accounts with Snapple, Coca-Cola, and Taco Bell. When those deals fell through, Songline discovered Ferndale's fundamental fault: content. As it turned out, the soap opera's quirky, provocative attitude scared away advertisers, and probably some visitors as well.

Ferndale's production team tried to keep the Web site afloat by downsizing and cost cutting. In the end, they simply could not stop the bleeding. Arriola attributes Ferndale's failure to miscalculations in finance and style. The original plan relied too heavily on revenue from AOL, and the content of the site did not follow the same recipe that AOL's other successful areas used. Perhaps Arriola could use the death of Ferndale as a plot for a murder scenario on Crime Scene. ■

Source: Art Jahnke, "Noble Failures," *WebMaster*, December 1996.

MANAGEMENT CHALLENGES

Failed projects such as Ferndale are not limited to initiatives on the World Wide Web and the Internet. There is a very high failure rate among conventional information systems projects as well. In nearly every organization, information systems projects take much more time and money to implement than originally anticipated, or the completed system does not work properly. Some of these problems are caused by information system technology, but many can be attributed to managerial and organizational factors. Implementing an information system is a process of organizational change, and you should be aware of the following management challenges:

1. **Organizational inertia.** In the absence of an organizational crisis, it is difficult to focus organizational attention and resources on developing new systems because organizations are so resistant to change. Much large-scale system development is initiated in periods of organizational crisis, and is not planned. These periods are not well suited to rational planning and implementation.

2. **Dealing with the complexity of large-scale systems projects.** Large-scale systems that affect large numbers of organizational units and staff members and that have extensive information requirements are difficult to oversee, coordinate, and plan for. Implementing such systems, which have multi-year development periods, is especially problem-ridden because the systems are so complex.

3. **Estimating the time and cost to implement a successful large information system.** There are few reliable techniques for estimating the time and cost to develop medium- to large-scale information systems. Few projects take into account the long-term maintenance costs of systems. Guidelines presented in this chapter are helpful but cannot guarantee that a large information system project can be precisely planned and given a projected budget.

When information systems fail to work properly or cost too much to develop, companies may not realize any benefits from their information system investment and the system may not be able to solve the problems for which it was intended. Because so many information systems are trouble-ridden, designers, builders, and users of information systems should understand how and why they succeed or fail. This chapter explores the managerial, organizational, and technological factors responsible for information system success and failure and examines the process of system implementation.

As many as 75 percent of all large systems may be considered to be operating failures. Although these systems are in production, they take so much extra time and money to implement or are so functionally deficient that businesses can't reap the expected benefits. A 1994 study by Standish Group International Inc. found that 31 percent of all corporate software development projects are canceled before completion. Fifty-one percent cost two to three times the amount budgeted and take three times longer than expected to finish (Bulkeley, 1996).

Many information **system "failures"** are not necessarily falling apart, but either they clearly are not used in the way they were intended, or they are not used at all. Users have to develop parallel manual procedures to make these systems work properly. For example, the employee benefits department of a multiunit manufacturing concern continues to maintain all the benefits data for the company's 20,000 employees manually, despite the presence of an automated, on-line system for pension and life insurance benefits. Users complain that the data in the system are unreliable because they do not capture the prior benefits plan data for employees from acquisitions and because payroll earnings figures are out of date. All pension calculations, preretirement estimates, and benefits analysis must be handled manually.

In some systems, nearly all reports put out for management are never read. They are considered worthless and full of figures of no consequence for decision making or analysis (Lucas, 1981). For instance, managers in a prominent commercial bank with branches throughout the United States and Europe found its batch loan account system virtually useless. Pages of reports were filled with zeros, making it practically impossible to assess the status of a client's loan. The amount of the loan, the outstanding balance, and the repayment schedule had to be tracked manually. The bank was also highly dissatisfied with its on-line client reporting system. Although the bank maintained files on all areas for client accounts (loans, savings, Individual Retirement Accounts, checking), only checking and savings account data were available on-line. Therefore, managers and analysts could not obtain complete client profiles when they needed them.

Other automated systems go untouched because they are either too difficult to use or because their data cannot be trusted. Users continue to maintain their records manually. For instance, a nationally known executive recruiting firm found that essential reports on search activity are routinely three months out of date. The firm has to develop statistics manually on the number of executive searches initiated in a given month. Recruiters have no way of tracking and coordinating searches among the company's branch offices in New York, Chicago, Houston, and Los Angeles.

Still other systems flounder because of processing delays, excessive operational costs, or chronic production problems. For instance, the batch accounts receivable system of a medium-sized consumer products manufacturer was constantly breaking down. Production runs were aborting several times a month, and major month-end runs were close to three weeks behind schedule. Because of excessive reruns, schedule delays, and time devoted to fixing antiquated programs, the information systems staff had no time to work out long-term solutions or convert to an on-line system.

In all of these cases, the information systems in question must be judged failures. Why do system failures occur?

system failure An information system that either does not perform as expected, is not operational at a specified time, or cannot be used in the way it was intended.

Information System Problem Areas

The problems causing information system failure fall into multiple categories, as illustrated by Figure 14.1. The major problem areas are design, data, cost, and operations. These problems can be attributed not only to technical features of information systems but to nontechnical sources as well. In fact, most of these problems stem from organizational factors.

FIGURE 14.1

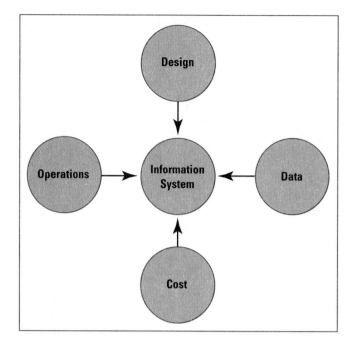

Design

The actual design of the system fails to capture essential business requirements or improve organizational performance. Information may not be provided quickly enough to be helpful; it may be in a format that is impossible to digest and use; or it may represent the wrong pieces of data.

The way in which nontechnical business users must interact with the system may be excessively complicated and discouraging. A system may be designed with a poor **user interface**. The user interface is the part of the system with which end users interact. For example, an input form or an on-line screen may be so poorly arranged that no one wants to submit data. The procedures to request on-line information retrieval may be so unintelligible that users are too frustrated to make requests. A graphical user interface that is supposed to be intuitively easy to learn may discourage use because display screens are cluttered and poorly arranged or because users don't understand the meaning and function of the icons. For example, most users of Microsoft Publisher did not understand an icon with arrows pointing in all four directions that was meant to designate that they could move boxes in any direction around the screen. The problem was solved when programmers embedded a moving truck with the word *move* on it within the four arrows (Bulkeley, 1992). A high percentage of business software developed or purchased by companies goes unused or underused because it lacks an appropriate user interface.

An information system will be judged a failure if its design is not compatible with the structure, culture, and goals of the organization as a whole. As pointed out in Chapter 3, management and organization theorists have viewed information system technology as closely interrelated with all the other components of organizations—tasks, structure, people, and culture. Because all these components are interdependent, a change in one will affect all the others. Therefore, the organization's tasks, participants, structure, and culture are bound to be affected when an information system is changed. Designing a system redesigns the organization.

Historically, information system design has been preoccupied with technical issues at the expense of organizational concerns. The result has often been information systems that are technically excellent but incompatible with their organization's structure, culture, and goals. Without a close organizational fit, such systems have created tensions, instability, and conflict.

user interface The part of the information system through which the end user interacts with the system; type of hardware and the series of on-screen commands and responses required for a user to work with the system.

Data

The data in the system have a high level of inaccuracy or inconsistency. The information in certain fields may be erroneous or ambiguous; or they may not be broken out properly for business purposes. Information required for a specific business function may be inaccessible because the data are incomplete.

Cost

Some systems such as the Ferndale on-line multimedia soap opera operate quite smoothly, but their cost to implement and run on a production basis is way over budget. Other systems may be too costly to compete. In both cases, the excessive expenditures cannot be justified by the demonstrated business value of the information they provide.

Operations

The system does not run well. Information is not provided in a timely and efficient manner because the computer operations that handle information processing break down. Jobs that abort too often lead to excessive reruns and delayed or missed schedules for delivery of information. An on-line system may be operationally inadequate because the response time is too long.

Measuring System Success

How can we tell whether a system is successful? This is not always an easy question to answer. Not everyone may agree about the value or effectiveness of a particular information system. Individuals with different decision-making styles or ways of approaching a problem may have totally different opinions about the same system. A system valued highly by an analytical, quantitatively oriented user may be totally dismissed by an intuitive thinker who is more concerned with feelings and overall impressions. Likewise, a junior sales manager with a new MBA in marketing may be more appreciative of information system reports on the demographic characteristics

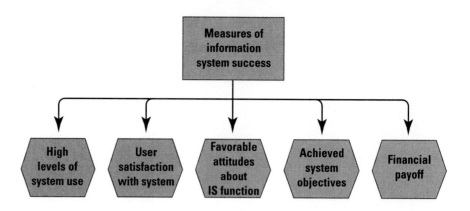

FIGURE 14.2

Measures of information system success. MIS researchers have different criteria for measuring the success of an information system. They consider the five measures in the figure to be the most important.

of his territory than a veteran representative who has worked the same territory for 15 years and knows it by heart. The perception and use of information systems can be heavily conditioned by personal and situational variables (Lucas, 1981). To further complicate the picture, what users say they like or want in a new information system may not necessarily produce any meaningful improvements in organizational performance (Markus and Keil, 1994).

Nevertheless, MIS researchers have looked for a formal set of measures for rating systems. Various criteria have been developed, but the following measures of system success, illustrated in Figure 14.2, are considered the most important.

1. *High levels of system use,* as measured by polling users, employing questionnaires, or monitoring parameters such as the volume of on-line transactions.

2. *User satisfaction with the system,* as measured by questionnaires or interviews. This might include users' opinions on the accuracy, timeliness, and relevance of information; on the quality of service; and perhaps on the schedule of operations. Especially critical are managers' attitudes on how well their information needs were satisfied (Ives et al., 1983; Westcott, 1985) and users' opinions about how well the system enhanced their job performance (Davis, 1989).

3. *Favorable attitudes* of users about information systems and the information systems staff.

4. *Achieved objectives,* the extent to which the system meets its specified goals, as reflected by improved organizational performance and decision making resulting from use of the system.

5. *Financial payoff* to the organization, either by reducing costs or by increasing sales or profits.

The fifth measure is considered to be of limited value even though cost-benefit analysis may have figured heavily in the decision to build a particular system. The benefits of an information system may not be totally quantifiable. Moreover, tangible benefits cannot be easily demonstrated for the more advanced decision-support system applications. And even though cost-benefit methodology has been rigorously pursued, the history of many systems development projects has shown that realistic estimates have always been difficult to formulate. MIS researchers have preferred to concentrate instead on the human and organizational measures of system success such as information quality, system quality, and the impact of systems on organizational performance (Lucas, 1981; DeLone and McLean, 1992).

14.2   CAUSES OF INFORMATION SYSTEM SUCCESS AND FAILURE

As described in Chapter 3, systems are developed in the first place because of powerful external environmental forces and equally powerful internal or institutional

APPROACHES	IMPLEMENTATION STAGES		
	Adoption	Management	Routinization
Actors' roles	XXXX	XXXX	
Strategy		XXXX	
Organizational factors		XXXX	XXXX

FIGURE 14.3

Approaches and implementation stages in the implementation literature. The *X*s indicate the stages of implementation on which the different approaches tend to focus. For instance, literature that uses an actor/role approach to implementation tends to focus on the early stages of adoption and management.

forces. Many systems fail because of the opposition of either the environment or the internal setting.

As many MIS researchers have pointed out, the introduction or alteration of an information system has a powerful behavioral and organizational impact. It transforms the way various individuals and groups perform and interact. Changes in the way information is defined, accessed, and used to manage the resources of the organization often lead to new distributions of authority and power (Lucas, 1975). This internal organizational change breeds resistance and opposition and can lead to the demise of an otherwise good system. An important characteristic of most information systems is that individuals are asked or required to change their behavior to make the system function.

But there are other reasons why a system may fail. Several studies have found that in organizations with similar environments and institutional features, the same innovation will be successful in some organizations but fail in others (Robey and Sahay, 1996). Why? One explanation focuses on different patterns of implementation.

The Concept of Implementation

Implementation refers to all organizational activities working toward the adoption, management, and routinization of an innovation. Figure 14.3 illustrates the major stages of implementation described in research literature and the major approaches to the subject (see also Tornatsky et al., 1983).

Some of the implementation research focuses on actors and roles. The belief is that organizations should select actors with appropriate social characteristics and systematically develop organizational roles, such as "product champions," to innovate successfully (see Figure 14.4). Generally, this literature focuses on early adoption and management of innovations.

A second school of thought in the implementation literature focuses on strategies of innovation. The two extremes are top-down innovation and grassroot innovation. There are many examples of organizations in which the absence of senior management support for innovation dooms the project from the start. At the same time, without strong grass roots, end-user participation and information system projects can also fail.

A third approach to implementation focuses on general organizational change factors as being decisive to the long-term routinization of innovations. Table 14.1

implementation All organizational activities working toward the adoption, management, and routinization of an innovation.

FIGURE 14.4

Actors in the innovation process. During implementation, the roles of actors include being product champions, bureaucratic entrepreneurs, and gatekeepers. To be successful in their roles as innovators and sponsors of change, actors should have certain demographic characteristics including social status in the organization, higher education, and social, technical, and organizational sophistication.

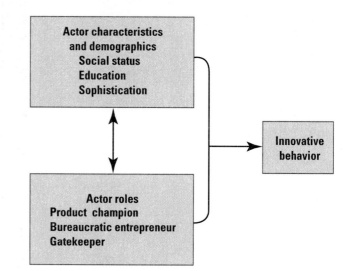

change agent In the context of implementation, the individual acting as the catalyst during the change process to ensure successful organizational adaptation to a new system or innovation.

illustrates some key organizational actions required for long-term, successful implementation, and indicators of success (Yin, 1981). Actions to increase organizational learning and overcome barriers to acquiring new knowledge and practices are also useful (Attewell, 1992).

In the context of implementation, the systems analyst is a **change agent**. The analyst not only develops technical solutions but also redefines the configurations, interactions, job activities, and power relationships of various organizational groups. The analyst is the catalyst for the entire change process and is responsible for ensuring that the changes created by a new system are accepted by all parties involved. The change agent communicates with users, mediates between competing interest groups, and ensures that the organizational adjustment to such changes is complete.

One model of the implementation process is the Kolb/Frohman model of organizational change. This model divides the process of organizational change into a seven-stage relationship between an organizational *consultant* and his or her *client*. (The consultant corresponds to the information system designer and the client to the user.) The success of the change effort is determined by how well the consultant and client deal with the key issues at each stage (Kolb and Frohman, 1970). Other models of implementation describe the relationship as one between designers, clients, and decision makers, who are responsible for managing the implementation effort to bridge the gap between design and utilization (Swanson, 1988). Recent work on im-

Table 14.1   Actions and Indicators for Successful System Implementation
Support by local funds
New organizational arrangements
Stable supply and maintenance
New personnel classifications
Changes in organizational authority
Internalization of the training program
Continual updating of the system
Promotion of key personnel
Survival of the system after turnover of its originators
Attainment of widespread use

Source: Yin (1981).

plementation stresses the need for flexibility and improvisation with organizational actors not limited to rigid prescribed roles (Markus and Benjamin, 1997; Orlikowski and Hofman, 1997).

Studies of the implementation process have examined the relationship between information system designers and users at different stages of systems development. Studies have focused on issues such as the following:

- Conflicts between the technical or machine orientation of information systems specialists and the organizational or business orientation of users

- The impact of information systems on organizational structures, work groups, and behavior

- The planning and management of systems development activities

- The degree of user participation in the design and development process

Causes of Implementation Success and Failure

Implementation research to date has found no single explanation for system success or failure. Nor does it suggest a single formula for system success. However, it has found that implementation outcome can be largely determined by the following factors:

- The role of users in the implementation process

- The degree of management support for the implementation effort

- The level of complexity and risk of the implementation project

- The quality of management of the implementation process

These are largely behavioral and organizational issues and are illustrated in Figure 14.5.

User Involvement and Influence

User involvement in the design and operation of information systems has several positive results. First, if users are heavily involved in systems design, they have more opportunities to mold the system according to their priorities and business requirements

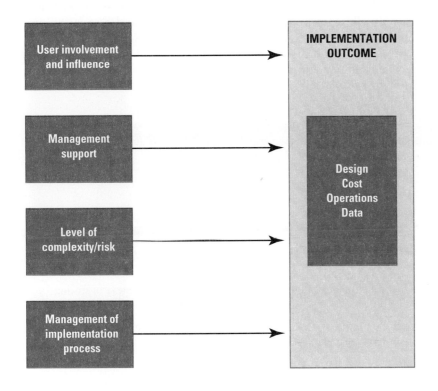

FIGURE 14.5

Factors in information system success or failure. The implementation outcome can be largely determined by the role of users; the degree of management support; the level of risk and complexity in the implementation project; and the quality of management of the implementation process. Evidence of success or failure can be found in the areas of design, cost, operations, or data of the information system.

and more opportunities to control the outcome. Second, they are more likely to react positively to the system because they have been active participants in the change process itself (Lucas, 1974).

Incorporating the user's knowledge and expertise leads to better solutions. However users often take a very narrow and limited view of the problem to be solved and may overlook important opportunities for improving business processes or innovative ways to apply information technology. The skills and vision of professional system designers are still required much in the same way that the services of an architect are required when building a new house. The outcome would most likely be inferior if people tried to design their houses entirely on their own (Markus and Keil, 1994).

THE USER–DESIGNER COMMUNICATIONS GAP. The relationship between consultant and client has traditionally been a problem area for information system implementation efforts. Users and information systems specialists tend to have different backgrounds, interests, and priorities. This is referred to as the **user–designer communications gap.** These differences lead to divergent organizational loyalties, approaches to problem solving, and vocabularies. Information systems specialists, for example, often have a highly technical or machine orientation to problem solving. They look for elegant and sophisticated technical solutions in which hardware and software efficiency is optimized at the expense of ease of use or organizational effectiveness. Users, on the other hand, prefer systems that are oriented to solving business problems or facilitating organizational tasks. Often the orientations of both groups are so at odds that they appear to speak in different tongues. These differences are illustrated in Table 14.2, which depicts the typical concerns of end users and technical specialists (information system designers) regarding the development of a new information system. Communication problems between end users and designers are a major reason why user requirements are not properly incorporated into information systems and why users are driven out of the implementation process.

Systems development projects run a very high risk of failure when there is a pronounced gap between users and technicians and when these groups continue to pursue different goals. Under such conditions, users are often driven out of the implementation process. Participation in the implementation effort is extremely time consuming and takes them away from their daily activities and responsibilities. Because they cannot comprehend what the technicians are saying, the users conclude that the entire project is best left in the hands of the information specialists alone. With so many implementation efforts guided by purely technical considerations, it is no wonder that many systems fail to serve organizational needs.

user–designer communications gap The difference in backgrounds, interests, and priorities that impede communication and problem solving among end users and information systems specialists.

Table 14.2	The User–Designer Communications Gap
User Concerns	**Designer Concerns**
Will the system deliver the information I need for my work?	How much disk storage space will the master file consume?
How quickly can I access the data?	How many lines of program code will it take to perform this function?
How easily can I retrieve the data?	How can we cut down on CPU time when we run the system?
How much clerical support will I need to enter data into the system?	What is the most efficient way of storing this piece of data?
How will the operation of the system fit into my daily business schedule?	What database management system should we use?

Management Support

If an information systems project has the backing and approval of management at various levels, it is more likely to be perceived positively by both users and the technical information services staff. Both groups will believe that their participation in the development process will receive higher-level attention and priority. They will be recognized and rewarded for the time and effort they devote to implementation. Management backing also ensures that a systems project will receive sufficient funding and resources to be successful. Furthermore, all the changes in work habits and procedures and any organizational realignments associated with a new system depend on management backing to be enforced effectively. If a manager considers a new system to be a priority, the system will more likely be treated that way by his or her subordinates (Doll, 1985; Ein-Dor and Segev, 1978).

However, management support can sometimes backfire. Sometimes management becomes overcommitted to a project, pouring excessive resources into a systems development effort that is failing or that should never have been undertaken in the first place (see the Window on Technology) (Newman and Sabherwal, 1996).

Management support may be somewhat less essential for small businesses that do not have the resources or highly developed bureaucracies of large organizations. Technical and methodological expertise from external sources such as consultants or information technology vendors may play a larger role in successful implementations, because small businesses do not have large, internal information systems staff from whom to draw (Thong, Yap, and Raman, 1996).

Level of Complexity and Risk

Systems differ dramatically in their size, scope, level of complexity, and organizational and technical components. Some systems development projects, such as the project described in the Window on Technology, are more likely to fail because they carry a much higher level of risk than others.

Researchers have identified three key dimensions that influence the level of project risk (McFarlan, 1981).

PROJECT SIZE. The larger the project—as indicated by the dollars spent, the size of the implementation staff, the time allocated to implementation, and the number of organizational units affected—the greater the risk. Therefore, a $5 million project lasting for four years and affecting five departments in 20 operating units and 120 users will be much riskier than a $30,000 project for 2 users that can be completed in two months. Another risk factor is the company's experience with projects of given sizes. If a company is accustomed to implementing large, costly systems, the risk of implementing the $5 million project will be lowered. The risk may even be lower than that of another concern attempting a $200,000 project when the firm's average project cost has been around $50,000.

PROJECT STRUCTURE. Some projects are more highly structured than others. Their requirements are clear and straightforward, so that the outputs and processes can be easily defined. Users know exactly what they want and what the system should do; there is almost no possibility of them changing their minds. Such projects run a much lower risk than those whose requirements are relatively undefined, fluid, and constantly changing; where outputs cannot be easily fixed because they are subject to users' changing ideas; or because users cannot agree on what they want.

EXPERIENCE WITH TECHNOLOGY. The project risk will rise if the project team and the information system staff lack the required technical expertise. If the team is unfamiliar with the hardware, system software, application software, or database management system proposed for the project, it is highly likely that one or all of the following will occur:

Time Warner's Bleeding-Edge Customer-Service System

In 1994, Time Warner Communications rolled the dice and decided to make a $1 billion investment in advanced information systems and networks so that it could break into the residential telephone business. It was a high-risk decision, and the gamble failed. Time Warner had to grapple with intense competition, regulatory uncertainty, and its own internal financial troubles. But the company's local telephone initiative also suffered because a leading-edge customer-service system couldn't deliver when it was needed most.

Time Warner Communications is a subsidiary of Time Warner Inc., the $10 billion media conglomerate and second largest provider of cable television in the United States. The Customer Management System was central to Time Warner's strategy for cracking the local telephone service market. Time Warner expected to link its cable and telephone systems to an integrated package of product offerings, with the Customer Management System providing better services and features than its competitors at a lower cost. In early 1994, Mohammed Fahim, then Time Warner Communications' director of information systems and services, decided to build a client/server infrastructure for the customer-service system and for monitoring its network operations.

The project combined account, product, and network data in a data repository. Fahim selected an expert system to implement the business rules as a means of coping with the volatile nature of the telecommunications industry. The choice allowed the company to make constant rule changes, such as what type of data is acceptable in ordering and billing forms, without having to rewrite applications.

Fahim chose object-oriented development languages to reduce development time. However, the company had to build an additional layer of software to link applications with its Sybase Inc. System 10 database. Time Warner Communications outsourced the writing of some of the program code to lower-priced developers in Pakistan.

A number of tools are commercially available today to link object-based applications to relational databases. Time Warner

Communications' homegrown software slowed response time. The system was so slow that employees were forced to handwrite information such as customer names and the types of service they ordered and later key it into the system. The company rushed to deploy the system, leaving insufficient time for testing.

Constant "tweaking" of the object-relational database management system eventually improved performance. At one time, opening an account took as long as eight seconds, storing the data in the database took an additional ten seconds, and creating a new account took up to four seconds. Now the system can perform all these steps in less than one second.

Other problems plagued Time Warner Communications as well. Regulatory delays forced the company to spend more money for equipment than what it anticipated. Rules and prices for entry into the telecommunications business are uncertain, making it difficult for companies unfamiliar with the telephone business to develop an accurate business model. The company will need to purchase additional hardware and filters to convert its one-way cable broadcast medium into a two-way telephone communication system.

Time Warner has canceled plans to expand its local residential telephone business and is trying to sell the Customer Management System.

To Think About: *Evaluate the level of complexity and risk in this project. What problems did the Customer Management System project encounter? What management, organization, and technology factors were responsible for those problems? Could those problems have been avoided? How?*

Source: Emily Kay and Larry Marion, "Failed Phone Venture Shows How Not to Build Software," *Computerworld*, May 5, 1997.

- Unanticipated time slippage because of the need to master new skills
- A variety of technical problems if tools have not been thoroughly mastered
- Excessive expenditures and extra time because of inexperience with the undocumented idiosyncrasies of each new piece of hardware or software

These dimensions of project risk will be present in different combinations for each implementation effort. Table 14.3 shows that eight different combinations are possible, each with a different degree of risk. The higher the level of risk, the more likely it is that the implementation effort will fail.

Table 14.3	Dimensions of Project Risk		
Project Structure	Project Technology Level	Project Size	Degree of Risk
High	Low	Large	Low
High	Low	Small	Very low
High	High	Large	Medium
High	High	Small	Medium-low
Low	Low	Large	Low
Low	Low	Small	Very low
Low	High	Large	Very high
Low	High	Small	High

Management of the Implementation Process

The development of a new system must be carefully managed and orchestrated. Each project involves research and development. Requirements are hard to define at the level of detail for automation. The same piece of information may be interpreted and defined differently by different individuals. Multiple users have different sets of requirements and needs. Costs, benefits, and project schedules must be assessed. The final design may not be easy to visualize. Because complex information systems involve so many interest groups, actors, and details, it is sometimes uncertain whether the initial plans for a system are truly feasible.

Often basic elements of success are forgotten. Training to ensure that end users are comfortable with the new system and fully understand its potential uses is often sacrificed or forgotten in systems development projects. In part because the budget is strained toward the end of a project, and at the very point of startup there are insufficient funds for training (Bikson et al., 1985).

The conflicts and uncertainties inherent in any implementation effort will be magnified when an implementation project is poorly managed and organized. As illustrated in Figure 14.6, a systems development project without proper management will most likely suffer these consequences:

- Cost overruns that vastly exceed budgets
- Unexpected time slippage
- Technical shortfalls resulting in performance that is significantly below the estimated level
- Failure to obtain anticipated benefits

How badly are projects managed? On average, private sector projects are underestimated by one-half in terms of budget and time required to deliver the complete system promised in the system plan. A very large number of projects are delivered with

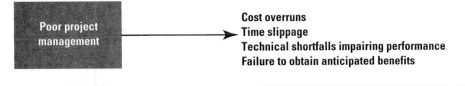

FIGURE 14.6

Consequences of poor project management. Without proper management, a systems development project will take longer to complete and most often will exceed the budgeted cost. The resulting information system will most likely be technically inferior and may not be able to demonstrate any benefits to the organization.

missing functionality (promised for delivery in later versions). Government projects suffer about the same failure level, perhaps worse (Laudon, 1989; Helms and Weiss, 1986).

Why are projects managed so poorly and what can be done about it? Here we discuss some possibilities.

IGNORANCE AND OPTIMISM.   The techniques for estimating the length of time required to analyze and design systems are poorly developed. There are no standards; there is little sharing of data within and across organizations; and most applications are "first time" (i.e., there is no prior experience in the application area). Academics generally do not study large-scale commercial systems but instead focus on small-scale, easily taught or learned software projects. The larger the scale of systems, the greater the role of ignorance and optimism. Very-large-scale systems (VLSS)—sometimes called *grand design systems*—suffer extraordinary rates of failure (Laudon, 1989; United States General Services Administration, 1988). The net result of these factors is that estimates tend to be optimistic, "best case," and wrong. It is assumed that all will go well when in fact it rarely does.

THE MYTHICAL MAN-MONTH.   The traditional unit of measurement used by systems designers to project costs is the **man-month.** Projects are estimated in terms of how many man-months will be required. However, while costs may vary as a product of people and months, the progress of the project does not, as pointed out by Frederick P. Brooks (Brooks, 1974). As it turns out, people and months are not interchangeable in the short run on systems projects. (They may be interchangeable in the long run, but we live in the short run.) In other words, adding more workers to projects does not necessarily reduce the elapsed time needed to complete a systems project.

Unlike cotton picking—when tasks can be rigidly partitioned, communication between participants is not required, and training is unnecessary—systems analysis and design involves *tasks that are sequentially linked, cannot be performed in isolation, and require extensive communications and training.* Software development is inherently a group effort, and hence communication costs rise exponentially as the number of participants increases. Moreover, when personnel turnover approaches 20 to 30 percent, many of the participants in software projects require much learning and communication.

Given these characteristics, adding labor to projects can often slow down delivery, as the communication, learning, and coordination costs rise very fast and detract from the output of participants. For comparison, imagine what would happen if five amateur spectators were added to one team in a championship professional basketball game. Chances are quite good that the team composed of five professional basketball players would do much better in the short run than the team with five professionals and five amateurs.

FALLING BEHIND: BAD NEWS TRAVELS SLOWLY UPWARD.   Slippage in projects, failure, and doubts is often not reported to senior management until it is too late. To some extent, this is characteristic of projects in all fields. The CONFIRM project, a very large-scale information systems project to integrate hotel, airline, and rental car reservations, is a classic example. It was sponsored by the Hilton Hotels, Budget Rent-A-Car, and Marriott Corporations and developed by AMR Information Services, Inc., a subsidiary of American Airlines Corporation. The project was very ambitious and technically complex, employing a staff of 500. Members of the CONFIRM project management team did not immediately come forward with accurate information when the project started encountering problems coordinating various transaction processing activities. Clients continued to invest in a project that was faltering because they were not informed of its problems with database, decision-support, and integration technologies (Oz, 1994).

Another example of this problem is the crash of the space shuttle *Challenger* in January 1986. The information that O-ring seals on the space shuttle might not perform well in the cold January weather and that engineers strongly objected to launch-

man-month   The traditional unit of measurement used by systems designers to estimate the length of time to complete a project. Refers to the amount of work a person can be expected to complete in a month.

ing the shuttle in cold weather did not reach the top National Aeronautics and Space Administration (NASA) management team, which ultimately decided to launch. The reasons, although not entirely clear, in part involve the well-understood principle that bearers of bad news are often not appreciated and that senior management wants schedules to be met.

Organizational hierarchy has a pathological and deadly side: Senior management is often kept in the dark (see Chapters 3 and 4). For systems projects, this seems to be especially true. Systems workers know that management has promised a delivery date to important user groups, that millions of dollars have been spent, and that careers depend on timely delivery of the whole system. As the project falls behind, one day at a time, no one wants to bother senior management with minor slippage details. Eventually, days add up to months and then to years. By then it is too late to save the project, no matter how many people are added to the team.

The Challenge of Business Reengineering

Given the challenges of innovation and implementation, it is not surprising to find a very high failure rate among business reengineering projects, which typically require extensive organizational change. A series of studies reinforce Michael Hammer's observation that 70 percent of all reengineering projects fail to deliver promised benefits. Many information systems to support business reengineering take too long to develop and don't deliver what the company wants. The Cambridge, Massachusetts, consulting firm of Arthur D. Little, Inc. found that only 16 percent of the 350 business executives they surveyed were "fully satisfied" with their business reengineering efforts. Moreover, 68 percent of the executives reported that their reengineering projects had unintended side effects, creating new problems instead of solving old ones (Caldwell, 1994).

In some cases, these problems stemmed from management's inability to identify the critical problems to be solved by reengineering or to distinguish between radical revamping of core business processes and incremental changes. In such instances, companies wound up only making incremental improvements in ongoing operations instead of radically redesigning their business processes. But in many cases, major hurdles to reengineering were caused by poor implementation and change management practices that failed to address widespread fears of change. Figure 14.7 summarizes Deloitte & Touche's findings about the greatest obstacles to successful business reengineering. Studies by CSC Index Inc. and others report similar results. Dealing with fear and anxiety throughout the organization, overcoming resistance by key managers, changing job functions, career paths, recruitment, and training pose even greater threats to reengineering than companies' difficulties with visualizing and designing breakthrough changes to their business processes (Maglitta, 1994). Reengineering problems are part of the larger problem of organizational implementation and change management.

The Implementation Process: What Can Go Wrong

The following problems are considered typical for each stage of systems development when the implementation process is poorly managed.

Analysis

- Time, money, and resources have not been allocated to researching the problem. The problem remains poorly defined. Objectives of the implementation project will be vague and ambiguous; benefits will be difficult to measure.

- Little or no time is spent in preliminary planning. There are no standards to use in estimating preliminary costs or the duration of the project.

- The project team is not properly staffed. Personnel are assigned on an "as available" basis and cannot dedicate themselves to the project. User groups to be served by the system are not represented on the team.

FIGURE 14.7

Obstacles to business reengineering.
Resistance to organizational change
poses the greatest obstacle to business
reengineering efforts.
*Adapted from: Bruce Caldwell, "Missteps,
Miscues," InformationWeek, June 20, 1994.*

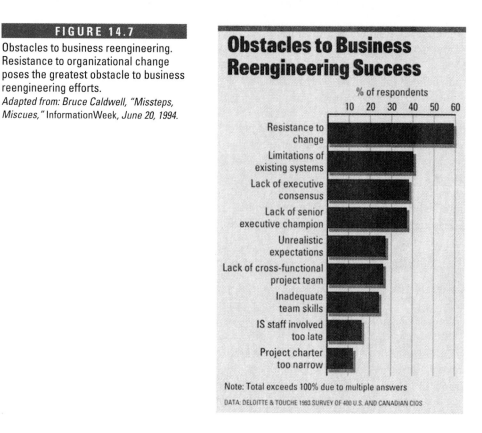

Obstacles to Business Reengineering Success

- The information services staff promises results that are impossible to deliver.
- Requirements are derived from inadequate documentation of existing systems or incomplete findings from systems study activities.
- Users refuse to spend any time helping the project team gather the requisite information.
- Project analysts cannot interview users properly. They do not know how to ask the right questions. They cannot carry on an extended conversation with users because they lack good communication skills.

Design

- Users have no responsibility for or input to design activities. The design, therefore, reflects the biases of the technical staff. It does not mesh well with the structure, activities, and culture of the organization or the priorities of management.
- The system is designed only to serve current needs. No flexibility has been built in to anticipate the future needs of the organization.
- Drastic changes in clerical procedures or staffing are planned without any organizational impact analysis.
- Functional specifications are inadequately documented.

Programming

- The amount of time and money required for software development is underestimated.
- Programmers are supplied with incomplete specifications.
- Not enough time is devoted to the development of program logic; too much time is wasted on writing code.

- Programmers do not take full advantage of structured design or object-oriented techniques. They write programs that are difficult to modify and maintain.
- Programs are not adequately documented.
- Requisite resources (such as computer time) are not scheduled.

Testing

- The amount of time and money required for proper testing is underestimated.
- The project team does not develop an organized test plan.
- Users are not sufficiently involved in testing. They do not help to create sample test data or review test results. They refuse to devote much time to the testing effort.
- The implementation team does not develop appropriate acceptance tests for management review. Management does not review and sign off on test results.

Conversion

- Insufficient time and money are budgeted for conversion activities, especially for data conversion.
- Not all the individuals who will use the system are involved until conversion begins. Training begins only when the system is about to be installed.
- To compensate for cost overruns and delays, the system is made operational before it is fully ready.
- System and user documentation is inadequate.
- Performance evaluations are not conducted. No performance standards are established, and the results of the system are not weighed against the original objectives.
- Provisions for system maintenance are inadequate. Insufficient information systems personnel are trained to support the system and to make maintenance changes.

14.3   MANAGING IMPLEMENTATION

Not all aspects of the implementation process can be easily controlled or planned (Alter and Ginzberg, 1978). However, the chances for system success can be increased by anticipating potential implementation problems and applying appropriate corrective strategies. Various project management, requirements gathering, and planning methodologies have been developed for specific categories of problems. Strategies have also been devised for ensuring that users play an appropriate role throughout the implementation period and for managing the organizational change process.

Controlling Risk Factors

One way implementation can be improved is by adjusting the project management strategy to the level of risk inherent in each project. If a systems development project is placed in the proper risk category, levels of risk can be predicted in advance and strategies developed to counteract high-risk factors (McFarlan, 1981).

Implementers must adopt a contingency approach to project management, handling each project with the tools, project management methodologies, and organizational linkages geared to its level of risk. There are four basic project management techniques:

1. External integration tools link the work of the implementation team to that of users at all organizational levels.

2. Internal integration tools ensure that the implementation team operates as a cohesive unit.

3. Formal planning tools structure and sequence tasks, providing advance estimates of the time, money, and technical resources required to execute them.

4. Formal control tools help monitor the progress toward goals.

The risk profile of each project will determine the appropriate project management technique to apply, as illustrated in Table 14.4.

External Integration Tools

external integration tools
Project management technique that links the work of the implementation team to that of users at all organizational levels.

Projects with relatively *little structure* must involve users fully at all stages. Users must be mobilized to support one of many possible design options and to remain committed to a single design. Therefore, **external integration tools** must be applied.

- Users can be selected as project leaders or as the second-in-command on a project team.
- User steering committees can be created to evaluate the system's design.
- Users can become active members of the project team.
- The project can require formal user review and approval of specifications.
- Minutes of all key design meetings can be distributed widely among users.
- Users can prepare the status reports for higher management.
- Users can be put in charge of training and installation.
- Users can be responsible for change control, putting a brake on all nonessential changes to the system once final design specifications have been completed.

Internal Integration Tools

internal integration tools
Project management technique that ensures that the implementation team operates as a cohesive unit.

Projects with *high levels of technology* benefit from **internal integration tools**. The success of such projects depends on how well their technical complexity can be managed. Project leaders need both heavy technical and administrative experience. They

Table 14.4	Strategies to Manage Projects by Controlling Risks			
Project Structure	Project Technology Level	Project Size	Degree of Risk	Project Management Tool
1. High	Low	Large	Low	High use of formal planning High use of formal control
2. High	Low	Small	Very low	High use of formal control Medium use of formal planning
3. High	High	Large	Medium	Medium use of formal control Medium use of formal planning
4. High	High	Small	Medium-low	High internal integration
5. Low	Low	Large	Low	High external integration High use of formal planning High use of formal control
6. Low	Low	Small	Very low	High external integration High use of formal control
7. Low	High	Large	Very high	High external integration High internal integration
8. Low	High	Small	High	High external integration High internal integration

This project team of professionals is using portable computing tools and documents to enhance communication, analysis, and decision making.

must be able to anticipate problems and develop smooth working relationships among a predominantly technical team.

- Team members should be highly experienced.
- The team should be under the leadership of a manager with a strong technical and project management background.
- Team meetings should take place frequently, with routine distribution of meeting minutes concerning key design decisions.
- The team should hold regular technical status reviews.
- A high percentage of the team should have a history of good working relationships with each other.
- Team members should participate in setting goals and establishing target dates.
- Essential technical skills or expertise not available internally should be secured from outside the organization.

Formal Planning and Control Tools

Projects with *high structure* and *low technology* present the lowest risk. The design is fixed and stable and the project does not pose any technical challenges. If such projects are large, they can be successfully managed by **formal planning** and **formal control tools**. With project management techniques such as PERT (Program Evaluation and Review Technique) or Gantt charts, a detailed plan can be developed. (PERT lists the specific activities that make up a project, their duration, and the activities that must be completed before a specific activity can start. A Gantt chart such as that illustrated in Figure 14.8 visually represents the sequence and timing of different tasks in a development project, as well as their resource requirements.) Tasks can be defined and resources budgeted. These project management techniques can help managers identify bottlenecks and determine the impact that problems will have on project completion times.

formal planning tools Project management technique that structures and sequences tasks; budgeting time, money, and technical resources required to complete the tasks.

formal control tools Project management technique that helps monitor the progress toward completion of a task and fulfillment of goals.

- Milestone phases can be selected.
- Specifications can be developed from the feasibility study.
- Specification standards can be established.
- Processes for project approval can be developed.

Standard control techniques will successfully chart the progress of the project against budgets and target dates, so that the implementation team can make adjustments to meet their original schedule.

- Disciplines to control or freeze the design can be maintained.
- Deviations from the plan can be spotted.

HRIS COMBINED PLAN-HR

Task	Da	Who
DATA ADMINISTRATION SECURITY		
QMF security review/setup	20	EF TP
Security orientation	2	EF JV
QMF security maintenance	35	TP GL
Data entry sec. profiles	4	EF TP
Data entry sec views est.	12	EF TP
Data entry security profiles	65	EF TP
DATA DICTIONARY		
Orientation sessions	1	EF
Data dictionary design	32	EF WV
DD prod, coordn-query	20	GL
DD prod. coord-live	40	EF GL
Data dictionary cleanup	35	EF GL
Data dictionary maint.	35	EF GL
PROCEDURES REVISION DESIGN PREP		
Work flows (old)	10	PK JL
Payroll data flows	31	JL PK
HRIS P/R model	11	PK JL
P/R interface orient. mtg.	6	PK JL
P/R interface coordn. I	15	PK
P/R interface coordn.	8	PK
Benefits interfaces (old)	5	JL
Ben. interfaces new flow	8	JL
Ben. communication strategy	3	PK JL
New work flow model	15	PK JL
Posn. data entry flows	14	WV JL

RESOURCE SUMMARY

Name		Who	1997 Oct	Nov	Dec	1998 Jan	Feb	Mar	Apr	May	Jun	Jul	Aug	Sep	Oct	Nov	Dec	1999 Jan	Feb	Mar	Apr
Edith Farrell	5.0	EF	2	21	24	24	23	22	22	27	34	34	29	26	28	19	14	4	3		
Woody Holand	5.0	WH	5	17	20	16	10	14	10	2											
Charles Pierce	5.0	CP		5	11	20	13	9	10	7	6	8	4	4	4	4	4				
Ted Leurs	5.0	TL		12	17	17	19	17	14	12	15	16	2	1	1	1	1				9
Toni Cox	5.0	TC	1	11	10	11	11	12	19	19	21	21	21	17	17	12	9	3	2		
Patricia Clark	5.0	PC	7	23	30	34	27	25	15	24	25	16	11	13	17	10	3				
Jane Lawton	5.0	JL	1	9	16	21	19	21	21	20	17	15	14	12	14	8	5				
David Holloway	5.0	DH	4	4	5	5	5	2	7	5	4	16	2								6
Diane O'Neill	5.0	DO	6	14	17	16	13	11	9	4											
Joan Albert	5.0	JA	5	6			7	6	2	1				5	5	1					
Marie Marcus	5.0	MM	15	7	2	1	1														
Don Stevens	5.0	DS	4	4	5	4	5	1													
Casual	5.0	CASL		3	4	3			4	7	9	5	3	2							
Kathy Manley	5.0	KM		1	5	16	20	19	22	19	20	18	20	11	2						
Anna Borden	5.0	AB					9	10	16	15	11	12	19	10	7	1					
Gail Loring	5.0	GL		3	6	5	9	10	17	18	17	10	13	10	10	7	17	14	13	3	1
UNASSIGNED	0.0	X											9	236	225	230	216	178	9	7
Co-op	5.0	CO		6	4				2	3	4	4	2	4	16						
Casual	5.0	CAUL							3	3	3										
TOTAL DAYS			49	147	176	196	194	174	193	195	190	181	140	125	358	288	284	237	196	12	23

FIGURE 14.8

Formal planning and control tools help to manage information systems projects successfully. The Gantt chart in this figure was produced by a commercially available project management software package. It shows the task, man-days, and initials of each responsible person, as well as the start and finish dates for each task. The resource summary provides a good manager with the total man-days for each month and for each person working on the project to successfully manage the project. The project described here is a data administration project.

- Periodic formal status reports against the plan will show the extent of progress.

Overcoming User Resistance

In addition to fine-tuning project management strategies, implementation risks can be reduced by securing management and user support of the implementation effort.

Section 14.2 has shown how user participation in the design process builds commitment to the system. The final product is more likely to reflect users' requirements. Users are more likely to feel that they control and own the system. Users are also more likely to feel satisfied with an information system if they have been trained to use it properly (Cronan and Douglas, 1990).

However, MIS researchers have also noted that systems development is not an entirely rational process. Users leading design activities have used their position to further private interests and to gain power rather than to promote organizational objectives (Franz and Robey, 1984). Users may not always be involved in systems projects in a productive way, as the Window on Management describes.

Participation in implementation activities may not be enough to overcome the problem of user resistance. The implementation process demands organizational change. Such change may be resisted because different users may be affected by the system in different ways. Whereas some users may welcome a new system because it brings changes they perceive as beneficial to them, others may resist these changes because they believe the shifts are detrimental to their interests (Joshi, 1991).

If the use of a system is voluntary, users may choose to avoid it; if use is mandatory, resistance will take the form of increased error rates, disruptions, turnover, and even sabotage. Therefore, the implementation strategy must not only encourage user participation and involvement, it must also address the issue of counterimplementation (Keen, 1981). **Counterimplementation** is a deliberate strategy to thwart the implementation of an information system or an innovation in an organization.

Researchers have explained user resistance with one of three theories (Markus, 1983; Davis and Olson, 1985):

1. **People-oriented theory.** Factors internal to users as individuals or as a group produce resistance. For instance, users may resist a new system or any change at all because they are fearful or do not wish to learn new ways of doing things.

2. **System-oriented theory.** Factors inherent in the design create user resistance to a system. For instance, users may resist a system because its user interface is confusing and they have trouble learning how to make the system work.

3. **Interaction theory.** Resistance is caused by the interaction of people and systems factors. For instance, the system may be well designed and welcomed by some users but resisted by others who fear it will take away some of their power or stature in the organization or even their jobs.

Strategies have been suggested to overcome each form of user resistance:

People oriented:	User education (training)
	Coercion (edicts, policies)
	Persuasion
	User participation (to elicit commitment)
System oriented:	User education
	Improve human factors (user/system interface)
	User participation (for improved design)
	Package modification to conform to organization when appropriate
Interaction:	Solve organizational problems before introducing new systems
	Restructure incentives for users
	Restructure the user–designer relationship
	Promote user participation when appropriate

Strategies appropriate for the interaction theory incorporate elements of people-oriented and system-oriented strategies. (An example can be found in the Window on Management.) There may be situations in which user participation is not appropriate. For example, some users may react negatively to a new design even though its overall benefits outweigh its drawbacks. Some individuals may stand to lose power as a result of design decisions (Robey and Markus, 1984). In this instance, participation in design may actually exacerbate resentment and resistance.

counterimplementation A deliberate strategy to thwart the implementation of an information system or an innovation in an organization.

people-oriented theory User-resistance theory focusing on factors internal to users.

system-oriented theory User-resistance theory focusing on factors inherent in the design of the system.

interaction theory User-resistance theory stating that resistance is caused by the interaction of people and systems factors.

More User Involvement, Please

How should a giant health maintenance organization (HMO) react when a new, crucial system is rejected by its users? This is the dilemma that Kaiser Permanente faced in 1996 when it installed enhancements to its clinical information presentation system (CIPS). The problem was enormous, and the system was absolutely critical. Kaiser Permanente is the largest HMO in the United States, serving more than 2.5 million people in Northern California alone. The system was a focus of medical activity, with more than 6500 log ons per day by doctors, nurses, and other health professionals. The system was so large that each log on, on average, resulted in 45 hits (screen accesses). When the new interface was installed, the Clinical Information Systems Group (CISG), the development team, was flooded with complaints. Many users even pleaded to have CISG pull the new system and return to the old one.

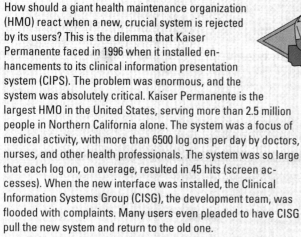

Fixing the new system was urgent. Yet the current system was really a secondary problem. The more fundamental issue was a management one that would affect all systems to be developed in the future: establishing a development methodology that would avoid such disasters and give the users a system they need and want. To accomplish this, the first task was determining what had gone wrong in the current disaster.

The first problem appeared to be the lack of user involvement. After all, the system was rejected by the user community. But that was not the case. On the contrary, it had been a user group that had developed the requirements for the system. Only after the user teams had completed their work were the requirements turned over to the information technology group for development. However, a deeper examination showed that the issue in fact was inadequate user involvement. The problem had two distinct facets.

The first facet was the computer experience of the members of the user teams that had drawn up the requirements. The same user teams had been performing the task of gathering systems development requirements for a number of years. Not surprisingly, their members had gained a great deal of expertise in computer use during these years. Although this might sound like ideal teams, the fact was the computer skill of the team members was far greater than the skills of the broader user communities they represented. The team members had lost touch with the less sophisticated skills of the broader user communities. The require-

ments documents were designed to meet the specialized needs of the team members on the faulty assumption that the needs of the larger community would thus be served. Most users represented by these teams did not have the opportunity to review the specifications. The result was that the average users' needs were not met. The design led to a system that was both too sophisticated for most users and focused primarily on the very specific needs of a few people.

To prevent this from happening in the future, CISG addressed this problem first by broadly identifying the stakeholders in a project and then broadening the teams gathering specifications to represent all stakeholders. Next they established procedures to involve the broader user communities in reviewing specifications as they were written. They made certain, for example, that both novice users and the more sophisticated users were consulted.

The second facet to the problem of inadequate user involvement was the lack of proper system testing as it was being developed. Most users did not see the system until it went live, and then it was too late to avoid the disaster. In the future, a broad base of users had to be involved in testing during development. Those designing the new development procedures decided that a broad base of users should test any new system in one-on-one sessions to take place at the workplace of the users. Thus, the developers were able to obtain immediate feedback from those who would be using the new system.

One result of broader user involvement at both the requirements and testing stages was the feeling of ownership of new systems that developed among the broader user community while the systems were still in development stage.

> **To Think About:** Describe the management problems in the development effort that resulted in such widespread rejection of the new system. What were the causes of these problems? Describe the management changes used to address the problems, and evaluate those changes.

Source: Steven Borenstein, M.D., Stephanie Sales, R.N.N.P., and Shoshanna Miller, "User Involvement," *Physicians and Computers*, April 1997.

Designing for the Organization

The entire systems development process can be viewed as planned organizational change, because the purpose of a new system is to improve the organization's performance. Therefore, the development process must explicitly address the ways in which the organization will change when the new system is installed, including installation of intranets (see the Window on Organizations). In addition to procedural changes, transformations in job functions, organizational structure, power relation-

Implementing Canada's Government-Wide Intranet

Implementation of an intranet within a large organization is usually not a major technical issue. Large organizations tend to have many robust networks already in place. The technical staffs already well understand the technical issues. Moreover, intranets are based on Internet and World Wide Web technology which is inexpensive and easy to install and maintain. For large organizations, the biggest problems with installing intranets are organizational, and the Canadian government is now facing that fact.

Canada is huge, crossing five time zones and encompassing the second largest area of any country in the world. The government has more than 260,000 employees spread across this vast land. Thus far, its many departments have been run rather autonomously. "All the departments of government are managed as separate entities," points out Chris Hughes, director of information delivery services for the Government Telecommunications and Informatics Services (GTIS), the government's in-house systems integration group. "There is no one organization that says 'You must do it this way." adds Hughes. This is particularly true of some large departments, such as Revenue and Defense. However, all the departments, including the small ones, are already using desktop computers and client server technology in sophisticated ways.

When GTIS decided to install a government-wide intranet, it had the same reasons as many other organizations, including high communications costs, a $2 billion annual printing bill, and the need to make more information available to its employees and citizens. The new network is based on Netscape Navigator and includes a Web home page that is an information resource for federal government employees. This site is only accessible to employees. It includes on-line policy manuals, House of Commons debate transcripts, information on travel to obscure places, and much more, all in both English and French. In addition it includes links to the home pages of various departments. The network also provides links to personnel, payroll, and financial systems databases. And, of course, it provides an e-mail system.

The problems faced by the establishment of this new intranet are mostly organizational. This intranet requires cooperation among the many departments that are used to working in almost total isolation. They must cooperate to determine what data are accessible and to whom. They must get used to the idea that other people will know more about their business than in the past. They must use the e-mail system if telephone bills are to be reduced. What the intranet means to the employees of the Canadian government is a change in culture.

Interestingly, although GTIS had the authority to build an intranet, it had no authority to require anyone to use it. When the intranet was set up, more than 80,000 employees had access should they choose to use it. "They'll use it if they see value," explained Hughes. Obviously, they did see value. As of mid-1996, 55 government agencies and departments were using it.

GTIS has also established a home page that is open to the Canadian public (http://canada.gc.ca). This site offers the public access to 70 government Web sites. When established, these sites offered only information, including millions of unclassified documents. However, the sites will soon allow users to transact business, such as filing income taxes, and corporate tending for government contracts.

To Think About: Do you think the intranet will change the way the employees of the Canadian government carry out their duties? Explain your answer. What steps do you think GTIS should have taken to address the organizational problems prior to the actual installation of the intranet?

Source: Gordon Arnaut, "Canadian Connection," *InformationWeek*, July 22, 1996.

---

ships, and behavior will all have to be carefully planned. When technology-induced changes produce unforeseen consequences, the organization can benefit by improvising to take advantage of new opportunities. Information systems specialists, managers, and users should remain open-minded about their roles in the change management process and not adhere to rigid narrow perceptions (Orlikowski and Hofman, 1997; Marcus and Benjamin, 1997). Figure 14.9 illustrates the organizational dimensions that would need to be addressed for planning and implementing office automation systems.

Although systems analysis and design activities are supposed to include an organizational impact analysis, this area has traditionally been neglected. An **organizational impact analysis** explains how a proposed system will affect organizational structure, attitudes, decision making, and operations. To integrate information systems successfully with the organization, thorough and fully documented organizational impact assessments must be given more attention in the development effort.

organizational impact analysis
Study of the way a proposed system will affect organizational structure, attitudes, decision making, and operations.

The Canadian government created an intranet which provides e-mail and extensive information resources to federal government employees. Its successful use depends on increased cooperation among departments and a more collaborative organizational culture.

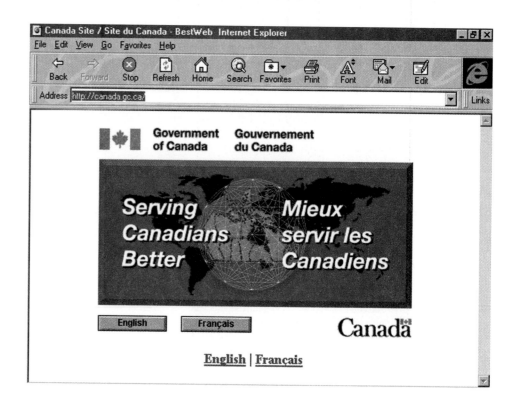

Allowing for the Human Factor

The quality of information systems should be evaluated in terms of user criteria rather than the criteria of the information systems staff. In addition to targets such as memory size, access rates, and calculation times, systems objectives should include standards for user performance. For example, an objective might be that data entry clerks learn the procedures and codes for four new on-line data entry screens in a half-day training session.

Areas where users interface with the system should be carefully designed, with sensitivity to ergonomic issues. **Ergonomics** refers to the interaction of people and machines in the work environment. It considers the design of jobs, health issues, and the end-user interface of information systems. The impact of the application system on the work environment and job dimensions must be carefully assessed. One noteworthy study of 620 Social Security Administration claims representatives showed that the representatives with on-line access to claims data experienced greater stress than those with serial access to the data via teletype. Even though the on-line interface was more rapid and direct than teletype, it created much more frustration. Representatives with on-line access could interface with a larger number of clients per day. This changed the dimensions of the job for claims representatives. The restructuring of work—involving tasks, quality of working life, and performance—had a more profound impact than the nature of the technology itself (Turner, 1984).

ergonomics The interaction of people and machines in the work environment, including the design of jobs, health issues, and the end-user interface of information systems.

Sociotechnical Design

Most contemporary systems-building approaches tend to treat end users as essential to the systems-building process but play a largely passive role relative to other forces shaping the system such as the specialist system designers and management. A different tradition rooted in the European social democratic labor movement assigns users a more active role, one that empowers them to codetermine the role of information systems in their workplace (Clement and Van den Besselaar, 1993).

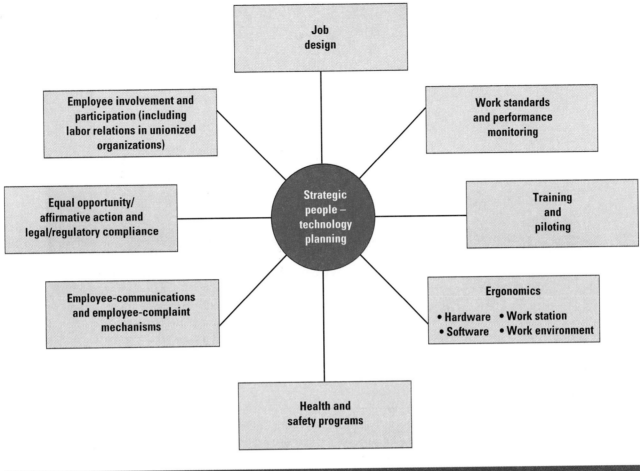

FIGURE 14.9

Key human organizational factors for office automation planning and implementation. For successful implementation, the planner must consider ergonomics, job design, work standards, health and safety, training, employee communications, employee participation, and legal/regulatory factors.

Reprinted with permission of G.K. Hall & Co., an imprint of Macmillan Publishing Company, from The Changing Workplace *by Alan F. Westin et al. Copyright © 1985 by G.K. Hall & Co.*

This tradition of participatory design emphasizes participation by the individuals most affected by the new system. It is closely associated with the concept of sociotechnical design. A **sociotechnical design** plan establishes human objectives for the system that lead to increased job satisfaction. Designers set forth separate sets of technical and social design solutions. The social design plans explore different work group structures, allocation of tasks, and the design of individual jobs. The proposed technical solutions are compared with the proposed social solutions. Social and technical solutions that can be combined are proposed as sociotechnical solutions. The alternative that best meets both social and technical objectives is selected for the final design. The resulting sociotechnical design is expected to produce an information system that blends technical efficiency with sensitivity to organizational and human needs, leading to high job satisfaction (Mumford and Weir, 1979). Systems with compatible technical and organizational elements are expected to raise productivity without sacrificing human and social goals.

sociotechnical design Design to produce information systems that blend technical efficiency with sensitivity to organizational and human needs.

MANAGEMENT

Two principal reasons for system failure are inadequate management support and poor management of the implementation process. Managers should fully understand the level of complexity and risk in new systems projects and provide realistic levels of support and resources.

ORGANIZATION

The reason why most information systems fail is that system builders ignore organizational behavior problems, especially organizational inertia and resistance to change. Eliciting user support and maintaining an appropriate level of user involvement at all stages of system building are essential.

TECHNOLOGY

Systems sometimes fail because the technology is too complex or sophisticated to be easily implemented or because system builders lack the requisite skills or experience to work with it. Managers and systems builders should be fully aware of the risks and rewards of various technologies as they make their technology selections.

For Discussion: If you were a member of your corporation's management committee to oversee and approve systems development projects, what criteria would you use in evaluating new project proposals? What would you look for to determine whether the project was proceeding successfully?

SUMMARY

1. Identify major problem areas in information systems. A high percentage of systems are considered failures because they are not used in the way they were intended. Some are not used at all. System failure is evidenced by problems with design, data, cost, or operations. The sources of system success or failure are primarily behavioral and organizational.

2. Determine whether a system is successful. Criteria for evaluating the success of an information system include (1) level of system use, (2) user satisfaction, (3) favorable user attitudes about the information system and its staff, (4) achieved objectives, and (5) financial payoff to the organization.

3. Describe the principal causes of information system failure. The principal causes of information system failure are (1) insufficient or improper user participation in the systems development process, (2) lack of management support, (3) high levels of complexity and risk in the systems development process, and (4) poor management of the implementation process. There is a very high failure rate among business reengineering projects because they require extensive organizational change.

4. Describe the relationship between the implementation process and system outcome. Implementation is the entire process of organizational change surrounding the introduction of a new information system. One can better understand system success and failure by examining different patterns of implementation. Especially important is the relationship between participants in the implementation process, notably the interactions between

system designers and users. Conflicts between the technical orientation of system designers and the business orientation of end users must be resolved. The success of organizational change can be determined by how well information systems specialists, end users, and decision makers deal with key issues at various stages in implementation.

5. Describe appropriate strategies to manage the implementation process. Management support and control of the implementation process are essential, as are mechanisms for dealing with the level of risk in each new systems project. Some companies experience organizational resistance to change. Project risk factors can be brought under some control by a contingency approach to project management. The level of risk in a systems development project is determined by three key dimensions: (1) project size, (2) project structure, and (3) experience with technology. The risk level of each project will determine the appropriate mix of external integration tools, internal integration tools, formal planning tools, and formal control tools to be applied.

Appropriate strategies can be applied to ensure the correct level of user participation in the systems development process and to minimize user resistance. Information system design and the entire implementation process should be managed as planned organizational change. Participatory design emphasizes the participation of the individuals most affected by a new system. Sociotechnical design aims for an optimal blend of social and technical design solutions.

System failure
User interface
Implementation
Change agent
User–designer
   communications gap

Man-month
External integration tools
Internal integration tools
Formal planning tools
Formal control tools
Counterimplementation

People-oriented theory
System-oriented theory
Interaction theory
Organizational impact
   analysis

Ergonomics
Sociotechnical design

REVIEW QUESTIONS

1. What do we mean by information system failure?

2. What kinds of problems are evidence of information system failure?

3. How can we measure system success? Which measures of system success are the most important?

4. Define implementation. What are the major approaches to implementation?

5. Why is it necessary to understand the concept of implementation when examining system success and failure?

6. What are the major causes of implementation success or failure? How are they related to the failure of business reengineering projects?

7. What is the user–designer communications gap? What kinds of implementation problems can it create?

8. List some of the implementation problems that might occur at each stage of the systems development process.

9. What dimensions influence the level of risk in each systems development project?

10. What project management techniques can be used to control project risk?

11. What strategies can be used to overcome user resistance to systems development projects?

12. What organizational considerations should be addressed by information system design?

GROUP PROJECT

Form a group with two or three other students. Write a description of the implementation problems you might expect to encounter for the information system you designed for the business process redesign project in Appendix A. Write an analysis of the steps you would take to solve or prevent these problems. Alternatively, you could describe the implementation problems that might be expected for one of the systems described in the Window boxes or chapter-ending cases in this text. Present your findings to the class.

CASE STUDY

What Went Wrong at FoxMeyer?

FoxMeyer Drug Co. of Carrollton, Texas, was the main unit of FoxMeyer Health Corporation. At that time FoxMeyer was the fourth largest drug wholesaler in the United States with 1995 sales of $5.1 billion. The drug wholesaler industry had been going through a rapid consolidation, and in the early- and mid-1990s, FoxMeyer management was faced with the question of how they would compete with larger competitors to ensure their survival.

FoxMeyer drugs were distributed through a system of warehouses in the areas of its major customers. Every day the company filled orders from thousands of pharmacies and hospitals, shipping up to 500,000 items in these orders. Keeping tight control over inventory is critical to the industry because the cost of maintaining a high enough inventory to support such daily shipments is so great. At the same time, the whole industry competes by operating on low profit margins. Quality customer service, including rapid, accurate shipment of orders, is also key to competition. FoxMeyer believed it had to underbid its competitors for the business of large drug-store chains of hospital organizations while offering its customers high-quality service. Otherwise it would be swallowed by one of its larger rivals.

In 1994 at the center of the company's information technology architecture was an aging Unisys mainframe computer and inflexible application systems common to such old hardware. Its inventory system was able to track inventory daily, but it could not track inventory minute by minute as shipments were received or sent. Its warehouses, like most in any industry, had not been modernized through installation of new packing and shipping technology.

In 1994 management decided it had to take strong action to preserve FoxMeyer's independence and help the company compete against larger companies. The strategy they decided to follow was to use technology to "leapfrog the competition" according to Kenneth Woltz, a Chicago-based consultant to FoxMeyer. The company announced a $56 million project to develop and install Delta Information System. The new computer system would be used to manage critical operations focusing particularly on inventory control. The plan included building a new warehouse in Washington Court House, Ohio, with computerized robots to fill most orders for FoxMeyer's Midwestern customers. The specific inventory goals of the project included speeding up inventory turnover through better inventory control, thus reducing inventory costs, and providing ways to better serve customers by giving FoxMeyer more detailed information about each customer's ordering patterns. Another key goal was that of cutting costs. Management projected that the new systems, once fully implemented, would result in annual savings of $40

million. "They featured computerizing as a highlight of increasing their efficiency," explains Christina Valauri who followed the company as an analyst for PaineWebber Inc. "We are betting our company on this," proclaimed Chief Information Officer Robert R. Brown to *ComputerWorld.*

To build its new 340,000-square-foot warehouse, FoxMeyer spent about $18 million. The company hired Anderson Consulting, a leading international information systems consulting firm, both to advise them about the project and to supply skilled personnel to work on it. Although the company has not released information on how much they paid Anderson, project sources claim that it amounted to tens of millions of dollars. The project purchased R/3, an inventory management software system from SAP AG, a giant German software company (see the ending case for Chapter 12). In recent years SAP software had become so highly touted that information systems professionals vie for the opportunity to gain SAP experience so that they can become more employable and demand higher wages. Although SAP had been designed to run on Digital Equipment Corporation hardware, FoxMeyer purchased a Hewlett-Packard Co. client/server system at a cost of $4.8 million.

The software was designed to run on client/server hardware and it had the reputation for working well, enabling its users to replace their old mainframes. The hardware choice proved to not be a serious problem as the software ultimately ran well on the Hewlett-Packard equipment. However, the company had serious problems because "it's a very difficult system to implement," claims Kenneth Woltz. Client/server software is quite complex and was still relatively new at the time. Some difficulties were expected. The real source of the software problems was that no large wholesaler had ever used it before. In fact, SAP had never been used for so many transactions, and FoxMeyer claims that their later experience showed that SAP could

only handle a few thousand items per day. In addition, according to Woltz, "SAP was originally designed for manufacturers and lacked many features for the wholesale distribution business." An SAP spokesperson claims that the company "did end up having people go on site to perfect some of the interfaces between SAP and legacy systems. That did cause some delays." Douglas Schwinn, FoxMeyer's current chief information officer, says that during development they "ran some simulations, but not with the level of data we have in an operating environment."

Reports indicate that once the company had committed to SAP, management did not want to hear about problems. A number of people claimed they were encouraged to minimize problems. One manager contends, "It wasn't appropriate to criticize SAP." A consultant to the project said, "Every time we showed something that didn't work, they'd say 'Is this a deal-breaker?'"—the implication being that if not, the project will continue. This same consultant added that "no one [problem] was a deal-breaker. But if you put enough cinder blocks on a rowboat, it's going to sink."

The software problems were magnified by changing business conditions. In May 1993, Phar-Mor Inc., a Midwestern pharmacy chain, filed for bankruptcy protection. About 15 percent of FoxMeyer's total business came from this one chain. FoxMeyer management was working on the assumption that it had to grow to survive, and when FoxMeyer executives realized that the Phar-Mor business was permanently lost, they became concerned that they would not be able to grow enough to remain independent. They launched an urgent search for new customers and eventually found University HealthSystem Consortium, a national alliance of major teaching hospitals. In July 1994 the company signed a five-year contract with deliveries scheduled to start in early 1995. Management announced that the contract would generate $4 to 5 billion in revenue over the five contract years. However, to meet the aggressive deadline set for handling University HealthSystem orders, the SAP software implementation had to be moved forward three months, that despite the serious problems that were occurring. One programmer commented, "I would never plan on moving implementation up by 90 days." FoxMeyer later said that they did begin filling University HealthSystems orders on time, but University HealthSystems declined to comment.

Once the new system was implemented, serious data problems came to light. One result was that FoxMeyer could not be used to monitor customer purchasing patterns, one of the major goals of the project. Programmers pointed out that the reason the problems were not found until they had gone live with the system was that the project team did not have time to test all of it. For example, they skipped testing any portions of the SAP software that they had not customized. Interestingly, although the system had minute-by-minute data problems, it did produce bills that accurately reflected the customer's order. The ironic result of the accurate billing is that it contributed to even greater problems because, as we shall see, the bills did not reflect what was actually shipped.

Major shipping problems arose from the new Ohio warehouse. The automated system was designed to pick 80 percent of all items automatically, as compared with an industry average of 33 percent. The high level of automation was to be a key to both FoxMeyer's improved service and to its lower costs. The system relied on bar coding, bar-code readers, and automated conveyors to pick the products and automatically convey them to the appropriate dock and truck. The system, when first installed, was full of bugs and kept shutting down such critical elements as carousels and conveyors. Also, the scanners often failed to read the bar codes on the boxes. The warehouse opened in

August 1995, three months late and with many of the same bugs still not worked out. The company was forced to open the new warehouse despite the buggy system, because of the departure of many experienced warehouse staff members in the old warehouses. They had been able to read the clear handwriting on the wall—most of them would be replaced by the new automated system. As they left, the company replaced them with temps until the new warehouse opened, but temps were not able to handle the job and service deteriorated terribly, forcing the opening of the new warehouse before the problems were corrected.

As the system at the new warehouse repeatedly failed during the busiest working hours, the operators had to stop and then restart it. Boxes did not reach their loading position on time. Much of the work had to be done manually with the data being entered into the computer manually later, leading to many errors in the system. The most significant problem was that many orders were shipped with items missing but with an invoice for a complete order. In most instances, the missing items had arrived at the dock late due to system problems, and they were then put on a follow-up truck. Customers saw service quality deteriorate as they did not receive invoiced items when the original shipment arrived. The customers called FoxMeyer's customer service which ordered the missing items shipped the next day. Later, the missing items would arrive on later trucks. The result was that when the shipment of missing items ordered by customer service arrived the next day, many customers had received many duplicate items. However, because the SAP inventory system produced accurate bills based only on the order, customers were not billed for the duplicate deliveries. The not unexpected result was that many of the customers did not bother reporting the overages. Schwinn claims, "The enormity of the duplicate orders

wasn't clear until we did an inventory," but the problem led to huge loses to FoxMeyer. The company was forced to announce a $34 million charge to cover the uncollectible losses from customer orders. The fact was, the company did not know to whom the duplicate orders were sent or the content of those orders.

Another aspect of the developing disaster was FoxMeyer management's eagerness to make ultra-low bids for contracts to gain customers based on the assumption that the automated systems would reduce costs dramatically. They even won the University HealthSystem Consortium contract with an aggressively low bid despite the fact that most of the hospitals were on the West Coast where FoxMeyer had no warehouses. When making the bid, FoxMeyer knew it would have to build six new warehouses in the region. Again, they expected efficiencies from the new automated systems to make such contracts profitable.

FoxMeyer's stock suffered heavily from the automation problems. The stock, which reached a high of $26 per share in 1994 when the Delta project was announced, dropped to about $3 per share by December of that year. The company eventually filed for court protection under Chapter 11 of the Federal Bankruptcy law. Wade Hyde, a spokesperson for FoxMeyer, claimed that "fundamentally, the computer-integration problems we had were a significant factor leading to the bankruptcy filing." Later, McKesson Corp. was able to purchase FoxMeyer Drug Co. for a mere $80 million in cash. FoxMeyer had indeed bet its company on the new system, and it lost.

Interestingly, those still involved claim that the automation system finally worked as expected once the problems were solved. Mr. Schwinn claims the whole automation project is saving the company a lot of money, although it is not achieving the $40 million goal because of the complications involved with the University HealthSystem contract. ∎

Source: William M. Bulkeley, "When Things Go Wrong," *The Wall Street Journal*, November 11, 1996.

Case Study Questions

1. Analyze FoxMeyer's situation using the competitive forces and value chain models. How well had FoxMeyer's information systems supported its business strategy and business processes?

2. Classify and describe the problems with the Delta project using the categories described in the section in this chapter on causes of information systems success and failure. What management, organization, and technology factors caused these problems?

3. What role did SAP's software play in the failure? Were the software problems the fault of SAP, FoxMeyer, or both? Explain your answer.

4. Assess the causes of the failure of the project. Who was responsible? For example, what role did FoxMeyer's information technology group play in the failure? Do you agree with Schwinn that "fundamentally, the computer-integration problems we had were a significant factor leading to the bankruptcy filing?"

5. What were the project risks that should have been seen at the beginning of the project but were not? Why do you think they were not seen? What changes would you make to prevent that from happening again?

REFERENCES

Alter, Steven, and Michael Ginzberg. "Managing Uncertainty in MIS Implementation." *Sloan Management Review* 20 (Fall 1978).

Attewell, Paul. "Technology Diffusion and Organizational Learning: The Case of Business Computing." *Organization Science,* no. 3 (1992).

Barki, Henri, and Jon Hartwick. "Rethinking the Concept of User Involvement." *MIS Quarterly* 13, no. 1 (March 1989).

Baroudi, Jack, Margrethe H. Olson, and Blake Ives. "An Empirical Study of the Impact of User Involvement on System Usage and Information Satisfaction." *Communications of the ACM* 29, no. 3 (March 1986).

Baroudi, Jack, and Wanda Orlikowski. "A Short Form Measure of User Information Satisfaction: A Psychometric Evaluation and Notes on Use." *Journal of Management Information Systems* 4, no. 4 (Spring 1988).

Batiste, John L. "The Application Profile." *MIS Quarterly* (September 1986).

Best, James D. "The MIS Executive as Change Agent." *Journal of Information Systems Management* (Fall 1985).

Bikson, Tora K., Cathleen Stasz, and D. A. Mankin. "Computer Mediated Work. Individual and Organizational Impact in One Corporate Headquarters." Santa Monica, CA: Rand Corporation (1985).

Brooks, Frederick P. "The Mythical Man-Month." *Datamation* (December 1974).

Bulkeley, William. "Programmers Need to Keep It Simple." *Wall Street Journal* (June 30, 1992).

Bulkeley, William. "When Things Go Wrong." *Wall Street Journal* (November 18, 1996).

Cafasso, Rosemary. "Few IS Projects Come in on Time, on Budget." *Computerworld* (September 12, 1994).

Caldwell, Bruce. "Missteps, Miscues." *InformationWeek* (June 20, 1994).

Clement, Andrew, and Peter Van den Besselaar. "A Retrospective Look at PD Projects." *Communications of the ACM* 36, no. 4 (June 1993).

Cooper, Randolph B., and Robert W. Zmud. "Information Technology Implementation Research: A Technological Diffusion Approach." *Management Science* 36, no. 2 (February 1990).

Corbato, Fernando J. "On Building Systems That Will Fail." *Communications of the ACM* 34, no. 9 (September 1991).

Cronan, Timothy Paul, and David E. Douglas. "End-user Training and Computing Effectiveness in Public Agencies: An Empirical Study." *Journal of Management Information Systems* 6, no. 4 (Spring 1990).

Davis, Fred R., "Perceived Usefulness, Ease of Use, and User Acceptance of Information Technology." *MIS Quarterly* 13, no. 3 (September 1989).

Davis, Gordon B., and Margrethe H. Olson. *Management Information Systems,* 2nd ed. New York: McGraw-Hill (1985).

DeLone, William H., and Ephrain R. McLean. "Information System Success: The Quest for the Dependent Variable." *Information Systems Research* 3, no. 1 (March 1992).

Delong, William H. "Determinants of Success for Computer Usage in Small Business." *MIS Quarterly* (March 1988).

Doll, William J. "Avenues for Top Management Involvement in Successful MIS Development." *MIS Quarterly* (March 1985).

Ein-Dor, Philip, and Eli Segev. "Organizational Context and the Success of Management Information Systems." *Management Science* 24 (June 1978).

Franz, Charles, and Daniel Robey. "An Investigation of User-Led System Design: Rational and Political Perspectives." *Communications of the ACM* 27 (December 1984).

Ginzberg, M. J. "The Impact of Organizational Characteristics on MIS Design and Implementation." Working paper CRIS 10, GBA 80-110. New York University Center for Research on Information Systems, Area Computer Applications and Information Systems Area (1980).

Ginzberg, Michael J. "Early Diagnosis of MIS Implementation Failure: Promising Results and Unanswered Questions." *Management Science* 27 (April 1981).

Gould, John D., and Clayton Lewis. "Designing for Usability: Key Principles and What Designers Think." *Communications of the ACM* 28 (March 1985).

Gullo, Karen. "Stopping Runaways in Their Tracks." *InformationWeek* (November 13, 1989).

Hammer, Michael, and Steven A. Stanton. *The Reengineering Revolution.* New York: HarperCollins (1995).

Helms, Glenn L., and Ira R. Weiss. "The Cost of Internally Developed Applications: Analysis of Problems and Cost Control Methods." *Journal of Management Information Systems* (Fall 1986).

Hirscheim, R. A. "User Experience with and Assessment of Participative Systems Design." *MIS Quarterly* (December 1985).

Ives, Blake, Margrethe H. Olson, and Jack J. Baroudi. "The Measurement of User Information Satisfaction." *Communications of the ACM* 26 (October 1983).

Joshi, Kailash. "A Model of Users' Perspective on Change: The Case of Information Systems Technology Implementation." *MIS Quarterly* 15, no. 2 (June 1991).

Keil, Mark, Richard Mixon, Timo Saarinen, and Virpi Tuunairen. "Understanding Runaway IT Projects." *Journal of Management Information Systems* 11, no. 3 (Winter 1994–95).

Keen, Peter W. "Information Systems and Organizational Change." *Communications of the ACM* 24 (January 1981).

Kolb, D. A., and A. L. Frohman. "An Organization Development Approach to Consulting." *Sloan Management Review* 12 (Fall 1970).

Laudon, Kenneth C. "CIOs Beware: Very Large Scale Systems." Center for Research on Information Systems, New York University Stern School of Business, working paper (1989).

Lederer, Albert L., Rajesh Mirani, Boon Siong Neo, Carol Pollard, Jayesh Prasad, and K. Ramamurthy. "Information System Cost Estimating: A Management Perspective." *MIS Quarterly* 14, no. 2 (June 1990).

Lederer, Albert, and Jayesh Prasad. "Nine Management Guidelines for Better Cost Estimating." *Communications of the ACM* 35, no. 2 (February 1992).

Lucas, Henry C., Jr. *Toward Creative Systems Design.* New York: Columbia University Press (1974).

Lucas, Henry C., Jr. *Why Information Systems Fail.* New York: Columbia University Press (1975).

Lucas, Henry C., Jr. *Implementation: The Key to Successful Information Systems.* New York: Columbia University Press (1981).

McFarlan, F. Warren. "Portfolio Approach to Information Systems." *Harvard Business Review* (September–October 1981).

McPartlin, John P. "Uncle Sam Calls in the Reserves." *InformationWeek* (April 27, 1992).

Maglitta, Joseph. "Rocks in the Gears." *Computerworld* (October 3, 1994).

Marcus, Aaron. "Human Communication Issues in Advanced UIS." *Communications of the ACM* 36, no. 4 (April 1993).

Markus, M. L. "Power, Politics and MIS Implementation." *Communications of the ACM* 26 (June 1983).

Markus, M. Lynne, and Mark Keil. "If We Build It, They Will Come: Designing Information Systems That People Want to Use." *Sloan Management Review* (Summer 1994).

Markus, M. Lynne, and Robert I. Benjamin. "Change Agentry—The Next IS Frontier." *MIS Quarterly* 20, no. 4 (December 1996).

Markus, M. Lynne, and Robert I. Benjamin. "The Magic Bullet Theory of IT-Enabled Transformation." *Sloan Management Review* (Winter 1997).

Miller, Steven E. "From System Design to Democracy." *Communications of the ACM* 36, no. 4 (June 1993).

Moore, Gary C., and Izak Benbasat. "Development of an Instrument to Measure the Perceptions of Adopting an Information Technology Innovation." *Information Systems Research* 2, no. 3 (September 1991).

Mumford, Enid, and Mary Weir. *Computer Systems in Work Design: The ETHICS Method.* New York: John Wiley (1979).

Newman, Michael, and Rajir Sabherwal. "Determinants of Commitment to Information Systems Development: A Longitudinal Investigation." *MIS Quarterly* 20, no. 1 (March 1996).

Nidumolu, Sarma R., Seymour E. Goodman, Douglas R. Vogel, and Ann K. Danowitz. "Information Technology for Local Administration Support: The Governorates Project in Egypt." *MIS Quarterly* 20, no. 2 (June 1996).

Orlikowski, Wanda J., and J. Debra Hofman. "An Improvisational Change Model for Change Management: The Case of Groupware Technologies." *Sloan Management Review* (Winter 1997).

Oz, Effy. "When Professional Standards Are Lax: The CONFIRM Failure and Its Lessons." *Communications of the ACM* 37, no. 10 (October 1994).

Raymond, Louis. "Organizational Context and Information System Success: A Contingency Approach." *Journal of Management Information Systems* 6, no. 4 (Spring 1990).

Robey, Daniel, and M. Lynne Markus. "Rituals in Information System Design." *MIS Quarterly* (March 1984).

Robey, Daniel, and Sundeep Sahay. "Transforming Work Through Information Technology: A Comparative Case Study of Geographic Information Systems." *Information Systems Research* 7, no. 1 (March 1996).

Singleton, John P., Ephraim R. McLean, and Edward N. Altman. "Measuring Information Systems Performance." *MIS Quarterly* 12, no. 2 (June 1988).

Swanson, E. Burton. *Information System Implementation.* Homewood, IL: Richard D. Irwin (1988).

Tait, Peter, and Iris Vessey. "The Effect of User Involvement on System Success: A Contingency Approach." *MIS Quarterly* 12, no. 1 (March 1988).

Thong, James Y. L., Chee-Sing Yap, and K. S. Raman. "Top Management Support, External Expertise, and Information Systems Implementation in Small Business." *Information Systems Research* 7, no. 2 (June 1996).

Tornatsky, Louis G., J. D. Eveland, M. G. Boylan, W. A. Hetzner, E. C. Johnson, D. Roitman, and J. Schneider. *The Process of Technological Innovation: Reviewing the Literature.* Washington, DC: National Science Foundation (1983).

Turner, Jon A. "Computer Mediated Work: The Interplay Between Technology and Structured Jobs." *Communications of the ACM* 27 (December 1984).

United States General Services Administration. "An Evaluation of the Grand Design Approach to Developing Computer-Based Application Systems." Washington, DC: General Services Administration (September 1988).

Westcott, Russ. "Client Satisfaction: The Yardstick for Measuring MIS Success." *Journal of Information Systems Management* (Fall 1985).

Westin, Alan F., Heather A. Schweder, Michael A. Baker, and Sheila Lehman. *The Changing Workplace.* White Plains, NY, and London: Knowledge Industry Publications, Inc. (1985).

White, Kathy Brittain, and Richard Leifer. "Information Systems Development Success: Perspectives from Project Team Participants." *MIS Quarterly* (September 1986).

Yin, Robert K. "Life Histories of Innovations: How New Practices Become Routinized." *Public Administration Review* (January–February 1981).

SYSTEM MODERNIZATION AT THE SOCIAL SECURITY ADMINISTRATION: 1982–1997

The Social Security Administration (SSA) consists of approximately 63,000 employees located in 1300 field offices, 10 regional offices, 37 teleservice centers, 7 processing centers, 4 data operations centers, and the Baltimore headquarters. SSA administers the major social insurance programs of the United States and several other related programs, which include:

- *Retirement and Survivors Insurance (RSI)*
- *Disability Insurance (DI)*
- *Supplemental Security Income (SSI)*

In order to administer these programs, SSA maintains 260 million names in its account number file (enumeration file), 240 million earnings records, and 50 million names on its master beneficiary file. In addition to keeping these files current, SSA annually issues 10 million new Social Security cards, pays out $170 billion, posts 380 million wage items reported by employers, receives 7.5 million new claims, recomputes (because of changes in beneficiary status) 19 million accounts, and handles 120 million bills and queries from private health insurance companies, carriers, and intermediaries. Virtually every living American has some relationship with SSA.

In the early 1980s, the long-term funding for Social Security payments in the United States was in serious jeopardy, and SSA's computerized administrative systems were nearing collapse. This was an unusual state of affairs for SSA. As the flagship institution of the New Deal, SSA had developed broad bipartisan support, and there was never any serious question about its long-term financial viability until the late 1970s. In addition, since its inception in 1935, SSA had been one of the leading innovators and implementors of advanced information technology in the United States. With a special long-term relationship with IBM from the mid-1930s to the late 1960s, SSA was a test site for many of the leading commercial hardware and software innovations of this period.

In 1982, SSA announced its Systems Modernization Plan (SMP), a $500 million five-year effort to completely rebuild its information systems and administrative processes. Since then, the SMP has been expanded to $1 billion and 10 years. The SMP was one of the largest civilian information system rebuilding efforts in history. Ten years later, SSA embarked on another ambitious round of technology modernization as it tried to create an information architecture for the twenty-first century.

SSA illustrates many central problems of management, information technology, and organization faced by private and public organizations in a period of rapid technical and social change. Although SSA operates in a unique federal government environment, many large private organizations have exhibited similar problems in this time period. The problems and solutions illustrated in this case are generic.

The case is organized into three sections. Section I describes the overall situation at SSA in the period before SMP, roughly 1972 to 1982. Section II describes the experience of SMP. Section III considers the long-term prospects of SSA.

SECTION I: ORGANIZATION, MANAGEMENT, AND SYSTEMS, 1972–1982

The overall system environment at SSA in 1982 could best be described as a hodgepodge of software programs developed over a 20-year period in four different machine environments. In the history of the agency, no one had ever conducted an information system requirements study to understand the overall requirements of the agency or the specific requirements of its subunits. There had been no planning of the information systems function for more than 20 years. Instead, as in many private organizations, systems drifted along from year to year, with only incremental changes.

Software

SSA software resulted from decades of programming techniques. The enumeration system, which supports the issuance of Social Security numbers, was designed in the late 1950s and had never been changed. The earning system was designed in 1975, the claims processing system was unchanged from the early 1960s, and other systems were also inherited from the late 1960s and 1970s. The software was a product of unplanned patchwork, with no regard given to its deterioration over time.

From the 1950s to the 1980s, there were four major equipment transitions. However, the software was not improved or redesigned at any of these transitions. All of SSA's files and programs were maintained on over 500,000 reels of magnetic tape, which were susceptible to aging, cracking, and deterioration. Because tape was the storage medium, all data processing was batch sequential.

In summary, there were 76 different software systems making up SSA's basic computer operations. These software systems were themselves congeries of programs that performed the primary business functions of SSA. There were more than 1300 computer programs encompassing over 12 million lines of COBOL and other code.

Most of the 12 million lines of code were undocumented. They worked, but few people in the organization knew how or why, which made maintenance extremely complex. In the 1960s and 1970s, Congress and the president made continual changes in the benefit formulas, each of which required extensive maintenance and changes in the underlying software. A change in cost-of-living rates, for instance, required sorting through several large interwoven programs, which took months of work.

Because of the labor-intensive work needed to change undocumented software and the growing operations crisis, software development staff were commonly shifted to manage the operations crisis. The result was little development of new programs.

It did not help matters that few people in Congress, the Office of the President, the Office of Management and Budget, or other responsible parties understood the deleterious impact of program changes on SSA systems capabilities. Unfortunately, SSA did not inform Congress of its own limitation.

What is unusual about SSA is that in the late 1970s it had not begun to make the transition to newer storage technology, file management and database technology, or more modern software techniques. In this respect, SSA was about five years behind private industry in making important technological transitions.

Hardware

By 1982, SSA was operating outdated, unreliable, and inadequate hardware, given its mission. Many of the computers had not been manufactured or marketed for 10 years or more. Eleven IBM 360/65 systems were no longer manufactured or supported. Although more modern equipment might have required $1 million annually for maintenance and operations expenses, SSA was spending more than $4 million to keep these antiquated machines in service.

The antiquated hardware forced SSA to rely on third-party maintenance services. Because of frequent breakdowns, over 25 percent of the production jobs ended before completion (abended jobs), and 30 percent of the available computer processing power was idle. As a result of hardware deficiencies, a number of specific program impacts became apparent in 1982:

- Earnings enforcement operations, which help detect overpayments, were more than three years behind schedule.

- The computation of benefit amounts to give credit for additional earnings after retirement was three years behind schedule.

- SSI claims and posteligibility redeterminations could be processed only three times a week rather than five times a week. This meant delays of several days or weeks for SSI beneficiaries.

- To process cost-of-living increases in 1982 for 42 million individuals, SSA had to suspend all other data processing for one week.

- In 1982, there was a three-month backlog of data needed to notify employers about incorrectly reported employee earnings. This created a suspense file with more than 2 million entries of unposted earnings and required additional manual work to handle employer correspondence.

SSA estimated that its gross computing capacity was deficient by more than 2000 CPU hours per month. SSA estimated that it needed 5000 central processing hours per month, but its capacity was only 3000 CPU hours per month.

Telecommunications

SSA depends heavily on telecommunications to perform its mission. Its 1300 field offices need timely access to data stored at the central computer facility in Baltimore. In 1982, however, SSA's telecommunications was the result of an evolving system dating back to 1966. The primary telecommunications system was called the Social Security Administration Data Acquisition and Response System (SSADARS), designed to handle 100,000 transactions per day. One year after it was built in 1975, the system was totally saturated. Each year teleprocessing grew by 100 percent. By 1982 the SSADARS network was frequently breaking down and was obsolete and highly inefficient.

One result of the saturated communications system was that senior SSA local executives working in field offices were forced to come in on the weekends to key in data to the SSADARS system, which was overloaded during the week. By 1982, there was little remaining CPU telecommunications capacity in the off-peak periods to handle the normal growth of current workloads. Entire streams of communications were frequently lost. At peak times, when most people wanted to use the system, it was simply unavailable. The result was telecommunications backlogs ranging from 10,000 to 100,000 messages at a time.

Database

The word *database* can be used only in a very loose sense to refer to SSA's 500,000 reels of magnetic tape on which it stored information on clients in major program areas. Each month SSA performed 30,000 production jobs, requiring more than 150,000 tapes to be loaded onto and off of machines. The tapes themselves were disintegrating, and errors in the tapes, along with their physical breakdown, caused very high error rates and forced a number of reruns. More than one-third of the operations staff (200 people) was required simply to handle the tapes.

As in many private sector organizations, data were organized at SSA by programs, and many of the data elements were repeated from one program to the next. SSA estimates that there were more than 1300 separate programs, each with its own data set. Because there was no data administration function, it was difficult to determine the total number of data elements, or the level of redundancy within the agency as a whole or even within program areas.

Management Information Systems

In 1982, SSA had a woefully inadequate capability in the MIS area. Because the data were stored on magnetic tape and were generally not available to end-user managers throughout the organization, all requests for reports had to be funneled through the information systems operations area.

But there was a crisis in operations, and this meant delays of up to several years in the production of reports crucial for management decision making. As long as all data were stored in a format that required professional computer and information systems experts to gain access to them, general management always had to deal with the information systems department. This group had a stranglehold over the organization. Their attitude, as one commentator noted, was summed up in the statement, "Don't bother us or the checks won't go out."

How Could This Happen?

There are two explanations for SSA's fall from a leading-edge systems position to near collapse in the early 1980s. First, there were internal institutional factors involving middle and senior management. Second, a sometimes hostile and rapidly changing environment in the 1970s added to SSA's woes.

In the 1970s, Congress had made more than 15 major changes in the RSI program alone. These changes increasingly taxed SSA's systems to the point that systems personnel were working on weekends to make required program changes.

In 1972 Congress passed the Supplemental Security Income (SSI) program, which converted certain state-funded and -administered income maintenance programs into federal programs. SSA suddenly found itself in the welfare arena, which was far removed from that of a social insurance agency. Unprepared local staffs suddenly faced thousands of angry applicants standing in line. Riots occurred in some cities. Other programs, such as Medicaid and changes in disability insurance, as well as cost-of-living (COLA) escalators, all severely taxed SSA's systems and personnel capacity. The 1978 COLA required changes in over 800 SSA computer programs.

The number of clients served by SSA doubled in the 1970s. But because of a growing economic crisis combining low growth and high inflation (stagflation), Congress was unwilling to expand SSA's work force to meet the demands of new programs. There was growing public and political resistance to expanding federal government employment at the very time when new programs were coming on-line and expectations of service were rising.

SSA management in this period consistently overstated its administrative capacity to Congress and failed to communicate the nature of the growing systems crisis. SSA pleas for additional manpower were consistently turned down or reduced by Congress and the White House. Workloads of employees dramatically increased, and morale and job satisfaction declined. Training was reduced, especially in the systems area, as all resources were diverted to the operations crisis.

Toward the end of the 1970s, the political environment changed as well. A growing conservative movement among Republicans and Democrats interested in reducing the size of all federal programs led to increasing pressure on SSA to reduce employment levels. In the long actuarial funding debate at the beginning of the 1980s, there was talk about "privatizing" Social Security and abolishing the agency altogether.

Complicating SSA's environment was the Brooks Act of 1965, which mandated competitive procurement of computing equipment and services. Up to 1965, SSA had had a longstanding and beneficial relationship with IBM. Virtually all of SSA's equipment was manufactured by IBM and purchased on a noncompetitive basis. IBM provided planning, technical support, software support, and consulting services to SSA as part of this relationship.

By the 1970s this close relationship had ended. IBM shifted its support and marketing efforts away from the federal arena because of the Brooks Act. SSA found itself in a new competitive environment, forced to do all of its own planning, development, and procurement work. As the workload rapidly expanded at SSA in the 1970s, the agency needed a well-planned, closely managed transition to new computing equipment and software. This transition never occurred.

A challenging environment might have been overcome by a focused and dedicated management group. Perhaps the most critical weakness of all in SSA's operation in the 1970s was its inability to gain management control over the information systems function and over the information resource on which the organization itself was based.

Senior management turnover was a critical problem. In its first 38 years, SSA had six commissioners with an average tenure of 6.5 years. Two men led the agency for 27 of its 38 years. But from 1971 to 1981, SSA had seven commissioners or acting commissioners with an average tenure of 1.1 years. None of these commissioners had any experience at SSA. The senior staff of the agency was also repeatedly shaken up in this period. Compared with earlier senior managers, those of the 1970s failed to realize the critical importance of information systems to SSA's operation. Long-range planning of the agency or systems became impossible. Authority slowly but inevitably devolved to operations-level groups, the only ones that knew what was going on.

With new senior management came four major reorganizations of the agency. Major SSA programs were broken down into functional parts and redistributed to new functional divisions. Program coherence was lost. Performance measures and management control disappeared as managers and employees struggled to adapt to their new functions.

Efforts at Reform

SSA made several efforts in this period to regain control and direction in the systems area on which its entire operation critically depended. In 1975, SSA created the Office of Advanced Systems (OAS) within the Office of the Commissioner. SSA hoped that this advanced, high-level planning group with direct access to senior management would develop a strategy for change. Unfortunately, this effort failed to reform SSA's manual and batch processes and was opposed by systems operations management and the union. There was no White House support for it and no suggestion from Congress or the White House that needed funding would be forthcoming. In 1979 the OAS was abolished by a new management team.

A second effort at reform began in 1979. This time the idea originated with new senior management. Called *partitioning*, the new reform effort sought to break SSA's internal operations into major program lines— similar to product lines—so that each program could develop its own systems. This plan was quickly rejected by the White House, Congress, and outside professionals.

A third reform effort also began in 1979. Here SSA sought to replace the aging SSADARS telecommunications network with new, high-speed communications terminals in the district offices and new telecommunications computers in the Baltimore headquarters. After a competitive procurement process, SSA contracted with the Paradyne Corporation for 2000 such terminals. Unfortunately, the first 16 systems failed all operational tests on delivery in 1981. Investigations produced charges of bidding fraud (selling systems to SSA that did not exist, "black boxes with blinking lights"), securities fraud, bribery, bid rigging, perjury, and an inadequate SSA systems requirements definition. By 1983 SSA took delivery of all the terminals, and they did perform for their expected life of eight years. But the procurement scandal further reduced SSA's credibility in Congress and the White House.

Senior management turnover, lack of concern, and failed efforts at reform took a severe toll in the systems area. Planning of information systems was either not done or was done at such a low operational level that no major changes in operations could be accomplished.

SECTION II: THE SYSTEMS MODERNIZATION PLAN

As the crisis at SSA became increasingly apparent to Congress, the General Accounting Office, and the President's Office, pressure was placed on SSA to develop a new strategy. In 1981 a new commissioner, John Svahn, a recently appointed former insurance executive with systems experience, began work on a strategic plan to try to move SSA data processing from collapse to a modern system. The result was a five-year plan called the Systems Modernization Plan (SMP). SMP was intended to bring about long-range, tightly integrated changes in software, hardware, telecommunications, and management systems. At $500 million, the original cost estimate in 1982, the SMP was one of the single most expensive information systems projects in history. The goals of the SMP were as follows:

- Restore excellence to SSA systems and return the agency to its state-of-the-art position.
- Avoid disruption of service.
- Improve service immediately by purchasing modern hardware.
- Improve staff effectiveness and productivity.
- Restore public confidence by enhancing accountability, auditability, and detection of fraud.

SMP Strategy

As a bold effort to secure a total change at SSA, the SMP adopted a conservative strategy. This strategy called for SSA to do the following:

- Achieve modernization through incremental, evolutionary change, given the unacceptable risks of failure.
- Build on the existing systems, selecting short-term, feasible approaches that minimize risks.
- Separate the modernization program from the operations and maintenance programs.

- Use an external system integration contractor to provide continuity to the five-year project.
- Utilize industry-proven, state-of-the-art systems engineering technology.
- Establish a single organizational body to plan, manage, and control SMP.
- Elevate systems development and operations to the highest levels of the agency.

SMP Implementation

The original plan foresaw a five-year effort broken into three stages: survival, transition, and state of the art. In the survival stage (18 months), SSA would focus on new hardware acquisition to solve immediate problems of capacity shortage. In the transition stage (18 months), SSA would begin rebuilding software, data files, and telecommunications systems. In the final state-of-the-art stage, SSA would finalize and integrate projects to achieve a contemporary level of systems. The SMP involved six interrelated programs.

1. Capacity Upgrade Program (CUP). CUP was developed to reconfigure and consolidate the physical computing sites around central headquarters in Baltimore; to acquire much higher-capacity and more modern computers; to eliminate sequentially organized magnetic tape files and switch over to direct access devices; and to develop a local computing network for high-speed data transfers.

2. System Operation and Management Program (SOMP). SOMP was intended to provide modern automated tools and procedures for managing and controlling SSA's main computer center operations in Baltimore. Included were automated job scheduling tools, job station monitoring and submission systems, operational job procedures, training, and a central integrated control facility to ensure that SSA would make a smooth transition to a modern data center environment.

3. Data Communications Utility Program (DCUP). DCUP was designed to reengineer SSA's major telecommunications system (SSADARS). What SSA wanted was a transparent conduit for the transmission of data between and among processing units of different manufacture using a single integrated network. More than 40,000 on-line terminals were to be used in the 1300 field offices.

4. Software Engineering Program (SEP). SEP was designed to upgrade the existing software and retain as much of it as possible so that entirely new code did not have to be written. A critical part of the SEP was a top-down, functional analysis (using the enterprise system planning method) of the Social Security process—all of the business and organizational functions of SSA. Hopefully, this top-down planning effort would provide the framework for the redesign of SSA's total system by establishing the requirements for improvements in existing software. A second key aspect of the software engineering effort was the implementation of new software engineering technology. This involved developing and enforcing programming standards, developing quality controls, and using modern computer-aided software development tools. Special emphasis was placed on the development of modern program documentation, standardization of programs, and conversion to higher-level languages when possible.

5. Database Integration. The database integration project involved four objectives. As a survival tactic, SSA wanted to reduce the current labor-intensive, error-prone magnetic tape operation by converting all records to high-speed disk, direct access storage devices (DASD). A second goal was to establish a data administration function to control the definition of data elements and files. A third goal was to eliminate the data errors by establishing data controls, validating files, and developing modern storage disk technology. A fourth objective was to integrate the variety of databases, making communication among them transparent.

6. Administrative Management Information Engineering Program (AMIE). SSA was fundamentally dependent on manual activities to conduct most of its administration. Requests for personnel actions, purchase requisitions, telephone service, travel orders, building modifications, training requests—all these administrative matters were processed manually. The AMIE program was designed to integrate MIS with other programmatic modernization activities: to automate and modernize labor-intensive administrative processes and to develop management MIS to improve the planning and administrative process.

The End of SMP: Success and Failure

SMP had become increasingly controversial: Critics claimed failure while the agency's leaders claimed success. By 1988 Dorcas Hardy, the new SSA commissioner, quietly ended SMP and announced a new plan called "2000: A Strategic Plan." What had the SMP accomplished in five years?

For much of the earlier years of SMP the environment was supportive of and sympathetic to the modernization program. By 1986, however, criticism was beginning to develop over the rising costs and seeming endless time frame. In large part the critics drew strength from the fact that the SMP project had been extended by SSA for an additional five years (to 1992) and had doubled in expected cost to $1 billion; no major software breakthroughs were apparent to the public or Congress; and the effort to modernize SSA's "backend" or database appeared to stall.

The White House increasingly pressed SSA to make plans for reducing its staff by one-quarter, or 20,000 positions. By the end of 1988, the SSA staff had been reduced by 17,000 workers, from 83,000 down to 66,000, mostly by attrition. These reductions were made in anticipation of sharp increases in productivity brought about by the SMP modernization efforts. There was little systematic effort to examine this hope.

Under pressure from the White House, the new commissioner abandoned the pact with the union. The union began a long, drawn-out battle with the management for control over the implementation process. This battle frequently resulted in public congressional testimony challenging management claims of enhanced service, quality, and productivity. In labor's view, SSA management put excessive pressure on employees to work faster to "make the modernization program look good." "The Unions and the employees looked forward to system modernization," according to Rose Seaman, an SSA claims representative and SMP oversight person for the American Federation of Government Employees (AFGE), but "systems modernization never delivered. Instead there is great pressure on claims reps to perform clerical functions the system cannot perform, and to alter records so that processing times are reduced."[1]

The General Accounting Office (GAO), responding to requests from the House Government Operations Committee (Rep. Jack Brooks, Democrat of Texas, chairman), issued many highly critical reports of SSA's procurement policies. In one report issued in 1986, GAO charged that SSA failed to redevelop software or to develop a true database architecture. In another 1987 report, GAO claimed that SSA's new Claims Modernization Software would handle only 2 percent of the workload (merely initial applications for retirement and not the application processing or postentitlement changes)! The report chided SSA for dropping modernization of the postentitlement process which accounts for 94 percent of daily SSA transactions.

SSA management heatedly denied GAO's allegations, but the backsliding in software became a major weapon of SMP opponents. GAO called for a halt in procurements. Hardy refused and began purchasing 40,000 full-color desktop terminals.

A review of SMP by the Office of Technology Assessment (OTA), a congressional research agency, concluded that the White House, Congress, and SSA were all to blame for SSA's failure. The White House was blamed for prematurely seeking huge workforce reductions before the new systems were in place. It was also blamed for continuing political interference in the agency and for failure to support senior management. Congress was blamed for failing to understand the complexity of SSA programs and the long-term nature of total systems change. In addition, OTA blamed new procurement laws for slowing down and complicating the purchase of new hardware.

OTA pointed to a number of faults at SSA. From the very beginning of SMP, SSA failed to rethink its method of doing business. SMP basically sought to automate an organizational structure and a way of doing business established in the 1930s. SSA failed, for instance, to question the role of 1300 field offices—are they really needed in a day of wide area networks and microcomputers? Should SSA's major data files be centralized in Baltimore? SSA failed to rethink its basic architecture of a centralized mainframe operation in Baltimore serving the entire country. Why not a more decentralized structure? Why not minicomputers in every district office? OTA also pointed to SSA's failure to develop new software on a timely basis and a new database architecture. It was felt these shortcomings, especially in software and database, would ultimately come to haunt SSA thereafter. In general, SMP lacked a vision for the future around which it could build a powerful new information architecture.[2]

GAO, OTA, and labor critics believed that whatever increases in productivity occurred from 1982 to 1988 resulted largely from workforce reduction, deterioration in service, and asking the remaining employees to work harder, rather than any result of technology per se. Although public surveys published by SSA showed the general public thought SSA did a fine job, surveys of field office employees and managers with direct knowledge of the situation showed declining service quality, employee performance, and morale.

As employee levels dropped, managers complained in interviews that the "work load is oppressive," recalling days in the 1960s when lines of clients surrounded SSA offices. Although managers praised the new claims modernization software, teleservice centers, and preinterviewing techniques which permit clericals to answer questions of clients using online queries, the overall reduction in labor force put a "crushing load on District Office personnel." Employees and managers reported many of the most capable managers and claims representatives were leaving SSA for the private sector or other government jobs as working conditions deteriorated.[3]

For the critics SSA had made some improvements in service and processing, but these resulted early in the SMP plan and were largely the result of hardware purchases and running the old software faster. Whatever progress in productivity occurred did so at the expense of employees and service to clients.

By 1988, SSA management conceded that SMP had indeed doubled in size to a projected $1 billion, but by 1988 the SMP plan had actually spent slightly less ($444 million) than the original estimate of $500 million. Management conceded that the time required to reach state-of-the-art processing had been extended to 1992; that "there was an excessive emphasis on hardware, that software development was slow, and that the agency carried over large balances of unbudgeted funds from year to year (indicating difficulty in managing projects and allocated funds).[4] In fact, software development was four years behind schedule, and the database redesign (the so-called "backend" of the system) was still being considered after five years. Nevertheless, SSA had documented steady improvement in a number of measures of services to beneficiaries, many of which are due to the SMP:

- A 25 percent decrease in RSI claims processing time.
- A small decrease in DI claims processing time (2.2 days).
- A high and improving rate of RSI claims accuracy (95.7 to 97.2 percent).
- A 41 percent decrease in SSI processing time.
- A 7 percent decrease in SSI blind/disabled processing time.
- A 47 percent decrease in RSDI (Retired Survivors Disability Insurance) change of status processing time.
- Stable administrative costs in RSI since 1980 (1.1 percent of benefits).

Management pointed to the following key changes brought about by the SMP: Management claimed that overall SMP brought about a 25 percent increase in productivity. The agency was now doing slightly more "work" in 1988 than it was in 1982 but with 17,000 fewer employees. SSA created a new deputy commissioner for systems development and raised the status of systems in the organization to the senior management level. Management noted that SMP had made great progress in its specific program areas:

Hardware Capacity Upgrade.

Between 1982 and 1988 SSA increased processing capacity twentyfold, from 20 MIPS to a total of 400

1982	Today
6 weeks to receive a Social Security card	Takes 10 working days
4 years to post annual wage reports	Done in 5 months
Over a month to process an RSI claim	Done in about 20 days
4 years to do annual recomputations for those entitled to higher benefits	Done in 6 months
3 weeks of computer processing for annual cost-of-living increases	Done in 25 hours
15 days for payments in emergency situations	Received in 5 days

MIPS, replacing outdated computers purchased without competitive bids with hardware supplied by three manufacturers on a competitive basis.

System Operation and Management Program (SOMP).

The central processing facility in Baltimore developed efficient job scheduling standards and procedures for handling tapes and documents so that 95 percent of its processing is completed on time.

Data Communications Utility Program (DCUP).

Under SMP a network of more than 50,000 devices was installed nationwide, with the objective of putting a terminal on every claims representative's desktop. Network capacity increased from 1200 characters per second in 1982 to 7000 characters per second in 1988.

Software Engineering.

SSA made major progress redesigning the software for the retirement program. Now millions of retired persons can initiate the claims process or inquire about their accounts using an 800-number teleservice or have a claims representative initiate the claim on-line from a district office. In 1982 this capability was not even imagined. Developing such interactive systems to deliver services required entirely new code; the old software could not be salvaged.

Database Integration.

SSA converted 500,000 reels of tape to more modern DASDs. All master files were converted to disk, making it possible to handle more than 2 million inquiries per day directly on-line. SSA developed its own inhouse data management system called the Master Data Access Method (MADAM) to handle all on-line and batch access to SSA master files. However, the data are still organized according to major program areas. SSA has yet to develop an integrated database for all or even some of its major programs that could provide a "whole person" view of SSA clients. A major difficulty is deciding on an overall database architecture that could integrate information from the major program areas.

SECTION III: SSA'S STRATEGIC PLAN AND INFORMATION SYSTEMS PLAN

SSA issued a new Agency Strategic Plan (ASP) in 1988. The plan was updated in 1991 to incorporate a wider vision of the agency's future. The new ASP strategic priorities called for improvements in client access to SSA, the appeals process, and the disability process; movement toward a "paperless agency"; and establishment of a decentralized data processing structure.

In August 1990 Renato A. DiPentima took over as deputy commissioner of systems. DiPentima initiated a seven-year Information Systems Plan (ISP) in September 1991 to support the Agency Strategic Plan. The ISP was updated in 1992 and late 1993.

The Information Systems Plan is SSA's long-range plan for managing information systems as the agency moves into the 1990s and beyond. Its primary goal is to support the Agency Strategic Plan by building a systems environment that improves service to the public and SSA users. Long-term strategic priorities include improving the disability process, the appeals process, and the public's access to SSA by turning SSA into a paperless agency with electronic claims folders and establishing a cooperative processing architecture. The Information Systems Plan was designed to be a continuous plan that could always be upgraded.

Both plans address the challenges faced by SSA as it moves into the twenty-first century. SSA's total workload is expected to increase by 26 percent between 1990 and 2005. There will be limited funding for new initiatives, coupled with increased demands for higher levels of service to the public. In the past, most SSA clients preferred to visit SSA field offices. Today, they prefer to conduct their business over the telephone and they expect the same fast, efficient service they receive in the private sector. SSA must enhance systems to handle increasing workloads without hiring more employees, keeping costs low because of scarce budgetary resources. The number of field and operational employees has already decreased substantially since the 1980s and the remaining employees require new technologies to handle the increased workload.

SSA still maintains a centralized mainframe system at its Baltimore headquarters linked to 39,000 dumb terminals in its field offices and teleservice centers via SSANet, the main SSA Network (the former Data Communications and Utility Program described earlier). The Information Systems Plan calls for moving SSA toward a distributed architecture, ending its total reliance on centralized mainframe computers for its programmatic applications that deliver services to SSA clients. Selected business functions are being distributed between headquarters and local processors. Most

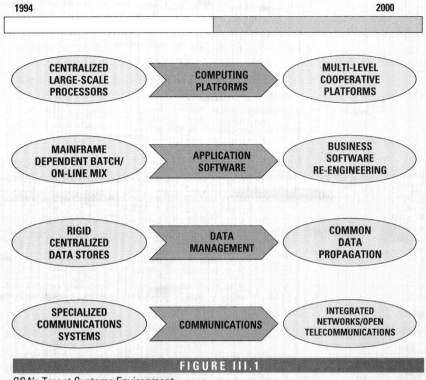

FIGURE III.1

SSA's Target Systems Environment.
Source: Social Security Administration, "Information Systems Plan." Baltimore, Maryland: Department of Health and Human Services, September 1994.

SSA employees will use LAN-based intelligent workstations with multiple levels of software running on platforms ranging from mainframes to microcomputers. Databases are being distributed. Greater efficiency will result from having processing close to the data source and information user. Figure III.1 illustrates SSA's target systems environment.

The SSA's technology modernization calls for an IWS/LAN (intelligent workstation and local area network) Technology Program. IWS/LAN is intended to move SSA to a more decentralized computing environment by replacing SSA's "dumb terminals" with 95,000 PCs arranged in token ring LANs. The LANs give SSA field staff more autonomous computing power and the ability to perform word processing, to share data, and to exchange e-mail messages. They are being linked to the agency's main network, SSANet (see Figure III.2).

By distributing processing and storing data at the level where the work is done, the number of data accesses and the volume of network traffic should be minimized, increasing the response time for many workloads. This arrangement will allow the automation of many functions that are presently not cost effective to do on a mainframe or practical to do on a standalone PC, giving SSA the computer capacity to handle increasing workloads.

The SSA's computer center in Baltimore will continue to supply mainframe processing power. SSA expects to use its existing mainframe software for programs such as retirement and supplemental security that are already automated, with the PCs emulating the old terminals. But as applications are rewritten, the PCs will perform more of the processing and the mainframe will gradually evolve into a database server role. SSA has argued that implementation of IWS/LAN is essential to provide an infrastructure for future electronic delivery and reengineering initiatives and to avoid problems and expenditures resulting from breakdowns in existing dumb terminals.

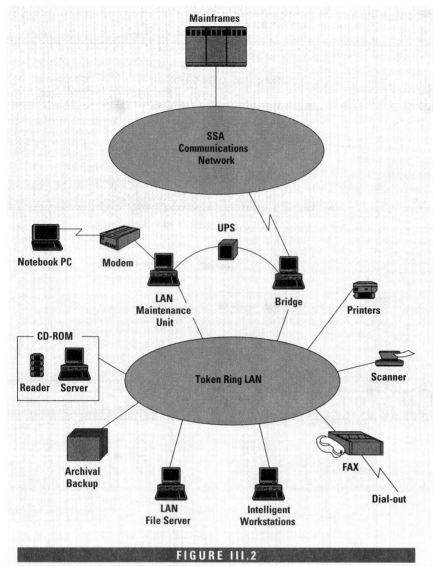

Mainframes

SSA Communications Network

UPS

Notebook PC **Modem**

LAN Maintenance Unit

Bridge

Printers

CD-ROM

Reader **Server**

Token Ring LAN

Scanner

Archival Backup

FAX

LAN File Server

Intelligent Workstations

Dial-out

FIGURE III.2

SSA's Target Distributed Processing System.
Source: Social Security Administration, "Information Systems Plan." Baltimore, Maryland: Department of Health and Human Services, September 1994.

SSA has replaced many batch applications with on-line interactive systems, starting with the Title II claims process. Eventually the Title XVI, disability, and Title II postentitlement processes will be handled online. By the year 2000, SSA expects to convert most of its major systems to an interactive environment using an "appearance of update" technique, which from the user perspective appears to update master records online. Expert systems, such as an application to provide answers to telephone inquiries, will help reduce manual processing.

Although databases will be distributed over SSA's multilevel telecommunications system, commercial DBMS are still not capable of handling SSA's specific requirements under a distributed processing environment. SSA plans to monitor the performance improvements of commercial DBMS as they mature for future consideration. The decision to distribute SSA's large databases will be based on cost/benefit and service improvement considerations.

SSA is reducing transmission costs by using telephone switching systems to integrate network access when possible. It will provide a common connection to be shared by voice services, video teleconferencing, fax, LAN interconnections, and SSANet. SSA communications planning will use OSI standards, specifying appropriate protocols, interfaces, and network technologies to obtain required intercommunication and interoperability.

SSA points to many service improvements that resulted from these systems initiatives. An 800 phone number now receives 300,000 calls a day. Seventy percent of babies in the United States are enumerated at birth, eliminating the need to make separate applications for Social Security numbers. Kiosks installed in some locations provide public information.

Is Distributed Technology Enough?

In the spring of 1994, the Office of Technology Assessment released a report stating that the SSA's $1.1 billion five-year migration from mainframe to client/server computing was technically sound, but ahead of the agency's understanding of how to use intelligent workstations and LANs to improve service delivery. The OTA report reiterated concerns raised by the GAO that SSA was unlikely to realize significant benefits because it had not linked its proposed technology strategy to specific service delivery improvements. GAO questioned SSA's plans to implement IWS/LAN before determining the service delivery improvements that could result from this technology. OTA noted that SSA had made a "good-faith effort" to restructure its service delivery but that the agency had "prioritized . . . installation according to current SSA operational and service delivery needs—essentially automating marginal improvements in the status quo." OTA believed that SSA needed to include its clients, labor representatives, and individuals with experience in electronic service delivery into its planning process and it needed to reengineer its business processes to dramatically improve service. OTA also believed SSA had not done enough analysis of the costs and benefits of automation, including IWS/LAN, and of the impact of automation against specific performance goals.

OTA pointed out that SSA's ever-increasing workload, coupled with staff reductions from further government downsizing, could again threaten SSA's ability to deliver the level of service expected by Congress and the public. The use of 800 telephone numbers, a key component of SSA's current service delivery strategy, is overloaded during peak periods. (Most callers receive a busy signal on their first attempt to call.)

OTA also questioned the feasibility of managing a massive distributed computing environment from a single facility in Baltimore. Deputy Commissioner DiPentima responded by noting that it was a big challenge to maintain such a large network and monitor it centrally. If SSA were to monitor the network locally, it would require 2000 LAN managers. The centrally managed network has been able to process 20 million transactions per day with 99.9 percent uptime.

OTA recommended that SSA receive funding for reengineering and service delivery planning and that the agency participate in government-wide electronic delivery pilots and projects such as:

- Increased use of toll-free 800 telephone numbers for service delivery.

- Electronic data interchange for filing earnings reports by business.

- Direct electronic deposit of benefits payments.

- Electronic bulletin boards and networks to provide the public with information about SSA.

- Multiprogram electronic benefits delivery in which a single card could be used to obtain payment for Social Security benefits, Medicaid, and food stamps.

- Integrated electronic records for SSA recipients, providing a single "electronic folder" instead of separate electronic and paper files.

- Automated disability determination to streamline determination of initial and ongoing medical qualifications for disability insurance benefits.

Determining eligibility for disability benefits is considered the most troubled SSA service. SSA must continually ensure that recipients are eligible based on their medical and financial condition. Candidates for disability benefits are currently evaluated by state Disability Determination Service (DDS) offices, which are funded by SSA but are run by the states. Initial disability determinations can take up to several months, with a backlog of 750,000 cases. The backlog of continuing reviews is even larger. The error rate for Disability Insurance (DI), resulting in overpayments to eligible recipients, payments to ineligible recipients, or denial of benefits to qualified people, is estimated to be around 3.5 percent, similar to the error rate for Supplemental Security Income (SSI) programs. SSA-sponsored studies have suggested that automation will play a small role in improving the disability process in comparison to radically changing the organization and the flow of disability work. SSA set up a reengineering task force in mid-1993, with the full support of top management, to focus on ways to radically improve the disability benefit determination process. The staff conducted over 1000 interviews and visited SSA offices and Disability Determination Service offices in a majority of states.

In its drive toward paperless processing, SSA is working with Pitney Bowes on a pilot electronic filing system for small businesses. Small businesses will be able to file their annual W2 tax forms on the Internet. If successful, this electronic filing effort could replace the 62 million paper forms SSA receives annually from small businesses and reduce the workload at SSA's Wilkes Barre data operations center. (Companies with over 250 employees already file electronically, although not over the Internet.)

Most requests for benefits estimates are made on paper forms that cost SSA about $5.23 each to process. Congress has ordered the agency to provide annual benefits estimates for every worker over age 25, amounting to 123 million people, by the year 2000. SSA is experimenting with using the Web to deliver this information on-line at almost no cost. Taxpayers could use the SSA Web site to obtain an on-line estimate of their retirement benefits.

Savings would be significant, but the initiative has come under fire for its potential threat to individual privacy. To access the data via the Web, individuals must provide their name, Social Security number, date and place of birth, mother's maiden name, and their e-mail address. They will then receive a verification code at their e-mail address. The verification code will be required to obtain an on-line benefits estimate. Although SSA officials believe their Web site is secure, they warned users that they could not guarantee that the information entered by users could not be intercepted by others and decrypted. Citizens can still receive their benefits estimates and history of reported earnings by mail.

Reengineering services is starting to pay off. SSA is being described as the federal agency providing the best service to its customers, winning praise from Vice President Al Gore and business reengineering expert Michael Hammer. But this high level of service could be compromised if the agency does not solve its Year 2000 problem.

SSA was one of the first government agencies to tackle date problems, having made date changes part of its regular maintenance since 1989. SSA prints about 45 million checks per month, representing $300 to 400 billion flowing yearly into the U.S. economy. According to Judy Draper, project director for the Year 2000, "We can't not fix it." But SSA does not operate in a vacuum. Even if all its programs are fixed, it feeds and accepts data from the Veteran's Administration and the Treasury Department. Its Year 2000 problem won't be solved until all related systems from other federal agencies are fixed.

Much has been learned by SSA about the difficulties of building systems that can meet ever-changing business needs. Management has learned that deploying new information technology does not automatically translate into fewer employees, especially when transaction volumes are increasing. Can SSA continue to decentralize? Will SSA's information systems infrastructure maintain the level of service the public and Congress expects? These are just some of the difficult questions facing SSA as it moves into the twenty-first century. ■

Sources: Robert Pear, "U.S. to Go Back on Internet with Social Security Benefits," *The New York Times,* September 4, 1997; "Social Security Unit to Close a Web Site for Security Review," *The Wall Street Journal,* April 10, 1997; Sharon Machlis, "Web Apps May Cut Costs at Social Security," *Computerworld,* April 7, 1997; Dale Buss, "Social Security Going Paperless," *Home-Office Computing,* February 1997; David Bank, "Social Security Plans to Test W2 Forms Filed on the Internet," *The Wall Street Journal,* October 25, 1996; Martha T. Moore, "Social Security Reengineers: Agency puts focus on its customers." *USA TODAY,* August 30, 1995; Social Security Administration, "Information Systems Plan," Baltimore, MD: Department of Health and Human Services (September 1994); Office of Technology Assessment, "The Social Security Administration's Decentralized Computer Strategy," Washington, D.C.: U.S. Government Printing Office (April 1994); and Office of Technology Assessment, "The Social Security Administration and Information Technology: A Case Study," Washington, D.C.: U.S. Congress (1986).

Case Study Questions

1. What were the major factors in SSA's past that made it a leading innovator in information systems technology? How did these supportive factors change in the 1970s?

2. Describe briefly the problems with SSA's hardware, software, data storage, and telecommunications systems prior to SMP.

3. What were the major environmental and institutional factors that created the crisis at SSA?

4. Why did SSA's reform efforts in the late 1970s fail?

5. What were the major elements of SSA's implementation strategy for SMP? Describe its major projects.

6. What successful changes in management and organizational structure have been brought about by SMP? How secure are these changes (what environmental factors could destroy them)?

7. In what areas has SMP had the greatest success? In what areas has SMP not succeeded? Why?

8. Evaluate SSA's IWS/LAN Technology Program in light of SSA's history of information system projects.

9. How successful has SSA been in creating an appropriate information system architecture for the year 2000? Justify your explanation.

[1]"Union Faults SSA Modernization Plan," *Federal Computer Week,* October 9, 1989.
[2]Office of Technology Assessment, "The Social Security Administration and Information Technology, a Case Study," Washington, D.C.: U.S. Congress (1986).
[3]Based on interviews in northeastern U.S. metropolitan area district offices by the authors and Alan F. Westin.
[4]Social Security Administration, "Report on Social Security Administration Computer Modernization and Related Expenditures," prepared for the Senate Appropriations Committee, February 1989, p. ii.

Management and Organizational Support Systems

Today's information economy and society puts a special premium on the management of information in the organization. Capturing and distributing intelligence and knowledge, leadership, collaboration, and group decision making have become vital to organizational innovation and survival. This section describes how information systems can foster these objectives and support new kinds of management decision making by individuals and groups.

CHAPTER 15

Managing Knowledge

Chapter 15 examines specific types of information systems that help organizations create, capture, and distribute knowledge and information. Some of these systems are based on the Internet. They include technologies for document management, collaborative work, and project management; customized knowledge work systems for skilled professionals and knowledge workers; and artificial intelligence systems that capture or codify knowledge and intelligence. Numerous examples of expert systems, neural networks, fuzzy logic, genetic algorithms, intelligent agents, and other intelligent techniques illuminate the capabilities and limitations of artificial intelligence applications in business.

CHAPTER 16

Enhancing Management Decision Making

Chapter 16 focuses on decision-support systems (DSS), group decision-support systems (GDSS), and executive support systems (ESS). These systems are more helpful to managers faced with unstructured and semistructured decisions than traditional information systems. Examples of individual, group, and organizational decision-support systems and of leading-edge executive support applications show how these systems enhance the management decision-making process.

PART FOUR CASE STUDY

Boeing Designs the Paperless Airplane

Boeing Corporation's 777 jet airplane made history because it was the first time an airplane was designed entirely on the computer. This paperless airplane represented a transformation in the company's design and production processes, one that was deemed vital to survival. This case explores the relationship between the strategy, business processes, and information systems at the Boeing Corporation as it grappled with new competitors and declining sales.

Managing Knowledge

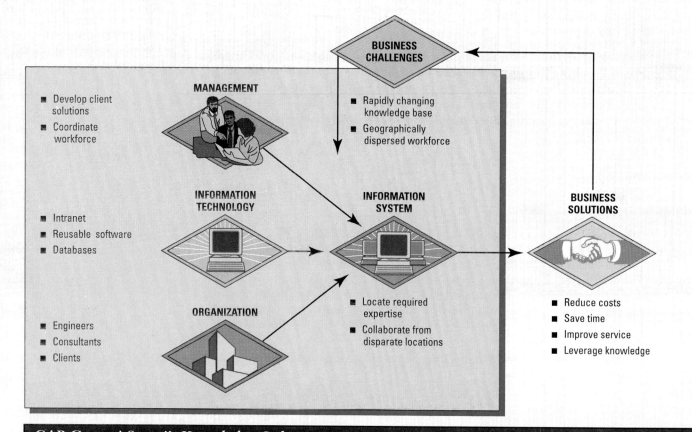

- Develop client solutions
- Coordinate workforce

MANAGEMENT

- Intranet
- Reusable software
- Databases

INFORMATION TECHNOLOGY

- Engineers
- Consultants
- Clients

ORGANIZATION

BUSINESS CHALLENGES

- Rapidly changing knowledge base
- Geographically dispersed workforce

INFORMATION SYSTEM

- Locate required expertise
- Collaborate from disparate locations

BUSINESS SOLUTIONS

- Reduce costs
- Save time
- Improve service
- Leverage knowledge

CAP Gemeni Sogeti's Knowledge Galaxy

One day CAP Gemeni Sogeti, the French computer services giant, received an urgent request from Exxon Chemical Co., one of its customers. Exxon needed a software development tool that would help it integrate off-the-shelf software packages with its custom business applications. Exxon had combed the market for five months and nothing had turned up. Ed Baugh, CAP Gemeni's project manager for Exxon, knew that building such a tool from scratch would take eighteen months, much too long for his client.

CHAPTER OUTLINE

LEARNING OBJECTIVES

After completing this chapter, you will be able to:

1. Explain the importance of knowledge management in contemporary organizations.
2. Describe the applications that are most useful for distributing, creating, and sharing knowledge in the firm.
3. Define artificial intelligence.
4. Explain how organizations can use expert systems and case-based reasoning to capture knowledge.
5. Describe how organizations can use neural networks and other intelligent techniques to improve their knowledge base.

In desperation, Baugh sent an electronic SOS across the company's intranet, Knowledge Galaxy. Within 48 hours, he received a response. An engineer in Hoskyns Group, PLC, CAP Gemeni's British unit, knew of a software tool that perhaps could be tailored for Exxon's needs. Baugh followed up and presented a solution to Exxon three weeks later, clinching a hefty development contract.

Knowledge Galaxy has helped CAP Gemeni in many ways by putting critical resources and expertise within every employee's reach. The intranet provides a storehouse of reusable software objects that employees can easily reference, so that CAP Gemeni does not have to reinvent the wheel for each project. The company has cut project time in half and can prepare sales bids much more quickly.

In addition to e-mail and filing capabilities, Knowledge Galaxy has areas for electronic chat groups, bulletin boards, a database of cur-

rent projects linked to employees working on them, and hundreds of Web pages to update CAP Gemeni's global work force on the latest technologies. The company is so pleased with its Internet capabilities that it has set up an Internet café for employees in its Paris headquarters to surf the Web while on break. ■

Source: Gail Edmondson, "One Electronic SOS Clinched the Deal," *Business Week*, February 26, 1996.

CAP Gemeni's experience shows why collaborating and communicating with other experts and sharing ideas and information have become essential requirements in business, science, and government. In an information economy, capturing and distributing intelligence and knowledge and enhancing group collaboration have become vital to organizational innovation and survival. Special systems can be used for managing organizational knowledge, but they raise the following management challenges.

1. **Designing information systems that genuinely enhance the productivity of knowledge workers.** Information systems that truly enhance the productivity of knowledge workers may be difficult to build because the manner in which information technology can enhance higher-level tasks such as those performed by managers and professionals (i.e., scientists or engineers) is not always clearly understood (Sheng et al., 1989–1990). High-level knowledge workers may resist the introduction of any new technology, or they may resist knowledge work systems because such systems diminish personal control and creativity. For instance, some architects may resist using computer-aided architectural rendering systems because they fear that the computer-generated representations of buildings cannot convey the individual artistry and imagination of hand-drawn renderings.

2. **Creating robust expert systems.** Expert systems must be changed every time there is a change in the organizational environment. Every time there is a change in the rules used by experts, they have to be reprogrammed. It is difficult to provide expert systems with the flexibility of human experts. Many thousands of businesses have undertaken experimental projects in expert systems, but only a small percentage have created expert systems that can actually be used on a production basis.

3. **Determining appropriate applications for artificial intelligence.** Finding suitable applications for artificial intelligence techniques is not easy. Some parts of business processes are rule based, others are based on patterns, and still others are based on exhaustive searching of manual files for the proverbial needle in the haystack. Identifying the business process, identifying the right technique, and determining how to build the system all require a focused effort.

This chapter examines information system applications specifically designed to help organizations create, capture, and distribute knowledge and information. First we examine information systems for supporting information and knowledge work. Then we look at the ways in which organizations can use artificial intelligence technologies for capturing and storing knowledge and expertise.

15.1 KNOWLEDGE MANAGEMENT IN THE ORGANIZATION

Chapter 1 described the emergence of the information economy, in which the major source of wealth and prosperity is the production and distribution of information and knowledge. For example, 55 percent of the U.S. labor force now consists of knowledge and information workers, and 60 percent of the gross national product of the United States comes from the knowledge and information sectors, such as finance and publishing. Knowledge-intensive technology is vital to these information-intense sectors but also plays a major role in more traditional industrial sectors such as the automobile and mining industries.

In an information economy, knowledge and core competencies—the two or three things that an organization does best—are key organizational assets. Producing unique products or services or producing them at lower cost than competitors is based on superior knowledge of the production process and superior design. Knowing how to do things effectively and efficiently in ways that other organizations cannot is a primary source of profit. Some management theorists believe that these knowledge assets are just as important—if not more important—than physical and financial assets in ensuring the competitiveness and survival of the firm.

As knowledge becomes a central productive and strategic asset, the success of the organization increasingly depends on its ability to gather, produce, maintain, and disseminate knowledge. Developing procedures and routines to optimize the creation, flow, learning, and sharing of knowledge and information in the firm becomes a central management responsibility. The process of systematically and actively managing and leveraging the stores of knowledge in an organization is called **knowledge management**. Information systems can play a valuable role in knowledge management, helping the organization optimize its flow of information and capture its knowledge base.

knowledge management The process of systematically and actively managing and leveraging the stores of knowledge in an organization.

Information Systems and Knowledge Management

All the major types of information systems described thus far facilitate the flow of information and have organizational knowledge embedded in them. However, office automation systems (OAS), knowledge work systems (KWS), group collaboration systems, and artificial intelligence (AI) applications are especially useful for knowledge management because they focus primarily on supporting information and knowledge work and on defining and capturing the organization's knowledge base.

Figure 15.1 illustrates the array of information systems specifically designed to support knowledge management. An office automation system (OAS) helps disseminate and coordinate the flow of information in the organization. A knowledge work system (KWS) supports the activities of highly skilled knowledge workers and

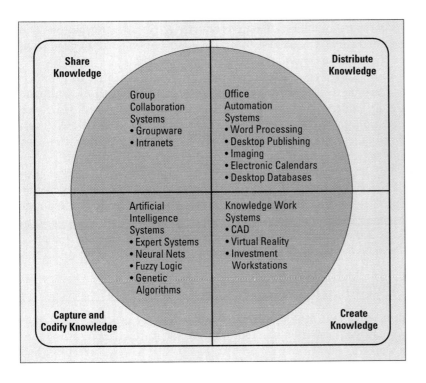

FIGURE 15.1

A number of contemporary information systems are designed to give close-in support to information workers at many levels in the organization.

professionals as they create new knowledge and try to integrate it into the firm. Group collaboration and support systems support the creation and sharing of knowledge among people working in groups. Artificial intelligence systems provide organizations and managers with codified knowledge that can be reused by others in the organization.

Knowledge Work and Productivity

In information economies, organizational productivity depends on increasing the productivity of information and knowledge workers. Consequently, companies have made massive investments in information technology to support information work. Information technology now accounts for 41 percent of total business expenditures on capital equipment in the United States (Roach, 1996). Much of that information technology investment has poured into offices and the service sector. Office automation and professional work systems are among the fastest-growing information system applications.

Although information technology has increased productivity in manufacturing, the extent to which computers have enhanced the productivity of information workers is under debate. Some studies show that investment in information technology has not led to any appreciable growth in genuine productivity among office workers. The average white-collar productivity gain from 1980 to 1990 was only 0.28 percent each year. Corporate downsizings and cost reduction measures have recently increased worker efficiency but have not yet led to sustained enhancements signifying genuine productivity gains (Roach, 1988 and 1996). Other studies suggest that information technology investments are starting to generate a productivity payback. Brynjolfsson and Hitt's (1993) examination of information systems spending at 380 large firms over a five-year period found that return on investment (ROI) averaged over 50 percent per year for computers of all sizes. It is too early to tell whether these gains are short term or represent a genuine turnaround in service sector productivity.

Productivity changes among information workers are difficult to measure because of the problems of identifying suitable units of output for information work (Panko, 1991). How does one measure the output of a law office? Should one measure productivity by examining the number of forms completed per employee (a measure of physical unit productivity), or by examining the amount of revenue produced per employee (a measure of financial unit productivity) in an information- and knowledge-intense industry? The debate about the contribution of IT to productivity is clouded by confusion about what question is being asked.

In addition to reducing costs, computers may increase the quality of products and services for consumers. These intangible benefits are difficult to measure and consequently are not addressed by conventional productivity measures. Moreover, because of competition, the value created by computers may primarily flow to customers rather than to the company so that the payback from information technology investments is not reflected in profits and revenue (Brynjolfsson, 1996).

Introduction of information technology does not automatically guarantee productivity. Desktop computers, e-mail, and fax applications can actually generate more drafts, memos, spreadsheets, and messages—increasing bureaucratic red tape and paperwork. Firms are more likely to produce high returns on information technology investments if they rethink their procedures, processes, and business goals.

15.2 INFORMATION AND KNOWLEDGE WORK SYSTEMS

information work Work that primarily consists of creating or processing information.

Information work is work that consists primarily of creating or processing information. It is carried out by information workers who are usually divided into two subcategories: **data workers,** who primarily process and disseminate information; and **knowledge workers,** who primarily create new knowledge and information.

Examples of data workers include secretaries, sales personnel, accountants, and draftsmen. Researchers, designers, architects, writers, and judges are examples of knowledge workers. Data workers can usually be distinguished from knowledge workers because knowledge workers usually have higher levels of education and membership in professional organizations. In addition, knowledge workers exercise independent judgment as a routine aspect of their work. Data and knowledge workers have different information requirements and different systems to support them.

Distributing Knowledge: Office Information Systems

Most data work and a great deal of knowledge work take place in offices, including most of the work done by managers. The office plays a major role in coordinating the flow of information throughout the entire organization. The office has three basic functions (see Figure 15.2):

- Managing and coordinating the work of data and knowledge workers
- Connecting the work of the local information workers with all levels and functions of the whole organization
- Connecting the organization to the external world, including customers, suppliers, government regulators, and external auditors

Office workers span a broad range of workers—professionals, managers, sales, and clerical workers working alone or in groups. Their major activities include the following:

- Managing documents, including document creation, storage, retrieval, and dissemination
- Scheduling, for both individuals and groups
- Communicating, including initiating, receiving, and managing voice, digital, and document-based communications for both individuals and groups
- Managing data, such as on employees, customers, and vendors

These activities can be supported by office automation systems (see Table 15.1). An **office automation system (OAS)** can be defined as any application of information technology that intends to increase productivity of information workers in the office. Fifteen years ago office automation meant only the creation, processing, and management of documents. Today professional knowledge and information work remains highly document centered. However, digital image processing is also at the core of today's systems, as are high-speed digital communications services. Because office work involves many people jointly engaged in projects, contemporary office automation systems have powerful group assistance tools such as networked digital

data workers People such as secretaries or bookkeepers who primarily process and disseminate the organization's paperwork.

knowledge workers People such as engineers, scientists, or architects who design products or services or create new knowledge for the organization.

office automation system (OAS) Computer system, such as word processing, voice mail, and videoconferencing systems, designed to increase the productivity of information workers in the office.

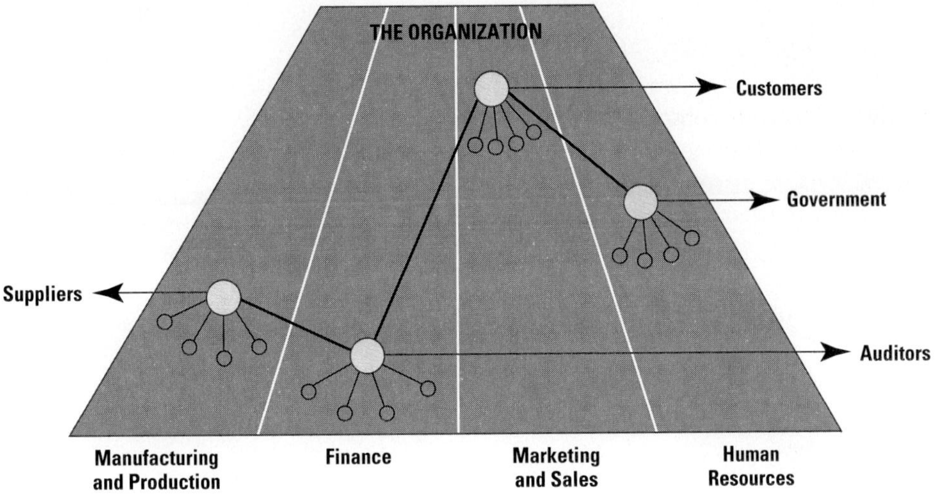

FIGURE 15.2

The three major roles of offices. Offices perform three major roles. [1] They coordinate the work of local professionals and information workers. [2] They coordinate work in the organization across levels and functions. [3] They couple the organization to the external environment.

Table 15.1	Typical Office Automation Systems
Office Activity	**Technology**
Managing documents	Word processing; desktop publishing; document imaging; workflow managers
Scheduling	Electronic calendars; groupware; intranets
Communicating	E-mail; voice mail; digital answering systems; groupware; intranets
Managing data	Desktop databases; spreadsheets; user-friendly interfaces to mainframe databases

calendars. An ideal contemporary office automation system would involve a seamless network of digital machines linking professional, clerical, and managerial work groups and running a variety of types of software.

Although word processing and desktop publishing address the creation and presentation of documents, they only exacerbate the existing paper avalanche problem. For instance, Ultramar Oil, a Long Beach, California, oil refinery, maintains about 20,000 material safety data sheets in huge notebooks; if an emergency chemical spill occurs, employees must manually search these notebooks for the appropriate sheet or sheets that contain the lifesaving and damage-control information they urgently need. Workflow problems arising from paper handling are enormous.

One way to reduce problems stemming from paper-based work flow is to employ document imaging systems. **Document imaging systems** are systems that convert documents and images into digital form so that they can be stored and accessed by the computer. Such systems store, retrieve, and manipulate a digitized image of a document, allowing the document itself to be discarded. The system must contain a scanner that converts the document image into a bitmapped image, storing that image as a graphic. With imaging systems the document will originally be stored on a magnetic disk, where it can be retrieved instantly. When it ceases to be active, it will be transferred to an optical disk, where it will be stored for as many months or years as is needed. Optical disks, kept on-line in a **jukebox** (a device for storing and

document imaging systems
Systems that convert documents and images into digital form so that they can be stored and accessed by the computer.

jukebox A device for storing and retrieving many optical disks.

Essex County Massachusetts implemented an automated document imaging and retrieval system for many of its records. Processing of mortgages, liens, deeds, and other land records has been streamlined and made more cost-effective.

retrieving many optical disks) require up to one minute to retrieve the document automatically. A typical large jukebox will hold more than 10 million pages (an 8 1/2-by-11-inch document usually requires about 50 kilobytes of storage after data compression).

An imaging system also requires an **index server** to contain the indexes that will allow users to identify and retrieve the document when needed. Once the document has been scanned, index data are entered so that the document can be retrieved in a variety of ways, depending on the application. For example, the index may contain the document scan date, the customer name and number, the document type, and some subject information. Finally, the system must include retrieval equipment, primarily workstations capable of handling graphics, although printers are usually included. USAA's imaging system in Chapter 2 illustrates the kinds of benefits imaging technology can provide.

To achieve the large productivity gains promised by imaging technology, organizations must redesign their work flow. In the past, the existence of only one copy of the document largely shaped work flow. Work had to be performed serially; two people could not work on the same document at the same time. Significant staff time had to be devoted to filing and retrieving documents. Once a document has been stored electronically, workflow management can change the traditional methods of working with documents (see Chapter 11).

Document management technology can be a source of competitive advantage, as the Window on Technology illustrates.

Creating Knowledge: Knowledge Work Systems

Knowledge work is that portion of information work that creates new knowledge and information. For example, knowledge workers create new products or find ways to improve existing ones. Knowledge work is segmented into many highly specialized fields, and each field has a different collection of **knowledge work systems (KWS)** that are specialized to support workers in that field. Knowledge workers perform three key roles that are critical to the organization and to the managers who work within the organization:

- Keeping the organization up to date in knowledge as it develops in the external world—in technology, science, social thought, and the arts
- Serving as internal consultants on the areas of their knowledge, the changes taking place, and the opportunities
- Acting as change agents evaluating, initiating, and promoting change projects

Knowledge workers and data workers have somewhat different information systems support needs. Most knowledge workers rely on office automation systems such as word processors, voice mail systems, and calendaring systems, but they also require more specialized knowledge work systems. Knowledge work systems are specifically designed to promote the creation of new knowledge and ensure that new knowledge and technical expertise are properly integrated into the business.

Requirements of Knowledge Work Systems

Knowledge work systems have special characteristics that reflect the special needs of knowledge workers. First, knowledge work systems must give knowledge workers the specialized tools they need, such as powerful graphics, analytical tools, and communications and document management tools. These systems require great computing power to handle rapidly the sophisticated graphics or complex calculations necessary to such knowledge workers as scientific researchers, product designers, and financial analysts. Because knowledge workers are so focused on knowledge in the external world, these systems must also give the worker quick and easy access to external databases.

Law Goes High-Tech

The 275-attorney Boston law firm of Hale and Dorr is among the most technologically sophisticated in the United States. Annual technology expenditures amount to $2 to 3 million, above average for law firms of that size. But Hale and Dorr believes they're worth it because they've boosted their bottom line. Here's why.

The firm believes in technology as a way of doing business. The firm chose UNIX workstations over PCs because of their expandability and flexibility. Its technology infrastructure includes 300 Sun SPARCStation 2 and 4 workstations, 4 Sun SPARC servers, 15 Tadpole SPARCbook 3 XP portable computers, 170 Hewlett-Packard LaserJet 4s printers, 30 Xerox 4220 copy machines, 5 Fujitsu scanners, 41 fax machines, and 3 videoconferencing systems (two in Boston and one in Washington). A Hewlett-Packard jukebox provides optical drive storage along with 10 Sun CD drives. Software tools include Evidence imaging software, enhanced Mosaic Web browsers, PageMaker for courtroom exhibits and presentations, and FrameMaker for internal document publishing. The firm maintains an extensive library of CD-ROMs, access to more than 100 on-line databases (including Lexis/Nexis and other legal databases), and a CD-ROM database updated weekly with information on rules, fees, and forms for security offerings in all 50 states.

Hale and Dorr's Boston headquarters and its branch offices in Manchester, New Hampshire, and Washington, D.C., are becoming paperless. All internal correspondence, including financial data, meeting announcements, and firm news, are transmitted through the firm's e-mail network. Other information such as partner profiles, law and court updates, and the firm's New England IPO Report is available through the firm's Web site, which was established in January 1995.

Imaging technology helps the litigation department prepare for large lawsuits, potentially saving clients millions of dollars. For example, Hale and Dorr was hired to defend Legent, a maker of mainframe operating system software that was acquired by Islandia, a branch of Computer Associates in August 1995. Legent was besieged by lawsuits charging management fraud when its stock fell by more than one-third the day after disappointing quarterly earnings were announced in July 1993.

The Legent case, like all securities suits, created a mountain of paperwork. At that time, the law allowed plaintiffs to fish through internal Legent documents. The company had to turn over 150,000 pages to the plaintiff's firms. Technology helped Hale and Dorr's litigators to prepare for the case on an accelerated schedule. All the documents for the case were scanned and stored on eight-inch Exabyte magnetic cartridge tapes. Paralegals then added critical information about each document, such as who read it, when it was written, and whether it contained handwritten notations. Hale and Dorr loaded the cartridges on its network hard drive, where they could use Evidence imaging software to search them from their own workstations. In two hours, one attorney completed the same search that would have taken nearly a week using traditional paper-based methods. No documents were lost and several attorneys could examine the same document simultaneously. Hale and Dorr could even pack documents for Legent executives to review on portable computers. Thanks to imaging technology Hale and Dorr prepared for trial in two weeks. The judge dismissed the case against Legent. Prices for imaging start at 50 cents per page, but it can cut the cost of paperwork management in large lawsuits by one-third or more.

To Think About: How is imaging technology related to this law firm's business strategy? What business processes has it changed?

Source: Mike France, "But Not Tech Converts Like Hale and Dorr," *Forbes ASAP*, April 8, 1996.

A user-friendly interface is important to a knowledge worker's system. User-friendly interfaces save time by allowing the user to perform the needed tasks and get to the required information without having to spend a lot of time learning how to use the computer. Saving time is more important for knowledge workers than for most other employees because knowledge workers are highly paid—wasting a knowledge worker's time is simply too expensive. Figure 15.3 summarizes the requirements of knowledge work systems.

Knowledge workstations are often designed and optimized for the specific tasks to be performed so that a design engineer will require a different workstation than does a lawyer. Design engineers need graphics with enough power to handle three-dimensional computer-aided design (CAD) systems. On the other hand, financial analysts are more interested in having access to a myriad of external databases and in optical disk technology so that they can access massive amounts of financial data very quickly.

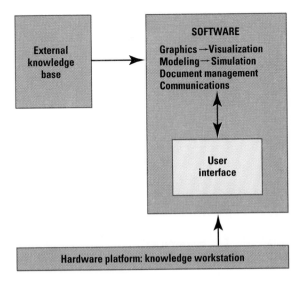

FIGURE 15.3
Requirements of knowledge work systems. Knowledge work systems require strong links to external knowledge bases in addition to specialized hardware and software.

Examples of Knowledge Work Systems

Major knowledge work applications include computer-aided design (CAD) systems, virtual reality systems for simulation and modeling, and financial workstations. **Computer-aided design (CAD)** automates the creation and revision of designs, using computers and sophisticated graphics software. Using a more traditional design methodology, each new design modification requires a mold to be made and a prototype to be physically tested. That process has to be repeated many times over, which is a very expensive and time-consuming process. Using a CAD workstation, the designer only needs to make a physical prototype toward the end of the design process because the design can be easily tested and changed on the computer. The ability of the CAD software to provide design specifications for the tooling and the manufacturing process also saves a great deal of time and money while producing a manufacturing process with far fewer problems. For example, the Maddox Design Group of Atlanta, Georgia, uses MicroArchitect CAD software from IdeaGraphix for architectural design. Designers can quickly put in the architectural background, popping in doors and windows, and then do the engineering layout. The software can generate door and window schedules, time accounting reports, and projected costs. Additional descriptions of CAD systems can be found in Chapters 2 and 13.

Virtual reality systems have visualization, rendering, and simulation capabilities that go far beyond those of conventional CAD systems. They use interactive graphics software to create computer-generated simulations that are so close to reality that users believe they are participating in a real-world situation.

Virtual reality is interactivity in such a way that the user actually feels immersed in the world that the computer creates. To enter the virtual world, the user dons special clothing, headgear, and equipment, depending on the application. The clothing contains sensors that record the user's movements and immediately transmit that information back to the computer. For instance, to walk through a virtual reality simulation of a house, you would need garb that monitors the movement of your feet, hands, and head. You would also need goggles that contain video screens and sometimes audio attachments and feeling gloves so that you can be immersed in the computer feedback.

Virtual reality is just starting to provide benefits in educational, scientific, and business work. Matsushita Electric Works in Japan has put virtual reality to work in its department stores. The stores sell kitchen appliances and cabinets. To promote these products Matsushita has created an application it calls Virtual Kitchen. The prospective buyers bring their kitchen layouts to the department store, where trained staff enters a copy of the design into the computer. The customers then don the

computer-aided design (CAD) Information system that automates the creation and revision of designs using sophisticated graphics software.

virtual reality systems Interactive graphics software and hardware that create computer-generated simulations that provide sensations that emulate real-world activities.

appropriate equipment and suddenly find themselves in their own kitchen. Now they can try out the appliances in various sizes, colors, and locations. They can test new cabinets, opening and closing the cabinet doors and drawers. They can place their existing table and chairs into the picture so the scene will be realistic. They can walk around and discover the feel and ambience of the new kitchen. With this technology the customer is able to buy with a great deal more confidence. Matsushita is able to make many more on-the-spot sales.

At General Electric's Research and Development Center in Schenectady, New York, GE scientists are working with a group of surgeons from Boston's Brigham and Women's Hospital to develop a virtual reality system to be used in surgery. One stated goal is to be able to superimpose a 3-D image of the patient onto the patient and then to operate on the image and the patient at the same time. The surgeon's actions on the large virtual image would be duplicated by computer-controlled instruments on the patient.

Although these are futuristic hopes, the GE research team is making progress. Currently, for example, they are able to use a magnetic resonance imaging (MRI) machine to make two-dimensional-slice pictures of a volunteer's brain. Using virtual reality goggles, and with those MRI images as input, they are able to view the virtual brain with superb, three-dimensional reality. They can peel off layers of the image to reveal the underlying parts. They have used these images to put a special cap on a volunteer, project the image of his own brain on the cap, and then sketch onto the cap the surgical pathway through the brain's furrows to a spot where they might need to perform surgery. Although the process of operating on the image itself remains a futuristic goal, the team does hope that within the next several years they will be able to create a virtual image that surgeons can have beside the operating table so that they can consult it during the operation (Naj, 1993).

The financial industry is using specialized **investment workstations** to leverage the knowledge and time of its traders and portfolio managers. New York–based Chancellor Capital Management, Inc. developed its own investment workstations to

investment workstation Powerful desktop computer for financial specialists, which is optimized to access and manipulate massive amounts of financial data.

Virtual reality helps medical schools teach anatomy and surgery by simulating the working of the human body, allowing students the options of 3-D viewing and unlimited removal and repositioning of tissues.

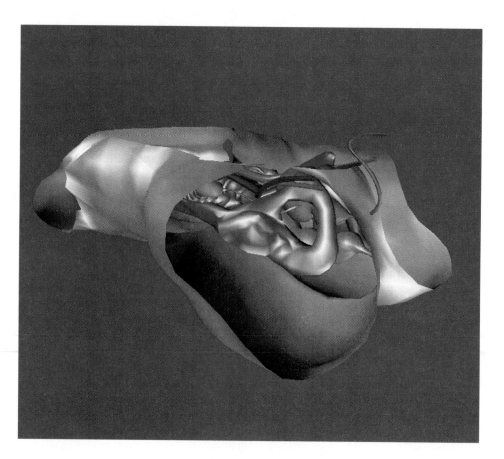

Table 15.2   Examples of Knowledge Work Systems

Knowledge Work System	Function in Organization
CAD/CAM (Computer-aided design/ computer-aided manufacturing)	Provides engineers, designers, and factory managers with precise control over industrial design and manufacturing
Virtual reality systems	Provide drug designers, architects, engineers, and medical workers with precise, photo-realistic simulations of objects
Investment workstations	High-end PCs used in financial sector to analyze trading situations instantaneously and facilitate portfolio management

help it manage $25 billion in assets for 300 clients. The workstations integrate the wide range of data required by portfolio managers from the firm's investment management systems and its portfolio accounting systems and make them available with the touch of a button. By providing one-stop information faster and with fewer errors, the workstations streamline Chancellor's entire investment process from stock selection to updating accounting records.

Previously, Chancellor's data were stored separately in its accounting, trading, research, and analytical systems. That not only meant a loss of data integrity, but also an increase in the difficulty the professional staff had in locating and accessing data. The professional staff had to use separate systems to access data on differing areas of investment.

Chancellor built software bridges between these systems with one feeding the other, thus reducing data integrity problems while making access easy. It installed a new user interface so that users have one friendly screen with a number of windows. Different users have different windows, depending on their own needs. Users can move from one window to another with ease, noting market trends in one window, checking a second window to determine the state of their assets, then to a third window to check analysts' reports on stocks in which they are interested, and finally moving to a fourth window to execute their chosen trades. In the past, each of these moves would have required the user to log off one system and on to another, a process that not only wastes time, but also is frustrating (Michaels, 1993).

Table 15.2 gives examples of the major types of knowledge work systems.

Sharing Knowledge: Group Collaboration Systems

Although many knowledge and information work applications have been designed for individuals working alone, organizations have an increasing need to support people working in groups. Chapters 9 and 10 have introduced key technologies that can be used for group coordination and collaboration: e-mail, teleconferencing, data-conferencing, videoconferencing, groupware, and the Internet. Groupware and the Internet are especially valuable for this purpose.

Groupware

Groupware consists of specialized software designed to promote information sharing. Groupware systems allow groups of people to work together on documents, schedule meetings, route electronic forms, access shared folders, develop shared databases, and send e-mail. Information-intensive companies such as consulting firms and law firms have found groupware a valuable tool for leveraging their knowledge assets.

For example, Ernst & Young, one of the Big Five accounting firms, hopes to improve its worldwide competitiveness by using Lotus Notes to create a communications infrastructure. In the past, Ernst & Young could not respond quickly to

groupware Software that recognizes the significance of groups in offices by providing functions and services that support the collaborative activities of work groups.

worldwide business opportunities because its international offices were often unaware of activities in the other branches and even in branches in the same country. The company's offices in the United States, the United Kingdom, Canada, the Netherlands, and Australia are linking Lotus Notes to Oracle relational databases, eliminating the need for multiple copies of files. Employees' desktop computers are tied into local area networks (LANs) that are connected regionally into a private, wide area network (WAN). Figure 15.4 illustrates the infrastructure created for the company's offices in the United Kingdom, so that staff can work together on projects that require regional teamwork. The eastern regional offices share an Oracle database containing staff demographic data that help Ernst & Young compile the best team for a specific job. Managers from these offices built a shared client and prospect database to help employees stay abreast of developments in other offices. Using Lotus Notes, employees can share a diary, which may be more effective than posting notices on bulletin boards (Black, 1995).

Groupware is becoming popular in traditional manufacturing companies because it promotes information sharing and coordination across the sales and production functions. For instance, Howmet, a manufacturer of jet aircraft and industrial gas turbine engine components, uses Lotus Notes for information sharing among geographically dispersed sales and production units. Howmet casts engine parts based on client specifications; its sales force must coordinate orders with factories in the United States, the United Kingdom, France, and Japan. Using groupware reduces the time to exchange this information and resolve the sales staff's questions about orders. Instead of spending so much time collecting information, Howmet's

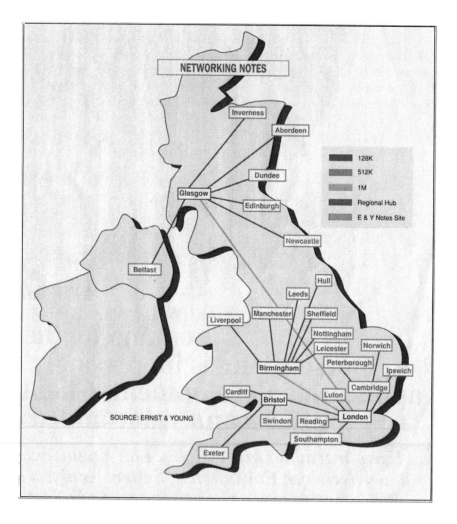

FIGURE 15.4

Ernst & Young's knowledge work infrastructure. Ernst & Young is developing a network linking its offices in the United Kingdom to speed up the pace of collaboration using groupware and other communications tools.

Adapted from: George Black, "Taking Notes, Big Sixer Aims for Head of the Class," Software Magazine, *March 1995, Sentry Publishing Company, Inc.*

sales and marketing managers can use that time to analyze it for competitive advantage (McCune, 1996).

Group Collaboration Via the Internet

Chapter 10 has described the multiple ways in which organizations can use the Internet for group collaboration and coordination, especially the Internet capabilities for e-mail, discussion groups, and intranets for corporate information sharing. (Intranet and Web technology allow collaborators in remote sites to display and exchange information that includes text, graphics, and sound about a common project or related projects using hypermedia links.) For simple tasks such as sharing documents or document publishing, an intranet is generally less expensive to build and maintain than applications based on proprietary products such as Lotus Notes. Information can be shared by people using different computer systems. Some companies such as CAP Gemeni Sogeti, described in the chapter-opening vignette, may find their communication and collaboration needs satisfied by the Web and intranets.

However, proprietary groupware software such as Notes has important capabilities that cannot yet be matched by Web technology. Notes is more flexible when documents have to be changed, updated, or edited on the fly. It can track revisions to a document as it moves through a collaborative editing process. Internal Notes-based networks are more secure than intranets (Web sites are more likely to crash or to have their servers overloaded when there are many requests for data). Notes is thus more appropriate for applications involving production and publication of documents by many authors, those with information requiring frequent updating and document tracking, and those that need high security and replication.

In contrast, the Web is best suited for applications with a central repository, a small number of authors, and relatively static information; Web documents cannot be easily updated every hour. However, Web capabilities for supporting group collaboration are continually improving. Netscape Communications' Communicator software bundles a Web browser with messaging and group collaboration tools, including e-mail, newsgroup discussions, a group scheduling and calendaring tool, Web-page composing software, and point-to-point conferencing. Microsofts Internet Explorer 4.0 has been enhanced with similar collaboration capabilities.

At the same time, Notes and other groupware products are being enhanced so that they can be integrated with the Internet. Domino 4.5, an Internet-enabled version of Notes, allows Notes to act as a Web server, providing an easy route for companies to take their document-based data to the Internet or an intranet. Notes clients can act as Web browsers to access information on the World Wide Web. Notes servers and data can be accessed by Web browsers as well as by Notes clients; Notes databases can contain HTML pages as well as Notes documents.

Group collaboration technologies alone cannot promote information sharing if team members do not feel it is in their interest to share, especially in organizations that encourage competition among employees. This technology can best enhance the work of a group if the applications are properly designed to fit the organization's needs and work practices.

15.3   ARTIFICIAL INTELLIGENCE

Organizations are using artificial intelligence technology to capture individual and collective knowledge and to codify and extend their knowledge base.

What Is Artificial Intelligence?

Artificial intelligence (AI) can be defined as the effort to develop computer-based systems (both hardware and software) that behave as humans. Such systems would be

artificial intelligence (AI)   The effort to develop computer-based systems that can behave like humans, with the ability to learn languages, accomplish physical tasks, use a perceptual apparatus, and emulate human expertise and decision making.

FIGURE 15.5

The artificial intelligence family. The field of AI currently includes many initiatives: natural language, robotics, perceptive systems, expert systems, and intelligent machines.

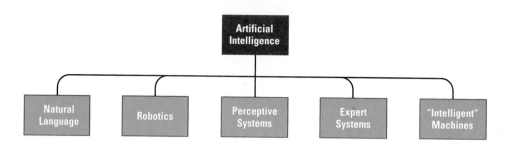

able to learn natural languages, accomplish coordinated physical tasks (robotics), utilize a perceptual apparatus that informs their physical behavior and language (visual and oral perception systems), and emulate human expertise and decision making (expert systems). Such systems would also exhibit logic, reasoning, intuition, and the commonsense qualities that we associate with human beings. Figure 15.5 illustrates the elements of the artificial intelligence family. Another important element is intelligent machines, the physical hardware that performs these tasks.

Successful artificial intelligence systems are based on human expertise, knowledge, and selected reasoning patterns but they do not exhibit the intelligence of human beings. Existing artificial intelligence systems do not invent new and novel solutions to problems. Existing systems extend the powers of experts but in no way substitute for them or capture much of their intelligence. Briefly, existing systems lack the common sense and generality of naturally intelligent machines such as human beings.

Human intelligence is vastly complex and much broader than computer or information systems. A key factor that distinguishes human beings from other animals is their ability to develop associations and to use metaphors and analogies such as *like* and *as*. Using metaphor and analogy, humans create new rules, apply old rules to new situations, and at times act intuitively and/or instinctively without rules. Much of what we call common sense or generality in humans resides in the ability to create metaphor and analogy.

Human intelligence also includes a unique ability to impose a conceptual apparatus on the surrounding world. Metaconcepts such as cause-and-effect and time, and concepts of a lower order such as breakfast, dinner, and lunch, are all imposed by human beings on the world around them. Thinking in terms of these concepts and acting on them are central characteristics of intelligent human behavior.

Why Business Is Interested in Artificial Intelligence

Although artificial intelligence applications are much more limited than human intelligence, they are of great interest to business for the following reasons:

- To preserve expertise that might be lost through the retirement, resignation, or death of an acknowledged expert

- To store information in an active form—to create an organizational knowledge base—that many employees can examine, much like an electronic textbook or manual, so that others may learn rules of thumb not found in textbooks

- To create a mechanism that is not subject to human feelings such as fatigue and worry. This may be especially useful when jobs are environmentally, physically, or mentally dangerous to humans. These systems may also be useful advisors in times of crises.

- To eliminate routine and unsatisfying jobs held by people

- To enhance the organization's knowledge base by suggesting solutions to specific problems that are too massive and complex to be analyzed by human beings in a short time

Capturing Knowledge: Expert Systems

In limited areas of expertise, such as diagnosing a car's ignition system or classifying biological specimens, the rules of thumb used by real-world experts can be understood, codified, and placed in a machine. Information systems that solve problems by capturing knowledge for a very specific and limited domain of human expertise are called **expert systems**. An expert system can assist decision making by asking relevant questions and explaining the reasons for adopting certain actions.

Expert systems lack the breadth of knowledge and the understanding of fundamental principles of a human expert. They are quite narrow, shallow, and brittle. They typically perform very limited tasks that can be performed by professionals in a few minutes or hours. Problems that cannot be solved by human experts in the same short period of time are far too difficult for an expert system. But by capturing human expertise in limited areas, expert systems can provide benefits to help organizations make higher-quality decisions with fewer people.

How Expert Systems Work

Human knowledge must be modeled or represented in a way that a computer can deal with it. The model of human knowledge used by expert systems is called the **knowledge base**. Two ways of representing human knowledge and expertise are by using rules and by using knowledge frames.

A standard structured programming construct (see Chapter 13) is the IF–THEN construct, in which a condition is evaluated. If the condition is true, an action is taken. For instance,

IF INCOME > $45,000 (condition)

THEN PRINT NAME AND ADDRESS (action)

A series of these rules can be a knowledge base. Any reader who has written computer programs knows that virtually all traditional computer programs contain IF–THEN statements. The difference between a traditional program and a **rule-based expert system** program is one of degree and magnitude. Artificial intelligence (AI) programs can easily have 200 to 10,000 rules, far more than traditional programs, which may have 50 to 100 IF–THEN statements. Moreover, in an AI program the rules tend to be interconnected and nested to a far larger degree than in traditional programs, as shown in Figure 15.6. Hence the complexity of the rules in a rule-based expert system is considerable.

Could you represent the knowledge in the *Encyclopedia Britannica* this way? Probably not, because the **rule base** would be too large, and not all the knowledge in the encyclopedia can be represented in the form of IF–THEN rules. In general, expert systems can be efficiently used only in those situations in which the domain of knowledge is highly restricted (such as in granting credit) and involves no more than a few thousand rules.

Knowledge frames can be used to represent knowledge by organizing it into chunks of interrelated characteristics. The relationships are based on shared characteristics rather than a hierarchy. This approach is grounded in the belief that humans use frames, or concepts, to make rapid sense out of perceptions. For instance, when a person is told, "Look for a tank and shoot when you see one," experts believe that humans invoke a concept, or frame, of what a tank should look like. Anything that does not fit this concept of a tank is ignored. In a similar fashion, AI researchers can organize a vast array of information into frames. The computer is then instructed to search the database of frames and list connections to other frames of interest. The user can then follow the various pathways pointed to by the system.

Figure 15.7 shows a part of a knowledge base organized by frames. A "CAR" is defined by characteristics or slots in a frame as a vehicle, with four wheels, a gas or diesel motor, and an action such as rolling or moving. This frame could be related to

expert system Knowledge-intensive computer program that captures the expertise of a human in limited domains of knowledge.

knowledge base Model of human knowledge that is used by expert systems.

rule-based expert system An AI program that has a large number of interconnected and nested IF–THEN statements, or rules, that are the basis for the knowledge in the system.

rule base The collection of knowledge in an AI system that is represented in the form of IF–THEN rules.

knowledge frames A method of organizing expert system knowledge into chunks; the relationships are based on shared characteristics determined by the user.

FIGURE 15.6

Rules in an AI program. An expert system contains a number of rules to be followed when utilized. The rules themselves are interconnected; the number of outcomes is known in advance and is limited; there are multiple paths to the same outcome; and the system can consider multiple rules at a single time. The rules illustrated are for simple credit-granting expert systems.

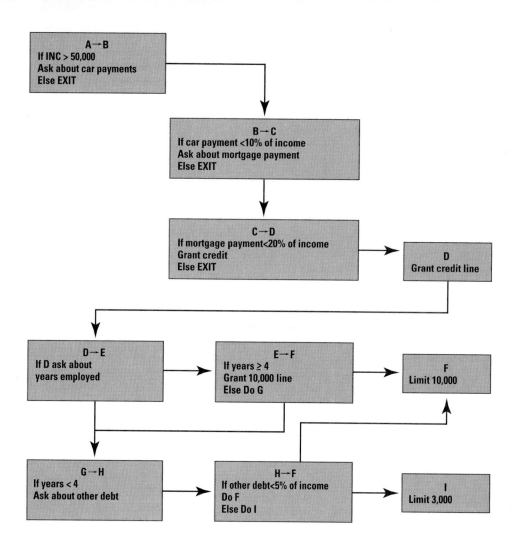

A→B
If INC > 50,000
Ask about car payments
Else EXIT

B→C
If car payment <10% of income
Ask about mortgage payment
Else EXIT

C→D
If mortgage payment<20% of income
Grant credit
Else EXIT

D
Grant credit line

D→E
If D ask about
years employed

E→F
If years ≥ 4
Grant 10,000 line
Else Do G

F
Limit 10,000

G→H
If years < 4
Ask about other debt

H→F
If other debt<5% of income
Do F
Else Do I

I
Limit 3,000

AI shell The programming environment of an expert system.

inference engine The strategy used to search through the rule base in an expert system; can be forward or backward chaining.

forward chaining A strategy for searching the rule base in an expert system that begins with the information entered by the user and searches the rule base to arrive at a conclusion.

backward chaining A strategy for searching the rule base in an expert system that acts like a problem solver by beginning with a hypothesis and seeking out more information until the hypothesis is either proved or disproved.

just about any other object in the database that shares any of these characteristics, such as the tank frame.

The **AI shell** is the programming environment of an expert system. In the early years of expert systems, computer scientists used specialized programming languages such as Lisp or Prolog that could process lists of rules efficiently. Today a growing number of expert systems use AI shells that are user-friendly development environments. AI shells can quickly generate user-interface screens, capture the knowledge base, and manage the strategies for searching the rule base.

The strategy used to search through the rule base is called the **inference engine**. Two strategies are commonly used: forward chaining and backward chaining (see Figure 15.8).

In **forward chaining** the inference engine begins with the information entered by the user and searches the rule base to arrive at a conclusion. The strategy is to fire, or carry out, the action of the rule when a condition is true. In Figure 15.8, beginning on the left, if the user enters a client with income greater than $100,000, the engine will fire all rules in sequence from left to right. If the user then enters information indicating that the same client owns real estate, another pass of the rule base will occur and more rules will fire. Processing continues until no more rules can be fired.

In **backward chaining** the strategy for searching the rule base starts with a hypothesis and proceeds by asking the user questions about selected facts until the hypothesis is either confirmed or disproved. In our example in Figure 15.8, ask the question, "Should we add this person to the prospect database?" Begin on the right of the diagram and work toward the left. You can see that the person should be added

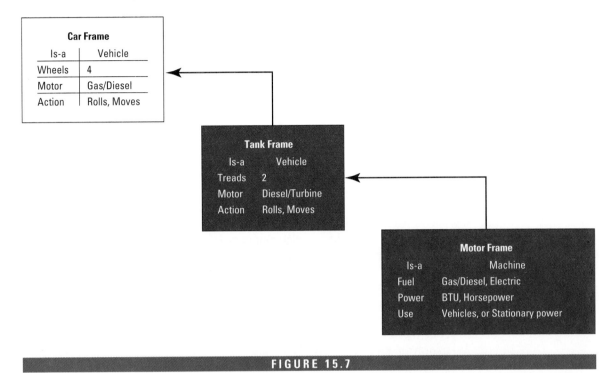

FIGURE 15.7

Frames to model knowledge. Knowledge and information can be organized into frames. Frames capture the relevant characteristics of the objects of interest. This approach is based on the belief that humans use "frames" or concepts to narrow the range of possibilities when scanning incoming information to make rapid sense out of perceptions.

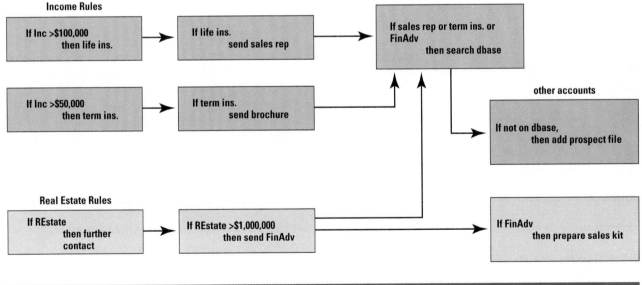

FIGURE 15.8

Inference engines in expert systems. An inference engine works by searching through the rules and "firing" those rules that are triggered by facts gathered and entered by the user. Basically, a collection of rules is similar to a series of nested "IF" statements in a traditional software program; however, the magnitude of the statements and degree of nesting are much greater in an expert system.

to the database if a sales representative is sent, term insurance is granted, or a financial advisor will be sent to visit the client.

Building an Expert System

Building an expert system is similar to building other information systems, although building expert systems is an iterative process with each phase possibly requiring several iterations before a full system is developed. Typically the environment in which an expert system operates is continually changing so that the expert system must also continually change. Some expert systems, especially large ones, are so complex that in a few years the maintenance costs will equal the development costs.

An AI development team is composed of one or more experts, who have a thorough command over the knowledge base, and one or more knowledge engineers, who can translate the knowledge (as described by the expert) into a set of rules or frames. A **knowledge engineer** is similar to a traditional systems analyst but has special expertise in eliciting information and expertise from other professionals.

The team members must select a problem appropriate for an expert system. The project will balance potential savings from the proposed system against the cost. The team members will develop a prototype system to test assumptions about how to encode the knowledge of experts. Next, they will develop a full-scale system, focusing mainly on the addition of a very large number of rules. Because the complexity of the entire system grows with the number of rules, the comprehensibility of the system may be threatened. Generally the system will be pruned to achieve simplicity and power. The system is tested by a range of experts within the organization against the performance criteria established earlier. Once tested, the system will be integrated into the data flow and work patterns of the organization. The Window on Management illustrates one company's experience building an expert system and the challenges it posed to management.

Examples of Successful Expert Systems

There is no accepted definition of a successful expert system. What is successful to an academic ("It works!") may not be successful to a corporation ("It cost a million dollars!"). The following are examples of expert systems that provide organizations with an array of benefits including reduced errors, reduced cost, reduced training time, improved decisions, and improved quality and service.

Countrywide Funding Corporation in Pasadena, California, is a loan underwriter with about 400 underwriters in 150 offices around the country. The company developed a PC-based expert system in 1992 to make preliminary creditworthiness decisions on loan requests. The company had experienced rapid, continuing growth and wanted the system to help ensure consistent and high-quality loan decisions.

Countrywide's Loan Underwriting Expert System (CLUES) has about 400 rules. Countrywide tested the system by having every loan application handled by a human underwriter also fed to CLUES. The system was refined until it agreed with the underwriter in 95 percent of the cases. However, Countrywide will not rely on CLUES to reject loans, because the expert system cannot be programmed to handle exceptional situations such as those involving a self-employed person or complex financial schemes. An underwriter will review all rejected loans and will make the final decision. CLUES has other benefits. Traditionally, an underwriter could handle six or seven applications a day. Using CLUES, the same underwriter can evaluate at least sixteen per day (Nash, 1993).

The Digital Equipment Corporation (DEC) and Carnegie-Mellon University developed XCON in the late 1970s to configure VAX computers on a daily basis. The system configures customer orders and guides the assembly of those orders at the customer site. XCON has been used for major functions such as sales and marketing,

Does AI Have a Role in Health Care?

Containing costs is vital in any business, but nowhere more so than in the health care industry where costs have been rising far faster than the inflation rate. Management at United HealthCare Corporation finds that cutting pennies can sometimes save them millions of dollars. This Minnetonka, Minnesota, health care giant took in $9 billion in 1995 and is primarily in the health insurance business, although it also is involved with health maintenance organizations and other services.

Insurance claims payments can generate a costly overhead. Traditionally all claims are handled manually. The simple claims can be handled by claims processors. The more complex ones required the involvement of medical analysts who are registered nurses (RNs). One measure the health care industry uses to determine how efficient its operations are is the metric known as the medical loss ratio (MLR). The MLR is a measure of the percentage of premium revenue that actually goes for medical costs. Too high and the conclusion is that the company is inefficient, too low and management concludes that not enough is going into health care. United HealthCare Senior Vice President Kathy Walstead-Plumb believes that the mid-1970s was good, but their ratio was actually in the 80 percent range in the early 1990s.

When processed manually, United HealthCare was spending $1.23 per claim. With millions of claims annually, cutting that cost a little could easily save millions of dollars and bring the MLR down. When claims were processed, many were immediately classified as payable and sent to claims processors. Others would have to be reviewed by medical analysts to determine if the billed service is covered, and if so, for how much. In some cases the RNs had to do a thorough search of the claimant's history.

In the mid-1990s United HealthCare's chief information officer (CIO), James P. Bradley, decided to find out if artificial intelligence could be used to cut the cost of claims processing. He established a separate unit, the advanced technology department, and named two programmers as comanagers. The two, J. P. Little and David Williams, had no managerial experience, but both had just completed masters degrees in artificial intelligence. The new system was to be an expert system.

Trouble began almost immediately. The first task of the unit was to identify the 1000 to 2000 rules the nurses used. To learn these rules, the programmers needed the full cooperation of the nurses, but the nurses were afraid that they would lose their jobs and be replaced by a computer. They felt that the new system, dubbed AdjudiPro, "would make them obsolete because its initial goal was to take over many of the review duties of the medical analysts and claims processors," according to Jean Toftely, a

medical analyst supervisor. In fact, claims Walstead-Plumb, management's plan was to free up the nurses to "do more of the investigative research work to find new trends." In addition, the company was growing so rapidly that it could not possibly lay off staff during this time. The issue for management was to communicate this to this staff in order to gain their understanding and cooperation. Once they realized the situation and addressed it, the project could proceed.

However, the project then ran into another problem. The nurses and programmers spoke different languages. According to Toftely, "There was a period when we did a lot of talking because they didn't know what they were looking for, and neither did we." This issue was overcome through a cooperative effort and by bringing Toftely over to the IS department so she could work full time on bridging the gap.

J. P. Little had worked on a previous project in which the technicians had programmed in isolation. His comment was, "We had wonderful software and no one wanted it." Little added, "I vowed then to never again do application development in a vacuum." With this in mind the project team of both programmers and RNs produced a prototype to prove to the claims processing community that the system could in fact process claims correctly. "That was the key moment in the project," claims Little. "We inspired enough confidence in the user community that they went to bat for us."

AdjudiPro was a success. It processes over half of the company's claims, handling part or all of one million claims per month. The system only sends 3 percent of the claims to the medical analysts due to complexity or incompleteness. The claims processed by AdjudiPro cost only 15 cents each to process, an immense savings of $13 million in 1995 alone. The project itself cost only $3.4 million, an excellent investment in health care cost containment. And United HealthCare's MLR has been reduced to 78 percent as a result.

To Think About: In your opinion, should management have anticipated the problems faced by the AdjudiPro project? What should they have done, and when, to prevent these problems from arising? What management, organization, and technology issues should have been addressed? How did AdjudiPro change United HealthCare's business processes?

Source: Anne Knowles, "A Bargain at 15 Cents," *CIO,* February 1, 1966.

Countrywide Funding Corporation uses an expert system called CLUES to evaluate the credit worthiness of loan applications. The system contains about 400 rules provided by loan underwriters.

manufacturing and production, and field service, and played a strategic role at DEC (Sviokla, 1990; Barker and O'Conner, 1989). It is estimated that XCON and related systems saved DEC approximately $40 million per year. XCON started out with 250 rules but has expanded to about 10,000.

Whirlpool uses the Consumer Appliance Diagnostic System (CADS) to help its customer-service representatives handle its 3 million annual telephone inquiries. The system expedites customer service by directing customers to a single source of help without delay. Previously, customers who had a problem or question about Whirlpool products might have been put on hold or directed to two or three different customer representatives before their questions could be answered. Whirlpool developed CADS using Aion's Development System for OS/2 as its expert system shell. Two knowledge engineers worked with one programmer and three of the company's customer-service experts to capture 1000 rules for 12 product lines. By 1999, Whirlpool expects to use CADS to respond to 9 million calls annually.

Problems with Expert Systems

Although expert systems lack the robust and general intelligence of human beings, they can provide benefits to organizations if their limitations are well understood. Only certain classes of problems can be solved using expert systems. Virtually all successful expert systems deal with problems of classification in which there are relatively few alternative outcomes and in which these possible outcomes are all known in advance. Many expert systems require large, lengthy, and expensive development efforts. Hiring or training more experts may be less expensive than building an expert system.

The knowledge base of expert systems is fragile and brittle; they cannot learn or change over time. In fast-moving fields such as medicine or the computer sciences, keeping the knowledge base up to date is a critical problem.

Expert systems can only represent limited forms of knowledge. IF–THEN knowledge exists primarily in textbooks. There are no adequate representations for deep causal models or temporal trends. No expert system, for instance, can write a textbook on information systems or engage in other creative activities not explicitly foreseen by system designers. Many experts cannot express their knowledge using an IF–THEN format. Expert systems cannot yet replicate knowledge that is intuitive, based on analogy and on a sense of things.

Contrary to early promises, expert systems do best in automating lower-level clerical functions. They can provide electronic checklists for lower-level employees in service bureaucracies such as banking, insurance, sales, and welfare agencies. The applicability of expert systems to managerial problems is very limited. Managerial

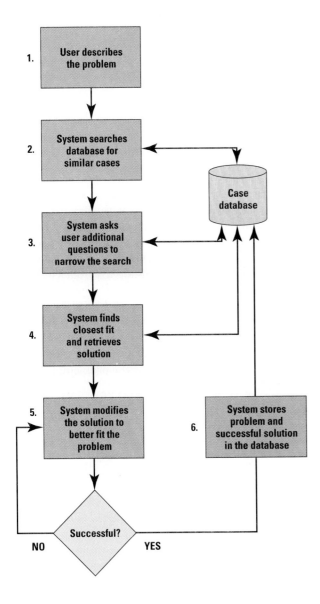

FIGURE 15.9
How case-based reasoning works. Case-based reasoning represents knowledge as a database of past cases and their solutions. The system uses a six-step process to generate solutions to new problems encountered by the user.

problems generally involve drawing facts and interpretations from divergent sources, evaluating the facts, and comparing one interpretation of the facts with another, and do not involve analysis or simple classification. Expert systems based on the prior knowledge of a few known alternatives are unsuitable to the problems managers face on a daily basis.

Organizational Intelligence: Case-Based Reasoning

Expert systems primarily capture the knowledge of individual experts. But organizations also have collective knowledge and expertise which they have built up over the years. This organizational knowledge can be captured and stored using case-based reasoning. In **case-based reasoning (CBR)**, descriptions of past experiences of human specialists, represented as cases, are stored in a database for later retrieval when the user encounters a new case with similar parameters. The system searches for stored cases similar to the new one, finds the closest fit, and applies the solutions of the old case to the new case. Successful solutions are tagged to the new case and both are stored together with the other cases in the knowledge base. Unsuccessful solutions are also appended to the case database along with explanations as to why the solutions did not work (see Figure 15.9).

case-based reasoning (CBR)
Artificial intelligence technology that represents knowledge as a database of cases.

Expert systems work by applying a set of IF–THEN–ELSE rules against a knowledge base, both of which are extracted from human experts. Case-based reasoning, in contrast, represents knowledge as a series of cases and this knowledge base is continuously expanded and refined by users.

For example, let us examine Compaq Computer of Houston, Texas, a company that operates in a highly competitive, customer-service-oriented business environment and is flooded daily with customer phone calls crying for help. Keeping those customers satisfied requires Compaq to spend millions of dollars annually to maintain large, technically skilled, customer-support staffs. When customers call with problems, they first must describe the problem to the customer-service staff, and then wait on hold while customer service transfers the call to an appropriate technician. The customer then describes the problem all over again while the technician tries to devise an answer—all in all, a most frustrating experience. To improve customer service while reining in costs, Compaq began giving away expensive case-based reasoning software to customers purchasing their Pagemarq printer.

The software knowledge base is a series of several hundred actual cases of Pagemarq printer problems—actual war stories about smudged copies, printer memory problems, jammed printers—all the typical problems people face with laser printers. Trained CBR staff entered case descriptions in textual format into the CBR system. They entered certain key words necessary to categorize the problem (such as *smudge, smear, lines, streaks, paper jam*). They also entered a series of questions that might need to be asked to allow the software to further narrow the problem. Finally, solutions were also attached to each case.

With the Compaq-supplied CBR system running on their computer, owners no longer need to call Compaq's service department. Instead they run the software and describe the problem to the software. The system swiftly searches actual cases, discarding unrelated ones and selecting related ones. If necessary to further narrow the search results, the software will ask the user for more information. In the end, one or more cases relevant to the specific problem are displayed, along with their solutions. Now, customers can solve most of their own problems quickly without even a telephone call while Compaq saves $10 to 20 million annually in customer support costs.

15.4 OTHER INTELLIGENT TECHNIQUES

Organizations are starting to utilize other intelligent computing techniques to extend their knowledge base by providing solutions to specific problems that are too massive or complex to be handled by people with limited time and resources. Neural networks, fuzzy logic, genetic algorithms, and intelligent agents are creating promising business applications.

Neural Networks

There has been an exciting resurgence of interest in approaches to artificial intelligence in which machines are designed to imitate the physical thought process of the biological brain. Figure 15.10 shows two neurons from a leech's brain. The soma, or nerve cell, at the center acts like a switch, stimulating other neurons and being stimulated in turn. Emanating from the neuron is an axon, which is an electrically active link to the dendrites of other neurons. Axons and dendrites are the "wires" that electrically connect neurons to one another. The junction of the two is called a *synapse*. This simple biological model is the metaphor for the development of neural networks. **Neural networks** consist of hardware or software that attempts to emulate the processing patterns of the biological brain.

neural network   Hardware or software that attempts to emulate the processing patterns of the biological brain.

The human brain has about 100 billion (10^{11}) neurons, each having about 1000 dendrites, which form 100,000 billion (10^{14}) synapses. The brain's neurons operate

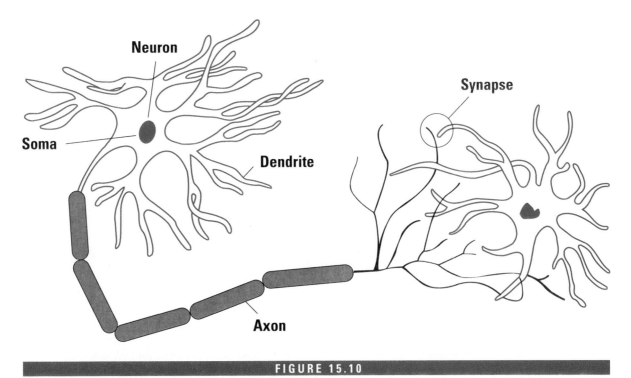

FIGURE 15.10

Biological neurons of a leech. Simple biological models, like the neurons of a leech, have influenced the development of artificial or computational neural networks in which the biological cells are replaced by transistors or entire processors.
Source: Defense Advance Research Projects Agency (DARPA), 1988. Unclassified. Hereinafter "DARPA, 1988."

in parallel, and the human brain can accomplish about 10^{16} or 10 million billion interconnections per second. This far exceeds the capacity of any known machine or any machine now planned or ever likely to be built with current technology.

But far more complex networks of neurons have been simulated on computers. Figure 15.11 shows an artificial neural network with two neurons. The resistors in the circuits are variable and can be used to teach the network. When the network makes a mistake (i.e., chooses the wrong pathway through the network and arrives at a false conclusion), resistance can be raised on some circuits, forcing other neurons to fire. If this learning process continues for thousands of cycles, the machine learns the correct response. The neurons are highly interconnected and operate in parallel.

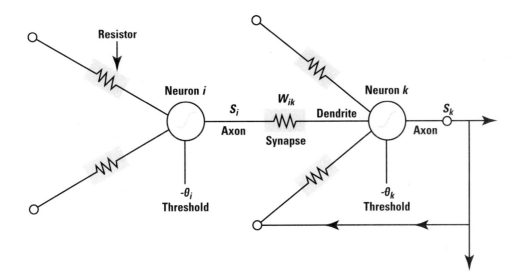

FIGURE 15.11

Artificial neural network with two neurons. In artificial neurons, the biological neurons become processing elements (switches), the axons and dendrites become wires, and the synapses become variable resistors that carry weighted inputs (currents) that represent data.
Source: Defense Advance Research Projects Agency DARPA, 1988 Unclassified Hereinafter "DARPA, 1988."

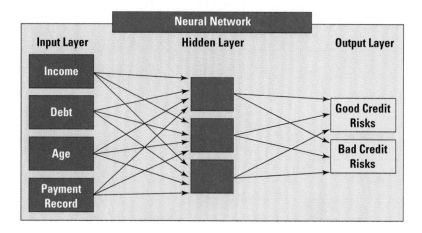

A neural net has a large number of sensing and processing nodes that continuously interact with each other. Figure 15.12 represents a neural network comprising an input layer, an output layer, and a hidden processing layer. The network is fed a training set of data for which the inputs produce a known set of outputs or conclusions. This helps the computer learn the correct solution by example. As the computer is fed more data, each case is compared with the known outcome. If it differs, a correction is calculated and applied to the nodes in the hidden processing layer. These steps are repeated until a condition, such as corrections being less than a certain amount, is reached. The neural network in Figure 15.12 has "learned" how to identify a good credit risk.

The Difference Between Neural Networks and Expert Systems

What is different about neural networks? Whereas expert systems seek to emulate or model a human expert's way of solving a set of problems, neural network builders claim that they do not model human intelligence, do not program solutions, and do not aim to solve specific problems per se. Instead, neural network designers seek to put intelligence into the hardware in the form of a generalized capability to learn. In contrast, the expert system is highly specific to a given problem and cannot be easily retrained.

Take a simple problem such as identifying a cat. An expert system approach would interview hundreds of people to understand how humans recognize cats, resulting in a large set of rules, or frames, programmed into an expert system. In contrast, a trainable neural network would be brought to the test site, connected to the television, and started out on the process of learning. Every time a cat was not correctly perceived, the system's interconnections would be adjusted. When cats were correctly perceived, the system would be left alone and another object scanned.

Neural network applications are emerging in medicine, science, and business to address problems in pattern classification, prediction and financial analysis, and control and optimization. Papnet is a neural net-based system to distinguish between normal and abnormal cells when examining Pap smears for cervical cancer, with far greater accuracy than visual examination by technicians. The computer is not able to make the final decision and so the technician will review the selected abnormal cells. Using Papnet, a technician requires one-fifth the time to review a smear while attaining perhaps ten times the accuracy of the existing manual method.

Neural networks are being used by the financial industry to discern patterns in vast pools of data that might help investment firms predict the performance of equities, corporate bond ratings, or corporate bankruptcies (Lin, 1993). Japanese firms are using neural networks for prediction of securities ratings, timing of stock buying and selling, prediction of future yield of securities, inspection of flaws in steel plate, classification

Visa Spots Credit Card Fraud

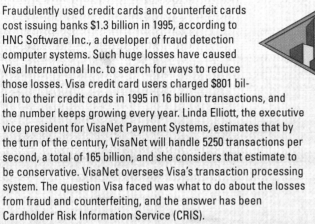

Fraudulently used credit cards and counterfeit cards cost issuing banks $1.3 billion in 1995, according to HNC Software Inc., a developer of fraud detection computer systems. Such huge losses have caused Visa International Inc. to search for ways to reduce those losses. Visa credit card users charged $801 billion to their credit cards in 1995 in 16 billion transactions, and the number keeps growing every year. Linda Elliott, the executive vice president for VisaNet Payment Systems, estimates that by the turn of the century, VisaNet will handle 5250 transactions per second, a total of 165 billion, and she considers that estimate to be conservative. VisaNet oversees Visa's transaction processing system. The question Visa faced was what to do about the losses from fraud and counterfeiting, and the answer has been Cardholder Risk Information Service (CRIS).

Visa spent $2 million to build CRIS, a neural network-based information system that is designed to monitor all Visa transactions looking for sudden changes in the buying patterns of cardholders. For example, if a cardholder uses her card to make only small purchases in Detroit but suddenly starts making large purchases, the system will alert employees at VisaNet who in turn notify the bank that issued the card. The bank will attempt to verify that the recent user is in fact the cardholder. Cathy Basch, who works in Foster City, California, is someone who uses both her card and her husband's Visa card for small purchases. Suddenly, during the Christmas season 1995, CRIS noticed unusually expensive items being charged against Basch's card. Her bank was notified and they in turn called Basch. She explained to the bank official that her husband was indeed making unusual charges because he was out Christmas shopping. She was grateful, however, because Visa had spotted the shift in the card's purchasing pattern that could have been the result of a lost or stolen card.

With the 50 million transactions worldwide, CRIS has plenty of data to help the neural network learn. If a cardholder's spending pattern changes, CRIS will produce a score. The higher the score, the higher the risk. The scores are reported to the banks, and they take whatever steps they deem appropriate. Many banks have their own systems to help spot fraud in credit card use, but their systems do not have access to the massive amounts of data CRIS has, making them less able to spot trends.

One key to the success of CRIS is its ability to react quickly to purchase events. The closer you get to the point of the transaction, the less money the bank stands to lose. Therefore, to make the system faster, Visa is in the process of changing the way it stores and accesses the data used by CRIS. The existing system is dependent on four networked mainframes, one each in McLean, Virginia, San Mateo, California, Basingstoke, England, and Yokohama, Japan. Data for these computers are stored on tape. Tapes are pulled from the mainframes 12 times a day and data are fed to CRIS. However, Visa is aiming at storing the previous four days of data in a data storehouse where it can be accessed instantly. A data storehouse resembles a data warehouse in that it stores large amounts of data on-line. However, it stores a more limited amount of data in that manner than a data warehouse. Using the new data storehouse, Visa expects that its mainframes will be able to process each transaction and notify the bank within minutes, thus enabling the bank to respond much more quickly to a shift in spending patterns.

The system is proving to be a good investment. In 1994 Visa member banks lost more than $148 million from use of counterfeit Visa cards. However, the loss in 1995 dropped by 16 percent to $124 million as a result of the use of CRIS. Visa has had such success with neural network technology applied that it is looking to apply it to other risk areas, such as bankruptcy risk.

To Think About: *How is neural network technology related to Visa's business strategy?*

Source: Bronwyn Fryer, "Visa Cracks Down on Fraud," *Information Week*, August 26, 1996.

---

of welding defects, sound analysis, and identification of parts on a lens production line (Asakawa and Takagi, 1994). The Window on Organizations illustrates how Visa International Inc. is using a neural network to help detect credit card fraud.

Unlike expert systems, which typically provide explanations for their solutions, neural networks cannot always explain why they arrived at a particular solution. Moreover, they cannot always guarantee a completely certain solution, arrive at the same solution again with the same input data, or always guarantee the best solution (Trippi and Turban, 1989–90). They are very sensitive, and may not perform well if their training covers too little or too much data. In most current applications, neural networks are best used as aids to human decision makers instead of substitutes.

Fuzzy Logic

fuzzy logic Rule-based AI that tolerates imprecision by using nonspecific terms called *membership functions* to solve problems.

Traditional computer programs require precision—on–off, yes–no, right–wrong. However, we as human beings do not experience the world this way. We might all agree that +120 degrees is hot and −40 degrees is cold; but is 75 degrees hot, warm, comfortable, or cool? The answer depends on many factors: the wind, the humidity, the individual experiencing the temperature, one's clothing, and one's expectations. Many of our activities are also inexact. Tractor-trailer drivers would find it nearly impossible to back their rig into a space precisely specified to less than an inch on all sides.

Fuzzy logic, a relatively new, rule-based development in AI, tolerates imprecision and even uses it to solve problems we could not have solved before. Fuzzy logic consists of a variety of concepts and techniques for representing and inferring knowledge that is imprecise, uncertain, or unreliable. Fuzzy logic can create rules that use approximate or subjective values and incomplete or ambiguous data. By expressing logic with some carefully defined imprecision, fuzzy logic is closer to the way people actually think than traditional IF–THEN rules.

Ford Motor Co. has developed a fuzzy logic application that backs a simulated tractor-trailer into a parking space. The application uses the following three rules:

IF the truck is *near* jackknifing, THEN *reduce* the steering angle.

IF the truck is *far away* from the dock, THEN steer *toward* the dock.

IF the truck is *near* the dock, THEN point the trailer *directly* at the dock.

This logic makes sense to us as human beings, for it represents how we think as we back that truck into its berth.

How does the computer make sense of this programming? The answer is relatively simple. The terms (known as *membership functions*) are imprecisely defined so that, for example, in Figure 15.13 cool is between 50 degrees and 70 degrees, although the temperature is most clearly cool between about 60 degrees and 67 degrees. Note that *cool is* overlapped by *cold* or *norm*. To control the room environment using this logic, the programmer would develop similarly imprecise definitions for humidity and other factors such as outdoor wind and temperature. The rules might include one that says, "*If the temperature is cool or cold and the humidity is low while the outdoor wind is high and the outdoor temperature is low, raise the heat and humidity in the room.*" The computer would combine the membership function

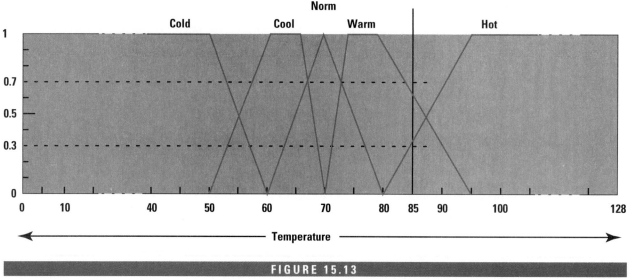

FIGURE 15.13

Implementing fuzzy logic rules in hardware. The membership functions for the input called temperature are in the logic of the thermostat to control the room temperature. Membership functions help translate linguistic expressions such as "warm" into numbers that can be manipulated by the computer.

Source: James M. Sibigtroth, "Implementing Fuzzy Expert Rules in Hardware," AI Expert, April 1992. © 1992 Miller Freeman., Inc. Reprinted with permission.

readings in a weighted manner and, using all the rules, raise and lower the temperature and humidity.

Fuzzy logic is widely used in Japan and is gaining popularity in the United States. Its popularity has increased partially because managers find they can use it to reduce costs and shorten development time. Fuzzy logic code requires few IF–THEN rules, making it simpler than traditional code. The rules required in the previous trucking example, plus its term definitions, might require hundreds of IF–THEN statements to implement in traditional logic. Compact code requires less computer capacity, allowing Sanyo Fisher USA to implement camcorder controls without adding expensive memory to its product.

Fuzzy logic also allows us to solve problems not previously solvable, thus improving product quality. In Japan, Sendai's subway system uses fuzzy logic controls to accelerate so smoothly that standing passengers need not hold on. Mitsubishi Heavy Industries in Tokyo has been able to reduce the power consumption of its air conditioners by 20 percent through implementing control programs in fuzzy logic. The auto-focus device in our cameras is only possible because of fuzzy logic. Williams-Sonoma sells an "intelligent" steamer made in Japan that uses fuzzy logic. A variable heat setting detects the amount of grain within, cooks it at the preferred temperature, and keeps food warm up to 12 hours.

Management has also found fuzzy logic useful for decision making and organizational control. A Wall Street firm had a system developed that selects companies for potential acquisition, using the language that stock traders understand. Recently a system has been developed to detect possible fraud in medical claims submitted by health care providers anywhere in the United States.

Genetic Algorithms

Genetic algorithms (also referred to as *adaptive computation*) refer to a variety of problem-solving techniques that are conceptually based on the method living organisms use to adapt to their environment—the process of evolution. They are programmed to work the way populations solve problems: by changing and reorganizing their component parts using processes such as reproduction, mutation, and natural selection. Thus, genetic algorithms promote the evolution of solutions to particular problems, controlling the generation, variation, adaptation, and selection of possible solutions using genetically based processes. As solutions alter and combine, the worst ones are discarded and the better ones survive to go on and produce even better solutions. Genetic algorithms breed programs that solve problems even when no person can fully understand their structure (Holland, 1992).

Genetic algorithms originated in the work of John H. Holland, a professor of psychology and computer science at the University of Michigan, who devised a genetic code of binary digits that could be used to represent any type of computer program with a 1 representing true and a 0 representing false. With a long enough string of digits, any object can be represented by the right combination of digits. The genetic algorithm provides methods of searching all possible combinations of digits to identify the right string representing the best possible structure for the problem.

In one method, a user first randomly generates a population of strings consisting of combinations of binary digits. Each string corresponds to one variable in the problem. A user applies a test for fitness, ranking the strings in the population according to their level of desirability as possible solutions. Once the initial population is evaluated for fitness, the algorithm then produces the next generation of strings (consisting of strings that survived the fitness test plus offspring strings produced from mating pairs of strings) and tests their fitness. The process continues until a solution is reached (see Figure 15.14).

Like neural networks, genetic algorithms are ideal applications for massively parallel computers. Each processor can be assigned a single string. Thus, the entire

genetic algorithms Problem-solving methods that promote the evolution of solutions to specified problems using the model of living organisms adapting to their environment.

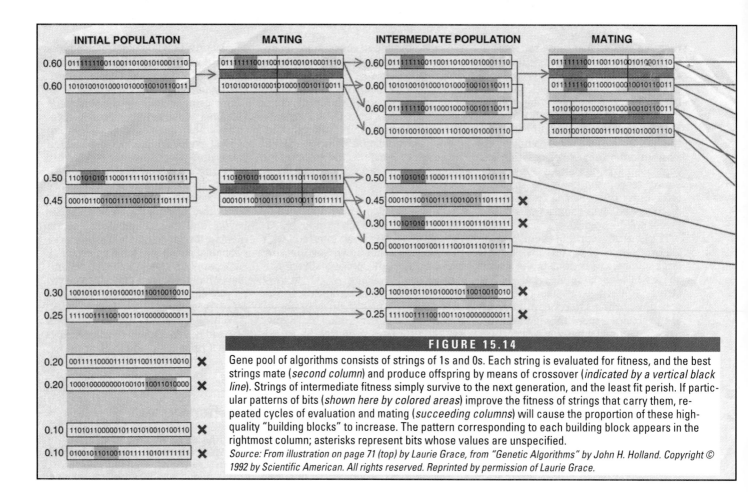

| INITIAL POPULATION | MATING | INTERMEDIATE POPULATION | MATING |

population of a genetic algorithm can be processed in parallel, offering growing potential for solving problems of enormous complexity.

Solutions to certain types of problems in areas of optimization, product design, and the monitoring of industrial systems are especially appropriate for genetic algorithms. Many business problems require optimization because they deal with issues such as minimization of costs, maximization of profits, most efficient scheduling, and use of resources. If these situations are very dynamic and complex, involving hundreds of variables or hundreds of formulas, genetic algorithms are suitable for solving them because they can attack a solution from many directions at once.

Commercial applications of genetic algorithms are emerging. Engineers at General Electric use a genetic algorithm to help them design jet turbine aircraft engines, a complex problem involving about 100 variables and 50 constraint equations. The engineers evaluate design changes on a workstation that runs a simulation of the engine in operation. Because each design change requires a new simulation to test its effectiveness, the designers can spend weeks on solutions that may or may not be optimal. Using an expert system reduced the time to produce a satisfactory design from several weeks to several days but would produce solutions only up to a point. Further improvements required simultaneous changes in large numbers of variables. At that point GE introduced a genetic algorithm that took the initial population of designs produced by the expert system and generated a design that contained three times the number of improvements over the best previous version in a period of only two days. Other organizations using genetic algorithms include the Coors Brewing Company, which uses genetic algorithms for scheduling the fulfillment and shipment of orders, and the U.S. Navy, which uses genetic algorithms for scheduling F-16 tryouts (Burtka, 1993).

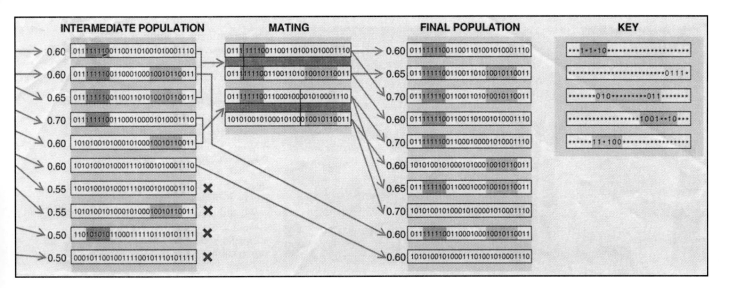

Hybrid AI Systems

GE's system for jet engine design achieved impressive results by combining genetic algorithm and expert system technology. Genetic algorithms, fuzzy logic, neural networks, or expert systems can be integrated into a single application to take advantage of the best features of these technologies. Such systems are called **hybrid AI systems.** Hybrid applications in business are growing. In Japan, Hitachi, Mitsubishi, Ricoh, Sanyo, and others are starting to incorporate hybrid AI into products such as home appliances, factory machinery, and office equipment. Matsushita has developed a "neurofuzzy" washing machine that combines fuzzy logic with neural networks. Nikko Securities has been working on a neurofuzzy system to forecast convertible-bond ratings.

hybrid AI system Integration of multiple AI technologies into a single application to take advantage of the best features of these technologies.

Intelligent Agents

Intelligent agents are software programs that work in the background to carry out specific, repetitive, and predictable tasks for an individual user, business process, or software application. The agent uses a built-in or learned knowledge base to accomplish tasks or make decisions on behalf of the user. Intelligent agents can be programmed to make decisions based on the user's personal preferences—for example, to delete junk e-mail, schedule appointments, or travel over interconnected networks to find the cheapest airfare to California. The agent can be likened to a personal digital assistant collaborating with the user in the same work environment. It can help the user by performing tasks on the user's behalf; training or teaching the user; hiding the complexity of difficult tasks; helping the user collaborate with other users; or monitoring events and procedures (Maes, 1994).

Intelligent agent A software program that uses a built-in or learned knowledge base to carry out specific, repetitive, and predictable tasks for an individual user, business process, or software application.

There are many intelligent agent applications today in operating systems, application software, e-mail systems, mobile computing software, and network tools. For example, the Wizards found in Microsoft Office software tools have built-in capabilities to show users how to accomplish various tasks, such as formatting documents or creating graphs, and to anticipate when users need assistance. (Search engines for locating information on the World Wide Web do not actually qualify as agents even though they are sometimes classified as such. These engines do not search the Internet for a query. They simply sort through a massive database of Web pages that the engine's company has gathered.)

At IBM's Almaden Research Center, Dr. Ted Selker created an agent that actually facilitates the learning process for computer programmers that are learning the programming language LISP. COACH (Cognitive Adaptive Computer Help) contains three knowledge components that enable it to function. One compiles information about the user's LISP abilities, including frequent mistakes, and which coaching techniques proved effective. Another component maintains information about LISP itself. The final component stores strategies for coaching. COACH ensures that students of LISP receive a more thorough learning experience than they would otherwise.

Of special interest are intelligent agents used to cruise networks, including the Internet, in search of information. AT&T pioneered in this area with its PersonaLink service. PersonaLink used an object-oriented remote programming language called Telescript from California's General Magic Inc. to establish an environment for e-mail, on-line news, and an electronic marketplace. AT&T hoped to attract all kinds of suppliers and consumers to its global electronic commerce service. The service never took off the ground because consumers found the Internet more accessible and affordable, but other intelligent agent products have been developed. Telescript applications are being developed by other companies.

Figure 15.15 illustrates how General Magic's Telescript technology could be used to send agents out on the Internet to perform tasks for users interested in financial and business information. Users can specify what information they want and the agent will draw the information from multiple Web sites.

Verity Inc. has developed server software that permits the release of an agent for the purpose of researching Web sites and databases. The product also provides means for the agent to then brief a user on its findings by way of a pager, e-mail, or Web page. The Verity agent rates the importance of its findings according to the user's preferences, and uses those ratings in its reports. It has already turned out customized editions of the San Jose Mercury's on-line newspaper in tests.

The Cambridge, Massachusetts company, Agents Inc., sells an agent that caters to consumers on the Internet. Users send critiques of movies and music to Agents' Web site, Firefly. When they want to select a new movie or buy a CD, they can supply data on their personal favorites, and Firefly will produce a list of similar items based on the critiques. The primary audience for Continuum's agent is companies with products to sell. The agent, known as a *machine learning tool*, provides sellers with a forum for displaying the latest data on their products for a monthly fee.

Agents are being used to facilitate virtual organizations because they can handle interactions among different organizations and database structures. Their roles include purchasing, selling, and communicating with other agents. For example,

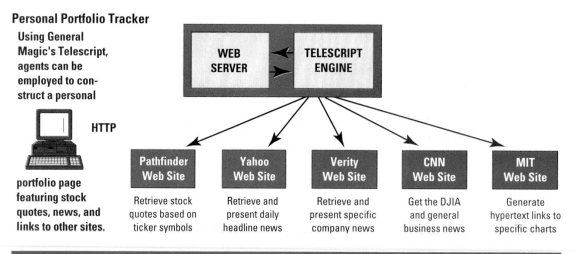

FIGURE 15.15

Intelligent agents for the Internet. Using General Magic's Telescript, agents can be employed to construct a personal portfolio page featuring stock quotes, news, and links to other sites.

Source: From Dean Tomasula "Agents to Represent Traders" in Wall Street and Technology, *Volume 14, No. 7, July, 1996. Copyright © 1996 Miller Freeman, Inc.*

SmartProcurement, developed jointly by the National Institute for Standards and Technology and Enterprise Integration Technologies, uses intelligent agents over the Internet or other networks to execute procurement electronically by locating information in different databases. After receiving an electronic or human request for quotation (RFQ), an agent acquires a list of agents who have been registered as vendors for the requested item and sends the RFQ to them. The agents can decide whether or not to bid. Each bid is sent to the purchasing agent which accumulates the bids for selection by a buyer. After a bid is selected, the winning vendor is notified. (O'Leary, Kuokka, and Plant, 1997).

MANAGEMENT WRAP-UP

MANAGEMENT

ORGANIZATION

TECHNOLOGY

Leveraging and managing organizational knowledge have become core management responsibilities. Managers need to identify the knowledge assets of their organizations and make sure that appropriate systems and processes are in place to maximize their utilization.

Systems for knowledge and information work and artificial intelligence can enhance organizational processes in a number of ways. They can facilitate communication and coordination, bring more analytical power to bear in the development of solutions, or reduce the amount of human intervention in organizational processes.

An array of technologies is available to support knowledge management, including artificial intelligence technologies and tools for knowledge and information work and group collaboration. Managers should understand the costs, benefits, and capabilities of each technology and the knowledge management problem for which each is best suited.

For Discussion: Select a business process and describe how it could be enhanced by a knowledge, information work, or artificial intelligence application.

SUMMARY

1. Explain the importance of knowledge management in contemporary organizations. Knowledge management is the process of systematically and actively managing and leveraging the stores of knowledge in an organization. Knowledge is a central productive and strategic asset in an information economy. Information systems can play a valuable role in knowledge management, helping the organization optimize its flow of information and capture its knowledge base. Office automation systems (OAS), knowledge work systems (KWS), group collaboration systems, and artificial intelligence applications are especially useful for knowledge management because they focus primarily on supporting information and knowledge work and on defining and codifying the organization's knowledge base.

2. Describe the applications that are most useful for distributing, creating, and sharing knowledge in the firm. Offices coordinate information work in the organization, link the work of diverse groups in the organization, and couple the organization to its external environment. Office automation systems (OAS) support these functions by automating document management, communications, scheduling, and data management. Word processing, desktop publishing, and digital imaging systems support document management activities. Electronic mail systems and groupware support communications activities. Electronic calendar applications and groupware support scheduling activities. Desktop data management systems support data management activities.

Knowledge work systems (KWS) support the creation of new knowledge and its integration into the organization. KWS require easy access to an external knowledge base; powerful computer hardware that can support software with intensive graphics, analysis, document management, and communications capabilities; and a friendly user interface. Knowledge work systems often run on workstations that are customized for the work they must perform. Computer-aided design (CAD) systems and virtual reality systems that create interactive simulations that behave like the real world require graphics and powerful modeling capabilities. Knowledge work systems for financial professionals provide access to external databases and the ability to analyze massive amounts of financial data very quickly.

Groupware is special software to support information-intensive activities in which people work collaboratively in groups. Intranets can perform many group collaboration and support functions.

3. Define artificial intelligence. Artificial intelligence is the development of computer-based systems that behave like humans. There are five members of the artificial intelligence family tree: (1) natural language, (2) robotics, (3) perceptive systems, (4) expert systems, and (5) intelligent machines. Artificial intelligence lacks the flexibility, breadth, and generality of human intelligence but it can be used to capture and codify organizational knowledge.

4. Explain how organizations can use expert systems and case-based reasoning to capture knowledge. Expert systems are knowledge-intensive computer programs that solve problems that previously required human expertise. The systems capture a limited domain of human knowledge using rules or frames. The strategy to search through the knowledge base, called the *inference engine,* can use either forward or backward chaining. Expert systems are most useful for problems of classification or diagnosis. Case-based reasoning represents organizational knowledge as a database of cases that can be continually expanded and refined. When the user encounters a new case, the system searches for similar cases, finds the closest fit, and applies the solutions of the old case to the new case. The new case is stored together with successful solutions in the case database.

5. Describe how organizations can use neural networks and other intelligent techniques to improve their knowledge base. Neural networks consist of hardware and software that attempt to mimic the thought processes of the human brain. Neural networks are notable for their ability to learn without programming and to recognize patterns that cannot be easily described by humans. They are being used in science, medicine, and business primarily to discriminate patterns in massive amounts of data.

Fuzzy logic is a software technology that expresses logic with some carefully defined imprecision so that it is closer to the way people actually think than traditional IF–THEN rules. Fuzzy logic has been used for controlling physical devices and is starting to be used for limited decision-making applications.

Genetic algorithms develop solutions to particular problems using genetically based processes such as fitness, crossover, and mutation to breed solutions. Genetic algorithms are starting to be applied to problems involving optimization, product design, and monitoring industrial systems.

Intelligent agents are software programs with a built-in or learned knowledge base that carry out specific, repetitive, and predictable tasks for an individual user, business process, or software application. Intelligent agents can be programmed to search for information or conduct transactions on networks, including the Internet.

KEY TERMS

Knowledge management	Knowledge work	Knowledge base	Case-based
Information work	system (KWS)	Rule-based expert system	reasoning (CBR)
Data workers	Computer-aided	Rule base	Neural network
Knowledge workers	design (CAD)	Knowledge frames	Fuzzy logic
Office automation	Virtual reality systems	AI shell	Genetic algorithms
system (OAS)	Investment workstation	Inference engine	Hybrid AI system
Document imaging systems	Groupware	Forward chaining	Intelligent agent
Jukebox	Artificial intelligence	Backward chaining	
Index server	Expert system	Knowledge engineer	

REVIEW QUESTIONS

1. What is knowledge management? List and briefly describe the information systems that support it.

2. What is the relationship between information work and productivity in contemporary organizations?

3. Describe the roles of the office in organizations. What are the major activities that take place in offices?

4. What are the principal types of information systems that support information worker activities of the office?

5. What are the generic requirements of knowledge work systems? Why?

6. Describe how the following systems support knowledge work: computer-aided design (CAD), virtual reality, investment workstations.

7. How does groupware support information work? Describe its capabilities and the Internet capabilities for collaborative work.

8. What is artificial intelligence? Why is it of interest to business?

9. What is the difference between artificial intelligence and natural or human intelligence?

10. Define an expert system and describe how it can help organizations use their knowledge assets.

11. Define and describe the role of the following in expert systems: rule base, frames, inference engine.

12. What is case-based reasoning? How does it differ from an expert system?

13. Describe three problems of expert systems.

14. Describe a neural network. For what kinds of tasks would a neural network be useful?

15. Define and describe fuzzy logic. For what kinds of applications is it suited?

16. What are genetic algorithms? How can they help organizations solve problems? For what kinds of problems are they suited?

17. What are intelligent agents? How can they be used to benefit businesses?

GROUP PROJECT

With a group of classmates, find a task in an organization (near your college or university) that requires some intelligence to perform and that might be suitable for an expert system. Describe as many of the rules required to perform this task as possible. Interview and observe the person performing this task. Consider changing the task to simplify the system. Report your findings to the class.

CASE STUDY

The United Nations Turns to Expert Systems

The United Nations has a payroll that would give most multinational corporations nightmares. Its 15,000 employees are in thousands of jobs in more than 100 locations worldwide. They must pay in dozens of currencies. Moreover, they have major operational centers in a number of cities around the world, from New York to Amman, Jordan, Bangkok, Thailand, Nairobi, Kenya, Santiago, Chile, and Vienna, Austria. However, the worst complication is not the salary itself but the entitlements that accompany the salary. Susan Graham, a Price Waterhouse consultant with the United Nations explains, "Pay for U.N. employees is determined by a base salary plus entitlements. These [entitlements] include benefits based on location of work and a staff member's contractual situation. All of these factors affect the type of entitlements each employee is eligible for, and they make up a significant portion of [an employee's] pay." The entitlements alone are so complex that they fill three volumes of several hundred pages each. Calculations of these entitlements have been manual and are often described as "tedious." The United Nations decided to address these and other administrative computing matters in 1990 with its new Integrated Management Information System (IMIS).

Until IMIS, computing at the United Nations was based on aging mainframe systems. When the United Nations decided to modernize, it went all the way and moved to a client/server system. The new system's infrastructure includes Windows and UNIX operating systems, and several thousand PC clients connected to HP 9000 servers. IMIS is a series of client/server application modules that integrate accounting, payroll, personnel management, procurement, and transportation functions. From the be-

ginning of the project and throughout its history, the project staff has included 30 to 60 developers. In addition, Price Waterhouse has supplied consultants to the entitlements project. All-in-all, it was a most ambitious project, covering five years and costing $70 million.

The first two years were spent gathering requirements, designing the system, and implementing the networks. In late 1993 they began to address the complex payroll system. For the entitlements portion they designed the Entitlements System. For this they decided they had to use object-oriented technology to build an expert system that was capable of interpreting the complex salary regulations. For its development tool, the project selected PowerModel of IntelliCorp of Mountain View, California. The tool fits well with the U.N.'s Windows—UNIX client/server environment. It integrates object-oriented programming, rule-based reasoning, a graphical user interface, and dynamic links to databases and other applications. It includes a fourth-generation tool for building both a rule base and a knowledge base.

The entitlements project very early had to face the enormous task of translating the three volumes of paper rules into a rules-based knowledge base. The developers first had to organize the requirements into a class structure of objects. According to another Price Waterhouse consultant, Luis Munoz, "Establishing the requirements was one of the most difficult parts of the project." He added that "Users in different locations see and apply the requirements in different ways." Once they had designed the rule base, the team then had to translate them into on-line rules.

The choice of PowerModel proved to be a good one. According to Graham, "PowerModel provided a flexible system for establishing the rule base since it incorporates features from both object-based and procedural languages." She added, "It allowed us to automate the parts of the system that were objectively quantifiable and also to build a waiving process into the system for exceptions."

The knowledge base for the system is on-line and is capable of applying entitlements automatically. The system also reassesses when a change to an employee's status is approved. Thus the system automates the tedious entitlement process and generates the appropriate salary for the next payroll once status changes are entered. According to Thomas Kamps, a systems analyst at the United Nations, "This philosophy led to the creation of the Entitlements System, which succeeded in automating manual processes that had defied automation for decades."

The new system had to be able to deal with time as a variable because promotions often do not reach the appropriate payroll office until long after it has been awarded. When a promotion is entered, the system must recalculate the entitlements based on the promotion date so that entitlements will be appropriate for the time between the promotion and the date it is finally entered into the system. According to Munoz, "Sometimes, events that merit a change in an individual's entitlements, such as a promotion, aren't actually recorded until months later. But adding that entitlement at a later date might negate or modify other changes made to that individual's personnel status since the time of the actual promotion."

One reason the project decided to use an object-oriented expert system is that the entitlement rules change so often. With traditional programming, each rule change would result in changes to program code followed by recompiling the whole program. However, given the software technology being used, all the support staff needs to do to implement a rule change is to go into the specific object and make the change there and then simply return the new object into the rule base.

The system has been a success. It maintains the data on all U.N. employees and their dependents. It automatically manages such relevant events as promotions, relocations, and dependency status changes. As a result, entitlement determination is more consistent than in the past, making the process more equitable. When IMIS processes a change to someone's entitlements, it offers an explanation of why the change, how it determined the change, and the current value of the entitlements. One result, according to Graham, is "The U.N.

now has much greater accuracy in the way entitlements are handled." In addition, she points out that whereas traditional systems usually compute entitlements when a payroll is run, "in IMIS, personnel officers can make changes and see immediately what effect those changes will have on a staff member's pay." The system also allows its users to generate reports on the data, perform what-if scenarios, and project costs, making it an important planning tool as well.

The IMIS system has been successful enough that the United Nations is now using PowerModel to develop other financial systems. For example they have developed an accounting transaction posting system that automatically posts according to posting rules. Graham points out, "With this new system, users don't need to know anything about the debits and credits." All they do is enter the data and "PowerModel analyzes that transaction to determine what the debit and credit entries should be." The system even includes rules on consolidating accounts into other accounts and on closing out books at the end of certain financial periods. ∎

Source: David Baum, "U.N. Automates Payroll with AI System," *Datamation*, November 1996.

Case Study Questions

1. Was an expert system an appropriate technology for the United Nations to use with its payroll system? Why or why not?

2. How did IMIS change the way the United Nations conducted its business? How important is it for the United Nations? Why?

3. What problems did IMIS solve for the United Nations?

REFERENCES

Allen, Bradley P. "Case-Based Reasoning: Business Applications." *Communications of the ACM* 37, no. 3 (March 1994).

Amaravadi, Chandra S., Olivia R. Liu Sheng, Joey F. George, and Jay F. Nunamaker, Jr. "AEI: A Knowledge-Based Approach to Integrated Office Systems." *Journal of Management Information Systems* 9, no. 1 (Summer 1992).

Applegate, Linda. "Technology Support for Cooperative Work: A Framework for Studying Introduction and Assimilation in Organizations." *Journal of Organizational Computing* 1, no. 1 (January–March 1991).

Asakawa, Kazuo, and Hideyuki Takagi. "Neural Networks in Japan." *Communications of the ACM* 37, no. 3 (March 1994).

Bair, James H. "A Layered Model of Organizations: Communication Processes and Performance." *Journal of Organizational Computing* 1, no. 2 (April–June 1991).

Bansal, Arun, Robert J. Kauffman, and Rob R. Weitz. "The Modeling Performance of Regression and Neural Networks." *Journal of Management Information Systems* 10, no. 1 (Summer 1993).

Barker, Virginia E., and Dennis E. O'Connor. "Expert Systems for Configuration at Digital: XCON and Beyond." *Communications of the ACM* (March 1989).

Beer, Randall D., Roger D. Quinn, Hillel J. Chiel, and Roy E. Ritzman. "Biologically Inspired Approaches to Robots." *Communications of the ACM* 40, no. 3 (March 1997).

Bikson, Tora K., J. D. Eveland, and Barbara A. Gutek. "Flexible Interactive Technologies for Multi-Person Tasks: Current Problems and Future Prospects." *Rand Corporation* (December 1988).

Black, George. "Taking Notes, Big Sixer Aims for Head of the Class." *Software Magazine* (March 1995).

Blanning, Robert W., David R. King, James R. Marsden, and Ann C. Seror. "Intelligent Models of Human Organizations: The State of the Art." *Journal of Organizational Computing* 2, no. 2 (1992).

Bobrow, D. G., S. Mittal, and M. J. Stefik. "Expert Systems: Perils and Promise." *Communications of the ACM* 29 (September 1986).

Bohn, Roger E. "Measuring and Managing Technological Knowledge." *Sloan Management Review* (Fall 1994).

Braden, Barbara, Jerome Kanter, and David Kopcso. "Developing an Expert Systems Strategy." *MIS Quarterly* 13, no. 4 (December 1989).

Brynjolfsson, Erik. "The Productivity Paradox of Information Technology." *Communications of the ACM* 36, no. 12 (December 1993).

Brynjolfsson, Erik. "The Contribution of Information Technology to Consumer Welfare." *Information Systems Research* 7, no. 3 (September 1996).

Brynjolfsson, Erik, and Lorin Hitt. "New Evidence on the Returns to Information Systems." MIT Sloan School of Management, October 1993.

Burtka, Michael. "Generic Algorithms." *The Stern Information Systems Review* 1, no. 1 (Spring 1993).

Busch, Elizabeth, Matti Hamalainen, Clyde W. Holsapple, Yongmoo Suh, and Andrew B. Whinston. "Issues and Obstacles in the Development of Team Support Systems." *Journal of Organizational Computing* 1, no. 2 (April–June 1991).

Byrd, Terry Anthony. "Implementation and Use of Expert Systems in Organizations: Perceptions of Knowledge Engineers." *Journal of Management Information Systems* 8, no. 4 (Spring 1992).

Carlson, David A., and Sudha Ram. "A Knowledge Representation for Modeling Organizational Productivity." *Journal of Organizational Computing* 2, no. 2 (1992).

Churchland, Paul M., and Patricia Smith Churchland. "Could a Machine Think?" *Scientific American* (January 1990).

Clifford, James, Henry C. Lucas, Jr., and Rajan Srikanth. "Integrating Mathematical and Symbolic Models through AESOP: An Expert for Stock Options Pricing." *Information Systems Research* 3, no. 4 (December 1992).

Cox, Earl. "Applications of Fuzzy System Models." *AI Expert* (October 1992).

Cox, Earl. "Solving Problems with Fuzzy Logic." *AI Expert* (March 1992).

Creecy, Robert H., Brij M. Masand, Stephen J. Smith, and Davis L. Waltz. "Trading MIPS and Memory for Knowledge Engineering." *Communications of the ACM* 35, no. 8 (August 1992).

Dhar, Vasant. "Plausibility and Scope of Expert Systems in Management." *Journal of Management Information Systems* (Summer 1987).

Dhar, Vasant, and Roger Stein. *Intelligent Decision Support Methods: The Science of Knowledge Work.* Upper Saddle River, NJ: Prentice-Hall (1997).

El Najdawi, M. K., and Anthony C. Stylianou. "Expert Support Systems: Integrating AI Technologies." *Communications of the ACM* 36, no. 12 (December 1993).

Feigenbaum, Edward A. "The Art of Artificial Intelligence: Themes and Case Studies in Knowledge Engineering." Proceedings of the IJCAI (1977).

Gelernter, David. "The Metamorphosis of Information Management." *Scientific American* (August 1989).

Gill, Philip J. "A False Rivalry Revealed." *Information Week* (May 20, 1996).

Giuliao, Vincent E. "The Mechanization of Office Work." *Scientific American* (September 1982).

Goldberg, David E. "Genetic and Evolutionary Algorithms Come of Age." *Communications of the ACM* 37, no. 3 (March 1994).

Grant, Robert M. "Prospering in Dynamically Competitive Environments: Organizational Capability as Knowledge Integration." *Organization Science* 7, no. 4 (July–August 1996).

Griggs, Kenneth. "Visual Aids that Model Organizations." *Journal of Organizational Computing* 2, no. 2 (1992).

Hayes-Roth, Frederick. "Knowledge-Based Expert Systems." *Spectrum IEEE* (October 1987).

Hayes-Roth, Frederick, and Neil Jacobstein. "The State of Knowledge-Based Systems." *Communications of the ACM* 37, no. 3 (March 1994).

Hinton, Gregory. "How Neural Networks Learn from Experience." *Scientific American* (September 1992).

Holland, John H. "Genetic Algorithms." *Scientific American* (July 1992).

"How Organizations Use Groupware to Improve a Wide Range of Business Processes." *I/S Analyzer* 35, no. 2 (February 1996).

Jacobs, Paul S., and Lisa F. Rau. "SCISOR: Extracting Information from On-line News." *Communications of the ACM* 33, no. 11 (November 1990).

Johansen, Robert. "Groupware: Future Directions and Wild Cards." *Journal of Organizational Computing* 1, no. 2 (April–June 1991).

Kanade, Takeo, Michael L. Reed, and Lee E. Weiss. "New Technologies and Applications in Robotics." *Communications of the ACM* 37 no. 3 (March 1994).

Lee, Soonchul. "The Impact of Office Information Systems on Power and Influence." *Journal of Management Information Systems* 8, no. 2 (Fall 1991).

Leonard-Barton, Dorothy, and John J. Sviokla. "Putting Expert Systems to Work." *Harvard Business Review* (March–April 1988).

Lieberman, Henry. "Intelligent Graphics." *Communications of the ACM* 39, no. 8 (August 1996).

Liker, Jeffrey K., Mitchell Fleischer, Mitsuo Nagamachi, and Michael S. Zonnevylle. "Designers and Their Machines: CAD Use and Support in the U.S. and Japan." *Communications of the ACM* 35, no. 2 (February 1992).

Lin, Frank C., and Mei Lin. "Neural Networks in the Financial Industry." *AI Expert* (February 1993).

Maes, Pattie. "Agents that Reduce Work and Information Overload." *Communications of the ACM* 38, no. 7 (July 1994).

Mann, Marina M., Richard L. Rudman, Thomas A. Jenckes, and Barbara C. McNurlin. "EPRINET: Leveraging Knowledge in the Electronic Industry." *MIS Quarterly* 15, no. 3 (September 1991).

Marsden, James R., David E. Pingry, and Ming-Chian Ken Wang. "Intelligent Information and Organization Structures: An Integrated Design Approach." *Journal of Organizational Computing* 2, no. 2 (1992).

McCarthy, John. "Generality in Artificial Intelligence." *Communications of the ACM* (December 1987).

McCune, Jenny C. "All Together Now." *Beyond Computing* (May 1996).

Meador, C. Lawrence, and Ed G. Mahler. "Choosing an Expert System Game Plan," *Datamation* (August 1, 1990).

Meyer, Marc H., and Kathleen Foley Curley. "An Applied Framework for Classifying the Complexity of Knowledge-Based Systems." *MIS Quarterly* 15, no. 4 (December 1991).

Michaels, Jenna. "Managing Technology." *Wall Street & Technology* (February 1993).

Motiwalla, Luvai, and Jay F. Nunamaker, Jr. "Mail-Man: A Knowledge-Based Mail Assistant for Managers." *Journal of Organizational Computing* 2, no. 2 (1992).

Munakata, Toshinori, and Yashvant Jani. "Fuzzy Systems: An Overview." *Communications of the ACM* 37, no. 3 (March 1994).

Mykytyn, Kathleen, Peter P. Mykytyn, Jr., and Craig W. Stinkman. "Expert Systems: A Question of Liability." *MIS Quarterly* 14, no. 1 (March 1990).

Naj, Amal Kumar. "Virtual Reality Isn't a Fantasy for Surgeons." *The Wall Street Journal* (March 3, 1993).

Nash, Jim. "Expert Systems: A New Partnership." *AI Expert* (December 1992).

Nash, Jim. "State of the Market, Art, Union, and Technology." *AI Expert* (January 1993).

Newquist, Harvey P. "AI at American Express." *AI Expert* (January 1993).

Newquist, Harvey P. "Virtual Reality's Commercial Reality." *Computerworld* (March 30, 1992).

O'Leary, Daniel, Daniel Kuokka, and Robert Plant. "Artificial Intelligence and Virtual Organizations." *Communications of the ACM* 40, no. 1 (January 1997).

Panko, Raymond R. "Is Office Productivity Stagnant?" *MIS Quarterly* 15, no. 2 (June 1991).

Porat, Marc. *The Information Economy: Definition and Measurement.* Washington, D.C.: U.S. Department of Commerce, Office of Telecommunications (May 1977).

Press, Lawrence. "Systems for Finding People." *Journal of Organizational Computing* 2, no. 3 and 4 (1992a).

Press, Lawrence. "Lotus Notes (Groupware) in Context." *Journal of Organizational Computing* 2, no. 3 and 4 (1992b).

Roach, Stephen S. *Industrialization of the Information Economy.* New York: Morgan Stanley and Co. (1984).

Roach, Stephen S. *Making Technology Work.* New York: Morgan Stanley and Co. (1993).

Roach, Stephen S. "Services Under Siege—The Restructuring Imperative." *Harvard Business Review* (September–October 1991).

Roach, Stephen S. "Technology and the Service Sector." *Technological Forecasting and Social Change* 34, no. 4 (December 1988).

Roach, Stephen S. "The Hollow Ring of the Productivity Revival." *Harvard Business Review* (November–December 1996).

Ruhleder, Karen, and John Leslie King. "Computer Support for Work Across Space, Time, and Social Worlds." *Journal of Organizational Computing* 1, no. 4 (1991).

Rumelhart, David E., Bernard Widrow, and Michael A. Lehr. "The Basic Ideas in Neural Networks." *Communications of the ACM* 37, no. 3 (March 1994).

Schatz, Bruce R. "Building an Electronic Community System." *Journal of Management Information Systems* 8, no. 3 (Winter 1991–1992).

Searle, John R. "Is the Brain's Mind a Computer Program?" *Scientific American* (January 1990).

Self, Kevin. "Designing with Fuzzy Logic." *Spectrum IEEE* (November 1990).

Sheng, Olivia R. Liu, Luvai F. Motiwalla, Jay F. Nunamaker, Jr., and Douglas R. Vogel. "A Framework to Support Managerial Activities Using Office Information Systems." *Journal of Management Information Systems* 6, no. 3 (Winter 1989–1990).

Sibigtroth, James M. "Implementing Fuzzy Expert Rules in Hardware." *AI Expert* (April 1992).

Simon, H. A., and A. Newell. "Heuristic Problem Solving: The Next Advance in Operations Research." *Operations Research* 6 (January–February 1958).

Sproull, Lee, and Sara Kiesler. *Connections: New Ways of Working in the Networked Organization.* Cambridge, MA: MIT Press (1992).

Starbuck, William H. "Learning by Knowledge-Intensive Firms." *Journal of Management Studies* 29, no. 6 (November 1992).

Stein, Eric W. "A Method to Identify Candidates for Knowledge Acquisition." *Journal of Management Information Systems* 9, no. 2 (Fall 1992).

Storey, Veda C., and Robert C. Goldstein, "Knowledge-Based Approaches to Database Design," *MIS Quarterly* 17, no. 1 (March 1993).

Stylianou, Anthony C., Gregory R. Madey, and Robert D. Smith. "Selection Criteria for Expert System Shells: A Socio-Technical Framework." *Communications of the ACM* 35, no. 10 (October 1992).

Sviokla, John J. "An Examination of the Impact of Expert Systems on the Firm: The Case of XCON." *MIS Quarterly* 14, no. 5 (June 1990).

Sviokla, John J. "Expert Systems and Their Impact on the Firm: The Effects of PlanPower Use on the Information Processing Capacity of the Financial Collaborative." *Journal of Management Information Systems* 6, no. 3 (Winter 1989–1990).

Tam, Kar Yan. "Automated Construction of Knowledge-Bases from Examples." *Information Systems Research* 1, no. 2 (June 1990).

Tank, David W., and John J. Hopfield. "Collective Computation in Neuronlike Circuits." *Scientific American* (October 1987).

Trippi, Robert, and Efraim Turban. "The Impact of Parallel and Neural Computing on Managerial Decision Making." *Journal of Management Information Systems* 6, no. 3 (Winter 1989–1990).

Turban, Efraim, and Paul R. Watkins. "Integrating Expert Systems and Decision Support Systems." *MIS Quarterly* (June 1986).

Wallich, Paul. "Silicon Babies." *Scientific American* (December 1991).

Waltz, David L. "Artificial Intelligence." *Scientific American* (December 1982).

Weitzel, John R., and Larry Kerschberg. "Developing Knowledge-Based Systems: Reorganizing the System Development Life Cycle." *Communications of the ACM* (April 1989).

Weizenbaum, Joseph. *Computer Power and Human Reason— From Judgment to Calculation.* San Francisco: Freeman (1976).

White, George M. "Natural Language Understanding and Speech Recognition." *Communications of the ACM* 33, no. 8 (August 1990).

Widrow, Bernard, David E. Rumelhart, and Michael A. Lehr. "Neural Networks: Applications in Industry, Business and Science." *Communications of the ACM* 27, no. 3 (March 1994).

Zadeh, Lotfi A. "Fuzzy Logic, Neural Networks, and Soft Computing." *Communications of the ACM* 37, no. 3 (March 1994).

Zadeh, Lotfi A. "The Calculus of Fuzzy If/Then Rules." *AI Expert* (March 1992).

Enhancing Management Decision Making

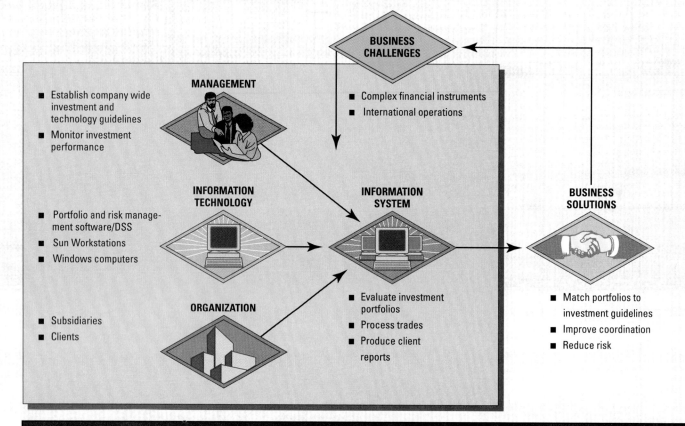

- **MANAGEMENT**
  - Establish company wide investment and technology guidelines
  - Monitor investment performance

- **INFORMATION TECHNOLOGY**
  - Portfolio and risk management software/DSS
  - Sun Workstations
  - Windows computers

- **ORGANIZATION**
  - Subsidiaries
  - Clients

- **BUSINESS CHALLENGES**
  - Complex financial instruments
  - International operations

- **INFORMATION SYSTEM**
  - Evaluate investment portfolios
  - Process trades
  - Produce client reports

- **BUSINESS SOLUTIONS**
  - Match portfolios to investment guidelines
  - Improve coordination
  - Reduce risk

Coutts & Co. Group Analyzes Risk

Coutts & Co. Group, the global private banking arm of NatWest Bank, consists of a diverse group of investment businesses under one umbrella. The group handles investments in the international equity, fixed income, and foreign exchange markets and has started to trade in derivatives. Regional subsidiaries have some latitude in decision making but must comply with broad investment and technology guidelines established at the Coutts Group's headquarters.

The Coutts Group decided it needed a structured investment process, which included software for managing risk. Without technol-

LEARNING OBJECTIVES

After completing
this chapter, you will
be able to:

1. Define a decision-support system (DSS) and a group decision-support system (GDSS).

2. Describe the components of decision-support systems and group decision-support systems.

3. Explain how decision-support systems and group decision-support systems can enhance decision making.

4. Describe the capabilities of an executive support system (ESS).

5. Describe the benefits of executive support systems.

ogy to measure risk, problems can arise in imposing the investment process or in managing certain investment portfolios within risk guidelines set for clients. The Group started looking for portfolio management software that could support local needs and market conventions while using a common set of tools to measure risks and returns of internationally diversified portfolios according to the organization's investment guidelines.

After much searching, the Coutts Group settled on Olivia (Online Investment Analyses), a portfolio and risk management software package developed by Promco, a Geneva-based company. Olivia is distributed worldwide by London-based Cray systems as an integrated fund management system which includes capabilities for processing trades and intranet client reporting. The system is object oriented in design and runs on Sun Microsystems workstations and other hardware with Windows interfaces. The Coutts Group worked with Sun and Promco to build additional risk control and analytic functions that it needed.

Olivia can interface with the Group's various back-office accounting systems in different countries that contain local client data. The back-office information is translated into a common set of standards which can be used by Olivia. Olivia helps Coutts & Co. Group enforce its structured investment process by letting management see how a portfolio is structured and whether it is in line with company-wide strategy. Olivia will issue a series of alerts to ensure that a manager remains in compliance with client and legal restrictions as well as the company's asset allocation strategies and policies. ■

Source: "In a Class of Its Own," *Open Finance*, Autumn 1996.

Coutts & Co. Group's portfolio management system is an example of a decision-support system (DSS). Such systems have powerful analytic capabilities to support managers during the process of arriving at a decision. Other systems in this category are group decision-support systems (GDSS), which support decision making in groups, and executive support systems (ESS), which provide information for making strategic-level decisions. These systems can enhance organizational performance, but they raise the following management challenges:

1. **Building information systems that can actually fulfill executive information requirements.** Even with the use of Critical Success Factors and other information requirements determination methods, it may still be difficult to establish information requirements for ESS and DSS serving senior management. Chapter 4 has already described why certain aspects of senior management decision making cannot be supported by information systems because the decisions are too unstructured and fluid. Even if a problem can be addressed by an information system, senior management may not fully understand its actual information needs. For instance, senior managers may not agree on the firm's critical success factors, or the critical success factors they describe may be inappropriate or outdated if the firm is confronting a crisis requiring a major strategic change.

2. **Integrating DSS and ESS with existing systems in the business.** Even if system builders do know the information requirements for DSS or ESS, it may not be possible to fulfill them using data from the firm's existing information systems. Various MIS or TPS may define important pieces of data, such as the time period covered by fiscal year, in different ways. It may not be possible to reconcile data from incompatible internal systems for analysis by managers even through data cleansing and data warehousing. A significant amount of organizational change may be required before the firm can build and install effective DSS and ESS.

Most information systems described throughout this text help people make decisions in one way or another, but DSS, GDSS, and ESS are part of a special category of information systems that are explicitly designed to enhance managerial decision making. This chapter describes the characteristics of each of these types of information systems and shows how each actually enhances the managerial decision-making process.

DSS, GDSS, and ESS can support decision making in a number of ways. They can automate certain decision procedures (for example, determining the highest price that can be charged for a product to maintain market share). They can provide information about different aspects of the decision situation and the decision process, such as what opportunities or problems triggered the decision process, what solution alternatives were generated or explored, and how the decision was actually reached. Finally, they can stimulate innovation in decision making by helping managers question existing decision procedures or explore different solution designs (Dutta, Wierenga, and Dalebout, 1997).

As noted in Chapter 2, a **decision-support system (DSS)** assists management decision making by combining data, sophisticated analytical models and tools, and user-friendly software into a single powerful system that can support semistructured or unstructured decision making. A DSS provides users with a flexible set of tools and capabilities for analyzing important blocks of data.

decision-support system (DSS) Computer system at the management level of an organization that combines data, analytical tools, and models to support semistructured and unstructured decision making.

DSS and MIS

DSSs are more targeted than MIS systems. An MIS provides managers with reports based on routine flows of data and assists in the general control of the organization. In contrast, a DSS is tightly focused on a specific decision or classes of decisions such as routing, queueing, evaluating, predicting, and so forth. In philosophy, a DSS promises end-user control of data, tools, and sessions. An MIS focuses on structured information flows, whereas a DSS emphasizes change, flexibility, and a quick response. With a DSS there is less of an effort to link users to structured information flows and a correspondingly greater emphasis on models, assumptions, ad hoc queries, and display graphics. Both the DSS and MIS rely on professional analysis and design. However, whereas an MIS usually follows a traditional systems development methodology, freezing information requirements before design and throughout the life cycle, a DSS is consciously iterative and never frozen.

Chapter 4 introduces the distinction between structured, semistructured, and unstructured decisions. Structured problems are repetitive and routine, for which known algorithms provide solutions. Unstructured problems are novel and nonroutine, for which there are no algorithms for solutions. One can discuss, decide, and ruminate about unstructured problems, but they are not solved in the sense that one finds an answer to an equation (Henderson and Schilling, 1985). Semistructured problems fall between structured and unstructured problems. A DSS is designed to support semistructured and unstructured problem analysis.

Chapter 4 also introduces Simon's description of decision making, which consists of four stages: intelligence, design, choice, and implementation. Decision-support systems are intended to help design and evaluate alternatives and monitor the adoption or implementation process.

A well-designed DSS can be used at many levels of the organization. Senior management can use a financial DSS to forecast the availability of corporate funds for investment by division. Middle managers within divisions can use these estimates and the same system and data to make decisions about allocating division funds to projects. Capital project managers within divisions, in turn, can use this system to begin their projects, reporting to the system (and ultimately to senior managers) on a regular basis about how much money has been spent.

Types of Decision-Support Systems (DSS)

The earliest DSS tended to draw on small subsets of corporate data and were heavily model driven. Recent advances in computer processing and database technology have expanded the definition of a DSS to include systems that can support decision making by analyzing vast quantities of data.

Today there are two basic types of decision-support systems, model driven and data driven (Dhar and Stein, 1997). Early DSS developed in the late 1970s and 1980s were model driven. **Model-driven DSS** were primarily standalone systems isolated from major organizational information systems that used some type of model to perform "what-if" and other kinds of analyses. Such systems were often developed by end-user divisions or groups not under central IS control. Their analysis capabilities were based on a strong theory or model combined with a good user interface that

model-driven DSS Primarily standalone system that uses some type of model to perform "what-if" and other kinds of analyses.

data-driven DSS A system that supports decision making by allowing users to extract and analyze useful information that was previously buried in large databases.

made the model easy to use. The voyage-estimating DSS described in Chapter 2 is an example of a model-driven DSS.

The second type of DSS is a **data-driven DSS**. These systems analyze large pools of data found in major organizational systems. They support decision making by allowing users to extract useful information that was previously buried in large quantities of data. Often data from various transaction processing systems (TPS) are collected in data warehouses for this purpose. On-line analytical processing (OLAP) and datamining can then be used to analyze the data.

Traditional database queries answer such questions as, "How many units of product number 403 were shipped in November 1997?" On-line analytical processing (OLAP), or multidimensional analysis, supports much more complex requests for information, such as, "Compare sales of product 403 relative to plan by quarter and sales region for the past two years." We described on-line analytical processing (OLAP) and multidimensional data analysis in Chapter 8. With OLAP and query-oriented data analysis, users need to have a good idea about the information for which they are looking.

Datamining is more discovery driven. **Datamining** provides insights into corporate data that cannot be obtained with OLAP by finding hidden patterns and relationships in large databases and inferring rules from them to predict future behavior. The patterns and rules can then be used to guide decision making and forecast the effect of those decisions. The types of information that can be yielded from datamining include associations, sequences, classifications, clusters, and forecasts (Edelstein, 1996).

Associations are occurrences linked to a single event. For instance, a study of supermarket purchasing patterns might reveal that when corn chips are purchased, a cola drink is purchased 65 percent of the time, but when there is a promotion, cola is purchased 85 percent of the time. With this information, managers can make better decisions because they have learned the profitability of a promotion.

In *sequences,* events are linked over time. One might find, for example, that if a house is purchased, then a new refrigerator will be purchased within two weeks 65 percent of the time and an oven will be bought within one month of the home purchase 45 percent of the time.

Classification recognizes patterns that describe the group to which an item belongs by examining existing items that have been classified and by inferring a set of rules. For example, businesses such as credit card or telephone companies worry about the loss of steady customers. Classification can help discover the characteristics of customers who are likely to leave and can provide a model to help managers predict who they are so that they can devise special campaigns to retain such customers.

Clustering works in a manner similar to classification when no groups have yet been defined. A datamining tool will discover different groupings within data, such as finding affinity groups for bank cards or partitioning a database into groups of customers based on demographics and types of personal investments.

Although these applications involve predictions, *forecasting* uses predictions in a different way. It uses a series of existing values to forecast what other values will be. For example, forecasting might find patterns in data to help managers estimate the future value of continuous variables such as sales figures.

Datamining uses statistical analysis tools as well as neural networks, fuzzy logic, genetic algorithms, or rule-based and other intelligent techniques (described in Chapter 15).

As noted in Chapter 4, it is a mistake to think that decisions are only made by individuals in large organizations. In fact, most decisions are made collectively. Chapter 4 describes the rational, bureaucratic, political, and "garbage can" models of organizational decision making. Frequently, decisions must be coordinated with several groups before being finalized. In large organizations, decision making is inherently a group process, and a DSS can be designed to facilitate group decision making. Section 16.2 deals with this issue.

datamining Technology for finding hidden patterns and relationships in large databases and inferring rules from them to predict future behavior.

Components of DSS

Figure 16.1 illustrates the components of a DSS. They include a database of data used for query and analysis, a software system with models, data mining, and other analytical tools and a user interface.

The **DSS database** is a collection of current or historical data from a number of applications or groups. It may be a small database residing on a PC that contains a subset of corporate data that has been downloaded and possibly combined with external data. Alternatively, the DSS database may be a massive data warehouse that is continuously updated by major organizational TPS. The data in DSS databases are generally extracts or copies of production databases so that using the DSS does not interfere with critical operational systems.

The **DSS software system** contains the software tools that are used for data analysis. It may contain various OLAP tools, datamining tools, or a collection of mathematical and analytical models that easily can be made accessible to the DSS user. A **model** is an abstract representation that illustrates the components or relationships of a phenomenon. A model can be a physical model (such as a model airplane), a mathematical model (such as an equation), or a verbal model (such as a description of a procedure to write up an order). Each decision support system is built for a specific set of purposes and will make different collections of models available depending on those purposes.

Perhaps the most common models are libraries of statistical models. Such libraries usually contain the full range of expected statistical functions including means, medians, deviations, and scatter plots. The software has the ability to project future outcomes by analyzing a series of data. Statistical modeling software can be used to help establish relationships, such as relating product sales to differences in age, income, or other factors between communities. Optimization models, often using linear programming, determine optimal resource allocation to maximize or

DSS database A collection of current or historical data from a number of applications or groups. Can be a small PC database or a massive data warehouse.

DSS software system Collection of software tools that are used for data analysis, such as OLAP tools, datamining tools, or a collection of mathematical and analytical models.

model An abstract representation that illustrates the components or relationships of a phenomenon.

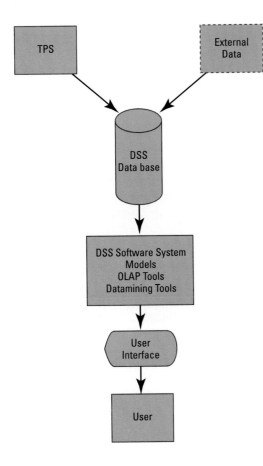

Overview of a decision-support system (DSS). The main components of the DSS are the DSS database, the DSS software system, and the user interface. The DSS database may be a small database residing on a PC or a massive data warehouse.

minimize specified variables such as cost or time. The Advanced Planning System (discussed in the next section) uses such software to determine the effect that filling a new order will have on meeting target dates for existing orders. A classic use of optimization models is to determine the proper mix of products within a given market to maximize profits.

Forecasting models are often used to forecast sales. The user of this type of model might supply a range of historical data to project future conditions and the sales that might result from those conditions. The decision maker could then vary those future conditions (entering, for example, a rise in raw materials costs or the entry of a new, low-priced competitor in the market) to determine how these new conditions may affect sales. Companies often use this software to attempt to predict the actions of competitors. Model libraries exist for specific functions, such as financial and risk analysis models.

Among the most widely used models are **sensitivity analysis** models that ask "what-if" questions repeatedly to determine the impact of changes in one or more factors on outcomes. "What-if" analysis—working forward from known or assumed conditions—allows the user to vary certain values to test results in order to better predict outcomes if changes occur in those values. "What happens if" we raise the price by 5 percent or increase the advertising budget by $100,000? What happens if we keep the price and advertising budget the same? Desktop spreadsheet software, such as Lotus 1-2-3 or Microsoft Excel, is often used for this purpose. Backward sensitivity analysis software is used for goal seeking: If I want to sell one million product units next year, how much must I reduce the price of the product?

The DSS user interface permits easy interaction between users of the system and the DSS software tools. A graphic, easy-to-use, flexible user interface supports the dialogue between the user and the DSS. The DSS users are usually corporate executives or managers, persons with well-developed working styles and individual preferences. Often they have little or no computer experience and no patience for learning to use a complex tool, so the interface must be relatively intuitive. In addition, what works for one may not work for another. Many executives, offered only one way of working (a way not to their liking), will simply not use the system. To mimic a typical way of working, a good user interface should allow the manager to move back and forth between activities at will.

Examples of DSS Applications

There are many ways in which DSS can be used to support decision making. Table 16.1 lists examples of DSS in well-known organizations. To illustrate the range of capabilities of a DSS, we will now describe some successful DSS applications. The Advanced Planning System and the Egyptian Cabinet DSS are examples of a model-driven DSS. Southern California Gas Co., ShopKo Stores, and Wal-Mart's systems are examples of a data-driven DSS.

The Advanced Planning System—A Manufacturing DSS

To support most kinds of manufacturing, companies use a type of software known as manufacturing resources planning (MRPII). The typical MRPII system includes such applications as master production scheduling, purchasing, material requirements planning, and even general ledger. Many thousands of these packages have been installed around the world. Although they are useful as far as they go, these packages usually run on a mainframe so that they can process massive amounts of data. As a result, they are too large and slow to be used for "what-if" simulations and too procedural to be modified into decision-support software. A Canadian company, Carp Systems International of Kanata, Ontario, sells the Advanced Planning System (APS) to give the user DSS functionality using the data from existing MRPII systems.

sensitivity analysis Models that ask "what-if" questions repeatedly to determine the impact of changes in one or more factors on outcomes.

Table 16.1   Examples of Decision-Support Systems

Organization	DSS Application
American Airlines	Price and route selection
Equico Capital Corporation	Investment evaluation
General Accident Insurance	Customer buying patterns and fraud detection
Bank of America	Customer profiles
Frito-Lay, Inc.	Price, advertising, and promotion selection
Burlington Coat Factory	Store location and inventory mix
National Gypsum	Corporate planning and forecasting
Southern Railway	Train dispatching and routing
Texas Oil and Gas Corporation	Evaluation of potential drilling sites
United Airlines	Flight scheduling
U.S. Department of Defense	Defense contract analysis

APS allows a range of "what-if" processing by pulling the relevant data from the manufacturing software and performing calculations based on user-defined variables. After Hurricane Andrew hit south Florida in 1992, Trane's Unitary Productions division in Fort Smith, Arkansas, was asked to quickly ship 114 five-ton air conditioning systems to small businesses in the affected area. Using APS, within minutes Trane's could determine not only how long it would take to build the units but also how the added production would affect its existing customer commitments. The company found that it was able to fit the added production in without disrupting existing orders. It delivered the units weeks before the competition did.

Pitney Bowes, the $3.3 billion business equipment manufacturer, uses the software to simulate supply changes. Pitney Bowes carries enough manufacturing inventory to satisfy demand for 30 days. Using APS, the firm asked to see the impact if it would reduce the inventory to 15 days. APS responded with an answer within five minutes, including an estimate of what Pitney Bowes would save. Similarly, Sikorsky Aircraft of Stratford, Connecticut, claims that over a three-year period, the company has been able to use this software to help halve its inventory even while its sales doubled.

APS is a complex piece of software costing from $150,000 to $1 million and requiring intensive computing power. It runs on an IBM RS/6000 workstation. As with any other software, users caution that APS (and similar packages) are only as good as the data. If the data are out of date or wrong, APS only allows the user to do wrong things more quickly (Rifkin, 1992).

The Egyptian Cabinet DSS

The Egyptian Cabinet is composed of the prime minister, thirty-two other ministers, and four ministerial-level committees with their staffs. Decision making here is, by its very nature, strategic because it involves questions of survival: balance of payments, deficit management, public sector performance, economic growth, and national defense.

Decision making at these high levels of governments, or corporations, is often portrayed as a rational decision process. But in fact, decision making involves managing issues that are forced on decision makers with varying and shifting priorities. Issues circulate continuously; they enter and exit through participants and are resolved in the sense that they dissolve or go away or are overtaken by other issues.

FIGURE 16.2

The cabinet decision-making process with IDSC.
Source: Reprinted with special permission from MIS Quarterly, Volume 12, Number 4, December 1988. Copyright 1988 by the Society for Information Management and the Management Information Systems Research Center at the University of Minnesota.

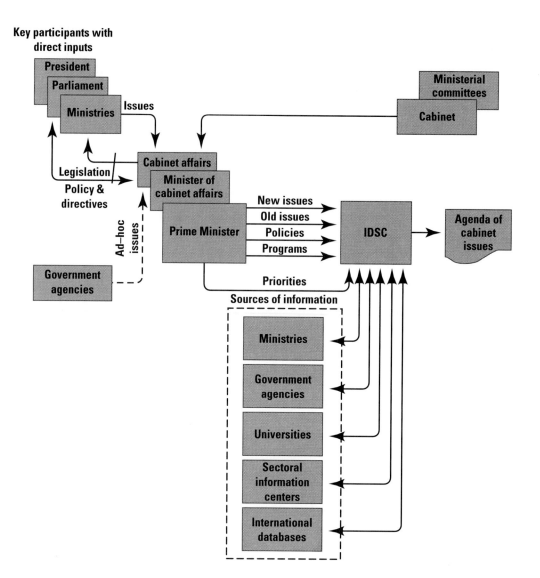

Key participants with direct inputs

The issues are themselves complex, poorly defined, interdependent, and related to many features of society. Information is voluminous but unreliable and qualitative.

In 1985, the Egyptian Cabinet developed a three-person Information and Decision Support Center (IDSC) to assist its own decision-making process (Figure 16.2). Today, 150 people work full time providing DSS services to the cabinet on critical issues. The IDSC system is based on a network of 110 PCs connected to a mainframe. Software includes standard desktop packages for database management, spreadsheet software, and FOCUS, a fourth-generation language and application generator, all of which have been fully converted to Arabic form. The electronic mail system is bilingual (Arabic/English).

One of the first uses of IDSC was to develop a new tariff structure to replace an inconsistent and complex structure that was thought to be impeding economic growth. The goal of the policy set forth by the cabinet was to create a consistent, simple tariff structure; increase revenues to the treasury; and promote economic growth without harming poor citizens. A PC based DSS model was built of the proposed new tariff structure, using a prototyping methodology.

The new policy activated many opposing groups. The Ministry of Industry, hoping to increase local production of auto parts, supported new tariffs on imported auto parts. This was supported as well by the Ministry of Economy, which supported local production. But the policy was opposed by the Ministry of Finance because it would reduce customs revenue.

The DSS was walked around, back and forth, from one ministry to another, making adjustments to the proposed tariffs, playing "what-if" games to see the impact of tariff changes on revenue and local employment. After one month of intensive effort, the groups reached agreement on the new tariff policy. Builders of the DSS felt the system reduced conflict by clarifying the trade-offs and potential impacts of tariff changes. Whereas early estimates of higher tariffs claimed $250 million in increased revenues would result, the DSS predicted $25 million. By 1987, the actual increased revenue was $28 million (El Sherif and El Sawy, 1988).

The Egyptian Cabinet's DSS illustrates the idea that a DSS is not only an application, but a generalized capability for addressing decision makers' needs. Unlike an MIS, a DSS does not simply involve a routine, steady flow of data, but instead can be flexibly responsive to new situations by using data and analytic models (even spreadsheets) to work through the consequences of decisions and assumptions.

Southern California Gas Company

Southern California Gas Company needed to be more competitive in a recently deregulated industry. It created a marketing department and used datamining to focus the company's marketing efforts. Southern California Gas created a data mart—a departmental data warehouse consisting of billing records combined with credit data from Equifax and U.S. census records. Using datamining techniques, the marketing department was able to identify a segment of customers most likely to sign up for a level payment plan.

Southern California Gas also used the system to decrease churn, or customers who were most likely to leave. Marketers learned that small, heating-only commercial customers were more sensitive to price increases than had been imagined. If the company were to raise its rates, this group of customers would switch to electric heating (mostly through space heaters). The company then performed a cost-benefit analysis to find out how much it cost to have such customers leave. Management decided that the company was not losing enough money from churn from this group of customers to warrant spending much money to keep them. It did, however, change its marketing approach to this group. It receives different literature that addresses the issue (Varney, 1996).

ShopKo Stores

ShopKo Stores, a $2 billion regional discounter, based in Green Bay, Wisconsin, competes head-to-head with Wal-Mart. The company started using datamining in about 1994 to discover cause-and-effect relationships between store items and customer buying habits. By using IBM's Intelligent Miner software across its advertising and merchandising departments, it discovered that customers who come in to purchase one product often buy another associated product, but that many associations are one-way streets. For example, a camera sale often triggers a film sale, but a film sale usually doesn't cause a camera sale.

ShopKo also learned that sales increased when merchandise was arranged in the store to match the way items were advertised in local circulars. Sometimes, however, the company ignores the results of datamining to maintain a high level of customer service. For example, ShopKo did increase sales by displaying baby formula next to baby clothes, but customers reported that they felt manipulated by that layout. ShopKo returned baby formula to its original location (Gerber, 1996).

In Chapter 2 we described Wal-Mart's strategic inventory replenishment system. Data from this system and from other sources are fed into Wal-Mart's data warehouse to feed data-driven decision-support systems. The Window on Technology describes some of these systems and their importance to the company.

Wal-Mart Mines for Details

At over 24 terabytes, Wal-Mart's data warehouse is the largest in the world. More than 30 applications run on the system, enabling the company to carefully analyze every cost and line item. Wal-Mart management can be more detailed than most of its competitors on what's going on with every product, in every store, every day—and act on it. The company's business strategy depends on having access to detailed data at every level.

The data warehouse contains point-of-sale, inventory, products in transit, market statistics, customer demographics, finance, product returns, and supplier performance data from Wal-Mart's 2900 stores. These data are analyzed in three broad areas of decision support: analyzing trends, managing inventory, and understanding customers. The information has helped Wal-Mart establish "personality traits" for each of its 3000 or so outlets, which can help managers make decisions about the product mix and presentation for each store.

Wal-Mart is starting to roll out a demand-forecasting application using neural network software and a 4000-processor parallel computer from Neo Vista Solutions Inc. The system maintains a year of data on the sales of 100,000 products. By examining individual items for individual stores, the system can create a seasonal sales profile of each item. This information will help the company predict which items will be needed in each store. Another application is market-basket analysis. Data are collected on items comprising a shopper's total purchase so that the company can analyze relationships and patterns in customer purchases. For example, Wal-Mart found that people who visit its stores on Thursdays to buy Huggies tend to purchase 19 additional items, while Thursday's beer buyers tend to buy only beer. Every Thursday Wal-Mart put Huggies on sale to entice customers to fill their shopping carts. Wal-Mart even changed its floor layout so that shoppers would bump into the 19 popular products.

Wal-Mart is working with Warner-Lambert Co. (the maker of Listerine) and several technology firms to create a collabora-

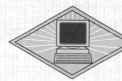

tive buyer–supplier system on the Internet that will improve the link between retail sales and manufacturing planning. The effort, called collaborative forecasting and replenishment (CFAR) could produce $179 billion in retail industry savings by cutting down idle inventory. Wal-Mart extracts data from its data warehouse relevant to Warner-Lambert product sales. The data are stored in Wal-Mart's CFAR server, which has been specifically configured to support collaborative forecasting. Wal-Mart buyers use a spreadsheet-like document with space for collaborative comments called a CFAR workbench to attach to the CFAR server so that they can take a first pass at a forecast for Listerine sales. A copy of the Listerine workbench appears automatically on Warner-Lambert's CFAR server. Warner-Lambert planners add their figures and comments, publishing the result for Wal-Mart to see. This process is repeated until Wal-Mart buyers and Warner-Lambert planners arrive at mutually acceptable figures. At that point, the workbench is finalized and shipped to Warner-Lambert's manufacturing planning system. The forecasts also factor in geographic and seasonal market trend and predicted store demands. When Wal-Mart and Warner-Lambert piloted CFAR for joint forecasting, they cut product supply cycle time for Listerine in half, from twelve weeks to six.

To Think About: How is Wal-Mart's data warehouse related to its business strategy? How does it support decision making? What business processes are affected?

Sources: "Mining the Largest Data Warehouse" in "*Data Mining: Plumbing the Depths of Corporate Databases,*" April 21, 1997; Bruce Caldwell, "Wal-Mart Ups the Pace," *InformationWeek,* December 9, 1996; and Charles B. Darling and J. William Semich, "Extreme Integration," *Datamation,* November 1996.

DSS can also be used as training instruments to teach managers how to make better decisions. The Window on Organizations describes how SmithKline Beecham uses simulation software that lets managers practice making decisions before they are faced with real-world decision making on the job.

Building DSS

Building a DSS is different from building a TPS or MIS. Developing a TPS or MIS results in systems that represent a response to a specific set of information needs. Development of DSS systems focuses on identifying a problem and a set of capabilities that users consider helpful in arriving at decisions about that problem. A DSS generally uses smaller amounts of data, does not need real-time transaction data, involves a smaller number of important users, and tends to employ more sophisticated analytic models than other systems. Because a DSS is customized to specific users and

Going to War over Competition

In some areas of life, such as sports and the military, we believe in the aphorism "practice makes perfect," and we put in a great effort honing our skills with nothing on the line. In other areas, such as parenting and business, we are expected to produce results without practice and often without much advanced learning. In parenting and business, all mistakes are for real and the learning that results can be expensive and even disastrous. Business has begun to understand, and so the idea of practice is beginning to catch on. One tool businesses use is computer simulation.

Business is taking a leaf from the pages of military manuals. The military regularly hold war games, attempting to give their staffs experience in warlike conditions. They also give personnel experience in working together as teams, in making quick decisions on their feet, and in facing the need to respond immediately to unexpected turns of events. Business now has software available that can simulate such conditions in the marketplace. Puerto Rican-born Adrian Cruz runs the Latin American unit for SmithKline Beecham, the $9 billion multinational pharmaceutical giant, and is a believer in simulations. Cruz, who was a decorated platoon leader in Vietnam, holds several simulations a year, using software developed by Advanced Competitive Strategies (ACS) of Portland, Oregon. His goals include practice and education, but in addition he hopes to create a sense of urgency and an esprit de corps among those who attend. As Cruz explained, "Nobody dies and no money is lost, but nobody comes out of a war game thinking the same way. You become more analytical, more comfortable by testing contingencies and scenarios." Sometimes he even achieves goals of immediate strategic importance.

ACS tailors its software for the specific client and for the specific simulation. For Cruz, ACS uses a "closed-loop" game which describes an established market with well-understood competitive dynamics. Such a model reflects actual conditions of the market in Mexico and of SmithKline's competitors. In 1996 SmithKline planned to introduce an important new consumer product into the rapidly growing Mexican market. Cruz decided on a "war game" prior to the introduction, spending more than $100,000 on preparation. Preparation included more than a month's time of one SmithKline manager to compile pertinent real-world data and feed them into the computer.

When the invited personnel arrived for the two-day simulation, they were divided into four teams, one representing SmithKline and one representing each of its three main competitors. Whatever move the SmithKline team made in introducing its product, the other three teams responded with the computer generating performance results based on the decisions of each team. To gain a foothold in the market, the SmithKline team tried a number of strategies, including lowering the product's price, changing packaging, and developing a new ad campaign.

When the four teams were developing their moves and countermoves, they used the computer to aid them in evaluating their actions and to project the results of their choices. In addition, from time to time Cruz threw in some surprises, such as devaluing the peso or making consumer behavior more price sensitive. The teams had to respond to these changes.

The results? Cruz certainly accomplished his goals. Teams came to understand the issues they will face when the new product is actually introduced. In addition, they gained confidence in their ability to deal with whatever will be thrown their way from the market or from each of the competitors. But the teams also came to a realization as to what strategy they needed to follow when introducing the new product. They agreed that if SmithKline should follow a strategy of price cutting, its established competitors will respond with massive price cuts, preventing SmithKline from gaining any kind of foothold in the market. Because the point of the strategy was not to trigger a price war, the teams decided to not launch a direct attack on the whole market. Instead, they agreed to position their new product as a niche product. They reasoned that if the company was only targeting a segment of the market, there would be less resistance from the competition because in the end they would lose more than SmithKline.

To Think About: *How did SmithKline Beecham's simulation software support decision making? How can using simulation systems help promote a firm's business strategy?*

Sources: Pete Carbonara, "Game Over," and David Diamond, "Business is War—So Lets Have a War Game," *Fast Company,* December–January 1997.

---

specific classes of decisions, it requires much greater user participation to develop. In addition, a DSS must be flexible and must evolve as the sophistication of users grows. Building a DSS must therefore use a changing, evolving method that is iterative. Iterative development utilizing prototyping is recommended (see Chapter 12).

Factors in DSS Success and Failure

As experience with DSS has grown, a number of factors have been identified as important to their success and failure. The success factors are not very different from those of the MIS and other systems. These factors are described in detail in Chapter 14. Several studies have noted that user training, involvement, and experience; top management's support; length of use; and novelty of the application were the most important factors in DSS success. *Success* is defined as perceived improvements in decision making and overall satisfaction with the DSS (Alavi and Joachimsthaler, 1992; Sanders and Courtney, 1985).

A smaller study of 34 DSS found that DSS orientation toward top management (assistance with making important decisions) and return on investment are the most important factors in the approval process for these systems (Meador and Keen, 1984; King, 1983). This important finding highlights what organizations are looking for when they develop DSS. Organizations need support for upper management decision making, which requires custom-built, flexible, and easy-to-use systems that address important organizational problems.

16.2 GROUP DECISION-SUPPORT SYSTEMS (GDSS)

The early work in DSS focused largely on supporting individual decision making. However, because so much work is accomplished in groups within organizations, during the late 1980s system developers and scholars began to focus on how computers can support group and organizational decision making. This work followed even earlier efforts to develop electronic aids to community and societal decision making in the 1970s, based largely on mainframes (see Laudon, 1977). As a result of the focus on computer support of group decision making, a new category of systems developed, known as the group decision-support system (GDSS).

What Is a GDSS?

group decision-support system (GDSS) An interactive computer-based system to facilitate the solution to unstructured problems by a set of decision makers working together as a group.

A **group decision-support system (GDSS)** is an interactive computer-based system to facilitate the solution of unstructured problems by a set of decision makers working together as a group (DeSanctis and Gallupe, 1987). The GDSS was developed in response to a growing concern over the quality and effectiveness of meetings. The underlying problems in group decision making have been the explosion of decision-maker meetings, the growing length of those meetings, and the increased number of attendees. Estimates on the amount of a manager's time spent in meetings range from 35 to 70 percent.

Meeting facilitators, organizational development professionals, and information systems scholars have been focusing on this issue and have identified a number of discrete meeting elements that need to be addressed (Grobowski et al., 1990; Kraemer and King, 1988; Nunamaker et al., 1991). Among these elements are the following:

1. *Improved preplanning,* to make meetings more effective and efficient.

2. *Increased participation,* so that all attendees will be able to contribute fully even if the number of attendees is large. Free riding (attending the meeting but not contributing) must also be addressed.

3. *Open, collaborative meeting atmosphere,* in which attendees from various organizational levels feel able to contribute freely. The lower-level attendees must be able to participate without fear of being judged by their management; higher-status participants must be able to participate without having their presence or ideas dominate the meeting and result in unwanted conformity.

4. *Criticism-free idea generation,* enabling attendees to contribute without undue fear of feeling personally criticized.

5. *Evaluation objectivity,* creating an atmosphere in which an idea will be evaluated on its merits rather than on the basis of the source of the idea.

6. *Idea organization and evaluation,* which require keeping the focus on the meeting objectives, finding efficient ways to organize the many ideas that can be generated in a brainstorming session, and evaluating those ideas not only on their merits but also within appropriate time constraints.

7. *Setting priorities and making decisions,* which require finding ways to encompass the thinking of all the attendees in making these judgments.

8. *Documentation of meetings* so that attendees will have as complete and organized a record of the meeting as may be needed to continue the work of the project.

9. *Access to external information,* which will allow significant, factual disagreements to be settled in a timely fashion, thus enabling the meeting to continue and be productive.

10. *Preservation of "organizational memory,"* so that those who do not attend the meeting can also work on the project. Often a project will include teams at different locations who will need to understand the content of a meeting at only one of the affected sites.

One response to the problems of group decision making has been the adoption of new methods of organizing and running meetings. Techniques such as facilitated meetings, brainstorming, and criticism-free idea generation have become popular and are now accepted as standard. Another response has been the application of technology to the problems resulting in the emergence of group decision-support systems.

Characteristics of GDSS

How can information technology help groups to arrive at decisions? Scholars have identified at least three basic elements of a GDSS: hardware, software tools, and people. *Hardware* refers first to the conference facility itself, including the room, the tables, and the chairs. Such a facility must be physically laid out in a manner that supports group collaboration. It must also include some electronic hardware, such as electronic display boards, as well as audiovisual and computer equipment.

A wide range of *software tools,* including tools for organizing ideas, gathering information, ranking and setting priorities, and other aspects of collaborative work are now being used to support decision-making meetings. We describe these tools in the next section. *People* refers not only to the participants but also to a trained facilitator and often to a staff that supports the hardware and software. Together these elements have led to the creation of a range of different kinds of GDSS, from simple electronic boardrooms to elaborate collaboration laboratories. In a collaboration laboratory, individuals work on their own desktop microcomputers. Their input is integrated on a file server and is viewable on a common screen at the front of the room; in most systems the integrated input is also viewable on the individual participant's screen. See Figure 16.3 for an illustration of an actual GDSS collaborative meeting room.

One can appreciate the potential value of a GDSS by examining the software tools. We describe the functions of several types of tools central to a full-blown collaboration laboratory. We then give an overview of a GDSS meeting so that you can understand its potential to support collaborative meetings. Finally, we examine how a GDSS affects the problems we have described, and its power to enhance group decision making.

GDSS Software Tools

Some features of the groupware tools for collaborative work described in Chapters 9 and 15 can be used to support group decision making. But a GDSS is considered more explicitly decision oriented and task oriented than groupware, as it focuses on

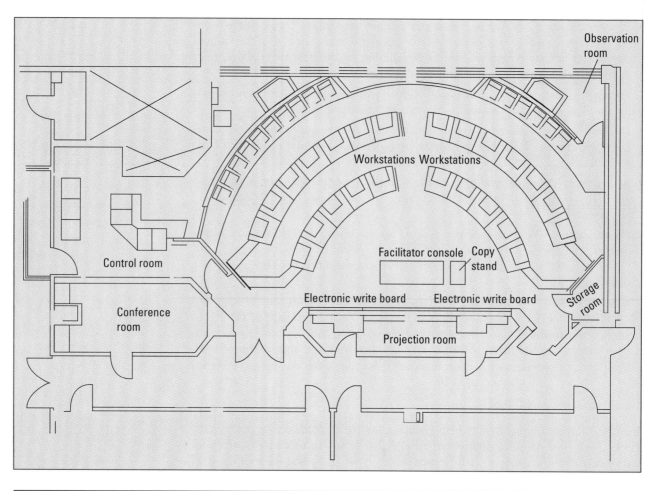

FIGURE 16.3

Illustration of PLEXSYS decision room. The large group room was opened in 1987, with 24 IBM PS/2 workstations. A gallery holds 18 observers. The room has 38 audio pick-up microphones and six video cameras with stereo audio. Two large-screen electronic displays and projectors permit playing of videotapes, discs, 35-mm slides, and computer graphics presentations.

Source: Reprinted with special permission from MIS Quarterly, *Volume 12, Number 4, December 1988. Copyright 1988 by the Society for Information Management and the Management Information Systems Research Center at the University of Minnesota.*

helping a group solve a problem or reach a decision (Dennis et al., 1988). Groupware is considered more communication oriented. Specific GDSS software tools include the following:

- *Electronic questionnaires* aid the organizers in pre-meeting planning by identifying issues of concern and by helping to ensure that key planning information is not overlooked.

- *Electronic brainstorming tools* allow individuals simultaneously and anonymously to contribute ideas on the topics of the meeting.

- *Idea organizers* facilitate the organized integration and synthesis of ideas generated during brainstorming.

- *Questionnaire tools* support the facilitators and group leaders as they gather information before and during the process of setting priorities.

- *Tools for voting or setting priorities* make available a range of methods from simple voting, to ranking in order, to a range of weighted techniques for setting priorities or voting.

- *Stakeholder identification and analysis tools* use structured approaches to evaluate the impact of an emerging proposal on the organization, and to identify

The Ventana Corporation demonstrates the features of its GroupSystems for Windows electronic meeting software, which helps people create, share, record, organize, and evaluate ideas in meetings, between offices, or around the world.

stakeholders and evaluate the potential impact of those stakeholders on the proposed project.

- *Policy formation tools* provide structured support for developing agreement on the wording of policy statements.

- *Group dictionaries* document group agreement on definitions of words and terms central to the project.

Additional tools are available, such as group outlining and writing tools, software that stores and reads project files, and software that allows the attendees to view internal operational data stored by the organization's production computer systems.

Overview of a GDSS Meeting

An **electronic meeting system (EMS)** is a type of collaborative GDSS that uses information technology to make group meetings more productive by facilitating communication as well as decision making. It supports any activity in which people come together, whether at the same place at the same time or in different places at different times (Dennis et al., 1988; Nunamaker et al., 1991). IBM has a number of EMSs installed at various sites. Each attendee has a workstation. The workstations are networked and are connected to the facilitator's console that serves as both the facilitator's workstation and control panel and the meeting's file server. All data that the attendees forward from their workstations to the group are collected and saved on the file server. The facilitator is able to project computer images onto the projection screen at the front center of the room. The facilitator also has an overhead projector available. Whiteboards are visible on either side of the projection screen. Many electronic meeting rooms are arranged in a semicircle and are tiered in legislative style to accommodate a larger number of attendees.

The facilitator controls the use of tools during the meeting, often selecting from a large tool box that is part of the organization's GDSS. Tool selection is part of the pre-meeting planning process. Which tools are selected depends on the subject matter, the goals of the meeting, and the facilitation methodology the facilitator will use.

electronic meeting system (EMS)
A collaborative GDSS that uses information technology to make group meetings more productive by facilitating communication as well as decision making. Supports meetings at the same place and time or in different places and times.

FIGURE 16.4

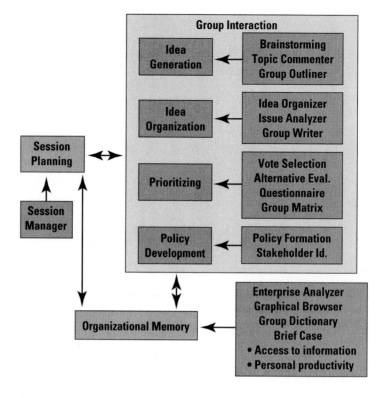

Group system tools. The sequence of activities and collaborative support tools used in an electronic meeting system (EMS) facilitates communication among attendees and generates a full record of the meeting.
Source: From Nunamaker, et al., "Electronic Meeting Systems to Support Group Work" in Communications of the ACM, *July, 1991. Copyright © 1991 Association For Computing Machinery.*

Attendees have full control over their own desktop computers. An attendee is able to view the agenda (and other planning documents), look at the integrated screen (or screens as the session progresses), use ordinary desktop PC tools (such as a word processor or a spreadsheet), tap into production data that have been made available, or work on the screen associated with the current meeting step and tool (such as a brainstorming screen). However, no one can view anyone else's screens so participants' work is confidential until they release it to the file server for integration with the work of others. All input to the file server is anonymous—at each step everyone's input to the file server (brainstorming ideas, idea evaluation and criticism, comments, voting, etc.) can be seen by all attendees on the integrated screens, but no information is available to identify the source of specific inputs. Attendees enter their data simultaneously rather than in round-robin fashion as is done in meetings that have little or no electronic systems support.

Figure 16.4 shows the sequence of activities at a typical EMS meeting. For each activity it also indicates the type of tools used and the output of those tools. During the meeting all input to the integrated screens is saved on the file server. As a result, when the meeting is completed, a full record of the meeting (both raw material and resultant output) is available to the attendees and can be made available to anyone else with a need for access.

How GDSS Can Enhance Group Decision Making

GDSSs are still relatively new. Nonetheless, scholars and business specialists have studied these systems, and the systems are now being used more widely, so that we are able at least to understand some of their benefits and even evaluate some of the tools. We look again at how a GDSS affects the 10 group meeting issues raised earlier.

1. *Improved preplanning.* Electronic questionnaires, supplemented by word processors, outlining software, and other desktop PC software, can structure planning, thereby improving it. The availability of the planning information at the actual meeting also can serve to enhance the quality of the meeting. Experts seem to feel that these tools add significance and emphasis to meeting preplanning.

2. *Increased participation.* Studies show that in traditional decision-making meetings without GDSS support the optimal meeting size is three to five attendees. Beyond that size, the meeting process begins to break down. Using GDSS software, studies show the meeting size can increase while productivity also increases. One reason for this is that attendees contribute simultaneously rather than one at a time, and can thus make more efficient use of the meeting time. Free riding is apparently decreased too, perhaps because the one or two individuals who are not working will stand out when everyone else in the room is busy at workstations. Interviews of GDSS meeting attendees indicate that the quality of participation is higher than in traditional meetings.

3. *Open, collaborative meeting atmosphere.* A GDSS contributes to a more collaborative atmosphere in several ways. First, anonymity of input is essentially guaranteed. Individuals need not be afraid of being judged by their boss for contributing a possibly offbeat idea. Anonymity also reduces or eliminates the deadening effect that often occurs when high-status individuals contribute. Even the numbing pressures of social cues are reduced or eliminated.

4. *Criticism-free idea generation.* Anonymity ensures that attendees can contribute without fear of personally being criticized or of having their ideas rejected because of the identity of the contributor. Several studies show that interactive GDSS meetings generate more ideas and more satisfaction with those ideas than verbally interactive meetings (Nunamaker et al., 1991). GDSS can help reduce unproductive interpersonal conflict (Miranda and Bostrum, 1993–1994).

5. *Evaluation objectivity.* Anonymity prevents criticism of the source of ideas, thus supporting an atmosphere in which attendees focus on evaluating the ideas themselves. The same anonymity allows participants to detach themselves from their own ideas and so they are able to view them from a critical perspective. Evidence suggests that evaluation in an anonymous atmosphere increases the free flow of critical feedback and even stimulates the generation of new ideas during the evaluation process.

6. *Idea organization and evaluation.* GDSS software tools used for this purpose are structured and are based on methodology. They usually allow individuals each to organize and then submit their results to the group (still anonymously). The group then iteratively modifies and develops the organized ideas until a document is completed. Attendees have generally viewed this approach as productive.

7. *Setting priorities and making decisions.* Anonymity helps lower-level participants have their positions taken into consideration along with the higher-level attendees.

8. *Documentation of meetings.* Evidence at IBM indicates that postmeeting use of the data is crucial. Attendees use the data to continue their dialogues after the meetings, to discuss the ideas with those who did not attend, and even to make presentations (Grobowski et al., 1990). Some tools even enable the user to zoom in to more detail on specific information.

9. *Access to external information.* Often a great deal of meeting time is devoted to factual disagreements. More experience with GDSS will indicate whether GDSS technology reduces this problem.

10. *Preservation of "organizational memory."* Specific tools have been developed to facilitate access to the data generated during a GDSS meeting, allowing nonattendees to locate needed information after the meeting. The documentation of a meeting by one group at one site has also successfully been used as input to another meeting on the same project at another site.

Experience to date suggests that GDSS meetings can be more productive, make more efficient use of time, and produce the desired results in fewer meetings. One problem with understanding the value of GDSS is their complexity. A GDSS can be configured in an almost infinite variety of ways. In addition, the effectiveness of the

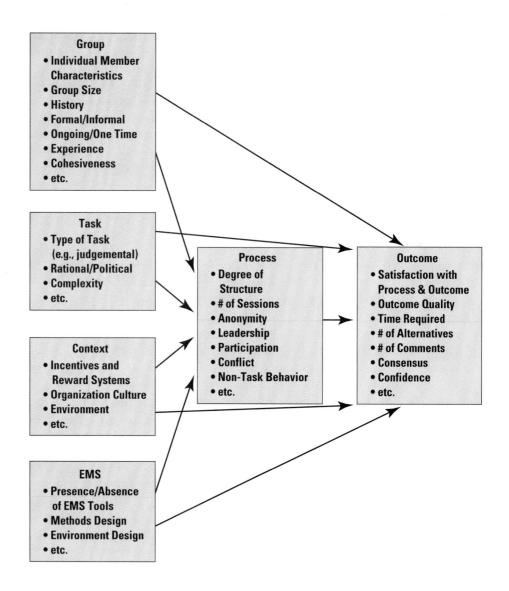

FIGURE 16.5

The research model for electronic meetings. For effective group meetings, include the nature of the group, the task to be accomplished, and the context of the meeting in the design of the EMS.

Source: Reprinted with special permission from MIS Quarterly, *Volume 12, Number 4, December 1988. Copyright 1988 by the Society for Information Management and the Management Information Systems Research Center at the University of Minnesota.*

Group
- Individual Member Characteristics
- Group Size
- History
- Formal/Informal
- Ongoing/One Time
- Experience
- Cohesiveness
- etc.

Task
- Type of Task (e.g., judgemental)
- Rational/Political
- Complexity
- etc.

Context
- Incentives and Reward Systems
- Organization Culture
- Environment
- etc.

EMS
- Presence/Absence of EMS Tools
- Methods Design
- Environment Design
- etc.

Process
- Degree of Structure
- # of Sessions
- Anonymity
- Leadership
- Participation
- Conflict
- Non-Task Behavior
- etc.

Outcome
- Satisfaction with Process & Outcome
- Outcome Quality
- Time Required
- # of Alternatives
- # of Comments
- Consensus
- Confidence
- etc.

tools will partially depend on the effectiveness of the facilitator, the quality of the planning, the cooperation of the attendees, and the appropriateness of tools selected for different types of meetings. GDSS can enable groups to exchange more information, but can't always help participants process the information effectively or reach better decisions (Dennis, 1996).

Researchers have noted that the design of an electronic meeting system is only one of a number of contingencies that affect the outcome of group meetings. Other factors, including the nature of the group, the task, the cultural setting, the manner in which the problem is presented to the group, and the context also affect the process of group meetings and meeting outcomes (Dennis et al., 1988 and 1996; Nunamaker et al., 1991; Watson, Ho, and Raman, 1994). Figure 16.5 graphically illustrates these relationships.

16.3 EXECUTIVE SUPPORT SYSTEMS (ESS)

We have described how DSS and GDSS help managers make unstructured and semistructured decisions. **Executive support systems (ESS)** also help managers with unstructured problems, focusing on the information needs of senior management. Combining data from both internal and external sources, ESS creates a generalized computing and communications environment that can be focused and applied to a changing array of problems. ESS helps senior executives monitor organizational performance, track activities of competitors, spot problems, identify opportunities, and forecast trends.

The Role of ESS in the Organization

Prior to ESS, it was common for executives to receive numerous fixed-format reports, often hundreds of pages every month (or even every week). The first systems developed specifically for executives in the early 1980s were mainframe systems designed to replace that paper, delivering the same data to the executive in days rather than in weeks. Executives had access to the same data, only it was on-line in the form of reports. Such systems were known as senior management **briefing books.** Using a briefing book, executives usually could **drill down** (move from a piece of summary data down to lower and lower levels of detail). Briefing books did not spread widely through the executive suites. The data that could be provided by briefing books were limited and the briefing books were too inflexible.

By the late 1980s, analysts found ways to bring together data from throughout the organization and allow the manager to select, access, and tailor them easily as needed. Today, an ESS is apt to include a range of easy-to-use desktop analytical tools. Use of the systems has migrated down several organizational levels so that the executive and any subordinates are able to look at the same data in the same way.

Today's systems try to avoid the problem of data overload so common in paper reports because the data can be filtered or viewed in graphic format (if the user so chooses). Systems have maintained the ability to drill down (even starting from a graph).

One limitation in an ESS is that it uses data from systems designed for very different purposes. Often data that are critical to the senior executive are simply not there. For example, sales data coming from an order entry transaction processing system are not linked to marketing information, a linkage the executive would find useful. External data are now much more available in many ESS systems. Executives need a wide range of external data, from current stock market news to competitor information, industry trends, and even projected legislative action. Through their ESS, many managers have access to news services, financial market databases, economic information, and whatever other public data they may require. Managers can also use the Internet for this purpose, as described in the Window on Management.

ESS today includes tools for modeling and analysis. For example, many ESS use Excel or other spreadsheets as the heart of their analytical tool base. With only a minimum of experience, most managers find they can use these common software packages to create graphic comparisons of data by time, region, product, price range, and so on. Costlier systems include more sophisticated specialty analytical software. (While DSS uses such tools primarily for modeling and analysis in a fairly narrow range of decision situations, ESS uses them primarily to provide status information about organizational performance.)

Developing ESS

ESS are executive systems, and executives create special development problems (we introduced this topic in Section 16.1). Because executives' needs change so rapidly, most executive support systems are developed through prototyping. A major difficulty for developers is that high-level executives expect success the first time. Developers must be certain that the system will work before they demonstrate it to the user. In addition, the initial system prototype must be one that the executive can learn very rapidly. Finally, if executives find that the ESS offers no added value, they will reject it.

One area that merits special attention is the determination of executive information requirements. ESSs need to have some facility for environmental scanning. A key information requirement of managers at the strategic level is the capability to

executive support system (ESS)
Information system at the strategic level of an organization designed to address unstructured decision making through advanced graphics and communications.

briefing books On-line data in the form of fixed-format reports for executives; part of early ESS.

drill down The ability to move from summary data down to lower and lower levels of detail.

Netting Information on Your Competition

Keeping track of the competition is probably as old as business itself. Companies are always anxious to learn anything they can about a change in strategy, the release of new products, a change in management, or anything else that will help get the jump on them. In the past, gathering competitive intelligence involved lots of legwork and reams of paper. Today, managers can find an astonishing amount of competitive intelligence without leaving their desktops—much of it for free—by using the Internet.

The Internet is quick to use, easy to search, and offers a breathtaking array of information. Many companies now have Web sites, enabling you to monitor them regularly. Companies often place more on their Web sites than they release publicly in any other way, making them a potentially rich source of information or at least providing clues to what is happening. Most sites also contain hypertext links to other related sites, enabling researchers to follow many threads in their search for important information. Net search engines allow the researcher to locate a great deal of information on corporate executives, often including some of their speeches and articles. Government sites on the Web provide public documents, such as patent applications, financial filings, and documents filed with regulatory agencies, that may be of value.

Usenet discussion groups often become a gold mine in the search for meaningful data. Usenet groups are specialized, allowing researchers to focus on specific issues of interest to the target companies. Participating in or just monitoring them might tell you much about your competition, and they are fully public. They even make available names and e-mail addresses to anyone interested. A new search tool, Deja News, allows individuals to search news groups by e-mail address, enabling researchers to determine which news groups the target person reads and all postings of that person to those groups. Thus, researchers can target an area of interest, locate individuals from companies about which they are interested, and trace all discussions of those people. Usenet groups can also lead researchers to individuals who have similar interests as themselves and so can be of help.

Benn R. Konsynski, Emory University business professor, tells of a company who visited a competitor's site and found a preview of a competitor's promotional campaign at a trade show coming in two weeks. The company was able rapidly to revise its own plans and outclass its competitor at the trade show. Staff at Fuld & Co. once noticed that a high-technology hardware producer was searching via Usenet for software engineers to hire. Fuld was able to conclude that the hardware company was making a strategic shift in its product line.

Many companies also keep up with customers and even business partners via the Net. Proper research can enable you to be knowledgeable about the issues your customers are facing. BellSouth Corporation's Leadership Institute started a market dynamics program that teaches executives how to study customers using the Internet before calling them.

One tactic being used by more companies is to have their information technology group build Web pages for their employees which include links that would be helpful in gathering information about competitors or customers. Thus, those with a need to know can gather much of the information themselves without delay and with no need to rely on others. For example, BBN Systems and Technologies built a Web page with links to statistics, published news accounts, press releases, Federal Communications Commission documents, a map of cable TV provider locations, and information about interactive cable TV trials. BBN employees could use this Web page to do their own research on the Internet and cable television from their desktops.

One warning about the process, however. Collecting data is only the beginning. The data will usually come in bits and pieces that require a major analytical effort. In addition, gathering data this way does have its problems. The information gathered on the Net is often stale, incomplete, tainted, or from questionable sources. Moreover, the huge quantities of data found on the Net, most of it irrelevant, can make the task of gathering useful information daunting and tedious. In addition, companies conducting this research under their corporate Internet account can be identified. The way around this last problem is to not use a corporate Net account but rather an account from a commercial service provider and use an e-mail address that cannot be linked to the firm.

To Think About: How important do you think competitive intelligence is to senior management and why?•How does it support decision making? What are the management benefits of using the Web for this purpose?

Sources: Anne Stuart, "Click & Dagger," *Webmaster,* July/August 1996.

detect signals of problems in the organizational environment that indicate strategic threats and opportunities (Walls et al., 1992). The ESS needs to be designed so that both external and internal sources of information can be used for environmental scanning purposes. The Critical Success Factor methodology for determining information requirements (see Chapter 11) is recommended for this purpose. Table 16.2 suggests steps for eliciting such requirements.

Because ESS could potentially give top executives the capability of examining other managers' work without their knowledge, there may be some resistance to ESS at lower levels of the organization. Implementation of ESS should be carefully managed to neutralize such opposition (see Chapter 14).

Cost justification presents a different type of problem with an ESS. Because much of an executive's work is unstructured, how does one quantify benefits for a system that primarily supports such unstructured work? An ESS is often justified in advance by the intuitive feeling that it will pay for itself (Watson et al., 1991). If ESS benefits can ever be quantified, it is only after the system is operational.

Benefits of ESS

How do executive support systems benefit managers? As we stated earlier, it is difficult at best to cost-justify an executive support system. Nonetheless, interest in these systems is growing, so it is essential to examine some of the potential benefits scholars have identified.

Table 16.2   Steps for Determining ESS Requirements
1. Identify a set of issue-generating critical events.
2. Elicit from the executive his assessment of the impact of the critical events on his goals and derive a set of critical issues.
3. Elicit from the executive three to five indicators which can be used to track each critical issue.
4. Elicit from the executive a list of potential information sources for the indicators.
5. Elicit from the executive exception heuristics for each indicator.

Reprinted by permission of Joseph G. Walls, George R. Widmeyer, and Omar A. El Sawy, "Building an Information System Design Theory for Vigilant EIS," *Information Systems Research* Vol. 3, No. 1 (March 1992), p. 56, The Institute of Management Sciences.

Comshare's Commander Decision Web system provides executives with easy-to-use graphics, planning, and financial analysis tools for scanning the external environment and for analyzing the performance of their firm. Decision Web users can drill down into a multi-dimensional database.

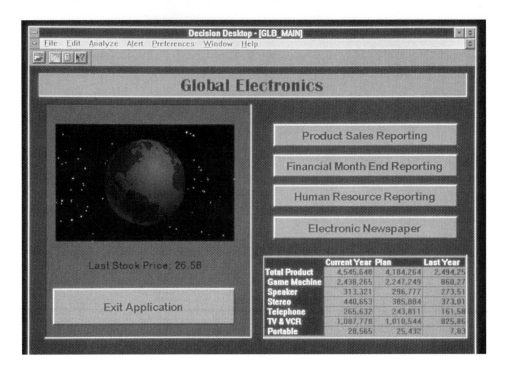

Much of the value of ESS is found in their flexibility. These systems put data and tools in the hands of executives without addressing specific problems or imposing solutions. Executives are free to shape the problems as they need, using the system as an extension of their own thinking processes. These are not decision-making systems; they are tools to aid executives in making decisions.

The most visible benefit of ESS is their ability to analyze, compare, and highlight trends. The easy use of graphics allows the user to look at more data in less time with greater clarity and insight than paper-based systems can provide. In the past, executives obtained the same information by taking up days and weeks of their staffs' valuable time. By using ESS, those staffs and the executives themselves are freed up for the more creative analysis and decision making in their jobs. ESS capabilities for drilling down and highlighting trends may also enhance the quality of such analysis and can speed up decision making (Leidner and Elam, 1993–1994).

Executives are using ESS to monitor performance more successfully in their own areas of responsibility. Some are also using these systems to monitor key performance indicators. The timeliness and availability of the data result in needed actions being identified and taken earlier. Problems can be handled before they become too damaging; opportunities can also be identified earlier.

Executive support systems can and do change the workings of organizations. Immediate access to so much data allows executives to better monitor activities of lower units reporting to them. That very monitoring ability often allows decision making to be decentralized and to take place at lower operating levels. Executives are often willing to push decision making further down into the organization as long as they can be assured that all is going well. ESS can enable them to get that assurance. A well-designed ESS could dramatically improve management performance and increase upper management's span of control.

We will close our examination of executive support systems by looking at actual examples of ESS in use.

Examples of ESS

To illustrate the various ways in which ESS can enhance management decision making, we now describe three executive support systems, one for private industry and two for the public sector. These systems were developed for very different reasons and serve their organizations in different ways.

Pratt & Whitney

Pratt & Whitney is a multibillion-dollar corporation located in East Hartford, Connecticut, whose Commercial Engine Business (CEB) produces jet engines. The firm's executives view customer service and product performance as the heart of their business and therefore the heart of their strategic plan to expand their market share. Walt Dempsey, a member of the company's business management and planning department, launched a study to assess the information needs that would support their strategic plan. The study led to the purchase of Commander EIS, a leading ESS package from Comshare. Commander EIS features colorful presentations and a pictorial menu that can be learned intuitively, with variances and exceptions highlighted in color. Users can access data with a touch screen, a mouse, or a keyboard and they can zoom in for deeper levels of detail either by navigating on their own or by following predefined paths.

Implementation began with a prototype built for the president of CEB, Selwyn Berson. Commander EIS allows Berson to track key quality and reliability measures for each jet engine model by customer. The data are shown from existing production systems and provide information on reliability, spare engine and parts availability, and deliveries. Using this system, CEB is able to answer customers' questions regarding repair status and can project how long repairs will take. Berson and others are able to drill down to determine reasons for repairs on specific engines. They also are capable of drilling down to specific data on service to an individual customer. Thus, CEB executives are able to determine where quality improvements need to be made in terms of both customer service and engine quality. CEB's ESS is helping them to meet their strategic plan objectives. The system was originally used by about 25 senior executives, although Pratt & Whitney expects the number of users to grow to over 200 ("The New Role," January 1992).

The United States General Services Administration

The General Services Administration (GSA) manages the vast real estate holdings of the United States government. In a period of tight federal budget restraints and as part of Vice President Gore's "reinventing government" initiatives, the organization needed to find ways to optimize the use of the government's multibillion-dollar inventory of 16,000 properties worldwide. Yet GSA managers facing this challenge had no system that would support them by making easily available to them the 4 gigabytes of data stored in their computers. The data were available only in old-fashioned printed reports and through slow, expensive custom programming. Analysis of the data was nearly impossible. GSA's response was GAMIS (Glenn Asset Management Information System), an executive support system based primarily on Lotus Notes that literally puts the needed data and analysis at the fingertips of the GSA's nontechnical managers.

The main purpose of the system was to give management quick and easy views of the organization's assets. Managers now can easily use ad hoc queries and perform "what-if" analysis, receiving the results on screen, in graphics format when desired. After indicating a specific office building, for example, the user will be offered 13 choices of data on that building, such as who occupies it, its financials, information on the congressional district it is in (if it is in the United States), and even a scanned photograph of the building. The data can be accessed via geographic information system (GIS) software from MapInfo Corp. (see Chapter 7). Through this software interface, the user begins with a national map and drills down into regional and city maps that show detail on location and type of property. Another click of the mouse and the user will pull up all the data on that piece of property. Users can limit the data at the outset, specifying, for example, that they want to look only at Justice

Department properties with more than 50,000 square feet of floor space. All data are available to about 100 GSA employees in Washington, while about 50 employees in each of the 10 regions have access to all data for their own region. Washington employees also have available a database of commercial properties with rental space available.

With GAMIS, nontechnical managers can access and analyze gigabytes of information that were formerly available only via printouts and custom programming. The system has received high marks from many officials, including John Glenn, Democratic senator from Ohio and long a vocal critic of the GSA's antiquated computer system. When Glenn first saw the system demonstrated, he was reported to have been so impressed that the GSA named the system after him. Observers have also praised the system because it was built from off-the-shelf software, making it quick and inexpensive to develop, providing high returns with minimum investments (Anthes, 1994).

New York State Office of General Services

The New York State Office of General Services (OGS) is responsible for servicing other state agencies throughout New York. Its services include (but are not limited to) design, construction, and maintenance of state buildings, food and laundry services to both correctional facilities and health-related institutions, statewide vehicle management, and centralized printing. With this diversity of services, an annual budget well over $500 million, and more than 4000 employees, executive oversight was a nightmare. Until 1986, OGS automatically received annual budget increases in line with inflation rates. Budget deficits were made up through supplemental allocations by the legislature. OGS felt no pressures to improve efficiency or stay within its budget. That changed in 1986 when a new administrative head of the agency was appointed. He decided that the organization had to operate in a more efficient, effective, and responsive manner. He also wanted to avoid year-end deficits. These objectives required better management at the top.

The first module of a new OGS ESS was implemented in 1988. The system allows the executives to monitor status by program, comparing budget with actual expenditures and showing estimated expenditures through the remainder of the fiscal year. Management can drill down to see specific details in any category. The system contains only raw data, allowing the users great flexibility in aggregating and analyzing it to meet their needs. For example, users are able to view a single expense category by month across organizations, or view several months of expenses for a given unit. Because the raw data are there, the executives can drill down to the source. The system includes exception reporting so that budget problems are highlighted and detected early. Executives are also using the system to compare budgetary control by units to spot personnel performance problems.

Because the system was developed for a government agency, the cost was of more than normal concern—the system had to be built inexpensively. The system uses ordinary PCs networked with the agency's mainframe and off-the-shelf, standard, inexpensive software tools. The total cost was less than $100,000. The system is menu driven and very easy to use. New users are trained through a 30-minute demonstration, and experience has shown that this is all that they need. No user manual is available.

One interesting byproduct of the system has been the need to develop productivity measures. Future development will focus on the area of performance analysis, attempting to answer such questions as how many people are required to work in specific units. The ESS called for OGS to measure something that it had never measured before. The work of developing these measures should in itself contribute to the drive for more efficiency (Mohan et al., 1990). This ESS is helping the Office of General Services enhance management control.

Management is responsible for determining where management support systems can make their greatest contribution to organizational performance and for allocating the resources to build them. At the same time, management needs to work closely with system builders to make sure that these systems effectively capture their information requirements and decision processes.

Management support systems can improve organizational performance by speeding up decision making or improving the quality of management decisions themselves. However, some of these decision processes may not be clearly understood. A management support system will be most effective when system builders have a clear idea of its objectives, the nature of the decisions to be supported, and how the system will actually support decision making.

Systems to support management decision making can be developed with a range of technologies, including the use of large databases, modeling tools, graphics tools, datamining and analysis tools, and electronic meeting technology. Identifying the right technology for the decision or decision process to be supported is a key technology decision.

For Discussion: As a manager or user of information systems, what would you need to know to participate in the design and use of a DSS or an ESS? Why?

MANAGEMENT

ORGANIZATION

TECHNOLOGY

SUMMARY

1. Define a decision-support system (DSS) and a group decision-support system (GDSS). A decision-support system (DSS) is an interactive system under user control that combines data, sophisticated analytical models and tools, and user-friendly software into a single powerful system that can support semistructured or unstructured decision making. There are two kinds of DSS: model-driven DSS and data-driven DSS. A group decision-support system (GDSS) is an interactive computer-based system to facilitate the solution of unstructured problems by a set of decision makers working together as a group rather than individually.

2. Describe the components of decision-support systems and group decision-support systems. The components of a DSS are the DSS database, the DSS software system and the user interface. The DSS database is a collection of current or historical data from a number of applications or groups that can be used for analysis. The DSS software system consists of OLAP and data mining tools or mathematical and analytical models that are used for analyzing the data in the database. The user interface allows users to interact with the DSS software tools directly.

Group decision-support systems (GDSS) have hardware, software, and people components. Hardware components consist of the conference room facilities, including seating arrangements and computer and other

electronic hardware. Software components include tools for organizing ideas, gathering information, ranking and setting priorities, and documenting meeting sessions. People components include participants, a trained facilitator, and staff to support the hardware and software.

3. Explain how decision-support systems and group decision-support systems can enhance decision making. Both DSS and GDSS support steps in the process of arriving at decisions. DSS provides results of model-based or data-driven analysis that help managers design and evaluate alternatives and monitor the progress of the solution that was adopted. GDSS helps decision makers meeting together to arrive at a decision more efficiently and are especially useful for increasing the productivity of meetings larger than four or five people. However, the effectiveness of GDSS is contingent on the nature of the group, the task, and the context of the meeting.

4. Describe the capabilities of executive support systems (ESS). Executive support systems (ESS) help managers with unstructured problems that occur at the strategic level of management. ESS provides data from both internal and external sources and provides a generalized computing and communications environment that can be focused and applied to a changing array of problems. ESS helps senior executives spot problems, identify opportunities, and forecast trends. These systems can filter out extraneous details for high-level overviews, or they can drill down to provide senior managers with detailed transaction data if required.

5. Describe the benefits of executive support systems. ESS helps senior managers analyze, compare, and highlight trends so that they more easily may monitor organizational performance or identify strategic problems and opportunities. ESS may increase the span of control of senior management and allow decision making to be decentralized and to take place at lower operating levels.

KEY TERMS

Decision-support system (DSS)	DSS database	Group decision-support system (GDSS)	Executive support system (ESS)
Model-driven DSS	DSS software system	Electronic meeting system (EMS)	Briefing books
Data-driven DSS	Model		Drill down
Datamining	Sensitivity analysis		

REVIEW QUESTIONS

1. What is a decision-support system (DSS)? How does it differ from a management information system (MIS)?

2. How can a DSS support unstructured or semistructured decision making?

3. What is the difference between a data-driven DSS and a model-driven DSS? Give examples.

4. What are the three basic components of a DSS? Briefly describe each.

5. In what ways is building decision-support systems different from building traditional MIS systems?

6. What is a group decision-support system (GDSS)? How does it differ from a DSS?

7. What are the three underlying problems in group decision making that have led to the development of GDSS?

8. Describe the three elements of a GDSS.

9. Name five GDSS software tools.

10. What is an electronic meeting system (EMS)?

11. For each of the three underlying problems in group decision making referred to in question 7, describe one or two ways GDSS can contribute to a solution.

12. Define and describe the capabilities of an executive support system.

13. Define *briefing books*. Explain why they were not adequate to support executive decision making.

14. In what ways is building executive support systems different from building traditional MIS systems?

15. What are the benefits of ESS? How do these systems enhance managerial decision making?

GROUP PROJECT

With three or four of your classmates, identify several groups in your university that could benefit from a GDSS. Design a GDSS for one of those groups, describing its hardware, software, and people elements. Present your findings to the class.

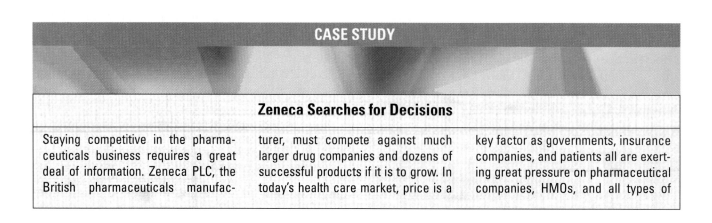

CASE STUDY

Zeneca Searches for Decisions

Staying competitive in the pharmaceuticals business requires a great deal of information. Zeneca PLC, the British pharmaceuticals manufacturer, must compete against much larger drug companies and dozens of successful products if it is to grow. In today's health care market, price is a key factor as governments, insurance companies, and patients all are exerting great pressure on pharmaceutical companies, HMOs, and all types of health care companies to lower their prices. To the deliverers of health care services, lower prices mean they must have lower costs. While remaining profitable, Zeneca must be able to compete with lower costs, while being more aggressive, creative, and innovative than its competitors in marketing its products.

Zeneca's U.S. facility in Wilmington, Delaware, has no shortage of data. In the early 1990s its IBM mainframe already held 6 million records which were the source of the six-inch thick reports that were distributed monthly to 200 marketing and sales managers. The paper reports contained current and historical details about customers, products, contracts, drug pricing, and sales. Given their size, the reports required great patience and perseverance to locate and identify specific information needed by a user. According to senior systems engineer Keith Magay, "It could take as long as two days for a manager to find the pertinent data" because of the size of the paper reports. Once the needed data were located (if they were), they were still paper-based static data and difficult to use and analyze.

Yet use of marketing and sales data is vital to Zeneca if it is to compete successfully. For example, Zeneca's prostate cancer treatment drug, Zolodex, has been outsold by its more expensive competitor, Lupron. Given the pressures by their customers to lower costs, one would expect that Zolodex would be the leader rather than Lupron. But Zeneca managers were only able to find out which drug was selling the most through analysis of their stored data, and that was a most daunting task when it was delivered in monthly paper reports.

To address the problem, Zeneca management decided to build a decision-support system which would enable managers to mine the data quickly. The system, known as ZICS (Zeneca Integrated Contracting System), draws its data from multiple mainframe databases as if those databases were a single data warehouse. Marketing and sales managers gain access to the data through their desktop computers or portable laptops. They can easily obtain information on account types, customers, product classes, contract terms, prescription drug pricing, and sales and contract histories.

The system itself is sophisticated, using a new technology known as online analytical processing (OLAP) that enables users to analyze multiple factors simultaneously. Zeneca business managers can obtain a multidimensional view of data to manipulate product and customer information. Because the system is interactive and supports complex many-to-many comparisons, users can find indirect correlations that would otherwise not be visible. The analysis takes place on-line and interactively. Users can view the data from several perspectives, including by product, by account type, or by broad market segment. A manager might tap into the system to see how much of a given prescription drug an HMO purchased over six months. The manager could click on a cell for the account name, then click on other cells to view the time period and sales information, then click on still other cells to view the products. The manager could use menu-based navigational tools to shop around for better data comparisons.

In 1995, using this system, managers at Zeneca discovered that Zolodex was being outsold by Lupron. Sales managers were then able to pull together sales data by customer so they would be able to demonstrate to their customers how many tens of thousands of dollars they could save by purchasing Zolodex rather than Lupron. According to Bob Bogle, Zeneca's vice president of information systems, "With this kind of system, we can analyze large volumes of data in ways that let us reach intelligent competitive decisions." The company intends to use the data to help its staff demonstrate to customers how a contract with Zeneca can increase the customers' profits. ZICS cost Zeneca only about $30,000 to build, although they also had to pay $200,000 for the underlying DSS software. However, that software can be used as the basis for other decision-support systems, and ZICS has garnered such glowing reports from its users that the company planned to build others in 1996, including one to serve their 27 corporate account managers and another to support the company's 50 national managers. ■

Sources: Stephen D. Moore, "Zeneca Says Profit Jumped Last Year; Warns About Costs," *The Wall Street Journal*, March 12, 1997; and Bronwyn Fryer, "Zeneca Take Its Medicine," *InformationWeek*, March 18, 1996.

Case Study Questions

1. What problems did Zeneca face in trying to make good decisions?

2. What was Zeneca's business strategy and how was decision making related to it?

3. What kind of decision-support system did Zeneca develop? What kinds of decisions did the DSS support?

4. What management, organization, and technology issues had to be addressed when building the new system?

REFERENCES

Alavi, Maryam, and Erich A. Joachimsthaler. "Revisiting DSS Implementation Research: A Meta-Analysis of the Literature and Suggestions for Researchers." *MIS Quarterly* 16, no. 1 (March 1992).

Anthes, Gary H. "Notes System Sends Federal Property Data Nationwide." *Computerworld* (August 8, 1994).

Bonzcek, R. H., C. W. Holsapple, and A. B. Whinston. "Representing Modeling Knowledge with First Order Predicate Calculus." *Operations Research* 1 (1982).

Brachman, Ronald J., Tom Khabaza, Willi Kloesgen, Gregory Piatetsky-Shapiro, and Evangelos Simoudis. "Mining Business Databases." *Communications of the ACM* 39, no. 11 (November 1996).

Chidambaram, Laku. "Relational Development in Computer-Supported Groups." *MIS Quarterly* 20, no. 2 (June 1996).

Chidambaram, Laku, Robert P. Bostrom, and Bayard E. Wynne. "A Longitudinal Study of the Impact of Group Decision Support Systems on Group Development." *Journal of Management Information Systems* 7, no. 3 (Winter 1990/1991).

Dennis, Alan R. "Information Exchange and Use in Group Decision Making: You Can Lead a Group to Information, but You Can't Make It Think." *MIS Quarterly* 20, no. 4 (December 1996).

Dennis, Alan R., Jay F. Nunamaker, Jr., and Douglas R. Vogel. "A Comparison of Laboratory and Field Research in the Study of Electronic Meeting Systems." *Journal of Management Information Systems* 7, no. 3 (Winter 1990/1991).

Dennis, Alan R., Joey F. George, Len M. Jessup, Jay F. Nunamaker, and Douglas R. Vogel. "Information Technology to Support Electronic Meetings." *MIS Quarterly* 12, no. 4 (December 1988).

Dennis, Alan R., Joseph S. Valacich, Terry Connolly, and Bayard E. Wynne. "Process Structuring in Electronic Brainstorming." *Information Systems Research* 7, no. 2 (June 1996).

DeSanctis, Geraldine, and R. Brent Gallupe. "A Foundation for the Study of Group Decision Support Systems." *Management Science* 33, no. 5 (May 1987).

DeSanctis, Geraldine, Marshall Scott Poole, Howard Lewis, and George Desharnais. "Computing in Quality Team Meetings." *Journal of Management Information Systems* 8, no. 3 (Winter 1991–92).

Dhar, Vasant, and Roger Stein. *Intelligent Decision Support Methods: The Science of Knowledge Work.* Upper Saddle River, NJ: Prentice-Hall (1997).

Dutta, Soumitra, Berend Wierenga, and Arco Dalebout. "Designing Management Support Systems Using an Integrative Perspective." *Communications of the ACM* 40, no. 6 (June 1997).

Easton, George K., Joey F. George, Jay F. Nunamaker, Jr., and Mark O. Pendergast. "Two Different Electronic Meeting Systems." *Journal of Management Information Systems* 7, no. 3 (Winter 1990/1991).

Edelstein, Herb. "Technology How To: Mining Data Warehouses." *InformationWeek* (January 8, 1996).

El Sawy, Omar. "Personal Information Systems for Strategic Scanning in Turbulent Environments." *MIS Quarterly* 9, no. 1 (March 1985).

El Sherif, Hisham, and Omar A. El Sawy. "Issue-Based Decision-Support Systems for the Egyptian Cabinet." *MIS Quarterly* 12, no. 4 (December 1988).

Etzioni, Oren. "The World Wide Web: Quagmire or Gold Mine?" *Communications of the ACM* 39, no. 11 (November 1996).

Fayyad, Usama, Gregory Piatetsky-Shapiro, and Padhraic Smyth. "The KDD Process for Extracting Useful Knowledge from Volumes of Data." *Communications of the ACM* 39, no. 11 (November 1996).

Gallupe, R. Brent, Geraldine DeSanctis, and Gary W. Dickson. "Computer-Based Support for Group Problem Finding: An Experimental Investigation." *MIS Quarterly* 12, no. 2 (June 1988).

Gerber, Cheryl. "Excavate Your Data." *Datamation* (May 1, 1996).

Ginzberg, Michael J., W. R. Reitman, and E. A. Stohr (eds.). *Decision Support Systems.* New York: North Holland Publishing Co., (1982).

Gopal, Abhijit, Robert P. Bostrum, and Wynne W. Chin. "Applying Adaptive Structuration Theory to Investigate the Process of Group Support Systems Use." *Journal of Management Information Systems* 9, no. 3 (Winter 1992–93).

Grobowski, Ron, Chris McGoff, Doug Vogel, Ben Martz, and Jay Nunamaker. "Implementing Electronic Meeting Systems at IBM: Lessons Learned and Success Factors." *MIS Quarterly* 14, no. 4 (December 1990).

Henderson, John C., and David A. Schilling. "Design and Implementation of Decision Support Systems in the Public Sector." *MIS Quarterly* (June 1985).

Hiltz, Starr Roxanne, Kenneth Johnson, and Murray Turoff. "Group Decision Support: Designated Human Leaders and Statistical Feedback." *Journal of Management Information Systems* 8, no. 2 (Fall 1991).

Ho, T. H., and K. S. Raman. "The Effect of GDSS on Small Group Meetings." *Journal of Management Information Systems* 8, no. 2 (Fall 1991).

Hogue, Jack T. "A Framework for the Examination of Management Involvement in Decision Support Systems." *Journal of Management Information Systems* 4, no. 1 (Summer 1987).

Hogue, Jack T. "Decision Support Systems and the Traditional Computer Information System Function: An Examination of Relationships During DSS Application Development." *Journal of Management Information Systems* (Summer 1985).

Houdeshel, George, and Hugh J. Watson. "The Management Information and Decision Support (MIDS) System at Lockheed, Georgia." *MIS Quarterly* 11, no. 2 (March 1987).

Imielinski, Tomasz, and Heikki Mannila. "A Database Perspective on Knowledge Discovery." *Communications of the ACM* 39, no. 11 (November 1996).

Jessup, Leonard M., Terry Connolly, and Jolene Galegher. "The Effects of Anonymity on GDSS Group Process with an Idea-Generating Task." *MIS Quarterly* 14, no. 3 (September 1990).

Jones, Jack William, Carol Saunders, and Raymond McLeod, Jr., "Media Usage and Velocity in Executive Information Acquisition: An Exploratory Study." *European Journal of Information Systems* 2 (1993).

Kasper, George M. "A Theory of Decision Support System Design for User Calibration." *Information Systems Research* 7, no. 2 (June 1996).

Keen, Peter G. W., and M. S. Scott Morton. *Decision Support Systems: An Organizational Perspective.* Reading, MA: Addison-Wesley (1982).

King, John. "Successful Implementation of Large-Scale Decision Support Systems: Computerized Models in U.S. Economic Policy Making." *Systems Objectives Solutions* (November 1983).

Kraemer, Kenneth L., and John Leslie King. "Computer-Based Systems for Cooperative Work and Group Decision Making." *ACM Computing Surveys* 20, no. 2 (June 1988).

Laudon, Kenneth C. *Communications Technology and Democratic Participation.* New York: Praeger (1977).

Le Blanc, Louis A., and Kenneth A. Kozar. "An Empirical Investigation of the Relationship Between DSS Usage and System Performance." *MIS Quarterly* 14, no. 3 (September 1990).

Leidner, Dorothy E., and Joyce L. Elam, "Executive Information Systems: Their Impact on Executive Decision Making." *Journal of Management Information Systems* (Winter 1993–1994).

Leidner, Dorothy E., and Joyce J. Elam. "The Impact of Executive Information Systems on Organizational Design, Intelligence, and Decision Making." *Organization Science* 6, no. 6 (November–December 1995).

Lewe, Henrik, and Helmut Krcmar. "A Computer-Supported Cooperative Work Research Laboratory." *Journal of Management Information Systems* 8, no. 3 (Winter 1991–92).

McLeod, Poppy Lauretta, and Jeffry R. Liker. "Electronic Meeting Systems: Evidence from a Low Structure Environment." *Information Systems Research* 3, no. 3 (September 1992).

Meador, Charles L., and Peter G. W. Keen. "Setting Priorities for DSS Development." *MIS Quarterly* (June 1984).

Miranda, Shaila M., and Robert P. Bostrum. "The Impact of Group Support Systems on Group Conflict and Conflict Management." *Journal of Management Information Systems* 10, no. 3 (Winter 1993–1994).

Mohan, Lakshmi, William K. Holstein, and Robert B. Adams. "EIS: It Can Work in the Public Sector." *MIS Quarterly* 14, no. 4 (December 1990).

Nidumolu, Sarma R., Seymour E. Goodman, Douglas R. Vogel, and Ann K. Danowitz. "Information Technology for Local Administration Support: The Governorates Project in Egypt." *MIS Quarterly* 20, no. 2 (June 1996).

Niederman, Fred, Catherine M. Beise, and Peggy M. Beranek. "Issues and Concerns about Computer-Supported Meetings: The Facilitator's Perspective." *MIS Quarterly* 20, no. 1 (March 1996).

Nunamaker, J. F., Alan R. Dennis, Joseph S. Valacich, Douglas R. Vogel, and Joey F. George. "Electronic Meeting Systems to Support Group Work." *Communications of the ACM* 34, no. 7 (July 1991).

Panko, Raymond R. "Managerial Communication Patterns." *Journal of Organizational Computing* 2, no. 1 (1992).

Post, Brad Quinn. "A Business Case Framework for Group Support Technology." *Journal of Management Information Systems* 9, no. 3 (Winter 1992–93).

Rifkin, Glenn. " 'What-If' Software for Manufacturers." *New York Times* (October 18, 1992).

Rockart, John F., and David W. DeLong. "Executive Support Systems and the Nature of Work." Working Paper: Management in the 1990s, Sloan School of Management (April 1986).

Rockart, John F., and David W. DeLong. *Executive Support Systems: The Emergence of Top Management Computer Use.* Homewood, IL: Dow-Jones Irwin (1988).

Sambamurthy, V., and Marshall Scott Poole. "The Effects of Variations in Capabilities of GDSS Designs on Management of Cognitive Conflict in Groups." *Information Systems Research* 3, no. 3 (September 1992).

Sanders, G. Lawrence, and James F. Courtney. "A Field Study of Organizational Factors Influencing DSS Success." *MIS Quarterly* (March 1985).

Sharda, Ramesh, and David M. Steiger. "Inductive Model Analysis Systems: Enhancing Model Analysis in Decision Support Systems." *Information Systems Research* 7, no. 3 (September 1996).

Silver, Mark S. "Decision Support Systems: Directed and Nondirected Change." *Information Systems Research* 1, no. 1 (March 1990).

Sprague, R. H., and E. D. Carlson. *Building Effective Decision Support Systems.* Englewood Cliffs, NJ: Prentice-Hall (1982).

Stefik, Mark, Gregg Foster, Daniel C. Bobrow, Kenneth Kahn, Stan Lanning, and Luch Suchman. "Beyond the Chalkboard: Computer Support for Collaboration and Problem Solving in Meetings." *Communications of the ACM* (January 1987).

"The New Role for 'Executive Information Systems.' " *I/S Analyzer* (January 1992).

Turban, Efraim. *Decision Support and Expert Systems: Management Support Systems.* New York: Macmillan (1993).

Turoff, Murray. "Computer-Mediated Communication Requirements for Group Support." *Journal of Organizational Computing* 1, no. 1 (January–March 1991).

Tyran, Craig K., Alan R. Dennis, Douglas R. Vogel, and J. F. Nunamaker, Jr. "The Application of Electronic Meeting Technology to Support Senior Management." *MIS Quarterly* 16, no. 3 (September 1992).

Varney, Sarah E. "Database Marketing Predicts Customer Loyalty." *Datamation* (September 1996).

Vogel, Douglas R., Jay F. Nunamaker, William Benjamin Martz, Jr., Ronald Grobowski, and Christopher McGoff. "Electronic Meeting System Experience at IBM." *Journal of Management Information Systems* 6, no. 3 (Winter 1989–1990).

Volonino, Linda, and Hugh J. Watson. "The Strategic Business Objectives Method for EIS Development." *Journal of Management Information Systems* 7, no. 3 (Winter 1990–1991).

Walls, Joseph G., George R. Widmeyer, and Omar A. El Sawy. "Building an Information System Design Theory for Vigilant EIS." *Information Systems Research* 3 no. 1 (March 1992).

Watson, Hugh J., Astrid Lipp, Pamela Z. Jackson, Abdelhafid Dahmani, and William B. Fredenberger. "Organizational Support for Decision Support Systems." *Journal of Management Information Systems* 5, no. 4 (Spring 1989).

Watson, Hugh J., R. Kelly Rainer, Jr., and Chang E. Koh. "Executive Information Systems: A Framework for Development and a Survey of Current Practices." *MIS Quarterly* 15, no. 1 (March 1991).

Watson, Richard T., Geraldine DeSanctis, and Marshall Scott Poole. "Using a GDSS to Facilitate Group Consensus: Some Intended and Unintended Consequences." *MIS Quarterly* 12, no. 3 (September 1988).

Watson, Richard T., Teck Hua Ho, and K. S. Raman. "Culture: A Fourth Dimension of Group Support Systems." *Communications of the ACM* 37, no. 10 (October 1994).

Zigurs, Ilze, and Kenneth A. Kozar. "An Exploratory Study of Roles in Computer-Supported Groups." *MIS Quarterly* 18, no. 3 (September 1994).

BOEING DESIGNS THE PAPERLESS AIRPLANE

The Boeing Company of Seattle is the single largest exporter in the United States and the number one commercial aircraft producer in the world, with 55 to 60 percent of the world market since the 1970s. Recently, it acquired new muscle in military and defense production when it purchased its longtime archrival, the McDonnell Douglas Corporation, and the aerospace and defense operations of Rockwell International. Boeing now appears to be flying high, but a few years ago, the company had started to nosedive. This case looks at the role played by information systems and the new production and design process for the 777 line of commercial aircraft in Boeing's turnaround.

For years, Boeing had no serious competitors. Then Airbus entered the commercial airplane market, commanding 28 percent of market share by 1994. Airbus's new A330 wide-body twinjet plane went into service in November 1994. In late 1994 Airbus announced a new four-engine double-decker plane, the A3XX, priced at about $200 million. This plane will carry 570 passengers up to 8400 miles, with operating costs projected to be 20 percent lower than Boeing's competing 747-400.

Although Airbus and Japanese companies have become troubling sources of competition, Boeing's major competition has been its own aircrafts, which are old but still in use. The cost of new planes has risen so dramatically that airlines are often choosing to refurbish older ones to make them last longer rather than placing orders for new aircraft. Boeing's airplane sales were unable to keep up given its high production costs.

Boeing has developed a multifaceted strategy to respond to these problems. The fundamental component of this strategy is to cut costs and prices. The company reduced its workforce by one-third over a six-year period. At the same time the company is making design changes so that new planes will be significantly cheaper to operate than are existing planes. Boeing plans to use the lowered costs to drop new-plane prices so dramatically that it becomes cheaper for an airline to purchase and operate a new plane rather than to refurbish and operate an aging one. Management established a goal of reducing production costs by 25 percent and defects by 50 percent between 1992 and 1998. They also wanted to radically reduce the time needed to build a plane, for example, lowering the production time of 747s and 767s from 18 months in 1992 down to 8 months in 1996. Reducing production time would result in major cost savings, for example, by reducing inventory expenses.

A second strategic decision was to hold tight and not attempt to compete head-on with the Airbus A3XX. Many airlines today prefer to fly smaller planes directly from point of departure to destination, such as Cincinnati to Zurich. By using smaller airplanes and avoiding hubs such as New York's Kennedy Airport, the airlines avoid both slot congestion and the high cost of flying in and out of such hubs.

A third element of Boeing's strategy is to upgrade its existing aircraft lines. Boeing has invested $2.5 billion to upgrade its 737 short-haul line. It is using custom-fitted 737s to expand into the corporate jet business.

Finally, the company introduced a new aircraft line—the 777—to compete in and hopefully dominate the twin-engine wide-body market that is just opening. The 777 class involves medium-sized, wide-body, twinjet, commercial passenger aircraft, carrying between 300 and 440 people. They are designed to fly with only two pilots, thus reducing the cost of operations. They use only two engines, which are the largest, most powerful aircraft engines ever built, each achieving from 74,000 to 100,000 pounds of thrust. Using only two engines reduces operating costs by saving on fuel, maintenance, and spare parts. Boeing claims that altogether the 777 will cost 25 percent less to operate than older Boeing models.

The planes use a number of new, lightweight, cost-effective structural materials, such as a new composite material for the floors and a new aluminum alloy used in wing skin that also improves corrosion and fatigue resistance. As a result of the lighter materials and fewer engines, a 777 weighs about 500,000 pounds, compared with 800,000 pounds for a four-engine 747. The planes will use a fly-by-wire flight-control system in which aircraft-control and maneuver commands are transmitted to the elevators, rudder ailerons, and flaps as electrical signals flowing through electrical wires rather than by mechanical steel cables.

Fly-by-wire control systems are easier to construct, weigh less and require fewer spare parts and less maintenance.

The 777 was designed to improve passenger comfort and service. Ceilings are higher, offering 6 feet 4 inches of headroom. Coach seats are the widest available, and broader aisles allow passengers to "squeeze past" when a flight attendant is pushing a food and beverage cart. All seats can have their own video screens and a small handset that serves as a telephone, program selector, and credit card reader and allows passengers to use their PCs to send and receive faxes and electronic messages.

The 777s are priced between $116 and $140 million. Industry analysts estimate that it will take about 300 aircraft and four years for Boeing to break even. They warn that if sales are slow and if this process is stretched over 20 years, Boeing will never make a profit on the planes.

Boeing management opted to reengineer the whole design and production process for the 777. Boeing had been making airplanes with a World War II–era production process. Inherent inefficiencies drove up costs and lengthened production times. It took 800 computers to manage the coordination of engineering and manufacturing and many did not communicate directly with each other. The list of parts produced by engineering for a given airplane was configured differently from the lists used by manufacturing and customer service. Therefore, the parts list had to be broken down, converted, and recomputed up to 13 times during production of a single plane.

The process had originally been used to coordinate the production of B-17s and other planes for the Army Air Corps. It kept track of the several million parts that go into each airplane rather than tracking the development of the airplane itself. The process worked well when Boeing was building 10,000 identical bombers but became quite a headache when major

airlines wanted planes that were slightly different.

Every order for a plane or group of planes is customized according to the customer's requirement so that, for example, the seating arrangements and the electronic equipment will differ from order to order. In such situations Boeing designers long ago realized that they would save much time and work if they reused existing designs rather than design the customized configuration from scratch. However, the process of design customization was manual and took more than 1000 engineers a year of full-time work to complete. The process was very paper intensive (a final design of the Boeing 747 consisted of 75,000 engineering drawings).

To reuse old, stored paper-aircraft configurations and parts designs, the engineers first needed to laboriously search through an immense amount of paper drawings to find appropriate designs to reuse for the configuration ordered. They then laboriously copied the old designs to use as a starting point for the new ones. Inevitably, errors crept into the new designs—large numbers of errors, given the large numbers of design sheets—because of unavoidable copying mistakes. The thousands of engineers who manually worked on these designs rarely compared notes. Planes were built in fits and starts, filling warehouses with piles of paper and years' worth of wasted byproducts.

A customer's identification number had to be placed individually on a drawing of every part of the plan. This was cumbersome enough but it created major bottlenecks when customers changed their specifications. For instance, if a customer changed its specification for a cockpit thrust-reverse lever from aluminum to titanium, Boeing employees had to spend 200 hours on design changes and another 480 hours retabbing the drawings with customer identification codes. Draftsmen required 2.5 years of training to fully understand the system

and even then one-third of their paperwork contained at least one error.

Another problem with manual design was that the staff needed to create life-size mock-ups in plywood and plastic to ensure that the pipes and wires which run through the plane are placed properly and do not interfere with other necessary equipment. They also needed to verify the accuracy of part specifications. This was a slow, expensive, laborious process. At production time, errors would again occur when part numbers of specifications were manually copied and at times miscopied onto order sheets, resulting in many wrong or mis-sized parts arriving.

Engineers worked in separate fiefdoms based on their field of specialization. Some engineers designed the plane's parts, others put them together, and others designed the packing crates for the parts. They rarely compared notes. If production engineers in Boeing's Auburn, Washington, factory built a mock-up of a new airplane and discovered a part that didn't fit, they sent a complaint back to the designers in Renton, Washington. The designers pulled out their drawings, reconfigured the part to make sure it matched drawings of surrounding parts, and sent the new design back to Auburn. Warehouses filled with paper.

All these challenges prompted Boeing to redesign its production process and move to paperless design and a team approach for building the 777. Boeing replaced half of its 800 computer systems with 4 new ones to reprocess most of the manufacturing and engineering data. Instead of treating airplane parts as unique, Boeing started grouping them into three categories according to their frequency of use. It assembled a single parts list that can be used by every division without modification and without tabbing. Instead of defining an airplane by its compiled parts, Boeing defined parts by the plane for which the parts are used.

Boeing established design–build teams that brought together designers and fabricators from a range of specialties throughout the whole process. In this way changes that were once made after production began are now made during design because of the presence of production staff on the design team, thus saving time and money. Boeing's primary aim in turning to a CAD system was to reduce the possibility of human error.

Boeing's CAD system is gigantic, employing nine IBM mainframes, a Cray supercomputer, and 2200 workstations, and ultimately storing 3500 billion bits of information. The hardware alone cost hundreds of millions of dollars. It is one of the world's largest networks. Fiber-optic links connect Boeing's Seattle-area plants with a plant in Wichita, Kansas, which is constructing the flight deck for the 777, and with plants in Japan that are building most of the 777's fuselage. Boeing engineers calculate that their system has exchanged more than 1.5 trillion bytes of production data with Japan alone.

The amount of data on the network is so vast—more than 600 databases in different software languages—that information is sometimes hard for users to find. Some engineers need four kinds of computers on their desks to obtain the information they need. Analysts have likened the network to the Tower of Babel warning that accessing data could be a major headache for Boeing over the next decade.

Boeing purchased three-dimensional graphics software called Catia, developed by France's Dassault Systems, a unit of Dassault Aviation SA, and sold by IBM. Catia stands for computer-aided three-dimensional interactive application. The system enables engineers to call up any of the 777's 3 million parts, modify them, fit them into the surrounding structure, and put them back into the plane's "electronic box" so that other engineers can make their own adjustments.

For instance, an engineer designing the rib of the aircraft's wing might find that the wing spar abutting the rib overlaps it by 11/100ths of an inch. The engineer could move the computer icon to the intruding spar, and the system would call up the name and telephone number of the designer for that piece. In the past, the clash would trigger a new pile of paperwork. With the new CAD system, engineers can alter the rib's design to fit snugly against the spar in 30 minutes. Boeing officials claim they could use the system to redesign large pieces of an airplane's fuselage in a matter of weeks. The system has cut the time spent reworking 777 parts by more than 90 percent, compared with the paper-based approach for earlier models.

The team set a specific goal of reducing engineering changes and ill-fitting components by 50 percent compared with the last major Boeing design project (767s). CAD software enables engineers to test how all parts fit together without having to build models and without having to solve most problems during the assembly of the first aircraft, at which time extensive redesign of the aircraft and of individual parts is very costly and time consuming. The designs stored in the CAD software system can be used to generate parts orders and fabrication specifications automatically without all the errors that result from hand copying. Finally, by electronically storing aircraft configurations and parts designs, those designs can quickly and easily be located, copied, and used as the basis for designing new plane orders. CAD technology helped Boeing break from the traditional method of building the whole plane sequentially. Boeing moved to parallel production, building selected sections of the plane simultaneously.

One major innovation was Boeing's decision to involve customers in design and testing. Four buyers—United, ANA, British Airways, and Japan Airlines—each kept a team of two to four engineers on site to work with the Boeing project team during the design, building, and testing phases. One result was that 80 items that in past lines had been optional equipment were made standard in response to users' requests, including satellite communications and global positioning systems.

Because during fabrication each airplane has to be individually configured to match customer specification, making optional equipment standard reduces variability during design and production of an order. The results are a lower cost of production and redesign and, ultimately, a lower sale price. In addition, other vital changes were made in response to customer requests. For example, the length of the wingspan of the 777 is far greater than previous Boeing planes. The users wanted the wingspan to be no greater than those of DC-10s and 767s so that the 777s would fit in existing airport gate and taxiway spaces. To accommodate this request, Boeing changed the wing design to incorporate a hinge that allows the wingtip to fold once the plane is on the runway, a feature that has long been common on military aircraft.

Boeing put in more engineering time on the project than originally planned because the software proved somewhat slow and complicated to manipulate. Some engineers had trouble making the transition from working two-dimensionally on paper to working three-dimensionally on the computer screen. Boeing is working with IBM and Dassault to improve the CAD system for advanced versions of the 777. Boeing management believes the ease with which the parts are going together will make up for the increased front-end costs.

The preliminary results have certainly been promising. The airplane was designed entirely on the computer screen, and it was assembled without initial mock-ups. Using electronic preassembly, many of the space conflicts were solved before any physical production took place. The value of electronic design software was proved, for example, when the wing flaps were designed and electronically tested in mid-1992 wholly on the computer. Later, in 1994, the actual tests on a live aircraft showed that the wing flaps worked perfectly.

The accuracy of the CAD design system is clear. In the past, the typical horizontal or vertical variances of any part were ⅜ to ½ inch. Using the CAD system to design the parts, the average variance was reduced to $^{23}/_{1000}$ of an inch vertically and $^{11}/_{1000}$ of an inch horizontally. The company reports that it exceeded its goal of cutting overall engineering design errors by 50 percent. Boeing has announced that the time to design and build a 777 order has already been reduced to 10 months compared with the 18 months initially required for 747 and 767 orders. Total cost to design and bring the 777 to production was $4 billion.

One final issue Boeing faced was that of testing and receiving governmental approval for operation from the United States Federal Aviation Administration (FAA). Standard certification testing has not been a problem. The main testing hurdle Boeing faced was the need to achieve extended-range twinjet operations (ETOPS) certification, which is granted by the FAA. It is needed before commercial long-range flights over water can occur. It is required for two-engine planes (four-engine planes are less vulnerable to problems from engine failure, because the failure of one or two engines will leave two or three still operating).

In the past ETOPS approval has come only after the plane has been in service two years so its performance could be evaluated under actual operational conditions. Boeing wanted approval for the 777 earlier than that to prevent Airbus from garnering too large a portion of the twin-engine wide-body market.

To obtain ETOPS approval at the same time the 777 aircraft went into service in the spring 1995, Boeing engaged in a far more extensive than normal testing program, working closely with the FAA. Boeing management asserted that the comput-erized design of the airplane, along with the heavy testing regimen, justi-fied an early award. On May 30, 1995, the FAA granted unprecedented approval for the 777 to begin over-water flights without two years of in-service tests.

Boeing made its first delivery of 777s on time to United Airlines on May 15, 1995, and the 777 commenced commercial service the following month. United complained that the 777 had too many mechanical problems that had disrupted departures twice as often as expected. Expectations for immediate reliability were high because Boeing management had so heavily promoted the advanced testing performed on the 777. Some FAA officials subsequently revealed that the pressure for early ETOPS certification led top-level officials to overrule safety concerns about a design flaw in the engine fan blades that might severely destabilize the plane.

Since winning ETOPS approval, Boeing has booked hundreds of orders for the new aircraft, with very strong demand from Asian carriers. Orders for Boeing planes have come so fast that Boeing has had trouble keeping up, especially while it is trying to complete the reengineering of its systems and production processes. The question is, "Can Boeing maintain its profitability over the long term?" During its lean years it offered discounts of up to 10 percent; the company doesn't want to turn away business now that it is finally arriving. Will Boeing's new efficiencies let it make money on all those planes sold at lower prices?

Sources: Adam Bryant, "Boeing Has Its Feet on the Ground," *The New York Times*, July 22, 1997; Jeff Cole, "Rivalry Between Boeing, Airbus Takes New Direction," *The Wall Street Journal*, April 30, 1997; "Onslaught of Orders Has Boeing Scrambling to Build Jets Faster," *The Wall Street Journal*, July 24, 1996; Jeff Cole and Michael J. McCarthy, "United Warns Boeing that Performance of New 777 Is 'Major Disappointment," *The New York Times*, March 6, 1996; Christina Del Valle and Michael Schroeder, "Did the FAA Go Easy on Boeing?" *BusinessWeek*, January 29, 1996; Rochele Garner, "Flight Crew," *Computerworld*, February 5, 1995; Alex Taylor III, "Boeing: Sleepy in Seattle," *Fortune*, August 7, 1995; John Holusha, "Can Boeing's New Baby Fly Financially?" *The New York Times*, March 27, 1994; Shawn Tully, "Why to Go for Stretch Targets," *Fortune*, November 4, 1994.

Case Study Questions

1. Analyze Boeing's competitive position in the early 1990s using the competitive forces and value chain models.

2. What management, organization, and technology problems did Boeing have? How did they prevent Boeing from executing its business strategy?

3. How did Boeing redesign its production process and information systems to support its strategy?

4. What role do knowledge work systems play in Boeing's business strategy? Evaluate the significance of that role.

5. How does the production of the Boeing 777 fit in with Boeing's strategy? What role did information systems play?

6. What management, organization, and technology problems do you think Boeing encountered in building the 777 and redesigning its production process? What steps do you think they did take, or should have taken, to deal with these problems?

7. How successful has Boeing been in pursuing its strategy? In what ways do you consider its strategy sound? Risky?

Managing Contemporary Information Systems

The pervasiveness and power of contemporary information systems and the wide-spread use of the Internet have made security, control, and development of global systems key management problems. Part Five concludes the text by examining the management, organization, and technology dimensions of these problems and by describing strategies, procedures, and technologies for meeting these challenges.

CHAPTER 17

Controlling Information Systems

Chapter 17 demonstrates why management must take special measures to ensure that information systems are secure and effectively controlled. Without proper safe-guards, information systems are highly vulnerable to destruction, abuse, error, and loss, especially in networked environments. Both general and application-specific controls can be applied to ensure that information systems are accurate, reliable, and secure. An appropriate control structure for information systems will consider costs and benefits. This chapter highlights the importance of information system security and auditing and the new security problems posed by the Internet.

CHAPTER 18

Managing International Information Systems

Chapter 18 analyzes the principal challenges confronting organizations that want to use information systems, including the Internet, on an international scale. Organizations need to design appropriate business strategies and information systems infrastructures for this purpose and they need to overcome significant management, organization, and technology obstacles to systems that transcend national boundaries.

PART FIVE CASE STUDY

Phantom Profits Haunt Kidder Peabody

On April 17, 1994, the Wall Street securities firm of Kidder Peabody sent shock waves throughout the financial community by firing Joseph Jett, its most successful bond trader. By posting phantom bond trades as profits, Jett had actually lost $90 million for the company. This case study examines the circumstances surrounding Jett's dismissal and asks students to assess the role played by information systems and the management control environment in Kidder's bond trading fiasco.

CHAPTER 17

Controlling Information Systems

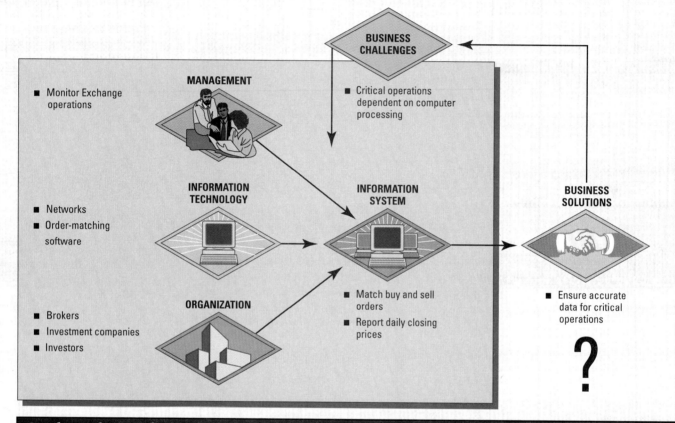

BUSINESS CHALLENGES
- Critical operations dependent on computer processing

MANAGEMENT
- Monitor Exchange operations

INFORMATION TECHNOLOGY
- Networks
- Order-matching software

ORGANIZATION
- Brokers
- Investment companies
- Investors

INFORMATION SYSTEM
- Match buy and sell orders
- Report daily closing prices

BUSINESS SOLUTIONS
- Ensure accurate data for critical operations

?

Stock Market Snafu Rattles Hong Kong Investors

When Franco Tong, a salesman at New China Hong Kong Securities Ltd., first turned on his computer on the morning of Thursday, December 12, 1995, he couldn't believe his eyes. His stock price screen said that blue-chip HSBC holdings had plunged 16 percent overnight. Across town, a Chinese investment company's computer said that the Hong Kong stock market, the sixth largest in the world, had dropped 3.9 percent in its first minute of trading. Yet some stocks seemed to soar. Sixteen companies looked like they were up more than 100 percent. Brokers were deluged with phone

LEARNING OBJECTIVES

After completing
this chapter, you will
be able to:

1. Show why automated information systems are so vulnerable to destruction, error, and abuse.
2. Describe the role of controls in safeguarding information systems.
3. Distinguish between general controls and application controls.
4. Describe the most important techniques for controlling information systems.
5. Identify the factors that must be considered when developing the controls for information systems.
6. Explain the importance of auditing information systems.

---

calls from panicked small investors who wanted to bail out.

Was it a bull market, or was it the Big Crash? It was neither. The Hang Seng index had dropped 1 percent on fears of rising U.S. interest rates (which affect Hong Kong's). No one was sure until hours later when they learned that the Hong Kong Stock Exchange had experienced a big computer glitch. When the market had opened, its automated order-matching system listed wildly incorrect stock closing prices for the previous day. An estimated 80 percent of the 1220 securities listed on the exchange had the wrong price.

Exchange officials learned about the problem before the market opened, and rushed to prevent panic. They issued warnings and manually installed the correct Wednesday closing prices for each stock. This painstaking process took until noon. Because the exchange's data are distributed by other vendors, many brokers didn't receive the correct numbers until much later, if at all. Franco Tong called his trader in the futures pit to make sure that the market hadn't really crashed.

Some dealers tried to take advantage of the snafu to make a quick buck. One offered to sell shares of underwear maker Top Form International for almost twice its correct price. No one took the offer.

While some brokers shrugged off the snafu, others worried when the official index figures for the first 20 minutes of trading hadn't been announced. "No one knows if the market really fell 500 points," said one nervous manager. "If you can't trust your Hang Seng index, who can you trust?"

Source: Erik Guyot, "Test of Nerves for Investors in Hong Kong," *The Wall Street Journal*, December 13, 1996.

The experience of the Hong Kong Stock Exchange illustrates one of many problems that organizations relying on computer-based information systems may face. Hardware and software failures, communications disruptions, natural disasters, employee errors, and use by unauthorized people may prevent information systems from running properly or running at all. As you read this chapter, you should be aware of the following management challenges:

1. **Controlling large distributed multiuser networks.** No system is totally secure, but large, distributed multiuser networks and the Internet are especially difficult to secure. Security becomes more problematic when networks are no longer confined to individual departments or groups or to centralized mainframe systems. It is very difficult to assert control over networks using heterogeneous hardware, software, and communications components when thousands of workers can access networks from many remote locations.

2. **Subjectivity of risk analysis.** Risk analysis depends on assumptions. For instance, the flawed Patriot missile system described at the end of Section 17.1 was originally designed to work under a much less stringent environment than that in which it was actually used during Operation Desert Storm. Subsequent analyses of its effectiveness were downgraded from 95 percent to 13 percent (Neumann, 1993). Because risks are only potential events, not certainties, they are often either overestimated or underestimated. Measures to avoid risk can also be used to stifle innovation or change.

3. **Designing systems that are neither overcontrolled nor undercontrolled.** The biggest threat to information systems is posed by authorized users, not outside intruders. Most security breaches and damage to information systems come from organizational insiders. If a system requires too many passwords and authorizations to access information, the system will go unused. Controls that are effective but that do not prevent authorized individuals from using a system are difficult to design.

Computer systems play such a critical role in business, government, and daily life that organizations must take special steps to protect their information systems and ensure that they are accurate and reliable. The Hong Kong Stock Exchange suffered a crisis because it had not taken all the proper steps to ensure the reliability of its order-matching system. This chapter describes how information systems can be *controlled* so that they serve the purposes for which they are intended.

17.1   SYSTEM VULNERABILITY AND ABUSE

Before computer automation, data about individuals or organizations were maintained and secured as paper records dispersed in separate business or organizational units. Information systems concentrate data in computer files that can potentially be accessed more easily by large numbers of people and by groups outside the organization. Consequently, automated data are more susceptible to destruction, fraud, error, and misuse.

When computer systems fail to run or work as required, firms that depend heavily on computers experience a serious loss of function. The longer systems are down, the more serious the consequences for the firm. Some firms relying on computers to

Table 17.1   Downtime Costs

| Business | Industry | Financial impact of system failure per hour | |
		Cost Range (per hour)	Average Cost (per hour)
Brokerage Operations	Finance	$5.6–7.3 million	$6.45 million
Credit Card/Sales Authorization	Finance	$2.2–3.1 million (seasonal)	$2.6 million
Pay-Per-View	Media	$67–233 thousand	$150 thousand
Home Shopping (TV)	Retail	$87–140 thousand	$113 thousand
Catalog Sales	Retail	$60–120 thousand	$90 thousand
Airline Reservations	Transportation	$67–112 thousand	$89.5 thousand
Tele-Ticket Sales	Media	$56–82 thousand	$69 thousand
Package Shipping	Transportation	$24.5–32 thousand	$28 thousand
ATM Fees	Finance	$12–17 thousand	$14.5 thousand

Source: Reprinted by permission of Contingency Planning Research, Livingston, NJ.
Downtime can cost you a lot. Exact costs, of course, depend on the business you're in, as well as the particular application affected.

process their critical business transactions may experience a total loss of business function if they lose computer capability for more than a few days. Table 17.1 shows the financial impact in various industries for each hour of computer downtime.

Why Systems Are Vulnerable

There are many advantages to information systems when they are properly safeguarded. But when large amounts of data are stored in electronic form, they are vulnerable to many more kinds of threats than when they exist in manual form. For example, an organization's entire recordkeeping system can be destroyed by a computer hardware malfunction. Table 17.2 lists the most common threats to computerized information systems. They can stem from technical, organizational, and environmental factors compounded by poor management decisions.

Computerized systems are especially vulnerable to such threats for the following reasons:

- A complex information system cannot be replicated manually. Most information cannot be printed or is too voluminous to be handled manually.

- There is usually no visible trace of changes in computerized systems because computer records can be read only by the computer.

- Computerized procedures appear to be invisible and are not easily understood or audited.

- The development and operation of automated systems require specialized technical expertise, which cannot be easily communicated to end users. Systems are

Table 17.2   Threats to Computerized Information Systems

Hardware failure	Fire
Software failure	Electrical problems
Personnel actions	User errors
Terminal access penetration	Program changes
Theft of data, services, equipment	Telecommunications problems

open to abuse by highly technical staff members who are not well integrated into the organization. (Programmers and computer operators can make unauthorized changes in software while information is being processed or can use computer facilities for unauthorized purposes. Employees may make unauthorized copies of data files for illegal purposes.)

- Although the chances of disaster in automated systems are no greater than in manual systems, the effect of a disaster can be much more extensive. In some cases, all the system's records can be destroyed and lost forever.

- Most automated systems are accessible by many individuals. Information is easier to gather but more difficult to control.

- On-line information systems are even more difficult to control because data files can be accessed immediately and directly through computer terminals. Legitimate users may gain easy access to computer data that were previously not available to them. They may be able to scan records or entire files that they are not authorized to view. By obtaining valid users' log ons and passwords, unauthorized individuals can also gain access to such systems. The chances of unauthorized access to or manipulation of data in on-line systems are considerably higher than in the batch environment.

New Vulnerabilities and the Internet

Advances in telecommunications and computer software have magnified these vulnerabilities. Through telecommunications networks, information systems in different locations can be interconnected. The potential for unauthorized access, abuse, or fraud is not limited to a single location but can occur at any access point in the network.

Additionally, more complex and diverse hardware, software, organizational, and personnel arrangements are required for telecommunications networks, creating new areas and opportunities for penetration and manipulation. Wireless networks using radio-based technology are even more vulnerable to penetration because radio frequency bands are easy to scan. The vulnerabilities of telecommunications networks are illustrated in Figure 17.1. Developing a workable system of controls for telecommunications networks is a complex and troubling problem. The Internet poses special problems because it was explicitly designed to be easily accessed by people on different computer systems. TCP/IP, the networking standard for the Internet, is inherently insecure.

The efforts of "hackers" to penetrate computer networks have been widely publicized. A **hacker** is a person who gains unauthorized access to a computer network for profit, criminal mischief, or personal pleasure. The potential damage from intruders is frightening. The Window on Organizations describes problems created by hackers for organizations that use the Internet.

Recently, there is rising alarm over hackers propagating **computer viruses,** rogue software programs that spread rapidly from system to system, clogging computer memory or destroying programs or data. More than 2100 viruses are known to exist, with 50 or more new viruses created each month. (Table 17.3 describes the characteristics of the most common viruses.) The most notorious virus outbreak occurred in November 1988, when Robert Morris, a brilliant computer science student, introduced a program through a Cornell University terminal that spread uncontrollably throughout the Internet, which at that time tied together numerous other networks, including National Science Foundation Network (NSF Net) which links universities, research labs, and other institutions. Morris intended his program to reside quietly on Internet computers, but it echoed throughout the network in minutes, tying up computer memory and storage space as it copied and recopied itself hundreds of thousands of times.

hacker   A person who gains unauthorized access to a computer network for profit, criminal mischief, or personal pleasure.

computer virus   Rogue software programs that are difficult to detect and that spread rapidly through computer systems, destroying data or disrupting processing and memory systems.

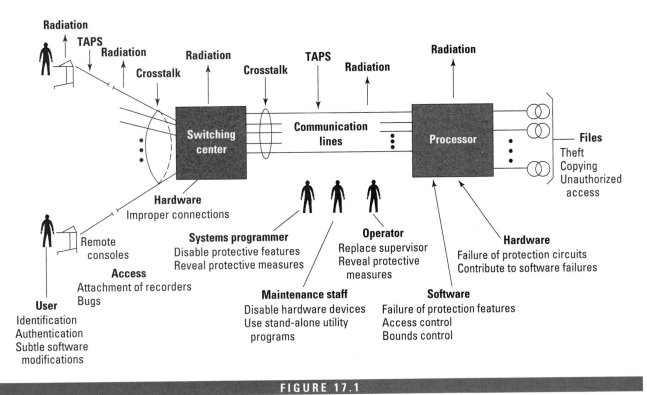

Telecommunication network vulnerabilities. Telecommunications networks are highly vulnerable to natural failure of hardware and software and to misuse by programmers, computer operators, maintenance staff, and end users. It is possible to "tap" communications lines and illegally intercept data. High-speed transmission over twisted wire communications channels causes interference called *crosstalk*. Radiation can disrupt a network at various points as well.

The virus was quickly detected, but hundreds of computer centers in research institutions, universities, and military bases had to shut down. Estimates of the number of systems actually infected ranged from 6000 to 250,000. A virus that was not intended to harm caused upward of $100 million in lost machine time, lost access, and direct labor costs for recovery and cleanup.

In addition to spreading via computer networks, viruses can invade computerized information systems from "infected" diskettes from an outside source, through infected machines, from files on software downloaded from other computers, or even

Table 17.3	**Common Computer Viruses**
Virus Name	**Description**
Concept	Macro virus that attaches itself to Microsoft Word documents.
Form	Makes a clicking sound with each keystroke but only on the 18th of the month. Contains a hidden reference to someone named Corrine.
Joshi	Activates on January 5, freezing your PC until the phrase "Happy Birthday Joshi" is typed on the keyboard.
Monkey-2	Hides in memory, infecting every disk it contacts and making some unusable.
Green Caterpillar	Launches a little worm that crawls around the screen rearranging characters and changing their color.
Michelangelo	Activates on March 6, the artist's birthday, and destroys most of your data by overwriting the hard disk drive with characters from system memory.
Stoned	Displays the message "Your PC is Stoned" and damages the system's directory and file allocation table.

Uprooting the Internet Hackers

Business use of the Internet has been growing rapidly over the past few years. But the Internet has no central authority or management and therefore no one to install the technology or establish network-wide security policies. Reports of Internet security breaches are rising, making many businesses reluctant to make heavy use of the Net.

The main concern comes from unwanted intruders—hackers—who use the latest technology and their skill to break into supposedly secure computers or disable them. Hackers have been trying to break into Rockwell International's systems via the Internet on a regular basis, even though the aerospace giant uses the latest firewall and encryption technology.

Panix, a pioneering Internet service provider that hosts nearly 1000 corporate Web sites, was virtually shut down for four days in September 1996 because a hacker bombarded its computer with requests for information. The intruder had alternately invaded Panix's computers that control pages on the Web, others that store e-mail, and still others that link Internet addresses to Panix subscribers, blocking them from receiving communications. The hacker used a special computer program to send up to 150 requests per second to Panix's computers, seeking to establish a connection or to obtain information. The requests contained fake Internet addresses, which Panix computers must sort out before they can reject them. Panix computers were overwhelmed by the deluge and thus could not handle legitimate Web or e-mail requests. Panix is trying to find the source of the attack, but there is no easy way to trace it.

Panix suffered another serious attack in October 1993 which forced it to shut down for three days. Hackers collected passwords from legitimate Panix users. With those passwords, they then were able to access other computers connected to the Internet to steal both data and more passwords. The security of the whole system had been compromised.

Government agencies have also suffered Internet attacks. Intruders have broken into the networks of the National Institutes of Health to observe traffic and to copy password files. In 1994, hackers broke into Pentagon computers and attached "sniffers" (programs monitoring data flowing across a network) to switches connecting U.S. Air Force computers to the Internet. The hackers were searching for passwords they could use to access U.S. Air Force databases.

Organizations such as the Computer Emergency Response Team (CERT) have been set up explicitly to address security on the Internet. CERT helps both to determine who is breaking into the Internet and to devise solutions to the method used for the break-in. When an Internet user reports a new break-in to CERT, they do not publicize it until they find a solution. With the increase in break-ins, the United States Defense Department's Advanced Research Projects Agency (ARPA) is planning to add funding to CERT in order to double their staff. The Federal Bureau of Investigation (FBI) also investigates computer crimes reported to them, 80 percent of which are on the Internet.

> **To Think About:** In light of these security problems, what management, organization, and technology issues would you consider in developing an Internet security plan?

Sources: Dean Tomasula, "Tighter Security Loosens the Constraints on Electronic Commerce," *Wall Street and Technology,* February 1997; Bart Ziegler, "Savvy Hacker Tangles Web for Net Host," *The Wall Street Journal,* September 12, 1996; Bob Violino, "Your Worst Nightmare," *InformationWeek,* February 19, 1996; David Bernstein, "Insulate Against Internet Intruders," *Datamation,* October 1, 1994; and Joseph C. Panettiere, "Guardian of the Net," *InformationWeek,* May 23, 1994.

from on-line electronic bulletin boards. The potential for massive damage and loss from future computer viruses remains (see Figure 17.2) (Anthes, 1993).

antivirus software Software designed to detect and often eliminate computer viruses from an information system.

Antivirus software is special software designed to check computer systems and disks for the presence of various computer viruses. Often the software can eliminate the virus from the infected area. However, most antivirus software is effective only against viruses already known when the software is written—to protect their systems, management groups must continually update their antivirus software.

Advances in computer software have also increased the chances of information system misuse and abuse. Using fourth-generation languages, end users can now perform programming functions that were formerly reserved for technical specialists. They can produce programs that inadvertently create errors, and they can manipulate the organization's data for illegitimate purposes. Chapter 5 contains a more detailed discussion of computer crime and abuse.

The growth of database systems, in which data are shared by multiple application areas, has also created new vulnerabilities. All data are stored in one common

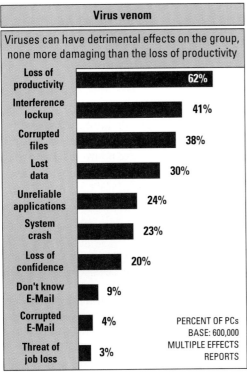

Virus venom

Viruses can have detrimental effects on the group, none more damaging than the loss of productivity

Effect	Percent
Loss of productivity	62%
Interference lockup	41%
Corrupted files	38%
Lost data	30%
Unreliable applications	24%
System crash	23%
Loss of confidence	20%
Don't know E-Mail	9%
Corrupted E-Mail	4%
Threat of job loss	3%

PERCENT OF PCs
BASE: 600,000
MULTIPLE EFFECTS
REPORTS

Source: Dataquest, San Jose, Calif.

FIGURE 17.2

Copyright January 28, 1993 by Computerworld, Inc., Framingham, MA 01701. Reprinted from Computerworld.

location, but many users may have the right to access and modify them. It may not be easy to identify who is using or possibly misusing the data in such circumstances. Because the data are used by more than one organizational unit, the effect of an error may reverberate throughout the organization. There may also be less chance of discovering errors. Each functional unit has less individual control over the data and has fewer grounds for knowing whether the computer is right.

Companies can detect and eliminate computer viruses in their systems by regularly using antivirus software.

Concerns for System Builders and Users

The heightened vulnerability of automated data has created special concerns for the builders and users of information systems. These concerns include disaster, security, and administrative error.

Disaster

Computer hardware, programs, data files, and other equipment can be destroyed by fires, power failures, or other disasters. Such disasters can disrupt normal operations and even bring an entire organization to a standstill. It may take many years and millions of dollars to reconstruct destroyed data files and computer programs. If an organization needs them to function on a day-to-day basis, it will no longer be able to operate. This is why companies such as Visa USA Inc. and National Trust, for example, employ elaborate emergency backup facilities.

Visa USA Inc. has duplicate mainframes, duplicate network pathways, duplicate terminals, and duplicate power supplies. Visa even uses a duplicate data center in McLean, Virginia, to handle half of its transactions and to serve as an emergency backup to its primary data center in San Mateo, California. National Trust, a large bank in Ontario, Canada, uses uninterruptable power supply technology provided by International Power Machines (IPM), a provider of power protection technology. The electrical power at National Trust's Mississauga location fluctuates frequently during the normal business day, largely due to a nearby shopping mall.

fault-tolerant computer systems
Systems that contain extra hardware, software, and power supply components that can back the system up and keep it running to prevent system failure.

Fault-tolerant computer systems contain extra hardware, software, and power supply components that can back the system up and keep it running to prevent system failure. Fault-tolerant computers contain extra memory chips, processors, and disk storage devices. They can use special software routines or self-checking logic built into their circuitry to detect hardware failures and automatically switch to backup devices. Parts from these computers can be removed and repaired without disruption to the computer system. Their increased reliability is the reason the European Community banks are using fault-tolerant computer systems to clear cross-border transaction trading in the new unified European currency, the European Currency Unit (ECU). Eventually the European Community countries expect to make the ECU their single currency for international trade, making the stability of this clearing function critical to the stability of the world economy.

on-line transaction processing
Transaction processing mode in which transactions entered on-line are immediately processed by the computer.

Fault-tolerant technology is used by firms for critical applications with heavy on-line transaction processing requirements. In **on-line transaction processing**, transactions entered on-line are immediately processed by the computer. Multitudinous changes to databases, reporting, or requests for information occur each instant.

Rather than build their own backup facilities, many firms contract with disaster recovery firms, such as Comdisco Disaster Recovery Services in Rosemont, Illinois, and Sungard Recovery Services headquartered in Wayne, Pennsylvania. These disaster recovery firms provide "hot sites," housing spare computers at various locations around the country where subscribing firms can run their critical applications in an emergency. Disaster recovery services now offer backup for client/server systems as well as traditional mainframe applications (see the Window on Management). Disaster recovery firms also offer "cold sites," special buildings designed to house computer equipment; they do not contain computers, but they can be made operational in one week.

Security

security Policies, procedures, and technical measures used to prevent unauthorized access, alteration, theft, or physical damage to information systems.

Security refers to the policies, procedures, and technical measures used to prevent unauthorized access or alteration, theft, and physical damage to information systems. Security can be promoted with an array of techniques and tools to safeguard computer hardware, software, communications networks, and data. We have already discussed disaster protection measures. Other tools and techniques for promoting security will be described in subsequent sections.

Reno Avoids Disaster with a Recovery Plan

In mid-December 1996 nearly four feet of water overflowed from the Truckee River, flooding downtown Reno. Water gushed into the basement of the Hampton Inn, where communications hardware for critical reservations data was stored. The equipment, which is shared by the Hampton Inn and Harrah's Hotel Casino, stayed dry and functional because it had been placed on racks that were high enough to avoid flood damage. Management and the information systems department had planned for such disasters.

Moving the hardware was one of the first steps in a comprehensive disaster recovery plan, which was recommended when the company installed new Windows NT servers two years earlier. The plan included procedures for bringing down the servers and for moving key departments to backup sites where they could continue critical business functions without disruption. When the flood started, the information systems department followed the plan to bring down the network in a controlled manner and to set up a designated server to continue processing reservations.

Reno Air Inc. had to work a little harder to save its systems. Duffy Mees, its director of information technology, had to drive a truck through flood-high water to rescue servers and networking hardware from the computer room. Mees and his staff then set up shop on higher ground at the Reno-Tahoe International Airport, resuming operations on the lower concourse. When water started flooding the concourse, the group moved the hardware again to a ticket counter upstairs, which soon flooded as

well. They moved the equipment a final time to the Peppermill Hotel Casino.

Although the flood cost Reno Air a router and two PCs, it did not destroy its data. Randy Reigal, the airline's systems engineer, was relieved. A critical server was in company headquarters. "If it had been a bigger flood, we might not have been so lucky," he said. Managers at both Harrah's and Reno Air said it might take months before they could calculate losses created by the unavailability of information systems. A spokesperson for the city of Reno said that flood damage to Reno and Sparks and to Washoe County amounted to an estimated $33 million.

Frank DeLuca, senior director of client services at Sungard Recovery Services Inc. in Wayne, Pennsylvania, recommends companies go through a comprehensive drill to test their disaster recovery plans at least once a year. Unfortunately, few companies follow this advice, believing it is too expensive to do a full disaster recovery plan test. However, the cost of an untested plan can outweigh the cost of a tested one. Rekeying data, banking, or accounting transactions can easily cost hundreds of thousands of dollars.

To Think About: What are the management benefits of a disaster recovery plan? What management, organization, and technology issues have to be addressed by a disaster recovery plan?

Source: Justin Hibbard, "Solid Plans Keep IS High and Dry," *Computerworld*, January 13, 1997.

Sungard Recovery Services provides mobile facilities where subscribers can run their critical computer applications in an emergency.

Errors

Computers can also serve as instruments of error, severely disrupting or destroying an organization's record keeping and operations. Errors in automated systems can occur at many points in the processing cycle: through data entry, program error, computer operations, and hardware. Figure 17.3 illustrates the points in a typical processing cycle where errors can occur. Even minor mistakes in automated systems can have disastrous financial or operational repercussions. For instance, on February 25, 1991, during Operation Desert Storm, a Patriot missile defense system operating at

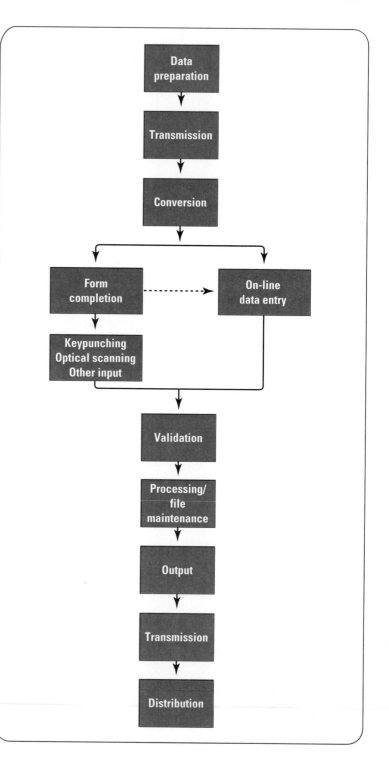

Dharan, Saudi Arabia, failed to track and intercept an incoming Scud missile launched by Iraq. The failure was traced to a software error in the system's weapons control computer. The Scud hit an army barracks, killing 28 Americans.

17.2 CREATING A CONTROL ENVIRONMENT

To minimize errors, disaster, computer crime, and breaches of security, special policies and procedures must be incorporated into the design and implementation of information systems. The combination of manual and automated measures that safeguard information systems and ensure that they perform according to management standards is termed *controls*. **Controls** consist of all the methods, policies, and organizational procedures that ensure the safety of the organization's assets, the accuracy and reliability of its accounting records, and operational adherence to management standards.

controls All the methods, policies, and procedures that ensure protection of the organization's assets, accuracy and reliability of its records, and operational adherence to management standards.

In the past, the control of information systems was treated as an afterthought, addressed only toward the end of implementation, just before the system was installed. Today, however, organizations are so critically dependent on information systems that vulnerabilities and control issues must be identified as early as possible. The control of an information system must be an integral part of its design. Users and builders of systems must pay close attention to controls throughout the system's life span.

Computer systems are controlled by a combination of general controls and application controls. **General controls** are those that control the design, security, and use of computer programs and the security of data files in general throughout the organization. On the whole, general controls apply to all computerized applications and consist of a combination of system software and manual procedures that create an overall control environment. **Application controls** are specific controls unique to each computerized application, such as payroll, accounts receivable, and order processing. They consist of both controls applied from the user functional area of a particular system and from programmed procedures.

general controls Overall controls that establish a framework for controlling the design, security, and use of computer programs throughout an organization.

application controls Specific controls unique to each computerized application.

General Controls

General controls are overall controls that ensure the effective operation of programmed procedures. They apply to all application areas. General controls include the following:

- Controls over the system implementation process
- Software controls
- Physical hardware controls
- Computer operations controls
- Data and network security controls
- Administrative controls

Implementation Controls

Implementation controls audit the systems development process at various points to ensure that the process is properly controlled and managed. The systems development audit should look for the presence of formal review points at various stages of development that enable users and management to approve or disapprove the implementation. (Examples of such review points are user and management sign-offs on the initial systems proposal, design specifications, conversion, testing, and the postimplementation audit described in Chapter 12.)

implementation controls Audit of the systems development process at various points to ensure that it is properly controlled and managed.

The systems development audit should also examine the level of user involvement at each stage of implementation and check for the use of a formal cost-benefit methodology in establishing system feasibility. The audit should also look for the use of controls and quality assurance techniques for program development, conversion, and testing. (These issues are discussed in Chapters 11 through 13).

An important though frequently neglected requirement of systems building is appropriate documentation. Without good documentation that shows how a system operates from both a technical and a user standpoint, an information system may be difficult, if not impossible, to operate, maintain, or use. Table 17.4 lists the various pieces of documentation that are normally required to run and maintain an information system. The systems development audit should look for system, user, and operations documentation that conforms to formal standards.

Software Controls

software controls Controls to ensure the security and reliability of software.

program security controls Controls designed to prevent unauthorized changes to programs in systems that are already in production.

Controls are essential for the various categories of software used in computer systems. **Software controls** monitor the use of system software and prevent unauthorized access of software programs, system software, and computer programs.

System software controls govern the software for the operating system, which regulates and manages computer resources to facilitate execution of application programs. System software controls are also used for compilers, utility programs, reporting of operations, file setup and handling, and library record keeping. System software is an important control area because it performs overall control functions for the programs that directly process data and data files. **Program security controls**

Table 17.4 Essential User and Technical Documentation for an Information System	
Technical Documentation	**User Documentation**
System flowchart	Sample reports/output layouts
File layouts	Sample input forms/screens
Record layouts	Data preparation instructions
List of programs/modules	Data input instructions
Program structure charts	Instructions for using reports
Narrative program/module descriptions	Security profiles
Source program listings	Functional description of system
Module cross references	Work flows
Error conditions/actions	Error correction procedures
Abnormal termination log	Accountabilities
Job setup requirements	Processing procedure narrative
Job run schedules	List/description of controls
Report-output distribution	Responsible user contact
Responsible programmer contact	
Job control language listings	
Backup/recovery procedures	
Run control procedures	
File access procedures	
Hardware/operating system requirements	

are designed to prevent unauthorized changes to programs in systems that are already in production.

Hardware Controls

Hardware controls ensure that computer hardware is physically secure and check for equipment malfunction. Computer hardware should be physically secured so that it can be accessed only by authorized individuals. Access to rooms where computers operate should be restricted to computer operations personnel. Computer terminals in other areas or PCs can be kept in locked rooms. Computer equipment should be specially protected against fires and extremes of temperature and humidity. Organizations that are critically dependent on their computers must also make provisions for emergency backup in case of power failure.

Many kinds of computer hardware also contain mechanisms that check for equipment malfunction. Parity checks detect equipment malfunctions responsible for altering bits within bytes during processing. Validity checks monitor the structure of on–off bits within bytes to make sure that it is valid for the character set of a particular computer machine. Echo checks verify that a hardware device is performance ready. Chapter 6 discusses computer hardware in detail.

hardware controls Controls to ensure the physical security and correct performance of computer hardware.

Computer Operations Controls

Computer operations controls apply to the work of the computer department and help ensure that programmed procedures are consistently and correctly applied to the storage and processing of data. They include controls over the setup of computer processing jobs, operations software and computer operations, and backup and recovery procedures for processing that ends abnormally.

Instructions for running computer jobs should be fully documented, reviewed, and approved by a responsible official. Controls over operations software include manual procedures designed to both prevent and detect error. These are composed of specified operating instructions for system software, restart and recovery procedures, procedures for the labeling and disposition of input and output magnetic tapes, and procedures for specific applications.

Human-operator error at a computer system at the Shell Pipeline Corporation caused the firm to ship 93,000 barrels of crude oil to the wrong trader. This one error cost Shell $2 million. A computer operator at Exxon Corporation headquarters inadvertently erased valuable records about the 1989 grounding of the Exxon *Valdez* and the Alaskan oil spill that were stored on magnetic tape. Such errors could have been avoided had the companies incorporated tighter operational safeguards.

System software can maintain a system log detailing all activity during processing. This log can be printed for review so that hardware malfunction, abnormal endings, and operator actions can be investigated. Specific instructions for backup and recovery can be developed so that in the event of a hardware or software failure, the recovery process for production programs, system software, and data files does not create erroneous changes in the system.

computer operations controls Procedures to ensure that programmed procedures are consistently and correctly applied to data storage and processing.

Data Security and Network Controls

Data security controls ensure that valuable business data files on either disk or tape are not subject to unauthorized access, change, or destruction. Such controls are required for data files when they are in use and when they are being held for storage. It is easier to control data files in batch systems, because access is limited to operators who run the batch jobs. However, on-line and real-time systems are vulnerable at several points. They can be accessed through terminals as well as by operators during production runs.

data security controls Controls to ensure that data files on either disk or tape are not subject to unauthorized access, change, or destruction.

When data can be input on-line through a terminal, entry of unauthorized input must be prevented. For example, a credit note could be altered to match a sales invoice on file. In such situations, security can be developed on several levels:

- Terminals can be physically restricted so that they are available only to authorized individuals.

- System software can include the use of passwords assigned only to authorized individuals. No one can log on to the system without a valid password.

- Additional sets of passwords and security restrictions can be developed for specific systems and applications. For example, data security software can limit access to specific files, such as the files for the accounts receivable system. It can restrict the type of access so that only individuals authorized to update these specific files will have the ability to do so. All others will only be able to read the files or will be denied access altogether.

Systems that allow on-line inquiry and reporting must have data files secured. Figure 17.4 illustrates the security allowed for two sets of users of an on-line personnel database with sensitive information such as employees' salaries, benefits, and medical histories. One set of users consists of all employees who perform clerical functions such as inputting employee data into the system. All individuals with this type of profile can update the system but can neither read nor update sensitive fields such as salary, medical history, or earnings data. Another profile applies to divisional managers, who cannot update their systems but who can read all employee data fields for their division, including medical history and salary. These profiles would be established and maintained by a data security system. A multilayered data security system is essential for ensuring that this information can be accessed only by authorized persons. The data security system illustrated in Figure 17.4 provides very fine-grained

FIGURE 17.4

Security profiles for a personnel system. These two examples represent two security profiles or data security patterns that might be found in a personnel system. Depending on the security profile, a user would have certain restrictions on access to various systems, locations, or data in an organization.

SECURITY PROFILE 1

User: Personnel Dept. Clerk

Location: Division 1

Employee Identification
Codes with This Profile: 00753, 27834, 37665, 44116

Data Field Restrictions	Type of Access
All employee data for Division 1 only	Read and Update
• Medical history data	None
• Salary	None
• Pensionable earnings	None

SECURITY PROFILE 2

User: Divisional Personnel Manager

Location: Division 1

Employee Identification
Codes with This Profile: 27321

Data Field Restrictions	Type of Access
All employee data for Division 1 only	Read Only

security restrictions, such as allowing authorized personnel users to inquire about all employee information except in confidential fields such as salary or medical history.

Although the security risk of files maintained off-line is smaller, data files on disk or tape can be removed for unauthorized purposes. These can be secured in lockable storage areas, with tight procedures so that they are released only for authorized processing. Usage logs and library records can be maintained for each removable storage device if it is labeled and assigned a unique identity number.

Linking to the Internet or transmitting information via intranets requires special security measures. Large public networks, including the Internet, are more vulnerable because they are virtually open to anyone and because they are so huge that when abuses do occur, they can have an enormously widespread impact. Chapter 10 described the use of *firewalls* to prevent unauthorized users from accessing private networks. As growing numbers of businesses expose their networks to Internet traffic, firewalls are becoming a necessity.

A firewall is generally placed between internal LANs and WANs and external networks such as the Internet. The firewall controls access to the organization's internal networks by acting like a "Checkpoint Charlie" that examines the users' credentials before they can access the network. The firewall identifies names, Internet Protocol (IP) addresses, applications, and other characteristics of incoming traffic. It checks this information against the access rules that have been programmed into the system by the network administrator. The firewall prevents unauthorized communication into or out of the network, allowing the organization to enforce a security policy on traffic flowing between its network and the Internet (Oppliger, 1997). Table 17.5 describes different categories of firewall products and compares their capabilities. Hybrid products are now being developed that combine these features.

To create a good firewall, someone must write and maintain the internal rules identifying the people, applications, or addresses that are allowed or rejected in very fine detail. Firewalls can deter, but not completely prevent, network penetration from outsiders, and should be viewed as one element in an overall security plan.

Table 17.5 Categories of Firewall Products	
Type of Firewall Product	Description
Packet-Filtering Firewall	A router examines each incoming Internet Protocol (IP) packet, checking its source or destination addresses or services. Access rules must identify every type of packet that the organization doesn't want to admit.
Application Gateway	Special software restricts traffic to a particular application, such as e-mail or Lotus Notes groupware.
Circuit-level Gateway	Connects an outside TCP/IP port to an internal destination such as a network printer. Acts as an intelligent filter that can distinguish a valid TCP or User Datagram Protocol session.
Proxy Server	Maintains replicated copies of Web pages for easy access by a designated class of users. Outside visitors can be routed to this information while more sensitive information can be kept away from this access point.
Stateful Inspection	Technology that derives information from the state of transmission and applies it to the organization's business rules. The state information is stored to provide a context for examining messages from similar sources.

Source: Richard H. Baker, "Fighting Fire with Firewalls," *InformationWeek,* October 21, 1996.

Administrative Controls

administrative controls Formalized standards, rules, procedures, and disciplines to ensure that the organization's controls are properly executed and enforced.

segregation of functions Principle of internal control to divide responsibilities and assign tasks among people so that job functions do not overlap to minimize the risk of errors and fraudulent manipulation of the organization's assets.

Administrative controls are formalized standards, rules, procedures, and control disciplines to ensure that the organization's general and application controls are properly executed and enforced. The most important administrative controls are (1) segregation of functions, (2) written policies and procedures, and (3) supervision.

Segregation of functions is a fundamental principle of internal control in any organization. In essence, it means that job functions should be designed to minimize the risk of errors or fraudulent manipulation of the organization's assets. The individuals responsible for operating systems should not be the same ones who can initiate transactions that change the assets held in these systems. Responsibilities for input, processing, and output are usually divided among different people to restrict what each one can do with the system. For example, the individuals who operate the system should not have the authority to initiate payments or to sign checks. A typical arrangement is to have the organization's information systems department responsible for data and program files and end users responsible for initiating input transactions or correcting errors. Within the information systems department, the duties of programmers and analysts are segregated from those of computer equipment operators. (The organization of the information systems department is discussed in Chapter 3.)

Written policies and procedures establish formal standards for controlling information system operations. Procedures must be formalized in writing and authorized by the appropriate level of management. Accountabilities and responsibilities must be clearly specified.

Supervision of personnel involved in control procedures ensures that the controls for an information system are performing as intended. With supervision, weaknesses can be spotted, errors corrected, and deviations from standard procedures identified. Without adequate supervision, the best-designed set of controls may be bypassed, short-circuited, or neglected.

Weakness in each of these general controls can have a widespread effect on programmed procedures and data throughout the organization. Table 17.6 summarizes the effect of weaknesses in major general control areas.

Application Controls

Application controls are specific controls within each separate computer application, such as payroll or order processing. They include both automated and manual procedures that ensure that only authorized data are completely and accurately processed by that application. The controls for each application should take account of the whole sequence of processing, manual and computer, from the first steps taken to prepare transactions to the production and use of final output.

Not all the application controls discussed here are used in every information system. Some systems require more of these controls than others, depending on the importance of the data and the nature of the application.

Application controls focus on the following objectives:

1. *Completeness of input and update.* All current transactions must reach the computer and be recorded on computer files.

2. *Accuracy of input and update.* Data must be accurately captured by the computer and correctly recorded on computer files.

3. *Validity.* Data must be authorized or otherwise checked with regard to the appropriateness of the transaction. (In other words, the transaction must reflect the right event in the external world. The validity of an address change, for example, refers to whether a transaction actually captured the right address for a specific individual.)

4. *Maintenance.* Data on computer files must continue to remain correct and current.

Table 17.6   Effect of Weakness in General Controls

Weakness Area	Impact
Implementation controls	New systems or systems that have been modified will have errors or fail to function as required.
Software controls (program security)	Unauthorized changes can be made in processing. The organization may not be sure of which programs or systems have been changed.
Software controls (system software)	These controls may not have a direct effect on individual applications. Because other general controls depend heavily on system software, a weakness in this area impairs the other general controls.
Physical hardware controls	Hardware may have serious malfunctions or may break down altogether, introducing numerous errors or destroying computerized records.
Computer operations controls	Random errors may occur in a system. (Most processing will be correct but occasionally it may not be.)
Data file security controls	Unauthorized changes can be made in data stored in computer systems or unauthorized individuals can access sensitive information.
Administrative controls	All the other controls may not be properly executed or enforced.

Application controls can be classified as (1) input controls, (2) processing controls, and (3) output controls.

Input Controls

Input controls check data for accuracy and completeness when they enter the system. There are specific input controls for input authorization, data conversion, data editing, and error handling.

INPUT AUTHORIZATION.   Input must be properly authorized, recorded, and monitored as source documents flow to the computer. For example, formal procedures can be set up to authorize only selected members of the sales department to prepare sales transactions for an order entry system. Sales input forms might be serially numbered, grouped into *batches*, and logged so that they can be tracked as they pass from sales units to the unit responsible for inputting them into the computer. The batches may require authorization signatures before they can be entered into the computer.

DATA CONVERSION.   Input must be properly converted into computer transactions with no errors as it is transcribed from one form to another. Transcription errors can be eliminated or reduced by keying input transactions directly into computer terminals from their source documents. (Point-of-sale systems can capture sales and inventory transactions directly by scanning product bar codes.)

    Batch control totals can be established beforehand for transactions grouped in batches. These totals can range from a simple document count to totals for quantity fields such as total sales amount (for the batch). Computer programs count the batch totals from transactions input. Batches that do not balance are rejected. On-line, real-time systems can also utilize batch controls by creating control totals to reconcile with hard copy documents that feed input.

input controls   Procedures to check data for accuracy and completeness when they enter the system, including input authorization, data conversion, and edit checks.

input authorization   Proper authorization, recording, and monitoring of source documents as they enter the computer system.

data conversion   Process of properly transcribing data from one form into another form for computer transactions.

batch control totals   A type of input control that requires counting batches or any quantity field in a batch of transactions prior to processing for comparison and reconciliation after processing.

edit checks Routines performed to verify input data and correct errors prior to processing.

EDIT CHECKS. Various routines can be performed to edit input data for errors before they are processed. Transactions that do not meet edit criteria will be rejected. The edit routines can produce lists of errors to be corrected later. The most important types of edit techniques are summarized in Table 17.7.

An advantage of on-line, real-time systems is that editing can be performed up-front. As each transaction is input and entered it can be edited, and the terminal operator can be notified immediately if an error is found. Alternatively, the operator may fail to correct the error on purpose or by accident. The system can be designed to reject additional input until the error is corrected or to print a hard copy error list that can be reviewed by others.

Processing Controls

processing controls Routines for establishing that data are complete and accurate during updating.

Processing controls establish that data are complete and accurate during updating. The major processing controls are run control totals, computer matching, and programmed edit checks.

run control totals Procedures for controlling completeness of computer updating by generating control totals that reconcile totals before and after processing.

Run control totals reconcile the input control totals with the totals of items that have updated the file. Updating can be controlled by generating control totals during processing. The totals, such as total transactions processed or totals for critical quantities, can be compared manually or by computer. Discrepancies are noted for investigation.

computer matching Processing control that matches input data with information held on master files.

Computer matching matches the input data with information held on master or suspense files, with unmatched items noted for investigation. Most matching occurs during input, but under some circumstances it may be required to ensure completeness of updating. For example, a matching program might match employee time cards with a payroll master file and report missing or duplicate time cards.

Edit checks verify reasonableness or consistency of data. Most edit checking occurs at the time data are input. However, certain applications also require some type of reasonableness or dependency check during updating. For example, consistency checks might be utilized by a utility company to compare a customer's electric bill with previous bills. If the bill were 500 percent higher this month compared with last month, the bill would not be processed until the meter was rechecked.

Table 17.7	Important Edit Techniques	
Edit Technique	**Description**	**Example**
Reasonableness checks	To be accepted, data must fall within certain limits set in advance, or they will be rejected.	If an order transaction is for 20,000 units and the largest order on record was 50 units, the transaction will be rejected.
Format checks	Characteristics of the contents (letter/digit), length, and sign of individual data fields are checked by the system.	A nine-position Social Security number should not contain any alphabetic characters.
Existence checks	The computer compares input reference data with tables or master files to make sure that valid codes are being used.	An employee can have a Fair Labor Standards Act code of only 1, 2, 3, 4, or 5. All other values for this field will be rejected.
Dependency checks	The computer checks whether a *logical* relationship is maintained between data for the *same* transaction. When it is not, the transaction is rejected.	A car loan initiation transaction should show a logical relationship between the size of the loan, the number of loan repayments, and the size of each installment.
Check digit	An extra reference number called a *check digit* follows an identification code and bears a mathematical relationship to the other digits. This extra digit is input with the data, recomputed by the computer, and the result compared with the one input.	See the check digit in Figure 17.5 for a product code using the Modulus 11 check digit system.

Output Controls

Output controls ensure that the results of computer processing are accurate, complete, and properly distributed. Typical output controls include the following:

- Balancing output totals with input and processing totals
- Reviews of the computer processing logs to determine that all the correct computer jobs were executed properly for processing
- Audits of output reports to make sure that totals, formats, and critical details are correct and reconcilable with input
- Formal procedures and documentation specifying authorized recipients of output reports, checks, or other critical documents

Security and Electronic Commerce

Security of electronic communications is a major control issue for companies engaged in electronic commerce. Not only must security problems be solved, but both individuals and managers of organizations must believe that these problems are solved before electronic commerce can reach its full potential.

It is essential that commerce-related data of buyers and sellers be kept private when it is transmitted electronically. For example, individuals want to protect their credit card numbers, while companies want to protect company secrets. The data being transmitted must also be protected against being purposefully altered by someone other than the sender, so that, for example, stock market execution orders or product orders accurately represent the wishes of the buyer and seller.

Many organizations rely on encryption to protect sensitive information transmitted over networks. **Encryption** is the coding and scrambling of messages to prevent unauthorized access to or understanding of the data being transmitted. A message can

output controls Ensure that the results of computer processing are accurate, complete, and properly distributed.

encryption The coding and scrambling of messages to prevent their being read or accessed without authorization.

Product Code:	2	9	7	4	3
Weight:	6	5	4	3	2
Multiply each product code number by weight:	12	45	28	12	6
Sum results:	12 + 45 + 28 + 12 + 6 = 103				
Divide the sum by modulus:	103/11 = 9 with remainder of 4				
Subtract remainder from modulus number to obtain check digit:	11 − 4 = 7				
Add check digit to original product code to obtain new code:	297437				

FIGURE 17.5

Check digit for a product code. This is a product code with the last position as a check digit, as developed by the Modulus 11 check digit system, the most common check digit method. The check digit is 7 and is derived by the steps listed in this figure. Errors in the transcription or transposition of this product code can be detected by a computer program that replicates the same procedure for deriving the check digit. If a data entry person mistakenly keys in the product number as 29753, the program will read the first five digits and carry out the Modulus 11 process. It will derive a check digit of 4. When this is compared with the original check digit on the last position of the product code, the program will find that the check digits do not match and that an error has occurred.

be encrypted by applying a secret numerical code called an *encryption key* so that it is transmitted as a scrambled set of characters. To be read, the message must be decrypted (unscrambled) with a matching key. A number of different encryption standards exist, including Data Encryption Standard (DES), which is used by the U.S. government, RSA (by RSA Data Security), SSL (Secure Sockets Layer), and S-HTTP (Secure Hypertext Transport Protocol). SSL and S-HTTP are used for Web-based traffic.

Encryption is especially useful to shield messages on the Internet and other public networks because they are less secure than private networks. Encryption helps protect transmission of payment data, such as credit card information and helps address problems of authentication and message integrity. **Authentication** refers to the ability of each party to know that the other parties in a transaction are who they claim to be. In the nonelectronic world, we use our signatures. Bank-by-mail systems avoid the need for signatures on checks they issue for their customers by using well-protected private networks in which the source of the request for payment is recorded and can be proved. **Message integrity** is the ability to be certain that the message that is sent arrives without being copied or changed. Experts are currently working on methods that involve encryption for creating agreed-upon certified digital signatures. Modern encryption methods are expected to be mathematically so complex that it becomes almost impossible to change a message and have the resulting message be understandable.

Much on-line commerce continues to be handled through private EDI networks, usually run over value-added networks (VANs). VANs have traditionally been used for electronic commerce because they are relatively secure and reliable, and because they offer additional desirable functions such as network auditing and tracking of communications. However, because they have to be privately maintained and run on high-speed private lines, VANs are expensive, easily costing a company $100,000 per month. They are also inflexible, being connected only to a limited number of sites and companies. As a result, the Internet is emerging as the network technology of choice. EDI transactions on the Internet equal one-half to one-tenth the cost of a VAN-based transaction (Knowles, 1997). Special electronic payment systems have been developed for the Internet. Their capabilities and security features are described in the Window on Technology.

Developing a Control Structure: Costs and Benefits

Information systems can make exhaustive use of all the control mechanisms previously discussed. But they may be so expensive to build and so complicated to use that the system is economically or operationally unfeasible. Some cost-benefit analysis must be performed to determine which control mechanisms provide the most effective safeguards without sacrificing operational efficiency or cost.

One of the criteria that determine how much control is built into a system is the *importance of its data*. Major financial and accounting systems, for example, such as a payroll system or one that tracks purchases and sales on the stock exchange, must have higher standards of controls than a system to inventory employee training and skills or a "tickler" system to track dental patients and remind them that their six-month checkup is due. For instance, Swiss Bank invested in additional hardware and software to increase its network reliability because it was running critical financial trading and banking applications.

Standing data, the data that are permanent and that affect transactions flowing into and out of a system (e.g., codes for existing products or cost centers) require closer monitoring than individual transactions. A single error in transaction data will affect only that transaction, whereas a standing data error may affect many or all transactions each time the file is processed.

The cost effectiveness of controls will also be influenced by the efficiency, complexity, and expense of each control technique. For example, complete one-for-one

authentication   The ability of each party in a transaction to ascertain the identity of the other party.

message integrity   The ability to ascertain that a transmitted message has not been copied or altered.

standing data   Data that are permanent and affect transactions flowing into and out of a system.

Securing Electronic Payments on the Internet

Almost everyone agrees that the biggest piece of the Internet commerce puzzle is how to get paid. Many companies and individuals are reluctant to use the Internet for electronic payments because Internet communication is so difficult to secure. Financial organizations such as Citibank continue to use private networks because the security and reliability of the Internet does not yet meet their strict standards. On the other hand, stock trading on the Internet is flourishing, and companies such as Virtual Vineyards or Amazon.com booksellers are busy selling their wares on-line with Internet electronic payment systems. Here's how the most popular payment processing systems work.

CyberCash/Checkfree Wallet gives away client software that encrypts and forwards transaction and credit card information to a Web-based merchant. The merchant in turn forwards the information to a CyberCash server. The server takes the information behind a firewall, decrypts it, and sends it to the merchant's bank. The merchant's bank then forwards an authorization request to the bank that issued the credit card. After verifying the information, the bank issuing the card forwards either an approval or denial of payment to CyberCash. CyberCash transmits this information back to the merchant, who notifies the customer. The chance of a security breach is lessened because the merchant on the Web never sees or stores a credit card number.

CyberCharge acts as an interface between banking networks and Microsoft Merchant Server, electronic commerce software developed by Microsoft for selling on the Web. It does not require users to have client software and complies with RSA, SET/SSL, and POS commercial encryption standards. CyberCharge connects users of Microsoft Merchant Server to the federal banking network using a high-speed connection. Web sites running Microsoft Merchant Server can route encrypted data through the CyberCharge backbone to authorize, collect, and deposit funds into their bank accounts directly. When a prospective customer purchases something on a Web site using Microsoft Merchant Server, that user enters payment information and clicks a button to submit it. The server accepts the order, encrypts it, and transmits it to CyberCharge's server, which in turn routes it directly to the banking network.

DigiCash uses electronic cash for anonymous on-line purchasing. *Electronic cash* or *e-cash* is money represented in electronic form which is moving outside the normal network of money (paper currency, coins, checks, credit cards) and for now is *not* under the purview of the Federal Reserve within the United States. Users are supplied with client software and can exchange money with another e-cash user over the Internet. When they make an on-line purchase, the e-cash software creates a "coin" in an amount specified by the user and sends it to the bank wrapped in a virtual "envelope." The bank withdraws the amount requested from the user's account, puts a validating stamp on the "envelope" to validate the "coin's" value, and returns it to the user. When the envelope comes back, the user can spend the "coin."

First Virtual Internet Payment System takes a different approach from the others. Instead of devising a secure way to transmit information over the Internet, they avoid it entirely. Prospective customers must first apply for a unique alphanumeric personal identification number called a *VirtualPIN* that can be used at any participating site. The VirtualPIN is stored with the user's credit card number off-line, on a secure computer, meaning that only First Virtual has access to sensitive data. Merchants using this system must obtain a Seller's VirtualPIN and set up an account. When a customer makes a purchase over the Internet, all that travels on the Internet is the customer's VirtualPIN number. To process a payment, the merchant submits its Seller's VirtualPIN along with the shopper's VirtualPIN to First Virtual. First Virtual then e-mails the customer to confirm the purchase. If the customer approves the transaction, First Virtual processes the transaction and sends confirmation to the seller. The seller then ships the purchased item to the buyer.

To Think About: What management, organization, and technology issues would you consider in selecting an Internet payment system?

Source: Robert Keenan, "Are We There Yet?: A Developer's Guide to Internet Commerce Solutions," *Interactivity*, February 1997.

---

checking may be time consuming and operationally impossible for a system that processes hundreds of thousands of utilities payments daily. But it might be possible to use this technique to verify only critical data such as dollar amounts and account numbers, while ignoring names and addresses.

A third consideration is the *level of risk* if a specific activity or process is not properly controlled. System builders can undertake a **risk assessment,** determining the likely frequency of a problem and the potential damage if it were to occur. For example, if an event is likely to occur no more than once a year, with a maximum of

risk assessment Determining the potential frequency of occurrence of a problem and the potential damage if the problem were to occur. Used to determine the cost-benefit of a control.

Table 17.8	On-Line Order Processing Risk Assessment		
Exposure	Probability of Occurrence (%)	Loss Range/ Average ($)	Expected Annual Loss ($)
Power failure	30	5000–200,000 (102,500)	30,750
Embezzlement	5	1000–50,000 (25,500)	1275
User error	98	200–40,000 (20,100)	19,698

This chart shows the results of a risk assessment of three selected areas of an on-line order processing system. The likelihood of each exposure occurring over a one-year period is expressed as a percentage. The next column shows the highest and lowest possible loss that could be expected each time the exposure occurred and an "average" loss calculated by adding the highest and lowest figures together and dividing by 2. The expected annual loss for each exposure can be determined by multiplying the "average" loss by its probability of occurrence.

a $1000 loss to the organization, it would not be feasible to spend $20,000 on the design and maintenance of a control to protect against that event. However, if that same event could occur at least once a day, with a potential loss of over $300,000 a year, $100,000 spent on a control might be entirely appropriate.

Table 17.8 illustrates sample results of a risk assessment for an on-line order processing system that processes 30,000 orders per day. The probability of a power failure occurring in a one-year period is 30 percent. Loss of order transactions while power is down could range from $5000 to $200,000 for each occurrence, depending on how long processing was halted. The probability of embezzlement occurring over a yearly period is about 5 percent, with potential losses ranging from $1000 to $50,000 for each occurrence. User errors have a 98 percent chance of occurring over a yearly period, with losses ranging from $200 to $40,000 for each occurrence. The average loss for each event can be weighted by multiplying it by the probability of its occurrence annually to determine the expected annual loss. Once the risks have been assessed, system builders can concentrate on the control points with the greatest vulnerability and potential loss. In this case, controls should focus on ways to minimize the risk of power failures and user errors.

In some situations, organizations may not know the precise probability of threats occurring to their information systems, and they may not be able to quantify the impact of events that disrupt their information systems. In these instances, management may choose to describe risks and their likely impact in a qualitative manner (Rainer, Snyder, and Carr, 1991).

To decide which controls to use, information system builders must examine various control techniques in relation to each other and to their relative cost effectiveness. A control weakness at one point may be offset by a strong control at another. It may not be cost effective to build tight controls at every point in the processing cycle if the areas of greatest risk are secure or if compensating controls exist elsewhere. The combination of all the controls developed for a particular application will determine its overall control structure.

17.3   AUDITING INFORMATION SYSTEMS

Once controls have been established for an information system, how do we know that they are effective? To answer this question, organizations must conduct comprehensive and systematic *audits*. Large organizations have their own internal auditing group charged with this responsibility.

Function: Personal Loans _____
Location: Peoria, Ill. _____
Prepared by: _____ J. Ericson _____
Preparation date: __ June 16, 1998 _____
Received by: _____ T. Barrow _____
Review date: _____ June 28, 1998 _____

Nature of Weakness and Impact	Chance for Substantial Error		Effect on Audit Procedures	Notification to Management	
	Yes/ No	Justification	Required Amendment	Date of Report	Mangement Response
Loan repayment records are not reconciled to borrower's records during processing.	Yes	Without a detection control, errors in individual client balances may remain undetected.	Confirm a sample of loans.	5/10/98	Interest Rate Compare Report provides this control.
There are no regular audits of computer-generated data (interest charges).	Yes	Without a regular audit or reasonableness check, widespread miscalculations could result before errors are detected.		5/10/98	Periodic audits of loans will be instituted.
Programs can be put into production libraries to meet target deadlines without final approval from the Standards and Controls group.	No	All programs require management authorization. The Standards and Controls group controls access to all production systems, and assigns such cases to a temporary production status.			

FIGURE 17.6

Sample auditor's list of control weaknesses. This chart is a sample page from a list of control weaknesses that an auditor might find in a loan system in a local commercial bank. This form helps auditors record and evaluate control weaknesses and shows the result of discussing those weaknesses with management, as well as any corrective actions taken by management.

The Role of Auditing in the Control Process

An **MIS audit** identifies all the controls that govern individual information systems and assesses their effectiveness. To accomplish this, the auditor must acquire a thorough understanding of operations, physical facilities, telecommunications, control systems, data security objectives, organizational structure, personnel, manual procedures, and individual applications.

The auditor should collect and analyze all the material about a specific information system, such as user and system documentation, sample inputs and outputs, and relevant documentation about integrity controls. The auditor usually interviews key individuals who use and operate the system concerning their activities and procedures. Application controls, overall integrity controls, and control disciplines are examined. The auditor should trace the flow of sample transactions through the system and perform tests using, if appropriate, automated audit software.

The audit lists and ranks all control weaknesses and estimates the probability of their occurrence. It then assesses the financial and organizational impact of each threat. Figure 17.6 is a sample auditor's listing of control weaknesses for a loan system. It includes a section for notifying management of such weaknesses and for management's response. Management is expected to devise a plan for countering significant weaknesses in controls.

MIS audit Identifies all the controls that govern individual information systems and assesses their effectiveness.

Data Quality Audits

An important aspect of information system auditing is an analysis of data quality. **Data quality audits** are accomplished by the following methods:

- Surveying end users for their perceptions of data quality
- Surveying entire data files
- Surveying samples from data files

data quality audit Surveys of end users, files, and samples of files for accuracy and completeness of data in an information system.

This data quality auditor is analyzing the quality of data for a client by conducting a survey of data files for accuracy in the information system.

Unless regular data quality audits are undertaken, organizations have no way of knowing to what extent their information systems contain inaccurate, incomplete, or ambiguous information. Some organizations, such as the Social Security Administration, have established data quality audit procedures. These procedures control payment and process quality by auditing a 20,000-case sample of beneficiary records each month. The FBI, on the other hand, did not conduct a comprehensive audit of its records systems until 1984. With few data quality controls, the FBI criminal record systems were found to have serious problems.

A study of the FBI's computerized criminal records systems found a total of 54.1 percent of the records in the National Crime Information Center system to be inaccurate, ambiguous, or incomplete, and 74.3 percent of the records in the FBI's semi-automated Identification Division system exhibited significant quality problems. A summary analysis of the FBI's automated Wanted Persons File also found that 11.2 percent of the warrants were invalid. A study by the FBI itself found that 6 percent of the warrants in state files were invalid and that 12,000 invalid warrants are sent out nationally each day. The FBI has taken some steps to correct these problems, but low levels of data quality in these systems have disturbing implications.

- More than 14,000 persons could be at risk of being falsely detained and perhaps arrested because of invalid warrants.

- In addition to their use in law enforcement, computerized criminal history records are increasingly being used to screen prospective employees in both the public and private sectors. This is the fastest growing use of these records in some states. Many of these records are incomplete and show arrests but no court disposition; that is, they show charges without proof of conviction or guilt. Many individuals may be denied employment unjustifiably because these records overstate their criminality.

- These criminal records systems are not limited to violent felons. They contain the records of 36 million people, about one-third of the labor force. Inaccurate and potentially damaging information is being maintained on many law-abiding citizens.

The level of data quality in these systems threatens citizens' constitutional right to due process and impairs the efficiency and effectiveness of any law enforcement programs in which these records are used (Laudon, 1986a).

Data that are inaccurate, untimely, or inconsistent with other sources of information can also create serious operational and financial problems for businesses. When bad data go unnoticed, they can lead to bad decisions, product recalls, and even financial losses. For instance, Geer DuBois, a New York advertising agency, lost a $2.5-million-a-year account after the agency's billing system failed to credit the client for a six-figure payment. Even though Geer DuBois repaid the client with interest, the client decided to use another advertising firm. First Financial Management Corporation of Atlanta had to restate its earnings for the first nine months of the year because a subsidiary had lost track of some records after changing its accounting system (Wilson 1992). Studies have found an error rate as high as 15% in purchases made using laser scanners at checkout counters. Overcharges often outnumber undercharges because many merchandise items have higher prices in the scanner's database than on the shelf (Yang and Stern, 1995; Betts, 1994).

Poor data quality can be attributed to multiple causes. It may stem from errors during data input or it may be the result of faulty information system and database design. Systems need to be designed so that data are represented to rigorously mirror the real world and to satisfy the needs of actual users of the data (Wand and Wang, 1996; Strong, Lee, and Wang, 1997).

MANAGEMENT WRAP-UP

Management is responsible for developing the control structure for the organization. Key management decisions include establishing standards for systems accuracy and reliability, determining an appropriate level of control for various organizational functions, and establishing a disaster recovery plan.

MANAGEMENT

Many security breaches, errors, and other control problems can be attributed to human and organizational factors—people working inside the organization who either misuse or abuse information systems. Controls must take these human factors into account, because adding extensive controls can make systems too difficult to use.

ORGANIZATION

Systems that depend on networks and the Internet are highly vulnerable to penetration or disruption, requiring special safeguards. Key technologies for creating a contemporary control environment include antivirus and data security software, firewalls, and preprogrammed procedures for various steps in the processing cycle.

TECHNOLOGY

For Discussion: It has been said that controls and security should be one of the first areas to be addressed in the design of an information system. Do you agree? Why or why not?

SUMMARY

1. Show why automated information systems are so vulnerable to destruction, error, and abuse. Organizations have become so dependent on computerized information systems that they must take special measures to ensure that these systems are properly controlled. With data easily concentrated into electronic form and many procedures invisible through automation, systems are vulnerable to destruction, misuse, error, fraud, and hardware or software failures. The effect of disaster in a computerized system can be greater than in manual systems because all the records for a particular function or organization can be destroyed or lost. On-line systems and those utilizing networks, including the Internet, are especially vulnerable because data files can be immediately and directly accessed through computer terminals or at many points in the communications network. Computer "viruses" can spread rampantly from system to system, clogging computer memory or destroying programs and data.

2. Describe the role of controls in safeguarding information systems. Controls consist of all methods, policies, and organizational procedures that ensure the safety of the organization's assets, the accuracy and reliability of its accounting records, and adherence to management standards. For computerized information systems, controls consist of both manual and programmed procedures. Controls that safeguard information system security are especially important in today's on-line networked environment.

3. Distinguish between general controls and application controls. There are two main categories of controls: general controls and application controls. General controls control the overall design, security, and use of computer programs and files for the organization as a whole. They include physical hardware controls; system software controls; data file and network security controls; computer operations controls; controls over the system implementation process; and administrative controls. Firewalls help safeguard private networks from unauthorized access when organizations use intranets or link to the Internet.

Application controls are controls unique to specific computerized applications. They focus on the completeness and accuracy of input, updating and maintenance, and the validity of the information in the system. Appli-cation controls consist of (1) input controls, (2) processing controls, and (3) output controls. Encryption is a widely used technology for securing electronic payment systems.

4. Describe the most important techniques for controlling information systems. Some principal application control techniques are programmed routines to edit data before they are input or updated; run control totals; and reconciliation of input source documents with output reports.

5. Identify the factors that must be considered when developing the controls for information systems. To determine what controls are required, designers and users of systems must identify all the control points and control weaknesses and perform risk assessment. They must also perform a cost-benefit analysis of controls and design controls that can effectively safeguard systems without making them unusable.

6. Explain the importance of auditing information systems. Comprehensive and systematic MIS auditing can help organizations to determine the effectiveness of the controls in their information systems. Regular data quality audits should be conducted to help organizations ensure a high level of completeness and accuracy of the data stored in their systems.

KEY TERMS

Hacker	General controls	Administrative controls	Computer matching
Computer virus	Application controls	Segregation of functions	Output controls
Antivirus software	Implementation controls	Input controls	Encryption
Fault-tolerant computer systems	Software controls	Input authorization	Authentication
	Program security controls	Data conversion	Message integrity
On-line transaction processing	Hardware controls	Batch control totals	Standing data
	Computer operations controls	Edit checks	Risk assessment
Security		Processing controls	MIS audit
Controls	Data security controls	Run control totals	Data quality audit

REVIEW QUESTIONS

1. Why are computer systems more vulnerable than manual systems to destruction, fraud, error, and misuse? Name some of the key areas where systems are most vulnerable.

2. Name some features of on-line information systems that make them difficult to control.

3. What are fault-tolerant computer systems? When should they be used?

4. What are controls? What distinguishes controls in computerized systems from controls in manual systems?

5. What is the difference between general controls and application controls?

6. Name and describe the principal general controls for computerized systems.

7. Describe how each of the following serve as application controls: batching, edits, computer matching, run control totals.

8. What kinds of edit techniques can be built into computer programs?

9. How does MIS auditing enhance the control process?

10. What is the function of risk assessment?

11. Why are data quality audits essential?

12. What is security? List and describe controls that promote security for computer hardware, computer

networks, computer software, and computerized data.

13. Why must special security measures be taken by businesses linking to the Internet?

14. Describe the role of firewalls and encryption systems in promoting security.

GROUP PROJECT

Form a group with two or three other students. Select a system described in one of the Window boxes or chapter-ending cases. Write a description of the system, its functions, and its value to the organization. Then write a description of both the general and application controls that should be used to protect the organization. Present your findings to the class.

CASE STUDY

NASD Files Do a Disappearing Act

The National Association of Securities Dealers (NASD) is the self-regulatory organization of the brokerage industry and the operator of NASDAQ, the over-the-counter stock trading system that has evolved into the second largest stock market in the United States and the third largest in the world. NASD maintains regulatory records on the nation's 535,000 stockbrokers in a central registration depository (CRD) system. In early 1997, NASD disclosed that as many as 20,000 pieces of regulatory data on stockbrokers had been inadvertently purged from this system.

NASD first said that only 1100 files had been purged, but later revised the figure to about 3000. State regulators, on the other hand, insist the number was 20,000. The NASD said the 20,000 figure represented only the potential number of purged filings as opposed to actual ones.

CRD information is used by investors and regulators to track disciplinary histories of stockbrokers and their firms and is the industry's first line of defense against bad brokers. Despite the leading-edge technology available to Wall Street, the CRD still works much like a library card catalogue. Material about brokers and firms must be keyed manually by NASD clerks.

The NASD reported that these clerks were following faulty guidelines, which were inadvertently issued when the deletions occurred. These guidelines, which NASD no longer uses, were spelled out in an internal memorandum obtained by *The Wall Street Journal*. The NASD memo informs staffers that "revised" guidelines allowed them to delete a broad range of disciplinary data from the CRD system, including instances when a customer, court, or arbitration panel withdraws or dismisses a broker as a named party in a lawsuit or arbitration filing before a judgment is entered. Most purged data dealt with such information.

Under a contract with state regulators, NASD is not allowed to delete such information, yet the states were not informed about the revised guidelines. Elisse Walter, chief operating officer at NASD's regulatory arm, admitted that "it was an error—a serious error at that," but she stated that NASD quickly established steps and controls to make sure the problem would not happen again.

While NASD restored the purged records, investors could call a NASD hotline to find out about pending and resolved disciplinary cases against brokers or firms. (State securities offices can give investors additional data about pending court cases and arbitration.)

Attorneys representing investors were not satisfied. The NASD, as a self-regulatory organization disseminating data, should at the minimum have been able to inform people that the information they provide may not be complete.

The problem was accidentally uncovered a year earlier by a state regulator. John Deden, a Colorado investigator, printed out a CRD report of a stockbroker he was investigating. When he tapped into the CRD files a few months later to update the investigation, he found that two complaints that were on the original printout had disappeared from the file. Checking on other investigatory files, Delden found that a felony conviction on another broker's record had vanished as well. As he dug further, he found more missing data.

In September 1996, a group of NASD executives and regulators developed a "restoration protocol" for correcting the purged files. The group examined 300 pieces of purged data and determined what needed to be restored. It found 20,000 pieces of regulatory data that had been deleted from a sample of records between January 1995 and August 1996.

Determining what data are missing can be difficult. For example, NASD purged a customer complaint that Joseph Kathrein, Jr., a broker from Quick and Reilly Group Inc., in Newport Beach, California, had conducted unauthorized options trading. NASD had purged the complaint because it did not allege fraud. Kathrein denied the allegation and stated that the case had been resolved in arbitration, with no finding of guilt on either side. But he noted that it was part of his record and that everything should be on file for investors and regulators to view.

The purged Kathrein data will be restored to the CRD system, but other purges will be more difficult to reinstate. NASD allowed disciplinary records of brokers to be expunged as part of private settlement pacts with investors. According to Denise Crawford, the Texas securities commissioner, this practice raises the issue of whether the states can rely on the CRD. "If we can't rely on this information, the public isn't being served," she said.

State regulators are negotiating with the NASD on ways to overhaul the CRD system, including instituting procedures to erase stale complaints against brokers. The NASD and the states have agreed that certain complaints could be excised, such as those settled in favor of a broker or those that were not resolved within two years. They are also working on expanding system capabilities to give investors access to CRD's electronic database directly on-line. ∎

Source: Michael Siconolfi, "NASD Error Results in a Purge of Broker Data," *The Wall Street Journal*, February 7, 1997.

Case Study Questions

1. Evaluate the importance of the CRD system for the NASD, for the financial community, and for investors.

2. Identify control weaknesses in the CRD system. What management, organization, and technology factors were responsible for those weaknesses?

3. Design controls for the CRD system to deal with these problems.

REFERENCES

Anderson, Ross J. "Why Cryptosystems Fail." *Communications of the ACM* 37, no. 11 (November 1994).

Anthes, Gary H. "Viruses Continue to Wreak Havoc at Many U.S. Companies." *Computerworld* (June 28, 1993).

Baker, Richard. "Fighting Fire with Firewalls." *Information Week* (October 21, 1996).

Betts, Mitch. "Human Error Trips Up Laser Scanner Accuracy." *Computerworld* (June 27, 1994).

Boockholdt, J. L. "Implementing Security and Integrity in Micro-Mainframe Networks." *MIS Quarterly* 13, no. 2 (June 1989).

Borning, Alan. "Computer System Reliability and Nuclear War." *Communications of the ACM* 30, no. 2 (February 1987).

Buss, Martin D. J., and Lynn M. Salerno. "Common Sense and Computer Security." *Harvard Business Review* (March–April 1984).

Charette, Ron. "Inside RISKS: Risks with Risk Analysis." *Communications of the ACM* 34, no. 5 (June 1991).

Chaum, David. "Security Without Identification: Transaction Systems to Make Big Brother Obsolete." *Communications of the ACM* 28 (October 1985).

Fithen, Katherine, and Barbara Fraser. "CERT Incident Response and the Internet." *Communications of the ACM* 37, no. 8 (August 1994).

Halper, Stanley D., Glenn C. Davis, Jarlath P. O'Neill-Dunne, and Pamela R. Pfau. *Handbook of EDP Auditing.* Boston: Warren, Gorham and Lamont (1985).

Hoffman, Lance. *Rogue Programs.* New York: Van Nostrand Reinhold (1990).

"Information Security and Privacy." *EDP Analyzer* (February 1986).

Kahane, Yehuda, Seev Neumann, and Charles S. Tapiero. "Computer Backup Pools, Disaster Recovery, and Default Risk." *Communications of the ACM* 31, no. 1 (January 1988).

King, Julia. "It's C.Y.A. Time." *Computerworld* (March 30, 1992).

Knowles, Ann. "EDI Experiments with the Net." *Software Magazine* (January 1997).

Laudon, Kenneth C. "Data Quality and Due Process in Large Interorganizational Record Systems." *Communications of the ACM* 29 (January 1986a).

Laudon, Kenneth C. *Dossier Society: Value Choices in the Design of National Information Systems.* New York: Columbia University Press (1986b).

Littlewood, Bev, and Lorenzo Strigini. "The Risks of Software." *Scientific American* 267, no. 5 (November 1992).

Loch, Karen D., Houston H. Carr, and Merrill E. Warkentin. "Threats to Information Systems: Today's Reality, Yesterday's Understanding." *MIS Quarterly* 16, no. 2 (June 1992).

Maglitta, Joe, and John P. Mello, Jr. "The Enemy Within." *Computerworld* (December 7, 1992).

McPartlin, John P. "The True Cost of Downtime." *InformationWeek* (August 3, 1992).

Needham, Roger M. "Denial of Service: An Example." *Communications of the ACM* 37, no. 11 (November 1994).

Neumann, Peter G. "Risks Considered Global(ly)." *Communications of the ACM* 35, no. 1 (January 1993).

Oppliger, Rolf. "Internet Security, Firewalls and Beyond." *Communications of the ACM* 40, no. 5 (May 1997).

Perrow, Charles. *Normal Accidents.* New York: Basic Books (1984).

Post, Gerald V., and J. David Diltz. "A Stochastic Dominance Approach to Risk Analysis of Computer Systems." *MIS Quarterly* (December 1986).

Rainer, Rex Kelley, Jr., Charles A. Snyder, and Houston H. Carr. "Risk Analysis for Information Technology." *Journal of Management Information Systems* 8, no. 1 (Summer 1991).

Straub, Detmar W. "Controlling Computer Abuse: An Empirical Study of Effective Security Countermeasures." Curtis L. Carlson School of Management, University of Minnesota (July 20, 1987).

Strong, Diane M., Yang W. Lee, and Richard Y. Wang. "Data Quality in Context." *Communications of the ACM* 40, no. 5 (May 1997).

Tate, Paul. "Risk! The Third Factor." *Datamation* (April 15, 1988).

Thyfault, Mary E., and Stephanie Stahl. "Weak Links." *InformationWeek* (August 10, 1992).

United States General Accounting Office. "Computer Security: Virus Highlights Need for Improved Internet Management." *GAO/IMTEC-89-57* (June 1989).

United States General Accounting Office. "Computer Security: DEA Is Not Adequately Protecting National Security Information." *GAO/IMTEC-92-31* (February 1992).

United States General Accounting Office. "Patriot Missile Defense: Software Problem Led to System Failure at Dharan, Saudi Arabia." *GAO/IMTEC-92-26* (February 1992).

Wand, Yair and Richard Y. Wang. "Anchoring Data Quality Dimensions in Ontological Foundations." *Communications of the ACM* 39, no. 11 (November 1996).

Weber, Ron. *EDP Auditing: Conceptual Foundations and Practice,* 2nd ed. New York: McGraw-Hill (1988).

Wilson, Linda. "Devil in Your Data." *InformationWeek* (August 31, 1992).

Yang, Catherine and Willy Stern. "Maybe They Should Call Them 'Scammers'." *Business Week* (January 16, 1995).

Managing International Information Systems

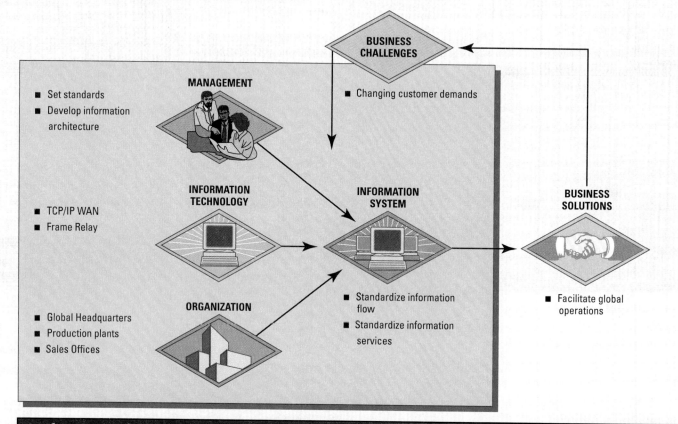

- Set standards
- Develop information architecture

MANAGEMENT

BUSINESS CHALLENGES

- Changing customer demands

- TCP/IP WAN
- Frame Relay

INFORMATION TECHNOLOGY

INFORMATION SYSTEM

BUSINESS SOLUTIONS

ORGANIZATION

- Global Headquarters
- Production plants
- Sales Offices

- Standardize information flow
- Standardize information services

- Facilitate global operations

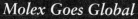

Molex Goes Global

When it comes to doing business around the world, Molex Corporation is a seasoned pro. This manufacturer of electrical connectors, headquartered in Lisle, Illinois, has been operating multinationally for more than 30 years. Molex runs 44 production plants in 21 countries and has sales offices in 35 nations.

Molex had been run using a decentralized international model. Each site operated independently.

CHAPTER OUTLINE

LEARNING OBJECTIVES

After completing this chapter, you will be able to:

1. Identify the main factors behind the growing internationalization of business.
2. Choose among several global strategies for developing business.
3. Understand how information systems support different global strategies.
4. Manage the development of international systems.
5. Understand the main technical alternatives in developing global systems.

But new customer demands called for a global business model where the company could present a single face in every worldwide location. Molex needed to find ways to standardize the flow of information and information services across the corporation.

Management stipulated that all the manufacturing and research and development centers around the world share cost data (to consoli-date financial information), production statistics (to allocate manufacturing resources more efficiently), and engineering and quality data (to promote a single quality standard). Information systems had to provide one level of support and one uniform set of services from Illinois to Tokyo. Molex is linking disparate desktop computers and computer centers into a TCP/IP wide area network backbone for global connectivity. It is contracting with a frame relay vendor for WAN services. Like Molex, many companies in a wide range of industries are searching for ways to link their multinational facilities into a single coherent information architecture. ■

Source: Mark Mehler, "Networking the World," *Beyond Computing*, May 1996.

Molex is one of many business firms moving toward global forms of organization that transcend national boundaries. But Molex could not make this move unless it reorganized its information systems. Molex improved its network connectivity and standardized some of its information systems so that the same information could be used by disparate business units in different countries. Such changes are not always easy to make, and raise the following management challenges:

1. **Lines of business and global strategy.** Firms will have to decide whether some or all of their lines of business should be managed on a global basis. There are some lines of business in which locale variations are slight, and the possibility exists to reap large rewards by organizing globally. PCs and power tools may fit this pattern, as well as industrial raw materials. Other consumer goods may be quite different by country or region. It is likely that firms with many lines of business will have to maintain a very mixed organizational structure.

2. **The difficulties of managing change in a multicultural firm.** Although engineering change in a single corporation in a single nation can be difficult, costly, and long term, bringing about significant change in very-large-scale global corporations can be daunting. Both the agreement on "core business processes" in a transnational context and the decision on common systems requires either extraordinary insight, a lengthy process of consensus building, or the exercise of shear power.

3. **The social and political role of "stateless" firms.** It is one thing to talk about a stateless transnational firm, but the people who work in these firms do have states, cultures, and loyalties; the operating divisions of these firms do in fact reside in various nation states with their own laws, politics, and cultures. It is unclear precisely how these stateless firms fit into the national cultures that they must serve. In reality, so-called stateless firms have had to be very careful to show local populations that they in fact do serve the interests of the state and broader culture.

The changes Molex made are some of the changes in international information systems infrastructure—the basic systems needed to coordinate worldwide trade and other activities—that organizations need to consider if they want to operate across the globe. This chapter explores how to organize, manage, and control the development of international information systems.

18.1 THE GROWTH OF INTERNATIONAL INFORMATION SYSTEMS

We have already described two powerful worldwide changes driven by advances in information technology that have transformed the business environment and posed new challenges for management. One is the transformation of industrial economies and societies into knowledge- and information-based economies. The other is the emergence of a global economy and global world order.

The new world order will sweep away many national corporations, national industries, and national economies controlled by domestic politicians. Much of the Fortune 500—the 500 largest U.S. corporations—will disappear in the next 50 years, mirroring past behavior of large firms since 1900. Many firms will be replaced by fast-moving networked corporations that transcend national boundaries. The growth of international trade has radically altered domestic economies around the globe. About $1 trillion worth of goods, services, and financial instruments—one-fifth of the annual U.S. gross national product—changes hands each day in global trade.

Consider a laptop computer as an example: The CPU is likely to have been designed and built in the United States; the DRAM (or dynamic random access memory, which makes up the majority of primary storage in a computer) was designed in the United States but built in Malaysia; the screen was designed and assembled in Japan, using American patents; the keyboard was from Taiwan; and it was all assembled in Japan, where the case was also made. Management of the project was located in Silicon Valley along with marketing, sales, and finance that coordinated all the myriad activities from financing and production to shipping and sales efforts. None of this would be possible without powerful international information and telecommunication systems, an international information systems infrastructure.

To be effective, managers need a global perspective on business and an understanding of the support systems needed to conduct business on an international scale.

Developing the International Information Systems Infrastructure

This chapter describes how to go about building an international information systems infrastructure suitable for your international strategy. An infrastructure is the constellation of facilities and services, such as highways or telecommunications networks, required for organizations to function and prosper. An **international information systems infrastructure** consists of the basic information systems required by organizations to coordinate worldwide trade and other activities. Figure 18.1 illustrates

international information systems infrastructure The basic information systems required by organizations to coordinate worldwide trade and other activities.

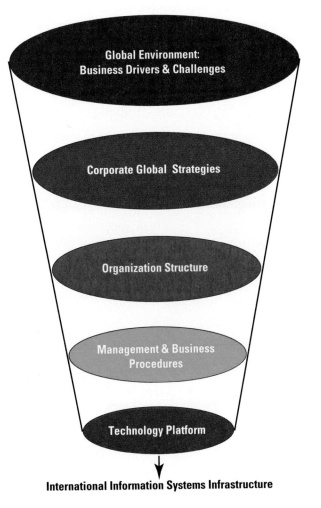

International Information Systems Infrastructure

FIGURE 18.1

International information systems infrastructure. The major dimensions for developing an international information systems infrastructure are the global environment, the corporate global strategies, the structure of the organization, the management and business procedures, and the technology platform.

the reasoning we will follow throughout the chapter and depicts the major dimensions of an international information systems infrastructure.

The basic strategy to follow when building an international system is first to understand the global environment in which your firm is operating. This means understanding the overall market forces, or business drivers, that are pushing your industry toward global competition. A **business driver** is a force in the environment to which businesses must respond and that influences the direction of the business. Likewise, examine carefully the inhibitors or negative factors that create *management challenges*—factors that could scuttle the development of a global business. Once you have examined the global environment, you will need to consider a corporate strategy for competing in that environment. How will your firm respond? You could ignore the global market and focus on domestic competition only, sell to the globe from a domestic base, or organize production and distribution around the globe. There are many in-between choices.

Once you have developed a strategy, it is time to consider how to structure your organization so it can pursue the strategy. How will you accomplish a division of labor across a global environment? Where will production, administration, accounting, marketing, and human resource functions be located? Who will handle the systems function?

Once you have designed an international organization, you will have to consider the management issues in implementing your strategy and making the organization design come alive. Key here will be the design of business procedures. How can you discover and manage user requirements? How can you induce change in local units to conform to international requirements? How can you reengineer on a global scale, and how can you coordinate systems development?

The last issue to consider is the technology platform. Although changing technology is a key driving factor leading toward global markets, you need to have a corporate strategy and structure before you can rationally choose the right technology.

Once you have completed this process of reasoning, you will be well on your way toward an appropriate international information infrastructure capable of achieving your corporate goals. Let us begin by looking at the overall global environment.

business driver A force in the environment to which businesses must respond and that influences the direction of business.

The Global Environment: Business Drivers and Challenges

Table 18.1 illustrates the business drivers in the global environment that are leading all industries toward global markets and competition.

Table 18.1 The Global Business Drivers
General Cultural Factors
Global communication and transportation technologies
Development of global culture
Emergence of global social norms
Political stability
Global knowledge base
Specific Business Factors
Global markets
Global production and operations
Global coordination
Global workforce
Global economies of scale

The global business drivers can be divided into two groups: general cultural factors and specific business factors. There are easily recognized general cultural factors driving internationalization since World War II. Information, communication, and transportation technologies have created a *global village* in which communication (by telephone, television, radio, or computer network) around the globe is no more difficult and not much more expensive than communication down the block. Moving goods and services to and from geographically dispersed locations has fallen dramatically in cost.

The development of global communications has created a global village in a second sense: There is now a **global culture** created by television and other globally shared media such as movies which permit different cultures and peoples to develop common expectations about right and wrong, desirable and undesirable, heroic and cowardly. A shared culture, with shared cultural artifacts such as news programs and movies, permits the emergence of shared societal norms concerning proper attire, proper consumption, and good and bad government. The collapse of the Eastern bloc has speeded up the growth of a world culture enormously, increased support for capitalism and business, and reduced the level of cultural conflict considerably.

global culture The development of common expectations, shared artifacts, and social norms among different cultures and peoples.

A last factor to consider is the growth of a global knowledge base. At the end of World War II, knowledge, education, science, and industrial skills were highly concentrated in North America, Europe, and Japan, with the rest of the world euphemistically called the *Third World*. This is no longer true. Latin America, China, Southern Asia, and Eastern Europe have developed powerful educational, industrial, and scientific centers, resulting in a much more democratically and widely dispersed knowledge base.

These general cultural factors leading toward internationalization result in specific business globalization factors that affect most industries. The growth of powerful communications technologies and the emergence of world cultures create the condition for *global markets*—global consumers interested in consuming similar products that are culturally approved. Coca-Cola, American sneakers (made in Korea but designed in Los Angeles), and CNN News (a television show) can now be sold in Latin America, Africa, and Asia.

Responding to this demand, global production and operations have emerged with precise on-line coordination between far-flung production facilities and central headquarters thousands of miles away. At Sealand Transportation, a major global shipping company based in Newark, New Jersey, shipping managers in Newark can watch the loading of ships in Rotterdam on-line, check trim and ballast, and trace packages to specific ship locations as the activity proceeds. This is all possible through an international satellite link.

The new global markets and pressure toward global production and operation have called forth whole new capabilities for global coordination of all factors of production. Not only production but also accounting, marketing and sales, human resources, and systems development (all the major business functions) can now be coordinated on a global scale. Frito Lay, for instance, can develop a marketing sales force automation system in the United States, and once provided, may try the same techniques and technologies in Spain. Micromarketing—marketing to very small geographic and social units—no longer means marketing to neighborhoods in the United States, but to neighborhoods throughout the world! In our laptop computer example described earlier in this chapter, design has become internationalized and coordinated through shared culture (defining what is good design) and dense communications networks. These new levels of global coordination permit for the first time in history the location of business activity according to comparative advantage. Design should be located where it is best accomplished, as should marketing, production, and finance.

Finally, global markets, production, and administration create the conditions for powerful, sustained global economies of scale. Production driven by worldwide global demand can be concentrated where it can be best accomplished, fixed resources can be allocated over larger production runs, and production runs in larger plants can be scheduled more efficiently and precisely estimated. Lower cost factors of production can be exploited wherever they emerge. The result is a powerful strategic advantage to firms that can organize globally. These general and specific business drivers have greatly enlarged world trade and commerce.

Not all industries are similarly affected by these trends. Clearly, manufacturing has been much more affected than services that still tend to be domestic—and highly inefficient. However, the localism of services is breaking down in telecommunications, entertainment, transportation, financial services, and general business services including law. Clearly those firms within an industry that can understand the internationalization of the industry and respond appropriately will reap enormous gains in productivity and stability.

Business Challenges

Although the possibilities of globalization for business success are significant, fundamental forces are operating to inhibit a global economy and to disrupt international business. Table 18.2 lists the most common and powerful challenges to the development of global systems.

particularism Making judgments and taking actions on the basis of narrow or personal characteristics.

At a cultural level, **particularism,** making judgments and taking action on the basis of narrow or personal characteristics, in all its forms (religious, nationalistic, ethnic, regionalism, geopolitical position) rejects the very concept of a shared global culture and rejects the penetration of domestic markets by foreign goods and services. Differences among cultures produce differences in social expectations, politics, and ultimately legal rules. In certain countries, such as the United States, consumers expect domestic namebrand products to be built domestically and are disappointed to learn that much of what they thought of as domestically produced is in fact foreign made.

Different cultures produce different political regimes. Among the many different countries of the world there are different laws governing the movement of information, information privacy of their citizens, origins of software and hardware in systems, and radio and satellite telecommunications. Even the hours of business and the terms of business trade vary greatly across political cultures. These different legal regimes complicate global business and must be considered when building global systems.

transborder data flow The movement of information across international boundaries in any form.

For instance, European countries have very strict laws concerning transborder data flow and privacy. **Transborder data flow** is defined as the movement of information across international boundaries in any form. Some European countries prohibit the processing of financial information outside their boundaries or the movement of employee information to foreign countries. The European Commission (the highest

Table 18.2	Challenges and Obstacles to Global Business Systems
General	
Cultural particularism: regionalism, nationalism	
Social expectations: brandname expectations; work hours	
Political laws: transborder data and privacy laws	
Specific	
Standards: different EDI, e-mail, telecommunications standards	
Reliability: phone networks not reliable	
Speed: data transfer speeds differ, slower than United States	
Personnel: shortages of skilled consultants	

planning body for the integration of Europe) is considering a digital services data protection directive that would restrict the flow of any information to countries (such as the United States) that do not meet strict European information laws on personal information. That means, for instance, that a French marketing manager may not be able to use a credit card in New York because the credit information cannot be forwarded to the United States, given its privacy laws. In response, most multinational firms develop information systems within each European country to avoid the cost and uncertainty of moving information across national boundaries.

Cultural and political differences profoundly affect organizations' standard operating procedures. A host of specific barriers arise from the general cultural differences, everything from different reliability of phone networks to the shortage of skilled consultants (see Steinbart and Nath, 1992). The Window on Organizations later in this chapter illustrates how such differences can affect efforts to conduct international business on the Internet.

National laws and traditions have created disparate accounting practices in various countries, which impact the way profits and losses are analyzed. German companies generally do not recognize the profit from a venture until the project is completely finished and they have been paid. British firms, on the other hand, begin posting profits before a project is completed, when they are reasonably certain they will get the money. Many European companies do not report per-share earnings, which is considered essential for U.S. and British firms.

These accounting practices are tightly intertwined with each country's legal system, business philosophy, and tax code. British, U.S., and Dutch firms share a predominantly Anglo-Saxon outlook that separates tax calculations from reports to shareholders to focus on showing shareholders how fast profits are growing. Continental European accounting practices are less oriented toward impressing investors, focusing on demonstrating compliance with strict rules and minimizing tax liabilities. These diverging accounting practices make it difficult for large international companies with units in different countries to evaluate their performance.

Cultural differences can also affect the way organizations use information technology. For example, Japanese firms fax extensively but are reluctant to take advantage of the capabilities of e-mail. One explanation is that the Japanese view e-mail as poorly suited for much intragroup communication and depiction of the complex symbols used in the Japanese written language (Straub, 1994).

Language remains a significant barrier. Although English has become a kind of standard business language, this is truer at higher levels of companies and not throughout the middle and lower ranks. Software may have to be built with local language interfaces before a new information system can be successfully implemented.

Currency fluctuations can play havoc with planning models and projections. Although a great deal of progress has been made in developing a common currency for the European economic community, occasionally this regime breaks down, evidenced by the British pound fluctuation in 1992 and 1993, or the U.S. dollar fluctuating against the Japanese yen and stronger European currencies. A product that appears profitable in Mexico or Japan may actually produce a loss due to changes in foreign exchange rates.

These inhibiting factors must be taken into account when you are designing and building an international infrastructure for your business. For example, companies trying to implement "lean production" systems spanning national boundaries typically underestimate the time, expense, and logistical difficulties of making goods and information flow freely across different countries (Levy, 1997).

State of the Art

Where do firms now have international applications and where do they plan expansion in the future? Figure 18.2 indicates the state of the art in terms of current applications and emerging areas of international systems infrastructure.

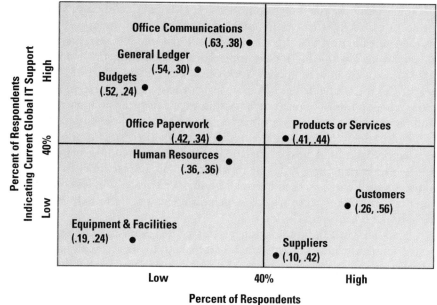

FIGURE 18.2

Frequency and type of business entities supported by global systems and databases. Most current IT applications are relatively simple office systems involving budgeting, communications, and general ledger financial coordination. Most corporations have local human resource and equipment/facilities systems. Global firms are expanding product support, customer service, and supplier systems to global stature.

Source: Adapted from Blake Ives and Sirkka Jarvenpaa, "Wiring the Stateless Corporation: Empowering the Drivers and Overcoming the Barriers," SIM Network, September/October 1991, p. 4C. Copyright © 1991 Society for Information Management.

One might think, given the opportunities for achieving competitive advantages as outlined previously and the interest in future applications, that most international companies have rationally developed marvelous international systems architectures. Nothing could be further from the truth. Most companies have inherited patchwork international systems from the distant past, often based on concepts of information processing developed in the 1960s—batch-oriented reporting from independent foreign divisions to corporate headquarters, with little on-line control and communication. At some point, corporations in this situation will face powerful competitive challenges in the marketplace from firms that have rationally designed truly international systems. Still other companies have recently built technology platforms for an international infrastructure but have nowhere to go because they lack global strategy.

As it turns out, there are significant difficulties in building appropriate international infrastructures. The difficulties involve planning a system appropriate to the firm's global strategy, structuring the organization of systems and business units, solving implementation issues, and choosing the right technical platform. Let us examine these problems in greater detail.

18.2   ORGANIZING INTERNATIONAL INFORMATION SYSTEMS

There are three organizational issues facing corporations seeking a global position: choosing a strategy, organizing the business, and organizing the systems management area. The first two are closely connected, so we will discuss them together.

Global Strategies and Business Organization

Four main global strategies form the basis for global firms' organizational structure. These are domestic exporter, multinational, franchiser, and transnational. Each of these strategies is pursued with a specific business organizational structure (see Table 18.3). For simplicity's sake, we describe three kinds of organizational structure or governance: centralized (in the home country), decentralized (to local foreign units), and coordinated (all units participate as equals). There are other types of governance patterns observed in specific companies (e.g., authoritarian dominance by

Table 18.3   Global Business Strategy and Structure

Business Function	Strategy			
	Domestic Exporter	Multinational	Franchiser	Transnational
Production	Centralized	Dispersed	Coordinated	Coordinated
Finance/Accounting	Centralized	Centralized	Centralized	Coordinated
Sales/Marketing	Mixed	Dispersed	Coordinated	Coordinated
Human Resources	Centralized	Centralized	Coordinated	Coordinated
Strategic Management	Centralized	Centralized	Centralized	Coordinated

one unit, a confederacy of equals, a federal structure balancing power among strategic units, and so forth; see Keen, 1991).

The **domestic exporter** strategy is characterized by heavy centralization of corporate activities in the home country of origin. Nearly all international companies begin this way, and some move on to other forms. Production, finance/accounting, sales/marketing, human resources, and strategic management are set up to optimize resources in the home country. International sales are sometimes dispersed using agency agreements or subsidiaries, but even here foreign marketing is totally reliant on the domestic home base for marketing themes and strategies. Caterpillar Corporation and other heavy capital equipment manufacturers fall into this category of firm.

The **multinational** strategy concentrates financial management and control out of a central home base while decentralizing production, sales, and marketing operations to units in other countries. The products and services on sale in different countries are adapted to suit local market conditions. The organization becomes a far-flung confederation of production and marketing facilities in different countries. Many financial service firms, along with a host of manufacturers such as General Motors, Chrysler, and Intel, fit this pattern.

Franchisers are an interesting mix of old and new. On the one hand, the product is created, designed, financed, and initially produced in the home country, but for product-specific reasons must rely heavily on foreign personnel for further production, marketing, and human resources. Food franchisers such as McDonald's, Mrs. Fields Cookies, and Kentucky Fried Chicken fit this pattern. McDonald's created a new form of fast-food chain in the United States and continues to rely largely on the United States for inspiration of new products, strategic management, and financing. Nevertheless, because the product must be produced locally—it is perishable—extensive coordination and dispersal of production, local marketing, and local recruitment of personnel are required. Generally, foreign franchisees are clones of the mother country units, yet fully coordinated worldwide production that could optimize factors of production is not possible. For instance, potatoes and beef can generally not be bought where they are cheapest on world markets but must be produced reasonably close to the area of consumption.

Transnational firms are the stateless, truly globally managed firms which may represent a larger part of international business in the future. Transnational firms have no single national headquarters but instead have many regional headquarters and perhaps a world headquarters. In a **transnational** strategy, nearly all the value-adding activities are managed from a global perspective without reference to national borders, optimizing sources of supply and demand wherever they appear, and taking advantage of any local competitive advantages. Transnational firms take the globe, not the home country, as their management frame of reference. The governance of these firms has been likened to a federal structure in which there is a strong central management core of decision making, but considerable dispersal of power

domestic exporter   A strategy characterized by heavy centralization of corporate activities in the home country of origin.

multinational   A global strategy that concentrates financial management and control out of a central home base while decentralizing production, sales, and marketing operations to units in other countries.

franchiser   A firm where product is created, designed, financed, and initially produced in the home country, but for product-specific reasons must rely heavily on foreign personnel for further production, marketing, and human resources.

transnational   Truly globally managed firms that have no national headquarters; value-added activities are managed from a global perspective without reference to national borders, optimizing sources of supply and demand and taking advantage of any local competitive advantage.

McDonald's offers Chinese diners a full selection of burgers, fries, and drinks. McDonald's patrons in other countries will find the same choices available to them.

and financial muscle throughout the global divisions. Few companies have actually attained transnational status, but Citicorp, Sony, Ford, and others are attempting this transition.

Information technology and improvements in global telecommunications are giving international firms more flexibility to shape their global strategies. Protectionism and a need to serve local markets better encourage companies to disperse production facilities and at least become multinational. At the same time, the drive to achieve economies of scale and take advantage of short-term local advantages moves transnationals toward a global management perspective and a concentration of power and authority. Hence, there are forces of decentralization and dispersal, as well as forces of centralization and global coordination (Ives and Jarvenpaa, 1991).

Global Systems to Fit the Strategy

The configuration, management, and development of systems tend to follow the global strategy chosen (Roche, 1992; Ives and Jarvenpaa, 1991). Figure 18.3 depicts the typical arrangements. By *systems* we mean the full range of activities involved in building information systems: conception and alignment with the strategic business plan, systems development, and ongoing operation. For the sake of simplicity, we consider four types of systems configuration. *Centralized systems* are those in which systems development and operation occur totally at the domestic home base. *Duplicated systems* are those in which development occurs totally at the home base but operations are handed over to autonomous units in foreign locations. *Decentralized systems* are those in which each foreign unit designs its own, totally unique solutions and systems. Last, *networked systems* are those in which systems development and operations occur in an integrated and coordinated fashion across all units. As can be seen in Figure 18.3, domestic exporters tend to have highly centralized systems in which a single domestic systems development staff develops worldwide applications. Multinationals offer a direct and striking contrast: Here foreign units devise their own systems solutions based on local needs with few if any applications in common with headquarters (the exceptions being financial reporting

SYSTEM CONFIGURATION	STRATEGY			
	Domestic Exporter	Multinational	Franchiser	Transnational
Centralized	X			
Duplicated			X	
Decentralized	x	X	x	
Networked		x		X

FIGURE 18.3

Global strategy and systems configurations. The large X's show the dominant pattern, and the small x's show the emerging patterns. For instance, domestic exporters rely predominantly on centralized systems, but there is continual pressure and some development of decentralized systems in local marketing regions.

and some telecommunications applications). Franchisers have the simplest systems structure: Like the products they sell, franchisers develop a single system usually at the home base and then replicate it around the world. Each unit—no matter where it is located—has the same identical applications. Last, the most ambitious form of systems development is found in the transnational: Networked systems are those in which there is a solid, singular global environment for developing and operating systems. This usually presupposes a powerful telecommunications backbone, a culture of shared applications development, and a shared management culture that crosses cultural barriers. The networked systems structure is most visible in financial services where the homogeneity of the product, money, and money instruments seem to overcome cultural barriers.

Reorganizing the Business

How should a firm organize itself for doing business on an international scale? To develop a global company and an information systems support structure, a firm needs to follow these principles:

1. Organize value-adding activities along lines of comparative advantage. For instance, marketing/sales functions should be located where they can best be performed, for least cost and maximum impact; likewise with production, finance, human resources, and information systems.

2. Develop and operate systems units at each level of corporate activity—national, regional, and international. To serve local needs, there should be *host country systems units* of some magnitude. *Regional systems units* should handle telecommunications and systems development across national boundaries that take place within major geographic regions (European, Asian, American). *Transnational systems units* should be established to create the linkages across major regional areas and coordinate the development and operation of international telecommunications and systems development (Roche, 1992).

3. Establish at world headquarters a single office responsible for development of international systems, a global chief information officer (CIO) position.

Many successful companies have devised organizational systems structures along these principles. The success of these companies relies not only on the proper organization of activities, but also on a key ingredient—a management team—that can understand the risks and benefits of international systems and that can devise strategies for overcoming the risks. We turn to these management topics next.

18.3 MANAGING GLOBAL SYSTEMS

The survey of 100 large global corporations described earlier found that CIOs believed the development and implementation of international systems were the most difficult problems they faced. Table 18.4 lists what these CIOs believed were the principal management problems posed by developing international systems.

It is interesting to note that these problems are the chief difficulties managers experience in developing ordinary domestic systems as well! But these are enormously complicated in the international environment.

A Typical Scenario: Disorganization on a Global Scale

Let us look at a common scenario. A traditional multinational consumer goods company based in the United States and operating in Europe would like to expand into Asian markets and knows that it must develop a transnational strategy and a supportive information systems structure. Like most multinationals it has dispersed production and marketing to regional and national centers while maintaining a world headquarters and strategic management in the United States. Historically, it has allowed each of the subsidiary foreign divisions to develop its own systems. The only centrally coordinated system is financial controls and reporting. The central systems group in the United States focuses only on domestic functions and production. The result is a hodgepodge of hardware, software, and telecommunications. The e-mail systems between Europe and the United States are incompatible. Each production facility uses a different manufacturing resources planning system (or different version with local variations), and different marketing, sales, and human resource systems. The technology platforms are wildly different: Europe is using mostly UNIX-based file servers and IBM PC clones on desktops. Communications between different sites are poor, given the high cost and low quality of European intercountry communications. The U.S. group is moving from an IBM mainframe environment centralized at headquarters to a highly distributed network architecture based on a national value-added network, with local sites developing their own local area networks. The central systems group at headquarters was recently decimated and dispersed to the U.S. local sites in the hope of serving local needs better and reducing costs.

What do you recommend to the senior management leaders of this company who now want to pursue a transnational strategy and develop an information systems infrastructure to support a highly coordinated global systems environment? Consider the problems you face by reexamining Table 18.4. The foreign divisions will resist efforts to agree on common user requirements—they have never thought about much other than their own units' needs. The systems groups in American lo-

Table 18.4 Management Issues in Developing International Systems	
Agreeing on common user requirements	88%
Inducing procedural business changes	79
Coordinating applications development	77
Coordinating software releases	69
Encouraging local users to take on ownership	58

Source: Adapted from Butler Cox, *Globalization: The IT Challenge,* 1991, Amdahl Executive Institute, Sunnyvale, CA.

cal sites, which have been recently enlarged and told to focus on local needs, will not easily accept guidance from anyone recommending a transnational strategy. It will be difficult to convince local managers anywhere in the world that they should change their business procedures to align with other units in the world, especially if this might interfere with their local performance. After all, local managers are rewarded in this company for meeting local objectives of their division or plant. Finally, it will be difficult to coordinate development of projects around the world in the absence of a powerful telecommunications network, or therefore difficult to encourage local users to take on ownership in the systems developed.

Strategy: Divide, Conquer, Appease

Figure 18.4 lays out the main dimensions of a solution. First, consider that not all systems should be coordinated on a transnational basis—only some core systems are truly worth sharing from a cost and feasibility point of view. **Core systems** are systems that support functions that are absolutely critical to the organization. Other systems should only be partially coordinated because they share key elements, but they do not have to be totally common across national boundaries. For such systems, a good deal of local variation is possible and desirable. A last group of systems are peripheral, truly provincial, and are needed to suit local requirements only.

core systems Systems that support functions that are absolutely critical to the organization.

Define the Core Business Processes

How do you identify *core systems?* The first step is to define a short list of truly critical core business processes. Business processes were defined in Chapter 3, which you should review. Briefly, business processes are sets of logically related tasks such as shipping out correct orders to customers or delivering innovative products to the

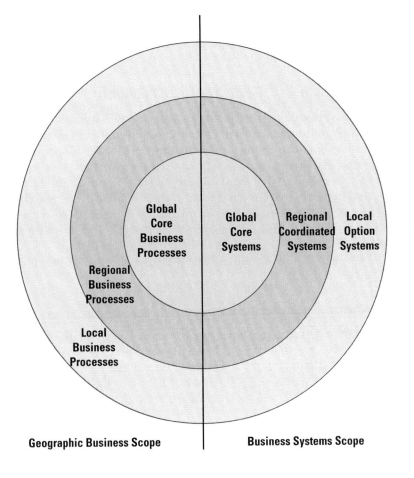

Global Core Business Processes

Global Core Systems

Regional Coordinated Systems

Local Option Systems

Regional Business Processes

Local Business Processes

Geographic Business Scope

Business Systems Scope

FIGURE 18.4

Agency and other coordination costs increase as the firm moves from local option systems toward regional and global systems. On the other hand, transaction costs of participating in global markets probably decrease as firms develop global systems. A sensible strategy is to reduce agency costs by developing only a few core global systems that are vital for global operations, leaving other systems in the hands of regional and local units.
Source: From Managing Information Technology in Multinational Corporations *by Roche, Edward M., © 1993. Adapted by permission of Prentice-Hall, Inc., Upper Saddle River, NJ.*

market. Each business process typically involves many functional areas, communicating and coordinating work, information, and knowledge.

The way to identify these core business processes is to conduct a workflow analysis. How are customer orders taken, what happens to them once they are taken, who fills the order, how are they shipped to the customers? What about suppliers? Do they have access to manufacturing resource planning systems so that supply is automatic? You should be able to identify and set priorities in a short list of 10 business processes that are absolutely critical for the firm.

Next, can you identify centers of excellence for these processes? Is the customer order fulfillment superior in the United States, manufacturing process control superior in Germany, and human resources superior in Asia? You should be able to identify some areas of the company, for some lines of business, where a division or unit stands out in the performance of one or several business functions.

When you understand the business processes of a firm, you can rank-order them. You can then decide which processes should be core applications, centrally coordinated, designed, and implemented around the globe, and which should be regional and local. At the same time, by identifying the critical business processes, the really important ones, you have gone a long way to defining a vision of the future that you should be working toward.

Identify the Core Systems to Coordinate Centrally

By identifying the critical core business processes, you begin to see opportunities for transnational systems. The second strategic step is to conquer the core systems and define these systems as truly transnational. The financial and political costs of defining and implementing transnational systems are extremely high. Therefore, keep the list to an absolute minimum, letting experience be the guide and erring on the side of minimalism. By dividing off a small group of systems as absolutely critical, you divide opposition to a transnational strategy. At the same time, you can appease those who oppose the central worldwide coordination implied by transnational systems by permitting peripheral systems development to progress unabated, with the exception of some technical platform requirements.

Choose an Approach: Incremental, Grand Design, Evolutionary

A third step is to choose an approach. Avoid piecemeal approaches. These will surely fail for lack of visibility, opposition from all who stand to lose from transnational development, and lack of power to convince senior management that the transnational systems are worth it. Likewise, avoid grand design approaches that try to do everything at once. These also tend to fail, due to an inability to focus resources. Nothing gets done properly, and opposition to organizational change is needlessly strengthened because the effort requires huge resources. An alternative approach is to evolve transnational applications from existing applications with a precise and clear vision of the transnational capabilities the organization should have in five years.

A global systems strategy should include a global security policy, as the Window on Management describes.

Make the Benefits Clear

What is in it for the company? One of the worst situations to avoid is to build global systems for the sake of building global systems. From the beginning, it is crucial that senior management at headquarters and foreign division managers clearly understand the benefits that will come to the company as well as to individual units. Although each system offers unique benefits to a particular budget, the overall contribution of global systems lies in four areas.

Global systems—truly integrated, distributed, and transnational systems—contribute to superior management and coordination. A simple price tag cannot be

Security Goes Global

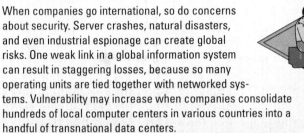

When companies go international, so do concerns about security. Server crashes, natural disasters, and even industrial espionage can create global risks. One weak link in a global information system can result in staggering losses, because so many operating units are tied together with networked systems. Vulnerability may increase when companies consolidate hundreds of local computer centers in various countries into a handful of transnational data centers.

According to Professor Edward Roche, author of *Managing Information Technology in Multinational Corporations* (1992), companies need to devise a security plan that addresses their global systems, and they need to rehearse coordination between headquarters and their local operations throughout the world.

Supporting this coordinated security policy approach, IBM and Comdisco, Inc. have developed global business recovery services. Companies can put their entire organization under one umbrella policy rather than contract disaster recovery services on a regional basis.

Forward-looking global organizations are setting up a small, central security team at company headquarters and then appointing someone to take charge of security for each business unit around the world. The central team conducts a risk analysis for the entire organization and then selects a methodology to use worldwide. For example, European operations might emphasize physical computer security, because computer theft is higher there than elsewhere.

The challenge is creating a security policy that can work across international boundaries. Only a small percentage of companies actually have security departments—as low as 18 percent among Asian-Pacific countries and 21 percent in Europe. There are different regional attitudes about the importance of security, making it difficult for employees to pay attention to the problem.

Less stringent security requirements in Europe and Asia allow banks to be less diligent about disaster recovery plans than in other parts of the world. The availability of software can also add to difficulties in implementing worldwide security strategies. Through a series of virus attacks, Otis Elevator learned that its European subsidiaries used antivirus software with a lower level of protection than that used by corporate headquarters in Farmington, Connecticut.

Global security planning paid off for Young & Rubicam Advertising. When the main server in its Sao Paulo, Brazil, office crashed one morning in December 1996, it could have created a catastrophe. Instead, it set off some well-laid plans. A copy of Lotus Notes (which this international advertising firm uses for its creative work, media plans, and strategy) was downloaded from its New York office on its wide area network (WAN). The Sao Paulo office was operational by the end of the business day. No data had been lost.

When Young & Rubicam launched its WAN in Latin America, it developed a single security plan for its diverse network needs in Argentina, Brazil, Mexico, and the United States. However, procedures differ slightly in each country. For example, in Brazil and Argentina, daily backup tapes are delivered to a storage vault, whereas in Mexico, backup tapes are delivered to the home of a Mexican executive because no similar pickup services exist.

> **To Think About:** What are the management benefits of having a global security plan? What are the management, organizational, and technology challenges to implementing such a plan?

Source: Tom Duffy, "Avoiding a Transnational Breakdown," *Computerworld Global Innovators*, March 10, 1997.

---

put on the value of this contribution, and the benefit will not show up in any capital budgeting model. It is the ability to switch suppliers on a moment's notice from one region to another in a crisis, the ability to move production in response to natural disasters, and the ability to use excess capacity in one region to meet raging demand in another.

A second major contribution is vast improvement in production, operation, and supply and distribution. Imagine a global value chain, with global suppliers and a global distribution network. For the first time, senior managers can locate value-adding activities in regions where they are most economically performed.

Third, global systems mean global customers and global marketing. Fixed costs around the world can now be amortized over a much larger customer base. This will unleash new economies of scale at production facilities.

Last, global systems mean the ability to optimize the use of corporate funds over a much larger capital base. This means, for instance, that capital in a surplus region can be moved efficiently to expand production of capital-starved regions; that cash can be managed more effectively within the company and put to use more effectively.

These strategies will not by themselves create global systems. You will have to implement what you strategize and this is a whole new challenge.

Implementation Tactics: Cooptation

cooptation Bringing the opposition into the process of designing and implementing the solution without giving up control over the direction and nature of the change.

The overall tactic for dealing with resistant local units in a transnational company is cooptation. **Cooptation** is defined as bringing the opposition into the process of designing and implementing the solution without giving up control over the direction and nature of the change. As much as possible, raw power should be avoided. Minimally, however, local units must agree on a short list of transnational systems and raw power may be required to solidify the idea that transnational systems of some sort are truly required.

How should cooptation proceed? Several alternatives are possible. One alternative is to permit each country unit the opportunity to develop one transnational application first in its home territory, and then throughout the world. In this manner, each major country systems group is given a piece of the action in developing a transnational system, and local units feel a sense of ownership in the transnational effort. On the downside, this assumes the ability to develop high-quality systems is widely distributed, and that, say, the German team can successfully implement systems in France and Italy. This will not always be the case. Also, the transnational effort will have low visibility.

A second tactic is to develop new transnational centers of excellence, or a single center of excellence. There may be several centers around the globe that focus on specific business processes. These centers draw heavily from local national units, are based on multinational teams, and must report to worldwide management—their first line of responsibility is to the core applications. Centers of excellence perform the initial identification and specification of the business process, define the information requirements, perform the business and systems analysis, and accomplish all design and testing. Implementation, however, and pilot testing occur in World Pilot Regions where new applications are installed and tested first. Later, they are rolled out to other parts of the globe. This phased roll-out strategy is precisely how national applications are successfully developed.

The Management Solution

We can now reconsider how to handle the most vexing problems facing managers developing the transnational information system infrastructures that were described in Table 18.4.

- *Agreeing on common user requirements:* Establishing a short list of the core business processes and core support systems will begin a process of rational comparison across the many divisions of the company, develop a common language for discussing the business, and naturally lead to an understanding of common elements (as well as the unique qualities that must remain local).

- *Inducing procedural business changes:* Your success as a change agent will depend on your legitimacy, your actual raw power, and your ability to involve users in the change design process. **Legitimacy** is defined as the extent to which your authority is accepted on grounds of competence, vision, or other qualities. The selection of a viable change strategy, which we have defined as evolutionary but with a vision, should assist you in convincing others that change is feasible and desirable. Involving people in change assuring them that change is in the best interests of the company and their local units, is a key tactic.

legitimacy The extent to which one's authority is accepted on grounds of competence, vision, or other qualities.

- *Coordinating applications development:* Choice of change strategy is critical for this problem. At the global level there is simply far too much complexity to attempt a grand design strategy of change. It is far easier to coordinate change by making small incremental steps toward a larger vision. Imagine a five-year plan of action rather than a two-year plan of action, and reduce the set of transnational systems to a bare minimum to reduce coordination costs.

■ *Coordinating software releases:* Firms can institute procedures to ensure that all operating units convert to new software updates at the same time so that everyone's software is compatible.

■ *Encouraging local users to take on ownership:* The key to this problem is to involve users in the creation of the design without giving up control over the development of the project to parochial interests. Recruiting a wide range of local individuals to transnational centers of excellence helps send the message that all significant groups are involved in the design and will have an influence.

Even with the proper organizational structure and appropriate management choices, it is still possible to stumble over technological issues. Choices of technology, platforms, networks, hardware, and software are the final elements in building transnational information system infrastructures. The Window on Technology describes how one global corporation has tackled these problems.

18.4 TECHNOLOGY ISSUES AND OPPORTUNITIES

Information technology is itself a powerful business driver for encouraging the development of global systems, but it creates significant challenges for managers. Global systems presuppose that business firms develop a solid technical foundation and are willing to continually upgrade facilities.

Main Technical Issues

Hardware, software, and telecommunications pose special technical challenges in an international setting. The major hardware challenge is finding some way to standardize the firm's computer hardware platform when there is so much variation from operating unit to operating unit and from country to country. Figure 18.5 illustrates the diverse hardware platforms that had been used by Citibank Asia-Pacific in various countries. (Citibank Asia-Pacific is centralizing some back-office applications, such as check and savings account processing, loan processing, and general ledger, and consolidating computer centers. One of the international case studies following this chapter is devoted to this topic.) Managers will need to think carefully about where to locate the firm's computer centers and about how to select hardware suppliers. The major global software challenge is finding applications that are user friendly and that truly enhance the productivity of international work teams. The major telecommunications challenge is making data flow seamlessly across networks shaped by disparate national standards. Overcoming these challenges requires systems integration and connectivity on a global basis.

Hardware and Systems Integration

The development of transnational information system infrastructures based on the concept of core systems raises questions about how the new core systems will fit in with the existing suite of applications developed around the globe by different divisions, different people, and for different kinds of computing hardware. The goal is to develop global, distributed, and integrated systems. Briefly, these are the same problems faced by any large domestic systems development effort. However, the problems are more complex because of the international environment. For instance, in the United States, IBM Corp. and IBM operating systems have played the predominant role in building core systems for large organizations, whereas in Europe, UNIX was much more commonly used for large systems. How can the two be integrated in a common transnational system?

Think Global and Act Local

What do business people mean when they say "think global and act local?" And how does a company's information technology contribute to instituting such a strategy? These are the questions that employees faced from DHL Worldwide Express, the Brussels-based shipment firm with more than 40,000 employees and a presence in 80,000 cities in 220 countries worldwide.

By acting locally, DHL means, for example, that its customers should be able to view their computer screens with their own language, that the computer databases will contain regulations that are important for every country where needed, that local information will be up to date on the computer and on the World Wide Web, and that all local (i.e., national) information will be under the control of the DHL units within each country. Acting globally means, for example, that the computer systems around the world be integrated, that customers anywhere in the world can check on the status and location of their packages and have that information be timely and accurate.

To meet both global and local requirements, DHL developed flexible global systems based on clear standards that also enable local units to meet their needs relatively easily. According to Nigel Green, a DHL Hong Kong–based information technology planning manager, central DHL provides "core applications services, accessible to all." These applications "sit on top of a messaging and communications infrastructure." The core global services offered by these applications include customer shipment, transit time, and billing details. They also contain electronic mail and intranet services. These global systems are built based on widely published standards so that all local DHL groups know how to customize to meet local needs. These systems are highly parametized, enabling local groups to set the parameters locally to meet their own needs, making it easy for them to customize as they require.

In addition, the flexibility of the global databases enables the local units to store only data needed locally. Some countries require additional data to support their local import regulations and their business practices. Thus, the common shipment database was specifically designed and built to enable local organizations to store local shipment data that will be seen only by the local unit that needs and stores it.

DHL standards also involve common application programming interfaces with local options which, for example, enable the Japanese group to display its DHL screens and information in Japanese characters rather than in some common "international" language such as English.

The second facet in global thinking and local action is dynamic systems that are automatically updated without requiring extra maintenance based on changing data in existing databases. DHL's Web site includes package tracking and a drop box and office locator. Originally, when it created its Web pages, DHL coded displayed data such as telephone numbers into the programs. The customer does not care how the data are stored, so long as they are there when needed. However, when most of the data the customers see are hard-coded into programs, the task of keeping up-to-date local information from all over the world is overwhelming. For instance, if a company should change its telephone number or address, that change would require a programmer to modify the program to update the data, a time-consuming and expensive task. Imagine if all the customers in a country had a telephone number change, as recently happened when the Australian telephone company added an extra digit to every telephone number in the country. The task would be overwhelming and perhaps too expensive to perform if programs had to be changed. So DHL switched to a programming approach that dynamically retrieves customer data from databases that are already being kept current to serve the other functions. Thus, when Australia made its massive telephone number change, no program updating was required. Now, as long as the local units keep their local customer data up to date in the proper place, no programming changes are needed and the local units can be served locally by an international system.

To Think About: *Suggest ways DHL could encourage the local units to follow these standards. What management, organization, and technology issues do you think DHL faced in introducing the "think global and act local" approach?*

Source: Anna Foley, "Global Shipper is Ready for World's Special Delivery Needs," *Computerworld Global Innovators,* March 10, 1997; and Natalie Engler, "Keeping Up with the Joneses," *Computerworld,* February 24, 1997.

The correct solution will often depend on the history of the company's systems and the extent of commitment to proprietary systems. For instance, finance and insurance firms have typically relied almost exclusively on IBM proprietary equipment and architectures, and it would be extremely difficult and cost ineffective to abandon that equipment and software. Newer firms and manufacturing firms generally find it much easier to adopt open UNIX systems for international systems. As pointed out in previous chapters, open UNIX-based systems are far more cost effective in the long run, provide more power at a cheaper price, and preserve options for future expansion.

Citibank Asia-Pacific's Conversion Schedule

Country	Conversion date
Australia	December '94
Guam	March '96
Hong Kong	April '95
India	October '97
Indonesia	November '96
Japan	No conversion
Malaysia	May '95
Pakistan	August '98
Philippines	June '96
Saudi Arabia	October '97
Singapore	March '95
South Korea	October '97
Taiwan	August '97
Thailand	August '96
Turkey	September '95
United Arab Emirates	January '97

- IBM mainframe
- AS/400
- Unix
- Unisys mainframe
- No current platform

DATA: CITIBANK ASIA–PACIFIC CONSUMER BANK

FIGURE 18.5

Citibank Asia-Pacific's hardware platforms. Citibank Asia-Pacific was using different hardware platforms in the various countries where it operates. It is consolidating its computer centers and standardizing core back-office applications to run on software at its Singapore IBM mainframe.

Source: Copyright © 1995 by CMP Publications, Inc., 600 Community Drive, Manhasset, NY 11030. Reprinted from InformationWeek *with permission.*

Once a hardware platform is chosen, the question of standards has to be addressed. Just because all sites use the same hardware does not guarantee common, integrated systems. Some central authority in the firm has to establish data, as well as other technical standards, with whom sites are to comply. For instance, technical accounting terms such as the beginning and end of the fiscal year must be standardized (review our earlier discussion of the cultural challenges to building global businesses), as well as the acceptable interfaces between systems, communications speeds and architectures, and network software.

Connectivity

The heart of the international systems problem is telecommunications—linking together the systems and people of a global firm into a single integrated network just like the phone system but capable of voice, data, and image transmissions. However, integrated global networks are extremely difficult to create (see Figure 18.6). For example, many countries cannot even fulfill basic business telecommunications needs such as obtaining reliable circuits, coordinating among different carriers and the regional telecommunications authority, obtaining bills in a common currency standard, and obtaining standard agreements for the level of telecommunications service provided.

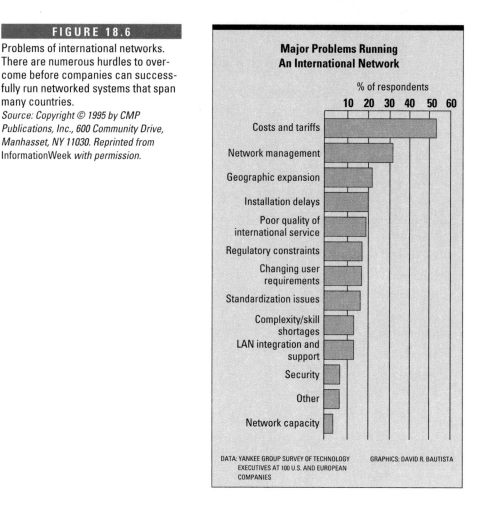

Major Problems Running An International Network

% of respondents

DATA: YANKEE GROUP SURVEY OF TECHNOLOGY EXECUTIVES AT 100 U.S. AND EUROPEAN COMPANIES

GRAPHICS: DAVID R. BAUTISTA

Despite moves toward economic unity, Europe remains a hodgepodge of disparate national technical standards and service levels. The problem is especially critical for banks or airlines that must move massive volumes of data around the world. Although most circuits leased by multinational corporations are fault-free more than 99.8 percent of the time, line quality and service vary widely from the north to the south of Europe. Network service is much more unreliable in southern Europe (Stahl, 1992).

Although the European economic community has endorsed EDIfact as the European electronic data interchange (EDI) standard, existing European standards for networking and EDI are very industry specific and country specific. Most European banks use the SWIFT (Society for Worldwide Interbank Financial Telecommunications) protocol for international funds transfer, while automobile companies and food producers often use industry-specific or country-specific versions of standard protocols for EDI. Complicating matters further, the United States standard for EDI is ANSI (American National Standards Institute) X.12. The Open Systems Interconnect (OSI) reference model for linking networks is more popular in Europe than it is in the United States. Various industry groups have standardized on other networking architectures, such as Transmission Control Protocol/Internet Protocol (TCP/IP), or IBM's proprietary Systems Network Architecture (SNA). Even standards such as ISDN (Integrated Services Digital Network) vary from country to country.

Firms have several options for providing international connectivity: Build their own international private network, rely on a network service based on the public switched networks throughout the world, or use the Internet and intranets.

One possibility is for the firm to put together its own private network based on leased lines from each country's PTT (post, telegraph, and telephone authorities).

With limited information technology resources, Frank Russell Co., a financial firm, created a powerful global network to link its headquarters in Tacoma, Washington, with offices in New York City, Toronto, London, Sydney, Tokyo, and Zurich.

Each country, however, has different restrictions on data exchange, technical standards, and acceptable vendors of equipment. These problems magnify in certain parts of the world. Despite such limitations, in Europe and the United States, reliance on PTTs still makes sense while these public networks expand services to compete with private providers.

The second major alternative to building one's own network is to use one of several expanding network services. With deregulation of telecommunications around the globe, private providers have sprung up to service business customers' data needs, along with some voice and image communications.

Although common in the United States, IVANs (International Value-Added Network Services) are expanding in both Europe and Asia. These private firms offer value-added telecommunications capacity usually rented from local PTTs or international satellite authorities, and then resell it to corporate users. IVANs add value by providing protocol conversion, operating mailboxes and mail systems, and offering integrated billing that permits a firm to track its data communications costs. Currently these systems are limited to data transmissions, but in the future they will expand to voice and image.

The third alternative, which is becoming increasingly attractive, is to create global intranets such as the World Bank's intranet described in the case study concluding this chapter, or to use the Internet for international communication. However, the Internet is not yet a worldwide tool because many countries lack the communications infrastructure for extensive Internet use. Countries face high costs, government control, or government monitoring.

Western Europe faces both high transmission costs and lack of common technology because it is not politically unified and because European telecommunications systems are still in the process of shedding their government monopolies. The lack of an infrastructure and high costs of installing one is even more widespread in the rest of the world. In South Africa, for instance, a slow (14.4 kbps) modem costs more than a month's average wages. Where an infrastructure exists, as in China and Pakistan, it is often outdated, lacks digital circuits, and has very noisy lines. Figure 18.7 shows the uneven distribution of Internet host computers throughout the world and the disparities in Internet access among developing and developed nations.

Many countries monitor transmissions. The governments in China and Singapore monitor Internet traffic and block access to Web sites considered morally or politically offensive. Corporations may be discouraged from using this medium. Companies planning international operations through the Internet will still have many hurdles.

Software

Compatible hardware and communications provide a platform but not the total solution. Also critical to global core infrastructure is software. The development of core systems poses unique challenges for software: How will the old systems interface with the new? Entirely new interfaces must be built and tested if old systems are kept in local areas (which is common). These interfaces can be costly and messy to build. If new software must be created, another challenge is to build software that can be realistically used by multiple business units from different countries when these business units are accustomed to their unique procedures and definitions of data.

Aside from integrating the new with the old systems, there are problems of human interface design and functionality of systems. For instance, to be truly useful for enhancing productivity of a global work force, software interfaces must be easily understood and mastered quickly. Graphical user interfaces are ideal for this but presuppose a common language—often English. When international systems involve knowledge workers only, English may be the assumed international standard. But as international systems penetrate deeper into management and clerical groups, a common language may not be assumed and human interfaces must be built to accommodate different languages and even conventions.

What are the most important software applications? Although most international systems focus on basic transaction and MIS systems, there is an increasing emphasis on international collaborative work groups. EDI—electronic data interchange—is a common global transaction processing application used by manufacturing and distribution firms to connect units of the same company, as well as customers and suppliers on a global basis. Groupware systems such as electronic mail, videoconferencing, Lotus Notes, and other products supporting shared data files, notes, and electronic mail are much more important to knowledge- and data-based firms such as advertising firms, research-based firms in medicine and engineering, and graphics and publishing firms. The Internet will be increasingly employed for such purposes.

New Technical Opportunities and the Internet

Major technical advances that should fall in price and gain in power over the next few years have importance to global networking and systems. After many years of stagnant development, PTTs in Europe and local Bell operating companies in the United States are finally moving ISDN (Integrated Services Digital Network) into the marketplace. Chapter 10 has described the benefits of using ISDN as an international standard for transmitting voice, images, and data over the public telephone network. ISDN will make networking services of all kinds as readily available as a phone jack in the wall.

Virtual private networks (VPNs) add features to the basic public telephone system that are usually available only to private networks. The basic idea of these services

virtual private network (VPN)
The ability to custom configure a network using a portion of the public switched network to create the illusion of a private network for a company.

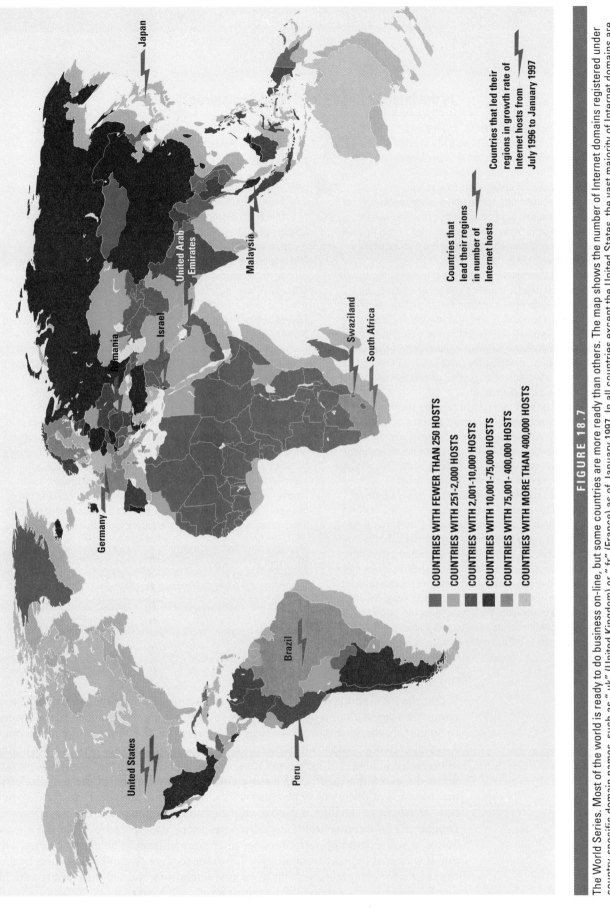

FIGURE 18.7

The World Series. Most of the world is ready to do business on-line, but some countries are more ready than others. The map shows the number of Internet domains registered under country-specific domain names, such as ".uk" (United Kingdom) or ".fr" (France) as of January 1997. In all countries except the United States, the vast majority of Internet domains are registered under country-specific domain names.

Source: From Christopher Koch, "It's Wired, Wired World" in Webmaster, March, 1997, pp. 52–53. Reprinted through the courtesy of CIO. © 1997 CIO Communications, Inc.

Legend (map):

- COUNTRIES WITH FEWER THAN 250 HOSTS
- COUNTRIES WITH 251–2,000 HOSTS
- COUNTRIES WITH 2,001–10,000 HOSTS
- COUNTRIES WITH 10,001–75,000 HOSTS
- COUNTRIES WITH 75,001–400,000 HOSTS
- COUNTRIES WITH MORE THAN 400,000 HOSTS

Countries that lead their regions in number of Internet hosts

Countries that led their regions in growth rate of Internet hosts from July 1996 to January 1997

Is the Internet Ready for Global Commerce?

When a Web site opens for business, anyone anywhere in the world can walk in, but actually selling abroad can be difficult. Global business operates in over 200 jurisdictions, each with its own mechanisms and regulations for distribution, freight handling, marketing, accounting, credit, and dispute resolution. Unlike conventional exporters, Web businesses cannot develop expertise by focusing on one country at a time. Anyone anywhere in the world can walk in, bringing a number of unresolved questions with them.

International Internet trade affects a range of political, economic, and cultural issues, including control of content, consumer protection, distributor licensing and regulation, enforcement of contracts, tax evasion, and libel and slander laws. Expectations and understandings that define a good business relationship vary widely among various cultures; often, they are unarticulated. Further complications arise when different parties in a transaction have different languages or different levels of competence in the same language.

What if completing a transaction requires supplementary services such as legal services, customs brokers, or fulfillment or advisory services? Where does the on-line merchant start? One solution is to contact a due-diligence service such as Standard and Poor's Corporation. Another is to order a World Trader's Data report from a regional office of the U.S. Department of Commerce. Neither solution is cheap (World Trader's Data reports cost about $100 each).

Outside the United States, both law and custom place the burden of complying with local import regulations upon the buyer rather than the seller. (To date, a seller is protected if the Web site and the purchase contract place sole responsibility for clearing customs with the buyer.) However, agreements to represent a product or service inside a foreign country carry some liability, opening exposure to taxation. Web merchants should be cautious about extending credit abroad, even to established customers, because it is difficult to collect debts in faraway jurisdictions. The

Small Business Foundation and the Export Legal Assistance Network maintain Web sites with more information on these issues.

The Global Business Alliance, a consortium including the U.S. Chamber of Commerce, Microsoft Corporation, General Electric Co., AT&T, Dun & Bradstreet Corporation, Digital Equipment Corporation, Chase Manhattan Bank, and SHL Systemhouse Inc., a Canadian software firm, started an on-line service called International Business Exchange (IBEX) to help companies master new business relations. IBEX walks members through the process of forming international business relationships one step at a time, with advice on building a company identity, preparing a buy–sell offer, defining the structure of interaction with interested parties, and negotiating.

Web sites need to be explicitly designed for international commerce. Because telephone service and Internet access are expensive in many countries outside the United States, Web pages should be kept simple and fast loading. The Web site should filter out intercultural references and should provide multicurrency price listings and unit-conversion tables. Addresses and telephone numbers for the business and its representatives should be complete and detailed. Special marketing and help files for shipping, currency, and payment information are recommended for customers with limited English language skills. Ideally, the Web site should present information in multiple languages. If this option is too costly, the Web site should at the minimum provide translations of the most important help files.

To Think About: What management, organization, and technology issues should be addressed with developing a Web site for international business? What business processes are affected?

Source: Fred Hapgood, "Foreign Entanglements," *Webmaster*, January–February 1996.

---

is that the local phone company provides each corporate user the ability to custom configure a network and use whatever portion of the public switched net is needed to do the job, charging only for services used. In a sense, the phone company becomes a digital network company, providing many features of a private network (including abbreviated dialing) for firms operating internationally. Firms using virtual private networks avoid the expense of leasing entire lines and many of the technical and maintenance problems of private networks. Throughout this text we have shown how the Internet facilitates global coordination, communication, and electronic commerce. As Internet technology becomes more widespread outside the United States, it will expand opportunities for international trade. The global connectivity and low cost of Internet technology will further remove obstacles of geography and time zones for companies seeking to expand operations and sell their wares abroad. Small companies may especially benefit (Quelch and Klein, 1996).

Sofware interfaces may have to be translated to accomodate users in East Asia or other parts of the world.

To use the Internet successfully for international commerce, organizations need to address a range of issues, as described in the Window on Organizations.

Finally, the variety of satellite systems described in Chapter 9 will revolutionize communications because they bypass existing ground-based systems. Thus, a salesperson in China could send an order confirmation request to the home office in London effortlessly and expect a reply instantly. The evolution of digital cellular phone and personal communications services will greatly increase the number of cellular communications units and wireless networks. These kinds of *communicate and compute anytime, anywhere* networks will be built throughout the next decade.

MANAGEMENT WRAP-UP

Managers are responsible for devising an appropriate organizational and technology infrastructure for international business. Choosing a global business strategy, identifying core business processes, organizing the firm to conduct business on an international scale, and selecting an international information systems infrastructure are key management decisions.

MANAGEMENT

Cultural, political, and language differences magnify differences in organizational culture and standard operating procedures when companies operate internationally in various countries. These differences create barriers to the development of global information systems that transcend national boundaries.

ORGANIZATION

The main technology decision in building international systems is finding a set of workable standards in hardware, software, and networking for the firm's international information systems infrastructure. The Internet and intranets will increasingly be used to provide global connectivity and to serve as a foundation for global systems, but many companies will still need proprietary systems for certain functions, and therefore international standards.

TECHNOLOGY

For Discussion: If you were a manager in a company that operates in many countries, what criteria would you use to determine whether an application should be developed as a global application or as a local application?

SUMMARY

1. Identify the major factors behind the growing internationalization of business. There are both general cultural factors and specific business factors to consider. The growth of cheap international communication and transportation has created a world culture with stable expectations or norms. Political stability and a growing global knowledge base that is widely shared contribute also to the world culture. These general factors create the conditions for global markets, global production, coordination, distribution, and global economies of scale.

2. Choose among several global strategies for developing business. There are four basic international strategies: domestic exporter, multinational, franchiser, and transnational. In a transnational strategy, all factors of production are coordinated on a global scale. However, the choice of strategy is a function of the type of business and product.

3. Understand how information systems support different global strategies. There is a connection between firm strategy and information systems design. Transnational firms must develop networked system configurations and permit considerable decentralization of development and operations. Franchisers almost always duplicate systems across many countries and use centralized financial controls. Multinationals typically rely on decentralized independence among foreign units with some movement toward development of networks. Domestic exporters are typically centralized in domestic headquarters with some decentralized operations permitted.

4. Manage the development of international systems. Implementing a global system requires an implementation strategy. Typically, global systems have evolved without conscious plan. The remedy is to define a small subset of core business processes and focus on building systems that could support these processes. Tactically, you will have to coopt widely dispersed foreign units to participate in the development and operation of these systems, being careful to maintain overall control.

5. Understand the main technical alternatives in developing global systems. The main hardware and telecommunications issues are systems integration and connectivity. The choices for integration are to go either with a proprietary architecture or with an open systems technology such as UNIX. Global networks are extremely difficult to build and operate. Some measure of connectivity may be achieved by relying on local PTT authorities to provide connections, building a system oneself, relying on private providers to supply communications capacity, or using the Internet and intranets. Public authorities and PTTs are moving forward rapidly with ISDN and other digital services to compete with private companies. The main software issue concerns building interfaces to existing systems and providing much needed group support software.

KEY TERMS

International information systems infrastructure	Particularism	Franchiser	Legitimacy
	Transborder data flow	Transnational	Virtual private network (VPN)
Business driver	Domestic exporter	Core systems	
Global culture	Multinational	Cooptation	

REVIEW QUESTIONS

1. What are the five major factors to consider when building an international information systems infrastructure?

2. Describe the five general cultural factors leading toward growth in global business and the four specific business factors. Describe the interconnection among these factors.

3. What is meant by a *global culture?*

4. What are the major challenges to the development of global systems?

5. Why have firms not planned for the development of international systems?

6. Describe the four main strategies for global business and organizational structure.

7. Describe the four different system configurations that can be used to support different global strategies.

8. What are the major management issues in developing international systems?

9. What are three principles to follow when organizing the firm for global business?

10. What are three steps of a management strategy for developing and implementing global systems?

11. What is meant by *cooptation*, and how can it be used to build global systems?

12. Describe the main technical issues facing global systems.

13. Describe three new technologies that can help firms develop global systems.

GROUP PROJECT

With a group of students, identify an area of emerging information technology and explore how this technology might be useful for supporting global business strategies. For instance, you might choose an area such as digital telecommunications (e.g., electronic mail, wireless communications, value-added networks) or collaborative work group software or new standards in operating systems or EDI or the Internet. It will be helpful to choose a business scenario to discuss the technology. You might choose, for instance, an automobile parts franchiser or a clothing franchise such as the Limited Express as example businesses. What applications would you make global, what core business processes would you choose, and how would the technology be helpful?

CASE STUDY

Banking on Technology To Lift Up Developing Countries

The World Bank, officially known as the International Bank for Reconstruction and Development, is a nongovernmental organization that works closely with such international organizations as the United Nations and its many agencies. It was established in 1944 (during World War II) by the renowned United Nations Monetary and Financial Conference at Bretton Woods in the United States. The bank's goal is "to reduce poverty and improve living standards by promoting sustainable growth and investments in people." It provides loans, technical assistance, and policy guidance, in the process giving away or lending billions of dollars every year to developing countries.

Most often the aid is aimed at helping the recipient countries improve their infrastructures, their health care, their education, and their environmental protection. One key World Bank expectation is that its projects will help reduce information and income inequalities. World Bank hopes to help these countries diversify into information-intensive industries, and to promote small and medium enterprises. Bank projects help the economies of these countries better mesh with the more advanced economies by promoting participation in global trade and competition.

Zambia is typical of the kinds of countries the World Bank is trying to help. It is a land-locked country slightly larger in size than Texas, located in southern Africa. It has a population of 9 million people and is growing at a rate approaching 4 percent. The life expectancy of infants at birth is only 36.3 years. Zambia's people have a literacy rate of 78 percent, which is high compared with many poor African countries. However, it has only one library, one university, and no television stations. Its economy is very limited, with copper mining accounting for over 80 percent of the country's foreign currency intake. It has an annual industrial growth rate of only 1 percent. The country is not self-sufficient in agriculture, and in addition has a consumer price inflation rate that was 46 percent in 1994. In 1995 its gross domestic product per capita was estimated at only $900. All in all, it is a poor and not very developed country.

In recent years, World Bank officials have been saying that even more important to countries like Zambia than the lack of money is the lack of information. Telecommunications infrastructure has become so vital that many economists now believe that telephone lines per capita better indicate a country's economic health than the more traditional per capita gross domestic product measure. In this area countries like Zambia have almost no telecommunications infrastructure. In many of these countries the cost of information is simply too high. For instance, in Tanzania, the cost of a call to New York is $7.50 per minute so that a 10-minute call costs $75, equaling the monthly wages of the average Tanzanian. Even more expensive, a two-page fax costs $50. Yet because faxes are sent through the telephone system, the quality is so poor that they rarely arrive complete and unaltered. Communication equipment is outdated and run-down so that quality cannot be improved. Given these kinds of telecommunications conditions, investment in these economies is usually so risky that few businesses dare take the plunge.

The World Bank itself also faced communications problems in recent years. At any one time 60 percent of its 10,000-member staff is out in the field, and for this staff, often being stationed in rural areas of countries such as Zambia and Tanzania, that can mean being totally out of touch and without modern methods of communications. As recently as 1994 the staff in the bank's Washington, D.C., headquarters kept up to date with developments in the field only through talking with colleagues who had returned from the field, supplemented with reports that were weeks out of date.

Since that time the bank has installed in all of its 97 offices around the world access to the bank's own network and its intranet. An enterprise network linking over 10,000 desktops uses TCP/IP and Netscape Navigator Web browsers, with plans to adopt Lotus Notes groupware. Intranet services are hosted on servers from Digital Equipment Corporation (DEC) and Sun Microsystems, along with Microsoft Windows NT servers.

Through the intranet, employees can do a full-text search of more than 10,000 of the bank's reports. They also have access to the databases on which investment decisions are made. In addition the bank has turned to the Web to help with all kinds of communications. Now, through the use of the Internet and its own intranet, communication within the organization has improved dramatically. Even in such countries as Zambia, Internet access has become available (often through the action of the World Bank), enabling its field and headquarters staffs to stay in touch.

From its own experience upgrading its telecommunications infrastructure, the bank has realized the clear benefits of the Internet in the less-developed countries. As a result, the World Bank has begun to focus more on financing the development of private Internet connections in its customers' countries. In September 1995, the bank created its Information for Development Program (InfoDev) division which is devoted to financing information technology infrastructure. In 1996 the bank member countries loaned only $4.4 million for InfoDev, tiny in comparison with the $21 billion loaned by them in that year. Nonetheless, that small amount is a beginning and a symbol of the World Bank's new understanding that Internet connectivity can play a potent role in raising the standard of living in the developing countries.

One challenge the World Bank is facing is how to build "local capacity," the economists' term for the ability of these countries to provide their own services. In Zambia a project devoted to building local telecommunications capacity provided by Zambians began in 1994 with a World Bank grant of $122,000 to establish ZamNet. The Zambian government made a major contribution by deregulating its dying telecommunications infrastructure, leaving ZamNet to take the steps it needed. ZamNet was set up as an independent, privately owned business. Project manager Mark Bennett was able to draw upon the University of Zambia's (Lasaka) existing network, originally using it as a backbone for ZamNet. It began offering Internet service provider (ISP) services for a fee, and it soon had 1500 subscribers paying a monthly fee of $50. The fee is high but the income is being used to build the network. As ZamNet's user base grows, the company plans to cut its monthly fee in half. The fee also helps subsidize the use of the Internet by the university, the country's health and public service sectors, and the government. Although current use of ZamNet remains far too expensive for most Zambians, the company is self-sufficient and growing. This is particularly significant given the $7000 per month cost of renting satellite time from Intelsat, a service owned by the countries it serves.

Problems exist, of course. To reach the Internet, data had to travel from ZamNet servers to the Zambian phone company's earth station, its link to the satellite. Although the distance is only five kilometers, the quality of the Zambian telephone ground service is so poor that data integrity cannot be protected. To deal with this problem, ZamNet is taking another route to the Internet. During 1997, ZamNet will switch to the PamAmSat Corporation satellite and will beam its own data directly from its own VSAT dish, thus bypassing the telephone company altogether. Using this approach offers a second benefit. ZamNet has been limited to the 9600 kps of bandwidth offered by the Zambian telephone company. Uploading its own data, it will be able to increase its own bandwidth at will.

In Zambia, the Internet has become important for much more than simply keeping the World Bank staffs in touch. A U.S. press official, on a recent trip to Zambia, was surprised to find that an American relief worker who had been laboring in isolated places for five years was keeping up with world events. When asked how, he replied, "Well, I read the *Washington Post* every morning on the Internet." This indicates that the Net is thus becoming a lifeline for information for residents of Zambia and other countries with poorly developed information systems. It can contribute significantly to improved education. Teachers and health care workers will be able to tap into Internet resources to further their own education through the use of distance learning. Health care workers can now obtain the knowledge they need to help them fight such diseases as AIDS—in Zambia over 25 percent of the children are malnourished and 25 percent are HIV positive. Given this new connectivity, Zambia expects to be able to attract doctors and teachers to remote areas where they would never have ventured in the past. Bennett, who is no longer employed by ZamNet, now plans to place laptop computers in remote hospitals, connecting them to the rest of the world.

The Internet is also becoming critical for the ability of developing countries to attract outside investment. "An Internet connection gives the countries of Africa a better chance of attracting companies," concludes Vincent Hovanec, the director of corporate communications for Global One, a joint venture of France Telecom, Deutsche Telekom, and Sprint. Hovanec explained, "If you have Internet connectivity, then global information access is not an issue." Many people now believe that the Internet may be the quickest and cheapest way for many African nations to achieve the level of communications they so badly need to attract foreign investment and develop a modern economy. ∎

Sources: Christopher Koch, "It's a Wired, Wired World," *Webmaster*, March 1997; The World Bank Group, http://www.worldbank.organization; Zambia, http://www.tbc.gov.gc.ca/cwgames/country/Zambia.

Case Study Questions

1. Describe the various barriers Zambia faces in modernizing its economy.

2. In what ways can the Internet help Zambia (and other African countries) attract the investment needed to help their economies modernize and grow?

3. What organization, management, and technology problems did the World Bank face in trying to establish locally owned and managed Internet links in less-developed African countries?

4. Suggest ways the World Bank can use the Internet to help develop the "local capacity" needed to make these countries self-reliant in telecommunications. In other fields such as medicine and education?

5. How did the Internet help the World Bank operate as an international organization?

REFERENCES

Cash, James I., F. Warren McFarlan, James L. McKenney, and Lynda M. Applegate. *Corporate Information Systems Management*, 4th ed. Homewood, IL: Irwin (1996).

Chismar, William G., and Laku Chidambaram. "Telecommunications and the Structuring of U.S. Multinational Corporations." *International Information Systems* 1, no. 4 (October 1992).

Cox, Butler. *Globalization: The IT Challenge*. Sunnyvale, California: Amdahl Executive Institute (1991).

Deans, Candace P., and Michael J. Kane. *International Dimensions of Information Systems and Technology*. Boston, MA: PWS-Kent (1992).

Deans, Candace P., Kirk R. Karwan, Martin D. Goslar, David A. Ricks, and Brian Toyne. "Key International Issues in U.S.-Based Multinational Corporations." *Journal of Management Information Systems* 7, no. 4 (Spring 1991).

Dutta, Amitava. "Telecommunications Infrastructure in Developing Nations." *International Information Systems* 1, no. 3 (July 1992).

Holland, Christopher, Geoff Lockett, and Ian Blackman. "Electronic Data Interchange Implementation: A Comparison of U.S. and European Cases." *International Information Systems* 1, no. 4 (October 1992).

Ives, Blake, and Sirkka Jarvenpaa. "Applications of Global Information Technology: Key Issues for Management." *MIS Quarterly* 15, no. 1 (March 1991).

Ives, Blake, and Sirkka Jarvenpaa. "Global Business Drivers: Aligning Information Technology to Global Business Strategy." *IBM Systems Journal* 32, no. 1 (1993).

Ives, Blake, and Sirkka Jarvenpaa. "Global Information Technology: Some Lessons from Practice." *International Information Systems* 1, no. 3 (July 1992).

Karin, Jahangir, and Benn R. Konsynski. "Globalization and Information Management Strategies." *Journal of Management Information Systems* 7 (Spring 1991).

Keen, Peter. *Shaping the Future*. Cambridge, MA: Harvard Business School Press (1991).

King, William R., and Vikram Sethi. "An Analysis of International Information Regimes." *International Information Systems* 1, no. 1 (January 1992).

Levy, David. "Lean Production in an International Supply Chain." *Sloan Management Review* (Winter 1997).

Mannheim, Marvin L. "Global Information Technology: Issues and Strategic Opportunities." *International Information Systems* 1, no. 1 (January 1992).

Nelson, R. Ryan, Ira R. Weiss, and Kazumi Yamazaki. "Information Resource Management within Multinational Corporations: A Cross-Cultural Comparison of the U.S. and Japan." *International Information Systems* 1, no. 4 (October 1992).

Neumann, Seev. "Issues and Opportunities in International Information Systems." *International Information Systems* 1, no. 4 (October 1992).

Palvia, Shailendra, Prashant Palvia, and Ronald Zigli, eds. *The Global Issues of Information Technology Management*. Harrisburg, PA: Idea Group Publishing (1992).

Quelch, John A., and Lisa R. Klein. "The Internet and International Marketing." *Sloan Management Review* (Spring 1996).

Roche, Edward M. *Managing Information Technology in Multinational Corporations*. New York: Macmillan (1992).

Sadowsky, George. "Network Connectivity for Developing Countries." *Communications of the ACM* 36, no. 8 (August 1993).

Stahl, Stephanie. "Global Networks: The Headache Continues." *InformationWeek* (October 12, 1992).

Steinbart, Paul John, and Ravinder Nath. "Problems and Issues in the Management of International Data Networks." *MIS Quarterly* 16, no. 1 (March 1992).

Straub, Detmar W. "The Effect of Culture on IT Diffusion: E-Mail and FAX in Japan and the U.S." *Information Systems Research* 5, no. 1 (March 1994).

Tractinsky, Noan, and Sirkka L. Jarvenpaa. "Information Systems Design Decisions in a Global Versus Domestic Context." *MIS Quarterly* 19, no. 4 (December 1995).

PHANTOM PROFITS HAUNT KIDDER PEABODY

On the morning of April 18, 1994, the Wall Street financial community awoke to headlines revealing that Joseph Jett, one of the most successful traders on Wall Street, had been fired. Jett, who at age 36 was the head of zero-coupon bond trading at Kidder Peabody Group Inc., had earned $210 million for Kidder in 1993, nearly half of the firm's total profit of $439 million. He personally had earned $9 million in salary, commission, and bonus and had been honored as Kidder's trader of the year for 1993.

Jett made his huge profits by trading government bond strips. Strips are created when the interest and principal portions of bonds are split into two separately traded instruments. The bond strips represent the bonds' interest payments—owners of strips have the right to the bonds' interest payments. Profits are made from buying strips in the open market and then reselling them at a higher price. The price of the strips will normally rise as the due date of the underlying bond approaches. The bonds, stripped of their interest portion, are known as zero-coupon bonds. Both the strips and the bonds are widely traded. Strips produce a very narrow profit on each trade, requiring a huge number of trades to make a large profit. However, many traders consider them to be risk free.

Once Jett had taken over the zero-coupon bond desk in early 1993,

he reported to Edward Cerullo, age 44, who was an executive managing director of Kidder and the head of its 750-person fixed-income securities group. Cerullo was widely considered to be Kidder's number two executive, after CEO Michael Carpenter. He was the person who had built Kidder's bond trading business, the foundation of Kidder's recent successes. Insiders report Cerullo made as much as $20 million in 1993, double his 1992 income. Much of that was a bonus based on the profits of Jett.

THE SCHEME UNCOVERED

In late March 1994, David Bernstein, who also reported to Cerullo, noticed that Jett's trading volume had been exploding, and he became suspicious. He began an intensive review of those trades and, at home over the weekend, he discovered that Jett had not been closing his trades. Jett had not actually booked any real profits. His profits were really fakes. Bernstein called in the Kidder accountants, and in early April they determined that Jett's legitimate trades had actually lost $90 million, whereas his fake trades had resulted in about $350 million in phantom profits. Bernstein took all of this to Cerullo, and on Sunday evening, April 17, Jett received a hand-delivered letter at his home informing him that he had been dismissed. Jett's scheme had apparently unraveled.

The next day Kidder notified the Securities and Exchange Commission (SEC) and the New York Stock Exchange (NYSE). The firm also reassigned six other bond traders and

trade-processing staff because they had not reported the scheme to management. Later, when asked why they were not fired, Carpenter explained, "Are they bad people? No. They just didn't catch it."

Jett's scheme was relatively simple. He would buy interest strips for forward delivery (delivery at a later date). However, when the contracts came due, he did not actually settle them. Instead he rolled them forward, closing the current strips and opening new ones due at a later date. Every time he rolled a position over, he booked a profit, but it was a fictitious profit, fictitious because nothing was ever settled, no cash ever changed hands, and Kidder never received any cash. Nor could Kidder ever collect accrued interest for strips it no longer owned. The so-called "profits" were actually only an agreement that Kidder would sell the strips back to the government in the future, and when Jett rolled the position over, the commitment was rolled over with it. Once the contracts were rolled over, Kidder no longer owned the earlier ones. To keep the scheme going, Jett had to keep writing the strips farther out in time and for larger amounts so the computerized accounting system would be fooled. The quantities became so large that Jett claimed to control more than twice the total amount of some bonds that had been stripped.

Jett told Kidder he had made trades involving $1.76 trillion in principal value in the first three months of 1994. Only $79 billion of those trades were real. The remaining $1.6 trillion, representing 95 percent, was never traded. Because Kidder officials apparently focused on the net profit of the department, not on individual types of trades, the phony trades obscured the losses. No one noticed the implausibility of what Jett was doing until the spring of 1994. It turned out that Jett never made any legitimate profits for Kidder—his trading actually lost $85,415,000 for the company (see Figure V.1).

Jett was able to take a bogus profit on the price of the strip, the interest portion of the bond, before it was "reconstituted," or turned back

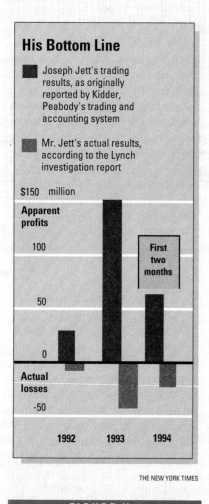

His Bottom Line

■ Joseph Jett's trading results, as originally reported by Kidder, Peabody's trading and accounting system

■ Mr. Jett's actual results, according to the Lynch investigation report

$150 million

Apparent profits

100

50

0

Actual losses

-50

1992   1993   1994

First two months

THE NEW YORK TIMES

FIGURE V.1

Apparent profits vs. actual losses at Kidder Peabody. Kidder Peabody's trading and accounting system recorded Joseph Jett's phantom trade as profits, when they actually produced losses for the firm.
Adapted from: Sylvia Nasar, "Kidder Scandal Tied to Failure of Supervision," in The New York Times, *August 5, 1994. Copyright © 1994 by The New York Times Co. Reprinted by permission.*

into the original bond because Kidder's trading system recognized a profit on the date that a forward "recon" was entered into the system. In other words, the system allowed Jett to report as "trades" what were really only a stated intention to make transactions in the future. The "profits" Jett reported reflected accrued interest that would never be received. Jett was rewarded with huge bonuses for the profits he claimed, when his trading was actually producing losses.

This accounting loophole, which allowed Jett to book a nonrealized profit at the time a trade was opened, resembled a giant ponzi scheme. According to Robert Dickey, a former Kidder trader, "You can make a temporary profit, but it's not real." He said the computer system defect was known by Jett's predecessors. In fact, it later came to light that in May 1993 Kidder accountant Charles Fiumefreddo noticed the critical flaw in the accounting system and suggested that it be fixed. His request was ignored. See Figure V.2 for a further explanation of the strips and Jett's scheme.

Kidder CEO Carpenter's public response was to claim that the trades were essentially harmless because they did not involve the mortgage or derivative markets and "involved no customers." He was correct that no customer was directly harmed because all these trades were for Kidder's own account. Carpenter also said that the scheme was "an isolated incident that happened despite the diligent efforts" to make Kidder's compliance control and risk management "state of the art." He announced that Kidder would take legal action against Jett. Giant conglomerate General Electric was also involved as the parent of Kidder Peabody.

GE CEO Jack Welch stated that the scheme "violates everything we believe in and stand for." Welch also announced that Kidder had hired Gary Lynch to "lead a comprehensive investigation into what went wrong and to recommend steps to prevent a re-

currence." Lynch was a partner at Kidder's outside law firm, Davis, Polk & Wardwell. He had an impeccable reputation for honesty and tenacity, and his background was perfect for the job. He had spent thirteen years at the SEC, the last four years as its enforcement chief. He was the lawyer who led the investigation and prosecution of the notorious insider trading case against Drexel Burnham Lambert and traders Ivan Boesky, Dennis Levine, Michael Milken, and Martin Siegel in the late 1980s.

Cerullo, Jett's boss, had not personally unearthed the problem. His public response was that Kidder's internal controls met industry standards. He added that he could not possibly have immersed himself in the financial records of the 750 traders that report to him. He further contended that Jett's profits had grown over an extended time, and at an appropriate growth rate, leaving no reason for him to be suspicious. Finally, he claimed that Jett's positions (holdings) were never as large as the reported $10 billion and were certainly within normal bounds. According to Alan Cohen, a New York defense lawyer who is a former head of the securities fraud unit of the Manhattan United States Attorney's office, "Traders have enormous discretion in what they buy and sell, and the more senior they are, the more discretion they have," meaning that large, successful traders are normally not closely monitored at Wall Street firms.

The size of the Kidder loss was difficult to determine at first. Despite Cerullo's claim, experienced traders estimated that Jett had to have been holding more than $10 billion in bonds to be able to record $350 million in profits, regardless if the profits were phony. Later, former government-bond desk traders estimated Jett's holdings to have been about $18 billion. The financial result of the discovery was that Kidder's income had been inflated by about $350 million over the previous 15 months. The investigation later

Conjuring Phantom Profits: A Scenario

Here is how Joseph Jett, who was dismissed as chief of Kidder Peabody's Government bond trading department, was said to be using quirks of the firm's accounting system to take credit for profits that existed only on paper.

FIGURE V.2

How Joseph Jett could fool Kidder Peabody's accounting system.

Adapted from: Floyd Norris, "Kidder, Peabody, Where Trading Went Awry," in The New York Times, *August 5, 1994. Copyright © 1994 by The New York Times Co., Reprinted by permission.*

STRIPPED AND RECONSTITUTED BONDS

A Treasury bond is a promise by the Treasury to make two kinds of payments: interest twice a year before the bond matures, and the principal (the face value of the bond) upon maturity.

When the Treasury issues the bond it is all in one piece, but the two components are often traded separately later: as a "strip" of coupons and the principal payment. The pieces can also be put back together, in a move called a recon.

Sometimes the bonds trade for slightly more in pieces than together, or vice versa; brokers routinely strip or reconstitute bonds to make arbitrage profits out of the small price differences.

30-year Treasury bond due in May 2007

Face value: **$1,000**
Interest rate: **12%**

Interest coupons
$60 every six months

+

Principal payment
$1,000 on maturity

FORWARD TRADES AND EPHEMERAL PROFITS

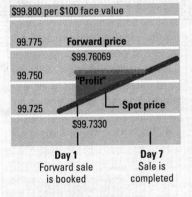

$99.800 per $100 face value

99.775   **Forward price**
$99.76069

99.750   **"Profit"**

99.725   **Spot price**
$99.7330

Day 1
Forward sale is booked

Day 7
Sale is completed

This forward sale of $8 million in strips was booked by Kidder Peabody as yielding $2,215 "profit" on the first day, falling to zero six days later.

A strip's principal payment component trades at a discount to face value that gradually shrinks in a predictable way as maturity approaches. Kidder Peabody's accounting system allows for this when assessing the value of forward trades.

When a broker records a forward sale—a deal struck today to sell a strip for a set price on a date in the future—the system notes that the forward price is higher than today's spot price, and books the difference as a profit. That profit is reduced each day as the spot price rises closer to the forward price, disappearing entirely the day the deal is completed.

If the deal were reversed and the broker was buying rather than selling, this temporary paper profit would be a paper loss instead.

OFFSETS THAT DIDN'T OFFSET

Apparently, Kidder's accounting system used different formulas to calculate the temporary gain or loss for different kinds of transactions.

Mr. Jett is said to have booked forward recon transactions with the Federal Reserve that offset each other exactly, leaving his net position in the market neutral and risk-free. The "trades" with the Fed were accounting fictions, since no money changed hands. But the complexities of the Kidder accounting system had the effect of crediting him with temporary paper profits on some of the trades that were larger than the paper losses on the offsetting trades. That made it appear the Mr. Jett was making profits for the firm without running any risk.

The paper profits on any one set of forward trades soon diminished to zero, but by then Mr. Jett booked yet more phantom profits on new trades.

The New York Times

found that Jett held $600 billion in phony strip positions at the end and had "booked" 60,000 trades that were actually never closed. Kidder's 1993 profits had to be reduced from $439 million to $89 million. Observers say the total loss, including the "profits" earned, made the scheme one of the biggest ever recorded on Wall Street.

BACKGROUND

The story of the loss goes back a number of years. General Electric purchased an 80 percent share of Kidder Peabody Group Inc., the 120-year-old New York–based investment banking firm, in April 1986 for $602 million. Jack Welch, the chairman of GE since 1981, has the reputation of being nearly obsessive about internal controls and says that the key to his management style is the avoidance of surprises. Under his guidance, GE became a highly profitable cash-rich company.

Financial analysts believe that one reason Welch was so successful was that he cut GE's bureaucracy and decentralized the company. To counterbalance the decentralization and remain consistent with his strong emphasis on control, he established a formidable team of internal auditors to keep tab on the various semi-independent units. Welch also is reputed to be very "results oriented," another oftcited reason for GE's success over the last few years.

GE purchased Kidder near the end of the era when junk bonds were hot. The insider trading scandal was about to break. The scandal led to the most famous Wall Street legal case of the 1980s, and to the collapse of Drexel Burnham Lambert and the conviction of two billionaire traders, Ivan Boesky and Michael Milken. One key figure in the junk bond scandal was Martin Siegel, a successful Kidder trader who had been secretly cooperating with Boesky in insider trading. In 1987, now under the spotlight of the insider trading investigation, Kidder and its parent GE settled civil insider trad-

ing charges and instituted a compliance system designed to help management detect the most complex trading crimes. Kidder placed compliance supervisors in every one of Kidder's departments and business units. The compliance officers and auditors were directed to analyze trading positions and transactions for different types of risks, including liquidity and interest rate moves.

Because Jett's transactions were risk free, they went undetected by the firm's compliance officers for a long time. And because securities firms execute thousands of trades each day, compliance officers may be able to check only a small sample of transactions. There's an assumption that most senior people are honest. Unless one has reason to believe that trades are bogus, the chances of catching fraudulent trades are very low. Traders have been able to outsmart lawyers and auditors because financial instruments are changing so rapidly that few compliance supervisors and auditors understand how they are traded.

In the 1990s Kidder's biggest success was in the field of repackaging mortgage-backed securities into complex bundles known as *collateralized mortgage obligations (CMOs)*. Mortgage-backed bonds are securities created by pooling home mortgages. CMOs are derivatives; that is, they are trading instruments that change value according to the change in the value of underlying financial instruments, in this case mortgage bonds. Bonds, in turn, are dependent on interest rates, rising in value when interest rates fall and falling when interest rates rise. In 1993 Kidder underwrote a total of $81 billion in home mortgage–backed securities, more than any other investment bank and fully 85 percent of Kidder's total underwriting that year. In other words, the company had all its eggs in one basket, a basket totally dependent on the behavior of interest rates.

During the early 1990s, interest rates in the United States fell sharply as the country struggled to come out

of a recession. Profits in fixed incomes were easy—all one had to do was to hold bonds and related instruments. However, by the end of 1993, an economic recovery was in full swing and the United States Federal Reserve Bank began to raise interest rates. During the first months of 1994, interest rates were rising at a fairly rapid rate. As rates rose, applications for new mortgages declined. Mortgage bond underwriting for the second quarter was down by 72 percent. This was particularly harmful at Kidder because it was far more dependent than other Wall Street firms on mortgage-backed securities.

Joseph Jett, the central figure in the success of Kidder in those years, came from the small Midwest town of Wickliffe, Ohio. On a scholarship to the Massachusetts Institute of Technology, Jett earned a bachelor's degree in chemistry in 1980 and a masters in 1982. He began his working career at GE as a senior process engineer in the plastics division and advanced to production engineer in 1985. Apparently unhappy with his choice of careers, he quit his job and enrolled in Harvard University, completing requirements for an MBA degree in 1987 (the degree was not awarded, apparently because he did not pay all of his university bills). He then turned to Wall Street where he was hired as a junior trader in mortgage-backed securities at Morgan Stanley & Co. He quickly graduated to a position of arbitrage trader. In 1989 when Morgan's structured-finance group was reorganized, he was laid off. He then moved to CS First Boston as a junior mortgage-backed securities trader. When the position was eliminated in 1991, he was hired by Kidder as a government bond trader, an area in which he had no trading experience. At the age of 33, his meteoric rise began.

Jett began contributing significantly to Kidder's profits almost immediately. In 1993 he was so successful that he was promoted to the position of chief of government bond trading (the zero-coupon bond desk) where he oversaw 16 traders plus a support staff. In 1993, because his trading had apparently contributed $210 million, or nearly half of the total published Kidder profits, he earned $9 million. In January 1994 he was honored with the Kidder "Chairman's Award" as the star 1993 Kidder employee. In accepting the honor at the annual Kidder retreat at Boca Raton, Florida, his speech focused on the importance of making money, preaching profit at all costs. "This is war," he was quoted as saying. "You do anything to win. You make money at all costs."

Signs of trouble at Kidder began in 1991 when Linda LaPrade sued Kidder claiming Cerullo pressured her to inflate bids on government securities to amass a larger share of the securities for later resale. She further alleged he told her "profits and performance were most important," threatening to fire her if she did not comply. Cerullo denied the charges, calling her a disgruntled former employee. The same year Cerullo was fined $5000 and censured by the National Association of Securities Dealers (NASD) for improperly supervising a bond trader named Ira Saferstein. Saferstein had created fake mortgage-backed bond trades. NASD said that Cerullo "did not object to Saferstein's execution of these transactions and failed to take steps to reverse or adjust" them. Cerullo explained, "The guy did something we told him not to do. He did it again and we fired him on the spot."

In 1992, according to several Kidder traders, Hugh Bush, a trader who worked next to Jett, was fired immediately after raising questions with Cerullo about what he considered to be improper trades by Jett. Bush apparently accused Jett of "mismarking"—misrecording—trading positions, which is illegal. According to reports, Bush was promptly fired and Cerullo never investigated the allegation. Later Cerullo would not say why Bush was fired but he did say that Bush "never came to me and made

any accusations about Jett or anyone." Also in 1992 Scott Newquist raised questions about Jett's trades. Newquist was a Kidder investment-banking chief and a member of the inventory committee, a group responsible for tracking the firm's trading positions. Newquist later claimed he brought allegations of problems with Jett's positions to Carpenter, telling him that the inventory committee was relying on "vague assertions" about Jett's huge trading positions. But, Newquist contends, Carpenter did nothing because of his (Carpenter's) narrow focus on profit. Carpenter denied that Newquist ever asked him to take any action and further denied being only concerned with the bottom line.

TURMOIL AND INSTABILITY AT KIDDER

In the weeks and months that followed the firing of Jett, both the business press and Lynch investigated Kidder Peabody, and a great deal of speculation ensued. A search of the various regulatory records found that there were no prior complaints about Jett; he had had no major disciplinary problems. In late April, word leaked out that GE had invested another $200 million into Kidder, making up 95 percent of the $210 million loss. On April 22 Kidder discharged Neil Margolin for concealing losses ("improperly valuing inventory positions") of about $10 million. Margolin was a 29-year-old, relatively green trader, who also reported to Cerullo. Mismarking positions is a fairly common problem on Wall Street and often leads to dismissal. A check of Margolin's record showed no history of disciplinary action. Kidder once again announced that the hidden losses did not result in losses for any Kidder customer or any other Wall Street firm, that Margolin's trades were all for Kidder's own account.

On May 10 at a preliminary court hearing, Kidder formally accused Jett of fraud. At that same hearing, Jett

asked Kidder to release to him a $5-million account that he claimed was his. The account contained part of Jett's 1993 earnings. Jett claimed he was unable to pay rent and his legal fees without access to his funds. Kidder did offer to release enough funds for Jett's living expenses and "reasonable" legal fees, which would leave Kidder in the position of being able to determine the size of Jett's defense.

As soon as the scandal was uncovered, a question arose as to the real value of the mortgage-based securities held by Kidder. Most investment banks value the price of their securities at the close of every trading day. However, because interest rates were rising fast in the spring of 1994, turbulence in the government bond market resulted, making pricing more difficult. Also, few trades of these securities were occurring with the number of new mortgages dropping precipitously, making legitimate daily prices impossible to obtain. Several former Kidder traders claimed that the value of Kidder mortgage-related positions were calculated far less often than at most firms, although Carpenter denied the assertion. On May 12, KPGM Peat Marwick, the third largest accounting firm in the United States, completed a review of Kidder's mortgage bond inventory and turned it over to Carpenter. According to Carpenter the report concluded that, "No adjustments [in pricing] have been suggested as a result." On the same day, Kidder also claimed its mortgage department had made money so far in 1994, despite having incurred losses since mid-March. Carpenter denied the rumors of large losses.

Throughout May and June, Kidder experienced the departure of a number of experienced traders. On June 22, GE CEO Welch announced that he had replaced Carpenter as Kidder CEO. Welch said that Carpenter's removal was not the result of any findings in the continuing investigation. Rather, he said, his purpose was to restore the confidence of Kidder's clients.

Carpenter was replaced by two GE executives. Dennis D. Dammerman, GE's chief financial officer, became Kidder's temporary CEO. The *Wall Street Journal* called him "Mr. Welch's most trusted lieutenant." Dennis J. Nayden, age 40, was named Kidder's chief operating officer and the person to replace Dammerman when he returned to his GE post. Nayden had been the executive vice president of GE Capital Services. He too had no background in the securities business. The *Wall Street Journal* called him "GE's top financial trouble-shooter."

Another leading figure in this drama was Melvin Mullin, age 46, a former professor of mathematics who came to Kidder in 1988 and became chief of the firm's government bond business. He was the person who hired Jett in 1991 and was his supervisor for several years. When Mullin moved on, Jett replaced him at the zero-coupon bonds desk. At one point Mullin hired his wife, Denise Mullin, as a bond trader. In 1993 Denise Mullin resigned after objections from executives at both GE and Kidder over the propriety of being supervised by her husband. When she left, auditors found errors in her account and had to reduce the value of her holdings by $2 million.

On July 11, Kidder announced it had fired Peter Bryant, a London-based Kidder options trader who also reported to Mullin. Hired in 1986 from Lazard Brothers & Co., he was considered a leading futures and options salesman and Kidder's top producer in the London office. The firm claimed he had hidden losses totaling $6 million on about a dozen option trades on French and Spanish government treasury bonds.

On July 23 Cerullo announced that he had resigned from Kidder. Cerullo's position supervising 750 traders was split, and he was replaced by two traders. Steven Baum had been the head of Kidder's commercial mortgages group. He came to Kidder from Salomon Brothers. Baum had been censured by the NASD (National Association of Securities Dealers) in 1991 for improperly supervising a bond trader who created fake mortgage-backed bond trades. William Watt was based in London where he had been responsible for Eurobond trading and sales. He had also been a supervisor of Bryant's. With Cerullo's departure, the newspapers speculated that many more traders would leave Kidder. Traders had liked working for Cerullo both because he gave his traders great freedom in their work and he rewarded them with large bonuses. For example, in 1993, Kidder had one of the highest compensation ratios on Wall Street, paying its traders and staff $882 million, more than half its net revenue. Kidder paid its sales force mainly on commission instead of salary plus bonuses.

Jett spoke to federal prosecutors again on July 25 and told them that he had been ordered to reduce his trading positions in early April, two weeks before he was fired. He stated that David Bernstein, acting for Cerullo, had told him that Kidder was in violation of net capital rules. The SEC requires brokerage houses to maintain a minimum ratio of net capital (cash plus other easily convertible assets) to debt. If accurate, this revelation suggested that Kidder's financial condition was worse than had been previously suspected. Kidder denied Jett's charges. In early August, Kidder revealed that for the month of July the company had a pre-tax loss of $56 million.

Mullin was the next to go. The announcement that he was fired was made on August 3. Mullin had earned $2.7 million in 1993, partly based on Jett's trades. During the Lynch inquiry, he had told the investigators that there was no way he could have reviewed 1500 to 2000 trade tickets per day.

CHARGES AND COUNTERCHARGES

Finally, on August 4, the long-awaited Lynch report on the Jett case was released. Its findings included the following conclusions:

- Jett, acting on his own, "knowingly manipulated Kidder's trading and accounting systems to generate" about $350 million in false profits. Although Kidder's internal auditors had conducted two reviews of Jett's trading desk in 1993, they never caught on because they were inexperienced and had been given "misrepresentations" by Jett.
- The scheme had actually generated $349.7 million in phony profits and $85.4 million in actual losses.
- The investigators calculated that, if settled, the total trades by Jett in bonds and strips would have been over $34 billion. It also pointed out that Jett had actually reported $1.7 trillion in phony trades.
- Kidder's 750-team bond trading group, under Cerullo's supervision, had operated as an independent fiefdom, uncontrolled by senior management.
- Richard O'Donnell, Kidder's senior vice president and chief financial officer (CFO), was exonerated from any blame, as CFO O'Donnell's responsibilities included overseeing the firm's accounting and control (audit) functions. In an interview, Lynch excused O'Donnell, saying "the accounting people got involved so late in the game." The report did say that there were "a string of misjudgments and missed opportunities." It also noted that O'Donnell did learn about anomalies in Jett's ledger but did not investigate them.
- Mullin was criticized for not reviewing trade tickets and other documents and for failing to respond to objections about Jett's trading from another trader. The report also noted that Mullin had championed Jett without understanding his trading activities.
- Much of the blame was directed at Cerullo. The report said he did

not examine Jett's trading, not even by sampling for information about settlement dates and counterparties, information that would have disclosed Jett's deceptions. The report concluded that Cerullo's supervision of Jett was "seriously deficient." However, the report did support Cerullo's denial that he had of any knowledge of the scheme.

- The investigators firmly rejected Carpenter's oft repeated contention that the Jett problem could have happened at any firm, that a clever crook will beat the system every time. Nonetheless, it concluded that Carpenter bore no direct responsibility for the affair, except that it happened on his watch.

- The report urged Kidder to institute new policies and procedures for trader supervision, including a manual or computer review of trade tickets.

The report concluded that the ultimate problem was the emphasis throughout Kidder on profits and greed. Although "Jett was provided the opportunity to generate false profits by trading and accounting systems," it was his supervisors who allowed Jett to use that opportunity for over two years because they never understood what Jett was doing in his day-to-day trading activity or the reason for his apparent profitability. "The door to Jett's abuses was opened as much by human failings as by inadequate formal systems," it concluded. It also said of Jett's supervisors, "Their focus was on profit and loss, and risk-management data provided no insight into the mechanics of Jett's trading."

Over the next few days, strong criticisms of the report emerged. Those criticisms included:

- It is hard to believe that Jett could have acted alone. Even an anonymous GE financial officer who did not work at Kidder was quoted as asking, "How could $350 million in profits go into the books when no money changed hands?" The implication is that Jett must have had help, even if that help was just purposeful inattention.

- The report did not address the issue of why questions were not raised earlier, given that the trading pattern persisted over a long time and involved such enormous sums of money. Where were the GE and Kidder auditors in 1991 and 1992?

- The report fails to deal with Jett's accusation that Cerullo was aware of his trading activities. In fact, a statement by Brian Finkelstein cited in the report seemed to indicate that Cerullo was aware of the trades, and yet this statement was never addressed.

- Many wondered how O'Donnell could be exonerated from responsibility. John Coffee, a Columbia University professor in securities law, asked, "How could the accountants not have insisted that whole time on being able to identify assets?" Many wanted to know why the report did not address the question of where the cash was. Not a penny had come into Kidder through Jett's trades, yet the auditors and accountants never examined the issue. Others point out that $1.7 trillion in trades in 1993, an amount equaling nearly half of all U.S. treasury securities in private hands, should have triggered the interest of the auditors.

- Many questioned how Carpenter could possibly be exonerated when Jett's profits constituted more than 20 percent of his company's profits—Jett was his biggest profit producer. Moreover, Carpenter awarded Jett the annual "Chairman's Award." Did Carpenter ever look into what Jett was doing, and if not, why not? Didn't this constitute a failure to supervise?

- The report fails to ask why Jett's superiors who had been fired or forced to retire were allowed to keep millions of bonus dollars based on the phantom "profit" of their supervisee. Even more, why had Cerullo been given a $10 million severance package?

However, the strongest criticism was reserved for Lynch himself. Lynch was filling multiple, conflicting roles for Kidder. First, he was hired by Kidder to investigate the whole affair to aid Kidder in improving its own procedures. In addition, he was representing the company in an arbitration claim against Jett. In a third role, Lynch was also representing Kidder with the Securities and Exchange Commission, the New York Stock Exchange, and the Manhattan United States attorney's office as they investigated Kidder in relation to the Jett affair. The question critics raised is, "How could Lynch 'zealously' represent his client in front of these legal entities while also fully revealing in his investigations the depth of the responsibility borne by Kidder and its management?" The conclusion of many observers was that the main purpose of the report was to be a bargaining chip with the SEC, NYSE regulators, and the government attorneys.

THE INEVITABLE END

The losses at Kidder continued. Losses for August amounted to about $30 million, with losses for year-to-date reaching nearly $250 million after taxes, already the worst in Kidder's 129-year history. On December 15, with 1994 net losses estimated at nearly $1 billion, GE sold most of Kidder's remaining assets to PaineWebber. The sale occurred at the worst possible time because Wall Street was undergoing its worst slump in years. A total of 2250 Kidder employees lost their jobs and Kidder ceased to exist. At the end of 1994, GE announced that it expected to report record profits for that year.

GE shareholders led by the Teachers' Retirement System of Louisiana filed suit in New York State against GE and its board of directors, trying to hold the company liable for failing to detect the Jett bond-trading scandal. The complaint pointed to the inattentiveness of GE's directors and a corporate culture that stressed making profits at any cost. New York Supreme Court Justice Ira Ganneman ruled that allegations that the defendant directors knew of the bond-trading scheme or profited from it "are insufficient to support findings of bad faith or intentional misconduct." GE and its board were cleared of liability in the Kidder case.

However, civil administrative proceedings were filed against Jett, Cerullo, and Mullin by the Securities and Exchange Commission. In January 1996 the SEC charged Jett with securities fraud and books and records violations, and Cerullo and Mullin with failure to supervise. Kidder and Carpenter were not charged. The SEC was persuaded that they both relied on existing systems and data from Jett and his superiors and weren't directly responsible for Jett's supervision.

At the SEC's administrative proceedings, Jett defended himself by saying that everything he did was on the basis of an accounting system that existed before his arrival at Kidder. He believes that it was not his responsibility to question profits credited to him by Kidder's trading system. He asserted that management knew about his bond-trading strategy, pointing to conversations he had with his superiors that he had recorded into his computer diary. The diary was entered into evidence over SEC objections. Jett said that Kidder officials concluded after a month-long internal inquiry that his strategy resulted in "early revenue recognition."

In December 1996, a securities arbitration panel ruled that Kidder was unable to prove that Jett engaged in "fraud, breach of duty, and unjust enrichment" and awarded Jett $1 million

of his bonuses that Kidder had frozen. Cerullo settled his SEC charge without admitting or denying guilt. He paid a $50,000 fine and was suspended from working as a supervisor in the securities industry for a year. Kidder paid him $9 million in deferred compensation and severance. Mullin settled for $25,000 and suspension for three months. An administrative law judge's ruling on the SEC complaint against Jett is imminent.

Consultants have pointed out that there are ways for companies to avoid the risks and losses suffered by Kidder Peabody. Merrill Lynch, for example, puts limits on the size of trades and trading positions. At Fidelity Investments, traders who violate any of several guidelines (such as buying a foreign stock for an account that is only supposed to hold U.S. stocks) are presented with red flames on their computer screens. A bulletin is then automatically sent to Fidelity's compliance department. Another money management firm doesn't tie compensation to the performance of a trader's account and it uses a special risk manager to oversee its trading floor. All companies can ensure that traders do not have any responsibility for bookkeeping functions, which should be handled only by the operations department.

Sources: Saul Hansell, "A Scoundrel or a Scapegoat?" *The New York Times,* April 6, 1997; John R. Dorfman, "Brokerage Firms Take Action to Detect Potential Rogue Traders in their Midst," *The Wall Street Journal,* November 29, 1995; Kurt Eichenwald, "Learning the Hard Way How to Monitor Traders," *The New York Times,* March 9, 1995; Michael Siconolfi, "Judge Clears GE of Liability in Kidder Case," *The Wall Street Journal,* April 22, 1996, "SEC Raises New Red Flag with Jett Case," *The Wall Street Journal,* January 10, 1996, "Fired Kidder Aide Tells U.S. He Acted on Orders, Firm Violated Capital Rules," *The Wall Street Journal,* July 26, 1994, "Jett Fires Back, Says Kidder Refuses Data," *The*

Wall Street Journal, September 7, 1994, "Kidder Says Review Approves the Way It Values Mortgage-Backed Bonds," *The Wall Street Journal,* May 13, 1994, "Kidder Trader in Bond Options Dismissed," *The Wall Street Journal,* July 12, 1994, "Lynch's Dual Role in Inquiry Prompts Question," *The Wall Street Journal,* August 5, 1995, "Report Faults Kidder for Laxness in Jett Case," *The Wall Street Journal,* August 5, 1995, "Saga of Kidder's Jett: Sudden Downfall of an Aggressive Wall Street Trader," *The Wall Street Journal,* April 19, 1994, and "Kidder Discloses Phony Trades, Fires a Trader," *The Wall Street Journal,* April 18, 1994; Douglas Frantz with Sylvia Nasar, "The Ghost in Kidder's Money-Making Machine," *The New York Times,* April 29, 1994; Saul Hansell, "Kidder, Peabody Jolted by Phantom Bond Trades," *The Wall Street Journal,* April 19, 1994; Linda Himelstein, "They Said, He Said, at Kidder Peabody," *Business Week,* August 8, 1994; Steve Lohr, "Kidder Dismisses 2nd Trader, Saying He Concealed Loss," *The New York Times,* April 23, 1994; Sylvia Nasar, "Kidder Scandal Tied to Failure of Supervision," *The New York Times,* August 5, 1994, "Kidder Trader Wants Funds Freed," *The New York Times,* May 30, 1994, "Kidder's No. 2 Executive Resigns," *The New York Times,* July 23, 1994, and "Multiple Motives for Kidder's Self-Examination," *The New York Times,* August 8, 1994; Sylvia Nasar and Douglas Frantz, "A Dramatic Rise, and a Nasty Fall," *The New York Times,* April 22, 1994; Floyd Norris, "Fool's Profits: Just How Dumb Was Kidder," *The New York Times,* August 7, 1994, and "Kidder, Peabody, Where Trading Went Awry," *The New York Times,* April 19, 1994; Joe Queenan, "A Sure Tip-Off," *Barrons,* May 2, 1994; Michael Quint, "G.E. Ousts Kidder, Peabody Chief," *The New York Times,* June 23, 1994; Michael Siconolfi, Laura Jereski, and Steven Lipin, "GE's Mr. Welch Ousts Kidder's Chairman, Names Financial Aides," *The Wall Street Journal,* June 23, 1994; Gary Weiss, "What Lynch Left Out," *Business Week,* August 22, 1994.

Case Study Questions

1. Describe the problem or problems that eventually caused the collapse of Kidder Peabody. What management, organization, and technology factors contributed to or caused the problems?

2. Who was responsible for the Jett bond-trading fiasco? Jett? His superiors? Kidder Peabody? The accounting and trading system? Justify your answer.

3. Why do you think Jett was not caught earlier?

4. Some have said that exploiting a dysfunctional information system such as Kidder's accounting and trading system can constitute fraud. It is like receiving 100 paychecks each week when you should get only one. One can't say, "The company meant to pay me 100 times." Do you agree? Why or why not?

5. Do you think computer information systems could have prevented the problems and prevented the collapse of Kidder? Why or why not?

6. Assume you have been assigned the task of designing a new computerized accounting information system that would address the underlying problems. Define your goals for such a system, the kind of data it should capture, where and how that data should be captured, the types of reporting it should include, who would receive those reports, what other computer systems should make use of the data, and the controls that would be required.

International Case Studies

From Geelong & District Water Board to Barwon Water:
An Integrated IT Infrastructure

Joel B. Barolsky and Peter Weill
University of Melbourne (Australia)

Ginormous Life Insurance Company

Len Fertuck
University of Toronto (Canada)

From Analysis to Interface Design-the Example of Cuparla

Gerhard Schwabe, Stephen Wilczek and Helmut Krcmar
University of Hohenheim (Germany)

Citibank Asia-Pacific: Rearchitecting Information Technology
Infrastructure for the Twenty-First Century

Boon Siong Neo and Christina Soh
Information Management Research Center (IMARC)
Nanyang Business School
Nanyang Technological University (Singapore)

Heineken Netherlands B.V.: Reengineering IS/IT to Enable
Customer-oriented Supply Chain Management

Donald A. Marchand, Thomas E. Vollmann, and Kimberly A. Bechler
International Institute for Management Development (Switzerland)

From Geelong & District Water Board to Barwon Water: An Integrated IT Infrastructure[1]

Joel B. Barolsky and Peter Weill, University of Melbourne (Australia)

Joe Adamski, the Geelong and District Water Board's (GDWB) executive manager of information systems, clicked his mouse on the phone messages menu option. Two messages had been left. The first was from an IT manager from a large Sydney-based insurance company confirming an appointment to "visit the GDWB and to assess what the insurance company could learn from the GDWB's IT experience." The second was from the general manager of another large water board asking whether Adamski and his team could assist, on a consultancy basis, in their IT strategy formulation and implementation.

The site visit from the insurance company was the thirty-fifth such request the Board had received since the completion of the first stage of their IT infrastructure investment strategy in January 1992. These requests were a pleasant diversion but the major focus of the GDWB's IT staff was to nurture and satisfy the increasing demands from the operational areas for building applications utilizing the newly installed IT infrastructure. The Water Board also faced the problem of balancing further in-house developments with external requests for consulting and demands from the GDWB's IT staff for new challenges and additional rewards.

ORGANIZATION BACKGROUND

The GDWB was constituted as a public utility of the Australian State of Victoria in July 1984 following an amalgamation of the Geelong Waterworks and Sewerage Trust and a number of other smaller regional water boards. The Board has the responsibility for the collection and distribution of water and the treatment and disposal of wastewater within a 1600 square mile region in the southwest part of the state. In 1991, the permanent population serviced by the Board exceeded 200,000 people, this number growing significantly in the holiday periods with an influx of tourists.

The GDWB financed all its capital expenditure and operational expenditure through revenue received from its customers and through additional loan borrowings. Any profits generated were reinvested in the organization or used to pay off long-term debt. For the financial year 1990–91 the Board invested over $35.3 million in capital works and spent over $25 million in operating expenditures. Operating profit for the year 1990–91 exceeded $62.4 million on total assets of $292.5 million.

In 1992, the GDWB was headed by a governing board with a state government–appointed chairperson and eight members, elected by the residents of the community, who each sat for a three-year term. Managerial and administrative responsibilities were delegated to the GDWB's Executive Group which consists of the CEO and executive managers from each of the five operating divisions,

namely Information systems, finance, corporate services, engineering development, and engineering operations. From 1981 to 1992, the number of GDWB employees across all divisions rose from 304 to 454.

The GDWB's head office, situated in the regional capital city of Geelong, housed most of the Board's customer service, administrative, engineering, IT, and other managerial staff. Complementing these activities, the GDWB operated five regional offices and a specialized 24-hour emergency contact service.

Commenting on the Board's competitive environment at the time, the GDWB's CEO, Geoff Vines, stated, "Although the organization operated in a monopolistic situation there still were considerable pressures on us to perform efficiently. Firstly, and most importantly, our objective was to be self-funding—our customers wouldn't tolerate indiscriminate rate increases as a result of our inefficiencies and we could not go cap in hand to the state government. Secondly, the amalgamation trend of water boards was continuing and the stronger the Board was the less likely it would be a target of a takeover. And thirdly, we did in a sense compare ourselves with private sector organizations and in some ways with other water boards. We had limited resources and we have to make the most of them."

KEY PROBLEM AREAS

Relating the situation up until the mid-1980s, Vines said that the Board faced a major problem in collectively identifying its largest assets—the underground pipes, drains, pumps, sewers, and other facilities. He explained that most of these facilities were installed at least two or three meters below the surface and therefore it was almost impossible to gain immediate physical access to them. The exact specifications of each particular asset could only be ascertained through a thorough analysis of the original installation documentation and other geophysical surveys and maps of the area.

The limitations on identifying these underground facilities impacted operational performance in a number of key areas:

- Most of the maintenance work conducted by the Board was based on reactive responses to leaks and other faults in the systems. It was difficult to introduce a coordinated preventative maintenance program because it was not possible to accurately predict when a particular pipe or piece of equipment was nearing the end of its expected life span.

- Only a limited number of hard copies of this facility information could be kept. This significantly reduced the productivity of the engineering and operations staff, especially in remote areas where they had to request this information from the central record-keeping systems. Backlogs and inaccuracies in filing also impacted efforts to repair, upgrade, or install new piping, pumps, and other equipment. On numerous occasions changes would be made to one set of plans without the same changes being recorded on the other copies of the same plans. Engineers designing improvements to existing facilities were often confronted with the problem of not being sure whether they were using the most up-to-date information of the facilities currently installed in the area concerned.

- The Board could not place realistic replacement values and depreciation charges on these underground assets.

With over 100,000 rateable properties in its area of responsibility, the GDWB maintained a centralized paper filing system containing more than a billion pages of related property information. The documents, most of which were of different sizes, quality, and age, were divided into 95,000 different files and sorted chronologically within each file. Access to the documents was made difficult as larger documents were cumbersome to copy and older documents were beginning to disintegrate. Having only one physical storage area significantly increased the potential exposure to fire and other risks and limited the wider distribution and sharing of the information. In the early 1980s, it was commonplace for a customer request for a statement of encumbrances placed at one of the GDWB's regional offices to take in excess of four weeks. The delays usually centered on finding the appropriate documents at the Property Services' central files, making the necessary copies, and transferring the documents back to the regional offices.

THE INFORMATION SYSTEMS DIVISION

In 1985, PA Consulting was commissioned to conduct a comprehensive review of the Board's strategy, management, operations structures, and systems. One recommendation made by the consultants was that the Board should institute a more systematic approach to strategic planning. A major outcome of the planning process that followed was to create a new division for computing services and to recruit a new manager for this new area who reported directly to the CEO. The EDP Division was created with the objectives of "satisfying the Board's Information System needs through the provision of integrated and secure corporate computer systems and

communication network." Vines said that the Board needed a stand-alone information services group that could be used as a resource center for all users and that could add value to the work conducted by each functional group within the Board.

In April 1987, Joe Adamski was employed to fill the new position of EDP manager (later changed to executive manager of information systems). At the time of his arrival, only a small part of the GDWB's work systems were computerized, the main components of which included:

- a "low-end" IBM System 38, primarily to run financial and other accounting software and some word processing applications. The system ran an in-house developed rate collection system which kept basic information on ratepayers including property details and consumption records;

- 19 "dumb" terminals—none of the Board's regional offices had terminal access to the central computer systems;

- a terminal link to the local university's DEC 20 computer to support the technical and laboratory services; and

- four stand-alone PCs, running some individual word processing packages as well as spreadsheet (Lotus 1-2-3), basic CAD, and data base applications.

Computer maintenance, support, and development was allocated to the finance division and delegated to an EDP supervisor (and three staff) who reported to the finance manager. Adamski noted, "The computer set-up when I joined was pretty outdated and inefficient. For example, the secretarial staff at Head Office were using the System 38's word processing facility and had to collect their dot matrix printouts from the computer room situated on the ground floor of the five-story building. In the technical area, some water supply network analysis data was available through the use of the DEC 20 system; however, hard copy output had to be collected from the University which was over five kilometers away. Most of the design engineers were using old drafting tables with rulers, erasers, and pencils as their only drafting tools."

Recognizing that some users required immediate solutions to problems they were facing, the Board purchased additional terminals, peripherals, and stand-alone microcomputers for the various areas thought to be in greatest need. Adamski said that these additional purchases further compounded some of the Board's computer-related problems. "We had a situation where we had at least four different CAD packages in use in different departments and we couldn't transfer data between them. There was a duplication of peripheral equipment with no sharing of printers, plotters, and other output devices. In addition, various managers began to complain that system expertise was too localized and that there was little compatibility between the various applications."

PLANNING THE NEW ROLE FOR IT

In July 1988, Adamski initiated a long-term computing strategy planning process with the establishment of a special planning project team with both IT and user representatives. The team embarked on a major program of interviews and discussion with all user areas within the Board. They investigated other similar public utilities across Australia to assess their IT strategies and infrastructures and made contact with various computer hardware and software vendors to determine the latest available technologies and indicative costs.

The Project Team developed a comprehensive corporate computing strategy that would provide, as Adamski put it, the "quantum leap forward in the Board's IT portfolio." Adamski said that central to the devised computing strategy was that there should be as much integration and flexibility as possible in all the

Board's technical and administrative systems. "Linked to this strategy was the notion that we should strive for an 'open systems' approach with all our applications. This meant that each system had to have publicly specifiable interfaces or 'hooks' so that each system could talk to each other. From the users' perspective an open systems approach meant that all the different applications looked pretty much the same and it was simple and easy to cross over from one to the other. It also meant that if we weren't happy with one particular product within the portfolio or we wanted to add a new one we could do it without too much disruption to the whole system."

He continued, "A key decision was made that we should build on our existing IT investments. With this in mind we had to make sure that the new systems were able to use the data and communicate with the System 38. We wanted only one hardware platform using only one operating system and only one relational data base management system (RDBMS). We also wanted only one homogenous network that was able to cater to a number of protocols and interfaces such as the network system for the microcomputers, workstations, and the Internet connection. There also had to be a high degree of compatibility and interaction with all the data files and applications that were proposed. In view of this, we chose a UNIX platform with a client/server architecture."

In addition to specifying the software components of the system, the Project Team outlined the hardware that was necessary to run the new systems and the additional staff that needed to be hired. To achieve the stated computing strategies and benefits, the Team also recommended that implementation take place over three key stages, with a formal progress review instituted at the end of each stage.

APPROVAL

In February 1989, the corporate computing strategy planning process was

completed and Adamski presented the key recommendations to the governing Board. In his presentation, Adamski stated that the infrastructure cost of implementing the strategy was estimated to be about $5 million for the entire project (excluding data capture costs) and that the project would take up to the end of 1995 for full commissioning.

Vines stated, "From my perspective, the proposed IT strategy took into account the critical functions in the organization that needed to be supported, such as customer services, asset management, and asset creation. These were fundamental components of the Board's corporate objectives, and the computer strategy provided a means to realize these objectives and provide both short- and long-term benefits. There were some immediate short-term benefits, such as securing property services data that had no backup, and productivity gains in design and electronic mail. From a long-term perspective, I believe you can never really do an accurate rate-of-return calculation and base your decision solely on that. If you did you probably would never make such a large capital investment in IT. We did try to cost-justify all the new systems as best we could but we stressed that implementing IT strategy should be seen as providing long-term benefits for the entire organization that were not immediately measurable and would come to fruition many years later. Until all the information was captured and loaded on the IT facilities from the manual systems, the full benefits could not be realized."

Following an extensive and rigorous tendering process, it was decided that the Board should follow a multivendor solution as no one vendor could provide a total solution. Sun Microsystems was selected as the major hardware vendor and was asked to act as "prime contractors" in implementation. As prime contractors Sun was paid one project fee and then negotiated separate contracts with all other suppliers.

IMPLEMENTATION

In April 1990, the implementation of the IT strategy commenced with the delivery of the Sun file servers and workstations and installation of a homogenous network throughout the Board. Adamski said that the implementation stage went surprisingly smoothly. "We didn't fire anybody as a direct result of the new systems, but jobs were changed. There was some resistance to the new technology—most of it was born out of unfamiliarity and fear of not having the appropriate skills. Some people were very committed in doing things 'their way.' When some of these people started to perceive tangible productivity benefits, their perspectives started to change. We tried to counsel people as best we could and encourage them to experiment with the new systems. Most peo-

ple eventually converted but there were still some objectors."

Adamski added that while they were implementing the new systems it was important for the IS Division not to lose sight of its key objectives and role within the organization. "We had to make sure that we didn't get carried away with the new whiz-bang technology and reduce our support and maintenance of the older, more conventional systems. For example, the Board went onto a new tariff system and we had to make significant changes to our rating system to accommodate this. Having an application generator in place significantly improved the systems upgrade time."

In May 1992, the Board's computer facilities included 4 Sun file servers, 80 Sun workstations, 100 microcomputers, 40 terminals, and the IBM System 38 Model 700. By this

time, the IS Division had implemented the following components of the systems (see Figure 1 for a schematic of the systems):

1. A **Document Imaging Processing System** (DIPS) used for scanning, storing, and managing all documents on each property within the GDWB region which were being kept in the 95,000 separate paper files. This system was also used for the storage, backup, and retrieval of 25,000 engineering plans and drawings. DIPS gave designated Head Office departments and regional offices real-time access to all property documentation and allowed them to print out scanned images when required. The system had a sophisticated indexing system that facilitated easy retrieval of stored images by users and access

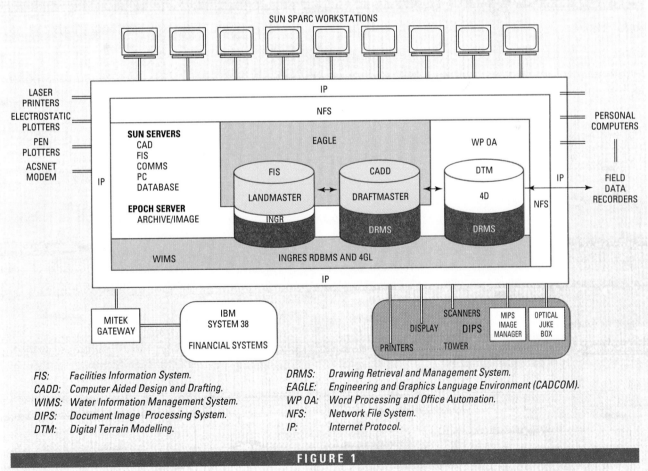

FIS: Facilities Information System.
CADD: Computer Aided Design and Drafting.
WIMS: Water Information Management System.
DIPS: Document Image Processing System.
DTM: Digital Terrain Modelling.

DRMS: Drawing Retrieval and Management System.
EAGLE: Engineering and Graphics Language Environment (CADCOM).
WP OA: Word Processing and Office Automation.
NFS: Network File System.
IP: Internet Protocol.

FIGURE 1

GDWB corporate computing system.

FIGURE 2

Example of a building plan kept for each rateable property.

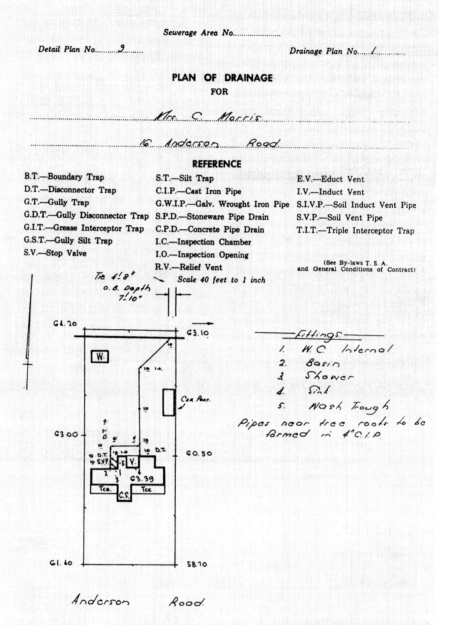

TORQUAY SEWERAGE AUTHORITY

Sewerage Area No...............

Detail Plan No......9.......

Drainage Plan No....1....

PLAN OF DRAINAGE
FOR

Mrs. C. Morris

16 Anderson Road

REFERENCE

B.T.—Boundary Trap

D.T.—Disconnector Trap

G.T.—Gully Trap

G.D.T.—Gully Disconnector Trap

G.I.T.—Grease Interceptor Trap

G.S.T.—Gully Silt Trap

S.V.—Stop Valve

S.T.—Silt Trap

C.I.P.—Cast Iron Pipe

G.W.I.P.—Galv. Wrought Iron Pipe

S.P.D.—Stoneware Pipe Drain

C.P.D.—Concrete Pipe Drain

I.C.—Inspection Chamber

I.O.—Inspection Opening

R.V.—Relief Vent

E.V.—Educt Vent

I.V.—Induct Vent

S.I.V.P.—Soil Induct Vent Pipe

S.V.P.—Soil Vent Pipe

T.I.T.—Triple Interceptor Trap

(See By-laws T. S. A. and General Conditions of Contract)

Scale 40 feet to 1 inch

Fittings

1. W.C. Internal
2. Basin
3. Shower
4. Sink
5. Wash Trough

Pipes near tree roots to be formed in 4" C.I.P.

Anderson Road

Examined...

Garlick & Stewart Engineer

Date.........10. 2. 72.......

by other programs. Figure 2 presents a copy of a scanned property plan from DIPS.

2. A digital mapping **Facilities Information System (FIS)** that provided for the storage, management, and ongoing maintenance of all graphic (map related) and nongraphic information relating to water and wastewater services, property information, property boundaries, and easements throughout the Board's region. The FIS provided a computerized "seamless" geographic map covering the entire GDWB region. The system encompassed the storing of all maps in digital form and attaching map coordinates to each digital point. Every point on a digital map was linked to a unique X and Y coordinate, based on the standard Australian Mapping Grid system, and had a specific address linked to it. Once each point on a map was precisely addressed and identified, specific attributes were attached to

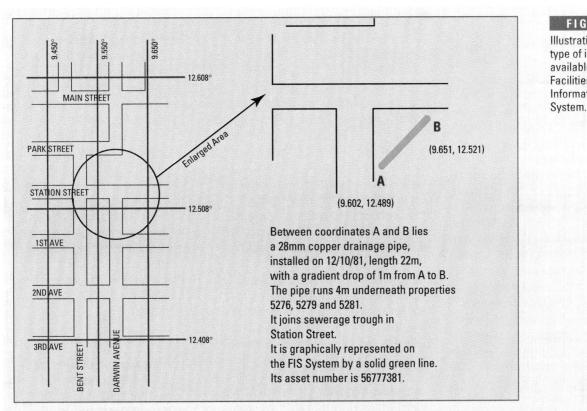

FIGURE 3

Illustration of the type of information available on the Facilities Information System.

Between coordinates A and B lies a 28mm copper drainage pipe, installed on 12/10/81, length 22m, with a gradient drop of 1m from A to B. The pipe runs 4m underneath properties 5276, 5279 and 5281. It joins sewerage trough in Station Street. It is graphically represented on the FIS System by a solid green line. Its asset number is 56777381.

it. These attributes were then used as methods of recording information or used as indexes for access to or by other programs, for example, sewer pipe details, property details, water consumption, and vertical heights above sea level. The selected map area with all the related attributes and information was then displayed graphically in full color on a high resolution workstation monitor (see Figure 3).

The FIS allowed cross referencing to financial, rating, and consumption data (through indexing) held on the System 38. It also enabled each underground facility to be numbered, catalogued, and identified as an asset with their associated data being integrated into other asset management systems. The FIS enabled data stored on a particular map to be "layered," with water pipes at one layer, sewer pipes at another, property boundaries at a third, future plans at another, and so on. This gave users the ability to recall maps in layers and to select the level and amount of detail they required. The system was centered around a mouse-driven graphic interface where the user zoomed in and out and/or panned around particular areas—at the broadest level, showing the whole of southern Victoria, and at the most detailed, the individual plumbing and drainage plan of one particular property (through cross-referencing to the DIPS).

3. A **Computer-Aided Design and Drafting (CADD)** system that provided an integrated programmable 3-D environment for a range of civil, mechanical, electrical, surveying, and general engineering design and drafting applications. It offered the following features:

- display manipulation, including multiple angle views, zooms, and pans;

- geometric analysis, including automatic calculation of areas, perimeters, moments of inertia, and centroids; and

- various customization features such as user-defined menus and prompts and a user-friendly macro language.

4. **Word Processing and Office Automation (WP/OA)** systems providing users the ability to prepare quality documentation integrating graphics, spreadsheets, mail merge, and databases, as well as other utilities such as electronic mail and phone message handling.

5. A **Relational Database Management System (RDBMS)** and a **Fourth-Generation Language** as a base foundation for the development of new applications. Some of the RDBMS applications included:

- a Drawing and Retrieval Management System (DRMS) to control the development, release, and revision of all CADD projects and files; and

- a Water Information Management System (WIMS) used for the storage and management of hydrographic engineering and laboratory data, both current and historical.

OUTCOMES

Vines said that one of the most important strategic outcomes of the changes introduced had been the way in which decision making at all levels with the organization had been enhanced. "This improvement is largely due to the fact that people have now got ready access to information they have never had before. This information is especially useful in enhancing our ability to forward plan. The flow and reporting of financial information has also speeded up and we now complete our final accounts up to two months earlier than we used to. In the areas that have come on-line there has been a definite improvement in productivity and in customer service. The CADD system, for example, is greatly enhancing our ability to design and plan new facilities. The turnaround time, the accuracy of the plans, and the creativity of the designers has been improved dramatically. In many departments there has been a change in work practices—some of the mundane activities are handled by the computer, allowing more productive work to be carried out, like spending more time with customers. Our asset management and control also started to improve. There was greater integrity in the information kept, and having just one central shared record meant that updating with new data or changes to existing data was far more efficient."

Adamski added that the initial reaction by Board staff to the whole corporate computing strategy "ranged from scepticism to outright hostility." He continued, "By the end of 1991, I would say that there had been a general reversal in attitude. Managers started to queue outside my office asking if we could develop specific business applications for them. They had begun to appreciate what the technology could do and most often they suddenly perceived a whole range of opportunities and different ways in which they could operate. One manager asked me, for example,

if we could use document imaging technology to eliminate the need for any physical paper flows within his office. Technically this was possible but it was not really cost justifiable and the corporate culture would not really have supported it. Putting together the IS Division budget is now a difficult balancing act with a whole range of options and demands from users. I now ask the users to justify the benefits to be derived from new application proposals and I help out with the cost side. Cost-benefit justification usually drives the decisions as well as the 'fit' with the existing IT and other corporate objectives. What also must be considered is that these objectives are not written in stone. They are flexible and can and should adjust to changes in both the internal and external environment."

A number of GDWB staff indicated that the new systems had enhanced their ability to fulfill their work responsibilities:

- A customer-service officer at one of the Board's regional offices stated that the DIPS had enabled her to respond to customer requests for encumbrance statements within a matter of minutes instead of weeks. She added that a number of customers had sent letters to their office complimenting them on the improvements in the service they received. She said that new DIPS had "flow on" benefits that weren't fully recognized. She cited the case in which local architects were able to charge their clients less because they had more ready access to information from the GDWB.

- A maintenance manager declared that the FIS had enabled his department to predict when pipes and drains should be replaced before they actually ruptured or broke down, by examining their installation dates and the types of materials used. He said this process over time

started to shift the emphasis of his department's maintenance work from being reactive to being more preventative. He added that the system also enabled him to easily identify and contact the residents that would be affected by the work that the Board was going to do in a particular area. He said that the FIS enabled him to plot out with his mouse a particular area of a map on his screen. It would then "pick up" all the relevant properties in the area and identify the names and addresses of the current ratepayers residing in those properties.

- A secretary to a senior head office manager said that despite being a little daunted at first by the new word processing system, she felt the system had helped her considerably. She said that besides the obvious benefits in being able to prepare and edit documents on a WYSIWYG screen, she also had the ability of viewing as well as integrating scanned property plans, correspondence, and other documents from the DIPS.

Adamski said that one of the flow-on benefits from the FIS in particular was that the Board had the potential of selling the information stored on the system to authorities such as municipal councils and other public utilities such as Telecom, the State Electricity Commission, and the Gas and Fuel Corporation. He added that they had also considered marketing the information to private organizations such as building managers, architects, and property developers, and that the return from these sales could significantly reduce the overall costs in developing the FIS.

THE FUTURE

Commenting on the future prospects for the Board's IS Division, Adamski said, "There are some very complex applications that we are developing but we now have the skills, the tools, and the infrastructure to develop them cost effectively and to ensure that they deliver results. I think one of the main reasons why we are in this fortuitous position is that we chose a UNIX platform with client/server processing and a strong networking backbone. It gives us the flexibility and integration that we set out to achieve and we will need in the future to realize both our long- and short-term objectives. It's a lot easier now to cost-justify requests for new applications. The challenges ahead lie in three areas. Firstly, it's going to be difficult to consistently satisfy all our users' needs in that their expectations will be increasing all the time and they will become more demanding. We have to recognize these demands and at the same time keep investing in and maintaining our infrastructure. Secondly, we still have some way to go in developing a total corporate management information system. There are still some 'islands of data' floating around and the challenge is to get it all integrated. And thirdly, as the most senior IT manager at the Board I have to make sure that we retain our key IT staff and we compensate them adequately, both monetarily and in providing them stimulating and demanding work."

The Geelong and District Water Board changed its name to Barwon Water in February 1994. The name change reflected the change in the organization's governance structure with the appointment by the state government of a professional, "skills-based" governing board to replace the community-elected members. This initiative was part of a broader government strategy to commercialize state-owned utilities and to strive for greater efficiencies and productivity across the whole public service.

Four months after the name change, Geoff Vines retired and was replaced by Dennis Brockenshire as Barwon Water's chief executive. Brockenshire, formerly a senior manager with the State Electricity Com-

mission, had considerable business and engineering experience relating to large-scale supply systems serving a large customer base. Commenting on Barwon Water's information technology (IT) infrastructure, Brockenshire stated, "Barwon Water has made and continues to make a significant investment in IT. The organization has spent something in the region of $7 to $10 million in building its IT infrastructure and has recurrent costs of 3 percent of total expenditure. I want to make sure we get an appropriate return for this investment. It is critical that IT delivers real business benefits. Since I've come into this role, I have insisted that my line managers justify any new IT investment on the grounds of the business value it will create."

From the period 1992 to 1995, Barwon Water's information systems (IS) department had focused most of its efforts in capturing all the relevant mapping, customer, and facilities data for its key systems. Significant resources were allocated to utilize the existing IT infrastructure to improve customer service and to streamline work flows. Improvements in security were also a major priority given the confidential and private nature of information stored on the various databases and the listing of Barwon Water's home page on the World Wide Web. In terms of hardware and software, the IBM System 38 was replaced by a Sun Sparcstation server running the Prophecy accounting package in a UNIX operating environment. The IS department had commenced work on an executive information system to assist with cost and performance measurement, particularly at the business unit level. This system would provide the core information to support a major benchmarking exercise in which Barwon Water compared its performance on key processes with other organizations, both within and external to the water industry.

Business processes were mapped and examined where steps could be eliminated or substituted by

new IT applications. An interesting example of this was the introduction of a paperless, encumbrance certificating system. In this system a solicitor handling a property matter could interact with Barwon Water via the fax machine without the need to actually visit an office. All documents sent to and from Barwon Water and those transferred within the organization were accomplished entirely on the system with no need to print a hard copy. Processing times for these applications were reduced from an average of 10 days to a few hours.

A number of other efficiency gains were realized with the utilization of the IT infrastructure. The productivity of the engineering design staff increased by 20 to 50 percent for most drawings and by 90 percent for redrawings. The systems distributed computing design also reduced design cycles by enabling staff to share files and work on a common file to avoid duplicated effort. Overall staff numbers with Barwon Water had dropped to 400 by July 1995. Adamski said that although the total reduction in staff numbers could not be directly attributed to the new systems, there were several areas where staff had been made redundant or redeployed. He said that in many cases the systems "freed-up" front-line service personnel to spend more time listening and being responsive to customer concerns.

Barwon Water continued to receive acclaim for its innovative IT systems. In 1994 it was awarded the Geelong Business Excellence Award in the Innovation Systems/ Development of Technology category. It also received a nomination for the award for innovation by the Washington-based Smithsonian Institute[2].

A major organizational restructure in early 1995 saw Joe Adamski take over the responsibility for strategic planning as well as information systems. Adamski said that this restructure ensured that IT developments would be closely aligned with broader business objectives and strategies. He added that having the senior IT executive responsible for business planning symbolized how essential IT had become to the organization's operations and its management and control systems. As part of the restructure new business units were formed with the managers of these units made accountable for both revenue and cost items.

Commenting on future challenges, Adamski outlined his vision for Barwon Water as the computing center for the Greater Geelong region. "Geelong and district covers 4000 square kilometers. Within this region, there has recently been an amalgamation of councils into two super-councils—the City of Greater Geelong and the Surf Coast Council. These two organi[z]ations, serve the same customers as ourselves. We have articulated what we see as benefits of using common databases, mapping, and other information to serve these customers. Suggested benefits include a service shopfront where customers could pay rates, water tariffs, and apply for property approvals at the same place. These systems we now have in place at Barwon Water would be a good starting point in building this regional concept. Data is our most valuable asset and there is no point in duplicating it."[3]

Source: Copyright © by Joel B. Barolsky and Peter Weill. Funding for this research was provided by IBM Consulting (USA). Reprinted by permission of Joel B. Barolsky and Peter Weill.

Case Study Questions

1. Describe the Geelong and District Water Board and the environment in which it operates. What problems did GDWB have before 1988? What were the management, organization, and technology factors that contributed to those problems?

2. Describe the role of information systems at GDWB and the GDWB's information system portfolio before July 1988.

3. Describe and critique the process of upgrading GDWB's information systems portfolio.

4. How did the Water Board justify its investments in new information system technology? What were the benefits?

[1] This case was prepared by Joel B. Barolsky and Professor Peter Weill as part of the Infrastructure Study funded by *IBM Consulting Group (International)*. It should be read in conjunction with the *Geelong and District Water Board Information Technology Management (CL298-1992)* case. Both of these cases were written as the basis of discussion rather than to illustrate either effective or ineffective handling of a managerial situation. Copyright © 1995 Joel B. Barolsky and Peter Weill, Melbourne Business School Limited, The University of Melbourne.

[2] The original case study written by Barolsky and Weill on Geelong and District Water Board was awarded the Australian Computer Society Prize for best IT Case Study in 1993.

[3] "IT Manager Leads Corporate Plan to Water," MIS April 1994, 41–46

Ginormous Life Insurance Company

Len Fertuck, University of Toronto (Canada)

Ginormous Life is an insurance company with a long tradition. The company has four divisions that each operate their own computers. The IS group provides analysis, design and programming services to all of the divisions. The divisions are actuarial, marketing, operations, and investment. All divisions are located at the corporate headquarters building. Marketing also has field offices in twenty cities across the country.

- **The Actuarial Division** is responsible for the design and pricing of new kinds of policies. They use purchased industry data and weekly summaries of data obtained from the Operations Division. They have their own DEC VAX minicomputer, running the UNIX operating system, to store data files. They do most of their analysis on PCs and Sun workstations, either on spreadsheets or with a specialized interactive language called APL.

- **The Marketing Division** is responsible for selling policies to new customers and for follow-up of existing customers in case they need changes to their current insurance. All sales orders are sent to the Operations Division for data entry and billing. They use purchased external data for market research and weekly copies of data from operations for follow-ups. They have their own IBM AS/400 minicomputer with dumb terminals for clerks to enter sales data. There are also many PCs used to analyze market data using statistical packages like SAS.

- **The Operations Division** is responsible for processing all mission-critical financial transactions including payroll. They record all new policies, send regular bills to customers, evaluate and pay all claims, and cancel lapsed policies. They have all their data and programs on two IBM ES/9000 mainframes running under the OS/390 operating system. The programs are often large and complex because they must service not only the fifteen products currently being sold but also the 75 old kinds of policies that are no longer being sold but still have existing policy holders. Clerks use dumb terminals to enter and update data. Applications written in the last five years have used a SQL relational database to store data, but most programs are still written in COBOL. The average age of the transaction processing programs is about ten years.

- **The Investment Division** is responsible for investing premiums until they are needed to pay claims. Their data consists primarily of internal portfolio data and research data obtained by direct links to data services. They have a DEC minicomputer to store their data. The internal data are received by a weekly download of cash flows from the Operations Division. External data are obtained as needed. They use PCs to analyze data obtained either from the mini or from commercial data services.

A controlling interest in Ginormous Life has recently been purchased by Financial Behemoth Corp. The management of Financial Behemoth has decided that the firm's efficiency and profitability must be improved. Their first move has been to put Dan D. Mann, a hotshot information systems specialist from Financial Behemoth in charge of the Information Systems Division. He has been given the objective of modernizing and streamlining the computer facilities without any increase in budget.

In the first week on the job, Dan discovered that only seven junior members of the staff of 200 information systems specialists know anything about CASE tools, End-User Computing, or LANs. They have no experience in implementing PC systems. There is no evidence of any formal Decision Support Systems or Executive Information Systems in the organization. New applications in the last five years have been implemented in COBOL on DB2, a relational database product purchased from IBM. Over two thirds of applications are still based on COBOL flat files. One of the benefits of using DB2 is that it is now possible to deliver reports quickly based on ad hoc queries. This is creating a snowballing demand for conversion of more systems to a relational database so that other managers can get similar service.

There have been some problems with the older systems. Maintenance is difficult and costly because almost every change to the data structure of applications in operations requires corresponding changes to applications in the other divisions. There has been a growing demand in other divisions for faster access to operations data. For instance the Investment Division claims that they could make more profitable investments if they had continuous access to the cash position in operations. Marketing complains that they get calls from clients about claims and cannot answer them because they do not have current access to the status of the claim. Management wants current access to a wide variety of data in summary form so they can get a better understanding of the business. The IS group says that it would be difficult to provide access to data in operations because of security considerations. It is difficult to ensure that users do not make unauthorized changes to the COBOL files.

The IS group complains that they cannot deliver all the applications that users want because they are short-staffed. They spend 90 percent of their time maintaining the existing systems. The programmers are mostly old and experienced and employee turnover is unusually low, so there is not likely to be much room for improvement by further training in programming. Employees often remark that the company is a very pleasant and benevolent place to work. At least they did until rumors of deregulation and foreign competition started to sweep the industry.

Dan foresees that there will be an increasing need for computer capacity as more and more applications are converted to on-line transaction processing and more users begin to make ad hoc queries. Dan is also wondering if intranets or the Internet should become part of any new software.

Dan began to look for ways to solve the many problems of the Information Systems Division. He solicited proposals from various vendors and consultants in the computer industry. After a preliminary review of the proposals, Dan was left with three broad options suggested by IBM, Oracle Corp. and Datamotion, a local consulting firm. The proposals are briefly described below.

IBM proposes an integrated solution using IBM hardware and software. The main elements of the proposal are:

- **Data and applications will remain on a mainframe.** The IBM ES/9000 series of hardware running their OS/390 operating system will provide mainframe services. Mainframe hardware capacity will have to be approximately doubled by adding two more ES/9000 series machines. The four machines will run under OS/390 with Parallel Sysplex clustering technology that allows for future growth. The Parallel Sysplex system can be scaled by connecting up to 32 servers to work in parallel and be treated as a single system for scheduling and system management. The OS/390 operating system can also run UNIX applications.

- **AS/400 minicomputers running under the OS/400 operating system** will replace DEC minicomputers.

- **RS/6000 workstations running AIX**—a flavor of the UNIX operating system—can be used for actuarial computations. All hardware will be interconnected with IBM's proprietary SNA network architecture. PCs will run under the OS/2 operating system and the IBM LAN Server to support both Microsoft Windows applications and locally designed applications that communicate with mainframe databases.

- **A DB2 relational database will store all data on line.** Users will be able to access any data they need through their terminals or through PCs that communicate with the mainframe.

- **Legacy systems will be converted using re-engineering tools,** like Design Recovery and Maintenance Workbench from Intersolv, Inc. These will have the advantage that they will continue to use the COBOL code that the existing programmers are familiar with. New work will be done using CASE tools with code generators that produce COBOL code.

- **Proven technology.** The IBM systems are widely used by many customers and vendors. Many mission-critical application programs are available on the market that address a wide variety of business needs.

Oracle Corp. proposed that all systems be converted to use their Oracle database product and its associated screen and report generators. They said that such a conversion would have the following advantages:

- **Over 90 hardware platforms are supported.** This means that the company is no longer bound to stay with a single hardware vendor. Oracle databases and application programs can be easily moved from one manufacturer's machine to another manufacturer's machine by a relatively simple export and import operation as long as applications are created with Oracle tools. Thus the most economical hardware platform can be used for the application. Oracle will also access data stored in an IBM DB2 database.

- **Integrated CASE tools and application generators.** Oracle has its own design and development tools called Designer/2000 and Developer/2000. Applications designed with Designer/2000 can be automatically created for a wide variety of terminals or for the World Wide Web. The same design can be implemented in Windows, on a MacIntosh, or on X-Windows in UNIX. Applications are created using graphic tools that eliminate the need for a language like COBOL. The designer works entirely with visual prototyping specifications.

- **Vertically integrated applications.** Oracle sells a number of common applications, like accounting programs, that can be used as building blocks in developing a complete system. These applications could eliminate the need to redevelop some applications.

- **Distributed network support.** A wide variety of common network protocols like SNA, DecNet, Novell, and TCP/IP are supported. Different parts of the database can be distributed to different machines on the network and accessed or updated by any application. All data are stored on line for instant access. The data can be stored on one machine and the applications can be run on a different machine, including a PC or workstation, to provide a client/server environment. The ability to distribute a database allows a large database on an expensive mainframe to be distributed to a number of cheaper minicomputers.

Datamotion proposed a data warehouse approach using software tools from Information Builders Inc. Existing applications would be linked using EDA, a middleware data warehouse server that acts as a bridge between the existing data files and the users performing enquiries. New applications would be developed using an application tool called Cactus. The advantages of this approach are:

- **Data Location Transparency** EDA Hub Server provides a single connection point from which applications can access multiple data sources anywhere in the enterprise. In addition, users can join data between any supported EDA databases—locally, cross-server, or cross-platform. Users can easily access remote data sources for enhanced decision-making capabilities.

- **The EDA server can reach most non-relational databases** and file systems through its SQL translation engine. EDA also supports 3GL, 4GL, static SQL, CICS, IMS/TM, and proprietary database stored procedure processing.

- **Extensive network and operating system support.** EDA supports 14 major network protocols and provides protocol translation between dissimilar networks. EDA also runs on 35 different processing platforms. EDA servers support optimized SQL against any RDBMS. And the EDA server can automatically generate the dialect of SQL optimal for the targeted data source. It is available on: Windows 3.x, Windows 95, Windows NT, OS/2, MVS, UNIX, CICS, VM, OpenVMS, Tandem, and AS/400.

- **Comprehensive Internet Support.** With EDA's Internet services, users can issue requests from a standard Web browser to any EDA supported data source and receive answer sets formatted as HTML pages.

- **Cactus promotes modern development methods.** Cactus allows the developer to partition an application, keeping presentation logic, business logic and data access logic separate. This partitioning of functionality can occur across a large number of enterprise platforms to allow greater flexibility in achieving scalability, performance and maintenance. Cactus provides all the tools needed to deal with every aspect of developing, testing, packaging and deploying client/server traditional applications or Web-based applications.

Dan is not sure which approach to take for the future of Ginormous Life. Whichever route he follows, the technology will have an enormous impact on the kinds of applications his staff will be able to produce in the future

and the way in which they will produce them. While industry trends toward downsizing and distribution of systems may eventually prove to be more efficient, Dan's staff does not have much experience with the new technologies that would be required. He is uncertain about whether there will be a sufficient payoff to justify the organizational turmoil that will result from a major change in direction. Ideally he would like to move quickly to a modern client/server system with minimal disturbance to existing staff and development methods, but fears that both of these are not simultaneously possible.

Source: Reprinted by permission of Len Fertuck, University of Toronto, Canada.

Case Study Questions

Dan must prepare a strategy for the renewal of the Information Systems Division over the next three years. As his assistant, prepare an outline, in point form, containing the following items:

1. A list of factors or issues that must be considered in selecting a technology platform for the firm.

2. Weights for each factor obtained by dividing up 100 points among the factors in proportion to their importance.

3. A score from 0 to 10 of how each of the three proposals performs on each factor.

4. A grand score for each proposal obtained by summing the product of the proposal score times the factor weight for each proposal.

5. The technology that you would recommend that Dan adopt and the reason for choosing the particular technology that you recommend.

6. The order in which each component of the technology should be introduced and the reason for selecting the order.

From Analysis to Interface Design—The Example of Cuparla

Gerhard Schwabe, Stephan Wilczek, and Helmut Krcmar
University of Hohenheim (Germany)

Like in other towns, members of the Stuttgart City Council have a large workload: In addition to their primary professions (e.g., an engineer at Daimler Benz) they devote more than 40 hours a week to local politics. This extra work has to be done under fairly unfavorable conditions. Only council sessions and party meetings take place in the city hall; the deputies of the local council do not have an office in the city hall to prepare or coordinate their work. This means, for example, that they must read and file all official documents at home. In a city with more than 500,000 inhabitants, they receive a very large number of documents. Furthermore, council members believe they could be better informed by the administration and make better use of their time. Therefore Hohenheim University and partners launched the Cuparla project to improve the information access and collaboration of council members.[1]

A detailed analysis of their work revealed the following characteristics of council work:

- Council members need support available to them any time and in any place as they are very mobile.

- Council members collaborate and behave differently in different contexts: While they act in-formally and rather open in the context of their own party, they behave more controlled and for-mal in official council sessions.

- A closer investigation of council work reveals a low degree of process structure. Every council member has the right of initiative and can inform and involve other members and members of the administration in any order.

- Council members rarely are power computer users. Computer support for them has to be straightforward and intu-itive to use.

When designing computer sup-port we initially had to decide on the basic orientation of our software. We soon abandoned a workflow model as there are merely a few steps and little order in the collaboration of local politicians. Imposing a new structure into this situation would have been too restrictive for the council members. We then turned to pure document ori-entation, imposing absolutely no structure on the council members' work. We created a single, large data-base with all the documents the city council ever needs. However, working with this database turned out to be too complex for the council members. In addition, they need to control the ac-cess to certain documents at all stages of the decision-making process. For example, a party may not want to reveal its proposals to other parties before it has officially been brought up in the city council. Controlling access to each document

individually and changing the access control list were not feasible.

Therefore, the working context was chosen as a basis of our design. Each working context of a council member can be symbolized by a "room." A private office corresponds to the council member working at home; there is a party room, in which the member collaborates with party colleagues, and a committee room symbolizes the place for committee meetings. In addition, there is a room for working groups, a private post of-fice, and a library for filed information. All rooms hence have an electronic equivalent in the Cuparla software. When opening the Cuparla software, a council member sees all the rooms from the entrance hall (see Figure 1).

The council member creates a document in one room (e.g., a private office) and then shares it with other council members in other rooms. If the member moves a document into the room of his party, the member shares it with his party colleagues; if he hands it on to the administration, he shares it with the mayors, administra-tion officials, all council members, and so forth.

The interface of the electronic rooms resembles the setup of the orig-inal rooms. Figure 2 shows the exam-ple of the room for a parliamentary party. On the left side of the screen are document locations, and on the right side are the documents of the se-lected location. Documents that are currently worked on are displayed on the "desk." These documents have the connotation that they need to be

FIGURE 1

Entrance Hall

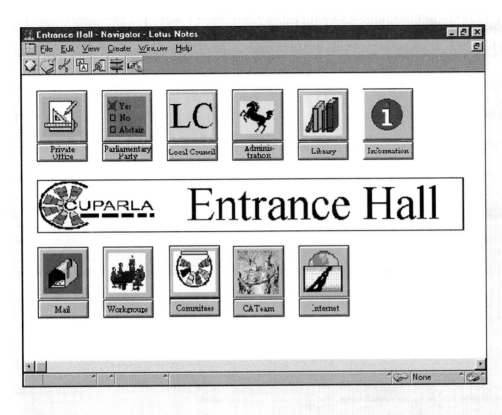

worked on without an additional outside trigger. If a document is in the files, it belongs to a topic that is still on the political agenda; however, a trigger is necessary to move it out of the shelf. If a topic is no longer on the political agenda, all documents belonging to it are moved to the archive.

The other locations support the collaboration within the party. The conference desk contains all documents for the next (weekly) party meeting. Any council member of the party can put documents there. When preparing for the meeting, the council member simply has to check the conference desk for relevant information. The mailbox for the chairman contains

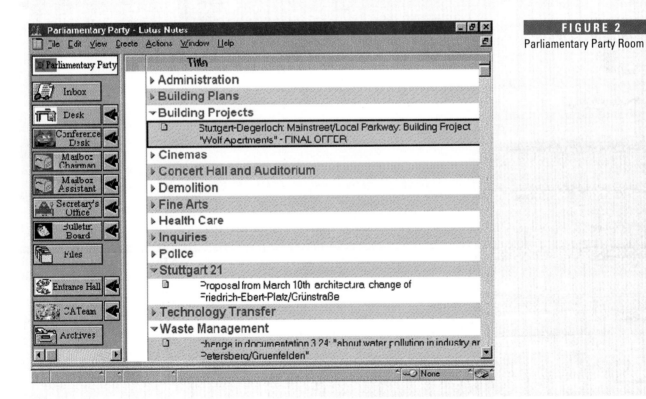

FIGURE 2

Parliamentary Party Room

all documents about which the chairman needs to decide. In contrast to the e-mail account, all members have access to the mailbox. Duplicate work is avoided as every council member is aware of the chairman's agenda. The mailbox of the assistant contains tasks for the party assistants—the mailbox for the secretary assignments for the secretary (e.g., a draft for a letter). The inbox contains documents that have been moved from other rooms into this room.

Thus, in the electronic room all locations correspond to the current manual situation. Council members do not have to relearn their work. Instead, they collaborate in the shared environment to which they are accustomed, with shared expectations on the other peoples' behavior. Feedback from the pilot users indicates that this approach is appropriate.

Some specific design features make the software easy to use. The software purposely does not have a fancy 3-D interface that has the same look as a real room. Buttons (in the entrance hall) and lists (in the rooms) are much easier to use and do not distract the user from the essential parts. Each location (e.g., the desk) has a small arrow. If a user clicks on this arrow, a document is moved to the location. This operation is much easier for a beginner than proceeding by "drag and drop."

Furthermore, software design is not restricted to building an electronic equivalent of a manual situation. If a user wants to truly benefit from the opportunities of electronic collaboration support systems, one has to include new tools that are not possible in the manual setting. For example, additional cross-location and room search features are needed to make it easy for the council member to retrieve information. The challenge of interface design is to give the user a starting point that is similar to a familiar situation. A next step is to provide users with options to improve and adjust their working behaviors to the opportunities offered by the use of a computer.

Source: The project partners are Hohenheim University (Coordinator), Datenz entraslie Baden-Wurttemburg, and Group Vision Softwaresysteme GmbH. The project is funded as part of its R&D program by Dete Berkom GmbH, a 100% subsidiary of German Telekom.

Case Study Questions

1. Analyze the management, organization, and technology issues that had to be addressed by the Cuparla project.

2. Analyze the interface and design of the Cuparla system. How easy is it to use? What problems does it solve? What organizational processes does the system support? How effective is it? Would you make any changes?

3. Could the Cuparla software be used for other applications in business? Why or why not? What modifications would be required?

[1]The project partners are Hohenheim University (Coordinator), Datenzentrale Baden-Württemberg, and Group Vision Softwaresysteme GmbH. The project is funded as part of its R&D program by DeTeBerkom GmbH, a 100 percent subsidiary of German Telekom.

Citibank Asia-Pacific: Rearchitecting Information Technology Infrastructure For the Twenty-First Century

Boon Siong Neo
Christina Soh
Information Management Research Center (IMARC)
Nanyang Business School
Nanyang Technological University
(Singapore)

I. CITICORP

Citicorp in 1991 recorded a net loss of $457 million,[1] suspended the dividend on its common stock, and saw the price of that stock fall to a long-time low before rebounding after year end. Nevertheless, and despite the magnitude of our problems, 1991 for Citicorp was in key respects a transitional, turnaround year.

John Reed, Citicorp's chairman, acknowledged Citicorp's problems in his letter to stockholders in the 1991 annual report. The bank had been struggling with a large third-world loan portfolio, as well as significant problems with its commercial property loans, and with its financing of highly leveraged transactions in the United States. The bank needed more equity but third-world debt costs prevented Citicorp from increasing its equity through retention of earnings.

The severe storms to which Citicorp had been subjected prompted significant changes. To combat the slowdown in revenue growth and the rise in consumer and credit write-offs,

Citicorp aggressively reduced expenses to improve the operating margin, and issued stock to improve their capital ratio. Structural changes were aimed at providing more focused direction to the business. John Reed articulated three requirements for being a "great bank in the 1990s"—meeting customer needs, having financial strength, and "marshalling human and *technological* resources . . . *more imaginatively and cost-effectively* than one's competitors."

In the midst of this organizational turbulence, one of Citicorp's undisputed strengths was its global presence. It is unrivaled in its network of banks in more than 90 countries. Its overseas consumer banking operations in particular were showing healthy growth. Global consumer banking includes mortgage and insurance business and non-U.S. credit card business. Citicorp only entered the field of consumer banking in the mid-70s. John Reed's vision was to pursue growth in the consumer banking area, and to pursue it through global expansion and leveraging IT.

The primary vision in consumer banking is "Citibanking"—combining relationship banking with technology that enables Citibank to serve its customers anywhere anytime with the same high standard of service that they receive in their home countries. Some examples of the manner in which tech-

nology enables the Citibanking vision include: having a one-stop account opening, paperless transactions, instant card and check issuance, and instant account availability; having a customer relationship database that supports cross-product relationships, creation of hybrid products and customized products, and relationship pricing that more closely matches the value to the customer. The Citicard is the key to Citibanking services such as checking, money market, and bankcard accounts. Consumer banking products are distributed through bank branches, Citicard centers, and Citiphone banking, which gives 24-hour, 7-day-a-week service. The global services available to customers were augmented in 1991 when Citibank joined the CIRRUS ATM network, allowing Citicard holders access to cash around the world.

The results of operating and structural changes, as well as the impact of the growing Asian consumer market, contributed to a turnaround at Citicorp, where the 1992 net earning was $772 million. This earned it an A-minus credit rating from *Standard and Poor,* which also upgraded the bank's outlook from negative to stable. Their performance continued to improve each year (see Figure 1). In early 1994, the bank was also given permission by the U.S. regulatory agency to resume issuing dividends. These improvements were reflected in Citicorp's

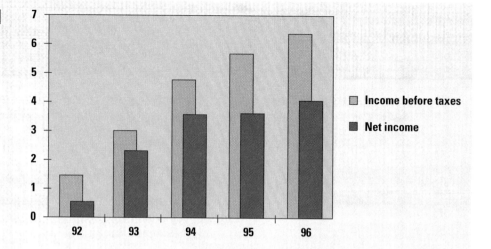

FIGURE 1
Income in Billions.
Source: Citicorp Annual Report, 1996.

Income before taxes

Net income

share price, which moved up to $36.88 during 1993, from a low of $23 in 1990. By 1997, the stock price was 10 times its low in 1990.[2]

II. CITIBANK IN ASIA-PACIFIC

Even in 1991, the profit that Citicorp made on its Asian business was a healthy $400m, if one excludes the loan write-offs for Australia and New Zealand, and their slow progress in the difficult Japanese retail banking market. This compares well with the $894m loss in the United States, and the $132m profit in Europe, Africa, and the Middle East.[3] The Asian market also has a high growth potential. Asian consumer deposits grew six-fold to $13.6 billion between 1983 and 1992, while loans grew seventeen-fold to $10.8 billion over the same period.[4] This growth is a reflection of the region's high gross savings rate (about 35 percent), and high GNP growth.

Citicorp has been in Asia since 1902 when it set up finance houses in a number of Asian ports, such as Shanghai and Singapore. It has built up an understanding of these local markets. Today, consumer banking in the Asia-Pacific is organized into three regions—North Asia (Korea, Taiwan, Hong Kong, and the Philippines), South Asia (Thailand, Malaysia, Singapore, Indonesia, and Australia), and Central Europe/Middle Eastern Asia (India, Pakistan, Saudi

Arabia, United Arab Emirates, Eastern Europe). The regional directors report to New York–based Executive Vice President De Sousa, who also heads the Private Bank. Besides the country managers, functions reporting to the regional directors include financial control, marketing and business development, technology and operations, treasury, credit, human resources, and service quality. Citicorp's major competitors in terms of established presence throughout Asia are Hong Kong Bank and Standard Chartered Bank, but neither has the global reach that Citicorp offers.

Citibank began pursuing consumer banking in Asia in earnest in 1986, and since then Asian accounts have increased from 1 million to 6 million in 1997 and are expected to reach 13 million by the year 2000. Critics suggest that Citicorp may run into credit problems because Asians have little experience with personal debt. Nonetheless, Citicorp continues to pioneer the concept of consumer credit in Asia—beside the usual mortgage and auto loans, Citicorp offers round-the-clock phone banking and automated teller cards that can be used in Singapore as well as New York.[5] Interestingly, some innovations such as phone banking were motivated by local regulations that severely restricted the number of branches that it may operate. To compete with the local banks, Citibank has had to be very focused in its customer base.

Citibank has made significant innovations in packaging financial services for the relatively rich customer, and has managed to corner the market. Part of the underlying philosophy is that its market position requires continual research into local customer needs—what one senior Citibank officer called the "let a hundred flowers bloom" approach. That approach has resulted in each country having its own IT infrastructure and unique applications. Although it has worked adequately in the past, the local markets approach does not allow Citibank to integrate its products, services, and information to serve its highly sophisticated, mobile, and increasingly demanding global customers. Further, there were substantial economies of scale that may be gained from standardizing and consolidating bank products and processing across the diverse countries of the Asia-Pacific region. The key to achieving these goals lies in rearchitecting the technology infrastructure that enables the consumer banking business.

III. TECHNOLOGY INFRASTRUCTURE IN CITIBANK ASIA-PACIFIC

In the early 1990s, each of Citibank's Asia-Pacific countries belonged to one of three automation platforms—MVS, AS/400, or UNIX—and had one of two consumer banking applications—COSMOS or CORE. COSMOS was an earlier set of applications, and was fairly typical of most U.S. banks' offshore banking applications. It was written in COBOL to provide flexibility in complying with varying regulatory reporting formats, and it provided back-office support for standard areas such as current accounts, general ledger, and some loans processing. Subsequently, Citibank began to replace COSMOS with CORE, which was to provide a comprehensive system to run on AS/400s. CORE was used in a number of countries with smaller operations, such as Indonesia. It was not suitable for countries, such as India, where IBM did not have a presence, and in countries with high volumes, such as Hong Kong. Both COSMOS and CORE were subject to many country-specific modifications over time, as each country operation responded to varying regulatory and business requirements. The result was significant differences in each country's basic banking software.

A two-pronged strategy was adopted: first, rearchitect the IT infrastructure by standardizing and centralizing all back-office banking functions, and second, develop centers of excellence by encouraging individual countries to take the lead in developing products and processes where they have significant leadership and competitive advantages in the marketplace. The only rule in the latter strategy is that the lead country should develop products and processes that meet the requirements for all countries in the region and must provide ongoing support for the systems in which such products and processes are embedded.

IV. REGIONAL CARD CENTER AS PROTOTYPE OF THE NEW STRATEGY

A significant piece of Citibank's Asian-Pacific IT infrastructure that provided the prototype for further subsequent consolidation in consumer banking is the Regional Card Center (RCC). The RCC was set up in Singapore in 1989 to support start-up credit card businesses in Southeast Asia. Country managers whose credit card data processing were to be centralized demanded exacting performance standards from the center because of its direct impact on their operating performance. Ajit Kanagasundram, who used to run the data center for Citibank Singapore, was given the mandate to set up and run the center:

The purpose of the RCC was to jump-start the credit card businesses in Citibank countries in Southeast Asia. Setting up the processing infrastructure before offering credit card services in each country would take too long and be too costly for start-up businesses. According to the sentiment at that time, we had planned the RCC for the initial three years, and then put processors in each country after that. The time constraint to make the RCC operational also dictated our approach, which was to get the operational software requirements from a couple of lead businesses, in this case, Citibank Hong Kong and Singapore. Trying to get requirements from all countries would be too time consuming and result in missed market opportunities. Further, 80 percent of credit card operational requirements are stipulated by the card associations and were common across countries. We recruited a few staff experienced in credit card operations, used our own production experience, plus onsite consultants to modify the software, and got the RCC operational in eight months.

By 1990, we had reduced the processing cost per credit card by 45 percent and we were given the mandate to extend our operations to cover the Middle East and North Asia, excluding Hong Kong. In 1991, a credit card software that had been developed by Citicorp in London and that was scheduled for implementation in Thailand was scrapped in favor of CARDPAC, the package used by the RCC. By 1994, in the midst of heightened cost consciousness because of corporate financial troubles, our cost per card was down to 32 percent of the 1989 cost. None of the country managers asked for decentralization of the credit card operations—who wants cost per card to triple overnight? We are now processing cards for 15 countries and the number of cards processed have increased from 230,000 in 1990 to 5 million in 1996. We have also decreased the time it took to launch a new business from 14 months to 3 months.

In 1993, Citibank beat out other regional rivals to become the issuer of affinity Visa and Mastercard for Passages, a joint frequent-flyer program of 15 Asian airlines. Citibank credits its ability to launch and support the cards regionally, enabled by the RCC, as being a key factor for being selected. By the end of 1996, the RCC was processing credit cards for 5 million customers in 15 countries from Japan in the north to New Zealand in the south, and from Turkey in the west to Guam in the east. The cost economies offered by the RCC made it obvious for countries to join it rather than go on their own. Citibank projects that, by 1999, its cost per card would drop by a further one-third from the current levels, the benefits of which would be reflected in each country's bottom line.

The RCC concept combines both centralization and decentralization ideas to meet specific local business needs and low costs of processing at the same time. The business strategy, marketing, credit evaluation, and customer service for credit cards continue to be decentralized in each country to cater to local market conditions and needs. The front-end data capture and printing of customer statements are also decentralized to each country. What is centralized is the back-end transaction processing and data repository. The control and active management of credit card businesses continue to be with country managers and the business gains are reflected in the financial performance of each country. The RCC provides the technology infrastructure for lowering operational costs, diffusing best practices, and attracting the needed technical talent. RCC's accumulated experience and infrastructure also enable Citibank to launch the card business in new countries within four months.

The strategic architecture of the RCC is shown in Figure 2. An IBM ES/9000 Model 821 designed for high-volume on-line and batch transaction processing formed the main platform for the system. Input/output operations performed at Citibank branches, ATMs, and other electronic systems include new account opening, collections, authorizations, printing of reports and monthly statements, and customer service. These input/output operations at individual countries are linked via leased lines of different capacities (2.4 kbps to 64 kbps). The databases and transaction history are stored centrally at the RCC.

The decreasing costs of telecommunications and the cost savings from standardizing hardware, software, and procedures enable RCC to reap ever-increasing economies of scale as each new country joins its fold, and as businesses of member countries grow. The centralization of credit card operations in the RCC provided other benefits as well:

- It could devote the necessary resources to ensure superior service levels round the clock (100 percent availability and four-second terminal response time 99 percent of the time).

- It could recruit and retain talent from the best in the region because of the size of its operations; its 60 professional staff have developed in-depth knowledge and expertise in credit card operations and operations of the IBM S/390 platform.

The major concern of the RCC is that of telecommunication costs. Although the RCC has employed advanced data compression techniques, the current costs of leased land/sea circuits are significantly higher than equivalent lines in the United States. Although costs are expected to come down when fiber-optic submarine cables are put in place, the RCC's heavy reliance on telecommunications makes it vulnerable to corporate pressure to locate network processing in areas that minimize its total operating costs. The RCC experience provided the experiential base for subsequent rearchitecting of the technology of the consumer bank. The experience and expertise that RCC had built up would be repositioned to serve the processing requirements of the Asia-Pacific Consumer Bank.

V. REARCHITECTING THE *IT* INFRASTRUCTURE

The fundamental changes in IT infrastructure were motivated by the need to enable the Citibanking vision. The appointment of George DiNardo as the new chief technology officer in 1993 signaled the bank's strategic intent to develop a new technology infrastructure for capitalizing the opportunities from rapid economic growth in Asian countries which is expected to continue well into the twenty-first century. Recipient of *Information Week's* CIO of the Year Award for 1988,

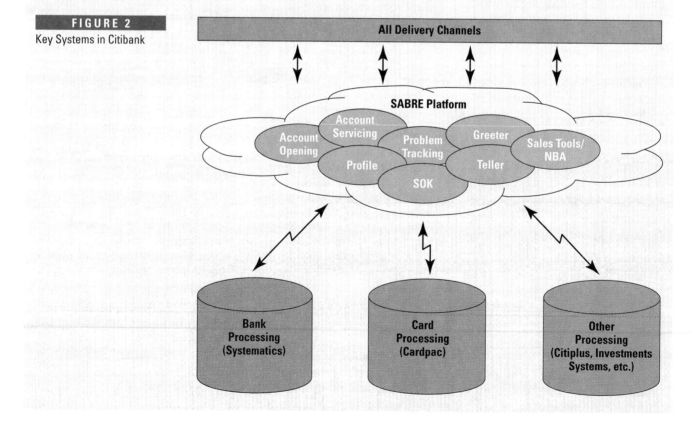

FIGURE 2
Key Systems in Citibank

DiNardo had been with Mellon Bank in Pittsburgh from 1969 to 1991, and was its executive vice president of information systems function from 1985 to 1991. Prior to joining Citicorp, he was a consulting partner for Coopers and Lybrand and a professor of information systems at a leading U.S. university. DiNardo's plan for IT in Citibank is to enable Citibanking, through standardization of the IT platform, to significantly reduce processing costs per transactions through economies of scale, to reduce product to market times by 50 percent, and to increase systems reliability. He crisply summed up his job portfolio at Citibank:

> My job is to introduce the most advanced technology possible in Asia and I spent 35 years doing that for other banks, Bankers Trust and Mellon Bank.[6] I am truly a bank businessman and a technologist. The vision requires that a customer going anywhere in the world be able to transact the same way wherever he goes. It is moving to (the concept of) Citibank recognizes you, and relationship manages you. If you have $100,000 with Citibank, you have certain services free, and it will be the same wherever you go. It's the ability to use the ATM wherever you are.

Moving toward this level of global banking requires that a Citibank branch anywhere in the world will have access to the customer's addresses, customary services, and relationships anywhere else in the world. It would have been costly to achieve this with the then decentralized computing structure, where each country in the Asia-Pacific has its own host computer and where each country has a different technology platform. It would also be difficult to ensure simultaneous rollout across countries of new products. Hence, the foundational changes to computing at Citibank Asia-Pacific began with the centralization of processing and a uniform back-office platform. The bank standardized on an IBM MVS platform. DiNardo explained the logic of centralization for Citibank Asia:

> The old days of having the computer center next to you are gone. Where should your computer center be—remote! Now, with fiber, put your console, command center in your main office, and your big box is remote. Our command center is here in Singapore . . . The telecommunications are improving enough that we can centralize. The economies of large IBMs are important to banking. I have promised that if we regionalize on a new single system, we will get savings. It will cost $50m to do this, but we will break even in year two. We will put the largest IBM box we can get in a center in Singapore. I have promised a 10 to 20 percent computing reduction every year. How am I going to do that? You buy the biggest building, so you can pull any computer in any time, backup for 100 percent up-time, 99.9 percent on-time completion of batch jobs. Then you don't need backup all over Asia. You put in all the other countries account processing, and transmit all the rest.

Initially, the major saving will come from avoiding the need to build a computer center in Hong Kong. Savings arise also from having all processing in one site, with only one other hot backup site, as compared with having processing distributed in 14 countries, and with each country having its own backup. Citibank will be leveraging off the networks that are already in place as a result of the regional card center. Another significant source of savings comes from the centralization of software development.

Citibank is aiming for uniformity in its back-room processing software. Previously, each country controlled its own systems development efforts, so that while each country started out with the same basic software, over time the plethora of systems development efforts resulted in significantly different systems. The advent of PCs and client/server computing compounded the rate of change. Citibank replaced individual country systems that have evolved over time with a $20-million integrated back-office banking applications package from Systematics.

The strength of the Systematics package is that it has evolved significantly through its sale to more than 400 banks, and therefore offers many functions and features. It uses a traditional design based on the MVS/CICS/COBOL platform and has been proved capable of supporting high volumes. According to DiNardo, the idea is to not reinvent the wheel by writing yet another in-house back-office processing system, but to take this package and "turn the 2000 Citibank systems professionals loose on innovation . . . its delivery and panache that counts . . . to create reusable modules to be called in through Systematics user exits. Systematics have promised to keep the exits constant through time." The plan also calls for eventual conversion of all other programs to the Systematics format, for example, using the same approach to data modeling, COBOL programming, and naming conventions.

A new Asia-Pacific data center running an IBM ES/9000 model 821 mainframe was set up in Singapore's Science Park on the western part of the island in October 1994. The hot-site backup running an IBM ES/9000 model 500 was located in Singapore's Chai Chee Industrial Park on the eastern part of the island. The intent is to relocate the backup site to another country to mitigate against country risks once the conversion is complete and the systems are running smoothly. Investments are also made to increase programmer productivity at development centers in Singapore, India, and the Philippines. Citibank is planning to spend $5 million on tools that will increase programmer productivity by 5 to 10 percent each year. Programmers in the centers will do remote TSO development using terminals with channel connects in all countries. Citibank is also considering putting in hyper channels if necessary.

By the first quarter of 1997, six countries have been converted to the Systematics platform—Australia, Singapore, Turkey, Guam, the Philippines, and Malaysia. The other countries are expected to be converted by 1998. By 1999 when the data center consolidation and regionalization are complete, Citibank expects to save about $17.6 million and reduce its staff by about 96 people. Its unit cost for banking transactions is expected to drop by 44 percent from 1996 levels.

VI. BUILDING COMMON FRONT-END SYSTEMS

Peter Mills, director for business improvement, is a 26-year Citibank veteran who has worked in most of the Citibank Asian divisions in his career and has oversight responsibilities for developing common processes for all Asia-Pacific businesses.

> Citibanking is our business vision. We have consolidated on a common platform for efficient back-room processing. My role is to create common business processes that may result in common front-end systems that are compatible with our back-end platforms. As part of the rearchitecting of Citibank's technology infrastructure, we initiated several process reengineering projects to develop new process templates for the Asia-Pacific. It is thus crucial that we manage our key reengineering projects very carefully.

A common thread that has emerged from both the reengineering and infrastructural change efforts is the idea of incorporating best practice—what Citibank calls "centers of excellence." In the area of software development, the emphasis on adopting best practice among the Citibank countries is a guard against the common trap of settling for the lowest common denominator in the process

of standardization. The commitment to develop a reengineering template incorporating the best redesigned processes from each country, for use in developing common systems, is another embodiment of this idea. DiNardo explains what is being practiced in Citibank Asia-Pacific:

> The purchase of the Systematics package provides the bank with increased functionality and standardized processing without significant systems development effort. In-house development effort will be focused on strategic products such as those for currency trading, Citiplus, and the SABRE front-end teller and platform systems. The approach to future systems development will no longer be one of letting "a hundred flowers bloom." There will no longer be systems development or enhancement only for individual countries. Any country requiring any change needs to convince at least two other countries to support it. Any changes made would then be made for all Citibank countries in Asia. Several countries have now been identified as likely centers of excellence for front-end software development: Taiwan for auto loans processing, Australia for mortgage products, Hong Kong for personal finance products, India, the Philippines, and Singapore will become centers for application software development, design, and the generation of high-quality code at competitive cost.

The reengineering of business processes in Singapore provides a glimpse of how Citibank intends to introduce best practices in banking products and service delivery, which would be built into common front-end systems. Citibank has been in Singapore for more than 90 years. It started out as a wholesale bank. The consumer bank business was started later in the 1960s. Being a foreign bank, it is allowed to set up only three branches in Singapore. Nonetheless,

Citibank has done very well in Singapore. Customer accounts have more than tripled since 1989, largely due to the successful introduction of Citibank's Visa card business. There has been an accompanying ten-fold increase in profit in the same period.

Citibank's retail customers in Singapore represent the more affluent segment of the population. The bank's fees and rates are not the lowest, but they feel that they are able to offer a higher level of service and more innovative banking products. This image of innovation and customer service is reinforced through a series of advertisements in print and on television. Innovative products include ready credit and Citiphone banking. The Citiphone service is Citibank Singapore's attempt to provide a high level of customer service despite the regulations that limit its number of branches to three. The vice president in charge of customer service, and the person responsible for implementing Citiphone, calls it their branch in the sky. This is a 24-hour, 7-day-a-week service, that is manned by accredited Citibank officers, who are empowered to make decisions on the spot.

The increase in account volume, however, has been accomplished without any major increase in staff or changes in processes. Staff, processes, and infrastructure that were originally designed to support about 50,000 accounts, were strained when they had to support an account volume of about 250,000. This has contributed to a drop in customers' perception of service levels. Annual surveys indicated that customer satisfaction has dropped from a high of 90 percent in 1987 to a low of 65 percent in 1993. Some departments are experiencing high overtime and employee turnover. A cultural assessment study conducted by consultants confirmed that some employees did not feel valued and trusted. Front-line operations were also paper intensive and perceived to have significant opportunities for improvements. In addition, there was the need to achieve the vision of Citibanking, which required cross-product integration as a basis for relationship banking.

The project was carried out in three phases: (1) building the case for action, (2) design, and (3) implementation. In the first two phases, the consultants worked closely with four Citibankers who were assigned full time to the reengineering project. After six months, the team completed phase two and composed a list of 28 recommended process changes. Three core processes were identified for change—delivery of services to the customer, marketing, and transaction processing. The delivery process included account opening and servicing, credit, and customer problem resolution. The team found that it was encumbered with many hand-offs, a "maker-checker" mindset where transactions had to be checked by someone other than the originating employee, and unclear accountability for problem resolution. The transaction processing process was basically the back-end processing for the transactions originating in the branches. The major observation here was that the processing was fragmented by product or system. The marketing processes were currently also product focused, and there was limited understanding of customer segments and individual customers.

The vision which the team presented included a streamlined front-end delivery process with clear accountability and quick turnaround on customer problem resolution, a unified approach to transaction processing, and segment-focused, cross-product marketing. They felt that the most radical change required would be that of the organizational culture. One aspect of culture manifested in the "maker-checker" was a legacy of the days when the bank was a wholesale bank, and each transaction value was very high while volume was relatively low. In the retail bank business, the high volume and low individual value of transactions required a different mindset. Other aspects of Citibank

culture that would need to change include the emphasis and the incentive system that rewarded product innovation and individuality. The process changes required a culture that focused more on relationships with customers and on team efforts.

The team also set detailed targets for each of the core processes. Among the many targets set for the delivery process, a rise in the percentage of customers who were highly satisfied from 64 to 80 percent, an increase in percentage of customers served within five minutes from 71 to 80 percent, and an improvement in transactions processing accuracy from 2 errors per 5000 transactions to 1 error per 5000 transactions. Detailed targets for productivity and cost improvements were also set. These targets that were in effect also listed measures that would be used to evaluate each process on a recurring basis.

Phase three involved the formation of three implementation teams—service delivery, operations, and product development and marketing—and many more employees. Each team was headed by the vice president in charge of the function. The role of the consultants in phase three was scaled back and they resisted some recommended changes. George DiNardo and Peter Mills addressed the problem of resistance by having discussions with key stakeholders of the processes to be reengineered, and by focusing on a number of projects. Before the end of the first year, the consultants had been phased out. The Citibank implementation teams were driving their own implementation.

A major part of implementation was to develop and implement the information systems needed to support the reengineered processes. Figure 3 is a representation of the key front-end systems within Citibank. One resulting new system is Strategic Asia-Pacific Branch Retail Environment (SABRE). SABRE consists of two complementary subsystems: SABRE I is at the teller level, and provides automated support

for signature verification, paperless teller transactions, and Citicard transactions. SABRE II includes the phone banking systems, together with facilities for telemarketing and cross-product marketing at the branches. The bank is developing the SABRE system in-house, because it considers this to be a strategic product.

The process change efforts, in tandem with the ongoing changes to the IT systems, have resulted in measurable improvements. Citibank tracks performance indicators before and after process changes (see Table 1) to assess the extent of the improvements.

VII. MANAGING IMPLEMENTATION AND CHANGE

It is evident that the structure of computing in Citibank is undergoing significant change. The changes are not trivial and will have "strategic impacts on the future business of the bank." The credibility and experience of George DiNardo were crucial in convincing senior officers of the bank in corporate headquarters and in Asia of the need for drastic change to the IT infrastructure. He has the backing of Citibank's top management and since taking the job, has already brought a different perspective to technology management. He starts from the premise that the IT infrastructure will be standardized to obtain the maximum benefit for the bank. Countries wanting to be different will have to justify it, quite a change from the days when country managers decide the types of technology they want for each country. The IT management team is charging ahead at great speed. When asked for the planned sequence of change activities, DiNardo replied that his approach was "to get all changes bubbling along at the same time … get a few good people who know what they are doing."

The RCC experience provides a useful model for the current consumer bank consolidation. The in-depth technical expertise gained from running a regional data center would be

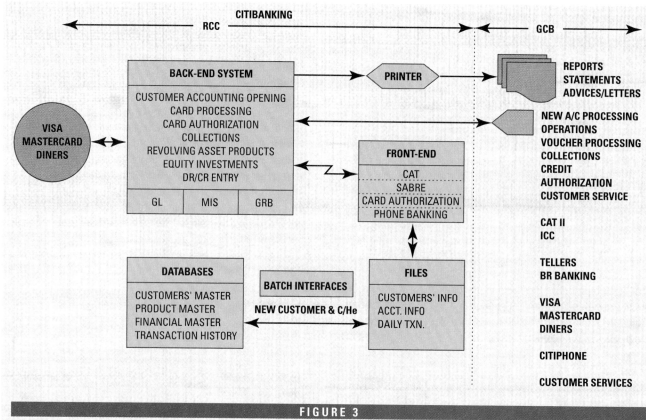

FIGURE 3

Strategic Architecture

directly relevant to the new infrastructure that Citibank is putting in place for consumer banking. Not surprisingly, Ajit now directs and runs the data center for the new Asian-Pacific Consumer Banking technology infrastructure. However, the new infrastructure is more than just scaling up to process more transactions. The business of Citibanking in Global Consumer Banking is more diverse and complex than Cards, and requires the internalization of many business parameters in developing software to support back-end banking operations. Correspondingly, the business impact is also far greater. Citibank, as an American bank operating in Asia, is subjected to restrictions in the number of branches allowed in each country. The reliance on an electronic interface with customers and for an electronic channel for delivery of banking services is significantly higher than many local banks. Citibank sees the new technological infrastructure as a key enabler for flexibility and integration in its product and service offerings throughout Asia at a competitive cost.

The conversion approach is to first bring the bank's internal processes into conformity with the

Table 1						
Results of Citicard Benchmarking Program						
	Cycle Time		No. of Hand-offs		Paperless	
	Before	After	Before	After	Before	After
Statement rendition	41 hrs	24 hrs	2	1	—	—
Duplicate charges	6 days	24 hrs	3	1	no	yes
Card not received charges	6 days	24 hrs	3	1	no	yes
Address change	24 hrs	instant	2	none	no	yes
Payment status inquiry	1–3 days	instant	3	none	no	yes
Account cancellation	24 hrs	instant	2	none	no	yes
Application status inquiry	1–2 days	instant	3	none	no	yes
Expired card charges	2 days	instant	2	1	—	—

Systematics process flow. Reengineering principles were applied to streamline and standardize these processes. The Systematics package also has a customer information systems module that will be used by the bank to support its relationship banking strategy. The conversion to a new technology infrastructure at Citibank Asia-Pacific spells some loss of control over computing for the Citibank country managers. Surprisingly, there has not been serious opposition to the changes, although country managers are understandably "nervous" about the sweeping changes. DiNardo offered a few reasons:

It's an idea whose time has come. The Asia Pacific high profit margin must be maintained! They all know this. They know the value of what we're doing. Computer costs will be down for them, it will affect their bottom line. There is no longer any desire for the sophisticated manager to have his/her own mainframe computer. They know that I have done it 700 times already. No one objects to the logic of the idea. We will insist on a postimplementation audit. The country managers in Asia did see that to survive the next 10 years something like this is necessary. It's all about customer service.

However, it is the level of service and support from the center that country managers are concerned about. The standardization and centralization strategy obviously restricted some flexibility in individual country operations. The strategy was adopted consciously and the gain in integrated customer service and economies of scale is substantial. From experience in other areas of business activities, there is a tendency for most centralized operations to develop a life of their own that over time makes it less responsive to the needs of the end users. Will the Citibank Asia-Pacific data

center go the same way eventually? Citibank is putting in place processes to ensure that country needs are not neglected. "Through the conversion and development, we know their needs very well. For example, we will even help them get support from the two other countries needed to justify enhancements," DiNardo explained. The issue of responsiveness to local needs is unlikely to go away despite such assurances. There is also a related concern about how priorities for enhancements will be handled if there are not enough resources and capacity to meet requests in a timely manner.

A number of factors may impede the progress of the plans. First is the risk that the Systematics conversion may surface unexpected technical problems, as Citibank experienced in converting operations in the Philippines. "We are learning as we go," commented one member of the technical staff. The conversion and implementation schedule may need to be stretched and the expected payback delayed. The Asia-Pacific conversion that was originally supposed to be completed by 1997 has already been pushed to 1998. Part of the reason is the shortage of technical personnel in the region. Further, those who have "cut their teeth" doing the technical implementation are being lured away by other international banks beginning to embark on similar strategies.

Second, the Asian technical staff, although skilled and highly motivated, are, in DiNardo's opinion, conservative. This makes it more difficult to push for the adoption of certain technologies that are perceived to be new in the region. "They tend to be too conservative in planning change— they are not aggressive in their time and payoff targets." DiNardo's experience and confidence have provided the needed leadership to his technical staff in setting the pace and standards for change. The question is whether the pace of change will continue at the same rate when DiNardo retires in about one year.

Third, the standardization and consolidation of technologies and systems have created a sophisticated but highly complex operation at Citibank's Asia-Pacific headquarters. For example, the Asia-Pacific data center has to deal with the integration of various operating systems such as MVS, Stratus, and UNIX. DiNardo admitted that "there are very few people able to run such massive data centers in the region." The high level of operational complexity presents challenges in maintaining consistently high availability, reliability, and quick response times.

Characteristically, DiNardo considers these minor problems that will not affect the overall success of the planned change. Although the implementation is still in progress, the plans have been well received by top management at Citicorp, and it is making plans for similar technology regionalization strategies for Europe, the United States, and Latin America. The Asia-Pacific Consumer Bank is setting the pace and direction for Citicorp in its technology strategy. The Citiplus multicurrency time deposits and Systematics product processes have now been adopted as standards for Citicorp worldwide. One important unanticipated gain accruing to Citibank as a result of the massive infrastructural change is that it has finessed its Year 2000 problem in the process. Once the 15 Asia-Pacific countries are converted by 1998, there will be no legacy systems and no Year 2000 problems to worry about, saving Citibank an estimated $60 million. The new architecture has also eliminated the need to find programmers with very rare operating system skills needed by the old systems. The successful implementation of the changes will reduce the cost of IT services and increase the ability of IT to support product innovation and integration. Today, Citibank services primarily the high-networth customers in Asia. IT may enable the bank to also offer its brand of services to the growing middle class.

Source: From Boon Siong and Christina Soh, Information Management Research Center (IMARC) Nanyang Business School, Nanyang Technological University, Singapore. Reprinted by permission.

Case Study Questions

1. What business strategy is Citicorp pursuing in Asia?

2. Evaluate Citibank's Asia-Pacific information systems in light of this strategy. How well do they support it?

3. Evaluate Citibank's strategy for managing its Asia-Pacific information systems infrastructure.

[1] All financial figures are in U.S. $ unless otherwise stated.

[2] "Citicorp Credit Card Chief to Retire," *Business Times,* April 21, 1997.

[3] "Citicorp in Asia: Eastward Look," *The Economist,* October 24, 1992, p. 90.

[4] "Thinking Globally, Acting Locally," *China Business Review,* May–June, 1993, pp. 23–25.

[5] "For Citibank, there's no place like Asia," *Business Week,* March 30, 1992, pp. 66–69.

Heineken Netherlands B.V.: Reengineering IS/IT to Enable Customer-Oriented Supply Chain Management

Donald A. Marchand, Thomas E. Vollmann, and Kimberly A. Bechler,
International Institute for Management Development
(Switzerland)

In June 1993, Jan Janssen, financial manager of Heineken Netherlands B.V. and the person responsible for Information Systems (IS) and Information Technology (IT), and his IS manager, Rob Pietersen, faced the challenge of developing an IS/IT configuration that would add value to the business and support the ongoing transformation of Heineken's supply chain management system. This system was extensive, not only supplying the Dutch home market, but also providing a significant part of the supply to more than 100 export countries served by the Heineken Group. Supply chain management was central to enterprise-wide transformation.

Management was committed to a process-driven organization, customer-service partnerships, 24-hour delivery lead time, major innovations in the transport system, and resulting changes in the way people worked. And Janssen knew that all of these—and more—required fundamental changes in the way this new work was to be supported by information systems and technology.

Janssen was convinced that the effective management of information as well as a more appropriate IT infra-structure were critical to achieving Heineken's goals of increased flexibility, greater coordination, and a sharper focus on customer needs.

In his mind, the change program initiated in 1990 in the IS/IT area had just been the beginning. Now, he and Pietersen needed to design an information systems and technology back-bone that would be flexible enough to evolve with the changing business needs and adapt to continuous changes in technology.

HEINEKEN NETHERLANDS B.V.

Heineken Netherlands B.V. was the principal operating company responsible for operations in Heineken's home market. It also accounted for a significant part of Heineken N.V.'s worldwide exports. Of the 60.4 million hectoliters[1] of beer produced worldwide under the supervision of the Heineken Group in 1994, a significant portion was produced in the company's two Dutch breweries—Zoeterwoude and 's-Hertogenbosch (Den Bosch). Likewise, 11 percent of the Heineken Group's sales took place in the domestic market, and more than 5400 employees worked for Heineken Netherlands.

Supply Chain Management

The supply chain at Heineken Netherlands began with the receipt of the raw materials that went into the brewing process, and continued through packaging, distribution, and delivery. Brewing took six weeks; it began with the malt mixture of barley and ended with the filtering of the beer after fermentation. Depending on the distribution channel, the beer was then packaged in "one-way" or returnable bottles or cans of different sizes and labels, put in kegs, or delivered in bulk.

The variety of outlets meant that the company had to manage differences in response time (beer for the domestic market was produced to stock, while exported beer was produced to order) and three distinct distribution channels. While each channel consisted mainly of the same steps from the receipt of raw materials through brewing, they differed greatly in packaging and distribution. Beer could be distributed to either on-premise outlets (hotels, restaurants, and cafes, where it was delivered in kegs or poured directly into cellar beer tanks), off-premise outlets (supermarkets, grocery and liquor stores, where it was sold in a variety of bottle and package sizes for home consumption), or to export markets (export deliveries were made to order).

Ongoing Transformation

With key customers requesting faster response times, the development of a process-driven view of Heineken's supply chain activities became critical. The company started the transformation of its supply chain management system by creating customer-service partnerships with its largest domestic customers. The overall objective was to improve the logistics chain dramatically for these customers. In response, delivery lead times were reduced and the transport system was changed. However, the supply chain transformation was seen as a never-ending process.

New Customer-Service Partnerships

In these new service partnerships, Heineken was requested to reduce the time from the placement of the product order to the actual delivery. Before, this delivery lead time had been three days, but the supermarket chains wanted Heineken to supply their warehouses in the Netherlands in 24 hours. Each of the warehouses carried only 8 hours of stock at any time, so the supermarket chains depended on quick and flexible delivery to maintain low inventories and fast response times.

To further enhance its close cooperation with customers, Heineken had embarked on a pilot test of a new logistics improvement called "Comakership" with Albert Heijn, the largest supermarket chain in the Netherlands. Comakership was part of Albert Heijn's Efficient Customer Response project, "Today for Tomorrow." The Albert Heijn retail stores sent their sales information as scanning data to the computer in their central head office. There, the data for Heineken products were scanned out and separated. The beer sales information was then relayed via a standard EDI system (provided by a value-added network operator) from the central office of Albert Heijn directly to Heineken's Zoeterwoude brewery. Heineken was usually able to deliver within 18 hours. Although the pilot had been initiated in only one of Albert Heijn's distribution centers (and the set of stores it served), it had already resulted in lower lead times, decreased costs, and less complexity in the distribution system.

Moving to a 24-Hour Delivery Lead Time

As a result of these successes, top management concluded that delivery lead time could be cut to 24 hours for most domestic customers. However, it would require major shifts in the company's stock levels, distribution centers, work organization, transport system, organizational structure, and information systems.

The 24-hour lead time allowed for greater stock turnover and for lower stock levels in the customer distribution centers. There was, however, more interdepot traffic and higher stocks of packaging material ("returnables") on the brewery premises (which had been located elsewhere along the supply chain). But management believed that as less total inventory was held in the system, these packaging material stocks might be reduced over time.

New Transport System

Until 1991, Heineken Netherlands had contracted out the transportation of its products from the two breweries to about 50 transporters. All of them used a lorry-trailer system with "dedicated" drivers—a driver and his "truck" could make an average of 2.1 deliveries per day. To meet the 24-hour lead time, Heineken had to completely change the fleet used for transport and reduce the number of transporters from 50 to 10. Heineken then contracted 4 cabin trucks from each transporter (40 cabin trucks in total) and paid them for the use of the trailers. The ability of the driver to move from one trailer to another without waiting for unloading meant that he could make an average of 2.4 deliveries per day (a cost reduction of approximately G1.5 million).[2]

New Information Management (IM) Needs

Heineken's customer-service partnership with Albert Heijn and the other changes Heineken had implemented in its supply chain activities brought new information requirements to support the more stringent delivery dictates. With the pilot testing of the Comakership logistics improvement, Heineken needed to implement systems which could manage this new transfer of information, and make appropriate modifications in work activities and organizational structure. Furthermore, the new IS/IT infrastructure needed to be flexible enough to handle and reflect individual retailer and customer beer purchasing patterns.

In the context of these changes in supply chain activities, Janssen reflected on the beginnings of the transformation of IS/IT:

> The transformation of IS/IT and the shifts occurring in our supply chain activities were concurrent without causality. That is very strange, but it just happened that way. I can't say to you that it is a "chicken and egg" kind of story. Of course, there was a link but not an explicit one. Somewhere in our minds, when you do one you do the other, too.

Janssen knew that the relationship between information management, information systems, and information technology had to be clearly defined to have optimum support for the new approaches to value creation. Information management focused on supporting customers and creating new "bundles of goods and services." Information systems focused on developing applications software, managing data, and supporting the new business processes. Finally, information technology related primarily to data and text services, and the underlying operating systems, interfaces, hardware, and networks.

PHASE I: RECOGNIZING THE NEED FOR CHANGE

In July 1989, at the beginning of all the changes at Heineken, Janssen (then at headquarters and responsible for IS/IT worldwide) received a request for a second mainframe at Heineken

Netherlands, costing G6 million (with another G6 million required in three to four years); Janssen brought in the consulting firm Nolan, Norton, Inc. to evaluate the IS/IT infrastructure, first at the corporate level and then at the operating company level for Heineken Netherlands:

> A proposal to purchase a second mainframe focused everybody on our IS/IT infrastructure. You have to have some kind of crisis to get people thinking.

IS/IT Benchmarking

Nolan, Norton, Inc. benchmarked Heineken's IS/IT cost structure against the beverage industry IS/IT average and it was clear that Heineken was indeed not competitive—the company was spending twice the money for half the functionality. "The Nolan, Norton report confirmed what a very wide group of the users thought," Janssen commented. In response, management recommended decentralizing the data center and having each business area manage its own computing resources.

At the same time, Janssen asked Heineken Netherlands, the largest operating company, to develop a new IS/IT plan based on new computer technology, "which meant looking for mid-range platforms, decentralized computing, and standard software packages, rather than developing customized programs for every new application—previously the standard practice." Before determining an appropriate IS/IT plan, Janssen made sure that information management scans were conducted in every functional area. Managers were asked, "What do you need and how can that support our business?" The results were used to create information plans. Working with KPMG Management Consultants and Nolan, Norton, Inc., Janssen developed a list of priorities for IS/IT and selected a new IT platform (IBM AS/400)—both were accepted in July 1990:

The AS/400 became the core of our new IT platform for two reasons: first, we had been a client with IBM for roughly 40 years, and it was not their fault that we used their mainframes in the wrong way; second, we already knew that huge masses of application software were being written for the AS/400, as a quick scan easily confirmed. Furthermore, we were starting to think about an appropriate IT architecture and we were considering the possibility of using personal computers as peripherals linked together through local area and wide area networks.

Implementation of the New IS/IT Plan

Before the end of 1990, Janssen was appointed financial manager. He became the person responsible for IS/IT at Heineken Netherlands and was to oversee the implementation of the new IS/IT plan. Janssen concluded that outsourcing would play a critical role in this process:

> The decision to outsource was part of the plan. When we came to the conclusion that a major change was necessary, that we should look for mid-range computers, that we should go for standard software, that we should not go for dumb terminals but for personal computers as peripherals, it became clear to us that this was a big operation and we could not evolve to it. We could not manage just to keep the old systems in the air with all the problems and have enough management attention for building up the new systems. So we told the organization, "Gentlemen, we are going to outsourcers, and we are going to freeze the applications to free up management time."

PHASE 2: OUTSOURCING TO DEVELOP THE NEW IS/IT INFRASTRUCTURE

Outsourcing enabled the IS group to keep the "old" mainframe applications running while it developed a new IT approach—focusing on the development of its client/server distributed processing infrastructure, the appropriate new IT architecture, and the IS people and skills to achieve these new objectives.

Outsourcing

In 1991, after scanning the outsourcers' market, Janssen chose Electronic Data Systems (EDS), the largest provider of computer services in the United States. EDS provided the *expertise* and *infrastructure* required to meet Heineken's information systems and technology needs, and *career possibilities* for Heineken's mainframe personnel, both vital to the successful transformation of its IS/IT infrastructure. Finally, the five-year contract (with declining involvement each year) provided "guaranteed continuity" while Heineken maintained control. The plan indicated that the last mainframe program would be replaced in 1996 and the contract with EDS would end.

Development of the New IT Architecture

The development of the new IT architecture took place almost concurrently:

> We moved in two directions— one, to outsource our operational concerns, and two, to focus on our new architecture development, eventually replacing everything which was on the mainframe with standard packages on AS/400s.

With the decision to downsize—to move off the mainframe platform—and to decentralize the information management and systems, Janssen chose a comprehensive client/server strategy using a combination of workstations, local and wide area networks, mid-range systems such as AS/400s and local area servers to complete the technology architecture. (Refer to Figure 1 for Heineken's IT architecture.) "Personal Computers" became "Heineken workstations" to eliminate

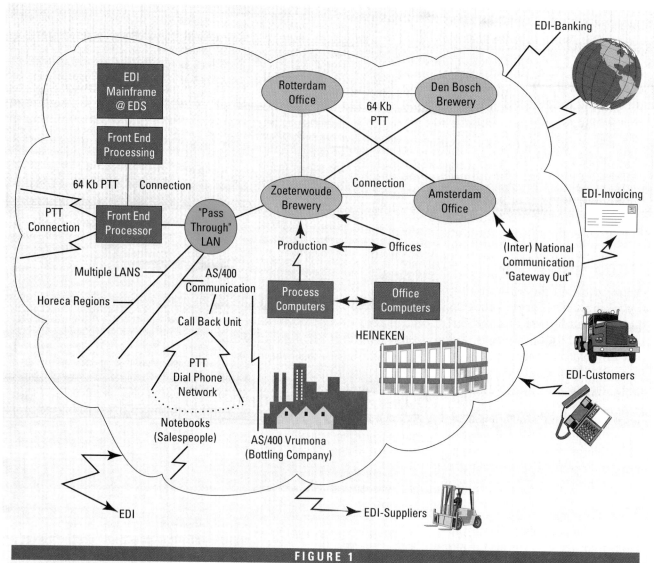

FIGURE 1

Heineken Network Era WAN/LAN

the confusion and "mess" of having 2000 "personal" workstations—in this way, every workstation had the same setup. Furthermore, the salesforce began using "Notebooks" for customer sensing and information sharing.

Changing Over to Standard Packages and Developing Greater Flexibility to Serve the Business

In 1993, Rob Pietersen became IS manager at Heineken Netherlands. He believed that the decentralized IS/IT operations gave more "computer power to the people," and enabled the "user" to become the process owner. Old mainframe programs were replaced

with new standard application packages that covered all the functions in the supply chain. Heineken started this "changeover" by focusing on the software applications dealing with clients: order entry, delivery, transport, invoicing, and accounts receivable.

Selecting Standard Software Packages

To increase flexibility and customer responsiveness, Pietersen knew that Heineken had to shift from the "waterfall approach" to the development of standard software packages:

> At that time in the mainframe world, we were developing soft-

ware applications using a methodology often referred to as the "waterfall." You started with a requirements definition from the users, developed a design and the code to implement that design (getting signoffs at each point along the way). You put the code in production, tested the code, released the code into operation and then you maintained it. When you adopted the code, you went back to the users and asked them if this was what they wanted, and often they said "What?" This waterfall process took 18–36 months or more, and by the time it was completed, the users' requirements often had changed.

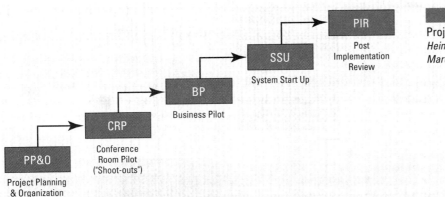

Pietersen began using the PILS (Project Integral Logistics)—named after the successful approach developed to select appropriate logistics software—to test and select standard software packages (refer to Figure 2). The PILS approach involved:

- identifying appropriate software packages;

- setting the top two package vendors against one another in a "shoot-out"—as in the American "Wild West"—where the specific elements of each software package were compared and contrasted;

- creating a business pilot;

- implementing it;

- evaluating its performance.

For IS people, this meant moving from COBOL programming to developing a thorough knowledge of the business.

Pietersen chose PRISM for the logistics area and JD Edwards for the financial area. Pietersen found that the new systems and policies better fit the information needs of the company:

> We needed more flexibility, more power, and less cost. Our current systems have scored high in each of those areas. Computer power is now where it belongs: not with the IT people, but in the hands of the people who need it.

IS Group Reconfiguration

Outsourcing the mainframe and mainframe applications to EDS led to a change in the configuration of the IS group as well. Contracts with employees from software houses were stopped, and many of the individuals working on the mainframe went with the mainframe systems to EDS while other

staff shifted to other areas of the IS group, such as systems management.

Pietersen was convinced that the competencies and capabilities of the IS group had to be expanded to align the use of IT with the evolving supply chain, rather than simply promoting IT solutions as "answers" to the company's information management "problems." Pietersen understood that this change in approach for the IS group required not only a deeper knowledge of business processes and strategy, but also an understanding of how people used the information.

Pietersen therefore transformed the IS department from units for application development, customer support, and operations (a functional structure) to teams servicing production, commercial, distribution, and customer-service areas—the "process owners" (a team-oriented business approach). (Refer to Figures 3 and 4 for the IS organization before and after

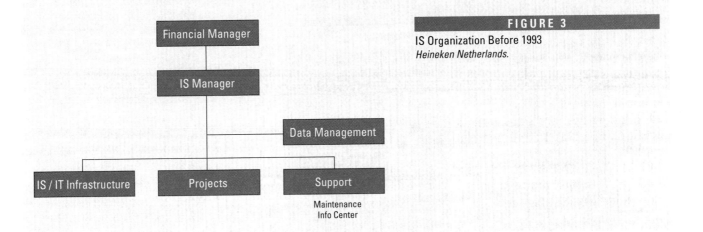

FIGURE 3

IS Organization Before 1993
Heineken Netherlands.

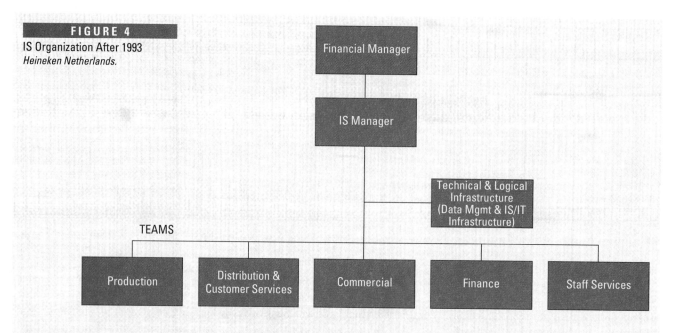

FIGURE 4

IS Organization After 1993
Heineken Netherlands.

Financial Manager

IS Manager

Technical & Logical
Infrastructure
(Data Mgmt & IS/IT
Infrastructure)

TEAMS

Production | Distribution & Customer Services | Commercial | Finance | Staff Services

1993.) The information management needs of the business areas were thus defined by people from both the business areas and IS. These *account teams* helped select standard application packages and, afterwards, adapt the business process to the software package *or* adapt the software package to the business process. These teams thus developed and implemented systems that gave the required support for the respective business processes and delivered information to enable a better control of the supply chain. Shrinking from 130 to 40 people, the IS group was now "doing what they had been doing differently."

Pietersen and Janssen believed that increasing overall access to information would support management's efforts to enhance the employees' empowerment. Client/server systems also fostered teamwork and horizontal decision making. They were fast, flexible, and permitted greater communication with customers and suppliers, which resulted in improved customer service. And they promoted the development of a "process view" (focusing on total processes rather than on discrete tasks). Furthermore, the new configuration of the IS group, with its more team-oriented business approach, also promoted a spirit of greater cooperation and communica-

tion. Pietersen commented, "If we still had the mainframe, all this would not be possible."

Evaluating IS Performance

In 1995, Pietersen and Janssen were still trying to determine how to measure the performance of the IS/IT department. They agreed that IS/IT needed to serve the business, and different service level agreements were to be negotiated with the different functional areas (as shown in Figure 5):

> What is our business? Is it information technology? No, our business is brewing and selling premium beer of high quality. We changed our IT policy to make it clear that IT *supports* the business, but doesn't *drive* the business. We started to focus on having a beautiful bottom line rather than beautiful IT applications.

Currently, IS performance was based on the timely and successful completion of projects. The most important *measure* was the improvement of the business process for which a system or service was meant. In the future, Pietersen and Janssen would be trying to develop criteria to measure the impact of an IS project on improving *overall business performance*.

PHASE 3: LEVERAGING INFORMATION ASSETS IN THE BUSINESS

Executive Information Systems (EIS)

By 1995, Heineken's operational supply chain system—from supplier to end customer—was in its final phase, and the company had begun to add the decision-support element. Decision-support or executive information systems would make it possible for managers to express their information requirements directly. Pietersen hoped that their ease of use would encourage managers to analyze past performance in greater depth and enable them to simulate the possible consequences of proposed actions more accurately. When it came to selecting the appropriate software, Pietersen had chosen EIS Express:

> I call it the technical infrastructure; the basic logical infrastructure of all these systems is in place, and now we come to enabling real improvement, not just the EDI links we have with our retailers, but also such things as installing executive information systems (EIS) to give our management team the control instruments they need to navigate us through the more turbulent business environments we will face in the coming

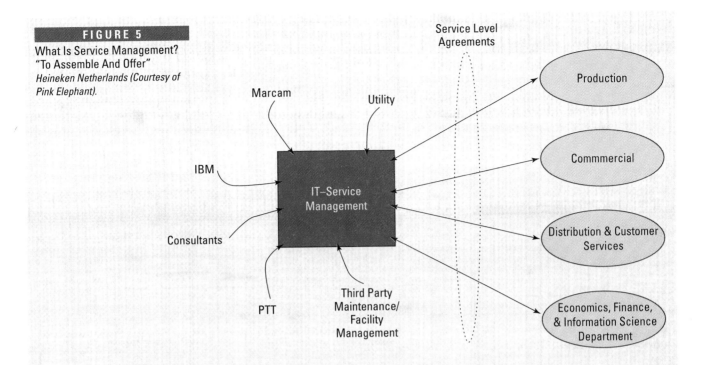

FIGURE 5

What Is Service Management?
"To Assemble And Offer"
*Heineken Netherlands (Courtesy of
Pink Elephant).*

years. The executive information systems gather their data from the data warehouses of the different business systems in all areas and can show this easily through different (graphical) viewpoints.

One of Janssen and Pietersen's goals for the use of executive information systems was to have unity in the data. Janssen explained:

> Having unity in our data is crucial. Only a few years ago we discovered some departments were using different unit volumes than we were. And that just should not happen in any organization.

Better Planning Tools

A key part of the IS/IT strategy was to develop an integrated set of systems to plan and control the overall supply chain, both in the short run (bottle-line scheduling and daily operations) and over a longer horizon (sales forecasts and long-term operations research). The aim was faster and more flexible control of supply chain activities. Jan Janssen elaborated:

What we are working toward is a coherent and consistent set of planning and scheduling tools which are more or less compatible and interconnectible so that you can build up or build down the basic data. Our goal is to be able to model business processes and to have the data, like sales forecasts, to support our decisions about capacity, bottling lines, and stocks. We want to be in a position where, if you have to make a decision, you can run simulations based on actual data.

The concept of supply chain management ultimately served as the driver for better planning tools. Management understood that an overall planning function with multiple time horizons was essential to optimize the supply chain activities as well as to ensure better information management. (Refer to Figure 6 for Heineken's information systems.)

Janssen and Pietersen had put in place information systems to collect and integrate information on Heineken's "on-premise" customer activity. Information on each hotel, restaurant, and cafe/pub that Hein-

eken Netherlands had contact with (as owner, financing agent, or product supplier) was included in these systems. In this way, Heineken Netherlands was able to provide the relevant sales force with an integrated view of their customers (large or small) as well as with information on competitors catering to the same establishments, beer sold, and contract terms. Janssen elaborated:

> We are thinking about what the "next stage of the rocket" will be. We have defined the baseline and are looking at workflow, EDI and planning information systems—how should these planning systems interrelate? We are in the process of defining the next phase of the vision for Heineken as a business in the Netherlands and for the IS/IT fit to that. The current debate is just how far to go.

This case is a condensed version of Heineken Netherlands BV A&B. It was prepared by Research Associate Kimberly A. Bechler under the supervision of Professors Donald A. Marchand and Thomas E. Vollmann, as a basis for class discussion rather than to illustrate either effective or ineffective handling

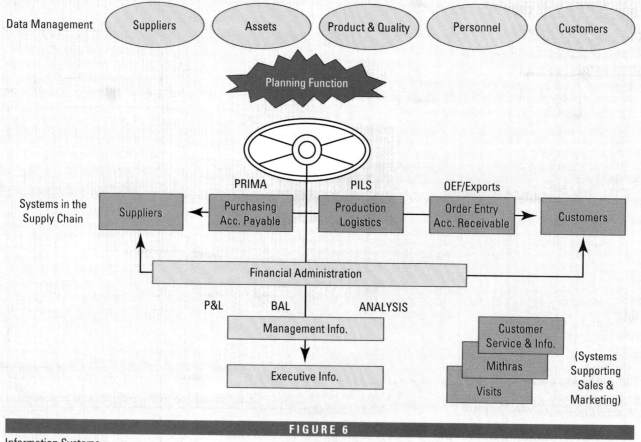

Data Management | Suppliers | Assets | Product & Quality | Personnel | Customers

Planning Function

PRIMA | PILS | OEF/Exports

Systems in the Supply Chain

Suppliers ← Purchasing Acc. Payable | Production Logistics | Order Entry Acc. Receivable → Customers

Financial Administration

P&L | BAL | ANALYSIS

Management Info.

Executive Info.

Customer Service & Info.
Mithras
Visits

(Systems Supporting Sales & Marketing)

FIGURE 6

Information Systems
Heineken Netherlands.

of a business situation. The names of the Heineken managers involved have been disguised. It was developed within the research scope of Manufacturing 2000, a research and development project conducted with global manufacturing enterprises. The authors wish to acknowledge the generous assistance of Heineken management, especially IS manager Gert Bolderman. Copyright © 1996 by **IMD**—International Institute for Management Development, Lausanne, Switzerland. Not to be used or reproduced without written permission directly from **IMD**.

Case Study Questions

1. Analyze Heineken Netherlands using the value chain and competitive forces models. Why did the company feel it needed to transform its supply chain?

2. Analyze all the elements of the new IT infrastructure that Heineken selected for its new business processes. Were Heineken's technology choices appropriate? Why or why not?

3. What management, organization, and technology issues had to be addressed when Heineken Netherlands reengineered its supply chain?

[1] 1 Hectolitre = 22 Imperial gallons = 26.418 US gallons; *Heineken 1994 Annual Report.*
[2] 1000 Guilders (G) = approximately £ 368 = US$ 575 (at December 31, 1994); *Heineken 1994 Annual Report.*

Business Process Redesign Project

HEALTHLITE YOGURT COMPANY

Healthlite Yogurt Company is a market leader in the expanding U.S. market for yogurt and related health products. Healthlite is experiencing some sharp growing pains. With the growing interest in low-fat, low-cholesterol health foods, spurred on by the aging of the baby boomers, Healthlite's sales have tripled over the past five years. At the same time, however, new local competitors, offering fast delivery from local production centers and lower prices, are challenging Healthlite for retail shelf space with a bevy of new products. Without shelf space, products cannot be retailed in the United States, and new products are needed to expand shelf space. Healthlite needs to justify its share of shelf space to grocers and is seeking additional shelf space for its new yogurt-based products such as frozen desserts and low-fat salad dressings.

Healthlite's biggest challenge, however, has not been competitors, but the sweep of the second hand. Yogurt is a very short shelf-life commodity. With a shelf life measured in days, yogurt must be moved very quickly.

Healthlite maintains its U.S. corporate headquarters in Danbury, Connecticut. Corporate headquarters has a central mainframe computer that maintains most of the major business databases. All production takes place in local processing plants, which are located in New Jersey, Massachusetts, Tennessee, Illinois, Colorado, Washington, and California. Each processing plant has its own minicomputer, which is connected to the corporate mainframe. Customer credit verification is maintained at the central corporate site where customer master files are maintained and order verification or rejection is determined. Once processed centrally, order data are then fed to the appropriate local processing plant minicomputer.

Healthlite has 20 sales regions, each with approximately 30 sales representatives and a regional sales manager. Healthlite has a 12-person marketing group in corporate headquarters and a corporate director of sales and marketing. Each salesperson is able to store and retrieve data for assigned customer accounts using a terminal in each regional office linked to the corporate mainframe. Reports for individual salespeople (printouts of orders, rejection notices, customer account inquiries) and for sales offices are printed in the regional offices and mailed to them.

Sometimes, the only way to obtain up-to-date sales data is for managers to make telephone calls to subordinates and then piece the information together. Data about sales and advertising expenses and customer shelf space devoted to Healthlite products are maintained manually at the regional offices. Each regional office maintains its own manual records of customer shelf space and promotional campaigns. The central computer contains only consolidated, companywide files for customer account data and order and billing data.

The existing order processing system requires sales representatives to write hard copy tickets, listing the amount of each product ordered by each customer account, to place orders through the mail. Approximately 100 workers at Healthlite corporate headquarters open, sort, and enter 500,000 order tickets per week into the computer by keypunching them. The order transactions are batched and transmitted each evening from the mainframe to a minicomputer at each of Healthlite's processing sites. These daily order data specify the total yogurt and yogurt product demand for each processing center. Each processing center then produces the amount and type of yogurt and yogurt-related products ordered and then ships the orders out. Shipping managers at the processing centers assign the shipments to various transportation carriers.

The rapid growth, fueled by Healthlite's "health" image, and the branching into new yogurt-based products has put pressures on Healthlite's existing information systems. By mid-1996, growth in new products and sales had reached a point where Healthlite was printing new tickets for the sales force every week. The firm was choking on paper. For each order, a salesperson filled out at least two forms per account. Some sales representatives have more than 80 customers.

As it became bogged down in paper, Healthlite saw increased delays in the processing of its orders. Because yogurt is a fresh food product, it could not be held long in inventory. Yet Healthlite had trouble shipping the right goods to the right places in time. It was taking between 4 and 14 days to process and ship an order, depending on mail delivery rates. Healthlite also found accounting discrepancies of $1.5 million annually between the sales force and headquarters.

Communication between sales managers and the sales representatives has been primarily through the mail or by telephone. For example, regional sales managers have to send representatives letters with announcements of promotional campaigns or pricing discounts. Sales representatives have to write up their monthly reports of sales calls and then mail this information to regional headquarters.

Healthlite is considering new information system solutions. First of all, the firm would like a system that expedites order processing. Management would also like to make better use of information systems to support sales and marketing activities and to take advantage of leading-edge information technology.

Sales and Marketing Information Systems: Background

Sales and marketing are vital to the operation of any business. Orders must be processed and related to production and inventory. Sales of products in existing markets must be monitored and new products must be developed for new markets. The firm must be able to respond to rapidly changing market demands, proliferation of new products and competing firms, shortened product life spans, changing consumer tastes, and new government regulations.

Firms need sales and marketing information for product planning, pricing decisions, devising advertising and other promotional campaigns, forecasting market potential for new and existing products, and determining channels of distribution. They must also monitor the efficiency and effectiveness of the distribution of their products and services.

The sales function of a typical business captures and processes customer orders and produces invoices for customers and data for inventory and production. A typical invoice is illustrated here.

```
Customer:

Highview Supermarket

223 Highland Boulevard

Ossining, NY 10562

Customer Number 00395

                                              Order Number 598422
                                              Order Date: 03/07/98
QTY ITEM NO.        DESCRIPTION      UNIT PRICE      AMOUNT
100  V3392          8 oz. Vanilla    $.44           $44.00
 50  S4456          8 oz. Strawberry $.44           $22.00
 65  L4492          8 oz. Lemon      $.44           $28.60
SHIPPING: $6.50
TOTAL INVOICE: $101.10
```

Data from order entry are also used by a firm's accounts receivable system and by the firm's inventory and production systems. The production planning system, for instance, builds its daily production plans based on the prior day's sales. The number and type of product sold will determine how many units to produce and when.

Sales managers need information to plan and monitor the performance of the sales force. Management also needs information on the performance of specific products, product lines, or brands. Price, revenue, cost, and growth information can be used for pricing decisions, for evaluating the performance of current products, and for predicting the performance of future products.

From basic sales and invoice data, a firm can produce a variety of reports with valuable information to guide sales and marketing work. For weekly, monthly, or annual time periods, information can be gathered on which outlets order the most, on the average order amount, on which products move slowest and fastest, on which salespersons sell the most and least, on which geographic areas purchase the most of a given product, and on how current sales of a product compare with last year's product.

With a group of three or four of your classmates, develop a proposal for redesigning Healthlite's business processes for sales, marketing, and order processing and related information systems to make the company more competitive. Your report should include the following:

1. An overview of the organization—its structure, products, and major business processes for sales, marketing, and order processing.

2. Problem analysis—What was the nature of Healthlite's problems? How are these problems related to existing business processes and systems? Include a diagram of the existing system showing the flows of data and business processes.

3. Solution description—What are the goals and objectives of a new solution? What technical, organizational, or financial feasibility issues should be considered? What alternative solutions should be considered? What are the costs and benefits of each alternative? (You can use computer magazines, the Internet, or industry information to find out approximate costs for developing a new system.) Which should be selected and why?

4. Solution design—How should Healthlite's business processes and systems be re-designed to support the solution selected? What pieces of information should the new system contain? How should this information be organized, stored, and captured? Your discussion should include the following:

- A diagram of your new system design showing new flows of data and re-designed business processes
- A description of the functions of the new system
- A sample data entry screen for the new system
- Report specifications
- File or database design
- Conversion procedures
- Quality assurance measures

5. Organizational impact analysis—Include a discussion of how your solution will impact the organization. Consider human interface issues, the impact on jobs and interest groups, and any risks associated with implementing your solution. How will you implement your solution to take these issues into account?

Glossary

Acceptance testing: Provides the final certification that the system is ready to be used in a production setting.

Accountability: The mechanisms for assessing responsibility for decisions made and actions taken.

Accounting rate of return on investment (ROI): Calculation of the rate of return from an investment by adjusting cash inflows produced by the investment for depreciation. Approximates the accounting income earned by the investment.

Ada: A programming language that is portable across different brands of hardware; is used for both military and nonmilitary applications.

Adhocracy: Task force organization, such as a research organization, designed to respond to a rapidly changing environment and characterized by large groups of specialists organized into short-lived multidisciplinary task forces.

Administrative controls: Formalized standards, rules, procedures, and disciplines to ensure that the organization's controls are properly executed and enforced.

Agency theory: Economic theory that views the firm as a nexus of contracts among self-interested individuals rather than a unified, profit-maximizing entity.

AI shell: The programming environment of an expert system.

American Standard Code for Information Interchange (ASCII): A 7- or 8-bit binary code used in data transmission, PCs, and some large computers.

Analog signal: A continuous waveform that passes through a communications medium. Used for voice communications.

Antivirus software: Software designed to detect and often eliminate computer viruses from an information system.

Application controls: Specific controls unique to each computerized application.

Application generator: Software that can generate entire information system applications; the user needs only to specify what needs to be done, and the application generator creates the appropriate program code.

Application software: Programs written for a specific business application to perform functions specified by end users.

Application software package: Set of prewritten, precoded application software programs that are commercially available for sale or lease.

Archie: A tool for locating data on the Internet that performs keyword searches on an actual database of documents, software, and data files available for downloading from servers around the world.

Arithmetic-logic unit (ALU): Component of the CPU that performs the principal logical and arithmetic operations of the computer.

Artificial intelligence (AI): The effort to develop computer-based systems that can behave like humans, with the ability to learn languages, accomplish physical tasks, use a perceptual apparatus, and emulate human expertise and decision making.

Assembly language: A programming language developed in the 1950s that resembles machine language but substitutes mnemonics for numeric codes.

Asynchronous transfer mode (ATM): A networking technology that parcels information into 8-byte cells, allowing data to be transmitted between computers from different vendors at any speed.

Asynchronous transmission: The low-speed transmission of one character at a time.

Attribute: A piece of information describing a particular entity.

Authentication: The ability of each party in a transaction to verify the identity of the other parties.

Backward chaining: A strategy for searching the rule base in an expert system that acts like a problem solver by beginning with a hypothesis and seeking out more information until the hypothesis is either proved or disproved.

Bandwith: The capacity of a communications channel as measured by the difference between the highest and lowest frequencies that can be transmitted by that channel.

Bar code: Form of OCR technology widely used in supermarkets and retail stores in which identification data are coded into a series of bars.

Baseband: LAN channel technology that provides a single path for transmitting either text, graphics, voice, or video data at one time.

BASIC (Beginners All-purpose Symbolic Instruction Code): A general-purpose programming language used with PCs and for teaching programming.

Batch control totals: A type of input control that requires counting batches or any quantity field in a batch of transactions prior to processing for comparison and reconciliation after processing.

Batch processing: A method of collecting and processing data in which transactions are accumulated and stored until a specified time when it is convenient or necessary to process them as a group.

Baud: A change in signal from positive to negative or vice versa that is used as a measure of transmission speed.

Behavioral perspective: Descriptions of management based on behavioral scientists' observations of how organizations actually behave and what managers actually do in their jobs.

Bit: A binary digit representing the smallest unit of data in a computer system. It can only have one of two states, representing 0 or 1.

Bit mapping: The technology that allows each pixel on the screen to be addressed and manipulated by the computer.

Bounded rationality: Idea that people will avoid new, uncertain alternatives and stick with tried-and-true rules and procedures.

Briefing books: On-line data in the form of fixed-format reports for executives; part of an early ESS.

Broadband: LAN channel technology that provides several paths for transmitting text, graphics, voice, or video data so that different types of data can be transmitted simultaneously.

Bugs: Program code defects or errors.

Bureaucracy: Formal organization with a clear-cut division of labor, abstract rules, and procedures, and impartial decision making that uses technical qualifications and professionalism as a basis for promoting employees.

Bureaucratic model: Model of decision making where decisions are shaped by the organization's standard operating procedures (SOPs).

Bus network: Network topology linking a number of computers by a single circuit with all messages broadcast to the entire network.

Business driver: A force in the environment to which businesses must respond and that influences the direction of business.

Business processes: The unique ways in which organizations coordinate and organize work activities, information, and knowledge to produce a valuable product or service.

Business reengineering: The radical redesign of business processes, combining steps to cut waste and eliminating repetitive, paper-intensive tasks to improve cost, quality, and service and to maximize the benefits of information technology.

Byte: A string of bits, usually eight, used to store one number or character in a computer system.

C: A powerful programming language with tight control and efficiency of execution; is portable across different microprocessors and is used primarily with PCs.

Cache: Memory area for high-speed storage of frequently used instructions and data.

Capital budgeting: The process of analyzing and selecting various proposals for capital expenditures.

Carpal tunnel syndrome (CTS): Type of RSI in which pressure on the median nerve through the wrist's bony carpal tunnel structure produces pain.

Case-based reasoning (CBR): Artificial intelligence technology that represents knowledge as a database of cases.

Cathode ray tube (CRT) terminal: A screen, also referred to as a video display terminal (VDT). Provides a visual image of both user input and computer output. Displays text or graphics as either color or monochrome images.

Cellular telephone: A device that transmits voice or data, using radio waves to communicate with radio antennas placed within adjacent geographic areas called *cells*.

Central processing unit (CPU): Area of the computer system that manipulates symbols, numbers, and letters, and controls the other parts of the computer system.

Centralized processing: Processing that is accomplished by one large central computer.

Change agent: In the context of implementation, the individual acting as the catalyst during the change process to ensure successful organizational adaptation to a new system or innovation.

Channels: The links by which data or voice are transmitted between sending and receiving devices in a network.

Chatting: Live, interactive conversations over a public network.

Choice: Simon's third stage of decision making, when the individual selects among the various solution alternatives.

Class: The feature of object-oriented programming so that all objects belonging to a certain class have all of the features of that class.

Client: The user point-of-entry for the required function. Normally a desktop computer, workstation, or laptop computer, the user generally interacts directly only with the client, typically through a graphical user interface, using it to input and retrieve data, and to analyze and report on them.

Client/server model: A model for computing that splits the processing between "clients" and "servers" on a network assigning functions to the machine most able to perform the function.

Coaxial cable: A transmission medium consisting of thickly insulated copper wire. Can transmit large volumes of data quickly.

COBOL (COmmon Business Oriented Language): The predominant programming language for business applications because it can process large data files with alphanumeric characters.

Cognitive perspective: Descriptions of management and organization which emphasize the role of knowledge, core competency, and perceptual filters.

Cognitive style: Underlying personality disposition toward the treatment of information, selection of alternatives, and evaluation of consequences.

Communications processors: Hardware that supports data transmission and reception in a telecommunications network.

Communications technology: Physical devices and software that link various computer hardware components and transfer data from one physical location to another.

Compact disk read-only memory (CD-ROM): Read-only optical disk storage used for imaging, reference, and database applications with massive amounts of data and for multimedia.

Competitive forces model: Model used to describe the interaction of external influences, specifically threats and opportunities, that affect an organization's strategy and ability to compete.

Compiler: Special system software that translates a higher-level language into machine language for execution by the computer.

Computer abuse: The commission of acts involving a computer that may not be illegal but are considered unethical.

Computer crime: The commission of illegal acts through the use of a computer or against a computer system.

Computer hardware: Physical equipment used for input, processing, and output activities in an information system.

Computer matching: Processing control that matches input data with information held on master files.

Computer mouse: Handheld input device whose movement on the desktop controls the position of the cursor on the computer display screen.

Computer operations controls: Procedures to ensure that programmed procedures are consistently and correctly applied to data storage and processing.

Computer software: Detailed, preprogrammed instructions that control and coordinate the work of computer hardware components in an information system.

Computer virus: Rogue software programs that are difficult to detect and that spread rapidly through computer systems, destroying data or disrupting processing and memory systems.

Computer vision syndrome (CVS): Eye strain condition related to cathode ray tube (CRT) use, with symptoms including headaches, blurred vision, and dry, irritated eyes.

Computer-aided design (CAD): Information system that automates the creation and revision of designs using sophisticated graphics software.

Computer-aided software engineering (CASE): The automation of step-by-step methodologies for software and systems development to reduce the amount of repetitive work the developer needs to do.

Computer-based information system (CBIS): An information system that relies on computer hardware and software for processing and disseminating information.

Concentrator: Telecommunications computer that collects and temporarily stores messages from terminals for batch transmission to the host computer.

Connectivity: A measure of how well computers and computer-based devices communicate and share information with one another without human intervention.

Context diagram: Overview data flow diagram depicting an entire system as a single process with its major inputs and outputs.

Control unit: Component of the CPU that controls and coordinates the other parts of the computer system.

Controller: A specialized computer that supervises communications traffic between the CPU and the peripheral devices in a telecommunications system.

Controls: All the methods, policies, and procedures that ensure protection of the organization's assets, accuracy and reliability of its records, and operational adherence to management standards.

Conversion: The process of changing from the old system to the new system.

Conversion plan: Provides a schedule of all activities required to install a new system.

Cooperative processing: Type of processing that divides the processing work for transaction-based applications among mainframes and PCs.

Cooptation: Bringing the opposition into the process of designing and implementing the solution without giving up control over the direction and nature of the change.

Copyright: A statutory grant which protects creators of intellectual property against copying by others for any purpose for a period of 28 years.

Core systems: Systems that support functions that are absolutely critical to the organization.

Cost-benefit ratio: A method for calculating the returns from a capital expenditure by dividing the total benefits by total costs.

Counterimplementation: A deliberate strategy to thwart the implementation of an information system or an innovation in an organization.

Critical success factors (CSFs): A small number of easily identifiable operational goals shaped by the industry, the firm, the manager, and the broader environment that are believed to ensure the success of an organization. Used to determine the information requirements of an organization.

Cultural theory: Behavioral theory stating that information technology must fit into an organization's culture or the technology will not be adopted.

Customization: The modification of a software package to meet an organization's unique requirements without destroying the integrity of the package software.

Cylinder: Represents circular tracks on the same vertical line within a disk pack.

Data: Streams of raw facts representing events occurring in organizations or the physical environment before they have been organized and arranged into a form that people can understand and use.

Data administration: A special organizational function for managing the organization's data resources, concerned with information policy, data planning, maintenance of data dictionaries, and data quality standards.

Data bus width: The number of bits that can be moved at one time between the CPU, primary storage, and the other devices of a computer.

Data conversion: Process of properly transcribing data from one form into another form for computer transactions.

Data definition language: The component of a database management system that defines each data element as it appears in the database.

Data dictionary: An automated or manual tool for storing and organizing information about the data maintained in a database.

Data element: A field.

Data flow diagram (DFD): Primary tool in structured analysis that graphically illustrates a system's component processes and the flow of data between them.

Data flows: The movement of data between processes, external entities, and data stores in a data flow diagram.

Data management software: Software used for creating and manipulating lists, creating files and databases to store data, and combining information for reports.

Data manipulation language: A language associated with a database management system that is employed by end users and programmers to manipulate data in the database.

Data mining: Technology for finding hidden patterns and relationships in large databases and inferring rules from them to predict future behavior.

Data quality audit: Surveys of end users, files, and samples of files for accuracy and completeness of data in an information system.

Data redundancy: The presence of duplicate data in multiple data files.

Data security controls: Controls to ensure that data files on either disk or tape are not subject to unauthorized access, change, or destruction.

Data stores: Manual or automated inventories of data.

Data warehouse: A database, with reporting and query tools, that stores current and historical data extracted from various operational systems and consolidated for management reporting and analysis.

Data workers: People such as secretaries or bookkeepers who primarily process and disseminate the organization's paperwork.

Database: A collection of data organized to service many applications at the same time by storing and managing data so that they appear to be in one location.

Database administration: Refers to the more technical and operational aspects of managing data, including physical database design and maintenance.

Database management system (DBMS): Special software to create and maintain a database and enable individual business applications to extract the data they need without having to create separate files or data definitions in their computer programs.

Dataconferencing: Teleconferencing in which two or more users are able to edit and directly modify data files simultaneously.

Data-driven DSS: A system that supports decision making by allowing users to extract and analyze useful information that was previously buried in large databases.

Datamining: Analysis of large pools of data to find patterns and rules that can be used to guide decision making and predict future behavior.

Debugging: The process of discovering and eliminating the errors and defects—the bugs—in program code.

Decision and control theory: Behavioral theory stating that the function of the organization is to make decisions under conditions of uncertainty and risk and that organizations centralize decision making and create a hierarchy of decision making to reduce uncertainty and to ensure survival.

Decisional roles: Mintzberg's classification for managerial roles where managers initiate activities, handle disturbances, allocate resources, and negotiate conflicts.

Decision-support system (DSS): Information system at the management level of an organization that combines data, analytical tools, and models to support semistructured and unstructured decision making.

Dedicated lines: Telephone lines that are continuously available for transmission by a lessee. Typically conditioned to transmit data at high speeds for high-volume applications.

Descartes' rule of change: A principle that states that if an action cannot be taken repeatedly, then it is not right to be taken at any time.

Design (in decision making): Simon's second stage of decision making, when the individual conceives of possible alternative solutions to a problem.

Design: Stage in the systems life cycle that produces the logical and physical design specifications for the systems solution.

Desktop publishing: Technology that produces professional-quality documents combining output from word processors with design, graphics, and special layout features.

Development methodology: A collection of methods, one or more for every activity within every phase of a development project.

Digital scanners: Input devices that translate images such as pictures or documents into digital form for processing.

Digital signal: A discrete waveform that transmits data coded into two discrete states as 1-bits and 0-bits, which are represented as on–off electrical pulses; used for data communications.

Digital video disk (DVD): High-capacity optical storage medium that can store full-length videos and large amounts of data.

Direct access storage device (DASD): Refers to magnetic disk technology that permits the CPU to locate a record directly, in contrast to sequential tape storage that must search the entire file.

Direct cutover strategy: A risky conversion approach in which the new system completely replaces the old one on an appointed day.

Direct file access method: A method of accessing records by mathematically transforming the key fields into the specific addresses for the records.

Direct or random file organization: A method of storing data records in a file so that they can be accessed in any sequence without regard to their actual physical order on the storage media.

Distributed database: A database that is stored in more than one physical location. Parts or copies of the database are physically stored in one location, and other parts or copies are stored and maintained in other locations.

Distributed processing: The distribution of computer processing work among multiple computers linked by a communication network.

Divisionalized bureaucracy: Combination of many machine bureaucracies, each producing a different product or service, under one central headquarters. Common form for Fortune 500 firms.

Document imaging systems: Systems that convert documents and images into digital form so that they can be stored and accessed by the computer.

Documentation: Descriptions of how an information system works from either a technical or end-user standpoint.

Domain name: The unique name of a collection of computers connected to the Internet.

Domestic exporter: A strategy characterized by heavy centralization of corporate activities in the home country of origin.

DOS: Operating system for 16-bit PCs based on the IBM personal computer standard.

Downsizing: The process of transferring applications from large computers to smaller ones.

Downtime: Periods of time in which an information system is not operational.

Drill down: The ability to move from summary data down to lower and lower levels of detail.

DSS database: A collection of current or historical data from a number of applications or groups. Can be a small PC database or a massive data warehouse.

DSS software system: Collection of software tools that are used for data analysis, such as OLAP tools, datamining tools, or a collection of mathematical and analytical models.

Due process: A process in which laws are well known and understood and there is an ability to appeal to higher authorities to ensure that laws are applied correctly.

Economic feasibility: Determines whether the benefits of a proposed solution outweigh the costs.

Edit checks: Routines performed to verify input data and correct errors prior to processing.

Electronic commerce: The process of buying and selling goods electronically by consumers and from company to company through computerized business transactions.

Electronic data interchange (EDI): The direct computer-to-computer exchange between two organizations of standard business transaction documents.

Electronic mail (e-mail): The computer-to-computer exchange of messages.

Electronic market: A marketplace that is created by computer and communication technologies that link many buyers and sellers via interorganizational systems.

Electronic meeting system (EMS): A collaborative GDSS that uses information technology to make group meetings more productive by facilitating communication as well as decision making. Supports meetings at the same place and time or in different places and times.

Encryption: The coding and scrambling of messages to prevent unauthorized access to or understanding of the data being transmitted.

End users: Representatives of departments outside the information systems group for whom information systems applications are developed.

End-user development: The development of information systems by end users with little or no formal assistance from technical specialists.

End-user interface: The part of an information system through which the end user interacts with the system, such as on-line screens and commands.

Enterprise analysis: An analysis of organization-wide information requirements by looking at the entire organization in terms of organizational units, functions, processes, and data elements; helps identify the key entities and attributes in the organization's data.

Enterprise networking: An arrangement of the organization's hardware, software, telecommunications, and data resources to put more computing power on the desktop and create a companywide network linking many smaller networks.

Entity: A person, place, thing, or event about which information must be kept.

Entity-relationship diagram: A methodology for documenting databases illustrating the relationship between various entities in the database.

Entrepreneurial structure: Young, small firm in a fast-changing environment dominated by a single entrepreneur and managed by a single chief executive officer.

Environmental factors: Factors external to the organization that influence the adoption and design of information systems.

Erasable programmable read-only memory (EPROM): Subclass of ROM chip that can be erased and reprogrammed many times.

Ergonomics: The interaction of people and machines in the work environment, including the design of jobs, health issues, and the end-user interface of information systems.

Ethical "no free lunch" rule: Assumption that all tangible and intangible objects are owned by someone else unless there is a specific declaration otherwise and that the creator wants compensation for this work.

Ethics: Principles of right and wrong that can be used by individuals acting as free moral agents to make choices to guide their behavior.

Executive support system (ESS): Information system at the strategic level of an organization designed to address unstructured decision making through advanced graphics and communications.

Expert system: Knowledge-intensive computer program that captures the expertise of a human in limited domains of knowledge.

Extended *Binary Coded Decimal Interchange Code* (EBCDIC): Binary code representing every number, alphabetic character, or special character with 8 bits, used primarily in IBM and other mainframe computers.

External entities: Originators or receivers of information outside the scope of the system portrayed in the data flow diagram. Sometimes called *outside interfaces.*

External integration tools: Project management technique that links the work of the implementation team to that of users at all organizational levels.

Extranet: A private intranet that is accessible to select outsiders.

Facsimile (fax) machine: A machine that digitizes and transmits documents with both text and graphics over telephone lines.

Fair information practices (FIP): A set of principles originally set forth in 1973 that governs the collection and use of information about individuals and forms the basis of most U.S. and European privacy laws.

Fault-tolerant computer systems: Systems that contain extra hardware, software, and power supply components that can back the system up and keep it running to prevent system failure.

Feasibility study: As part of the systems analysis process, the way to determine whether the solution is achievable, given the organization's resources and constraints.

Feedback: Output that is returned to the appropriate members of the organization to help them evaluate or correct input.

Fiber-optic cable: A fast, light, and durable transmission medium consisting of thin strands of clear glass fiber bound into cables. Data are transmitted as light pulses.

Field: A grouping of characters into a word, a group of words, or a complete number, such as a person's name or age.

File: A group of records of the same type.

File Transfer Protocol (FTP): Tool for retrieving and transferring files from a remote computer.

Firewall: Hardware and software placed between an organization's internal network and an external network to prevent outsiders from invading private networks.

Floppy disk: Removable magnetic disk storage primarily used with PCs.

Focused differentiation: Competitive strategy for developing new market niches for specialized products or services where a business can compete in the target area better than its competitors.

Formal control tools: Project management techniques that help monitor the progress toward completion of a task and fulfillment of goals.

Formal planning tools: Project management technique that structures and sequences tasks; budgeting time, money, and technical resources required to complete the tasks.

Formal system: System resting on accepted and fixed definitions of data and procedures, operating with predefined rules.

FORTRAN (FORmula TRANslator): A programming language developed in 1956 for scientific and mathematical applications.

Forward chaining: A strategy for searching the rule base in an expert system that begins with the information entered by the user and searches the rule base to arrive at a conclusion.

Forward engineering: The final step in reengineering when the revised specifications are used to generate new, structured program code for a structured and maintainable system.

Fourth-generation language: A programming language that can be employed directly by end users or less skilled programmers to develop computer applications more rapidly than conventional programming languages.

Frame relay: A shared network service technology that packages data into bundles for transmission but does not use error-correction routines. Cheaper and faster than packet switching.

Franchiser: A firm where product is created, designed, financed, and initially produced in the home country, but for product-specific reasons must rely heavily on foreign personnel for further production, marketing, and human resources.

Front-end processor: A small computer managing communications for the host computer in a network.

Full-duplex transmission: A transmission in which data can travel in both directions simultaneously.

Function point analysis: Software output metric that measures the number of inputs, outputs, inquiries, files, and external interfaces used in an application. Used to assess developer productivity and software efficiency.

Fuzzy logic: Rule-based AI that tolerates imprecision by using nonspecific terms called *membership functions* to solve problems.

Garbage can model: Model of decision making that states that organizations are not rational and that decisions are solutions that become attached to problems for accidental reasons.

Gateway: A communications processor that connects dissimilar networks by providing the translation from one set of protocols to another.

General controls: Overall controls that establish a framework for controlling the design, security, and use of computer programs throughout an organization.

Genetic algorithms: Problem-solving methods that promote the evolution of solutions to specified problems using the model of living organisms adapting to their environment.

Gigabyte: Approximately one billion bytes. Unit of computer storage capacity.

Global culture: The development of common expectations, shared artifacts, and social norms among different cultures and peoples.

Gopher: A tool for locating information stored on Internet gopher servers through a series of easy-to-use, hierarchical menus.

Graphical user interface (GUI): The part of an operating system that users interact with that uses graphic icons and the computer mouse to issue commands and make selections.

Graphics language: A computer language that displays data from files or databases in graphic format.

Group decision-support system (GDSS): An interactive computer-based system to facilitate the solution to unstructured problems by a set of decision makers working together as a group.

Groupware: Software that recognizes the significance of groups in offices by providing functions and services that support the collaborative activities of work groups.

Hacker: A person who gains unauthorized access to a computer network for profit, criminal mischief, or personal pleasure.

Half-duplex transmission: A transmission in which data can flow two ways but in only one direction at a time.

Hard disk: Magnetic disk resembling a thin steel platter with an iron oxide coating; used in large computer systems and in many PCs.

Hardware controls: Controls to ensure the physical security and correct performance of computer hardware.

Hierarchical data model: One type of logical database model that organizes data in a treelike structure. A record is subdivided into segments that are connected to each other in one-to-many parent-child relationships.

High-level language: Programming languages in which each source code statement generates multiple statements at the machine-language level.

Home page: A World Wide Web text and graphical screen display that welcomes the user and explains the organization that has established the page.

Hybrid AI system: Integration of multiple AI technologies into a single application to take advantage of the best features of these technologies.

Hypermedia database: An approach to data management that organizes data as a network of nodes linked in any pattern established by the user; the nodes can contain text, graphics, sound, full-motion video, or executable programs.

Hypertext Markup Language (HTML): A programming tool that uses hypertext to establish dynamic links to other documents stored in the same or remote computers.

Immanuel Kant's Categorical Imperative: A principle that states that if an action is not right for everyone to take it is not right for anyone.

Implementation: All organizational activities working toward the adoption, management, and routinization of an innovation.

Implementation (in decision making): Simon's final stage of decision making, when the individual puts the decision into effect and reports on the progress of the solution.

Implementation controls: Audit of the systems development process at various points to ensure that it is properly controlled and managed.

Incremental decision making: Choosing policies most like the previous policy.

Index: A table or list that relates record keys to physical locations on direct access files.

Index server: In imaging systems, a device that stores the indexes that allow a user to identify and retrieve a specific document.

Indexed sequential access method (ISAM): A file access method to directly access records organized sequentially using an index of key fields.

Inference engine: The strategy used to search through the rule base in an expert system; can be forward or backward chaining.

Information: Data that have been shaped into a form that is meaningful and useful to human beings.

Information architecture: The particular form that information technology takes in a specific organization to achieve selected goals or functions.

Information center: A special facility within an organization that provides training and support for end-user computing.

Information partnership: Cooperative alliance formed between two corporations for the purpose of sharing information to gain strategic advantage.

Information policy: Formal rules governing the maintenance, distribution, and use of information in an organization.

Information portability: The sharing of computer files among different hardware platforms and software applications.

Information requirements: A detailed statement of the information needs that a new system must satisfy; identifies who needs what information, and when, where, and how the information is needed.

Information rights: The rights that individuals and organizations have with respect to information which pertains to themselves.

Information superhighway: High-speed digital telecommunications networks that are national or worldwide in scope and accessible by the general public rather than restricted to use by members of a specific organization or set of organizations such as a corporation.

Information system: Interrelated components working together to collect, process, store, and disseminate information to support decision making, coordination, control, analysis, and visualization in an organization.

Information systems department: The formal organizational unit that is responsible for the information systems function in the organization.

Information systems managers: Leaders of the various specialists in the information systems department.

Information systems plan: A road map indicating the direction of systems development: the rationale, the current situation, the management strategy, the implementation plan, and the budget.

Information work: Work that primarily consists of creating or processing information.

Informational roles: Mintzberg's classification for managerial roles where managers act as the nerve centers of their organizations, receiving and disseminating critical information.

Inheritance: The feature of object-oriented programming in which a specific class of objects receives the features of a more general class.

Input: The capture or collection of raw data from within the organization or from its external environment for processing in an information system.

Input authorization: Proper authorization, recording, and monitoring of source documents as they enter the computer system.

Input controls: Procedures to check data for accuracy and completeness when they enter the system, including input authorization, data conversion, and edit checks.

Installation: Systems life cycle stage consisting of testing, training, and conversion; the final steps required to put a system into operation.

Institutional factors: Factors internal to the organization that influence the adoption and design of information systems.

Intangible benefits: Benefits that are not easily quantified; they include more efficient customer service or enhanced decision making.

Integrated Services Digital Network (ISDN): International standard for transmitting voice, video, and data to support a wide range of service over the public telephone lines.

Integrated software package: A software package that provides two or more applications, such as word processing and spreadsheets, providing for easy transfer of data between them.

Intellectual property: Intangible property created by individuals or corporations which is subject to protections under trade secret, copyright, and patent law.

Intelligence: The first of Simon's four stages of decision making, when the individual collects information to identify problems occurring in the organization.

Intelligent agent: A software program that uses a built-in or learned knowledge base to carry out specific, repetitive, and predictable tasks for an individual user, business process, or software application.

Interaction theory: User-resistance theory stating that resistance is caused by the interaction of people and systems factors.

Internal integration tools: Project management technique that ensures that the implementation team operates as a cohesive unit.

Internal rate of return (IRR): The rate of return or profit that an investment is expected to earn.

International information systems infrastructure: The basic information systems required by organizations to coordinate worldwide trade and other activities.

Internet: International network of networks that is a collection of over 100,000 private or public networks.

Internet service provider (ISP): A commercial organization with a permanent connection to the Internet which sells temporary connections to subscribers.

Internetworking: The linking of separate networks, each of which retains its own identity, into an interconnected network.

Interoperability: The ability of a single piece of software to operate on two different machine platforms showing users an identical interface and performing the same tasks.

Interorganizational systems: Information systems that automate the flow of information across organizational boundaries and link a company to its customers, distributors, or suppliers.

Interpersonal roles: Mintzberg's classification for managerial roles where managers act as figureheads and leaders for the organization.

Interpreter: A special translator of source code into machine code that translates each source code statement into machine code and executes it, one at a time.

Intranet: An internal network based on Internet and World Wide Web technology.

Intuitive decision makers: Cognitive style that describes people who approach a problem with multiple methods in an unstructured manner, using trial and error to find a solution.

Investment workstation: Powerful desktop computer for financial specialists, which is optimized to access and manipulate massive amounts of financial data.

Iteration construct: The logic pattern in programming in which certain actions are repeated while a specified condition occurs or until a certain condition is met.

Iterative: Process of repeating the steps to build a system over and over again.

Java: An object-oriented programming language that can deliver only the software functionality needed for a particular task as a small applet downloaded from a network; can run on any computer and operating system.

Joint application design (JAD): A design method which brings users and IS professionals into a room together for an interactive design of the system.

Jukebox: A device for storing and retrieving many optical disks.

Key field: A field in a record that uniquely identifies instances of that record so that it can be retrieved, updated, or sorted.

Kilobyte: One thousand bytes (actually 1024 storage positions). Used as a measure of PC storage capacity.

Knowledge- and information-intense products: Products that require a great deal of learning and knowledge to produce.

Knowledge base: Model of human knowledge that is used by expert systems.

Knowledge engineer: A specialist who elicits information and expertise from other professionals and translates it into a set of rules, frames, or semantic nets for an expert system.

Knowledge frames: A method of organizing expert system knowledge into chunks; the relationships are based on shared characteristics determined by the user rather than a hierarchy.

Knowledge management: The process of systematically and actively managing and leveraging the stores of knowledge in an organization.

Knowledge work system (KWS): An information system that aids knowledge workers in the creation and integration of new knowledge in the organization.

Knowledge workers: People such as engineers, scientists, or architects who design products or services or create new knowledge for the organization.

Knowledge-level decision making: Evaluating new ideas for products, services, ways to communicate new knowledge, and ways to distribute information throughout the organization.

Knowledge-level systems: Information systems that support knowledge and data workers in an organization.

Legitimacy: The extent to which one's authority is accepted on grounds of competence, vision, or other qualities.

Liability: The existence of laws that permit individuals to recover the damages done to them by other actors, systems, or organizations.

LISTSERV: On-line discussion groups using e-mail mailing list servers instead of bulletin boards for communications.

Local area network (LAN): A telecommunications network that requires its own dedicated channels and that encompasses a limited distance, usually one building or several buildings in close proximity.

Logical design: Lays out the components of the information system and their relationship to each other as they would appear to users.

Logical view: A representation of data as they would appear to an application programmer or end user.

Low-orbit satellite: Satellites that travel much closer to the earth than traditional satellites and so are able to pick up signals from weak transmitters while consuming less power.

Mac OS 8: Operating system for the Macintosh computer that supports multi-tasking and access to the Internet and has powerful graphics and multimedia capabilities.

Machine bureaucracy: Large bureaucracy organized into functional divisions that centralizes decision making, produces standard products, and exists in a slow-changing environment.

Machine cycle: Series of operations required to process a single machine instruction.

Machine language: A programming language consisting of the 1s and 0s of binary code.

Magnetic disk: A secondary storage medium in which data are stored by means of magnetized spots on a hard or floppy disk.

Magnetic ink character recognition (MICR): Input technology that translates characters written in magnetic ink into digital codes for processing.

Magnetic tape: Inexpensive and relatively stable secondary storage medium in which large volumes of information are stored sequentially by means of magnetized and nonmagnetized spots on tape.

Mainframe: Largest category of computer, used for major business processing.

Maintenance: Changes in hardware, software, documentation, or procedures to a production system to correct errors, meet new requirements, or improve processing efficiency.

Management control: Monitoring how efficiently or effectively resources are utilized and how well operational units are performing.

Management information system (MIS): Information system at the management level of an organization that serves the functions of planning, controlling, and decision making by providing routine summary and exception reports.

Management-level systems: Information systems that support the monitoring, controlling, decision-making, and administrative activities of middle managers.

Managerial roles: Expectations of the activities that managers should perform in an organization.

Man-month: The traditional unit of measurement used by systems designers to estimate the length of time to complete a project. Refers to the amount of work a person can be expected to complete in a month.

Mass customization: Use of software and computer networks to finely control production so that products can be easily customized with no added cost for small production runs.

Massively parallel computers: Computers that use hundreds or thousands of processing chips to attack large computing problems simultaneously.

Master file: A file that contains all permanent information and is updated during processing by transaction data.

Megabyte: Approximately one million bytes. Unit of computer storage capacity.

Megahertz: A measure of cycle speed, or the pacing of events in a computer; one megahertz (MHz) equals one million cycles per second.

Message integrity: The ability to ascertain that a message that is sent arrives without being copied or changed.

Microeconomic model: Model of the firm that views information technology as a factor of production that can be freely substituted for capital and labor.

Microprocessor: Very large-scale integrated circuit technology that integrates the computer's memory, logic, and control on a single chip.

Microsecond: One-millionth of a second.

Microwave: A high-volume, long-distance, point-to-point transmission in which high-frequency radio signals are transmitted through the atmosphere from one terrestrial transmission station to another.

Middle managers: People in the middle of the organizational hierarchy who are responsible for carrying out the plans and goals of senior management.

Millisecond: One-thousandth of a second.

Minicomputer: Middle-range computer.

MIS audit: Identifies all the controls that govern individual information systems and assesses their effectiveness.

Mobile data networks: Wireless networks that enable two-way transmission of data files cheaply and efficiently.

Model: An abstract representation that illustrates the components or relationships of a phenomenon.

Model-driven DSS: Primarily standalone system that uses some type of model to perform "what-if" and other kinds of analyses.

Modem: A device for translating digital signals into analog signals and vice versa.

Module: A logical unit of a program that performs one or a small number of functions.

Muddling through: Method of decision making involving successive limited comparisons where the test of a good decision is whether people agree on it.

Multimedia: Technologies that facilitate the integration of two or more types of media such as text, graphics, sound, voice, full-motion video, or animation into a computer-based application.

Multinational: A global strategy that concentrates financial management and control out of a central home base while decentralizing production, sales, and marketing operations to units in other countries.

Multiplexer: A device that enables a single communications channel to carry data transmissions from multiple sources simultaneously.

Multiprocessing: An operating system feature for executing two or more instructions simultaneously in a single computer system by using multiple central processing units.

Multiprogramming: A method of executing two or more programs concurrently using the same computer. The CPU executes only one program but can service the input/output needs of others at the same time.

Multitasking: The multiprogramming capability of primarily single-user operating systems, such as those for microcomputers.

Nanosecond: One-billionth of a second.

Net present value: The amount of money an investment is worth, taking into account its cost, earnings, and the time value of money.

Network: Two or more computers linked to share data or resources such as a printer.

Network computer: Simplified desktop computer that does not store software programs or data permanently. Users download whatever software or data they need from a central computer over the Internet or an organization's own internal network.

Network data model: A logical database model that is useful for depicting many-to-many relationships.

Network economics: Model based on the concept of a network where adding another participant entails zero marginal costs but can create much larger marginal gain. Used as a model for strategic systems at the industry level.

Network operating system: Special software that manages the file server in a LAN and routes and manages communications on the network.

Neural network: Hardware or software that attempts to emulate the processing patterns of the biological brain.

Normalization: The process of creating small stable data structures from complex groups of data when designing a relational database.

Object code: Program instructions that have been translated into machine language so that they can be executed by the computer.

Object-oriented database: An approach to data management that stores both data and the procedures acting on the data as objects that can be automatically retrieved and shared; the objects can contain multimedia.

Object-oriented programming: An approach to software development that combines data and procedures into a single object.

Object-oriented software development: Approach to software development that deemphasizes procedures and shifts the focus from modeling business processes and data to combining data and procedures to create objects.

Office automation system (OAS): Computer system, such as word processing, electronic mail system, and scheduling system, that is designed to increase the productivity of data workers in the office.

On-line analytical processing (OLAP): Capability for manipulating and analyzing large volumes of data from multiple perspectives.

On-line processing: A method of collecting and processing data in which transactions are entered directly into the computer system and processed immediately.

On-line transaction processing: Transaction processing mode in which transactions entered on-line are immediately processed by the computer.

Open systems: Software systems that can operate on different hardware platforms because they are built on public nonproprietary operating systems, user interfaces, application standards, and networking protocols.

Open Systems Interconnect (OSI): International reference model for linking different types of computers and networks.

Operating system: The system software that manages and controls the activities of the computer.

Operational control: Deciding how to carry out specific tasks specified by upper and middle management and establishing criteria for completion and resource allocation.

Operational feasibility: Determines whether a proposed solution is desirable within the existing managerial and organizational framework.

Operational managers: People who monitor the day-to-day activities of the organization.

Operational-level systems: Information systems that monitor the elementary activities and transactions of the organization.

Optical character recognition (OCR): Form of source data automation in which optical scanning devices read specially designed data off source documents and translate the data into digital form for the computer.

Organization (behavioral definition): A collection of rights, privileges, obligations, and responsibilities that are delicately balanced over time through conflict and conflict resolution.

Organization (technical definition): A stable, formal social structure that takes resources from the environment and processes them to produce outputs.

Organizational culture: The set of fundamental assumptions about what products the organization should produce, how and where it should produce them, and for whom they should be produced.

Organizational impact analysis: Study of the way a proposed system will affect organizational structure, attitudes, decision making, and operations.

Organizational model: Model of decision making that takes into account the structural and political characteristics of an organization.

OS/2: Powerful operating system used with the 32-bit IBM/Personal System/2 PC workstations that supports multitasking, networking, and more memory-intensive applications than DOS.

Output: The distribution of processed information to the people or activities where it will be used.

Output controls: Ensure that the results of computer processing are accurate, complete, and properly distributed.

Outsourcing: The practice of contracting computer center operations, telecommunications networks, or applications development to external vendors.

Packet switching: Technology that breaks blocks of text into small, fixed bundles of data and routes them in the most economical way through any available communications channel.

Page: A small fixed-length section of a program, which can be easily stored in primary storage and quickly accessed from secondary storage.

Paging system: A wireless transmission technology in which the pager beeps when the user receives a message; used to transmit short alphanumeric messages.

Paradigm shift: Radical reconceptualization of the nature of the business and the nature of the organization.

Parallel processing: Type of processing in which more than one instruction can be processed at a time by breaking down problems into smaller parts and processing them simultaneously with multiple processors.

Parallel strategy: A safe and conservative conversion approach in which both the old system and its potential replacement are run together for a time until everyone is assured that the new system functions correctly.

Particularism: Making judgments and taking actions on the basis of narrow or personal characteristics.

Pascal: A programming language used on PCs and to teach sound programming practices in computer science courses.

Patent: A legal document that grants the owner an exclusive monopoly on the ideas behind an invention for 17 years; designed to ensure that inventors of new machines or methods are rewarded for their labor while making widespread use of their inventions.

Payback method: A measure of the time required to pay back the initial investment of a project.

Pen-based input: Input devices such as tablets, notebooks, and notepads consisting of a flat-screen display tablet and a penlike stylus that digitizes handwriting.

People-oriented theory: User-resistance theory focusing on factors internal to users.

Personal communication services (PCS): A new wireless cellular technology that uses lower-power, higher-frequency radio waves than does cellular technology and so can be used with smaller-sized telephones inside buildings and tunnels.

Personal computer (PC): Small desktop or portable computer.

Personal digital assistant (PDA): Small, pen-based, handheld computers with built-in wireless telecommunications capable of entirely digital communications transmission.

Phased approach strategy: Introduces the new system in stages either by functions or by organizational units.

Physical design: The process of translating the abstract logical model into the specific technical design for the new system.

Physical view: The representation of data as they would be actually organized on physical storage media.

Pilot study strategy: A strategy to introduce the new system to a limited area of the organization until it is proven to be fully functional; only then can the conversion to the new system across the entire organization take place.

Pixel: The smallest unit of data for defining an image in the computer. The computer reduces a picture to a grid of pixels. The term *pixel* comes from picture element.

PL/1 (Programming Language 1): A programming language developed by IBM in 1964 for business and scientific applications.

Plotter: Output device using multicolored pens to draw high-quality graphic documents.

Pointer: A special type of data element attached to a record that shows the absolute or relative address of another record.

Political model: Model of decision making where decisions result from competition and bargaining among the organization's interest groups and key leaders; the desires of any one member.

Political theory: Behavioral theory that describes information systems as the outcome of political competition between organizational subgroups for influence over the policies, procedures, and resources of the organization.

Portfolio analysis: An analysis of the portfolio of potential applications within a firm to determine the risks and benefits and select among alternatives for information systems.

Postimplementation: The final stage of the systems life cycle in which the system is used and evaluated while in production and is modified to make improvements or meet new requirements.

Postindustry theory: Behavioral theory stating that the transformation of advanced industrial countries into postindustrial societies creates flatter organizations dominated by knowledge workers where decision making is more decentralized.

Present value: The value, in current dollars, of a payment or stream of payments to be received in the future.

Primary activities: Activities most directly related to the production and distribution of a firm's products or services.

Primary storage: Part of the computer that temporarily stores program instructions and data being used by those instructions.

Printer: A computer output device that provides paper hard copy output in the form of text or graphics.

Privacy: The claim of individuals to be left alone, free from surveillance or interference from other individuals, organizations, or the state.

Private branch exchange (PBX): A central switching system that handles a firm's voice and digital communications.

Process specifications: Describe the logic of the transformations occurring within the lowest-level processes of the data flow diagrams.

Processes: Portray the transformation of input data flows to output data flows in a data flow diagram. Each has a unique reference number and is named with a verb–object phrase.

Processing: The conversion, manipulation, and analysis of raw input into a form that is more meaningful to humans.

Processing controls: Routines for establishing that data are complete and accurate during updating.

Product differentiation: Competitive strategy for creating brand loyalty by developing new and unique products and services that are not easily duplicated by competitors.

Production: The stage after the new system is installed and the conversion is complete; during this time the system is reviewed by users and technical specialists to determine how well it has met its original goals.

Production or **service workers:** People who actually produce the products or services of the organization.

Professional bureaucracy: Knowledge-based organization such as a law firm or hospital that is dominated by department heads with weak centralized authority; operates in a slowly changing environment.

Profitability index: Used to compare the profitability of alternative investments; it is calculated by dividing the present value of the total cash inflow from an investment by the initial cost of the investment.

Program: A series of statements or instructions to the computer.

Program security controls: Controls designed to prevent unauthorized changes to programs in systems that are already in production.

Program-data dependence: The close relationship between data stored in files and the software programs that update and maintain those files. Any change in data organization or format requires a change in all the programs associated with those files.

Programmable read-only memory (PROM): Subclass of ROM chip used in control devices because it can be programmed once.

Programmers: Highly trained technical specialists who write computer software instructions.

Programming: Stage in the systems life cycle that translates the design specifications produced during the design stage into software program code.

Project definition: Stage in the systems life cycle that determines whether the organization has a problem and whether the problem can be solved by launching a system project.

Protocol: A set of rules and procedures that govern transmission between the components in a network.

Prototype: Preliminary working version of an information system for demonstration and evaluation purposes.

Prototyping: Process of building an experimental system quickly and inexpensively for demonstration and evaluation so that end users can better determine information requirements.

"Push" technology: Method of obtaining relevant information on the Internet by having a computer broadcast information directly to the user based on prespecified interests.

Quality: Conformance to producer specifications and satisfaction of customer criteria such as quality of physical product, quality of service, and psychological aspects.

Query language: A high-level computer language used to retrieve specific information from databases or files.

Random access memory (RAM): Primary storage of data or program instructions that can directly access any randomly chosen location in the same amount of time.

Rational model: Model of human behavior based on the belief that people, organizations, and nations engage in basically consistent, value-maximizing calculations or adaptations within certain constraints.

Rationalization of procedures: The streamlining of standard operating procedures, eliminating obvious bottlenecks so that automation makes operating procedures more efficient.

Read-only memory (ROM): Semiconductor memory chips that contain program instructions. These chips can only be read from; they cannot be written to.

Record: A group of related fields.

Reduced instruction set computing (RISC): Technology used to enhance the speed of microprocessors by embedding only the most frequently used instructions on a chip.

Redundant array of inexpensive disks (RAID): Disk storage technology to boost disk performance by packaging more than 100 smaller disk drives with a controller chip and specialized software in a single large unit to deliver data over multiple paths simultaneously.

Reference model: A generic framework for thinking about a problem.

Register: Temporary storage location in the ALU or control unit where small amounts of data and instructions reside for thousandths of a second just before use.

Relational data model: A type of logical database model that treats data as if they were stored in two-dimensional tables. It can relate data stored in one table to data in another as long as the two tables share a common data element.

Repetitive stress injury (RSI): Occupational disease that occurs when muscle groups are forced through repetitive actions with high-impact loads or thousands of repetitions with low-impact loads.

Report generator: Software that creates customized reports in a wide range of formats that are not routinely produced by an information system.

Request for Proposal (RFP): Detailed list of questions submitted to vendors of packaged software or other computer services to determine if the vendor's product can meet the organization's specific requirements.

Resource allocation: Determination of how costs, time, and personnel are assigned to different activities of a systems development project.

Responsibility: Accepting the potential costs, duties, and obligations for the decisions one makes.

Reverse engineering: The process of taking existing programs' code, file, and database descriptions and converting them into corresponding design-level components that can then be used to create new applications.

Ring network: A network topology in which all computers are linked by a closed loop in a manner that passes data in one direction from one computer to another.

Risk assessment: Determining the potential frequency of occurrence of a problem and the potential damage if the problem were to occur. Used to determine the cost-benefit of a control.

Risk Aversion Principle: Principle that one should take the action that produces the least harm or incurs the least cost.

Rule base: The collection of knowledge in an AI system that is represented in the form of IF–THEN rules.

Rule-based expert system: An AI program that has a large number of interconnected and nested IF–THEN statements, or rules, that are the basis for the knowledge in the system.

Run control totals: Procedures for controlling completeness of computer updating by generating control totals that reconcile totals before and after processing.

Satellite: The transmission of data using orbiting satellites to serve as relay stations for transmitting microwave signals over very long distances.

Satisficing: Choosing the first available alternative to move closer toward the ultimate goal instead of searching for all alternatives and consequences.

Scoring model: A quick method for deciding among alternative systems based on a system of ratings for selected objectives.

Search engine: A tool for locating specific sites or information on the Internet. Primarily used to search the World Wide Web.

Secondary storage: Relatively long-term, nonvolatile storage of data outside the CPU and primary storage.

Sector: Method of storing data on a floppy disk in which the disk is divided into pie-shaped pieces or sectors. Each sector is assigned a unique number so that data can be located using the sector number.

Security: Policies, procedures, and technical measures used to prevent unauthorized access, alteration, theft, or physical damage to information systems.

Segregation of functions: Principle of internal control to divide responsibilities and assign tasks among people so that job functions do not overlap to minimize the risk of errors and fraudulent manipulation of the organization's assets.

Selection construct: The logic pattern in programming in which a stated condition determines which of two or more actions can be taken depending on which satisfies the stated condition.

Semiconductor: An integrated circuit made by printing thousands and even millions of tiny transistors on a small silicon chip.

Semistructured decisions: Decisions where only part of the problem has a clear-cut answer provided by an accepted procedure.

Senior managers: People occupying the topmost hierarchy in an organization who are responsible for making long-range decisions.

Sensitivity analysis: Models that ask "what-if" questions repeatedly to determine the impact of changes in one or more factors on outcomes.

Sensors: Devices that collect data directly from the environment for input into a computer system.

Sequence construct: The sequential single steps or actions in the logic of a program that do not depend on the existence of any condition.

Sequential file organization: A method of storing data records in which the records must be retrieved in the same physical sequence in which they are stored.

Server: The computer in a client/server network that stores various programs and data files for users of the network. Determines access and availability in the network.

Server computer: Computer specifically optimized to provide software and other resources to other computers over a network, with large memory and disk storage capacity, high-speed communications capabilities, and powerful CPUs.

Simplex transmission: A transmission in which data can travel in only one direction at all times.

Sociological theory: Behavioral theory stating that organizations develop hierarchical bureaucratic structures and standard operating procedures to cope in unstable environments and that organizations cannot change routines when environments change.

Sociotechnical design: Design to produce information systems that blend technical efficiency with sensitivity to organizational and human needs.

Software: The detailed instructions that control the operation of a computer system.

Software controls: Controls to ensure the security and reliability of software.

Software metrics: Objective assessments of the software used in a system in the form of quantified measurements.

Software package: A prewritten, precoded, commercially available set of programs that eliminates the need to write software programs for certain functions.

Software reengineering: Methodology that addresses the problem of aging software by salvaging and upgrading it so that the users can avoid a long and expensive replacement project.

Source code: Program instructions written in a high-level language that must be translated into machine language to be executed by the computer.

Source data automation: Input technology that captures data in computer-readable form at the time and place the data are created.

Spreadsheet: Software displaying data in a grid of columns and rows, with the capability of easily recalculating numerical data.

Standard: Approved reference models and protocols as determined by standard-setting groups for building or developing products or services.

Standard operating procedures (SOPs): Precise, defined rules, procedures, and practices developed by organizations to cope with virtually all expected situations.

Standing data: Data that are permanent and affect transactions flowing into and out of a system.

Star network: A network topology in which all computers and other devices are connected to a central host computer. All communications between network devices must pass through the host computer.

Storage technology: Physical media and software governing the storage and organization of data for use in an information system.

Stored program concept: The idea that a program cannot be executed unless it is stored in a computer's primary storage along with required data.

Strategic decision making: Determining the long-term objectives, resources, and policies of an organization.

Strategic information systems: Computer systems at any level of an organization that change the goals, processes, products, services, or environmental relationships to help the organization gain a competitive advantage.

Strategic transitions: A movement from one level of sociotechnical system to another. Often required when adopting strategic systems that demand changes in the social and technical elements of an organization.

Strategic-level systems: Information systems that support the long-range planning activities of senior management.

Structure chart: System documentation showing each level of design, the relationship among the levels, and the overall place in the design structure; can document one program, one system, or part of one program.

Structured: Refers to the fact that techniques are instructions that are carefully drawn up, often step-by-step, with each step building on a previous one.

Structured analysis: Top-down method for defining system inputs, processes, and outputs and for partitioning systems into subsystems or modules that show a logical graphic model of information flow.

Structured decisions: Decisions that are repetitive, routine, and have a definite procedure for handling them.

Structured design: Software design discipline, encompassing a set of design rules and techniques for designing a system from the top down in a hierarchical fashion.

Structured programming: Discipline for organizing and coding programs that simplifies the control paths so that the programs can be easily understood and modified. Uses the basic control structures and modules that have only one entry point and one exit point.

Structured Query Language (SQL): The emerging standard data manipulation language for relational database management systems.

Supercomputer: Highly sophisticated and powerful computer that can perform very complex computations extremely fast.

Supply chain: A collection of physical entities, such as manufacturing plants, distribution centers, conveyances, retail outlets, people, and information, which are linked together into processes supplying goods or services from source through consumption.

Supply chain management: Integration of supplier, distributor, and customer logistics requirements into one cohesive process.

Support activities: Activities that make the delivery of the primary activities of a firm possible. Consist of the organization's infrastructure, human resources, technology, and procurement.

Switched lines: Telephone lines that a person can access from a terminal to transmit data to another computer, the call being routed or switched through paths to the designated destination.

Switching costs: The expense a customer or company incurs in lost time and expenditure of resources when changing from one supplier or system to a competing supplier or system.

Synchronous transmission: The high-speed simultaneous transmission of large blocks of data.

System failure: An information system that either does not perform as expected, is not operational at a specified time, or cannot be used in the way it was intended.

System flowchart: Graphic design tool that depicts the physical media and sequence of processing steps used in an entire information system.

System residence device: The secondary storage device on which a complete operating system is stored.

System software: Generalized programs that manage the resources of the computer, such as the central processor, communications links, and peripheral devices.

System testing: Tests the functioning of the information system as a whole to determine if discrete modules will function together as planned.

Systematic decision makers: Cognitive style that describes people who approach a problem by structuring it in terms of some formal method.

System-oriented theory: User-resistance theory focusing on factors inherent in the design of the system.

Systems analysis: The analysis of a problem that the organization will try to solve with an information system.

Systems analysts: Specialists who translate business problems and requirements into information requirements and systems, acting as liaison between the information systems department and the rest of the organization.

Systems design: Details how a system will meet the information requirements as determined by the systems analysis.

Systems development: The activities that go into producing an information systems solution to an organizational problem or opportunity.

Systems life cycle: Traditional methodology for developing an information system that partitions the systems development process into six formal stages that must be completed sequentially with a very formal division of labor between end users and information systems specialists.

Systems Network Architecture (SNA): Proprietary telecommunications reference model developed by IBM.

Systems study: Stage in the systems life cycle that analyzes the problems of existing systems, defines the objectives to be attained by a solution, and evaluates various solution alternatives.

Tangible benefits: Benefits that can be quantified and assigned monetary value; they include lower operational costs and increased cash flows.

Technical feasibility: Determines whether a proposed solution can be implemented with the available hardware, software, and technical resources.

Technical–rational "classical" perspective: Descriptions of management and organizations that focus on the mechanistic aspects of organization and the formal management functions of planning, organizing, coordinating, deciding, and controlling.

Technostress: Stress induced by computer use whose symptoms include aggravation, hostility toward humans, impatience, and enervation.

Telecommunications: The communication of information by electronic means, usually over some distance.

Telecommunications software: Special software for controlling and supporting the activities of a telecommunications network.

Telecommunications system: A collection of compatible hardware and software arranged to communicate information from one location to another.

Teleconferencing: The ability to confer with a group of people simultaneously using the telephone or electronic mail group communication software.

Telnet: Network tool that allows someone to log on to one computer system while doing work on another.

Test plan: Prepared by the development team in conjunction with the users; it includes the preparations for the series of tests to be performed on the system.

Testing: The exhaustive and thorough process that determines whether the system produces the desired results under known conditions.

Time sharing: The sharing of computer resources by many users simultaneously by having the CPU spend a fixed amount of time on each user's program before proceeding to the next.

Topology: The shape or configuration of a network.

Total quality management (TQM): A concept that makes quality control a responsibility to be shared by all people in an organization.

Touch screen: Input device technology that permits the entering or selecting of commands and data by touching the surface of a sensitized video display monitor with a finger or a pointer.

Track: Concentric circle on the surface area of a disk on which data are stored as magnetized spots; each track can store thousands of bytes.

Trade secret: Any intellectual work or product used for a business purpose that can be classified as belonging to that business provided it is not based on information in the public domain.

Traditional file environment: A way of collecting and maintaining data in an organization that leads to each functional area or division creating and maintaining its own data files and programs.

Transaction cost theory: Economic theory that states that firms exist because they can conduct marketplace transactions internally more cheaply than they can with external firms in the marketplace.

Transaction file: In batch systems, a file in which all transactions are accumulated to await processing.

Transaction processing system (TPS): Computerized system that performs and records the daily routine transactions necessary to conduct the business; these systems serve the operational level of the organization.

Transborder data flow: The movement of information across international boundaries in any form.

Transform algorithm: A mathematical formula used to translate a record's key field directly into the record's physical storage location.

Transmission Control Protocol/Internet Protocol (TCP/IP): U.S. Department of Defense reference model for linking different types of computers and networks. Used in the Internet.

Transnational: Truly globally managed firms that have no national headquarters; value-added activities are managed from a global perspective without reference to national borders, optimizing sources of supply and demand and taking advantage of any local competitive advantage.

Tuple: A row or record in a relational database.

Twisted wire: A transmission medium consisting of pairs of twisted copper wires. Used to transmit analog phone conversations but can be used for data transmission.

Unit testing: The process of testing each program separately in the system. Sometimes called *program testing*.

UNIX: Operating system for PCs, minicomputers, and mainframes, which is machine independent and supports multi-user processing, multitasking, and networking.

Unstructured decisions: Nonroutine decisions in which the decision maker must provide judgment, evaluation, and insights into the problem definition; there is no agreed-upon procedure for making such decisions.

Usenet: On-line forums in which people share information and ideas on a defined topic through large electronic bulletin boards where anyone can post messages on the topic for others to see.

User interface: The part of the information system through which the end user interacts with the system; type of hardware and the series of on-screen commands and responses required for a user to work with the system.

User–designer communications gap: The difference in backgrounds, interests, and priorities that impede communication and problem solving among end users and information systems specialists.

Utilitarian Principle: Principle that assumes one can put values in rank order and understand the consequences of various courses of action.

Utility program: System software consisting of programs for routine, repetitive tasks, which can be shared by many users.

Value chain model: Model that highlights the primary or support activities that add a margin of value to a firm's products or services where information systems can best be applied to achieve a competitive advantage.

Value-added network (VAN): Private, multipath, data-only third-party-managed networks that are used by multiple organizations on a subscription basis.

Vendor-managed inventory: Approach to inventory management that assigns the supplier the responsibility to make inventory replenishment decisions based on order, point-of-sale data, or warehouse data supplied by the customer.

Veronica: Capability for searching for text that appears in gopher menus by using key words.

Very high-level programming language: A programming language that uses fewer instructions than conventional languages. Used primarily as a professional programmer productivity tool.

Videoconferencing: Teleconferencing with the capability of participants to see each other over video screens.

Virtual organization: Organization using networks linking people, assets, and ideas to create and distribute products and services without being limited by traditional organizational boundaries or physical location.

Virtual private network (VPN): The ability to custom configure a network using a portion of the public switched network to create the illusion of a private network for a company.

Virtual reality systems: Interactive graphics software and hardware that create computer-generated simulations that provide sensations that emulate real-world activities.

Virtual storage: A way of handling programs more efficiently by the computer by dividing the programs into small fixed- or variable-length portions with only a small portion stored in primary memory at one time.

Visual programming: The construction of software programs by selecting and arranging programming objects rather than by writing program code.

Voice input device: Technology that converts the spoken word into digital form for processing.

Voice mail: A system for digitizing a spoken message and transmitting it over a network.

Voice output device: A converter of digital output data into spoken words.

WAIS: A tool for locating data on the Internet that requires the name of the databases to be searched based on a key word.

Walkthrough: A review of a specification or design document by a small group of people carefully selected based on the skills needed for the particular objectives being tested.

Web browser: An easy-to-use software tool for accessing the World Wide Web and the Internet.

Web site: The World Wide Web pages maintained by an organization or individual.

Wide area network (WAN): Telecommunications network that spans a large geographical distance. May consist of a variety of cable, satellite, and microwave technologies.

Windows: A graphical user interface shell that runs in conjunction with the DOS PC operating system. Supports multitasking and some forms of networking.

Windows 95: A 32-bit operating system, with a streamlined graphical user interface that can support software written for DOS and Windows but can also run programs that take up more than 640 K of memory. Features multitasking, multithreading, and powerful networking capabilities.

Windows 98: New version of the Windows operating system that is more closely integrated with the Internet.

Windows NT: Powerful operating system developed by Microsoft for use with 32-bit PCs and workstations based on Intel and other microprocessors. Supports networking, multitasking, and multiprocessing.

Word length: The number of bits that can be processed at one time by a computer. The larger the word length, the greater the speed of the computer.

Word processing: Office automation technology that facilitates the creation of documents through computerized text editing, formatting, storing, and printing.

Word processing software: Software that handles electronic storage, editing, formatting, and printing of documents.

Workstation: Desktop computer with powerful graphics and mathematical capabilities and the ability to perform several tasks at once.

World Wide Web: A system and set of standards for storing, retrieving, formatting, and displaying information in a networked environment.

Write once/read many (WORM): Optical disk system that allows users to record data only once; data cannot be erased but can be read indefinitely.

Name Index

Organizations Index

International Organizations Index

Subject Index

Drag-and-drop, visual programming and, 250, 251
Drill down, 607
DSS (decision-support systems), *See* Management decision making
Due process
    ethical issues and, 154
    privacy and, 158
Duplicated systems, for international information systems, 664
DVDs, *See* Digital video disks

EAMs, *See* Electronic accounting machines
EBCDIC, *See* Extended Binary Coded Decimal Interchange Code
EC, *See* Electronic commerce
Echo checks, 637
Economic feasibility, 401
Economic theories, *See* Organizations
EDI, *See* Electronic data interchange
EDIfact, 361, 674
EDI networks, electronic commerce and, 644
Edit checks, 642
EDP, *See* Electronic data processing
Efficient customer response systems, 56–59, 61
Electromagnetic spectrum, wireless transmission and, 305, 306
Electronic accounting machines (EAMs), 49, 90, 91
Electronic brainstorming tools, as group decision-support system tools, 602
Electronic cash (e-cash), 645
Electronic clearinghouses, as Internet business model, 356
Electronic commerce, 24–25
    Internet and, 22, 24–25, 349–55, 356, 376–79, 644, 645
    security and, 643–44, 645
Electronic Communications Privacy Act of 1986, 159, 321
Electronic data interchange (EDI), 324–25
    international information systems and, 674, 676
Electronic data processing (EDP), 49
Electronic mail (e-mail), 440
    address, 140, 343
    cultural differences and, 661
    electronic commerce and, 351
    international information systems and, 676
    Internet and, 341–43
    security and, 368
    work separated from location by, 20
Electronic market, 22, 24–25
    See also Internet
Electronic meeting system (EMS), 603–4, 606
Electronic payment systems, Internet and, 354, 644, 645
Electronic questionnaires, as group decision-support system tools, 602
Employment, reengineering and, 173
EMS, *See* Electronic meeting system
Encryption, 643–44
Encryption key, 644
End users, 92
    international information systems and, 670, 671
    prototyping and, 435–37
    systems development and, 405, 444–50, 451, 457
    See also Controls; Fourth-generation languages; *under* Users
Engineering Magazine, 117

Enhanced CU-SeeMe, 323
Enterprise analysis, for database management systems, 290, 386–89
Enterprise networking, 337–40
    business drivers of, 340
    client/server model of computing in, 338–40
    implementation of, 366–69
    problems posed by, 366–68, *see also* Connectivity
        costs, 366–67
        data administration, 369
        management control, 366
        organizational change, 366, 368–69, 391
        reliability, 367–68
        security, 368
        training, 369
Entity, 265, 266
Entity order, 265, 266
Entity-relationship diagram, 280
Entrepreneurial structure, of organizations, 80
Environment
    management and, 142
    organization and, 81–83, 125
    systems development and, 93
Environmental scanning, 81
EPROM, *See* Erasable programmable read-only memory
Equity, participation in digital age and, 173–74
Erasable programmable read-only memory (EPROM), 198–99
Ergonomics, information systems and, 530
Error-control software, 311
Errors
    information system vulnerability and, 634–35
    input controls for, 642
ESS (executive support systems), *See* Management decision making
Ethernet, 315
Ethical analysis, 155
Ethical issues, 151, 155–56
    accountability, 154
    due process, 154
    ethical analysis process and, 155
    ethical principles and, 155–56
    liability, 154, 167
    piracy, 164
    privacy, 159
    professional codes of conduct and, 156, 157, 176–77
    real-world, 156–57
    responsibility, 154
    system quality, 169
    technology and, 153–54
    See also Moral dimensions; Political issues; Social issues
Ethical "no free lunch" rule, 156
Ethics, 151
    See also Ethical issues
European Currency Unit (ECU), 632
Excel, 247, 248, 251, 594, 607
Execution cycle, of machine cycle, 199, 200
Executive support systems (ESS), *See* Management decision making
Existence checks, 642
Expert systems, *See* Artificial intelligence
Explicit knowledge, 126
Extended Binary Coded Decimal Interchange Code (EBCDIC), 193, 194, 195
External entities, in data flow diagram, 485

External integration tools, 524
Extranets, 364–65

Facsimile (fax) machines, 320
    cultural differences and, 661
Fair Credit Reporting Act of 1970, 159, 291
Fair information practices (FIP), 158
Fair Information Practices Doctrine, 158
Family, boundaries between work and, 170–71
Family Educational Rights and Privacy Act of 1978, 159
Fault-tolerant computer systems, 632
FDDI, 361
Feasibility study, in systems analysis, 401–2
Federal Copyright Act of 1790, 161
Federal Managers Financial Integrity Act of 1982, 159
Feedback, 8
Fiber-optic cable, 305, 310
Field, 265
Fifth-generation computers, 215, 218–21
File, 265, 266
File management, 265–71
    accessing records in, 266–68
        direct file method, 268
        indexed sequential method, 267
    problems with, 268–71
        data redundancy, 269–70
        inflexibility, 270–71
        program-data dependence, 270
        security, 271
        sharing, 271
    terms and concepts in, 265–66
File transfer protocol (FTP), 342, 344
Finance, as organizational function, 11
Financial models (capital budgeting), *See* Information systems
FIP, *See* Fair information practices
Firewalls, 639
    intranet and, 361
Firm-level strategy, 51, 59–61
    core competencies and, 60–61
    Internet and, 63, 64
    synergy and, 59
First Amendment
    liability and, 166
    privacy and, 158
First-generation computers, 200
First-generation programming language, 239
Flat file organization, 269
Flattened organization, 19–20, 99
Floating point operation, 220
Floppy disks, 206, 208
Flowchart, *See* System flowchart
FOCUS, 239, 243
Focused differentiation, 54
Forecasting models, 594
Forecasts, datamining and, 592
Form (computer virus), 629
Formal control tools, 524, 525–26
Formal organizations, 11
Formal planning tools, 524, 525–26
Formal system, 8, 9
Format checks, 642
FORTRAN (FORmula TRANslator), 230, 233, 239, 240, 241, 272, 432
Forward chaining, 566, 567
Forward engineering, 499, 500

Fourth Amendment, privacy and, 158
Fourth-generation computers, 201–3
Fourth-generation languages, 230, 239–40, 242–49
    application generators, 243, 244
    end-user development and, 444–47, 448
    graphics languages, 242, 243–44
    PC tools, *see* Personal computer
    query languages, 239, 242–43
    report generators, 242, 243
    system misuse and abuse and, 630
    very high-level programming languages, 242, 243, 244
    See also Application software packages
Frame relay, 318
Frames of reference, decision making and, 134, 136–37
Franchisers, for international information systems, 663, 665
Freedom of Information Act, 159
Front-end CASE tools, 496
Front-end processor, 311
FTP, *See* File transfer protocol
Full-duplex transmission, 311
Function point analysis, 481–82
Future shock, 99n
Fuzzy logic, 576–77

Gantt charts, 525, 526
"Garbage can" model, of decision making, 137, 139
Gateways, 315, 357
GDSS (group decision-support systems), *See* Management decision making
General controls, 635
Genetic algorithms, 577–79
Geographic information system (GIS) software, 245, 246
Gigabyte, 196
GIS, *See* Geographic information system software
Globalization
    business and system requirements of, 26
    connectivity and, 356, 358–59
    information systems and, 5, 20, *see also* International information systems
    Internet and, 348, 350, 355
    time-based competition and, 170
Global markets, international information systems and, 659–60
Global networks, organizational change and, 391
Global village, 659
Global worker, 26
Golden Rule, 155
Gopher, 342, 344–45
Gossip networks, 9
Grand design systems, *See* Very-large-scale systems
Graphical user interface (GUI), 234
    organizational change and, 391
Graphics languages, 242, 243–44
Grassroot innovation, 513
Green Caterpillar (computer virus), 629
Group decision-support systems (GDSS), *See* Management decision making
Group dictionaries, as group decision-support system tools, 603
Groupware, 325–26, 561–63
    international information systems and, 676
    Lotus Notes, 325, 326, 338, 365, 397, 561–62, 563, 676
GUI, *See* Graphical user interface

Hackers, 172, 628, 630
Half-duplex transmission, 311
Handwith, 310
Hard disks, 206–7
Hardware, *See* Computer hardware
Harvard Graphics, 243
Health, computer-related disorders and, 174–76
Hertz, 310
Hierarchical data model, 276, 278–79
Hierarchical organization, 19
High-density diskette, 207
High-level languages, 239
    See also Fourth-generation languages
Home page, 345
Host country systems, for international information systems, 665
HTML, *See* Hypertext Markup Language
Human relations school, 118, 120
Human resources, as organizational function, 11
Hybrid AI system, 579
Hybrid object-relational systems, 284
Hypermedia database, 284
Hypertext Markup Language (HTML), 345

Icons, 234
Idea organizers, as group decision-support system tools, 602
Imaging systems, *See* Document imaging systems
Implementation, 508, 512–32
    actors and roles in, 513, 514
    business reengineering and, 521, 522
    as decision-making stage, 131, 132
    of international information systems, 670
    management of, 523–31
        external integration tools for, 524
        formal control tools for, 524, 525–26
        formal planning tools for, 524, 525–26
        human factor and, 530
        implementation process and, 519–21
        internal integration tools for, 524–25
        organizational change for, 528–29, 530, 531
        risk and, 523–24
        sociotechnical design for, 530–31
        support and, 517, 518
        user resistance and, 526–28
    models of, 514–15
    organizational change and, 513–15
    stages of, 513
    strategies of innovation and, 513
    success and failure of
        analysis and, 521
        conversion and, 523
        design and, 522
        programming and, 522–23
        risk/complexity level and, 517–19, *see also* management of, *above*
        testing and, 523
        user involvement and, 515–16
    success and failure of, 515–23, *see also* management of, *above*
Implementation controls, 635–36
IMS (Information Management System), 276, 279
Inbound logistics, 52
Incremental decision making, 134
Index, to files, 267
Indexed sequential access method (ISAM), 267
Index server, 557

Industrial economies, information systems and transformation of, 5, 6–7
Industry-level strategy, 51, 61–63
    competitive forces model and, 62–63
    information partnerships and, 61–62
    Internet and, 63, 64
    network economics and, 63
Inference engine, 566, 567
Informal information systems, 9
Information, 8, 49–50
    See also under Data
Informational roles, of managers, 121, 122–23
Information architecture, 26–28, 90, 91, 337
    See also Computer hardware; Computer software; Enterprise networking; Telecommunications
Information brokers, as Internet business model, 356
Information centers, for end-user computing, 449
Information partnerships, 61–62
Information policy, database management systems and, 290
Information portability, 357
Information repository, in CASE tool kit, 495, 496–97
Information requirements, for systems analysis, 402–3
Information revolution, 6
Information rights, as moral dimension, 151, 152, 158–61, 176
Information superhighway, 302
Information systems
    application backlog and, 228
    behavioral approach to, 14
    building new, *see* Systems development
    business value of, 9, 11–13, 28, 408–21, *see also* capital budgeting analysis of; nonfinancial and strategic analyses of, *below*
    capital budgeting analysis of, 409–17
        accounting rate of return on investment for, 413, 415
        cash flows and, 409, 415
        cost-benefit ratio for, 415, 416
        example of, 411–13, 414, 415
        intangible benefits and, 410
        internal rate of return for, 415, 416
        limitations of, 409–10
        net present value for, 415–16
        payback method for, 413, 415
        profitability index for, 415, 416
        results of, 417
        tangible benefits and, 410
    as capital project, 410–11, *see also* capital budgeting analysis of, *above*
    catastrophes and, 171
    changing conceptions of, 49–50
    computing power and, 16–17
    control and, 28
    costs and benefits of, 410
    decision-support systems, *see* Management decision making
    definition of, 7–9
    dependence on, 171–72
    ergonomics and, 530
    executive support systems, *see* Management decision making
    failure of, 509–11, 512–13, *see also* Implementation
    formal, 8, 9
    functions of, 8
    informal, 9
    knowledge-level, 37, 38, 39
    knowledge work systems, 39, 40, 42–43, 48

Track, 207–8
Trade secrets, 161
Traditional file environment, 269, 270
Transaction brokers, as Internet business model, 356
Transaction cost theory, 94, 96–97
Transaction file, 214
Transaction processing systems (TPS), 39, 40–42, 48, 130
    data-driven DSS and, 592
    systems life cycle for, 433
Transborder data flow, international information systems and, 660–61
Transform algorithm, 268
Transistors, for second-generation computers, 200
Transmission Control Protocol/Internet Protocol (TCP/IP), 341, 358, 361, 674
Transmission control software, 311
Transnational strategy, for international information systems, 663–64, 665
Transnational system units, for international information systems, 663–64, 665
Tuple, 277, 278
Twisted wire, 304–5, 310

Uncontrolled data
    end-user computing tools and, 448, 450, 451
    World Wide Web and, 450, 451
Unit testing, 406
UNIX, 235, 237, 242, 340, 357, 360, 361, 460, 671, 672
Unstructured decisions, 129, 130
Usenet groups, 342, 343, 608
User acceptance, 118, 120
User-designer communications gap, 516
User-developed systems, See End users
User exits, 244
User interface
    implementation and, 515–16
    international information systems and, 676, 679
    system failure and, 510, 511
User resistance, implementation and, 526–28
User satisfaction
    system quality and, 477
    system success and, 512
Utilitarian Principle, 156
Utility programs, 229, 230, 233

Vacuum tubes, for first-generation computers, 200
Validity, application controls and, 640
Validity checks, 637
Value-added networks (VANs), 317–18
    electronic commerce and, 644

international, see IVANS
Value chain analysis, 118, 119
Value chain model, 51–52, 64–65
Value chains, 64–65
VANs, See Value-added networks
VAX minicomputers, 338, 361
VAX/VMS operating system, 460
VDT (video display terminal), See Cathode ray tube terminal
Vendor-managed inventory, 64
Veronica, 342, 345
Very high-level programming languages, 242, 243, 244
Very large-scale integrated circuits (VLSIC), for fourth-generation computers, 201–3
Very-large-scale systems (VLSS), 520
Videoconferencing, 322–23
    international information systems and, 676
    work separated from location by, 20
Video display terminal (VDT), See Cathode ray tube terminal
Video Privacy Protection Act of 1988, 159
Virtual offices, 99, 100, 101
Virtual organizations, 20, 21, 118, 120
Virtual private networks (VPNs), international information systems and, 676, 678
Virtual reality systems, 559–60, 561
Virtual storage, 232
Virtual storefront, as Internet business model, 356
Viruses, See Computer viruses
Visual Basic, 338
Visual programming, 250, 251
VLSIC, See Very large-scale integrated circuits
VLSS, See Very-large-scale systems
Voice input devices, 213
Voice mail, 320
Voice output device, 215
Von Neumann architecture, 219
Voting tools, as group decision-support system tools, 602
Vulnerability, See Controls

WAIS (Wide Area Information Servers), 342, 345
Walkthrough, 482
WANs, See Wide area networks
Web, See World Wide Web
Web browsers, 248–49, 345–47
Web site, 18, 345
Wide area networks (WANs), 312, 316–17
Windows, 235
    95, 235, 236, 321, 360
    98, 235, 236
    NT, 235, 236, 338, 339, 460

Wireless transmission, 305–10
Word length, 202
WordPerfect, 243, 246, 251
Word processing software, 43, 246, 247
Work flows, information systems and, 25
Workflow software, 84, 142, 397, 398
Work groups, information systems and, 88
    See also Office automation systems
Workstations, 203, 204
    investment, 560–61
Work teams, 128
World Wide Web, 18, 345–47
    banking via, 53
    Catalog Site on, 2–4
    datamining and, 55
    electronic commerce and, 22, 351
    ethics and, 321
    failure and, 506–8
    geographic information system software on, 245, 246
    group collaboration via, 563
    information architecture and, 91
    intellectual property protection and, 163–64
    internal databases linked to, 291, 292
    intranet and, 360, 361–65
    liability on, 168
    Mac OS 8 and, 237
    management and, 127, 128
    multimedia on, 216, 217
    organizations and, 102
    privacy and, 160
    "push" technology for, 346–47
    search engines for, 579
    searching for information on, 346–47
    stocks traded on, 24
    strategic uses of, 58–59, 60, 63, 73
    uncontrolled information and, 450, 451
    web browsers for, 248–49
    Windows 98 and, 236
    See also Internet
WORM, See Write once/read many
Write once/read many (WORM), 210

X.12, 361
X.25, 361
X.400, 361
X Windows, 361

Zero defects, 169, 479
Zero-level data flow diagram, 486, 487

Photo Credits

Contributors

 AUSTRALIA
Joel B. Barolsky, University of Melbourne
Peter Weill, University of Melbourne

CANADA
Len Fertuck, University of Toronto

GERMANY
Helmut Krcmar, University of Hohenheim
Gerhard Schwabe, University of Hohenheim
Stephen Wilczek, University of Hohenheim

SINGAPORE
Boon Siong Neo, Nanyang Technological
    University
Christina Soh, Nanyang Technological
    University

SWITZERLAND
Kimberly A. Bechler, International
    Institute for Management Development
Donald A. Marchand, International
    Institute for Management Development
Thomas E. Vollmann, International
    Institute for Management Development

Consultants

AUSTRALIA
Robert MacGregor, University of
    Wollongong
Alan Underwood, Queensland
    University of Technology
Peter Weill, University of Melbourne

CANADA
Wynne W. Chin, University of Calgary
Len Fertuck, University of Toronto
Robert C. Goldstein, University of
    British Columbia
Rebecca Grant, University of Victoria
Kevin Leonard, Wilfrid Laurier University
Anne B. Pidduck, University of Waterloo

GREECE
Anastasios V. Katos, University of
    Macedonia

HONG KONG
Enoch Tse, Hong Kong Baptist University

INDIA
Sanjiv D. Vaidya, Indian Institute of
    Management, Calcutta

ISRAEL
Phillip Ein-Dor, Tel-Aviv University
Peretz Shoval, Ben Gurion University

MEXICO
Noe Urzua Bustamante, Universidad
    Tecnológica de México

NETHERLANDS
E.O. de Brock, University of Groningen
Theo Thiadens, University of Twente
Charles Van Der Mast, Delft University
    of Technology

PUERTO RICO, **Commonwealth**
of the United States
Brunilda Marrero, University of Puerto
    Rico

SWEDEN
Mats Daniels, Uppsala University

SWITZERLAND
Andrew C. Boynton, International
    Institute for Management Development